MW01104365

The Law *and* Business Administration *in Canada*

Twelfth Edition

J. E. SMYTH
Late Professor of Commerce
Faculty of Management Studies
University of Toronto

D. A. SOBERMAN
Faculty of Law
Queen's University

A. J. EASSON
Late Professor of Law
Faculty of Law
Queen's University

S. A. McGILL
School of Business & Economics
Wilfrid Laurier University

Pearson Canada
Toronto

Library and Archives Canada Cataloguing in Publication

The law and business administration in Canada / J.E. Smyth . . . [et al.].—12th ed.

Previous eds. by J.E. Smyth, D.A. Soberman and A.J. Easson.
Includes bibliographical references and index.
ISBN 978-0-13-514170-0

1. Commercial law—Canada—Textbooks. 2. Commercial law—Canada—Cases. I. Smyth, J. E. (James Everil), 1920–1983

KE919.S69 2010   346.7107   C2008-908124-2

ISBN-13: 978-0-13-514170-0
ISBN-10: 0-13-514170-2

Vice President, Editorial Director: Gary Bennett
Editor-in-Chief: Ky Pruesse
Acquisitions Editor: Don Thompson
Sponsoring Editor: Alexandra Dyer
Marketing Manager: Leigh-Anne Graham
Senior Developmental Editor: Pamela Voves
Production Editors: Laura Neves, Richard Di Santo
Copy Editor: Laura Neves
Proofreaders: Ron Jacques, Maria Jelinek
Production Coordinator: Sarah Lukaweski
Compositor: Macmillan Publishing Solutions
Permissions Researcher: Sandy Cooke
Art Director: Julia Hall
Cover and Interior Designer: Michelle Bellemare
Cover Image: Getty Images

2 3 4 5   13 12 11 10 09

Printed and bound in the United States of America.

This book is dedicated to the memory of Alex Easson—
a great teacher and a highly respected scholar and author.

BRIEF TABLE OF CONTENTS

TABLE OF CONTENTS

PART 6
Business Organizations: Their Forms, Operation, and Management 579

PART 7
Creditors and Debtors 687

ABOUT THE AUTHORS

J.E. Smyth

James Everil (Ev) Smyth (1920–1983) studied commerce at University of Toronto, where he earned a B.A. and an M.A. He also became a Chartered Accountant and a Fellow of the Institute of Chartered Accountants. He taught at Queen's University from 1946 to 1963, and then returned to University of Toronto where he taught until 1983. He was an outstanding teacher and also served a term as head of the Department of Political Economy and then as head of the School of Business at University of Toronto. He was the author of *Introduction to Accounting Methods* (Kingston: Jackson Press, 1951) and *The Basis of Accounting* (Toronto: Ryerson Press, 1954). In 1983, he was posthumously given the L.S. Rosen Award for Outstanding Contribution to Canadian Accounting Education by the Canadian Academic Accounting Association.

Dan Soberman

Dan Soberman studied law at Dalhousie University and at Harvard University. He began teaching at Dalhousie in 1955, and in 1957 moved to Queen's University to help start the law faculty. He was dean of the faculty from 1968 to 1977, taught full-time until retirement in 1993, and continued to teach part-time there and in the School of Business until 1999. In the late 1960s, he was a member of a federal Business Corporations Task Force that drafted the Canada Business Corporations Act. In the autumn term of 2000, he was visiting professor at Kwansai Gakuin University in Japan. From 1977 until 2000, he was an adjudicator on human rights tribunals in Ontario and federally, and also acted as an arbitrator in labour disputes. He has authored, or co-authored, chapters in various legal books and articles in law journals.

Alex Easson

Alex Easson (1936–2007) studied law in England, at Oxford University and the London School of Economics. Prior to coming to Canada, he practised law as a solicitor in London and taught at the University of Southampton. He was appointed Professor of Law at Queen's University in 1976 and remained at Queen's until he retired from full-time teaching in 2000. He then concentrated on his consulting practice, working principally for international organizations such as the IMF and the OECD, and specializing in international taxation, foreign investment, and economic reform. His work took him to more than 40 countries on five continents. He authored, or co-authored, more than a dozen books, the most recent being *Tax Incentives for Foreign Direct Investment* (The Hague: Kluwer Law International, 2004). We at Pearson Canada appreciate his contributions over several editions to this highly-acclaimed text

Shelley McGill

Shelley McGill earned her LL.B. at the University of Western Ontario and her LL.M. at Osgoode Hall Law School at York University. Prior to joining Wilfrid Laurier University, she was a partner in the Ontario law firm of Sims Clement Eastmen (now Miller Thomson). In 1992, she became a faculty member at Laurier's School of Business and Economics where she teaches business law to graduate and undergraduate business students. Also in 1992, Mrs. McGill was appointed a Deputy Judge of the Ontario Small Claims Court and she continues to preside on a part-time basis. Recently, her research has focused on consumer protection issues and she has been published in a variety of Canadian and international law journals.

PREFACE

We are excited to introduce the 12th edition of *The Law and Business Administration in Canada*! Over the past four decades, this text has been studied by thousands of business students. It has shaped today's business leaders and given them an introduction to the integral relationship between law and business.

More so today than ever before, law plays a part in every facet of day-to-day business activities. Although contractual relationships remain the foundation of most business dealings with customers, suppliers, and lenders, other pressing legal issues continuously emerge. Throughout the previous 11 editions, this text has responded to the quick pace of change in the business and educational environments with new content, features, and resources. This 12th edition incorporates the traditional study of contractual principles with a new focus on current legal issues surrounding corporate governance, e-commerce, privacy, and globalization.

The 12th edition is a perfect fit for the needs of today's business student. It combines an unsurpassed commitment to in-depth legal content with a new integrated approach to international and ethical content. Each chapter identifies relevant international and ethical issues so students will study these concepts in context throughout the text.

The introductory chapters have been revised to expand the discussion of two key components. First, the relationship between business, law, and ethics is examined in the context of corporate social responsibility. Students are introduced to the concepts they will use when considering the ethical issues presented in each chapter. Second, the components of an effective legal risk-management strategy are reviewed. Identifying legal risk management as a key part of the effective management of every business helps students understand the relevance of their legal education.

Corporate governance has attracted worldwide attention over the last decade and the law has changed to incorporate safeguards and adopt ethical standards. Chapters 28 and 29 have been significantly revised to cover the new domestic and international standards of corporate governance.

Finally, we are happy to introduce a new chapter on privacy. Technology use and *misuse* have raised the profile of privacy law and it concerns every business stakeholder. Privacy law transcends legal disciplines and is heavily regulated. Students will benefit from the consolidation of the many privacy issues into one chapter.

In short, the 12th edition presents a comprehensive overview of traditional and current business law topics in a readable yet thorough format.

Shelley McGill
July 2008

Summary of Changes to This Edition

We have raised the profile of five key business issues:

■ risk management,

■ ethics,

■ internationalization,

■ corporate governance, and

■ privacy.

Risk management is a recognized discipline within business education. Legal risk management requires that a manager apply basic legal principles and concepts to business operations. If this practical application of legal knowledge is emphasized at the outset of a law course, students will appreciate the context of everything that comes afterwards. Since most instructors deal with legal risk management at the outset of their courses, we have raised the profile of legal risk management by redesigning Chapter 1 and, to a lesser extent, Chapter 2.

International business and ethics are cornerstones of business education. AACSB accreditation requires an accredited school to demonstrate how these topics are covered. Usually, each course in the program must demonstrate coverage of ethics and international issues. We have increased coverage of these two topics by including **an ethical and international application in each chapter**. This will make it easy for instructors to demonstrate how their course meets AACSB requirements. With this integrated format, instructors will be able to meet AACSB standards regardless of which chapters are taught.

Recent corporate governance scandals and reform have made it mandatory for managers to understand the legal aspects of corporate governance. We have **raised the profile of corporate governance** by reorganizing the content and language in Chapters 28 and 29 in a way that connects with current themes in corporate governance.

Finally, **privacy law** is developing into its own area of specialization and privacy obligations are a daily concern for business. Therefore, we have added a **new chapter on privacy**.

All chapters have been thoroughly updated and Ethical Issue and International Issue boxes have been added and revised. We have made every effort to simplify the writing style while maintaining the book's in-depth coverage and level of explanation.

Extensive revisions have been made to the following chapters.

Part 1: The Law in Its Social and Business Context

This part has undergone significant organizational and content changes to place greater emphasis on business context through legal risk-management strategies.

Chapter 1: Law, Society, and Business

- **Added** a new section, "How Does Law Influence Behaviour?"
- **Revised** "The Significance of Law for the Business Environment" to include a discussion of civil, regulatory, and criminal exposure. The concept of legal risk has also been introduced (the duty to conduct business in compliance with standards set and the potential of liability for non-compliance). Proactive and reactive elements of law and business are also discussed.
- **Added** a "Legal Risk Management" section covering the components of a legal risk-management plan and what legal knowledge is necessary to undertake the plan.
- **Revised** the material on law and conscience to focus on the connections and disconnections between law and ethics. The chapter discusses whether a proactive approach to risk management requires a higher standard than mere legal compliance. This section also explains why ethics and law are different, the difficulty of legislating ethics, and the influence of ethical principles on the development of law. Codes of conduct are relevant here. The Ethical Issue boxes in subsequent chapters continue this focus on ethics.
- **Added** a "Law and International Business" section to demonstrate the limits of the law in a jurisdictional context. Conflicting laws and forum shopping are also discussed. NGO's and professional standards are connected. International Issue boxes in subsequent chapters provide further international discussions.
- **Expanded** the "Who Makes Law?" section to include the role of the courts in making and interpreting the law, arbitrating private disputes, and setting policy. Content on the law-making function of passing legislation and granting regulatory power is also expanded.
- **Revised** coverage of the Charter of Rights and Freedoms. New content deals with the s. 96 division of powers and the contents of the Charter. Further discussion addresses why business might want to challenge a statute and how they would use the constitution to do it.

Chapter 2: The Machinery of Justice
Some of the content of this chapter has been moved to Chapter 1 to fit in the overall discussion of who makes law.

- **Moved** discussion of public versus private law to Chapter 1.
- **Revised** the section "The Sources of Law": legislative content was moved to Chapter 1. Simplified the discussion of the history of judge-made law. The "Administrative Law" section has been moved to Chapter 1.

- **Expanded** the content on alternative dispute resolution.
- **Reduced** legal aid coverage since its relevance to business is limited.
- **Revised** the section "The Legal Profession" and added a subsection titled "Business and the Legal Profession" addressing the role of in-house counsel, retainers, paralegals, and compliance officers.
- **Added** an Ethical Issue box on consumer class-action waivers and an International Issue box on appointing versus electing judges in the U.S. Court system.

Part 5: Property

Chapter 22: Intellectual Property

- **Added** coverage of recent copyright legislation and international intellectual property framework.

Chapter 23: Interests in Land and Their Transfer

- **Reduced** historical content and **added** modern principles of land transfer and electronic registration, previously in Chapter 26.

Chapter 25: Mortgages of Land and Real Estate Transactions

- **Added** coverage of title fraud and key Ontario Court of Appeal decisions.

Part 6: Business Organizations: Their Forms, Operation, and Management

This part has undergone significant changes to organization and language, primarily in Chapters 28 and 29, in order to increase coverage of corporate governance.

Chapter 28: Corporate Governance: The Internal Affairs of Corporations

- **Added** discussion of organizing and managing a corporation to meet its internal objectives and external responsibilities. The discussion of affairs and business has been retained in a revised format. The topic has been presented as applicable to all corporations, public and private, and references universal standards from CBCA.
- **Added** a new section, "Corporate Governance of Publicly Traded Corporations," identifying the nature of shareholders in public corporations and the resulting increased concern over the protection of investors and the public. The new corporate governance regulations applicable to internal operations of public companies have been introduced with references to securities legislation and the Sarbanes-Oxley Act of 2002. Discussion of private corporations has also been incorporated, as many private corporations choose to organize their internal operations to meet higher standards before going public.
- **Added** discussion of the legal role of the accounting profession and auditors.
- **Revised** the section "The Structure of the Modern Business Corporation" to more clearly delineate the various types of shareholders, directors (board and chair) and officers (CEO and senior management).
- **Revised** the discussion of corporate directors to include conflict of interest and independence and what a director can do to protect himself from liability.
- **Added** a section on corporate officers to make it clear to students that they have many of the same responsibilities as directors. Further discussion of the CEO and Chairman roles and the concept of independence has also been added.

Chapter 29: Corporate Governance: External Responsibilities

■ **Revised** the section "Changing Nature of Business Responsibilities" to "Liability Arising from Business Responsibilities." The discussion adds employees to the list of stakeholders affected by a corporation's business and provides a clearer description of potential liability for failure to meet obligations. It also adds a refresher on civil, regulatory, and criminal liability. Coverage of corporate liability versus personal liability of directors and officers has also been added.

■ **Revised** the "Protection of Investors" section to more thoroughly cover new securities regulations regarding audit committees, regulation of the accounting profession, disclosure requirements, independence, and codes of conduct. Secondary market liability is also discussed.

■ **Added** a brief section on protection of employees that refers to Chapter 20 for greater discussion.

■ **Updated** the "Protection of the Public Interest" section to include environmental and consumer regulations.

■ **Updated** the discussion of criminal liability to include new *mens rea* and whistle-blower retaliation topics.

■ **Updated** the discussion of personal liability to include auditors.

Part 8: The Modern Legal Environment for Business

This part has undergone significant change, including the revision of e-commerce and international and government regulation material, and the addition of a new chapter on privacy.

Chapter 32: Government Regulation of Business

■ **Added** coverage of privacy and corporate governance.

Chapter 33: International Business Transactions

■ **Updated** the language of the chapter to reflect the globalized language of business.

■ **Added** content on the international role of non-governmental organizations, including international codes of conduct.

■ **Expanded** the coverage of commercial arbitration to recognize the various processes currently in place.

Chapter 34: Electronic Commerce

■ This chapter has been thoroughly revised and updated.

■ **Added** coverage of consumer protection and a section on employment (misuse of company technology).

■ **Updated** content on intellectual property.

Chapter 35: Privacy (new to this edition)

This new chapter provides coverage of legal privacy issues in both the private and public sectors.

■ Private-sector coverage includes employer issues (data collection, confidentiality, trade secrets, customer lists, insider trading, etc.), employee issues (personal data collection, use, distribution and security; performance evaluation; human rights protections; and workplace surveillance), and consumer issues (personal data collection, use, distribution, and security).

■ Public-sector coverage discusses government institutions, including the various levels of government, education, and health care.

■ Under each topic, civil liability, criminal liability, and government regulations are identified where appropriate.

Authors' Acknowledgments

Over the years we have been fortunate in the helpful advice and encouragement we have received from many of our colleagues. In particular, our thanks are due to Stuart Ryan, Hugh Lawford, Richard Gosse, Donald Wood, David Bonham, Bruce McDonald, Gordon Simmons, Marvin Baer, David Mullan, Kenneth Swan, William Lederman, Robert Land, Nicholas Bala, Stanley Sadinsky, and Donald Stuart. We have also had the assistance of a number of excellent student researchers, notably Ib Petersen, Don Luck, Darryl Aarbo, Colleen Dempsey, Rebecca Lovelace, Grace Pereira, Ryan Mills, Samia Alam, and Allison Ostafew. Additionally, we have had the benefit of the many helpful and constructive suggestions that have been passed on to us by our publishers from the reviewers of each new edition. To all of these we express our thanks.

We appreciate the insights and suggestions of the following individuals who provided feedback on the 11th edition or reviewed the manuscript for the 12th edition:

Dr. Bruce Anderson, Saint Mary's University

Peter Macdonald, York University

Sandra Malach, University of Calgary

Ellen J. McIntosh, University of British Columbia

Douglas H. Peterson, University of Alberta

Joe Radocchia, University of Waterloo

Jerome A. Tholl, University of Regina

Kenneth Wm. Thornicroft, University of Victoria

We would like to also thank all those at Pearson Education Canada who worked so diligently to bring this text into print. Among others, thanks go to Alexandra Dyer, Sponsoring Editor; Don Thompson, Acquisitions Editor; Pamela Voves, Developmental Editor; Leigh-Anne Graham, Marketing Manager; Richard Di Santo and Laura Neves, Production Editors; and Sarah Lukaweski, Production Coordinator.

Features

A careful effort has been made to develop features that will facilitate learning and enhance an understanding of business applications:

- An Explanation of Abbreviations is printed on the inside back cover.

- A Table of Statutes and a Table of Cases are provided on pages xxi and xxx, respectively.

- The opening section of each chapter summarizes the focus of the material to follow and lists some of the questions that will be considered.

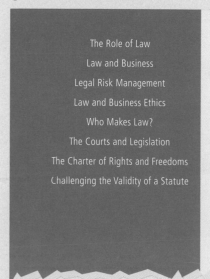

The Role of Law

Law and Business

Legal Risk Management

Law and Business Ethics

Who Makes Law?

The Courts and Legislation

The Charter of Rights and Freedoms

Challenging the Validity of a Statute

What do we mean when we use the word "law"? Since a simple definition is not adequate, we begin by examining the role of law in society, how it relates to morals and ethics, and how it applies to the business environment.

In this chapter we examine such issues as:

- How does law reflect society's attitudes?

- What is the significance of the law to the business environment?

- How should business approach the management of legal risks?

- What is the relationship between the law and business ethics?

- Who makes law?

- How do courts decide whether the legislation is valid under the Constitution?

- What else do courts do?

■ Case boxes throughout the book provide examples based on actual cases.

> ## CASE 35.3
>
> A dismissed employee requested access to her employment file and complained to the Privacy Commissioner when the employer refused to make full disclosure. The Privacy Commissioner ordered production of all documents, even those for which solicitor–client privilege was claimed; section 12 of PIPEDA gives the Commissioner power to order production in the same manner as a court. The Federal Court of Appeal overturned the production order and the Supreme Court of Canada agreed. It held that solicitor–client privilege was a fundamental part of the Canadian justice system, and section 12 does not confer a right of access to solicitor–client documents.[27]

■ Illustration boxes throughout the book provide other realistic examples.

> ## ILLUSTRATION 28.1
>
> Brown holds a large number of shares in each of World Electric and Universal Shipbuilding, and is a director of each of these corporations. Universal Shipbuilding requires expensive turbo-generator sets for two large ships under construction. World Electric is one of several manufacturers of
>
> Brown is faced with an obvious conflict of interest: can she encourage or even support a contract between the two corporations? On one side, it is in Brown's interest to see Universal Shipbuilding obtain the equipment at the lowest possible price. On the other side, it is in her interest to see World

■ Checklists in most chapters summarize important points to facilitate understanding and review.

> ## CHECKLIST   Forms of Intellectual Property
>
> Canadian law recognizes the following basic forms of intellectual property:
>
> ■ trademarks
> ■ copyright
> ■ patents

■ A Contemporary Issue box in most chapters highlights a current legal issue in light of changing business practices.

> ## CONTEMPORARY ISSUE
>
> ### BCE and the Ontario Teachers' Pension Fund
>
> The Ontario Teachers' Pension Fund (OTPF) sought approval for a $51.7 billion purchase and privatization of BCE Inc., the country's largest telecommunications company and Bell Canada's parent

■ An International Issue box in most chapters provides students with an application of the chapter topics.

> ## INTERNATIONAL ISSUE
>
> ### Outsourcing and Transborder Data Flow
>
> In the global business environment, outsourcing specialized operational tasks has become a common practice. When outsourcing involves the transfer of personal information, issues of security and privacy are raised. Customers may consent to the collection of personal data without realiz-

■ An Ethical Issue box in most chapters reinforces the role of ethics in business.

ETHICAL ISSUE

Money Laundering and Solicitor–Client Privilege

As part of a federal anti-terrorism initiative, the federal government enacted the Proceeds of Crime (Money Laundering) and Terrorist Financing Act. Under the federal legislation, profession-

■ Key terms are boldfaced and concise definitions are given in the margins. A complete glossary can be found at the end of the book.

THE MEANING OF CAPACITY TO CONTRACT

legal capacity
competence to bind oneself
legally

repudiate
reject or declare an intention

When we enter into a contract, we usually assume that the other party has the capacity to make a contract and is bound by it, but this is not always so. We would not expect a four-year-old child to be able to bind herself to pay $100 for a computer game; at that age she would lack the competence—the **capacity**—to enter into legally binding contracts. Although the requirements of Chapters 5 and 6 were met, as a matter of *policy* the law may excuse one party, such as the four-year-old child, from her obligations. Of course, in most cases, a lack of capacity is not so obvious; one party reasonably assumes the other has capacity to enter into a contract.

In practice, it is remarkable how little litigation arises as a result of minors attempting to

■ Diagrams are provided in some chapters to enhance specific explanations.

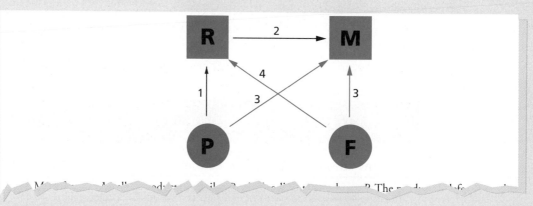

■ Questions for Review near the end of each chapter provide students with an opportunity to check their understanding of main issues and to review the related parts of the chapter.

QUESTIONS FOR REVIEW

1. What are the three key components of modern privacy?
2. What is the constitutional authority for declaring the right to privacy a human right?
3. What is the standard of protection that the Charter gives to privacy?

■ Cases and Problems at the end of each chapter ask students to apply concepts and principles from the chapter to realistic scenarios and actual cases.

CASES AND PROBLEMS

1. KDP Limited operates a pool-servicing business in Vancouver. In the summer, KDP has 8 service vans on the road; each van has 2 employees and 12 of the employees are students. It seems that fewer and fewer service calls are being completed each day and the manager is concerned about productivity. The employees say it is the increased traffic in the city; it just takes longer to get to and from each call. It also seems

■ A list of useful websites relevant to each Part is provided at the end of the book (p. 846). Key websites, such as those for federal and provincial statutes, are listed on the inside front cover for easy reference.

■ A Bibliography of selected sources is presented at the end of the book (p. 842).

■ For convenience, an explanation of "How to Read Citations" is printed on the inside back cover.

Supplements

The following supplements have been carefully prepared to aid instructors and students in using this edition:

■ *Instructor's Resource CD-ROM* (ISBN-10: 0-13-715192-6; ISBN-13: 978-0-13-715192-9): This resource CD includes the following instructor supplements:

• **Instructor's Resource Manual:** This manual provides lecture suggestions, a summary of the major changes from the 11th edition, additional information about the cases cited in the text, notes on the various Issue boxes, and suggested answers to all the Questions for Review and Cases and Problems.

• **Pearson TestGen:** TestGen is testing software that enables instructors to view and edit the existing questions, add questions, generate tests, and distribute the tests in a variety of formats. Powerful search and sort functions make it easy to locate questions and arrange them in any order desired. TestGen also enables instructors to administer tests on a local area network, have the tests graded electronically, and have the results prepared in electronic or printed reports. TestGen is compatible with Windows and Macintosh operating systems, and can be downloaded from the TestGen website: **www.pearsoned.com/testgen**. Contact your local sales representative for details and access.

• **PowerPoints:** A collection of transparencies, culled from the textbook or specifically designed to complement chapter content, is also available electronically in PowerPoint format on the Instructor's Resource CD-ROM.

■ *Companion Website* (**www.pearsoned.ca/smyth**): This website includes chapter outlines, multiple-choice questions (with answers), short-answer questions (with answers), and links to other relevant websites for each part of the text. We have created a new, robust Companion Website for this edition of the book. This protected website is designed for students and instructors and provides **provincially specific material** relating to topics in each chapter. This material is focused on the following regions of the country:

• British Columbia

• Alberta

• Manitoba/Saskatchewan

• Ontario

■ Pearson Education Canada supports instructors interested in using **online course management systems**. We can provide text-related content in WebCT, Blackboard, and our own private-label version of Blackboard called CourseCompass. To find out more about creating an online course using Pearson content in one of these platforms, contact your local Pearson Education Canada representative.

PEARSON
Education
Canada

The Pearson Education Canada

COMPANION WEBSITE

A Great Way to Learn and Instruct Online

The Pearson Education Canada Companion Website is easy to navigate and is organized to correspond to the chapters in this textbook. Whether you are a student in the classroom or a distance learner you will discover helpful resources for in-depth study and research that empower you in your quest for greater knowledge and maximize your potential for success in the course.

Companion
Website

[www.pearsoned.ca/smyth]

Enter

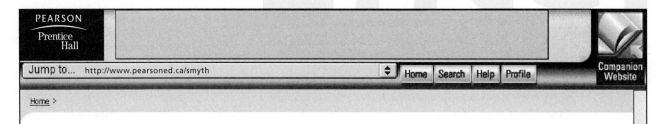

PEARSON
Prentice
Hall

Companion
Website

Jump to... http://www.pearsoned.ca/smyth ⧩ Home | Search | Help | Profile

Home >

Companion Website

The Law and Business Administration in Canada, Twelfth Edition, by Smyth, Soberman, Easson, and McGill

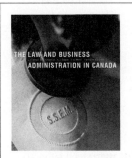

Student Resources

The modules in this section provide students with tools for learning course material. These modules include:

- Chapter Objectives
- Destinations
- Quizzes
- Glossary
- Internet Application Exercises
- Provincial Resources

In the quiz modules, students can send answers to the grader and receive instant feedback on their progress through the Results Reporter. Coaching comments and references to the textbook may be available to ensure that students take advantage of all available resources to enhance their learning experience.

Instructor Resources

This module links directly to additional teaching tools. Downloadable PowerPoint Presentations and an Instructor's Manual are just some of the materials that may be available in this section.

TABLE OF STATUTES

Note: The page numbers in italics at the end of each entry refer to pages in this book.

TABLE OF CASES

Note: The page numbers in italics at the end of each entry refer to pages in this book.

The Law in Its Social and Business Context

L aw cannot be reduced to a simple set of rules and instructions, to be memorized and applied mechanically. It must be viewed from a larger perspective involving societal values and priorities. Through the press, radio, and television, we are constantly exposed to the complexity and uncertainty of legal disputes involving competing priorities. In order to gain an understanding of the legal system, we must learn something about its history and evolution, and about the goals and theories that underlie its principles and rules.

Law provides the framework for virtually all business arrangements. Parties to a contract, investors in a corporation, owners of land and buildings—all need reliability and predictability in their relations with others. While the legal system provides much of the certainty that business relations require, parties may still disagree about their respective rights and obligations and end up before the courts. The role of the courts is not only to settle disputes, but also to explain the rules—that is, to give reasons that justify their decisions. These explanations are very important in helping others to understand the law, adjust their behaviour, and avoid disputes. So, while only a very small proportion of business arrangements end up in court, the courts play a much larger role in society by providing reliable guidelines for business arrangements. Chapter 1 gives an overview of the role of law in society, its special importance in the regulation of business, and the continuing debate about its values.

Law comes from many sources—the legislatures, administrative bodies, and the courts. To the non-lawyer, the structure of the court system is confusing; an overview helps in understanding how disputes get before the courts and are ultimately resolved. Chapter 2 explains how the courts operate and how parties utilize them. We describe the court system in England (where ours originated), Canada, and the United States. We also describe alternative forms of dispute resolution, which sometimes lead to more satisfactory outcomes for both parties than could be achieved by resorting to the courts.

1

Law, Society, and Business

What do we mean when we use the word "law"? Since a simple definition is not adequate, we begin by examining the role of law in society, how it relates to morals and ethics, and how it applies to the business environment.

In this chapter we examine such issues as:

- How does law reflect society's attitudes?

- What is the significance of the law to the business environment?

- How should business approach the management of legal risks?

- What is the relationship between the law and business ethics?

- Who makes law?

- How do courts decide whether the legislation is valid under the Constitution?

- What else do courts do?

- How does the Charter of Rights and Freedoms protect our human rights?

- Why is the Charter relevant for business?

- What is the purpose of a code of conduct?

- How does law impact international business activities?

THE ROLE OF LAW

How Do We Define Law?

A simple definition would be misleading because law is so diverse and complex. It is helpful to begin with a brief description of what law does: it sets basic standards of behaviour that are enforced by government, and also by individuals and groups with the help of government. The law binds all of us; we cannot opt out of the legal system as we may from a club's rules by simply resigning—a club's rules are not law. Who makes law and how it is made are discussed later in this chapter and in Chapter 2.

Why do we have—and need—law? First, law is needed to protect persons, property, and society as a whole; it prohibits conduct that society believes to be harmful to others. For example, we must not assault another person or steal that person's property. The law punishes someone who is found guilty of illegal conduct. However, it does much more than forbid harmful conduct: it also prescribes simple but vital rules that allow us to get on with our everyday lives—for example, by requiring all types of vehicles to drive on the right-hand side of the road. There is no moral reason to drive on the right side rather than on the left, as a number of countries require. But clearly, we must have just one rule in a particular country that all drivers obey.

Second, law gives government the power to act for the benefit of society in general. It authorizes government to provide policing, fire fighting, education, and health care—and to raise taxes to pay for those activities. We expect our government to operate in accordance with the **rule of law**. Law involving the government is labelled as **public law**.

Third, law regulates individuals' interaction with each other; for example, it enables us to make legally binding agreements enforceable in the courts. This is known as **private law**, also sometimes referred to as *civil law*. It allows us to plan and organize our affairs, and we can bargain with others for mutual advantages. The essential feature is that we can *rely* on such arrangements because they are enforceable: we can book in advance a flight across the Pacific, accept a long-term employment contract or a lease of business offices, or buy an interest in a partnership or a corporation. The law provides an element of *certainty* in determining contractual and property rights—something that is essential for the efficient carrying on of business.

> **rule of law**
> established legal principles that treat all persons equally and that government itself obeys
>
> **public law**
> law that regulates the conduct of government and the relations between government and private persons
>
> **private law**
> law that regulates the relations between private persons and groups of private persons

---

CHECKLIST   What Does Law Do?

- It influences and controls the behaviour of individuals in society.
- It empowers, influences, and controls the actions of government.
- It influences and controls interaction between individuals.

How Is Law Linked to Morals and Ethics?

Law, morals, and ethics are interrelated. Individuals "must" comply with the law—it is not optional. Therefore, laws must be *just* so that the majority of society views them as achieving a fair result and voluntarily complies. Most laws naturally evolve from basic moral principles that all people accept.[1]

---

1. Natural law theory has two streams. One stream involves a foundation of religious principles linked to ancient societies where religious leaders held law-making powers. The 17th-century Dutch philosopher Grotius revived the second theory of natural law based on fundamentally rational moral principles independent of religion. One of the most eloquent expressions that combines these two views of natural law, based on the teachings of the 17th-century English philosopher John Locke, is found in the Declaration of Independence of the United States: "We hold these truths to be self-evident: that all men are created equal, that they are endowed by their Creator with certain unalienable rights, that among these are life, liberty and the pursuit of happiness" (italics added).

Still, law often reflects only a minimum standard acceptable to most people. Morals, on the other hand, are *optional* standards of behaviour that people "ought" to observe even though they are not compulsory. Similarly, ethical behaviour is generally considered to be a higher standard than the law involving concepts of integrity, trust, and honour. Although legal philosophers try to create clear distinctions, the categories overlap.[2] For example, lying is always unethical and immoral and sometimes against the law. The law imposes ethical obligations of trust and integrity on some positions, such as directors of corporations, lawyers, and doctors. When unethical and immoral behaviour are recognized by the majority of society as unacceptable, it is likely that a law will be introduced to regulate the conduct. Therefore, the moral and ethical values of society as a whole shape the development and direction of the law.

Is It Ever Right to Break the Law?

Even an effective, democratic legal system still leaves us with a number of difficult issues: Is it ever right to break the law? Is "law" the same thing as "justice"? What if a law is unjust? Intelligent, moderate men and women generally agree that there are times when an individual is justified in breaking the law, although they would add that, generally speaking, the law should be obeyed. They would also agree that there are unjust laws, but even these ought to be obeyed because of the chaotic consequences for society if many people failed to obey them. Even while trying to get unjust laws changed by normal, lawful means, we should still comply with them.

ILLUSTRATION   1.1

Mary Brown was at home tending her sick 18-month-old baby. He had a high temperature caused by an undetermined virus. Suddenly she realized that the child had lapsed into a coma. Fearing that he was in a state of convulsion and might die, she rushed him to her car and drove to the nearest hospital. Within a few moments she was driving 110 km/h in a 50 km/h zone. On arrival at the hospital, the child was placed in emergency care, and the doctor commended her for having saved the life of her child. A police officer arrived on the scene and presented her with a summons for dangerous driving.

Mary Brown drove her car far in excess of the speed limit—a speed limit designed to promote safety. She endangered the lives of other users of the streets, but she did so in order to save the life of her own child. She would not argue that the 50 km/h speed limit was unreasonable or unjust, but only that in the circumstances she was justified in breaking the law or, possibly, that the law should not apply to that particular situation. Nonetheless, the law was apparently broken.

Law and justice, then, may not always coincide. But, one may ask, "Is an unjust law really law?" In some rare circumstances, it has been argued that a law is so atrociously unjust that it need not be obeyed by anyone. Conversely, is there any point in having a law that no one will obey, such as prohibition or music downloading? These perplexing questions demonstrate the link between law and ethics. Law must be rooted in the ethical and moral values of the society in order to be effective.

How Does Law Influence Behaviour?

First, we hope that individuals voluntarily comply with the law simply because it is the law and the vast majority of us instinctively understand the need to "obey the rules."

---

2.   The 18th-century philosopher David Hume pioneered the theory of *positive law* which clearly distinguishes between those laws one must comply with and moral obligations that one "ought" to observe. Those that require clear distinctions between these two categories are known as legal positivists. John Austin, a 19th-century philosopher, advanced the theory of legal positivism by designating law as that proclaimed by the sovereign ("the King of Parliament"). Modern legal thinkers have abandoned the sovereign source of law in favour of a *basic law* (a constitution or founding document) that is recognized by citizens and empowers lawmakers.

However, to further encourage compliance most laws trigger penalties or consequences when they are broken. When a person breaks the law they are held responsible for the consequences; this is often described as **legal liability**. How offensive society finds the conduct determines what area of the law regulates it and therefore what type or types of legal liability it will attract. If lawmakers view the conduct as extremely offensive to society as a whole, such as murder, they will consider it a matter of public law, require the government to enforce the law, and impose the most serious consequences, that of **criminal liability**. If society views the conduct as less offensive but still necessary for an orderly society, such as proper driving habits, it may only expose the conduct to **regulatory or quasi-criminal liability** and the government will generally ticket offenders. Alternatively, if lawmakers designate the conduct as primarily a private matter affecting only the parties involved, such as a tenant failing to pay rent, it will be considered a matter of private law and persons harmed by the conduct will be responsible for enforcing the law through private or civil lawsuits. This type of liability is known as **civil liability**. These three forms of liability are the tools used by lawmakers to encourage people to abide by the law.

legal liability
responsibility for the consequences of breaking the law

criminal liability
responsibility arising from commission of an offence against the government or society as a whole

regulatory or quasi-criminal liability
responsibility arising from breaches of less serious rules of public law often enforced through specialized regulatory tribunals set up by the government for specific purposes

civil liability
responsibility arising from a breach of a private law enforced through a lawsuit initiated by the victim

CHECKLIST What Types of Legal Liability Do Lawmakers Use to Control Individual Behaviour?

- Criminal liability
- Regulatory or quasi-criminal liability
- Civil liability

ILLUSTRATION 1.2

In 2004 the federal government announced plans to decriminalize possession of recreational use marijuana. This sparked a debate about whether society's attitude towards marijuana use had changed. Some people misunderstood the plan as one that would legalize marijuana use when, in fact, the conduct was to remain illegal as a regulatory offence.

It is possible for one event to attract all three types of liability.

ILLUSTRATION 1.3

A business releases chemicals into the groundwater contrary to the environmental emissions standards. Local residents drink the contaminated water and die. The company would face criminal liability if charged by the government with the offence of criminal negligence causing death. It could also be fined for breach of the particular environmental regulations and it would also likely be sued by the victims' families for the losses associated with the deaths of their loved ones.

LAW AND BUSINESS

The Significance of Law for the Business Environment

Law is part of every facet of doing business. It is central to a business's interaction with its customers, suppliers, competitors, and government. Law outlines what to do, how to do it, and what not to do. Businesses may face criminal, regulatory, and/or civil liability if they do not comply. It is sometimes said that there are too many laws—that business is over-regulated. Laws may be resented because they add to the cost of doing business. Too much regulation can restrict economic freedom and make a country's businesses less competitive.

There is no doubt, however, that modern society cannot function without laws, and businesses cannot succeed without understanding them. Indeed, business executives identify legal certainty as one of the key factors that determine whether or not they decide to invest in a particular country. To have a good environment for business, a country must provide an adequate legal infrastructure that clearly defines rights and responsibilities and properly enforces them. Over-regulation may be a severe inconvenience—but it is far less of an obstacle to business than is the complete absence of regulation.

Law and International Business

Generally, law regulates conduct within a country's jurisdictional boundaries, but business is not restricted to the borders of a single country. Increasingly, the world is becoming a single giant marketplace in which firms from different countries carry on business; they make agreements, and they compete against and sometimes co-operate with each other. For Canada, more than for most countries, the international dimension of business is especially important; foreign trade and foreign investment result in a wide variety of legal relationships between parties in two or more countries. Accordingly, the law is a significant element in the international business environment.

Businesses may be faced with different rules for each country in which they do business. Determining which laws apply to any given situation can lead to a conflict of laws. As will be discussed in later chapters, governments and **non-governmental organizations** are trying to harmonize laws in order to address these conflicts through the use of treaties, conventions, and model laws. Model laws are recommended templates for domestic laws that are developed by advisory organizations such as law reform commissions. Treaties and conventions are international agreements between governments in which countries agree to pass similar laws. These agreements are often brokered through **super-governmental organizations** such as the United Nations. The success of these initiatives depends on the willingness of countries to implement the agreed-upon treaty rules. Most chapters of this book will identify an international issue.

LEGAL RISK MANAGEMENT

Businesses must understand the laws that affect them, the relevant compliance requirements, and the risks of legal liability associated with their activities. Some may question why business managers need to familiarize themselves with the law, properly suggesting that lawyers are the experts in this field. However, business managers are the experts in the activities of their businesses and they must understand the **legal risks** associated with the everyday choices they make. Business managers cannot effectively use lawyers unless they know what to ask and when to ask it and then understand the advice they receive.

Early identification of a legal risk is vital to its effective management. Businesses must develop **legal risk management plans** that anticipate possible legal liability and provide preventive and remedial strategies. The involvement of lawyers is only part of the overall plan.

Developing a Legal Risk Management Plan

Developing a legal risk management plan requires five distinct steps involving every facet of the organization as well as experts in law, finance, and insurance. It is a continuous process that includes ongoing revision as law evolves, business expands and diversifies, and personnel changes.

non-governmental organizations
voluntary non-profit associations of private individuals or groups working together to influence policy, raise awareness, or affect change

super-governmental organizations
non-profit associations of governments from around the world working to find common approaches to international issues, such as the World Trade Organization or United Nations

legal risk
business activities, conduct, events, or scenarios that could expose a business to any type of legal liability

legal risk management plan
a plan developed by a business that identifies potential legal liability and provides preventive and remedial strategies

First, managers must undertake a **legal audit** of the operation. This involves an examination of every area, action, and interaction of the business in order to identify potential legal liability and legal compliance risks. This requires the participation of those most familiar with the functional areas of the business, and these managers must be conversant in the principles of legal liability. This book focuses on the important business law principles of legal liability.

Second, after a comprehensive list of legal risks is developed, the risks must be prioritized. What is the most serious legal risk facing the business? Prioritization involves assessing the likelihood or frequency of the event occurring and the magnitude of the consequences if the event occurs. Risks should be addressed in order of their priority. This book reviews important business law cases that will help value and assess risks.

Third, managers must develop effective strategies to deal with each risk. The strategy must have proactive and reactive elements; in other words, there must be a plan to prevent the risk from occurring and also a plan to deal with the risk in a way that minimizes its consequences if it does occur. Prevention is important because there are consequences even with a successful legal dispute. A legal dispute is expensive and time-consuming to process, it drains energy, focus, and resources from other areas of the business, and it attracts negative publicity. Reaction is important because you cannot prevent every eventuality. For example, a nuclear power plant puts safety measures in place to prevent an accident, but there is still an evacuation plan in case there is an accident. This book will identify legal strategies for risk management.

Fourth, the business must implement the plan. Implementation involves more than just announcing the plan. There must be education, training, testing, and monitoring. Employees must be aware of the plan and capable of complying with it. Management must undertake regular monitoring to ensure that the plan is followed. It is worse for a business to have a plan and not follow it than to have no plan at all.

Finally, the plan must be revised regularly. New legal risks must be added to the plan. Legal risks change every day as new laws are introduced and cases are decided. As businesses expand to new jurisdictions, different laws apply. New products and processes bring new risks. Personnel restructuring mean responsibilities may shift. A plan must reflect current organizational structures so everyone performs their responsibilities.

legal audit
a review of each area, action, and interaction of the business to identify potential legal liability and legal compliance risks

CHECKLIST Steps in the Development of a Legal Risk Management Plan

- Identify potential legal risks.
- Assess and prioritize each legal risk based on likelihood and magnitude.
- Develop a strategy to address each risk from both proactive and reactive perspectives.
- Implement the plan.
- Regularly review and update the plan.

Strategies to Manage Legal Risks

As noted, every legal risk management plan involves preventive and reactive strategies. There are four general categories for managing legal risk:

- Avoid the risk: this strategy involves discontinuing the conduct or finding another way to achieve the result.
- Reduce the risk: this strategy includes quality control initiatives that decrease the likelihood of the risk or minimize its damage.

- ■ Transfer the risk: this strategy accepts that the risk may occur and shifts the consequences to someone else. It may be an insurance company or a consumer through contracts that assumes responsibility.
- ■ Absorb the risk: this strategy accepts that the risk may occur and budgets for the expenses. This is done with remote risks or small-valued risks. The potential cost is factored into the price of the product. This is known as self-insuring.

A business will use all of these strategies in combination.

ILLUSTRATION   1.4

Illustration 1.3 describes the legal liability risks associated with water contamination. A manufacturing business may *avoid* the most serious risks by selecting the safest chemicals for its manufacturing process. It will further *reduce* the likelihood of the risk by implementing strong quality control measures and warning those nearby of the use of chemicals. Naturally, it will also carry insurance to *transfer* the costs of an environmental cleanup. However, this insurance is very expensive, so the business may *absorb* some of the risk by choosing a high deductible.

LAW AND BUSINESS ETHICS

Business Ethics

corporate social responsibility
a concept that suggests business decision-makers consider ethical issues including the interests of customers, employees, creditors, the public, and other stakeholders, in addition to legal and financial concerns

code of conduct
a common standard of behaviour that may take the form of a values statement or a prescribed set of rules

We have struggled to determine if it can ever be right to break the law. We should also consider whether it is always sufficient merely to abide by the law: are there occasions when a higher standard of behaviour is required? In a commercial context, this raises the issue of business ethics and **corporate social responsibility**. As shown in Figure 1.1, corporate social responsibility can be thought of as having three domains: ethical, legal, and economic. In the wake of recent corporate scandals, businesses are encouraged to live up to a higher ethical standard than is imposed on them by law. One way to promote an ethical climate in a business is to introduce a **code of conduct** that requires behaviour in line with ethical values such as honesty, trust, loyalty, and responsibility.[3]

Why should a firm commit itself to observing a higher ethical standard than is required by law? The answer may be quite straightforward: a firm behaves ethically because that is how its owners or managers believe it should behave. More often, however, ethical behaviour is a matter of enlightened self-interest. A firm that respects its employees is more likely to have a stable, contented, and productive work force; a firm that operates a liberal "returns" policy is more likely to create consumer loyalty; a firm that shows concern for the environment and the community in which it is located will benefit from an improved public image; and a firm with transparent and independent leadership will benefit from the trust and confidence of the public investor. Finally, as we have noted, the ethical values of society shape the development of the law; proactive legal risk management anticipates where the law may go in the future and prepares for it now. Today's voluntary ethical standard may be tomorrow's mandatory obligation. Most chapters of this book will identify an ethical issue.

Codes of Conduct

Codes of conduct take a variety of forms and may fill gaps that law cannot reach:

(a) *Binding codes*—some activities, particularly of professionals, are regulated by a code of conduct, or a similar set of rules, laid down by a governing body or trade association. Professional codes of conduct are considered further in Chapter 4. Although these rules

---

3. Mark S. Schwartz, "A Code of Ethics for Corporate Codes of Ethics" (2002), 41 *Journal of Business Ethics* 27–43; Mark S. Schwartz and Archie B. Carroll, "Corporate Social Responsibility: A Three Domain Approach" (2003), 13(4) *Business Ethics Quarterly* 503–30.

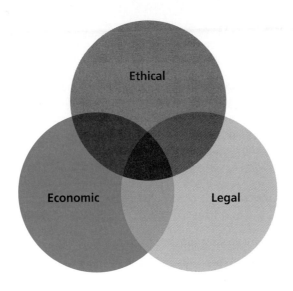

Source: Mark S. Schwartz and Archie B. Carroll, "Corporate Social Responsibility: A Three Domain Approach" (2003), 13(4) *Business Ethics Quarterly* 509.

FIGURE 1.1

Corporate Social Responsibility: A Three Domain Approach

are not law, their effect is often similar. A member of a profession or trade association who breaches the code of conduct may face disciplinary proceedings and may even be expelled from that body—a very severe sanction, since often it will deprive the offender of the right to work in the profession. These bodies may cross jurisdictional boundaries that the law does not.

(b) *Voluntary codes*—some industries have established voluntary codes of conduct for their activities. Although voluntary, they often have a strong persuasive effect. A voluntary code may even be used as a substitute for government regulation: there is an implicit threat that, if an industry—for example, the advertising industry—does not regulate itself satisfactorily, the government will step in and legislate standards. In other cases, voluntary codes are adopted where there is no effective power to legislate. A well-known example is the United Nations Code of Conduct for Transnational Corporations. Multinational enterprises are urged to observe certain minimum standards—for example, on employment of child labour—even though there are no legal restrictions in countries in which they operate.

(c) *Self-imposed codes*—some firms have adopted and published their own codes of conduct, especially in relation to employment conditions and environmental protection. Codes may be a response to public criticism—for example, to criticism of working conditions in overseas factories of manufacturers of clothing and sporting goods; sometimes they may be used to impress and attract particular groups of consumers. In other cases they simply reflect the philosophy of the owners or managers of the firm. The contents of the code may form part of employment contracts, and employees may be disciplined for violations.

ILLUSTRATION   1.5

Students attending a university are governed by an academic code of conduct that forbids cheating. Cheating is unethical. The code allows the university to expel or suspend a student for cheating. The university does not have to establish that the student broke the law, only that he or she violated the academic code of conduct that forms part of the contractual relationship between the university and the student.

WHO MAKES LAW?

Law comes from a variety of sources:

basic law
a constitution that is habitually obeyed by the citizens of a country and that they regard as legitimate and binding

statute
a piece of legislation passed by government

regulations
administrative rules implemented by government as a result of authorization given in a statute

case law
a collection of individual cases decided by the courts that develop and shape legal principles

(a) *The Constitution*—the **basic law** from which all other laws draw their power. It may be created by a sovereign, such as a monarchy or a government. A constitution is a "higher" law by which all other laws are governed; all other laws must comply with the constitution in order to be valid and enforceable. 制定法

(b) *Legislation*—also known as **statute law, statutes**, or acts, is passed by Parliament and by provincial legislatures in compliance with the Constitution.

  (i) *Subordinate legislation*—rules passed under authorization of a statute by a body designated in the statute, such as the federal or a provincial cabinet, or by a cabinet minister, or by an administrative body such as the Canadian Radio-television and Telecommunications Commission. These rules are referred to as **regulations**.

  (ii) *Administrative rulings*—rulings handed down by administrative bodies created by the legislation to hear complaints and applications by individuals and groups, according to the terms of the legislation.

(c) *Court decisions*—judgments handed down by single judges or a panel of judges after hearing a case before the court. These decisions are collectively referred to as **case law**. Sometimes a decision impacts only the parties involved, but other times the decision includes explanations and opinions that shape the law and have relevance beyond the specific parties. We will deal with this type of law in more detail in Chapter 2.

Courts play a very special role in our society: whenever the government itself or any private citizen or group tries to gain the benefit or protection of a law against the will of another, the complaining party may resort to the courts. Accordingly, courts are central to law enforcement. Under a legal system such as ours, derived from the English common law, legislation has historically played only a small part in resolving legal disputes between private parties—individuals, corporations, or other organized groups not connected with the government. There are large areas of the law unaffected by legislation. In these areas, the courts apply principles from case law that they themselves have developed in their long history of delivering written decisions, and in novel situations of developing new principles. These activities of the courts are important and complex. We shall discuss the evolution and continuing importance of court decisions based on principles developed by the courts themselves in the next chapter. This chapter will review legislation and the courts.

CHECKLIST   What Do Courts Do?

- They determine the validity of legislation.
- They interpret legislation.
- They protect human rights.
- They develop case law, creating new principles to resolve disputes.

THE COURTS AND LEGISLATION

Even in areas where there is legislation, courts play an important role. It will be the court that decides if a statute is valid and enforceable. If it is valid, the court must decide what the words of the statute mean and whether that interpretation covers the subject of the dispute. In Canada, validity depends on the Constitution.

Federalism and the Constitution

In a federal country such as Canada (and also the United States), there are two distinct levels of government—federal and provincial; under the Constitution Act, 1867[4] each level has an independent existence and its own sphere of activity. Our national Parliament cannot alter the structure of provincial governments.[5] The division of legislative power, mainly under sections 91 and 92 of the Constitution, allocates certain areas to the federal Parliament and others (including power over municipalities) to the provincial legislatures. When conflict arises, the courts determine if legislation is within the jurisdiction of the enacting government. Whenever an act—or any provision in an act—is found by the court to be *outside* the legislature's jurisdiction and therefore beyond its powers (***ultra vires***), that act or provision is void. The Constitution also gives **residual powers** to the federal government, so that all fields not expressly allocated to the provinces are within federal jurisdiction. Examples are new activities developed after 1867, such as air traffic and radio and television broadcasting.

All federations face the same difficulty: practical problems refuse to divide themselves into well-defined subjects that fall clearly within either federal or provincial jurisdiction. Many problems overlap both jurisdictions, and often both levels of government seem to have **concurrent powers** to regulate an activity. When both levels pass legislation and conflict arises between the statutes, the federal legislation prevails; the provincial law is nullified because of the need for uniformity across Canada in areas of federal jurisdiction. For example, the federal government has jurisdiction over radio and television broadcasting, and the provincial governments have jurisdiction to regulate advertising in order to protect consumers. May a province still regulate advertising on television? Who should answer this question?

Problems of jurisdiction arose in the United States before Canada was founded. In the early 19th century, the Supreme Court of the United States held that neither the federal nor the state governments could have the last word on interpreting the U.S. Constitution; to give one level the power to interpret the document (doubtless in its own favour) would be to confer supremacy upon it. Instead, the court declared that it must itself be the final arbiter of the Constitution, the umpire between the two levels of government.[6] This position was accepted by the states and by Congress. In Canada, the Supreme Court has come to play the same key role as constitutional umpire.

ultra vires
beyond the powers and therefore void

residual powers
powers that fall within federal jurisdiction because they are not expressly allocated to the provinces by the Constitution

concurrent powers
overlapping powers of both levels of government to regulate the same activities

---

CASE 1.1

The Quebec Consumer Protection Act prohibits advertising directed at persons under the age of 13. The provisions of the act apply to all forms of advertising—newspapers, magazines, television. There already existed extensive federal regulations of television broadcasting. After receiving warnings from the Quebec government about its television advertising for children, Irwin Toys Limited asked that the court declare the provisions in the provincial act to be void because they interfered with the federal government's jurisdiction to regulate television. The court disagreed; it found that the purpose of the act was to protect children, "a valid provincial objective," and while it did have an "incidental" effect on television advertising, it was not incompatible with existing federal regulations. "Neither television broadcasters nor advertisers are put into a position of defying one set of standards by complying with the other."[7] Consequently, the court held that the provisions of the Quebec Consumer Protection Act were not in conflict with federal regulations and, so, not void.

---

4. This act was formerly known as the British North America Act, but was officially renamed The Constitution Act, 1867 by the Constitution Act, 1982. Both of these acts and all intervening amendments are now referred to as the Constitution.

5. Such changes may be done only by amending the Constitution, a difficult task that requires approval of the provinces themselves.

6. *Marbury* v. *Madison*, 5 U.S. 137 (1803).

7. *Irwin Toy Ltd.* v. *Quebec (Attorney-General)*, [1989] 1 S.C.R. 927 at 964. This case raised other issues under the Canadian Charter of Rights and Freedoms, noted later in this chapter.

The court's decision was consistent with the principle that it should not easily strike down legislation—that it should respect the intent of the legislatures—unless the legislation was clearly inconsistent with the constitutional division of powers.

THE CHARTER OF RIGHTS AND FREEDOMS

A constitution often does more than allocate jurisdiction between levels of government: it may also prohibit all government interference in certain areas; it may remove them from the legislative power of both levels. In 1982, the Charter of Rights and Freedoms became part of the Constitution; it places limits on many aspects of government action and protects **human rights**.[8]

The popular American term "civil rights" has a peculiar meaning in Canadian constitutional law. Section 92 of the Constitution designates "property and civil rights" as an area of provincial responsibility. Our courts have generally taken the term to mean something like "**private rights**" relating to the ownership of property, contract law, and family relations. The Charter refers to "rights and freedoms" and our reference to human rights avoids confusion.

First, we should note that the Charter is *entrenched* in the Constitution: it cannot be repealed by an ordinary act of Parliament or of provincial legislatures in each of the areas where formerly they were able to pass and repeal laws at their will. Section 52(1) states:

> The Constitution of Canada is the supreme law of Canada, and any law that is inconsistent with the provisions of the Constitution is, to the extent of the inconsistency, of no force or effect.

Any change in the Charter can only be by way of amendment as provided for in the Constitution Act—that is, by consent of the Parliament of Canada and the legislatures of at least two-thirds of the provinces containing at least 50 percent of the population of all the provinces. We can see then that the Charter is much more difficult to change than is an ordinary statute.

Second, subject to the important qualifications in the following paragraphs, rights entrenched in the Charter cannot be infringed by ordinary legislation: to the extent that a statute offends a right in the Charter, it will be declared invalid. The legislature cannot interfere with those rights that are founded on the "higher law" of the Constitution. The idea of rights based on a higher law was a major departure from British Parliamentary supremacy, and is more like the theory of the United States Constitution.

Although prior to the Charter our courts had not dealt with entrenched human rights, they did have wide experience in deciding whether a piece of legislation is within the competence of the federal Parliament or of provincial legislatures under section 91 or 92 of the Constitution; they struck down legislation when they concluded that it went beyond the powers granted. The Supreme Court of Canada has shown that it is prepared to strike down those provisions in statutes that offend the rights and freedoms guaranteed in the Charter.[9] Indeed, the Supreme Court has gone further: it has "read into" a human rights act (rather than striking down a part of the act) words prohibiting discrimination on the basis of sexual orientation, words that the legislature had not chosen to include as part of the act.[10]

human rights
recognized entitlements encompassing traditional freedoms associated with civil liberty and basic human necessities

private rights
individual rights arising from private law

---

8. The terms "human rights," "civil liberties," and "civil rights" are synonyms. "Civil liberties" and "civil rights" are the older terms, dating from as far back as the 18th century, and referring primarily to freedom of the individual in politics and religion. They include freedom of expression (both of speech and of the press), freedom of association and assembly, freedom to practise and preach one's religion, freedom from arbitrary arrest and detention, and the right to a fair trial. The horrors of the Second World War—deportation, starvation, and genocide—heightened awareness of human needs beyond the traditional freedoms mentioned above and this led to the term "human rights."

9. See, for example: *R.* v. *Big M Drug Mart Ltd.* (1985), 18 D.L.R. (4th) 321, striking down the Lord's Day Act of Canada as a form of compulsory religious practice; and *A.G. of Quebec* v. *Quebec Association of Protestant School Boards et al.* (1984), 10 D.L.R. (4th) 321, nullifying certain sections of Quebec's Charter of the French Language as violating minority language rights under section 23 of the Charter of Rights and Freedoms.

10. *Vriend et al.* v. *The Queen in the Right of Alberta et al.* (1998), 156 D.L.R. (4th) 385.

(3) **Third,** the Charter includes section 33, which permits a legislature to override certain other sections. That is, if a statute states expressly that it "shall operate notwithstanding" those specified sections, a legislature may infringe some of the most important rights guaranteed by the Charter. Section 33 also contains a so-called sunset clause: the overriding section of the statute expires five years after it comes into force unless it is re-enacted by the legislature—and continues to expire after each further five years. The reasoning behind these provisions seems to be as follows: the declaration of certain rights in our Constitution gives them great moral and political force; governments will rarely dare to pass legislation expressly overriding the Charter, and very likely for only limited purposes—and they will have to produce strong reasons for continuing the override beyond the first five years. In the years since the Charter, legislatures have operated within these constraints; in general they have not found it politically easy to avoid the Charter and to use the override section.

(4) **Fourth,** none of the rights set out in the Charter is absolute; section 1 states that they are all subject "to such reasonable limits prescribed by law as can be demonstrably justified in a free and democratic society." The problem of what amounts to "reasonable limits" arises whenever a complainant claims that a right entrenched in the Charter, such as the freedom of expression, has been infringed.

In general, a statute is *presumed to be valid*—that is, to be within the power of a legislature passing it: a person attacking it must show why it is invalid. However, a person need show only that one of his constitutionally guaranteed rights has been infringed by a provision in a statute; the provision would then be *presumed invalid* unless the government could persuade the court that the infringement was "demonstrably justified." So, the **burden** shifts to the government to show that the section of a statute that interferes with constitutional rights is justified. It is difficult to predict in a general way how deferential the courts will be to the legislatures. In what circumstances will judges say, "Since the elected majority think this infringement is justified, we will not interfere" rather than "The will of the majority does not justify this interference with individual rights"?

(5) **Fifth,** the Charter applies to governments and governmental activities; it has limited application between private persons. In the private sector, the protection of human rights has been a matter for human rights codes, passed by each of the provinces and by Parliament (to cover those activities that are under federal jurisdiction). These codes are not entrenched and may be amended from time to time by the legislature, or even repealed entirely, although complete repeal is highly unlikely. The Charter itself states that it applies "in respect of all matters within the authority of Parliament . . . [and] . . . of the legislature of each province." These words make the Charter applicable to all statutes, to regulations under statute law, to municipal laws, and to Crown corporations. However, the Supreme Court of Canada has refused to extend Charter requirements to corporations and even to our publicly funded universities because they are considered to be independent of the government.[11] This matter has been left to human rights codes.

burden
the requirement that, unless a party can establish facts and law to prove its case, it will lose

The Rights and Freedoms Protected by the Charter

Several of the most important protections given by the Charter are reproduced here beginning with those rights and freedoms that may be overridden by Parliament or a provincial legislature through use of section 33.

Fundamental Freedoms

2. Everyone has the following fundamental freedoms:

    (a) freedom of conscience and religion;

    (b) freedom of thought, belief, opinion and expression, including freedom of the press and other media of communication;

    (c) freedom of peaceful assembly; and

    (d) freedom of association.

---

11. *McKinney* v. *University of Guelph*, [1990] 3 S.C.R. 229, at 266, ". . . the mere fact that an entity is a creature of statute . . . is in no way sufficient to make its actions subject to the Charter."

Legal Rights

7. Everyone has the right to life, liberty and security of the person and the right not to be deprived thereof except in accordance with the principles of fundamental justice.

8. Everyone has the right to be secure against unreasonable search or seizure.

9. Everyone has the right not to be arbitrarily detained or imprisoned.

10. Everyone has the right on arrest or detention

    (a) to be informed promptly of the reasons therefor;

    (b) to retain and instruct counsel without delay and to be informed of that right; and

    (c) to have the validity of the detention determined by way of habeas corpus and to be released if the detention is not lawful.

Sections 11 to 14 deal in detail with the rights of persons accused of crimes during Criminal proceedings against them.

Equality Rights

15. (1) Every individual is equal before and under the law and has the right to the equal protection and equal benefit of the law without discrimination and, in particular, without discrimination based on race, national or ethnic origin, colour, religion, sex, age or mental or physical disability.

    (2) Subsection (1) does not preclude any law, program or activity that has as its object the amelioration of conditions of disadvantaged individuals or groups including those that are disadvantaged because of race, national or ethnic origin, colour, religion, sex, age or mental or physical disability.

Two aspects of section 15 deserve comment. First, subsection (2) permits "affirmative action" (or "reverse discrimination")—that is, programs aimed at assisting disadvantaged people such as the aged, those who have disabilities, or those who, because of racial or ethnic background, have lived in impoverished conditions. Without such a provision, it might have been possible for a person not a member of a disadvantaged group to complain that he was not receiving equality of treatment if a disadvantaged person were given an extra benefit such as special funding to obtain higher education or training for a job.

Second, section 28 of the Charter states:

> Notwithstanding anything in this Charter, the rights and freedoms referred to in it are guaranteed equally to male and female persons.

This section is not subject to being overridden by Parliament or a legislature; it deals with equality of treatment between the sexes—as does section 15(2)—and it states that equality is guaranteed "notwithstanding anything in the Charter" including, presumably, section 15(2). Does this phrase then mean that affirmative action for the benefit of women offends section 28, so that a man may complain of unequal treatment if a woman is given special benefit?

The following rights and freedoms are also not subject to a legislative override:

Democratic Rights

3. Every citizen of Canada has the right to vote in an election of members of the House of Commons or of a legislative assembly and to be qualified for membership therein.

Mobility Rights

6. (1) Every citizen of Canada has the right to enter, remain in and leave Canada.

    (2) Every citizen of Canada and every person who has the status of a permanent resident of Canada has the right

        (a) to move to and take up residence in any province; and

        (b) to pursue the gaining of a livelihood in any province.

(3) The rights specified in subsection (2) are subject to

  (a) any laws or practices of general application in force in a province other than those that discriminate among persons primarily on the basis of province of present or previous residence; and

  (b) any laws providing for reasonable residency requirements as a qualification for the receipt of publicly provided social services.

(4) Subsections (2) and (3) do not preclude any law, program or activity that has as its object the amelioration in a province of conditions of individuals in that province who are socially or economically disadvantaged if the rate of employment in that province is below the rate of employment in Canada.

Section 6(4) is an affirmative action provision permitting programs of employment that give preference to local workers in a province with higher-than-average unemployment in Canada.

The Significance of the Charter for Business

As noted above, the Charter of Rights and Freedoms applies to government and not the private sector, so why is it relevant to business? The answer lies in the fact that government regulates and controls the business environment through legislation. If that legislation violates the Charter of Rights and Freedoms, it can be declared invalid, and business will be free of the regulation. The retail industry was revolutionized by just such a Charter argument.

CASE 1.2

The Lord's Day Act was a federal statute dating back to 1906 that required businesses to remain closed on Sundays. In 1982, an Alberta-based pharmacy, Big M Drug Mart Ltd., remained open on a Sunday and was charged with a violation of the act. In defence, they claimed that the law was invalid because it violated the Charter of Rights and Freedoms, specifically freedom of religion. They felt the Lord's Day Act forced non-Christians to honour the Christian religious practice of not working on Sunday. The Supreme Court agreed, held the Lord's Day Act invalid for offending the Charter, and found Big M Drug Mart Ltd. not guilty because no one can be convicted of an offence under an unconstitutional law.[12]

Now Sunday shopping is the rule rather than the exception and the retail industry is forever changed.

CHALLENGING THE VALIDITY OF A STATUTE

As we have seen, the court will declare a statute invalid if:

■ the subject matter is outside the constitutional jurisdiction of the government, or
■ it violates the Charter of Rights and Freedoms.

In order to make this determination, the court must investigate the purpose and effect of the statute. What does it do and why? What do the words mean? Interpreting the legislation in a narrow way may mean that it falls inside the power of the government, while a broad interpretation may lead to invalidity.

12. *R. v. Big M Drug Mart Ltd., supra*, n. 9.

株式市場　ブローカー　　　　　　　　　　　（発言の）意味

ILLUSTRATION 1.6

The Canadian Parliament receives a report of a special study of abuses in the stock market that cause investors to lose their savings. In response, it passes a statute prohibiting certain kinds of advertising of securities as misleading, and making them criminal offences. A broker who specializes in these transactions claims that his activity is lawful, and carries on in defiance of the statute. He is charged with an offence and raises the following arguments in defence: (a) that the law is unconstitutional because it purports to make changes in an area that is exclusively within the jurisdiction of the provinces under the Constitution Act, 1867; and (b) that even if his first argument is wrong, the government as prosecuting authority has placed an unreasonable interpretation upon the statute and has applied it too broadly in charging him with an offence. He argues, in other words, that under any reasonable interpretation of the statute his activity would remain lawful.

挑戦

We can see from Illustration 1.6 that a legislature faces a double problem in attempting any type of reform. First, it knows that if its entire statute is ruled unconstitutional, it will be void and make no change at all in the law. (The broker in the illustration would then be subject to no new regulation whatsoever.) Indeed, even were the Supreme Court to interpret the statute as not being completely beyond federal powers, it might still restrict its application to areas within federal jurisdiction and so limit the statute that it would fail to accomplish the desired reform. In effect, the court would be saying: "If these words were given a broad meaning, they would attempt to regulate activity beyond the powers of the federal Parliament. Clearly, Parliament could not have meant to do such a thing. If, however, we restrict their meaning to 'such and such,' the regulation will be within federal jurisdiction and valid. We will assume that Parliament meant to do only what is possible under the Constitution, and accordingly find that these words have a restricted meaning." (Once again the broker would escape regulation if his activity were outside federal jurisdiction.)

Second, and apart from the constitutional hurdle, courts have sometimes been criticized for interpreting statutes narrowly so as to interfere as little as possible with existing private rights. Such an interpretation may in large measure frustrate an intended reform. (Again, in this event, the broker might be saved by the narrow interpretation of the statute.)

We can see that a constitutional defeat in the courts is more serious than a narrow interpretation. Parliament cannot overcome a decision by the Supreme Court that a statute is unconstitutional unless the Constitution itself is amended—a process that requires a high degree of provincial agreement as well as the consent of Parliament.[13] However, if the problem is simply one of interpretation, the government can then introduce an amendment to broaden the application of the statute. The trouble with relying on the ability to amend legislation is that except for emergencies or extraordinary pressure on government, the wheels of Parliament "grind exceeding slow," and a year or several years may pass in the normal course of events before an amendment is enacted.

When the Supreme Court nullifies legislation on constitutional grounds, it can arouse strong feelings and sometimes vehement attacks, both for and against the judges as individuals and the idea that a court can have so much authority. A variety of cries can be heard: "The Court is a reactionary bastion standing in the way of badly needed reform"; "The Court is nine elderly lawyers, neither elected nor representative of the people, defeating the wishes of a democratically elected legislature"; "The Court has prevented one level of government from running roughshod over the jurisdiction of the other"; "The Court has stopped the government from making an unwarranted

踏みつける

---

13. A constitution, whether it is of a small social club or a large nation, almost always contains provisions for its own amendment. A "simple majority"—that is, any number more than 50 percent (for example, 50.01 percent)—may pass an appropriate motion to change any earlier motion or law also passed by a simple majority. But the provisions of a constitution are usually "*entrenched*": only a "special majority" may amend them. Typically a special majority is two-thirds or three-quarters of the ballots cast, but sometimes there are quite complex special majorities, giving a specified group the power of veto. Unless *that* group, even if it comprises a very small minority, approves of a proposed amendment, the amendment will be lost.

to treat with brutal force

intrusion on individual liberties." Judges of the Supreme Court cannot escape making decisions that play a critical role in political, social, and economic change. As a result, the role and the personality of Supreme Court judges in particular, and of judges generally, have become subjects of great interest to legal theorists, sociologists, psychologists, and the media, as well as to the practising lawyers who appear before them.

CHECKLIST Three Ways to Challenge the Validity of a Statute

- Argue that the subject matter of the legislation is not within the jurisdiction of the relevant government.
- Argue that the legislation violates the Charter of Rights and Freedoms.
- Argue that the interpretation of the legislation is wrong.

CONTEMPORARY ISSUE

The Role of Judges

Have judges become too "political"? Are they "usurping" the powers of Parliament and the provincial legislatures? Should the political views of judges be explored during appointment?

Earlier in this chapter, we discussed the role of our courts in interpreting the Constitution. The traditional role of the courts in a federation has been to act as umpire in jurisdictional disputes involving legislation affecting levels of government. However, since the Charter of Rights and Freedoms became part of our Constitution in 1982, increasingly the courts have been asked to interpret and strike down legislation of both levels as being inconsistent with rights entrenched in the Charter. Two cases, in 1998 and 1999, added to the controversy about whether our courts have become too "activist." The very public and politicized confirmation process for United States Supreme Court judges is a stark contrast to the private appointment of Canadian Supreme Court judges.

In *Vriend* v. *Alberta*[14] in 1998, the Supreme Court of Canada went further than simply striking down a provision in a statute; it in effect ordered the legislature of Alberta to amend its human rights legislation to prohibit discrimination based on a person's sexual orientation. In 1999, our courts upheld the decision of a federal Human Rights Tribunal.[15] The Tribunal had ordered the federal government to pay several billion dollars in compensation to current federal employees and to former employees—almost entirely women—who were discriminated against because they were not paid fairly for work of equal value usually performed by male counterparts.

Some critics have complained that such court activism is depriving elected legislators of the power to make policy decisions and to enact legislation based on their value judgments and

continued

---

14. *Vriend v. Alberta*, supra, note 10.
15. *Supra*, n. 10.

what they believe their constituents want. Others have defended the courts on the basis that our federal and provincial governments together made a basic decision in 1981–82 to entrench Charter rights: ever since, legislatures must abide by the consequences because the courts have no alternative but to interpret statutes in the light of the Charter. In response, the critics claim that the courts have not shown enough deference to legislatures and to their values as implemented in statutes; instead the courts are imposing their own values. This has led to calls for the reform of the judicial appointment process.

In 2004, the Supreme Court handed down two decisions that appeared to recognize the central role of legislatures.[16] In October 2004, the Court deferred to a decision by the government of Newfoundland and Labrador not to honour a deal reached in 1988 with its public sector workers to end pay discrimination against female hospital workers. By 1991, the government claimed it could not deliver on the deal because of the "severe" fiscal crisis hitting the province. The Court agreed that such a denial of Charter rights could only be justified by "extraordinary" circumstances, but it accepted the position taken by the province. This decision has generated criticism that the Supreme Court has become too deferential to government decisions.

In December 2004, the Supreme Court gave its opinion in the reference on the controversial subject of same-sex marriages,[17] in which it stated that the power to change the definition of marriage lies exclusively with the federal government. Although it appeared that the Court was showing deference to the legislature, it did declare that churches could not be forced to perform same-sex marriages. This was after the Ontario Court of Appeal had already effectively legalized same-sex marriage by striking down the marriage licence rules that prevented same-sex couples from obtaining a licence.[18] The Court refused to state whether it agreed with lower courts that the traditional man–woman definition of marriage offends the Charter rights of same-sex couples because the judgment was not appealed by the government.

QUESTIONS TO CONSIDER

1. When a court determines that a particular provision in a statute is contrary to the Charter of Rights and Freedoms, what alternative does it have apart from striking down the provision?

2. What option may legislatures use to overcome the power of the courts? Why do they not utilize this option frequently?

3. Assuming that a sufficient majority of provincial legislatures along with the federal Parliament could be formed to amend the constitution, what form of amendment would you suggest to limit the powers of the judges?

4. Should Canada adopt a more American-style appointment process for Supreme Court judges where political views are publicly examined?

Sources: Roger Kerans, "Don't Blame the Judges," *Globe and Mail,* March 22, 2000; Raj Anand, "Vriend Will Affect Charter Equality Rights and Remedies" (June 1988), 18(7) *Lawyers Weekly;* see also Craig Bavis, "The Latest Steps on the Winding Path to Substantive Equality" (August 1999), 37 *Alberta Law Review* 683; "Money Beats Rights; Supreme Court ruling says budget concerns are more important than Charter rights," *Hamilton Spectator,* October 29, 2004; Tonda MacCharles, "Same-Sex Marriage is Upheld," *Globe and Mail,* December 10, 2004; Campbell Clark and Kirk Makin, *Chaouilli* v. *Quebec (Attorney General),* 2005 SCC 35.

16. *Newfoundland (Treasury Board)* v. *N.A.P.E.,* (2004) 244 D.L.R. (4th) 294.

17. *Reference re: Same-Sex Marriage,* (2004) 246 D.L.R. (4th) 193.

18. *Halpern* v. *Attorney General of Ontario et al.,*(2003), 65 O.R. (3d) 161 (C.A.)

QUESTIONS FOR REVIEW

1. Describe the three main roles of law in our society.

2. How is the legal infrastructure of a country significant for business?

3. What is legal liability?

4. Distinguish between criminal liability and civil liability.

5. Are law and ethics the same thing?

6. What are the features of a legal risk management plan?

7. Why have business enterprises adopted codes of conduct?

8. What is the special role of the courts in a federal country?

9. What are residual powers? Concurrent powers?

10. What makes a "constitutional defeat" before the courts so serious for a legislature?

11. What strategies does business use to manage legal risk?

12. What is the special meaning of "public law" as distinct from "private law"?

13. Describe the special significance of sections 91 and 92 of the Constitution Act. What problems do these sections encompass?

14. If a citizen claims a provision in a statute to be unconstitutional because it is contrary to the Canadian Charter of Rights and Freedoms, must the government then show it is constitutional? Explain.

15. Which activities are governed by the Charter and which are not? Describe the distinction.

16. "We have a parliament to pass laws, a government to administer laws, and a police department to enforce laws. Ironically, these potent instruments for the restriction of liberty are necessary for the enjoyment of liberty." (A.A. Borovoy, *The Fundamentals of Our Fundamental Freedoms* [Toronto: The Canadian Civil Liberties Education Trust, 1974] at 5.) Comment on the meaning of this quotation.

ADDITIONAL RESOURCES FOR CHAPTER 1 ON THE COMPANION WEBSITE *(www.pearsoned.ca/smyth)*

In addition to self-test multiple-choice, true–false, and short essay questions (all with immediate feedback), application exercises, and links to useful web destinations, the Companion Website provides the following resources for Chapter 1:

- **British Columbia:** Administrative Tribunals; British Columbia's Electoral System; British Columbia's Legislative Process; Government Lobbyists; Judicial Review; Municipal By-laws; Statutory Interpretation

- **Alberta:** Adult Interdependent Relationships Act; Alberta Human Rights Code; Privacy; Same Sex Marriage; Tobacco Reduction Act

- **Manitoba/Saskatchewan:** Charter Cases; Human Rights

- **Ontario:** Agreements to Share Power; Charter of Rights and Freedoms; Human Rights; Jurisdiction; Legislation; Same-Sex Marriage

The Machinery of Justice

This chapter provides the basic information necessary to effectively use the legal system and develop risk management strategies. Chapter 1 identified the sources of law and considered the key role of the constitution. In this chapter we identify the various ways in which law is classified. We revisit the sources of law—judge-made, legislation, and administrative rulings—and examine how each type develops and evolves over time. In this chapter we examine such questions as:

■ What is the difference between substantive and procedural law? Public and private law? The civil and common law legal systems?

■ The theory of precedent—how do we meet the need for certainty as well as for flexibility and change in the law?

■ How are the systems of courts organized?

■ What are the procedures for using the courts and making out-of-court settlements?

■ What costs are associated with going to court and who pays them?

■ What alternative methods of resolving disputes are available?

■ What is a class action?

■ How is the legal profession organized and governed?

CLASSIFYING LAW

Dividing law into broad categories helps us to understand, organize, and explain the many laws that govern us. In Chapter 1 we explained that laws fall into two basic categories: public law (dealing with government) and private law (dealing with non-government relationships). Each of these categories is subdivided into specific topics. Subcategories of public law include constitutional law, criminal law, and taxation. Private law covers topics such as contracts, torts, and property law. Business law draws on topics from both public and private law. This book emphasizes contract law as it is the foundation of every business transaction.

Laws are also divided into two other basic categories: **substantive law** and **procedural law**. When lawmakers decide to address particular conduct they designate the acceptable conduct and then identify a process to enforce it. The rules that define the acceptable conduct or the rights and duties of each person are substantive laws. Some examples are: the *right* to own property, to vote, to enter into contracts, and to sell or give away property; the *duty* to avoid injuring others and to perform contractual obligations, and to obey traffic laws, customs regulations, and other laws. Rules that deal with how the rights and duties may be protected and enforced are procedural laws. Put quite simply, substantive law is "what" the law is and procedural law deals with "how" the law is enforced.

substantive law
the rights and duties that each person has in society

procedural law
law that deals with the protection and enforcement of substantive rights and duties

WHO MAKES LAW?

Chapter 1 identified the two key sources of law:

- the government through legislation: legislation is made by federal, provincial, and even local governments and includes, for instance, regulations passed by a licence committee of a town council. The committee's authority can be traced to provincial legislation, but as a practical matter, the committee is creating new law;
- the courts through case decisions.

As noted, the Constitution is the foundation of all legislation and its role in establishing and enforcing the law was reviewed in Chapter 1. This chapter will examine how legislation and case law develop and evolve. The development, evolution, and relative importance of these laws varies from jurisdiction to jurisdiction depending on the legal system adopted by the jurisdiction.

LEGAL SYSTEMS: CIVIL LAW AND COMMON LAW

Regions of the World Under Each System

Two great systems of law developed in Western Europe, and they have been inherited by most parts of the world colonized by European nations. The older of the two systems is called the civil law. It covers the whole of continental Europe and to a large extent Scotland, much of Africa, and the whole of South and Central America. In North America it applies in Quebec, Mexico, and to some degree in several of the southern United States, but particularly in Louisiana, which was a French territory until early in the 19th century. When the English conquered French Canada, they guaranteed the people of Quebec the continued use of French civil law in most areas of private law. To this day, most of the private law of the province of Quebec is civil law.

The other legal system is called the **common law** and originated in England at the time of the Norman Conquest. It covers most of the English-speaking world including Canada, the United States, and Australia, and it is a significant part of the law of many non-English-speaking countries

common law
the case-based system of law originating in England and covering most of the English-speaking world—based on the recorded reasons given by courts for their decisions

that were part of the British Empire, notably India, Pakistan, Bangladesh, and the former colonies in Africa and the Caribbean. The common law is based on case law—the recorded reasons given by courts for their decisions and adapted by judges in later cases. This book focuses on common law, and we describe the theory of common law in the following sections: "The Theory of Precedent" and "The Sources of Law."

civil law
the system of law involving a comprehensive legislated code, derived from Roman law that developed in continental Europe and greatly influenced by the Code Napoléon of 1804

Roman law
the system of law codified by the Eastern Roman Emperor Justinian in the 6th century

The **civil law** has its roots in **Roman law**, in particular in Justinian's Code, drafted in the a.d. 6th century for the famous emperor of the Eastern Roman Empire. The code was inherited by the whole of continental Europe and formed the foundation for most of its legal systems. Napoléon ordered a new French version in 1804, known as the Code Napoléon; it was adopted in or greatly influenced the development of codes in Italy, Spain, Germany, Switzerland, and Belgium. Civil law theory requires that all law be collected into a consolidated body of legislation known as the civil code, and this code is far more important than any case decision. The court always refers to the code to settle a dispute. If the code does not seem to cover a new problem, then the court is free to reason by analogy to settle the problem from general principles in the code. In theory, a later court need not follow the earlier reasoning in a similar case; the second court may decide that, in its view, a just result of the law ought to be the reverse of the earlier decision. Simply put, civil law values legislation over case law and common law gives case law the same or sometimes greater value than legislation.

The Need for Consistency and Predictability

For consistency and fairness, we need *like cases to be treated alike.* This also reduces the number of disputes that go to court because parties can anticipate how a case will turn out based on prior outcomes.

ILLUSTRATION   2.1

A contracts to build a house for *B* but does not carry out the agreement. Their contract specifies that *B* is only entitled to $50 if *A* defaults. *B* sues *A* and collects only $50 for the breach. *X* makes a similar contract with *Y* and fails to carry out the contract. *Y* sues *X* for damages, but the court awards *Y* $10 000 in the suit, refusing to enforce the $50 cap on damages.

Either decision, examined entirely separately, might seem reasonable enough: some people might well believe that the builder should only pay $50; others might favour the owner's true losses. But if we place the two decisions side by side, for example, in adjoining courtrooms on the same day, there would be two *very* unhappy litigants. *X* would complain because *A*, in a similar situation, escaped without paying any real damages; *B* would be angry because she obtained virtually nothing while *Y* got substantial damages for breach of a similar contract. *X* and *B* would both feel unjustly treated, and most people would agree with them—the law should be either one way or the other but not consist of two contradictory rules at the same time.

Equal and consistent treatment in like situations is a central concern of justice and hence of law as well. Therefore, whether in civil law or in common law countries, judges must be interested in, and influenced by, what other judges have decided in similar cases.

A second major element of law is *predictability.* Suppose, after the contrary decisions we have just discussed, *P* wishes to make a similar contract with *Q. Q* asks a lawyer whether the contractual limit on damages is a binding one: if *P* backs out, will he be liable to pay damages to *Q* for any loss caused by failing to carry out the bargain or will he only need to pay $50? *Q's* lawyer would have to say, "Maybe yes, maybe no; it depends on whether the court prefers the result in the case of *A* against *B* or that in *X* against *Y.*" One can well imagine the state of confusion if this were the normal advice a client was to receive! If people are to be able to find out where they stand and to act with reasonable certainty, *the law itself must be fairly predictable*—another strong reason why like cases ought to be decided alike.

In order to explain how cases are linked, judges develop principles that describe their connection to one another. These principles build into a body of doctrine—a framework of predictable rules that serves as background for the vast majority of legal relations.

As a result, in civil-law countries, judges try to decide similar cases in the same way most of the time, although they are under *no binding* rule to do so. Today, in such countries as France and Germany, reports of decisions are regularly published so that lawyers and judges can learn what the courts are deciding and how they are interpreting the civil code in modern disputes.

COMMON LAW: THE THEORY OF PRECEDENT

Certainty Versus Flexibility

Consistency and predictability became primary goals of the common law judges in England as early as the 13th century. They adopted the custom of following already decided cases, which is called the theory of precedent. The Latin phrase for the rule is **stare decisis**—to stand by previous decisions. However, for many years the judges followed previous decisions quite slavishly, even when in changed circumstances the results were nonsensical or clearly unjust. Such a practice, while it has the merits of certainty and uniformity, can become inflexible and harsh.

Therefore *stare decisis* is not an ironclad rule or, put another way, the theory of precedent is not absolute. First, although judges may be influenced by all prior decisions, they are only bound to follow decisions of a higher level court. Decisions of lower courts have influential value only. Second, in order to be fair, precedents only bind the same circumstances. Since many words have imprecise or uncertain meanings, their vagueness permits judges to draw distinctions between similar problems and so refuse to follow obsolete precedents. In addition, no two sets of facts are identical in every respect—even when the same parties are involved, the time must be different. Judges, when they feel it to be truly necessary, can **distinguish** the current case from an earlier precedent by dwelling upon minor differences. In this way they are able to adjust the law rather slowly to changing circumstances and values. Even so, the spirit of the common law system is bound to the theory of precedent: we look to past decisions to find principles and to apply them to new situations. Accordingly, a large part of the study of law is the study of decided cases.

Despite some flexibility, the theory of precedent does make it difficult for judges to respond to rapid change in society. A decision that seemed quite acceptable in 1985 may be entirely out of step with current social standards. A court may only be able to cope with a major change by directly overruling an earlier decision.

Accommodating Change

Generally speaking, in order to **overrule** an established precedent, the matter must be addressed by a court higher than the one establishing the initial precedent. As will be discussed under the sections on Systems of Courts, courts are organized into a hierarchy involving three basic categories: courts of first instance (trial courts); appeal courts that hear appeals from the trial divisions, and the Supreme Court, which is the highest level of appeal. Courts are reluctant to overrule precedents established at the same level. The danger in overruling decided cases too freely is that doing so would undermine the needed consistency and predictability in law. Obviously Supreme Courts must be able to overrule themselves; otherwise, old precedents could never change without legislative intervention. The Supreme Court of the United States has never considered itself bound to follow its own previous decisions when the result would be manifestly unjust. The House of Lords (the English equivalent of the Supreme Court) reversed its traditional position in 1966 when it announced that it would no longer consider itself bound to follow its own decisions—so recognizing the need to

stare decisis
to stand by a previous decision

distinguish
identification of a factual difference that renders a prior precedent inapplicable to the case before the court

overrule
to declare an existing precedent no longer binding or effective

move on from older decisions when contemporary standards call for change. Similarly, the Canadian Supreme Court accepts this needed flexibility.[1] In 2007, the Ontario Court of Appeal took the unusual step of overruling its own 2005 precedent on title fraud, candidly describing the 2005 case as "incorrectly decided."[2]

It is important to understand these significant changes to *stare decisis* when proposing answers to the "Cases and Problems" offered for discussion at the end of Chapters 3 to 35. When one finds a reported case with facts that seem to be the same as those in a case under discussion, it would be a mistake to assume that the conclusion in a reported case is the only possible outcome. It is much more useful to consider the case offered for discussion on its legal and social merits and then look at a reported case to see what light it may shed on the problem. Some reported cases have been severely criticized both by learned writers and by other courts in later cases.

Although both civil and common law often reach similar conclusions in most areas of the law, there are some important differences. This book deals only with principles of the common law. Much of what is written here does not necessarily apply to the civil law of Quebec.

THE SOURCES OF LAW

The Variety of Sources

Historically, judge-made law is the oldest form of law, but it is important to remember that even in a common law legal system the government also makes law. The government source of law consists of the statutes passed by Parliament and by provincial legislatures, and this source has many subcategories. For example, Cabinet, in its formal role of adviser to the monarch, can also "legislate" within certain limited areas by issuing orders-in-council.[3] Every province has also passed statutes providing for the creation of municipal governments and for their supervision. These statutes give municipalities the power to make law and to raise revenue for the benefit of their citizens. Municipal by-laws and regulations are a form of statute law. There is a vast area of **subordinate legislation** usually known as administrative law: statutes grant authority to various administrative agencies of government to make rules and regulations in order to carry out the purposes set out in the legislation.

subordinate legislation
law created by administrative agencies whose authority is granted by statute in order to carry out the purposes of the legislation

Statutes

As already discussed in Chapter 1, sometimes legislatures enact statutes to **codify** existing case law precedents in an area rather than to change it, as, for example, in the passing of the Bills of Exchange Act, the Sale of Goods Act, and the Partnership Act. Before these acts were passed, the related law was to be found in a staggering number of individual cases. The acts did away with the labour and uncertainty of searching through so many cases.

codify
set down and summarize in a statute the existing common law rules governing a particular area of activity

Courts are often called on to interpret a statute in order to decide what the language means, whether it applies to the facts of a case, and, if it does, to decide also on its consequences. Their decisions then form a precedent referred to in subsequent cases. Therefore, judge-made law and statutes are frequently interrelated. The traditional attitude of the courts towards case law is quite different from their attitude towards statutes. While case law is the creation of the courts themselves, statute law, as one writer put it, is "an alien intruder in the house of common law."

---

1. See statement by Cartwright, J. in *R. v. Binus*, [1968] 1 C.C.C. 227 at 229: "I do not doubt the power of the court to depart from a previous judgment of its own. . . ." It should be noted, however, that the court did not overrule itself in this case.

2. *Lawrence* v. *Maple Trust Co. et al.* (2007) 84 O.R. (3d) 94 overruled *Household Realty Corp. Ltd.* v. *Liu* (2005) 261 D.L.R. (4th) 679 (C.A.).

3. An order-in-council is issued by the Privy Council (in effect, the Cabinet) in the name of the monarch, either in exercise of the royal prerogative or under authority of a statute.

When deciding a case using case law, the courts regularly use principles from earlier decisions, even though the facts may be quite different. On the other hand, the courts are much less likely to apply the provisions of a statute unless the facts of the case are covered specifically by the statute. This attitude of the courts is called the **strict interpretation** of statutes.

Statutory interpretation takes a variety of approaches. Courts may take a literal approach by adopting the dictionary meaning of the word when the meaning appears plain and obvious. A **liberal approach** involves consideration of the context, the custom and trade usage of the language, as well as the intent or purpose of the government when it passed the law. This will involve looking at the state of the law at the time of the passage of the statute and the language used when the bill was introduced and debated.

Canadian courts are encouraged to take a liberal approach to statutory interpretation. The federal Interpretation Act directs the court to take a "fair, liberal and large" interpretation of statutes.[4]

strict interpretation
courts apply the provisions of a statute only where the facts of the case are covered specifically by the statute

liberal approach
statutory interpretation that considers the legislative intent, purpose, and history of the statute, as well as the context of the language

Legislation Framework

There are two main classes of legislation: passive and active. The first and simplest consists of those statutes that change the law: they prohibit an activity formerly permitted or else remove a prohibition, so enabling people to carry on a formerly illegal activity. This type of legislation is essentially passive because although it provides a legal framework for people to go about their business, it does not presume to supervise and regulate their activities. Passive legislation leaves it to an injured party or a law-enforcement official to complain about any activity that has violated a statute of this kind and to begin court proceedings.

"Active" Legislation: Administrative Law and Government Programs

The second class of "active" legislation gives the government itself power to carry on a program—to levy taxes and to provide revenue for the purpose stated in the statute, such as building a hospital and paying pensions to the elderly. The statute may authorize the government to offer subsidies to encourage a particular economic activity, and to create an agency to supervise and to regulate the related trade or activity. Parliament itself is not the right body to run any program requiring continual supervision. Its members from across the country have diverse talents and interests, and their primary responsibilities are to represent their ridings and to enact legislation.

From early times in England, Parliament passed legislation to authorize the monarch to levy taxes, pay and equip the armed forces, and construct public works. Projects *authorized* by Parliament were *executed* by the monarch and his officials—the term "executive" describes the agencies of government that carry out Parliament's will. Translated into modern terms, this process means that every government department, agency, and tribunal is established by the legislature in a statute. For example, the Canadian Radio-television and Telecommunications Commission was established under the Broadcasting Act, which sets out the Commission's purposes and grants it regulatory powers to carry them out.[5]

Subordinate Legislation

In exercising its regulatory powers and acting in its executive capacity, an administrative agency creates new law, which we described earlier as regulations or "subordinate legislation." Some subordinate legislation sets down broad criteria, such as regulating the type of guarantee that a licence applicant must supply to carry on a particular activity, and the amount and type of investment required as a precondition. Other subordinate legislation may be detailed and technical (fees for applications, location of transmitters).

---

4. Interpretation Act, R.S.C. 1985, c. I-21, s. 12.
5. Broadcasting Act, R.S.C. 1985, c. B-9, s. 5.

Important regulations, such as those setting out broad standards, require the approval of the Cabinet in the form of an order-in-council. The agency itself drafts these regulations, and the minister responsible for the agency brings them before the Cabinet. Lesser regulations may be authorized by the minister, the head of the agency, or even a designated officer of the agency.

As we noted in Chapter 1, the growing complexity of society and government has increased the need for specialized knowledge and control in such areas as environmental protection, energy, transportation, communications, education, and welfare; and the list includes a growing number of business and professional activities that are believed to affect the public interest. Although administrative law is not the main concern in this book, we will discuss it with respect to such business-related topics as labour relations, consumer protection, and the financing and operation of corporations, areas in which government agencies and their regulations play important roles.

Case Law: Judge-Made Law

The Common Law[6]

Although the volume of statute law continues to grow, case law precedents remain the bulk of our private law and, in particular, of the law of contracts. Since the common law is based on the theory of precedent, it depends on a flow of reported cases from an organized national **system of courts**: cases need to be decided by courts with a recognized position within the system in order for their decisions to influence judges in subsequent cases. This collection of case law precedents is also referred to as common law.

The earliest decisions were made, of course, without the benefit of previous precedent so courts looked to a variety of outside sources for direction. Established local customs clearly played an important role in those years. As well, early common law precedents borrowed from **canon law**, Roman law, **feudal law**, and **merchant law**.

As the number of precedents increased and the courts developed into a settled order of importance, the courts' own precedents became more and more important and the need to draw on outside sources was reduced.

Equity

As the body of reported decisions grew, the common law rules became more precise and increasingly strict. Judges applied these precedents rigidly. Eventually the common law became very formal, with much of its cumbersome procedure rooted in ancient customs and superstitions. An aggrieved party had to find one of the ancient forms, called a **writ,** to suit his particular grievance. If he could not find an appropriate writ, the court would not grant a remedy. As England developed commercially, the old writs did not provide relief for many wrongs suffered by innocent parties, often resulting in great hardship. Aggrieved parties without a remedy began to petition the king, who, in the age of the divine right of the monarchy, looked upon himself as the source of all law and justice. The king considered the hearing of petitions an important duty to his subjects and often granted relief that was inconsistent with the existing common law precedent.

As the number of petitions increased, the king's chancellor (his chief personal adviser, usually a cleric) took over the task of administering them. Soon another whole system of courts was growing: the courts of the chancellor, or the **courts of chancery** as they became known. These courts created exceptions to the common law rules when they felt the precedent was too harsh. They became known as *courts of equity*, and the rules that they developed created new precedents called

system of courts
the organization of courts into a hierarchy that designates the responsibilities of the court and determines the importance of the precedent; the standard system has three levels: trial, appeal, and final appeal

canon law
law created by the Church, which had its own jurisdiction and courts in matters pertaining to itself, family law, and wills

feudal law
a system of land ownership rooted in sovereign ownership: land was handed down to lords who gave possession of parcels of land to lesser "royals" in exchange for military service and loyalty

merchant law
rules and trade practices developed by merchants in medieval trade guilds and administered by their own courts

writ
an ancient form required in order to take a grievance to court

courts of chancery
a system of courts under the king's chancellor and vice-chancellors developed from the hearing of petitions to the king—courts of equity

6. Confusingly, the term "common law" has three possible meanings: (a) common law as opposed to equity; (b) judge-made law (including equity) as opposed to statute law; and (c) the legal system of a common law country as opposed to a civil law country.

the *principles of equity* or, simply, **equity**. Equity and the common law contribute equally to the legal system developed by our judges.

equity
rules developed by the courts of equity as exceptions to existing rules of common law

The courts of common law were very narrow in the kinds of remedies they offered; they would award only money damages to a party injured by a breach of contract. Yet sometimes money alone was not adequate compensation.

ILLUSTRATION 2.2

B owned two separate lots of land and agreed to buy the middle lot between them from *S* in order to erect a large building on the three pieces once they were joined.

S changed his mind and refused to convey the middle lot. If *B* sued for breach of contract in a common law court, he would be awarded only money damages, an inadequate remedy since his building project would be frustrated.

By contrast, the courts of equity were prepared, if they thought fit, to grant **equitable remedies** such as **specific performance**—that is, to order the defendant to convey the land. If the defendant refused, he would be jailed for **contempt of court** until he gave in and carried out the order. The threat of a medieval jail was highly persuasive!

equitable remedies
new remedies created by the courts of equity to address situations where money damages did not solve the problem

In summary, the approach of the chancery courts was different from that of the common law courts. "Equity was a gloss on common law; it was a set of rules which could be invoked to supplement the deficiencies of common law or to ease the clumsy working of common law actions and remedies."[7] Remedies in equity were discretionary; the relative innocence of the petitioner and the hardship he suffered determined whether the individual could hope for equity's special type of intervention. It was equity that pioneered key legal concepts of trust and loyalty and it was equity that considered the relative position of the parties when applying the law. As equity developed over many years, its principles became as accepted as those of the common law.

specific performance
an order by a court of equity to carry out a binding obligation

contempt of court
a finding by a court that a party has refused to obey it and will be punished

CHECKLIST   Three Meanings of Common Law

The phrase "common law" refers to three interrelated topics:

1. The English-based legal system—common law system—as opposed to the French-based civil law system;
2. The original body of precedents developed by common law courts as opposed to the body of precedents known as equity developed by the courts of chancery;
3. The entire collection of case law or judge-made law as opposed to statutes or legislation.

Merger of the Courts

In 1865 the British Parliament passed an act merging the two systems of courts into the single system we know today where one set of courts applies principles from both common law and equity.[8] The Canadian provinces passed similar acts shortly afterwards.

---

7. R.M. Jackson, *The Machinery of Justice in England*, 8th ed., J.R. Spencer, ed. (Cambridge: The University Press, 1989), p. 7.

8. For convenience, the division of labour has been preserved in England by having two divisions within the High Court of Justice: a Chancery Division and a Queen's Bench Division.

Amalgamating the courts of common law and equity did not result in abandoning the philosophy of equity. Every judge now is supposed to have two minds, one for equity and one for common law precedent. Judges exercise their discretion to apply an equitable principle when it appears warranted in the circumstances of a case. Equity continues to provide a "conscience" for our modern common law; it prevents the law when applied to particular facts from straying too far from reason and fairness. Today, equity is often viewed as pivotal in the link between law and ethics.

THE SYSTEM OF COURTS IN ENGLAND

As we have seen, the courts are very important in a common law legal system. A major part of business law continues to be created by judges. Accordingly, we should be familiar with the system of courts and their rules of procedure. Figure 2.1 illustrates the basic court system.

Two reasons make it useful to begin by studying the English courts. First, much of our own law is derived from English case law, and these cases will be easier to understand if we are familiar with the structure of the courts that decided them. Second, the English system affords a good starting place because England has a single government, and its system of courts is easier to grasp than the more complicated federal structure existing in Canada. The role of the three levels—courts of first instance, appeal courts, final court of appeal—is much the same in England as in Canada.

The Courts of First Instance—Trial Courts

Courts of first instance are also sometimes called courts of original jurisdiction because actions begin and trials take place in this court. This is the place where witnesses are called and an initial judgment is rendered.

The Court of Appeal

appellant
the party who petitions for an appeal

respondent
the party who defends on an appeal

The Court of Appeal is the next level. Actions do not originate in this court, but a party who is dissatisfied with the decision of a court of first instance may appeal to the Court of Appeal to reconsider the decision. The party who petitions for an appeal is called the **appellant**; the other party, the **respondent**. The appeal is not a new trial and no witnesses are called: the court does not listen to questions of fact because they were for the trial judge to decide. The Court of Appeal proceeds on the basis of the written trial record, and lawyers for each side argue only questions of law—the

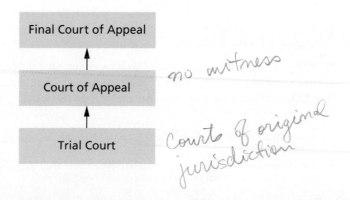

FIGURE 2.1
Basic Court System

appellant claiming that the trial judge erred in interpreting the law, and the respondent arguing to uphold the decision of the trial judge. The court may do one of four things:

- agree with the trial judge and *dismiss* the appeal
- agree with the appellant and *reverse* the trial judgment
- vary the trial judgment in part
- declare that the trial judge erred in failing to consider certain facts and *send the case back* for a **new trial** in the lower court

new trial
a case sent back by the appeal court for retrial by the lower court

The Court of Appeal usually hears cases in a panel of three judges, but occasionally five judges may hear a very important case. The outcome is determined by a simple majority.

The House of Lords

Parties dissatisfied with a decision of the Court of Appeal have one more chance before the House of Lords, the ultimate court of appeal and the highest court in the land. It is somewhat surprising to learn that the House of Lords, more widely known as the upper house of the British Parliament, is also the final court of appeal in Britain. Originally, any member of the House of Lords (members of the peerage) could sit with the House when it was convened as a court, but since the mid-19th century only great lawyers and judges who have been elevated to the peerage actually hear and decide appeals. The court usually consists of the Lord Chancellor and up to nine Lords of Appeal in Ordinary, who are full-time salaried judges.

THE SYSTEM OF COURTS IN CANADA

We noted in Chapter 1 that the Canadian Constitution divides legislative powers between the federal and provincial governments. It gives the provinces jurisdiction over the administration of justice—the organization and operation of police forces and the system of courts. It also gives the federal government jurisdiction over trade and commerce, banking, bankruptcy, and criminal law—matters frequently litigated before the courts—as well as the exclusive right to appoint, and the obligation to pay, all county court and superior court judges.[9]

Why this peculiar division in the administration of the legal system? It is due, at least in part, to the fact that at the time of discussions on Confederation in Canada, the United States had just been through a terrible civil war. Many Canadians believed that biased local state legislatures and locally elected judges (sometimes without any legal training) had fanned internal division in the United States by passing discriminatory laws and often by administering laws unfairly against "outsiders" (citizens of other states). The Canadian Constitution sought to avoid the problem of local bias by placing jurisdiction over matters that might be affected by local influence in the hands of the national government. Our Constitution also requires that only qualified lawyers be appointed to the county and superior court benches. Until retirement, they hold office conditional on good behaviour, and superior court judges can be removed only by "joint address"—that is, a vote taken before both the House of Commons and the Senate. These provisions are designed to keep judges as unbiased and immune from local pressures as possible.

Generally there are three tiers of courts in the Canadian system: the courts of first instance or trial divisions, the intermediate provincial courts of appeal, and the final court of appeal, the Supreme Court of Canada. In the late 1980s and the 1990s, the court systems in all provinces went through a reorganization that merged a number of the courts and simplified the court structure. The names and jurisdictions of the courts differ somewhat from province to province, but in general they follow the same pattern as set out below. Figure 2.2 illustrates the structure of the Canadian Court System.

---

9. The Constitution Act, 1867, ss. 91, 92, 96 and 100. As we note below, in all provinces these courts have been merged.

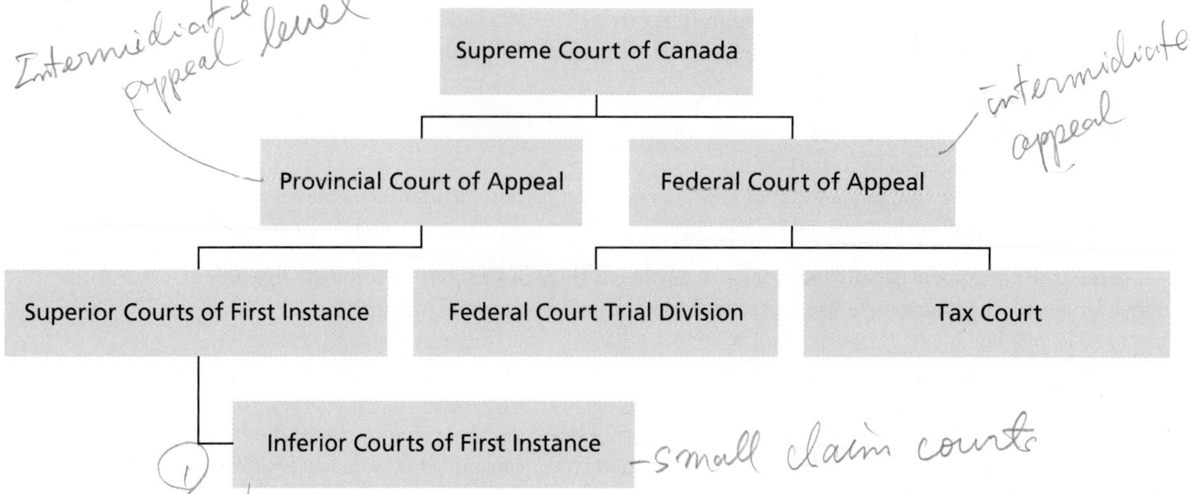

FIGURE 2.2
Canadian Court System

The Provincial Court System

This system is the primary system of courts that deals with most matters of private and public law. As will be noted below, a federal court system exists to deal with a relatively small percentage of matters including tax and intellectual property.

THE COURTS OF FIRST INSTANCE

The courts of first instance are trial courts where witnesses give evidence and initial judgments are made. The topic of the dispute will determine in which trial court the dispute belongs. There are two branches of trial courts. The inferior trial courts are courts created by provincial legislation for a particular purpose. The superior trial courts are the constitutionally created courts presided over by federally appointed judges. Individual provinces designate branches at each level to deal with specific topics. Most of the time inferior trial court judgments are appealed to the superior trial court before they move to the intermediate appeal level. The names of each court may vary from province to province.

Inferior Trial Courts

Small Claims Court

The court handles private disputes for smaller amounts of money. The maximum amounts have been increased in recent years but may vary considerably from one province to another.[10] Its

continued

10. British Columbia, Nova Scotia, Alberta \$25 000; Ontario \$10 000 but is considering \$25 000. In Ontario and Manitoba, Small Claims Court is a division of General Division (Superior Court) while other provinces maintain Small Claims Court as a civil division of the Provincial Court.

procedure is quite simple and informal, so that the cost of taking action is small. The court is important to business because most consumer or client disputes and collections are handled in this court. Despite its small monetary limit, it is the busiest civil court.

Provincial Division

The court decides very little, if any, private law. It hears criminal cases of almost every type except for the most serious offences such as murder, treason, sexual assault, and manslaughter. It may hold preliminary hearings in prosecution of these crimes to decide whether there is enough evidence to proceed to a superior court trial. No jury trials are held before Provincial Division judges. If an accused person elects (as one may) to have a jury trial, the case must be heard in superior court. Anyone charged with a criminal offence for which there can be a prison sentence of five years or more has the right to a trial by jury: in some cases where the prison sentence is less than five years, an accused person may also choose a jury.

A different division of this court hears family questions of custody and support but not divorce. Some provinces set up a separate criminal division to act as a Youth Court where children and adolescents can be dealt with by special youth court judges rather than in the adult criminal courts.

Superior Trial Courts

Surrogate Court (or Probate Court)

This court supervises the estates of deceased persons. It appoints an administrator to wind up the affairs of anyone who dies intestate (without leaving a will), settles disputes over the validity of wills and the division of assets, and approves the accounts of executors and administrators. Four provinces maintain separate probate courts,[11] while the remaining five common law provinces have merged them into the superior court system but with separate divisions.

General Division or Superior Court

This court has unlimited jurisdiction in civil (private) and criminal actions. Federally appointed judges sit in this court that deals with divorce and the most serious criminal matters, as well as all civil (private law) disputes outside the jurisdiction of Small Claims Court. The Court may also serve as a court of appeal for less serious criminal matters heard in Provincial Division. In Ontario, the Divisional Court is a branch of the General Division (known in Ontario as Superior Court of Justice) and it hears appeals from Small Claims Court, interim orders, and other administrative tribunals. Judges of the Superior Court of Justice also act as Divisional Court judges.

INTERMEDIATE APPELLATE COURT

The Court of Appeal

Each province has one intermediate appellate court, called variously the Appellate Division, the Supreme Court *en banc* (the whole bench), and Queen's Bench Appeals, as well as the Court of Appeal. It performs the same function as the Court of Appeal in England. All matters arising in the courts of first instance are appealed to the Provincial Court of Appeal.

---

11. Alberta, New Brunswick, Nova Scotia, and Saskatchewan.

The Federal Courts

Supreme Court of Canada

The Supreme Court is the final court of appeal in Canada, the equivalent of the House of Lords in England. It consists of nine judges and hears appeals from both the provincial courts of appeal and the Federal Court of Canada. In addition, it has special jurisdiction under the Supreme Court Act[12] to rule on the constitutionality of federal and provincial statutes when they are referred to the court by the federal Cabinet. In private actions, the appellant must obtain special leave from the Supreme Court to appeal.[13] Relatively few private matters are granted leave, so for many disputes the provincial Court of Appeal is the last resort.

THE FEDERAL COURTS

Courts of First Instance

Tax Court of Canada

The Tax Court hears appeals of taxpayers against assessments by the Canada Customs and Revenue Agency. The court hears only tax appeals and with relatively simple procedures. Either the taxpayer or the department may appeal its decisions to the Federal Court of Appeal.

The Federal Court of Canada   The federal government maintains the Federal Court of Canada in two divisions, a Trial Division and an Appeal Division. The Federal Court has exclusive jurisdiction over such matters as disputes concerning ships and navigation, and many sorts of lawsuits against the federal government itself. In the rather complicated areas of patents, copyright, and trademarks, the Federal Court has exclusive jurisdiction in some portions but in others there is  concurrent jurisdiction with provincial courts. And there also remains a large area of concurrent jurisdiction where a plaintiff may sue in either a provincial or the Federal Court. For example, a person injured by the careless operation of a government motor vehicle may sue in a provincial court.

Intermediate Level Appeal

Federal Court of Appeal   This court hears appeals from the Federal Tax Court and the Federal Court of Canada Trial Division. As noted above, matters from the Federal Court of Appeal are appealed to the Supreme Court of Canada.

INTERNATIONAL ISSUE

The System of Courts in the United States

Both Canada and the United States have federal systems of government and common law legal systems, but there are major differences between their constitutions. In the United States, the individual states—at least theoretically—have more autonomy, and have the residual power that in Canada rests with the federal government. Although under the Constitution the Canadian government has the power to create a full system of three-tier federal courts throughout Canada, Parliament has felt content to allow the provincial governments to organize one centralized set of

continued

12. R.S.C. 1985, c. S-26, s. 53.

13. *Ibid.*, s. 40.

provincial courts using their constitutional power over the administration of justice. The provincial courts decide cases of first instance (with the exception of the fields reserved exclusively to the Federal and Tax Courts) with federally and provincially appointed judges deciding matters falling within their respective constitutional authorities.

On the other hand, the United States has set up a full system of federal courts—including a court of final appeal, the U.S. Supreme Court—that handles a large portion of litigation, although much less than the total handled by the state courts. Criminal law, for example, is a state matter, except in cases involving specific fields of federal jurisdiction, such as national defence, or in cases where an offence is committed in more than one state, such as moving stolen goods across state boundaries. The federal courts have jurisdiction in the following areas: bankruptcy; postal matters; federal banking laws; disputes concerning maritime contracts or wrongs; prosecution of crimes punishable under federal laws of the United States or committed at sea; actions requiring an interpretation of the U.S. Constitution, federal statutes, and treaties; and disputes between citizens of different states.

Most states also have an independent three-tier system of courts, with a final state appellate court. Unlike in Canada, there is no integration of the state and federal courts. Rarely, appeals are accepted by the U.S. Supreme Court when the appellant can convince the Supreme Court that a "substantial constitutional issue" is involved in a state matter.

Another fundamental difference between the two systems lies in their judicial selection processes. In Canada, all judges are appointed to a life term. Although the process varies somewhat for provincial and federal judges, most appointments begin with an application from a lawyer. The applicant is then screened by a selection committee; selected applicants are often interviewed by the committee. A list of acceptable candidates is then turned over to the Minister of Justice (or the provincial equivalent) who makes the final selection after consultation with Cabinet.

As noted in Chapter 1, the United States Supreme Court judges are appointed to a life term by the President with a public confirmation process through the Senate. This is the system for appointment of all federal judges. However, selection of state judges, which are by far the majority of American judges, varies widely on a state-by-state basis. Most state trial judges are selected for a limited term using some form of election. In New York, the Democratic and Republican parties each select one candidate to represent their party in the state election so that only two names appear on the ballot. On January 16, 2008, the United States Supreme Court upheld this "partisan voting" process in *New York State Board of Elections* v. *Lopez Torres*.[14] In other states, any candidate may run but the electoral district may be so wide that minority voices are suppressed. This system has been criticized in Georgia, Mississippi, and Louisiana. In other states, the governor appoints the judge for the first term and thereafter the judge must face the electorate to be renewed. This is known as retention election. Critics of retention elections worry that judges are tempted to make popular decisions in order to win re-election.

QUESTIONS TO CONSIDER

1. What are the arguments in favour of elected judges?
2. What are the disadvantages of judicial elections?
3. Discuss the pros and cons of life-term appointment.
4. In Chapter 1 we discussed the Ontario Court of Appeal decision that opened the door for same-sex marriage and the subsequent reference sent by Parliament to the Supreme Court of Canada. Why do you think the elected members of Parliament looked to the courts for direction on this issue?

Sources: Randolph N. Jonakait, Chapter 2 in *Checking Abuses of Power: The American Jury System* (New Haven, CT: Yale University Press, 2006); Gordon Van Kessell, "Adversary Excesses in the American Criminal Trial" (1992), 67 *Notre Dame Law Review* 427; Adam Liptak, "Rendering Justice, With One Eye on Re-election," *New York Times*, May 25, 2008, at 1, 13.

14. 2008 U.S.

PROCEDURAL LAW: USING THE COURTS

The following is a general description of the procedures involved in a civil (private) lawsuit. Each province enacts regulations setting out the steps in a lawsuit, including forms, fees, and timelines. These regulations are known as the **rules of civil procedure**. Public law disputes have different procedures.

rules of civil procedure
the provincial regulations that set out the steps in a private lawsuit, including forms, fees, and timelines

Who May Sue?

Not everyone has the capacity to start an action. An adult citizen of Canada has the broadest capacity—virtually unlimited access to the courts for any type of action. Generally speaking, non-Canadians may also sue as freely as citizens. But during hostilities any person found to be an enemy alien loses the right to sue. A child (a person under the age of 18 or 19, depending on the province) is not permitted to bring an action alone but must be represented by an adult person. If a child begins an action not knowing that an adult representative is required, and the error is discovered, the court will "stay" proceedings until a parent or "litigation guardian" (also known as a "next friend") is appointed. Children are presumed not to have the sound judgment needed to undertake the risks of court proceedings; they must rely on an adult person to act on their behalf. Similarly, an insane person cannot sue without a court-appointed representative.

Generally speaking, corporations (bodies incorporated by using procedures under a statute) may sue and be sued, although foreign corporations may be subject to strict regulation and be required to obtain a provincial licence before bringing an action.

In each of these cases, an action is brought by a "person," either for that person's own benefit or for the benefit of another person. For this purpose, a corporation is considered to be a legal "person" or "entity." We refer to an incorporated body as "it" rather than "they"; in other words, it is not thought of as a group of persons but as a single unit. Greater difficulties arise when an action is brought by or against an **unincorporated collectivity**, a group of persons such as a social club, a church, a political party, and perhaps most important, a trade union. In most cases, unincorporated groups are not recognized by the courts and may not sue or be sued. The position of trade unions varies: in some jurisdictions, it is possible to sue and be sued by a trade union, while in others it is not.

unincorporated collectivity
a group of persons that in most cases is not recognized by the courts and that may not sue or be sued

Standing to Sue

Suppose a careless landowner pollutes a stream that runs through a municipal park. If the municipality is reluctant to sue the owner, may an individual resident of the city sue on behalf of herself and all other residents for injury to the park? Suppose a board of censors bans a controversial film. May a resident of the province sue on behalf of himself and other residents who are denied the opportunity to view the film? Do individuals in these circumstances acquire "standing" before the court, and can they establish a right that should be recognized by the court? Generally speaking, courts have been reluctant to permit actions by individuals when their rights are not specifically affected. The courts are concerned that especially litigious and cantankerous members of the public may choose to litigate many matters in which they have no direct interest. An ordinary citizen may be a member of several organizations including a trade union, hold shares in a company, vote as a taxpayer in a community, own land adjacent to public waterways, and be a user of a park and a movie fan. One can imagine many other roles in which an individual might be considered a member of a large group. The judiciary has worried that the courts could become clogged by such actions.

On the other hand, with growing awareness of damage to our environment through pollution and failure to practise conservation, and with the growing complexity of pharmaceutical products, prepared foods, and mechanical devices sold to the public, the risk of serious injury to large groups of persons has grown. Effective means must be available to the public to protect itself from careless and unscrupulous enterprises, especially if it appears that no governmental body is taking adequate steps to protect the public interest.

Some decisions of the Supreme Court of Canada have recognized the right of a taxpayer to sue when he believes public revenues are being improperly used, and the right of a movie viewer to bring an action when he believes his right to see a film has been taken away by a provincial censorship body.[15] This area is in a state of flux, and it is likely to be many years before satisfactory rules have been worked out by the legislatures and the courts to achieve a balance between protecting the public interest and minimizing abuse of the judicial process.

Class Actions[16]

Suppose the owner of a car wishes to sue the manufacturer to recover loss caused by a serious defect in the car, and the defect is known to exist in several thousand other cars of the same model. Should the owner sue not only on his own behalf, but also as representative of a class—that is, on behalf of all the other owners—or must each owner bring his own lawsuit? If he fails in his action, will all other owners necessarily fail, or vice versa? Courts are reluctant to take away an individual's right to litigate his own claim. On the other hand, it would be unfortunate to clog the courts with hundreds, perhaps thousands, of repetitive claims in which all the essential facts and applicable laws had already been clearly established. Sometimes the amount in dispute is individually minor and not worth the cost of a lawsuit unless multiple **plaintiffs** can pool their resources. Grouping parties with similar claims into one action is known as a **class action** and the benefits include avoiding multiple actions and inconsistent results, allowing economic access to justice and deterring wrongful behaviour.

A court must approve the idea of a class action before it can proceed. The court hears argument about whether there is an identifiable class or group, whether there are common issues, and whether a class action would be the preferable procedure. If the court so decides, then the class action is certified and the matter proceeds to trial as one action. The resulting judgment binds all members of the class; it makes the matter ***res judicata*** and the case cannot be brought before the court again to contest legal liability. In our example of the defective car, if liability has already been established, other owners still have the right to have the court assess the amount of damage if the parties could not settle on an amount.[17]

Most provinces have passed legislation to clarify the rules and make it easier to bring class actions.[18] The British Columbia and Ontario acts permit either a plaintiff or a defendant to apply to a court to have himself and others in his group declared to be a "class." However, most class actions are brought by plaintiffs. Defendants complain that class actions encourage frivolous lawsuits that are so expensive to defend, even through just the certification process, that unfounded claims are often settled.

Settlement Out of Court

Advantages

Disagreements, injuries to persons and property, and breaches of many laws give rise to legal claims and they take place daily in vast numbers, but aggrieved parties litigate only a small proportion of them. Even when parties start court proceedings, the disputes rarely go to trial. (In the City of London, England, fewer than 1 percent of legal proceedings continue to trial.) Do all the remaining

plaintiff
the party that commences a private (civil) legal action against another party

class action
an action in which an individual represents a group of possible plaintiffs and the judgment decides the matter for all members of the class at once

res judicata
a case that has already been decided by a court and cannot be brought before a court again

---

15. *Nova Scotia Board of Censors v. MacNeil* (1975), 55 D.L.R. (3d) 632; *Minister of Justice of Canada v. Borowski* (1981), 130 D.L.R. (3d) 588; Finlay v. Minister of Finance, [1986] 2 S.C.R. 607; *Canadian Council of Churches v. Canada*, [1992] 1 S.C.R. 236.

16. W.K. Branch, *Class Actions in Canada* (Vancouver: Western Legal Publications, 1996); C. Jones, *Theory of Class Actions* (Toronto: Irwin Law, 2003).

17. The difficulties in maintaining a class action in such circumstances are well illustrated by the decision of the Supreme Court of Canada in *Naken* v. *General Motors of Canada Ltd.* (1983), 144 D.L.R. (3d) 385. For comment, see Fox, (1984), 6 S.C.L.R. 335.

18. Class Proceedings Act, R.S.B.C. 1996, c. 50; S.M. 2002, c. 130; S.O. 1992, c. 6; S.S. 2001, c. 12.01.

settlement

an out-of-court procedure by which one of the parties agrees to pay a sum of money or perform an act in return for a waiver by the other party of all rights arising from the grievance

aggrieved persons simply abandon their rights? On the contrary, the great majority of serious grievances are resolved by **settlement**.

Settlement is an out-of-court procedure by which one of the parties agrees to pay a sum of money or do certain things in return for a waiver by the other party of all rights arising from the grievance. This process has always been important as it is speedy and definite and avoids the expense of litigation. Each party to a settlement also avoids the risk that the court will find against him. Since there are two sides to a story, and since the issues are rarely black and white, almost always there is some uncertainty in predicting which side will win. Of course, the stronger one party's claim appears to be, the more advantageous a settlement it will demand and usually obtain. Often a person starts legal proceedings to convince her adversary that she will not put up with delays or an inadequate settlement. As a result, many actions are settled soon after they are started.

Why then are the courts and the relatively small body of decisions resulting from an enormous number of disputes so important? There are two main reasons: first, the decided cases supply the principles by which aggrieved parties may gauge the relative merit of their claims, predict the outcome of a possible court action, and strike a value for their claims; second, the court is the last resort, the decisive tribunal when all compromise fails. It settles the issue when the parties themselves cannot.

Growing Delay in the Court System

Despite the obvious advantages of settling disputes out of court, the number of cases going to trial has increased steadily over the years, indeed much faster than the growth in population. There are a number of reasons suggested for more frequent resort to the courts, such factors as the higher general level of education and the greater awareness of one's rights, especially since the Charter of Rights and Freedoms became part of our Constitution; the increased complexity of society and of the legal system generally; and the need for many new regulatory schemes. The large increase in the number of cases has led to a backlog causing very long delays in actually getting most cases heard. In the 1950s, cases were generally heard within a few months; rarely did a year pass without a case going to trial. In contrast, currently delays of several years have become the norm. Even trials for relatively small claims that take little time to be heard often wait many months—sometimes more than a year—to be heard. Many provinces have designed simplified procedures and case management systems to move matters to trial more quickly.[19]

Delay often creates hardship: a plaintiff who has suffered serious injury may wait many years to be compensated; it may become much more difficult for witnesses to recall evidence; indeed sometimes one of the parties may die before the case is heard. As a result, new rules have been enacted to encourage settlement.[20] The rules penalize parties who do not accept a reasonable offer of settlement. So, if a party rejects a reasonable offer to settle from the other party and the court's subsequent judgment shows that the offer was a good one—that is, it orders substantially the same remedy as the offer made—the first party will be ordered to pay the costs (as discussed under that heading later in this chapter) incurred by the other party.

Parties have themselves become increasingly aware of the advantages of avoiding court battles and, since the 1970s, often choose to utilize "alternative dispute resolution," discussed under that heading later in this chapter.

Procedure Before Trial

Most business people will gratefully concede that the intricacies of procedure are properly the responsibility of lawyers. Even so, an overall understanding of what the various steps in legal procedure aim

19. Ontario has a simplified procedure for matters under $50 000. British Columbia has a pilot project testing a simplified procedure for Small Claims under $5 000. Case management systems set timelines for completion of each step of the process failing which the matter is dismissed.

20. Rule 57 (18), B.C. Rules of the Supreme Court; Rule 49, Rules of Civil Procedure, Ont.; Rule 49, Rules of Court, N.S.

to accomplish should help business administrators to work more effectively with their legal advisers. In addition, business law students may be needlessly puzzled when they study cases by the occasional reference to procedure if they do not have a general idea of its function.

Rules of procedure remain an important part of the law because a well-defined procedure is necessary to permit the courts to work efficiently. Procedure has now been simplified and the number of steps in legal proceedings greatly reduced. Special procedures are still used to interpret wills, contracts, and other documents and for certain proceedings under statutes. Most litigation, however, proceeds through the courts in a form called an action, and most actions are begun by **issuing** and **serving** a writ or a statement of claim.[21] The statement of claim describes the reason for the action or the **cause of action**. A cause of action is an event or set of events that gives rise to legal liability. The statement of claim must describe both the facts and the legal principles that impose liability.

issuing
commencing the lawsuit by filing a copy of the statement of claim with the court office

serving
providing a copy of the issued claim to each defendant

cause of action
an event or set of events that gives rise to legal liability

ILLUSTRATION 2.3

Tom buys an apple from a farmer, eats it, and becomes ill. Tom may commence an action for compensation for his suffering, lost time from work, and cost of medicine. The statement of claim must describe the facts of the event and the particulars of his loss. When, where, and from whom was the apple purchased? These would be the relevant facts. In addition, the claim must refer to the legal principles that apply to the situation and create liability. In Tom's case, the claim would refer to the rules of contract law, product liability, and sale of goods that require a product to be fit for the purpose that it was sold.

A trial does not follow automatically from a decision to start an action. After a plaintiff decides to sue and has a writ or statement of claim issued by the court, the document is then served on the defendant. In this way, the defendant learns by whom and for what he is being sued, so that he can prepare to defend himself; the plaintiff cannot proceed until the notice has been served. It is obvious that as soon as one is served with a writ or statement of claim one should immediately consult a lawyer. It is a well-known saying that "he who acts on his own behalf has a fool for a client." Lawyers have learned that people are so mesmerized by their own cause that they cannot properly evaluate their claims; in personal matters, one lawyer almost always has another lawyer act as representative.

Once a plaintiff has formally commenced an action and served the required documents on the defendant, why should they not go to trial immediately? For one thing, court trials are expensive; the time of the plaintiff and defendant, their **counsel** (lawyers), the judge, and other officers of the court is valuable. It would be wasteful to use time in court to do things that can be done more quickly and cheaply out of court. It is worthwhile to try to discover exactly what the disagreement is about; otherwise the parties waste time arguing about some things on which they agree. Pre-trial procedure attempts to narrow the trial precisely to those matters on which the parties are at odds. The necessary steps are as follows:

counsel
lawyer representing a plaintiff or defendant

(a) If the action was started by a writ, the defendant gives notice both to the clerk of the court and to the plaintiff that he intends to contest the action by **entering (filing) an appearance**. The plaintiff then delivers a statement of claim. (In the current Ontario procedure, an action begins with a statement of claim—eliminating the need for the first two documents, a writ and an appearance.) In the statement of claim, the plaintiff sets out in detail the facts that she alleges have given rise to her cause of action and the damages suffered by her. The defendant replies with a **statement of defence**, admitting those facts not in dispute in the statement of claim and denying all others, and in addition setting out any other facts that the defendant intends to prove in court in support of his

entering (filing) an appearance
filing notice of an intention to contest an action

statement of defence
a reply to a statement of claim, admitting facts not in dispute, denying other facts, and setting out facts in support of the defence

---

21. Several provinces have simplified the process by abolishing the writ as a means of starting an action. The process now begins with issue of a statement of claim.

defence. Referring to Illustration 2.3, the farmer may admit to selling the apple but deny that it was the apple that made Tom sick. The statement of defence may also dispute the law. The plaintiff may then deliver a reply countering the added facts alleged by the defendant and adding any further facts believed necessary to cope with the defence. Often the defendant may have a claim of his own arising from the same facts. He will then **counterclaim** as well as defend. In turn the plaintiff will defend the counterclaim. Both claims will then be tried together.

counterclaim
a claim by the defendant arising from the same facts as the original action by the plaintiff to be tried along with that action

(b) The documents are assembled to form the main body of **pleadings**. Their purpose is to make clear exactly what each party intends to prove in court so that an adequate counter-attack can be prepared if available. The Hollywood element of surprise is contrary to the principle of law that each side should have sufficient notice to put its view of the facts before the court. If a party attempts to introduce surprise evidence, the court may refuse to hear it; or if it admits the evidence, it will usually delay proceedings to give the other side an opportunity to reply and will also penalize the party with loss of costs. Pleadings often reveal an aspect of the claim of which the other side was unaware. For example, the plaintiff may claim to have an important receipt book in her possession. The rules of procedure compel the plaintiff upon demand to surrender it to the defendant for inspection. In some circumstances a party may demand further particulars of a claim so that it can be evaluated more clearly.

pleadings
documents filed by each party to an action providing information it intends to prove in court

examination for discovery
processes allowing either party to examine the other in order to narrow the issues

(c) Some provinces provide for various forms of **examination for discovery**, processes allowing either party to examine the other in order to narrow the issues further and to decide whether to proceed with a trial. Discovery allows a party to learn about the strength of the other party's case so that an informed decision about settlement can be made. Each party must also produce their list of witnesses and relevant documents. Discovery of documents involves locating documents, preserving them, reviewing them for relevance, and producing them to the other side. Increasingly relevant documents are in electronic form, and production of these documents has become known as e-discovery.

Once both sides have satisfied themselves that the action should go to trial, they ask court officials to place the case on the docket for the next sitting of the court.

(d) Most provinces require a pre-trial or settlement conference with a judge or mediator after discovery is complete. During this meeting, the issues in dispute are reviewed in an attempt to settle as many as possible or at least narrow the issues so that any eventual trial will be shorter.

The Trial

The trial is the culmination of the action. Parties bring their evidence of all facts in dispute before the court. In private actions the burden of proof is on the plaintiff to prove her case. The standard of proof is the balance of probabilities or more likely than not. This is done by bringing all the evidence of favourable facts before the court. The plaintiff must be prepared to argue that these facts, once established, prove the claim in law. (Of course, counsel for the plaintiff must decide beforehand what facts she must prove in support of the claim.) The defendant, on the other hand, must attempt to establish another version of the facts or at least to minimize the value of the evidence submitted by the plaintiff. The gap between the versions of the two parties is often astonishing. Sometimes the defendant will argue that even if the facts are as the plaintiff claims, they do not support the claim in law. For example, suppose the defendant had swerved his car off the road at night because of oncoming lights. He might argue that although his conduct was as the plaintiff claimed, it did not constitute negligence but on the contrary had been quite reasonable under the circumstances.

Evidence is brought before the court by examining witnesses. Counsel for the plaintiff calls as witnesses those persons whose testimony is favourable to the client. Counsel for the defendant may then cross-examine those witnesses to bring out any aspects of their testimony that were neglected and that may serve the defendant's position. Counsel for the plaintiff may then re-examine the witnesses to clarify any points dealt with in the cross-examination. Counsel for the defendant may also call witnesses of his own.

Certain types of evidence are not **admissible** because they are prejudicial without adding anything to the facts in dispute or because they are **hearsay**; that is, they are words attributed by the witness to a person not before the court. The basis for the hearsay rule is the view that the credibility of oral evidence cannot be properly assessed when it is secondhand, and that one who is alleged to have made an assertion should testify in person and be subject to cross-examination and the scrutiny of the court. The rules of admissibility of evidence are intended to winnow bad evidence from good. Unfortunately, in the process they have become technical, more so in the United States than in Canada.

When the court has heard all the evidence, counsel then present the arguments in law favouring their respective clients. In simple cases the judge may give the decision at once or after a short recess, but in complicated and important cases the judge usually **reserves judgment** in order to have time to study the notes of the facts and legal arguments, and to compare the opinions in decided cases and textbooks. The judgment is often given orally in the court; decisions in important cases are always given in written form as well and are reprinted in the law reports.

Appeals

If either or both parties wish to appeal, they must make up their minds and serve notice within a time limit, usually 30 days or less.

As we have seen, most appeals take the form of a review by an appeal court of evidence forwarded to it from the trial courts. An appeal court also reviews proceedings of the trial court when a party contends that the trial judge erred in instructing the jury or in admitting or excluding certain evidence; if it agrees, the appeal court may order the case sent back to a new trial, directing the judge to correct the shortcomings of the first trial.

Costs

Who Provides Funds for the Court System?

Quite apart from the time and effort of the parties who are adversaries in the court—their time away from employment and the lost energy—a lawsuit occupies the time of highly trained and expensive judges and court officials, lawyers, and their staffs.

In an important sense, the courts provide a public service, a forum for peacefully settling disputes with the aid of government supervision and enforcement. The courts provide an essential alternative to parties taking matters into their own hands, with the probable risks of violence. Our governments pay the expenses of sustaining the court system, including the salaries of judges, registrars, clerks, and other employees, as well as the maintenance of court buildings. Litigants pay a portion of these overhead **costs** through charges made for specific items, such as issuing a writ or registering a judgment against a losing defendant in order to enforce a claim.

Solicitor–Client Fees

Litigants themselves pay the costs of hiring their own lawyers, although, as we shall see, an important development has been the system of **legal aid**, where the government pays for many legal services provided to low-income litigants. A client pays a lawyer a **solicitor–client fee**—payment for time the lawyer spends discussing the case with the client, helping the client decide whether to pursue or defend the action, and agreeing to be retained—that is, to represent the client in negotiations to settle or in a court action. As well, there are usually various expenses associated with a court case, such as time required to prepare for trial, court charges, travel costs when the case is heard or when

---

admissible evidence
evidence that is acceptable to the court

hearsay
words attributed by a witness to a person who is not before the court

reserve judgment
postpone giving a decision after the hearing ends

costs
funds paid by litigants to cover a portion of the government's expenses in maintaining the court system

legal aid
a system where the government pays for many legal services provided to low-income litigants

solicitor–client fee
payment for the time and expenses of a lawyer in preparing a case and representing the client in negotiations to settle or in court

evidence must be obtained at another location, and the usual array of out-of-pocket costs, all of which must be paid by the litigant. These direct costs of litigation are often substantial, especially if the original hearing is followed by an appeal, and, as we shall discuss below, they play an important part in an individual's decision whether to proceed with a lawsuit.

Party and Party Costs

Suppose a person is sued and defends himself successfully, with the court dismissing the action brought by the plaintiff. Should he be left with all the expense of defending an action that the court rejected?

Or suppose a party demands payment for an injury wrongfully inflicted on her; the other party denies any liability; she then sues successfully. Should she have to bear the expense of a court action to recover a sum that the other party ought to have paid without making it necessary to go to court?

English and Canadian law subscribe to the "loser pays" rule. This means that at least part of the winning party's legal costs should be shifted to the losing side by an award known as **party and party costs**.[22] In each province there is a published scale of costs, varying with the level of court in which the case is heard, for the preparation of court documents by the lawyer and for standard payment for each hour of preparation for presenting a case and for each appearance or day in court. Accordingly, when a plaintiff wins a case for, say, damages in a traffic accident, the court will award "x dollars damages, plus costs," against the defendant. If the defendant successfully defends the action, the court will dismiss the claim "with costs"—that is, party and party costs against the plaintiff. If the result of the action is a mixed one—for example, a plaintiff's claim succeeds in part and is rejected in part—the costs may be apportioned, or each party may be left to pay its own costs.

party and party costs
an award that shifts some of the costs of litigation to the losing side according to a published scale of fees

Total Costs of Litigation

A solicitor–client fee is almost always greater than an award of party and party costs. Therefore, even when a client wins a case with an award of costs in her favour, these costs will ordinarily cover only a portion of the fee charged by her lawyer; she will have to pay an amount over and above the costs recovered from the losing side. But she is considerably better off than the losing side with respect to the costs of the litigation; the loser must pay *both* party and party costs to the other side *and* a solicitor–client fee to his own lawyer, as well as, of course, the amount of the judgment. In rare cases, when a judge believes the losing party behaved unreasonably, solicitor–client costs will be awarded. This means that the loser must pay the winner's entire solicitor–client fees.

Occasionally a client may believe that his lawyer has charged too high a fee for representing him in a court action, and the two are unable to reach a satisfactory settlement of the bill. If necessary, the client can have the matter referred to an officer of the court to assess the bill—that is, to set a fair fee for the service rendered in the action.

Legal Aid

Legal services, like all other services available in our society, require time and resources and cost money. Some services, such as public education and police and fire protection, have long been available without fee. Since the 1960s, basic medical and hospital services have also been provided to every resident in each province of Canada. Our view of what basic services ought to be available to everyone has enlarged over the years, especially in times of prosperity. However, there has been a growing concern—indeed controversy—about whether our economy can continue to support all the public services offered in recent decades; a number of services, including legal aid, have been cut back, and the level of services that will be available in the future is uncertain.

---

22. See G.D. Watson, and W. Bogart et al., *Civil Litigation*, 4th ed. (Toronto: Emond Montgomery, 1991) at Chapter 4.

Until the late 1960s, legal services had been available almost exclusively to those who could afford to pay. Low-income earners could not afford legal services; what services they did receive were usually in the form of charity from lawyers who were willing to provide assistance free of charge to persons in dire circumstances. Ontario began a large-scale, publicly funded legal aid scheme in 1967, and most other provinces followed suit within a few years. Legal aid is of limited importance to business law because legal aid will not cover business disputes nor most private law matters.

There are two different models of legal aid, both used extensively in Canada and often in combination. The Ontario model—sometimes known as the **judicare** model—has been adopted by several other provinces as the dominant method of delivering legal services. Under this model, the names of lawyers willing to work for "legal aid rates" are placed on a list. Approved legal aid clients choose their lawyers from this list and the government pays the lawyer at a substantially reduced legal aid rate regulated by the legal aid legislation. The client must apply to legal aid and obtain a certificate to qualify for the program. Only criminal, quasi-criminal, and family law matters typically qualify for legal aid certificates.[23]

The second model—known as the **community legal services** or **legal clinic model**—is used in Saskatchewan. In this model the government funds clinics staffed with full-time lawyers who spend all of their time providing legal services to qualified low-income clients. Both models have advantages and disadvantages so provinces tend to use a combination.[24]

The Economics of Civil Litigation

The subject of costs raises the question of the economics of litigation: is it worthwhile to start an action? This is a key business law risk management question. First, there is always a risk of losing: a plaintiff who loses is not only denied the remedy sought, but also must pay costs of the defendant. Even if the party seems certain of winning, it would generally be unwise to proceed with a claim that would occupy the time of the courts and incur heavy expenses in retaining a lawyer in order to collect a minor sum, pursue an impecunious defendant, or, conversely, to defend an insignificant claim.[25]

Second, even apart from legal costs, businesses must examine the business costs of litigation. Often it may not be worth a business's time and effort to fight. For instance, a supplier of perishable goods such as potatoes might be offered payment of a reduced price by a buyer who claims that the potatoes had not arrived in as good condition as promised. The supply firm might decide that it is not worth the trouble to sue for the difference in price of, say, $200; nor, for that matter, would it wish to alienate the buyer, a good customer. It simply accepts the reduced price in full payment. On the other hand, the supply firm may think it necessary to fight the minor claim in order to discourage other claims.

A strategy should be developed considering the impact of the litigation on all segments of the business. If the supply firm has had several similar complaints from customers and is concerned that the carrier has been careless in transporting the potatoes, it may decide to change carriers or to claim against the carrier. If the carrier should deny liability, the supplier would find it necessary to sue the carrier and "join" the buyer in the same suit in order to obtain a ruling from the court about the degree of care that the carrier is bound to show, as well as what amounts to satisfactory condition of the potatoes on delivery. In other words, a party may have additional reasons besides the actual recovery of an award of damages for bringing an action for a relatively small sum.

judicare
a model of legal aid in which lawyers agree to be paid according to government fee schedules for serving clients who qualify for legal aid

community legal services or legal clinic
a model of legal aid where legal services are delivered by community law offices with full-time staff lawyers and managed by boards elected by residents of the community

23. G.D. Watson and N.J. Williams, *Canadian Civil Procedure*, 2nd ed. (Toronto: Butterworths, 1977), pp. 2–70. See also 4th ed. (1991), Supplement (1997), pp. 231–70.

24. F. Zemans, "Legal Aid and Legal Advice in Canada" (1978) 16 Osgoode Hall L.J. 633.

25. For discussion about the costs of litigation, see P. Puri, "Financing of Litigation by Third-Party Investors: A Share of Justice?" (1998) 36 Osgoode Hall L.J. 515 (the Introduction).

Contingent Fees 成功報酬

Origins in the United States

In the United States, most courts do not follow the "loser pays" rule; a party, whether winner or loser, is required to pay only his own lawyer's fees. As a result **contingency fees** were developed to give access to justice to impecunious litigants who might otherwise be denied the chances to pursue their claims.

Critics argue that prospective litigants clog American courts with large claims even when the chances of success are poor; a plaintiff who fails does not risk having to pay the defendant's costs. At the same time, the American system of costs "fails to compensate justly the winner whose claim has been vindicated, and it discourages the litigation of small claims."[26]

Under a contingency fee arrangement, "the lawyer agrees to act on the basis that if the client is successful the lawyer will take as a fee a certain percentage of the proceeds of the litigation, and in the event that the client is unsuccessful the lawyer will make no charge for the services rendered."[27] From a prospective litigant's point of view—especially in a case where there may be a fairly poor chance of winning, but if an award is made, it will likely be for a large sum—a contingent fee arrangement may be the only practical way of bringing an action. A lawyer may take several cases and will be content to win one; the single contingent fee will cover his expenses in all the cases and leave him with substantial compensation for his work.

contingent or contingency fee
a fee paid for a lawyer's services only if the client is successful; there is no charge if the client is unsuccessful

ILLUSTRATION 2.4 スキーハイか

A is injured very seriously while skiing on an open slope. She complains that the accident was caused by an unmarked obstacle. Very likely, a court would find either that she accepted the risks voluntarily or that she was the author of her own misfortune through personal carelessness. Even so, if *A* is in a jurisdiction where a contingent fee agreement is available to her, she might well find it practical to bring an action on the small chance that the court would find the resort owner liable for the injury. She would probably not be able to afford the expense of litigation under the traditional Anglo-Canadian scheme for charging fees.

The Use of Contingent Fees in Canada

Canada was slow to adopt contingency fees as a result of concerns that such arrangements

- encourage unnecessary and even frivolous litigation;
- expose defendants to the costs of defending themselves against claims that have no merit;
- encourage some clients to agree to unconscionably large percentage fees demanded by their lawyers;
- drive up the cost of settlements and court awards and thus affect insurance premiums;
- cloud the judgment of the lawyer who becomes a stakeholder in the litigation.

However, access to justice arguments prevailed, and most Canadian provinces now accept contingency fee arrangements, subject to supervision by the courts.[28] In 2004, Ontario was the last province to endorse contingency fees; the cap in Ontario states that the fee cannot exceed the amount of the plaintiff's recovery.[29] Although no statistics are available, it is generally agreed that contingency fees are most often used in class actions and the combination has led critics to lament

---

26. *Supra*, note 22, p. 265.

27. *Ibid.*, p. 253.

28. Justice Statute Law Amendment Act, 2002, S.O. 2002 c. 24; O. Reg. 195/2004; Solicitors Act, R.S.O. 1990, c. S-15 as amen. See also: M. Trebilcock, "The Case for Contingent Fees: The Ontario Legal Profession Rethinks Its Position" (1985) 15 *Can. Bar L.J.* 360–8.

29. "A slice of the settlement: contingency fees across Canada," Vol. 13, No. 9, October 1986, *National* 12. Ottawa: The Canadian Bar Foundation.

the explosion of American-style litigation. Criticism has focused on class actions involving individually minor claims where it appears that the lawyers make millions.[30]

ALTERNATIVE DISPUTE RESOLUTION 解决方式

For many years, there have been informal ways to resolve disputes rather than resorting to the courts and, by the 1970s, the rising costs and delays involved in using the court system encouraged a new emphasis on the alternatives. Today, many parties to disputes agree not to go to court and instead to use the private procedures of *alternative dispute resolution*, known as **ADR**. The oldest form of ADR is **arbitration**—referring a dispute to an arbitrator who will **adjudicate** the matter; the arbitrator will hear the parties, much as in a court case but usually with less formality and more promptly, and will deliver a decision with reasons. The decisions bind only the parties involved and are confidential. Arbitration was developed specifically with the business disputant in mind. The goal is party auton- 自治 omy; parties design their own process by selecting the rules, the forum, the arbitrator, and even the law that will be applied to the dispute. Often parties agree, through a term in their contract, to refer to an arbitrator any dispute that may arise under the agreement. In the absence of a pre-dispute term they may agree after a dispute arises to refer the matter to arbitration. Arbitration is also used in public sector disputes, in such areas as labour relations, workers' compensation, and international commerce (as discussed in Chapter 33). Normally, the parties agree in advance to be bound by the arbitrator's decision, but under some plans, a party may appeal to the courts.[31] 调解 师

An increasingly important form of ADR is **mediation**. In mediation, a neutral third party acceptable to both sides acts as mediator during settlement negotiations. The mediator has no power to make a binding decision, but assists the parties in reaching a settlement. This is the ultimate form of party autonomy where parties not only design the process like arbitration but also design their own settlement. The mediator hears both parties, identifies and clarifies the issues, and explores middle ground that might be acceptable. Mediation can be evaluative—where the mediator offers an opinion on the substance of the dispute—or it may be facilitative—where the mediator guides the process only. It may focus on the rights of the parties but it will often include an interest-based discussion. Mediation allows imaginative settlements not possible in courts and considers interests and factors beyond who would win in a courtroom.

The process usually begins with the mediator and both sides present, and after preliminary remarks by the mediator, each side presents its position; the mediator usually asks questions and tries to clarify those areas where the parties may agree and disagree. Separate meetings may be held with each side to explore the prospects of agreement. All parties must adhere to basic rules of respect and confidentiality for an effective mediation. 促进方式

While informal mediation has been used to settle disputes for many years, in the last two decades it has developed into a sophisticated procedure, and the success rate of reaching settlement is relatively high. There is now a very large volume of literature on the subject.[32] As well, there are training courses available across Canada at universities and through associations of mediators.

ADR
alternative dispute resolution—using private procedures instead of the courts to resolve disputes

arbitration
a form of ADR where a dispute is referred to an arbitrator who adjudicates the matter and the parties agree to be bound by the arbitrator's decision, although there may be a right to appeal to the courts

adjudicate
hear parties and deliver a decision with reasons

mediation
a form of ADR where a neutral third party who is acceptable to both sides acts as a mediator, assisting the parties to reach a settlement

30. S.G. McKee, *The Canadian Challenge Class Actions in Canada A Potentially Momentous Change to Canadian Legislation, Law and Markets: Is Canada Inheriting America's Litigious Legacy* (J. Robson, O. Libbert, ed., The Fraser Institute, Vancouver, Canada, 1997), available online at: http://oldfraser.lexi.net/publications/books/laws_markets/canadian_challenge.html (accessed February 13, 2008).

31. John C. Carson, "Dispute Resolution, Negotiation, Mediation and Arbitration in Ontario" (1993) 10(1) Business and the Law 1.

32. The 2001 Ministry of the Attorney General Evaluation of the Ontario Mandatory Mediation Program reported a 40% settlement rate, online at: www.attorneygeneral.jus.gov.on.ca/english/courts/manmed/exec_summary_recommend.pdf (accessed February 13, 2008). The following three recent books are high-quality examples: G. Adams, *Mediating Justice: Legal Dispute Negotiations* (Toronto: CCH Canadian Ltd., 2003); R.M. Nelson, *Nelson on ADR* (Scarborough: Thomson Carswell, 2003); C. Picard et al., *The Art and Science of Mediation* (Toronto: Emond Montgomery Publications Ltd., 2004); A.J. Pirie, *Alternative Dispute Resolution Skills, Science and The Law* (Toronto: Irwin Law, 2000).

To be effective, a mediator must have the respect and confidence of both parties; key qualities are impartiality, sensitivity to each side's concerns, the ability to understand and analyze the disagreement, and the ability to present a creative approach to suggesting solutions.

Mediation has become very attractive to parties in disputes although sometimes it can be abused: a party who does not really want to settle the dispute may agree to mediation in order to gain time by delay. When mediation fails, the parties ordinarily resort to arbitration or the courts.

The advantages of ADR, both arbitration and mediation, are:

- *speed*—cases are resolved by mediation or arbitration much more promptly than through the courts
- *cost*—promptness in itself saves money; in addition, since the parties themselves have chosen this method, they usually co-operate to avoid delays and keep the hearing as short as they can
- *choice of adjudicator or mediator*—unlike the courts, the parties can choose a person whom they believe is especially suited to resolve the issue because of her experience and expertise in the area of the dispute
- *confidentiality*—the parties can agree to keep the dispute private to minimize harm to their business through disclosure of confidential information or encouraging others to bring similar complaints
- *preserving ongoing relations*—since ADR is usually less adversarial than litigation, it is less likely to foster antagonism between the parties, and will allow them to continue to work together afterwards[33]

ADR has become important to legal risk management not only because of the forgoing advantages but also because of its wide availability and enforceability. The ADR movement, in particular arbitration, grew out of commercial business disputes and was driven by the inability of domestic legal systems to handle international business disputes. Federal and provincial arbitration legislation was passed to promote arbitration and recognize and enforce arbitration awards through the courts.[34] Since the early 1990s Canadian courts have followed a policy in favour of arbitration by upholding and enforcing arbitration agreements.[35] Organizations such as the International Chamber of Commerce facilitate arbitration among private sector international business partners. Domestically, private sector providers are widely available through organizations such as ADR Chambers and American Arbitration Forum, to name just a couple. Better Business Bureaus around the country offer ADR services to their members. By placing an ADR clause in a business agreement, businesses can take a proactive approach to legal risk management and ensure that if a dispute does arise it will not be resolved in the courts.

Mediation is also being embraced by the court systems. In Ontario, every civil (private) and estate action commenced in Toronto, Ottawa, and Windsor must undergo a three-hour mandatory mediation session before it may be set for trial. Saskatchewan also has a mandatory mediation program for civil actions filed in the Court of Queen's Bench. In Alberta, all Small Claims Court actions are screened and selected actions must enter mandatory mediation; civil actions in the

33. For a general overview, see D. Paul Emond, *Commercial Dispute Resolution: Alternatives to Litigation* (Aurora, ON: Canada Law Book, 1989) or A. J. Pirie, *supra* note 32.

34. Commercial Arbitration Act, R.S.B.C. 1996, ch. 55 (CAA); Arbitration Act, R.S.A. 2000, c. A-43; Arbitration Act, 1992, S.S. 1992, c. A-24.1; Arbitration Act, C.C.S.M. c. A120; Arbitration Act, R.S.Y. 2002, c. 8; Arbitration Act, R.S.N.W.T. 1988, c. A-5; Arbitration Act, S.N.B. 1992, c. A-10.1; Arbitration Act, R.S.N.S. 1989, c.19; Arbitration Act, R.S.P.E.I., 1988, c. A-16; Arbitration Act, R.S.N.L. 1990, c.A-14; Quebec Code of Civil Procedure, R.S.Q. c. C-25, art. 940—951.2. (Arbitration legislation).

35. *Ontario Hydro* v. *Denison Mines Ltd,* [1992] O.J. No. 2948 at para. 8; See *Deluce Holdings Inc.* v. *Air Canada,* [1992] O.J. No. 2382; *Buck Bros. Ltd.* v. *Frontenac Builders,* [1994] O.J. No. 37; *Onex Corp.* v. *Ball Corp* (1994), 12 B.L.R. (2nd) 151; *Canadian National Railway Co.* v. *Lovat Tunnel Equipment Inc.*(1999), 174 D.L.R. (4th) 385 (Ont C.A.); *Diamond & Diamond* v. *Srebrolow,* [2003] O.J. No. 4004.

Alberta Court of Queen's Bench may be moved to mediation by either party upon the filing of a notice. These provinces maintain rosters of approved mediators.[36]

Still, ADR has its limits and its critics. It is not right for every dispute. Situations that involve an imbalance of power between the parties can result in abuse. Parties may be forced unwillingly into ADR or they may be bullied into undesirable settlements in mediation. Therefore, restrictions and protections have been put in place for certain types of conflicts. Family disputes cannot be arbitrated in Quebec, and Ontario has created a specially regulated and supervised form of family arbitration.[37] Consumers are another group that are being protected from mandatory ADR processes with several provinces refusing to enforce pre-dispute arbitration clauses.[38]

ETHICAL ISSUE

Access to Justice

One fundamental tenet in democratic nations is that all people should have access to justice, or, as one popular maxim states: "Everyone is entitled to their day in court." What does this mean? Is it enough that courts exist and are available for use? Are courts synonymous with justice? What about alternative dispute resolution processes? Several topics in this chapter raise questions such as "What is access to justice?" and "When has it been denied?" If courts and lawyers are too expensive, is access to justice denied?

Some of the provinces have taken steps to reduce the cost of litigation. For example, British Columbia has simplified rules of procedure for claims of $100 000 or less and Ontario is considering raising the limit of its simplified procedure from $50 000 to $100 000. Simplified procedures expedite the path to trial with early disclosure requirements, limited pre-trial procedures, and reduction in the length of trials. Alberta has raised its Small Claims Court limit to $25 000. Ontario has undertaken some mandatory mediation pilot projects. The hope is that many cases will be settled in mediation, at less cost to the parties and to the public. The Alberta Provincial Court—Civil Division may refer parties to mediation of its own accord or at a party's request. The British Columbia Superior Court promotes the use of settlement conferences conducted by a judge or a master (a judicial officer who presides over certain types of proceedings).

What if disputants cannot access these simplified initiatives? Over the last decade it has become common for big companies to insert mandatory arbitration clauses and waivers of class actions into consumer contracts so that consumers must arbitrate their disputes. Dell Computers and Rogers Cable have both had such clauses upheld by the courts, effectively preventing consumers from processing lawsuits against them.[39] Is this effective legal risk management or a denial of consumer access to justice or both? Balancing the interests of business and consumer is not easy.

continued

---

36. Rule 24.1 and 75.1 Ontario Rules of Civil Procedure; Alberta Civil Practice Note No.11; The Queen's Bench Act, 1998, S.S. 1998, c. Q-1.01, s. 42.

37. Article 2639, *Civil Code of Quebec*, S.O. 1991, c. 64; Family Statute Law Amendment Act, 2006, S.O. 2006 c.1.; O. Reg. 134/07.

38. Ontario banned pre-dispute consumer arbitration clauses and class action waivers on July 31, 2005: Consumer Protection Act, 2002, S.O. 2002, c. 30, ss. 7, 8. Quebec banned them on December 14, 2006: Consumer Protection Act, R.S.Q. c. P-40.1, s. 11.1. Alberta has legislation requiring government approval of consumer arbitration clauses: Fair Trading Act, R.S.A. 2000, C. F-2, s. 16.

39. *Dell Computers* v. *Union des consommateurs* 2007 SCC 34; *Kanitz* v. *Rogers Cable Inc.* (2002) 58 O.R. (3d) 299 (ON. S.C.J.).

THE LEGAL PROFESSION

solicitor
an "office" lawyer in England who interviews clients, carries on legal aspects of business and family affairs, and prepares cases for trial

barrister
a lawyer in England who accepts cases from solicitors and presents them in court, and also acts as consultant in complex legal issues

brief
a case handed by a solicitor to a barrister

notary
a solicitor in Quebec

advocate
a barrister in Quebec

attorney
a lawyer in the United States, encompassing the roles of both barrister and solicitor

disbarred
expelled from the law society and deprived of the privilege of practising law

solicitor–client privilege
a client's right to have all communications with his or her lawyer kept confidential

Every legal risk management plan involves the use of legal experts. In England, the legal profession is divided into two groups, *solicitors* and *barristers*. **Solicitors** are "office" lawyers. They spend most of their time interviewing clients and carrying on the legal aspects of business and family affairs. They look after the drafting of wills, deeds, and contracts, the incorporation of companies, arrangements for adoption of children, and other domestic documents. They also prepare cases for trial, draft pleadings, complete research, interview witnesses, and make extensive notes for trial. In addition, they argue cases in some of the lower courts. **Barristers** take **briefs**—that is, cases handed to them by solicitors—and present them in court. They also give opinions with respect to potential litigation and are consulted by solicitors on a wide variety of more complex legal issues such as corporate mergers and tax planning.

In the Canadian common law provinces, all lawyers are qualified as both barristers and solicitors; they may carry out the duties of both professions and often do so, especially in smaller cities and towns. In larger cities, lawyers tend to specialize in particular areas of the law; lawyers who specialize in private (civil) trials are known as "litigation" lawyers. Under the civil law of Quebec, the profession is divided in approximately the same way as in England. Quebec has **notaries** (solicitors) and **advocates** (barristers). In the United States the distinction has broken down completely. A lawyer is not even called "barrister and solicitor" as in Canada, but is simply an **attorney**.

The legal profession is organized on a provincial basis in Canada. Each province has its own "bar" (barristers' society or law society), and by provincial statute one must qualify and be licensed as a member in order to practise law. Membership in one provincial bar does not permit a lawyer to practise in another province. A member in one province must meet the standards and pay the fees of the provincial bar in another province before practising in that province. Most provincial law societies allow out-of-province lawyers to carry on some minor activity within the province. A member of any provincial bar, however, may appear before the Supreme Court of Canada.

Law societies set professional standards of behaviour for all their members and discipline lawyers who violate the standards. The standards—including honesty, integrity, confidentiality, and competency—govern the lawyer's relationship with clients, the courts, the administration of justice, and the public. The most serious violations result in a lawyer being **disbarred**—expulsion from the law society and loss of the privilege of practising law. When a client hires a lawyer, the relationship is governed by these professional standards as well as the historic protection of **solicitor–client privilege**. This privilege requires the lawyer to keep confidential all communications between the lawyer and the client. The lawyer cannot be forced to reveal such communication to a court unless the client approves. This privilege protects the client and allows the client to speak candidly to the lawyer, ultimately ensuring the best possible legal advice.

The most recent development affecting the legal profession is the emergence of the **paralegal**—a non-lawyer who provides some form of legal service. For many years, lawyers have hired non-lawyers, trained them in a specific area, and then delegated clerical responsibilities to the paralegal. In this model, they work under the supervision of a lawyer and the lawyer is responsible to the client for the work. As lawyers' fees increased, paralegals began offering clerical services directly to the public in such areas as incorporations, uncontested divorces, and simple wills. Now paralegals assist people in all sorts of areas including minor court matters such as highway traffic tickets, landlord and tenant disputes, and Small Claims Court matters. Although some paralegals offer exceptional service, unregulated paralegals present risks to the public: the quality of service varies widely; they are not subject to educational requirements, licensing, professional standards, or discipline; and they do not have to carry liability insurance. Ontario is the first jurisdiction in North America to regulate paralegals. In order to offer services directly to the public, Ontario paralegals must be licensed by the Law Society of Upper Canada, carry insurance, meet competency standards, and are subject to discipline.[40]

> **paralegal**
> a non-lawyer who provides some form of legal service to the public

Business and the Legal Profession

Should a business hire a lawyer to deal with a problem when it arises or should it **retain** a lawyer in advance of any particular need? Should a business hire or retain one lawyer or law firm to handle all its needs? Should the business retain multiple lawyers with specific specialties? Is the best solution an in-house lawyer? These are difficult questions that every business must answer. The answer depends on the size of the business, the type of legal risks, and the resources available. The development of a legal risk management plan, as discussed in Chapter 1, will help the business to identify its legal needs.

> **retain or retainer**
> the contract between a lawyer and client that describes the work that will be done and the fee that will be charged

Most businesses use some **outside counsel**—self-employed lawyers who work alone, in small partnerships, or in large national firms, and bill the business for services rendered. Using this type of lawyer allows a business to select the specific specialty needed for the job. However, it is also valuable for a business to have a long-term relationship with one lawyer or firm that becomes familiar with its business and legal needs. Sometimes this is accomplished by hiring a large firm, building a relationship with one contact lawyer, and referring work as needed to various lawyers within the firm.

> **outside counsel**
> self-employed lawyers who work alone, in small partnerships, or in large national firms, and bill the business for services rendered

Businesses with regular legal needs sometimes hire a lawyer as a full-time employee of the business, known as **in-house counsel**. The in-house counsel may need to hire outside counsel for matters beyond his or her capabilities, but in such circumstances the in-house counsel can communicate and supervise the outside counsel in a way that minimizes the cost. In addition, the in-house counsel often supervises a team of paralegals working as compliance officers in various areas of the business. **Compliance officers** monitor regulatory and legislative requirements applicable to the business and ensure that the business complies. The role of in-house counsel is expanding to include a proactive role in the management and strategy of the business. An in-house counsel can be a valuable member of the management team and the decision to hire such a lawyer should not be undertaken as a purely mathematical calculation of saved legal fees.

> **in-house counsel**
> a lawyer who provides legal services to a business as a full-time employee of the business

> **compliance officers**
> employees that monitor regulatory and legislative requirements applicable to the business and ensure that the business complies

---

40. Law Society Act, R.S.O. 1990, c. L-8 as amen. See also the criticism of the Ontario model contained in Chapter 4 of the Federal Competition Bureau Report *Self-regulated Professions Balancing Competition and Regulation*, December 2007, online at www.competitionbureau.gc.ca/epic/site/cb-bc.nsf/en/02523e.html (accessed February 13, 2008).

QUESTIONS FOR REVIEW

1. Distinguish the civil law system from the common law system.
2. Explain the theory of precedent and its values.
3. Describe the relationship between the courts of common law and equity.
4. What is the purpose of codifying law in a statute?
5. Why has subordinate legislation come to prominence?
6. How does the operation of an appeal court differ from that of a trial court?
7. Motion pictures and television programs are responsible for a misconception about the way in which trials proceed. Explain.
8. Describe the basic difference between the systems of courts in the United States and in Canada.
9. What are the advantages of a settlement over a court trial?
10. Define appellant; respondent; counterclaim; counsel; bench; writ; settlement; pleadings; party and party costs; *res judicata.*
11. What is a "class action" and when do parties use them?
12. How does a judge decide a case when there is no precedent available in earlier decisions?
13. Explain why a legal rule in one province may differ from that in another province.
14. One of the major purposes of private law is to settle disputes between businesses. How can the settlement of a particular private dispute make a contribution to the business community as a whole?
15. "I was never ruined but twice; once when I won a lawsuit and once when I lost one." How can a successful litigant lose?
16. Explain the nature of a "contingency fee." How are contingent fees used in Canada?
17. What are the advantages that make ADR an attractive way of settling disputes?
18. Distinguish between judicare and community legal services.
19. What considerations will influence the decision to hire in-house counsel?

ADDITIONAL RESOURCES FOR CHAPTER 2 ON THE COMPANION WEBSITE *(www.pearsoned.ca/smyth)*

In addition to self-test multiple-choice, true–false, and short essay questions (all with immediate feedback), application exercises, and links to useful web destinations, the Companion Website provides the following resources for Chapter 2:

- **British Columbia:** Class Action Lawsuits; Commercial Arbitration Mediation Center for the Americas; Court Structure in British Columbia; The Federal Court; International Arbitration; Juries for Civil Actions; The Law Society of British Columbia; Lawyers' Fees; Limitation Fees; Litigation Guardian; Mediation and Arbitration; Notaries; Paralegals; Practice of Law; Proceedings Against the Crown; Sheriffs and Bailiffs; Small Claims Court; Supreme Court of British Columbia Self Help Centre (SHC)

- **Alberta:** ADR; Civil Enforcement; Class Actions; Class Proceedings Act; Contingency Fees; Costs; Judgment Interest; Jurisdiction; Legal Aid; Limitation Periods; Small Claims Court

- **Manitoba/Saskatchewan:** ADR; Courts in the Province; Court Rules; Pre-Trial Process; Small Claims; Who Makes the Law?

- **Ontario:** Administrative Law; ADR; Arbitration; Case Management; Class Actions; Contingency Fees; Costs; Court System; Legal Aid; Legal Profession; Mandatory Mediation; Paralegals; Simplified Procedure; Small Claims Court; Solicitor–Client Privilege; Trial Process

Torts

The contract part of this book is concerned with business arrangements that are entered into on a voluntary basis, by contract, but there are also important aspects of the law that create rights or impose obligations without there having been any agreement or consent. For example, property rights might arise through inheritance, and criminal law creates rules of behaviour that everyone must follow. Government regulation of business activities will be discussed in Chapter 32 and in other chapters throughout the book.

In Part 2 we discuss legal risks arising from an important area of "non-consensual" law: the law of torts. The law of torts recognizes situations when an injured party should be compensated for the harm caused by another person. A manufacturer's goods may be defective and injure a consumer. A newspaper may publish a story that destroys someone's reputation. A driver delivering goods may carelessly injure a pedestrian. An accountant's negligent audit of a business may cause loss to an investor. In these and other situations, the person who is harmed may claim a remedy against the one who caused the harm.

A business may suffer injury—for example, by a fire carelessly started on adjoining premises that spreads and damages its property, or because it receives negligent advice from its lawyer. All of these situations raise important issues that are determined under principles of the law of torts.

In Chapter 3 we consider the essential characteristics of tort law that impose a duty to take care. We concentrate on the most important tort—negligence—and also examine more briefly other torts, such as nuisance and those that contain an element of deliberate conduct, such as defamation and false imprisonment.

Chapter 4 discusses the problems of professional liability. In modern society there is increasing need for specialized knowledge. Those without special skills rely on "professionals," and those who hold themselves out as being qualified are held to higher standards of care and skill than are members of the general public. When harm is caused they are held accountable.

The law of torts is a broad subject that impacts many aspects of everyday life. The aim of the following two chapters is to concentrate upon those aspects of tort law that most directly affect business. A business person needs to be aware of the potential risks, and accompanying legal liability, associated with his or her activities, as well as of the remedies available when actions of others harm the interests of the business.

The Law of Torts

The word "tort" derives from the French, meaning "wrong." A tort is a wrong, that is to say, an injury, done by one person to another, sometimes intentionally but more often unintentionally. The injury may be physical—to the person or property of the victim— or it may just be financial.

This chapter examines the circumstances in which the law requires the person who causes an injury to compensate the victim. In this chapter we examine such questions as:

- What is the basis for tort liability?
- What constitutes "negligence"?
- How does the law of negligence apply to particular situations, such as the liability of manufacturers and of the owners or occupiers of premises?
- In what other circumstances does the law of torts provide remedies?
- What remedies are provided?

THE SCOPE OF TORT LAW

The role of the law of **torts** is to *compensate* victims for harm suffered from the activities of others. In theory *punishment* is left to the criminal law, if the conduct in question happens also to amount to a crime.[1] For example, when a person punches a neighbour in the nose, the neighbour may sue him in tort for compensation and the state may also charge him with the criminal offence of assault causing bodily harm.

    While there is no entirely satisfactory definition of "tort," it is not difficult to compile a list of separate "torts." As a general proposition, tort law identifies those circumstances that create a right to compensation.

    The basic issue for society when dealing with such causes of harm as automobile accidents, industrial accidents, or pollution of the environment is to determine who should bear the loss—the victim, the person whose act caused the harm, the group that benefits most directly from a common activity, such as all motor vehicle owners, or an even larger group, such as taxpayers generally. Tort law is one instrument for apportioning loss, along with other instruments such as insurance and government compensation schemes.[2]

tort
a wrongful act done to the person or property of another

DEVELOPMENT OF THE TORT CONCEPT

In the early stages of development, societies usually had simple rules for imposing liability for injurious conduct: anyone who caused direct injury to another had to pay compensation. No inquiry was made into the reasons for the injury or whether the conduct of the injurer was justified. This type of liability is called **strict liability**. Gradually, the idea developed that a person should not be responsible for harm caused to another if he acted without *fault*. The courts also began to consider the way in which the harm had arisen. At first, only direct injuries were recognized by the courts—running down another person or striking a blow. Gradually the courts began to recognize indirect or consequential injuries. For example, suppose *A* carelessly dropped a log in the road and did not bother to remove it although it was near sunset. After dark, *B*'s horse tripped over the log and was seriously injured. In early law, *B* would have been without a remedy. Later, however, the courts recognized that *A*'s act was as much responsible for the injury to *B*'s horse as if *A* had struck the horse by throwing the log at it. They allowed *B* to recover damages.[3]

strict liability
liability that is imposed regardless of fault

    Therefore, early tort law evolved in two ways: the law took into account the *fault* of the defendant and it also took into account *causation*—whether the defendant's conduct could be considered the cause of the harm. Both these developments present difficult problems, which we will examine more closely.

THE BASIS FOR LIABILITY

Fault

Fault, in the context of tort law, refers to blameworthy or culpable conduct—conduct that in the eyes of the law is unjustifiable because it intentionally or carelessly disregards the interests of others. One justification for basing liability upon fault is a belief in its deterrent effect: people will be more inclined to be careful if they must pay for the consequences of their carelessness. There is little hard evidence

---

1. In some cases the courts award "punitive damages"; see the discussion later in this chapter under the heading "Remedies."

2. For a fuller discussion of the purposes of tort law, see especially J. Fleming, *The Law of Torts*, 9th ed. (Sydney: Law Book Company, 1998). See also A.M. Linden, *Canadian Tort Law*, 6th ed. (Toronto: Butterworths, 1997).

3. This example was discussed by Fortesque, J. in *Reynolds* v. *Clarke* (1726), 93 E.R. 747, and has been cited many times since by both the courts and leading writers as a classic statement of the law.

to support this theory, although it is reasonable to suppose that large, highly publicized awards of damages have had an effect upon the standards and practices of manufacturers, surgeons, and similar persons affected by those awards. But the modern reality is that many of the activities where tort liability arises—driving a car, operating a factory or store, practising medicine—are covered by insurance. Carelessness is more likely to be deterred by the likelihood of criminal penalties (for example, for dangerous driving) and of increased insurance premiums than by the possibility of being sued in tort.

A compensation system based on fault also has its defects. Accident victims who cannot establish fault on the part of some other person go uncompensated, and the costs and delays of litigation deter many other claims. At the same time, when fault is established there is a tendency for the victim to be over-compensated, especially where the defendant is a large corporation and its conduct is considered particularly blameworthy.[4]

Strict Liability

Not all tort liability is based upon fault. As already noted, early tort law took a narrow approach, imposing the burden of compensation upon the person who caused the injury regardless of whether he was at fault. That offends modern ideas of fairness. However, strict liability persists in some areas of modern tort law. For example, a person who collects potentially dangerous substances or materials on his land, from which they subsequently escape, is liable for any resulting damage even if he were blameless.[5]

ILLUSTRATION 3.1

A manufacturer stored acid in a large container on his property. The container was accidentally punctured by a visitor's truck. The acid leaked out and damaged a neighbouring farmer's crops. The manufacturer is liable to compensate the farmer. The risk of that type of damage is a burden that the manufacturer must bear as the price for storing dangerous chemicals on his land. (The truck driver may also be liable for the damage if he is found to be at fault.)

Some activities are inherently dangerous regardless of the amount of care taken—for example, transporting high explosives. A strong argument may be made that a person carrying on an inherently dangerous activity should be strictly liable for damage, regardless of fault. In other words, a person who undertakes a dangerous activity should charge for his services according to the degree of risk, and should carry adequate insurance to compensate for possible harm done to others. Most often strict liability is imposed by legislation, although some United States courts have done it. In the absence of legislation, Canadian courts still apply the principles of negligence. However, they have raised the standard of care as the danger increases. As a result, in many cases involving hazardous activities the defendant finds that the standard of care is so high that it is virtually impossible for him to show that he has satisfied it. The effect is much the same as if he were strictly liable.

Social Policy

Whether liability should be based on fault, on strict liability, or on some other principles is an important question of policy. Policy objectives change as our social standards change. These standards force the law to adapt in many ways, ranging from direct legislative intervention to more subtle influences on judge and jury in determining liability and the amounts of damages awarded.

The most radical proposals would eliminate lawsuits for all personal injuries and compensate victims through a government scheme. A step in that direction has been taken in Canada with the virtual elimination of fault as the basis for automobile accident claims through a system of compulsory

---

4. This is especially so in the United States, where jury trials and awards of punitive damages are more common. That has been the main focus for the recent calls there for "tort law reform."
5. *Rylands* v. *Fletcher* (1868), L.R. 3 H.L. 330. In Canada, the *Rylands* v. *Fletcher* rule requires a non-natural use of the land and damage caused by escape. See John *Campbell Law Corporation* v. *Owners, Strata Plan 1350*, 2001 BCSC 1342.

"no-fault" insurance. Another example of an alternative to the tort approach is found in the scheme governing **workers' compensation** in Canada. Under this scheme, industrial accidents are seen as the inevitable price of doing business. Employers must contribute to a fund that is used to compensate workers injured in industrial accidents, even when the employer is blameless and the injury is the result of the employee's own carelessness.

But between comprehensive "no-fault" schemes on the one hand and strict liability on the other, there are many circumstances where liability based on fault is still considered to be the fairest principle. In most areas of tort law, liability is imposed on a fault basis.[6]

Vicarious Liability

One area in which the law has responded to the pressure of social needs relates to torts committed by employees in the course of their employment. In some cases an employer may be personally at fault for an act committed by an employee: for example, he may instruct an employee to perform a dangerous task for which he knows the employee is not trained. In such a case the employer personally is at fault, and it may be that there is no fault on the part of the employee.[7]

But should an employer be liable when the employee alone is at fault? Over the years the courts developed a basis for holding the employer liable for harm caused by the acts of an employee when those acts arose in the course of employment. Now, the employer may be found liable even when he has given strict instructions to take proper care or not to do the particular act that causes the damage, and he may be held liable for criminal, as well as negligent, acts of an employee.[8]

There are two main justifications for taking this strict approach. First, although an employee is personally liable for the torts he commits while acting for himself or his employer, employees often have limited assets available to pay compensation for the potential harm they can cause—a train driver may injure hundreds of passengers. Second, there is an argument based on fairness: the person who makes the profit from an activity should also be liable for any loss. This is called the principle of **vicarious liability**, by which an employer is liable to compensate persons for harm caused by an employee in the course of employment.[9] (See Figure 3.1.)

"no-fault" insurance
a system of compulsory insurance that eliminates fault as a basis for claims

workers' compensation
a scheme in which employers contribute to a fund used to compensate workers injured in industrial accidents regardless of how the accident was caused

vicarious liability
the liability of an employer to compensate for harm caused by an employee

The victim, *V*, is injured by *A* while *A* is acting in the course of his employment. *V* can sue *A* [1]. *V* can also sue the employer, *B* [2], who will normally have a greater ability to pay. (In practice, *V* is likely to sue both *A* and *B*.) If *V* does sue *A*, it is possible that *A* will have a right to be indemnified by *B* [3]. Or, if *B* has to compensate *V*, *B* may be able to sue *A* [4]. These rights [3 and 4] could arise under the contract of employment.

FIGURE 3.1
Vicarious Liability

---

6. See, for example, *Fiala* v. *Cechmanek* (2001), 201 D.L.R. (4th) 680, where the defendant suffered from a mental illness of which he was unaware. During a manic outburst, he damaged the plaintiff's automobile. The Alberta Court of Appeal held that he was not liable for the damage: there could be no liability without fault.

7. See *Edgeworth Construction Ltd.* v. *N.D. Lee & Associates Ltd.* (1993), 107 D.L.R. (4th) 169.

8. *British Columbia Ferry Corp.* v. *Invicta Security Service Corp.* (1998), 167 D.L.R. (4th) 193.

9. For a review of the policy issues underlying the vicarious liability principle, see the decision of the Supreme Court of Canada in *671122 Ontario Ltd.* v. *Sagaz Industries Canada Inc.* (2001), 204 D.L.R. (4th) 542. As that case demonstrates, one difficulty is to determine whether the primary tortfeasor was an employee or an independent contractor. As we shall see in Chapter 19, the principle of vicarious liability is not restricted to acts of employees; in some circumstances a person may be held liable for the torts committed by an agent.

NEGLIGENCE

negligence
the careless causing of injury to the person or property of another

By far the most common basis for legal actions in tort, and the one that best illustrates the fault theory of liability, is **negligence**. The concept of negligence is quite simple: anyone who carelessly causes injury to another should compensate the victim for that injury. As it has developed in the courts, negligence has become a complex and sophisticated body of law, covering a wide variety of situations.

CHECKLIST Elements of a Negligence Action

In establishing the right to recover compensation, a plaintiff must prove three things:
1. The defendant owed the plaintiff a duty of care.
2. The defendant breached that duty.
3. The defendant's conduct caused injury to the plaintiff.

All three of the above requirements must exist for the plaintiff to succeed. The first element requires a *value judgment* by the court—is the activity complained of one that *ought* to create a duty? The second question is a mixed question of policy and fact—did the defendant's conduct fall below the standard of behaviour required in the circumstances? The third question involves difficult philosophical issues as well as fact—what is meant by "cause," and what is "injury"?

Duty of Care

duty of care
a relationship so close that one must take reasonable steps to avoid causing harm to the other

In order to establish liability in negligence a plaintiff must establish a **duty of care** owed to her by the defendant. What is the nature of that duty? Duty focuses on the relationship between the parties.

The principal question is whether the defendant should have foreseen that his actions might do harm to the victim. Another way of putting it, since the defendant cannot be expected to anticipate all the possible consequences of his actions, is to ask, "Would a normally intelligent and alert person—a reasonable person—have foreseen that those actions would likely cause harm?" But the plaintiff must go further: she must establish that the defendant owed a duty of care to *her*. As a general rule, the duty will arise only where the defendant could reasonably have foreseen a risk of harm to the plaintiff or to someone in the plaintiff's position.

CASE **3.1**

A courier company contracted with the Province of British Columbia to deliver an envelope to a land registry office in Prince George. Unknown to the courier company, the envelope contained a document relating to land owned by the plaintiff. If delivered on time, the document would have enabled the plaintiff to complete the sale of its land. The courier company was unreasonably slow and delivered the document too late. As a result, the plaintiff was unable to perform the contract of sale, and it suffered a loss of $77 000.

The Supreme Court of Canada held that the courier company was not liable to the plaintiff. It owed no duty of care to the plaintiff since it could not reasonably have foreseen that the delay would cause a loss to some third person outside its relationship with its client, the Province.[10]

---

10. *B.D.C. Ltd.* v. *Hofstrand Farms Ltd.* (1986), 26 D.L.R. (4th) 1. For a recent example see *Esser* v. *Luoma* (2004), 242 D.L.R. (4th) 112.

Two years earlier, in *City of Kamloops* v. *Nielsen*, the Supreme Court of Canada ruled that, to determine the existence of a duty of care, a court must ask:

> . . . is there a sufficiently close relationship between the parties (the [defendant] and the person who has suffered the damage) so that, in the reasonable contemplation of the [defendant], carelessness on its part might cause damage to that person? If so, are there any considerations which ought to negative or limit (a) the scope of the duty and (b) the class of persons to whom it is owed or (c) the damages to which a breach of it may give rise?[11]

Recently, the Supreme Court of Canada summarized the test for duty of care in one sentence: "Whether such a relationship exists depends on foreseeability, moderated by policy concerns."[12] Policy concerns consider the effect that recognizing a duty of care will have on other legal obligations, the legal system, and society more generally.[13] Concerns include such things as the proliferation of lawsuits or the ability to insure against a huge new potential legal risk.

The courts have sometimes held that a duty of care is owed to persons other than the individual who is directly injured. For example, a negligent driver was held to be liable to a parent who suffered severe nervous shock when she saw her own child, who was standing nearby, run down and killed.[14] In that case the court considered that the type of injury suffered by the parent was foreseeable.

In recent years more and more duties have been imposed by statute, especially upon the operators of businesses—as we shall see further in Chapters 29 and 32. In addition to statutory penalties, breach of these duties may give rise to liability in tort to persons who are injured as a result. The courts have also shown increasing willingness to hold public bodies liable for the negligent performance of their statutory duties. Municipalities have been held liable to homeowners for issuing building permits for defective designs or for not carrying out proper inspections of construction works.[15] A public body may be liable even where the statute imposes no duty but merely confers a discretionary power on it—for example, to maintain a highway—if it is negligent in the exercise of that power.[16]

Standard of Care

The **standard of care** refers to the level of care that a person must take in the circumstances. The law places a general duty on every person to take *reasonable care* to avoid causing foreseeable injury to other persons and their property. What constitutes a reasonable standard of care? It is often said that the standard demanded is that of the ordinary reasonable person, or "the person on the Yonge Street subway."[17] However, the standard of care necessarily varies according to the activity in question: the standard expected of a brain surgeon is that of a competent brain surgeon rather than of the person in the subway.

standard of care
the level of care that a person must take in the circumstances

11. [1984] 2 S.C.R. 2 at 10 (per Wilson, J.). This test was cited with approval by LaForest, J. in *Hercules Managements Ltd.* v. *Ernst & Young* (1997), 146 D.L.R. (4th) 577 (S.C.C.), in a judgment that provides a comprehensive review of the Canadian law on the duty of care. That case is examined further in Chapter 4.
12. *Mustapha* v. *Culligan of Canada Ltd.*, 2008 SCC 27 at para. 4, relying on the seminal case of *Anns* v. *Merton London Borough Council*, [1978] A.C. 728 (H.L.).
13. *Cooper* v. *Hobart*, [2001] 3 S.C.R. 537.
14. *Hinz* v. *Berry*, [1970] 1 All E.R. 1074. Contrast with *Schlink* v. *Blackburn* (1993), 18 C.C.L.T. (2d) 173, where the plaintiff was at home, asleep in bed, when his wife was injured in a motor accident; his nervous shock occurred some time later when he was told of the accident.
15. *City of Kamloops* v. *Neilsen, supra*, n. 11; *Rothfield* v. *Manolakos* (1989), 63 D.L.R. (4th) 449.
16. See, for example, *Bisoukis* v. *City of Brampton* (1999), 180 D.L.R. (4th) 577 (failure to sand a stretch of road where black ice was known to form). The courts will normally not interfere with policy decisions taken by the appropriate body, but once a policy decision has been taken (for example, to guard against rock falls onto a highway), the body will be liable if it is negligent in carrying out that policy: *Just* v. *British Columbia* (1989), 64 D.L.R. (4th) 689; contrast with *Gobin* v. *British Columbia*, (2002) 214 D.L.R. (4th) 328.
17. Linden, *Canadian Tort Law, supra*, n. 2, at 126–7.

In addition, the court must balance competing interests. On the one hand the court considers the degree of likelihood that harm will result from the activity in question and the potential severity of the harm. On the other hand it considers the social utility of the activity and the feasibility of eliminating the risk. It may be permissible not to take every possible precaution where the risk of serious damage or injury is small, but where there is danger of a major catastrophe, it would be unreasonable not to take every known precaution.

Legislation not only imposes duties but also sets out the appropriate standard of care for particular activities. For example, safety standards for the food industry are prescribed by statute, and those standards are frequently a good indication of where a court will set the negligence threshold. But it must be remembered that the tort of negligence is based on fault, and the fact that a person may be guilty of a breach of a statutory standard does not of itself make him civilly liable to a person injured as a result of the breach—at least if he can show that the offence occurred without fault on his part.[18]

Causation

causation
injury resulting from the breach of the standard of care

For an action in negligence to succeed, it is necessary for the plaintiff to show not only that a duty of care was owed to her and that duty has been breached, but also that she has been injured as a result of the breach; that is to say, the breach of duty is the cause of the injury. **Causation** is a complex subject about which whole volumes have been written. An extreme view of the theory of causation can link one act to every other act in the world.

ILLUSTRATION 3.2

PQR Inc. were having some renovations done to part of their factory building by *STU* (Contractors) Ltd. One of the *STU* workmen negligently sliced through a cable, causing an electric motor to burn out. The motor was an essential part of the factory's cooling system; without it, the factory could continue in operation for only a few hours. The factory manager, *X*, immediately decided to drive to the nearby town to obtain a replacement motor. On the way, his car was struck by a vehicle carelessly driven by *Y*, and *X* suffered slight injuries and concussion. By the time *PQR* were able to get the motor back to the factory, the cooling system had overheated and it had been necessary to close down operations. As a result, four hours of production were lost. Worse, *X*'s injury caused him to miss a meeting with an important client, as a result of which *PQR* lost the opportunity of a lucrative contract.

In Illustration 3.2 it could be argued that the negligence of *STU*'s worker "caused" (1) the shutdown at the factory, (2) the injury to *X*, and (3) the loss of the contract. But for his slicing through the cable, none of those consequences would have followed. The same might be argued with respect to *Y*'s careless driving. Yet it would seem unreasonable to hold *STU* liable for items (2) and (3), or to hold Y liable for items (1) and (3). Clearly, the "but for" approach to causation does not always provide a satisfactory solution.

For the most part the courts have avoided philosophical discussion and have adopted a common-sense approach. No matter how blameworthy a person's conduct may be, he will not be held liable for damage that he did not cause. In a famous case, a passenger in a small boat accidentally fell overboard into ice-cold water and died. The boat's operator was under a duty to try to rescue him. He was negligent in the attempt at rescue, but was held not liable because, even if he had used proper rescue procedures, the passenger would have been dead before he could have been pulled from the water.[19]

---

18. *R.* v. *Saskatchewan Wheat Pool*, [1983] 1 S.C.R. 205.

19. *Matthews* v. *MacLaren*, [1969] 2 O.R. 137, affirmed in *Horsley* v. *MacLaren*, [1972] S.C.R. 441.

Again, a person will not be held liable for consequences of his acts that are considered to be too **remote** or unrelated. Generally speaking, the closer in time the occurrence of an injury is to a person's careless conduct, the less chance there is of some significant intervening act happening, and the more likely he is to be found the "cause" of the injury.

remote
unrelated or far removed
from the conduct

CASE 3.2

B and his wife were involved in an automobile accident. *B* received relatively slight injuries but his wife was severely injured. Two years later, *B* was in another accident and some time after that he was diagnosed as suffering from severe depression. In the action arising out of the first accident, *B* claimed damages in respect of the depression.

The claim was rejected. The court held that, if *B*'s depression had resulted from the stress of seeing his wife suffer, day after day, the damage might have been foreseeable. However, the length of time between the first accident and the onset of the depression (more than two years later) cast doubt on the causal relationship. The depression might have been the result of the second accident.[20]

As both Case 3.2 and Illustration 3.2 demonstrate, an injury may be the result of two or more negligent acts by different defendants. In such a case, which of them should be held liable? At one time the courts attempted to determine which of the acts was the "proximate cause" of injury. That sometimes produced an unfair result, and the modern tendency is to hold both defendants liable.[21]

CASE 3.3

An innkeeper allowed a customer to drink too much and then turned him out to walk home along a country road, where he was hit by a careless motorist. Both the innkeeper and the motorist were held to have contributed to the accident.[22]

Remoteness of Damage

Foreseeability is a major element, as we have seen, both in establishing whether or not a duty of care exists and in determining what is the appropriate standard of care. It reappears again when the question of the *extent* of liability for negligence is considered.

Until the 1960s the position seemed to be that, once some sort of damage was reasonably foreseeable as a consequence of a negligent act, the actor was liable for *all* damage resulting directly from that act, however unlikely that damage was.[23]

---

20. *Beecham* v. *Hughes* (1988), 52 D.L.R. (4th) 625.
21. For an example, see *Economy Foods & Hardware Ltd.* v. *Klassen* (2001), 196 D.L.R. (4th) 413, where a fire was caused by the negligence of one defendant but spread, causing additional damage, due to the failure of the second defendant to install an adequate system of sprinklers.
22. *Menow* v. *Honsberger and Jordan House Ltd.*, [1974] S.C.R. 239. See also *Murphy* v. *Little Memphis Cabaret Inc.* (1998), 167 D.L.R. (4th) 190; *Renaissance Leisure Group Inc.* v. *Frazer* (2004), 242 D.L.R. (4th) 229. By contrast, the Supreme Court of Canada held that a restaurant serving alcohol to a party of people, knowing that they had arrived by car, owed a duty to the driver and passengers, but since some members of the party were not drinking, it was entitled to assume that a non-drinker would be driving; consequently, it was not responsible for the accident: *Mayfield Investments Ltd.* v. *Stewart* (1995), 121 D.L.R. (4th) 222. It is still unclear whether "social hosts" (for example, at a private party), will be held liable in the same way as "commercial hosts": see *Childs* v. *Desormeaux* (2004), 239 D.L.R. (4th) 61.
23. *Re Polemis*, [1921] 3 K.B. 560.

CASE 3.4

Employees of the defendants, who were charterers of a ship called *Wagon Mound*, negligently allowed a large quantity of oil to escape from the ship into Sydney Harbour, Australia. Some of the oil washed up against the plaintiff's dock. Workers on the dock were carrying on welding operations. A spark from a welder ignited some cotton waste floating on the surface of the water and this, in turn, ignited the oil. A severe fire resulted, causing considerable damage to the dock.

The Australian trial judge held the defendants liable. They had been negligent in allowing the oil to escape, and it was foreseeable that some damage to the plaintiff's dock might result from the leakage, though the judge found that damage by fire was not foreseeable. Nevertheless, the actual damage was a direct result of the defendants' breach of their duty to the plaintiff.

The defendants appealed and the Privy Council allowed the appeal, holding that liability existed only in respect of the sort of damage that was reasonably foreseeable.[24]

The *Wagon Mound (No. 1)* decision (Case 3.4) restricted liability to damage that was reasonably foreseeable. A follow-up case known as *Wagon Mound (No. 2)* defined "reasonably foreseeable" as a real risk: "one which would occur to the mind of a reasonable man in the position of the defendant . . . which he would not brush aside as far fetched."[25] A court undertakes an objective assessment of what a *reasonable* defendant would foresee as likely injury to the *average* defendant. The damage is considered from the perspective of the "normal" victim—a person of "ordinary fortitude." It is not based on the actual circumstances of the particular plaintiff.

CASE 3.5

A consumer saw a dead fly in a bottle of water as he replaced a canister in his home. The observation was so upsetting that he developed serious mental disorders including anxiety and phobias. The trial judge found that the mental injuries were caused by the incident and awarded damages of approximately $340 000. The judgment was overturned by the Court of Appeal and leave to the Supreme Court of Canada was granted. The Supreme Court did not interfere with the trial judge's finding that the mental illness was caused by the incident but found that mental illness was not a reasonably foreseeable type of damage in the circumstances. The average person would not suffer a mental disorder as a result of seeing a fly in a water bottle. This was an extreme reaction by a plaintiff with particular vulnerabilities. The same reaction would not be expected in a person of ordinary fortitude. The plaintiff could not recover because the damage was too remote.[26]

However, there is some element of subjectivity in the valuation of the damage. If the type of damage is considered reasonably foreseeable, the court will compensate the victim for his *actual* damage. When a teenager negligently started his father's snowmobile, which escaped from his control, crossed a schoolyard, and collided with a gas pipe just outside the school causing gas to escape into the school and explode, he was held liable for all the resulting damage. The damage was considered to be of a general type that might have been foreseen even if the actual extent of the damage was unusually high.[27]

Economic Loss

damages
a sum of money awarded as compensation

As we noted at the beginning of this chapter, the purpose of tort law is to compensate for loss suffered as a consequence of the wrongful act of another. As we shall see, the remedy given in cases of negligence is a sum of money by way of **damages**. A plaintiff injured in an automobile collision

24. *Overseas Tankship (U.K.) Ltd.* v. *Morts Dock & Engineering Co.* (*The Wagon Mound No. 1*), [1961] A.C. 388.
25. *Overseas Tankship (U.K.) Ltd.* v. *Miller Steamship Co. Pty. Ltd.* (*The Wagon Mound No. 2*), [1967] A.C. 617 at p. 643; *Hughes* v. *Lord Advocate*, [1963] A.C. 837.
26. *Mustapha, supra*, n. 12.
27. *Hoffer* v. *School Division of Assiniboine South*, [1973] W.W.R. 765 (S.C.C.). The father and the gas company that installed the pipe were also held liable.

may be compensated not only for her physical injuries and for the cost of repairing her car, but also for *economic loss*, such as wages lost due to an enforced absence from work and the cost of renting a replacement car.

There are two types of cases. In the first type, economic loss is caused without there being any physical damage at all. A classic example is the leading case of *Hedley Byrne* v. *Heller and Partners,*[28] in which the House of Lords established that financial loss suffered as a result of a negligent misstatement may be recovered. This subject is discussed further in Chapter 4. In the second type of case there is physical damage, but not to the plaintiff or her property.

CASE 3.6

B negligently operated a tugboat and it collided with a railway bridge owned by *C*. The bridge was closed for several weeks for repairs. As a result, the railway company, which was the principal user of the bridge, suffered a loss of profit because it had to reroute traffic.

The Supreme Court of Canada held that the railway company could recover its loss.[29]

The decision turned in part on the close relationship that existed between the owner of the bridge and the railway company and, while it established that there *may* be recovery for pure economic loss in some situations, it left open the question of when the courts will hold that a duty is owed to a plaintiff or when the particular damage is not too remote. The answer turns on the particular circumstances of the case. For example, where a supplier sold a quantity of polyethylene resin to a corporation, knowing the resin to be defective and also knowing that the purchaser was part of a group of wholly owned subsidiaries that operated in an interdependent manner, the supplier was held liable to the entire group.[30]

A somewhat different issue was raised in Case 3.7:

CASE 3.7

A land developer contracted with the defendant construction company to build an apartment building, which was later sold to the plaintiffs. About 10 years later, a section of cladding fell from the ninth floor. On examination, defects in the construction were found and the plaintiffs had the entire cladding replaced. They successfully sued the defendants for the cost of the repairs.

Although no damage had been suffered, apart from the cladding on the ninth floor, the Supreme Court of Canada held that it was foreseeable that without the repairs there was a strong likelihood of physical harm to persons or to property. It was right that the defendants should be liable for the cost of replacing the rest of the cladding. In reaching that conclusion, the court recognized the strong underlying policy justification of providing an incentive to prevent accidents before they happen.[31]

Burden of Proof

Like plaintiffs in most court proceedings, a plaintiff in a tort action must prove all the elements of her case. In certain kinds of cases, however, the plaintiff does not know why or how the accident

28. [1964] A.C. 465.
29. *Canadian National Railway Co.* v. *Norsk Pacific Steamship Co.* (1992), 91 D.L.R. (4th) 289.
30. *Plas-Tex Canada Ltd.* v. *Dow Chemical of Canada Ltd.* (2004), 245 D.L.R. (4th) 650. The supplier was also liable for breach of contract.
31. *Winnipeg Condominium Corp. No. 36* v. *Bird Construction Co.,* [1995] 1 S.C.R. 85.

happened. For example, a pedestrian knocked down by a car, or a consumer poisoned by a dangerous substance in a jar of food, may have no way of knowing exactly how the defendant driver's or manufacturer's conduct caused her injury. The car might suddenly have swerved out of control because of some hidden mechanical defect, or the poisonous substance might have been deliberately inserted into the jar after it had left the manufacturer.

The law takes these difficulties of proof into account. A plaintiff may initially meet his burden of proof using circumstantial evidence. If the plaintiff establishes that the behaviour of the defendant is the most likely cause of the injury, the burden of proof then shifts to the defendant to show that he was not at fault. Once the burden has been shifted to him, he will be found liable unless he produces evidence to satisfy the court that, on balance, he was not at fault. Historically, this principle was known as *res ipsa loquitur,* or, translated, "the facts speak for themselves." It emerged in a 19th-century English case[32] in which the plaintiff, standing in a street, was struck by a barrel of flour falling from the upper window of the defendant's warehouse. Not unreasonably, the court concluded that, unless the defendant could prove otherwise, the most likely cause was the negligent conduct of the defendant or one of his employees.

In 1998, the Supreme Court of Canada dispensed with use of the Latin phrase, concluding that the principle was really just an application of the circumstantial evidence rules.[33]

res ipsa loquitur
the facts speak for themselves

The Plaintiff's Own Conduct

Early in the development of the principles of negligence the courts recognized that, even if the defendant had been negligent, the plaintiff might be largely responsible for her own injury. The courts at one time took a rather narrow and mechanical approach to the question. If the defendant could establish that the plaintiff contributed in any way to her own loss, the plaintiff would fail even if the defendant was mainly at fault. The harshness of the **contributory negligence** rule was changed by legislation pioneered in Canada.[34] These statutes required courts to apportion damages according to the respective degree of responsibility of the parties. The statutes do not set out in detail the basis for making the apportionment, but leave it to be decided by judges and juries according to their opinion of what is fair in the circumstances.

contributory negligence
negligence of an injured party that contributes to her own loss or injury

CASE	3.8

The plaintiff, a passenger in a truck, was injured when the driver failed to negotiate a sharp curve on a rural access road. The plaintiff had been aware that the driver had been drinking when he accepted the lift. The trial judge held the plaintiff 15 percent to blame, the driver 50 percent, for driving too fast and while impaired, and the municipality 35 percent, for not having erected a sign warning of the dangerous bend.[35]

By applying an appropriate standard of care to the plaintiff as well as to the defendant, the courts have also taken account of changing social standards. For example, it is now common to find that a person injured in a motor vehicle accident has contributed to some extent to her own injuries by failure to wear a seat belt.[36]

---

32. *Byrne* v. *Boadle* (1863), 159 E.R. 294.

33. In *Fontaine* v. *Loewen Estate* (1998), 1 S.C.R. 424, the Supreme Court of Canada held that the *res ipsa loquitur* principle was an unnecessarily confusing approach to the circumstantial evidence rule. There was no presumption of negligence simply because a vehicle left the road in a single-vehicle accident.

34. Ontario passed the first statute in the field: Negligence Act, S.O. 1924, c. 32.

35. The Supreme Court of Canada upheld the trial judge's determination: *Housen* v. *Nikolaisen* (2002), 211 D.L.R. (4th) 577.

36. A driver of a vehicle may be held negligent for failure to ensure that a child passenger is wearing a seat belt: *Galaske* v. *O'Donnell* (1994), 112 D.L.R. (4th) 109 (S.C.C.); see also *Heller* v. *Martens* (2002), 213 D.L.R. (4th) 124.

Another problem arises when the victim is not to blame for the accident itself but her own *subsequent* conduct contributes to the *extent* of her original injuries—for example, where a plaintiff refuses to undergo safe and simple surgery or refuses to accept blood transfusions,[37] and thus aggravates her condition. In some cases, the courts have decided that part of the damages were due to the plaintiff's unreasonable conduct and were therefore not recoverable.[38] This result may be justified on the ground that the plaintiff's own conduct has contributed to the seriousness of the injury. Alternatively, it may be regarded as an application of the principle that a plaintiff is expected to act reasonably to minimize, or **mitigate**, any damage suffered. This principle is discussed further, in the context of contract law, in Chapter 15.

It is important to note that the statutory defence of contributory negligence may be raised only in actions based in tort law.[39] A farmer whose crops were destroyed sued the manufacturer and supplier of a pesticide. He successfully claimed that the instructions for use did not contain an adequate warning of the risks involved; the alleged negligence of the farmer himself was held to be no defence since the action was based on breach of contract.[40]

mitigate
duty to act reasonably and quickly to minimize the extent of damage suffered

The Relevance of Insurance

The modern reality is that in many tort cases the actual loss falls on an insurance company. In the case of automobile collisions, for example, both plaintiff and defendant are normally insured. But suppose that *A* decides not to take out collision insurance on her automobile and it is damaged in an accident caused by the negligence of another driver, *B*. Since *A* is expected to mitigate her loss, should it follow that she has contributed to the loss by failing to take out insurance against the risk? Can *B* successfully defend an action by *A* for negligence on the grounds that *A* might have avoided her loss by taking out adequate insurance coverage? The answer is no. Courts do not admit evidence about the existence or amount of insurance coverage in negligence actions because their decisions must be based strictly on the merits of the dispute being tried and be free from any suspicion that their judgment has been biased by a knowledge of the amount of insurance protection that the plaintiff has chosen to purchase. So, in our example, the failure of the plaintiff to have insured her car against damage by collision would not be admitted as evidence and would not affect the amount of damages.

Suppose, however, that in our example *A* had taken out collision insurance. Will *A* be compensated twice—once by her insurance company and again by the defendant? The answer, again, is no. When an insured party recovers first from her insurance company, her right to claim against the wrongdoer passes to the insurance company. It "stands in the insured person's shoes"; that is, it becomes **subrogated** to the insured party's rights and may itself sue the defendant and collect (see Figure 3.2). But if *A* recovers her loss, or part of it, by suing *B*, then to that extent she cannot afterwards recover from her own insurance company.

subrogation
where one person becomes entitled to the rights and claims of another

In practice it is normally simpler for *A* to recover under her insurance policy, leaving the company to decide whether or not to sue *B*. One reason is that under the policy *A* may be entitled to recover the full extent of her loss, even though she may have been partly at fault, and, if she sued *B*, the damages might be reduced on account of her own contributory negligence. Another reason is that *B* might have insufficient funds to pay the claim. If *B* also has insurance, the two insurance

---

37. *Hobbs* v. *Robertson* (2004) 243 D.L.R. (4th) 700.

38. See *Janiak* v. *Ippolito* (1985), 16 D.L.R. (4th) 1 (S.C.C.).

39. It also seems that the defence is not available in strict liability torts, such as conversion; see *Boma Manufacturing Ltd.* v. *Canadian Imperial Bank of Commerce* (1996), 140 D.L.R. (4th) 463 (S.C.C.). However, where the breach of duty is identical in both contract and tort, some courts have allowed the defence of contributory negligence to be raised against both claims: see *Crown West Steel Fabricators* v. *Capri Insurance Services Ltd.* (2002), 214 D.L.R. (4th) 577.

40. *Caners* v. *Eli Lilley Canada Inc.* (1996), 134 D.L.R. (4th) 730 (Man. C.A.). This aspect of contractual liability is discussed in Chapter 16.

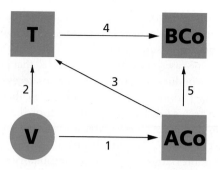

FIGURE 3.2

Insurance

Victim *V* is injured in an accident, caused by the negligence of tortfeasor *T*. *V* is insured by *ACo*, and *T* by *BCo*. V may claim under her policy with *ACo* [1], or may sue *T* [2]. If *V* claims under her policy, *ACo* may bring proceedings (in *V*'s name) against *T* [3]. T could then claim under his policy with *BCo* [4]. Alternatively, *ACo* might settle with *BCo* [5].

companies will usually settle the question of payment between themselves, without resorting to expensive litigation. There may be cases, however, where the amount that the insurance company offers to pay under the policy is less than the sum the plaintiff considers a court would likely award.

PRODUCT LIABILITY

One of the most important areas of tort law, for many businesses, is the liability of manufacturers for injury or loss caused by defects in their products. Consider the four cases below. Who should bear the loss in each one?

CASE 3.9

X runs a small refreshment booth at a beach and buys his supplies from *Y* Bottling Co. Ltd. He sells a dark-green bottle of ginger ale to *A*, who gives it to her friend, *B*. *B* drinks half the contents and becomes violently ill. The balance is found to contain a decomposed snail. *B* is hospitalized and is unable to return to work for several weeks.

CASE 3.10

P buys a *Q* Company sports car from Dealer *R*. On being driven away from the showroom, the car loses a defective front wheel and collides with a parked vehicle, injuring the occupant, *S*.

CASE 3.11

M buys from the *N* Ski Shop a set of thermal underwear manufactured by *O* Company. The underwear contains a toxic acid and when it comes in contact with perspiration causes *M* to have a severe skin burn.

CASE 3.12

J buys a bottle of cough medicine, manufactured by the *K* company, from her local drugstore. To try to get rid of her cold she drinks two stiff whiskies, takes a dose of the medicine, and goes to bed. During the night she has a heart attack. The cough medicine is extremely dangerous if taken with alcohol, but there was no warning to that effect on the bottle or package.

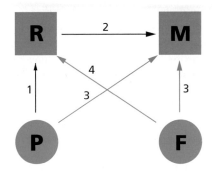

Manufacturer *M* sells a product to retailer *R*, which sells it to purchaser *P*. The product is defective and injures *P* and her friend, *F*. *P* can sue *R* in contract [1], and *R* can sue *M* for its loss, also in contract [2]. *P* and *F* can sue *M* in tort [3]. *F* might also be able to sue *R* in tort, if *R* should have discovered the defect.

FIGURE 3.3
Product Liability

As we shall see in Chapter 16, the retailer in each of our examples may be liable to the buyer for breach of an implied *contractual* undertaking that a product is not defective. But in Case 3.9, *X* sold the soft drink to *A* rather than to *B*, the injured party: there was no contract with *B*. Similarly, in Case 3.10, the injured person, *S*, has no contractual relationship with Dealer *R*. In these circumstances, contractual remedies are not available. If the injured parties are going to be compensated, it must be by imposing liability in tort law or by providing a special statutory remedy. (See Figure 3.3.)

It was not until 1932 that the British courts recognized the duty of manufacturers to the ultimate consumers of their products as an obligation in tort law. The House of Lords did so in the famous case of *Donoghue* v. *Stevenson*,[41] in which the facts were similar to those in Case 3.9. Case 3.10 is drawn in part from the United States case *MacPherson* v. *Buick Motor Co.*,[42] decided by the New York Court of Appeals in 1916, a decision that may have influenced the later House of Lords decision.

In the years since *Donoghue* v. *Stevenson*, its principle has been applied by the courts in a wide variety of circumstances to protect consumers and other members of the public. The complexity and sophistication of modern manufactured products makes it increasingly difficult for consumers and distributors to detect dangers in those products, and places manufacturers in a position of growing responsibility for the safety of consumers. In Case 3.5, dealing with the fly in the water bottle, the Supreme Court of Canada declared that it is well established that a manufacturer of consumable goods owes a duty of care to the ultimate consumer.[43] This duty also extends to other businesses in the chain of distribution.[44]

To hold that manufacturers owe a duty of care to consumers and others who might be injured is only a partial solution to the problem. Normally, an injured party will have no way of proving that the manufacturer was negligent. However, if the product is defective, then it may be reasonable to assume that there has been negligence in some stage of its design, production, or inspection, unless there is evidence of some other reason for the defect. The circumstantial evidence principle (discussed earlier in this chapter) will be applied. The manufacturer will be liable unless it can show that the cause of the defect was not something for which it should be held responsible, or at least that it had taken all reasonable precautions to prevent defective goods from reaching the distribution system.[45]

41. [1932] A.C. 562.

42. 111 N.E. 1050 (1916).

43. *Mustapha*, *supra*, note 12 at para. 6.

44. New Brunswick has made this duty abundantly clear by codifying it in the Consumer Product Warranty and Liability Act, S.N.B. 1978, c. C-18.1.

45. United States courts have gone further. They tend to favour a principle of strict liability, under which the manufacturer impliedly warrants its products to be free of defects regardless of negligence. However, the end result is probably not very different.

In Case 3.11, based on the leading case of *Grant* v. *Australian Knitting Mills*,[46] the manufacturing company was placed in the following dilemma: if the inspection process permitted the underwear to pass through undetected, the system was inadequate and the company was therefore negligent. If the inspection process was virtually foolproof, as the manufacturer claimed, then one of its employees must have been personally at fault, making the manufacturer vicariously liable. As a result, manufacturers are liable for injuries resulting directly from all product defects of which, given the present state of technology, they can reasonably be expected to be aware.[47] Manufacturers who choose to reduce costs by omitting necessary safety features, or by using a system of sampling inspection rather than inspecting every item, become responsible for harm that results. In the long run, the savings in production cost may be outweighed by increased insurance premiums for product liability.

Case 3.12 takes us a stage further. Even though a product is not defective in any way, there may be dangers if the product is not properly used. Courts have ruled that manufacturers owe a duty to consumers to give proper warning of such dangers.[48]

duty to warn
to make users aware of the risks associated with the use of the product

The **duty to warn** is a continuing one, owed to consumers of the product. If, after a product has been placed on the market, the manufacturer becomes aware of potential dangers in its use, it must issue appropriate warnings to the public.[49] Sometimes, however, the duty may be met by issuing the warning to a "learned intermediary." In *Hollis* v. *Dow Corning Corp.*[50] the Supreme Court of Canada considered that the warning of the dangers of silicone breast implants should have been given to the physicians who would perform the implant operation. Had this been done, a direct warning to the public might not have been necessary.[51]

A plaintiff whose claim is based on a failure to warn must also satisfy the court that, had a proper warning been given, she would not have used the product or would not have used it in the way she did; that is, the failure to warn must have been a cause of the injury.[52]

CONTEMPORARY ISSUE

Tobacco Litigation

Astronomical awards of damages in the United States against tobacco manufacturers have received a lot of publicity. Individual smokers who have become ill as a result of smoking have received large sums in compensation. In July 2000, in Florida, for example, a court awarded US $145 billion in punitive damages in a class action on behalf of 700 000 smokers and former smokers.

continued

46. [1936] A.C. 85.

47. The situation may be different where the defective item is merely a component that is incorporated into the product of another manufacturer. In that case, the second manufacturer has the opportunity, and duty, to test the component for defects: see *Viridian Inc.* v. *Dresser Canada Inc.* (2002), 216 D.L.R. (4th) 122.

48. *Lambert* v. *Lastoplex Chemical Co. Ltd.*, [1972] S.C.R. 569 (inflammable lacquer); *Buchan* v. *Ortho Pharmaceutical (Canada) Ltd.* (1984), 28 C.C.L.T. 233 (Ont.) (side effects of contraceptive pills); *Plas-Tex Canada Ltd.* v. *Dow Chemical of Canada Ltd.*, supra, n. 30 (defective resin). The duty to warn may be excluded by an express contractual provision; see *Bow Valley Husky (Bermuda) Ltd.* v. *Saint John Shipbuilding Ltd.* (1997), 153 D.L.R. (4th) 385 (S.C.C.). For an interesting analysis of the duty to warn see D.W. Boivin, "Factual Causation in the Law of Manufacturer—Failure to Warn" (1998–99) 30 Ottawa Law Rev. 47.

49. *Nicholson* v. *John Deere Ltd.* (1989), 57 D.L.R. (4th) 639.

50. (1995), 129 D.L.R. (4th) 609.

51. The physician might then be liable if he operated without explaining the risk to the patient; this is discussed in Chapter 4.

52. In *Hollis* v. *Dow Corning Corp.*, supra, n. 50, the Supreme Court of Canada preferred a subjective approach to causation in product liability cases; would the plaintiff have used the product if she had known of the risk? See also *Arndt* v. *Smith* (1997), 148 D.L.R. (4th) 48 (S.C.C.).

Two years later a Los Angeles court awarded US $28 billion in punitive damages to a single plaintiff (though this was reduced on appeal to a mere US $28 million). State governments have also launched proceedings to recover the extra health-care costs that they have incurred in treating tobacco-related illnesses. In 1998, a settlement was reached under which the major tobacco companies agreed to pay a group of states a total of US $246 billion over a 25-year period.

Tobacco litigation in Canada is a more recent development. Claims for compensation have been brought both by individuals[53] and in the form of class actions.[54]

Canadian governments, too, have joined in the action. The federal government brought an action to recover health-care costs in New York State, presumably in the expectation of obtaining much larger damages than a Canadian court was likely to award. The action was dismissed on a technicality, having cost the government about $13 million in legal fees. Meanwhile, British Columbia passed a statute specifically entitling the government to recover health-care costs.[55] The first statute was declared unconstitutional by the B.C. Supreme Court.[56] A replacement statute was promptly enacted[57] and declared constitutional by the Supreme Court of Canada.[58]

QUESTIONS TO CONSIDER

1. Should individual smokers be compensated for smoking-related illnesses? How can one prove the illness was caused by smoking? Are smokers responsible for their own misfortunes? Should they be held contributorily negligent?

2. What is the basis for the claims to recover health-care costs? Should governments that have permitted the sale of cigarettes, knowing the health risks, and that have collected vast amounts of tax on their sale be entitled to compensation for the costs of providing health care?

3. Is it appropriate for a government to enact a statute for the specific purpose of allowing it to bring a claim? Is that a form of retroactive legislation?

(For an interesting review of these issues relating to tobacco liability, see G. Edinger, "The Tobacco Damages and Health Care Costs Recovery Act" [2001], 35 *Canadian Business Law Journal* 95.)

OCCUPIER'S LIABILITY

What is the duty that is owed by an owner or occupier of land[59] and buildings to visitors to those premises? The common law developed in a rather complicated manner: distinctions were made between different categories of visitors—invitees, licensees, and trespassers—and the degree of the duty owed differed with each category. The highest duty was owed to an **invitee**—that is, a person permitted by the occupier to enter for business purposes (for example, a shopper). The duty owed

invitee
a person permitted by an occupier to enter premises for business purposes

---

53. See *McIntyre Estate* v. *Ontario* (2003), 218 D.L.R. (4th) 193. That case is notable in that the Ontario Court of Appeal permitted the action to be brought on a contingency-fee basis.

54. *Caputo* v. *Imperial Tobacco Limited* (2004), 236 D.L.R. (4th) 348. The action was dismissed for failure to establish an identifiable class.

55. Tobacco Damages and Health Care Costs Recovery Act, S.B.C. 1998, c. 45.

56. *JTI-Macdonald Corp.* v. *British Columbia* (2000), 184 D.L.R. (4th) 335.

57. Tobacco Damages and Health Care Costs Recovery Act, S.B.C. 2000, c. 30. The government of Newfoundland and Labrador has enacted a similar statute: Tobacco Health Care Costs Recovery Act, S.N.L.2001, c. T-4.2.

58. *British Columbia* v. *Imperial Tobacco Canada Ltd.*, [2005] 2 S.C.R. 473, 2005 SCC 49.

59. An owner is not necessarily the "occupier" for the purposes of the legislation. In *Beheyt* v. *Chrupalo* (2004), 244 D.L.R. (4th) 688, the owners' daughter had taken full responsibility for the premises for the previous eight years, and was the landlord of the plaintiff and the person responsible under the Occupier's Liability Act.

by an occupier to an invitee is to take care to prevent injuries from hazards of which the occupier is aware and also those of which as a reasonable person he ought to be aware. By contrast, the duty owed to a **licensee**—any other visitor entering with the express or implied permission of the occupier—was simply to remove concealed dangers of which the occupier had actual knowledge.

licensee
a visitor (other than an invitee) who enters premises with the consent of the occupier

The distinction between invitee and licensee has been abolished by statute in most Canadian provinces,[60] and a common duty of care is now owed by an occupier to all visitors lawfully on the premises. Essentially, the general principles of negligence now apply.

CASE 3.13

A had been shopping at *B*'s milk store in a shopping plaza owned by *C*. On his way back to his car he tripped over an uneven paving stone just outside the store, fell, and was injured. He sued both *B* and *C*. Applying the common law rules, it was held that the plaintiff was an invitee of both defendants.[61] The owner of the plaza was negligent in its duty to maintain the sidewalk, and the milk store had failed in its duty to provide safe access for its customers. Under the modern statutory rules, both defendants would have been held liable for negligence.

trespasser
a person who enters premises without the permission of the occupier

A **trespasser** is someone who enters premises unlawfully. She enters without an invitation from or the permission of the occupier and is either unknown to the occupier or, if known to him, would be refused permission. The duty owed in these circumstances is minimal—the occupier must not set out deliberately to harm the trespasser or recklessly disregard the possibility that his acts might injure a trespasser. Thus, he must not set traps or fire a gun in the general area where he knows a trespasser to be. It is sometimes said that even a trespasser is owed a duty of "common humanity."

CHECKLIST Negligence

The elements of basic negligence are:

- a duty of care is owed
- standard of care is breached
- injury is caused

The elements have been refined to address common situations:

- product liability
  - defective products causing injury
  - dangerous products triggering a duty to warn
- occupier's liability

Defences to negligence include:

- contributory negligence
- failure to mitigate damage

---

60. For example, R.S.A. 2000, c. O-4, s. 5; R.S.B.C. 1996, c. 337, s. 3; R.S.M. 1987, c. O-8; S.N.S. 1996, c. 27; R.S.O. 1990, c. O.2, s. 1(a). In Newfoundland and Labrador, much the same result has been achieved through the courts by "restating" the common law to the effect that an occupier now owes a duty to all lawful visitors to take reasonable care: see *Gallant* v. *Roman Catholic Episcopal Corp. for Labrador* (2001), 200 D.L.R. (4th) 643.
61. *Snitzer* v. *Becker Milk Co.* (1977), 15 O.R. (2d) 345.

OTHER TORTS

One Tort or Many?

Tort law is continually changing and expanding.[62] New activities and technologies are developed, bringing new risks to the public. The law eventually creates standards for carrying on those activities and grants remedies to parties injured by conduct failing to meet those standards. As a result, the list of torts is always growing. The torts discussed below do not constitute an exhaustive list. Some torts are examined in other chapters, in the context of other subjects. We shall discuss them as they arise and mention them only briefly here.

Most of the torts we will discuss in this section differ from negligence in that they are **intentional torts**. This means that the conduct was not accidental: it was done on purpose. It does not mean that the damage was intended. For example, someone who incites a person to break an existing contract commits a tort known as **inducing breach of contract**. As we see in Chapter 7, any contract pursuing such a result is illegal as being against public policy. The tort of **deceit** takes the form of knowingly making a false statement with a view to inducing another to act upon it to her detriment. We discuss it in Chapters 4 and 9 under the heading of *misrepresentation*. The tort of **conversion** is the wrongful exercise of control over goods, inconsistent with the ownership or against the wishes of the party entitled to them. We encounter the tort of conversion in Chapters 16, 17, and 30.

intentional torts
torts involving conduct that was not accidental

inducing breach of contract
intentionally causing one person to breach his contract with another

deceit
knowingly making a false statement with a view to its being acted upon by another person

conversion
dealing with the goods of another in a manner that is inconsistent with the other's ownership

Nuisance

A small group of offences, known as **public nuisances**, includes such actions as blocking public roads, interfering with the use of public amenities such as marketplaces or parks, and emitting dangerous substances in public places. Actions against the wrongdoer may ordinarily be brought only by a government agency on behalf of the public as a whole. Occasionally, however, an individual who is able to show a special injury that is substantially greater than that suffered by other members of the general public may bring an action for compensation against the wrongdoer.[63]

On the other hand, the common law recognizes an occupier's right to the normal use and enjoyment of her land, free from interference from **private nuisances**, such as noxious fumes, excessive noise, or contaminating liquids poured into rivers or percolating through the soil. The term "occupier" includes not only the owner of land but tenants as well.

The law does not give an occupier a right to absolute freedom from these various annoyances. The courts must weigh competing interests and consider two main issues: the degree of interference with the occupier's use and enjoyment of the land, and the economic importance of the offending activity.[64] The level of interference that a community as a whole already tolerates, and that individual members of it can be expected to tolerate, as *reasonable use*, also varies according to local conditions. The standard of reasonable use of adjoining lands in an industrial area might be quite unreasonable and amount to tortious use in a holiday resort area. These are questions that are difficult to resolve in the context of private litigation. Increasingly, they have become the subject of government regulation.

public nuisance
interference with the lawful use of public amenities

private nuisance
interference with an occupier's use and enjoyment of her land

---

62. For example, some cases suggest that there is a tort of "unlawful appropriation of personality." Such cases, however, are more likely to fall within copyright law: see *Gould Estate* v. *Stoddart Publishing Co.* (1998), 161 D.L.R. (4th) 321, and the discussion in Chapter 22.

63. It seems it is also possible for the same activity to be both a public and a private nuisance: see *Sutherland* v. *Canada* (2002), 215 D.L.R. (4th) 310.

64. For an interesting illustration of this balancing of interests, see *Rideau Falls Generating Partnership* v. *City of Ottawa* (1999), 174 D.L.R. (4th) 160. The defendant municipality operated an annual ice management system to control upstream spring flooding. It broke up river ice and sent it over the falls, causing flooding to the plaintiff's generating station. The Ontario Court of Appeal held that the plaintiff should not have had its rights sacrificed to benefit the other upstream interests.

A major problem confronting modern society is pollution of the atmosphere and water resources. In common law, the discharge of noxious substances into the atmosphere or into water is not itself a breach of duty, either to the community at large or to individuals who may subsequently be harmed by those substances, although a person who suffers injury as a result may be able to establish liability in negligence. But it is usually very difficult to prove that the conduct of any one person or industry has caused harm. People who breathe carbon monoxide fumes over an extended period of time may suffer serious injury to health, but it is impossible to show that any one automobile is responsible for the harm. For these reasons, control over pollution is most effectively exercised through legislation that defines standards and that prescribes penalties for failure to comply with those standards. We consider these issues further in Chapters 29 and 32.

Trespass

trespass
unlawful entering, or remaining, on the land of another

The most ancient tort of all is that of **trespass**, the act of entering on the lands of another without consent or lawful right or, after a lawful entry, refusing to leave when ordered to do so by the occupier. An owner may fence her lands and use reasonable force to eject a trespasser. She may also bring an action against the trespasser, but she will often get little more than nominal damages unless she can prove that actual harm was done to her property. A brief discussion of this tort arises in Chapter 24 in relation to the rights of landlord and tenant against one another.

Assault and Battery

assault
the threat of violence to a person

battery
unlawful physical contact with a person

Another of the earliest torts recognized by English law is that of *trespass to the person*. The present-day legal terms are **assault** (the threat of violence) and **battery** (the actual physical contact), although the word "assault" is frequently used by itself to include battery. Assaults often constitute a crime and the attacker may be fined or imprisoned. He may also be liable (in tort) to compensate his victim, though assault and battery cases are rarely litigated as private actions. There is, however, one important exception. Since the essence of a battery is the unlawful touching of a person without consent, a surgeon who operates on a patient without consent commits a battery. This problem is discussed in the next chapter.

False Imprisonment and Malicious Prosecution

false imprisonment
unlawfully restraining or confining another person

false arrest
causing a person to be arrested without reasonable cause

A more interesting aspect of trespass to the person—and one that has far more importance from a business perspective—is the tort of **false imprisonment**. (**False arrest**, a phrase often used in the same context, ordinarily includes a false imprisonment, but has the additional feature of holding the victim with the intention of turning him over to the police for prosecution.) False imprisonment consists of intentionally restraining a person, without lawful justification, either by causing his confinement or by preventing him from leaving the place in which he is.

It is not necessary that there be actual physical restraint, or even the threat that it will be applied: a reasonable fear that a store detective might shout "Stop, thief!" would be enough restraint to amount to an imprisonment. There is therefore a real risk in confronting a member of the public with the charge of a crime without strong evidence. For example, the store detective who detains a suspected shoplifter when no shoplifting has in fact occurred has no defence against an action for false imprisonment, even if he reasonably believed the suspect had stolen goods.

malicious prosecution
causing a person to be prosecuted for a crime without an honest belief that the crime was committed

But someone who honestly makes a complaint to the police about a suspected crime is not liable for false imprisonment if the person is arrested by the police as a result of the complaint, even if the complaint turns out to be unfounded. So if a store detective reports a suspected shoplifter to a police officer and the police officer arrests the alleged shoplifter, the store detective is not liable for false imprisonment. However, if he did not have an honest belief that a crime had been committed he would be guilty of **malicious prosecution**. It is therefore much safer to report suspicious activities to the police, and let them decide whether an arrest is reasonably justified, than to attempt a citizen's arrest and learn too late that no crime has been committed.

Defamation

The tort of **defamation** is better known in each of its two forms, **libel** (written defamation) and **slander** (spoken defamation). In either case it consists of a statement that causes injury to the private, professional, or business reputation of another person. In defamation cases, the courts will not award damages unless the plaintiff can demonstrate that the defendant has made serious allegations about her character or ability, causing real and significant injury to her reputation. Defamation requires *publication*—that is, communication of the offending (written or oral) statement to someone other than the person defamed.

A defence against a charge of defamation is that the alleged defamatory statements are true, though it is for the defendant to prove the truth of the statements. In some circumstances there is immunity from defamation suits. Words spoken in parliamentary debate, in proceedings in law courts and inquests, and before royal commissions are subject to **absolute privilege**. The aim is to promote candid discussion; as a result, even intentional and malicious falsehoods uttered in Parliament are immune from action in the courts.

In other cases a qualified privilege applies. For example, a person may be asked to disclose information or give an opinion about another, as in a letter of reference from a former employer or a bank manager. The person supplying the letter would be reluctant to express an honest opinion if he might later have to prove everything he had stated in a court of law. Consequently, the law gives a **qualified privilege** to anyone giving such information. Provided he gives it in good faith with an honest belief in its accuracy, he is not liable for defamation even if the statements turn out to be untrue.

defamation
making an untrue statement that causes injury to the reputation of another person

libel
written defamation

slander
spoken defamation

absolute privilege
complete immunity from liability for defamation

qualified privilege
immunity from liability for defamation provided a statement was made in good faith

Economic Torts

Finally, there is a group of torts sometimes referred to collectively as "economic torts" that are of growing importance to the business community.[65] These torts fall into two main categories.

First, there are those torts that relate to the carrying on of business. Intentional interference with contractual relations, or inducing a breach of contract, is a tort whose origins can be traced back to the 14th century. Usually if *A* induces *B* to break his contract with *C*, *C* will sue *B* for the breach of contract.[66] As discussed below, this tort is becoming increasingly popular in the employment context where *C* may have limited resources as compared to *A*.

The tort of **unlawful interference with economic relations** is committed, for example, when *A* threatens *B* with violence if *B* continues to do business with *C*. It is not necessary that there be an actual breach of contract, but the tort requires more than just an intention to interfere—unlawful means must be used.[67] Until fairly recently the law in this area was mainly concerned with the activities of labour unions, and now falls within the sphere of labour relations legislation.

unlawful interference with economic relations
attempting by threats or other unlawful means to induce one person to discontinue business relations with another

---

CASE 3.14   The plaintiff corporation was one of the principal suppliers of car seat covers to Canadian Tire. A marketing company retained by one of its competitors bribed an employee of Canadian Tire to switch suppliers, with the result that the plaintiffs lost future business. The Supreme Court of Canada held the marketing company liable for unlawful interference with the plaintiffs' economic interests.[68]

---

65. For an example see *Verchere* v. *Greenpeace Canada* (2004) 241 D.L.R. (4th) 327, in which environmental protesters chained themselves to loggers' equipment, causing them to stop work. The protestors were held liable for lost wages.

66. For examples of actions brought in tort, see *Ernst & Young* v. *Stuart* (1997), 144 D.L.R. (4th) 328; *Gainers Inc.* v. *Pocklington Holdings Inc.* (2000), 194 D.L.R. (4th) 109. In certain circumstances, the conduct of the parties may be reviewable under the Competition Act, R.S.C. 1985, c. C-34; see *Harbord Insurance Services Ltd.* v. *Insurance Corp. of British Columbia* (1993), 9 B.L.R. (2d) 81.

67. *1175777 Ontario Ltd.* v. *Magna International Inc.* (2001), 200 D.L.R. (4th) 521. Those unlawful means may, themselves, also constitute a tort; see, for example, *Tran* v. *Financial Debt Recovery Ltd.* (2000), 193 D.L.R. (4th) 168.

68. *671122 Ontario Ltd.* v. *Sagaz Industries Canada Inc.*, *supra*, note 9. The competitor was held not to be vicariously liable, since the marketing company acted as an independent contractor.

product defamation
making false and damaging statements about the products of another person

passing off
representing one's own goods as those of another

A second category of torts relates to false advertising in relation to another's products.[69] A person commits the tort of injurious falsehood, or **product defamation**, when he intentionally makes false and disparaging statements about the products of another person—for example, a business competitor. A dishonest trader may also try to cash in on an established reputation by **passing off** his own goods as those of a competitor—for example, by using a similar label or form of packaging. Passing off is considered further in Chapter 22. Breaches of copyright, and of patent or trademark rights, are also forms of tort; they, too, are dealt with in Chapter 22. Another tort, unfair competition, is considered in Chapter 32.

ETHICAL ISSUE

Employee Recruitment

Every employer seeks skilled and experienced employees. Ads are placed and recruitment consultants (also known as headhunters) are hired, all with a view to enticing attractive applicants. The usual result is an employee quitting her current job to join a new employer. In such a case, has the new employer committed the tort of inducing breach of contract? No—provided the employee gave the current employer proper notice, no tort has been committed. However, liability could attach if the new employer encourages the employee to ignore notice or other obligations.

Recent focus has been on confidentiality obligations. It is common for employers to include confidentiality requirements in employment contracts. If an employee leaves to join a competitor, the former employer may be concerned that the employee will breach the confidentiality agreement. In addition to suing the employee, it is becoming common to sue the competitor for inducing breach of contract.[70]

In 2007, Microsoft commenced a lawsuit alleging "executive poaching" (inducing breach of employment contract) against Google. Microsoft claimed that Google was well aware of the confidentiality and non-competition requirements in the employee's contract and "encouraged" the employee to violate them.

QUESTION TO CONSIDER

1. How can an employer hire experienced employees without being accused of inducing breach of contract?

Sources: C. Noon, "Microsoft Sues Google for Alleged Exec Poaching," *Forbes.com*, May 20, 2007, www.forbes.com/2005/07/20/microsoft-google-china-cx_cn_0720autofacescan01.html; J.R. Sproat, *Wrongful Dismissal Handbook* (Toronto: Thomson Carswell, 2004), pp. 7.9–7.11; "Sprint Is Sued by BellSouth and Cingular," *New York Times*, February 8, 2003, http://query.nytimes.com/gst/fullpage.html?res=9C05E6D7123BF93BA35751C0A9659C8B63 (accessed June 27, 2008); M. Richtel, "Sprint's New Boss Is Handcuffed by His Past Job," *New York Times*, May 26, 2003, http://query.nytimes.com/gst/fullpage.html?res=9504E1D91231F935A15756C0A9659C8B63&sec=&spon=&pagewanted=all (accessed June 27, 2008).

---

69. False advertising of one's own products is considered under the heading "Consumer Protection" in Chapter 32.
70. In 2003, BellSouth and Cingular Wireless sued Sprint for luring vice-chairman Gary Forsee to Sprint. They obtained a temporary injunction blocking Mr. Forsee's move to Sprint. Ultimately, Mr. Forsee was allowed to join Sprint subject to restrictions on the activities he could undertake.

REMEDIES

Since the purpose of the law of torts is to compensate an injured party, the usual remedy is an award of a sum of money by way of damages. The concept of damages is discussed in greater detail in Chapter 15, but since there are some differences in the principles that govern damages in tort and in contract, a few observations will be helpful in this chapter.

Generally, the purpose of damages is to restore the plaintiff, so far as is possible, to the position she would have been in if the tort had not been committed. The object of awarding damages is not to punish the wrongdoer, though **punitive or exemplary damages** may be awarded in rare cases, such as a deliberate libel or malicious false imprisonment.

Tort damages are often classified in two categories: **special damages** and **general damages.** Special damages refer to items that can be more or less accurately quantified—medical bills, the cost of repairing a car, or actual lost wages. General damages include more speculative items, such as future loss of earnings due to disability, and non-pecuniary losses, such as awards for the "pain and suffering" of losing a limb or one's sight. Obviously, it is impossible to put a money value on health and happiness, but the courts must attempt to do so. They have thousands of precedents to guide them.

In some cases, remedies other than damages may be available, although they are rarely granted. Where a defendant has wrongfully converted the plaintiff's property, the court may order its specific **restitution** to the plaintiff, since to restrict the remedy to damages would in effect allow the defendant to compel a sale of the property. Courts may also grant an **injunction**—that is, order the defendant to refrain from committing further acts of a similar nature under threat of imprisonment for contempt of court if he disregards the order. For example, an injunction may restrain the defendant from committing a nuisance or from trespassing on the plaintiff's land. Less frequently, courts grant a **mandatory injunction**, ordering the defendant to take some positive action, such as removing a fence blocking the plaintiff's right-of-way to her property.

punitive or exemplary damages
damages awarded with the intention of punishing a wrongdoer

special damages
damages to compensate for quantifiable injuries

general damages
damages to compensate for injuries that cannot be expressed in monetary terms

restitution
an order to restore property wrongfully taken

injunction
an order restraining a person from doing, or continuing to do, a particular act

mandatory injunction
an order requiring a person to do a particular act

INTERNATIONAL ISSUE

Tort Reform

In the United States, tort reform is a hot political topic. Attention focuses on large damage awards and their impact on insurance premiums and availability of services. One of the major concerns is medical malpractice (physician's negligence). Large judgments affect the supply of physicians in high-risk specialties such as obstetrics, and the affordability of medical insurance. Another concern is the use of class actions to pool claims. They often result in huge contingency fees for the lawyers and small compensation for individual plaintiffs.

There are a number of reasons why tort judgments tend to be higher in the United States than in other jurisdictions around the world, including:

- the popularity of juries,
- the common use of punitive damages,
- the absence of a public health-care system, and
- the popularity of class actions and contingency fees.

Among the reform measures being considered are:

- capping the size of damage awards,

continued

■ limiting the use of juries,

■ adopting the "loser pays" rule, and

■ abolishing contingency fees.

As we have noted, some Canadian jurisdictions have undertaken targeted tort reform. Some injuries arising from negligent use of a motor vehicle are now handled by "no fault" schemes.

QUESTIONS TO CONSIDER

1. Should Canada consider capping the size of all damage awards?

2. Do you think tobacco industry litigation would have occurred without class actions and contingency fees?

Sources: R.L. Miller and G.A. Jentz, *Business Law Today: Standard Edition*, 7th ed. (Mason, OH: West Legal Studies in Business, 2006), p. 118; S.D. Sugarman, "United States Tort Reform Wars" (2002) 25(3) *The University of New South Wales Law Journal* 849–53; L. Dobbs, "Tort reform important to U.S. future," *CNN.com*, January 6, 2005, www.cnn.com/2005/US/01/06/tort.reform/index.html (accessed June 27, 2008).

MANAGING LEGAL RISK

legal risk
a business risk that may involve legal proceedings

Businesses are exposed to numerous risks of different types in the course of their operation. Some of these risks may be termed **legal risks** in that they have important legal implications—in particular, they may involve the business in being sued or in having to commence legal proceedings in order to enforce its rights.

As a general rule, the legal risk involved in contract and property law is, or should be, predictable, and appropriate steps may be taken in advance to reduce, or manage, those risks. Tort risks, by contrast, are often unpredictable or, where some risk can be predicted, the extent of the risk may be very difficult to estimate. The potential tort liability of a business is wide-ranging, as this chapter has illustrated. The business may be vicariously liable for the negligent, or even the intentionally wrongful, acts of its employees. It may be liable for injuries caused by defects in the products it sells. It may be liable for injuries sustained by visitors to its premises, or caused by harmful substances escaping from those premises.

On the other hand, it may be the business that suffers the harm. Its property may be damaged by the negligent act of some other person, or a competitor may unlawfully interfere with its economic interests.

Legal risks of this nature cannot be entirely eliminated, but they can be reduced by following a risk management strategy, as discussed in Chapter 1, in particular by

■ increasing business awareness of potential legal problems;[71]

■ assessing the legal risks and obtaining professional legal advice *before* undertaking new ventures;[72]

■ considering all risk management strategies, including avoiding, reducing, and transferring the risk;

■ transferring the risk by insuring against damage to one's own property and against liability to others. (Insurance is considered in more detail in Chapter 18.)

71. That is one of the main aims of this book.

72. Failure to obtain legal advice may even amount to contributory negligence in some circumstances: see *M. Tucci Construction Ltd.* v. *Lockwood* [2000] O.J. No.3192.

QUESTIONS FOR REVIEW

1. What is the origin of the word "tort," and what does it mean?

2. What is the principal purpose of tort law?

3. What is meant by "strict liability"? Should liability ever be "strict"?

4. Who should bear the loss resulting from an automobile accident? What are the alternatives?

5. What is the main justification for the principle of vicarious liability?

6. What must a plaintiff prove in order to succeed in an action based on negligence?

7. In what circumstances may a public authority be held liable for damage resulting from its failure to carry out a statutory duty imposed on it?

8. How do the courts determine the appropriate standard of care to be expected of a defendant?

9. Is the "but for" test an appropriate way of determining causation?

10. What is meant by "economic loss"? What are the two types of economic loss?

11. Should an injured party be able to recover damages despite the fact that her own conduct was negligent and contributed to the injury?

12. Is it relevant, in a tort action, that the injured party has taken out insurance against the loss sustained?

13. When is a manufacturer under a duty to warn?

14. What is the test, in most Canadian provinces, for establishing the liability of occupiers for injury to lawful visitors? Are trespassers treated differently?

15. What is the difference between a public and a private nuisance?

16. What constitutes false imprisonment?

17. Distinguish between libel and slander. What is meant by "privilege" in the context of defamation?

18. What are the requirements for establishing that the tort of unlawful interference with economic interests has been committed?

19. What are "punitive damages"? Should they be awarded in tort actions?

20. What is an injunction?

21. What are the main steps that can be taken to reduce legal risk?

CASES AND PROBLEMS

1. Western Ferries Inc. entered into a contract with Invincible Security Services Ltd. to provide security for its dockyard buildings. One of Invincible's employees, DeSage, was employed to patrol the premises during the night. For reasons unknown, DeSage deliberately set fire to one of the buildings, causing damage amounting to $65 000.

   Western brought an action against Invincible, claiming that Invincible was liable for the actions of their employee, DeSage. Invincible responded that DeSage had come to them with good references and had been properly instructed and trained by them to do the job.

   Should Invincible be held liable?

2. Sullivan and his friend Williams were having a quiet drink together one evening in the Tennessee Tavern when they got into an argument with four men at the next table, who had obviously had a fair amount to drink and were looking for a fight. There was a brief scuffle when one of the four men attacked Sullivan. The scuffle was broken up by two members of the tavern staff.

The tavern owner had the four men ejected by the back door of the tavern. He then told Sullivan and Williams to leave by the front door. They did so, only to be confronted by the four, who viciously attacked them, causing serious injury to Sullivan. Sullivan brought an action against the owner of the tavern, alleging that he was partly responsible for causing the injuries.

Should Sullivan succeed?

3. Smiley, a buyer for Carrefour Fashions, entered the store of a rival firm, Boulevard Boutique, in order to find out what were the latest lines they were carrying. He was recognized by Maldini, the manager of Boulevard. Maldini called the store detective, Rocco, and ordered him to "keep an eye" on Smiley while he (Maldini) called the police.

Maldini called the police, informing them that he had a "suspected shoplifter" on the premises. Smiley did not attempt to leave before the police arrived, assuming that Rocco would prevent him if he tried to do so.

Smiley accompanied the police officers to the police station, where they accepted his explanation of why he was in the store and released him.

What claim might Smiley have against Boulevard, Maldini, or Rocco? Does Boulevard have any cause of action against Smiley?

4. Prentice, an encyclopedia salesman, telephoned Hall and arranged to visit her at her apartment to show her his firm's latest volumes. When he entered the apartment building, owned by Newman, Prentice found the staircase lighting was out of order. He attempted to climb the stairs in the dark and fell on a loose step, breaking his leg. Hall knew of the faulty light and the loose step but had not thought to warn Prentice. No one had told Newman of either defect.

What claim does Prentice have against either Hall or Newman?

5. Princess Properties Inc. are the owners of a large office building originally constructed in the 1930s. Renovations were carried out by Fundamental Construction Ltd. in 1975, during which fireproofing material, containing asbestos, was installed. Princess did not know that the material contained asbestos and had relied on Fundamental to select appropriate insulating material.

In the course of further renovations in 1987, the existence of the asbestos material was discovered. Princess had it removed because it was considered a health hazard.

Princess brought an action for the cost of removing the material and for lost rent against

(a) Fundamental Construction Ltd.

(b) the architects, who had specified the use of the material in 1975

(c) the manufacturers of the material

On what basis might Princess have a valid claim against each of these defendants, and what are the principal issues that would have to be determined at trial?

6. Taylor had a student loan that was in arrears. Collection of the loan had been transferred from the original lender to Kneecap Collections Inc., a collection agency. When Kneecap demanded payment, Taylor questioned the amount that was being claimed, which was substantially larger than the amount of the original loan. Kneecap did not provide any explanation and made a further demand for immediate payment. Taylor replied that he would not pay unless he received a satisfactory explanation.

Kneecap then started a campaign of harassment. They made violent threats to Taylor, and repeatedly telephoned his employer, making various false statements about Taylor. They told his employer that Taylor had defrauded them, that he had a court order against him, and that he was secretly working part time for a competitor firm. As a result, even though Taylor denied all of these allegations, he was fired by his employer.

What remedies might Taylor have against Kneecap?

7. Brown is a farmer who raises chickens on a large scale. The baby chicks require a continuous supply of oxygen to survive, and the necessary equipment for that purpose was connected to the electric power supplied to the farm. Brown had installed an auxiliary battery-operated power generator in the barn to be available as an emergency backup. He also had a battery-operated power failure detector installed in his bedroom so that if the power in the farmhouse failed, a warning signal would alert him to the danger of loss of power to his operation.

Chauncey is a driver for Gardiner Transport Ltd. While driving the company's tractor-trailer, Chauncey allowed the vehicle to wander on to the shoulder of the road where the upper part struck overhead wires. As a result, electric power service in the area was interrupted for a period of five hours. The interruption extinguished the supply of oxygen to Brown's barn and several thousand chickens died. Unfortunately, Brown had failed to replace the battery in the alarm detector in his bedroom, and so, on the one occasion he needed it, it did not work.

Brown brought an action for damages of $30 000 against both Chauncey and Gardiner Transport Ltd. to compensate him for the loss of his chickens. At the trial a witness estimated that about 50 percent of chicken breeders used power failure detectors.

Discuss the merits of Brown's case. Explain with reasons what the court's decision would probably be.

ADDITIONAL RESOURCES FOR CHAPTER 3 ON THE COMPANION WEBSITE *(www.pearsoned.ca/smyth)*

In addition to self-test multiple-choice, true–false, and short essay questions (all with immediate feedback), application exercises, and links to useful web destinations, the Companion Website provides the following resources for Chapter 3:

- **British Columbia:** The Apology Act; Contributory Negligence; Defamation; Good Samaritans; Insurance Corporation of British Columbia (ICBC); Motor Vehicle Insurance; Occupiers' Liability; Parental Liability; Trespass to Land; Workers' Compensation; WorkSafeBC

- **Alberta:** Auto Insurance Act; Automobile Insurance; Charitable Donation of Food Act; Contributory Negligence; Defamation; Emergency Medical Aid Act; Maternal Tort Liability Act; Occupiers' Liability; Social Hosts; Trespass

- **Manitoba/Saskatchewan:** Contributory Negligence; Defamation; Farming and Nuisance; No-Fault Insurance; Occupiers' Liability—Trespass to Land; Vicarious Liability

- **Ontario:** Causation; Contributory Negligence; Defamation; Duty of Care; No-Fault Liability Insurance; Occupiers' Liability; Parental Liability; Private Investigators and Security Guards; Reverse Onus; Strict Liability; Trespass; Vicarious Liability; Workers' Compensation

Professional Liability:
THE LEGAL DILEMMA

This chapter describes three different ways the law imposes legal liability on professionals: contract, fiduciary duty, and tort. Its primary focus is the application of tort law to professionals—persons such as accountants, architects, doctors, engineers, lawyers, and pharmacists.

In this chapter we examine such questions as:

■ What are the special duties owed by professionals to their clients and to others?

■ How do the duties differ when they derive from contract? Fiduciary relationship? Tort law?

■ What is the appropriate standard of care expected of professionals?

■ How is causation determined when a loss is suffered?

■ What is the role of professional organizations in setting standards for professional conduct?

PROFESSIONAL LIABILITY: THE LEGAL DILEMMA

As business becomes more complex, professional services have become one of the fastest growing and most important sectors of the economy; at the same time, the potential for economic harm caused by negligent or fraudulent conduct of professionals has also grown considerably.

We use the term "professionals" here to apply to people who have specialized knowledge and skills that their clients rely on and are prepared to pay for. Usually they belong to some professional body and are licensed by that body to offer their services to the public. Professional opinions, obviously, are not infallible. Their value lies in assisting in clients' decisions and in increasing the likelihood that those decisions will be sound. The purchase of professional services reduces risk. But when a client pays for and relies on professional advice and it turns out to be wrong, the question arises whether the professional is liable for the loss or harm suffered by the client, or even by someone else, who relies on the advice. As we shall discuss, tort is one way to assign liability to a professional. In addition, a professional may be found liable under the contract to supply the advice. Finally, the law may require the professional to honour a fiduciary duty separate from her tort or contractual obligations.

As in other areas of tort law, the courts face a problem in determining when liability for professional incompetence or negligence arises. In theory, there is a persuasive argument to be made in favour of widened liability of professionals. The benefits (or utility) gained by a plaintiff who recovers damages will exceed the losses (or reduced utility) of a professional defendant who has to pay them but who can recoup the loss by increasing fees and by purchasing insurance protection to safeguard against liability. However, if the courts go too far and award damages to compensate everyone who relies on bad advice, the increased costs will likely discourage people from entering the profession and increase the price of advice beyond reach.

In practice, the greater exposure to liability for professional negligence has led to extensive use of liability insurance. Because of uncertainty concerning liability and the risk of heavy damages, insurance premiums have been rising. Professional fees, in turn, increase to cover insurance costs. As fees rise, clients expect more for their money, and when they are disappointed are more likely to sue. The process is something of a vicious circle and striking a fair balance can be a challenge for the courts.[1]

LIABILITY OF PROFESSIONALS

Professional liability may be considered under three headings:

- contractual duty
- fiduciary duty
- duty in tort

In most cases, the professional stands in a contractual relationship with her client. Because of the professional's skill and experience, a special relationship of trust usually also exists between professional and client, giving rise to a fiduciary duty. And a professional, like anyone else, owes a duty of care under tort law to persons who may foreseeably be injured by her negligence.

---

1. The dilemma is well summarized by Professor Brian Cheffins regarding the potential liability of auditors for incorrect statements in a corporation's financial statements: B.R. Cheffins, "Auditors' Liability in the House of Lords: A Signal Canadian Courts Should Follow" (1991), 18 C.B.L.J. 118 at 125–7; this passage was quoted with approval by LaForest, J. in the Supreme Court of Canada *Hercules Managements Ltd.* v. *Ernst & Young* (1997), 146 D.L.R. (4th) 577 at 593.

Contractual Duty

An agreement to provide professional services to a client contains a promise, whether stated expressly or not, to perform those services with due care. A breach of that promise is a breach of the contract, and the client may then sue for damages. The next part of this book is devoted to the law of contracts, and subsequent chapters will discuss liability for breach of a contractual promise, including a promise to perform with due care.

Fiduciary Duty

fiduciary duty
a duty imposed on a person who stands in a special relation of trust to another

A professional's duty often extends beyond her contractual duty in an important way. A principle of equity imposes a **fiduciary duty** where a person is in a special relationship of trust, such as often exists in professional–client relations.[2] This fiduciary duty can arise even when the professional donates services free of charge, so that no contract exists.

The first step to imposing liability for breach of fiduciary duty is establishing that the relationship is one to which the duty applies. According to the judgment of Wilson, J. in the Supreme Court of Canada, in *Frame* v. *Smith*,[3] relationships in which a fiduciary obligation exists possess three general characteristics:

- The fiduciary has scope for the exercise of some discretion or power.
- The fiduciary can unilaterally exercise that power or discretion so as to affect the beneficiary's legal or practical interests.
- The beneficiary is peculiarly vulnerable to or is at the mercy of the fiduciary holding the discretion or power.

The law has long recognized some professional relationships as inherently fiduciary including lawyer/client and doctor/patient. But not every professional relationship is a fiduciary one. For example, the broker and client relationship depends on the particular facts of the case. Five factors applicable to the assessment of a financial advisor/client relationship are: vulnerability, trust, reliance, discretion, and the standards expressed in a professional code of conduct.[4]

CASE 4.1

Mr. and Mrs. Hunt, a retired couple in their 70s, set up an investment account with Mr. Schram of TD Evergreen. Mr. Schram considered Mr. Hunt a person of average investment knowledge. Prior to his retirement, Mr. Hunt was a vice-president and director of a large footwear manufacturer.

The account was "non-discretionary," that is, no trade was to be completed without Mr. Hunt's express authorization. Mr. Schram sold 1349 of the Hunts' 1472 shares in BCE. By the time Mr. Hunt learned of the sale, the BCE stock price had risen and the Hunts sued for the lost profit. The Hunts claimed breach of contract and breach of fiduciary duty. The Court of Appeal found that the unauthorized sale amounted to a breach of contract but disallowed the claim for breach of fiduciary duty. The Court found that the relationship was not a fiduciary one. It lacked the necessary degree of discretion, reliance, and trust; Schram could not exercise unilateral power over the account and all other trades were directed by Mr. Hunt. Although there were some health and age issues, these did not amount to vulnerability in the context of the relationship.[5]

---

2. *Nocton* v. *Lord Ashburton*, [1914] A.C. 932 at 943–58; *Hedley, Byrne & Co. Ltd.* v. *Heller & Partners Ltd.*, [1964] A.C. 465 at 486.

3. [1987] 2 S.C.R. 99 at 136. See also *Air Canada* v. *M & L Travel Ltd.* (1993), 108 D.L.R. (4th) 592.

4. *Hodgkinson* v. *Simms*, [1994] 3 S.C.R. 377.

5. *Hunt* v. *TD Securities Inc.*, (2003) 229 D.L.R. (4th) 609 (Ont. C.A.).

If a fiduciary duty is found to exist, it imposes a wider range of obligations on a professional than is expressly stated in the contract or required under tort law. The professional must act honestly, in good faith, and only in the best interests of the client. The second step to imposing liability involves determining if the professional's behaviour meets the fiduciary duty. For example, a lawyer who entered into a business arrangement with a client of long standing and failed to disclose his own precarious financial situation was held to be in breach of his fiduciary duty to the client.[6] And an accountant may not use information obtained from a client to make an investment without the consent of the client.

Liability for breach of fiduciary duty may arise without any negligence.

CASE 4.2

Hodgkinson, a stockbroker, was inexperienced in tax planning. He wanted an independent professional to advise him in respect to tax planning and tax shelter needs. He retained Simms, an accountant who specialized in these areas. On Simms' advice, Hodgkinson invested in a number of MURBs (multiple unit residential buildings) as tax shelters and lost heavily when the value of the MURBs fell during a decline in the real estate market. The advice was perfectly sound at the time it was given. Unknown to Hodgkinson, Simms was also acting for the developers in structuring the MURBs and did not disclose that fact to Hodgkinson. The Supreme Court of Canada accepted the client's claim that he would not have undertaken the investment had he known of the adviser's conflict of interest. Simms was held to be in breach of his fiduciary duty to Hodgkinson and consequently liable to compensate Hodgkinson for his loss.[7]

Case 4.2 illustrates the principle that a fiduciary should not place herself in a position of **conflict of interest** and has a duty not to profit, or attempt to profit, at the client's expense. A fiduciary obligation requires complete loyalty to the other party to the relationship. Consequently, a professional who acts on behalf of two or more clients who have competing interests (for example, the vendor and the purchaser of a piece of property) may well find it impossible to fulfill her duty to them both. In one recent case, the Ontario Court of Appeal made an order prohibiting a law firm, one of whose lawyers had represented two book stores in an amalgamation five years earlier, from acting for a prospective purchaser of the amalgamated company.[8] The law firm possessed confidential information that it had acquired in the earlier transaction. The firm was placed in a potentially impossible position: its duty to its previous clients forbade it to disclose the information, which in turn made it difficult to represent the new client effectively.

conflict of interest
a situation where a duty is owed to a client whose interests conflict with the interests of the professional, another client, or another person to whom a duty is owed

ETHICAL ISSUE

Lessons from Enron

Enron was the seventh-largest public corporation in the United States. The energy giant's collapse into bankruptcy cost investors billions of dollars and was accompanied by revelations of fraud and impropriety on a massive scale.

The Enron affair highlighted the many conflicts of interest that arise when a corporation's external auditors also act as its accountants, business advisers, or management consultants. In theory, a corporation's auditors are appointed by its shareholders: their task is to supervise the

continued

6. *Korz v. St. Pierre* (1987), 61 O.R. (2d) 609; *Strother v. 3464920 Canada Inc.*, [2007] 2 S.C.R. 177.
7. *Hodgkinson v. Simms, supra*, n. 4. See also *Martin v. Goldfarb* (1998), 163 D.L.R. (4th) 639 and *Strother* at note 6.
8. *Chapters Inc. v. Davies, Ward & Beck LLP.* [2000] O.J. No. 4973.

financial management of the corporation's affairs by the directors and management and to report any irregularities. In reality, the auditors are usually selected by the management and their appointment is a formality. They consequently owe their position to the very people they are meant to supervise, an obvious conflict of interest.

A second conflict of interest arises when the auditors are themselves members of a firm that has lucrative contracts to supply accounting and management services to the corporation that they are required to audit. If they judge the directors too harshly, they may jeopardize those contracts and lose an important source of income for their firm.

To address these and other governance problems, the United States passed the Sarbanes-Oxley Act of 2002 (SOX), which introduced a number of changes, including:

■ prohibiting a company from hiring one accounting firm to provide both auditing and consulting services, and

■ placing auditor selection under the control of directors who do not work at the company.

The application of SOX was not limited to American companies—it applied even to foreign companies trading on an American exchange. As we will discuss in Chapters 28 and 29, Canada immediately felt the impact of SOX and has now adopted many of the SOX provisions.

QUESTIONS TO CONSIDER

1. What other possible solutions would you propose to minimize conflicts of interest?

2. Is it appropriate for American legislation to apply to Canadian corporations?

3. Accountants have always been under a duty to avoid conflicts of interest. Why was this existing duty not sufficient to prevent the auditor/consultant conflict?

Sources: New York State Society of Certified Public Accountants, "The Sarbanes-Oxley Act of 2002," *The Website of the New York Society of CPAs*, www.nysscpa.org/oxleyact2002.htm; L. McCallum and P. Puri, *Canadian Companies' Guide to Sarbanes-Oxley Act*, (Markham: LexisNexis Butterworth, 2004).

Duty in Tort

Until the 1980s the courts appeared to favour the view that a professional's liability to her client should be governed by the duties owed under the contract.[9] They limited a client's right to sue for the tort of negligence to special circumstances where the professional's conduct did not fall within her contractual obligations. Subsequent decisions suggested that a plaintiff might choose to sue either in contract or in tort, and this approach has been confirmed by the Supreme Court of Canada. In a case where a solicitor was negligent in arranging a mortgage that was later found to be void, the Court held that the client was entitled to sue in either contract or tort.[10] The common law duty of care is not confined to relationships that arise apart from contract—it exists independently of the duty owed under the contract.

Of greater importance, usually, is the fact that a duty may be owed in tort to persons other than the client who is paying for the services. Many people may rely on a professional opinion given to a single client, as for example:

■ when an auditor expresses an opinion on the fairness and accuracy of the client firm's financial statements

■ when engineers or architects recommend design specifications for structures that, if faulty, may present risks to occupiers and others

9. *Nunes Diamonds* v. *Dominion Electric Co.* (1972), 26 D.L.R. (3d) 699 at 727–8.
10. *Central Trust Co.* v. *Rafuse* (1986), 31 D.L.R. (4th) 481.

- when bankers or credit analysts give assessments of creditworthiness for their customers which come to the attention of other lenders
- when accountants provide a corporation with a valuation of the business or its shares, and the valuation is intended for the use of a third party
- when a lawyer prepares a will for a client who intends to leave property to a beneficiary under the will
- when one doctor gives a professional opinion to another doctor concerning the patient of the second doctor

Potential **third-party liability** also exists for insurance agents and real estate agents. The contractual duty of a real estate agent is normally owed to the vendor of the property; that of an insurance agent is usually owed to the insurance company with which she arranges insurance.[11] In the course of their work for their principals, however, these agents develop close relations with persons to whom they may refer as "clients"—applicants for insurance and prospective purchasers of houses. While in a strict sense their commissions are paid by their principals, the persons with whom they deal in the course of their work provide them with the opportunity of earning the commissions and frequently rely on their advice.

third-party liability
liability to some other person who stands outside a contractual relationship

As we shall see, one of the most difficult questions that the courts have had to answer in recent years is where, precisely, to draw the line in deciding when a professional incurs liability to a non-client for a negligent or inaccurate statement.

CASE 4.3

A credit union was investigated by the government agency responsible for supervision. The investigation revealed that, over a number of years, the credit union had made various unauthorized and unsecured loans, and its loans department had committed various other irregularities. The credit union brought an action against its former auditors, claiming that they ought to have discovered the irregularities if their audits had been conducted with proper care. The auditors were found to have been negligent and were held liable for losses sustained by the credit union. However, the credit union was held to have been contributorily negligent, in failing to exercise proper supervision over its loan manager, and was held to be 30 percent to blame.[12]

The Choice of Action

Before turning to the tort liability question, one other issue needs to be addressed. As we have seen, sometimes a professional may be liable in tort but not in contract, or may be liable for breach of fiduciary duty without having been negligent. But there will frequently be cases where the professional is liable in both contract and in tort, and perhaps for breach of fiduciary duty as well. Does it matter whether the client sues for breach of contract, breach of fiduciary duty, or for negligence?

The choice may be important. The rules governing the time limits for bringing an action might make it advantageous to sue in tort.[13] On the other hand, in a tort action a client's own contributory negligence may be raised as a defence, though the defendant may still rely upon any term of

11. By contrast, an insurance broker usually acts as agent for the insured: see the discussion in *Adams-Eden Furniture Ltd.* v. *Kansa General Insurance Co.* (1996), 141 D.L.R. (4th) 288, and see Chapter 18.

12. *Capital Community Credit Union Ltd.* v. *BDO Dunwoody* [2001] O.J. No. 4249.

13. The time limit for a tort action is normally calculated from the moment when the breach is discovered, rather than when it occurs, as is the rule in contract. In *Central Trust Co.* v. *Rafuse, supra*, n. 10, the invalidity of the mortgage was not discovered until some years after it was executed. This difference in time limits is also important in cases of negligence by an architect or builder, where a defect may only be discovered many years after construction has been completed and it would be too late to sue in contract.

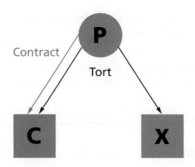

FIGURE 4.1

Contractual and Tort
Liability

The professional (*P*) owes both a contractual duty and a duty in tort to client (*C*). The only duty owed to a third party (*X*) is a duty in tort. (There may be occasions when a fiduciary duty is owed to *C* or to *X*.)

the contract that excludes or limits liability.[14] As we saw in Case 4.1, the problem can often be avoided by pleading both, or all three, causes of action in the alternative.[15]

The form of the action may also affect the amount of damages awarded in some cases. The principles for determining the measure of damages are not exactly the same in contract as in tort.[16] In the case of breach of fiduciary duty, a defendant may be under a **duty to account** for any profit derived from the breach in addition to or as an alternative to damages. However, in *Hodgkinson* v. *Simms*,[17] the Supreme Court of Canada held that damages for breach of a fiduciary duty should place the plaintiff in the position he would have been in if the breach had not occurred. In *Martin* v. *Goldfarb*, Finlayson, J.A., delivering the judgment of the Ontario Court of Appeal, expressed the view that, regardless of the doctrinal underpinning, plaintiffs should not be able to recover higher damage awards merely because their claim is characterized as breach of fiduciary duty as opposed to breach of contract or tort.[18]

duty to account
the duty of a person who commits a breach of trust to hand over any profits derived from the breach

LIABILITY FOR INACCURATE STATEMENTS

Misrepresentation

deceit
the making of a false statement with the intention of misleading another person

If a person makes an untrue statement, knowing it to be untrue, or at any rate without an honest belief in its truth, and with the intention to mislead some other person, the misrepresentation is fraudulent and amounts to the tort of **deceit**. A victim who relies reasonably on the statement and suffers a loss may recover from the person who made it. The tort of deceit may also be committed when a person deliberately conceals or withholds information.

---

14. *Central Trust Co.* v. *Rafuse*, supra, n. 10; *London Drugs Ltd.* v. *Kuehne & Nagel International Ltd.* (1992), 97 D.L.R. (4th) 261.

15. Where the plaintiff sues in both contract and in tort, it seems that the defence of contributory negligence can be raised against both claims; see *Crown West Steel Fabricators* v. *Capri Insurance Services Ltd.* (2002), 214 D.L.R. (4th) 577: contrast *Caners* v. *Eli Lilley Canada Inc.* (1996), 134 D.L.R. (4th) 730, where the action was brought only in contract.

16. See Chapter 3, under the heading "Remedies," and Chapter 15, under the heading "The Measurement of Damages."

17. *Supra*, n. 4; see Case 4.1.

18. (1998), 163 D.L.R. (4th) 639 at 652. Clearly, some uncertainty remains: see Waddams, "Fiduciary Duties and Equitable Compensation" (1996), 27 C.B.L.J. 466.

CASE 4.4

A bank allowed a customer to invest in a company that owed a substantial debt to the bank. The bank's employees knew that the company was on the verge of insolvency but did not disclose this fact to the customer. The bank was held guilty of fraud and liable to compensate the customer.[19]

Whereas deceit or **fraudulent misrepresentation** requires at least some guilty knowledge or willful disregard of the falsity of information provided, **negligent misrepresentation** requires only a breach of the duty of care and skill.

As we saw in Chapter 3, one of the most significant developments in the law of torts has been the extension of liability to include negligent acts causing purely economic loss, as distinguished from those causing injury to persons or property.[20] For a long time the courts drew back from holding persons liable for negligent misrepresentation except when there was a contract with the injured party or when they were subject to a fiduciary duty. The courts were especially reluctant to impose liability for negligent misrepresentation, in the absence of a direct contractual or fiduciary relationship, on professionals giving financial advice and information such as accountants, bankers, trust company officers, and stockbrokers, whose statements often reach large numbers of the public. They feared that to extend liability to third persons, for advice given to and intended only for a client, would make the risk so wide as to limit severely the reasonable freedom of professionals to practise their occupations. In a case in 1951, the English Court of Appeal held that an accountant who carelessly audited a misleading financial statement, knowing that it would be shown to a prospective investor, was not liable to the investor for the loss caused by reliance on the audited statement.[21] Lord Justice Denning, who dissented from the majority opinion, considered that such risks were greatly exaggerated: the duty of care need not be owed to every conceivable person, but should be confined to the particular person.

fraudulent misrepresentation
an incorrect statement made knowingly with the intention of causing injury to another

negligent misrepresentation
an incorrect statement made without due care for its accuracy

The *Hedley Byrne* Principle

Twelve years later, Lord Denning's position was accepted by the House of Lords in the famous case of *Hedley Byrne* v. *Heller & Partners*.[22]

CASE 4.5

Easipower asked Hedley Byrne, an advertising agency, to handle its account in placing ads in magazines and commercials on radio and TV. Since Hedley Byrne would have to extend credit to Easipower in arranging the advertising, it first decided to ask its own bank to obtain credit information on Easipower, and in particular about whether Easipower would be good for a line of credit up to certain limits. The bank manager made inquiries from Heller & Partners (Easipower's bankers) about Easipower's creditworthiness, without revealing Hedley Byrne's identity. Heller sent the following letter in reply:

CONFIDENTIAL

For your private use and without responsibility on the part of the bank or its officers

19. *Sugar* v. *Peat Marwick Ltd.* (1988), 55 D.L.R. (4th) 230.

20. Negligent misstatements causing physical injury have long been actionable—for example, where an architect's negligent design causes a building to collapse.

21. *Candler* v. *Crane, Christmas & Co.*, [1951] 2 K.B. 164.

22. *Hedley Byrne* v. *Heller & Partners*, [1964] A.C. 465.

Dear Sir:

In reply to your inquiry we advise that Easipower is a respectably constituted company, considered good for its ordinary business obligations. Your figures are larger than we are accustomed to see.

Yours truly,

Heller & Partners.

At no time did Hedley Byrne communicate directly with Heller, but its own bank did inform it of the full contents of the letter, including the disclaimer of responsibility. Hedley Byrne then accepted Easipower as an account and placed extensive advertising for it, running up a large balance. Shortly afterwards Easipower became insolvent and was unable to pay Hedley Byrne more than a small portion of the debt. Hedley Byrne sued Heller for the resulting loss, claiming it was caused by Heller's negligent misrepresentation of Easipower's creditworthiness.

disclaimer
an express statement to the effect that the person making it takes no responsibility for a particular action or statement

The House of Lords found that although Heller neither dealt with nor even knew the identity of Hedley Byrne, Heller should have foreseen that its information would be used by a customer of the other bank. It therefore owed that customer a duty to take reasonable care in expressing an opinion about the financial state of Easipower. On the facts, however, the court held that, because of the **disclaimer** of responsibility, Hedley Byrne could not rely on the information. Nevertheless, the *Hedley Byrne* decision established the principle of liability to third parties for negligent misrepresentation.

The result is that a person who makes such a misstatement may be held liable for losses suffered by a wider group than those with whom she has a direct contractual or fiduciary relationship. The crucial question is, "How wide is that group?"

Limits to the *Hedley Byrne* Principle

If the test of liability for negligent misrepresentation turned entirely on who could foreseeably be harmed, banks, public accountants, and other financial analysts might be faced with an almost unlimited liability. For example, the auditors of a corporation whose financial statements are made public know that the statements will be relied upon by many people who are unknown to them. They could be liable then to anyone who might happen to read the financial statements.[23]

CASE 4.6

Shareholders in two corporations brought an action against a firm of accountants, alleging that audits of the corporations' financial statements had been negligently prepared, and that in consequence, they had incurred investment losses and losses in the value of their shareholdings. Their claim failed.

The Supreme Court of Canada held that (a) there was no contractual relationship between the auditors of a corporation and its shareholders; (b) the purpose of the auditor's report was to oversee the management and affairs of the corporation, and (c) the auditors owed shareholders no duty of care in respect of their personal investments.[24]

---

23. This fear is largely responsible for the enactment in Ontario of legislation allowing for the creation of limited liability partnerships by accounting and other professional firms: see Chapter 26.
24. *Hercules Managements Ltd.* v. *Ernst & Young* (1997), 146 D.L.R. (4th) 577.

As to the existence of a duty of care, the court applied a two-part test, expressed as follows.[25]

> First one has to ask whether, as between the alleged wrongdoer and the person who has suffered
> damage there is a sufficient relationship of proximity or neighbourhood such that, in the reason-
> able contemplation of the former, carelessness on his part may be likely to cause damage to the
> latter—in which case a *prima facie* duty of care arises. Secondly, if the first question is answered
> affirmatively, it is necessary to consider whether there are any considerations which ought to neg-
> ative, or to reduce or limit the scope of the duty or the class of person to whom it is owed or the
> damages to which a breach of it may give rise. . . .[26]

The first branch of the test requires an inquiry into whether there is a sufficiently close relationship between the plaintiff and the defendant that in the reasonable contemplation of the defendant,
carelessness on its part may cause damage to the plaintiff. The court held that a *prima facie* duty of
care did exist in the *Hercules* case: the possibility that the shareholders would rely on the audited
financial statements of the corporation in conducting their affairs, and that they may suffer harm if
the reports were negligently prepared, must have been reasonably foreseeable to the auditors.

The second branch of the test raises what is essentially a policy issue. On this issue, LaForest,
J. said:

> I would agree that deterrence of negligent conduct is an important policy consideration with
> respect to auditors' liability. Nevertheless, I am of the view that, in the final analysis, it is
> outweighed by the socially undesirable consequences to which the imposition of indeterminate
> liability on auditors might lead.[27]

Liability, consequently, should be restricted to the use of the information for the same purpose
as that for which it was prepared. As a matter of law, the only purpose for which shareholders
receive an auditor's report is to provide them with information in order to be able to oversee the
management and affairs of the corporation—not for the purpose of guiding their personal investment decisions. Therefore, no duty of care was owed to them in that regard.

It would seem from this test that eligible plaintiffs must not only be "foreseeable" in a general
sense, but also more specifically "foreseen" in relation to a contemplated transaction. So when, in
an earlier case, an auditor negligently prepared accounts for a corporation, knowing that they were
to be shown to a potential purchaser of the corporation, the Supreme Court of Canada held that
he was liable for the loss suffered by the purchaser.[28] Securities legislation creates a statutory cause
of action for damages arising from misrepresentations contained in financial statements of publicly
traded companies, as well as other documents including a prospectus.[29]

Liability for negligent misrepresentation is not restricted to financial information provided by
professionals such as accountants and bankers.[30] A municipality has been held liable for loss suffered
by purchasers of land who relied on incorrect information given to them by the zoning department

---

25. The test was first enunciated by Lord Wilberforce in the *House of Lords in Anns* v. *Merton London Borough Council*,
[1978] A.C. 728 at 751–2 (H.L.). It was quoted with approval in the *Hercules* case, by LaForest, J., at 586, and has
been followed and applied in a number of other important Canadian decisions; for example, *Kamloops (City)* v.
Nielsen (1983), 10 D.L.R. (4th) 641; *Winnipeg Condominium Corp. No. 36* v. *Bird Construction Co.* (1995), 121
D.L.R. (4th) 193.

26. Just as LaForest, J. intended, this test now applies to all negligence cases, not merely those involving negligent misrepresentation: *Mustapha* v. *Culligan of Canada Ltd.*, 2008 SCC 27 and *Hill* v. *Hamilton-Wentworth Regional Police
Services Board*, 2007 SCC 41.

27. At 593.

28. *Haig* v. *Bamford* (1976), 72 D.L.R. (2d) 68.

29. Securities Act, R.S.O. 1990, c. S.5, ss. 130–138.14; R.S.B.C. 1996, c. 418, ss. 131–140; R.S.A. 2000, c. S-4,
ss. 203–211.095. For a discussion of the statutory liability see *Kerr* v. *Danier Leather Inc.*, 2007 SCC 44.

30. In one recent case a law firm was held liable for a negligent statement regarding the secured status of a loan: 347671
B.C. Ltd. v. *Heenan Blaikie* [2002] B.C.J. No. 347.

regarding permissible use of the land.[31] An engineering firm that was negligent in preparing drawings and specifications for a provincial construction project was held liable for loss suffered by the construction company that had bid successfully for the contract in reliance on the specifications.[32] Although the scope of the *Hedley Byrne* principle has been gradually widened over the years, the courts remain cautious about extending the principle too far. For example, in one recent case the British Columbia Court of Appeal held that a government department, which had negligently certified to a leasing corporation that a piece of contaminated land had been fully cleaned, was not liable to an investor who bought shares in the leasing corporation. There was insufficient proximity between the Crown and the plaintiff to establish a duty of care and, even if a duty of care was owed, it would be negated by the policy consideration of indeterminate liability.[33] In another case the Ontario Court of Appeal refused to extend liability for a defective smoke alarm system to the organization that set the safety standards and approved the product as safe. The parties did not have the necessary close and direct relationship to justify imposing a duty of care. Even if a *prima facie* duty of care did exist, policy considerations would negate the duty, since to do so would effectively create an insurance scheme for dissatisfied purchasers, for which the purchasers had paid nothing.[34]

A further requirement of the *Hedley Byrne* principle, apart from the existence of a duty, is that the plaintiff's reliance on the misrepresentation must have been reasonable. An interesting issue was raised in *Avco Financial Services Realty Ltd.* v. *Norman.*[35] At trial, the defendant finance company was held liable for a negligent misrepresentation by failing to point out to the plaintiff that he would need to renew a life insurance policy if he wished to renew his mortgage: the plaintiff was held to have been contributorily negligent by not inquiring further into the terms of the mortgage. On appeal, it was argued that the two findings were mutually inconsistent. If the plaintiff's reliance on the misrepresentation was reasonable, then he could not have been negligent himself. Alternatively, if he was negligent, his reliance on the statement would not have been reasonable. The Ontario Court of Appeal rejected both arguments. The two findings could co-exist: it could be reasonable to rely on a statement, but negligent to rely exclusively upon it.[36]

Omissions

The duty to take reasonable care includes the duty not to omit essential steps in providing professional services. It applies to sins of omission as well as sins of commission.

CASE 4.7

Fine's Flowers Ltd. sustained a serious loss from the freezing of flowers and plants in its greenhouse. The freezing conditions were caused by failure of a water pump, which interrupted the supply of water to boilers that heated the greenhouse. Fine's had arranged its insurance with the same agent for many years and its coverage and premium costs were extensive. It relied on the agent to recommend appropriate coverage and paid the necessary premiums without question. An inspector for the insurance company had advised the agent that the insurance policy with Fine's did not cover such matters as the failure of water pumps but the agent did not report this gap in insurance coverage to Fine's.

Since the policy provided no right of recovery from the insurance company, Fine's brought an action against the agent for breach of his duty of care in failing to notify it of the insufficient

---

31. *Bell* v. *City of Sarnia* (1987), 37 D.L.R. (4th) 438.

32. *Edgeworth Constructions Ltd.* v. *N.D. Lea & Associates Ltd.* (1993), 107 D.L.R. (4th) 169. Interestingly, the individual engineers employed by the firm, who prepared the drawings, were held not to owe a duty to the contractor.

33. *Border Enterprises Ltd.* v. *Beazer East Inc.* (2002), 216 D.L.R. (4th) 107.

34. *Hughes* v. *Sunbeam Corp. (Canada) Ltd.* (2003) 219 D.L.R. (4th) 467.

35. (2003) 226 D.L.R. (4th) 175.

36. See also *M. Tucci Construction Ltd.* v. *Lockwood* [2000], O.J. No. 3192, where an investor was misled by his accountant as to the nature of an agreement, but was held contributorily negligent for making no effort to have the agreement explained to him and for not taking legal advice.

coverage. The agent defended on the grounds that such a duty of care was so broad and sweeping as almost to make him strictly liable and that it was not part of his duty to know everything about a client's business in order to be in a position to anticipate every conceivable form of loss. The court nevertheless held that on the facts of the case a duty of care did exist, and Fine's succeeded in recovering damages from the agent. The grounds for recovery could equally be classified as negligent omission or breach of a special fiduciary relationship between Fine's Flowers and the insurance agent.[37]

As we noted in Chapter 3, a surgeon who operates on a patient without the patient's consent commits the tort of battery. In this context, "consent" means informed consent: before operating, the surgeon should explain the procedure and the possible risks to the patient. The modern tendency has been to hold a doctor liable in battery only when it can be said that there has been no genuine informed consent at all. However, the courts have recognized a patient's right to full information about the risks inherent in a treatment and the omission of relevant information normally amounts to negligence.[38] The court also considers a second question: would a reasonable person in the position of the plaintiff have decided against the procedure upon a proper disclosure of the risks?[39] If the court is satisfied that the answer is "yes," then it is also saying that the failure to inform was not only a breach of duty but also caused the harm—and the patient will be awarded damages in compensation. But where the court is satisfied that the patient would still have consented even if the risk had been explained, the physician will not be liable.[40] The question of causation is discussed more fully later in this chapter.

THE STANDARD OF CARE FOR PROFESSIONALS

In Chapter 3 we noted that the standard of care applied in ordinary negligence actions is that of "the person on the Yonge Street subway." That standard is obviously inappropriate when judging the work of an accountant, a lawyer, or a surgeon. But how should one determine what is an appropriate and acceptable standard?

CASE 4.8

Hodgins wished to add an extension with an indoor swimming pool to his house. Through his contractor, he sought the advice of the local hydro-electric commission on heating the addition. An employee of the commission, Runions, provided an estimate of the cost of heating by electricity. In reliance on the estimate, Hodgins specified electric heating for the extension. The estimate proved to be much below the actual costs. Hodgins sued the hydro-electric commission for negligent misrepresentation, on the authority of *Hedley Byrne*. Runions was found not to have been negligent.[41]

In reaching that conclusion, the Ontario Court of Appeal explicitly rejected a hindsight approach. Mr. Justice Evans observed:

. . . the Court is required to consider the information available in 1967 to one in the position of Runions. The question then arises: Did Runions exercise reasonable skill, competence and diligence in the preparation of the cost estimate or did he not? In the opinion of the expert, Runions calculated the heat loss in the same manner as anyone similarly expert in the art would have done in 1967. In the light of that uncontradicted evidence, it would appear that Runions prepared his estimate according to the skill and knowledge available to those engaged in that particular field. If Runions met the standard then he was not negligent and no liability can be imputed to the defendant. That the estimate was incorrect is not questioned, but it is not sufficient that the plaintiff establish merely that Runions' estimate was wrong, he must go further and establish that the incorrect estimate resulted from a lack of skill, competence or diligence on the part of Runions.[42]

---

37. *Fine Flowers Ltd.* v. *General Accident Assurance Co. et al.* (1974), 49 D.L.R. (3d) 641; affirmed (1977), 81 D.L.R. (3d) 139. See also *Martin* v. *Goldfarb* (1998), 163 D.L.R. (4th) 639.

38. Alternatively, it may be treated as a breach of fiduciary duty: see *Seney* v. *Crooks* (1998), 166 D.L.R. (4th) 337.

39. *Hopp* v. *Lepp* (1980), 112 D.L.R. (3d) 67; *Reibl* v. *Hughes* (1980), 114 D.L.R. (3d) 1. Contrast the "subjective" test applied in product liability cases, in *Hollis* v. *Dow Corning Corp.* (1995), 129 D.L.R. (4th) 609, considered in Chapter 3.

40. *Kitchen* v. *McMullen* (1989), 62 D.L.R. (4th) 481.

41. *Hodgins* v. *Hydro-Electric Commission of the Township of Nepean* (1975), 60 D.L.R. (3d) 1.

42. *Ibid.*, at 4.

The approach taken in the *Hodgins* case was to compare the quality of professional work done or advice given with the standards of the profession prevailing at the time. This approach tends to assess the adequacy of professional work without reference to the consequences of relying on it. However, simply complying with normal professional standards is not always an adequate defence. When the case was appealed to the Supreme Court of Canada, Chief Justice Laskin agreed that the action should be dismissed, but added:

> In my opinion, the care or skill that must be shown by the defendant must depend, as it does here, on what is the information or advice sought from him and which he has unqualifiedly represented that he can give. He may assume to act in a matter beyond his then professional knowledge or that of others in the field and, if he does, he cannot then so limit the plaintiff's reliance unless he qualifies his information or advice accordingly or unless the plaintiff knows what are the limitations of the defendant's competence when seeking the information or advice.[43]

Consequently, there seem to be two tests. A professional must exercise the same degree of skill and possess the same level of knowledge as is generally expected of members of that profession: that is to say, she must live up to the standards of the profession.[44] The courts will normally consider two types of evidence in determining what those standards are. Many professions publish a code of conduct for their members, or guidelines to be followed in particular types of work. These can usually be taken as laying down an appropriate standard. Frequently, the courts also hear the testimony of practitioners who state what they consider a proper standard. Sometimes, of course, professional opinion is divided—for example, about the best medical treatment in a particular circumstance. In such a case it will normally be sufficient that the defendant has followed a well-recognized practice, even though some other procedure might arguably have been better.[45]

But established standards alone should not be allowed to become a means for protecting members of a profession from liability.[46] As Chief Justice Laskin pointed out in the *Hodgins* case, sometimes a professional undertakes a task that is beyond the usual skills of her profession; she cannot then rely on the normal professional standard. The degree of skill and knowledge must be commensurate with the particular task undertaken.

CAUSATION

In Chapter 3 we defined the elements of negligence, meaning the conditions that must be met before compensation will be awarded to an injured party. The court must find that: the defendant owed a duty to the injured party, the defendant breached that duty, and the breach of duty caused the injury. We have discussed the first two of these conditions in this chapter in relation to the liability of a professional and now turn to the special problems of satisfying the requirement of causation.

The essence of causation, in professional–client relationships, is reliance. Did the client rely and act upon the advice of the professional? Would the client have acted in that way if he had not received that advice?[47]

---

43. *Hodgins* v. *Hydro-Electric Commission of the Township of Nepean* (1975), 60 D.L.R. (3d) 1.

44. No allowance appears to be made for experience: a newly qualified professional is held to the same standard as an experienced one. However, within a profession, a higher standard may apply to a specialist than to a general practitioner.

45. *Belknap* v. *Meekes* (1989), 64 D.L.R. (4th) 452; *ter Neuzen* v. *Korn* (1995), 127 D.L.R. (4th) 577.

46. See, for example, the decision of the Supreme Court of Canada in *Roberge* v. *Bolduc*, [1991] 1 S.C.R. 374, in which a notary was held to have been negligent in conducting a title search despite having followed the common practice in the profession.

47. As we have already noted, a surgeon will not be held liable for failure to fully inform a patient of all known risks if it is clear that the patient would have agreed to the procedure in any event.

CASE 4.9 An investment company became interested in acquiring control of an apparently prosperous family business. The company commissioned a report on the proposed acquisition from a well-known firm of investment analysts. The report estimated the family business to be worth more than $4 million and considered it to be a sound investment. Without having read the report, the directors of the investment company decided that they should move quickly—they had heard rumours that there was another prospective purchaser. They purchased all the shares in the family business for $3.5 million. Subsequently, they learned that the major asset of their acquisition was almost worthless and that they had paid several times what the shares were worth.[48]

Despite their negligence, the analysts were not found liable since their conduct was not in any way a cause of the loss.

THE ROLE OF PROFESSIONAL ORGANIZATIONS

Responsibilities and Powers

Most major professions—medicine, nursing, dentistry, accounting, law, engineering, and architecture—are governed by professional organizations established under, and to some extent regulated by, provincial statutes. A typical professional organization has a governing council composed mainly of elected representatives of the profession, but it may also have external lay representatives appointed by the government to provide an impartial voice in decision-making and to represent the public interest. Professional bodies have a number of special responsibilities:

- to set educational and entrance standards for candidates wishing to become members
- to examine and accredit educational institutions that prepare candidates for membership
- to set and adjust standards of ethical conduct and professional competence
- to hear complaints about and administer discipline to members who fail to live up to the established standards
- to defend the profession against attacks that it considers unfair, and to look after the general welfare of the profession

The governing statute typically gives members of the organization the exclusive right to use a professional designation to identify themselves and often also gives members the exclusive right to practise their profession.[49] Anyone who identifies himself as a member or attempts to practise when not accredited as a member may be—and usually is—prosecuted for committing an offence under the provincial statute.

Two important consequences flow from these powers. First, the right to discipline gives the organizations great power over individual members—expulsion, or suspension for any extended period, may destroy a member's means of livelihood. Second, exclusivity gives these self-governing professions great power over the quality and cost of their services to the public, and there is consequently a strong public interest in the affairs of the organizations.

48. Case 4.9 is based in part on the decision in *Toromont Industrial Holdings* v. *Thorne, Gunn, Helliwell & Christenson* (1977), 14 O.R. (2d) 87 (some damages were awarded, however, on other grounds.). See also *Martin* v. *Goldfarb* (1998), 163 D.L.R. (4th) 639.

49. For example, the exclusive right to practise applies to medicine and law, but not to some areas of accounting.

CASE 4.10

Schilling had entrusted $600 000 to an accountant, Hofman, to invest for him. Hofman absconded with the money. Hofman was a former member of the Association of Certified General Accountants of British Columbia, and having recently been disciplined for other offences, had been forced to resign from the Association, and had been deprived of the right to describe himself as a "CGA." Schilling sued the Association alleging negligence in not preventing Hofman from continuing to practise—as a result of which Hofman had been able to defraud Schilling.

The British Columbia Court of Appeal held that the Association was not liable. There was no private law duty of care that required the Association to bring a criminal prosecution against a former member or to inform potential clients of his resignation.[50]

The Supreme Court of Canada was faced with a rather similar issue in *Cooper* v. *Hobart.*[51] In that case, an investor who had entrusted funds to a mortgage broker, who dealt with those funds in an unauthorized manner, brought an action claiming damages against the Registrar (appointed by a statute regulating the mortgage broking profession). The plaintiff claimed that the Registrar, who had been investigating the broker, should have acted more promptly and suspended his licence earlier. The court held that the Registrar owed no duty of care to individual investors. The regulatory scheme required the Registrar to balance a number of competing interests in order to protect the public as a whole. The decision whether to suspend a broker involved both policy and quasi-judicial elements that were inconsistent with a duty of care to investors. To impose a duty of care in such circumstances would be to create an insurance scheme for investors at the cost of the tax-paying public.[52]

Codes of Conduct

code of conduct
rules of a professional organization setting out the duties and appropriate standards of behaviour to be observed by its members

Many professional bodies require their members to observe a **code of conduct**. As already noted, such codes may be important as evidence of what constitutes an appropriate standard of professional care, and may thus help to determine the extent of the duty owed by members to their clients. Additionally, codes of conduct may impose ethical standards on their members over and above any legal requirements. See the following example of a typical code of conduct.

Uniform Code of Professional Conduct

Canadian Association of Management Consultants

Purpose

The purpose of this Code is to identify those professional obligations that serve to protect the public in general and the client in particular. The Code is also designed to identify clearly the expectations of members with respect to other members and the profession.

continued

---

50. *Schilling* v. *Certified General Accountants Assn. of British Columbia* (1996), 135 D.L.R. (4th) 669.

51. (2001), 206 D.L.R. (4th) 193. The court reached a similar conclusion in *Edwards* v. *Law Society of Upper Canada* (2001), 206 D.L.R. (4th) 211, holding a law society not liable for failure to issue a warning that an investigation was being conducted into the handling of a lawyer's trust account.

52. The governing statute of the professional organization may provide for immunity in respect of acts done in good faith in the performance of a duty or exercise of a power under the statute; see, for example, Regulated Health Professions Act, 1991, S.O. 1991, c. 18, s. 38, considered in *Rogers* v. *Faught* (2002), 212 D.L.R. (4th) 366.

Definitions

"Council" is the Council or Board of any provincial or regional institute of Certified Management Consultants affiliated with the Canadian Association of Management Consultants (CAMC). "Member" is any individual registered and in good standing with a provincial or regional Institute of Certified Management Consultants in Canada.

Responsibilities to the Public

Legal: A member shall act in accordance with the applicable legislation and laws.

Representation: A member shall make representation on behalf of provincial, regional, or national Institute members only when authorized.

Public Protection: A member shall be liable for suspension or expulsion from membership where that member has behaved in a manner unbecoming to the profession, as judged by Council.

Responsibilities to the Profession

Knowledge: A member shall keep informed of the applicable Code of Professional Conduct and the profession's Common Body of Knowledge. A member shall strive to keep current with developments in any area of the profession where specific expertise is claimed.

Self-Discipline: A member shall recognize that the self-disciplinary nature of the profession is a privilege and that the member has a responsibility to merit retention of this privilege. Therefore, a member shall report to Council unbecoming professional conduct by another member.

Responsibilities for Others: A member shall ensure that other management consultants carrying out work on the member's behalf are conversant with, and abide by, the applicable Code of Professional Conduct.

Image: A member shall behave in a manner that maintains the good reputation of the profession and its ability to serve the public interest. A member shall avoid activities that adversely affect the quality of that member's professional advice. A member may not carry on business that clearly detracts from the member's professional status.

Responsibilities to Other Members

Review of a Member's Work: A member who has been requested to review critically the work of another member shall inform that member before undertaking the work.

Responsibilities to the Client

Due Care: A member shall act in the best interest of the client, providing professional services with integrity, objectivity, and independence. A member shall not encourage unrealistic client expectations.

Business Development: A member shall not adopt any method of obtaining business that detracts from the professional image of the Institute or its members.

Competence: A member shall accept only those assignments that the member has the knowledge and skill to perform.

Informed Client: A member shall, before accepting an assignment, reach a mutual understanding with the client as to the assignment objectives, scope, workplan, and costs.

Fee Arrangement: A member shall establish fee arrangements with a client in advance of any substantive work and shall inform all relevant parties when such arrangements may impair or may be seen to impair the objectivity or independence of the member. A member shall not enter into fee arrangements that have the potential to compromise the member's integrity or the quality of services rendered.

continued

Conflict: A member shall avoid acting simultaneously for two or more clients in potentially conflicting situations without informing all parties in advance and securing their agreement to the arrangement. A member shall inform a client of any interest which may impair or may be seen to impair professional judgment. A member shall not take advantage of a client relationship by encouraging, unless by way of an advertisement, an employee of that client to consider alternate employment without prior discussion with the client.

Confidentiality: A member shall treat all client information as confidential.

Objectivity: A member shall refrain from serving a client under terms or conditions that impair independence and a member shall reserve the right to withdraw from the assignment if such becomes the case.

Source: Canadian Association of Management Consultants, www.camc.com.

Discipline

One of the most important responsibilities of professional bodies is to maintain and improve standards. That may involve disciplining members of the profession. Most professions inevitably have a minority of members who act in an unprofessional, unethical, or illegal manner. The usual response of governing bodies is to punish serious cases of unethical conduct by expulsion or suspension. (There may also be provision for some form of compensation to the injured client by the governing body itself.) These actions are quite apart from any criminal prosecution of the wrongdoer or from private (civil) liability actions.

The more pervasive and difficult cases are those arising from alleged breaches of professional standards of skill and care. In what may be considered isolated cases of negligence, governing bodies ordinarily leave the matter to the regular courts, where an aggrieved client may bring an action. However, in repeated cases of violations, or where the conduct of the professional is such that her competence to remain in practice is called into question, the governing body will take disciplinary action in the same manner as it would for unethical conduct.

For the conduct of disciplinary proceedings against members, a professional organization usually has a standing discipline committee consisting of experienced members of the profession. In addition, the governing council usually designates one or more other members or a separate committee to act as "prosecutor." Both the prosecutor and the accused member may be represented by lawyers at the disciplinary hearing. Ordinarily, the finding of a discipline committee takes the form of a recommendation to the governing council of the organization, which then acts on the recommendation to expel, suspend, reprimand, or acquit. Disciplinary proceedings of this nature are subject to a general duty to act fairly[53] and are subject to review by the regular courts.

Conflict of Duty Towards Clients and the Courts

A member of a professional body faces a dilemma when required to testify in court proceedings affecting a client or patient. On the one hand, the member is expected to reply to questions under oath when examined and cross-examined in court; on the other hand, the member's testimony may appear to be a breach of confidence in the professional relationship with the client. A member or

---

53. For a discussion of this duty see *Mondesir* v. *Manitoba Assn. of Optometrists* (1998), 163 D.L.R. (4th) 703. Where the disciplinary body is established by statute, its procedures are also subject to the Charter: see *Costco Wholesale Canada Ltd.* v. *British Columbia* (1998), 157 D.L.R. (4th) 725.

student member of a professional organization probably has a duty to ask the court for a ruling before divulging any information obtained in a confidential capacity.

A professional who learns that a client may be engaged in or is contemplating possibly illegal activities may experience a further problem of interpreting her professional duties to the client. Needless to say, the professional must not assist the client (except to advise on possible illegality), and, in dissociating herself from the client's activities, may have to terminate the relationship. It appears to be generally conceded, however, that a professional would not normally be obliged to reveal confidential knowledge to prosecuting authorities: such information is said to be covered by **privilege**. However, where keeping silent would create a serious threat to public safety, the public interest requires disclosure.[54]

privilege
the right of a professional to refuse to divulge information obtained in confidence from a client

---

INTERNATIONAL ISSUE

International Issue

As discussed earlier, the United States' Sarbanes-Oxley Act of 2002 (SOX) was enacted in response to major corporate scandals including that of Enron. It gave the Securities and Exchange Commission the power to regulate the conduct of attorneys. One measure adopted is known as "up the ladder" reporting.[55] This measure requires very specific conduct from lawyers acting for public corporations. If a lawyer becomes aware of improper activities within the corporation, he or she must report the activity up the chain of command, all the way to the board of directors.

The most controversial part of the reporting requirement is known as "noisy withdrawal." If a corporation refuses to discontinue the improper activity, then the lawyer must withdraw her services AND report the improper activity to the Securities and Exchange Commission.

The American Bar Association raised strong objections to the "noisy withdrawal" proposal. To date the SEC has only implemented the rule in voluntary form. Lawyers *may* report violations to the SEC.[56]

QUESTIONS TO CONSIDER

1. Why would the American Bar Association object to "noisy withdrawal"?

2. Is there a public interest argument to counter the position of the Bar Association?

Sources: U.S. Securities and Exchange Commission, "Final Rule: Implementation of Standards of Professional Conduct for Attorneys," 17 CFR Part 205, September 26, 2003, www.sec.gov/rules/final/33-8185.htm; American Bar Association, "Independence of the Legal Profession: Section 307 of the Sarbanes-Oxley Act," December 1, 2004, www.abanet.org/poladv/priorities/sarbanes.html.

MULTI-DISCIPLINARY PARTNERSHIPS

Traditionally, professions have carried on their practice either alone or in partnership with fellow members of the same profession. Many professions forbid their members to incorporate. In the case of some professions—in particular, law—it has, in the past, been unlawful for a lawyer to practise in partnership with a non-lawyer. However, these rules are now changing.

---

54. *Smith* v. *Jones* (1999), 169 D.L.R. (4th) 385 (S.C.C.). The case concerned conversations between a psychiatrist and an alleged serial rapist. See *Canada (Privacy Commissioner)* v. *Blood Tribe Department of Health* 2008 SCC 44 where the Supreme Court prioritized solicitor–client privilege over access rights.

55. Title 17, Code of Federal Regulations, Part 205, s. 205.3.

56. *Ibid.*, s. 205.3(6)(d)(2).

In the past few years, legislation has been adopted in a number of provinces to permit the creation of "professional corporations"; we discuss these further in Chapter 27. The other major development is the changing attitude towards "multi-disciplinary partnerships" (MDPs). The main focus of the current debate on MDPs is on the combining of accountants and lawyers into a single firm. MDPs of this type are common in Europe, where the major international accounting firms have established their own legal departments. Several provincial law societies have set up working groups to study the implications of allowing their members to participate in MDPs. Advocates of MDPs claim a number of advantages—they benefit clients whose problems cannot readily be compartmentalized into legal and non-legal, and they provide a more efficient "one-stop shop" for business clients who require both accounting and legal services. By working together as a team, the quality of service provided by both professions is improved. There are, however, also concerns. There is a possibility that professional duties and codes of conduct may conflict,[57] and the increased sizes of firms and diversity of services provided may more readily give rise to conflicts of interest.

Although the legal profession has tended to oppose MDPs, it may well be that the fundamental freedom of association, in the Charter, gives a right to establish such partnerships.[58] So far, only Ontario and Quebec allow lawyers to participate in MDPs.[59]

QUESTIONS FOR REVIEW

1. What are the arguments in favour of imposing a wide liability on professionals?
2. What is the main effect of increased use of liability insurance?
3. What is the nature of the fiduciary duty owed by a professional? In what way can that duty be wider than a contractual duty?
4. Can a client choose to sue a professional adviser in either contract or tort? What difference might it make?
5. What is the principal basis of a professional's potential liability to persons who are not clients?
6. Why were the courts initially reluctant to impose liability for negligent misstatements?
7. What was the decision reached by the House of Lords in *Hedley Byrne* v. *Heller & Partners*?
8. What is the test now applied in Canada to determine whether a person is liable for a negligent misstatement?
9. Why might it be difficult to establish contributory negligence as a defence in a case involving negligent misrepresentation?
10. How can a person be liable for an omission?
11. What are the objections to a "hindsight" approach in determining the appropriate standard of professional care?
12. What is the essence of causation in most professional–client relationships?
13. What are the main responsibilities imposed or assumed by professional bodies?
14. Should professional bodies be allowed to discipline their members, or should that be left to the courts?
15. What are the potential advantages, and possible disadvantages, of multi-disciplinary partnerships?

57. For example, an accountant may be required to report certain financial information where a lawyer has a duty of confidentiality. These concerns have increased since the "Enron affair."
58. In *Black* v. *Law Society of Alberta* [1989] 1 S.C.R. 591, the Supreme Court of Canada struck down a rule that Alberta lawyers could not enter into partnership with lawyers from outside the province. The decision was based on the mobility rights provisions of the Charter, but arguably the right of association would have been equally applicable.
59. A 2007 Competition Bureau report supported MDPs for lawyers: "Self Regulated Professions – Balancing Competition and Regulation," December 11, 2007, www.competitionbureau.gc.ca/epic/site/cb-bc.nsf/en/02523e.html. See also, M. Rappaport, "Competition Bureau's Study Draws Tepid Reaction from Legal Community," *The Lawyers Weekly*, January 11, 2008, www.lawyersweekly.ca/index.php?section=article&articleid=599.

CASES AND PROBLEMS

1. Mitchell was the owner of a thriving restaurant business. He came to know "Simpson," an apparently successful businessman who engaged in various speculative investments. In reality, "Simpson" was a former lawyer whose real name was Anderson, and who had been disbarred and convicted of a number of offences involving fraud.

    Mitchell and Anderson became friendly and Anderson persuaded Mitchell to join him in a number of investments, which at first seemed to be successful. In the course of their business dealings, Mitchell said that he thought it would be sensible for him to retain the services of a lawyer: Anderson recommended him to see a lawyer named Gordon.

    Gordon quickly realized that Mitchell's business associate, "Simpson," was actually Anderson, whom he had known before Anderson's conviction. Gordon acted for Mitchell in a number of transactions, but despite his knowledge of Anderson's background, he said nothing about it to Mitchell.

    A year or so later, Mitchell discovered that most of the investments that he had undertaken with Anderson (both before and after becoming a client of Gordon) had turned out to be complete failures. Apparently, Anderson had siphoned off most of the value of the properties they had bought.

    Mitchell brought an action against Gordon, claiming that Gordon should have told him of Anderson's history and that, if he had done so, Mitchell would have terminated the relationship.

    Should Mitchell succeed?

2. Hedgeways Construction Inc. is a company specializing in highway construction. In response to a public invitation from the government of British Columbia to tender for an important road construction project, it submitted what turned out to be the winning bid.

    The detailed description of the project in the tender invitation document contained a number of important inaccuracies. As a result, the cost of completing the project was substantially greater than Hedgeways had estimated and it ended up making a loss on the project.

    The tender invitation document issued by the province contained a statement to the effect that any representations made therein were "general information" only and were not guaranteed by the province. The actual specifications and engineering drawings in the document had been prepared by Brown and Green, two qualified engineers employed by the firm Black and Associates Ltd., who had contracted with the province to provide the specifications.

    What claim, if any, does Hedgeways have against (a) the provincial government; (b) Black and Associates; and (c) Brown and Green?

3. Hopkins Steel Ltd. was a long-established corporation operating in Ontario. A few years ago it decided to change its bank and moved its account to the Canadian Business Bank. Before accepting the account, the bank made various enquiries and, in particular, examined the audited accounts of Hopkins over the preceding three years. The accounts showed a consistent record of profitability, growing steadily over the years. With this information the bank agreed to extend a line of credit to Hopkins and, over the following year or so, made advances to it totalling more than $2 million.

    Shortly thereafter, Hopkins ran into serious trouble and eventually was forced into bankruptcy with debts in excess of $2 million.

    The bank brought a claim against Cross, Jones and Sparrow, the accounting firm that had audited the annual accounts of Hopkins during the years in question. The bank claimed that the accounts for the preceding years, which it had examined before granting the loans, were inaccurate and had been negligently prepared and that Hopkins was already in serious trouble before the bank took them on as clients.

    In each case, the audited accounts contained the following statement:

    We have examined the balance sheet of Hopkins Steel Limited as at [date] and the statements of earnings, retained earnings, and changes in financial position for the year then ended. Our examination was made in accordance with generally accepted auditing standards, and accordingly included such tests and other procedures as we considered necessary in the circumstances.

According to the evidence, during the years in which Cross, Jones and Sparrow provided services to Hopkins, it also from time to time provided further information with respect to Hopkins to third parties, such as creditors and a bonding insurer for the company, and provided Hopkins with a number of copies of its financial statements and audit reports.

Does the bank have any claim against the accounting firm?

4. Sauguet broke her wrist and was treated by an orthopedic surgeon, Chen. Sauguet was an active sports-woman and was anxious to obtain proper treatment so that she might continue her sporting activities, though she did not specifically inform Chen of this. The wrist did not heal properly, and she eventually had to have surgery. The surgery was not fully successful and she was left with a permanent disability that, though relatively minor, prevented her from playing the sports she had enjoyed.

Sauguet brought an action against Chen, alleging negligent treatment. She claimed that Chen had failed to advise of an alternative treatment that was available. The alternative treatment was well known in the profession and, though more intrusive than the treatment that Chen had performed, was possibly more suitable for a patient in Sauguet's position, for whom making a complete recovery was very important. Sauguet claimed that if had Chen informed her of the alternative, that was the procedure she would have chosen.

Does Sauguet have a claim against Chen?

5. Hansen had practised for a number of years as an investment counsellor, advising clients on how to invest their savings. He had qualified as a Member of the Association of General Investment Counsellors, which entitled him to use the letters "M.A.G.I.C." after his name.

Over the years, the Association (AGIC) had received numerous complaints about Hansen. Many of his suggested investment schemes turned out to be disastrous, and there were strong suspicions that he was not only wholly incompetent but that he was also defrauding some of his clients.

Two years ago, after one particularly serious complaint, Hansen was called to attend a meeting of the disciplinary committee of AGIC. The committee informed him that, in view of the long history of complaints against him, it proposed to deprive him of his membership and to inform the Attorney-General's Department of the most recent complaint, about which there was at least a suspicion of fraud.

Hansen, who was a very persuasive talker, eventually convinced the committee not to report him, and to allow him to resign from the Association rather than being dismissed. He signed an undertaking that he would not practise again as an investment counsellor and would no longer describe himself as "M.A.G.I.C."

Despite the undertaking, Hansen very soon resumed his practice, in his old office, and continued to use his title. Soon afterwards, he was consulted by Thaler, who said she had heard excellent reports about him from a friend. Hansen quickly talked Thaler into entrusting her life savings to him. It appears now that Hansen has disappeared to an island in the South Pacific, taking Thaler's money with him.

Thaler has commenced proceedings against AGIC, claiming that if they had reported Hansen to the proper authorities and had taken steps to see that he abided by his undertaking to them, Hansen would not have been in a position to defraud her.

What claim does Thaler have against AGIC?

6. Gupta had a new pavilion and solarium constructed at his lakeside motel complex. He contacted Sanchez, the insurance broker through whom he had previously arranged all of his property insurance, told him of the addition, and asked him to arrange the necessary insurance. Sanchez informed him that he had informed the insurance company of the addition and its value, and that it would be covered under Gupta's existing policy, with an increase in premium to take account of the increase in value of the property covered.

Some months later, following unusually heavy rains, the new pavilion and its contents were severely damaged by flooding. (The rest of the motel, being further from the water's edge, was not affected.) When Gupta claimed on the policy, the insurance company pointed out a clause in the policy that stated clearly that it did not cover damage by flooding if the property affected was within 50 feet of any body of water (which the new pavilion was). Gupta had not looked at the policy when arranging the new coverage.

Does Gupta have a claim against Sanchez?

ADDITIONAL RESOURCES FOR CHAPTER 4 ON THE COMPANION WEBSITE *(www.pearsoned.ca/smyth)*

In addition to self-test multiple-choice, true–false, and short essay questions (all with immediate feedback), application exercises, and links to useful web destinations, the Companion Website provides the following resources for Chapter 4:

- **British Columbia:** The Law Society of British Columbia; Self-Regulating Professional Bodies
- **Alberta:** Podiatrists Act; Professional Liability; Professional Liability Insurance
- **Manitoba/Saskatchewan:** Codes of Professional Conduct
- **Ontario:** Codes of Conduct; Conflict of Interest; Disclaimers; Fiduciary Duty; Lawyers; Multi-Disciplinary Partnerships; Limited Liability Partnerships; Professional Discipline; Professional Organizations; Public Liability Insurance

Contracts

I n Chapter 2, we noted that, for business purposes, the largest areas of private law are contracts, torts, property, and trusts. Contracts are the foundation of virtually all business arrangements, whether for employment, for the sale of goods, services, or land, for the formation of a partnership or corporation, or for the settlement of a dispute. An understanding of contract law is essential to an understanding of business arrangements. Chapters 5 to 15 are devoted to a comprehensive overview of contractual arrangements, from their formation, to a discussion of the various things that can go wrong, to their ultimate discharge, either by performance, by mutual agreement among the parties, or by an aggrieved party resorting to the courts for a remedy.

Chapters 5, 6, and 7 discuss the formation of a contract—the various elements needed to make an arrangement legally binding: Chapter 5, the procedures, formal or informal, that the parties to a contract must follow; Chapter 6, the nature of a bargain and the elements required to make a promise binding; Chapter 7, classes of persons who may bind themselves to a contract, and why certain kinds of contracts are not binding. Chapters 8 and 9 consider the things that can "go wrong"— a court may conclude that what seemed like a valid contract does not bind the parties because there is a serious flaw. Chapter 10 discusses the requirement that certain kinds of contracts must be in writing, and the sometimes surprising consequences when such contracts are oral. Chapter 11 describes the process of interpreting terms of a contract when parties disagree about what they mean. Chapter 12 explains how rights under a contract may be acquired by persons who were not originally parties to it. Chapters 13, 14, and 15 discuss, respectively, the ways in which contracts come to an end, the consequences of breach by one party, and the remedies available to an aggrieved party.

5

Formation of a Contract:
OFFER AND ACCEPTANCE

In this chapter we describe the essential qualities of a contract, in particular, why it is enforceable in law and how a contract is formed. In this chapter we examine such questions as:

- Why is a contract enforceable in law?

- How is a contract formed?

- When forming a contract, what is the nature of an offer and how is it communicated to an offeree?

- How do we determine the terms of a contract?

- Why are standard form contracts used? What are their benefits and dangers?

- How does an offer come to an end—by lapse, revocation, rejection, or by "ripening" into a contract through acceptance by the offeree?

- What is the difference between unilateral and bilateral contracts?

- What are the consequences of a failed attempt to form a contract?

THE ROLE OF CONTRACT LAW

In Chapter 1, we noted that the law restrains our conduct in order to protect society, but it also expands our freedom of choice: it enables us to bargain with others for mutual advantages. We also pointed out that many legal rules work as guidelines for voluntary legal relationships such as business partnerships. Law becomes a framework within which parties can decide upon and bargain for their own legal obligations. People make rules for themselves and express their individual preferences. Contracts are a prime example of voluntary legal relationships.

On the other hand, there is often great inequality between parties to contracts in terms of bargaining power, expertise, and intelligence, and in some situations there is no opportunity whatever to bargain: many unfair contracts are made. On the whole, however, contract law responds well—perhaps better than most areas of the law—to the individual's needs and wishes, and it accommodates most relationships with a minimum of conflict.

THE NATURE OF A CONTRACT

Contracts generally begin with a promise, but not all promises become contracts. Although there may be a moral obligation to keep all promises, it does not follow that there is a legal obligation. Contract law is concerned with legally binding promises. "The most popular description of a contract that can be given is also the most exact one, namely that it is a promise or set of promises which the law will enforce."[1] Which promises will the law enforce? This question needs to be examined before we discuss how the law "enforces" contracts. In the next 11 chapters we examine, first, the nature of the promise or promises that may form a contract, and second, how they may be enforced. We start with the basic requirements of offer and acceptance in this chapter, and look at consideration and intention in Chapter 6.

THE NATURE OF AN OFFER

A contract does not come into existence until an offer has been made by one party and accepted by the other party. An **offer** is a *tentative* promise made by one party, the **offeror**, subject to a condition or containing a request to the other party, the **offeree**. When the offeree accepts the offer by agreeing to the condition or request, the offer is transformed into a contract. The promise is no longer tentative: the offeror is bound to carry out his promise while the offeree is bound to carry out the condition or request.

A mere *invitation* to do business is not an offer to make a contract. The display of a coat in a store window does not amount to an offer to sell; a mail-order catalogue does not guarantee that the goods pictured or described will be delivered to all who try to order them. These are simply merchandising or advertising devices to attract customers and to start negotiations for a contract of sale. A prospective customer, acting in response to the invitation, may make an offer and the merchant may in turn accept or refuse. Or the merchant may make an offer as soon as the customer shows interest.

Newspaper advertisements to sell goods at a certain price are generally mere invitations to the public to visit the place of business with a view to buying. A business is not expected to sell the goods to everyone who reads its advertisement: its supply is limited, and it cannot accurately predict the number of readers who will be seriously interested. If the advertisement were taken to be an offer and too many people accepted it, the business would be liable for breach of contract to all those who accepted and to whom it could not supply the advertised goods.

offer
a tentative promise made by one party, subject to a condition or containing a request to the other party

offeror
the person making the offer

offeree
the person to whom the offer is made

1. P.H. Winfield, *Pollock's Principles of Contract*, 13th ed. (London: Stevens & Sons Limited, 1950), at 1.

On the other hand, this does not mean that advertisements can never be offers; the courts have sometimes held them to be offers when their wording reasonably favoured this interpretation. An advertisement to sell a fixed number of items at a fixed price to those who accept first, an offer of a reward for information or for the return of a lost object, or a reward to any person using a preventive medicine who still catches an illness all may be valid offers. This group of advertisements forms a very small proportion of newspaper advertisements—they are the exception rather than the rule.

CASE 5.1

When self-service supermarkets and drugstores arrived in England, the courts had to decide whether the display of merchandise in itself amounted to an offer—and the act of the customer in taking the merchandise from the shelf amounted to an acceptance—or whether the display was merely an invitation to the customer to make an offer by taking the merchandise to the cashier. The question was important, because an English statute made it unlawful to sell certain medicinal products unless the sale was supervised by a registered pharmacist.[2]

The court held that the statute was not violated because a registered pharmacist was at hand near the cashier and could refuse a customer's offer to purchase any drug. The judge said:

> The mere fact that a customer picks up a bottle of medicine from the shelves in this case does not amount to an acceptance of an offer to sell. It is an offer by the customer to buy, and there is no sale effected until the buyer's offer to buy is accepted by the acceptance of the price.[3]

THE COMMUNICATION OF AN OFFER

The form of an offer is not important as long as its sense is understood. The offeror could say, "I offer to sell you my car for $500," or, "I will sell you my car for $500," or even, "I'll take $500 for my car." All are equally good offers, containing a tentative promise to sell the car if the buyer agrees to pay the stated price.

In most situations, an offeror communicates orally or in writing, but she can also express an offer by conduct without words. A taxi driver opening the door of her cab, a bidder raising his finger at an auction, and the gestures of floor traders at a stock exchange may also be offers.

An offeree cannot accept an offer until she is aware of it. This principle has an unexpected twist. A person may find and return a lost article to its owner and afterwards learn that a reward has been offered for its return. The finder is not entitled to the reward because she did not act in response to the offer, and therefore did not accept it.

Crossed offers provide a further example of this rule, as shown in Illustration 5.1.

ILLUSTRATION 5.1

A tells B she is interested in selling her car. The next day, A writes to B offering to sell her car for $1500; B has also written a letter crossing A's letter in the mail offering to buy the car for $1500. *There is no contract: B was unaware of A's offer when he wrote and so his letter could not be an acceptance; similarly, A was unaware of B's offer—A's letter, too, could not be an acceptance. Unless either A or B sends a subsequent acceptance, no contract will be formed.*

---

2. *Pharmaceutical Society of Great Britain* v. *Boots Cash Chemists (Southern) Ltd.*, [1952] 2 All E.R. 456.

3. *Ibid.*, per Lord Goddard, at 458.

Similarly, we cannot be required to pay people who do work for us without our knowledge. We are entitled first to receive an offer to do the work, which we may then accept or reject. A person for whom work has been done without his request, and without his knowledge, may well benefit from it; but as he has not accepted any offer to do the work, he has no contractual obligation to pay for it.

Suppose, however, that goods or services are provided to a person without his request but in circumstances where he has an opportunity to reject them. At common law, if he accepts the services or uses the goods, he is presumed to have accepted the offer and to have promised to pay the price. This rule was found inadequate in dealing with unconscionable selling practices that tempt consumers to bind themselves to pay for goods they did not request. Many provinces have passed legislation to reverse the rule, at least as it relates to goods. For example, section 12 of the Business Practices and Consumer Protection Act[4] states:

(1) A consumer has no legal obligation in respect of unsolicited goods or services unless and until the consumer expressly acknowledges to the supplier in writing his or her intention to accept the goods or services.

(2) Unless the consumer has given the acknowledgment referred to in subsection (1), the supplier does not have a cause of action for any loss, use, misuse, possession, damage or misappropriation in respect of the goods or services or the value obtained by the use of the goods or services.

AN OFFER MADE BY TENDERING A WRITTEN DOCUMENT TO THE OFFEREE

Standard Form Contracts: Their Risks and Benefits

Businesses that deal with the general public often present the terms of their offers in written documents handed to their customers, or they post notices containing terms on their business websites. Sometimes both methods are used together, the delivered document referring to the terms posted in the notice. Common examples are tickets for theatres, railways, and airlines, receipts for dry cleaning, parking, watch repairs, and checked luggage, as well as insurance policies and bills of lading.

Almost without exception, a person receiving any one of these documents is neither asked nor expected to read or approve of its terms. If he were to take time to read it and suggest changes, the agent of the offeror would probably become very annoyed. She would say, "Take it or leave it." As a practical matter, an offeree cannot change any terms of such a **standard form contract**: there is no real element of bargaining. He must accept the offer as is or not at all. Often, as when travelling by railway or airline, there may be no other practical means of transportation between two points; an offeree does not have the choice of refusing—he *must* accept if he is to make his journey. In this situation an offeror business is strongly tempted to disregard the interests of its offerees, the general public, and give itself every advantage; it rarely resists the temptation.

On the other hand, in many situations the standard form contract is essential: imagine waiting in line at a railway ticket office while each would-be passenger bargains separately for each term in his contract!

> . . . Too often, the standard form is presented as an evil. The form is part of efficiency and standardizing in modern business; in some situations a form may be the result of experience and

standard form contract
an offer presented in a printed document or notice, the terms of which cannot be changed by the offeree, but must be accepted as-is or rejected

---

4. S.B.C. 2004, c. 2.

a thorough job of drafting that could not be put together for just one deal alone. But the concentration of economic power, and in particular the rise of the large business corporation, has led to many situations in which bargaining power is grossly unequal. Power corrupts. Forms are often used in situations where a truly bargained contract is distorted or denied. They are dictated, not negotiated.[5]

There are three means of protection from this inequality in bargaining. First, if the business falls within an area regulated by a government board, the terms of such contracts are subject to board approval. When boards operate effectively, the public is usually well protected and unreasonable terms are excluded. Second, some segments of the public are offered special protection, such as consumers. Consumer protection legislation provides disclosure requirements and cancellation options. Finally, in the vast range of unregulated activity, the public receives only as much protection as the courts can find in the general law of contract.

Required Notice of Terms

Courts begin by presuming that an unqualified acceptance of an offer is an acceptance of every term of that offer. Suppose, however, that an offeree does not know that the offer contains a certain term. She purchases a ticket to attend a baseball game. A clause on the ticket states that the management reserves the right to remove the ticket-holder at any time without giving reasons. She does not know or suspect that the ticket contains such a term. Is she bound by it? If she satisfies the court that she did not know of it, then the court will ask what steps the management took to bring the term to the attention of its customers generally. If the court decides that the steps were insufficient, the ticket-holder is not bound by the term; and if she has been wrongfully ejected from the baseball park, she will have the same remedy as if the term had not been on the ticket.

On the other hand, if the court finds that the management had done what was reasonably necessary in the circumstances to bring the term to the notice of its customers, then the ticket-holder is bound by the term whether she knew of it or not. Each "ticket case" is decided on its own facts, and it is difficult to set down firm guidelines of what is or is not sufficient notice. It will help us to understand the courts' reasoning if we look at some of the leading cases.

CASE   5.2

In *Parker* v. *South Eastern Railway Co.*,[6] Parker deposited his suitcase in the luggage room of a railway station, paid a fee, and received a ticket on the face of which were the words, "See back." On the reverse side of the ticket it was stated that the railway was not liable for loss in excess of £10. The bag was lost, and Parker sued the railway for his loss, £24. On appeal, the court decided that the issue was whether the railway had done what was reasonably necessary to notify customers of the term. The court ordered a new trial because the trial judge had not asked the jury to decide this question.

The fact that the ticket contained on its face the words, "See back" is important. If a ticket—or other document given to the customer at the time of purchase—contains a short and clear reference to other terms appearing either on the reverse side, or posted on a nearby wall in the form of a notice or sign, it is more likely that "reasonably sufficient notice" of those terms has been given.

A sign in a parking lot disclaiming liability for loss or damage to car or contents may not in itself be reasonably sufficient notice to bind those who park their cars there: we have to ask whether the ticket or voucher received when a customer parks her car contains a clear reference to the sign and whether, in the circumstances, a customer *ought* to recognize the term stated on the sign as part of the contract she is making with the operator of the lot. A printed ticket or receipt containing the

---

5. Risk, *Recent Developments in Contracts, Special Lectures* (Toronto: Law Society of Upper Canada, 1966) at 256.
6. (1877), 2 C.P.D. 416.

words "subject to the conditions as exhibited on the premises" may be enough to tie the sign to each contract. The sign must, of course, be displayed prominently, but this in itself may not be sufficient; it must be brought home to the customer *at the time of making the contract*. The operator of the parking lot, garage, or other place of storage cannot safely assume that he may exempt himself from liability merely by putting up a sign.[7] Lord Justice Denning has summed up the law on this subject:

> People who rely on a contract to exempt themselves from their common law liability must prove that contract strictly. Not only must the terms of the contract be clearly proved, but also the intention to create legal relations—the intention to be legally bound—must be clearly proved. The best way of proving it is by a written document signed by the party to be bound. Another way is by handing him, before or at the time of the contract, a written notice specifying certain terms and making it clear to him that the contract is in those terms. A prominent public notice which is plain for him to see when he makes the contract would, no doubt, have the same effect, but nothing short of one of these three ways will suffice.[8]

Unusual or Unexpected Terms

An offeree may be willing to accept terms printed on a ticket or displayed on a poster because she assumes, reasonably, that the risk relates closely to the bargain she has made—for instance, a term denying any liability for damage to her car while parked in a parking lot. She would understand that the cost of parking would be higher if the car park operator had to insure against the risk of damage to her vehicle. But she would be surprised to find that the terms also exempted the operator from liability for personal injuries suffered by her as she walked to and from her parked car. Such unexpected terms need to be brought directly to the attention of the offeree; indeed, she might then decide to park elsewhere. In other words, a court may well find that there was adequate notice of usual, expected terms that the offeree chose not to read, but *not* of a surprising and therefore unreasonable term.

We have discussed situations where the offeree receives a ticket, a policy, or some other form of notice of the terms of the contract but where she does not sign a document containing the terms. If the offeree signs a document, a stronger presumption arises that she has accepted all the terms it contains; it becomes much more difficult for her to avoid the consequences.[9] However, the prospects of persuading a court to disregard onerous terms imposed in a written and signed document have improved somewhat,[10] as we shall see in our discussion of misrepresentation and unconscionability in Chapter 9.

THE LAPSE AND REVOCATION OF AN OFFER

Lapse

When an offer has lapsed, the offeree can no longer accept it even if he is unaware that it has lapsed; it has become void and no longer exists. An offer may **lapse** in any of the following ways:

(a) when the offeree fails to accept within a time specified in the offer
(b) when the offeree fails to accept within a reasonable time, if the offer has not specified any time limit
(c) when either of the parties dies or becomes insane prior to acceptance

lapse
the termination of an offer when the offeree fails to accept it within a specified time, or if no time is specified, then within a reasonable time

---

7. *Watkins* v. *Rymill* (1883), 10 Q.B.D. 178. It may be more difficult for the operator of a parking lot to exempt himself from liability when the customer leaves the keys in the car at the request of the parking lot operator, because a bailment for storage and safekeeping is implied. See Chapter 17, *infra*. See also: *Brown* v. *Toronto Auto Parks Ltd.*, [1954] O.W.N. 869; *Samuel Smith & Sons Ltd.* v. *Silverman* (1961), 29 D.L.R. (2d) 98; *Hefferon* v. *Imperial Parking Co. Ltd.* (1973), 46 D.L.R. (3d) 642.

8. *Olley* v. *Marlborough Court Ltd.*, [1949] 1 All E.R. 127, per Denning, L.J., at 134.

9. See *978011 Ontario Ltd.* v. *Cornell Engineering Co.* (2001) 12 B.L.R. (3d) 240 (Ont. C.C.).

10. *Tilden Rent-A-Car Co.* v. *Clendenning* (1978), 18 O.R. (2d) 601; *D.J. Provencher Ltd.* v. *Tyco Investments of Canada Ltd.* (1997), 42 B.L.R. (2nd) 45.

It is often difficult to predict what amounts to a "reasonable time." To say "it depends upon the circumstances of each case" may not seem helpful. The Supreme Court of Canada discussed how the subject-matter of the contract may provide a clue for deciding whether a reasonable length of time has elapsed in an offer to buy or sell:

> Farm lands, apart from evidence to the contrary . . . are not subject to frequent or sudden changes or fluctuations in price and, therefore, in the ordinary course of business a reasonable time for the acceptance of an offer would be longer than that with respect to such commodities as shares of stock upon an established trading market. It would also be longer than with respect to perishable goods such as food products. The fact that it was land would tend to lengthen what would be a reasonable time but other circumstances must also be considered.[11]

The "other circumstances" include the manner in which an offer is made and whether its wording indicates urgency. Often when a prospective purchaser makes an offer to buy property, she specifies that the offer must be accepted within 24 hours. The restriction is in her interest because it gives the vendor very little time to use this "firm offer" as a means of approaching other possible purchasers and bidding up the price.

Revocation

Notice of Revocation

An offeror may be able to revoke (that is, withdraw) an offer at any time before acceptance, even when it has promised to hold the offer open for a specified time. The offeror must provide notice of revocation to make it effective.

ILLUSTRATION 5.2

A Inc. sends a letter by courier on January 15 to B offering to sell its warehouse to B for $800 000, stating that the offer is open only until January 19 and that it must have heard from B by then. B receives the letter on January 16, and immediately prepares a letter of acceptance. Before B sends his reply on the morning of January 17, A Inc. changes its mind and telephones B saying that it withdraws its offer.

The revocation is valid because it has reached B before he has accepted. Accordingly, B can no longer accept A's offer.

In Illustration 5.2, the offeror clearly revoked the offer before its acceptance: its direct communication of the revocation left no doubt about the offeree's knowledge of it. The legal position of the parties is less certain if the offeree merely hears rumours that the offeror has revoked, or hears that the offeror has made it impossible to carry out the offer because it has sold the property to someone else. The court will consider the offer revoked if it would be unreasonable for the offeree to suppose that the offeror still intended to stand by its offer.[12] Nevertheless, it is always poor business practice to make an offer to sell a particular item to one party and then sell it to another without having directly withdrawn the offer to the first party. Quite apart from damage to goodwill, the offeror runs the risk of the first offeree accepting and of then being in breach when unable to fulfill both contracts.

11. *Barrick* v. *Clark*, [1950] 4 D.L.R. 529, per Estey, J., at 537.
12. See *Dickinson* v. *Dodds* (1876), 2 Ch. D. 463. See also *Hughes* v. *Gyratron Developments Ltd.*, [1988] B.C.J. No. 1598.

Options

An offeree may bind an offeror to keep its offer open for a specified time in one of two ways: (1) she may obtain a written offer under seal; (2) she may make a contract called an **option** to keep the offer open. We shall consider the use of a seal in the next chapter. In an option, the offeree makes a contract with the offeror in the following general terms: the offeree agrees to pay a sum of money; in return the offeror agrees (1) to keep the offer open for a specified time (that is, not to revoke the offer); and (2) not to make contracts with other parties that would prevent it from fulfilling its offer (that is, to give the offeree the exclusive right to accept the offer). The exclusive right to such an offer may be very valuable to an offeree, even though she may eventually decide not to accept.

option
a contract to keep an offer open for a specified time in return for a sum of money

exercise an option
to accept the offer contained in an option

ILLUSTRATION 5.3

PreciseComp Inc. purchases a number of options from property owners whose lots would, together, provide a suitable location for a new plant. PreciseComp pays $3000 to A for the right to buy her farm within three months for $350 000 and also buys similar option agreements from other farmers in the vicinity. In this way, PreciseComp can find out at a modest cost whether all the necessary property will be available and what the total cost will be. It need not *take up* or **exercise the options**—that is, accept the offers to sell the farms; it would simply chalk up the price of the relatively small sums paid for the option agreements as the cost of a feasibility study for the projected plant. On the other hand, PreciseComp would be within its rights to require each of the farmers who had sold it these options to sell at the agreed price—provided it accepts the offers contained in the options within the specified time.

In Illustration 5.3, the farmers are in the position of offerors who, for an agreed period of time, are not free to withdraw their offers without being in breach of contract. The parties are really contemplating two contracts: first, the option agreement itself and, second, the actual sale that will take place if the option is exercised.

REJECTION AND COUNTER-OFFER BY THE OFFEREE

In business negotiations the parties often make a number of offers and counter-offers, but until an offer by one side is accepted without qualification by the other, there is no contract; the parties have no legal obligation to one another. When an offeree receives an offer and, though interested, chooses to change some of its terms, he has not accepted; rather, he has made a counter-offer of his own and this amounts to rejecting the offer. The initiative in bargaining may shift back and forth until one party finds the last proposal of the other satisfactory and accepts it without qualification. Only then is a contract formed.

The making of a counter-offer necessarily amounts to rejecting the earlier offer and brings it to an end. If the offeror in turn rejects the counter-offer, the original offer does not revive. Only if the offeror agrees to renew it may the offeree accept the original offer. The courts have held, however, that when an offeree merely inquires whether the terms offered are the best he can expect, it does not amount to a rejection.

ILLUSTRATION 5.4

A sent a fax to B offering to sell her car for $2000. B replied by fax, "I will give you $1900 for the car." Two days later B sent a fax again to A saying, "I have been reconsidering. I will accept your offer to sell for $2000 after all."

In Illustration 5.4, there is no contract. *B*'s counter-offer of $1900 brought the original offer to sell for $2000 to an end. While *B* has phrased her final statement in the form of an acceptance, she is doing no more than making a fresh offer of her own that *A* may or may not wish to accept. Perhaps someone else has offered *A* $2100 for the car in the meantime. If, when *A* made the offer to sell for $2000, *B* had simply inquired whether this was the lowest *A* would go, the offer would have continued to stand. *B* would continue to be free to accept it within a reasonable period of time, provided *A* did not withdraw her offer first.

ETHICAL ISSUE

Is There a Duty to Negotiate in Good Faith?

Suppose a party enters into negotiations to purchase a business only for the purpose of gaining insight on how best to launch a successful competing business. What if a television network enters negotiations over the purchase of programming not with a view to completing a contract but in order to satisfy the regulator that no purchase is possible?[13] In these situations, a party may be accused of failing to negotiate in "good faith." What should be the consequences?

Tendering is one area of contract law where obligations of good-faith negotiations exist. Bidders must be treated fairly and equally but the law falls short of imposing a negligence duty of care.[14] Another example is the negotiation of options to renew an existing contractual relationship.[15]

QUESTIONS TO CONSIDER

1. Should the law recognize a duty to negotiate all contracts in good faith?

2. How could a business protect its competitive information during sale negotiations?

THE ELEMENTS OF ACCEPTANCE

Positive Nature

Acceptance must be made in some positive form, whether in words or in conduct, with one exception that we note below. If acceptance is by conduct, the conduct must refer unequivocally to the offer made—for example, shaking hands at the conclusion of negotiations is generally regarded as an acceptance of the last offer.

On the other hand, one's conduct may happen to comply with the means of acceptance set out in an offer and yet not amount to an acceptance. Suppose *A* always walks her dog around the park each evening. *B* leaves *A* a note saying that she will have accepted *B*'s offer to buy her car for $2000 if she walks her dog in the park that evening. *A* need not abandon her normal conduct to avoid accepting the offer and having the contract forced upon her.

---

13. *Westcom TV Group Ltd.* v. *CanWest Global Broadcasting Inc.*, [1997] 1 W.W.R. 761 (B.C.S.C.).

14. *Ron Engineering & Construction Eastern Ltd.* v. *Ontario* [1981] 1 S.C.R. 111; *Martel Building Ltd.* v. *Canada* [2000] 2 S.C.R. 860; *Design Services Ltd.* v. *Canada* 2008 SCC 22.

15. *Empress Towers Ltd.*, v. *Bank of Nova Scotia*, (1990) 73 D.L.R. (4th) 400 (B.C.C.A.). For a discussion of the duty to negotiate in good faith (if any) see J. D. McCamus, *The Law of Contracts*, (Toronto: Irwin Law Inc, 2005).

For the same reason, an offeror cannot insist on silence as a mode of acceptance, and so require the offeree to act in order to reject the offer.

ILLUSTRATION 5.5

Sanger, a sales representative for Ion Electric Supply Inc., demonstrated a new high-speed Auto-analyzer for Glover, the owner of a car repair service. The price was $2500. Glover thought the device was useful but overpriced: "At $1500 I might consider buying it." Sanger said that he could not reduce the price and removed the machine.

Two weeks later, an Auto-analyzer arrived with a letter from Sanger stating: "When I reported how impressed you were with our analyzer to the manager, he said it would be worth selling one even at a loss just to break into the market in your city. We know what an excellent reputation you have and it would be a good move to have our product in use in your shop. Our price is reduced, only to you, to $1750. That is below cost. If we don't hear from you in 10 days we shall assume you have accepted this exceptional buy and will expect payment of our invoice."

There will be no contract even if the offeree, Glover, does not reply and simply allows the machine to sit idle; but he may well be bound if he takes the risk of using the machine, even to experiment with it.

Silence can be a sufficient mode of acceptance only if the parties have habitually used this method to communicate acceptance in previous transactions, or have agreed between themselves in advance that silence is sufficient, as where books are regularly delivered under a contract for membership in a publisher's book club. Provincial consumer protection legislation regulates the use of unsolicited goods and negative option billing. If a consumer mistakenly pays for unrequested services he may request a refund.[16]

Communication to the Offeror

Generally speaking, an offeree must communicate acceptance to the offeror. Some types of offers, however, can be accepted without communication because the offeror asks only that the offeree perform an act, implying that the act will amount to acceptance. The offeror may, in other words, do away with receiving notice of acceptance, and be bound to the terms of the proposal as soon as the offeree has performed whatever was required of him in the offer.

CASE 5.3

Carbolic Smoke Ball Company placed an advertisement in a newspaper promising to pay £100 to anyone who used one of its smoke balls three times daily for two weeks and still contracted influenza. Mrs. Carlill bought a smoke ball and used it following the instructions supplied and contracted influenza. She sued the Smoke Ball Company on its promise to pay £100. As a part of its defence, the company pleaded that Mrs. Carlill had never communicated her intention to accept its offer. The court found in favour of Mrs. Carlill.[17] It held that the offer had implied that notice was not necessary because the company had asked only that readers should buy and use the smoke balls. Performance of the conditions set out was a sufficient acceptance without notifying the company.

The *Carlill* case also established that an offer may be made to an indefinite number of people who remain unknown to the offeror even after they have accepted. This result simply follows from the nature of the offer, a newspaper advertisement read by thousands of people. If the offer had been addressed to a particular group of persons, then only members of that group could have accepted.

---

16. See (for example) Business Practices and Consumer Protection Act, S.B.C. 2004, c. 2, ss. 12–14. Provincial

17. *Carlill* v. *Carbolic Smoke Ball Co.*, [1892] 2 Q.B. 484. See also *Grant* v. *Prov. of New Brunswick* (1973), 35 D.L.R. (3d) 141, and *Dale* v. *Manitoba* (1997), 147 D.L.R. (4th) 605.

The Moment of Acceptance

Business Negotiations: Tenders

The moment a contract is formed by acceptance of an offer, each party is bound to its terms. Accordingly, we must be able to analyze business negotiations so that we can identify:

- who made the offer,
- when it was communicated, and
- when the offer was accepted.[18]

inviting tenders
seeking offers from suppliers

The common business practice of **inviting tenders** illustrates the need for analyzing the various stages in a business deal to determine the point at which acceptance takes place. The purpose of inviting tenders may be either to obtain firm offers from the tenderers for a fixed quantity of goods and services over a stated period, or it may be to explore the market of available suppliers and develop the best terms for proceeding with a project. When the object is to obtain firm offers, the most satisfactory tender should become the basis for a contract between the inviter of the tenders and the successful bidder. This is normal practice when a government or business calls for tenders for the construction of a large project. In fact, the Supreme Court of Canada has considered the tender process as two contracts. It held that inviting tenders amounted to an offer to enter into a construction contract if selected according to the established criteria.[19] Submission of a bid was considered acceptance and formed a contract. Any refusal to honour the bid would be breach of contract. The party inviting the tenders promises—in return for the tenderer taking the trouble to prepare and submit its tender—to consider the tender and not ignore it entirely; if the inviting party fails to consider the tender it will be liable since it has breached the "tender contract."[20] If all goes well, the parties enter into a second contract for the construction project.

In other circumstances, however, no intention to form a contract upon the receipt of tenders is implied; the purpose of inviting tenders is nothing more than to identify a supplier as the appropriate source of work to be done or goods to be supplied, as required for a future project. For example, a municipal corporation may invite tenders by private trucking firms for the removal of snow from city streets during the coming winter. The selection of the successful bidder need not be followed up by a contract for a fixed sum, to remove whatever snow may fall—no one knows how severe the winter may be. The successful bidder has made a **standing offer** and the municipality may then make specific requisitions for snow removal as needed over the winter season. Each requisition becomes an acceptance by the municipality of the standing offer of the trucking company; to that extent the trucking company will have a contractual duty to perform for the price specified in its bid. The trucking company remains free to withdraw from the standing agreement if it finds the agreement unsatisfactory, and it will have no liability to do further work after its revocation.[21]

standing offer
an offer that may be accepted as needed from time to time

Whose Offer Has Been Accepted?

Buying an automobile from a car dealer provides a good example of the importance of knowing when, precisely, a contract is formed. Car sales agents employed by a dealer normally have no

---

18. In an English decision, the House of Lords resisted a tendency in some earlier cases to find that a contract is formed when the parties have substantially agreed on all the material terms, though the explicit acceptance of an offer remains outstanding: *Gibson* v. *Manchester City Council*, [1979] 1 W.L.R. 294.

19. *Ron Engineering, supra* note 14. The Supreme Court affirmed the two-stage contract approach in *Design Services Inc., supra* note 14, while rejecting a negligence duty of care.

20. See *Martel*, supra note 14. *Blackpool and Fylde Aero Club Ltd.* v. *Blackpool Borough Council*, [1990] 1 W.L.R. 1195. For further obligations that may be implied on inviting tenders, see *M.J.B. Enterprises Ltd.* v. *Defence Construction (1951) Ltd. et al*, [1999] 1 S.C.R. 619.

21. See *Powder Mountain Resorts Ltd.* v. *British Columbia*, [2001] 11 W.W.R. 488 (B.C.C.A.); *Mellco Developments Ltd.* v. *Portage Le Prairie (City)* (2002), 222 D.L.R. (4th) 67 (Man. C.A.).

authority to enter into contracts with customers. The management of the dealership retains the final word on both price and credit terms; the agent's task is to persuade any prospective buyer to submit an offer at a specified price. When the agent takes the offer to the sales manager, the manager may strike out the proposed price and insert a higher one with a request that the prospective buyer initial the change. In so doing, the manager rejects the customer's offer by making a counter-offer. No contract is formed unless and until the customer accepts the counter-offer.

CHECKLIST The Ways in Which an Offer May Come to an End

Once an offer has been made, it can come to an end in any one of a number of different ways:

- The offer may lapse when the offeree fails to accept within the time stated in the offer, or if no time limit is stated, within a reasonable time.
- The offeror revokes the offer before the offeree has accepted.
- The offeree rejects the offer or makes a counter-offer (which is in effect a rejection).
- The offeree accepts before any of the three above has occurred (in which case the offer ends and is replaced by a contract between the parties).

TRANSACTIONS BETWEEN PARTIES AT A DISTANCE FROM EACH OTHER

Modes of Acceptance

When the parties are at a distance, an offeree may accept only in the way proposed by the offeror. An offer made by mail may reasonably be taken as inviting acceptance by mail unless the offeror requests another mode of acceptance. Ordinarily, a faster mode may be used: a fax, e-mail, or telephone call in response to a letter can be valid acceptance.

The ordinary rule is that acceptance by mail is complete when a properly addressed and stamped letter of acceptance is dropped in the mail.[22] This "postal rule" is as practical and convenient as any alternative; otherwise, during the time required for a letter to reach its destination there would be a period of uncertainty when neither party would know whether a contract exists. The justification for the rule is that an offeror who chooses to use the post office to send an offer is assumed to be willing to have the same means used for acceptance, and to take a chance that the post office will be efficient in delivering it. An offeror who invites acceptance by mail must also be prepared to take the risk that the letter of acceptance may go astray; harsh though this may seem, it follows that the offeror would be bound by the contract without notice of its existence.

An offer may invite acceptance by post even though it was not sent through the mail itself, so long as acceptance by mail is a reasonable response to the offer. It may be reasonable that an offer

---

22. S.M. Waddams, *The Law of Contracts*, 4th ed. (Toronto: Canada Law Book Company, 1999) at 76–7; also *Sibtac Corporation Ltd.* v. *Soo; Lienster Investments Ltd., Third Party* (1978), 18 O.R. (2d) 395 at 402.

made orally in the presence of the offeree be accepted by letter; acceptance is complete at the time of mailing.[23] The English courts have held:

> Where the circumstances are such that it must have been within the contemplation of the parties that, according to the ordinary usages of mankind, the post might be used as a means of communicating the acceptance of an offer, the acceptance is complete as soon as it is posted.[24]

If the offeror has stated expressly how acceptance should be communicated, then it must be completed in the described manner. However, if he merely states a *preference* for acceptance by some means other than post as, for example, by telephone or in person, the offeree may still accept by post. But for all other forms of acceptance, the offeror is not bound unless and until the acceptance reaches him—and it must reach him before the offer has lapsed. When his stated preference is for a mode speedier than mail, there is increased risk that his offer will have lapsed before the letter of acceptance arrives. In these circumstances, the acceptance is not valid when dropped in the mailbox (as it would be if acceptance by mail were reasonably contemplated), but only when received. Even when an offeror invites acceptance by mail, he may state that it will be effective *only* if received. Indeed, he may state that acceptance by letter is invalid—it must be made in person. Such requirements are effective, and unless the offeree complies, she cannot bind the offeror.

When instantaneous means of communication such as telephone (or radio) are used, the offeror must receive the acceptance before he is bound. An English court considered what would be the result if the telephone line were to go dead so that the offeror did not hear the offeree's words of acceptance. The court concluded that the acceptance would be ineffective and that the offeror would have no contractual liability.[25] The common sense of this rule is that the offeree would know that the line went dead and that his acceptance might not have been heard. He must then verify that his acceptance was received.

Similarly, faxed acceptance is not effective until received, and one would expect this same rule to apply to e-mail.[26] E-commerce legislation establishes that acceptance may be completed by electronic mail and that e-mail is deemed to be received when it is capable of being retrieved by the recipient.[27] The legal issues that may arise generally in e-commerce are discussed more fully in Chapter 34.

Modes of Revocation

Revocation by instantaneous means of communication is subject to the same rules as acceptance, discussed above.

However, the rule concerning withdrawal of an offer by post differs from the usual rule concerning the time of acceptance. Revocation by post is effective only when notice is actually received

---

23. The same principle applies when correspondence is sent by courier service: *R. v. Weymouth Sea Products Ltd.* (1983), 149 D.L.R. (3d) 637.

24. *Henthorn v. Fraser*, [1892] 2 Ch. 27, per Lord Herschell, at 33. The law in Canada is probably accurately represented by this case, though there is some confusion caused by a Supreme Court of Canada decision on appeal from the Quebec courts where the post office is referred to as an "agent." See *Charlebois v. Baril*, [1928] S.C.R. 88. See also *Loft v. Physicians' Services Inc.* (1966), 56 D.L.R. (2d) 481, where a letter posted in a mailbox but never received was held to be adequate notice to the defendant.

25. *Entores, Ltd.* v. *Miles Far East Corporation*, [1955] 2 Q.B. 327, per Denning, L.J., at 332.

26. See *Eastern Power Ltd.* v. *Azienda Communale Energia & Ambiente* (1999), 178 D.L.R. (4th) 409 (Ont. C.A.); *Brinkibon Ltd.* v. *Stahag Stahl Und Stahlwarenhandelsgesellschaft mbH* [1983] 2 A.C. 34 (H.L.).

27. Most provinces have adopted legislation in conformity with the Uniform Electronic Commerce Act prepared by the Uniform Law Conference of Canada, see for example: Electronic Commerce Act, 2000, S.O. 2000, c. 17, s. 22(3).

by the offeree, not when it is dropped in the mailbox. As a result, the offeree may accept and a binding contract be formed after revocation of the offer has been mailed but not yet received.

ILLUSTRATION 5.6

Chen, in a letter posted January 15, offered to sell his business to Baker for $70 000. The letter was received by Baker on January 17. On January 19, Baker posted her letter of acceptance, which did not reach Chen until January 21. On January 18, however, Chen had decided to withdraw his offer and posted a letter to Baker revoking it. This letter did not reach Baker until January 20.

Chen's revocation arrived too late. There was a valid contract on January 19 when the acceptance was posted. Chen was bound from the moment the letter was dropped into the mailbox.

What is meant by the requirement that a revocation be "actually received"? Is it "received" when delivered to the place of business or residence of the offeree, or must it reach her in person? The general rule is that, unless the offeror knows or ought to know that the revocation will not reach the offeree at her usual address, delivery at that address establishes the fact and time of revocation, and the offeree is deemed to have notice from that time. This rule applies to other means of communication; if an offeror can establish that his revocation by courier or fax arrived at the offeree's usual address, it will be effective. We cannot be certain of an e-mail revocation: is it necessary for the offeree to have turned on her computer and checked her inbox?

Determining the Jurisdiction Where a Contract Is Made

Parties to a contract are often in different provinces or countries at the time they enter into the arrangement. If a dispute arises it may be important to know where the contract was formed, since the law in the two places may well be different. The place—the **jurisdiction**—where the contract was formed is an important factor in deciding which law applies. The general rule is that a contract is formed at the place where the acceptance becomes effective. That place is determined by the moment in time when the contract is effective. When an offeror invites an acceptance by mail, the contract is formed at the moment *when*—and so at the place *where*—the acceptance is dropped into the mailbox. When an instantaneous means of communication such as fax, e-mail, or telephone is used, the contract is not formed until the offeror receives the acceptance, and that is at the place where he receives it.

jurisdiction
the province, state, or country whose laws apply to a particular situation

UNILATERAL AND BILATERAL CONTRACTS

The Offer of a Promise for an Act

As we have seen in the *Carlill* case, an offer may invite acceptance simply by the offeree performing its conditions without communicating acceptance. Indeed, we would not have expected Mrs. Carlill to have telephoned or written to the Smoke Ball Co. to inform it that she intended to accept its offer when she bought the smoke ball!

An offer of a reward is accepted by anyone to whom the offer is made if she performs the required conditions, such as providing information or returning a lost article. When the reward is for providing information, the person who first gave the information is deemed to have accepted and is usually entitled to the reward.[28] However, in a 1997 case, a person gave a limited amount of

---

28. *Lancaster* v. *Walsh* (1838), 150 E.R. 1324.

unilateral contract
a contract in which the offer is accepted by performing an act or series of acts required by the terms of the offer

information that ultimately led to a lengthy investigation and conviction for murder (the *Bernardo* case), and the provider of the information was awarded only a portion of the reward originally offered.[29]

In the above examples, the offers are of a type that requires *acceptance by performance* of an act. Once the offeree has performed, she need not do anything more—except, of course, to request payment. All obligation now rests with the offeror to perform his half of the bargain. These contracts are often called **unilateral contracts.** Some offers require the offeree to perform a series of acts over a long period.

ILLUSTRATION 5.7

Brown offers to pay $4000 to Carson if she will build and deliver a trailer to the offeror in 60 days. Carson may accept only by actually delivering by that date, and until then there is no contract. Consequently, during that 60 days Carson may abandon performance at any time without being in breach. What about Brown—could he simply revoke his offer the day before delivery?

The strict rule used to be that the offeror could always revoke before acceptance, and judges seemed to accept this view. It was apparent that the offeree might suffer considerable hardship, but the answer was, "She knew the risk of revocation was present and accepted the risk." Since, however, parties often do not think about such possibilities, the hardship still occurs. Courts began avoiding this unfairness where possible by treating offers "as calling for bilateral rather than unilateral action when the language can be fairly so construed."[30] The advantage of treating an agreement as bilateral is that both parties are bound from the moment the offeree indicates the intention to perform.

subsidiary promise
an implied promise that the offeror will not revoke once the offeree begins performance in good faith and continues to perform

Where the courts do not find it possible to construe an offer as bilateral, they may still try to help the offeree by implying a **subsidiary promise** that the offeror will not revoke once the offeree begins performance in good faith and continues to perform. On this basis, in Illustration 5.7, as soon as Carson starts performance, a subsidiary contract may be formed in which Brown undertakes not to revoke while Carson proceeds reasonably with performance. A court might well hold that revocation would be a breach of the subsidiary contract.[31] Of course, the subsidiary promise is merely implied, and it may be excluded by an express term to the contrary in the offer: if *A* offers to pay *B* $800 for the delivery of a computer to her son provided it is delivered at exactly 10 p.m. at a birthday party and provided *A* does not change her mind, *A* may revoke the offer before delivery.

The Offer of a Promise for a Promise

While unilateral contracts are important, most offers require a promise from the offeree rather than performance as the means of acceptance. For example, if *A* Motors offers to sell a truck to *B* Inc. for $32 500 and *B* Inc. replies accepting the offer, a contract is formed though neither party has as yet performed anything. In effect, *A* Motors has promised to sell the truck for $32 500, and *B* Inc. in return has promised to buy it for $32 500; the two parties have traded promises. If either party should refuse to perform its promise, then the other would have a right to sue: both parties are bound to perform. This type of contract is called a **bilateral contract**.

bilateral contract
a contract where offeror and offeree trade promises and both are bound to perform

---

29. *Smirnis* v. *Sun Publishing Corp.* (1997), 3 O.R. (3d) 440.

30. *Dawson* v. *Helicopter Exploration Co. Ltd.*, [1955] 5 D.L.R 404, per Rand, J., at 410.

31. See *Brackenbury* v. *Hodgkin*, 102 A. 106, 116 Me. 399 (1917), and *Errington* v. *Errington*, [1952] 1 All E.R. 149.

The most common business transaction, the credit sale, is an example of the bilateral contract: at the time of the contract, and often for some time afterwards, the goods may be neither delivered by the seller nor paid for by the buyer. Similarly, in a contract of employment the employer promises to pay a wage or salary and the employee promises to work for a future period.

In bilateral contracts each party is both a **promisor** and a **promisee**; each has an obligation to perform as well as a right to performance by the other. In a court action, the party who sues as the promisee alleges that she has not received the performance to which she is entitled. The promisor may offer one or more defences as a reason or reasons why his conduct should be excused and why he should not be ordered to pay damages for breach of contract.

promisor
a party who accepts an obligation to perform according to the terms of the contract

promisee
a party who has the right to performance according to the terms of the contract

UNCERTAINTY IN THE WORDING OF AN OFFER

A vague offer may prove to be no offer at all, and the intended acceptance of it cannot then form a contract. If the parties enter into a loosely worded arrangement, a court may find the agreement too ambiguous and uncertain to be enforced.

CASE 5.4

Phibbs agreed to sell farmland to Choo for a price, "half [of which was] to be cash on possession of clear titles, the balance to be half the crop." Some time later, Phibbs refused to complete the deal and Choo sued him for the land.

The court found the agreement was too uncertain to be enforceable. It was unclear whether the land was to be transferred at once, leaving Phibbs without security for the unpaid balance of the price, or what would be the terms of a mortgage if one were to be given, or whether Phibbs was to wait for full payment before making the transfer. Nor was it clear how the crop-sharing provisions would be applied to a section of the land in which Phibbs owned only a part interest. Choo was not permitted to waive terms, even if for his own benefit, unless he could establish an enforceable agreement in the first place.[32]

Other examples of lack of certainty in the terms of a contract are a promise to give a "fair" share in the profits of a business; a promise to "favourably consider" the renewal of the present contract "if satisfied with you";[33] and a promise made by the buyer of a race horse to pay an additional amount on the price "if the horse is lucky."[34]

Even when the wording of a contract seems uncertain, a clear enough meaning may be found in evidence of local customs or trade usage that gives a new precision to the terms. The courts have a policy of making contracts effective wherever possible; they hold that (1) anything is certain that is capable of being calculated or ascertained, and (2) where a contract may be construed as either enforceable or unenforceable, they will favour the interpretation that will see the contract enforced. We shall examine these problems in greater detail in Chapter 11, when we discuss the interpretation of contracts.

---

32. *Phibbs* v. *Choo* (1976), 69 D.L.R. (3d) 756.
33. *Montreal Gas Co.* v. *Vasey*, [1900] A.C. 595.
34. *Cuthing* v. *Lynn* (1831), 109 E.R. 1130.

THE EFFECT OF AN INCOMPLETE AGREEMENT

What are the consequences when parties proceed on the basis of an incomplete agreement?

CASE 5.5

In *Brixham Investments Ltd.* v. *Hansink*,[35] both parties signed a letter providing for incorporation of the company and for entering into a further agreement. The letter did not set out the share allocation of the parties in the proposed company. When one party decided not to proceed with the project, the other sued for breach.

The Court considered whether the document was binding despite the lack of an agreement about share allocation. It held

that, although a court will imply certain terms that arise by necessary inference (for instance, if the letter referred to the parties as "equal partners"), where the document did not deal in any way with this crucial question of share allocation, the court will not construct an agreement between the parties. Accordingly, the document did not constitute a binding contract.

In other words, "The law does not recognize a contract to enter into a contract."[36]

A contract for the sale of goods is different from a contract for the sale of land or shares in a proposed corporation. Where the parties have agreed on the quantity, the Sale of Goods Act provides that the price in a contract of sale of goods "may be left to be fixed in manner thereby agreed, or may be determined by the course of dealing between the parties" and that "[W]here the price is not determined in accordance with the foregoing provisions the buyer must pay a reasonable price."[37]

FORMATION OF INTERNET CONTRACTS

Internet contracts are most pervasive in the consumer context. Businesses selling online use standardized terms and conditions just as in the physical world. As will be discussed in more detail in Chapter 34, two key types of legislation govern the formation of online contracts; e-commerce and consumer protection. The e-commerce legislation has modernized contract formation rules to allow "clicking an icon" to satisfy the acceptance and communication requirements of contract formation.[38]

Consumer protection legislation deals with the problems surrounding long detailed standard terms linked to an order webpage. Most provinces (most notably Alberta, British Columbia and Ontario) regulate Internet consumer agreements. However, these new statutory provisions may in fact alter the traditional rules of offer and acceptance to Internet contracts.

Section 38 of the Ontario Consumer Protection Act, 2002 states that before a consumer enters into an Internet agreement, the supplier shall disclose specific information about, among other things, the total price of the good or service, the terms of payment, and warranties. Subsection 38(2) states: "The supplier shall provide the consumer with an express opportunity to accept or decline the agreement. . . ." This suggests that the Internet consumer is the offeree, and it seems to

35. (1971), 18 D.L.R. (3d) 533.

36. *Von Hatzfeldt-Wildenburg* v. *Alexander*, [1912] 1 Ch. 284, per Parker, J., at 289. See also *National Bowling and Billiards Ltd.* v. *Double Diamond Bowling Supply Ltd. and Automatic Pinsetters Ltd.* (1961), 27 D.L.R. (2d) 342; Re Pigeon et al. and Titley, Pigeon, Lavoie Ltd. (1973), 30 D.L.R. (3d) 132. For a fuller discussion, see M.P. Furmston, Cheshire and Fifoot's *Law of Contract*, 13th ed. (London: Butterworths) at 39–43.

37. See, for example: R.S.B.C. 1996, c. 410, s. 12; R.S.O. 1990, c. S.1, s. 9; R.S.N.S. 1989, c. 408, s. 11.

38. Section 19(1) of the (Ontario) Electronic Commerce Act, 2000 (OECA) states that an offer or acceptance of a contractual offer "may be expressed, . . . (b) by an act that is intended to result in electronic communication, such as, (i) touching or clicking on an appropriate icon . . . on a computer screen. . . ."

contradict the general rule discussed in this chapter: that a retailer advertising goods for sale is making only an invitation to consumers to make offers—and typically in retail sales the consumer is the offeror.

Since an Internet consumer is considered the offeree, and after seeing the terms required to be disclosed by the supplier, she will be bound by the terms of the Internet contract at such time as she clicks an "I accept" icon on her computer screen. However, some e-retailers specifically design their websites with multiple acceptances before a "submit" icon is finally clicked. This would appear to satisfy the legislative "agreement to terms" requirement before the entire offer to purchase is submitted. In this context, the contract may not be formed until the retailer communicates acceptance with a confirmation number.

INTERNATIONAL ISSUE

Jurisdiction and Internet Contracts

The ability to contract over the Internet has greatly increased the number of international contracts in which the offeror is in one jurisdiction while the offeree is in another. As we have already described, the laws may be different in each location and jurisdiction is often determined by the place of acceptance. To reduce the likelihood that the rules relating to the formation of electronic contracts might be different in each jurisdiction, the United Nations has undertaken a number of initiatives:

- The United Nations Convention on the Use of Electronic Communications in International Contracts (2005)
- The United Nations Commission on International Trade Law (UNCITRAL) Model Law on Electronic Signatures (2001)
- The UNCITRAL Model Law on Electronic Commerce (1996)

Still, international variation exists. For example, Canadian consumer protection legislation extends protection to Canadian consumers even when they are involved in international contracts governed by a foreign jurisdiction.

QUESTIONS TO CONSIDER

1. Should Canadian provinces co-ordinate their legislation to avoid international inconsistency?
2. How can a business use its online contractual terms and conditions to ensure that foreign consumers are aware of the law that applies to the contract?

QUESTIONS FOR REVIEW

1. Distinguish an offer from a promise.
2. What is a standard form contract? Describe the different ways in which it may be accepted.
3. Explain the importance of notice of terms in a standard form contract. To what extent does the law protect the interest of the public in standard form contracts?
4. Describe the ways in which an offer may come to an end.

5. What is the legal effect of a counter-offer?

6. "We cannot be obligated by people who do work for us without our knowledge." Why?

7. What elements are required for an acceptance to be effective?

8. What does it mean to "purchase an option"?

9. What does it mean to "invite tenders"? When is a contract normally created in the tendering process?

 10. Can acceptance be effective from the moment a letter of acceptance is mailed even when the offer was not itself made through the mail?

11. Explain the different rules that apply to offer and acceptance when, rather than using the postal system, the parties communicate by telephone.

12. Should the same offer and acceptance rules apply to the sending of responses by fax or e-mail? Why?

13. Explain the difference between unilateral and bilateral contracts.

14. Did the *Carlill* case concern a unilateral or a bilateral contract?

15. What is the effect of an agreement in which the parties state that certain terms will be discussed and agreed upon at a later date?

16. Give an example of circumstances in which the rule "An offer must be communicated before it can be accepted" would operate.

17. Is it true that an acceptance must be communicated before a contract can be formed?

18. May a person withdraw a bid he makes at an auction sale before the fall of the hammer?

CASES AND PROBLEMS

1. Friday evening after closing, Sackett's Appliances placed an ad in its window, "This weekend only, five Whirlwind Dishwashers, reduced from $1199 to $599! Shop Early!" Martens saw the ad later that evening. She appeared the next morning at 9 a.m. when Sackett's opened its doors and stated to the clerk she would take one of the Whirlwind Dishwashers. The clerk replied that the ad was a mistake; the price should have been $999. Martens demanded to speak with the manager and insisted on Sackett's honouring its offer to sell at $599. The manager said, "I'm sorry, madam, but that machine cost us more than $800. We cannot sell it at $599." Martens said Sackett's was in breach of contract and she would see her lawyer about it.

   Is Martens right? Explain.

2. Garrett is the manager of Aristo Condos Inc. and is in charge of selling vacant units in the Aristo Towers. On October 4, Heilman examined several of the units with Garrett and said that he thought the prices a bit high but would think about it. Several days later, on October 7, Garrett sent Heilman an e-mail stating, "I will sell you any one of the units we examined together (numbers 14, 236, 238, or 307) for $275 000. I am sending you all the details by courier." Garrett then sent by courier to Heilman a formal offer containing all of the necessary terms, including the required down payment and acceptable mortgage financing. Later that day after he had received the e-mail message but before he had received the letter, Heilman e-mailed Garrett, "I accept your offer with respect to unit 307."

   Has a binding contract been formed by Garrett's e-mail? In what circumstances might this question become the basis of a dispute between the parties?

3. Last year, Lambert bought a car on August 15 and insured it with the Reliable Insurance Company, for whom Drake was the local agent. On the following July 29, Drake telephoned Lambert about renewing

her policy and learned she was on vacation at her summer cottage. Acting on behalf of Reliable Insurance, Drake wrote to Lambert at her cottage: "As you know, your car insurance policy with us expires on August 15. We will renew this policy on the same terms unless notified to the contrary by you. You may sign the application form and pay after you return to the city."

On her way back from her holidays on August 16, Lambert struck and injured a pedestrian with her car. The pedestrian claimed $100 000 damages from Lambert, and on referring the matter to the Reliable Insurance Company, Lambert was informed that her policy of insurance had expired without renewal on August 15.

Discuss Lambert's legal position.

4. A province and its largest university created a program by which the province would give funding to disadvantaged students. Students were told by the university that they would receive funding over four years and, on that basis, they enrolled in the program. The students dealt only with the university. In the third year of the program, the province restructured it so that students had to obtain their maximum Canada Student Loan before being eligible for funding.

The students sued for a declaration requiring the province to pay them at the original funding level for the full four years on the basis of a binding contract with the province. They claimed that they reasonably believed that they had a contractual arrangement with the province not to alter the terms and conditions of the funding arrangement. The province defended by stating that there was no contract with the students because they had not communicated their acceptance to it, but dealt only with the university; if anyone was bound, it was the university.

Discuss the merits of each party's argument. Who do you think should succeed?

5. Purcell was in failing health and advertised to sell his retail computing equipment business. Quentin was familiar with Purcell's business operations; he sent Purcell a detailed offer to buy for $450 000, paying $75 000 as a cash down payment, with the balance payable in instalments over two years. Purcell promptly sent an e-mail to Quentin stating: "The price and all the other terms seem fair, except that I need substantially more cash by way of down payment—say $125 000. Tell me how high you are willing to go." Quentin replied by e-mail, "There is no way I can increase the cash payment."

Purcell replied the next day, "Okay. I've thought about it, and given the state of my health, I have decided to accept your offer." By then, Quentin had heard that the business had suffered because of Purcell's declining health and he refused to go through with the purchase. He asserted that since Purcell had refused his offer, there was no deal. Is Quentin right? Has Purcell any basis for claiming that there is a binding contract with Quentin?

6. McKight wanted to buy from Chang a lot to build a retail outlet in Waverley, several kilometres north of the city of Halifax. McKight lives in Halifax and Chang lives in Waverley.

In May, McKight went to Waverley and offered Chang $135 000. Chang refused the offer. On July 7 McKight went again to see Chang, and this time Chang handed her an offer to sell the property for $155 000 and said he would hold the offer open for 14 days at that price.

Late in the evening of July 8, another person called to see Chang and offered him $150 000 for the property. Chang accepted, subject to a condition for avoiding the contract if he found he could not withdraw from his arrangement with McKight. The next morning at about 10:30 a.m., Chang went to McKight's home and knocked on the door. No one answered and he left a letter stating, "Please take notice that my offer to you of July 7 is withdrawn."

McKight did not see the letter of revocation until she came home for lunch at 12:30 p.m. She was not at home earlier because she had an appointment with her lawyer at 9:30 a.m. She requested her lawyer to write to Chang as follows: "I am instructed by Ms. McKight to accept your offer of July 7, to sell at the price of $155 000. Kindly have the contract prepared and forwarded to me." This letter was handed to a courier at 10 a.m. that morning (July 9) and delivered to Chang at about 2 p.m. When Chang received it, he replied stating that the offer had been withdrawn.

McKight brought an action for breach of contract against Chang. State with reasons what you think the court's decision would be.

7. Daly, a United States citizen, began negotiations with Stevens of Vancouver to investigate and stake mineral claims at the head of the Leduc River in British Columbia. Daly had discovered evidence of deposits there some 20 years earlier.

On January 13, Daly wrote, "A large mining company in Boise is showing an interest. To protect my interest it will be necessary for me to arrive at some definite arrangement soon." Stevens replied on January 17, "Perhaps we can make some arrangement this summer to finance you in staking claims for which I would give you an interest. I would suggest that I should pay for your time and expenses and carry you for a 10 percent interest in the claims." Daly replied on January 22, "Your proposition appeals to me as being a fair one."

Soon after, Daly was called to active duty in the United States Naval Reserve Engineering Corps and was sent to the Marshall Islands. Correspondence continued with some difficulty, but on February 28, Daly wrote, "As I informed you in a previous letter, your offer of a 10 percent interest for relocating and finding these properties is acceptable to me, provided there is a definite agreement to this effect in the near future."

On March 5, Stevens wrote, "I hereby agree that if you will take me in to the showings, and I think they warrant staking, I will stake the claims and give you a 10 percent interest. The claims would be recorded in my name and I will have full discretion in dealing with them—you are to get 10 percent of the vendor interest. I can arrange to get a pilot here." Daly replied on April 12, "If you will inform me when you can obtain a pilot, I will immediately take steps for a temporary release in order to be on hand."

On June 6, Stevens wrote, "I was talking to a prospector who said he had been over your showings at the head of the Leduc River, and in his opinion it would be practically impossible to operate there, as the showings were behind ice fields that, along with the extreme snowfalls, make it very doubtful if an economic operation could be carried on. I now have so much work lined up that I doubt if I would have time to visit your showings and do not think I would be warranted in making the effort to get in there due to the unfavourable conditions. I must advise you, therefore, not to depend on making this trip, and suggest if you are still determined to go in, to make some other arrangements."

Daly did not reply. On his return from the Marshall Islands the following year, he did, however, follow up his interest in the property. He discovered that in July, Stevens had sent prospectors into the area and, as a result of their investigations, had staked claims in his own name and later sold them to a mining development company. Daly brought an action against Stevens claiming damages for breach of contract. Should Daly succeed in his action? Explain.

8. The city of Cameron had grown substantially in the past decade and needed to expand its water purification plant. For this purpose it proposed to buy two hectares of land adjacent to the purification plant from Margot Nurseries, a thriving fruit and vegetable business owning 40 hectares of prime land. As the two hectares were particularly important to Margot, she bargained for a substantial price to pay for the relocation of her business's sorting and packaging area.

The city bargained very hard, and threatened to expropriate the land—as it had power to do under the provincial Expropriation Act—if a deal could not be reached. Finally, in exasperation, Margot handed the director of the purification plant a detailed written statement of the terms upon which she would sell, the offer to be open for 10 days. She asked for a price of $200 000, with $50 000 paid on acceptance. She would permit the city to begin excavation on the nearest one-quarter hectare, but it must delay moving onto the remainder of the land for 60 days so that she could make the needed relocation. When Margot handed the director the offer, she stated that if the city began excavations on the one-quarter hectare, that would be acceptance of her offer.

Within a week, city workers began excavating about 20 metres into Margot's land, and two days later she was served with a notice of expropriation under the Expropriation Act, offering her a price of $80 000.

Under the Act, if the parties do not reach a settlement, a court will hear evidence about the market value of the land and the costs caused by compulsory displacement to the owner; it then awards a sum in compensation and orders the owner to give up possession.

Margot, claiming that the city had accepted her offer before the expropriation proceedings were started, sued the city for damages for breach of the contract. Discuss the arguments of each side and give your opinion on who should succeed. What general issue of public policy arises when a legislature grants powers of expropriation to municipalities?

ADDITIONAL RESOURCES FOR CHAPTER 5 ON THE COMPANION WEBSITE *(www.pearsoned.ca/smyth)*

In addition to self-test multiple-choice, true–false, and short essay questions (all with immediate feedback), application exercises, and links to useful web destinations, the Companion Website provides the following resources for Chapter 5:

- **British Columbia:** Cooling-off Period; Electronic Transactions; Government Procurement and Tenders
- **Alberta:** Cooling Off Period; Electronic Contracts; Form of Contract
- **Manitoba/Saskatchewan:** Internet Consumer Contracts and the Consumer Protection Act; Negative Marketing
- **Ontario:** Acceptance; Consumer Agreements; Cooling-Off Periods; Consumer Protection Act 2002; Electronic Contracts; Exemption Clauses; Standard Form Contracts; and Terms Requiring Notice

6

Formation of a Contract:

Consideration, and Intention to Create Legal Relations

Before an agreement is binding in law, certain essentials must be present; first, there must be consideration, although in some instances there may be something else in its place. In this chapter we examine such questions as:

■ What is the nature of consideration, and what is required for it to be adequate to bind the parties?

■ How do we distinguish consideration from a gratuitous promise? from motive for making a promise? from an existing legal duty to perform?

■ What is equitable estoppel?

■ What other ways are there to make a promise binding?

■ Why is it essential that parties must intend their promises to be binding, and how may this normal presumption be missing?

THE MEANING OF CONSIDERATION

An accepted offer will not be recognized as an enforceable contract unless it has consideration. In essence, the accepted offer must form a **bargain**—where each party pays a price for the promise obtained from the other party. In a unilateral contract the price paid for the offeror's promise is the act done by the offeree. In a bilateral contract, the price paid for each party's promise is the promise of the other. This price is called *consideration*. In short, **consideration** is "the price for which the promise [or the act] of the other is bought."[1]

A promisor usually bargains for a benefit to himself, such as a promise to pay money, deliver goods, or provide services; but it need not be directly for his own benefit. So long as the promisor bargains for the other party to do something—or to promise to do something—that she otherwise would not do, the promisor will have received consideration.

bargain
each party pays a price for the promise of the other

consideration
the price for which the promise of the other is bought

ILLUSTRATION 6.1

Adams, a creditor of Brown, threatened to sue Brown for an overdue debt. Brown's friend, Cox, then promised to pay Adams Brown's debt if Adams would refrain from suing Brown, and Adams agreed.

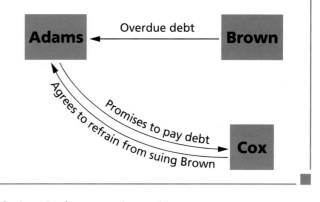

If Cox failed to pay Adams as agreed and Adams sued him for breach of contract, she would succeed. To establish consideration she need only show that she changed her conduct—that is, that she refrained from suing Brown, in return for Cox's promise. The "price" she agrees to pay for Cox's promise need not confer a direct benefit on him.

GRATUITOUS PROMISES

With some qualifications to be discussed later, consideration is essential to make a contract binding in law. A person may, of course, make a promise to another without bargaining for anything in return. A promise made in the absence of a bargain is called a **gratuitous promise** and, although accepted by the person to whom it is made, does not become a contract and is not enforceable in law. A promise to make a gift and a promise to perform services without remuneration are common examples of gratuitous promises. Such "contracts" are void for lack of consideration, which is another way of saying that they never amounted to a contract.

The law does nothing to prevent performance of a gratuitous promise. It simply states that if the promisor does not perform, the promisee has no legal remedy—he cannot seek compensation because he did not obtain the benefit he was promised. As a matter of honour, most people do perform their gratuitous promises.

What about charitable donations? Charities seldom find it in their interest to sue those who have made pledges but do not perform. They rely upon their prospective donors' sense of honour to a large extent, but in their budgeting they are wise to discount a small percentage as non-performers. They understand that people might become reluctant to give pledges if charities were likely to sue them for non-payment.

gratuitous promise
a promise made without bargaining for or accepting anything in return

---

1. P.H. Winfield, *Pollock's Principles of Contract*, 13th ed., at 133.

We can see, then, that if one person promises to reward another who has *previously* done an act gratuitously or given something of value, the promise is not binding. That promise is gratuitous—just like the benefit that the promisee had earlier conferred upon the promisor. Another approach is to say that the motive of the promisor was to return the kindness of the promisee, and, of course, motive and consideration are not the same thing. The benefit previously conferred upon the promisor is often called **past consideration**. Since there is no element of bargain—that is, of the benefit being performed *in return for* the promise—the expression is really contradictory, for "past consideration" is no consideration.

past consideration
a gratuitous benefit previously conferred upon a promisor

moral cause
moral duty of promisor to perform his promise

ETHICAL ISSUE

Promises

Ethically, we may believe it is wrong to break *any* promise seriously made and that every promisor has a moral duty to perform. If every promise were legally enforceable simply because the promisor had a moral duty to do as he said he would, we would not need the doctrine of consideration. In civil law legal systems, where **moral cause** may be sufficient to make a promise binding, courts must probe internally into a promisor's motive in order to establish moral obligation. While the doctrine of consideration has been attacked as causing unfair decisions in some instances (and undoubtedly it does, as we shall see), it has the benefit of being an objective test.

QUESTIONS TO CONSIDER

1. What difficulties arise when evaluating motives to establish moral obligations?
2. Is moral cause a more appropriate standard than consideration?

RELATION BETWEEN EXISTING LEGAL DUTY AND CONSIDERATION

Where *A* has an existing contractual duty to *B*, a later promise by *B* to pay *A* something extra to perform that obligation is not binding. Performance by *A* is not good consideration for the later promise because *A* was already bound to perform. Indeed, *A*'s failure to do so would have been a breach of contract. For example, a promise to members of a crew to increase their pay if they did not desert their ship was held to be unenforceable.[7] The existing contracts of employment between the crew and the employer bound the crew to perform their duties faithfully. On the other hand, a term of such contracts is that the ship be seaworthy. If it proves unseaworthy, the crew are released from their obligation, and then, of course, there will be consideration for the promise to increase their pay if the crew stays with the ship.[8]

The situation sometimes arises where one party threatens to default on its obligation to perform and leave the other party to sue for breach. A common example occurs in construction projects.

7. *Stilk* v. *Myrick* (1809), 70 E.R. 1168.
8. *Turner* v. *Owen* (1862), 6 E.R. 79.

ILLUSTRATION 6.3

A Inc. has tendered and won the contract to erect an office building for land developer *B*. During construction, *A* Inc. runs into unexpected difficulties and informs *B* that it is thinking of abandoning the project. However, *B*, relying upon completion at the agreed date, has already leased out large parts of the building. If *A* Inc. abandons the job, *B* will lose valuable time finding another builder to complete the project and will likely be in breach of leases he has made with prospective tenants.

To avoid these difficulties, *B* offers to pay *A* Inc. an extra $500 000 to enable it to hire extra workers and pay overtime wages in order to complete construction on time. *A* Inc. accepts and completes on the agreed date. However, *B* refuses to pay the additional sum on the grounds that he received no new consideration for his promise: *A* Inc. was already bound by its contract to complete on time.

Some U.S. courts have taken the view that a building firm is at liberty to abandon the job if it chooses, and to pay damages. In this view a fresh promise to proceed—that is, not to abandon the job—is good consideration for an additional sum and the owner is bound to pay it on completion. Most courts, including all English and Canadian courts, take the view that this conduct smacks of unfair pressure—a form of economic blackmail—by the party threatening to abandon the contract, and so they hold that there is no consideration for the promise to pay an extra sum.[9] However, a supplier intent on economic blackmail can still exact a legally enforceable promise from its customer to pay an increased price by delivering a "peppercorn" or a paperclip (or any other item of negligible value) to her in return for the promise, or by insisting that the customer make her promise under seal (as discussed later in this chapter).

We can see shortcomings in the doctrine of consideration when parties try to modify an existing contract. Not every change in contractual terms amounts to an unfair exploitation of the promisor. For instance, a promisor may believe it is in its best interests to pay the promisee more in order to ease the promisee's hardship and thus obtain better performance. So far, the Canadian courts have been reluctant to recognize this reality,[10] although an English case has allowed a construction company to recover a promised extra sum for completion.[11] The court was satisfied that there was no economic duress; the construction company had not exerted undue pressure and both parties benefited from performance.

A related problem arises when a stranger—a "third party" to a contract—promises to pay a sum to the promisor for his promise to perform already existing obligations to the promisee.

ILLUSTRATION 6.4

As in Illustration 6.3, *A* Inc. has made a contract to construct an office building for *B*. *C*, who has a lease as principal tenant in the building, promises to pay *A* $100 000 if *A* completes the building on time. Is there consideration for *C's* promise?[12] Since *A* is already under a duty to *B* to construct the building on time, what further price does *A* give for *C's* promise?

This problem has seldom arisen in the courts, but when it does they seem to agree that *A* can enforce *C's* promise, and further, that if *A* failed to perform, *A* would be liable to actions by *both B* and *C*.[13] *A* has given new consideration by promising *C* to complete on time and making himself

---

9. *See Gilbert Steel Ltd.* v. *University Construction Ltd.* (1976), 67 D.L.R. (3d) 606.

10. See Reiter, "Courts, Consideration and Common Sense" (1977), 27 U.T.L.J. at 439–512, especially at 459.

11. *Williams* v. *Roffey Brothers & Nicholls (Contractors) Ltd.*, [1990] 1 All E.R. 512. For a useful commentary, see Dan Halyk, "Consideration, Practical Benefits and Promissory Estoppel" (1991), 55(2) Sask. L. Rev. 393.

12. *Shadwell* v. *Shadwell* (1860), 142 E.R. 62.

13. *Scotson* v. *Pegg* (1861), 158 E.R. 121; *Pao On* v. *Lau Yiu Long*, [1979] 3 W.L.R. 435.

liable to *C* if he fails to do so. Accordingly, we must distinguish between the situation where the later promise is made by the promisee in the original contract, and where it is made by a third party to that contract.

Suppose instead that *A*'s duty to perform is a public duty required by law, as where *A* is a police officer. If *B* promises to pay *A* for services as a police officer, the court is confronted with two problems—the question of public policy *and* of consideration. If police officers have been asked to do something that they are already bound to do or something that will interfere with their regular duties, the court worries that the promise to pay them tends to corrupt public servants and it will likely find the promise unenforceable on grounds of public policy. On the other hand, if the court finds that the officers have been requested to do something beyond their duties and *not* in conflict with them, it will likely find consideration and hold the promise binding, as in *Glasbrook Brothers v. Glamorgan County Council*,[14] where a company agreed to pay for a special police guard during a strike and was held to be bound by its promise.

GRATUITOUS REDUCTION OF A DEBT

The requirement for consideration to make a promise binding can lead to other unsatisfactory results, especially in business transactions.

CASE 6.3

In the leading English case of *Foakes* v. *Beer*, a debtor owed a large sum of money to his creditor and payment was overdue. The creditor agreed to accept a series of instalments of the principal, and to forgo her right to interest, if the debtor paid promptly and regularly. The debtor paid the full principal as agreed, but the creditor then sued for the interest. She succeeded on the grounds that her promise to accept less than the total sum to which she was entitled—that is, principal plus accrued interest—was a gratuitous promise and did not bind her.[15]

This rule is unrealistic. For a number of sensible reasons, a creditor, *C*, may find it more to its benefit to settle for a reduced amount than to insist on payment in full. First, the compromise may avoid placing a debtor in bankruptcy where, by the time all other creditors' claims have been recognized, *C* might end up with less money than if it had accepted a reduced sum. Second, the proposed reduction may enable the debtor to persuade friends to lend him enough money to take advantage of it and make a fresh start. Third, the debtor may simply not have the assets to enable him to pay in full, so that a court judgment against him would not in any event realize more than the reduced amount. Finally, *C* may well need urgently at least part of the sum owed it for other commitments: it may be happier to take the lesser amount at once, instead of later collecting the full account with all the delays inherent in a legal action.

The rule in *Foakes* v. *Beer* may be avoided in several ways. In the first place, payment before the due date is sufficient consideration to make an agreed reduction in the debt binding on the creditor. So if the debtor pays $600 one day in advance in settlement of a $1000 debt due the next day, the agreement to accept $600 is binding. As we have seen, the court will not inquire into the adequacy of the consideration; if the creditor chooses to reduce the debt by $400 in order to receive payment one day in advance, it may bind itself to do so.

Second, the rule in *Foakes* v. *Beer* applies *only* to payments of money. It does not apply to the transfer of goods or to the provision of services. Since an individual may make a contract for a

---

14. [1925] A.C. 270.

15. (1884), 9 App. Cas. 605.

clearly inadequate consideration if he so desires, he may agree to pay $1000 for a trinket, a cheap watch, or a package of cigarettes. Similarly, he may agree to cancel a $1000 debt on receiving any one of these objects. In effect, he is trading the debt for the object, and such an agreement is valid, provided he agrees to it voluntarily. The result of this reasoning creates a paradox: if a person agrees to accept $900 in full settlement of a $1000 debt, he may later sue for the balance successfully; if a person accepts $500 and a string of beads worth 10 cents in full settlement of a $1000 debt, he will fail if he sues for the balance.

Third, the rule in *Foakes* v. *Beer* applies only to agreements between a creditor and debtor. A third party, who is not bound to pay anything to the creditor, may offer to pay the creditor a lesser sum if it will cancel the debt. A creditor that accepts such an offer is bound by its promise and will fail if it later sues the debtor.[16] The result is the same as if the third person had purchased the debt from the creditor.

ILLUSTRATION 6.5

A Co. Ltd. has an account receivable from *B* for $1000 and sells (assigns) it to *X* for $800. *A* Co. Ltd. no longer has any rights against *B*. It would not matter whether *X* was purchas-ing the account receivable as a business proposition and intended to hold *B* to her promise for full payment, or whether he wished merely to help her. *X*'s motive is irrelevant. If he deals directly with the creditor, the debt for $1000 can be bought for $800.

The result would have been different, however, if *X* had lent $800 to *B* and *B* had then paid the $800 to *A* Co. Ltd. apparently in full settlement of the account of $1000. So long as *B* deals directly with *A* Co. Ltd., the source of *B*'s funds used to pay *A* is irrelevant: *A* Co. Ltd. would not be bound by the settlement and could later sue *B* for $200 (apart from the statutory exceptions discussed below).

Finally, as we shall see shortly, the rule in *Foakes* v. *Beer* is avoided if the creditor agrees in writing and under seal to reduce the debt.

The rule in *Foakes* v. *Beer* has been restricted by statute in British Columbia, Alberta, Saskatchewan, Manitoba, and Ontario.[17] Under any of these acts, if a creditor agrees to accept part performance (that is, a lesser sum of money) in settlement of a debt, it is bound once it has accepted this part performance. On the other hand, it may be able to go back on its promise to accept a lesser sum of money before the sum is actually paid; the cases are unclear on this point.

EQUITABLE ESTOPPEL

Evolution of the Principle

Suppose a person makes a gratuitous promise to another, fully intending to keep it, but later finds it inconvenient to perform. Meanwhile, the promisee has quite reasonably relied on the promise and has incurred expenses he would otherwise not have made. What happens if the promisor subsequently defaults? According to the strict rules of common law, the answer is "nothing at all." The gratuitous promise remains gratuitous, the promise cannot be enforced, and the promisee suffers the burden of his expenses.

---

16. *Hirachand Punamchand* v. *Temple*, [1911] 2 K.B. 330.
17. Law and Equity Act, R.S.B.C. 1979, c. 224, s. 40; Judicature Act, R.S.A. 1980, c. J-1, s. 13 (1); Queens Bench Act, 1998, S.S. 1998, c. Q-1.01, s. 64; Mercantile Law Amendment Act, R.S.M. 1987, c. M-120, s. 6; and Mercantile Law Amendment Act, R.S.O. 1990, c. M.10, s. 16. For cases interpreting this section see *Rommerill* v. *Gardener* (1962), 35 D.L.R. (2d) 717 and others referred to therein.

ILLUSTRATION 6.6

A, who has just ordered a new 90-horsepower outboard motor, tells his friend B that he will give him his old 35-horsepower motor as soon as the new one arrives. To make use of A's old engine, B will have to make expensive modifications to his small boat. Instead, at A's suggestion he buys a new boat for $3000. Subsequently, A's brother reminds him that he had promised the old motor to him, and rather than promote a family quarrel, A tells B he cannot carry out his promise. B has no right in contract law to enforce A's promise.

Estoppel Based on Fact

estopped
prevented

When one person asserts as true a certain *statement of fact* and another relies on that statement to his detriment, the maker of the statement will be **estopped** (prevented) from denying the truth of his original statement in a court of law, even if it turns out to have been untrue.

ILLUSTRATION 6.7

A purchased a retail shoe business from X in rented premises owned by B. After a few months, A mentions to her landlord, B, that the business does not have an adequate sales area and that she would like to turn a back room into a display and fitting salon. The room contains a number of pieces of old furniture that she believes belong to B and that she would like to get rid of. B says, "That furniture belonged to X and you acquired it when you bought the business. You can do as you like with it." A replies, "I thought it was yours. That's what X told me." "No, it's yours," B answers. The tenant next door to A is present and hears the conversation.

That evening, when B reports the incident to his wife, she becomes furious and reminds B that several antique pieces given to them by her grandmother are stored in the back room of the store. When B arrives at the shoe store the next morning he discovers that the furniture has been taken away to the city dump and compressed by a bulldozer. He then sues A for the value of the antique furniture.

B would fail because A can prove in her defence that B said that the furniture was A's, and the court would estop B from asserting the true state of the facts.

Estoppel applies to an assertion of existing fact; but does it also apply to a promise of future conduct? This question has presented a problem for the courts. The truth of existing facts is an objective matter that can easily be determined by evidence. Future promises are a different matter.

Despite their problems with the idea of estoppel, the courts eventually found themselves unable to ignore the plea of an innocent party who had relied in good faith on a gratuitous promise only to find later that the promisor had changed his mind. On the grounds of fairness, courts exercised their equitable jurisdiction to estop *the promisor* from claiming that he was not bound by his gratuitous promise. This reasoning extended the idea of factual estoppel to promises. The principle has been called **promissory estoppel,** but the more common term is **equitable estoppel** because the court is acting as a court of equity to override a common law rule.

promissory estoppel or equitable estoppel
the court's exercise of its equitable jurisdiction to estop a promisor from claiming that she was not bound by her gratuitous promise where reliance on that promise caused injury to the promisee

The English doctrine of equitable estoppel is presently limited to a *defence* against a claim by the promisor where a legal relationship already exists between the parties. The English courts have not recognized that a gratuitous promisee's claim of equitable estoppel makes the promise to him a binding one. (Hence, in our Illustration 6.6, of the gratuitous promise of an outboard motor, the promisee would not succeed in an English court.)

The doctrine of equitable estoppel originated well over a century ago in the leading case of *Hughes* v. *Metropolitan Railway Co.*[18]

CASE 6.4

Metropolitan Railway, a tenant under a 99-year lease of a large block of buildings, was required to keep the building in good repair. The penalty for failure to honour a notice to repair from the landlord, Hughes, would be forfeiture of possession—the lease would be terminated. Hughes served notice that repairs were needed and the tenant had six months to make them. The tenant then suggested that Hughes might be interested in buying back the remaining years of the tenant's 99-year lease. The lease was a valuable one as rents to subtenants had risen greatly over the long years of the master lease. When Hughes expressed interest in the proposal, the two sides began serious negotiations. With Hughes' acquiescence, all repairs were delayed, since they would have increased the tenant's investment in the property and so raised the sale price of the lease.

After several months, negotiations broke down and the tenant then proceeded with the repairs. They were not finished within six months of the original notice, but were complete within six months of the end to negotiations. Hughes sued for forfeiture of the lease, and had he succeeded he would have obtained the remaining years free.

In refusing Hughes' claim, the House of Lords stated that by entering into negotiation Hughes had impliedly agreed to a suspension of the notice during negotiations; he could not later go back on his word and revert to his strict legal rights in the lease. The notice became effective again only on negotiations being broken off, when the tenant could no longer rely on Hughes' implied promise not to pursue his strict rights.

While a gratuitous promise may still be withdrawn, its withdrawal is not allowed to prejudice the promisee in respect of any reliance he has already placed on it. Notice of withdrawal (or an end to circumstances in which the promise is implied) may restore the promisor's rights to any future performance still owed by the promisee. In the *Hughes* case, the landlord was entitled, *after* the negotiations had broken down, to require repairs to be made within the six-month period provided in the lease.

The *Hughes* case illustrates the classic situation in which equitable estoppel arises:

(1) some form of legal relationship already exists between the parties;

(2) one of the parties promises (perhaps by implication only) to release the other from some or all of the other's legal duties to him; and

(3) the other party in reliance on that promise alters his conduct in a way that would make it a real hardship if the promisor could renege on his promise.

In these circumstances, if the promisor were to ignore his promise and sue to enforce his original rights, the promisee could successfully plead equitable estoppel to defeat the action against him.

The period immediately after the Second World War saw a flurry of cases in England in which Lord Denning sought gradually to develop the use of this doctrine.[19] Canadian courts have followed these developments: the Supreme Court of Canada in *Conwest Exploration Co.* v. *Letain*[20] pushed the doctrine quite far indeed. It can even be argued that the decision conceded that equitable estoppel might be used as a cause of action.[21] The facts were complicated, but the essential ones for our purposes can be summarized as follows.

---

18. (1877), 2 App. Cas. 439.

19. See, for example: *Central London Property Trust, Ltd.* v. *High Trees House, Ltd.*, [1947] K.B. 130.

20. (1964), 41 D.L.R. (2d) 198. See also: *Re Tudale Exploration Ltd. and Bruce et al.* (1978), 20 O.R. (2d) 593, per Grange J., at 597 and 599.

21. See, for example: *Crabb* v. *Arun District Council*, [1976] Ch. 179.

CASE 6.5

A held an option to purchase certain mining claims. Before the date of expiry of the option, *B*, the grantor of the option, impliedly agreed to its extension. (As in the *Hughes* case, it appeared to be in his own interest to do so.) As a result, *A* did not hurry to complete the required task under the option before the original expiry date, but he did try to exercise the option shortly afterwards, before *B* had given any notice that he wished to return to his strict legal rights. In an action brought by A asking the court to permit him to exercise his option, the court did not allow *B* to revert to the original expiry date, and *A*'s action succeeded.

B implicitly promised to extend the period during the original option period, while legal relations existed between the parties. On the one hand, it can be argued that this decision amounts to no more than an application of the *Hughes* case. On the other hand, the opposing view is that once the original option had expired, without an extension having been granted for additional consideration, no existing legal relationship between *A* and *B* remained; they were as strangers. Accordingly, to permit *A* to succeed is to permit him to use equitable estoppel as a cause of action. It remains to be seen whether the Canadian courts will favour this second view in future cases.

Injurious Reliance

injurious reliance
loss or harm suffered by a promisee who, to his detriment, relied reasonably on a gratuitous promise

In the United States, some states have expanded the principle of equitable estoppel to allow the injured party to force the promisor to perform the promise.[22] Courts in these states assert that since *the promisor* by his conduct *induced the injured party* to rely on his promise, the promisor must honour his promise to prevent an injustice. This principle, known as **injurious reliance**, is a cause of action, not just a defence.[23]

The U.S. term "injurious reliance" and the English term "equitable estoppel" are essentially two sides of the same coin: injurious reliance looks at the situation from the point of view of the promisee, while equitable estoppel views it from the position of the promisor.

INTERNATIONAL ISSUE

Will Injurious Reliance Be Adopted by the Canadian Courts?

We have just learned about the American doctrine of injurious reliance, where a promisee may have a cause of action against a promisor who makes and then breaks a gratuitous promise on which the promisee has relied to his detriment. The Canadian courts have been prepared to recognize some gratuitous promises as binding, but only to prevent a promisor from breaking a gratuitous promise and then suing the promisee. It is often said that Canadian courts accept the doctrine of promissory (equitable) estoppel as a "shield" (that is, a defence), but not a "sword" (that is, a cause of action). Recent decisions of Canadian appeals courts make one wonder if the Canadian common law will ever fully embrace the American notion of injurious reliance.

In the Supreme Court of Canada decision which examined these legal principles in detail, *Maracle v. Travellers Indemnity Co. of Canada*,[24] Mr. Justice Sopinka summarized the principles of promissory estoppel:

continued

22. *Ricketts* v. *Scothorn*, 77 N.W. 365 (1898).
23. American Law Institute, *Restatement of Contracts*, Section 90, Washington, 1932.
24. (1991), 2 S.C.R. 50.

The principles of promissory estoppel are well settled. The party relying on the doctrine must establish that the other party has, by words or conduct, made a promise or assurance which was intended to affect their legal relationship and to be acted on. Furthermore, the representee must establish that, in reliance on the representation, he acted on it or in some way changed his position.[25]

In *Maracle*, while it did not expressly adopt the doctrine of injurious reliance, the Supreme Court of Canada did not seem to limit the doctrine to its traditional place as a defence. Professor Waddams has since written: "It may therefore be suggested that the Commonwealth law is moving, though rather slowly, in the direction of [the American position in the Restatement of Contracts] towards the protection of promisees by reason of and to the extent of subsequent reliance."[26]

However, evidence in court opinions of this trend to adopt injurious reliance or promissory estoppel as a cause of action remains limited.[27] In a 2003 decision[28] of the British Columbia Court of Appeal, Madam Justice Huddart wrote:

While it may be, as Professor Waddams suggests, that the law is moving slowly toward a more generous approach to promissory estoppel than that said by Sopinka J. in *Maracle* v. *Travellers Indemnity Co.* to be well settled, I can see little evidence of that movement in Canadian authorities. . . .

Some evidence of movement is apparent in the 2008 Ontario Superior Court decision of *Hepburn* v. *Jannock Limited*,[29] where an employee's claim for a promised wage increase was allowed on a number of grounds including promissory estoppel.

QUESTIONS TO CONSIDER

1. Why do you think the Canadian courts seem slow to widen the scope of the doctrine of promissory estoppel to allow for injurious reliance as a cause of action?

2. Do you think the next time the Supreme Court of Canada has the opportunity to address the subject of promissory estoppel, it should endorse the American principle of injurious reliance as a cause of action?

Source: S.F. Waddams, *The Law of Contracts* (4th ed.) 1999, pp. 141–2 and 154–5.

THE EFFECT OF A REQUEST FOR GOODS OR SERVICES

When one person requests the services of another and the other performs those services, the law implies a promise to pay. Such a promise is implied between strangers or even between friends, if the services are rendered in a customary business transaction. But a promise to pay is not usually implied when the services are performed between members of a family or close friends; although the services were requested, the circumstances may show that the parties expected them to be given gratuitously because of friendship, kindness, or family duty.

---

25. *Maracle*, at 57.
26. S.F. Waddams, *The Law of Contracts* (4th ed); Canada Law Book: 1999, pp. 141–2 and 154–5.
27. An Ontario Court of Appeal decision, *Doef's Iron Works Ltd.* v. *MCCI*, [2004] O.J. No. 4358 states in paragraph 2 "It is well established that promissory estoppel can be used only as a shield and not as a sword. See: *Canwest Exploration Co.* v. *Letair*, [1964] S.C.R. 20, 41 D.L.R (2d) 198; *Reclamation Systems Inc.* v. *The Honourable Bob Rae* 1996 CanLII 7950 (ON S.C.), (1996), 27 O.R. (3d) 419."
28. *N.M* v. *A.T.A.*, 2003 BCCA 297.
29. (2008) 63 C.C.E.L. 3d. 101, at para 109–126.

quantum meruit
the amount a person merits to be paid for goods or services provided to the person requesting them

Even though neither party mentions price, the implied promise is for payment of what the services are reasonably worth—that is, for payment *quantum meruit*. Difficult though it may be when the services are not usual professional services with a recognized scale of fees, the court will still fix a fee that it considers to be reasonable.

After the requested services have been performed, the parties may agree on what they consider to be a reasonable price. If so, neither of them can later change his mind and ask the court to fix a reasonable price. In effect, by agreeing to a price each party has given up his right to refer the matter to the court.

ILLUSTRATION 6.8

A asks computer programmer *B* for technical assistance. Afterwards, *A* asks *B* what her fee is and *B* suggests a certain sum. *A* refuses to pay it. In an action for payment for services performed, the court may give judgment in favour of *B* in the amount she requested or for some other amount that it finds reasonable.

If instead, *A* had agreed to the figure suggested by *B* but later changed his mind about paying, the court would not concern itself with what it considered reasonable: it would give judgment in favour of *B* for the amount earlier agreed upon by the parties.

The performance of requested services creates an *existing obligation* to pay a reasonable price for them, and by later agreeing upon a fixed price, the parties have done away with the need for an implied price. Subsequent payment of the fixed price satisfies all obligations owed by the party who requested the services.

We must be careful to distinguish this position from that arising when a promise is made for a past consideration.[30] If, for example, *A* promises to pay *B* $100 because *B* has given her and her family an excellent dinner, *A* is not bound, since she is under no existing legal obligation at the time she makes her promise. If, however, *A* promises to pay *B* $100 because *B* has catered a dinner for her at her request, *A* would be bound; in fact, *A* was already bound to pay *B* a reasonable price, and she and *B* have simply agreed later upon what this price should be.

The principle of *quantum meruit* applies to goods supplied on request as well as to services rendered. Generally, a court has less difficulty ascertaining the reasonable worth of goods than of services.

covenant
a serious promise

covenantor
one who makes a covenant

document under seal
a covenant recorded in a document containing a wax seal, showing that the covenantor adopted the document as his act and deed

deed
a document under seal, which today is usually a small, red, gummed wafer

THE USE OF A SEAL

In medieval times, when few people could read or write, a serious promise or **covenant** was often recorded by a cleric. He would read the covenant to the **covenantor**, who would then show his consent by impressing his coat of arms into a pool of hot sealing wax poured at the foot of the document. Usually the coat of arms was worn on a signet ring. By impressing his seal in this way, the covenantor adopted the document as *his act and deed*. To this day a **document under seal** is still called a **deed**. Other methods of sealing a document evolved over time, including embossing the coat of arms directly on the paper. Today the usual method is to affix a small, red, gummed wafer to a document, but almost any mark identifiable as a "seal" will do, even the word "seal" simply written in.

---

30. *Lampleigh* v. *Braithwait* (1615), 80 E.R. 255.

A seal must be affixed (or the word "seal" written) on the document *at the time* the party signs it. The word "seal" printed on the document in advance presents difficulties: it may simply indicate the place where the parties are to place a red paper wafer. In *Royal Bank of Canada* v. *Kiska*[31] the bank used a printed form of guarantee that included the word "seal" and also the words "Given under seal at . . ." and "Signed, sealed and delivered in the presence of . . . ." The bank manager did not affix a red paper wafer, however, until some time after the promisor had signed and without the promisor's instructions to do so. Laskin, J. (later Chief Justice of the Supreme Court of Canada) commented:

> The respective words are merely anticipatory of a formality which must be observed and are not a substitute for it. I am not tempted by any suggestion that it would be a modern and liberal view to hold that a person who signs a document that states it is under seal should be bound accordingly although there is no seal on it. I have no regret in declining to follow this path in a case where a bank thrusts a printed form under the nose of a young man for his signature. Formality serves a purpose here and some semblance of it should be preserved. . . .[32]

Although, some lower courts[33] have held that the words "given under seal" are sufficient without the need to affix a red paper wafer, the Supreme Court endorses the role of the seal in Canadian common law:

> To create a sealed instrument, the application of the seal must be a conscious and deliberate act. At common law, then, the relevant question is whether the party intended to create an instrument under seal. . . .[34]

A promise made properly under the seal of the promisor does not require consideration to make it binding. Historically, signing under seal was considered an act done with great care. It is still considered so today. The seal says in effect, "I fully intend to be bound by this promise." Its presence means that the court will not, as it otherwise would, insist upon consideration to hold the promisor bound.

Although a seal is an alternative way to make a promise binding, it does not do away with any of the other requirements needed to make a promise enforceable. Other essentials for a binding contract (its legality, for example) remain the same.

Any offer may be made under seal and so becomes irrevocable. When a business firm or public body invites tenders and requires them to be submitted under the seal of the tenderer, the legal effect is much the same as when an option is given: the tenderer cannot withdraw without being liable in damages.[35]

Certain documents, such as a deed of land and a mortgage, traditionally required a seal even if there was consideration. Electronic registration of these documents has changed some of the seal requirements. These documents will be explained as they arise in later chapters.

AN INTENTION TO CREATE LEGAL RELATIONS

Even when an apparently valid offer has been accepted and consideration is present, there is no contract in law unless both sides also intended to create a legally enforceable agreement. Of course, parties do not ordinarily think about the legal effects of their bargains, and the law *presumes* that the necessary intention is present in almost all instances where an agreement appears to be seriously made.

---

31. (1967), 63 D.L.R. (2d) 582.

32. *Ibid.*, at 594.

33. *Canadian Imperial Bank of Commerce* v. *Dene Mat Construction Ltd.* and others, [1988] 4 W.W.R. 344 (N.W.T.S.C.); *Hongkong Bank of Canada* v. *New Age Graphic Design Inc.* [1996] B.C.J. No. (B.C.S.C.)

34. *Friedmann Equity Developments Inc.* v. *Final Note Ltd.*, [2000] 1 S.C.R. 842 at para 36.

35. See *Sanitary Refuse Collectors Inc.* v. *City of Ottawa*, [1972] 1 O.R. 296 at 308–9.

THE BURDEN OF PROVING ESSENTIAL ELEMENTS OF A CONTRACT

We have seen that once a plaintiff has shown that there was offer and acceptance and consideration for the promise, the court will ordinarily presume an intention to create legal relations—the elements we discussed in Chapters 5 and 6. At that point, and in the absence of evidence to the contrary, the court will presume that two further elements are present: (1) the defendant had the capacity to make a contract, and (2) the contract is legal. It is up to the defendant to show that she did not have the capacity to enter into the contract or that the contract was not legal, with the result that it would be unenforceable against her. First, we examine the question of capacity.

THE MEANING OF CAPACITY TO CONTRACT

When we enter into a contract, we usually assume that the other party has the capacity to make a contract and is bound by it, but this is not always so. We would not expect a four-year-old child to be able to bind herself to pay $100 for a computer game; at that age she would lack the competence—the **capacity**—to enter into legally binding contracts. Although the requirements of Chapters 5 and 6 were met, as a matter of *policy* the law may excuse one party, such as the four-year-old child, from her obligations. Of course, in most cases, a lack of capacity is not so obvious; one party reasonably assumes the other has capacity to enter into a contract.

In practice, it is remarkable how little litigation arises as a result of minors attempting to **repudiate** their contracts. An important non-legal sanction is very persuasive: if minors should repudiate on grounds of incapacity, they would all but eliminate their chances of finding others willing to give them credit. Even so, it is important to be aware of the rights and remedies available to both sides in such contracts.

MINORS (OR INFANTS)

Contracts Creating Liability for a Minor

A **minor** or an **infant** is a person who has not attained the **age of majority** according to the law of her province. At common law the age was deemed to be 21, but it now varies according to the legislation in each province.[1] The general rule is that a contract made by a minor is unenforceable against her but enforceable *by* her against the other side, whether or not the other person is aware that he is dealing with a minor. So a minor may simply ignore contractual promises. When a minor owns considerable assets, her father or mother is ordinarily empowered to look after her affairs or, with supervision of the court, may make contracts concerning her property; if her parents are deceased or are unable to manage her affairs, the court will appoint a **guardian** to do so.

While the purpose of these rules is to protect minors, if there were no exceptions that very purpose would be defeated and could cause great hardship: a minor in need of food or clothing—**necessaries**—might be unable to find a merchant willing to sell her these things on credit because she could not bind herself to pay for them. Accordingly, the courts regard contracts for necessaries as exceptions to a minor's immunity from liability.

---

legal capacity
competence to bind oneself legally

repudiate
reject or declare an intention not to be bound by

minor or infant
a person who has not attained the age of majority according to the law of his or her province

age of majority
the age at which a person is recognized as an adult according to the law of his or her province

guardian
a person appointed to manage the affairs of a minor in the place of his or her parents

necessaries
essential goods and services

---

1. It is usually 18 or 19 years. See, for example: Age of Majority Act, R.S.B.C. 1996, c. 5 (19 years); S.N.S. 1989, c. 4 (19 years); R.S.M. 1987, c. A-4 (18 years); Age of Majority and Accountability Act, R.S.O. 1990, c. A.7, s. 6 (18 years).

By contrast, the legal status of business corporations as employers is clearly settled. The differences between the two make uncertain the enforceability of collective agreements between corporations and labour unions. However, most provinces do have statutes[24] that provide for arbitration in the event of a dispute arising out of the collective agreement. If an employer does not implement the decision of the arbitrator, the union may apply to a labour relations board for permission to prosecute and for this purpose is given legal status. If a union rejects the arbitrator's decision and causes an illegal strike, damages have occasionally been awarded against the union; the enforceability of such decisions is a matter of debate. In those provinces where an employer may seek permission to prosecute a union for such a strike, the union's liability derives from a statutory provision and not from the union's contractual capacity.

Despite their indefinite status, labour unions may bring actions or defend against them when they so wish. By a legal technique known as a **representative action**, a union may expressly or impliedly authorize one or more persons to represent it in court simply as a group of individuals having a common interest in a particular case. As a result, union officials may bring or defend a representative action on behalf of its members.

representative action
an action brought by one or more persons on behalf of a group having the same interest

ENEMY ALIENS

Ordinarily, an **alien** has the same rights as a citizen in making contracts and in all other matters of private law. In the event of a declaration of war, however, an enemy alien loses all contractual capacity, apart from any special licence granted by the Crown. For the purposes of contracts, an *enemy* alien is identified not by citizenship but by the fact that either his residence or business interests are located in enemy territory.

alien
non-citizen

Any evidence that a contract made with an enemy alien is detrimental to the public interest will make the contract void as being against public policy, and the rights and liabilities created by the contract are wholly dissolved. In a few exceptional instances where the public interest is thought not to be affected, a contract may be regarded as being merely suspended for the duration of hostilities.

ABORIGINAL PEOPLES

In Canada, the definition of **Aboriginal peoples** includes native Indian, Inuit, and Métis peoples of Canada.[25] Native Indians living on reservations are still considered wards of the Crown. The property comprising the reservation is held by the Crown in trust for the benefit of the Indian band. It is not available as security for the claims of creditors, and any attempt to dispose of such property to an outside party is void unless the transaction has been approved by the Minister of Indian Affairs and Northern Development. Indians living on reservations may manufacture and sell chattels to outsiders, although in the prairie provinces, sales of produce must have the approval of a superintendent under the Minister. The legal position of Indians on reservations is set out in detail in the Indian Act.[26] Indians not living on a reservation have the same contractual capacity as that of any other citizen.

Aboriginal peoples
Indian, Inuit, and Métis peoples of Canada

24. See, for example: Labour Relations Code, R.S.B.C. 1996, c. 244, s. 82(2); The Labour Relations Act, S.O. 1995, c. 1, Sch. A. s. 405; The Trade Union Act, R.S.N.S. 1989, c. 475, s. 19(1).
25. Constitution Act, 1982, s. 35(2).
26. R.S.C. 1985, c. I-5. Section 4 excludes Inuit people from the application of the Act.

CASE 7.3

A judgment creditor tried to collect its judgment by garnishing the bank account of the debtor, God's Lake Indian Band, an Indian band on a reserve in Northern Manitoba. The bank account was with a financial institution in Winnipeg. The Supreme Court of Canada allowed the garnishment to proceed.

It held that the bank account was not actually situated on the reserve, nor was it "deemed to be" situated on the reserve within the meaning of the Indian Act. The creditor was entitled to collect.[27]

BANKRUPT DEBTORS

A bankrupt debtor, until he receives a discharge from the court, is under certain contractual disabilities. We will discuss these disabilities more fully in Chapter 31.

THE ROLE OF LEGALITY IN THE FORMATION OF A CONTRACT

legal
not offensive to the public good and not violating any law

The object or purpose of a contract must be **legal**: it must not offend the public good (that is, it must not be contrary to public policy) or violate any law. We noted at the beginning of this chapter that in the absence of evidence to the contrary, the courts presume that transactions are legal. However, a defendant may introduce evidence to show that this presumption is wrong. If he succeeds, the contract will at least be *void*; it was never formed at all. In some circumstances the courts will go further and find that the contract is also *unenforceable*.

THE DIFFERENCE BETWEEN A VOID AND AN ILLEGAL CONTRACT

No stigma attaches to the parties if their contract is simply void; they have just not succeeded in creating a binding agreement. If they have partly performed their promises, the court will do its best, taking all the circumstances into account, to restore them to their respective positions before the contract was attempted. It may order the return of money paid or of property transferred if the party complaining can show cause why it should be returned. In addition, each party is released from the performance of any further obligations under the agreement. A court may find that only a term of a contract is void and that the remaining parts are valid. If it decides that the void term can be **severed** without doing injustice to the parties, it will uphold the remainder of the contract.

severed
removed from the contract

When a contract is not only void but also illegal, the contract is unenforceable. The court will refuse to aid a party who knowingly agreed to an illegal arrangement. Not only may he not sue for money promised, but also if he has transferred property to the other party, he is not permitted to recover it. When both parties are tainted with knowledge of the illegal object, the fact that a court will assist neither of them leaves the plaintiff without a remedy and so assists the defendant. The legal maxim is: where both parties are equally in the wrong, the position of the defendant is the stronger. Under the policy towards illegal contracts, a court will not allow a part of the contract that might otherwise be legal to be severed and enforced.

27. *McDiarmid Lumber Ltd.* v. *God's Lake First Nation*, [2006] 2 S.C.R. 846.

The law is not very helpful in providing standards for deciding when a contract is illegal as well as void. Generally, the more reprehensible its purpose, the more likely the contract will be regarded as illegal and a plaintiff will be denied any remedy.

CONTRACTS AFFECTED BY STATUTE

Significance of the Wording of a Statute

A statute may simply prevent a particular type of contract from having any legal effect by stating that such agreements shall be void. Or it may go further and express positive disapproval by describing such agreements as "unlawful" or "illegal." A statute may even declare that performance of the agreement shall be a criminal offence, subject to prescribed penalties of a fine or imprisonment.

Contracts Void by Statute

Agreements Contrary to the Purpose of Legislation

Workers' compensation legislation, for example, states that any provision in an agreement between employer and employee purporting to deprive the employee of the protection of the Act is void.[28] Other statutes declare particular types of transfers of property to be void: ownership does not pass from the transferor and the property may be recovered from the transferee and applied according to the terms of the statute. For instance, the Bankruptcy and Insolvency Act contains a provision that if a person transfers property either by gift or for an obviously inadequate compensation and becomes bankrupt within one year, the transfer is void and the property is available to the trustee in bankruptcy.[29] The trustee may recover the property and apply it to the claims of the bankrupt person's creditors. The same statute provides that a transfer of property by an insolvent person to one of several creditors with a view to giving that creditor a preference over the others is "fraudulent and void" if it occurs within three months preceding bankruptcy.[30]

Promises to Pay a Betting Debt

At common law, debts resulting from bets were not considered against public policy and accordingly were not void. Nevertheless, the English courts did not like enforcing wagers that were based simply on speculation about an unknown result, with the winner collecting from the loser, so the courts searched for reasons to refuse them. Sometimes they looked at the subject-matter of the bet and found it to be against public policy, such as "bribing voters"—a wager with voters as to the outcome of an election in their constituency.[31]

---

28. See, for example: Workplace Safety and Insurance Act, S.O. 1997, c. 16, s. 16; Workers' Compensation Act, R.S.B.C. 1996, c. 492, s. 13; S.N.S. 1994–95, c. 10.

29. R.S.C. 1985, c. B-3, s. 91 of the Bankruptcy and Insolvency Act, as amended by S.C. 1992, c. 1 and c. 27. Section 3 of the Act also provides, "For the purposes of this Act, a person who has entered into a transaction with another person otherwise than at arm's length shall be deemed to have entered into a reviewable transaction." Under s. 100 a court may give judgment in favour of the trustee against the other party to such a transaction for the difference between the actual consideration given or received by the bankrupt and the fair market value of the property or services concerned. The provisions of the Bankruptcy and Insolvency Act are in the process of being reformed and are dealt with in more detail in Chapter 31.

30. Section 95(1).

31. *Allen* v. *Hearn* (1875), 1 T.R. 56. They even refused a remedy because an "idle wager" wasted the court's time: *Gilbert* v. *Sykes* (1812), 16 East 150 at 162.

This distaste for betting contracts, as well as a more general concern that gambling was harmful to society, led to early English statutes prohibiting certain types of betting, and eventually the Gaming Act of 1845 made all bets void and unenforceable, but they are not a criminal offence: there was no fine or imprisonment for those who make bets. It simply made it impossible for a winner to collect through court action.

Betting in Canada

In Canada, the Criminal Code[32] does make certain betting activities illegal. Activities such as betting on horse races are expressly declared legal (s. 204), but it is a criminal offence to keep a gaming house (s. 201) or to operate a pool (s. 202) or a lottery (s. 206) unless they fall under specified exceptions within the Act. Major exceptions include lotteries operated by a province or by an organization licensed by a province (s. 207).

Provincial gaming legislation evolved from the historic statutes of the United Kingdom. Now all provinces have gaming commissions that supervise the issuing of licenses for lotteries, race courses, and casinos.[33] Some statutes make specific reference to the enforcement of gambling contracts:

> No person may use civil proceedings to recover money owing to the person resulting from participating in or betting on a lottery scheme within the meaning of section 207 of the Criminal Code (Canada) conducted in Ontario unless the lottery scheme is authorized under subsection 207(1) of the Code.[34]

The Criminal Code does address the ability to pass title to an asset through an unlicensed lottery:

> Every sale, loan, gift, barter or exchange of any property, by any lottery, ticket, card or other mode of chance depending on or to be determined by chance or lot, is void, and all property so sold, lent, given, bartered or exchanged is forfeited to Her Majesty. (s. 206(5))

There is quite a large body of Canadian case law regarding betting. Most of it refuses to enforce debts, although some decisions allowed a creditor to succeed, usually one who has lent money to the debtor but who himself did not participate in the game.

wager
an agreement between two persons in which each has some probability of winning or losing

stakeholder
a person or organization that manages a betting arrangement for a fee and redistributes winnings

The parties to a **wager**—an agreement between two parties in which each has at the time some probability of winning or losing—must be distinguished from a **stakeholder** who manages a betting arrangement for a fee and redistributes winnings. Organizations that manage lotteries, racetracks, and casinos are stakeholders and therefore not a party to a wagering agreement. They do, however, remain legally accountable for performing their task as stakeholders.[35] A number of contracts commonly regarded as being of a legitimate business nature have a significant element of speculation in them—insurance contracts, stock exchange transactions, and "futures" transactions in commodities. Insurance statutes, in particular, require that contracts of insurance not be regarded as wagering contracts if they are to be enforceable.

Contracts Exempt from the Betting Prohibition

Insurance Contracts

Contracts of insurance form a large and important class of commercial transactions. In a true insurance contract one does not, of course, hope to win the "bet" with the insurance company, but rather that should the feared loss occur, one will receive a measure of compensation. The fear of loss is

---

32. Criminal Code, R.S.C. 1985, c. C-46, ss. 201–209.
33. See for example the Gaming Control Act, S.B.C. 2002, c. 14; Gaming Control Act, S.N.S. 1994–95, c. 4.
34. Gaming Control Act, S.O. 1992, c. 24, s. 47.1.
35. *Ellesmere* v. *Wallace*, [1929] 2 Ch. 1; *Tote Investors Ltd.* v. *Smoker*, [1968] 1 Q.B. 509.

expressed in the idea of **insurable interest**. For a person to have an insurable interest, he must have a financial benefit from the continued existence of the property or life insured or suffer some financial detriment from its loss or destruction. Provincial insurance acts state that an insurance contract is invalid unless the party making the contract has an insurable interest in the property or life insured.

Insurance statutes describe the circumstances where an insurable interest exists. With respect to life insurance, for policies on one's own life or on certain members of one's family, it is not necessary to show a financial interest—a detriment is presumed to exist in the loss of that life. But for all other persons, a policy holder must show that he has a financial interest in the person whose life is insured, such as a debtor or a business partner. The acts waive the requirement of an insurable interest only when the person whose life is insured consents in writing to placing the insurance.[36] We discuss insurance contracts more fully in Chapter 18.

insurable interest
an interest where a person has a financial benefit from the continued existence of the property or life insured or would suffer financial detriment from its loss or destruction

Stock Exchange Transactions

Stock exchange transactions are among the more speculative business contracts. While they are no doubt often explained by a difference of opinion between the buyer and the seller about the future price of the shares traded, the contract itself is an actual sale of personal property. Bona fide contracts for the purchase and sale of shares are therefore valid and enforceable. If, however, the subject of an agreement is a wager about what the price of a particular security will be at a specified future time, "without a bona fide intention of acquiring, selling or taking delivery" of the shares, such an agreement is an offence under the Criminal Code and accordingly it is illegal.[37]

Contract for the Future Delivery of Goods

Whenever goods are purchased or sold for future delivery at a price agreed upon in advance, one contracting party may gain at the expense of the other because of price changes between the time of the contract and the time of delivery. Again, the speculative element in these contracts is incidental to a larger purpose of selling goods, and the contracts cannot be successfully attacked on the ground that they amount to wagers. However, the prohibition against wagers on the price of shares, described above, applies equally to goods.

INTERNATIONAL ISSUE

Internet Gambling

As noted above, provinces control gambling within their borders by licensing specific types of gambling for particular purposes. Naturally, this power to control gambling and issue licences has jurisdictional limits. Internet gambling makes it easy for gamblers to access sites outside a province and beyond the control of provincial gaming authorities. Therefore, private sector online gambling sites located (wholly or partially) within a province are illegal.[38] However, at present, foreign online gambling sites whose entire operations are outside Canada, are not illegal.

Calls to regulate or prohibit offshore gambling focus on the risks associated with addiction, underage access, and criminal behaviour and, of course, lost government revenues. Prohibition may be difficult in any event. The United States' legislative attempts to prevent offshore gambling sites

continued

---

36. See, for example: Insurance Act, R.S.B.C. 1996, c. 226, s. 36(2)(b); R.S.O. 1990, c. I.8, s. 178(2)(b); R.S.N.S. 1989, c. 231, s. 180(2)(b).

37. Criminal Code, R.S.C. 1985, c. C-46, ss. 382, 383.

38. Those sites that are operated or sponsored by the Province itself are legal. See *R. v. Starnet Communications International Inc.* (August 17, 2001) Vancouver 125795-1 (B.C.S.C.); Criminal Code, R.S.C. 1985, c. C-46, ss. 201–209.

from accessing American gamblers has been the subject of an international trade dispute. The World Trade Organization (WTO) held that the American prohibition violated the General Agreement on Trade in Services (1995) and authorized sanctions of (a modest) US$21 000 000 against the United States.

QUESTIONS TO CONSIDER

1. Should Internet gambling be illegal?

2. Should the Criminal Code be amended to apply to offshore gambling sites that offer services to Canadian gamblers?

Sources: C.I. Kyer and D. Hough, "Is Internet Gaming Legal in Canada: A Look at Starnet," (2002) 1(1) *Canadian Journal of Law and Technology,* http://cjlt.dal.ca; T. L. Mackay, "Internet Gambling in Canada Waits in Legal Purgatory," *National Policy Working Group Policy Discussion Document,* July 2004, Canadian Center on Substance Abuse, www.ccsa.ca/NR/rdonlyres/9367E3DE-504F-476E-9F02-CBA1BB733C84/0/ ccsa0111282004.pdf; B.S. Klapper, "WTO Clears $21 million US in Sanctions Vs. U.S.," Associated Press, December 21, 2007, www.antiguawto.com/wto/AP_WTOClears21MSanctionsVSUS_21Dec07.pdf.

Agreements Illegal by Statute

We have noted that some statutes describe certain types of agreements as illegal. An example is the Competition Act, discussed in a separate section below. A number of other statutes do not deal directly with contracts but impose penalties for certain kinds of conduct. While the most important of these statutes is the Criminal Code, other examples are the Income Tax Act, which imposes penalties for false returns and evasion,[39] and the Customs Act, which exacts penalties for smuggling.[40] Any contract that involves such conduct is itself illegal, not because the statute refers directly to contracts, but because the common law holds that when the *object* of a contract is illegal by statute, then the contract itself is illegal.

Provincial statutes and municipal by-laws require the licensing or registration of various classes of business and professional people, ranging from taxicabs and local building trades to moneylenders, trading partnerships, real estate agents, investment advisers and stockbrokers, optometrists, and public accountants.[41] When such a person sues to collect for services provided, the defendant may raise as a defence that the plaintiff has not been properly registered for his trade.

CASE 7.4

K, an electrician, sued for work done and materials supplied to *A*, who pleaded in defence that *K* was not licensed as an electrical contractor as required by the local by-law. The court stated that the object of the by-law was to protect the public against mistakes and loss that might arise from work done by unqualified electricians and accordingly held that the contract was unlawful. The court would not assist *K* in his attempt to collect the account.[42]

---

39. S.C. 1970–71–72, c. 63, s. 239, as amended, S.C. 1980–81–82–83, c. 158, s. 58, S.C. 1988, c. 55, s. 182.

40. S.C. 1986, c. C-1, ss. 110–16, 153–61.

41. See, for example, the following Ontario statutes: Business Names Act, R.S.O. 1990, c. B.17, s. 7(1); Real Estate and Business Brokers Act, R.S.O. 1990, c. R.4, s. 3; Securities Act, R.S.O. 1990, c. S.5, s. 25; Drug and Pharmacies Regulation Act, R.S.O. 1990, c. H.4, s. 139; Public Accountancy Act, R.S.O. 1990, c. P.37, s. 14; and others.

42. *Kocotis* v. *D'Angelo* (1957), 13 D.L.R. (2d) 69. But see *Sidmay Ltd. et al.* v. *Wehttam Investments Ltd.* (1967), 61 D.L.R. (2d) 358, affirmed (1968), 69 D.L.R. (2d) 336, for a case in which a mortgagor was required to honour his mortgage obligations even though the mortgagee was a corporation not authorized to lend on mortgages under the Loan and Trust Corporations Act (Ontario).

Another decision held that a person in the electrician's position would be entitled to recover for the materials supplied, though not the fee for the services provided.[43]

We should note that when an action is brought *against* a person who has not been licensed, the defendant cannot use his own misconduct in not complying with a statute as a defence to an action by an innocent person. This result is an application of the general principle that a person (whether as plaintiff or defendant) is not permitted to use evidence of his own wrongdoing for his advantage before the courts.

The courts have also become more flexible and sympathetic towards entirely innocent breaches of a statutory requirement.

CASE 7.5

S, an American citizen, was lawfully admitted to Canada and applied for permanent residence status. While waiting for her status to be granted, she accepted a position without first obtaining a work permit as required under immigration regulations; *S* was unaware of the requirement. She and her employer paid premiums under the Employment Insurance Act. *S* was laid off and applied for benefits but they were denied on the basis that her contract of employment was void for illegality.[44]

The court rejected the "classic common law model of illegality" and stated that the consequences of declaring a contract illegal could often be too extreme. It was preferable to adopt a general principle rather than a rigid rule, and to refuse to give relief only where it would be contrary to public policy to do so. To allow this claim would not offend the policy of making benefits available to a person innocently unemployed. Nor would it encourage illegal immigrants to come to Canada to work illegally. *S* was not an illegal immigrant and she acted in good faith. The Act only imposed sanctions against those who knowingly obtained work without a permit. The court gave *S* the right to collect employment benefits.

CONTRACTS ILLEGAL BY THE COMMON LAW AND PUBLIC POLICY

The Common Law

Over the years, the common law has condemned certain types of conduct and has granted remedies, usually in the form of damages, to persons harmed by that conduct. Generally the conduct is considered a private wrong or tort, and whenever a contract contemplates the commission of a tort, the contract is illegal.

Among the private wrongs or torts that may be contemplated in an agreement are slander and libel, trespass, deceit (fraud), and, in particular, incitement to break an existing contract with someone else.

CASE 7.6

The Wanderers Hockey Club learned that Johnson had signed a contract to play for the following season with another club managed by Patrick. The Wanderers' manager persuaded Johnson to enter into a second contract with it for the same season by offering him a higher salary. Johnson tore up his contract with Patrick, but as things turned out, he failed to perform his new contract with the Wanderers, which then sued him for breach of contract.

The action failed on the grounds that no cause of action can arise out of a wrongdoing; it had been obvious to both parties that the second contract with the Wanderers could not be performed without breaking the earlier contract with Patrick.[45]

43. *Monticchio* v. *Torcema Construction Ltd.* (1979), 26 O.R. (2d) 305.
44. Re Still and Minister of National Revenue (1997), 154 D.L.R. (4th) 229.
45. *Wanderers Hockey Club* v. *Johnson* (1913), 14 D.L.R. 42. See also: *Fabbi et al.* v. *Jones* (1972), 28 D.L.R. (3d) 224.

An agreement may not have as its primary purpose the commission of a wrongful act, but suppose it contains an undertaking by one party to indemnify the other against damages arising from any private wrong committed in the course of performing the contract.

CASE 7.7

W.H. Smith & Son had agreed to print a weekly newspaper, *Vanity Fair*, for Clinton on the terms that it should have a letter of indemnity from Clinton against claims arising out of publication of libellous matter in the paper. In June 1907, the paper published an article containing statements libellous to Parr's Bank. W.H. Smith settled the claim against it by paying Parr's Bank a sum of money; in turn it sued to recover the money from Clinton. The action failed because the court refused to assist in the recovery of money to indemnify a wrongdoer, W.H. Smith, which had printed the libellous paper.[46]

There are important exceptions to this rule for contracts of insurance. For example, an insurance policy that promises to indemnify a motorist for the damages he may have to pay to third parties as a result of his negligent driving is neither void nor illegal; automobile insurance for public liability and property damage is valid. Similar policies of insurance are designed to protect professional people against the consequences of their negligence in the course of practice and such policies are also valid. However, the insurance protects the policy holder from negligence *only*—that is, from inadvertent wrongdoing, and *not* from deliberate acts of harm, such as fraud.

In addition, a person or a business may exempt itself from liability for negligence by the terms of a contract. A railway or other carrier may state in its standard form contract for the shipment of goods (bill of lading) that it shall not be liable for damage to goods in excess of a stated amount, whether caused by the negligence of its employees or not. The temptation to include such exemption clauses is great, and as a result these contracts are often subject to government regulation.

Public Policy

Even though a contract does not contemplate the commission of a crime or of any of the recognized private wrongs, it may still be regarded as illegal because it is contrary to public policy. If the court decides that a particular contract is prejudicial to the interests of Canada, its relations with foreign countries, its national defence, its public service, or the administration of justice within the country, the court will declare the contract illegal although its performance is neither a tort nor a crime in itself.

CASE 7.8

In *Symington* v. *Vancouver Breweries and Riefel*,[47] the plaintiff, Symington, promised the defendants (who were anxious to see a person named Ball convicted of illegal manufacture of alcohol) to give evidence that would assure Ball's conviction. The defendants promised to pay Symington $1000 for each month of imprisonment in Ball's sentence. Symington gave testimony and Ball was sentenced to 12 months' imprisonment. Symington received only part payment and sued for the balance.

---

46. *Smith* v. *Clinton* (1908), 99 L.T. 840.
47. [1931] 1 D.L.R. 935.

Symington failed on grounds of public policy that the agreement tended to pervert justice. In summarizing his reasons, Mr. Justice Martin said in part:

> There is a peculiar and sinister element in this case . . . it provides for remuneration upon a sliding scale corresponding in amount to the amount of the sentence secured by the informer's evidence. This is so direct and inevitable an incentive to perjury and other concomitant nefarious conduct that it cannot be in the public interest to countenance a transaction which is dangerous to such an exceptional degree to the administration of criminal justice.[48]

The arrangements by which a person accused of a crime may be released under bail are intended to be fair and humane.[49] However, they require that the party putting up the bail shall forfeit the bail money should the prisoner abscond. Accordingly, a promise either by the accused or by a third party to indemnify the party putting up bail is illegal.[50]

A common crime committed within the business world is embezzlement, the so-called white-collar crime. It is often committed by persons without previous criminal records who succumb to temptation or personal misfortune and "borrow" funds without permission. On discovery, the embezzler usually repents and promises to repay every cent if he is not turned over to the police. In many cases, either through sympathy or in the hope of recovering the loss, the victim of the embezzler agrees to the arrangement.

As charitable as the motives of the injured party may be, we must remember that the embezzler has committed a crime for which the law demands conviction. An agreement to withold information is wrong; the agreement obstructs justice and is illegal.[51] By agreeing to cover up the commission of the crime, the victim may also be in breach of the criminal law. The most a victim can do legally is to assure the embezzler that if restitution is made, he will testify to that effect as a mitigating factor in the court's assessment of the crime. The court considers restitution in these cases to be of great weight in arriving at a just punishment. In any event, the victim retains the right to recover the loss from an embezzler by suing for breach of trust or for wrongful conversion in tort.

Agreements that promote unnecessary litigation are also considered to be attempts to obstruct the course of justice. They take up the time of the law courts when more serious matters are awaiting a hearing. A party may wish to stir up litigation because of its advertising value, on the theory that any kind of publicity is good publicity. In *Dann* v. *Curzon*,[52] a theatre manager promised to pay a party for intentionally creating a disturbance in a theatre and then suing the manager for assault. The party did create a disturbance and his action for assault was dismissed. When the theatre manager failed to make the promised payment, the party sued him. The second action failed on grounds of public policy.

ETHICAL ISSUE
Confidentiality Clauses and Public Policy

Employment contracts and research contracts often contain clauses that require the employee or the funded researcher to maintain confidentiality about sensitive information. Such information might include the company's financial affairs, its marketing plans, the products it is developing, or

continued

48. *Ibid.*, at 937.
49. See M.L. Friedland, *Detention Before Trial* (Toronto: University of Toronto Press, 1965); Criminal Code, R.S.C. 1985, c. C-46, ss. 763–71.
50. *Herman* v. *Jeuchner* (1885), 15 Q.B.D. 561; Consolidated Exploration and Finance Co. v. Musgrave, [1900] 1 Ch. 37.
51. See J.W. Turner, *Russell on Crime*, 12th ed. (London: Stevens & Sons Ltd., 1964) at 339–41; also *U.S. Fidelity and Guarantee Co.* v. *Cruikshank and Simmons* (1919), 49 D.L.R. 674; *Keir* v. *Leeman* (1846), 115 E.R. 1315.
52. (1911), 104 L.T. 66.

the progress of research it is sponsoring. There are good reasons for these clauses. Businesses do not want their competitive position undermined by having private information end up in the hands of their rivals. They do not want the price of their stock or the reputation of their products to be affected by rumours and gossip. Courts award damages and sometimes grant injunctions for breach of confidentiality clauses.

However, what if the clause prevents a person from disclosing information that shows that a company's products place consumers or patients at risk? In that case, ethical and public policy concerns arise.

Dr. Nancy Olivieri, a professor of medicine at the University of Toronto and leading researcher at the Hospital for Sick Children, received funding from Apotex, a drug manufacturer, to conduct clinical trials on a new drug. The drug, called L1 or deferiprone, was designed to remove the excess iron that builds up in the bodies of patients who require frequent blood transfusions over long periods.

A few years into the trial, Dr. Olivieri became concerned that the drug was not effective and that dangerously high levels of iron were building up in the livers of some of the patients in the trial. When she reported her concern to the drug company and the hospital research ethics board, the company terminated the trial at the Toronto site. When she made her findings public, Apotex accused her of violating the confidentiality agreement she had signed and threatened to sue her. The company also asserted that her methods were suspect and her findings were unsupported by other researchers. While Dr. Olivieri published her research findings in the highly respected *New England Journal of Medicine*, Apotex did not submit its data for publication.

In her conflicts with the drug company, Dr. Olivieri had strong moral support from a number of her colleagues, many of whom thought the hospital had not properly supported and defended her. Eventually, Dr. Olivieri and the hospital reached a settlement of their differences.

QUESTIONS TO CONSIDER

1. Should the courts refuse to enforce confidentiality agreements if upholding them would mean that risks to the public are not disclosed? How can the proper balance be established between a company's interest in protecting sensitive information and the public's interest in knowing about risks to health and safety?

2. What sort of legislation, if any, do we need to protect employees and researchers who disclose information about products or activities that pose a risk to consumers or patients?

Sources: Susan Jeffrey, "Research Conflict," *The Medical Post*, January 21, 1997; Michael Valpy, "Science Friction," *Elm Street*, December 1998; University of Toronto Faculty Association Press Release, December 17, 1998; Joint Release, The Hospital for Sick Children and Dr. Nancy Olivieri, January 26, 1999; Marina Jimenez, "Olivieri, Foes Take Battle Over Drug to Ottawa," *National Post*, October 5, 1999.

AGREEMENTS IN RESTRAINT OF TRADE

Perhaps the most common reason for business agreements being challenged on grounds of public policy is that they may be in restraint of trade or reduce competition. The courts have long considered competition a necessary element of our economic life and regard agreements that diminish competition as undesirable. Some agreements in restraint of trade are simply unenforceable, while others may violate the Competition Act and trigger regulatory or criminal sanctions.

restrictive covenant
a term in restraint of trade

Even if a contract contains a **restrictive covenant** (a term in restraint of trade) that is found to be against public policy, the term may not invalidate the entire contract. The courts may refuse to enforce the offending term while treating the remainder of the contract as valid. The courts initially presume that any term in restraint of trade is against public policy, but the party seeking to enforce the covenant may **rebut** the presumption if it can demonstrate that it is a reasonable arrangement between the parties and does not adversely affect the public interest.

rebut
overcome

In this chapter, we shall examine the consequences of two of the classes of contracts in restraint of trade:

(a) Agreements between the vendor and the purchaser of a business in which the vendor undertakes not to carry on a similar business in competition with the purchaser.
(b) Agreements between employer and employee in which the employee undertakes that after leaving her present employment she will not compete against the employer, either by setting up her own business or by taking a position with a competing business.

A third class, agreements among manufacturers or merchants to restrict output or fix the selling price of a commodity or service, will be examined in Chapter 32, "Government Regulation of Business."

The courts begin by presuming that any term in restraint of trade is against public policy and is void and unenforceable, but this presumption is not absolute. It may be rebutted by the party seeking to enforce the covenant if it can demonstrate that it is a reasonable arrangement between the parties and does not adversely affect the public interest. In the two types of contracts discussed below, the courts put great weight on the interests of the parties themselves.

Agreements Between Vendor and Purchaser of a Business

Often, an important asset of a business is its goodwill—that is, the trade and commercial connections that it has established through years of carrying on business under its name and in a particular location. The vendor of a business can persuade the purchaser to pay for the goodwill only if he can make a binding promise that he will do nothing in the future to diminish or destroy the value of what he is selling. To do so, he must be free to covenant with the purchaser that he will not enter into any business that is likely to compete with the business he is selling: there will then be no danger of his attracting old customers away and so diminishing its value. After the sale, it is important that the law enforce reasonable undertakings of this kind made by the vendor, or else the purchaser, fearing she will be deprived of a valuable part of the asset she has purchased, will refuse to pay the vendor's price.

Accordingly, the law recognizes that both purchaser and vendor of a business may find a mutual advantage in a restrictive covenant and that such a restraint need not be against the public interest. As well, the parties usually deal with each other on a more or less equal footing in striking a bargain with respect to both the price and the protection asked for by the purchaser. The vendor's covenant not to compete with the purchaser as a term of an agreement for the sale of a business may be enforced if it can be shown that the restrictions placed on the vendor are reasonable in view of the nature of the trade or practice sold.

Whether a particular restriction is so broad that it offends the public interest is for the court to decide. On the one hand, a clause forbidding the vendor ever to enter business again anywhere would, for most types of business, be more than is needed to protect the purchaser and would be considered to deprive the public of the benefits of the vendor's abilities: accordingly, it would be void. On the other hand, a term by which the vendor undertakes for a stated period of time (or perhaps even within his lifetime) not to set up business again within a specified area that reasonably describes the area of competition may well be reasonable in the opinion of a court, and consequently valid. The size of the area and the period of time denied to the vendor vary with the nature of the business.

ILLUSTRATION 7.1

A dentist in Saskatoon sells his practice to a young graduate, promising that he will not practise again anywhere in Canada. The retiring dentist has a change of heart, however, and two years later sets up a practice in the same city. The other dentist brings action to obtain a court injunction restraining him from doing so.

In these circumstances a restrictive clause that denies the seller a right to practise anywhere in Canada is more than is necessary to protect the interests of the purchaser. To argue that a covenant in restraint of trade is not against public policy, it is necessary to show at least that it is reasonable between parties. The scope of this covenant, in view of the nature of a dental practice, is unreasonable, and it is therefore void. The purchaser would fail to obtain the injunction, although if the covenant had been confined to the city of Saskatoon for, say, a period of three years, it would probably have been valid.

With rare exceptions, the courts have refused to take on the task of narrowing to a "reasonable scope" the area within which the seller is not to set up business.[53] The basic objection to narrowing a covenant is that it discriminates in favour of one of the parties: it gives a purchaser who has demanded an unreasonable restriction the benefit of the court's opinion about the allowable maximum area not considered detrimental to the public interest. It would also discourage the vendor from taking the risk of opening a new business. If a restrictive clause is held to be too wide, it is highly unlikely that courts will narrow it to a reasonable scope; the clause will be void and a vendor who might otherwise have been bound by a reasonable restriction is free of the restraint. The lesson for the purchaser is that he should demand no more than a reasonable restriction, erring on the conservative side rather than demanding too much.

The case of *Nordenfelt* v. *Maxim Nordenfelt Guns and Ammunition Co. Ltd.*[54] illustrates how the nature of a business may be important in determining what is a reasonable restriction on its vendor.

CASE 7.9

Nordenfelt had been a manufacturer of guns and ammunition. He transferred his patents and business to Maxim Nordenfelt Guns and Ammunition Co. Ltd. for £287 500 and covenanted that for 25 years he would not engage, except on behalf of this company, either directly or indirectly in the business of a manufacturer of guns or ammunition or in any other business competing or liable to compete in any way with the business of the company. Later, Nordenfelt entered into an agreement with other manufacturers of guns and ammunition, and the plaintiff company brought an action to enforce the covenant.

The House of Lords decided that the clause could be broken into two parts: first, the promise not to engage in the manufacture of guns or ammunition, and second, the promise not to engage in *any other business* competing or liable to compete with the plaintiff company. The court held that the second promise was an unreasonable restriction and declared it void. But it also held it could sever the second promise from the first and that the first promise was a reasonable restriction. Accordingly, it granted an injunction to restrain Nordenfelt from working for any other business that manufactured guns and ammunition.

We can see, then, that although the courts will not save unreasonable restrictions by redrafting them or narrowing their effect, they will sever an unreasonable restriction from one that is reasonable—even if the restrictions occur in the same sentence—provided they are two distinct ideas and can be severed without changing the meaning of the reasonable restraint. In enforcing the restraint concerning guns and ammunition, the court pointed out that improved communications and transportation facilities had enabled orders to be directed to and filled from distant sources of

---

53. See *Goldsoll* v. *Goldman*, [1915] 1 Ch. 292, and *Attwood* v. *Lamont*, [1920] 3 K.B. 571. See also *Canadian American Financial Corp.* v. *King* (1989), 60 D.L.R. (4th) 293.

54. [1894] A.C. 535.

supply, and had greatly broadened the market in which competition might be effective in certain lines of business. The decision, though handed down in 1894, recognized that the whole world had become a market in the munitions business. In expressing the opinion of the court, Lord MacNaghten set the law in its present mould:

> All interferences with individual liberty of action in trading, and all restraints of trade of them-selves, if there is nothing more, are contrary to public policy and therefore void. That is the general rule. But there are exceptions: restraints of trade . . . may be justified by the special circumstances of a particular case. It is sufficient justification, and indeed it is the only justification, if the restriction is reasonable—reasonable, that is, in reference to the interests of the public, so framed and so guarded as to afford adequate protection to the party in whose favour it is imposed, while at the same time it is in no way injurious to the public.[55]

Agreements Between Employee and Employer

It is more difficult to convince courts that covenants between employee and employer restricting the future economic freedom of the employee are reasonable and not in restraint of trade.[56] Frequently there is no equality of bargaining power, and an employer is able to impose terms on an employee that the latter must accept if he wants the position. Later he may find that the covenant, if valid, makes it virtually impossible for him to leave his employer in order to accept another position in the vicinity: he would have to sell his house and become established in another city. In protecting employees by striking down unreasonable restraints, the courts at the same time serve a second public interest—they protect the mobility of labour and so encourage more efficient allocation of human resources.

We must distinguish agreements that try to govern an employee's means of livelihood *after* he leaves his present employment from those in which the employee undertakes not to compete directly or indirectly *while* he remains in the service of the employer. The law recognizes a full-time employee's primary duty of loyalty to the employer, and an absolute promise not to engage in any other business during the term of the employment is valid, whether that business competes with the employer or not. Similar agreements between partners that are operative during the life of the partnership are also binding.

A plaintiff seeking to enforce a restrictive covenant usually asks the court for the equitable remedy of an injunction to restrain the defendant. A restrictive covenant may be enforced if it can be shown to be reasonable between the parties and not injurious to the public.

The courts more readily accept as reasonable certain restraints placed upon an employee who has access to valuable trade secrets or a knowledge of secret processes in his employment[57] or who has acted as the personal representative of the employer in dealings with the customers of the business.[58] In such circumstances, a promise by the employee not to work for a competing business or to set up a business of his own after leaving his present employment is more likely to be binding upon him, particularly if the employer has evidence that its former employee is acting in a way that is depriving it of its proprietary interest in trade secrets or customer goodwill. Still, the clause must be reasonable as to the activity restricted, the geographic area covered, and the duration of the restriction. Courts will consider whether a less onerous form of *non-solicitation clause*—a restriction on marketing to a previous employer's customers—would suffice in the circumstances. If so, a complete ban on competition will be unenforceable.[59]

---

55. *Ibid*, at 565.

56. *Mason* v. *Provident Clothing & Supply Co. Ltd.*, [1913] A.C. 724.

57. *Reliable Toy Co. and Reliable Plastics Co. Ltd.* v. *Collins*, [1950] 4 D.L.R. 499. For an interesting case that compares covenants both during employment and after termination, see *Robinson (William) & Co. Ltd.* v. *Heuer*, [1898] 2 Ch. 451.

58. *Fitch* v. *Dewes*, [1921] 2 A.C. 158.

59. *J.G. Collins Insurance Agencies Ltd.* v. *Elsley*, [1978] 2 S.C.R. 916 at 926; *Lyons* v. *Multari* (2000), 50 O.R. (3d) 526 (C.A.).

QUESTIONS FOR REVIEW

1. Is a minor bound to pay the agreed contract price for necessaries? Explain.

2. What element is necessary for a contract of employment to bind a minor?

3. What obligation does a minor have when she repudiates a contract for non-necessary goods? Explain the policy reason for the rule.

4. Are minors' contracts for non-necessaries always voidable when the minors attain majority?

5. What two types of minors' contracts must be distinguished for the purpose of determining the liability of the minors after they become of age?

6. Give examples of persons of diminished contractual capacity. What special problems do such persons face when they want to deny responsibility under a contract?

7. Under what circumstances may a contract voidable at the option of one of the parties cease to be voidable?

8. What is the nature of the legal problem that adds to the uncertainty of an action against a trade union?

9. (a) When Jones was 17 years old, she took her stereo into the Mariposa Service Centre for an extensive repair job that cost $175. If she does not pay, can the Mariposa Service Centre sue her successfully?

   (b) After Jones becomes of age, she picks up the repaired stereo and does nothing to repudiate her liability to the Mariposa Service Centre. Can the Mariposa Service Centre recover the money now?

   (c) Upon becoming of age, Jones tells the manager of the Mariposa Service Centre in a telephone conversation that she will pay the $175. Can the Mariposa Service Centre recover now?

10. For what types of organization is a representative action important? Explain.

11. Why may it be important to a party to a dispute to show that a void contract is not also illegal?

12. How can we tell whether the intention of the legislature is to make a certain type of agreement illegal as well as void?

13. What are "wagering" contracts and are they legal? What government legislation should be considered when answering this question?

14. What quality must an insurance contract possess to prevent it from being a wager and therefore void?

15. What kinds of business contract may have an element of wagering incidental to the main purpose of the transaction?

16. Explain how restrictive covenants play a role in the sale of an active business.

17. What exception is there to the rule that an agreement is illegal if it purports to indemnify a person against the consequences of his own wrongdoing?

18. What factors does a court consider when determining if a restrictive covenant in an employment contract is legal and enforceable?

19. Discuss the courts' attitude towards the subsequent use of trade secrets acquired by a former employee.

CASES AND PROBLEMS

1. West was 17 years of age and obtained his driver's licence. He went to Drive-Yourself Ltd., showed his licence, and signed for the hiring of a car. The Drive-Yourself clerk did not notice West's age as being under 18, the minimum age required by the firm to agree to hire. The contract contained clauses requiring the hirer to observe all laws regulating the use of motor vehicles, not to enter the car in any competition, to indemnify the hiring company for any fines imposed in respect of the operation of the automobile, and to return it in good condition.

West then gathered up seven friends and took them for a drive. While attempting to pass another car at 20 km/h above the speed limit, he lost control and wrecked the car against a stump. At the time there were three passengers in the front seat in addition to West, the driver.

Drive-Yourself Ltd. brought an action against West for the value of the wrecked car. What scope, if any, would the plaintiff company have for countering West's defence of infancy? Indicate with reasons whether its action is likely to succeed.

2. For most of a year, Harrison acted as agent for the purpose of obtaining options on property on an island in British Columbia on behalf of the Western Development Company, which planned to develop the island industrially. These plans became known to the property owners on the island, and some of them, believing their holdings to be indispensable to the plan, sought to obtain prices much higher than the market value established there for farm or residential purposes.

Harrison obtained, for a consideration of $1, an option to purchase within one year the property of Mrs. Foy for $200 000. Harrison had negotiated the price with a Miss Foy and a widow, Mrs. Sheridan; he had offered $1000 a hectare, which was the maximum he had been authorized to offer, but the two women had insisted upon $2000 a hectare. He had then reluctantly agreed to take an option at the price demanded, explaining that his principals would not likely take up the option at such an exorbitant price. Miss Foy had next insisted that a further $10 000 be added to the price for the barn; Harrison had agreed to that, too.

It was only when the option agreement was prepared for signing that Harrison learned that he had not been dealing with the registered owner of the property, but with her daughters, both of whom resided there. They told him that Mrs. Foy was a very old lady and was bedridden. Harrison was taken to the bedroom where he explained, carefully and accurately, the terms and effect of the option. Mrs. Foy appeared to understand what he was saying, nodding and smiling and from time to time saying, "Yes." At that point Harrison turned to Miss Foy, who was standing at the foot of the bed, and asked her, "Do you really think your mother understands the difference between an option and an agreement to sell her land?" Miss Foy replied, "Yes, I think she understands." Then Mrs. Sheridan asked Harrison if, before getting her mother to sign, he would wait until they could get the family lawyer to be present. Harrison, exasperated with the way negotiations had been proceeding, replied testily that he was not prepared to put up with any further delay or discussion of terms. He asked Mrs. Foy to sign the option agreement. She did not sign her name but made a cross under the direction of one of her daughters who explained to Harrison that her mother used to be able to sign her name but that her hand was now too unsteady.

Harrison's principals did, in fact, elect to take up the option within the year to obtain property at the agreed price of $200 000; they had taken up the options on the adjoining properties and needed Mrs. Foy's property to complete the land they required. The two daughters said that the option agreement was "not worth the paper it was written on" because Mrs. Foy was insane at the time of her signing. The principals sued to have the option agreement enforced. It was brought out in evidence that Mrs. Foy was, indeed, insane, a fact of which Harrison denied any knowledge at the time; it was also shown that the fair market value of the property as a farm at the date of the option agreement was about $140 000.

Express an opinion about the likelihood that the action will succeed.

3. During the 1997–98 season Harvey ("Ace") Tilson played hockey for the Medicine Hat Broncos of the Western Junior Hockey League, scoring 30 goals and assisting on another 35 goals. In recent years many players in this league had been offered contracts to play professional hockey upon completion of their junior eligibility. They remain eligible to play in the League until the year in which they reach the age of 21.

In October 1996, Tilson signed a two-year contract with the Medicine Hat Broncos Hockey Club that was to terminate before the start of the hockey season in the early fall of 1998. However, at the beginning of training camp in September 1997, the manager of the Broncos presented Tilson and the other players with a new three-year contract. This contract contained a new set of standardized conditions of employment prescribed by the league and, by agreement among the clubs, was presented to all players in the league on a "take it or leave it" basis; the players understood that if they did not agree to waive their existing contracts and sign the new one they would not be able to play in the league and their professional prospects would be severely harmed. The new contract included the following clauses:

1. This contract supersedes all previous contracts between the Club [Medicine Hat Broncos Hockey Club] and the Player [Harvey J. Tilson].

2. The Club employs the Player as an apprentice hockey player for the term of three years commencing 1998 and agrees, subject to the terms of this contract, to pay the Player a salary of $150.00 per week plus an allowance for room and board of $200.00 per week, these payments to terminate at the last scheduled game of the Club each year.

3. The Player acknowledges that if his hockey skills and abilities develop to the degree that he is tendered and accepts a contract of employment with a professional hockey club, then the Club shall be entitled to compensation for its contribution to his development and, in consideration for such contribution by the Club, the Player agrees to pay the Club a sum equal to 20 percent (20%) of his gross earnings attributable to his employment with such professional hockey club during a period of three (3) years beginning on the date at which he first represents and plays for that professional hockey club.

4. The Player agrees that during the term of this contract he will loyally discharge his obligations to the Club and that he will not play for or be directly or indirectly employed by or interested in any other amateur or professional hockey club. The Player agrees that the Club shall have the right, in addition to any other legal remedies that the Club may enjoy, to prevent him by appropriate injunction proceedings from committing any breach of this undertaking

5. The Player acknowledges that, if in breach of his obligations under section 4, the Player plays for any other hockey club, the Club will lose his services as a skilled hockey player and will suffer a loss of income from reduced paid attendance at hockey games and broadcasting rights and that a genuine estimate of the amount of this loss would be the salary that the Player can earn as a hockey player for any other amateur or professional club.

The manager of the Broncos advised the players to take their copies of the contract home and discuss them with their parents. He added that a signed copy must be in his hands by the beginning of the following week. Tilson's parents actively encouraged him to sign the contract, and Tilson returned a signed copy to the manager on September 5, 1997.

Tilson played for the Broncos in the 1997–98 season until March 21, 1998. On that day he became 18 years of age, the age of majority in Alberta. On March 22, 1998, in a letter to the club written by his lawyer, Tilson repudiated the contract "without in any way acknowledging the validity thereof." On the same day, in the company of his lawyer, he signed a Pan-American Hockey Conference contract with the Calgary Whippets Hockey Club Ltd. for three seasons commencing September 1 of each of 1998, 1999, and 2000, providing for annual salaries of $70 000, $80 000, and $90 000, respectively.

At the time, the 1997–98 season was almost over, and the Broncos had qualified for the playoffs and were the favourite to win the Junior Cup. Tilson offered to stay with the team at his regular weekly salary and allowance during the 1998 playoffs if the Broncos Club would sign an agreement that Tilson's three-year hockey contract with it would expire when the playoffs ended. The Broncos refused and brought an action against Tilson, seeking an injunction to restrain him from breaking his contract or, in the alternative, damages of $150 000 representing the measure of its loss for being deprived of his services for the next two years.

Explain the legal issues raised in this dispute and offer with reasons an opinion about the probable outcome of the action.

4. Assume the facts of Problem 3 above, with the exception that the Broncos Club did sign the agreement proposed by Tilson in March 1998; that Tilson had played with the team during the 1998 playoffs; and

that the Broncos Club had then brought its action against Tilson. What line of reasoning might the Broncos use to support its argument that the March 1998 agreement was not binding on it? Would it be a good argument? Cite any relevant case or cases.

5. Marbett noticed that the ceiling on the upper floor of her house had become damp from water seepage. She mentioned the problem to her neighbour who remarked that Marbett's house was 25 years old and probably needed new roofing; he recommended her to contact Riley, who recently repaired his roof. Marbett phoned Riley and he came promptly to inspect the roof. He said he would replace it for $1800 within a few days. Marbett signed a contract to have the job done.

   The day the work was being completed Marbett was told by a friend that Riley did not have the required municipal licence for a roofing contractor. The friend said she believed Marbett did not have to pay Riley for the roofing work because the contract was illegal. Is the friend correct? Give reasons for your opinion.

6. Flanders & Co., a Montreal firm of wine importers, chartered the ship Bacchus from its owners, Swan Ltd., to transport a cargo of wine from Madeira to Montreal. The contract of charter party included a term to the effect that the charterer, Flanders & Co., should be liable for an additional $2500 for each additional day at the port of destination if the unloading of the ship were delayed for any reason. Unknown to either party, the wine was a prohibited product under the federal Food and Drugs Act because of a preservative used in its production.

   When the ship reached Montreal, customs officers refused permission to unload pending determination of the cargo's compliance with the federal act. The investigation and report from the government laboratory in Ottawa took 10 days; it was determined by customs officials that it would be illegal to import the wine, and the cargo was finally transferred at dockside to another ship for shipment to New York.

   When Flanders & Co. refused to pay the additional $25 000 caused by the delay, Swan Ltd. sued for the amount. What defence might Flanders & Co. offer? Would Swan Ltd. succeed?

7. John Gifford and his friend, Karl Holtz, were enthusiastic followers of the commodities market, the market in which such products as wheat, cotton, tobacco, and coffee are bought and sold for future delivery. However, they did not have sufficient capital to engage in the market themselves and so they played a game: they would "buy and sell" futures in various commodities under three-month contracts for delivery and then "settle" their fictional gains and losses on the delivery date. Karl did very well in the game and over a two-year period "earned" over $100 000 at John's expense.

   One day John finally said to Karl, "I think I have a real winner here: the price of coffee is going to rise sharply in the next three months. At what price do you want to sell to me?"

   Karl disagreed with John's prediction and replied, "I'll sell you $20 000 worth of coffee at today's price. The price is going to drop and you'll lose as usual."

   "For once, not only am I right, I'm prepared to back up my words. Are you?" asked John. "Let's make this a real transaction. If the price goes up, you pay me the difference. If it goes down, I pay you."

   "Okay, it's your funeral. It's a deal," Karl replied, and they shook hands on it.

   Three months later, the price of $20 000 worth of coffee had risen by 30 percent, making John richer by $6000. When John demanded payment, Karl said he didn't have that much in the bank but grudgingly gave John three cheques for $2000 each, one payable immediately and the other two post-dated one month and two months, respectively.

   John cashed the first cheque at Karl's bank at once. A month later, he used the second cheque to buy a used car from Grace Bukowsky. She has not yet presented it to Karl's bank for payment. John still has the third cheque.

   Karl has heard from a friend studying law that the whole transaction might be "illegal." Give him your opinion with reasons.

ADDITIONAL RESOURCES FOR CHAPTER 7 ON THE COMPANION WEBSITE *(www.pearsoned.ca/smyth)*

In addition to self-test, multiple-choice, true–false, and short-essay questions (all with immediate feedback), application exercises, and links to useful web destinations, the Companion Website provides the following resources for Chapter 7:

- **British Columbia:** Adult Guardianship; Business Corporations; Committee; Mentally Incompetent Persons; Minors; Parental Liability; Power of Attorney; Public Guardian and Trustee; Representation Agreements; Societies and Associations
- **Alberta:** Guardianship; Legality; Limited Capacity; Minors/Infants; Personal Directives; Powers of Attorney
- **Manitoba/Saskatchewan:** Age of Majority; Necessities; Parental Responsibility
- **Ontario:** Age of Majority; Confidentiality Agreements; Incompetence; Insurance Legislation; Lotteries; Necessaries; Non-Competition Clauses; Powers of Attorney

Grounds Upon Which a Contract May Be Impeached:

Mistake

In this chapter we discuss what happens when a party realizes that the contract is not the one that was intended. A party may have made any one of several errors. We examine such questions as:

■ What are the legal consequences of a mistake

- in recording an agreement?

- about the meaning of the words?

- about the existence or qualities of the subject-matter?

- about unforeseen future events?

- in performing a contract?

■ What are the legal consequences for innocent third parties in cases of void and voidable contracts and of *non est factum*?

THE RESTRICTED MEANING OF MISTAKE

We may enter into a contract only to regret it later—perhaps it turns out to be quite different from what we intended, or we decide that it was unwise—we made a "mistake" and wish we could be freed from it. However, the prospects for avoiding a contract because one has made a mistake are quite limited.

We must not confuse "legal mistake" with "mistake" in its more general, non-legal meaning: to say, "I made a mistake going for a walk without my umbrella" or "She made a mistake agreeing to work over the weekend" is simply to say that a person later believes she made an error in judgment when she acted in a particular way. Such errors in judgment do not legally justify avoiding one's obligations under a contract. To excuse performance too easily would undermine certainty in contractual arrangements: parties would be reluctant to rely on their contracts. While there are circumstances in which the courts will recognize a mistake and provide **equitable relief**, such circumstances are very limited. In the words of a United States court:

equitable relief
a discretionary remedy first developed by the courts of equity to undo an injustice

> Contracts are the deliberate and voluntary obligations of parties capable of contracting and they must be accorded binding force and effect. . . . The owner of property is supposed to know what it is worth and at least know what he is willing to take for his property. The purchaser may likewise exercise his free will and choice as to whether he will purchase property at a given price. After he has received the property, understanding that he is to pay a fixed price for it, he cannot be compelled to pay a different and greater price simply because the vendor was careless and negligent in the transaction of his own business [and had sold it for too little].[1]

ILLUSTRATION 8.1

A leaves a note for B, stating, "I will sell you my car for $5400 cash." B delivers $5400 to A, and obtains possession and a transfer of the registration. A immediately realizes that he had made an error in his note; he had intended to write $6400 rather than $5400. However, B was unaware of the error; she simply thought the price was an attractive one.

While in one sense there is a mistake, it is entirely A's doing, and B reasonably relied on it: if a remedy were granted to A, either to increase the price of the car or to require its return, B's reasonable expectations would be defeated. A reasonable bystander reading the note and observing B's acceptance would conclude that there was a contract in the terms of the note as written. Accordingly, A would not have a remedy.

ILLUSTRATION 8.2

L signs a five-year lease to rent a shop on a busy main street. He has misread a street map and believes that a city bus route uses the street and that a bus stop is close to the shop. In fact, the bus route runs along a parallel route two blocks to the south. The landlord is completely unaware of the lessee's erroneous belief. Here also, the contract is binding on the lessee despite his innocent and mistaken assumption.

There are two main types of mistake: *mistake about the terms* of a contract and *mistakes in assumptions* about important facts related to a contract although not part of the contract itself.[2]

---

1. *Tatum* v. *Coast Lumber Co.* (1909), 101 P. 957 at 960. See also *Scott* v. *Littledale* (1858), 120 E.R. 304.

2. Problems relating to mistake are difficult to classify and analyze. Many different frameworks have been tried, and none is entirely satisfactory in explaining the great diversity of problems that can and do arise. We believe that the approach adopted in this chapter, based in part on the work of G.E. Palmer, *Mistake and Unjust Enrichment* (Columbus: Ohio State U. Press, 1962), is the most helpful. For a careful, detailed analysis, see, S.M. Waddams, *The Law of Contracts*, 4th ed. (Toronto, Canada Law Book, 1999), Chapters 10, 11, and 12.

While sometimes courts grant relief on grounds we are about to consider, frequently they refuse to do so. Illustrations 8.1 and 8.2 above are examples, respectively, of the two types of mistake where relief would be denied because the mistaken parties would be found solely responsible for their own misfortunes. We shall also examine cases where relief has been granted.

MISTAKES ABOUT THE TERMS

Words Used Inadvertently

As Illustration 8.1 shows, one party may inadvertently use the wrong words in stating the terms of a contract. We should ask how those words ought reasonably to have been understood by the other party. If, in the circumstances, it was reasonable for the second party to rely on them and enter into the contract, then the terms of the contract are binding on the first party. It seems only fair that the consequences of the error should fall on the one who caused the problem.

On the other hand, suppose it is clear to a reasonable bystander that the first party made a mistake in expressing the terms of the contract: the price may be absurdly low or quite unrelated to the range of prices quoted by both sides during negotiations.

CASE 8.1

In *Webster* v. *Cecil*[3] the parties had been negotiating about the sale to Webster of land owned by Cecil. Initially Cecil had refused Webster's offer of £2000. Later Cecil wrote to Webster mistakenly offering the land for £1250. Immediately after he had mailed his letter, Cecil realized his error and sent a second letter stating that the price should have been £2250, but the second letter arrived after Webster had posted his acceptance. Webster sued to enforce the contract and failed, the court finding that he could not possibly have believed that £1250 was the intended offer price.

How does the court exercise its discretion to grant relief? It considers the behaviour of each party and the potential hardship to each party should it decide against him. In *Paget* v. *Marshall*,[4] the court adopted an imaginative approach to deal with this dilemma.

CASE 8.2

Paget had offered to lease out the third floor of a warehouse and a large portion of the second floor as well, reserving to herself only that portion of the second floor that was above a store she retained at ground level. Paget's brother explained these conditions to Marshall, who found them satisfactory. However, after the lease was drawn up and signed by both parties, Paget discovered that it included the portion of the second floor that she had wished to keep for herself. Paget sued to have the lease corrected to exclude the second floor portion over the store.

The court concluded that no reasonable person could have believed such an offer to have been made intentionally; the attempted acceptance is akin to fraud ("snapping up an offer") and the contract is voidable by the first party. However, it is not always easy to decide whether a party could have relied reasonably on the words used in an offer. Perhaps the offeree should have questioned the offeror to ask whether he really meant them; on the other hand, the offeree could have believed that the offeror simply intended to make the offer so attractive that the offeree would find it hard to resist accepting. After all, there may have been a change in the offeror's circumstances.

---

3. (1861), 54 E.R. 812.
4. (1884), 28 Ch. D. 255.

In giving judgment, Bacon, V.C., said:

> I must in charity and justice to the Defendant believe [him], because I cannot impute to him the intention of taking advantage of any incorrect expression . . . but . . . it is plain and palpable that the Plaintiff was mistaken and had no intention of letting . . . [leasing her own premises] . . . the Defendant should have an opportunity of choosing whether he will submit . . . to have the lease rectified . . . or . . . choose to throw up the thing entirely, because the object of the Court is, as far as it can, to put the parties into the position in which they would have been if the mistake had not happened. . . . The Plaintiff does not object, if the agreement is annulled, to pay the Defendant any reasonable expenses to which he may have been put by reason of the Plaintiff's mistake. . . .[5]

Perhaps not surprisingly, the defendant elected to keep the lease, as amended by the court, and to return to the plaintiff the portion over the store.[6]

Errors in Recording an Agreement

Sometimes parties may reach agreement—either orally, intending later to turn it into written form, or first written informally, and later to be put into a more formal contract—but the final written form does not accurately reflect the original agreement: a term may have been left out or important figures may be wrong. The party who stands to benefit from the mistake may insist that the final version represents the bargain and so resist any attempt to revert to the original terms. He may claim that the first agreement was too vague, or that it was subject to any further changes made before finally being *reduced* to writing or to a sealed instrument. Indeed, the defendant so argued, unsuccessfully, in the *Paget* case, above.

rectification
correction of a written document to reflect accurately the contract made by the parties

A party claiming that the arrangement was improperly recorded may ask the court for **rectification** of the contract. The request will succeed if the following conditions are met:

(a) The court is satisfied that there was a complete agreement between the parties, free from ambiguity and not conditional on further adjustments.
(b) The parties did not engage in further negotiations to amend the contract.
(c) The change in the written document may be fraudulent or innocent.
(d) When the document was signed the defendant knew or should have known of the mistake and the plaintiff did not.
(e) Any subsequent attempt to enforce the inaccurate written document is equivalent to fraud.[7]

CASE 8.3

In *U.S.A. v. Motor Trucks, Ltd.*,[8] the Government of the United States had agreed to pay a large sum of money in compensation for cancellation of war contracts at the end of the First World War. The payments were to reimburse a Canadian manufacturing company for equipment and buildings acquired to carry out the contracts and also in settlement of all contractual obligations of the U.S. Government. In return, the manufacturer agreed to give up all claims under the contract and to transfer certain lands to the U.S. Government. Transfer of the lands was somehow left out of the final formal settlement.

The manufacturer resisted the U.S. Government claim to the land on the grounds that it had originally consented to their inclusion while labouring under an "error as to [its own] legal rights."

The Privy Council rejected the manufacturer's claim that the original settlement was not binding and accordingly ordered the final formal settlement rectified to include the lands. There was no evidence that the parties had engaged in further bargaining before the final formal settlement, nor could the omission be explained except on the basis of an error.

---

5. *Ibid.*, at 266–7.
6. It is interesting to note how the court disposed of the costs in the action. "The Plaintiff is not entitled to costs, because [s]he has made a mistake, and the Defendant ought not to have any costs, because his opposition to the Plaintiff's demand has been unreasonable . . . ," per Bacon, V.C., *ibid.*, at 267.
7. *Sylvan Lake Golf & Tennis Club Ltd.* v. *Performance Industries Ltd.* (2002), 209 D.L.R. (4th) 318 (S.C.C.) at para 31. See also *Hepburn* v. *Jannock Limited* (2008), 63 C.C.E.L. (3d) 101.
8. [1924] A.C. 196. See and compare *R.* v. *Ron Engineering Construction Eastern Ltd.* (1981), 119 D.L.R. (3d) 267; *Belle River Community Arena Inc.* v. *W.J.C. Kaufman Co. Ltd.* (1978), 87 D.L.R. (3d) 761.

It is not easy to establish the conditions necessary for rectification: if the terms were ambiguous in the original agreement or if the parties carried on subsequent negotiations, a court is very reluctant to alter the final agreement. Rectification will not correct an error in judgment nor is it a substitute for due diligence.[9] In one English case, Lord Denning said, "In order to get rectification it is necessary to show that the parties were in complete agreement upon the terms of their contract, but by an error wrote them down wrongly."[10]

CASE 8.4

In *Lindsey* v. *Heron*,[11] the seller asked the buyer, "What will you give me for 75 shares of Eastern Cafeterias of Canada?" The buyer said he would make inquiries and then make an offer. Later in the day he replied, "I will give you $10.50 a share for your Eastern Cafeterias." The seller replied, "I accept your offer." The seller delivered the shares for his Eastern Cafeterias of Canada Ltd. and received a cheque in full payment. The buyer then realized that Eastern Cafeterias Ltd. and Eastern Cafeterias of Canada Ltd. were two different companies, and that he had the former company in mind when he made his offer to buy the shares. He stopped payment on his cheque. In defending against an action by the seller, the buyer claimed that his offer to buy "Eastern Cafeterias" was ambiguous, as he could have meant either company. He argued that since he and the seller were talking about different companies in ignorance of the misunderstanding between them, there was never any agreement and no contract was formed.

MISUNDERSTANDINGS ABOUT THE MEANINGS OF WORDS

Both parties to a contract may have agreed to the words actually used—neither party put them forward accidentally nor were any of the terms subsequently recorded incorrectly. Nevertheless, the parties may place quite different meanings on those words. In most instances, such disagreements can be treated as questions of interpretation: a court will decide which meaning is the more reasonable in light of the circumstances, including those things each party ought to have known about the subject-matter of the contract and about the intentions of the other party. In some cases it will decide that the meaning given by an offeror to her own words was the more reasonable one. If so, the offeree will be bound by the terms as understood by the offeror. In other cases the court will decide that the offeror was unwise to use the words as she did and that the offeree interpreted them more reasonably. In that event, the offeror will be bound by the contract as the offeree understands it.

In Case *Lyndsey* v. *Heron*, the court held that in view of the unambiguous statement of the seller when he referred to Eastern Cafeterias of Canada, the offer must be construed as referring to those shares. In giving the decision of the court, Mr. Justice Middleton said:

> I think that, judged by any reasonable standard, the words used by the defendants manifested an intention to offer the named price for the thing which the plaintiff proposed to sell, i.e., stock in the Eastern Cafeterias of Canada Limited. Had the plaintiff spoken of "Eastern Cafeterias," the words used would have been ambiguous, and I should find no contract, for each might have used the ambiguous term in a different sense; but the defendants, by use of these ambiguous terms in response to the plaintiff's request couched in unambiguous language, must be taken to have used it in the same sense.[12]

---

9. *Supra*, n. 7.
10. *Rose* v. *Pim*, [1953] 2 All E.R. 739 at 747; *Brisebois* v. *Chamberland et al.* (1991), 77 D.L.R. (4th) 583.
11. (1921), 50 O.L.R. 1.
12. *Ibid.*, at 9.

In rare cases the court is faced by an insoluble set of facts: both parties have been equally reasonable (or unreasonable) in the meaning they gave to the words, and it would be unjust to hold one party to the other's interpretation. The contract is void. The classic example occurred in the case of *Raffles* v. *Wichelhaus*.[13]

CASE 8.5

The contract was for the sale of cotton that was to arrive in England from Bombay on board the ship *Peerless*. By a remarkable coincidence two ships called *Peerless* were sailing from Bombay, one in October, the other in December. Neither party was aware that there were two ships: the seller believed that he contracted to sell cotton on the later ship; the buyer believed that he contracted to buy cotton on the earlier ship.

A delay of two months in the shipment of a commodity subject to market fluctuations is a major difference in terms. When the cotton arrived on the later ship the buyer refused to accept it or pay for it. The seller sued for breach of contract, and the buyer pleaded mistake in defence. The defence succeeded because the court could not decide which ship *Peerless* was meant. A reasonable person would have been unable to decide that the contract was for cotton on one ship rather than the other.

As suggested by Mr. Justice Middleton in *Lindsey* v. *Heron*, two parties, both equally careless, may use an ambiguous phrase, and the court will refuse to decide between the two conflicting interpretations. The practical result, then, is that the position of the defendant is the stronger: the party who tries to enforce the contract will fail. In *Falck* v. *Williams*,[14] a Norwegian ship owner communicated by cable with an Australian ship broker arranging contracts of carriage for the Norwegian's ships. The ship owner sent an ambiguous message in code, and each party interpreted it differently. In rejecting the ship owner's action for breach of contract, Lord MacNaghten said:

> In their Lordships' opinion, there is no conclusive reason pointing one way or the other. . . . It was the duty of the appellant as plaintiff to make out that the construction that he put upon it was the true one. In that he must fail if the message was ambiguous, as their Lordships hold it to be. *If the respondent had been maintaining his construction as plaintiff he would equally have failed* [italics added].[15]

MISTAKES IN ASSUMPTIONS

About the Existence of the Subject-matter of a Contract

The most fundamental of mistakes is a mistake about the very existence of the subject-matter. If at the time the contract was made the subject-matter, such as goods in the hold of a ship at sea, had been destroyed unknown to either party, it is hard to imagine a fair way to enforce the contract. Is the buyer required to pay the price for goods that cannot be delivered? Is the seller liable for breach for non-delivery? In *Couturier* v. *Hastie*,[16] the parties arranged for the sale of a cargo of corn believed to be en route from Greece to England. Unknown to them, the cargo had become overheated and was in danger of spoiling: the ship put into the port of Tunis where the corn was sold. The seller sued for the price of the cargo but failed; the contract was held to be void.

---

13. (1864), 159 E.R. 375. See also *Angevaare* v. *McKay* (1960), 25 D.L.R. (2d) 521, and *Staiman Steel Ltd.* v. *Commercial & Home Builders Ltd.* (1976), 71 D.L.R. (3d) 17.

14. [1900] A.C. 176.

15. *Ibid.*, at 181 (italics added).

16. (1852), 155 E.R. 1250, affirmed by the House of Lords (1856), 10 E.R. 1065.

This rule, as it applies to the sale of goods, has been incorporated in the Sale of Goods Act, which provides that "where there is a contract for the sale of specific goods and the goods without the knowledge of the seller have perished at the time the contract is made, the contract is void."[17] Of course, if the seller was aware that the goods had perished, his attempt to sell them would be fraudulent and the buyer could recover damages by suing in tort for deceit.

About the Value of the Subject-matter: Allocation of Risk

Finding a solution that is fair to both parties is much more difficult when the subject-matter of a contract is still in existence but its qualities are radically different from those contemplated by the parties. One party may be paying far too much for what he will receive. The other party may receive a windfall. The willingness of a court to grant relief varies according to the reasonable expectations of the parties.

In some types of transactions the parties are expected to know that the subject-matter may quickly rise or fall in value. Indeed, the contract can be thought of as primarily allocating risk. *A* may be willing to pay $5 per share for 10 000 shares in a corporation she believes is about to make large profits, while *B* is content to accept $5 per share for them in the belief that the price is more likely to drop. If, unknown to either of them, the financial position of the company has already declined or risen sharply before the contract is formed, the court will not grant relief to the party adversely affected: the change of circumstance is one of the risks expected in the contract.

It cannot always be so easily inferred that the parties intended to accept a particular risk: the court may conclude it would be unfair to allow the bargain to stand and will grant relief.

CASE 8.6

In *Hyrsky et al.* v. *Smith*,[18] the plaintiffs purchased a parcel of land for future commercial development. Foolishly, they failed to have a qualified person investigate the title to the property, as is the normal practice; as a result, they took some risk that the land was subject to "defects," that is, to claims by other parties. More than four years later, when they prepared to develop the property, they discovered that almost half of it had not been owned by the defendant and consequently had not been transferred to them. The remainder was too small to be developed commercially. The plaintiffs sued to have the contract **set aside** or **rescinded**, the purchase price repaid, and the land returned to the defendant.

The defendant resisted, claiming that the plaintiffs had taken the risk of not investigating title. In response, Lieff, J. said:

> If the mistake as to quantity is so substantial that in essence it changes the quality of the subject-matter, then a proper case for **rescission** may exist.

Later, he stated:

> It is true that under our present-day system of conveyancing [transferring land], the purchaser has ample opportunity to inquire and to inspect before he is compelled to close the transaction. . . . However that may be and notwithstanding the need for certainty and permanency in the law of . . . [transferring land], these policy considerations must yield to the desirability of doing equity where there has been . . . [a substantial error].[19]

set aside or rescinded cancelled or revoked to return the parties as nearly as possible to their original positions

rescission an order by a court to rescind

17. R.S.N.S. 1989, c. 408, s. 9; R.S.O. 1990, c. S.1, s. 7; R.S.B.C. 1996, c. 410, s. 10.
18. (1969), 5 D.L.R. (3d) 385.
19. *Ibid.*, at 392.

Lieff, J. considered requiring the plaintiffs to accept the smaller parcel of land, but he concluded that would be outside any risk that ought to have been assumed by the plaintiffs. Denying any relief to the plaintiffs would leave them with a piece of land too small for their purposes and leave the defendant with a windfall, a much higher price than the land was actually worth. Nor would it make sense for the court to order a reduction in price proportional to the land actually transferred to the plaintiffs; they would still have land they could not use. Accordingly, the court ordered the contract set aside as requested by the plaintiffs. However, it refused to award costs, because "had the plaintiffs searched the title as a prudent purchaser should have done, all of this litigation would never have arisen."[20]

We can see that the above analysis focuses on the reasonable expectations of each of the parties and the fairness of upholding the contract or setting it aside. A 1971 judgment stated:

> . . . if the Court finds that there has been honest, even though inadvertent mistake, it will afford relief in any case where it considers that it would be unfair, unjust or unconscionable not to correct it. . . . [21]

There is general approval of this broad approach, attempting to do justice and to minimize the effects of a mistake. Asking whether a party to a contract ought to bear the risk of a change in the subject matter is the main element in deciding whether it would be unfair to deny a remedy, when the change becomes known.

The Challenge of Achieving a Fair Result

Problems resulting from mistakes—situations in which one or both of the parties may have changed their position or given up other opportunities—may be especially difficult for the courts to resolve.

CASE 8.7

In *Solle* v. *Butcher*,[22] a landlord had substantially renovated a building containing five flats. A surveyor, who had been the landlord's partner in the business of buying and renovating residential buildings, was himself interested in renting one of the flats. He investigated the rental status of the property and concluded that, because of the renovations, rent controls no longer applied: the flat that formerly was limited to an annual rent of £140 could now be rented for £250 at fair market value.

On that basis the parties entered into a seven-year lease. In fact, they were mistaken: the property was still subject to rent control—although the landlord might have obtained permission for a rent higher than £140 if he had reported the reconstruction of the flat to the rent control authorities and applied for and received consent to increase the rent *before* entering into a lease. The parties had a falling out, and the tenant brought an action to recover his overpayments and for a declaration that only the £140 maximum was owed for the remainder of the lease.

Both parties had believed they were dealing with a flat exempt from rent control while the flat was actually subject to controls—a serious mistake in assumption about the subject-matter of the contract, because rent control made the £250 rent unenforceable. The court found that it would be unfair to hold the landlord to a seven-year lease at a low, uneconomical rent of £140, but also unfair to the tenant to declare the lease void and force him to vacate the flat. Instead, the court gave the tenant a choice: either he could vacate the flat and bring the contract to an end, or he could stay—but then the court would temporarily suspend the lease, enabling the landlord to make an application to the rent control authority to charge the full rent the authority would permit for the remainder of the lease, subject to a maximum of £250 as originally agreed.

---

20. *Ibid.*, at 393.

21. *McMaster University* v. *Wilchar Construction*, [1971] 3 O.R. 801, per Thompson, J., at 810. See also *256593 B.C. Ltd.* v. *456795 B.C. Ltd. et al.* (1999), 170 D.L.R. (4th) 470.

22. [1950] 1 K.B. 671

Case 8.7 required an imaginative approach in order to reach a fair solution. A court's willingness to grant relief will be influenced by its ability to create a result that seems reasonably fair to both parties. If it cannot see its way clear to a solution, it may simply refuse a remedy and leave the loss to lie where it has fallen.

Unforeseen Future Events

A party to a contract may fail to foresee a crucial change in conditions under which it is to perform. Performance may become physically or legally impossible—as when new government regulations prohibit delivery of a pharmaceutical product to a pharmacy. Or performance may have become pointless—as in paying for a seat reserved to watch a play that is cancelled. From the time the contract is formed until the unforeseen event occurs, there exists a valid, binding contract between the parties. However, a court may find that the event frustrated the basic purpose of the contract and declare both parties to be discharged from the moment the event occurred. We shall discuss discharge by frustration when we deal with discharge of contracts generally, in Chapter 13. We should note, however, that frustrating events are quite different from mistakes in assumption. Such mistakes concern the actual state of affairs at the time a contract is formed, while a frustrating event is one that takes place *after* formation and could not be known to either party.

MISTAKE AND INNOCENT THIRD PARTIES

How the Problem Arises

Suppose a party to a contract is a rogue who deceives a rather gullible—or at least imprudent—second party; the rogue gains possession of goods or obtains a valuable signed document. Whether the mistake is about assumptions (as where the victim is misled about the identity of the rogue) or about the terms (as where the victim is misled about the terms of a document he signs) does not matter: the rogue has lied and a court would willingly grant the victim relief; the victim would be able to recover the goods or the document. Unfortunately, this would happen only if the victim regained his senses quickly enough to pursue his remedies against the rogue. Usually the rogue profits quickly from his deception and absconds. The contest then remains between the victim and an innocent third party who has paid the rogue and in return received the goods or document that the rogue extracted from the victim.

Void and Voidable Contracts

Consequences of a Void Contract

To understand the law in this area we must consider the difference between void and voidable contracts. This distinction was first discussed with regard to infants' contracts, and is important generally in the law of contracts. As we have noted, to decide that a contract is void is to say that in law it was never formed at all: in this sense calling an agreement a void contract is a contradiction in terms—if it is void, it is no contract. Nevertheless, through custom and convenience the term has long been used to describe agreements that are void from the beginning.

The results flowing from a declaration that a contract is void are logical enough and usually fair when only the two original parties are concerned: if *A* sells goods to *B* and the sale is declared void, it follows that ownership never passed from *A* to *B*; if *B* still has the goods, *A* recovers them and repays any part of the purchase price already received.

However, the consequences are more far-reaching if *B* has already resold the goods (which in law he does not own) to *C*, an innocent third party. The second sale is equally void because, under common law, *B* had no right to the goods. As a result, the third party, *C*, has not acquired ownership although he has paid fair value for the goods and was unaware of the void sale between *A* and *B*.

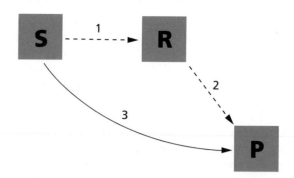

Figure 8.1
Void Contract

1. *S* "sells" goods to a rogue, *R*. *R* does not gain title.
2. *R* purports to sell the goods to *P*, the innocent purchaser. *P* does not gain title.
3. *S* may sue and recover the goods from *P*.

C must restore the goods to *A*, and, if he cannot, he will be liable to *A* (in the tort of conversion) for damages equal to their value (see Figure 8.1).

The common law recognizes no half measures: either the contract between *A* and *B* is void or it is not—and if the court decides it is not void, then despite *B*'s deceit, he has acquired title (ownership) to the goods and can transfer title to a third party. *A* will have no rights against the innocent third party; any claim for damages would be only against *B*, who has likely vanished. Unless the third party, *C*, participated in the fraud, the common law rules ignore the relative fault of *A* in carelessly selling on credit to a rogue, and of the third party in risking to buy from that rogue.

On the whole, declarations that a contract is void—with the harsh consequences that follow—are more unfair to third persons than to sellers of goods: those who take the risk of selling goods on credit make it easier for rogues in possession of the goods to dupe innocent third persons.

Consequences of a Voidable Contract

voidable
a contract that a court may set aside in an attempt to restore the parties to their original positions

The principles of equity are more flexible: between the original parties to a contract, equity will often declare a contract to be **voidable** and will order that it be set aside or rescinded, restoring the property to the seller and requiring him to return any benefit he might have received from the rogue (such as a down payment). So, while equity recognizes that at common law title has passed to the rogue, it will order him to restore both title and possession to the victim.

ILLUSTRATION 8.3

A Co., the sole distributor of a certain brand of imported office machines, has received an advance sample of a revolutionary new copier. *B* persuades *A* Co. to sell and deliver the machine to her on the basis that she will test it, and, if it proves satisfactory, will be prepared to buy at least 1000 units for her distribution chain. In fact, *B* has lied: she has no such distribution chain and intends to resell the machine to the highest bidder among several clients who may be interested in dismantling it and copying the innovations as quickly as possible. Fortunately, the next day one of the firms to whom *B* has offered the machine informs *A* Co. about *B*'s scheme. *A* Co. serves *B* with a statement of claim at once, demanding that the contract be set aside for deceit and the machine returned, on repayment of the purchase price by *A*. The court, in exercising its equitable powers, would grant *A* Co. its remedies.

However, equity also recognizes that new issues of fairness enter the picture as soon as the rights of an innocent third party are affected. Equity will not deprive an innocent purchaser of goods obtained from the rogue. The seller duped by the rogue is limited to an action for damages against the rogue for the unpaid price of the goods or for the tort of deceit. Unfortunately, the rogue is usually penniless or has absconded and cannot be found. Between the seller and the innocent purchaser, equity does not choose; it lets the loss lie where it had fallen—invariably on the duped seller who has parted with his property on the strength of the rogue's misrepresentations.

It is important to note that a third-party purchaser, to receive this protection, must be *innocent* and have paid *value* for the goods. A seller's attempt to recover goods will not be frustrated by someone who buys from the rogue knowing about the rogue's fraud; equity considers such a person as having no greater rights than the rogue himself. Accordingly, in Illustration 8.3, above, if *B* resold and delivered the copier to one of her "clients," who intended to dismantle the machine and was aware of *B*'s deception, *A* Co. could recover it from that client. If, however, the purchaser innocently bought the machine for its own use, *A* would have no claim against it (see Figure 8.2). But innocence alone is not enough; the third party must have paid a price for the item. Equity will not permit a party who has received the machine as a gift, even without knowledge of the fraud, to retain it against *A* Co.

In summary, we can see that where a contract concerns only the two original parties, it may not matter whether the court declares it void or merely voidable. In either event, the court may order the return of property that has passed between the parties. But if the property has been transferred to an innocent purchaser, the original owner may recover it only if the original contract is declared void.

Mistake About the Identity of a Party to a Contract

The dire consequences of a court finding a contract void are well illustrated by the classic English case of *Cundy* v. *Lindsay*.[23]

CASE 8.8 Lindsay, a manufacturer in Ireland, was persuaded to send goods on credit to a thief, Alfred Blenkarn. Blenkarn had signed an order for goods with an indistinct signature that appeared to be "Blenkiron & Co.," a reputable firm with offices on the same street but at a different number from that of Blenkarn. Lindsay did not check the street number, but simply shipped the goods to Blenkarn, who then sold the goods to Cundy for cash and absconded. Cundy was unaware of the fraud. Lindsay learned the true facts when he attempted to collect payment from Blenkiron & Co.; he then sued Cundy for the goods, claiming that the sale to Blenkarn was void.

The House of Lords accepted this argument. It held that as Lindsay intended to sell to "Blenkiron & Co." and only to them, Blenkarn obtained the goods entirely without Lindsay's consent. The court decided that a mistake by the duped seller about the identity of the other party made the contract void. Since there was no contract between Lindsay and Blenkarn, ownership of the goods remained with Lindsay: Cundy was required to return them or pay damages.

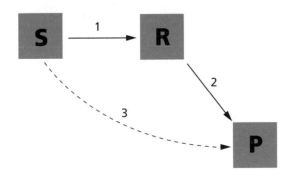

1. *S* "sells" goods to a rogue, *R*. *R*, despite his deceit, obtains title.
2. *R* purports to sell the goods to *P*, the innocent purchaser. *P* obtains title to the goods.
3. *S* cannot recover the goods from *P*.

FIGURE 8.2
Voidable Contract

---

23. (1878), 3 App. Cas. 459.

The decision in *Cundy* v. *Lindsay* offends the general principle that between two innocent parties, both victims of a fraud, the loss should be borne by the more careless of the two. Lindsay had shipped goods on credit without a careful check of the street address of Blenkiron & Co.; as a result of Lindsay's carelessness, Blenkarn gained possession of the goods. But Cundy was blameless. Between the two we should have expected that Lindsay would bear the loss; yet the decision that the contract was void led to a hardship upon Cundy. It is not surprising that the courts attempted to limit the application of this case.

The year after *Cundy*, in *King's Norton Metal Co.* v. *Edridge*,[24] a thief once again obtained goods on credit, working more cleverly than had Blenkarn.

CASE 8.9

Using an impressive but fake letterhead with the picture of a large factory and the name of a *non-existent* firm—Hallam & Co.—Wallis sent an order for goods to the plaintiffs, a firm of metal manufacturers. The plaintiffs sent Wallis the goods; he resold them and absconded. The plaintiffs, claiming that their contract with Hallam & Co. was void, sought to recover the goods from the innocent purchaser.

The action failed. The court held that they must have intended to contract with someone, and since there was no "Hallam & Co.," it could only be with the writer of the letter, even though he was a very different person from the party they had in mind. Accordingly, although the contract was voidable for fraud, title to the goods had passed to Wallis! The plaintiff could recover the goods from Wallis so long as he still had them, but meanwhile Wallis could pass title to an innocent purchaser.

The decision is distinguishable from *Cundy* v. *Lindsay* because in the *King's Norton* case there was only one party with whom the vendor might have contracted (Wallis, alias Hallam & Co.); the assumed identity was non-existent. Two separate entities existed in *Cundy* v. *Lindsay* (Blenkarn and Blenkiron & Co.). Though an innocent purchaser may be excused for failing to see the significance of this distinction, the *King's Norton* case has the virtue of limiting the application of *Cundy* v. *Lindsay* to situations where the rogue assumes an existing identity.

In both cases, the parties dealt by mail at a distance. The same difficulty about identity can occur when the innocent party and the rogue confront each other in person, but the law is clearer in this context.

CASE 8.10

In 1918, in *Phillips* v. *Brooks*[25] the English Court of Appeal held that the plaintiff jeweller intended to sell pearls to the man who appeared in his shop, even though the man falsely identified himself as a reputable and wealthy member of the community—whom the jeweller knew by name,

but not in person. The contract was voidable and not void. Consequently, an innocent purchaser from the rogue was protected and able to keep the pearls, despite the jeweller's claim that he intended to deal only with the reputable named person and not the rogue who had appeared in his shop.

The Court reaffirmed this reasoning in *Lewis* v. *Averay*,[26] where a rogue had obtained a car by paying for it with a bogus cheque while impersonating a well-known English movie actor. It held that since the contract was merely voidable, an innocent purchaser who acquired the car from the rogue was protected.

---

24. (1879), 14 T.L.R. 98.

25. [1918–19] All E.R. 246.

26. [1971] 3 All E.R. 907.

Canadian courts have followed the English cases. The Supreme Court of Canada held that a car-rental company had "consented" to the rental of a car to a rogue who gave a false identity.[27] Subsequent purchasers are probably better protected when the first transaction takes place face to face than when the transaction takes place by post.

INTERNATIONAL ISSUE

Identity Theft

Mistake as to identity is now a worldwide epidemic commonly known as *Identity Theft*. Billions of dollars are stolen each year when thieves steal personal data and assume the identities of credit-worthy people.

The discussion in this chapter has focused on the legal entitlement of the duped vendor to retrieve his goods from the party who has subsequently purchased them from the thief. In reality, legal entitlement is not the biggest issue. The goods involved are often shipped across borders and become untraceable. Businesses cannot seek return of the goods because they cannot find them. Instead, a business may try to enforce the contract by suing the true identity-holder for the unpaid account. Innocent parties are then surprised by large judgments and destroyed credit ratings.

QUESTIONS TO CONSIDER

1. What risk management strategies should a business put in place to reduce the possibility of mistake as to identity?

2. How will a court achieve a fair solution when considering the circumstances of the duped vendor and the true identity-holder?

Mistake About the Nature of a Signed Document

Non Est Factum

By signing a document that has been misrepresented to him either innocently or fraudulently, a person may induce an innocent third party to rely on the document. The person who signed may raise the plea known as ***non est factum*** ("it is not my doing"). If the court accepts the plea, it is good even against the third party who believes she has acquired rights under the document. In this respect the effect of a successful plea of *non est factum* is similar to the result in *Cundy* v. *Lindsay*: an innocent third party may suffer.

The plea originated in medieval times when most people could not read or write. A person would bind himself to a written document by making a mark or impressing his family seal, but he had to rely on the honesty of the literate party who presented the document to him. If he were later sued for breach of the terms of the document, he could plead that it was not his deed, because of a serious misrepresentation. In medieval times the result was reasonable. It would still be reasonable today if its application were limited to illiterate and blind persons and those who read and write only in a foreign language—persons who must rely on the honesty of others.

non est factum
"it is not my doing"

---

27. *Terry* v. *Vancouver Motors U-Drive Ltd. and Walter*, [1942] 1 W.W.R. 503.

CHAPTER

9

Grounds Upon Which a Contract May Be Impeached:

MISREPRESENTATION, UNDUE INFLUENCE, AND DURESS

Misrepresentation and Torts

Misrepresentation and Contracts

Consequences of Misrepresentation in Contracts

Opinion Versus Fact

Signed Documents and Misrepresentation by Omission

Silence as Misrepresentation: Contracts Requiring Disclosure

Undue Influence

Duress

Misrepresentations occur in situations other than contractual relations, but in this chapter, we are primarily concerned with the consequences of a misrepresentation by one party to a contract made to the other party. In this chapter we examine such questions as:

- Why is it important to determine whether a misrepresentation is material?

- What is the difference between "opinion" and "fact"?

- What are the implications of signing a document purporting to contain all the terms of a contract when one party claims that one or more important terms have been unintentionally omitted?

- When should the requirement of utmost good faith be applied?

- What remedy is available to the innocent party when the other party is found to have exerted undue influence or duress?

quasi-contract
an obligation that m
not as a result of cor
relations, but becaus
party has received ar
benefit at the expens
other

unjust enrichme
an unfair benefit

restitution
repayment or recove
loss

MISREPRESENTATION AND TORTS

As we have noted in Chapters 3 and 4, a misrepresentation may amount to a tort when it is made fraudulently[1] or negligently.[2] A victim who relies reasonably on such an assertion and suffers loss may recover from the wrongdoer. However, when a person makes a statement neither fraudulently nor negligently but nevertheless it proves to be false, no tort has been committed.

ILLUSTRATION 9.1

Andrews asks Barton, a stockbroker acquaintance, whether *X* Corporation is in sound financial condition, and Barton replies that she believes it to be very sound. Andrews then buys $25 000 worth of the shares in *X* Corporation. Unknown to either Andrews or Barton, the company's president had just been charged with embezzling $2 000 000 and the company was insolvent at the time Barton gave her evaluation. Andrews' newly acquired shares are worthless and he has lost $25 000, but unless Barton should have known of *X* Corporation's difficulties, Andrews will have no claim against her.

A person who innocently makes a misstatement and later learns that it is false is under a duty to inform the other party of the true situation as soon as she can. An innocent misrepresentation becomes fraudulent or negligent if the party responsible fails to correct it when in a position to do so.

MISREPRESENTATION AND CONTRACTS

Misrepresentation most often occurs during bargaining before a contract is formed. If a misrepresentation is **material**—that is, if it is a statement that could reasonably be expected to influence the decision of a party hearing (or reading) it in favour of entering into a contract—a court may set the contract aside at the request of the innocent party. In addition, if the maker of the misrepresentation also acted fraudulently or negligently, the court will grant damages against the wrongdoer. However, if he made the misrepresentation innocently and without negligence, no damages will be awarded; the aggrieved party's remedy is restricted to the right to **rescind**.

As we shall see in Chapter 15,[3] the right to rescind is limited by the rules of equity. In particular, if an aggrieved party cannot restore the subject-matter of the contract to the other party—for instance, the goods have been resold, consumed, or even have substantially deteriorated—the aggrieved party loses the right to rescind. As a result, a party who has received less than fair value because of an innocent misrepresentation may be left without any remedy.

An injured party may claim that a misrepresentation became a term of the subsequent contract, and if the court agrees, the party is entitled to a remedy based on breach of contract. At one time, the courts distinguished sharply between pre-contract representations and express terms of a contract.[4] However, they gradually became more willing to consider representations as having been incorporated into a contract as part of the contractual obligation of the maker of the statement. If the statement was an important inducement to enter into the contract, if the aggrieved party has suffered a substantial loss—and if there would otherwise be no remedy for an innocent misrepresentation because rescission is unavailable in the circumstances—a court is more willing to find that

material
could reasonably be expected to influence the decision of a party to enter into a contract

rescind
set the contract aside and put the party back in her pre-contract position

---

1. See section in Chapter 3 on "Deceit."
2. See section in Chapter 4 on "Misrepresentation."
3. Under "Equitable Remedies." Also: Waddams, *The Law of Contracts*, 4th ed., at 444–54.
4. For example: *Heilbut, Symons & Co.* v. *Buckleton*, [1913] A.C. 30.

the statement had indeed become a term. If the misrepresentation was made shortly before or at the time of entering into the agreement, it is easier for a court to conclude that it has become a term.[5]

So, too, courts have occasionally found statements about goods and services in advertisements and sales promotion material, read by a prospective buyer before making a contract, to be incorporated in the contract.[6] It is now common for standard form contracts to specifically declare that representations are not terms of the contract.

Remedies for breach of contract are separate from, and frequently broader than, rescission for misrepresentation.[7] We should note that a general rule of law is that a plaintiff will not be granted a remedy he does not expressly claim. Since it can be difficult to predict whether a court will find one set of remedies or the other to be appropriate, a party may seek each remedy in the alternative with the choice left to the court.[8] Occasionally, the court may find both remedies available and give the injured party a choice.

CONSEQUENCES OF MISREPRESENTATION IN CONTRACTS

When a party has relied upon an innocent misrepresentation and learns the true facts, the contract is voidable at the option of the victim. She must renounce the agreement promptly. If she allows an unreasonable length of time to pass without repudiating or she takes further benefits under the contract, she will lose her right to rescind. If she has sustained out-of-pocket expenses in performing the contract or has paid money to the other party before becoming aware of her right to rescind, she may be entitled to a money award known as an **indemnity** or **compensation** as a supplement to rescission.[9] Such loss must arise directly out of the performance of the contract—the indemnity does not cover nearly as wide a variety of loss as does an award of damages.

indemnity or compensation
a money award given as a supplement to rescission for loss sustained in performing a contract

CASE 9.1

Appell hired a sales agent to arrange a sale of his business. The agent gave Corbeil, a prospective purchaser, an estimate of the daily gross receipts of the business. When Corbeil asked if there were any records showing the daily turnover, the agent replied that Appell did not have any, but that the former owners of the business did. On meeting with Corbeil, the former owners were unable to produce the records, but they confirmed in a general way the information given by the sales agent. Corbeil then purchased the business, delivering his car to Appell at the agreed value of $1000 as a down payment, and began operating the business as of February 2, 1949. When he discovered that its revenue did not approach the amount indicated, he repudiated the purchase by letter dated February 8, 1949. He then sued for recovery of his car and damages for loss of its use, alleging fraud.[10]

rescission
setting aside or rescinding a contract in order to restore the parties as nearly as possible to their pre-contract positions

The court held that fraud was not proven but that the contract might still be rescinded for innocent misrepresentation. The purpose of **rescission** is to restore the parties as nearly as possible to their position before they entered into the contract. Hence Corbeil was entitled to the return of his car and also to *compensation* for depreciation in its value.

5. *Dick Bentley Productions Ltd.* v. *Harold Smith Motors Ltd.*, [1965] 2 All E.R. 65. See also *Esso Petroleum Co. Ltd.* v. *Mardon*, [1976] 2 All E.R. 5 (C.A.).

6. *Goldthorpe* v. *Logan*, [1943] 2 D.L.R. 519; *Murray* v. *Sperry Rand Corp.* (1979), 96 D.L.R. (3d) 113.

7. See Chapter 15, sections on "Implications of Breach" and "Damages."

8. For a discussion of alternative remedies, see *1018429 Ontario Inc.* v. *Fea Investments Ltd.* (1999), 179 D.L.R. (4th) 269.

9. *Whittington* v. *Seale-Hayne* (1900), 82 L.T. 49.

10. *Corbeil* v. *Appell*, [1950] 1 D.L.R. 159. When the court finds that the misrepresentation is not sufficiently serious, it may refuse rescission and limit the innocent party's remedy to damages. See *Field* v. *Zien*, [1963] S.C.R. 632; *Taggart* v. *Brancato Construction Ltd.* (1998), 16 R.P.R. (3d) 22.

In contracts for the sale of land, the right to rescission for innocent misrepresentation is generally lost once title to the property is transferred and the transaction is completed. There are two main reasons for this rule. First, purchasers are expected to "search the title" and to satisfy themselves by inspection of the property that it is as represented in the contract. If they are not satisfied, they are expected to exercise a right to rescind *before* the time for completion of the transaction. Second, there is the danger that an outstanding right to rescission would not be apparent to a third party who investigated the ownership of the land and relied on the registered title, for example, to extend credit on the security of a mortgage. When a misrepresentation is not fraudulent, only rarely will a court grant rescission after completion.[11]

ETHICAL ISSUE

Employment Resumé

In February 2006, David J. Edmondson resigned from his position as President and CEO of RadioShack Corp. after it was discovered that he lied on his resumé. His resumé indicated that he received a psychology degree from Pacific Coast Baptist College. After the College denied granting the degree, Mr. Edmondson acknowledged the error.

A resumé (and its corresponding covering letter) introduce an employment candidate to the employer. It describes the educational experience and work history of the candidate. An employer often decides whether or not to interview a candidate based on the information contained in the resumé. Most prospective employees design their resumés to emphasize their strengths and minimize their weaknesses. However, the resumé must fairly and accurately present the background of the candidate or it becomes a misrepresentation.

QUESTIONS TO CONSIDER

1. Is it acceptable to omit past employment if it is not relevant to the current employment sought? What if the candidate was fired from the previous employment?

2. What types of resumé "inaccuracies" should allow an employer to rescind the employment agreement?

3. Should Mr. Edmondson be entitled to his contractual severance package?

Sources: Associated Press, "RadioShack CEO David J. Edmondson Resigns," *CBS News*, February 21, 2006, www.cbsnews.com/stories/2006/02/21/ap/business/mainD8FTEJ480.shtml; Associated Press, "RadioShack CEO's Resume Raises Questions," *MSNBC Business*, February 14, 2006, www.msnbc.msn.com/id/11354888/.

OPINION VERSUS FACT

A false assertion is a misrepresentation only if it is made as a statement of fact. Most statements of opinion do not amount to misrepresentation and give no remedy for those who rely on them. The law is lenient towards sellers who rhapsodize about their wares: a bookseller's claim that "this is the best textbook in its field" would leave a disillusioned purchaser without any remedy.

---

11. For an exception, see *Northern & Central Gas Corp. Ltd.* v. *Hillcrest Collieries Ltd.* (1975), 59 D.L.R. (3d) 533. See also *Hyrsky et al.* v. *Smith* (1969), 5 D.L.R. (3d) 385, discussed in Chapter 8 under "Mistakes in Assumptions." Chapter 23 deals with the law relating to land.

We can see the distinction between an expression of opinion and one of fact by contrasting two statements. If *A* says to *B*, "That property is worth at least $50 000 today," her remarks are just an expression of opinion. But if she says instead, "That property cost me $50 000," she has made a representation of fact.

Unfortunately, it is not always so easy to distinguish between statements of fact and opinion. Suppose a merchant wishing to sell some foreign goods says, "In my opinion these goods can be imported under the lower tariff rate in section X of the statute." The buyer later finds that they cannot be imported under that section. The court might hold that the seller merely gave his opinion, but if the court finds that the merchant is an *expert* in marketing these goods, or has purported to be one, it may find that he made a misrepresentation. In this context an **expert opinion** is equivalent to a statement of fact.

expert opinion
an opinion given by a person who purports to have specialized knowledge of a subject

We normally expect an assertion of fact to be made in words, whether oral or written. However, conduct not expressed in words may also amount to an assertion of fact. If a prospective buyer asks to see goods of a certain specification and in response a seller shows him some goods without commenting on them, the seller's conduct alone may be an assertion of fact that the goods meet the buyer's specifications.

SIGNED DOCUMENTS AND MISREPRESENTATION BY OMISSION

We noted in Chapter 5 that the act of signing a document creates a presumption that the signer accepts all its terms. That presumption may be rebutted when a party (often a consumer) is expected to sign a document hurriedly and without an opportunity to read or understand it and when the other party has good reason to suspect that the signer may not fully comprehend the implications of signing the document. In the words of Professor Waddams (quoted with approval by the Ontario Court of Appeal):

> These cases suggest that there is a special onus on the supplier to point out any terms in a printed form that differ from what the consumer might reasonably expect. If he fails to do so, he will be guilty of a 'misrepresentation by omission', and the court will strike down clauses which 'differ from the ordinary understanding of mankind' or (and sometimes this is the same thing) clauses which are 'unreasonable or oppressive'. If this principle is accepted the rule about written documents might be restated as follows: the signer is bound by the terms of the document if, and only if, the other party believes on reasonable grounds that those terms truly express the signer's intention. This principle retains the role of signed documents as a means of protecting reasonable expectations; what it does not allow is that a party should rely on a printed document to contradict what he knows, or ought to know, is the understanding of the other party. Again this principle seems to be particularly applicable in situations involving the distribution of goods and services to consumers, though it is by no means confined to such situations.[12]

Usually, a party who has not signed a document can more easily rebut a presumption that he agreed to all the terms in it, and so he can avoid being bound by them, as discussed in the "ticket" cases in Chapter 5.

---

12. Waddams, "Contracts Exemption Clauses Unconscionability Consumer Protection" (Comments) (1971), 49 *Can. Bar Rev.* 578 at 590–1; cited *in Tilden Rent-A-Car Co.* v. *Clendenning* (1978), 18 O.R. (2d) 601, per Dubin, J.A. at 609. See also *Trigg* v. *MI Movers International Transport Services Ltd.* (1991), 4 O.R. (3d) 562.

SILENCE AS MISREPRESENTATION: CONTRACTS REQUIRING DISCLOSURE

When One Party Has Special Knowledge

The concept of misrepresentation also includes failure to disclose pertinent information because one of the parties has access to such information not available to the other. When a relationship between parties leads to a special measure of trust by one party in the other, it is unconscionable for the one to withhold information he knows to be material to the other's decision about entering into a contract.[13] The party "in a superior position of knowledge" has a duty to inform the other so that he may have an idea of the risks he would be taking under the proposed contract. Although the courts have gradually widened the scope of this duty, the **utmost good faith** does not require disclosure simply because one party knows something the other does not. The facts of each case will determine the court's view.

utmost good faith
a duty owed when a special measure of trust is placed in one party by the other

The requirement of utmost good faith almost always exists in a continuing business relationship. Partnership depends on mutual trust, and accordingly, partners owe a general duty of utmost good faith to each other in all their transactions. Similarly, directors and officers owe a duty of good faith towards their corporation.

Contracts of Insurance

An important type of contract requiring utmost good faith is the contract of insurance: a party seeking insurance must disclose to the insurance company all pertinent aspects of the risk she is asking it to assume. This information enables the insurer to make an informed judgment about whether to provide the insurance coverage requested and to fix a rate that is consistent with the risk. A person who applies for life insurance, for example, must disclose everything about her state of health that will be of value to the insurer in deciding whether to accept or reject her application. The insurer can refuse to pay the insurance money to her estate or beneficiaries if the insured person withheld information—such as having diabetes—when applying for the insurance. Similarly, an applicant's failure to disclose that she has been refused life insurance by other companies amounts to a breach of good faith and a misrepresentation.

The requirement of utmost good faith in applying for fire insurance is governed by statute in each province.[14] In *Sherman* v. *American Institute Co.*[15] the policy holder, when applying for fire insurance, failed to disclose that he had had a previous fire and that the insurance company affected had then refused to continue the insurance protection. The insured property was damaged by fire again, and when these facts came to light the insurance company refused to pay. It was held that the insured's conduct amounted to a fraudulent omission within the terms of the Insurance Act: the insurance company was not required to pay the insurance money.

Public liability insurance—for motor vehicles, for example—presents a special difficulty. Suppose an insured, who failed to disclose important information when applying for insurance, has an accident: on the one hand, this appears to justify his insurer refusing to pay a claim; on the other hand, an innocent third party, say a passenger injured by the negligence of the insured, would be unable to claim from the insurer. If the insured did not have sufficient assets to pay the passenger's claim, the innocent passenger would be the one to suffer the loss as a result of the insured party's non-disclosure *and* his negligence. Accordingly, there are strong public policy reasons why insurance should cover harm to third parties despite a breach of utmost good faith by the insured. The

---

13. *Lloyd's Bank Ltd.* v. *Bundy*, [1974] 3 All E.R. 757 at 765.

14. See, for example: Insurance Act, R.S.B.C. 1996, c. 226, s. 126; R.S.O. 1990, c. I.8, s. 148; R.S.N.S. 1989, c. 231, Sch. to Part VII, s. 1.

15. [1937] 4 D.L.R. 723.

insurer itself must then take greater precautions to investigate the safety record of the insured before agreeing to insure. Courts recognize an obligation to investigate in circumstances where the misrepresentation is "self-evidently false to a reasonable insurer."[16] However, the burden of truthfulness generally remains with the insured and automobile insurance legislation makes coverage of third parties mandatory only to the statutory minimum levels.[17]

Sale of Corporation Securities

prospectus
a statement issued to inform the public about a new issue of shares or bonds

A situation in which one party typically has special access to information arises in a subscription for the purchase of shares or bonds in a corporation. The promoters or directors naturally know more about the corporation's affairs and prospects than do the investing public from whom they are soliciting subscriptions. The corporation usually gives the investing public information about a new issue of shares or bonds in a statement called a **prospectus**, or sometimes in other documents such as circulars, letters, or notices published in newspapers.

All these documents present tempting opportunities for misrepresentation of a corporation's financial position by non-disclosure. Consequently, our various corporations and securities statutes now require disclosure of information in such documents in sufficient detail that directors, by simply omitting pertinent information, are more likely to be liable for violating the statute than for violating the common law.[18] As we shall see in Chapter 29, the securities acts of most provinces require that in many instances prospectuses be approved by the provincial securities commission or another government body before shares can be offered to the public.

Sale of Goods Compared with Sale of Land

caveat emptor
let the buyer beware

Generally a buyer of goods must take them with their defects unless some fact about their quality has been misrepresented. Certain qualifications to this doctrine of ***caveat emptor*** are discussed in Chapter 16 on the sale of goods. For example, *caveat emptor* applies only to the quality or condition of the goods, not to ownership. Simply by offering goods for sale, a seller implies that he has the right to sell them and to transfer full ownership free from any claims. Failure to disclose an outstanding claim entitles the buyer to rescission. Although the buyer's right to rescind arises from a breach of an implied term rather than from a duty to disclose, the result is the same as if utmost good faith about ownership had been required of the seller.

A purchaser of an interest in land has even less protection against undisclosed faults of the property. If the vendor has made no representations, in most cases the purchaser must take it with all its faults.[19] Even if the vendor's ownership is subject to the claims of other persons, he need not disclose these claims. In the absence of representations by the vendor, the law presumes that the vendor offers to sell only the interest he has in the land. The purchaser can protect himself only by making a thorough investigation of title. In a few instances, however, a court may imply a misrepresentation if non-disclosure amounts to fraud. For example, *A* purports to sell a piece of land to *B*, when in fact she occupies it only as a tenant and is not the owner. The court would find that *A* impliedly represented herself as owner and would grant rescission to *B*.

---

16. *Armstrong* v. *Northwest Life Insurance Co. of Canada* (1990), 72 D.L.R. (4th) 410, 414; *State Farm Mutual Automobile Insurance Co.* v. *General Accident Assurance Co. of Canada*, [1995] N.B.J. No. 405 (C.A.); *Coronation Insurance Co.* v. *Taku Air Transport* (1991), 85 D.L.R. (4th) 609; *Campanaro* v. *Kim* (1998), 112 O.A.C. 171.

17. *Schoff* v. *Royal Insurance Company of Canada*, [2004] 10 W.W.R. 32 (Alta. C.A.); Insurance Act. R.S.A. 2000, c. I-3, s. 613, 630, 635(11); R.S.O. 1990, c. I 8, s. 258 (10)(11). The statutory minimum coverage is $200 000 in Alberta and Ontario.

18. See, for example: Securities Act, R.S.O. 1990, c. S.5, s. 1(1) paras. 25, 38, 56, 122, 130, 130.1, 138.3. The legislation creates a civil cause of action against many of the individuals involved in the preparation of the prospectus.

19. In recent years the courts have gradually increased protection to purchasers with regard to serious defects that it would be impossible for them to discover. See, for example, *Sevidal* v. *Chopra* (1987), 64 O.R. (2d) 169, where the court held that the vendor had a duty to disclose that radioactive soil had been found on the property after the contract was made but before completion date.

UNDUE INFLUENCE

Special Relationships

Undue influence is the domination of one party over the mind of another to such a degree as to deprive the weaker party of the will to make an independent decision. A contract formed as a result of undue influence is voidable at the option of the victim. The victim may avoid the contract only if he acts promptly after he is freed from the domination. If he acquiesces or delays, hoping to gain some advantage, the court will refuse to assist him.

Undue influence is often an issue in disputes not involving contracts, as when a gift has been made and the donor wants to recover the gift, and perhaps more often when a bequest has been made under a will. Generally speaking, the principles governing undue influence in these circumstances are the same as in contract.

Usually undue influence arises where the parties stand in a special relationship to each other: one party has a special skill or knowledge causing the other to place confidence and trust in him. Typical examples of this relationship are doctor and patient, lawyer and client, minister and parishioner, parent and child.

undue influence
the domination of one party over the mind of another to such a degree as to deprive the weaker party of the will to make an independent decision

Dire Circumstances

Sometimes undue influence arises when one party is temporarily in dire straits and will agree to exorbitant and unfair terms because he is desperate for aid.

CASE   9.2   A whaling ship three years at sea sailed into a thick Arctic fog near the Bering Strait and ran onto rocks. The coast was barren and the ocean navigable only two months in the year: winter was expected within two or three weeks. Another ship came along, rescued the crew, and bought the cargo of whale oil at a bargain price, to which the captain of the wrecked ship readily agreed. The owners of the wrecked ship later successfully repudiated the contract for the sale of the whale oil.[20]

Burden of Proof

A party alleging undue influence must satisfy the court that in the circumstances domination was probable. It is easier to persuade the court when a special relationship has existed: the law presumes that undue influence was exerted in contracts advantageous to the party in the dominant position, as, for example, in a contract between a doctor and a patient in which the patient promises to sell the doctor an asset for a small fraction of its value. In the absence of a special relationship, it is more difficult for a party to demonstrate undue influence, but he still may be able to show, for instance, that he was in a desperate financial state at the time of the contract.

Once the alleged victim shows that circumstances likely to lead to undue influence existed, the burden shifts to the dominant party to prove that undue influence was *not* exerted by him. He will often find the task almost impossible; the courts are concerned that a dominant position should not be used as a device to exploit the weaker party. Sometimes the advantage taken by the stronger party is referred to as *fraud* or **constructive fraud**, but as Lord Selborne has put it:

constructive fraud
the unconscientious use of power by a dominant party to take advantage of the weakness of the other party

> Fraud does not here mean deceit or circumvention; it means an unconscientious use of the power arising out of these circumstances and conditions; and when the relative position of the parties

---

20. *Post v. Jones*, 60 U.S. 618 (1856).

prima facie
at first sight; on the face of it

is such as ***prima facie*** to raise this presumption, the transaction cannot stand unless the person claiming the benefit of it is able to repel the presumption by contrary evidence, proving it to have been in point of fact fair, just and reasonable.[21]

The most important factors in determining whether there is undue influence are the degree of domination of the stronger party and the extent of the advantage he has received (that is, the unfairness of the bargain). The degree of domination is often difficult to ascertain, because it involves questions of personality; by contrast, unfairness can generally be measured against the market value of the goods or services traded in a contract and is more easily judged.

Arrangements Between Husband and Wife

Undue influence is somewhat more difficult to prove between husband and wife than in the other relationships, because the law presumes that at various times either party may well desire to confer a benefit on the other without obtaining a good "price" in return. However, undue influence may arise, especially if one spouse is experienced in business and has persuaded the other, who has had little or no business experience, to pledge her separate assets as security or act as guarantor for his business transactions. Two cases illustrate how undue influence may be found in the husband–wife relationship.

CASE 9.3

A broker to whom a sum of money was owing either suggested to the husband or acquiesced in a representation made by him to his wife that the husband obtain promissory notes from his wife and make them payable to the broker. The wife later avoided her liability on the notes.[22]

CASE 9.4

A wife surrendered to a bank all her large separate estate to settle her husband's debts, in a series of transactions extending over a period of eight years. She was a confirmed invalid who had never had any advice that could be called independent—the only lawyer with whom she had any dealings was the solicitor of the bank and of her husband. She had acted in passive obedience to her husband. The transfers of the wife's property were set aside and recovered for the benefit of her estate.[23]

Importance of Independent Legal Advice

Sometimes a promisor chooses of his own free will to confer a benefit on another by contract, but subsequent events bring a change of heart and he claims undue influence; or the promisor may die, and his executor or heirs may then try to avoid the contract on grounds of undue influence. After the benefit has been promised but before it is actually conferred, the alleged dominant person, relying on the contract, may enter into further obligations. He may, for example, make a contract with a builder to erect a house on a piece of land, relying on an earlier contract in which a friend agreed to sell him the land at a very low price. If a court set aside the contract for the sale of the land because of undue influence, the dominant party would have to break the second contract for the construction of the house, and would become liable for payment of damages to the builder.

To avoid such risks whenever undue influence is a possibility, the dominant party would be wise to ask the other party to obtain independent legal advice about his rights and duties before making

---

21. *Aylesford* v. *Morris* (1873), L.R. 8 Ch. 484, at 490.

22. *Cox* v. *Adams* (1904), 35 S.C.R. 393.

23. *Bank of Montreal* v. *Stuart*, [1911] A.C. 120. See also *Bertolo* v. *Bank of Montreal* (1986), 57 O.R. (2d) 577; *Bank of Montreal* v. *Duguid* (2000),185 D.L.R. (4th) 458.

the agreement. Not only will the suggestion to get advice help refute a claim of undue influence, but testimony of the independent lawyer, not associated with the transaction, that he explained the nature of the transaction and that the other party freely and with full knowledge made the commitment, will usually be conclusive evidence against the claim.

A lawyer confronted with a situation in which undue influence may exist will almost always send the weaker party to some other completely independent lawyer. This situation often arises when a husband brings his wife to sign documents in which she is to guarantee proposed loans for her husband's business. The lawyer will usually suggest several lawyers' names and ask the wife to choose one at random. She will then visit the other lawyer *alone* with all relevant documents, have them explained carefully, pay the lawyer for his time, and return with a certificate signed by the lawyer stating exactly what took place in his office. Although this procedure seems overly cautious, it is the fair thing to do—and it may save the husband or the creditor untold difficulties if later a claim of undue influence is made. Occasionally, after receiving independent legal advice, a wife may well have second thoughts and refuse to sign the documents.

Threat of Prosecution

Undue influence may also arise through fear of prosecution of a near relation.[24] Parents may be prepared to go to great lengths to save their child from prosecution for a relatively minor offence: sometimes they promise money to a person in possession of the necessary evidence if he does not press for prosecution. The matter is very close to the criminal offence of blackmail even though no express threat may have been made; such activities might only come to light if the parent dies and the executor refuses to pay, or the child dies and the possibility of prosecution ceases.

Inequality of Bargaining Power

Courts have gradually become more willing to rescind a category of **unconscionable contracts**, either as an application of the law relating to undue influence or as an extension of the concept of utmost good faith. Unconscionable contracts are those that arise between parties of unequal bargaining power and that result in an unfairly advantageous deal for the powerful party. In an English case on this question, Lord Denning said:

unconscionable contracts
contracts between parties of unequal bargaining power that result in an unfairly advantageous bargain for the powerful party

> . . . through all these instances there runs a single thread. They rest on 'inequality of bargaining power'. By virtue of it, the English law gives relief to one who, without independent advice, enters into a contract on terms which are very unfair or transfers property for a consideration which is grossly inadequate, when his bargaining power is grievously impaired by reason of his own needs or desires, or by his own ignorance or infirmity, coupled with undue influences or pressures brought to bear on him by or for the benefit of the other. When I use the word 'undue' I do not mean to suggest that the principle depends on proof of any wrongdoing. The one who stipulates for an unfair advantage may be moved solely by his own self-interest, unconscious of the distress he is bringing to the other.[25]

Although inequality of bargaining power has become an important consideration before the courts, we must emphasize that by no means has it replaced the need for sophisticated legal analysis and careful understanding of the business setting of transactions. Courts insist first on a clear understanding of the problem under consideration; *only then* will they apply, with restraint, the general principle of unconscionability. And for good reason: it is essential that courts do not lightly upset

---

24. *Kaufman* v. *Gerson*, [1904] 1 K.B. 591.
25. *Lloyds Bank Ltd.* v. *Bundy, supra*, n. 13, quoted with approval in *McKenzie* v. *Bank of Montreal* (1975), 55 D.L.R. (3d) 641 at 652. The relationship between bank and borrower is one of debtor and creditor, and barring unusual circumstances, is not a fiduciary relationship: *Baldwin* v. *Daubney* (2006), 83 O.R. (3d) 308 (C.A.), para 12.

normal habits of reliance on bargains seriously made. Just the fact that with hindsight a contract looks like a "bad deal" does not make it unconscionable.

Loan Transactions

Unconscionable contracts often arise in loan contracts. The borrower may be in a financial crisis and desperate for money: he agrees to any exorbitant rate of interest at the time. Later he finds he cannot repay the debt because the interest is so high: it is all he can do to pay the interest regularly. The common law remedies discussed above are available, of course, as the transaction is often unconscionable. In addition, many jurisdictions have recognized that loans present a special problem and have passed statutes to provide additional remedies.[26]

It is especially important to note that the Criminal Code[27] makes it an offence to charge a rate of interest in excess of 60 percent per annum on a loan. In practice, criminal prosecutions for this offence are very rare. However, in civil cases, the courts refuse to allow recovery of interest where the "criminal" rate of interest has been exceeded. The loan contract itself is not void: the principal sum may still be recovered, but the illegal interest provision is *severed* from the contract. The courts have not been consistent in the method of severance. One approach has been their "blue pencil" test; for example, in *Mira Design* v. *Seascape Holdings*[28] a clause that provided for an increase in the principal of the loan after one month was struck out, and this ruling lowered the effective rate of interest below the criminal limit. In other cases the courts have simply held that the principal only is recoverable—the lender may not recover any interest.[29] This is more effective, since the risk of being deprived of any interest acts as a deterrent to lenders who might otherwise attempt to charge an exorbitant rate.

INTERNATIONAL ISSUE

Payday Loans

As discussed above, unconscionable loans with excessive interest provisions have been the subject of provincial legislation for a long time. However, the North American explosion of "payday" loans have revealed the vagueness of the existing legislation and prompted action.

Payday loans are short-term (daily or weekly) advances of small amounts of money (usually under $1000). Lenders charge not only interest but also application fees and service charges. When calculated on an annualized basis, the total charges often exceed 300% of the principal borrowed, well above the criminal rate of interest.

In the United States, payday loans are governed by state legislation. Common restrictions include:

- capping the charges on a fixed basis rather than a percentage basis (for example, Iowa describes the maximum interest charge as $15 per $100 over the term of the loan),

continued

26. Unconscionable Transactions Act, R.S.A. 2000, c. U-2; R.S.N.B. 1973, c. U-1; Unconscionable Transactions Relief Act, R.S.M. 1987, c. U20; R.S.N.L. 1990, c. U-1; R.S.O. 1990, c. U-2; R.S.P.E.I. 1988, c. U-2.
27. R.S.C. 1985, c. C-46, s. 347. See *Garland* v. *Consumer's Gas Co.*, [1998] 3 S.C.R. 112.
28. [1982] 1 W.W.R. 744 (B.C.S.C.). For an interesting review of this issue see Waldron (1994), 73 *Can. Bar Rev.* 1.
29. See *Kebet Holdings Ltd.* v. *351173 B.C. Ltd.* (1991), 25 R.P.R. (2d) 174 (B.C.S.C.); *Milani* v. *Banks* (1997), 145 D.L.R. (4th) 55.

- capping the principal amount that can be borrowed (for example, Illinois describes the maximum amount that can be borrowed as $1000 or 25 percent of a borrower's monthly gross income), and

- capping the number of renewals.

In Canada, seven provinces have passed legislation that will regulate the payday loan industry.[30] Common restrictions include:

- licence requirements for lenders,

- cost of borrowing (all charges) disclosure requirements,

- cooling-off periods during which a consumer can cancel the agreement, and

- capping cost of borrowing (the Quebec cap of 35 percent has discouraged the growth of the payday loan industry).

In Ontario, an independent advisory board will recommend the appropriate cap on the cost of borrowing. The lenders argue that this cap must exceed the criminal rate of interest because the default rate on payday loans is extremely high.

QUESTIONS TO CONSIDER

1. Should Canadian limits adopt the American approach of capping the cost of borrowing on a fixed rather than percentage basis?

2. What is the rationale behind the American limit on the number of renewals?

3. How should the cap relate to the criminal rate of interest?

Sources: National Conference of State Legislatures, "Payday Lending," *National Conference of State Legislatures,* May 1, 2008, www.ncsl.org/programs/banking/paydaylend-intro.htm; K. Daubs, "Poverty Activists Cheer Payday Loan Legislation," *Ottawa Citizen,* April 2, 2008, www.canada.com/ottawacitizen/news/city/story.html?id=4d74f667-a307-4545-beda-22f0aa5defa9.

DURESS

Duress consists of actual or threatened violence or imprisonment as a means of coercing a party to enter into a contract. The effect of duress is similar to that of undue influence: the contract is voidable at the option of the victim. The threat of violence need not be directed against the party being coerced—it may be a threat to harm the victim's spouse, parent, or child.

    Historically, duress was a concept recognized by the common law courts and was narrowly interpreted by them. Today duress is not strictly confined by the courts to the circumstances described above. Sometimes, the concepts of duress and undue influence appear to overlap. The concept of economic duress is one example; it focuses on **coercion** and an illegitimate or inappropriate application of pressure.[31]

duress
actual or threatened violence or imprisonment as a means of coercing a party to enter into a contract

coercion
improperly forced payment under protest

---

30. Quebec, Manitoba, British Columbia, Alberta, Nova Scotia, New Brunswick, and Ontario: Manitoba was the first (Consumer Protection Amendment Act [Payday Loans], S.M. 2006, c. 31) and Ontario was the most recent (Payday Loans Act, 2008, S.O. 2008, c. 9).

31. Coercion involves four factors: (a) protest, (b) available alternative, (c) lack of independent advice, (c) post-contract steps to avoid it. See *Pao On* v. *Lau Yiu Long,* [1980] A.C. 614 (P.C.).

CASE 9.5

Stott was a securities salesman employed at Merit Investments Corp. A term of his contract required him to "cover" all bad debts of his clients. In the case of one client, Stott's boss ordered him to close out the account. Stott took the position that he should not have to cover the loss because he was ordered to close the account. Stott was called into the boss's office and asked to sign a written promise to pay the debt in instalments. When Stott argued that he was not responsible, the boss replied "You are probably right, but if you don't sign, it won't go well with you at the firm and it would be very difficult for you to find employment in the industry."[32] Stott signed the promise to pay. The Ontario Court of Appeal found that there was coercion and Merit applied illegitimate pressure. The conduct would justify rescinding the agreement based on economic duress if Stott had acted immediately to repudiate it. Unfortunately, Stott complied with the agreement and did not complain until 2 years later when he left Merit's employment.

The concept of undue influence is still wider and more flexible than duress and includes almost any circumstances that would not otherwise be called fraud.

QUESTIONS FOR REVIEW

1. What factors might persuade a court to consider an innocent misrepresentation to be a term of the contract?

2. What are the consequences of an innocent misrepresentation in contract as compared with tort?

3. In what circumstances will a court find that an "opinion" is a misrepresentation of fact?

4. Felix owns and operates a bookshop. He has just learned from a friend who is a real estate agent that one of the large "super bookstores" has purchased a site and will be establishing a branch in 12 months just across the street from his store. There will be a public announcement in three months. Felix immediately advertises his business for sale and is approached by Gulliver. Felix bargains for a price based on his sales and income over the last three years, but does not mention the almost certain new competition that will arrive across the street. Gulliver makes an offer and Felix accepts it. Before the transaction is completed, Gulliver learns about the new bookstore. What rights, if any, does he have?

5. *D* applies for a car insurance policy from *E* Auto Ins. Co., without disclosing that he has been convicted of driving violations and was involved in three collisions in another province. The company issues the policy. *D* subsequently causes a collision in which he injures *F*. The insurance company then learns about *D*'s failure to disclose his bad record and it cancels the policy. What problem does this situation raise for *F*?

6. Under what circumstances does a victim of misrepresentation lose the right to rescind?

7. Describe the implied representation that arises from offering goods for sale.

8. In what circumstances does the burden of proof in claims based on undue influence shift to the party who is alleged to have exerted such an influence?

9. *H*'s business is in financial difficulties and he needs his wife, *W*, to guarantee a loan from a friend *T*. Before *T* accepts *W*'s guarantee, what precaution should he take?

10. Suppose *X*, who is in dire financial straits, borrows $10 000 from *Y* at an annual interest rate of 65 percent. *X* defaults on his first payment of interest and *Y* sues. How will the courts respond?

11. What factors will a court consider before it allows a party to rescind a contract that is a "bad deal"?

32. *Stott v. Merit Investment Corp.* (1988), 63 O.R. (2d) 545 (Cont. C.A.), at para.12.

CASES AND PROBLEMS

1. Smart was Hull's lawyer for many years and not only handled legal matters for Hull, but gave him important advice on business matters as well. At one stage, Hull owed Smart about $8500 for professional services; Smart suggested to Hull that the account could be conveniently settled in full if Hull would transfer his new 10-metre sailboat to Smart. Hull hesitated at first, but realizing how indispensable his relationship with Smart had been and how important it was that Smart should continue to respect the confidential nature of his private business affairs, he transferred the sailboat to Smart.

   A few months later Hull's daughter, who greatly enjoyed sailing, returned from graduate studies in Europe and persuaded her father to sue for recovery of the sailboat. Explain how the onus of proof will operate in the resulting legal action and indicate the probable outcome.

2. Condor Investments Inc. published the following ad to sell its residential apartment building.

   > Newly renovated Condor Suites for sale: 45 high-quality one- and two-bedroom residential units in a prime location, $2 300 000.

   Dollefson inspected the building and believed it would be a good investment. After negotiating with Condor's manager, the two parties signed a deal for $2 100 000 and Dollefson paid a deposit of $100 000.

   In the course of preparing to complete the transaction, his lawyer checked with the city, and she learned that while there were indeed 45 units, the city had issued an occupancy permit for only 41 units; four units at the basement level were occupied without a permit. Dollefson decided that he did not want the property and commenced an action for rescission of the contract on the ground of fraudulent misrepresentation. He asked for the return of his deposit with interest as well as the legal, appraisal, and auditing fees that he had incurred.

   What are the main arguments for both sides, and which one should succeed?

3. In response to an advertisement offering a free trial lesson in modern dancing, Galt, a graduate nurse, entered into a contract with the Modern Dancing Studios for 15 two-hour lessons for $350. Before she had taken all the lessons, the dancing instructor, Valentino, told her that she would become a wonderful dancer if she went on and that if she agreed to more lessons she would "probably get the bronze medal for dancing." On St. Valentine's Day he gave her a rose, and in the course of a lesson whispered in her ear how wonderfully she danced. She eventually signed a second contract to take another 35 hours of dancing lessons for $650. A new instructor was then assigned to her, and all compliments and personal attention ceased. Galt brought action for rescission of the contract and return of the $650.

   On what ground might such a contract be voided? Should the action succeed?

4. Amberton Realty Inc. purchased a small apartment building with four units, each leased as a private dwelling. It renewed the insurance policy of the previous owners with Eagle-eye Insurance Co. Three months later the two ground-floor units became vacant and Amberton leased them to a charitable organization, Help-Our-Youth, which used the space a few hours each day to hold social gatherings. Help-Our-Youth managed the unit with care and the other tenants did not complain. However, after six months a fire started in the hallway and the entire building was destroyed.

   Eagle-eye refused to compensate Amberton because the use of the insured premises was changed without its knowledge. Under the terms of the insurance policy, only buildings described in the policy and occupied as a private dwelling were covered at a lower premium. Amberton's manager had not read the terms of the policy, and was not aware of the difference.

   Amberton sued Eagle-eye. Give your opinion, with reasons, whether Amberton should succeed.

5. On arriving at Vancouver Airport, Mr. Clemson, a frequent traveller, rented a car from Tilford Car Rentals Ltd., as he had done many times before. The clerk asked him whether he wanted additional collision insurance coverage and, as usual, he said, "Yes." The clerk added a fee of $10 a day for this coverage. She then handed the contract to Clemson and he signed it in her presence. She was aware that he did not read the terms of the contract before signing it.

Clemson's signature appeared immediately below a printed statement that read, "I, the undersigned, have read and received a copy of above and reverse side of this contract." On the back of the contract, in small type and so faint on Mr. Clemson's copy as to be hardly legible, there was a series of conditions, one of which read:

> Notwithstanding the payment of an additional fee for limitation of liability for collision damage to the rented vehicle, customer shall be fully liable for all collision damage if vehicle is used, operated or driven off highways serviced by federal, provincial or municipal governments and for all damages to vehicle by striking overhead objects.

The clerk placed Clemson's copy of the contract in an envelope and gave him the envelope and car keys. He got in the car, placed the contract in the glove compartment, and drove to a nearby shopping plaza to buy a gift. While driving in the plaza parking lot, he collided with another car, causing damage of $2500 to his rented car. The car rental agency claimed that he was personally liable for repairs under the terms of their contract. Clemson refused to pay for the car repairs and Tilford Car Rentals Ltd. sued him for breach of contract.

Outline the nature of the arguments available to Tilford Car Rentals Ltd. and of the defences available to Clemson. Express an opinion, with reasons, about whether the action is likely to succeed.

6. GasCan Ltd. is an integrated oil refining and distributing company that sells its products through a chain of service stations. It owns the land on which the service stations are located and leases them to tenants through its real estate department. As is normal in these arrangements, tenants agree to buy all their gasoline and other products from GasCan.

GasCan wanted to find a tenant for one of its service stations that had become vacant. Barcza expressed an interest in leasing it. The manager of GasCan's real estate department told Barcza that the company's sales division had made a forecast of the estimated annual sales of gasoline at the station: 900 000 litres. Barcza made a rough cash flow projection and signed a five-year lease of the station at a rental of $10 000 a year.

The company's estimate proved to be entirely wrong. The annual volume of the service station proved to be only about 200 000 litres. It appeared that the real estate department of GasCan had consulted with the sales division and that between them they had honestly but foolishly made "a fatal error." A new clerk in the sales division had checked sales made by the former tenant, but had assumed that the figures were in gallons whereas they had already been converted to litres. He converted them a second time, making the figures four and a half times higher than they should have been.

Barcza, who was an experienced and diligent station operator, tried hard to make a success of the business, but there was nothing he could do to raise gasoline sales close to the estimate. Over a three-year period he lost money steadily and finally became insolvent.

What remedies could Barcza seek in an action against GasCan Ltd.? What defences would GasCan raise? Who should succeed? Explain.

7. Virginia McGraw inherited a fruit farm in the Okanagan Valley when her aunt died five years ago. Two years ago, she befriended Val Lawton, a used-car sales agent, and allowed him to operate the fruit farm on the understanding they would live there together when they were married.

Lawton operated the farm at a loss but concealed the mounting debts from McGraw by intercepting her mail. He did his business at the Tower Bank, where he periodically filed statements of largely fictitious assets as a basis for increasing loans. His main assets seem to have been an affable and suave appearance, McGraw's affection for him, and his long friendship with the bank manager.

The bank took possession of McGraw's car when, finally, Lawton defaulted on his bank loan: he had offered her car as collateral security, asserting that it was his. The bank manager soon learned that the car was in fact owned by McGraw but refused to return it to her until Lawton's loan was repaid. McGraw was sympathetic when the matter was explained to her at the bank, and she then applied to her credit union to borrow enough money to repay the bank and recover her car. Three weeks later she returned to the bank with her fiancé and the money required to get her car back. Before handing over the keys to her, the bank manager asked her to sign "this bunch of papers." He advised her that her signature was required "as a matter of formality only." She then signed the papers and was given the car keys.

Six months afterwards, the bank claimed from McGraw a half-year's interest on a mortgage on her fruit farm, and she then discovered that the mortgage document had been among the papers she had signed at the bank. The bank proposed to use the mortgage in substitution for other amounts still owed by Lawton.

At this point McGraw broke off her relations with Lawton and on the advice of her lawyer sued the Tower Bank. In her action she asked to have the mortgage set aside and, in addition, claimed $1000 damages in tort as compensation for costs incurred from the wrongful seizure of her car and the loss of its use.

Explain with reasons whether, in your opinion, this action should succeed.

ADDITIONAL RESOURCES FOR CHAPTER 9 ON THE COMPANION WEBSITE *(www.pearsoned.ca/smyth)*

In addition to self-test, multiple-choice, true–false, and short-essay questions (all with immediate feedback), application exercises, and links to useful web destinations, the Companion Website provides the following resources for Chapter 9:

- **British Columbia:** International Investment
- **Alberta:** Fair Trading Act; Gift Cards; Unconscionable Transactions; Undue Influence
- **Manitoba/Saskatchewan:** Unconscionable Transactions
- **Ontario:** Consumer Protection Act 2002; Independent Legal Advice; Misrepresentation; Unconscionable Transactions; Unfair Business Practices

10

The Requirement of Writing

Not only does it make good sense to keep a written record of contracts, but there can also be serious legal consequences for failing to do so. The ancient Statute of Frauds, which still applies substantially in all common law provinces, requires that many contracts be in writing to be enforceable. In this chapter we examine such questions as:

- What types of contracts are affected by the Statute?

- What elements need to be in writing in order to comply with the Statute?

- What is the effect of the Statute on contracts that do not comply with the writing requirement?

- What is the doctrine of "part performance"? How have the courts used it to limit the scope of the Statute?

- How does the requirement of writing under the Sale of Goods Act differ from that in the Statute of Frauds?

- What are the writing requirements under other consumer protection legislation?

THE DISTINCTION BETWEEN SUBSTANCE AND FORM

The Benefits of a Written Record

When we speak of the "formation" of a contract, we mean it in a substantive legal sense, not in a physical sense. The parties must have agreed to the terms of their contract. The contract may exist only in their recollection of the spoken words, or it may be recorded in a written document or stored electronically on a CD or in a computer. So the *substance*—the terms of the contract—may have a variety of physical *forms* or even no form at all, other than in the minds of the parties. The distinction between the substance of the contract and the form in which it is known to the parties is crucial: we must not confuse the two. For the purpose of this chapter, the following categories of form are important:

(a)   contracts whose terms are entirely oral

(b)   contracts whose terms are part oral and part written

(c)   contracts whose terms are entirely in writing, whether all in one document or spread through several documents, such as a series of letters

In good business practice, some record is kept of even the simplest transaction at the time it is made. Of course, the more complicated a contract becomes, the better it is to have a written record. Human memories are fallible, especially when burdened with many details, and common sense tells us that it is better to rely on written records than on mere memory. However, in some circumstances business records alone may not satisfy the legal requirement of writing, which we are about to discuss.

When a contract is wholly oral, the first problem for the court is to determine what exactly the parties agreed to; written evidence will aid a judge in deciding what the terms are and in resolving conflicting testimonies. But written evidence does not resolve all problems. Even when a court has ascertained the exact words of the contract, the words themselves may be open to several interpretations—and the court must decide their meaning in the particular contract in dispute. We shall discuss the interpretation of contracts in the next chapter.

The Statute of Frauds

At common law, once the terms are ascertained, a contract is equally effective whether it is in writing or merely oral. However, in 1677 the English Parliament passed the Statute of Frauds. It was concerned mainly with settling ownership and the transfer of ownership in land after the turmoil of the Civil War. The Statute required written evidence to eliminate perjured testimony in suits concerning land—which explains the use of the word "frauds" in the title.[1] The two sections in the Statute that particularly affected contracts made judges unhappy almost immediately. They were poorly drafted and did not accomplish their vague purposes. Unfortunately, the Statute became so much a part of the law that it was re-enacted or adopted virtually unchanged in most common law jurisdictions around the world, including those of Canada and the United States. A notable change in the law occurred in 1954 when England amended the Statute. British Columbia replaced the Statute with the Law and Equity Act,[2] and Manitoba repealed it entirely.[3] In the remaining common law provinces, the Statute is in force in substantially its original form.

---

1.   See Furmston, *Cheshire, Fifoot and Furmston's Law of Contract*, 13th ed., at 209–33. For a recent discussion, see Fridman, "The Necessity for Writing in Contracts Within the Statute of Frauds" (1985), 35 U.T.L.J. 43.

2.   Law Reform Amendment Act, S.B.C. 1985, c. 10, s. 8 repealed the Statute of Frauds, and s. 7 revised the requirements for writing by adding a new s. 54 to the Law and Equity Act, R.S.B.C. 1979, c. 224.

3.   R.S.M. 1987, c. F-158.

Consequences of the Statute of Frauds

The effect of the Statute of Frauds is to make certain types of contracts unenforceable unless they are in writing. Despite the fact that an oral contract is otherwise valid, if it falls within the Statute, it is unenforceable; neither party may sue on the contract. We shall discuss the effects of the Statute in more detail later in this chapter.

Parties to oral contracts are often able to avoid their obligations solely because these contracts have been held to come within the scope of the Statute: the contracts might be perfectly valid in every other respect. It has often been said that by defeating the reasonable expectations of parties, the Statute of Frauds promotes more frauds than it prevents. For this reason the courts have tried to limit the application of the Statute wherever possible. The results have not always been logical, but the application of the Statute has certainly been restricted by exceptions.

The problem of deciding whether a contract is affected by the Statute of Frauds arises only when an otherwise valid contract has been made. The mere fact that a promise is in writing as required by the Statute does not make the promise binding. There is no contract even to be considered unless all the requirements for the formation of a contract, as discussed in earlier chapters, are met.

THE TYPES OF CONTRACT AFFECTED BY THE STATUTE OF FRAUDS

The types of contract selected in the 17th century do not make much sense to us today. For example, the first class of contract listed, "A promise by an executor or administrator to answer damages out of his own estate," rarely occurs. An executor or administrator of an estate may find that a debt owed by the deceased is due, but it is not yet practical for him to pay it out of the estate assets. A creditor may press him to pay the debt from his own resources (later to be reimbursed from the estate) rather than merely give a promise to pay from the estate assets. If the executor or administrator should make a promise to pay the debt himself, the creditor will be unable to enforce it unless it is in writing.

A Promise to Answer for the Debt, Default, or Miscarriage of Another

Distinction Between Guarantee and Indemnity

guarantee
a conditional promise to pay only if the debtor defaults

indemnity
a promise by a third party to be primarily liable to pay the debt

In order to limit the application of the Statute, the courts have narrowed the definition of a promise "to answer for the debt, default, or miscarriage of another." They distinguish between two similar types of promises, a promise of **guarantee** and a promise of **indemnity**. A guarantee is a conditional promise to pay only if the debtor defaults: "If he does not pay you, I will." The creditor must look first to the debtor for payment, and only after the debtor has defaulted may the creditor claim payment from the guarantor.

In contrast, a person who makes a promise to indemnify a creditor makes herself *primarily* liable to pay the debt. Accordingly, when the debt falls due, the creditor may ignore its claim against the original debtor and sue the person who gave the promise to indemnify. "Give him the goods and I will see to it that you are paid," would usually be a promise to indemnify.[4] A promise by a purchaser of a business to its employees to pay back wages owed by the former owner would be a promise to indemnify.

---

4. As Furmston points out in *Cheshire, Fifoot and Furmston's Law of Contract*, 13th ed., at 212, it is the intention of the parties and not their language that determines whether the promise is a guarantee or an indemnity.

The courts have applied this part of the Statute of Frauds *only* to guarantees. A guarantee must be made in writing to be enforceable, but a promise to indemnify is outside the Statute and is enforceable without being in writing.

Subsidiary Promises of Guarantee

Even the class of guarantees that falls within the Statute has been narrowed: the courts have excluded those guarantees incidental to a larger contract where the element of guarantee is only one among a number of more important rights and duties created by the contract.

CASE 10.1

Sutton & Co. were stockbrokers and members of the London Stock Exchange with access to its facilities. Grey was not a member, but he had contacts with prospective investors. The parties made an oral agreement by which Grey was to receive half the commission from transactions for his clients completed through Sutton and was to pay half of any bad debts that might develop out of the transactions.

When a loss resulted from one of the transactions and Grey refused to pay his half, Sutton & Co. sued him. Grey pleaded that his promise to pay half the loss was a guarantee and was not enforceable against him because it was not in writing. The court ruled that the whole arrangement between Sutton and Grey had been a much broader one than merely guaranteeing the payment of a debt owing by a particular client, and that the Statute of Frauds should not apply. Accordingly, the agreement was enforceable, and Sutton & Co. obtained judgment against Grey for half the loss.[5]

Amendments to the Statute of Frauds

In amending the Statute of Frauds in recent years, England and British Columbia have retained the requirement of writing for contracts of guarantee. In addition, British Columbia has done away with the judge-made distinction between indemnity and guarantee by requiring that both types of promise be in writing.[6]

The Meaning of "Miscarriage"

In contrast to the restricted meaning given to the words "debt" and "default," the courts have given the word "miscarriage" a fairly wide meaning. They have interpreted a promise to "answer for the **miscarriage** of another" to mean "to pay damages for loss caused by the tort of another person," for example, by that person's negligence or fraud. Accordingly, to be enforceable, the promise "I will pay you for the injury *B* caused you if *B* doesn't settle with you" must be in writing. On the other hand, the promise "I will pay you for the injury *B* caused you if you will give up absolutely any rights you have against *B*" is a promise of indemnity and need not be in writing to be enforceable.[7]

miscarriage
an injury caused by the tort of another person

An Agreement Made in Consideration of Marriage

This section has always been interpreted as applying not to a promise to marry but to such related matters as arrangements about assets brought into a marriage as common property. The section has been replaced in all provinces by extensive family law reform legislation that recognizes a wide variety of enforceable arrangements in marriage and in cohabitation relations.[8] The legislation does

---

5. *Sutton & Co.* v. *Grey*, [1894] 1 Q.B. 285; *Bassie* v. *Melnychuk* (1993), 14 Alta. L.R. (3d) 31.
6. Law Reform (Enforcement of Contracts) Act, 1954, 2 & 3 Eliz. 2, c. 34, s. 1 (U.K.), and Statute of Frauds, R.S.B.C. 1996, c. 128, s. 48.
7. *Kirkham* v. *Marter* (1819), 106 E.R. 490; *Read* v. *Nash* (1751), 95 E.R. 632.
8. For example: Family Relations Act, R.S.B.C. 1996, c. 128, s. 61; Family Law Act, R.S.O. 1990, c. F.3, s. 52; Matrimonial Property Act, R.S.N.S. 1989, c. 275, s. 23.

require that these arrangements, since they are expected to apply to relationships over a long time, be in writing to be enforceable. Independent legal advice is another common requirement.

A Contract Concerning an Interest in Land

This provision is still regarded as necessary to protect interests in property. The special qualities of land, in particular its virtual indestructibility and permanence, make it important to be able to ascertain the various outstanding interests and claims against land. It is essential to have verified written records of transactions affecting interests in land, and these records must be available over many years for inspection by interested persons. And so we have systems of public records where interested parties may "search" and discover who owns or claims to own the interests in land.

Still, we must distinguish between contracts concerning land to which the Statute applies and others considered to be too remotely connected with land to be under the Statute. The courts have held that agreements to repair or build a house, or to obtain room and board, are outside the Statute, while agreements to permit taking water from a well, to lease any land, house, or other building, or even a portion of a building, are within the Statute. Landlord and tenant statutes make oral residential leases enforceable. We discuss the enforceability of leases again in Chapter 24.

England and British Columbia have retained the requirement of writing for contracts concerning interests in land.[9]

An Agreement Not to Be Performed by Either Party Within One Year

The purpose of this provision seems clear enough: Memories may fail over a long period and so Parliament chose an arbitrary one-year limit. Unfortunately, the choice of any definite cut-off date in itself creates difficulties. The injustice of denying enforcement of a contract lasting a year plus a day quickly became evident to the judges.

Once more they tried to cut down the effect of the Statute by holding that it did not apply to a contract, though it might well extend beyond a year, unless the terms of the contract specified a time for performance clearly longer than a year. The effect of this ruling is to exclude from the Statute contracts for an *indefinite* period.

ILLUSTRATION 10.1

Ajax Co. Ltd. hires Singh as a supervisor for setting up an electronic data-processing system without specifying a schedule. Although the parties expect the project to take longer than a year, it is not certain to do so. Accordingly, their oral contract is outside the Statute and need not be in writing.

On the other hand, if a contract is, by its terms, to extend beyond one year, it is governed by the Statute even though those terms state that it may be brought to an end in less than one year.

ILLUSTRATION 10.2

In an oral contract, the Trojan Co. Ltd. has hired Bergsen as general manager for two years, provided that either party may bring the contract to an end by giving three months' notice to the other. Bergsen has been working for the company for some months when he receives one month's notice of dismissal. He will be unable to enforce the term entitling him to three months' notice.

9. Law of Property Act, 1925, 15 & 16 Geo. 5, c. 20, s. 40 (U.K.), and Law and Equity Act, R.S.B.C. 1996, c. 253, as amended by Law Reform Amendment Act, S.B.C. 1985, c. 110, s. 7.

The courts have also held that the Statute does not apply even though *one* party will necessarily require more than a year to perform, provided that the contract also shows an intention that the other party will wholly perform within a year.

ILLUSTRATION 10.3

Grigorian agrees to repair promptly a leaking roof on Brown's warehouse for $15 000, with $5000 to be paid on completion of the repairs, plus $10 000 in two annual instalments of $5000 each. Grigorian completes the repairs within five weeks. At the end of the year Brown refuses to pay the first instalment, claiming that their oral agreement is unenforceable because payment could not be wholly performed within one year. Even so, Grigorian can enforce the contract. The court again excludes the Statute where it can find the slimmest reason for doing so, in this case because the parties intended that one of them, Grigorian, should complete performance within a year, and did so.

Where the obligations of one party clearly extend beyond one year, the intention that the other should wholly perform within one year must be clear from the terms of the contract or from the surrounding circumstances: it is not enough that the party *might* perform within one year. Therefore, an oral promise by *A* to pay *B* a sum of money in three years' time if *B* will tutor *A*'s daughter in accounting until she obtains a professional qualification will not be enforceable, unless it can clearly be shown from the surrounding circumstances that the tutoring was to be done within a few weeks or months and not to continue beyond one year.

The provision of the Statute of Frauds concerning agreements not to be performed within one year illustrates better than any other how far the courts have gone to prevent the Statute from working an injustice. They cannot always avoid the Statute, however, and injustice results when the plaintiff fails only because the Statute of Frauds bars him. Amending the Statute, as British Columbia has done, would alleviate this problem in other provinces.

Ratification of Infants' Contracts

Contracts requiring ratification by infants upon coming of age (that is, contracts that are not for a permanent interest in property) must in some jurisdictions be ratified in writing to be enforceable.[10] The requirement of writing does not, however, apply to the class of minors' contracts that are valid unless rejected: for these contracts, merely acquiescing is sufficient to bind infants after coming of age.

REQUIREMENTS FOR A WRITTEN MEMORANDUM

Suppose that a contract falls clearly within the scope of the Statute of Frauds. What must the memorandum contain to satisfy the Statute and permit a party to maintain an action upon the contract? The Statute requires a "note or memorandum" of the contract "signed by the party to be charged" or the party's authorized agent.

By the 1980s, courts had to consider whether newer forms of transmitting documents such as facsimile (or fax) satisfy the statutory requirement of being in "writing." Subsequent decisions of

---

10. See, for example: Statute of Frauds, R.S.O. 1990, c. S.19, s. 7; R.S.N.S. 1989, c. 442, s. 9; see also Chapter 8 of this book.

Canadian courts have assumed that facsimile transmissions are sufficient to satisfy the writing requirement of the Statute of Frauds.[11] The rapidly growing field of electronic commerce has had an even greater impact on the traditional statutory requirements of writing for commercial transactions. However, these amendments to statute law are in transition, and it remains important to be aware of the traditional writing requirements in order to comprehend the nature and effects of the changes described in Chapter 34 under the heading "Formal Requirements."

All Essential Terms Must Be Included

The memorandum must contain all the essential terms of the contract, including the identity of the parties. If the contract is for the sale of land, for example, the memorandum must name the parties, adequately describe the subject-matter (the land), and set out the consideration to be given for it.

CASE 10.2

Wayne and Janet Gretzky made a written offer to purchase a cottage property including a main house, guest house, and a two-storey boat house for $1 860 000. All the terms and conditions were acceptable to the vendor except the date for vacant possession of the boat house. The offer was rejected and a counter-offer was made. At this point, oral discussions took place between the various agents and their clients and a mutually agreeable date was established. However, the new terms were not placed in the agreement and no written memorandum of the boat house possession term was made. Subsequently, the vendors declined to complete the deal and the Gretzkys sued. The court found that vacant possession of the boat house was obviously an important issue between the parties and therefore it was an essential term. The contract failed to satisfy the Statute of Frauds and was unenforceable. The Gretzkys did not get the cottage.[12]

The Statute of Frauds makes an exception for contracts of guarantee by stating that the consideration for that type of promise need not appear in the writing.[13]

The memorandum need not be wholly within a single document; several written notes may be taken together to satisfy the requirements of the Statute. No problem arises when one or more of the documents refer directly to the others. The plaintiff will have considerably more trouble if there are no cross-references within the documents. The courts have gone as far as to hear evidence that a signed letter beginning with "Dear Sir" was contained in a particular envelope that bore the name and address of the plaintiff, and in this way to link the two pieces of paper as a sufficient memorandum.[14] The court justified its decision on the grounds that even without oral evidence, it could reasonably assume that the letter was delivered in an envelope: it admitted oral evidence merely to identify the envelope. On this basis, the court did not have to rely solely on

---

11. See *Rolling* v. *William Investments* (1989), 63 D.L.R. (4th) 760. The Ontario Court of Appeal decided that a facsimile transmission of acceptance of an option was a satisfactory acceptance, even though when the parties made the agreement in 1974, they "could not have anticipated delivery of a facsimile of the [accepted] offer by means of a telephone transmission. . . ." The court concluded:

> Where technological advances have been made which facilitate communications and expedite transmission of documents we see no reason why they should not be utilized. Indeed, they should be encouraged and approved. . . . [The defendant] suffered no prejudice by reason of the procedure followed.

12. *Hunter* v. *Baluke* (1998), 42 O.R. (3d) 553 (Ont. S.C.J.)

13. See, for example: R.S.O. 1990, c. S.19, s. 6; R.S.N.S. 1989, c. 442, s. 8.

14. *Pearce* v. *Gardner*, [1897] 1 Q.B. 688; *Harvie and Hawryluk* v. *Gibbons* (1980), 12 Alta. L.R. (2d) 72.

the testimony of the parties—something it rarely, if ever, will agree to do. In the words of Baron Blackburn:

> If the contents of the signed paper themselves make reference to the others so as to show by internal evidence that the papers refer to each other, they may be all taken together as one memorandum in writing . . . but if it is necessary, in order to connect them, to give evidence of the intention of the parties that they should be connected, shown by circumstances not apparent on the face of the writings, the memorandum is not all in writing, for it consists partly of the contents of the writings and partly of the expression of an intention to unite them and that expression is not in writing.[15]

ILLUSTRATION 10.4

A wrote to *B* on May 4 offering to pay $2000 for *B*'s computer and at the same time stating the terms in detail. *B* wrote back in a signed letter addressed to *A*, "I will accept your offer of May 4." The agreement is enforceable by either party. The two letters may be taken together as providing the necessary written evidence because they relate to each other and contain all the necessary terms.

Signed by the Defendant

The Statute requires that the note or memorandum be signed by the party to be charged—the defendant—and only that person, not the plaintiff. The plaintiff's own signature is irrelevant; if the defendant has not signed, the plaintiff's signature on the document does not help and he cannot enforce the contract against the other party.

The courts have been lenient in prescribing what amounts to a sufficient signature; it need not be in the handwriting of the defendant. A printed name will suffice as long as it is intended to validate the whole of the document. For example, a letterhead on an invoice is designed to verify the sale of the goods described below without a signature and is sufficient. E-commerce legislation now expands the notion of signature to include electronic signatures, as will be discussed in Chapter 34.

THE EFFECT OF THE STATUTE ON CONTRACTS WITHIN ITS SCOPE

What do we mean when we say that the Statute of Frauds makes an oral contract unenforceable? The courts recognize that an **unenforceable contract** still exists even though neither of the parties is able to obtain a remedy under it through court action. Is this not the same as saying it is void? The answer is a definite "no," for although no action may be brought on the contract itself, it may still affect the legal relations between the parties in several ways.

unenforceable contract
a contract that still exists for other purposes but neither party may obtain a remedy under it through court action

Recovery of Money Paid Under a Contract

First, both parties to an unenforceable contract may, of course, choose to perform under it, but if they do not, recovery of any down payment made will depend upon which party repudiates the contract.

---

15. Blackburn, *A Treatise on the Effect of the Contract of Sale* (London: W. Benning & Co., 1845) at 47, as quoted in *North Staffordshire Railway Co.* v. *Peek* (1863), 120 E.R. 777, per Williams, J., at 782.

ILLUSTRATION 10.5

P orally agrees to buy Blackacre from *V* for $50 000 and gives a down payment of $5000, the balance to be paid in 30 days.

Suppose that *P* then sees a more suitable property and refuses to pay the balance. The Statute of Frauds applies and *V*

cannot enforce the contract. On the other hand, *P* cannot by court action require *V* to return the payment. Although the contract is unenforceable, it is still valid and existing: *V* may retain the payment by claiming that it was properly owing and was paid under the contract.

ILLUSTRATION 10.6

Suppose instead it is *V* who refuses either to complete the sale or to return the payment. *P* can sue successfully for the

return of the payment. The court in these circumstances will not permit *V* to repudiate the contract and yet keep the payment received under its terms.

In the above illustrations we can see that the court will not permit the party who repudiates the contract to gain a further advantage, in Illustration 10.5 by allowing *P* to recover her payment after her own breach, and in Illustration 10.6 by permitting *V* to retain *P*'s payment after his breach. If the contract were found instead to be void, the problem of breach would not arise: there cannot be a "breach" of a void contract. For example, if the contract had been void for, say, uncertainty (so that the requirement of offer and acceptance was not met), *P* could recover her payment whether it was she or *V* who refused to complete the transaction.

Recovery for Goods and Services

Second, a party who has accepted goods and services under a contract that is unenforceable because of the Statute is not permitted to retain the benefit received without paying for it.

ILLUSTRATION 10.7

In an oral agreement, *A* promised to do certain work for *B* over 18 months, and *B* promised to pay *A* $60 000 on completion. Since the contract would not be performed by either party within one year, it would be "caught" (affected) by the Statute. Before *A* began work, *B* could repudiate with impunity and *A* would have no right to sue *B*.

However, if after *A* had started working, *B* repudiated and refused to give *A* access to *B*'s premises where the work was being done, *A* could sue *B* *quantum meruit* for the value of the work done to that point. Although *B* could still repudiate the oral contract (and *A* would have no right to enforce the contract in court), *B* had nevertheless requested the work to be done and would be liable to pay a reasonable price for it, as was explained in Chapter 6.

ILLUSTRATION 10.8

Suppose that under the oral agreement in Illustration 10.7, *A* completed the work as agreed, with *B*'s acquiescence. The court would view *B*'s original promise to pay for the work as a continuing offer of a unilateral contract, which *A* accepted by completing performance. No contract was formed until *A* actually completed performance, but at that moment the price became immediately payable.

In this view of the facts, the contract is clearly completed in less than a year after its formation—completion of the

work—and it is not caught by the Statute. *A* could, therefore, sue *B* successfully for the agreed price of $60 000—another example of the lengths to which the courts will go in their reasoning to prevent the Statute from working an injustice. We should also note that the agreed price would bind both parties, as it would in any enforceable contract. *A* could not refuse *B*'s tender of $60 000 and sue *quantum meruit* simply because *A* believed the work to be worth more than the agreed price. The enforceable oral contract, now outside the Statute, governs the price *A* may recover.

Effect of a Subsequent Written Memorandum

Third, a written memorandum may come into existence *after* the contract has been formed and the memorandum will still satisfy the Statute. As long as the memorandum comes into existence before the action is brought on the contract, it provides the necessary evidence.

ILLUSTRATION 10.9

P agrees orally to buy Blackacre from *V*. *P* then refuses to complete the contract, and *V* sends her a letter outlining the contract and demanding that she carry out her obligations. *P* replies by letter saying that she has decided not to go through

with the contract referred to in *V*'s letter and that she is not bound since the contract is not in writing. Even though the statements in *P*'s letter were intended to deny liability, the two letters taken together would amount to a sufficient memorandum to satisfy the Statute and make the contract enforceable.

Defendant Must Expressly Plead the Statute

Fourth, a defendant who is sued upon an oral contract must expressly plead the Statute as a defence to the action. If he fails to plead it, the court will decide the case without reference to the Statute. The plaintiff will then succeed if he establishes that the contract, though oral, was validly formed.

ETHICAL ISSUE

Injustice

The Statute of Frauds was passed during a particular period in history and was meant to deal with problems arising in that time. Over the three centuries since it was passed, the courts have seen injustices created by the application of a statute intended to prevent injustice. They have gone to considerable lengths to limit the Statute and soften its impact. Their efforts have created a confusing and seemingly contradictory set of exceptions and qualifications.

The reluctance of the courts to enforce this statute demonstrates the complicated relationship between the two law-making bodies (courts and legislature) when it comes to setting policy.

QUESTIONS TO CONSIDER

1. Is it ethical to allow individuals to avoid responsibility for obligations only because of a technical inadequacy?

2. Alternatively, is it ethical to force a party to honour an obligation that the Statute of Frauds declares unenforceable just because that party failed to mention the Statute?

3. Should a court be free to ignore a statute that appears to be outdated or unjust?

Effect on a Prior Written Contract

Fifth, an oral contract may effectively vary or dissolve a prior written contract even though the oral contract could not itself be enforced. An oral contract within the Statute is effective as long as a party does not have to bring an action to have it enforced.

ILLUSTRATION 10.10

P agrees to buy Roselawn from V under a written contract containing a promise by V to give vacant possession on a certain day. V then has unexpected difficulty in removing his tenants and tells P that he will not be able to give vacant possession. P finds another property equally suitable to her and available with vacant possession. Rather than get into a dispute, the parties make a mutual oral agreement to call off the contract: P releases V from his promise to transfer Roselawn with vacant possession in return for a release by V of P's promise to pay the purchase price. Afterwards V succeeds in removing his tenants and sues P to enforce the original written contract. P may successfully plead that the subsequent oral contract validly terminated the written contract.

However, the oral contract cannot be sued upon directly. Suppose that in addition to terminating the prior contract V had orally agreed to give P an option on another property in settlement of V's default in not giving vacant possession. Although the oral contract effectively dissolved the prior written contract, P could not sue upon the promise to give an option because otherwise the court would be enforcing an oral promise for an interest in land.[16]

Only the Party Who Has Signed Can Be Sued

Finally, as we have seen, a party to a contract who has signed a memorandum can be sued, but she cannot sue the other party who has not signed a memorandum; if the contract were void, neither party would have any rights under it.

THE DOCTRINE OF PART PERFORMANCE

part performance
performance begun by a plaintiff in reliance on an oral contract relating to an interest in land, and accepted by the courts as evidence of the contract in place of a written memorandum

We have seen how the courts have struggled to cut down the scope of the Statute of Frauds, severely limiting the circumstances in which it would apply. Nevertheless, in the common law courts even strict interpretation did not prevent the Statute from thwarting a large number of contracts. The courts of equity were prepared to go further than the common law courts to enforce contracts concerning interests in land. Plaintiffs often sued in equity because of the courts' special power to grant the remedy of specific performance when they felt the circumstances warranted it.[17] Shortly after the Statute of Frauds was passed, the courts of equity developed and applied the doctrine of **part performance** to contracts concerning land: if the plaintiff could show that he had begun performance of the contract in reliance on it, the court would accept that performance as evidence of the contract in place of a written memorandum. Our modern courts still employ the doctrine in cases concerning an interest in land.

Not every act of performance under a contract qualifies as a substitute for a written memorandum. The following conditions must be satisfied before the court will enforce the contract:

(a) The contract must be one concerning land.
(b) The acts of performance must suggest quite clearly the existence of a contract respecting the land in question; they must not be ambiguous and just as readily explained as part of a quite different transaction. In Canada, a payment of a deposit on the price of land, by itself, while certainly an act of part performance, is not a sufficient substitute for writing: the payment could refer to almost any kind of contract between the parties—such as a

---

16. See *Morris* v. *Baron*, [1918] A.C. 1 for a similar result.
17. See Chapter 2 and Chapter 15.

contract for the sale of goods or services.[18] (Illustration 10.6 shows that the purchaser may at least obtain the return of the deposit.) However, if a plaintiff has taken possession of the land with the acquiescence of the defendant and has begun to make improvements on it, the court considers this a sufficient act of part performance to satisfy the Statute. It would be extraordinary for an owner to allow a stranger to enter on his land and make improvements unless there was a contract in relation to the land to explain this behaviour.

(c) The plaintiff, not the defendant, must perform the acts, and must suffer a loss by the performance if the contract is not enforced. The plaintiff's performance in reliance on the oral contract and the defendant's refusal to carry out the contract combine to create a hardship that equity recognizes and seeks to remedy.[19]

Once an act of part performance is accepted by the court as sufficient evidence, the contract will be enforced. Even though the act of part performance does not disclose all the terms of the contract, the court will enforce the contract according to the terms orally agreed.

CASE 10.3

Brownscombe entered into an oral contract with an ailing farmer. Brownscombe agreed to work the farm provided that he would inherit the farm when the farmer died. Brownscombe laboured for 26 years on the farm for only nominal financial payment. When the farmer died there was no will leaving the property to Brownscombe. The Supreme Court of Canada held that working for low wages alone would not satisfy the part performance test. However, the fact that Brownscombe spent his own money to build a house on the farm at the suggestion of the farmer was conduct that met the part performance test. It was conduct inequitably referable to a sale agreement and inconsistent with an employment or tenancy relationship. Brownscombe was entitled to enforce the oral contract.[20]

In Case 10.2, Gretzky did not convince the court that payment of the deposit combined with waiver of the other conditions in the contract amounted to part performance.[21]

INTERNATIONAL ISSUE

Should the Statute of Frauds Be Repealed?

The Statute of Frauds was passed over three centuries ago and it has been argued that the historical reasons for creating the Statute of Frauds no longer exist. In Canada, more detailed consumer protection writing requirements nullify its impact. As previously noted, the Statute has been repealed (for example, in Manitoba) or amended (for example, in Ontario and British Columbia) in some common law jurisdictions. Perhaps it is time to replace or amend it throughout Canada. When the province of Ontario amended its Sale of Goods Act to remove the writing requirements (see note 23, below), it did so for the express purpose of facilitating electronic commerce.

continued

18. See *Ross* v. *Ross, Jr. et al.* (1973), 33 D.L.R. (3d) 351; *Brownscombe* v. *Public Trustee of Alberta*, [1969] S.C.R. 658; *Booth* v. *Knibb Developments Ltd.*, 2002 ABCA 180; *Varma* v. *Donaldson*, 2008 ABQB 106. Canada adheres to a strict interpretation of the part performance test despite the fact that in England, it is sufficient that the acts of part performance merely indicate the existence of a contract: *Steadman* v. *Steadman*, [1976] A.C. 536.

19. See *Thompson* v. *Guaranty Trust Co. of Canada*, [1974] S.C.R. 1023. The plaintiff had worked the farm of the deceased for over 40 years, receiving practically no remuneration during that time. On several occasions the deceased had stated to third persons that everything would go to the plaintiff if he remained with the deceased. The Supreme Court found that the years of work put in by the plaintiff were sufficient part performance to satisfy the Statute of Frauds.

20. *Brownscombe* v. *Public trustee of Province of Alberta*, *supra* n. 18.

21. *Supra note* 12, at para. 64–75.

On the other hand, consider this statement from Mr. Justice Côté of the Alberta Court of Appeal:

> Over 20 years ago, it was fashionable to attack the Statute of Frauds, and indeed a number of jurisdictions have repealed large chunks of it. But Alberta has not touched s. 4. In my view, the trend of modern legislation is actually to call for more writing in contracts and commercial transactions. The idea that one can validly sell a valuable piece of land entirely by oral discussions runs contrary to the expectations of most lay people; one can almost say that absence of writing casts into doubt intention to create binding legal relations. So I feel no compulsion to undermine the Statute.

Interestingly, provincial electronic commerce legislation like the Ontario Electronic Commerce Act addresses the issues of writing and signatures in electronic documents, not by avoiding the effect of legislation like the Statute of Frauds, but by seeking practical equivalents to those requirements in forming a contract.

Internationally, the trend may be different. Civil law jurisdictions, such as France, never had the Statute of Frauds. Even common law countries are moving away from writing requirements. England has repealed most of the Statute of Frauds. Article 11 of the *United Nations Convention on Contracts for the International Sale of Goods* reads:

> A contract for sale need not be concluded in or evidenced by writing and is not subject to any other requirements as to form. It may be proved by any means including witnesses.[22]

QUESTIONS TO CONSIDER

1. How are business relationships and commercial activity affected by complex legal rules about the enforceability of oral contracts?

2. Are there sound policy reasons for requiring some contracts to be in writing?

3. Are amendments adequate to address the problems arising from the Statute of Frauds, or would it be better to repeal the Statute and replace it with legislation that meets contemporary needs?

4. Can the Statute of Frauds co-exist with e-commerce legislation?

Sources: *Austie* v. *Aksnowicz*, [1999] 10 W.W.R. 713, 70 Alta. L.R. (3d) 154 (C.A.), at para. 55; Law Reform Commission of British Columbia, *Report on the Statute of Frauds* (1997), available online at www.bcli.org/pages/publications/lrcreports/reports(html)/Lrc33text.html; Manitoba Law Reform Commission, *Report on the Statute of Frauds* (1980); University of Alberta Institute of Law Research and Reform, *Background Paper No. 12: Statute of Frauds* (1979); *Report No. 44* (1985); S.O. 2000, c.17.

REQUIREMENTS OF THE SALE OF GOODS ACT

Until 1893, a provision of the English Statute of Frauds required as evidence of contracts for the sale of goods priced at £10 or more, either a written memorandum or one of three types of conduct. In that year, the provision was repealed and replaced by a similar one in the new Sale of Goods Act. When the Canadian provinces adopted the Sale of Goods Act, they followed the English example.

In 1954, when the English Parliament amended the Statute of Frauds, it also repealed the section in the Sale of Goods Act requiring special types of evidence to enforce contracts for the sale of

---

22. (1980), www.uncitral.org/pdf/english/texts/sales/cisg/CISG.pdf.

interest deprives her of the ability to reach an objective conclusion about that meaning: she needs unbiased advice. A court, in searching for the objective meaning of words, seeks the advice of the mythical reasonable person—the informed, objective bystander. The business person's closest, if imperfect, substitute for this legendary figure[7] must be her lawyer. If she finds her interpretation of a contract challenged, she should immediately obtain legal advice. By doing so she will have the benefit of an unbiased external opinion when it will be of most help to her. Her protection will be twofold: if her interpretation of the contract is correct, she will learn how best to enforce it; if it is incorrect, she may avoid a costly breach of contract.

The Goal of the Courts: To Give Validity to Contracts

Courts must make decisions, difficult though they may be. Frequently, it may seem easier for them to declare an agreement unenforceable because its wording is ambiguous; but if they took this attitude, the courts would not be performing their role of encouraging reliance on seriously made agreements. Instead, they lean towards keeping an agreement alive rather than brushing it aside as not binding. If at all possible, courts assign to ambiguous words a meaning that makes a contract enforceable. Lord Wright, one of the most respected of English judges in commercial law, gave a classic statement of the rule in a House of Lords decision:

> The object of the court is to do justice between the parties, and the court will do its best, if satisfied that there was an ascertainable and determinate intention to contract, to give effect to that intention, looking at substance and not mere form. It will not be deterred by mere difficulties of interpretation. Difficulty is not synonymous with ambiguity, so long as any definite meaning can be extracted.[8]

INTERNATIONAL ISSUE

Interpreting International Contracts

International contracts involve parties and issues from different countries and this can complicate the resolution of "interpretation" disputes. Two common strategies to encourage smooth resolution are standardized language and a clear choice of law.

First, adopting standardized language will reduce the likelihood of disputes. The International Chamber of Commerce developed 13 terms, known as "Incoterms," which are now in wide use around the world. They are designed to ensure a common understanding of risk allocation during the transportation and delivery of goods. For example, FOB (free on board) means the seller must clear the goods through customs and load the goods on the purchaser's chosen ship. Once the goods are on the ship, they are at the risk of the purchaser.

Second, it is imperative that international contracts contain a clause stating the choice of law. This clause designates the law that will be applied to resolve any future disputes. It is common to designate the law of one of the parties' countries and this will include the country's rules of interpretation.

Increasingly, however, parties are designating a neutral body of principles as the criteria to determine the dispute. One such body of principles is the *UNIDROIT Principles of International Commercial Contracts*. The principles represent a consolidation of the general rules of contract law. They are not associated with any one nation but were designed after considering of a number of

continued

---

7. For an amusing account of all the attributes of the "reasonable person," see A.P. Herbert, *Uncommon Law* (London: Methuen & Co., 1948), in the fictitious case of *Fardell* v. *Potts*.

8. *Scammel* v. *Ouston*, [1941] 1 All E.R. 14 at 25.

countries' laws, including the United States Uniform Commercial Code and the Quebec Civil Code. Chapter 4 of the Principles of Commercial Contracts specifically addresses interpretation issues and adopts a number of principles that we have considered, including:

Article 4.6 Contra Proferentem

If contract terms supplied by one party are unclear, an interpretation against that party is preferred.

Chapter 4 also includes rules focused on the international environment:

Article 4.7 Linguistic Discrepancies

Where a contract is drawn up in two or more language versions which are equally authoritative, there is, in case of discrepancy between the versions, a preference for the interpretation according to a version in which the contract was originally drawn up.

QUESTIONS TO CONSIDER

1. What would be the rationale for selecting a neutral body of principles rather than the law of a particular country?

2. Do you see anything contradictory between articles 4.6 and 4.7?

Sources: M.J. Bonell, "The UNIDROIT Principles of International Commercial Contracts and the Principles of European Contract Law: Similar Rules for the Same Purposes?" 26 *Uniform Law Review* (1996) 229–246, www.cisg.law.pace.edu/cisg/biblio/bonell96.html; International Institute for the Unification of Private Law (UNIDROIT), *UNIDROIT Principles of International Commercial Contracts 2004*, www.unidroit.org/english/principles/contracts/principles2004/blackletter2004.pdf; International Chamber of Commerce, *Incoterms*, www.iccwbo.org/incoterms/id3040/index.html.

THE PAROL EVIDENCE RULE

The Meaning of the Rule

Before a deal is made, the parties very often spend time bargaining and negotiating, making offers and counter-offers, with both sides making concessions until finally they reach a suitable compromise. The bargaining may be carried on orally or in writing. In important contracts, the parties usually put their final agreement into a more formal document signed by both sides. A party may later discover that the formal document does not contain one or more terms she believed were part of the agreement. The omission may have been due to a mistake in writing down the terms actually agreed upon—a typing error, for example. The equitable remedy of rectification, as explained in Chapter 8, may then be available.

parol evidence rule
a rule preventing a party to a contract from later adding a term previously agreed upon but not included in the final written contract

When, however, there is no clear evidence that a term was omitted by error, she will be held to the contract as it is written. According to the **parol evidence rule**, a party cannot later add a term previously agreed upon between the parties but not included in the final form of the contract. In this context the word "parol" means *extrinsic to* or *outside of* the written agreement.[9] The rule applies both to an oral agreement that has been reduced to writing and to a written agreement that has been set out in a more formal document.

---

9. For a more extensive discussion of the meaning of the parol evidence rule, see R. Cross and C. Tapper, *Cross on Evidence*, 9th ed. (London: Butterworths, 1999) at 651ff; John D.McCamus, *The Law of Contracts*,(Toronto: Irwin Law, 2005) at 193–207.

The parol evidence rule operates to exclude terms that one party claims should be added to the contract. It does not exclude evidence about the formation of the contract such as its legality, the capacity of the parties, mistake, duress, undue influence, or fraud. In other words, it does not affect evidence of any of the circumstances surrounding the contract: it operates only to exclude the addition of terms not found in the written document. As an example, we have seen that a court will admit oral evidence to prove that one of the parties made a material misrepresentation.

The Consequences of the Rule

Sometimes parties agree to omit a term from the final form of the contract, still intending it to be part of their whole agreement. They are most likely to do so when they are using a standard form contract, such as a conditional sale agreement, a short-term lease, a mortgage, or a grant of land. One party may persuade the other to leave a term out because it will be confusing or because his employer may object to it.

ILLUSTRATION 11.2

Sung offers to lease a computer system to Jeans, Inc., a small but prosperous manufacturer. An attractive part of the deal for Jeans is the promise by Sung that her firm will provide without charge a new software program for inventory and accounts receivable records. Sung explains that the contract contains no reference to this new software program because it is in its final stage of development and has yet to be publicly announced; her firm plans to introduce it with an advertising campaign.

Jeans' manager signs the contract without a term referring to the provision of the new software. The equipment is delivered several weeks later along with the promised program, but the program does not function properly and proves to be a failure.

Jeans, Inc. would be unlikely to succeed in an action against Sung's firm for breach of her oral promise. It is doubtful that Jeans would be entitled to rescission for misrepresentation since Sung did not state as a fact that the program was fully developed and available at the time the contract was formed.

The courts have been reluctant to relax the parol evidence rule even in circumstances where a party suffers hardship; they fear that to do so would tempt parties who are unhappy with their contracts to claim that favourable terms—discussed during negotiations but not agreed upon—are part of their contracts. The courts worry that they would create serious difficulties for the business community if they showed any tendency to upset written agreements deliberately made. For this reason, it is unwise to allow any term of importance to be omitted from the final written form of an agreement. If the term is important and the other side insists on excluding it from the final document, it is better to break off negotiations than to enter into the contract with that term excluded.

The Scope of the Rule

Does the Document Contain the Whole Contract?

We have seen that once the parties have reduced their agreement to a document in its final form, the parol evidence rule precludes either party from adding terms not in that final agreement. While at first sight the rule seems to apply, sometimes the court may find that the written document was not intended to embody the whole contract. In Chapter 10, we learned that the terms of a contract may be partly in writing and partly oral; if a party can show that the writing was not intended to contain the whole contract but was merely a part of it, then she may introduce evidence of those oral terms.[10]

---

10. *DeLasalle* v. *Guilford*, [1901] 2 K.B. 215, shows the lengths to which the courts will go in avoiding the parol evidence rule on these grounds. See also *Gallen* v. *Allstate Grain Co.* (1984), 9 D.L.R. (4th) 496, for a comprehensive review of the exceptions to the rule. For a contrasting view, see *Norman Estate* v. *Norman*, [1990] B.C.J. No. 199 (B.C.S.C.).

ILLUSTRATION 11.3

A, the owner of a fleet of dump trucks, agrees orally with *B*, a paving contractor, to move 3000 cubic metres of gravel within three months from Harrowsmith to Yarker for $18 000 and to provide any related documents that *B* may require for financing the project. To finance her paving operations *B* applies for a bank loan, and the bank requests evidence that the paving work can be started immediately. *B* therefore asks *A* to sign a statement to the effect that he will deliver 1000 cubic metres of gravel from Harrowsmith to Yarker within the next month for $6000. Soon after *A* starts to make the deliveries, he discovers that he has quoted too low a price per cubic metre. He claims that his agreement with *B* has been reduced to writing and that he need move only the 1000 cubic metres of gravel referred to in the writing.

The parol evidence rule does not apply. The written document for the bank was not intended to be a complete statement of the contract. Rather, it was drawn up as part of *A*'s performance of his obligation under it. Accordingly, *B* may sue *A* for damages if *A* refuses to perform the balance of the contract, and for this purpose *B* may offer evidence of the terms of the original oral agreement.

Interpretation of the Contract

The parol evidence rule does not affect the interpretation of express terms already in a contract. As noted in the preceding section, the court does accept evidence to explain the meanings of the words used in a written contract—to determine the meaning of the word "build" in the contract to build cabinets, for example. As Justice Freedman of the Manitoba Court of Appeal put it:

> If language of the written contract is clear and unambiguous, then no extrinsic parol evidence may be admitted to alter, vary or interpret in any way the words used in the writing.... Where a contract is ambiguous, however, and that ambiguity cannot be resolved contextually within the four corners of the contract, the court may suspend the parol evidence rule and allow extrinsic evidence to be admitted.[11]

Subsequent Oral Agreement

The parol evidence rule does not exclude evidence of an oral agreement that the parties may reach after they have entered into the written agreement. The subsequent oral agreement may change the terms of the written agreement[12] or, as we saw in Chapter 10, may even rescind the prior contract altogether.[13] When such a claim is made, the court will hear evidence of a subsequent oral contract.

Collateral Agreement

collateral agreement
a separate agreement between the parties made at the same time as, but not included in, the written document

An argument often used by a party is that there was a **collateral agreement** (sometimes called a collateral term or promise)—an entirely separate undertaking agreed on by the parties but not included in their written contract, probably because the written contract seemed an inappropriate place for it. The argument is that a collateral agreement may be enforced as a separate contract quite independent of the written document. If given much weight, this argument would easily avoid the parol evidence rule. Our courts seem willing to accept such a claim only when a separate consideration can be found for the collateral promise.

---

11. *Financial Security Life Assurance. Co.*, [2005] M.J. No. 448 (Man. C.A.).

12. See *Johnson Investments* v. *Pagritide*, [1923] 2 D.L.R. 985.

13. *Morris* v. *Baron*, [1918] A.C. 1.

ILLUSTRATION 11.4

A offers to sell his residence, Rainbow End, to *B* for $90 000. *B* replies that she will buy Rainbow End for that price only if *A* repairs or replaces a damaged, electronically operated garage door; *A* agrees. The parties draw up a written contract for the sale of Rainbow End but do not mention the garage door in it because they believe they should not do so in a formal contract. *A* fails to perform his promise regarding the garage door.

The consideration for the garage door repair or replacement is the payment of the $90 000 purchase price for Rainbow End, and so the promise to include the item appears as an integral part of the contract: unless the promise is mentioned in the written agreement, it is very likely to be excluded by the parol evidence rule.

If, instead, *B* had agreed to pay *A* an extra $750 for the garage door, there would be a separate consideration for it. In effect there would be two separate contracts: a written contract for the sale of Rainbow End for $90 000 and a collateral oral contract for the repair of the garage door for $750. Because of the separate consideration, the court would very likely consider the oral agreement outside the scope of the parol evidence rule and would enforce it.

Condition Precedent

A surprising historical exception to the parol evidence rule is the recognition of a separate understanding about a condition precedent. A **condition precedent** is any set of circumstances or events that the parties stipulate must be satisfied or must happen before their contract takes effect. It may be an event beyond the control of either party, such as a requirement that a licensing board approve the transfer of a business. And it need not be in writing. If the party claiming that a condition precedent was agreed on and not met can produce evidence to support the claim, a court will recognize it despite the existence of a complete and unconditional written form of the contract, and will declare the contract void. The courts are prepared to recognize and enforce a condition precedent agreed to orally even when the subject-matter of the contract falls within the scope of the Statute of Frauds or the Sale of Goods Act.

> **condition precedent**
> any set of circumstances or events that the parties stipulate must be satisfied or must happen before their contract takes effect

ILLUSTRATION 11.5

B offers to sell a car to *A* for $14 000. *A* agrees orally to buy it provided he can persuade his bank to lend him $10 000. The parties agree orally that the contract will operate only if the bank makes the loan, and that otherwise the contract will be void. They then make a written contract in which *A* agrees to pay *B* $14 000 in 10 days, and *B* agrees to deliver the car to *A* at that time. The writing does not mention that the contract is subject to *A* obtaining the bank loan. The bank refuses to lend the money to *A*, who then informs *B* that the sale is off. *B* sues *A* for breach of contract and contends that their oral understanding about the bank loan is excluded by the parol evidence rule.

The parol evidence rule does not apply, and *B* will fail in his action. In his defence, *A* must show that there was an oral understanding suspending the contract of sale unless and until he could obtain the necessary bank loan.

The courts will admit evidence of an oral understanding about a condition precedent even when the written contract expressly states that the parties' rights and duties are governed exclusively by the written terms. Once a court accepts a contention that the parties did indeed intend to suspend the operation of their contract subject to a condition precedent, then the whole of the contract is suspended, including any term attempting to exclude the admission of such evidence. In support of this view, a court has said:

> This assertion as to the whole being in writing cannot be used as an instrument of fraud; the plaintiff cannot ignore the means by which he obtained the contract sued upon, falsify his own undertaking, and, by the help of the court, fasten an unqualified engagement on the defendant.[14]

---

14. *Long* v. *Smith* (1911), 23 O.L.R. 121, per Boyd, C., at 127.

Summary

It is not easy to convince a court that the parol evidence rule does not apply: usually, when one party has misunderstood the effect of an agreement and her later evidence about the alleged oral terms is in sharp conflict with the evidence of the other party, the court will limit the contract to the written terms. Although the rule has been relaxed recently in cases in which there is clear evidence that an orally agreed term is in conflict with the final written version,[15] it remains hazardous for a contracting party to count on the possibility of an exception to the rule. He will be taking a substantial risk either at the time a contract is being formed and put in writing or at a later time when he must decide whether to go to court over a difference of opinion about the terms of the contract.

CHECKLIST   Exceptions to the Parol Evidence Rule

A court will admit parol evidence about a missing term when
- the written agreement does not contain the whole agreement,
- the missing term is part of a subsequent oral agreement,
- the missing term is part of a collateral agreement for which there is separate consideration, or
- the missing term is a condition precedent to the written agreement.

IMPLIED TERMS AS A METHOD OF INTERPRETATION

Comparison with Interpretation of Express Terms

Parties often present the courts with disagreements that they did not foresee when they made their contract. As discussed earlier in this chapter, one approach the courts use in resolving these disagreements is to determine the most reasonable interpretation of express terms.

A second approach is to consider whether the intention of the parties can be achieved only by admitting the existence of an **implied term**—that is, a term not expressly included by the parties in their agreement but which, in the opinion of the court, they would as reasonable people have included had they thought of the possibility of the subsequent difficulty arising. A term will be implied if it is obviously necessary to accomplish the purpose of the contract.

Sometimes, the two approaches are simply different aspects of the same problem. In Illustration 11.1, about the contract to build cabinets, the court might choose to concentrate on the meaning of the express words "to build," or it might instead consider whether the contract taken as a whole implies a term that the carpenter is to supply the lumber necessary to build the cabinets. Here, the distinction between these two approaches is more apparent than real—the meaning of the word "build" is likely to be an important factor in deciding whether a term can reasonably be implied.

implied term
a term not expressly included by the parties in their agreement but which, as reasonable people, they would have included had they thought about it

Terms Established by Custom or Statute

Implied terms usually result from long-established customs in a particular trade or type of transaction. They exist in almost every field of commerce and came to be recognized among business people because they made good sense or because they led to certainty in transactions without the

---

15. *Corey Developments Inc.* v. *Eastbridge Developments* (Waterloo) *Ltd.* (1997), 34 O.R. (3d) 73.

need to spell out every detail. In time, the courts fell into line with this business practice: when a party failed to perform in compliance with an implied term, the courts would recognize its existence and enforce the contract as though it had been an express term.

ILLUSTRATION 11.6

A asks *B*, a tire dealer, to supply truck tires for his five-tonne dump truck. *B* then shows *A* a set of tires and quotes a price. *A* purchases the tires. The sale slip merely sets out the name and the price of the tires. Later *A* discovers that these tires are not safe on trucks of more than three tonnes' capacity and claims that *B* is in breach of the contract.

On these facts, there was no express undertaking by *B* that the tires would be safe for a five-tonne truck or any other type of truck. Nevertheless, the court would hold that under the circumstances there was an implied term that the tires should be suitable for a five-tonne truck. It would say that in showing *A* the tires after he had made his intended use of them clear, *B*, as a regular seller of such tires, implied that they would be suitable for *A*'s truck.

This approach applies to all kinds of contracts, but in some fields, especially the sale of goods, insurance, partnership, and landlord and tenant relations, a large and complex body of customary terms has developed. In many jurisdictions, these customary terms have been codified in a statute that sets out in one place all the implied terms previously established by the courts for a particular field of law. For instance, court decisions in cases similar to Illustration 11.6 led to a specific provision in the Sale of Goods Act. We will discuss implied statutory terms relating to insurance in Chapter 18, partnership in Chapter 26, and landlord and tenant in Chapter 24.

Reasonable Expectation of the Parties

Apart from those fields where customary terms are implied, the question remains: in what circumstances are the courts likely to find an implied term to be appropriate to the interpretation of a contract? As a rule, the courts will imply terms reasonably necessary to make a contract effective; if not, the fair expectations of a party would be defeated.

On the other hand, the court will not go further than is necessary and will not make a new contract for the parties. Nor will it imply a term that is contrary to the expressed intent of the agreement. A term will be implied on grounds of business efficacy. Parties should therefore consider carefully what unstated assumptions are needed for performing their contract; they need to bring as many of the important possibilities as they can think of into the terms of the written contract.

As a general rule, when parties deal expressly with a matter in their contract, a court will not find an implied term that deals with the same matter in a different way. If the parties have been diligent in canvassing the foreseeable possibilities for future dispute, a court may conclude that they intended to deal in a comprehensive way with all future events, so that no further terms should be implied.[16]

However, even in lengthy and complex contracts, the parties may not have dealt with what later turns out to be a crucial matter. Courts will sometimes come to the conclusion that a term may be implied, so that the purpose of the contract will not be defeated.

---

16. See *Cooke* v. *CKOY Ltd.* (1963), 39 D.L.R. (2d) 209; *Shaw Cablesystems (Manitoba) Ltd.* v. *Canadian Legion Memorial Housing Foundation (Manitoba)* (1997), 143 D.L.R. (4th) 193.

CASE 11.1

Nickel Developments Limited (Nickel), the owner and developer of a shopping centre in Thompson, Manitoba, had collaborated with Canada Safeway Limited to design, build, and operate the shopping centre, which had been built substantially to the specifications of Safeway. Safeway signed a formal lease containing renewal options with Nickel for the use and operation of the shopping centre. It agreed to lease and use as a supermarket slightly more than half of the centre. The rest contained 12 other non-competing retail units. Safeway was the sole "anchor" tenant; without it or a similar major retailer, the project would not have been viable for Nickel.

All went well for 30 years, until just prior to the final renewal option, when Safeway, without notice, closed its supermarket but continued to occupy the space. For some time, Safeway had been operating another supermarket in a competing shopping centre in Thompson. It decided that it could not continue operating the two in a town that had gone through a lengthy recession; it would be better to close down the premises leased from Nickel. Rather than allow its lease to expire, leaving open the prospect of unwanted competition, Safeway chose to exercise its option to renew the lease for a final term of five years and go on paying the rent in order to keep the space vacant. It already knew that one of its supermarket competitors was interested in taking over the space and was communicating with Nickel.

Nickel served notice on Safeway, demanding possession of the leased space, claiming that Safeway had failed to comply with the implied term to use the leased premises "only as a supermarket" and for no other purpose. It stated that "vacancy by design" was not the kind of use intended. Safeway defended by stating there was no term in the lease expressly requiring it to keep operating its supermarket or prohibiting it from leaving the space vacant during the lease.

The Court of Appeal agreed with Nickel. It stated:

A lessee which effectively shuts down half of a shopping centre and fundamentally alters the original concept cannot, absent very unequivocal language, unilaterally alter the arrangement between the landlord and the tenant which had been followed through the entire term of the lease and through two renewal periods.

Safeway is in its present position within the shopping centre because it wanted to be and intended to be. The situation has not changed over the years. In these circumstances it was entirely reasonable for the motions judge to have found that there must be "continuous use" as a supermarket, and that promise does not include the right to intentionally maintain and renew long-term "non-use."[17]

In this case we can see how far the court would go when it found the conduct of Safeway to be clearly contrary to the intention of both parties in signing the contract.

QUESTIONS FOR REVIEW

1. Why does a dictionary definition of a word not always clarify its meaning in a contract? Give an example.
2. Explain and give an example of special usage of a word.
3. What are the primary goals of a court in interpreting a contract?
4. Describe some of the risks that may arise when parties have reached agreement orally about a contract and subsequently record it in writing. What role does the parol evidence rule play?
5. Name four ways in which a party may persuade a court that the parol evidence rule does not apply to the term or terms it asserts were part of the contract.
6. What is an implied term? Give an example.
7. Explain the purpose of a statutory implied term.

17. *Nickel Developments Ltd.* v. *Canada Safeway Ltd.* (2001), 199 D.L.R. (4th) 629.

8. When a contract is subject to a condition precedent, does the contract, nevertheless, still exist? May either party simply withdraw from the contract before the condition precedent has been met?

9. *B* wishes to have a patio roof installed at the back of his house, facing west and overlooking a city park. In the Yellow Pages of his telephone directory, he finds an advertisement by Patio Specialists Inc. stating, "We have the expertise to design and build just what you need." *B* contacts the firm; they inspect his property and recommend a specific design. *B* signs a contract provided by the firm. On the reverse side of the document, in faint print, there is a clause stating, "Patio Specialists Inc. gives no warranties about the safety or otherwise of our product as installed." Three weeks after the patio roof is completed, a strong wind lifts a portion of the roof and the structure is substantially ruined. The strength of the wind was unusual but does occur once every two or three years. Does *B* have a claim against Patio Specialists Inc. that might succeed?

10. What did Lord Wright mean in his judgment in *Scammel* v. *Ouston* when he said, "Difficulty is not synonymous with ambiguity"?

11. "The normal contract is not an isolated act, but an incident in the conduct of business or in the framework of some more general relation." (Furmston, *Cheshire and Fifoot's Law of Contract* [8th ed.], at 122.) Show how the idea expressed in this quotation is applied in the interpretation of contracts.

12. Clifton and Dealer sign a written contract in which Dealer is to deliver five fork-lift tractors to Clifton within two months, at the price stated in the contract. One month later, Dealer telephones Clifton to say that because of a prolonged strike at the manufacturing plant in the United States, he will be able to deliver only three of the vehicles within the two months. He offers to deduct $4000 from the price if Clifton will accept three vehicles immediately with the other two to follow within the third month. Clifton agrees. The three vehicles are delivered at once, but one week after the two months have expired Clifton decides that he does not like the vehicles. He returns them to Dealer with a note stating that because of failure to deliver on time, Dealer is in serious breach of their written contract, which is the only arrangement binding them, and Clifton is justified in cancelling it and returning the vehicles. Do you agree?

CASES AND PROBLEMS

1. Chalmers had been employed full-time as an auto mechanic by Pelham Motors for 16 years. He was 56 years of age and had been a certified mechanic for 20 years when Pelham's business suffered as a result of a downturn in the economy. He was laid off "temporarily," but his employer gave no specific duration for the layoff. Grudgingly Chalmers left work, but when he heard nothing for two weeks, he felt that the layoff amounted to wrongful dismissal and he sued Pelham Motors for severance pay.

    In defence, Pelham Motors claimed that it was an implied term of Chalmers' contract of employment that he could be laid off periodically as a consequence of insufficient business. It claimed that such a term was normal in the auto mechanic trade. In reply, Chalmers asserted that: (a) there had never been any discussion of such a term of his employment with his employer, neither when he was first hired nor afterwards; (b) in 16 years he had never been laid off; (c) he was not aware of such a custom in the trade, even if it was the practice in some auto repair shops.

    Should Chalmers succeed in his claim for severance pay? Explain.

2. Campbell offered to buy from Pym a three-eighth's share in a machine invented by Pym, provided that two engineers, Ferguson and Abernethie, recommended the invention. They arranged a meeting with the engineers to have them examine the machine and have Pym explain it to them. As a result of confusion about the time of the meeting, Abernethie did not attend; after waiting for some time, they went ahead with the meeting without him. The other engineer, Ferguson, approved of the machine, and the three

agreed that, since they might find it difficult to meet quickly with Abernethie, they would draft and sign an agreement that, if Abernethie later gave his approval, should be the final agreement. They drafted an agreement for the purchase of the three-eighth's share and Campbell signed it: the agreement made no reference to the need for Abernethie's approval of Pym's invention.

Abernethie later refused to recommend the machine when he saw it and Campbell refused to proceed with the purchase. Pym sued Campbell to enforce the contract as written. Should he succeed?

3. To assist John Lees & Sons in buying cotton on credit from Haigh, Brooks gave the following guarantee to Haigh:

Messrs. Haigh:

In consideration of your being in advance to Messrs. John Lees & Sons in the sum of $10 000 for the purchase of cotton, I do hereby give you my guarantee for that amount on their behalf.

John Brooks

When the question of the validity of Brooks' guarantee arose at a later time, the court had to interpret the meaning of the words "in consideration of your being in advance." If the words "being in advance" meant "already being in advance" or "already having a sum owing to you from past credit purchases by John Lees & Sons," the guarantee would have been given for a past consideration (assuming, at any rate, that its purpose was not to obtain Haigh's forbearance from suing). If, on the other hand, the words "being in advance" meant "becoming further in advance," the debt to be guaranteed was a future debt, and there was consideration for the guarantee because Haigh, without the guarantee, might not have supplied goods to John Lees & Sons.

If no further evidence is offered to clarify the meaning of these words, what rule will the court follow in choosing between the two possible meanings?

4. Atkinson advertised her house for sale, and Kirby made a written offer to purchase it for $124 000. The parties discussed the offer several days later, and Atkinson said that she would also like to sell her furniture. After discussion about the amount of furniture for sale and its price, Atkinson accepted, in writing, Kirby's offer to purchase the house. The offer had made no reference to the furniture and simply required Kirby's certified cheque for $8000 as an immediate payment towards the agreed price for the house. In fact, Kirby gave Atkinson a cheque for $24 950, the additional $16 950 being the price they had agreed upon orally for the furniture.

When Kirby took possession of the house, he found that Atkinson had taken the grand piano with her. He sued for breach of contract, alleging that their oral agreement about the furniture had specifically included the grand piano, and that he had even tried it out in her presence. In defence, Atkinson pleaded that she had never intended to sell the piano, and that, in any event, evidence of the oral agreement about the furniture would be inadmissible.

What issues must the court deal with before reaching a decision? Should Kirby's action succeed? Give reasons for your opinion.

5. In July, Saunders and Dimmock entered into a partnership for carrying on a grocery and butcher business on Dundee Street in Vancouver. They dissolved the partnership two years later: Dimmock sold his share to Saunders and agreed that Saunders would continue to operate the business by himself. Dimmock wrote out the agreement dissolving the partnership, and included his covenant as retiring partner that he would not "during a term of five years from the date hereof commence and carry on a butcher and grocery

business, neither directly nor indirectly, nor . . . work as an employee in such business within a radius of one kilometre from said premises at 346 Dundee Street, in the City of Vancouver."

Shortly after, Dimmock opened a grocery and butcher business at 258 Dundee Street, less than one kilometre away, and operated it as sole proprietor. Saunders brought an action to restrain Dimmock from continuing to break the covenant. In defence, Dimmock admitted that the one-kilometre restriction on employment was a reasonable restraint. He also conceded that if the restriction on carrying on business (owning a business) were also limited to one kilometre, it would be a reasonable restraint, but he argued that the words "one kilometre" applied only to employment and that there was no geographic limit to his covenant not to carry on business. Therefore, the first half of the covenant was void because it was an unreasonable restraint, and accordingly he was free to carry on business as owner. Did Dimmock break the contract?

6. Provinco Grain Inc. was in the business of selling seeds and buying and reselling the crops grown from the seeds they sold. Its sales manager approached Quinlan, a farmer in the Lower Fraser Valley in British Columbia, to grow an early crop of buckwheat for the Japanese market. Quinlan, who was an experienced farmer, was interested because it would be a valuable market. However, he had never grown the crop before and said he was worried about weeds; he understood they could be a serious problem. The sales manager replied that he need not worry—the buckwheat would smother any weeds. Quinlan bought seeds and signed a printed document stating that Provinco Grain Inc. gave no warranty as to "the productiveness or any other matter pertaining to the seed . . . and will not in any way be responsible for the crop."

Quinlan planted the seeds but weeds destroyed the crop and he suffered a substantial loss. He sued Provinco for damages on the basis that the sales manager's statement was a collateral warranty and a deliberate, material misrepresentation. With regard to the misrepresentation, the court found that the sales manager believed it to be true: he came from Saskatchewan where buckwheat did indeed suppress the weeds. Provinco further defended by claiming that the signed contract exempted it from all liability pertaining to the seeds and subsequent crop. Accordingly, any statement on this subject by the sales manager would be excluded by the parol evidence rule.

In reply, Quinlan's lawyer claimed that the sales manager's warranty was about the risk of weeds, and it did not contradict the terms of the signed contract pertaining to the seed itself. It was on the basis of that warranty that Quinlan signed the contract.

Give your view of each party's position and what the likely result would be.

7. Chénier sold the surface and minerals in her land in Alberta for $104 000 to Werner under an agreement for sale (an instalment sale that reserved Chénier's ownership in the property until a specified amount of the price was paid). Werner defaulted payment, giving Chénier the right to recover possession by court action. Chénier started proceedings, but they were not yet complete when it became apparent that the land was very valuable. Werner entered into a petroleum and natural gas lease with Imperial Oil Ltd. and received a cash bonus of $110 000, which he intended to use to settle his debt to Chénier. About the same time Chénier, anticipating the recovery of her property by court order, entered into a similar lease of the same property with California Standard Oil Co. At the time Chénier gave her lease to California Standard Oil Co., she told the company's agent that her ability to lease the property depended upon winning her court action against Werner and that she could give the lease only if the company's agent gave her a signed statement acknowledging that she (Chénier) did not have any right to lease the mineral rights until the court action against Werner went through. The agent gave her a statement to that effect, and Chénier and California Standard Oil Co. entered into a lease of the mineral rights that made no reference to the statement signed by the company's agent and also contained a paragraph stating that the lease contained the whole of the agreement.

Werner tendered the balance of the purchase price to Chénier, but she refused it and proceeded with the court action. The court dismissed Chénier's petition for recovery of the property. She was, therefore, unable to lease the property to California Standard Oil Co. and that company sued her for breach of contract. Should the action succeed?

8. For several years, John Conrad Kent operated a very successful "pop" radio station, CROC, in Calgary. At the same time, a separately owned station in Edmonton, CRED, was languishing. Its policy of broadcasting classical music and book reviews to a small but higher-than-average-income audience was attracting very little advertising revenue. Finally, the desperate owner and principal shareholder of CRED Radio Limited approached John Conrad Kent to inquire whether he would act as a consultant in the operation of CRED. Soon afterwards the parties made a contract, in the form of the letter below.

Kent had a free hand in the management of CRED, in making staff changes, in program planning, and in policy making. He introduced radical changes that resulted in a complete turnover in the station's audience. To banish its former image, the station's call letters were changed to CROL. At first, Kent went to Edmonton at least once a month and spent two or three days at the radio station; his visits were less frequent after the station was operating profitably, but he was always available and never refused his advice or presence when requested. Over the six-year period ending December 31, 1999, operating profits of CROL Radio Limited were $950 000.

At hearings of the Canadian Radio-television and Telecommunications Commission (CRTC) in October 1999, criticisms were made about CROL's program format and its non-local "absentee" form of management. As a result, the CRTC approved a renewal of the station's licence for only one year instead of the usual three years.

In January 2000, Kent moved to St. John's, Newfoundland, to work with offshore oil-drilling interests there. CROL Radio Limited then decided to terminate its contract with him. It sent him a letter stating that his services would no longer be used after June 30, 2000.

Kent protested that he was still available to perform the contract, that when the contract was being negotiated he had resisted a suggestion that it contain a provision for termination on reasonable notice and would have refused to sign a contract containing such a term, and that none of the specific events had occurred for which the contract might, by its express terms, be terminated. He sued for breach of contract against CROL Radio Limited, claiming damages of $400 000, his estimate of the present value of his annual earnings from the contract for the balance of his expected active business career.

Develop a line of argument for the defendant company, CROL Radio Limited, and speculate on Kent's chances for success in his action.

CRED RADIO LIMITED

Edmonton, Alberta,
December 15, 1993

Mr. J.C. Kent,
400 Foothills Road,
Calgary, Alberta

Dear Mr. Kent:

This letter will confirm our recent discussions in which you expressed a willingness to act as a consultant to this Company on the terms set out below. If these terms continue to be acceptable to you, please acknowledge your agreement at the bottom of this letter and return one of the two enclosed copies to us.

1. You are to give us upon request such services and advice as we shall require and will consult with us in Edmonton at such times as may be reasonably required and are consistent with your duties elsewhere.

continued

2. We are to pay you as remuneration for such services 40 percent of the operating profits of the Company. Operating profits shall mean the gross revenue from whatever sources before deducting your remuneration but after deducting all other operating and financial expenses, including depreciation expense and licence fees and taxes other than corporation income tax.

    Company's auditors shall prepare and deliver a statement of operating profits to you and to us as promptly as possible after December 31 each year, which statement shall be binding upon the Company and you. Payment of your remuneration shall be made by the Company within 30 days after the receipt of the auditor's statement.

3. Your employment shall be effective from January 1, 1994 and shall continue until terminated in the events and in the manner following:

    (i)   Should the Company become bankrupt or go into voluntary liquidation, your employment shall forthwith be terminated without notice.

    (ii) In the event that the Company's broadcasting licence is cancelled for any cause whatever, your employment may be terminated forthwith by the Company by written notice to that effect.

    (iii) In the event that the annual net profits of the Company for the three business years preceding the year in which such notice is given are on the average less than $20 000, your employment may be terminated by the Company at the end of the current business year by six months' written notice. "Net profits" shall mean the operating profits of the company as defined above after deducting your remuneration and corporation income tax.

Yours truly,

CRED Radio Limited

Rosanna Smith

President

Approved and accepted:

John Conrad Kent

December 21, 1993

ADDITIONAL RESOURCES FOR CHAPTER 11 ON THE COMPANION WEBSITE *(www.pearsoned.ca/smyth)*

In addition to self-test multiple-choice, true–false, and short essay questions (all with immediate feedback), application exercises, and links to useful web destinations, the Companion Website provides the following resources for Chapter 11:

- **British Columbia:** Terms Implied by Statute
- **Alberta:** Implied Terms; Legislative Interpretation
- **Manitoba/Saskatchewan:** Sale of Goods Act Implied Terms
- **Ontario:** Credibility; Consumer Protection Act 2002; Exemption Clauses; Implied Terms; Interpretation Act; Sale of Goods Act

12

Privity of Contract and the Assignment of Contractual Rights

A contract creates rights and duties between the parties who enter into the agreement; the rights may have an economic value that one party wishes to transfer to an outsider—a person who was not a party to the contract. Or, a party may wish to arrange for her duties under the contract to be performed by another person. In this chapter we look at how the law of contracts accommodates these important needs, and we examine such questions as:

■ Who can enforce the obligations described in a contract?

■ Vicarious performance—how may an outsider perform a party's obligations under a contract?

■ Trusts—how may rights be created for the benefit of an outsider to a contract?

■ In what other circumstances or special types of contracts do outsiders have the right to enforce a contract?

■ How may rights be assigned and what are the consequences?

■ What are negotiable instruments and why are they important in business?

PRIVITY OF CONTRACT

Limits on the Scope of Contractual Rights and Duties

When parties make a contract, they create a small body of law for themselves. It seems reasonable that the scope of a contract—its power to affect relations—be confined to the parties who agreed to it; persons outside the contract, who had no say in bargaining for its terms, should have neither rights nor duties under it.

In theory, this reasoning seems sound, and represents the general attitude of the common law as well as of other legal systems. But in practice, many situations arise where, for reasons of justice, and especially for business convenience, a contract must be allowed to affect persons outside it. In the law of contract, a person who is not a party to a contract is called a *third person* or **third party**, or sometimes a *stranger* to the contract. In this chapter, we explore the effect of contracts on third persons.

third party
a person who is not one of the parties to a contract but is affected by it

The general rule is that a contract does not confer any benefits or impose any obligations on a stranger to the contract. To succeed in an action in contract, the plaintiff must prove **privity of contract** with the defendant—that is, he must show that they are both parties to the same contract.

privity of contract
the relationship that exists between parties to a contract

ILLUSTRATION 12.1

A, a carpenter, owes $4000 to *B*. *A* offers to renovate *C*'s kitchen if *C* promises to pay off *A*'s debt to *B*. *C* accepts the offer, and *A* completes the renovation. As a third party to the contract for renovation, *B* cannot enforce *C*'s promise; there is no privity of contract between them.[1] Consequently, if *C* fails to pay *B*, she cannot sue *C*, but may still sue *A* for the debt *A* owes her; *A* may then sue *C* for his failure to carry out his promise to pay *B*, and will recover damages of $4000 plus any costs he suffered as a result of *B* suing him. This relationship is illustrated in Figure 12.1.

Another argument against permitting a third person to sue on a contract is that she has not given consideration for the promise. Suppose in Illustration 12.1 that *B* also signed as a party to the contract between *A* and *C* to renovate the kitchen. There would now be privity of contract between *B* and *C* because *C* would have made his promise of payment to *B* as well as to *A*. However, *B* still could not sue *C* because she would not have given consideration for *C*'s promise. Not only must consideration for a promise be given by a party to the contract, it must be given by the party seeking to enforce the promise.

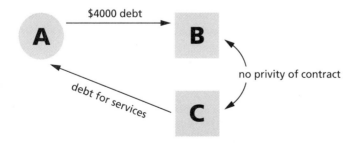

FIGURE 12.1
Privity and Consideration

---

1. *Price* v. *Easton* (1883), 110 E.R. 518.

The privity of contract rule can have harsh consequences when it prevents a third person from enforcing a contract when the whole object was to benefit him. Yet this was the decision in *Tweddle* v. *Atkinson*.[2]

CASE 12.1

The two fathers of a young married couple made a contract: the father of the husband promised the father of the bride that he would pay £100 to the couple, and in return the father of the bride promised that he would pay them a further £200.

Before he had paid the £200, the father of the bride died and his executor, Atkinson, refused to pay it.

The husband, Tweddle, brought an action to enforce the promise. He failed because he was a stranger to the contract between the two fathers. The court rejected the argument that the plaintiff's kinship to one of the contracting parties made him something more than a "stranger" to the contract.

Comparison with Rights and Duties in Tort

Liability of Sellers of Goods

We have seen in Chapter 11 that a consumer who purchases goods from a merchant receives the benefit of an implied term that the goods are reasonably suited for the purpose for which they are sold. If a person buys a can of salmon that turns out to be poisonous and that seriously harms her, she may successfully sue the merchant for breach of the implied term that the fish was suitable to eat. But members of her family who were also harmed by eating the salmon cannot recover damages against the merchant because the contract of sale was with the buyer, and only she can sue successfully for breach of contract. Other members of the family have no privity of contract with the merchant and no rights under the contract. New Brunswick has passed legislation that gives the user of a consumer product a right to sue the seller.[3]

Liability of Manufacturers

As we saw in Chapter 3, although members of the family have no rights against the merchant, the manufacturer may well be liable for negligence. After all, it is the manufacturer who caused the product to be poisonous, and the merchant has no way of knowing that sealed goods are not up to standard. The buyer, too, may sue in tort since she has no contract with the manufacturer.[4] In perhaps the most famous case of the 20th century, *Donoghue* v. *Stevenson*,[5] the House of Lords decided that manufacturers are liable in tort for damages caused by their products when the products will likely be used without intermediate examination. In these circumstances, manufacturers are under a high duty of care to make their products safe. If they fail to meet the standards, they must pay damages for the loss suffered.

As noted above, New Brunswick's Consumer Product Warranty and Liability Act extends contractual liability throughout the distribution chain.

2. (1861), 121 E.R. 762. The court based its decision on the rule that consideration must move from the promisee and that since the husband, Tweddle, could not show that he had given any consideration, his action must fail. But our definition of consideration also implies that the plaintiff to an action (in this case, Tweddle) must be a party to the contract; since he was not a party, he could not have given consideration in any event.

3. Consumer Product Warranty and Liability Act, S.N.B. 1978, c. C-18.1.

4. The idea of a "collateral warranty" that we shall shortly refer to in *Shanklin Pier, Ltd.* v. *Detel Products, Ltd.* is still regarded as a special concession in particular circumstances.

5. [1932] A.C. 562. Recently, the Supreme Court of Canada reiterated its acceptance of the manufacturer duty of care: *Mustapha* v. *Culligan of Canada Ltd.*, 2008 SCC 27 at para. 6.

VICARIOUS PERFORMANCE

How It Occurs

A promisor cannot escape his liability to the promisee by appointing a substitute for himself without the consent of the promisee. In other words, he cannot transfer or "assign" his liability by finding someone willing to assume the liability for him.

Nevertheless, in many situations it is normal for a party, without altering the terms of his contract, to arrange for someone else to carry out his duties, though he remains responsible to the promisee for proper performance. Performance of this type is known as **vicarious performance**; typically, an employee of the promisor performs vicariously (that is, on behalf of the promisor). If the work is not done satisfactorily, the promisee may seek a remedy for breach of contract against the promisor, but not against his employee. In turn, the employee can look only to the employer (and not to the promisee) for payment for the work he has done under his employment contract with the employer. The results are consistent with the rule of privity of contract.

vicarious performance
a third party performs on behalf of the promisor who remains responsible for proper performance

When Is Vicarious Performance Allowed?

When may a promisor employ a third party to perform the work vicariously? He may do so when personal performance by him was not the reason why the promisee entered into the contract.[6] The party entitled to performance generally cannot complain if someone other than the promisor turns up and does the work equally well. However, it would be unacceptable when personal performance is expected, as, for example, when a pianist makes a contract to perform at a concert.

In many contracts, the understanding is that by their very nature they must be performed by a large number of persons who are not parties to the contract: contracts for the construction of buildings, the manufacture of goods, and the transport of people or goods. Moreover, when goods are shipped to a destination that requires the services of more than one carrier, both parties understand that not only employees of the first carrier but also of another carrier will perform: a shipment by rail from Toronto to New York City may be made by Canadian National Railways (CN) and the New York Central. The shipper contracts with CN, whose franchise area includes the point of shipment, and CN arranges for completion of the shipment with the connecting carrier operating beyond the CN area of franchise.

It may not always be clear, as in Illustration 12.2, whether a party is expected to perform personally or whether she may employ someone to perform vicariously.

ILLUSTRATION 12.2

A Co. Ltd. contracts with a public accountant, *B*, to have its accounts audited. *B* sends *C*, a senior accountant, to carry out the audit program. May A Co. Ltd. object? This is a type of work that can be carried out competently by a qualified accountant and ordinarily would not require *B*'s personal performance unless A Co. Ltd. had expressly bargained for it. Consequently, the vicarious performance by *C* is permissible, and A Co. Ltd. is not entitled to reject the tender of such performance. (We may, of course, assume that a final review of the audit would always be made by *B*.)

Sometimes a party arranges for its obligations to be performed vicariously when it should have performed personally, but the other party may have no opportunity to protest until the work is finished. In this situation, the promisor breached a term in the contract (the implied or express promise to perform personally). The promisee may sue for damages to compensate for whatever loss he can show resulted from vicarious, rather than personal, performance.

---

6.   As we shall see in Chapter 27, corporations have no physical existence—personal performance is not possible, so all contracts with them must be carried out by their agents or employees.

Tort Liability

Suppose that in performing a contract vicariously, an employee commits a tort: he negligently damages a valuable instrument belonging to the promisee. As we noted in Chapter 3 on torts, the promisee may sue both the employer for vicarious liability and the employee personally. Since the employer ordinarily has a "deeper pocket" than its employee, the promisee almost always sues the employer, but may sue the employee as well, in case the court should find that the employer is not liable because the damage did not occur *in the course of employment.*

ILLUSTRATION 12.3

Suppose that in Illustration 12.2 above, *C* does such an inadequate job that he fails to detect a material error in the accounts, and, as a result, *A* Co. Ltd. suffers a loss. *A* Co. Ltd. must look to *B* for damages for breach of contract. In addition, if *C*'s poor work amounted to negligence, he would be personally liable to *A* Co. Ltd. in tort, and *B* would also be vicariously liable in tort for *C*'s negligence.

If, while working in the offices of *A* Co. Ltd., *C* stole some valuable client records to sell to a competitor of *A* Co. Ltd., *C* would, of course, be guilty of a crime as well as of committing a tort. However, the theft would not be considered conduct in the course of employment, and *B* would not be liable for *C*'s misconduct.

Exemption Clauses

exemption clause
a clause in a contract that exempts a party from liability

Employers often protect themselves from tort liability. For example, carriers and storage companies usually insert **exemption clauses** in their standard form contracts to exclude or limit liability for negligence. By allocating the risk of loss to the promisee, a storage company lowers its costs and so reduces its price to the promisee, which in turn obtains its own insurance against loss. While an exemption clause protects the storage company from liability for negligence,[7] until the 1990s its employees who were not parties to the contract were unable to claim its protection because of the traditional privity rule. In 1992, the Supreme Court of Canada reversed that position and granted protection to employees if they could show that the clause was intended to be for their benefit and the damage occurred in the course of their employment.[8]

TRUSTS

trust
an arrangement that transfers property to a person who administers it for the benefit of another person

trustee
a person or company who administers a trust

How a Trust Is Created

Suppose a mother wishes to provide for her son in case she should die while he is still an infant. In her will, she leaves a fund to be invested in securities, and directs that the income be used to care for her son. The fund will require someone to administer it—that is, to see that it is properly invested and that the income is paid out for the child's care. The fund is called a **trust**; the person—or perhaps a trust company—who looks after the fund is called a **trustee**. A trust has been defined

---

7. For a fuller discussion of the effect of exemption clauses, see Chapter 14.

8. *London Drugs* v. *Kuehne & Nagel International* (1992), 97 D.L.R. (4th) 261. See also *M.A.N.-B. & W. Diesel* v. *Kingsway Transports Ltd.* (1997), 33 O.R. (3d) 355.

as "any arrangement whereby property is transferred with the intention that it be administered by a trustee for another's benefit."[9] In this definition and in the above example, the trust is created by the transfer of some kind of *property* to the trustee in the will.

Suppose that the mother dies and the fund is handed over to the trustee, but the trustee refuses to pay out the income for the benefit of the son. We know that the trust fund was set up by the mother for his benefit and not for that of the trustee. What rights has the child as **beneficiary** of the trust? Although under common law rules the trustee becomes the legal owner of the trust, the rules of equity recognize that the son has an interest: he is the fund's *true* owner—the **beneficial owner**—and equity has developed procedures by which a beneficiary may compel a trustee to carry out its duties under the **trust agreement** diligently and faithfully. A trust may be created not only in a will (on death) but in any agreement that conveys property to a trustee on the understanding that it will be used for the benefit on a third party beneficiary.

The trust concept has important applications in business. For example, income trusts have become a popular form of business association where the business transfers its assets to a trustee for the benefit of the unit holders. Unit holders must be able to compel the trustee to comply with the terms of the trust. This will be discussed in Chapter 26.

A trust is created by operation of law when the creditors of a business convince the court that their debtor is no longer capable of paying its debts as they fall due. The court will order that the property of the bankrupt debtor be transferred to a trustee in bankruptcy who will sell the assets and distribute the proceeds to the creditors.

beneficiary
a person who is entitled to the benefits of a trust

beneficial owner
a person who, although not the legal owner, may compel the trustee to provide benefits to him

trust agreement
the document that conveys property to a trustee to be used for the benefit of a third party beneficiary

The Relation of the Trust Concept to Third Parties: Constructive Trusts

How is the concept of a trust related to contracts and the rights of third parties? The beneficiary of a trust is in a third party to a contract, being neither the person who created the trust nor the person who is appointed to administer it; yet, as we have seen, the beneficiary may enforce the trust in his favour. The rules of equity gradually developed an ingenious extension of the idea of the trust by recognizing that the legal right to demand performance of a promise in a contract is a thing of value—a type of property, in other words. Sometimes the contract containing the promise is not expressly described as a trust and the promise may be only one part of a larger deal. In some circumstances equity recognizes that a promisee who has obtained a promise for the benefit of a third person is a trustee. This would permit a third party to enforce the contract in his or her favour. A trust of this kind is called a **constructive trust**. When a court accepts this argument, the restrictions of the privity of contract rule are avoided.

constructive trust
a relationship that permits a third party to obtain performance of a promise included in a contract for his benefit

CASE 12.2 *A*, *B*, and *C* entered into a partnership agreement, a term of which stated that if one of the partners should die, his widow would receive a share of the future profits of the firm. On the death of *A*, the surviving partners, *B* and *C*, refused to pay a share of the profits to *A*'s widow. Would she be successful in enforcing the term?

These facts are based on *Re Flavell*,[10] where the court held that while the widow was not a party to the partnership agreement, that agreement had created a trust in her favour. It decided that her husband as promisee of the term in the partnership agreement had become a trustee of her interest. On his death, his executor became the trustee in his place, and the executor was successful in obtaining the share for the widow.

9. *Black's Law Dictionary*, 8th ed. (St. Paul, MN: West Publishing Co., 2004).
10. (1883), 25 Ch. D. 89. For an interesting later case, see *Beswick* v. *Beswick*, [1968] A.C. 58.

Unfortunately, parties to a contract are not likely to be aware of the subtleties of a constructive trust, nor are they likely to create a trust expressly to ensure that a third party beneficiary will have rights enforceable in court.[11] As a result, the constructive trust has not become a reliable means for avoiding the privity of contract rule.

OTHER EXCEPTIONS TO THE PRIVITY OF CONTRACT RULE

Insurance

Typically, in a contract (or policy) of life insurance, a person pays a premium in exchange for a promise from the insurance company to pay a sum of money on his or her death to a specified person, a spouse, say, who is not a party to the insurance contract. Each province has a statute that gives a beneficiary a right against the insurance company to enforce the insurance contract.[12] Similarly, in a contract of automobile insurance, the company may promise to indemnify not only the owner but also anyone driving with his consent. If a person driving with consent injures a pedestrian and is required to pay damages, she may in turn sue the insurance company for indemnity against her loss, even though she was not a party to the insurance contract.[13]

The Undisclosed Principal

undisclosed principal
a contracting party who, unknown to the other party, is represented by an agent

A further exception to the rule requiring privity of contract occurs when one of the contracting parties, unknown to the other, proves to be an agent of someone else: the person for whom the agent was acting, known as an **undisclosed principal**, may sue or be sued on the contract. The subject is discussed more fully in Chapter 19.

Contracts Concerning Land

The limits of privity of contract do not apply generally in land law. If the owner of land leases it to a tenant who promises to pay rent and keep the property in good repair, and the owner then sells it, the tenant must perform the promises for the new owner. The value of the land on the market would be substantially lowered if the tenant could ignore promises made to the former owner. Similarly, the new owner must respect the tenant's rights to remain on the property until the lease expires. Otherwise, tenants would always be in jeopardy of being evicted when land is sold. Accordingly, persons who acquire interests in land often do so subject to earlier contracts that both create obligations and give benefits in relation to the property. Land law will be discussed in Chapters 23, 24 and 25.

Special Concessions to Commercial Practice

Collateral Contracts

Courts have sometimes been prepared to enlarge the scope of a contract so that persons who are closely associated with a business transaction, though not strictly a party to it, may nevertheless find themselves subject to its terms.

11. Courts find it difficult to infer an intention to create a trust when the party to the contract has died. Courts will not infer a constructive trust unless the contract cannot be revoked or revised at a later date: see *Re Schebsman*, [1944] Ch. 83.
12. See, for example: Insurance Act, R.S.O. 1990 c. I.8, s. 195; R.S.B.C. 1996, c. 206, s. 146; R.S.N.S. 1989, c. 231, s. 197.
13. See, for example: Insurance Act, R.S.O. 1990, c. I.8, s. 239; Insurance (Vehicle) Act, R.S.B.C. 1996, c. 231, s. 76.

CASE 12.3

Shanklin, the owner of a pier, consulted Detel Products, Ltd., paint manufacturers, about the best type of paint to use in repainting the pier. Detel recommended one of its own paints and promised that the paint would have a life of 7 to 10 years. Shanklin then made a contract with a contractor to do the work requiring it to use the paint recommended by Detel. The contractor purchased the paint from Detel. The paint proved unsatisfactory; it lasted only about three months. Shanklin sued Detel for breach of warranty regarding the quality of the paint.[14]

While there was an express contract between Shanklin and the contractor, and another between the contractor and Detel, there was no express contract between Shanklin and Detel. Nevertheless, the court found that there was an *implied* **collateral contract** between Shanklin and Detel on the following terms: Detel warranted that its paint was suitable for the pier in return for Shanklin requiring the contractor to purchase the paint from Detel. Shanklin recovered extensive damages.

In applying the principle of the *Shanklin Pier* decision, a Canadian court found that a manufacturer of farm machinery made a representation to farmers in the form of a "collateral warranty" when it published a promotional sales brochure used by dealers for the purpose of inducing farmers to buy its products.[15] Accordingly, a farmer recovered damages from the manufacturer for breach of warranty. Mr. Justice Reid of the Ontario High Court of Justice said:

> I can see no legal basis for differentiating between dealer and manufacturer in relation to collateral warranties. The manufacturer initiated the affirmations; it was the manufacturer who apparently prepared and certainly published the brochure. The dealer would perforce have to rely on the manufacturer.[16]

collateral contract
an implied contract that binds a party who made a representation or promise that induced a person to enter into a contract with another party

Exemption Clauses and the Allocation of Risk

We have seen that an exemption clause between the owner of goods and a storage or a transportation company may protect the employees who are not parties to a contract.[17] A related problem arises when an exemption clause is intended to allocate risk by protecting one or more other parties who may participate in the shipment of goods. For example, goods sent from Japan to Canada not only travel by ship but also are moved on and off ships by stevedore firms in Japan and Canada, are perhaps stored for a short time in a warehouse, and then transported by rail or road carriers to their destination inland.

In these arrangements, the buyer usually obtains a single insurance policy to cover any loss that may occur after the goods leave the manufacturer until their arrival. The contract between the buyer and the principal carrier exempts the carrier—and all other carriers—from liability. In turn, the other carriers agree to perform their roles and set their fees on the understanding that they are exempt from negligence. These arrangements are cost efficient and avoid the need for intermediate carriers to obtain insurance. But there is no contract between the intermediate carriers and the buyer. Can these carriers claim the benefit of the exemption clause if the buyer sues them?

The courts have struggled with this problem, and the results are not entirely consistent. However, the prevailing opinion is that the intermediate carriers may successfully claim the protection of an exemption clause when the contract expressly states that they should be its "beneficiaries" and should be entitled to the protection of the clause, as set out in international rules (known as The Hague rules).[18]

---

14. *Shanklin Pier, Ltd.* v. *Detel Products, Ltd.*, [1951] 2 K.B. 854.

15. *Murray* v. *Sperry Rand Corp. et al.* (1979), 23 O.R. (2d) 456, 96 D.L.R. (3d) 113. See also *Cummings* v. *Ford Motor Co. of Canada*, [1984] O.J. No. 431.

16. *Ibid.*, at 466. See also: *Andrews* v. *Hopkinson*, [1957] 1 Q.B. 229; *Brown* v. *Sheen and Richmond Car Sales Ltd.*, [1950] 1 All E.R. 1102.

17. See *supra*, n. 8.

18. See *New Zealand Shipping Co. Ltd.* v. *A.M. Satterthwaite & Co. Ltd.*, [1975] A.C. 154 (P.C.), followed by the Supreme Court of Canada in *ITO-International Terminal Operators Ltd.* v. *Miida Electronics Inc. and Mitsui O.S.K. Lines Ltd.*, [1986] 1 S.C.R. 752.

CASE 12.4

A marine insurance policy included a waiver of the ship owner's right of subrogation against, among others, "any charterer." This meant that neither the owner nor the insurer would have the right to sue a charterer for damages caused by a charterer's negligence. The insured vessel was sunk by the negligence of a charterer, and the insurer paid the owner for the loss. The insurer and the owner then agreed that the owner would "waive any right it may have pursuant to the waiver of subrogation clause . . . ," and the insurer brought a subrogated action in the owner's name against the charterer.

The insurer won at trial but lost on appeal. The Supreme Court of Canada held that since the insurer had clearly intended to benefit the charterer in precisely the circumstances that had occurred, it was consistent with the parties' intention—and also with commercial reality—to recognize an exception to the doctrine of privity of contract. Accordingly, the agreement between the insurer and owner was ineffective to revoke the charterer's rights, which had crystallized when the loss occurred.[19]

The cases illustrate how the courts are becoming more sensitive to the essentials of commercial transactions and are more willing to grant appropriate remedies.

INTERNATIONAL ISSUE

Has Privity of Contract Lost Its Relevance?

Exceptions to the privity of contract principle allow some non-parties to enforce the obligations of a contract. In most of Canada, these exceptions are limited to specific types of contracts or specific clauses with identified non-party beneficiaries. As noted earlier, insurance contracts and trust agreements are such exceptions. The Supreme Court of Canada extended the *protection* of contractual exemption clauses to non-parties identified by the exemption clause, as we saw in Case 12.4.[20]

However, some jurisdictions have made sweeping changes to the privity of contract rule. In the United States, an *intended* beneficiary's right to sue has been recognized since 1859. In *Lawrence v. Fox*,[21] Fox promised Halley that he would pay Halley's debt. When Fox failed to make the payment, the New York Court of Appeal allowed the unpaid creditor (Lawrence) to sue Fox directly.

In 1999, England enacted the Contracts (Rights of Third Parties) Act 1999,[22] which allows non-parties to enforce any contractual obligation if the contract benefits them or specifically authorizes them to do so. Similar legislation exists in Australia and New Zealand.

New Brunswick's privity of contract rules were partially changed by the passage of the Consumer Product Warranty and Liability Act in 1978.[23] In 1994, the privity rule was abolished in favour of the *identified* beneficiary concept: Section 4(1) of the Law Reform Act reads:

> A person who is not a party to a contract but who is identified by or under the contract as being intended to receive some performance or forbearance under it may, unless the contract provides otherwise, enforce that performance or forbearance by a claim for damages or otherwise.[24]

continued

19. *Fraser River Pile & Dredge Ltd.* v. *Can-Dive Services Ltd.* (1999) 176 D.L.R. (4th) 257.
20. *Ibid.*; *London Drugs, supra,* n. 8.
21. 20 N.Y. 268 (1859).
22. 1999, c. 31 (Eng.)
23. *Supra,* n. 3. This Act entitled non-parties to sue for breach of the statutory warranties implied into a contract of sale. The exception is not limited to consumers but includes any organization involved in the chain of distribution such as retailers, wholesalers, and importers.
24. S.N.B. 1993, c. L-1.2. The Act was proclaimed in force on June 1, 1994.

QUESTIONS TO CONSIDER

1. Should all provinces abandon the privity of contract rule in favour of a "third party beneficiary" rule?
2. Should the law make a distinction between an intended beneficiary and an incidental beneficiary?
3. Should the law make a distinction between defendants and plaintiffs?

Sources: R.L. Miller and G.A. Jentz, *Business Law Today*, Standard Edition, 7th ed. (Florence, KY: South-Western College/West, 2006) at 325–344; J. Edelman, "Taking Promises Seriously" (2007), 45(3) *Canadian Business Law Journal* 399–413. Karl Dore, "Privity and Products Liability," *Consumer Products Warranty Law: Legal Guide*, August 24, 2000, www.law.unb.ca/cpwala/privity.htm.

ASSIGNMENT OF RIGHTS

The Nature of an Assignment

We have seen that, apart from land law, an assignment of liabilities to a third person is not possible. An assignment of contractual rights is, however, a common business transaction. Assignments are, in fact, the most important and long-established concession to commercial practice that our courts have recognized. Historically, such assignments became enforceable only as the courts became more willing to relax the privity of contract rule.

ILLUSTRATION 12.4

A Ltd., a building contractor, has erected a building for *B*. Under the terms of their contract, *B* still owes *A* Ltd. $10 000, to be paid one month after the completion of the building.

Meanwhile, *A* Ltd. has purchased $12 000 worth of materials from *X* Corp. In settlement of its debt to *X* Corp., *A* Ltd. pays $2000 in cash and assigns in writing its rights to the $10 000 still owing by *B*. *X* Corp. then notifies *B* that she should pay the money to it rather than to *A* Ltd. when the debt falls due.

In Illustration 12.4, the contractor *A* Ltd. is the **assignor** of its right to the payment of $10 000. It has assigned the right to *X* Corp., its **assignee**, for a valuable consideration. The consideration is *X* Corp.'s promise to accept the **assignment** in satisfaction of the balance of its claim against *A* Ltd. Given proper notice, the promisor *B* must perform for the assignee *X* Corp. instead of for the original promisee *A* Ltd.

Contractual rights are often valuable and may be considered a type of personal property along with the ownership of goods. The main difference is that tangible property, such as goods, may be possessed physically—it has a concrete existence; whereas a right to demand performance of a contract has no concrete existence—it is valuable only because it is enforceable in the courts. The rights to tangible property that may be possessed physically are known as **choses in possession**; the rights to intangible property—to things that have value only because they may be enforced by action in the courts—are called **choses in action**. There are many types of choses in action, including such things as patents, copyrights, stocks, bonds, funds deposited in a bank account, rights to collect the proceeds of an insurance policy, rights of action against persons who have caused injury, and rights under contracts generally.

The Importance of Assignments

A willingness to accept the ownership of choses in action as a form of personal wealth is an important mark of a modern industrial society. Choses in action give people the means of accumulating savings

assignor
a party that assigns its rights under a contract to a third party

assignee
a third party to whom rights under a contract have been assigned

assignment
a transfer by a party of its rights under a contract to a third party

choses in possession
rights to tangible property that may be possessed physically

choses in action
rights to intangible property such as patents, stocks, and contracts that may be enforced in the courts

in bank accounts and also, through the ownership of shares and bonds, to put those assets to work as capital of corporations. In other words, this device links personal saving to business investment. In some less-developed countries, where citizens have little confidence in their legal system, it has been a major problem to persuade those who have assets to abandon their preference for investment in gold, jewels, and real estate and to accept a portfolio of mortgages, shares, and bonds as an alternative form of property. As a result, active capital markets in these countries have been slow to develop.

In this chapter, we are concerned with the assignment of rights arising under contracts generally; a discussion of the specific features of such choses in action as mortgages, shares, bonds, and negotiable instruments is reserved for later chapters.

The Role of Equity

An assignment of rights (choses in action) and a sale of goods (choses in possession) are similar. In an assignment, the subject-matter is the transfer of contractual rights; in a sale, the subject-matter is the transfer of ownership in goods. Unfortunately, the common law rules failed to give equal recognition to an assignment; unlike choses in possession, the common law viewed choses in action as personal rights that could not be transferred. But the need for recognition grew as commerce increased, and the courts of equity stepped in to recognize and enforce assignments of contractual rights.

Equity required only that a clear intention to assign a benefit be shown either orally or in writing by the assignor, and it would then permit the assignee to recover the benefit from the promisor. Because of the conflict between the rules of the common law courts and those of equity, the courts of equity required in every action by an assignee of contractual rights that the assignee make the assignor a party as well. The action then had three parties—the assignee, the assignor, and the promisor.

CHECKLIST Third Parties Who May Play a Role in a Contract

There are many ways in which a third party to the original contract may acquire rights under it and become subject to duties to perform:

- by vicarious performance, such as an employee carrying out the obligations of one of the parties to the contract
- by accepting responsibility as a trustee to confer benefits on a third party
- by an insurance contract under which the insurer promises to pay a third party in the event that a particular risk occurs, such as a motor vehicle accident
- by an agent making a contract on behalf of an undisclosed principal
- by a party acquiring an interest in land subject to rights and duties owed to a third person
- by a commercial contract containing an implied collateral contract binding a third party who made representations relied on by a party to the contract
- by an assignment of rights to a third party by a party to the contract

EQUITABLE ASSIGNMENTS

A basic principle of law is that a court will not decide a dispute unless all the persons directly affected by its decision have been made parties to the court proceedings and have had an opportunity to argue on their own behalf. Accordingly, if an assignor assigns part of her rights only, she remains vitally interested in the result of an action by the assignee against the promisor: if the court should decide that the promisor is not bound to perform any part of his obligations, its decision would adversely affect the assignor as well as the assignee.

ILLUSTRATION 12.5

A owes B $10 000 under a contract. At the same time, B owes $6000 to X Finance Co. B assigns $6000 of her account

receivable from A to satisfy X. Subsequently, A refuses to pay X; X sues A for the $6000.

If the court were to decide that A was not bound to pay anything on the debt because, say, the contract between A

Assignment of Part of a Debt

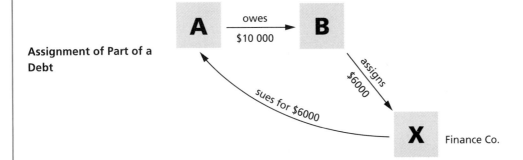

and B was within the Statute of Frauds and there was an insufficient memorandum of it, B would also be affected for she could not claim her remaining $4000 of the debt either.

The court requires that B be made a party to the action by X so that she may take part in it. In an assignment of part of a debt, both the assignee and the assignor are equally anxious that the court find the debtor (that is, the promisor)

liable. Accordingly, the assignor B must have her own chance to argue and to introduce evidence. For example, it might well be that she would have in her possession a memorandum sufficient to comply with the Statute of Frauds, and her evidence might be decisive in holding the debtor liable.

Similarly, in an action brought by B against A, the court would require that X Finance Co. also be made a party.

For the purposes of Illustration 12.6 below, let us assume that the assignor assigns only part of its rights; the promisor is willing to perform his obligation, but he does not know what part he should perform for the benefit of the assignee and what part for the benefit of the assignor.

ILLUSTRATION 12.6

A owes $100 000 to B Inc., due in 12 months. B Inc. needs short-term financing and borrows $80 000 from X Bank, repayable in 12 months. Under their loan agreement, B Inc. gives X Bank a conditional assignment of its account receivable from A as security for repayment of the loan under the following terms:

> As long as B Inc. pays the interest on its loan every three months, the bank will not be entitled to notify A of the assignment; but if B Inc. fails to pay the interest or fails to pay the $80 000 on the due date, the bank may advise A to pay it that sum plus unpaid interest, in reduction of his debt to B Inc. In other words, the

assignment is conditional upon the default of the borrower, B Inc.

If, at the end of the year, the bank notifies A that B Inc. has assigned his account and demands that A pay the bank, A cannot afford to do so until he has verified the default and the amount owing. He must check with B Inc. Suppose B Inc. claims that it has paid the bank $60 000 of the debt. A is in a quandary: he is aware of the competing claims and fears that if he pays one party and guesses wrong, the other may sue him successfully and collect the amount in dispute a second time. In such a case, A should hand the sum claimed by the bank over to the court as custodian and let B Inc. and the bank settle their dispute before a judge.

An equitable assignment also occurs when the subject of the assignment is an aggregate of book debts whose balances fluctuate over time.

ILLUSTRATION 12.7

Fribble Corp. owes $160 000 to Tower Bank under a demand loan. Fribble is required to make regular monthly payments on the loan and to provide the bank with semi-annual financial statements. Fribble reported substantial losses six months ago and was slow in making two subsequent interest payments. The bank threatened to call the loan unless it received additional security. Fribble then gave the bank a conditional assignment of its accounts receivable, including several large accounts, some of them running to tens of thousands of dollars.

Fribble receives frequent payments on these accounts from its customers, and also ships its products to them from time to time so that the account balances fluctuate substantially. Fribble promised to make its monthly interest payments without fail; otherwise, the bank would call the loan and notify Fribble's customers of the assignment.

In these circumstances the assignment is conditional, not only because it depends on a future event (default by Fribble), but also because the value of the accounts receivable varies according to the state of accounts between Fribble and each of its customers at any given moment.

In Illustrations 12.5, 12.6, and 12.7, all the parties have a vital interest in the assignment, and it is necessary that all be bound by the same court decision: the requirement of equity that the assignor and the debtor(s) be made parties to the assignee's action is fair in cases where the assignor retains an interest in the contract.

STATUTORY ASSIGNMENTS

The Need for Reform

In many business transactions, an assignor does not want to retain any rights under the contract; he assigns them entirely to the assignee. If later the assignee were to sue the promisor for failure to perform, the court-imposed requirement of making the assignor a party would be inconvenient and indeed might cause considerable hardship: the assignor might reside far away, or worse still, if he has died, it would be necessary to make his personal representative a party. In any event, the requirement increases the expense of the action by bringing in a party who has no real interest.

statutory assignment
an assignment that complies with statutory provisions enabling the assignee to sue the other party without joining the assignor to the action

equitable assignment
an assignment other than a statutory assignment

The British Parliament remedied this defect in the 19th century when the Judicature Act amalgamated the courts of common law and equity. The Act permits an assignee to sue the promisor without joining the assignor to the suit provided: (a) the assignment was absolute (*unconditional* and *complete*), (b) it was in writing, and (c) the promisor received notice of it in writing.[25] Assignments that comply with these requirements are known as **statutory assignments**. All other assignments are called **equitable assignments**. Note that the statute did not create a new type of assignment; it merely provided a streamlined procedure for hearing actions that meet the requirements laid down by statute.

---

25. See, for example: Conveyancing and Law of Property Act, R.S.O. 1990, c. C.34, s. 53; Law and Equity Act, R.S.B.C. 1996, c. 253, s. 36; Judicature Act, R.S.A. 2000, c. J-2; R.S.N.S. 1989, c. 240, s. 43(5). The statutory provisions are somewhat different in certain provinces. See, for example: Choses in Action Act, R.S.S. 1978, c. C-11, s. 2 and the Law of Property Act, R.S.M. 1987, c. L90, s. 31(1) and (5).

Meeting the Requirements of the Statute

It is not always convenient in business to meet the requirements of the statute, and many assignments remain equitable rather than statutory. For instance, with regard to requirement (a), an assignment is not *complete* if a balance remains to be paid to the assignor after the assignee is paid—the assignor still has an interest in the contract. Nor is an assignment *unconditional* when the amount assigned varies according to the state of accounts between the assignor and his debtor; this situation exists when the balance of the account assigned fluctuates because the assignor continues to sell goods or services on credit to the debtor (the customer) or the debtor reduces the balance assigned by making payments on account to the assignor—the balance assigned is not fixed and may need to be verified from the assignor's records. In neither of these situations is the assignment "absolute."

The need for (b)—writing in support of the statutory assignment—is reasonable: if the assignment were oral, the assignee would have to call the assignor as a witness to prove that the assignment was actually made. As we noted in Chapter 2, evidence given by other persons of what the assignor said is *hearsay*, and for this reason the court will not allow such evidence when the assignor himself is able to testify. In most cases, a written assignment signed by the assignor is as good as his personal appearance in court. Only if there is a rare allegation of serious fraud, such as forgery, will further evidence be required to prove the assignment. Similarly, (c)—the requirement of the promisor receiving the notice of assignment in writing—simplifies proving that the promisor knew of the assignment. It is good business practice and common sense to send written notice by registered letter when important rights are in question in any transaction.

NOTICE TO THE PROMISOR

The Effect of Notice on the Promisor

To be effective, *all* assignments require that notice be given to the promisor. But that does not mean the promisor's consent is required. A promisor ignores a notice of an assignment at his peril. Confronted with a demand for payment from one who claims to be an assignee, the promisor should, of course, require proof of the assignment to protect himself against a possible fraud, but once he has had an opportunity to satisfy himself that there has been an assignment, he must make further payments to the assignee. If he persists in making payment to his original creditor, he can be sued by the assignee and required to pay the amount a second time.

CASE 12.5

Brian Wholesalers Ltd. buys a large quantity of goods on credit from Akron Manufacturing Inc. and defaults payment. Brian offers to pay Akron by assigning certain of its accounts receivable owed by retail merchants with excellent credit ratings. Akron agrees to this settlement and takes an absolute assignment of the debts, the largest of which is owed by Woolridge's Department Store. Akron sends to Woolridge's a notice, signed by an officer of Brian, stating that the account has been assigned to Akron, and encloses a request that Woolridge's pay Akron. Woolridge's inadvertently ignores the notice and request and pays Brian, which shortly afterwards becomes bankrupt. Akron sues Woolridge's for payment of the debt again.

In these circumstances Akron would succeed in its action; Woolridge's paid Brian at its peril after receiving valid notice of the assignment.[26]

---

26. See *Brandt's Sons & Co.* v. *Dunlop Rubber Co. Ltd.*, [1905] A.C. 454.

The Effect of Notice from Contending Assignees

The ability to assign contractual rights is an important exception to the doctrine of privity of contract: someone other than the original party to a contract is permitted to claim the benefit of rights under the contract. Indeed, more than one person may claim to be the assignee of the same right: an unscrupulous creditor might sell the right to collect the same debt to two different persons by assigning it to each of them. The debtor is then faced with two demands for payment. Which of the two innocent assignees is entitled to payment? And which is left only with an action for fraud against the assignor?

The law is clear: the assignee who first gave notice to the debtor is the one entitled to payment. This rule, like the rule that the debtor must receive notice of assignment before it affects him, offers the only fair treatment to the debtor. Otherwise, a debtor would be in a very insecure position, never being sure when he makes payment whether someone else to whom he should have paid the money may turn up later. An assignee who receives his assignment first may be slow in notifying the debtor, and the second assignee notifies the debtor first.

We should note that the second assignee is entitled to payment by the debtor, unless he knows of the prior assignment at the time of the assignment to him. If he knows of that prior assignment, he is a party to the fraud and cannot take payment ahead of the first assignee without becoming liable to him. In order to determine who is entitled to the debtor's performance, the court must ascertain the validity and extent of every right claimed by contending assignees.

Mercifully, the debtor need perform his obligation only once—provided he acts prudently when it is unclear whose claim should prevail. As is suggested in Illustration 12.6, it may be necessary to pay the money into court and leave it to decide the validity and extent of the claims by contending assignees.

THE ASSIGNEE'S TITLE

An Assignee "Takes Subject to the Equities"

A fundamental rule is that an assignee can never acquire a better right to sue the promisor than the assignor himself had. In legal terms, the assignee's claim is "subject to the equities": her claim is subject to any rights the promisor had against the assignor before the promisor received notice of the assignment. The assignee cannot avoid any defence that the promisor had against the assignor, with whom he originally contracted.

If a person takes an assignment of rights under a contract originally induced by the fraudulent misrepresentation of the assignor, the assignee will have no better chance to enforce her claim than if she had been the perpetrator of the fraud herself. In other words, if a debtor is the victim of fraudulent misrepresentation, the contract remains voidable at his option despite any assignment of the contractual rights. (The debtor cannot, however, sue the assignee for damages for the tort of deceit: he must sue the assignor, the person actually guilty of the fraud.) In addition to fraudulent misrepresentation, a promisor may use as a defence against an assignee: mistake, undue influence, duress, and the fact that he received no consideration for his promise.

The position of an assignee of a chose in action is in marked contrast to the position of a person who obtains title to goods under a similarly flawed contract. For instance, we have seen that, in spite of his fraud, a person may obtain title to goods so that, in turn, he may pass on valid title to a subsequent innocent purchaser, who may retain the goods against the claim of the person fraudulently persuaded to part with them.[27] But a person who obtains contractual rights by fraud does not, by assigning these rights, give an innocent assignee the right to enforce them against the defrauded promisor. Consequently, an innocent assignee of a chose in action is in a much more vulnerable position than is an innocent purchaser of goods.

---

27. This result follows because fraud makes the contract voidable, not void. See Chapter 9 and *King's Norton Metal Co. v. Edridge* (1897), 14 T.L.R. 98; *Lewis* v. *Averay,* [1971] 3 All E.R. 907.

The Right to Set Off

An important defence of a promisor is his right to **set off** a debt owed to him by the assignor at the time the assignment is made:

set off

the right of a promisor to deduct an existing debt owed to it by the promisee

---

ILLUSTRATION 12.8

A is employed by *B* at a salary of $550 per week, payable at noon Saturdays when the business closes. On Thursday, *A* borrows $200 from *B*. On Saturday, *A* fails to appear at work on time. When he telephones an hour late, they argue, and *B* informs *A* that he is fired and tells him not to bother coming back. On Monday, *A* sues *B* for $550 in the small claims court. *B* may set off both the $200 loan and the $50 *A* would have earned had he come to work on Saturday morning. *A* obtains a court judgment for $300.

Suppose, instead of suing *B*, *A* had assigned his claim for salary to his neighbour *X* for $500. *X* would take the claim subject to the equities between *A* and *B*. Even though *X* did not know of *B*'s loan to *A* and of *A*'s failure to work on Saturday, *B* would be able to set off these amounts if *X* sued him: *X* would recover $300 from *B*, the same amount as *A* could recover.[28]

Until an assignee gives the promisor notice of the assignment, acts of either the assignor or the promisor or their agents may prejudice the assignee's rights. So it is important for an assignee to give notice as soon as possible. If he delays, his rights may well deteriorate.

ILLUSTRATION 12.9

Williams owes Mehta $900. Mehta assigns the debt to Young on May 1. Young neglects to notify Williams, and on May 11 Williams, unaware of the assignment, pays Mehta $300 on account. Because of her failure to notify Williams, Young, the assignee, may now recover from Williams only $600 and must look to Mehta for the $300 already paid.

When a creditor—a building contractor, say—assigns rights to partial payment before it has completed performance, the assignee may be subject to an additional risk. Even when the assignee has given notice to the debtor (the party entitled to completion of the project), the debtor may be able to use defences based upon developments *after* the time of notice. The assignor's (builder's) subsequent failure to complete performance may cause the debtor damages, which he can set off against the assignee's claim. In other words, an assignee's rights under a contract still incomplete are imperfect and subject to proper completion of the contract.[29]

A general assignment of book debts is an important business device for securing credit. The common law provinces each have statutes making such assignments void against the assignor's creditors unless the assignment is registered in a public office where its terms are available for inspection. The purpose of these statutes is to protect prospective creditors: they may inspect the registry to discover whether some assignee has a prior claim against the assets of a person who has applied to them for credit. We shall consider the reasons for providing public notice more fully in Chapters 23 and 30.

---

28. Provincial legislation may provide that an assignment of wages, or any portion, to secure payment of a debt is invalid. See, for example: Wages Act, R.S.O. 1990, c. W.1, s. 7(7); Assignment of Wages Act, R.S.S. 1978, c. A-30, s. 3; Labour Standards Code, 1972, R.S.N.S. 1989, c. 246, s. 89. In the authors' opinion, the reference is to amounts of wages coming due in future and not to wages already owing at the time of assignment. The policy underlying such a rule seems to be to prevent a creditor from depriving an employee of the means of livelihood, diminishing the employee's incentive to work, and so undermining the employment relationship.

29. *Young* v. *Kitchen* (1878), 3 Ex. D. 127.

ETHICAL ISSUE

Credit Cards

Credit cards have become one of the most common forms of payment for goods and services. There are several ways of setting up a credit card arrangement and organizing the legal relationships among the parties. Three-party credit card transactions (except when the card is issued by the merchant itself, such as a department store) are assignments of contractual rights: a business accepts a credit card and assigns its right to payment for goods or services purchased on credit to the credit card company. The credit card issuer pays the business for goods purchased with its card. The customer, by entering into a contract with the credit card company, consents to the assignment and agrees to pay the credit card issuer, rather than paying the business directly.

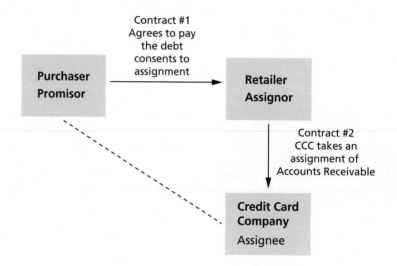

The credit card industry is well financed by charging businesses a small percentage of credit card sales (2 to 10 percent, depending on volume), by charging cardholders an annual fee, and by collecting interest on unpaid balances. Retailers are subject to merchant agreements that prevent them from surcharging credit card transactions to cover this fee. When considering the anti-competitive nature of the prohibition, one scholar wrote:

> This means that merchants who accept credit cards are forced to charge *all* customers the same higher prices in order to cover the costs of accepting credit card transactions. As a result, non-credit consumers (food stamps, cash, checks, debit) end up subsidizing credit card consumers and, indirectly subsidizing the entire credit card industry.[30]

Australia allows merchants to charge credit card customers a higher price.

continued

---

30. E. Warren, "Antitrust Issues in Credit Card Merchant Restraint Rules," *Discussion Paper for The Tobin Project Risk Policy Working Group*, May 6, 2007, www.tobinproject.org/downloads/RP_Merchant_Restraint_Rules.pdf, at para. 2.

QUESTIONS TO CONSIDER

1. Should cash customers be charged the same price as credit card customers when credit card customers cost the retailer more?

2. Why should credit card companies get to collect fees from both the customer and the retailer?

3. Who should bear the loss in the case of online credit card fraud: the consumer, the retailer, or the credit card issuer?

Sources: A.G. Guest and Eva Lomnicka, *An Introduction to the Law of Credit and Security* (London: Sweet & Maxwell, 1978), at para. 366; E. Warren, "Antitrust Issues in Credit Card Merchant Restraint Rules," *Discussion Paper for The Tobin Project Risk Policy Working Group*, May 6, 2007, www.tobinproject.org/downloads/RP_Merchant_Restraint_Rules.pdf.

ASSIGNMENTS BY OPERATION OF LAW

Upon the Death of a Party

When a person dies, the law automatically assigns his or her rights and obligations under outstanding contracts to a personal representative. If the deceased person leaves a will naming a representative, the representative is called an **executor**. If he or she fails to name an executor in the will (or the executor refuses to assume the position) or else leaves no will (that is, dies **intestate**), the court will appoint a personal representative called an administrator. A representative does not have to perform a contract requiring personal services; the skill of the deceased cannot be demanded of the representative. We need only think of the executor of a deceased violinist to understand the reason for this rule.

The task of an executor or **administrator** is to pay all just claims against the deceased's estate, to complete performance of any outstanding contractual obligations of the deceased not requiring personal skill, to pursue all claims the deceased had against others, and then to distribute the assets according to the will—or in the case of an intestate person, to distribute them to the heirs according to statutory provisions.[31]

executor
the personal representative of a deceased person named in his or her will

intestate
when a person dies without leaving a will

administrator
the personal representative of a person who dies intestate

Bankruptcy

A person carrying on business, who becomes insolvent, may realize that his position is hopeless, and may voluntarily apply for bankruptcy proceedings to avoid further loss to his creditors and injury to his name. Or it may be creditors who begin bankruptcy proceedings against a reluctant debtor by petitioning the court for an order known as a **receiving order**. If the creditors satisfy the court that their debtor is insolvent, the court will declare him **bankrupt** and appoint a licensed trustee to take charge of his property. It is then the duty of the trustee to liquidate the assets and to settle the creditors' claims.

We shall deal with bankruptcy again in Chapter 31. We raise the topic at this point simply to explain the relationship between a bankrupt person and the trustee in bankruptcy. In the proceedings, the court assigns to the trustee the bankrupt person's assets, including his contractual rights and his liabilities.[32]

receiving order
a court order to commence bankruptcy proceedings

bankrupt
declared insolvent by the court

---

31. The way in which the estate of an intestate person will be distributed to the heirs is set down in provincial statutes. See, for example: Estates Administration Act, R.S.O. 1990, c. E.22; Intestate Succession Act, R.S.N.S. 1989, c. 236, s. 153; Estate Administration Act, R.S.B.C. 1996, c. 122, Part 7.

32. A licensed trustee may, however, with the permission of inspectors appointed by the creditors, disclaim any lease of property of the bankrupt debtor. Bankruptcy and Insolvency Act, R.S.C. 1985, c. B-3 (as amended), s. 30(1)(k).

Assignments resulting from death and from bankruptcy proceedings started by creditors differ from other assignments in that they are involuntary; they take place "by operation of law." One's affairs are seldom completely in good order when either of these events occurs, and an assignment creates an artificial extension of the assignor's legal existence until his affairs can be wound up.

NEGOTIABLE INSTRUMENTS

Their Nature and Uses

negotiable instrument
a written contract containing a promise, express or implied, to pay a specific sum of money to the order of a designated person or to "bearer"

Chapter 21 of this book examines the law affecting negotiable instruments in more detail. Since, however, negotiable instruments are a special type of assignment, we can better understand both concepts by reviewing their differences here. A **negotiable instrument**—for example, a draft, promissory note, or cheque—is a written contract containing a promise, express or implied,[33] to pay a specific sum of money to the order of a named person or to "bearer."

Generally speaking, a negotiable instrument arises from a prior contract: a buyer delivers a negotiable instrument in payment for goods or services received. But delivery of the instrument does not complete the promisor's obligation. If he does not honour the instrument when it falls due and is presented to be paid, the promisee has the choice of suing under the original contract or for failure to honour the instrument. Often a promisee chooses to sue on the negotiable instrument because the procedure is somewhat simpler.

The unique aspects of the law of negotiable instruments arise when a promisee assigns an instrument to a third party.

Negotiability Compared with Assignability

negotiation
the process of assigning a negotiable instrument

endorse
sign one's name on a negotiable instrument

holder
a party who acquires a negotiable instrument from the transferor

The process of assigning a negotiable instrument is known as **negotiation**. A promisee or payee of an instrument may negotiate it in one of two ways: if the instrument is payable to bearer, he need only deliver it to a third party; if the instrument is payable in his name, he must **endorse** his name upon it and then deliver it. Negotiation is really a special type of assignment in which the new **holder** of the instrument acquires from the transferor the rights that the instrument has to convey.

In a sense, negotiation is a privileged type of assignment that, for reasons of business convenience, is freed from certain of the restrictions that apply to an ordinary assignment of contractual rights. It differs from an assignment of rights generally in the following important respects.

Notice to the Promisor

We have seen that notice plays two important roles in assignment generally: first, written notice is necessary before an assignee may take advantage of a statutory assignment; second, notice protects an assignee against the risk of the promisor being unaware of the assignment and paying the assignor or other assignees. However, notice does not affect the transfer of a negotiable instrument—indeed, it is irrelevant—because the promisor is liable to pay only one person, the holder of the instrument for the time being. Even if the promisor receives notice of the assignment, neither she nor her bank will pay the assignee unless and until the assignee presents the instrument. The promisor pays her debt only once—to the holder of the instrument for the time being and in exchange for the instrument. In effect she pays for the return of her negotiable instrument. "The

33. According to the wording of a cheque, the drawer does not directly promise to pay its amount, but he does promise by implication that sufficient funds will be available in his account to pay it when it is presented.

idea of 'embedding' legal rights in a document, such that the abstract rights move in unison with the physical certificate, has been very potent in commercial law, especially in regard to debt obligations."[34]

ILLUSTRATION 12.10

Steele receives his monthly paycheque of $3500 from Union Foundry Co. Ltd. He negotiates it to Comfy Furniture Mart for $2700 worth of furniture and $800 cash. Steele then tells his employer that he has inadvertently destroyed the cheque by throwing the envelope containing it into a fire, and he persuades Union to pay him a second time. When Comfy presents the original cheque for payment, Union must honour it even though Comfy gave no notice of the assignment.

If instead Steele had assigned to Comfy a claim against Union for arrears of wages (a contractual right not represented by any negotiable instrument) and if Comfy did not immediately notify Union of the assignment, Union could defeat the claim of Comfy, as assignee, by establishing that it had already paid Steele before receiving notice.

Defences of the Promisor

An assignee for value of a negotiable instrument may succeed in an action against the promisor where the assignor himself would not have succeeded. For example, even when a promisor is induced to sign a negotiable instrument because of fraud or undue influence, he may be sued successfully by a subsequent innocent holder who has given consideration for the instrument to the party guilty of the fraud; yet the rogue could not himself enforce the promise in the instrument.[35]

A defrauder may transfer enforceable rights under a negotiable instrument in much the same way that he can pass valid title to goods to an innocent purchaser. Similarly, a person who has given a negotiable instrument in payment for an illegal consideration loses the defence of illegality against an innocent holder of the instrument for value. By contrast, in an ordinary assignment of rights, the assignee never acquires a better right than the assignor had; the debtor retains her defences against the assignee.

ILLUSTRATION 12.11

Bacchus contracted with Hermes for the illegal transportation of liquor into Saskatchewan and gave Hermes his cheque for $2000 for services rendered. The police discovered and confiscated the liquor, and Bacchus then asked his bank to stop payment on the cheque to Hermes.

In the meantime, Hermes had used the cheque to pay a debt to an innocent trade creditor, Argus, who knew nothing of the illegal contract for which the cheque had been issued. Argus learned that payment of the cheque had been stopped when he attempted to cash it at the bank. Argus sued Bacchus on the dishonoured instrument.

Bacchus might have used the defence of illegality successfully in an action brought against him by the party with whom he contracted—Hermes. But he must pay the holder of the cheque, Argus, if (as appears probable) Argus can prove he took the instrument unaware of its illegal origin and gave value for it.

By contrast, if Hermes' claim for $2000 against Bacchus had remained simply in the form of an account receivable, no one to whom Hermes might have assigned the debt would have obtained a better right to collect it than Hermes himself had.

---

34. Baxter and Johnston, "New Mechanics for Securities Transactions" (1971), 21 U.T.L.J. 358.

35. Consumers are protected from the harshness of this rule, see The Bills of Exchange Act, R.S.C. 1985, c. B-4, restricting the rights of finance companies to assert the status of a holder in due course.

Form of Action

A holder of a negotiable instrument can sue in her own name; it is not necessary for her to join in the action any of the other parties who have signed the instrument.

Commercial Importance of Negotiability

For hundreds of years, merchants have found it to their advantage to recognize negotiable instruments as a special class of readily assignable promise, free from the formalities and many of the risks of an ordinary assignment of contractual rights. Business experience has shown that negotiability has a convenience far outweighing any cost of its abuse. We have noted that the law restricts the possibility of abuse in the face of such defences as fraud, undue influence, duress, and illegality by requiring a holder of a negotiable instrument to show that he was unaware of the origin of the tainted instrument, and that he or some previous holder of the instrument must have given value for it.[36]

Modern banking practice is based upon the relatively secure position of an innocent holder for value of a negotiable instrument. Banks are able to cash cheques or accept them for deposit without exhaustive inquiry into the background of the transactions out of which they arose since, as innocent holders for value, they are immune from the earlier flawed nature of the transaction. Without such a rule, banking facilities would be much less accessible to business and the public generally.

Currency

The familiar Bank of Canada note is a special type of instrument authorized by statute and designed to circulate with maximum ease of transferability. We shall refer to it again briefly in Chapter 21.

QUESTIONS FOR REVIEW

1. Define the following terms: third party; assignor; novation; constructive trust; beneficiary; chose in action.

2. Give an example of vicarious performance by a party other than an employee.

3. How has the privity of contract rule been modified with respect to insurance?

4. Describe the significance of exemption clauses in contracts for the storage and transportation of goods.

5. *P* contracted with *Q* to move equipment from one of *Q*'s buildings to another site. *R*, an employee of *P*, damaged some of the equipment. What facts must *Q* establish in order to hold *P* liable for *R*'s conduct?

6. Describe a collateral contract and the circumstances in which it may arise.

7. A debtor owed his creditor $2000. The creditor assigned her right to collect this debt to another person, *X*. The assignee, *X*, delayed in sending notice to the debtor that he was now the party entitled to payment. Before receiving any notice of assignment, the debtor paid his original creditor $750 on account. How have *X*'s rights been affected?

---

36. The requirements are somewhat more technical than we can conveniently describe here: the holder must be a *holder in due course*. See *infra*, Chapter 21.

8. Anderson, a skilled mechanic, agreed to do some car repair work for Bartlett. Anderson was busy when the car was delivered for repair and gave his friend Gauche the work to do, without consulting Bartlett. Gauche sent Bartlett a bill for the repair work. Bartlett refused to pay. Is he justified?

9. Give two examples of involuntary assignments.

10. What are the requirements for a statutory assignment? Describe the business advantages associated with such assignments.

11. Explain the two types of assignment by operation of law.

12. Is notice required to assign a negotiable instrument? Explain.

CASES AND PROBLEMS

1. King, a building contractor, completed the construction of a house for Harris. At completion, Harris owed King a balance of $15 000. King then borrowed $10 000 from the Brandon Bank. In consideration for this loan, King assigned to the bank as much of his account receivable from Harris as should be necessary to repay the sum borrowed plus interest and any further sums for which he might become indebted to the bank. Is the bank, as assignee, entitled to sue Harris without the assistance of King's testimony?

   Suppose instead that King had borrowed $20 000 from the Brandon Bank and in partial settlement assigned the whole of the $15 000 due to him from Harris. Are these changed facts in themselves sufficient to entitle the bank to sue Harris without joining King in the action?

2. The University of Ashcroft Business School offers one-week executive courses. For its October program on marketing strategies, Ashcroft's dean managed to make a deal with Professor Bertoff, a famous specialist in the field, to give the opening lecture and remain at the business school for two full days. Less than a week before the program was to begin, Bertoff sent an e-mail to the dean that his country's government had requested him to chair a crucial international meeting on trade policy; he would send his associate, Professor Colbert, a more junior but quite well-known person in the marketing field, to deliver the lecture prepared by Bertoff himself, and to remain on campus for the two days.

   The dean is quite upset: he has no alternative but to allow Colbert to fill in. He wishes to know whether he has a good case against Bertoff. Give your opinion with reasons.

3. Garbutt was dismissed by her employer, Carter Computers Inc., for allegedly dishonest conduct. She hired Harkin to be her lawyer and represent her in grievance arbitration for wrongful dismissal. Harkin was successful; the arbitrator found that Garbutt had been wrongfully dismissed and that she was entitled to be compensated for her losses.

   During negotiations to settle the amount of compensation, Garbutt gave Harkin a signed direction to Carter Computers to pay 30 percent of the settlement proceeds to Harkin. He delivered a photocopy of the direction to Carter Computers' in-house lawyer, but she told him that Carter Computers would honour only an original signed copy.

   The next day the parties reached a settlement of $20 000. Before the in-house lawyer received the original copy of the direction, she instructed the payroll department to issue a cheque to Garbutt for the full amount of the settlement proceeds. Harkin sued the defendant for failure to pay him the $6000.

   Summarize the arguments of each side, and give your opinion of whether Harkin should succeed.

4. Keirson sold his taxi business to Martens, covenanting neither directly nor indirectly to carry on or be engaged in another taxi business within five miles of the place of business for five years from the date of

sale. The agreement contained the usual clause extending the benefit of the contract to the "assigns" (assignees) of the parties. Two years later, Martens resold the taxi business to Nelman, and shortly afterwards Keirson entered into another taxi business within the five-mile area. Nelman brought an action against Keirson for an injunction to restrain him from operating a competing business within the five-mile area. Should Nelman succeed?

5. B. Flatt and F. Major made a $50 wager about the spelling of Cavalleria Rusticana. Flatt lost and he gave Major a cheque for $50. When Major attempted to deposit the cheque in her bank account, she learned that Flatt had instructed his bank to stop payment on it. What are Major's rights?

   Would it make any difference if Major had cashed Flatt's cheque with her corner pharmacist and the pharmacist was then confronted with Flatt's stop-payment order?

6. Glashov purchased on credit from Brown a building for business purposes. In their agreement, Glashov covenanted that he would insure the property and assign the insurance to Brown, the vendor, as security for the amount that remained owing on the purchase price.

   Glashov insured the property with the Standard Insurance Company but neglected to inform the company that the proceeds in the event of a claim should be paid to Brown. The building was later destroyed in a fire.

   Immediately after the fire, three of Glashov's trade creditors sought payment of their claims and agreed to accept from him an assignment to them of the proceeds of the fire insurance. The trade creditors gave notice to Standard Insurance Company at once, before the amount of the loss had been established and before that company had admitted any liability under the policy. Brown, after learning what had happened, informed the insurance company that she wished to claim the insurance money due, and supported her claim by showing to the company the terms of the agreement for sale. The insurance company paid the money into court for settlement of the dispute.

   What is the nature of the trade creditors' argument that they should have the insurance money instead of Brown? What possible defence or defences might Brown offer against this claim? To whom would a court order the payment of the insurance money?

7. York Bridge Co. Ltd. undertook construction work for the City of Vancouver. A month later, when the construction work was partly completed, York Bridge assigned to Southern B.C. Foundries & Steel Co. Ltd. the amount of $68 000 due to it for work completed by that time. When it took the assignment, the management of Southern B.C. Foundries was aware that the claim its company was acquiring arose from an uncompleted contract. Southern B.C. Foundries immediately notified the City of the assignment but delayed in pursuing its rights when the City was slow in paying.

   York Bridge abandoned the contract in the following September, and its non-performance caused a loss to the City of $125 000. When Southern B.C. Foundries then attempted, as assignee, to collect $68 000 from the City, the City defended by claiming it no longer owed money for the construction work because the damages it had suffered from the breach of contract exceeded the sum owing for the part of the work that had already been done. Southern B.C. Foundries contended that the sum of $68 000 was due and payable at the time the City had been notified of the assignment.

   Explain the issues raised by these facts and the applicable rules of law, and express an opinion whether Southern B.C. Foundries should be able to recover $68 000 from the City of Vancouver. Explain also whether this would appear to be an equitable or a statutory assignment, and indicate the significance that the type of assignment would have in this case.

8. Norton responded to a campaign for funds by the National Association for the Preservation of Wildlife (NAPW) by signing the following statement, which she gave to a canvasser for NAPW:

$1250.00 Charlottetown, Nov. 2, 2001

To assist in the purchase of conservation area sites and in consideration of the subscriptions of others, I promise to pay to the Treasurer of the National Association for the Preservation of Wildlife the sum of twelve hundred and fifty dollars, payable $500 on February 1, 2002 and $750 on August 1, 2002.

Joan I. Norton

This and other similar agreements permitted the Association to acquire property for use as conservation areas.

In order to obtain cash immediately from some of the pledges made to it, including Norton's, NAPW sold (assigned) them to Simpson for an undisclosed cash sum. Simpson's secretary telephoned Norton to advise her of the assignment of her promise, and Norton confirmed that she had made the pledge. Norton failed, however, to pay either of the instalments to Simpson. Simpson brought an action against Norton for payment of the $1250.

Express, with reasons, an opinion about the probable outcome of this action.

ADDITIONAL RESOURCES FOR CHAPTER 12 ON THE COMPANION WEBSITE *(www.pearsoned.ca/smyth)*

In addition to self-test multiple-choice, true–false, and short essay questions (all with immediate feedback), application exercises, and links to useful web destinations, the Companion Website provides the following resources for Chapter 12:

- **British Columbia:** Credit Cards; Statutory Assignment
- **Alberta:** Credit Cards; Statutory Assignment; Trusts
- **Ontario:** Consumer Credit; Death Without a Will; Executors; Statutory Assignments; Trusts

13

The Discharge of Contracts

When a contract comes to an end—is discharged—neither party has any obligations under it. Apart from breach, which is examined in the next chapter, we examine here the various ways in which a contract may be discharged. We discuss also the consequences of an event that makes performance impossible or pointless—a frustrating event—and its effects. In this chapter we examine such questions as:

- What is "tender of performance," and what are its requirements and consequences?

- What are the various ways in which a contract may be discharged by agreement?

- How may a contract provide for its own termination?

- What are the shortcomings of common law rules in their ability to deal with frustration?

- How have statutory reforms dealt with these problems?

- What special problems arise from frustration as it applies to the sale of goods?

- What is meant by "discharge by operation of law"?

THE WAYS IN WHICH A CONTRACT MAY BE DISCHARGED

To **discharge a contract** means "to cancel the obligation of a contract; to make an agreement or contract null and inoperative."[1] In this chapter, we shall consider four ways in which the discharge of a contract may occur: by performance, agreement, frustration, and operation of law. In addition, a contract is sometimes said to be "discharged" by its breach, but this topic is reserved for separate treatment in the following chapter.

discharge a contract
cancel the obligations of a contract; make an agreement or contract null and inoperative

DISCHARGE BY PERFORMANCE

The Nature of Discharge by Performance

Parties who enter into a contract expect it to be discharged by performance. Their contract ends when they have performed all their respective obligations satisfactorily. For a contract to be fully discharged, both parties—not merely one of them—must complete performance. A bilateral contract, formed by the offer of a promise for a promise, goes through three stages: first, when neither party has performed its promise; second, when one but not the other party has performed; and third, when both have performed. Only at the final stage is the contract discharged by performance. In a unilateral contract, formed by the offer of a promise for an act, the first stage is eliminated because the second takes place in the very formation of the contract through one party's performance; the last stage remains necessary for discharge by performance.

Performance may take several forms, depending on the contract. It may be services rendered, goods delivered, a cash payment made, or any combination of these.

Tender of Performance

One party may attempt to perform, but the other party refuses to accept the performance. An attempt to perform is called a **tender of performance**, whether accepted or rejected by the other party.

If a seller properly tenders delivery of goods and the buyer refuses to accept them, the seller is under no obligation to attempt delivery again and may immediately sue for breach of contract.

A debtor who makes an unsuccessful but reasonable attempt to pay will be free from further liability for interest on the amount owing, and generally will not have to pay court costs if he is later sued for the debt.

tender of performance
an attempt by one party to perform according to the terms of the contract

---

ILLUSTRATION 13.1

S agrees in writing to sell $10 000 worth of flour to B, cash on delivery. Before the date of delivery, the price of flour rises substantially. S becomes anxious to discover a means of avoiding the contract; hearing a rumour that B is in financial difficulties, he uses the argument that B may be unable to pay as an excuse for notifying B that he is terminating the contract. B, of course, wishes to proceed with the sale at the agreed price. She takes the contract to her bank and borrows sufficient cash (legal tender) to pay the purchase price. She then tenders the money to S in the presence of a witness. If S does not deliver the flour and B sues him for breach of contract, S cannot claim in defence that B was unable to pay.

---

1. *Black's Law Dictionary*, 6th ed., at 463.

However, refusing a tender of payment does not extinguish an existing debt. There is a legal principle that the debtor must seek out her creditor. She is not excused from tendering payment because her creditor is slow or hesitant about asking for it: the onus is on the debtor to find and pay her creditor.

DISCHARGE BY AGREEMENT

Waiver

waiver
an agreement not to proceed with the performance of a contract already in existence

The parties may agree between themselves not to perform their contract and so discharge it. A **waiver** is an agreement not to proceed with the performance of a contract already in existence. If neither party has performed fully at the time both agree to call off the bargain, there is automatically consideration for the waiver of each party: each still has rights and obligations outstanding, and a promise by one party to waive its rights is sufficient consideration for it being released from obligations to the other.

On the other hand, if one party has already fully performed its part but the other has not, the first party receives no consideration for giving a waiver of the other party's duty to perform. To be binding, its promise to release the other party should be under seal.

ILLUSTRATION 13.2

Atwater agrees to install a sound system in the Kent Theatre for $5500. Kent's right, under the contract, is to receive the benefits of the work, and Kent's obligation is to pay for the work. Atwater's right is to receive the price, and his obligation is to do the work required. If they should mutually agree to call off their contract before Atwater completes the work, there is consideration for the waiver. Atwater promises to abandon a claim for payment; in return, Kent Theatre promises to abandon a claim for services. Each party's promise is the price paid for the promise of the other.

But suppose that Kent has paid Atwater the $5500 and that to date Atwater has only partly installed the system. At this stage, any undertaking by Kent that it will "require neither completion of the work nor a return of any money" is without consideration and, therefore, not binding unless under seal.[2]

Of course, neither party can impose a waiver on the other. A party who fails to perform without securing a waiver by the other commits a breach of the contract. As we shall see in the next chapter, the consequences of breach are quite different from discharge by agreement.

Substituted Agreement

Accord and Satisfaction

accord and satisfaction
a compromise between contracting parties to substitute a new contractual obligation and release a party from the existing one

Sometimes a promisor finds that it cannot perform its obligation according to the terms of the contract or that performance has become very difficult. It may offer the promisee a money payment or some other substitute if the promisee discharges it from its original obligation. For example, a seller may find that it cannot obtain certain imported goods to fill an order and may offer other goods of equal quality, perhaps at a lower price, if the buyer releases it from its original promise. A promisee may be preparing to sue the promisor before a settlement is agreed on. **Accord and satisfaction** often takes the form of a compromise out of court.

---

2. This statement remains subject to the discussion in Chapter 6, concerning the "Gratuitous Reduction of a Debt" and "Injurious Reliance."

The distinction between a material alteration of the terms and accord and satisfaction is in the purpose of the arrangement: in a material alteration, the parties are primarily concerned with a new arrangement—the discharge of the old contract is incidental; in accord and satisfaction the parties are seeking a way to discharge their existing contract—the new arrangement is for that very purpose.

A party may concede liability for damages, but the other party disagrees about the amount of the damages it should receive. Suppose the party admitting liability tenders payment of an amount in settlement but the other refuses it, claiming that it is insufficient. The first party may then pay into court the amount offered. If the other party sues and the court awards it no more than the sum tendered in settlement, it will have to pay the court costs as a penalty for insisting upon litigation; in addition, the defendant will not be liable for interest on the sum due from the time it tendered the settlement. On the other hand, if the damages awarded are greater than the sum paid into court by the defendant, the judge may apportion the court costs between the parties, or if the sum tendered was unreasonably low, the judge may order the defendant to pay all the costs.

Novation

Novation is another method of discharge. It occurs when the parties to a contract agree to terminate it and substitute a new contract. There are two types of novation:

novation
the parties to a contract agree to terminate it and substitute a new contract

- a material change in terms
- a change in parties

If parties agree to a material alteration of the terms, one that goes to the root of the contract, they have, in effect, agreed to discharge their original contract and replace it with a new one. One material change would be to change the subject matter of the contract. For instance, car dealer *B* may inform *A* that he cannot deliver the car *A* has ordered without a lengthy delay. They agree to cancel the contract and substitute a new one: for a favourable price offered by *B*, *A* buys a car that *B* has in stock. It is not always easy to decide whether an agreed alteration leaves the original contract intact or amounts to novation.

CASE 13.1

P, a building contractor, agreed to pay a penalty if he did not have the construction work completed by a certain date. Before completion, *P* and the owner, *Q*, agreed that *P* should do some additional work on the same project. The changes made it impossible for *P* to complete the building by the original date. *Q* insisted that the penalty clause allowed him to deduct the penalty from the amount he still owed to *P*. The court held that the new agreement had discharged the old and that the penalty clause had disappeared with it.[3]

When one of the parties to the contract "leaves" and the remaining parties agree that another party replaces her, they have discharged the original contract and replaced it with a new one. A common example occurs when a party purchases a going business and assumes its outstanding liabilities as a part of the purchase price for the assets acquired. If the creditors accept the new owner as their debtor, either by an express agreement with it or by applying to the new owner for payment of claims against the former owner, the liability of the former owner is discharged and replaced by the liability of the purchaser. In the words of Mr. Justice Fisher:

> Where the business of a partnership is taken over by a new company [new owner] and the creditor of the partnership applies to the new company for payment, his claim is admitted and they

---

3. *Thornhill* v. *Neats* (1860), 141 E.R. 1392. See also *Amirault* v. *M.N.R.* (1990), 90 D.T.C. 1330. See *Jedfro Investments (U.S.A.) Ltd.* v. *Jacyk* 2007 SCC 55: the parties must arrive at a new agreement, not merely enter into negotiations.

promise to pay the debt, that is sufficient in my opinion to make the new company liable, as slight circumstances are sufficient to show an adoption by the creditors of the new company as their debtor.[4]

There must be evidence of intention and agreement to abandon the original contract on the part of *both* the creditors and the new owner.[5] The evidence need not be in the form of an express agreement; it may be shown by examining the conduct of the parties. However, the burden is upon the party claiming that there was novation to show that the other party has assumed all liabilities under a pre-existing contract and has acted on that contract.[6]

In good business practice, neither the vendor nor the purchaser of a business relies on implied novation with creditors. The two parties to the sale agree on what debts the new owner should assume and then call in the creditors to obtain their express consent to the substitution of a new debtor. In addition, to protect itself, the purchaser of a business makes a careful examination of public records, requires the vendor to provide a declaration setting out the names of all its creditors and the amounts owing to them, and publicizes the sale. We shall examine the statutory reasons for these procedures more fully in Chapters 30 and 31, which discuss creditors' rights.

A Contract Provides for Its Own Dissolution

Before agreeing to a contract, one party may express concern about a possible event affecting its ability or willingness to perform. If the other party is agreeable, they may include an express term to allow for this event occurring. Sometimes, a similar term may be implied by trade usage or by the surrounding circumstances of the agreement. The term may be a condition precedent, a condition subsequent, or an option to terminate.

Condition Precedent

In Chapter 11, we noted that a condition precedent is a future or uncertain event that must have occurred before the promisor's liability is established. (The "occurrence" may be a "non-event," that is, a condition that the thing not happen before the time stipulated.) In that chapter, because we were concerned with the interpretation of contracts and the operation of the parol evidence rule, we referred to a condition precedent as the result of an oral understanding. It may, of course, be a term in a written contract.

ILLUSTRATION 13.3

A Co. Ltd., located in Moncton, writes to *B* in Winnipeg offering him a good employment position. *B* replies by letter that he will take the position if *A* Co. Ltd. will first find satisfactory living accommodation in Moncton for him and his family. *A*

Co. Ltd. accepts *B*'s counter-offer by mail. The employer's act of finding the accommodation is a condition precedent.

Alternatively, *B* might reply that he will take the position if his wife, who works for a different firm, is not offered a promotion for which she has already applied. The failure to receive the promotion is a condition precedent.

It has sometimes been argued that a contract does not even come into existence when there is a condition precedent, and that to be capable of discharge, a contract must first have existed. Yet there is a real sense in which a contract is formed from the time of the offer and the acceptance, even though a condition precedent is not resolved until later. A contract subject to a condition precedent

---

4. Re *Star Flooring Co. Ltd.*, [1924] 3 D.L.R. 269 at 272.
5. *Toronto Star* v. *Aiken*, [1955] O.W.N. 613.
6. See *Pacific Wash-A-Matic Ltd.* v. *R.O. Booth Holdings Ltd.* (1979), 105 D.L.R. (3d) 323.

does have a binding force from the outset, and the parties are not free to withdraw from their promises unless and until the condition precedent becomes impossible to fulfill. The arrangement is, therefore, much more than an outstanding offer that can be revoked prior to acceptance. Accordingly, in Illustration 13.3, if immediately after *B* received *A* Co. Ltd.'s acceptance he changed his mind and took a position with a different firm, he would be in breach of contract.

A contract may contain a series of conditions precedent:

ILLUSTRATION 13.4

Grey, the owner of a construction site, stipulates in her contract with the builder, Brown, that as work progresses on their construction project it must be approved at specified stages by a designated architect, Greene. If, after any stage of the work is completed, Greene states that he is not satisfied with the quality of performance, Grey's obligation to pay for that stage and for further work under the contract ceases: Greene's approval is a condition precedent to payment for the work completed and for continuing with the remaining stages.

A party that agrees to do work on these terms exposes itself to the judgment and reasonableness of a designated person who assesses the work. Unless it can show that there has been fraud or collusion between that person and the party for which it is to do the work, it is bound by the verdict reached; it cannot claim a breach of contract if the work is brought to an end prematurely when the designated person, acting in good faith, refuses to approve what has been done.

A promisor is in an even more difficult position if it gives the right to approve or disapprove of performance to the promisee itself rather than to a third party such as an engineer or architect. The promisee's opinion of what is satisfactory is far more likely to be prejudiced in its own favour. The courts have held that a promisee given such a power can withhold approval and avoid liability under the contract. It does not matter that the promisee's judgment is unreasonable, or that the judge or jury believe that in the circumstances they themselves would have approved of the performance: so long as they find that the promisee is honestly dissatisfied, the promisor has no rights against it.[7]

Condition Subsequent

A **condition subsequent** is an uncertain event that brings a promisor's liability to an end automatically if it happens. Liability is established when the contract is formed but one of the parties has reserved for itself an "out" in certain circumstances. A buyer of a ticket for a baseball game has the benefit of a term in his contract that if the game is rained out before a stated inning, he will be given a ticket for another game.

condition subsequent
an uncertain event that brings a promisor's liability to an end if it happens

ILLUSTRATION 13.5

Norton is the holder of a baseball season's ticket that, because of some of his bad habits known to the management, was sold to him on terms that he must watch his conduct at the games.

Norton attends a game and his conduct annoys not only the operators of the ballpark but also other fans and those selling tickets. He has a loud, booming voice and insists on telling other fans things they do not want to know, and by moving about he obstructs the view of others. The management informs him that it is cancelling his season's ticket and tenders him a refund for the remaining games. Norton sues the management for breach of contract.

The contract contains a term relating to a condition subsequent—Norton's objectionable conduct. It is, therefore, discharged by agreement rather than by breach, and Norton's action will fail.[8]

---

7. *Truman* v. *Ford Motor Co.*, [1926] 1 D.L.R. 960.
8. See *North* v. *Victoria Baseball & Athletic Co.*, [1949] 1 W.W.R. 1033.

act of God
the raging of the natural elements

In contracts for the shipment of goods, an "**act of God**" (the raging of the natural elements) may be a condition subsequent if it results in the destruction of the shipment. When a railway, trucking line, airline, or marine shipping company accepts goods for shipment, it undertakes to be liable for any damage if the goods arrive at their destination in a poorer condition than they were received by the carrier; but there is also a term discharging the carrier from this liability if the goods are destroyed by an act of God. If the goods are only partly destroyed, the contract is not discharged completely; instead, the carrier is absolved from liability to the extent that the damage was caused to the goods by an act of God and the carrier must deliver them as they are. Such a term is implied by trade custom, but most carriers take the added precaution of expressly stating the term in their bills of lading. Accordingly, it is wise, when shipping goods at the owner's risk, to buy insurance against such loss.

Option to Terminate

A contract may include a term that gives one party, or perhaps both, the option of bringing the contract to an end before its performance has been completed, usually by giving notice. Exercising the option results in discharge by agreement because the means of discharge was agreed upon when drawing up the contract. For example, a contract of employment of indefinite duration usually contains an option clause, either express or implied, entitling the employer to dismiss an employee on giving the required notice, as explained in Chapter 20. Many mortgages have an option clause entitling the mortgagor to pay off the principal sum before maturity by tendering an additional payment of interest.

In a contract for the purchase of a business, a buyer may insist on a proviso allowing it to rescind the agreement if a current audit of the financial statements of the business should result in the auditor being unable to give an unqualified opinion on their fairness. In these circumstances, an auditor's qualified opinion (or unwillingness to express any opinion) would give the purchaser an option to terminate the contract.

INTERNATIONAL ISSUE

Will the NHL Come to Hamilton?

The story of Jim Balsillie's (as yet unfulfilled) dream to buy an NHL team and move it to Canada is a tale of conditions precedent, conditions subsequent, and options to terminate.

His 2006 bid to buy the Pittsburgh Penguins failed because Balsillie was unwilling to promise that the team would remain in Pittsburgh. The agreement of purchase and sale contained a league-required condition that the purchase be approved by the NHL Board of Governors. The NHL approval would only be granted if Balsillie agreed to a variety of terms, including the Pittsburgh location. As a result, Balsillie gave notice that he would not proceed with the purchase.

In 2007, negotiations with Nashville Predator owner Craig Leipold became trapped in a circle:

> What is known is that [Leipold] inexplicably took the position that Balsillie needed league consent for the purchase before Leipold would sign any such agreement. The effect was to cast Balsillie into a kind of feedback loop: to get league approval for his purchase, he needed a binding agreement; to get a binding agreement, he needed league approval.[9]

continued

9.   C. Gillis and J. Intini, "Shut Out of the NHL," *Maclean's* July 23, 2007, www.macleans.ca/culture/sports/article.jsp?content=20070723_107266_107266, at page 3.

League approval again focused on whether Balsillie would immediately move the Predators to Canada. NHL Commissioner Gary Bettman was vocal in his opposition to such a move. Two contracts figured prominently in the ability to make such a move:

1. The current lease of the Nashville arena: The lease included a term that allowed the Predators to end the lease early if average fan attendance at the games fell below 14 000. The City of Nashville felt that the tenant could not take advantage of this term because it was in default under the lease.

2. A new lease (and management agreement) with the City of Hamilton for the use of Copps Coliseum: This agreement was entered into during the Predator negotiations. The deal contained a condition that it would automatically expire if Balsillie did not buy a team by December 30, 2007.

The publicity surrounding the Hamilton lease, and the acceptance of deposits on season's tickets, drew the ire of the Commissioner. In the end, the Board of Governors did not even consider the approval question as it never made the agenda of a meeting. The Predators completed a deal with a group of Nashville investors for much less than the Balsillie offer.

Richard Rodier, Balsillie's lawyer, suggested that the deal failed because of a bias against Canada:

". . . to take money hand over fist and then give us the back of their hand when we offer significantly more money than anyone else for one of their franchises is, I think, insulting to the Canadian people."[10]

QUESTIONS TO CONSIDER

1. What kind of term was attached to the league approval of the Penguins sale: a condition precedent, subsequent, or option to terminate?

2. What kind of term was included in the City of Hamilton agreement: a condition precedent, subsequent, or option to terminate?

3. What kind of term was included in the Nashville arena lease: a condition precedent, subsequent, or option to terminate?

Sources: S. Brunt, "Balsillie Still in the Game," *Globe and Mail*, May 8, 2008, www.globesports.com/servlet/story/RTGAM.20080508.brunt09/GSStory/GlobeSportsHockey/home; D. Schoaltz, "Predators Inch Closer to Hamilton," *Globe and Mail*, June 13, 2007, www.globesports.com/servlet/story/RTGAM.20070613.wsptpredators13/GSStory/GlobeSportsHockey/home; D. Schoaltz, "Tickets? Who needs tickets?" *Globe and Mail*, June 14, 2007, www.globesports.com/servlet/story/RTGAM.20070613.wsptpreds13/GSStory/GlobeSportsHockey/home; C. Gillis and J. Intini, "Shut Out of the NHL," *Maclean's*, July 23, 2007, www.macleans.ca/culture/sports/article.jsp?content=20070723_107266_107266; P. Waldie and S. Stewart, "RIM Boss Buys NHL's Penguins," *Globe and Mail*, October 5, 2006, www.theglobeandmail.com/servlet/story/RTGAM.20061004.wbalsillie04/BNStory/GlobeSportsHockey/home; B. McKenzie, "Balsillie Pulls his Bid to Purchase Penguins," *TSN*, December 15, 2006, www.tsn.ca/nhl/story/?id=188556.

DISCHARGE BY FRUSTRATION

Effect of Absolute Promises

The common law originally held a party absolutely responsible for a failure to perform her promise—even when the failure was not her fault. Of course, she could avoid such consequences, if she foresaw them, by insisting on an express term in the contract absolving her from liability if

10. C. Gillis and J. Intini, "Shut Out of the NHL," *Maclean's* July 23, 2007, www.macleans.ca/culture/sports/article.jsp?content=20070723_107266_107266, at page 3.

the event should occur. Indeed, the argument for holding her responsible was that she could have provided for the discharge in the contract but did not do so. As a practical matter it is not possible to foresee all risks. As well, it would take too much time and money to negotiate long lists of unlikely events that would excuse performance.

As the next section will explain, the courts now excuse parties for failure to perform their contracts in a wide variety of circumstances where they are not at fault. Even so, courts remain reluctant to excuse performance in some types of contracts; historically, they have regarded these kinds of promises as absolute regardless of the reason for which they could not be performed.[11] Tenants' covenants in commercial leases to keep the property in good repair and to pay rent are promises of this kind. The result is that tenants have found themselves liable for damages caused by fire, storms, and enemy action, and liable for rent for the duration of the lease when the property was no longer of use to them.[12] However, in extreme cases where the whole point of the contract has disappeared, courts have become more willing to yield.[13]

Several provinces have enacted legislation to overrule the common law and provide that the doctrine of frustration apply to tenancy agreements for residential premises.[14] The legislation does not, however, extend the doctrine to leases of commercial, as opposed to residential, premises.

Doctrine of Frustration

As we have seen, it is an essential principle that contracts in general should have binding force and effect. If the courts excused a failure to perform for any flimsy excuse, there would be tremendous uncertainty in business affairs. Therefore, judges have carefully considered the scope of the doctrine and when it should be applied. Sometimes the parties may have included in their contract a term to deal with the particular risk that has occurred; if so, the courts will not accept the event as frustrating the parties' contract and will give only the limited protection provided in the contract.[15]

The courts have offered a variety of definitions of the **doctrine of frustration**. In *Davis Contractors Ltd.* v. *Fareham*, Lord Radcliffe said:

doctrine of frustration
the law excuses a party from performance when external causes have made performance radically different from that contemplated by the parties

> Frustration occurs whenever the law recognizes that without default of either party a contractual obligation has become incapable of being performed because the circumstances in which performance is called for would render it a radically different thing from that which was undertaken by contract. . . . It is not hardship or inconvenience or material loss itself which calls the principle of frustration into play. There must be as well such a change in the significance of the obligation that the thing undertaken would, if performed, be a different thing from that contracted for.[16]

In another case, Mr. Justice Goddard said:

> If the foundation of the contract goes, either by the destruction of the subject-matter or by reason of such long interruption or delay that the performance is really in effect that of a different contract, and the parties have not provided what in that event is to happen, the performance of the contract is to be regarded as frustrated.[17]

---

11. *Budgett & Co.* v. *Binnington & Co.*, [1891] 1 Q.B. 35; *Hills* v. *Sughrue* (1846), 153 E.R. 844. It is tempting to compare absolute liability for contractual promises with strict liability in tort law as discussed in Chapter 3. We should note, however, that their historical development and the policy underlying them vary greatly.

12. *Paradine* v. *Jane* (1647), 82 E.R. 897; *Redmond* v. *Dainton*, [1920] 2 K.B. 256; *Foster* v. *Caldwell*, [1948] 4 D.L.R. 70.

13. *Cricklewood Property & Investment Trust, Ltd.* v. *Leighton's Investment Trust, Ltd.*, [1945] A.C. 221; *Capital Quality Homes Ltd.* v. *Colwyn Construction Ltd.* (1975), 9 O.R. (2d) 617, per Evans, J.A., at 629. The application of the doctrine of frustration to these cases still remains limited: see *Victoria Wood Development Corp. Inc.* v. *Ondrey* (1977), 14 O.R. (2d) 723, Aff'd (1978), 92 D.L.R. (3d) 229 (Ont. C.A.).

14. See, for example: Residential Tenancies Act, S.O. 2006, c. 17, s. 19; The Residential Tenancies Act, 2006, S.S. 2006, c. R-22.0001, s. 11.

15. *Teleflex Inc.* v. *I.M.P. Group Ltd.* (1996), 149 N.S.R. (2d) 355.

16. [1956] A.C. 696 at 729. See also *KBK No. 138 Ventures Ltd.* v. *Canada Safeway Ltd.* (2000), 185 D.L.R. (4th) 651.

17. *Tatem Ltd.* v. *Gamboa*, [1939] 1 K.B. 132 at 139.

Lord Sumner put it this way:

> It is really a device by which the rules as to absolute contracts are reconciled with a special exception which justice demands.[18]

A decision that a contract has been discharged by frustration is viewed as a practical and reasonable solution imposed by a court under circumstances that were not anticipated by the parties.[19]

The simplest cases are those where performance becomes literally impossible, which explains why they were the ones first used by the courts to develop the doctrine of frustration.

CASE 13.2

The producer of a concert hired a music hall, but it was destroyed by fire before the scheduled date of the concert. No one was found to blame for the fire. The producer sued the owner of the hall for damages to compensate for losses sustained in having to cancel the concert.

The court held that the contract had been discharged by frustration and refused to award damages. Had the court found instead that the owner of the music hall had broken the contract, it would have ordered him to pay damages.[20]

CASE 13.3

Robinson had engaged Davison, a pianist, to give a concert on an agreed date. Robinson incurred expenses in preparing for the concert: advertising, selling tickets, and hiring staff for the evening. At about 9 a.m. on the morning of the concert date, he received word from Davison that a sudden illness would prevent her from performing. Robinson had further expenses in cancelling the concert. When he sued Davison for damages for his loss, the court held that the contract had been discharged by frustration, and the action failed.[21]

The doctrine was carefully adapted in later cases when actual performance remained physically possible but would have a very different meaning from the expectations of the parties when they made their agreement.

CASE 13.4

In July 1914 in England, the contractors Dick, Kerr & Co. agreed to construct certain reservoirs for a local water board within six years at a specified price; they started work immediately. In February 1916, during World War I, the Minister of Munitions, acting under wartime statutes, ordered the contractors to cease work. Most of their plant and materials were then sold under the Minister's directions.

After the war ended, the water board insisted that the contractors resume their work under the original terms, but the contractors refused to comply. Prices and conditions of supply had changed drastically from what they had been in 1916. The court held that the contract had been discharged by frustration and the water board failed in its action.[22]

---

18. *Hirji Mulji* v. *Chong Yue Steamship Co.*, [1926] A.C. 497 at 510.
19. The theories underlying the doctrine of frustration are discussed in Furmston, *Cheshire, Fifoot and Furmston's Law of Contract*, 13th ed., Chapter 20; and in Guest, *Anson's Law of Contract*, 27th ed., Chapter 14.
20. *Taylor* v. *Caldwell* (1863), 122 E.R. 309. See also *Laurwen Investments Inc.* v. *814693 N.W.T. Ltd.* (1990), 48 B.L.R. 100.
21. *Robinson* v. *Davison* (1871), L.R. 6 Ex. 269.
22. *Metropolitan Water Board* v. *Dick, Kerr & Co.*, [1918] A.C. 119.

On the other hand, even substantial hardship may not be a sufficient excuse for failing to perform. The fact that contractual obligations prove to be more onerous than anticipated will not, by itself, discharge a contract by frustration. A business is not excused from performance just because the most convenient or inexpensive method of performance is not available. To excuse a promisor in these circumstances would:

> impair the authority of written contracts . . . by lax or too wide application of the doctrine of frustration. Modern English law has recognized how beneficial that doctrine is when the whole circumstances justify it, but to apply it calls for circumspection.[23]

Lastly, we note that for a contract to be discharged by frustration, its performance must become impossible or purposeless *after the agreement was made* for reasons beyond the control of the parties. We must distinguish this situation from one in which performance was impossible or purposeless at the very time the agreement was made. If the subject-matter has ceased to exist at the time of the agreement, the agreement is void for mistake, as Chapter 8 has shown; it is not discharged by frustration.

Self-induced Frustration

self-induced frustration
a party wilfully disables itself from performing a contract in order to claim that the contract has been frustrated

A party that wilfully disables itself from performing cannot then claim successfully that the contract has been frustrated. Such **self-induced frustration** is a breach of the contract. In many circumstances, the distinction between true frustration and self-induced frustration is readily apparent.

ILLUSTRATION 13.6

(a) *A* Inc. contracts to transport earth for *B*. On realizing that it has made a bad bargain, *A* Inc. sells its sole dump truck and claims that it cannot fulfill the contract because of frustration. We have no difficulty in deciding that *A* Inc. has broken the contract.

(b) *A* Inc. contracts to transport earth for *B* in an isolated northern community. Shortly after the contract is made, its truck (the only available one in the area) is stolen and wrecked. The contract is discharged by frustration, and *A* Inc. is freed from its obligation to perform.

(c) *A* Inc. contracts to transport earth for *B*. Its dump truck breaks down because of an employee's negligence, and there will be a long delay in its repair as the parties are in a small northern community. Because the situation is attributable to *A* Inc.'s negligence, it will be liable for breach of contract.

Not every degree of fault or irresponsibility, however, will bar a party from claiming that the contract has been frustrated. As Lord Russell said in his judgment in a leading House of Lords case:

> The possible varieties are infinite, and can range from the criminality of the scuttler who opens the sea-cocks and sinks his ship, to the thoughtlessness of the prima donna who sits in a draught and loses her voice.[24]

---

23. *Twentsche Overseas Trading Co.* v. *Uganda Sugar Factory Ltd.* (1945), 114 L.J.P.C. 25 at 28. See also *Graham* v. *Wagman* (1976), 14 O.R. (2d) 349: "I have never heard that impecuniosity is an excuse for non-performance of a promise," per Weatherston, J., at 352.

24. *Joseph Constantine Steamship Line Ltd.* v. *Imperial Smelting Corp. Ltd.*, [1942] A.C. 154 at 179. See also *Kendall* v. *Ivanhoe Insurance Managers Ltd.*, [1985] O.J. No. 1725; *Atcor Ltd.* v. *Continental Energy Marketing Ltd.*, [1996] 6 W.W.R. 274.

ETHICAL ISSUE

Multiple Customers

Supposing a business has many contracts requiring the same performance and only limited ability to perform. Which contracts should be performed and which customers should go unsatisfied? It is up to the business to choose which contract will not be performed. This is considered by the courts as a form of self-induced frustration.

A classic case involves applications for fishing licences from the Ministry of Fisheries.[25] The business had four boats that were each rented out for the season. The Ministry granted the company only three licences, which could be allocated to any of the four boats. When sued by the fourth customer, the court rejected the business's defence of frustration because the business decided to breach the contract with the fourth customer.

QUESTIONS TO CONSIDER

1. Is this a fair result for the business? Would the doctrine of frustration apply if the business had not received any licences?

2. What factors should the business consider when deciding which contract(s) to perform?

3. What condition should the business place in the rental agreement to protect itself from this potential breach of contract liability?

The Effect of Frustration

Harshness of the Common Law

Until now, we have assumed that frustration discharges the contract and frees both parties from the duty of further performance. In the simple situation where neither party has performed at all, a complete discharge of both parties is a fair settlement. But often the circumstances are not so simple, and discharging both parties may lead to injustice. When, for example, performance is spread over a period of time and is to be paid for on completion, frustration of the contract before its completion may cause serious hardship for the performer or his estate. The harsh results in the old case of *Cutter* v. *Powell*[26] are a useful illustration. A seaman was to be paid on completion of a voyage from Jamaica to Liverpool. He died en route when the voyage was nearly three-quarters complete. An action by his widow to recover a proportionate part of his wages failed on the grounds that he had not performed as promised.[27]

Early decisions concerning frustration were harsh in another respect: the frustrating event was considered to terminate the contract and future obligations under it from the time of the frustrating event, but any performance already due was still enforceable. An example of another harsh decision was that in *Chandler* v. *Webster*.[28]

---

25. *Maritime National Fish Ltd.* v. *Ocean Trawlers Ltd.*, [1935] 3 D.L.R. 12.

26. (1795), 101 E.R. 573.

27. The harshness of this rule has since been mitigated to some extent by the doctrine of substantial performance, discussed in the next chapter.

28. [1904] 1 K.B. 493.

CASE 13.5

In London in 1902, the plaintiff rented a room to view the coronation procession of Edward VII. It was the first coronation in over 60 years (since that of Queen Victoria); the demand and price for locations with a view were very high—for this room, £141 payable at once. The plaintiff was able to pay only £100 at the time and owed the remaining £41. The contract was frustrated when the king became ill and the procession was cancelled. The plaintiff not only failed to recover his £100, but the court held that since the remaining £41 was due and owing before the frustrating event occurred, he was still liable for that sum, too! The "solution" in this decision was to let the loss lie where it had fallen at the time of the frustrating event.

The Court's Attempt to Soften the Harshness

The 1943 decision of the House of Lords in the *Fibrosa* case[29] altered the rule in *Chandler* v. *Webster*; it permitted a purchaser that had made an advance payment on equipment to recover its money since it had received no benefit from the other party before the frustrating event, the Second World War, began. This solution seems reasonable from the purchaser's point of view—but is it always so from the point of view of the other party? While a seller may not have delivered any of the fruits of its labour, it may well have done considerable work towards the completion of the contract at its own expense. According to the *Fibrosa* decision, the buyer can still demand the return of its deposit in full. In the *Fibrosa* case, the defendant company had partially completed expensive, custom-built machinery, and not only was it unable to require the buyer to share in its loss, but it had to return the entire deposit it had received.

It follows from the reasoning in *Fibrosa* that if a seller cannot retain a deposit on the ground that it has incurred expenses, it certainly cannot recover these expenses from a buyer that has made no deposit. On the other hand, the judgment stated that if the seller had conferred even the slightest benefit on the buyer (for example, if the seller had delivered a small advance shipment of spare parts), the seller could retain the whole deposit! The common law would do nothing to apportion the loss between the parties: it was a matter either of retaining the whole of the deposit or of returning it entirely.

Statutory Reform

At this point, it became clear that only legislation could correct the law. In 1943, during the Second World War, the English Parliament passed the Frustrated Contracts Act in an attempt to remedy the inequities. Subsequently, Prince Edward Island, New Brunswick, Ontario, Manitoba, Alberta, and Newfoundland passed similar acts with some improvement on the original English Act.[30] British Columbia passed its own act to the same effect but with major differences, discussed below.[31]

When a frustrating event occurs, the acts provide for the allocation of losses between parties where money was paid on account by one party to the other or was due but had not yet been paid.

> If, before the parties were discharged . . . [a party] incurred expenses in connection with the performance of the contract, the court, if it considers it just to do so having regard to all the circumstances, may allow the party to retain or to recover, as the case may be, the whole or any part of the sums paid or payable.[32]

29. *Fibrosa Spolka Akcyjna* v. *Fairbairn Lawson Combe Barbour, Ltd.*, [1943] A.C. 32.

30. Frustrated Contracts Act, R.S.P.E.I. 1988, c. F-16; R.S.N.B. 1973, c. F-24; R.S.O. 1990, c. F-34; R.S.M. 1987, c. F-190; R.S.A. 2000, c. F-27; R.S.N. 1990, c. F-26; R.S.N.W.T. 1988, c. F-12; R.S.Y. 2002, c. 96.

31. Frustrated Contract Act, R.S.B.C. 1996, c. 166.

32. Frustrated Contracts Act, R.S.O. 1990, c. F.34, s. 3(2).

In neither of these situations may the performing party retain or recover any sum in excess of the payment made or already due, even when its loss has been greater. The other party may recover any amount by which its payment exceeds the performing party's allowed loss. In addition, the acts authorize a court to award the performer a just proportion of any valuable benefit received by the other party regardless of whether a deposit has been paid.

Unfortunately, when a party has expended time and money in performance of a contract, but the other party, which was eventually to have received the benefit of the work, has (a) made no deposit and (b) has not yet received any benefit—except in British Columbia—the first party is still without remedy and must bear the loss wholly itself.[33] The British Columbia Act states, "a 'benefit' means something done in the fulfilment of contractual obligations, whether or not the person for whose benefit it was done received the benefit."[34] Therefore, in British Columbia,, expenditures made by the first party can be taken into account, and to the extent that the other party has received no benefit from them, the loss is divided equally.[35] This solution seems fair to both parties.

The Sale of Goods

Where the Sale of Goods Act Applies

In a contract for the sale of goods, where we might expect the doctrine of frustration to apply, we must first examine the Sale of Goods Act to see whether it deals directly with the particular situation. The Act states:

> Where there is an agreement to sell specific goods and subsequently the goods without any fault on the part of the seller or buyer perish before the risk has passed to the buyer, the agreement is thereby avoided.[36]

Three conditions must be present for this section to apply:

- First, the goods must be *specific*—that is, "they must be identified and agreed upon at the time the sale is made."
- Second, the risk must still be with the seller—that is, the seller must still be responsible for the safety of the goods.
- Third, the cause of the frustration must be the perishing of the goods.

ILLUSTRATION 13.7

A sends a fax to *B* offering to sell "the carload of number one flour sitting at our rail siding for $10 000, risk to pass to you on delivery of the shipping documents in seven days' time." *B* accepts by return fax. Three days later a shunting locomotive on adjacent tracks is derailed and knocks over the freight car containing the flour. The contents are spilled out and ruined by rain, frustrating the contract.

Both parties are immediately discharged from liability under the contract: *A* cannot sue for the price, nor can *B* sue for failure to deliver. *B* can recover any deposit it has made. *A's* only remedy is against those responsible for the accident.

---

33. The point may be illustrated by the facts in *Appleby* v. *Myers* (1867), L.R. 2 C.P. 651, discussed in Chapter 15 under "*Quantum Meruit.*" Even if the Frustrated Contracts Act had been passed at that time, it presumably would not have altered the decision.

34. Frustrated Contracts Act, R.S.B.C. 1996, c. 166, s. 5(4).

35. *Ibid.*, s. 5(3).

36. R.S.B.C. 1996, c. 410, s. 11; R.S.O. 1990, c. S.1, s. 8; R.S.N.S. 1989, c. 408, s. 10.

In Illustration 13.7, all three elements mentioned in the Sale of Goods Act are present and the Act applies; consequently the Frustrated Contracts Act does not.[37] But if any one of these elements is missing, the Sale of Goods Act does not apply.[38] The Frustrated Contracts Act applies in those provinces having the Act; in the remaining provinces the parties are left with the common law position up to and including the *Fibrosa* case. We now discuss the position of the parties in each of these circumstances.

In Provinces Where the Frustrated Contracts Act Applies

The application of the Act is more easily understood if we begin with some examples.

ILLUSTRATION 13.8

(a) *A* sends a fax to *B* offering to sell "one thousand sacks of number one flour from our warehouse stock for $5000, risk to pass to you on delivery of the shipping documents in seven days' time." *B* accepts by return fax. Three days later, the warehouse and contents are destroyed by fire without any negligence on *A*'s part. The goods are not specific because they have not been segregated from the larger stock and earmarked for the buyer.

(b) *A* sends a fax to *B* offering to sell "the carload of number one flour sitting at our rail siding for $10 000, risk to pass to you on delivery of the shipping documents in seven days' time." *B* accepts by return fax. Three days later, the government requisitions all of *A*'s flour, including the carload sold to *B*, in order to help feed the victims of a flood disaster. Here the contract is frustrated by an event other than the perishing of the goods.

In neither of the above examples does the Sale of Goods Act apply. Under the Frustrated Contracts Act, if *B* had made a deposit and sued for its return, the court would consider whether *A* had incurred any expenses towards the completion of the contract and would take them into account in determining how much of the deposit *B* would recover. If *B* had made no deposit, *A* could only recover the value of any benefit already conferred upon *B*.[39] So, if *A* had delivered one sack of flour to *B* as a sample, it could recover the price of that sack, but no more.

The Frustrated Contracts Act also states that the courts shall give effect to any special provisions made by the parties in anticipation of a frustrating event.

ILLUSTRATION 13.9

A sends a fax to *B* offering to sell "the carload of number one flour sitting at our rail siding for $10 000, risk to pass to you upon acceptance of this offer. Delivery in seven days' time." *B* accepts by return fax. Three days later the flour is destroyed in a derailment accident. The risk has already passed to the buyer when the frustrating event takes place.

In the above example, the parties have agreed expressly that the risk should pass to the buyer, which seems to indicate that the buyer would be liable for any loss caused by a frustrating event after the risk has passed. The buyer must then pay the price to the seller. While both the Act and the express terms of the contract indicate this result, there are no reported cases directly on point. Ordinarily, buyers arrange to insure valuable goods not in their possession when the risk passes to them.

---

37. Except in British Columbia, where s. 1(b) of the Frustrated Contracts Act states expressly that the Act applies even in these circumstances.

38. See, for example: R.S.O. 1990, c. S.1, s. 2(2)(c).

39. Except, as already noted, in British Columbia, where the court could give recovery for part or all of the expenses incurred, whether or not a benefit was conferred.

Where the Common Law Applies

Consider Illustrations 13.8 and 13.9 again as if they had occurred in a province without the Frustrated Contracts Act. In examples (a) and (b) of Illustration 13.8, the *Fibrosa* decision applies. If *B* had made a deposit, it could recover it in full regardless of whether *A* had incurred any expenses towards the completion of the contract. If, however, *B* had received the slightest benefit, such as one sack of flour as a sample, it could recover none of its deposit.

The *Fibrosa* case did not consider situations where the seller had conferred a benefit on the buyer (for instance, by an advance delivery of part of the goods) and where no deposit had been made. In these circumstances, the older cases would likely govern: both parties would be immediately discharged by the frustrating event, and the seller would have no right of recovery against the buyer for the goods already delivered when, by the contract, none are to be paid for until all are delivered. This result conforms to the law as stated in *Cutter* v. *Powell* and shows the value of the Frustrated Contracts Act in avoiding a harsh result.

The result in Illustration 13.9 is the same under the common law as under the statute; the common law rule as well as the statute respect the intention of the parties as contained in their contract of sale.

When the Source of the Goods Is Destroyed

Another way in which frustration may affect the sale of goods arises when the source of the goods, rather than the goods themselves, is destroyed. In a contract of sale containing no terms about how the goods shall be produced, the destruction of the source of the subject matter will not frustrate the contract. If, for example, the parties do not specify where the goods will be made but the factory expected to be the source is destroyed by fire, the supplier will probably not be excused from liability for failing to deliver goods according to the contract.[40] The supplier must either purchase the goods elsewhere for delivery to the buyer or pay damages for non-delivery. On the other hand, if the parties specify a particular source and the source is destroyed, the contract will be frustrated, and the buyer cannot demand delivery. In *Howell* v. *Coupland*[41] the contract was for the sale of 200 tonnes of a crop to be grown in a particular field. The crop failed. When the buyer sued for damages for non-delivery, the court held that the contract had been frustrated, and the action failed.

The general rule is that a frustrating event must defeat the common intention of both parties. In *Blackburn Bobbin* v. *Allen*,[42] it was held that a contract of sale is not frustrated when the seller only (and not the buyer) has a particular source of supply in mind and that source fails.

CASE 13.6

Shortly before the outbreak of the First World War the buyer had ordered a quantity of Finnish birch timber to be delivered at Hull, England. He presumed, not unreasonably, that the seller would supply him from existing stocks in England; he was unaware that the seller had to obtain it directly from Finland and there was no discussion of the subject by the parties. The outbreak of war made it impossible for the seller to fill the order. In an action for damages for non-delivery, the English Court of Appeal held that there had not been frustration and that the action should succeed.

---

40. See *Twentsche Overseas Trading Co., supra*, n. 23. But see also Dow Votaw, *Legal Aspects of Business Administration*, 3rd ed. (Englewood Cliffs: Prentice-Hall, 1969) at 165. The author notes that in the United States, "there is an increasing trend in the courts towards implying an agreement that goods are to be manufactured in a particular factory which the parties reasonably understand is to be the source of the subject-matter of the contract."
41. (1876), 1 Q.B.D. 258.
42. [1918] 2 K.B. 467.

An interesting Canadian decision falls between the *Howell* and the *Blackburn Bobbin* cases.[43]

CASE 13.7

A trucker in Parkhill contracted with a Toronto corn merchant to deliver a quantity of corn to shipping points in the Parkhill area specified by the corn merchant. The parties appeared to have understood that the trucker was to purchase the corn from certain Parkhill farmers when the crop matured. Unfortunately, the trucker was unable to obtain the required quantity of corn because of a local drought. The corn merchant sued for damages for failure to deliver according to the contract. The Court of Appeal agreed with the defendant trucker that if the source of the goods formed a term of the contract, the failure of the crop would have amounted to a frustrating event, excusing the trucker from performance. The majority of the court found that the contract had not expressly stated that the corn should be from a particular source and it was unwilling to find an implied term to that effect. It held that the trucker should have obtained the corn from other suppliers and that it was accordingly in breach of contract.

Justice Laskin disagreed with the majority and would have recognized the failure of their mutual *assumptions* as a form of frustration.[44]

DISCHARGE BY OPERATION OF LAW

The Bankruptcy and Insolvency Act operates to discharge a bankrupt debtor from contractual liabilities after the processes of bankruptcy have been completed. The debtor is discharged, however, only if he qualifies for a certificate stating that the bankruptcy was caused by misfortune and without any misconduct on his part.[45]

statute barred
an action that may no longer be brought before a court because the party wishing to sue has delayed beyond the limitation period in the statute

A debt or other contractual obligation that has been neglected by a creditor for a long time becomes **statute barred**—that is, the creditor loses the right to bring an action on it. Each province has a Limitations Act setting out the time at which a creditor loses its remedy.[46] The Limitations Act "bars" (rather than completely discharges) a right of action if the promisee fails to pursue it within the time specified. The statute gives effect to the legal principle that the public interest requires a definite end to the opportunity to sue. The effect of the statute is really to banish the right of action from the courts rather than to extinguish it. The distinction is important because a claim may be rehabilitated and made enforceable by certain conduct of the promisor, as we shall see in Chapter 31. The time period begins to run at the point when the cause of action arises or is discoverable by a reasonably diligent plaintiff.[47]

43. *Parrish & Heimbecker Ltd.* v. *Gooding Lumber Ltd.*, [1968] 1 O.R. 716.

44. *Ibid.* at 719–20.

45. R.S.C. 1985, c. B-3, s. 175.

46. See, for example: Limitation Act, R.S.B.C. 1996, c. 266, Limitations Act, R.S.O. 1990, c. L.15; Limitation of Actions Act, R.S.N.S. 1989, c. 258. For an explanation of the policy considerations underlying limitations, see "Adverse Possession" in Chapter 23 and "Limitations Statutes" in Chapter 31.

47. Limitation legislation (*ibid*) usually defines when the cause of action arises or is discoverable. See *Canada (Attorney General)* v. *Lamerman* 2008 SCC 14.

QUESTIONS FOR REVIEW

1. What are the consequences for a creditor who refuses a tender of performance by the debtor?

2. Describe the nature of the consideration given by the parties to a waiver.

3. When a party admits liability for breach, what is his best course of action? Explain.

4. In what respect does the arrangement known as accord and satisfaction involve a discharge of a contract?

5. Describe the role of novation in the purchase of a going business.

6. Does a contract exist at all before a condition precedent has been satisfied? Explain.

7. Why may an "option to terminate" clause be described as a condition subsequent?

8. The principles of mistake and discharge by frustration may both relate to contracts in which the subject matter is non-existent. How do these principles and their remedies differ?

9. What else, apart from physical destruction of the subject matter of a contract, can result in frustration of the contract?

10. Is substantial hardship in performing sufficient to excuse a promisor from performing? Explain.

11. James had contracted to give a talk and demonstration on resolving human relations conflicts in small organizations for a management consulting firm. After dinner with his hosts the evening before his talk, he accepted a dare to slide down a lengthy banister on the main staircase of the hotel. James fell off part-way down and suffered a concussion and a badly sprained ankle. He was unable to give his talk and has been sued for breach of contract. Give a brief opinion of the likely result.

12. Give two examples of the shortcomings in the *Fibrosa* case.

13. In what important respect has the British Columbia Frustrated Contract Act provided a fairer solution when a contract is frustrated?

14. What three conditions are required for the Sale of Goods Act to apply to a frustrated contract? Does the Act apply to a case where the goods have been impounded by the government?

15. Suppose *P* contracts to buy 10 tonnes of corn grown in the county of Haldimand from *S*. Because of a local drought there is insufficient corn, but *S* can quite easily obtain corn of the same quality from the adjacent county of Frontenac. Has the contract been frustrated? Give reasons.

16. In what respect may bankruptcy bring about the discharge of contracts?

CASES AND PROBLEMS

1. Urban Construction Co. contracted with Mandel to build a small two-storey office building for $240 000. The contract contained a clause stating that the agreed price would be reduced by $500 for every business day the building was not completed after April 1. The price was to be paid on completion of the building.

   During construction, Mandel asked Urban Construction Co. to alter certain specifications so that a complete air-conditioning system might be installed at a later time with a minimum of inconvenience and so that there would be an additional washroom on the second floor.

   The building was completed April 17. Urban Construction Co. refused Mandel's tender of a cheque for $243 500 (comprising $240 000 less $6500 for 13 business days, plus $10 000, the agreed price for the extra work). Urban Construction Co. brought action for $250 000, the full price without deduction. Examine the validity of the arguments Mandel might use in defending the action.

2. Twilight Properties agreed to purchase land on the Vancouver waterfront from the Harbour Commission, conditional upon no changes being made to the zoning by-law that permitted high-density development for building condominium units. Twilight then began negotiations with the city for a site plan for 650 units. Its chief executive officer, Moon, was very optimistic and immediately offered 500 units for sale. (He had a fallback plan to build only that number if the zoning and site plans were restricted by municipal authority.) Moon obtained agreements to purchase 110 units from individual purchasers, who paid deposits to Twilight of $20 000 per unit. Each contract contained a clause stating

> if the development does not proceed in accordance with Twilight Properties' plans, Twilight retains the right to terminate the contract without liability on or before June 30, 1998.

This date corresponded with the closing date in the agreement with the Harbour Commission. Units were to be available, and the deals closed one year later.

On June 30, 1998, Twilight completed the purchase of the lands, but the date passed without any approval of the site plan by the city. At the end of July, the Planning and Development Department of the city approved the site plan and sent it on to the city council. However, in October the city council refused to approve the plan and stated that it intended to reduce the number of units permitted on the property. The council instructed its secretary to write to Twilight and ask it whether it would be willing to provide a guarantee to the original condominium purchasers that it would perform its commitments to sell the units should the development be approved. Twilight replied that the city's request was inappropriate and an interference with its private contract rights. At its November meeting the city passed a more restrictive rezoning by-law that would permit only 400 units to be built.

Immediately afterwards Twilight returned the deposits of the purchasers and stated that their agreements were terminated; it was not possible to proceed with the project as planned. The unit purchasers sued for breach of contract. Twilight defended by claiming that their contracts were frustrated by the actions of the city. Summarize the arguments for each side, and give your opinion about who should succeed.

3. In 1994, the Dryden Construction Co. contracted with the Ontario Hydro Electric Power Commission to build an access road seven miles long from its Manitou Falls generating station to provincial Highway No. 105. The contract contained the following clause:

> The contractor agrees that he is fully informed regarding all of the conditions affecting work to be done and labour and materials to be furnished for the completion of the contract and that his information was secured by personal investigation and research and not from the Commission or its estimates and that he will make no claim against the Commission.

In fact, the area over which the road was to be built was under heavy snow at the time, and the temperature was very low. The description of the property proved to be inaccurate, there being much more muskeg than indicated. After these facts became known, the contractor claimed to be excused from the contract, alleging that it had been frustrated and that what was required amounted to an entirely different contract.

Is there a binding contract to build the road?

4. Howard rented a room to Kennedy along the route scheduled for the procession of the Royal Family for the day on which they would appear in Halifax. The agreement was in writing, and the rent for the room was for a substantial sum, payable at the time of the procession. In the meantime, Howard redecorated the room for the occasion. Later it was announced that the route of the Royal Family through the city had changed and would not pass Howard's building. Kennedy then refused to pay the rent for the room, and Howard sued for the amount. Should Howard succeed? How would it affect the outcome if at the time Kennedy undertook to rent the room she had paid a $100 deposit?

Suppose that the place in which these events occurred had been Saint John, New Brunswick, instead of Halifax, Nova Scotia; would the result be different?

5. Gilman Steel Ltd. is a large fabricator of reinforcing steel. It makes its product from steel bars purchased from steel mills in accordance with engineers' specifications for particular projects. Universal Construction Corp. is an apartment construction company.

In September 1998, Gilman and Universal signed a contract for the supply of fabricated steel at a price of $253 per tonne for use in three apartment buildings to be built consecutively by Universal at different sites.

At the first building site, deliveries were made and paid for as agreed and construction of that building was completed. Then in July 1999, steel mill companies announced increases in the price of unfabricated steel, to take effect in two stages. The price to Gilman would increase on August 1, 1999, by $8.50 per tonne and a second increase of a then-unspecified amount would become effective as of March 1, 2000.

In the changed circumstances, Gilman suggested a new contract for the second and third apartment buildings. Universal agreed to reconsider because it found that it would not require as much fabricated steel for the remaining two buildings as it had initially contracted for. The parties signed a new contract for the supply of fabricated steel at a price of $257 per tonne, a price that only partially passed on the increase to Gilman. Universal had thus agreed to pay a higher unit price for a smaller quantity of steel. The parties did not include in the contract a clause providing for an escalation of price because Universal expected to complete the remaining buildings before the next round of price increases in March 2000.

Construction of the second apartment building began in August 1999, and Gilman made numerous deliveries of steel. Universal accepted all steel delivered and regularly paid the amount billed on each invoice at $257 per tonne. The second building was completed in January 2000, and construction of the third was started.

On March 1, while the third apartment building was still far from completion, the steel mills announced the anticipated second price increase. Officers of Gilman, hoping to agree on another new contract, met with a senior officer of Universal. They asked Universal to consider a new contract since construction had not progressed as expected. Universal agreed to accommodate Gilman on the understanding that Universal would be given favourable consideration in the supply of steel for the construction of additional apartment buildings.

Gilman then prepared an agreement dated March 1, 2000, and mailed it to Universal. It was a duplicate of the preceding contract in July except that the price of the steel was increased. Universal did not sign or return the document, but it did accept deliveries of steel invoiced at the new rates without protest. Universal adopted a new method of payment, however, after March 1, 2000. It no longer paid by cheques based on the invoice amounts but in round figures that tended at first to overpayment; however, by the end of the construction this procedure led to a net balance of some $25 000 owing by Universal.

As construction of the third apartment building neared completion, the comptroller of Gilman asked for payment in full of the account. Universal informed him that it expected some new mortgage money to become available enabling it to pay the account in full soon. At about the same time, officers of Universal met with Gilman's officers to discuss a contract for the supply of steel for a new apartment complex. Universal reminded Gilman that it had twice agreed to new contracts and asked whether Gilman could offer a good price. Gilman made an offer and Universal said it would consider it. The meeting was conducted and concluded in an atmosphere of goodwill without complaint about the March price increase. Shortly afterwards, Universal decided that the new offer was not attractive enough to accept and indicated for the first time that it would not pay the portion of the past due account that represented the increase in the March 2000 agreement.

Gilman Steel Ltd. sued Universal Construction Corp. for the balance owing according to its invoices.

(a) Outline the nature of the defence or defences available to Universal.

(b) Explain the nature of the argument or arguments that could be advanced for the plaintiff.

(c) Indicate with reasons what the court's decision would likely be. (If you perceive any difference between what the law is and what it ought to be in a case of this kind, set out your reasoning separately from your prediction of what the decision is likely to be.)

6. Parker's Automatic Laundry Services Inc. installed coin-operated washing machines and dryers in an apartment building owned by Mountbatten Estates Ltd. under a five-year contract. The contract gave Parker's the exclusive right to install and maintain any laundry machines in the building. No one other than the employees of the laundry service company would be permitted to repair, remove, or replace any of the machines. A clause in the contract read:

> In the event the Proprietor [Mountbatten] sells or assigns its interest in the said premises, such Successor shall be fully bound by the terms of this agreement and before the Proprietor sells or assigns it shall obtain the consent in writing of the grantee or assignee to the terms of this agreement.

In return, Mountbatten was to receive 20 percent of the gross receipts collected from the use of the laundry equipment.

Six months later Mountbatten sold the apartment building to Baldoon Holdings Ltd. for $2 500 000. The lawyer acting for Baldoon drew up the agreement of sale, one clause of which read:

> The Vendor [Mountbatten] warrants to the Purchaser [Baldoon] that the 10 washing machines and 10 clothes dryers located in the apartment building have been placed there by Parker's Automatic Laundry Service Inc. pursuant to an agreement with a five-year term, a copy of which is attached hereto.

Following its purchase of the apartment building, Baldoon continued for a time to operate the building much as before and retained the same manager. Parker's made the first quarterly payment to Baldoon three months after the purchase. At that time, Baldoon approached Parker's with a view to purchasing the 10 washing machines and 10 dryers and operating them itself, as owner of the building. Parker's refused and Baldoon then instructed Parker's to remove its machines within two weeks. When Parker's failed to do so, Baldoon moved the machines to a locked storage area in the basement of the apartment building and replaced them with new washing machines and clothes dryers of its own.

Parker's Automatic Laundry Services Inc. brought an action against Baldoon Holdings Ltd. for breach of contract. Indicate with reasons what the result of this action will likely be, leaving aside the question of what the amount of damages should be, if awarded.

7. Diehl owned some land on which she planned to have a house built that would be suitable for her retirement the following year. She made a contract with Summers, a building contractor, to build a house for $80 000, the price to be paid in full on completion. The contract contained an unqualified promise by the contractor to complete the house at that price. When the house was about three-quarters finished, Diehl stored some expensive furniture in a completed part and took out a $20 000 fire insurance policy on the furniture.

Two weeks later, before the house was completed, lightning caused a serious fire that did considerable damage to both the building and the furniture. Summers learned that Diehl would receive about $16 000 in insurance money. When Diehl asked him to go ahead and complete the house, Summers said, "I believe I'm no longer bound to go on and if you do not pay me the insurance money, I will ask a court to declare that the contract has been frustrated. I'm willing to compromise if you pay me the insurance money." Diehl protested that she had lost considerably from the destruction of her furniture but finally said, "All right, go ahead and do the work."

When the house was completed Diehl paid Summers $80 000 but refused to pay anything more. Summers sued her for $16 000 on the ground that he had been led to believe he would receive this additional sum and would not otherwise have completed the contract.

At the trial, evidence was submitted that in contracts of this kind, builders frequently require an undertaking by the owner to insure the building during its construction against loss by fire and have the insurance company include a clause agreeing that, in the event of a claim, it would pay the insurance money first to the builder "insofar as his interest may appear." A copy of the written contract between Summers and Diehl was produced and showed that the contract did not include a term of this kind. The parties testified that neither of them had insured the building itself, as distinct from the contents. It was acknowledged that the contractor, Summers, would have had an insurable interest and could have insured the house himself to the value of the contract.

Develop the arguments for the plaintiff and the defendant, and offer an opinion about whether the action should succeed.

8. *M* Inc. chartered a vessel from *Q* Corp. under a five-year agreement that gave *M* an option to purchase the vessel at the end of the five-year term subject to "full performance of all its obligations under the agreement, including delivery of prompt payments in accordance with the schedule in the agreement." The agreement required seven monthly instalments each year on specified dates, "in cash, by way of Bank Transfer and/or certified cheques." The parties subsequently agreed informally that *M* would deliver seven post-dated, uncertified cheques to *Q* at the beginning of each operating season and they would be deposited on the specified dates.

There were no problems with the cheques for the first four years, but the cheque for the first payment in the fifth year was returned by reason of insufficient funds. The bank's refusal to honour *M*'s cheque was due to an error by a bank employee. *Q* immediately wrote to M stating that the option to purchase was void and of no further effect because of *M*'s failure to make the payment as required. *Q* also gave *M* instructions on how to remedy its late payment. *M* promptly made the payment with interest in accordance with *Q*'s instructions. All remaining payments were made on time.

As prescribed in the terms of their agreement, *M* gave notice to exercise the option to purchase the vessel. *Q* insisted that the failure to make the first payment in the fifth year on time was a precondition to exercising the option and that accordingly the option was void. *M* Inc. sued *Q* Corp. to enforce the option agreement. Give your opinion of which side should succeed.

ADDITIONAL RESOURCES FOR CHAPTER 13 ON THE COMPANION WEBSITE *(www.pearsoned.ca/smyth)*

In addition to self-test multiple-choice, true–false, and short essay questions (all with immediate feedback), application exercises, and links to useful web destinations, the Companion Website provides the following resources for Chapter 13:

- **British Columbia:** Frustrated Contracts; Limitation Periods; Sale of Goods Act; Tender of Payment; Tender of Performance
- **Alberta:** Frustration; Limitation Periods
- **Manitoba/Saskatchewan:** Limitations Act
- **Ontario:** Effect of Frustration; Limitation Periods; Options to Terminate; Sale of Goods Act

14

The Effect of Breach

Not all breaches are of the same importance or have the same consequences. When one party commits a breach, the aggrieved party may have choices to make, and those choices depend on how the breach occurs and how serious it is. In this chapter we examine such questions as:

- What options are available to an aggrieved party when the other party

  - expressly repudiates the contract?

  - simply fails to perform at the agreed time?

  - makes it impossible for itself to perform?

- How serious must the breach be to trigger various options?

- What role do exemption clauses play in affecting the aggrieved party's rights?

- What is the business significance of breach?

IMPLICATIONS OF BREACH

In our discussion of the ways in which a contract may be discharged, we noted that breach may sometimes become a method of discharge. We must qualify this statement in two ways: *First*, not every breach may discharge a contract. *Second*, breach does not discharge a contract automatically (as does frustration or completed performance, for example); even when a breach is sufficient to discharge the contract, only if the party that suffered the breach elects to treat it so will it be discharged.

An injured party cannot elect to treat every breach as discharging the contract and freeing it from its own obligation to perform. The breach must be of either the whole contract or an essential term of the contract so that the purpose of the agreement is defeated and performance by the aggrieved party becomes pointless. Breach of a minor term may entitle an aggrieved party to damages, but does not entitle it to abandon its obligations. It would do so at its peril, and the other party could, in turn, sue it successfully for failure to carry out its promises.

ILLUSTRATION 14.1

(a) *A* agrees to sell 10 000 bags of potatoes to *B* Wholesale Grocers and to deliver them in yellow paper bags with green labels. Through a mistake, the labels are printed in blue rather than green. The management of *B* may feel annoyed and believe that their merchandise display will not be as effective. *B* may sue *A* and collect damages for such loss as it can show the breach has caused, but it cannot reject the potatoes without itself committing a breach that might make it liable for heavy damages.

(b) *A* agrees to sell 10 000 bags of potatoes to *B* Wholesale Grocers and to deliver them to *B*'s warehouse on Wednesday in time for *B* to distribute them to its supermarket chain for a weekend special. *A* makes no delivery until late Friday afternoon. By this delay *A* has committed a breach of an essential term of the contract—delivery on Wednesday. *B* may reject the potatoes and discharge the contract, freeing itself from any obligation to pay for them. In addition, it may sue *A* for damages caused by failure to deliver on time. In the alternative, *B* may decide it still wants the potatoes and it may accept them. In this event, the contract is not discharged: *B* is liable to pay the price for the potatoes, subject to a deduction for damages caused by the failure to deliver them on time. If *B* should accept the potatoes and then refuse to pay for them, *A* could sue *B* for the price, and *B* could counterclaim for its damages.

We can see, then, that breach itself does not discharge a contract: if the breach is of a minor term, the contract is still binding on both parties; if the breach is of a fundamental term, the party committing the breach is still bound, but the injured party may elect to discharge the contract and free itself, or to affirm the contract so that it continues to bind both parties.

We should note also that a major term may be broken in only a minor respect. Suppose in Illustration 14.1 that *A* delivers on time but is short by 5 bags. The quantity to be delivered is a major term, but delivering 9995 bags of 10 000 promised would be only a **minor breach** of that term and would not entitle *B* to reject the shipment. If, however, *A* had delivered only 5000 bags there would be a **major breach**, and *B* could elect to reject them.

It is not always easy to decide whether a term of a contract is essential to it or of lesser importance, or whether the breach of an essential term is a serious one. Nevertheless, in any dispute concerning a breach, the first task is to determine to which class the term in question belongs.

We must note an unfortunate development in terminology concerning essential and non-essential terms: for a variety of reasons stemming from 19th-century developments in contract law, essential terms became known as **conditions** and non-essential terms as **warranties**. These names are unfortunate because "condition" may easily become confused with "condition precedent" (where the word "condition" means a happening or event rather than a term of an agreement), and

minor breach
a breach of a non-essential term of a contract or of an essential term in a minor respect

major breach
a breach of the whole contract or of an essential term so that the purpose of the contract is defeated

condition
an essential term of a contract

warranty
a non-essential term of a contract

"warranty" may be confused with its special meaning in a sale of goods (where it means a guarantee of quality of the goods or of their ownership—usually an essential term). Despite the confusion, the use of "condition" and "warranty" to distinguish essential from non-essential terms has now become common.

INTERNATIONAL ISSUE

Online Pharmacies

Canadian prescription drug prices are controlled by the Patented Medicine Prices Review Board. This means that Canadian prescription drugs are cheaper (often significantly) than the same drugs in the United States. Online pharmacies offer Canadian pricing to American consumers. Several American states no longer block access to online Canadian pharmacies.

Not surprisingly, drug manufacturers are unhappy with the potential for reduced profits. Currently, only 4 percent of Americans buy drugs online from all sources (Canadian, American, and others). The agreements under which the drugs are sold to the pharmacies prohibit the export of the drugs. Beginning in 2004, several drug manufacturers, including Merck and Pfizer Inc., took the position that the online pharmacies were in substantial breach of their sale agreements and the manufacturers were entitled to refuse to supply further drugs to the pharmacies.

QUESTIONS TO CONSIDER

1. Do you think the prohibition against exporting is a major term? If yes, what volume of drugs would amount to a major breach?

2. Are there reasons why the Canadian government should object to the exportation of Canadian prescription drugs?

Sources: "Canadian Internet Pharmacies: Buying Drugs from Canada – Small but Growing," *Senior Magazine Online*, www.seniormag.com/canadianpharmacy/articles/growing-use.htm (accessed June 26, 2008); "Canadameds Upset With Power Struggle of Drug Companies to Stop Mail Order Pharmacy Industry in Canada," *Medical News Today*, January 18, 2005, www.medicalnewstoday.com/articles/18997.php; "Merck Cuts Off Net Pharmacies," *Canadian Press*, January 21, 2005.

HOW BREACH MAY OCCUR

A party to a contract may break it

- by expressly repudiating its liabilities,
- by acting in a way that makes its promise impossible to perform, or
- by either failing to perform at all or tendering an actual performance that falls short of its promise.

EXPRESS REPUDIATION

express repudiation
a declaration by one of the contracting parties to the other that it does not intend to perform as promised

An **express repudiation** is a declaration by one of the contracting parties to the other that it does not intend to perform as it promised. The promisee is entitled to treat the contract as being immediately at an end, to find another party to perform, and to sue for whatever damages it sustains in delay and higher costs because the original contract will not be performed. Before substituting a new party to proceed with performance, it is prudent for the promisee to inform the repudiating party that it is treating the contract as terminated at once and is reserving its rights to sue for damages for breach.

Alternatively, a promisee may continue to insist on performance. If it chooses this option and does not receive performance by the time stated in the contract, it is still entitled to damages for breach of contract, but it takes a chance that intervening events may provide the promisor with an excuse for not performing. *Avery* v. *Bowden*[1] shows what can happen when a promisee insists upon performance.

CASE 14.1

The defendant chartered a ship in England to pick up a cargo at Odessa. On arrival, the ship's master requested the cargo, but the charterer's agent refused to provide it. By custom a charterer was entitled to a period of grace to provide a cargo, but as soon as the charterer repudiated the contract, the ship's master could have treated himself as freed from further liability; he could have sailed immediately for England. Instead, he elected to wait out the usual grace period and to continue to demand a cargo. Before the period expired, war broke out between England and Russia, and it became impossible to complete the contract. The ship's owner was unsuccessful when he sued the charterer for damages caused by the futile trip: the court held that the contract had been discharged by frustration and not by breach. It noted that the decision would have been different had the ship's master elected to treat the express repudiation as an immediate breach of contract.

Whenever breach occurs before the time agreed for performance, it is known as **anticipatory breach**.

anticipatory breach
a breach that occurs in advance of the time agreed for performance of a contract

ILLUSTRATION 14.2

A Co. contracts with *B* Ltd. for the delivery to *A* Co. in six months of well-drilling equipment at an agreed price. A week later, *B* Ltd. discovers that it has agreed to a price that is much too low and informs *A* Co. that it will not deliver the equipment as promised. *B* Ltd. has committed an anticipatory breach of its contract with *A* Co., and *A* Co. need not wait until the delivery date to sue *B* Ltd.

The courts have recognized that, as a promisee, *A* Co. is entitled not only to performance of the contract in six months' time but also to a continuous expectation of performance in the period between formation of the contract and its performance. During that period, *A* Co. may have entered into a drilling contract relying on delivery of the equipment. (In *Avery* v. *Bowden*, the charterer's repudiation was also an example of anticipatory breach.) The concept is a basic one; it asserts that a contract exists and has legal effect from the time of its formation, and not just from the time of its performance.

Major breach amounting to repudiation may also occur after performance has begun, and it will free the aggrieved party from further obligations.

1. (1855), 119 E.R. 647.

CASE 14.2 Atkinson's employment contract contained a clause that he would not work in competition with his employer, a billposting company, in the same town for two years after the termination of his employment. The employer dismissed him without cause in breach of the contract. Atkinson recovered damages for wrongful dismissal and then began to work within the district as a self-employed bill-poster. His former employer sought an injunction to restrain him from competing but failed. The court held that the company had by its dismissal repudiated the employment contract and entitled Atkinson to consider his own contractual obligations at an end.[2]

In these examples, repudiation takes the form of a declaration or of conduct affecting performance of the whole contract. In some business situations, however, one party simply ignores the contract or repudiates only a minor term of the contract. Such a breach does not entitle the other party to treat the contract as discharged. While considering the issue of repudiation the Supreme Court of Canada held that having "little regard" for an agreement does not establish that a party is repudiating the agreement. Ordinary, non-repudiatory breach is consistent with ignoring the terms of an agreement. More is required to establish repudiation."[3]

Whenever a business is unable to perform exactly as promised, a wise manager, as soon as she is aware of the situation, will notify the other party so that it may take immediate steps to reduce any loss that the breach may cause.

ILLUSTRATION 14.3

X Inc., a wholesale distributor of electronic equipment, has agreed to supply B Ltd., a chain of retail stores selling home entertainment components, with a large quantity of new Blu-ray players, along with sample demonstration discs of spectacular sound effects and advertising for the new product. Several days before delivery, the manager of X Inc. discovers that the Blu-ray players are in stock but that the demonstration discs have not arrived and appear to have been lost during shipment. Knowing that B Ltd. plans to feature the new product, X Inc.'s manager would be wise to notify B Ltd. at once of the expected breach of this minor term. B Ltd. might then be able to arrange in advance for an alternative supply of good demonstration discs. If X Inc. were to deliver the Blu-ray players without prior notice of its inability to supply the discs, B Ltd. might suffer a greater loss for which X Inc. would be liable.

ONE PARTY RENDERS PERFORMANCE IMPOSSIBLE

Under this heading, only a willful or negligent act of the promisor constitutes a breach of contract—it does not include an act that is an involuntary response to forces beyond its control. A deliberate or negligent act that makes performance impossible amounts to repudiation: the promisor may not have said so in words, but it is implied by her conduct—a form of the self-induced frustration considered in the preceding chapter. As with express repudiation, conduct that makes performance impossible may take place either before or during performance.

2. *General Billposting Co. v. Atkinson,* [1909] A.C. 118. This decision was followed in a preliminary hearing before trial in *Gerrard v. Century 21 Armour Real Estate Inc.* (1991), 4 O.R. (3d) 191, even where it was unclear whether there had been repudiation of the contract by the employer.
3. *Jedfro Investments (U.S.A.) Ltd. v. Jacyk* 2007 SCC 55.

ILLUSTRATION 14.4

A agrees to sell her Ferrari sports car to B for $30 000, with car and registration to be delivered in three weeks. A few days later, X, unaware of the agreement between A and B, offers A $35 000 for the car. A accepts and delivers the car to X that day. A is in breach of the contract with B the moment she makes the sale to X, and B may sue her as soon as he learns of it. A is not permitted to argue that she can still deliver the car on time by buying it back from X; B is entitled to a continuous expectation of A's performance until the day agreed for delivery arrives. The result would be the same if A's agent negligently sold the car to X.

ETHICAL ISSUE

Good Faith Performance

Civil law jurisdictions, including Quebec, recognize a general duty of good-faith performance. The Civil Code of Quebec states:

> The parties shall conduct themselves in good faith both at the time the obligation is created and at the time it is performed or extinguished. (art. 1375)

The United States also recognizes a generalized duty of good faith. The United States Restatement of Contracts describes it this way:

> Every contract imposes upon each party a duty of good faith and fair dealing in its performance and its enforcement. (s. 205)

Although difficult to define, good faith is thought to include concepts of fairness, honesty, and consideration for the interests of the other party.

So far, common law jurisdictions, including Canada, have not recognized a generalized duty of good faith. The Ontario Court of Appeal put it this way:

> Canadian courts have not recognized a stand-alone duty of good faith that is independent from the terms expressed in a contract or from the objectives that emerge from those provisions. The implication of a duty of good faith has not gone so far as to create new, unbargained-for, rights and obligations. Nor has it been used to alter the express terms of the contract reached by the parties. Rather, courts have implied a duty of good faith with a view to securing the performance and enforcement of the contract made by the parties, or as it is sometimes put, to ensure that parties do not act in a way that eviscerates or defeats the objectives of the agreement.[4]

One particular example of this specialized, narrow approach to good faith is increased damages when employers wrongfully dismiss an employee in bad faith.[5]

QUESTIONS TO CONSIDER

1. Should Canada recognize a general duty of good faith in contractual performance and enforcement? How does a generalized duty of good faith differ from an implied duty of good faith performance of the particular terms of the contract?

2. How would a good-faith duty be distinguished from a fiduciary duty?

Sources: J.D. McCamus, *The Law of Contracts* (Toronto: Irwin Law Inc., 2006), at pp. 780–805; W. Tetley, "Good Faith in Contract Particularly in Contracts of Arbitration and Chartering" (2004), 35 *JMLC* 561–616, available online at www.mcgill.ca/files/maritimelaw/goodfaith.pdf.

4. *Transamerica Life Canada Inc.* v. *ING Canada Inc.* (2003), 68 O.R. (3d) 457 (C.A.) at para 53.
5. *Wallace* v. *United Grain Growers Ltd.* (1997), 152 D.L.R. (4th) 1 (S.C.C.). For a discussion of a distributor's duty of good faith, see *1193430 Ontario Inc.* v. *Boa-Franc Inc.* (2005), 78 O.R. (3d) 81 (C.A.).

FAILURE OF PERFORMANCE

Types of Failure

Unlike the other two types of breach, failure of performance usually becomes apparent only when the time for performance arrives or during performance. The degree of failure may vary: it may be a total failure to perform, it may be a grossly inadequate performance, or it may be very minor. There may also be satisfactory performance of all but one of the terms of the contract or of only part of a main term. The extent of a failure always has an important effect on the nature of the remedies available to the injured party.

The problems created by failure to perform arise typically when the party accused of the breach is required, either by the terms of the contract or by usual trade practice, to perform its part first. It becomes necessary to decide whether the injured party is excused from performing its own part of the bargain. The question often arises in contracts requiring the delivery of goods by instalments when the quantity delivered fails to meet the amount called for in the contract. The issue is whether what is left undone amounts to a sufficient breach to free the injured party from its part of the bargain, or whether the breach is minor and entitles the injured party only to damages, while the agreement still continues to bind it. Partial delivery may be merely inconvenient, or it may be completely unsatisfactory.

ILLUSTRATION 14.5

(a) The seller contracts to deliver 6000 tonnes of coal in 12 monthly instalments of about 500 tonnes each. One of the terms is that the buyer is to provide the trucks to take the coal away. In the first month, the buyer sends sufficient trucks to take away only 400 tonnes. The buyer's default would not likely be sufficient to discharge the seller from its obligation to stand ready to provide the remaining 5600 tonnes over the following 11 months.[6]

(b) The seller agrees to deliver 150 tonnes of iron per month but delivers only 21 in the first month. Its default is very likely sufficient to discharge the buyer, which may then turn to another source of supply and sue for damages resulting from the breach.[7]

Often, an innocent party is left in a quandary. If she is really concerned about the seriousness of continuing defective performance, it is wise for her to seek legal advice before claiming to be discharged of her own obligations; otherwise, she risks being held liable for wrongful repudiation should a court find that the seller's default was only a minor breach.[8]

In a contract where one party is to perform by instalments, the other may consider itself freed from liability only if it can offer convincing affirmative answers to both of these questions:

(a) Is there good reason to think that future performance will be equally defective?
(b) Is either the expected deficiency or the actual deficiency to date important relative to the whole performance promised?

substantial performance

performance that does not comply in some minor way with the requirements of the contract

The Doctrine of Substantial Performance

The doctrine of **substantial performance** states that a promisor is entitled to enforce a contract when it has substantially performed, even though its performance does not comply in some minor way with the requirements of the contract. The promisor's claim is, however, subject to a reduction

---

6. See *Simpson* v. *Crippin* (1872), L.R. 8 Q.B. 14, where, in a similar situation, the buyer took delivery of only 158 tonnes in the first month, and yet the seller was held to the contract.

7. *Hoare* v. *Rennie* (1859), 157 E.R. 1083.

8. For an example of the difficulties that a party claiming a major breach may encounter, see *Agrifoods International Corp.* v. *Beatrice Foods Inc.*, [1997] B.C.J. No. 393.

for damages caused by its defective performance. The effect of the doctrine is that a promisee cannot seize upon a trivial failure of performance to avoid its own obligations.[9] There can often be substantial disagreement about how serious or trivial a failure in performance turns out to be.[10]

When the Right to Treat the Contract as Discharged Is Lost

Even when an aggrieved party would ordinarily have the right to treat its obligations as discharged by a serious breach, in two situations it will be entitled only to damages. The first occurs when the aggrieved party has decided to proceed with the contract and accept benefits under it despite the breach. In the second, the aggrieved party may have received the benefit of the contract and not learned of the breach until performance was complete.

CASE 14.3

A chartered a ship from *B* for £1550, for a voyage from Liverpool to Sydney. The contract specified that the ship should have a cargo capacity of at least 1000 tons. The vessel was unable to carry that amount of cargo, but *A* allowed it to load what it could and made an advance payment on the freight. Subsequently, *A* refused to pay the balance, claiming the contract had been discharged for breach of a major term. In an action by *B* for the balance of the price, the court noted that while *A* could have treated the contract as discharged, refused to load the ship, and sued for its loss, *A*'s acceptance of performance by the smaller ship closed the earlier option. Instead, *A* had to pay the agreed price, less any counterclaim for damages it could establish.[11]

CASE 14.4

X Farms purchased seed from *Y* Nurseries, described by *Y* as "common English sainfoin." After it was sown, it proved to be "giant sainfoin," an inferior type. However, *X* could not have learned of the breach until after the seed had been planted and came up, a time when it would be too late to reject the seed and treat the contract as discharged. *X*'s only remedy was to sue for damages for the breach.[12]

Cases 14.3 and 14.4 show that the right to consider a contract at an end may depend on an aggrieved party still being able to reject the substantial benefit of the contract. If it cannot, it will remain bound to perform its obligations, subject to a right to claim damages.

Exemption Clauses

Their Purpose

In business, a party that runs a significant risk of harm to the other party through some failure in the course of performing the contract must plan to cover its potential liability. There are several alternatives when striking a bargain:

(a) The party may obtain insurance against the risk and raise its price accordingly.
(b) It may "self-insure"—that is, charge a higher fee and build up a reserve fund to pay any claim that arises later from harm to a customer.
(c) It may include an **exemption clause** in the contract, in effect excluding itself from any liability for the risk and transferring the risk of harm to its customer.

exemption clause
a clause in a contract that exempts a party from liability

---

9. *Dakin & Co. Ltd.* v. *Lee*, [1916] 1 K.B. 566.
10. See *Miller* v. *Advanced Farming Systems Ltd.*, [1969] S.C.R. 845; *Sail Labrador Ltd.* v. *Challenge One*, [1999] 1 S.C.R. 265.
11. *Pust* v. *Dowie* (1863), 122 E.R. 740 and 745.
12. *Wallis* v. *Pratt*, [1911] A.C. 394. The buyer's remedy is confined to money damages "where a contract of sale is not severable and the buyer has accepted the goods or part thereof," by virtue of the Sale of Goods Act, R.S.O. 1990, c. S.1, s. 12(3); R.S.B.C. 1996, c. 410, s. 15(4); R.S.N.S. 1989, c. 408, s. 14(3).

As we noted in our discussion of the ticket cases in Chapter 5 on Offer and Acceptance, the last alternative is often the most attractive. We also discussed the use of exemption clauses in various business settings under the headings "Special Types of Contracts" in Chapter 11 and "Vicarious Performance" in Chapter 12.

There are several advantages that make exemption clauses attractive—and widely used. First, they permit a supplier of goods and services to keep its prices low, since the supplier need not increase them to protect itself against the risk of liability to its customer. Second, if the supplier is sued for damages despite the exemption clause, it will completely disclaim liability and so seek to avoid the difficult question of the extent of its liability for the harm done. Finally, if the supplier is in the position of using a standard form contract (especially if the contract is a detailed printed form with many other terms), it will, in most circumstances, have a distinct advantage over its customer. The customer may be quite knowledgeable about competitive pricing and drive a hard bargain, but may have little or no expertise in legal issues. A customer may gladly accept a lower price without fully realizing the implications of an exemption clause.

Exemption clauses usually make good sense and work reasonably well when the bargaining power and knowledge of the law is relatively equal between the parties. For example, one party may willingly assume a risk in return for a lower price; that party may already have adequate blanket insurance coverage. Or the activity may be extremely hazardous; a charter airline may be unwilling to fly a client into northern mountain regions in winter except at the client's own risk. Generally speaking, however, the party preparing the standard form contract drafts exemption clauses clearly to its own advantage, and the courts have developed techniques to cut this advantage down in unfair cases.

Attitude of the Courts: Requirement of Adequate Notice

When an exemption clause appears in a document that a customer does not sign—such as a ticket, a receipt, or a sign displayed on a wall—the first claim against it is to deny adequate notice of the term. If this claim succeeds, then the term is not considered to be part of the bargain between the parties.

Even if a person signs a document, in the circumstances described in Chapter 8 on Mistake, he may plead *non est factum*; although such cases are rare, if the party is successful, the entire document, including any exemption clause it may contain, is void. More often, as discussed in Chapter 9, a person may not be bound by a clause that is so unexpected and unfair that a reasonable signer would not think the contract contained such a term. This result is more likely if the contents of the document were misrepresented to the signer. The Ontario Court of Appeal has further enlarged the protection to apply to exemption clauses that absolve a defendant from liability for negligence, or limit its liability to a small portion of the harm suffered:

> . . . *the defendant must establish* that it has specifically drawn the onerous limitation clause to the plaintiff's attention or has accurately stated its legal effect to the plaintiff *before* he signs the contract[13] [italics added].

This decision shifts the burden to the defendant to demonstrate that it adequately informed the plaintiff. However, where a person signs a contract that does not contain an unexpectedly onerous clause, he will be bound by all the terms it contains; this is true even with a document he is not expected to sign, if he actually knew or should reasonably have known its terms.

Strict Interpretations of Exemption Clauses

When adequate notice has been given, what effect does an exemption clause have if, apart from the clause, the party who has drafted it fails in some significant way to perform the contract as agreed? Exemption clauses are typically drawn in very wide terms. A supplier of machinery might exempt

---

13. *Trigg* v. *MI Movers International Transport Services* (1991), 84 D.L.R. (4th) 504, per Tarnopolsky, J.A., at 508.

itself from "all liability for defects in the product supplied, for any negligence of its employees, and for any guarantees implied by custom or trade usage—except for guarantees expressly set out in the contract, such as replacing any defective parts for three months." Courts have taken the view that exemption clauses should be very strictly construed *against* the party that draws them because they permit parties to evade legal responsibility ordinarily placed on suppliers of goods and services.[14]

Even so, the courts respect the theory of freedom of contract, and in the absence of special rules (such as exist for common carriers) or special statutory protection (as in consumer protection legislation), they will not make a new contract for the parties to protect the one in a weaker position. If an exemption clause squarely excludes liability for the breach that has occurred, the injured party—subject to the discussion that follows—has no remedy. Accordingly, if one day after an express guarantee expires a piece of machinery breaks down for the first time, the supplier is not liable, even if at common law it would, in the absence of the clause, have been liable under an implied warranty of fitness. The burden is on the **drawing party** to prove the actual cause of the loss is covered by the clause.[15]

drawing party
the contracting party that prepared the agreement and/or the particular clause

Exemption clauses are strictly construed by the courts in ways that are not at first apparent: for example, a clause exempting a supplier from liability under the contract has been held not to exempt it from liability in tort.[16] Similarly, if a clause exempts a carrier from liability for negligence by its employees, the carrier will escape vicarious liability; however, the customer who has suffered injury or loss may still sue employees personally for their negligence unless, as decided in a 1990s Supreme Court of Canada case, the employees can show that the clause was clearly intended to protect them as well.[17] Moreover, the courts will narrowly define the failure covered by an exemption clause.

CASE 14.5

Purolator undertook to deliver a tender document from Cathcart's office to the office of Ontario Hydro. The bill of lading contained a clause stating that Purolator would not be liable for "any special, consequential or other damages for any reason including delay in delivery." The tender document was never delivered to Ontario Hydro.

In an action by Cathcart to recover lost profits, Purolator admitted that had the bid been received, it would have been accepted and that the loss of profit by Cathcart was $37 000, but Purolator claimed that the clause exempted it from any liability. However, Cathcart succeeded in its action. The court construed the clause strictly against the drafter of the term, Purolator, even though the parties were of equal bargaining power: the clause, on its "true construction," covered only damages rising from delay, not from a complete failure to deliver.[18]

Fundamental Breach

The most difficult cases for the courts arise when a breach has been so serious as to defeat the purpose of the contract; in the absence of the exemption clause, the aggrieved party could immediately have treated the contract as discharged and sued for damages. However, the exemption clause may be so broad that it appears to protect the wrongdoer from any liability. In a number of cases, courts have been reluctant to allow defendants to shelter behind such exemption clauses. They have

14. *Hunter Engineering* v. *Syncrude*, [1989] 1 S.C.R. 426 (S.C.C.).

15. *StarLine Inc.* v. *Hydro-Mac Inc.*, 2008 N.L.T.D. 73 (N.L.S.C.).

16. *White* v. *John Warrick & Co. Ltd.*, [1953] 2 All E.R. 1021.

17. *London Drugs* v. *Kuehne & Nagel International* (1992), 97 D.L.R. (4th) 261, discussed in Chapter 12, Privity of Contract, under "Vicarious Performance." Traditionally, employees were third parties who were unable to claim the benefit of an exemption clause in the contract between carrier and customer, but under the *London Drugs* case, employees may be protected. *London Drugs* has been followed in a number of cases. See *Madison Developments Ltd.* v. *Plan Electric Co.* (1997), 36 O.R. (3d) 80.

18. *Cathcart Inspection Services Ltd.* v. *Purolator Courier Ltd.* (1982), 34 O.R. (2d) 187.

fundamental breach
a breach that is so significant that it deprives the innocent party of most (if not all) of the benefit of the contract

labelled the default a "**fundamental breach**" and found that such a breach nullifies any exemption clause.[19] To treat an exemption clause as excusing one party entirely from performance would be repugnant to the very idea of a binding contract. Therefore, the clause must be struck down and the aggrieved party given a remedy in order to preserve the idea of a binding bargain. Once a court "identifies" a fundamental breach, it treats any exemption clause as ineffective to excuse that breach.

The above approach was questioned by the English Court of Appeal. Instead, it considered fundamental breach an extension of the existing rules of interpretation, involving consideration of the parties' intentions and expectations in the context of the whole agreement.[20]

On this basis, an exemption clause may effectively protect a defendant from liability for fundamental breach if, in all the circumstances, it ought to be inferred that the parties so agreed. This analysis was followed by the Supreme Court of Canada in a case where the defendant telegraph company failed to deliver a telegraphed tender, and the plaintiff contractor lost a construction contract it would otherwise have won.[21] The Court held that despite its failure to perform, the telegraph company was protected by the broad exemption clause printed on the telegram form.

The principle, stated as a rule of interpretation in the context of the whole agreement, is a sensible one, especially in transactions between businesses that agree to apportion the risks of a contract through the use of an exemption clause. For instance, a contractor for a large construction project may obtain insurance coverage at a better price than would be possible if each of its subcontractors had to take out separate policies. The subcontractors are able to make lower bids by exempting themselves from liability, with the agreement of the contractor. In these circumstances, if a court were to hold an exemption clause ineffective to protect a subcontractor, it would be defeating the bargain freely made by the parties.[22] We should note, however, that courts continue to examine these clauses very carefully, and to interpret them as not protecting the defendant when it would appear manifestly unfair or unconscionable to give protection.[23]

POSSIBLE CRIMINAL CONSEQUENCES OF BREACH

A breach of contract may be criminal when a party breaks the contract with the knowledge that the action will: endanger human life; cause bodily harm; expose valuable property to damage; deprive the inhabitants of a place of their supply of light, power, gas, or water; or delay or prevent the operation of a train by a common carrier.[24]

---

19. For a discussion of the five factors used to determine if a breach is fundamental, see *Shelanu Inc.* v. *Print Three Franchising Corp.* (2003), 64 O.R. (3d) 533 (C.A.), *Place Concorde East Limited Partnership* v. *Shelter Corp.* (2006), 211 O.A.C. 141, and *Spirent Communcations of Ottawa Limited* v. *Quake Technologies (Canada) Inc.* 2008 ONCA 92.

20. *U.G.S. Finance Ltd.* v. *National Mortgage Bank of Greece, S.A.*, [1964] 1 Lloyd's Rep. 446, per Pearson, L.J., at 453. This approach was generally approved by the House of Lords in *Suisse Atlantique Société D'Armement Maritime S.A.* v. *N.V. Rotterdamsche Kolen Centrale*, [1967] 1 A.C. 361. Now, England's Unfair Contracts Terms Act, 1977, (U.K.) 1977, c. 50, limits the application of exemption clauses.

21. *Linton* v. *C.N.R.* (1974), 49 D.L.R. (3d) 548. Four of the justices dissented vigorously, protesting that the effect of the majority decision was to leave the telegraph company substantially without any obligation. Subsequently, the House of Lords also allowed a very broad exemption clause to protect a defendant against liability for a deliberate act of destruction by one of its employees: *Production Ltd.* v. *Securicor Transport Ltd.*, [1980] 2 W.L.R. 283. The Supreme Court of Canada upheld a waiver of liability covering even the negligence of the snowmobile race operator, finding that the waiver was not unreasonable for a sporting activity with obvious dangers: *Dyck* v. *Manitoba Snowmobile Association* [1985] 1 S.C.R. 589.

22. For a full discussion of the problems raised with respect to the allocation of risk, see Waddams, *The Law of Contracts*, 4th. ed., at 338–51. In particular, at pp. 346–9, there is an interesting discussion of Harbutt's Plasticine case, in which the court disregarded an exemption clause protecting a defendant, and as a result, there was further litigation against an insurer that contested the unexpected liability of the defendant. See Harbutt's *"Plasticine" Ltd.* v. *Wayne Tank & Pump Co. Ltd.*, [1970] 1 Q.B. 447, and *Wayne Tank & Pump Co. Ltd.* v. *Employers Liability Assurance Corp. Ltd.*, [1974] Q.B. 57.

23. *Monta Arbre Inc.* v. *Inter-Traffic* (1983) Ltd. (1989), 71 O.R. (2d) 182. See also *Hunter, supra* n. 14.

24. Criminal Code, R.S.C. 1985, c. C-46, s. 422.

CONTEMPORARY ISSUE

Online Contracts and Exemption Clauses

Most online retailers attempt to protect themselves by including limitation of liability and exemption clauses on their sites as part of the terms of sale. An example might be: "The retailer makes no representations or warranties about the condition or quality of these goods, and expressly disclaims any covenant, representation, or warranty that may be implied into this contract of sale, whether by statute or otherwise." Often these clauses will be accompanied by a clause that limits the retailer's liability to the cost of the purchased good and no more.

As we saw in Chapter 5, exemption clauses are common in standard form consumer contracts, and they are often the reason that such contracts are one-sided in favour of the retailer. Online consumer contracts vary somewhat from the typical standard form contracts for a number of reasons: not only because of the oft-cited reasons that they typically cross jurisdictions and because of the inability of the consumer to inspect the goods, but also because the exemption clauses are presented to the purchasing consumer in a different manner. Some web retailers simply include a link on their ordering page to the "terms and conditions" of the purchase contract (including the exemption clause); others require the purchaser to scroll through all such terms and indicate her acceptance before she may complete an order. In a leading Ontario case, *Microsoft* v. *Rudder*, where the consumer plaintiffs complained about the terms of Microsoft's standard form online licence, the Ontario Superior Court likened scrolling through terms of an online contract to flipping through the pages of a multi-page paper contract. The judge in Rudder concluded that if a consumer clicked "I agree" at the end of a series of standard-form terms, she would be bound by those terms, including, presumably, any exemption clause.

However, recent revisions to Ontario's consumer protection laws require Internet retailers to provide written copies of their "Internet agreement" to consumers, including disclosure of any "restrictions, limitations and conditions that would be imposed by the supplier." Failure to disclose the prescribed information will allow the consumer to rescind the Internet contract; consequently, one could argue that while exemption clauses in online consumer contracts may be binding, they cannot be "hidden" from consumers.

QUESTIONS TO CONSIDER

1. Are exemption clauses potentially more disadvantageous to consumers in online contracts than in other contracting media (that is, storefronts, contracts through the mail, etc.)?

2. Do you think the law affecting the enforcement of standard form contracts should be altered to better reflect the online medium? Does the revised consumer protection legislation in Ontario go far enough to protect consumers?

3. Should it be a requirement of all online consumer contracts that consumers must expressly agree to the terms, including exemption clauses, before consumers are allowed to complete a purchase order? How might retailers obtain express agreement?

Sources: *Microsoft* v. *Rudder* [1999] O.J. No. 3778; Michael Erdle and Heather Watts, "Recent Developments in Online Contracting," *Internet and E-Commerce Law in Canada*, Vol. 2, number 10, December 2001. Consumer Protection Act, 2002, S.O. 2002, c. 30, ss. 38–39; Consumer Protection Act, 2002 Regulations, O.Reg.17/05, s. 32.

THE BUSINESS SIGNIFICANCE OF BREACH

The vast majority of contracts are performed not because there are legal rules and courts to enforce them, but because the contracts make sense to the parties themselves. The parties very likely saw a mutual economic advantage in forming their contract in the first place, or they would not have done so; the same advantage survives throughout the duration of most contracts to provide each side with an incentive to complete it. Few parties ever enter into a contract if they seriously suppose that they may later have to seek one of the remedies for breach through court action. Of course, the expected advantages from the bargain do not always materialize, and the benefits for one party may turn out to be losses. The remedies for breach that we examine in the next chapter play two roles: they encourage the performance of contracts and assist the other party in obtaining compensation if performance is not forthcoming.

QUESTIONS FOR REVIEW

1. Why does a major breach not automatically discharge a contract? Give an example.

2. Describe two ways in which anticipatory breach may occur.

3. In what types of contracts does it become particularly difficult to ascertain whether a breach is sufficient to allow the injured party to be freed from its part of the bargain? Explain.

4. Describe why the doctrine of substantial performance is of practical importance.

5. Even in the case of very serious breach, the aggrieved party may be unable to insist that he is discharged from his obligations. How does this occur?

6. What useful purpose is served by exemption clauses? Give an example.

7. Explain the attitude of the courts towards exemption clauses.

8. Give an example of strict interpretation of an exemption clause.

9. Explain the difficulties created by the doctrine of fundamental breach.

10. How have the courts applied the doctrine of fundamental breach?

11. What do you think Professor Macneil meant when he wrote, "The most important support for contractual relationships is not a sanction at all, but a continuation of the exchange motivations which led the parties to enter the relationship in the first place"? ("Whither Contracts" (1969), 21 *Journal of Legal Education* 403 at 410.)

CASES AND PROBLEMS

1. Stellar Construction Inc. agreed to build a new Olympic swimming pool for the Thomson Aquatic Centre for $450 000. The completion date was May 1. Thomson visited the pool on April 23, and was very disappointed with the quality of the tiles and caulking on the edges of the pool. She complained at once to Urqhart, Stellar's on-site manager.

   Urqhart said that the tiles and caulking complied with the specifications, but if Thomson wanted them replaced there would be a delay of two weeks for completing the project. Thomson insisted that the quality was inadequate but that she needed to have the pool ready by May 3 when she had scheduled the grand opening celebration of the renovated Centre. Urqhart replied that she would have to choose between a delayed opening and accepting the tiles as is. Thomson then said, "Leave it. We'll settle it later."

Stellar continued its work and completed the project on May 2, in time for the grand opening. The final payment of $100 000 to Stellar was due May 15, but Thomson refused to pay it. She claimed that she had an independent appraisal of the tile work, that it would cost at least $50 000 to have the work done, and that the pool would have to be closed for two weeks, causing substantial losses in revenue to the Aquatic Centre.

Stellar sued Thomson for the $100 000, denying that Thomson's complaint was valid. It was established that the tiles failed to meet the specifications in the contract between the parties, and that replacing them would indeed cost $50 000 plus the cost of business disruption. However, the diminished appearance of the pool caused by the tiles reduced the value of the pool by no more than $15 000.

Give your opinion whether it was Thomson's choice to replace or leave the tiles. In either case would Stellar's failure to perform amount to a minor or major breach?

2. O. Leander owns extensive greenhouses in which she grows flowers and plants for retail florists. On October 25, Jason, a retail florist, agrees to buy from Leander 1000 poinsettias for the Christmas trade, the plants to cost $1.00 each and to be available between December 10 and December 20. Jason requests delivery on December 11. At that time Leander advises him that she will not perform the contract, since she can obtain $1.25 each for the plants elsewhere. Jason refuses to pay more than $1.00 a plant and continues to insist upon delivery. On December 16, an extreme cold spell arrives, Leander's heating system breaks down, and all the poinsettias she has on hand freeze. Jason then purchases the 1000 poinsettias from another wholesale florist but has to pay $1.30 a plant.

Has Jason any remedy? Discuss the arguments in his favour and the defences that Leander might offer. Would it make any difference if the contract had provided instead that the plants be available between December 10 and December 15?

3. Fowler Engineering Co. agreed to supply Supreme Soap Co. with a specific machine for the manufacture of soap-chips from liquid soap. The essential terms of the contract were as follows:

Fowler agrees: To supply the machine and supervise its installation; to supervise the installation of all motors and pipes supplied by Supreme Soap; to test the machine and put it in good working order.

Supreme Soap agrees: To supply all necessary motors and pipes and labour; to pay $10 000 on delivery of the machine by Fowler; to pay the balance of $15 000 on completion of the installation.

When the machine was fully installed but had not yet been tested, Fowler demanded payment of the balance of $15 000. The manager of Supreme Soap Co. refused to pay until the machine had had a trial run and had proved satisfactory. Fowler said it did not want payment held up just because there might be some minor adjustments. Both parties were adamant. Supreme Soap Co. then employed another engineering firm to test the machine. The machine did not operate satisfactorily, although it was agreed that the defect could be remedied for about $250. The test also indicated that a different type of equipment would be better for the purposes of the soap company.

Supreme Soap Co. brought an action for return of the $10 000 deposit and for damages for breach of contract including the value of the floor space occupied by the machine, the value of the materials and labour it had supplied towards its completion, and the fees of the other engineering firm employed for the trial run. Fowler Engineering Co. counterclaimed for the balance owing on the price. What should the result be?

4. Three containers of equipment purchased by Bombardier Inc. in Japan arrived in Vancouver. Bombardier entered into a contract of carriage, using the standard bill of lading, with Canadian Pacific Ltd. (CP) to ship the containers by rail to Montreal. The contract contained a clause limiting CP's liability to $20 000 per container for any damage caused to the containers and their contents by CP's negligence while in transit.

The train carrying the containers derailed en route, but the accident was not caused by any negligence of CP. Two of the three containers were damaged by the derailment, but not seriously. (The third was unharmed.) However, during the salvage operation, CP's employees negligently set the two damaged containers on fire, causing much greater damage to their contents.

CP offered to pay $40 000 for the damage to the equipment in the two containers pursuant to the terms of the bill of lading. Bombardier rejected the payment and sued CP for $250 000, claiming that the damage done during the salvage operations was outside the contract of carriage; it argued that once the containers were thrown off the rails and were lying on the ground they were no longer "in transit." CP replied that salvage operations are an inherent part of a contract of carriage in case of accident, and that the clause limiting liability still applied.

Give your opinion of the arguments by each side and which would be likely to succeed.

ADDITIONAL RESOURCES FOR CHAPTER 14 ON THE COMPANION WEBSITE *(www.pearsoned.ca/smyth)*

In addition to self-test multiple-choice, true–false, and short essay questions (all with immediate feedback), application exercises, and links to useful web destinations, the Companion Website provides the following resources for Chapter 14:

- **Alberta:** Disclosure Requirements; Fundamental Breach; Substantial Performance
- **Manitoba/Saskatchewan:** Consumer Protection Legislation
- **Ontario:** Exemption Clauses; Fundamental Breach; Substantial Performance

Remedies for Breach

Apart from treating a contract as discharged, an injured party may need additional remedies to compensate it for any harm caused by breach of contract. The usual remedy is an award of damages. However, when damages are not sufficient, other remedies may be available. In this chapter, we examine such questions as:

- What is the purpose of an award of damages?

- What are the limits placed on an award by the requirement that the aggrieved party minimize the harm it has suffered?

- What factors are taken into account in measuring the loss?

- What are the main problems involved in measuring non-economic losses?

- What approaches are used in measuring loss?

- What is the significance of, and the limits on, obtaining remedies of

  - specific performance—ordering the wrongdoer to correct his wrong?

  - injunction—ordering the wrongdoer to cease his wrongful conduct?

  - rescission—returning the parties to a situation as if the contract had not existed?

  - *quantum meruit*—ordering payment for the value of goods or services received by the wrongdoer?

TYPES OF REMEDIES

In the last chapter, we discussed the remedy of termination—that is, the right to treat the contract as discharged as a result of breach. In addition, the injured party may have several other remedies available, depending on the type of breach and the subject matter of the contract. They are as follows:

(a) damages
(b) equitable remedies—specific performance, injunction, and rescission
(c) *quantum meruit*

DAMAGES

The Purpose of an Award of Damages

damages
a money award to compensate an injured party for the loss caused by the other party's breach

An award of **damages** aims to place the injured party in the same position as if the contract had been completed. The award is intended to compensate an injured party for the loss caused by failure to perform, not to punish the party liable for the breach. Of course, knowing that the injured party can force it to pay compensation usually deters a party from committing any breach it can avoid. In this respect, the purpose of an award of damages in contract is similar to that in the law of torts—that is, compensation and not punishment. The simple fact of liability acts as an economic deterrent.

The consequences of a solely economic approach may in some instances seem surprising. One can imagine circumstances in which a party to the contract could increase its total profits by deliberately breaking a contract.

ILLUSTRATION 15.1

X Inc. contracts to supply 100 000 widgets at $2.00 each to *Y* Corp. It expects to earn a profit of $20 000 on the contract. Shortly afterwards, *X* Inc. receives an offer to supply a different item to *Z* Ltd. at a profit of $60 000—but if it accepts the offer from *Z* Ltd., it will be unable to produce the 100 000 widgets for *Y* Corp.

X Inc. learns that a competing manufacturer can supply widgets of equal quality to *Y* Corp. at $2.25—that is, for $25 000 more than its own price. In these circumstances, *X* Inc. would gain financially if it were to forgo its profit of $20 000 on the contract with *Y* Corp. and pay that company $25 000 in damages for breach while earning $60 000 on the new contract—a net gain of $15 000.

A strictly economic analysis of the purpose of damages leads to a morally neutral view of contractual liability. This is controversial because it disregards any moral element in the legal obligation to perform one's promises. As we will discuss later in this chapter, modern courts are beginning to award damages to compensate for non-economic injury (such as mental distress) and to punish bad faith or malicious behaviour.[1]

We should note also that using a purely mathematical calculation, as in Illustration 15.1, narrows and oversimplifies the nature of the decision that must be made. Additional intangible costs of a decision to break a contract risk harming continuing good relations with the affected customer[2] as well as one's general reputation for honouring commitments.

---

1. J.C. McCamus, *The Law of Contracts* (Toronto: Irwin Law Inc., 2005), at p. 882–896.
2. The existence of this intangible cost is recognized by R.A. Posner, *Economic Analysis of Law*, 3rd ed. (Boston: Little, Brown & Co., 1977) at p. 81.

Mitigation of Damages

A party that has suffered a loss as a result of breach of contract is expected to do what it can to mitigate the extent of the loss: the damages it can recover at law will not include what it might reasonably have avoided. In this respect, **mitigation** in contract law is similar to the principle of contributory negligence in the law of torts. A business that has contracted to sell perishable goods and had them rejected will only prejudice itself by letting the goods spoil. Instead, it should re-sell them at the best obtainable price as quickly as it can if it wishes to recoup any resulting loss in an action for damages. Similarly, when a business has agreed to buy goods and the seller fails to deliver, the buyer should move to replace the goods from other suppliers as soon as possible. The same rule applies when a contract of employment is broken by the employer. An employee, in suing for damages for wrongful dismissal, should be able to show that he or she made every reasonable effort to find suitable alternative employment as a means of mitigating personal financial losses.

mitigation
action by an aggrieved party to reduce the extent of loss caused by the breach of the other party

In other words, an injured party can recover only for the losses resulting from the breach *that could not be reasonably avoided.* It follows that if a party acts in a manner that aggravates or increases the resulting loss, it will be denied recovery for the additional damages. A by-product of the mitigation rule is that it removes the incentive for conduct that is wasteful of economic resources.[3]

Prerequisites for an Award of Damages

To qualify for recovery, damage arising from breach of contract must "flow naturally from the breach." This principle has been interpreted to mean that a loss resulting from breach must be within the foreseeable limits of what the parties would have expected as a likely consequence of a failure to perform—had they thought about it when they drew up their contract. Damages are not generally awarded to compensate an injured party for some unusual or unexpected consequence of breach.

CASE 15.1

A carrier failed to deliver a vital piece of machinery promptly to a sawmill as instructed by an employee of the mill; as a result, the sawmill had to suspend operations until the part arrived. The sawmill company sued the carrier for the losses suffered by the shutdown, but the court refused to award damages because the employee had not told the carrier about the vital nature of the machinery when the carrier agreed to transport it, and the carrier had no reason to foresee the loss.

If the carrier had been told of the importance of the item, it would likely have been liable for the loss—unless it exempted itself from liability and suggested that the sawmill insure the shipment against risk of delay or loss. Or it would have placed the item in a higher category of freight to ensure greater care in delivery and charged a higher rate for its services.[4]

Sometimes a party does enter into a contract with knowledge of special liability if it fails to perform.

CASE 15.2

An engineering company contracted to make a machine and deliver it by a given date. It then made a subcontract with the defendant firm to manufacture an essential part, clearly stating the date that the entire machine had to be completed for its customer. The defendant subcontractor did not manufacture the part on time and

because of the delay, the buyer refused to accept the machine. The engineering company sued the subcontractor for damages, including the loss of profit on the main contract and the expenses incurred uselessly in making the machine. It succeeded; the court agreed that the subcontractor should have foreseen the risk when the contract was made.[5]

---

3. See Waddams, *The Law of Contracts*, 4th ed., at 553–63.

4. *B.C. Saw Mill Co.* v. *Nettleship* (1868), L.R. 3 C.P. 499. See also *Hadley* v. *Baxendale* (1854), 156 E.R. 145; *Koufos* v. *C. Czarnikow, The Heron II*, [1969] 1 A.C. 350; *Cornwall Gravel Co. Ltd.* v. *Purolator Courier Ltd.* (1978), 18 O.R. (2d) 551.

5. *Hydraulic Engineering Co.* v. *McHaffie Goslett* (1878), 4 Q.B.D. 670. See also *Telecommander Corp.* v. *United Parcel Service Canada Ltd.*, [1996] O.J. No. 4664.

In general, a seller or manufacturer of goods has a better idea of the consequences of late supply to the buyer than does a carrier of the goods. A supplier is more likely to know the needs of its customers in order to sell to them; a carrier usually knows only that the goods are to be picked up at one point and delivered to another according to the terms of the contract of carriage.[6]

A breach of contract may spark a chain of events that results in a significant "consequential" loss for the promisee. To an outsider, the relationship between the breach and the type of loss may be difficult to see. The critical test, however, is to ask whether, from the past business dealings between the parties and the actual and supposed knowledge of the promisor at the time of the contract—not at the time the breach occurs—its managers should reasonably have expected such a loss to be a result of breach by the promisor. If so, damages may be awarded against it to compensate for the loss.

THE MEASUREMENT OF DAMAGES

Expectation Damages

Differences Between Tort and Contract

We have just noted that the moment for determining whether damages were foreseeable is the time of making the contract and not when the breach occurs. Similarly, the moment for determining the amount of damages that were foreseeable is also the time of making the contract. There is an important distinction between assessing damages for tort and assessing damages for breach of contract. In tort, the only conceivable time for measuring damages is the time of wrongdoing—that is, the moment the tort is committed. In breach of contract, the reason for referring to the earlier moment of formation is that from that moment, a promisor becomes liable to uphold the promise and the promisee becomes entitled to a continuous expectation of performance until the time for performance arrives; it is on the basis of this reasonably foreseeable liability that the promisor has bargained for the price.

Should a court include in its award of damages for breach an amount equal to the *expected* profits on the aborted transaction? The answer is yes, because that result is part of the objective of placing an aggrieved party in the position it would have enjoyed had the contract been performed.

expectation damages
an amount awarded for breach of contract based on expected profits

An award of **expectation damages** for breach of contract often contrasts sharply with the measurement normal in tort, where recovery is limited to harm suffered as a result of the tort.

ILLUSTRATION 15.2

While examining a set of sketches in an art gallery, Jansen recognizes Took, a magazine art critic, and asks him what he thinks of the sketches. Took replies, "I like this one. I'm certain it is by Tom Thomson." As a result, Jansen immediately buys the sketch from the gallery at the asking price of $500. Took's assertion was a negligent misrepresentation and Jansen soon discovers the sketch is worth, at most, $100. Had it been a genuine Thomson, its value would have been at least $5000. In a tort action against Took, the measure of damages would be Jansen's loss, the $400 extra she paid above the market value of the sketch. However, she could not recover the potential profit of $4500 that she could have earned on resale had Took's representation been true.

Suppose instead that Took was the gallery owner and sold the sketch to Jansen describing it on the bill of sale as a work by Tom Thomson. In these circumstances, Jansen could sue for the expectation loss of $4500.

---

6. See *Victoria Laundry (Windsor) Ltd.* v. *Newman Industries Ltd.*, [1949] 2 K.B. 528, per Asquith, J., at 537; *United Oilseed Products Ltd.* v. *North American Car* (Canada) Ltd., [1984] B.C.J. No. 409.

Opportunity Cost

Why should there be this difference in the basis for recovery of damages? The main reason is the high value we place in our society on being able to rely on contracts from the moment we make them. If a contract breaker were liable to pay compensation only for losses actually suffered by the other party (such as out-of-pocket expenses), it could often ignore its obligations with relative impunity; the other party may not yet have made any actual expenditures, even though it may have forgone the opportunity to make a similar contract elsewhere. Indeed, the **opportunity cost**—the lost chance of making a similar contract with a different promisor—is an important reason for using expectation loss as a measure of damages. Many, if not most, business arrangements would otherwise be without adequate sanction in law: a "deal" would not be a deal in any binding sense. In other words, the liability for expectation damages provides the essential background remedy for an effective system of contract law.[7]

opportunity cost
the lost chance of making a similar contract with a different promisor

Contracts of Sale

Contracts for the sale of goods provide a useful example of the approach taken by the courts in measuring expectation damages when one party is in breach. Suppose, first, that a buyer is in breach by refusing to accept delivery of the goods purchased. In an action for damages[8] the first thing that we need to know is whether the seller's supply of goods exceeds the demand for them—that is, whether the seller can supply goods to all prospective customers. If so, the buyer's breach results in the seller losing the profit on one sale, regardless of the resale of those same goods to a second buyer: the seller would still have made the second sale even if the first buyer had accepted the goods, and would have made two sales instead of one. Accordingly, the seller may recover damages from the first buyer amounting to the lost profits on their contract of sale.

However, when the seller's supply is limited and it could not have filled a second order if the first buyer had accepted the goods, the seller's damages will be measured by, first, its additional expenses in taking reasonable steps to find a second buyer, and second, by any loss in revenue as a result of having to accept a lower sale price to dispose of the goods. The seller may suffer no damages at all if it resells for the full contract price (or more) without additional selling expenses.[9]

Suppose, instead, a seller breaks its contract by failing to deliver on time. If the buyer can obtain the goods elsewhere, the damages will be those reasonable expenses incurred in seeking an alternative supply and any additional price the buyer has had to pay above the original contract price. Of course, if the buyer obtains an alternative supply for the same or a lower price than that in the original contract, there will be no damages without added expenses in seeking the new supply.

These principles for measuring damages are based on the principle that when buyer and seller agree on a price and time for delivery, each has taken into account, and assumes, the risk of changes in the market price between the time of making the contract and the time of delivery. Whether the market price goes up or down in the interval, the seller must deliver and the buyer must accept delivery of the goods at the agreed time—or pay damages for failure to perform; they allocated the risk of change in price between them when they made the contract.

Consequential Damages

Consequential damages are in a sense secondary, one stage removed from the immediate effects of breach. Nevertheless, they may be both serious and reasonably foreseeable, so that a defendant will be liable to compensate for them. In our example of a seller that fails to deliver goods on time, suppose

---

7. See Waddams, *The Law of Contracts*, 4th ed., at 515–6. Also, *West Coast Finance Ltd. and Booth* v. *Gunderson, Stokes, Walton & Co.*, [1974] 2 W.W.R. 428 at 434–5, and [1975] 4 W.W.R. 501.

8. As we shall see in Chapter 16, the Sale of Goods Act provides special rules that set out when title to goods passes to a buyer before delivery. (See section on "Title to Goods.") If title has passed, a seller may sue for the price instead of for damages.

9. In one sense, the first buyer's breach enabled the seller to make the second sale. See *Apeco of Canada Ltd.* v. *Windmill Place* (1978), 82 D.L.R. (3d) 1.

the buyer is unable to obtain suitable replacements from another source in time to use them for the intended purpose—for instance, to resell them or to use them as components in another product. The seller will be liable for those kinds of damages that it knew or ought to have known would flow "naturally" from the breach—that is, were reasonably foreseeable by the seller at the time the contract was formed. The measure is the lost profits on any resale transactions and may also include damage claims against the buyer by its own customers as a result of its unavoidable default on contracts with them.

ILLUSTRATION 15.3

A Dairies Ltd. makes a written contract with *B* to supply *B*'s restaurant with ice cream twice weekly, on Tuesdays and Fridays. *A* Dairies fails to deliver on a Friday at the beginning of a hot summer weekend. Other suppliers are busy servicing their own customers and refuse to supply ice cream to *B*. *B* runs out of ice cream Saturday morning and cannot obtain a fresh supply until Monday. *B*'s loss is not the extra cost of obtaining ice cream elsewhere (which *B* was unable to obtain in any event); it is the loss of profits on ice cream sales over the weekend.

Instead of non-delivery, a seller's breach of contract may be in delivering defective goods. If so, other tests must be applied to assess the damages that would place the buyer in the same position as if the seller had performed the contract.

CASE 15.3

Lakelse Dairy Products purchased a new bulk-milk tank truck from General Dairy Machinery (GDM) to transport milk to its production facility. GDM was specialized in building such vehicles and warranted that it was fit for the purpose. However, the truck had serious flaws—there were cracks in the tank where milk remained in sufficient quantities; when the tank deteriorated and went bad, it infected new shipments of milk. Lakelse hired experts to find the source of the problem but it was confusing: Was it the milk from the farms? Was it the machinery in the production facility? Was it the truck?

It took several months to uncover the source of the problem. Meanwhile, a substantial amount of milk had to be discarded, and some had to be taken back from customers. When the source of the problem was discovered, Lakelse had to lease another tank truck. It sued GDM successfully, not only for the direct loss in value of the defective tank truck and the cost of leasing another truck, but also for the lost profits that would have been made on the discarded milk if it had been sold by Lakelse at market value.[10]

Consequential damages may arise from breach of a wide variety of contracts, not just the sale of goods. For instance, failure to repair the heating system of a concert hall as promised in time for a performance in midwinter could lead to the cancellation of the program, making the heating contractor liable for the losses due to cancellation, as well as for damage to the building by frozen pipes, since both are foreseeable harms.

General Damages

The term "general damages" describes an estimated amount that a court may award, over and above specific losses for harm, that cannot be calculated in precise monetary terms, but that the court believes necessary to compensate the aggrieved party fairly. For example, if a surgeon

---

10. *Lakelse Dairy Products Ltd.* v. *General Dairy Machinery & Supply Ltd.* (1970), 10 D.L.R. (3d) 277.

undertook to improve the appearance of a professional entertainer by performing plastic surgery on her nose, but the result was to disfigure the nose, a court would have to decide what general damages, over and above specific out-of-pocket medical and hospital expenses, would compensate the plaintiff for the effects of this failure on her state of mind and professional morale. A U.S. court has, in fact, awarded general damages for breach of contract in such circumstances.[11]

Reliance Damages

Suppose that a management consultant contracts to spend three months advising a manufacturing firm on the reorganization of its operations. The contract term is to start two weeks later, and in preparation for the project, the consultant spends the time assembling and preparing materials and reading the latest literature on the specialized business of the client firm. Just as she is about to start the consulting project on site, her client cancels the contract, saying it has decided to make no changes for the indefinite future. Fortunately, the consultant is able to take advantage of another consulting opportunity that can be easily substituted at the same fee. She could not, therefore, recover expectation damages for the fee she would have received if the manufacturing company had not cancelled the contract. However, she has still lost the time, effort, and expenditures involved in two weeks' preparation. Now it is merely wasted effort—not needed for the substituted job—effort she could have used more productively for other contracts. In these circumstances the consultant may recover as reliance damages the costs of all expenditures and wasted effort that were reasonably made in preparation for the first job.[12]

Liquidated Damages

Parties to a contract may agree in advance to terms stating an amount to be paid in damages if a breach should occur. The actual loss from breach may bear no relation to the agreed sum: it may turn out to be far greater or far less. Nevertheless, if the terms were a genuine attempt by the parties to estimate a loss, those terms will conclusively govern the amount of damages recoverable. Such provisions for **liquidated damages** can provide an economic incentive both to the promisor to perform (and so avoid incurring liability for the stated amount) and to the promisee to minimize its actual loss (since it will be entitled in any event to the stated amount and any savings will accrue directly to it).

liquidated damages
an amount agreed to be paid in damages by a party to a contract if it should commit a breach

---

ILLUSTRATION 15.4

P Inc. agrees to construct an office building for *Q* Properties Inc., with a completion date of May 31. Both parties agree that any delay will cause a loss in revenue to *Q* from prospective tenants. A term of the contract states that for any delay in completion, *Q* may deduct $600 per day from its final payment of $100 000 to *P*, payable one month after *Q* obtains possession of the building. Such a term is binding upon both parties whether *Q* Properties Inc. suffers a larger or smaller loss because of delay.

We must distinguish between a genuine attempt to anticipate or "liquidate" the consequences of a breach of contract and a **penalty clause**. If a term in the contract specifies an exorbitant amount, out of all relation to the probable consequences of breach, a court may find that it is intended merely to frighten a party into performance. Accordingly, the court will hold that it is a penalty clause and will disregard it in awarding damages based on an assessment of the actual loss suffered.

penalty clause
a term specifying an exorbitant amount for breach of contract, intended to frighten a party into performance

---

11. *Sullivan* v. *O'Connor*, 296 N.E. 2d 183 (1973). Damages of $13 500 were awarded. For a Canadian decision in which the plaintiff sued unsuccessfully in tort, see *Lokay* v. *Kilgour* (1984), 31 C.C.L.T. 177.
12. *Anglia T.V.* v. *Reed*, [1971] 3 All E.R. 690; *Lloyd* v. *Stanbury*, [1971] 2 All E.R. 267.

A sum paid as a deposit on the formation of a contract, to be forfeited on failure to perform, is a common type of liquidated damages provision, but it is treated somewhat differently. Partly because the money has already been paid as a guarantee of performance and partly because of a long history of deposits being forfeited, courts are reluctant to overturn such provisions even when they seem harsh: they are rarely recoverable. If, however, the sum is described as a part payment or a down payment, the courts are more willing to examine whether its forfeiture would be a penalty.

At the other extreme, a term limiting liquidated damages to a very small sum may be tantamount to an exemption clause. For instance, if a term states that $1 shall be payable as full compensation for breach, the issue for a court may be whether there has been a fundamental breach making the clause ineffective, as discussed in Chapter 14; it is clearly not a penalty. We should note also that any clause that limits the maximum recovery but also allows a lesser recovery according to the damage suffered can never be a penalty clause, although it may amount to an exemption clause.

Nominal Damages

Occasionally, a court may award nominal damages to acknowledge a breach of contract where the loss sustained by the promisee is negligible. A court award of $1 will at least establish the validity of the plaintiff's claim where a question of principle is at stake. In general, when the amount in dispute is nominal, the likelihood that a "successful" plaintiff will still have to pay or share court costs discourages such litigation.

PROBLEMS IN MEASURING DAMAGES

Mental Anguish

The main basis for awarding damages is, of course, compensating for economic loss. There is, however, a range of contractual interests that are, at least in part, non-economic—illustrated in the preceding section by the case involving plastic surgery. As we noted in Chapter 3 on Tort Law, courts came gradually to recognize pain, suffering, nervous shock, and humiliation as harms for which they will grant limited recovery. The courts have now begun to follow this trend in contract in an increasing number of cases that recognize mental distress resulting from breach as a form of non-economic harm entitled to compensation. Courts initially awarded this type of damage for contracts that promised some form of pleasure such as vacations or luxury items. Now damages for mental distress may be awarded in any breach of contract action if this type of damage was reasonably foreseeable by the parties at the time the contract was created.[13]

Wrongful Dismissal

Mental anguish often occurs when an employee is wrongfully dismissed, especially after long years of service. Apart from direct financial loss, for which he or she is entitled to compensation, the dismissed employee may feel humiliated and suffer a serious loss of confidence. Recently, the Supreme Court of Canada considered this type of damage and confirmed that although "normal distress and hurt feelings resulting from dismissal are not compensable . . . [mental anguish damages may be awarded] when the employer engages in conduct during the course of dismissal that is unfair or in bad faith such as [behaviour that is] untruthful, misleading or unduly insensitive."[14] Examples of behaviours that meet this test are lying about the reason for dismissal or defaming the reputation of the employee.[15] The plaintiff must prove the psychological harm for which mental anguish

---

13. *Fidler* v. *Sun Life Assurance Co. of Canada*, [2006] 2 S.C.R. 3, para 42.
14. *Honda Canada Inc.* v. *Keays* 2008 SCC 39, paras 56–57, referring to *Wallace* v. *United Grain Growers Ltd.* (1997), 152 D.L.R. (4th) 1 (S.C.C.) para 98.
15. *Ibid* para 59.

damages are claimed; it will not be presumed by the court. We discuss this issue more fully in Chapter 20.

Lost Holidays

There are many contracts, such as those for holiday travel and accommodation, that cost substantial sums of money but are not intended to confer an economic benefit on the vacationer. Unless courts take into account disappointment caused by the loss of an anticipated holiday, a vacationer would be without remedy apart from the return of any money paid. A return of that money would hardly be ample compensation to a vacationer who discovers at the airport that there is neither a flight nor any possibility of arranging an alternative holiday at the last minute. In 1973, an English court held, in the words of Lord Denning, "that damages for the loss of a holiday may include not only the difference in value between what was promised and what was obtained, but also damages for mental distress, inconvenience, upset, disappointment and frustration caused by the loss of the holiday."[16] This reasoning has been followed by Canadian courts.[17] A different example of recovery for mental distress arose in an action against an airline for breach of contract in transporting the plaintiffs' dogs.[18] The plaintiffs recovered damages for the mental suffering endured when they learned that their dogs suffocated while being carried in the baggage compartment of an airplane.

Attitude of the Courts

Apart from claims arising from wrongful dismissal, the relatively modest amounts that Canadian and English courts have awarded as damages for mental distress in actions for breach of contract[19] suggest that they hesitate to award large sums for highly subjective reactions that vary widely from person to person; they seem to have come to terms with their uncertainty by awarding damages, but only for limited amounts. In proposing a limit to the amount a plaintiff in a British Columbia case could recover for pain and suffering, the Supreme Court of Canada has stated that the purpose of recognizing mental distress in an award of damages is "to substitute other amenities for those that have been lost, not to compensate for the loss of something with a money value . . . [and] to provide more general physical arrangements above and beyond those directly relating to the injuries, in order to make life more endurable."[20]

We have noted that a U.S. court awarded general damages for mental distress to a professional entertainer for the "wasted" pain and suffering she experienced when plastic surgery was unsuccessful.[21] Although the plaintiff also claimed compensation for disappointment in not obtaining the anticipated enhancement in her beauty, the court rejected such expectation damages as being too speculative. It relied on the opinion of noted authorities in contract law to the effect that, "the reasons for granting damages for broken promises to the extent of the expectancy are at their strongest when the promises are made in a business context, when they have to do with the production or distribution of goods or the allocation of functions in the marketplace."[22]

---

16. *Jarvis* v. *Swan Tours Ltd.*, [1973] Q.B. 233. The quotation is Lord Denning's explanation of that decision in *Jackson* v. *Horizon Holidays*, [1975] 1 W.L.R. 1468 at 1472.

17. *Elder* v. *Koppe* (1974), 53 D.L.R. (3d) 705; *Keks* v. *Esquire Pleasure Tours Ltd.*, [1974] 3 W.W.R. 406; *Murray* v. *Triton Airlines Inc.* (1994), 365 A.P.R. 131.

18. *Newell* v. *C.P. Air* (1976), 74 D.L.R. (3d) 574.

19. Five hundred dollars for each of the two expelled union members; £125 for mental distress from loss of a holiday in the Jarvis case and £500 in the Jackson case; $500 for mental distress of the owners of the suffocated dogs.

20. *Lindal* v. *Lindal* (1981), 129 D.L.R. (3d) 263, per Dickson, J., at 272 and 273. See also *Wilson* v. *Sooter Studios Ltd.* (1988), 55 D.L.R. (4th) 303; *McIsaac* v. *Sun Life Co. of Canada* (1999), 173 D.L.R. 645.

21. *Sullivan* v. *O'Connor, supra*, n. 11.

22. The reference is to Fuller and Perdue, "The Reliance Interest in Contract Damages: 1" (1936), 46 Yale L.J. 52, especially at 60–3. The authors offer as justifications for expectation damages "the loss of opportunity to enter other contracts" and "a policy in favor of promoting and facilitating reliance on business agreements."

Cost of Performance Versus Economic Loss

The U.S. case *Peevyhouse* v. *Garland Coal & Mining Company*[23] provides a striking example of the difficulty in deciding on the appropriate standards for measuring damages in circumstances that fall outside traditional categories of economic loss.

CASE 15.4

Owners of a farm containing coal deposits leased it to a mining company for five years. The operation was strip mining, in which coal is scooped from open pits on the surface, scarring the land. The owners insisted on including a term in the lease requiring the company to restore the surface at the expiration of the lease by moving earth in order to level the pits. At the end of the lease, the company vacated without restoring the land and the owners sued for damages.

Breach was admitted by the company. However, the court was faced with the following dilemma: the cost of restoring the land as promised would be $29 000, but the market value of the farm would increase by only $300 as a result of the restoration. The owners claimed damages of $29 000, measured by the "cost of performance," and the company countered that it was liable only for damages of $300, measured by the "diminution in economic [market] value" caused by the breach.

The majority of the court held that:

> . . . under the "cost of performance" rule plaintiffs might recover an amount about nine times the total value of their farm. Such would be unconscionable and grossly oppressive damages, contrary to substantial justice . . . also, it can hardly be denied that if plaintiffs here are permitted to recover under the "cost of performance" rule they will receive a greater benefit from the breach than could be gained by full performance. . . . [24]

Accordingly, the court found that an award of $29 000 to the plaintiffs would have given them a windfall of $28 700; it awarded damages of only $300.

The position taken by the majority of the court is supported by the following economic analysis: it encourages parties to decide whether to perform or break their contracts in strictly economic terms. Thus, it would discourage the coal company from committing $29 000 of labour, materials, and equipment to a project that would result only in an increase of $300 in value. If, instead, "cost of performance" was used to measure the damages, the company might have chosen to perform in order to avoid litigation.[25]

On the other hand, this strictly economic analysis ignores the owners' subjective interest in having the farm restored. For sentimental or esthetic reasons—suppose the farm had been in their family for generations and they occupied an adjacent farm—they may have bargained expressly for restoration. Was it legally impossible for them to bargain successfully for such a promise? Suppose that after losing their case, the owners nevertheless decided to proceed with restoration, and they paid a contracting firm $29 000 in advance to do the job. Could the contracting firm, having accepted the money, then refuse to perform, offering to pay damages of $300 as the measure of its breach? The *Peevyhouse* decision suggests that it could.

Even the economic argument can be stated differently: the approximate cost of restoration was known more or less accurately when the lease was entered into; this cost must have been taken into account in setting the price for access to the coal; the owners would probably have charged a higher price for the coal had they realized that the company could not be made to pay the cost of restoration;

---

23. 382 P.2d 109 (Okla. 1963). See also *James* v. *Hutton & J. Cool & Sons Ltd.*, [1950] 1 K.B. 9.

24. *Ibid.*, per Jackson, J., at 113.

25. See Posner, *Economic Analysis of Law*, 3rd ed., at 109.

they could then have done the restoration using the extra revenue. In this sense, it is the company that has obtained a windfall of $28 700 in not having to pay the cost of what it had originally promised to do as part of the price of the lease.

It can be seen then that the *Peevyhouse* decision is debatable. The court was not unanimous in its opinion, and an opposite view was taken by another U.S. court.[26] While economic analysis is an important tool in both understanding and applying contract principles, it does not provide the only basis for analysis. The legitimate expectations of parties may include non-economic interests, which are also entitled to the protection of the law.

ETHICAL ISSUE

Should Courts Award General or Punitive Damages in Contract?

Should damages in contract solely reflect the model of compensation for economic loss or should they punish "bad" behaviour? Just as we have seen the debate in Part 2 about the appropriateness of awarding damages in tort for pure economic loss, we are now observing that common law courts are departing from their traditional reluctance in breach of contract cases to award damages for anything that is not purely economic and compensatory in nature. Consider, for instance, the English decision in *Jarvis* v. *Swan's Tours Ltd.* to "compensate" for the value of a lost vacation (see footnote 16).

In recent years, Canadian courts have considered the issue of awarding damages for mental distress when there has been breach of an employment contract—typically in cases where the employee alleges that she has been terminated for "no just cause." Historically in such cases, the damage awards granted by courts to the aggrieved employees have been based on the amount of salary in lieu of the proper amount of notice of termination the employee should have been given. In some circumstances, however, plaintiffs have argued that they are entitled to further compensation for the mental anguish, humiliation, and loss of self-esteem that were a direct result of the employer's breach of the employment contract and bad faith. In a recent Ontario case, *Ribeiro* v. *CIBC*, the court awarded $20 000 in general damages for mental distress and $50 000 in punitive damages to a former employee of the bank who had been wrongfully discharged. This result was confirmed by the Court of Appeal, and the Supreme Court of Canada chose not to hear CIBC's appeal.

There have also been several recent examples of Canadian courts awarding punitive damages to a plaintiff who has proven breach of contract. In *Whiten* v. *Pilot Insurance Company*, the Supreme Court of Canada confirmed the trial judge's award of $1 000 000 in punitive damages in a case concerning the defendant's breach of its obligations under a property insurance policy (or contract). In its decision, the Court held that while punitive damages in contract law are exceptional, they are appropriate if there has been "high-handed, malicious, arbitrary or highly reprehensible misconduct that departs to a marked degree from ordinary standards of decent behaviour."

This kind of "values-based" assessment of behaviour may lead to inconsistent and unpredictable results. In *Fidler* v. *Sun Life Assurance Co. of Canada*, the British Columbia Court of Appeal awarded mental distress and punitive damages arising from the arbitrary denial of long-term disability benefits for over *five* years. The mental distress award was upheld by the Supreme Court of Canada but the punitive damage award was set aside because the court found that the conduct was not malicious or oppressive.

continued

---

26. See *Groves* v. *John Wunder Co.*, 286 N.W. 235, 123 A.L.R. 502 (1939). This decision is questioned by Posner, *supra*, n. 25, at 108–9.

Some commentators have argued that "bad faith" is not relevant when assessing whether or not there has been a breach of contract, and consequently punitive damages for misconduct are inappropriate in contract law.

QUESTIONS TO CONSIDER

1. Should courts award damages for mental distress in any type of case where there has been a breach of contract?

2. Should courts award punitive damages in contract cases where the defendant, in breaching the contract, has behaved "reprehensibly"? What are the definitions of "reprehensible," "oppressive," and "malicious"?

3. Are employment and insurance contracts analogous to contracts for lost vacations and therefore suitable for an award of damages for mental distress?

Sources: Waddams, *The Law of Contracts*, 4th ed. (Aurora, ON: Canada Law Book, 1999), paras. 747–54; *Ribeiro* v. *Canadian Imperial Bank of Commerce* (1992), 13 O.R (3d) 278; and *Wallace* v. *United Grain Growers Ltd.* (1997), 152 D.L.R. (4th) 1 (S.C.C.); *Whiten* v. *Pilot Insurance Company*, [2002] 1 S.C.R. 595; *Fidler* v. *Sun Life Assurance Co. of Canada*, [2006] 2 S.C.R. 3.

EQUITABLE REMEDIES

Reasons for the Intervention of Equity

The old common law courts gave money damages as the sole remedy for breach of contract. But there are circumstances where money damages alone are inadequate. For example, suppose a purchaser wishes to construct a large factory and for that purpose enters into contracts to buy adjoining lots from five different vendors. If one vendor, who owns a crucial middle lot, repudiates the agreement to sell, the purchaser will be left with four lots, now of no use, and will be unable to proceed with building. Damages suffered by the purchaser may be very large, perhaps many times the sale price of the lot the vendor refuses to transfer. The most sensible remedy would be to order the vendor to transfer the lot to the purchaser on payment of the purchase price. And that is exactly what the old courts of chancery (equity) did. They recognized the inadequacy of the common law remedy and intervened to grant one of their special **equitable remedies**, such as *specific performance* (discussed below). Failure to comply with an equitable remedy places a defendant in "contempt of court" and can lead to a fine or imprisonment.

Reasons for Denying a Remedy

Equitable remedies are discretionary; that is, the court decides whether, in view of all the circumstances, there are good reasons to go beyond the ordinary common law remedy of damages. However, the principles governing the exercise of this discretion have become well settled, and a remedy is granted almost automatically to a plaintiff that complies with the established principles of equity. The following are among the more important requirements:

(a) A plaintiff must come to court with "clean hands"—that is, he must not himself be found to have acted unethically; if there is an element of sharp practice on his part, the court will leave him, at best, with his claim for money damages.

(b) If, after learning of the defendant's breach, a plaintiff delays unreasonably in bringing an action, perhaps lulling the defendant into believing that no action will be brought, a court will deny an equitable remedy.

equitable remedies
special non-monetary remedies given only when damages alone will not adequately compensate for a loss

(c) As we noted in Chapter 8 on Mistake, a court will refuse to intervene on equitable principles when to do so would affect an innocent purchaser.

(d) A court will not grant a remedy in equity when the plaintiff has not paid a substantial consideration for the defendant's promise; if the promise is simply given under seal or in exchange for a nominal sum, money damages alone will be awarded.

(e) Finally, a plaintiff must ordinarily be a party against whom the remedy would be awarded were he the defendant instead; for example, because a court will not grant an equitable remedy against an infant defendant when a contract is voidable at his option, neither will it grant that remedy *in his favour* as a plaintiff. This insistence on symmetry is an ancient principle, hard to justify on grounds of fairness, and is no longer followed when an employee seeks reinstatement, as we shall see in Chapter 20.

Specific Performance

A judgment for **specific performance** is an order requiring a defendant to do a specified act, most often to complete a transaction. For example, in a real estate sale agreement the court orders the vendor to complete and deliver all documents necessary to the transfer of ownership, and to vacate the premises so that the purchaser may take possession on payment of the purchase price.

specific performance
an order requiring a defendant to do a specified act, usually to complete a transaction

In situations where the court might be obligated to supervise a defendant, specific performance will not be granted. As a result, performance that depends on the personal skill or judgment of a defendant does not lend itself to an order for specific performance. An artist who repudiates a contract to give a concert will not be ordered to perform; to do so would be to invite a disgruntled performance. The plaintiff will have to be content with an award of money damages.

The remedy of specific performance is most often applied to contracts for the sale of land. Courts granted specific performance originally on the argument that each piece of land is unique, and that consequently money damages are an inadequate remedy. Today the uniqueness of the property must be proven to the court. In *Semelhago* v. *Paramadevan* in 1996, Mr. Justice Sopinka of the Supreme Court of Canada put it this way:

> While at one time the common law regarded every piece of real estate to be unique, with the progress of modern real estate development this is no longer the case. Both residential, business and industrial properties are mass produced much in the same way as other consumer products. If a deal falls through for one property, another is frequently, though not always, readily available. . . .
>
> . . . It cannot be assumed that damages for breach of contract for the purchase and sale of real estate will be an inadequate remedy in all cases. . . .
>
> . . . Specific performance should, therefore, not be granted as a matter of course absent evidence that the property is unique to the extent that its substitute would not be readily available.[27]

The *Semelhago* decision has had a significant effect on legal claims for specific performance: in the time since it was decided, several dozen decisions have referred to it—some courts relying on it to refuse specific performance and others finding that the land in question was sufficiently unique to decree specific performance. There is now much greater uncertainty whether specific performance will be granted.

It may seem surprising that a vendor of land may also be entitled to specific performance. The reasons are, first, that the general principle giving parties mutual remedies wherever possible is followed; and second, that damages may be an inadequate remedy to a vendor. If damages were awarded, the vendor would still be left with the land; she would have to look after the land, pay

---

27. [1996] 2 S.C.R. 415. For a critique of this case, see O.V. Da Silva, "The Supreme Court of Canada's Lost Opportunity: *Semelhago* v. *Paramadevan*" (1998), 23 Queen's L.J. 475.

taxes, maintain buildings, and would have to find another purchaser in order to rid herself of these burdens. Therefore, the court may order the purchaser to specifically perform the contract—that is, to pay the vendor the full sale price and accept the land.

Courts rarely grant specific performance of a contract for the sale of goods—damages are considered adequate compensation. Courts might grant specific performance of a contract for the sale of a one-of-a-kind item. Antiques, heirlooms, rare coins, and works of art are possible examples. Shares in a corporation may also be considered property for which specific performance is an appropriate remedy, especially when a plaintiff's primary purpose is to obtain a controlling or substantial interest in the firm.

Injunction

injunction
a court order restraining a party from acting in a particular manner, such as committing a breach of contract

negative covenant
a promise not to do something

An **injunction** is a court order restraining a party from acting in a particular manner; in relation to contract, it prohibits a party from committing a breach. For the remedy to be available, the courts require the contract to contain a **negative covenant**: a promise not to do something. However, the covenant need not be stated expressly as a prohibition but may simply be a logical consequence of an express promise. Accordingly, an *express promise* by a tenant to use leased premises for office space would likely be construed to contain an *implied promise* not to use them for a nightclub; the landlord could obtain an injunction prohibiting their use for a nightclub.

Sometimes a court may grant an injunction when it would not order specific performance, although the effect of the injunction may be almost the same as that of an order for specific performance. The court is willing to do so because it does not have the problem of continuing supervision when it grants an injunction; it simply orders the defendant to stop committing further breaches. So, when a hotelkeeper promised to buy all the beer he required exclusively from one supplier and then purchased some elsewhere, the court granted an injunction restraining him from making further purchases from other suppliers.[28] The court did not say, "You must buy all your supply from this source, and we will see that you do." Instead, it said in effect, "In future you must not buy from any other source, and if we hear of your doing so, you will be in serious trouble."

Interlocutory Injunction

Contracts of the kind just described are common, and breach can lead to serious consequences for both supplier and buyer. In the typical case, the supplier is the one seeking an injunction. However, in *Sky Petroleum Ltd.* v. *VIP Petroleum Ltd.*,[29] the position was reversed.

CASE 15.5

The buyer, an owner of a chain of service stations, contracted for a long-term supply of petroleum products at fixed prices and promised to take all its requirements from the one supplier. The contract was entered into shortly before the 1973 energy crisis, which created a shortage of fuel and a sharp rise in prices. During the crisis, the supplier claimed that the buyer was in default in payment and, by alleging breach, it tried to free itself from the obligation to continue delivering to the buyer's stations. Because of the severe shortage, the supplier's conduct would have left the buyer without any source of supply and forced it out of business before the courts could hear the dispute.

The buyer asked the court to take the exceptional step of granting a temporary injunction prohibiting the supplier from refusing to continue to deliver petroleum products to it, in effect compelling specific performance by the supplier in the interval before the full trial of the dispute. The court granted the injunction to prevent the bankruptcy of the buyer before it had a chance to present its case.

28. *Clegg* v. *Hands* (1890), 44 Ch. D. 503.
29. [1974] 1 W.L.R. 576. See also *Bentall Properties Ltd.* v. *Canada Safeway Ltd.*, [1988] B.C.J. No. 775.

We can see that, in some circumstances, a court will grant an **interlocutory injunction**—a temporary injunction—to restrain immediate harm from being done by a breach of contract, pending formal resolution of the dispute at trial. Courts are reluctant, however, to grant even a temporary injunction of this kind in personal service contracts.

interlocutory injunction
a temporary restraining order

Injunction Against an Employee

In contracts of employment, granting an injunction at the request of an employer against a former employee may have unacceptable consequences. If an injunction prohibits an employee from working for any other employer, it may leave the person with the harsh alternatives of returning to work for the plaintiff in an atmosphere of hostility, or being without any means of earning a living. Accordingly, a court is reluctant to grant an injunction against an employee who has promised exclusive services to one employer but has broken the contract by working elsewhere.

Injunctions have been granted, however, when an employee in possession of valuable trade secrets left his employer in breach of his employment contract and went to work for a competitor in the same line of business,[30] and when a singer promised her exclusive services to an employer for a limited period and expressly undertook not to sing anywhere else.[31] The granting of such injunctions should be viewed as an exception to the general rule that a court will not grant the remedy where the subject matter of the contract is personal services and where the effect would be to leave the employee no alternative but to work for the original employer or remain unemployed.

Rescission

The Choice Between Damages and Rescission

Generally speaking, the primary purpose of remedies for breach is to place an aggrieved party, as nearly as is practicable, in the position she would have been *had the contract been completed*. But in some situations another approach may be preferred by a plaintiff: she would wish to return as nearly as she can to the position that would have existed *had the contract not been made at all*. In other words, she would prefer **rescission**—to have the contract *set aside* or *rescinded*.

rescission
setting aside or rescinding a contract in order to restore the parties as nearly as possible to their pre-contract positions

If a breach is serious enough to discharge the plaintiff from her own obligations, she may elect rescission, provided that it is feasible to return the parties substantially to their pre-contract positions. An aggrieved party must choose between an action for damages to obtain the benefit of the contract and one for rescission to return her to the position that she would have been in if a contract had never existed at all; she cannot have both remedies since they have contradictory purposes. Rescission is usually denied if the subject matter of a contract cannot be returned by the plaintiff to the defendant, as when it has been consumed or incorporated into other goods or sold to innocent third parties.

Perhaps the most common claim for rescission occurs when durable goods—equipment, machinery, or consumer products such as refrigerators or television sets—fail to perform as required in a contract of sale. A buyer who is unhappy with the goods rarely wants damages for their diminished value or even a replacement of the same brand; he would much prefer to return them and get his money back. If goods to be returned have been damaged or have deteriorated in value, a court may refuse to order rescission and instead leave a plaintiff with the remedy of damages. Since there may have been substantial use or deterioration of the goods while in the hands of the buyer, the remedy is often unavailable.

A less common but nonetheless important situation where rescission may be the preferred remedy arises in the sale of a valuable asset, such as land, when the purchaser defaults.

---

30. *Robinson (William) & Co. Ltd.* v. *Heuer*, [1898] 2 Ch. 451; *C.B. Constantini Ltd.* v. *Slozka*, 2006 BCSC 1210, leave to appeal refused 2006 BCCA 473.

31. *Lumley* v. *Wagner* (1852), 42 E.R. 687; also *Warner Bros. Pictures* v. *Nelson*, [1937] 1 K.B. 209.

execution order
an order that gives the sheriff authority to levy execution

garnishee order
an order requiring the debtor's employer to retain a portion of the debtor's wages each payday and surrender the sum to the creditor

execution order gives the sheriff authority to seize and sell various chattels and arrange for a sale of the debtor's lands after an appropriate grace period.[34] More complicated procedures are necessary to seize a bank account, the contents of a safety-deposit box, or an income from a trust fund. A creditor may also obtain a **garnishee order** against a debtor's wages. The order requires the employer to retain a portion of the debtor's wages each payday and surrender the sum to the creditor to be applied against the judgment.

Besides money damages, a court may make two other types of money awards for breach of contract. As we shall see in Chapter 16, a seller may be awarded the price of goods sold instead of damages for non-acceptance. And a lender of money may be awarded the amount of the money lent plus accrued interest. Each of these awards is similar to a decree of specific performance in which the performance is to take the form of a payment of money owed, except that the judgment debtor's failure to pay will not amount to contempt of court; a judgment creditor is left with the usual remedies described above.

INTERNATIONAL ISSUE

Enforcement of Foreign Judgments

Sometimes the assets of a judgment debtor are located in a foreign jurisdiction. A judgment creditor must seek the foreign court's recognition of its judgment before it may seize the asset. In Canada, common law provinces recognize each others' judgments (and those of the United Kingdom) through a simple registration process. An enforcing court will recognize the judgment provided that the granting court had a real and substantial connection to the matter and followed its own jurisdictional rules. It does not matter if the defendant participated or agreed to the jurisdiction of the granting court.[35] Within Canada, there is confidence that the judicial systems offer procedural fairness and there is no need for examination of the correctness of the decision.

Recently, the Supreme Court extended the application of this narrow procedural fairness and jurisdiction test to foreign judgments from other countries such as the United States. In *Beals* v. *Saldanha*,[36] the Court recognized a judgment from Florida that granted damages of $210 000 plus $50 000 of punitive damages. This was somewhat controversial because circumstances of the case stemmed from an $8000 real estate transaction and there was no evidence to support punitive damages. The dissent felt that the excessive damages and the lack of notice associated with this potential outcome was a barrier to the recognition of the judgment. However, the majority disagreed and the judgment was recognized.

QUESTIONS TO CONSIDER

1. Should foreign judgments containing excessive damage awards be recognized by Canadian courts if the same damages would not be recoverable here?

2. Is it relevant to consider whether the foreign court easily recognizes Canadian judgments?

Sources: H.S. Fairley, "Open Season: Recognition and Enforcement of Foreign Judgments in Canada After *Beals* v. *Saldanha*" (2005), 11(2) *ILSA Journal of International and Comparative Law* 305–318; J.S. Ziegel, "Enforcement of Foreign Judgments in Canada, Unlevel Playing Fields and *Beals* v. *Saldamha*: A Consumer Perspective" (2003), 38 *Canadian Business Law Journal* 294–308.

34. For a description of property exempt from seizure, see, for example: Execution Act, R.S.O. 1990, c. E.24, s. 2; Court Order Enforcement Act, R.S.B.C. 1996, c. 78, s. 71.

35. *Morguard Investments* v. *De Savoye* [1990] 3 S.C.R. 1077.

36. [2003] 3 S.C.R. 416

QUESTIONS FOR REVIEW

1. Describe the limitations of a strictly economic view of the purpose of damages.

2. What is the reasoning behind the requirement that an injured party mitigate its losses?

3. Explain why the consequence of a breach generally affects the liability of a carrier of goods differently from a manufacturer of the same goods.

4. Define expectation damages, opportunity cost, consequential damages, reliance damages, and specific performance.

5. When a buyer refuses to accept delivery of goods, explain the significance of supply and demand in determining the damages suffered by the seller.

6. Describe the nature of liquidated damages and how they are distinguishable from a penalty clause.

7. Jim goes to the airport at the peak of the holiday season to catch his flight for a one-week Caribbean holiday he has already paid for. His travel agent made an error in booking his flight: it left two days earlier and Jim is unable to obtain another flight. His agent offers to refund the cost of his holiday. Has Jim any additional claim? Explain.

8. Do you agree or disagree with the decision in *Peevyhouse*? Give reasons.

9. When will a court refuse to grant the remedy of specific performance to a purchaser of land?

10. In what circumstances might a court grant an interlocutory injunction?

11. When may it be to the advantage of a plaintiff to ask for rescission rather than damages?

12. When a judgment debtor refuses to pay his debt, what recourse does the judgment creditor have?

CASES AND PROBLEMS

1. Complicated Machinery Co. Ltd. manufactures and assembles heavy equipment for industry. It accepted an order from Northern Paper Co. for a large machine that would automate certain processes; one of the terms of the order was that the machine was to be completed by October 31. The contract further stated that if the machine was not completed by October 31, Complicated Machinery Co. Ltd. would pay Northern Paper Co. "liquidated damages" at the rate of $1000 a week for the duration of the delay. The manager of Northern Paper Co. had written in a letter accompanying the offer: "Until the machine is in full operation it is hard to say what our savings will be. A thousand dollars a week is a rough guess."

   Complicated Machinery Co. Ltd. failed to deliver until December 26, eight weeks late. It billed the paper company for the full price less $8000 (eight weeks at $1000). The paper company discovered that the machine actually saved $2400 weekly in production costs. It therefore tendered as payment the full price less $19 200 (eight weeks at $2400). Which party is correct and why?

2. In December, Carvel Estates Ltd., a real estate developer, contracted to buy 24 large suburban lots from Dalquith Enterprises Inc., the transaction to close May 15. Carvel had hired an architect and intended to build expensive "up-market" homes. The plans for each house were at an advanced stage by late March, when, without any prior notice, Dalquith sent Carvel a cheque refunding Carvel's down payment. Dalquith informed Carvel that it could not go through with the deal because Dalquith's parent corporation had applied for a zoning change and wished to construct luxury condominiums on the site. Dalquith also stated it had discussed the situation with the owner of land adjacent to the site Carvel had purchased, and the owner was willing to discuss selling an equivalent number of lots to Carvel.

Carvel's manager was very upset because the firm would have been ready to begin work immediately after the May 15 closing date. Dalquith refused to reconsider its repudiation when asked by Carvel. Carvel commenced an action, requesting specific performance and damages for any additional costs as a result of delay in the project. Explain whether it is likely that Carvel will succeed in its request for specific performance, and if not, what other remedies might be available to Carvel.

3. Malvern Enterprises Inc. invited tenders for a construction project. The invitation included an often-used "privilege" clause to the effect that "the lowest or any tender shall not necessarily be accepted." Granite Construction Ltd. submitted a tender that, as it turned out, was the second lowest submitted. Another construction company made the lowest tender, to which it added a condition that was not part of the invitation to tender. However, Malvern considered the condition to be a minor change and it accepted the tender.

When Granite learned of the change made in the tender by the added condition, it sued Malvern for breach of contract, for damages amounting to the profit Granite would have made had its tender been accepted. Granite claimed that upon submitting a tender, each of the tenderers entered into a customarily implied contract with Malvern that it would consider only tenders that conformed to the invitation. Malvern responded that the privilege clause protected it from having to accept any particular tender and, therefore, it was not in breach of any implied contract. It also claimed that, in any event, it was free to accept any other conforming tender—not just that submitted by Granite.

During the trial, evidence given supported the usual practice that if the lowest tender had been disqualified, the contract would probably have been awarded to the second lowest tenderer. The court found that there was an implied contract that only fully conforming tenders would be considered by Malvern, and also that the privilege clause did not excuse accepting a non-conforming tender. The problem remained whether Granite was in a stronger position than all the remaining tenderers and whether it was entitled in the circumstances to damages amounting to a lost profit or, indeed, to any other damages.

Give your opinion of the likely outcome with reasons.

4. In November, Tanton agreed orally with Marsh to cut and haul to Marsh's mill approximately 500 000 board feet of lumber at a price of $20 per thousand board feet delivered to the mill. The contract also stated that on completion of the contract, Tanton should be reimbursed for the cost of the construction of camps and roads necessary for the lumbering operations.

In January next, after Tanton had delivered 200 000 board feet to the mill, he found himself in financial difficulties and unable to pay his employees. At the time Tanton had been paid for the logs delivered to date, but had not been paid for the camps and roads he had had to construct for the purpose. Tanton told Marsh that he was quitting and that he considered the contract as having been frustrated by his inability to pay his staff. He then sued to recover the value of the work done in the construction of camps, roads, and bridges during the lumbering operations up to January.

Should Tanton succeed?

5. Two students are trying after class to see what they can make of the legal significance of exemption clauses.

Harvey: *Exempting clauses are a cop-out. A promisor manages to put one in a contract and then is obligated to do nothing—only the other party is obligated.*

Lise: *But maybe the other party got a lower price because of the exemption clause.*

Harvey: *Often that's not so. Suppose the other party is a new Canadian and the exemption clause is in a standard form contract he's unfamiliar with?*

Lise: *But that must depend on whether the parties had equal bargaining power. Isn't that what the instructor said? One of the parties doesn't have to be exploited. Suppose the contract is between two established businesses?*

Harvey: *Then I still say there's no consideration on one side. What price does the business protected by an exempting clause pay for the other's promise?*

Lise:	*The business may not be opting out of all its obligations. Then there's still consideration. Don't you remember, "It is not for the courts to concern themselves with the adequacy of consideration"?*
Harvey:	*But suppose we're talking about a fundamental breach. Then what we have, in effect, is a total failure of consideration, even if technically we could find a little bit of consideration still there. Since you're quoting legal aphorisms, "The law does not concern itself with trivialities," either.*
Lise:	*I think you have to assume business people know what they're doing and that such one-sided contracts are the exception. Maybe with a novice, yes, but with an established business, no.*
Harvey:	*I'm beginning to get worried. Suppose a court decides an exemption clause shouldn't count because the breach is fundamental. If its reasoning is that there was a total failure of consideration, maybe there won't be any contract at all. Will that give the plaintiff what he wants? I thought he was suing for damages for breach.*
Lise:	*Maybe we should go ask the instructor.*

Comment briefly on Harvey's last point. Would the remedies available to the plaintiff business be different if the court found that there was no consideration instead of there being a claim for damages for breach of contract?

6. On June 30, Sinkiewicz, a professional football player, signed a three-year contract with the Mariposa Football Club Ltd. The contract contained the following clause:

The Player promises and agrees that, during the term of his contract, he will not play football or engage in activities related to football for any other person, firm, corporation, or institution, except with the prior written consent of the Club, and that he will not, during the term of this contract, engage in any game or exhibition of basketball, baseball, wrestling, boxing, hockey, or any other sport that endangers his ability to perform his services hereunder without the prior written consent of the Club.

In July of the following year, Sinkiewicz accepted an offer from another professional football club, the Orillia Wildcats, and moved to Orillia intending to play with that club for the coming football season. He also arranged to play hockey in Orillia after the football season ended.

After learning about Sinkiewicz's breach, the officials of the Mariposa Football Club sued for damages and for an injunction restraining Sinkiewicz from continuing to break his contract. The Mariposa Club alleged that it had sustained irreparable injury in having to locate another player of Sinkiewicz's calibre, and that it had in the past spent considerable money in training Sinkiewicz as a professional football player. In defence, Sinkiewicz testified that he would be unable to earn his livelihood if prevented from playing football and hockey. Discuss the legal issues the court will consider in reaching its decision.

7. Brown, a painting contractor, made an oral contract with Hilton to paint the interior of Hilton's house for $1600, to be paid on completion of the work. Brown ran into difficulty when he painted the walls of the living room because the paint was pulled into the wall by the porous plaster. He had the same problem when he applied a second coat. He then realized what was causing the trouble and applied what is known as a "sealer," so that the next coat would adhere properly. Leaving the living room until the sealer was dry, he began painting the dining room.

At that point, Hilton inspected the work and complained to Brown that the colour of the paint was not the colour she had selected. Brown became very annoyed and emphatically announced he would quit the job. Hilton urged him not to abandon the work without first seeing her husband, but in a huff he removed his materials and equipment. When he abandoned the work, Brown still had to finish painting the living room and had not begun to paint several other rooms in the house. It also appeared that the woodwork had been painted without having been sanded, and would have to be stripped and repainted. Brown brought an action against Hilton for $890, claiming $230 for materials and $660 for 33 hours' work. Should he succeed?

8. On September 2, the Department of Government Services published an invitation to submit tenders for the supply of materials for construction of a large administrative building. Its advertisement specified that tenders were to be delivered on or before 3 p.m. on November 6 at the office of the Contracts Officer of the Department of Government Services in Ottawa.

Buttonville Brick, Inc. prepared an estimate of the cost of supplying brick for the project and then made out a tender for delivery to the Department of Government Services. The tender was for the supply of all the brick required at a price of $556 000—a price on which the company could expect to earn a profit of about $75 000.

On the morning of November 5, Buttonville's manager, Hodson, telephoned Bulldog Couriers Inc. to inquire whether it could deliver an important document in Ottawa by noon of the following day. He said, "A lot is at stake for us—maybe $100 000—and if you can't deliver our envelope by tomorrow noon, either I or one of the other people here is going to have to drive directly to Ottawa with it." Hodson was assured there would be no problem with delivery.

Bulldog sent a station wagon at once to pick up the envelope. Buttonville Brick completed a bill of lading on a form supplied by Bulldog, which can be seen on the following page.

The van that took the envelope to Ottawa on its regular run was delayed because of a mechanical breakdown, and the envelope was not delivered to its destination until 3:21 p.m. on November 6. As a result, it was rejected as an eligible tender. The contract was given to another bidder who, as it turned out, had submitted a bid of $590 000—$34 000 more than Buttonville's. Buttonville sued Bulldog Couriers Inc. for consequential damages of $75 000.

At the trial the following excerpts from the Public Commercial Vehicles Act were cited:

12n (1) Except as provided in the regulations, every holder of an operating licence . . . shall issue a bill of lading to the person delivering or releasing goods to the licensee for transportation for compensation.

(2) A bill of lading shall contain such information as may be prescribed and shall include an acknowledgement of receipt by the carrier . . . therein described and an undertaking to carry such goods for delivery to the consignee or the person entitled to receive the goods and shall be signed by, or on behalf of, the issuing carrier . . . and by the consignor.

(3) The conditions set out in Schedule A shall be deemed to be a part of every contract for the transportation of goods for compensation. . . .

SCHEDULE A

1. The carrier of the goods herein described is liable for any loss thereof or damage or injury thereto, except as herein provided.

5. The carrier is not liable for loss, damage, or delay to any of the goods described in the bill of lading caused by an act of God, the Queen's or public enemies, riots, strikes, defect or inherent vice in the goods, the act or default of the shipper or owner. . . .

7. No carrier is bound to transport the goods by any particular public commercial vehicle or in time for any particular market or otherwise than with due despatch, unless by agreement specifically endorsed on the bill of lading and signed by the parties thereto.

9. Subject to paragraph 10, the amount of any loss, damage or injury for which the carrier is liable, whether or not the loss, damage or injury results from negligence, shall be computed on the basis of,

   (a) the value of the goods at the place and time of shipment including the freight and other charges if paid; or

   (b) where a value lower than that referred to in clause a has been represented in writing by the consignor or has been agreed upon, such lower value.

10. . . . the amount of any loss or damage computed under clause a or b of paragraph 9 shall not exceed $1.50 per pound [approximately $3.00 per kilogram] unless a higher value is declared on the face of the bill of lading by the consignor.

   Develop arguments for the plaintiff and for the defendant in this action and express an opinion about the probable outcome.

BULLDOG COURIERS INC.

BILL OF LADING

Date: November 5, 1999

Received at the point of origin on the date specified, from the shipper mentioned herein, the goods herein described, in apparent good order, except as noted (contents and conditions of contents of packages unknown) marked, consigned, and destined as indicated below, which the carrier agrees to carry and deliver to the consignee at the said destination. For other terms, see reverse side.

Point of origin
Buttonville Brick Ltd.,
100 Industrial Lane,
Buttonville, ON

Destination
Contracts Officer,
Department of Government Services,
100 Carling Drive,
Ottawa, ON

Contents	No. Pcs.	Weight	Charges
"Envelope—tender" "Deliver before 12 noon Nov. 6."	"1"	"400 g"	"$15.00"

Declared value
(Maximum liability $3.00 per kg unless declared valuation states otherwise. If a value is declared see conditions on reverse hereof.)

(signed) "*Bernard Colley*
for Bulldog Couriers Inc."

(signed) "*S. Hodson*
for Buttonville Brick Ltd."

On the reverse side, the bill of lading stated:

VALUE

Unless otherwise specifically agreed to in writing, the carrier will not transport any goods declared to have a value in excess of $250. Enquiries for such service should be directed to the carrier's closest regional office.

APPLICABLE LAW

It is agreed that every service to be performed hereunder shall be subject to the laws relating to the terms and conditions to be contained in bills of lading applicable in Ontario under the Public Commercial Vehicles Act.

ADDITIONAL RESOURCES FOR CHAPTER 15 ON THE COMPANION WEBSITE *(www.pearsoned.ca/smyth)*

In addition to self-test multiple-choice, true–false, and short essay questions (all with immediate feedback), application exercises, and links to useful web destinations, the Companion Website provides the following resources for Chapter 15:

- **British Columbia:** Enforcement of Judgments; Garnishment; Injunction; Seizure and Sale; Specific Performance; Writ of Execution
- **Alberta:** Enforcement of Judgments; Garnishment; Limitations of Actions
- **Manitoba/Saskatchewan:** Collection of Judgments
- **Ontario:** Debt Collection Process; Equitable Remedies; Executions; Garnishment; Judgment Debtor Examination

Special Types of Contract

T he study of contract law in Part 3 shows how important the use of contracts is in almost every aspect of business. Some types of contracts have developed in areas that are particularly important to business and deserve to be examined separately. We have selected a number of them for discussion in this part.

In Chapter 16, we discuss the nature of sales contracts and their legal effects, and examine in particular the risks assumed by the parties to a contract, the consequences of breach of contract, and the remedies available—for example, if a buyer fails to pay or if a seller delivers defective goods.

As Chapter 16 demonstrates, ownership of goods does not always coincide with possession. In Chapter 17, we examine two important types of contract in which ownership and possession are necessarily separate—leasing and bailment. In recent years, leasing has become big business, and the leasing of expensive equipment and items such as automobiles has become an important alternative to sale. Bailment, of which leasing is but one special form, occurs in many business activities—for example, when articles are delivered to a person other than the owner for transportation, storage, or repair.

Chapter 18 discusses insurance law—an important method of managing the risks that are inherent in the operation of a business. The later part of the chapter deals with the related topic of guarantee—that is, where a third person promises to perform a contract if the original promissor defaults.

In Chapter 19 we examine two types of arrangement that are commonly used to expand a business—agency and franchising. Businesses, except the very smallest sole proprietorships, have always employed agents—to sell their goods, purchase supplies, and negotiate other types of contract. Franchising, by contrast, is a quite recent development but one that is of growing importance.

Most businesses (again, excepting the smallest sole proprietorships) have employees. In Chapter 20 we concentrate on the employment relationship, the respective rights and duties of employers and employees, and the effects their conduct may have on third parties. We also examine the various laws that regulate employment relationships, such as workers' compensation, pay equity, and human rights.

Almost all business contracts involve one party making payment to the other. To conclude this part, Chapter 21 examines the use of negotiable instruments—cheques, promissory notes, and bills of exchange—and other methods of money transfer.

16

Sale of Goods

Contracts for the sale of goods are the most common type of contract and the most readily understood. They have generated a vast amount of case law, which was eventually codified into a statute—the Sale of Goods Act.

Unlike the chapters in Part 3, which were primarily concerned with the *common law* of contracts, this chapter concentrates on the provisions of a *statute*. In it we examine such questions as:

- What is the scope of the Sale of Goods Act?

- What are the terms that it implies in a contract of sale?

- How is the ownership of goods transferred?

- To what extent is the seller liable for defective or unsatisfactory goods?

- What are the remedies available to buyers and sellers?

Seller's Title

Caveat emptor applies to the qualities of goods, not their ownership. Inspection by the buyer normally does nothing to indicate who owns the goods. In offering to sell goods, the seller impliedly represents that he has the right to do so. The (Ontario) Sale of Goods Act states:

In a contract of sale, unless the circumstances of the contract are such as to show a different intention, there is

(a) An implied condition on the part of the seller that in the case of a sale the seller has a right to sell the goods, and that in the case of an agreement to sell the seller will have a right to sell the goods at the time when the property is to pass;

(b) An implied warranty that the buyer will have and enjoy quiet possession of the goods; and

(c) An implied warranty that the goods will be free from any charge or encumbrance in favour of any third party, not declared or known to the buyer before or at the time when the contract is made.[11]

An example of the **implied term as to title** is provided in Illustration 16.1.

implied term as to title
it is implied that the seller has a right to sell the goods

ILLUSTRATION 16.1

Alberti purchases a second-hand refrigerator from Blake. It later turns out that Cowan, not Blake, was the owner of the refrigerator. Cowan retakes possession of the refrigerator from Alberti.

In the contract of sale between Alberti and Blake, there was an implied undertaking by Blake that he had a right to sell the refrigerator, that Alberti should have quiet possession of it (that is, not have physical possession of it interrupted), and that it would be free from any encumbrance in favour of a third person (that is, no third person would have a right to the property). None of these requirements was satisfied. Alberti is therefore entitled to sue Blake for breach of an *implied condition of title*.

Description

The Act sets out the circumstances in which there is an **implied term as to description**, as follows:

Where there is a contract for the sale of goods by description, there is an implied condition that the goods will correspond with the description, and, if the sale is by sample as well as by description, it is not sufficient that the bulk of the goods corresponds with the sample if the goods do not also correspond with the description.[12]

implied term as to description
it is implied that goods sold by description will conform to the description

The word "description" applies to a generic characteristic of the goods (for example, that blouses offered for sale are cotton blouses instead of, say, nylon blouses) and not to words of praise about how good the blouses are (for example, that they will last a lifetime).

---

11. R.S.O. 1990, c. S-1, s. 13. The corresponding provisions in the Alberta, British Columbia, and Newfoundland and Labrador acts are: R.S.A. 2000, c. S-2, s. 14; R.S.B.C. 1996, c. 410, s. 16; R.S.N.L. 1990, c. S-6, s. 14.

12. Ont., s. 14: see also Alta., s. 15; B.C., s. 17; Nfld., s. 15.

ILLUSTRATION   16.2

Bridges bought from ProMotors an electric motor for use in his workshop. The motor was described in ProMotors' catalogue as "heavy-duty, double bearing." In fact, the motor supplied had only a single bearing, although that was not apparent without taking the motor apart, and it burned out after only three months of use.

Bridges may sue ProMotors based on the breach of an implied term to the effect that the goods will correspond with the description. While the expression "heavy-duty" may be a matter of opinion, "double bearing" is clearly a factual description within the meaning of the Act.

Where a sample is provided, the characteristics of the sample can be considered to form part of the description.

CASE   16.3

A hotel chain ordered a large number of sets of quality tableware, after having inspected samples. The tableware was delivered over a period of three years. The purchasers had no complaint regarding the earlier deliveries but discovered that the sets delivered later did not have the same manufacturer's embossed stamp on the back. They rejected the goods and sued for damages. The court held that the stamp, which had been on the sample, formed part of the description of the goods and the vendor was in breach of the implied warranty.[13]

Suitability and Quality

The Sale of Goods Act makes two exceptions to the general rule that the buyer must exercise care as to the suitability and quality of the goods:

> Subject to this Act and any statute in that behalf, there is no implied warranty or condition as to the quality or fitness for any particular purpose of goods supplied under a contract of sale, except as follows:
>
> 1.   Where the buyer, expressly or by implication, makes known to the seller the particular purpose for which the goods are required so as to show that the buyer relies on the seller's skill or judgment, and the goods are of a description that it is in the course of the seller's business to supply (whether he is the manufacturer or not), there is an implied condition that the goods will be reasonably fit for such purpose, but in the case of a contract for the sale of a specified article under its patent or other trade name, there is no implied condition as to its fitness for any particular purpose.
>
> 2.   Where the goods are bought by description from a seller who deals in goods of that description (whether he is the manufacturer or not), there is an implied condition that the goods shall be of merchantable quality, but if the buyer has examined the goods, there is no implied condition as regards defects that such examination ought to have revealed.[14]

implied term of fitness
it is implied that the goods are of a type that is suitable for the purpose for which they are bought

The **implied term of fitness** offers protection to a buyer who has a particular purpose in mind for the goods. To have the advantage of this provision, the buyer should declare this purpose specifically if it is not one of the general uses for such goods.

---

13.   *Coast Hotels Ltd.* v. *Royal Doulton Canada Ltd.* [2000] B.C.S.C. 1545.

14.   Ont., s. 15: see also Alta., s. 16; B.C., s. 18; Nfld., s. 16. See *Borgo Upholstery Ltd.* v. *Canada* [2004] N.S.J. No. 7 (N.S.C.A.).

ILLUSTRATION 16.3

Slack buys 30 m of clothesline wire from a hardware store and uses it as a cable for a homemade elevator in his barn. The wire breaks with him in the elevator, causing him injury. He sues the hardware dealer for damages.

Slack will not succeed because (1) he did not expressly state the particular purpose for which he intended to use the wire and so did not rely on the seller's skill and judgment, and (2) the use to which he put the wire was not a normal use for clothesline wire.

A purpose need not be stated in so many words if it is obvious. When buying cakes in a bakery, one need not state, "I propose to eat these." The essential requirement for Part 1 of section 15 noted above is that the buyer relied upon the seller's skill and judgment.[15]

CASE 16.4

Lavalin ordered 57 000 kilograms of welding electrodes from Carbonic for use in a project involving the fabrication of a cross-country gas transmission line. The electrodes turned out to be incapable of producing a satisfactory weld in a vertical position. Lavalin had made known to Carbonic the fact that the electrodes were to be used in a gas transmission line, apparently assuming that Carbonic's engineers would know that the electrodes would

have to be capable of functioning in a vertical position. In fact, Carbonic had no experience of pipeline work.

The court held that Carbonic had implied that it was familiar with pipeline work and that Lavalin had relied on Carbonic's skill and judgment. Lavalin was entitled to damages for the costs incurred with respect to the acquisition and handling of the useless electrodes.[16]

The Act provides that the implied condition of fitness does not apply when an article is sold under its trade name. In *Baldry* v. *Marshall*, the court had to consider this provision. Lord Justice Bankes said:

> The mere fact that an article sold is described in the contract by its trade name does not necessarily make the sale a sale under a trade name. Whether it is so or not depends upon the circumstances. . . . In my opinion the test of an article having been sold under its trade name within the meaning of the proviso is: did the buyer specify it under its trade name in such a way as to indicate that he is satisfied, rightly or wrongly, that it will answer his purpose, and that he is not relying on the skill or judgment of the seller, however great that skill or judgment may be?[17]

Part 2 of the section states when a seller is responsible for the *quality* of goods rather than for their suitability for any particular purpose. Under this part, to establish a breach of condition by the seller, the buyer need not show that she relied on the seller's skill and judgment.[18]

The **implied term of merchantable quality** needs explanation: to paraphrase an Australian decision, goods of merchantable quality should be in such a state that a buyer, fully acquainted with the facts and having found the goods in reasonably sound condition, would buy them without

implied term of merchantable quality
it is implied that the goods are in reasonable condition and free from defects that would make them unsuitable for use

---

15. *Chaproniere* v. *Mason* (1905), 21 T.L.R. 633; *McCready Products Ltd.* v. *Sherwin Williams Co. of Canada Ltd.* (1985), 61 A.R. 234. The seller's failure to provide adequate instructions as to use of the product and to warn of possible dangers may constitute a breach of the warranty: see *Caners* v. *Eli Lilley Canada Inc.* (1996), 134 D.L.R. (4th) 730.

16. *SNC-Lavalin International Inc.* v. *Liquid Carbonic Inc.* (1996), 28 B.L.R. (2d) 1.

17. [1925] 1 K.B. 260 at 266–7.

18. *Wren* v. *Holt,* [1903] 1 K.B. 610.

reduction below the current market price and without special guarantees.[19] The word "reasonably" needs to be emphasized; especially in the case of the sale of used goods, there is no warranty that the goods are entirely free from defect.

One problem is that the implied condition relates to the quality of the goods at the time of the contract, yet it may be some time later that the defect is discovered. Or it may be that the defect did not exist at the time of the sale but developed subsequently, perhaps due to misuse by the buyer or to some other reason. It is, consequently, a question of fact whether an article that ceases to function properly was defective at the time of sale. A new car that develops transmission problems within a few months is likely to have been defective all along; one that runs well for several years before developing a fault may well have been in satisfactory condition at the time of sale.

CASE 16.5

McCann bought an electric blanket from Sears. More than 10 years later it caught fire, causing damage to McCann's bedroom. McCann brought action for breach of contract on the ground that there was an implied condition that the electric blanket was reasonably free from defect. The court held that, in view of the time that had elapsed (during which the blanket had functioned without any problems), the buyer had failed to satisfy the burden of proving that the defect existed when the blanket was bought.[20]

In practice, it is often difficult to tell which part of the section is the more relevant to a buyer's complaint, as the two parts tend to overlap in their application.[21]

Sale by Sample

implied term that goods correspond with sample
it is implied that, when a sample of the goods to be sold has been provided, the actual goods supplied will correspond to that sample in type and quality

The last of the implied terms recognized in the Act is the **implied term that goods correspond with sample**. The Act provides:

In the case of a contract for sale by sample, there is an implied condition

(a) that the bulk will correspond with the sample in quality;

(b) that the buyer will have a reasonable opportunity of comparing the bulk with the sample; and

(c) that the goods will be free from any defect rendering them unmerchantable that would not be apparent on reasonable examination of the sample.[22]

ILLUSTRATION 16.4

The plant supervisor at High Grade Printing Company examined a sample of choice quality paper supplied by Universal Paper Co. Ltd. and approved its purchase. When the paper was used in one of the books printed by High Grade, it turned yellow and the entire run had to be done again. High Grade sued Universal Paper for damages for its loss. In defence, Universal Paper pleaded that the paper supplied was exactly the same as the sample on which the purchase was based, and that a chemical test of the sample would have revealed the defect.

The printing company should succeed in its action if it can show that the defect would not have been apparent on an ordinary examination, and that an ordinary examination would not include a chemical test.

---

19. *Australian Knitting Mills Ltd.* v. *Grant* (1933), 50 C.L.R. 387, per Dixon, J., at 418; also *Bristol Tramways* v. *Fiat Motors*, [1910] 2 K.B. 831, per Farwell, L.J., at 841.

20. *McCann* v. *Sears Canada Ltd.* (1998), 43 B.L.R. (2d) 217, Aff'd. (1999) 122 O.C.C. 91.

21. Nevertheless, the two warranties are not identical. In *Wharton* v. *Tom Harris Chevrolet Oldsmobile Cadillac Ltd.* [2002] B.C.J. No. 233, the B.C.C.A. held that a defective stereo system in a luxury car was a breach of the fitness warranty, although it did not render the car unmerchantable.

22. Ont., s. 16: see also Alta., s. 17; B.C., s. 19; Nfld., s. 17.

> **CHECKLIST** Implied Terms in a Contract for the Sale of Goods

Subject to certain exceptions and qualifications, the Sale of Goods Act implies the following contractual terms:

- an implied condition that the seller has (or will have) a right to sell the goods
- an implied warranty that the buyer will have and enjoy quiet possession of the goods
- an implied warranty that the goods will be free from any undisclosed charge or encumbrance
- an implied condition that the goods will correspond with the description under which they are sold
- an implied condition that the goods will be reasonably fit for the purpose for which they are required if that purpose was made known to the seller
- an implied condition that the goods will be of merchantable quality
- in the case of a sale by sample, an implied condition that the bulk will correspond with the sample

Exemption Clauses

The Sale of Goods Act contains the following provision:

> Where any right, duty or liability would arise under a contract of sale by implication of law, it may be negatived or varied by express agreement or by the course of dealing between the parties, or by usage, if the usage is such as to bind both parties to the contract.[23]

As a result, a seller may insist that a contract of sale contains an express term relieving it from the liability normally imposed by the implied terms. A prospective buyer may, of course, refuse to enter into a contract containing such an exemption clause. In some provinces, if she agrees to the clause, she loses the protection given to a buyer by the Act.[24]

The courts have restricted the circumstances in which a seller may excuse himself from liability under the Act. Clear and direct language must be used to contract out of the statutory protections.

> **CASE 16.6**
>
> Syncrude ordered 32 gearboxes from Hunter, a manufacturer, to drive its conveyor belts in the Alberta tar sands project. Syncrude provided specifications of what the gearboxes were required to do, and Hunter designed them to meet those specifications.
>
> The contract contained an express term guaranteeing the gearboxes for two years. When the period had expired, the gearboxes developed faults that were found to be due to faulty design. Syncrude could not succeed in an action on the express term because the two-year period had elapsed, but the Supreme Court of Canada held that the implied term of fitness under the Act could still be relied on. The existence of an express warranty was not inconsistent with the statutory warranties.[25]

If the words used in an exemption clause do not precisely describe the type of liability disclaimed, the courts will normally find that the implied liability is still part of the contract. If a seller includes an

23. Ont., s. 53: see also Alta., s. 54; B.C., s. 69; Nfld., s. 56.
24. As noted earlier, in British Columbia, New Brunswick, and Saskatchewan the warranties cannot be contracted out of in the case of retail sales.
25. *Hunter Engineering Co.* v. *Syncrude Canada Ltd.* (1989), 57 D.L.R. (4th) 321. See also *Fording Coal Ltd.* v. *Harnischfeger Corp. of Canada* (1991), 6 B.L.R. (2d) 157.

express term that "all warranties implied by statute are hereby excluded," the seller will avoid liability under all those implied terms that are *warranties* but not under those that are *conditions*.[26] Moreover, if the seller expressly promised that the goods would be of a certain quality or type, an exemption clause that refers only to implied terms will not free him from obligations under this express term.

CASE 16.7

Allan agreed to purchase a car from Lambeth Motors Ltd. In the contract the car was described as "a new, 190-horsepower, six-cylinder sedan." There was also a clause, inserted by the seller, that "all conditions, warranties, and liabilities implied by statute, common law, or otherwise are hereby excluded." After taking delivery, Allan discovered that the car was not new and had only four cylinders, and he sued for damages.

The exempting clause referred only to implied terms. The undertaking that the car was new and had six cylinders was an express term in the contract of sale. The seller had therefore failed to exempt itself from liability.[27]

The courts have also held that a seller cannot so completely exempt himself from liability that he may default on his bargain entirely. They will not give effect to an exemption clause that gives a seller immunity from action if he delivers goods that are totally different from those contracted for by the buyer or if he delivers goods to which he does not have good title.[28] In effect, the courts have held that a contract for the sale of goods would be deprived of all meaning if a seller's obligation were merely to deliver the goods "if he felt like it." (We have already discussed the doctrine of fundamental breach in relation to exemption clauses in contracts generally in Chapter 14.)

ETHICAL ISSUE

Exemption Clauses

Exemption clauses are an important tool used by businesses to limit their exposure to liability. As the forgoing discussion indicates, the Sale of Goods Act recognizes and preserves the role of an exemption clause. This position prioritizes the value of freedom to contract over the protective policy reflected in the implied terms. In Case 16.6, the Supreme Court seemed willing to accept the possibility that a properly worded exemption clause could protect a business even in cases of fundamental breach.

However, it may not be possible to contract out of the implied terms in the consumer context. In a complete reversal of the Sale of Goods Act, the Ontario Consumer Protection Act voids any "term or acknowledgement, whether part of the consumer agreement or not, that purports to negate or vary any implied condition or warranty under the Sale of Goods Act . . . " (s. 9(3)). This places the retailer in a precarious situation. Few retailers manufacture their own goods; the chain of distribution usually involves a manufacturer and a wholesaler. The retailer is bound by the implied terms of the Sale of Goods Act when dealing with consumers, but unable to rely on them when pursing the manufacturer or wholesaler of the goods.

QUESTIONS TO CONSIDER

1. Does this represent a fair result in today's marketplace?
2. Which legislation should be changed?

---

26. *Gregorio* v. *Intrans-Corp.* (1994), 115 D.L.R. (4th) 200 (Ont. C.A.).

27. *Andrews Bros. Ltd.* v. *Singer & Co. Ltd.*, [1934] 1 K.B. 17.

28. *Pinnock Brothers* v. *Lewis and Peat Ltd.*, [1923] 1 K.B. 690; *Karsales (Harrow) Ltd.* v. *Wallis*, [1956] 2 All E.R. 866; *Canadian-Dominion Leasing Corp. Ltd.* v. *Suburban Superdrug Ltd.* (1966), 56 D.L.R. (2d) 43.

Payment

Many contracts of sale set out the time of payment expressly—in others it may be implied from the terms of the contract and the particular circumstances. When the contract itself gives no guidance about when the buyer is to pay, the courts assume that delivery and payment are concurrent conditions; the transaction is presumed to be a cash sale. But this presumption may be rebutted by the circumstances in which the contract is made. For example, when payment from a customer is accepted by credit card, the buyer is normally entitled to delivery of the goods immediately, before payment by the credit card company.

The courts interpret the time set for payment as a warranty unless the parties have expressed themselves otherwise. Consequently, a seller is not entitled to rescind the contract of sale and have the goods back simply because payment is not made on time. He must be content with an action for the price of the goods. But the parties may agree on other terms. A seller may insist on a term entitling him to retake possession in the event of non-payment. This provision is characteristic of the instalment sale, to be considered separately in Chapter 30.

Delivery

The terms in a contract of sale relating to delivery are mainly of three kinds: terms relating to the quantity to be delivered, the time of delivery, and the place of delivery.

A term specifying the quantity of goods to be delivered is a condition. If the term is broken— that is, if the seller delivers a substantially different quantity—the buyer is free to reject the goods. Her right to do so exists whether a greater or lesser quantity than promised is delivered. The buyer may, of course, choose to take all or part of what is delivered. If she does so, she must pay for what she takes at the contract rate.

The time specified for delivery is also usually a condition, so that if the goods are not delivered on time the buyer may rescind the contract. She is free to look elsewhere for the goods she needs as soon as she learns they will not be available on time. If the parties agree that the goods are to be delivered as soon as they are available, without specifying a time, then delivery must occur within a reasonable time, taking into account all the circumstances.

The place of delivery is normally either the seller's place of business or wherever the goods happen to be located at the time of the contract. The parties may, however, express a different intention— for example, that the goods should be delivered to the buyer's home—or their intention may be implied from trade custom.

An offer for sale sometimes states, along with the asking price, the terms of delivery. It may, for example, quote wheat at so much per bushel *FOB Winnipeg*, or steel at so much per tonne *CIF Hamilton*. FOB means that the seller will place the goods at that location "free on board" the type of transportation specified. When a CIF (cost, insurance, freight) price is quoted, the seller undertakes to arrange insurance and to ship the goods to the buyer. (These and other standard terms are widely used in international trade and are discussed further in Chapter 33.) Another common type of contract is the COD (cash on delivery) contract in which the seller undertakes to deliver the goods at the buyer's place of business or residence.

Risk of Loss

If the buyer and seller do not expressly agree when the risk of loss (caused by damage to or destruction of the goods) passes from the seller to the buyer, it becomes necessary to imply such a term. For example, in FOB and CIF contracts it is normally implied that the goods remain at the risk of the seller until they have been delivered to the carrier, and in COD contracts, until the seller or the carrier has delivered them to the buyer. Parties may not think to include an express term concerning the passing of risk, and it may often be impossible to discover an implied term from the terms of the contract. Such an omission, though unfortunate, is understandable, since the great majority of contracts of sale proceed without any loss occurring between the time of making the agreement and the receipt of the goods by the buyer.

When a loss does occur, however, it is possible that both parties may disclaim any interest in or responsibility for the goods. The reason for their disclaimers is that the risk of loss follows the *title* to the goods unless the parties have agreed otherwise: the party that has title ordinarily suffers the loss.[29]

TITLE TO GOODS

Who May Pass Title?

Nemo Dat Quod Non Habet

nemo dat quod non habet
no one can give what he does not have

The Latin maxim ***nemo dat quod non habet***—literally, no one can give what he does not have—expresses a fundamental principle governing the passing of title to property. The principle finds expression in the Sale of Goods Act:

> Subject to this Act, where goods are sold by a person who is not the owner thereof and who does not sell them under the authority or with the consent of the owner, the buyer acquires no better title to the goods than the seller had, unless the owner of the goods is by conduct precluded from denying the seller's authority to sell. . . . [30]

That is, only the owner, or a person authorized by the owner, can pass a good title to goods. To this principle, the Act allows two main exceptions: certain sales made by an agent (considered below) and sales made under any special common law or statutory power of sale or under a court order.

The Effect of Agency

When a business ships goods to its agent for the agent to sell, the effect of the consignment is to give the agent (the consignee) the appearance of ownership in the eyes of the public. Statutes in the various provinces give the agent the same authority to deal with the goods as their owner has.[31] The agent may, therefore, validly pass title to anyone who purchases the goods in good faith, even though the sale may not be authorized or is on terms forbidden by the owner (the consignor).

Seller or Buyer in Possession

Difficult situations arise when a seller sells the same goods twice, or where a buyer sells goods before she actually owns them. The Act protects an innocent purchaser who "buys" the goods in the normal course of business without notice of the seller's defect in title.[32]

CASE 16.8

An Oklahoma corporation, Western Environmental, had acquired the assets of a Canadian oil refinery that was being closed down. It proceeded to sell off various assets of the refinery, including a quantity of pipe, which it sold to the plaintiff, Epscan, for $260 000. It was agreed that Epscan would cut and remove the pipe over the following three months. Before it could do so, Western sold the same pipe to another Canadian corporation, Bartin, and was paid $162 000. Epscan learned that Bartin was removing the pipe and sued Bartin for conversion. Meanwhile, Western and its employees has absconded.

At trial, Epscan was awarded damages for the conversion. On appeal, the Alberta Court of Appeal held that Bartin was protected under the Sale of Goods Act.[33] The vendor, Western, had remained in possession, there were no suspicious circumstances, and Bartin had no knowledge of Epscan's interest.[34]

29. For an example of this rule, see *A.M.S. Equipment Inc.* v. *Case*, [1999] B.C.J. No. 124.
30. Ont., s. 22; Alta., s. 23; B.C., s. 26; Nfld., s. 23.
31. See, for example, Factors Act, R.S.O. 1990, c. F.1, s. 2; R.S.A. 2000, c. F-1, s. 2; Sale of Goods Act, R.S.B.C. 1996, c. 410, s. 59.
32. Ont., s. 25; Alta., s. 26; B.C., s. 30; Nfld., s. 27. An exception may apply where the situation is governed by the Personal Property Security Act (discussed in Chapter 30).
33. Alta., s. 27(1), now s. 26(1).
34. *Bartin Pipe & Piling Supply Ltd.* v. *Epscan Industries Ltd.* (2004), 236 D.L.R. (4th) 75.

A buyer who does not take possession of goods when title passes consequently runs the risk that a fraudulent seller may resell them to an innocent third party who will obtain a good title. There is a similar risk where a seller allows the buyer to take possession of goods before title has passed.[35]

When Does Title Pass?

Specific Goods

As we have already noted, the risk—of loss or damage—generally passes with the title to goods. It is therefore essential to know *when* title passes. The first four rules set down in the Sale of Goods Act[36] for the passing of title relate to **specific goods**—that is, to goods that are already in existence and are identified and agreed on as the subject-matter of the sale at the time the contract is formed. These rules apply unless a contrary intention of the parties can be inferred from their conduct or from customary trade practice.

specific goods
goods in existence and agreed on as the subject-matter of the sale

Rule 1

Where there is an unconditional contract for the sale of specific goods in a deliverable state, the property in the goods passes to the buyer *when the contract is made*, and it is immaterial whether the time of payment or the time of delivery or both are postponed.

ILLUSTRATION 16.5

Maple Leaf Appliances Ltd. was having its annual January sale. Late on a Saturday afternoon, Haag bought a new television set displayed on the floor and paid for it by a cheque post-dated five days later. The set was to be delivered on Monday. The parties never discussed which of them should take the risk of loss before delivery of the set.

On the Sunday, burglars broke into the seller's premises and stole the television set. Haag stopped payment on the cheque. Maple Leaf Appliances sued Haag for the price of the set.

According to traditional analysis, title and risk are assumed to pass to the buyer at the same time, and the seller's action in Illustration 16.5 would succeed—title passed to Haag on Saturday, and the loss would be hers. This traditional analysis is based on a typical transaction between two businesses, and the purchaser would generally have insurance coverage for newly acquired goods. It bears little relation, however, to a modern consumer sales transaction. A consumer might think of the television set as being "hers" when she left the store and would object if the store were to resell it, but she would probably assume that the retailer remained entirely responsible for the set until it was safely delivered. In other words, in the mind of a typical consumer, title and risk of loss or damage would be separate concepts. This separation is not unreasonable, but the extent to which the courts will recognize it is uncertain.

Rule 2

Where there is a contract for the sale of specific goods and the seller is bound to do something to the goods for the purpose of putting them into a deliverable state, the property does not pass until such thing is done and the buyer has received notice.

---

35. Usually fraud is involved, but that is not necessarily so; see *Sun Toyota Ltd.* v. *Granville Toyota Ltd.* [2002] B.C.J. No. 807.

36. Ont., s. 19: see also Alta., s. 20; B.C., s. 23; Nfld., s. 20.

ILLUSTRATION 16.6

During the same January sale described in Illustration 16.5, another customer, Oliveira, agreed to buy a second-hand television set that Maple Leaf was displaying, but a term of the agreement was that Maple Leaf would replace the picture tube. It had not done so when the set was also stolen, along with Haag's. The title had not passed to Oliveira, and she would not be liable for the price.

Even if Maple Leaf Appliances had replaced the picture tube shortly after Oliveira left the store, she would not have the title unless she had also been *notified* that the replacement had been done before the set was stolen. Often, when a seller undertakes to deliver the goods, he will not communicate separately with the buyer to say that the goods are now in a deliverable state but will simply deliver them. In these circumstances, the required notice to the buyer is satisfied by delivery, and the title passes at the time of delivery.

Rule 3

Where there is a contract for the sale of specific goods in a deliverable state but the seller is bound to weigh, measure, test, or do some other act or thing with reference to the goods for the purpose of ascertaining their price, the property does not pass until such act or thing is done and the buyer has received notice.

ILLUSTRATION 16.7

McTavish, Frobisher & Co. agreed to buy a pile of beaver skins from Pond, a trapper, at an agreed price per skin. Before Pond counted the skins, most of them disappeared mysteriously. Here, the title had not passed to the buyer, and in the absence of any special agreement between the parties, the loss is Pond's.

Rule 4

When goods are delivered to the buyer on approval or on "sale or return" or other similar terms, the property passes to the buyer

(a) when he signifies his approval or acceptance to the seller or does any other act adopting the transaction.
(b) if he does not signify his approval or acceptance to the seller but retains the goods without giving notice of rejection, then, if a time has been fixed for the return of the goods, on the expiration of such time, and if no time has been fixed, on the expiration of a reasonable time, and what is a reasonable time is a question of fact.

We can see from this rule that a buyer may accept goods and acquire ownership without having expressly communicated that intention to the seller. As our discussion of bailment in Chapter 17 will show, a prospective buyer who has custody of goods on approval owes a duty of care in looking after them. A possibility of liability therefore exists, but since there is as yet no agreed price under a contract of sale, the amount would have to be fixed by the court.

unascertained goods
goods that have not been set aside and agreed upon as the subject of a sale

future goods
goods that have not yet been produced

Unascertained Goods

The Act sets out a separate rule for deciding when title passes in goods that are *unascertained* at the time of the contract. One example of **unascertained goods** occurs when they have not yet been produced—that is, when they are **future goods**. But goods may also be unascertained even when they are in existence, provided they have not yet been selected and related to a particular contract.

Goods are ascertained once they have been set aside or earmarked and have been agreed on as the subject matter of the sale. When unascertained goods are the subject of a contract, by definition the contract must be an agreement to sell, for title cannot pass to a buyer until the goods are ascertained.

Rule 5

(a) Where there is a contract for the sale of unascertained or future goods by description and goods of that description and in a deliverable state are unconditionally appropriated to the contract, either by the seller with the assent of the buyer or by the buyer with the assent of the seller, the property in the goods passes to the buyer, and such assent may be expressed or implied and may be given either before or after the appropriation is made.

(b) Where in pursuance of a contract the seller delivers the goods to the buyer or to a carrier or other bailee (whether named by the buyer or not) for the purpose of transmission to the buyer and does not reserve the right of disposal, he is deemed to have unconditionally appropriated the goods to the contract.

ILLUSTRATION 16.8

Prentice ordered from Hall's automotive supply store four truck tires, size 750 × 20. Hall had a large number of such tires in his stockroom. Later in the day, a clerk removed four of them from the rack where Hall kept his stock. He set them aside in the stockroom, attaching a note, "For Prentice." The clerk's act of separating the tires from the larger bulk does not amount to an unconditional appropriation of the goods. If the contents of the stockroom were to be destroyed in a fire, the loss of the tires would still be the seller's because title has not yet passed to the buyer.

Unconditional appropriation of goods to a contract does not take place until a seller can no longer change his mind and substitute other goods for delivery to the buyer. In other words, some act must be done that conclusively determines what goods are appropriated to the contract. It seems that nothing less than delivery of the goods—or at least an act that virtually amounts to delivery—will constitute unconditional appropriation. If, in the above example, the tires had been installed on the truck, that would amount to delivery and title—and risk would have passed to the buyer.

Where the seller appropriates goods to the contract, Rule 5 requires that the buyer assents to the appropriation. The buyer's assent, however, may be implied from the nature of the contract, and title may pass to the buyer even before she receives notice of the unconditional appropriation. For example, in Illustration 16.8 there would seem to be no need for the buyer's express assent when the seller installs the particular tires that have been selected. In this respect, then, the rule for unascertained goods differs from some of the rules we discussed earlier for specific goods.

Rule 5 above refers to the possibility of a seller reserving "the right of disposal." We shall consider this right in the following section when we deal with bills of lading.

CHECKLIST   The Passing of Title

Unless otherwise agreed, the Sale of Goods Act provides that title to goods passes from the seller to the buyer

- where there is an unconditional contract for the sale of specific goods in a deliverable state, when the contract is made.
- where there is a contract for the sale of specific goods and the seller is bound to do something to the goods to put them into a deliverable state, when the buyer has received notice that it has been done.

continued

- where there is a contract for the sale of specific goods in a deliverable state but the seller is bound to do something to ascertain their price, when the buyer has received notice that it has been done.

- where goods are delivered to the buyer on approval or on "sale or return," when the buyer signifies his approval, or does some other act adopting the transaction, or when the buyer retains the goods beyond a reasonable time.

- where there is a contract for the sale of unascertained or future goods by description, when goods of that description and in a deliverable state are appropriated to the contract by one party with the assent of the other.

Bills of Lading

bill of lading
a document signed by a carrier acknowledging that specified goods have been delivered to it for shipment

A **bill of lading** is still an essential part of many commercial sales transactions. Recently, however, the written bill of lading has increasingly been replaced by computer transactions. A broadly similar result to that discussed below is now achieved through a process known as Electronic Data Interchange.[37]

We can best understand the nature of a bill of lading by considering its purposes:

- It is a receipt issued and signed by a carrier, acknowledging that specified goods have been delivered to it for shipment.
- It provides evidence of the terms of the contract between the shipper and the carrier to transport the described goods to a stated destination.
- It may be evidence of title to the goods.

A bill of lading may be made out to the order of a specified party that has title to the goods in the course of transit and that may thus transfer title of the goods to someone else by endorsing it. More commonly, the seller makes out the bill of lading to his own order (or leaves the proposed transferee blank), thereby retaining the right of disposal during transit and enabling him to withhold title from the proposed buyer until the buyer makes satisfactory arrangements for payment. When this is done, the seller endorses the bill over to the buyer. A bill of lading is, consequently, a useful device for transferring ownership of goods independently of their physical possession.

REMEDIES OF THE SELLER

Lien

lien
a right of a person in possession of property to retain that property until payment

The primary objective of a business selling goods is to recover the contract price. One way of ensuring recovery is to withhold delivery until payment is made. While the goods remain in an unpaid seller's possession, the seller has a **lien** on the goods regardless of whether title has passed to the buyer. The seller has a claim or charge on them for their agreed price, and can refuse to part with them until the debt is satisfied. Once the seller delivers the goods to the buyer, however, he normally loses this special right to possession unless the buyer obtains them by theft or trickery. The right of lien is based upon possession and is extinguished when possession passes in good faith to the buyer.[38]

---

37. See the discussion of Electronic Commerce in Chapter 34.

38. An exception to this rule applies when an unpaid seller repossesses goods under the provisions of the Bankruptcy and Insolvency Act; this exception is discussed below under the heading "Repossession."

Not every contract of sale creates a right of lien for the seller. The remedy exists only in the following situations:

(a) where the contract does not state that the buyer is to have credit, so that payment may be required upon delivery

(b) where the goods have been sold on credit, the term of credit has expired without payment being made and the seller still has possession of the goods

(c) where the buyer becomes insolvent before delivery

In (c), a seller who refuses to deliver is excused only if the buyer is insolvent. A seller should be sure of the facts before exercising the right of lien; otherwise, he takes the risk that the buyer may subsequently sue for breach of the promise to deliver. It is not enough simply to hear that the buyer's financial position is questionable—it is necessary to be more specific and to show that the buyer is definitely unable to meet current debts as they come due. Otherwise, the seller must deliver as promised and will become an unsecured creditor of the buyer for the price of the goods.

A seller may waive his right of lien—and rely on the buyer's credit—in two ways. He may waive the right by implication, as in the usual credit sale, simply by agreeing to deliver before payment is due. Second, he may voluntarily deliver the goods before he needs to do so.

Stoppage in Transit

If a buyer becomes insolvent after an unpaid seller has delivered goods to a carrier, the seller may still have time to order the carrier to withhold the goods from the buyer. If given notice in adequate time, the carrier is bound to obey these instructions. If the carrier delivers to the buyer in spite of notice, it is liable for damages for conversion.

The right of **stoppage in transit** is an extraordinary one because it allows a seller who may have neither title nor possession to goods to exercise control over them.

stoppage in transit
the right of a seller to order a carrier not to deliver to the buyer

A seller takes the same risk in exercising a right of stoppage in transit as he does in asserting a right of lien. If, as matters turn out, he has mistakenly assumed that the buyer is insolvent, the buyer may sue for damages for non-delivery.

Repossession

As stated above, once possession passes in good faith to a buyer, the seller loses the right to repossess the goods even if the buyer fails to pay for them. An important exception to the rule was introduced in 1992 by an amendment to the law of bankruptcy.[39] Where a seller has delivered goods to a buyer and the buyer, before having paid in full for the goods, becomes bankrupt or insolvent, the seller may make a written demand for the return of the goods. The demand must be presented, within 30 days after the goods were delivered, to the trustee in bankruptcy or receiver appointed to manage the debtor's affairs. The right to repossess applies only to goods that were delivered in relation to the buyer's business, not to consumer goods. The goods must still be in the possession of the buyer, must be identifiable, and must be in the same condition as they were when sold. If the price has been partly paid, the seller has a choice between repossessing a portion of the goods in proportion to the amount still owing and repossessing all of the goods and refunding the amount already paid. The right of repossession ranks above any other claim to the goods, except those of a subsequent purchaser who has bought the goods for value and in good faith, without notice of the unpaid seller's claim.

Resale

After exercising a right of lien or of stoppage in transit under the Sale of Goods Act, an unpaid seller may give notice to the buyer and resell the goods to a third party. The new purchaser obtains good

---

39. Bankruptcy and Insolvency Act, R.S.C. 1985, c. B-3, s. 81.1, as added by S.C. 1992, c. 27.

title to them. Although not expressly authorized under the Bankruptcy and Insolvency Act, it seems that an unpaid seller who repossesses goods under that Act also has the right to resell them. The right of resale is especially helpful when the goods are perishable, but is not confined to such emergencies.

The right of resale extends to other circumstances and is not limited to a lien or stoppage in transit. The right arises whenever a buyer commits a breach by refusing to accept goods. Resale is then the means by which a seller mitigates his loss. If the seller has made a reasonable effort to obtain a good price on resale but obtains a lower price than that promised in the original contract, he may sue the original buyer for the deficiency.

Damages for Non-Acceptance

We used the contract of sale to illustrate the measurement of expectation damages in Chapter 15. Our discussion assumed that the title to the goods had not passed to the buyer at the time of the buyer's breach. We saw that a critical factor in determining the appropriate amount of damages is whether the seller is in a position to supply more goods than prospective customers might order. If so, the seller's damages are measured by the profits lost due to the buyer's breach; if not, damages are generally measured by any deficiency in the resale price of the rejected goods compared with the original contract price.

ILLUSTRATION 16.9

Read examined a used accordion for sale in Crescendo Music Stores Ltd. She agreed in writing to buy it for $600 provided the bellows were repaired and gold monogram initials were affixed to it. Before the repairs were made, Read informed Crescendo that she had decided to take up the saxophone instead and refused to accept the accordion. Crescendo sued Read.

The appropriate action would be for damages for non-acceptance because the title had not passed to Read at the time of her repudiation. If the music store had more used accordions in stock than it had customers wanting to buy them, it would have sustained damages equal to the profit it would have made had Read purchased the instrument as she promised.

If the store had no other used accordions and was able to resell the accordion, but for less than $600, it would have sustained damages equal to the difference between the two prices. If the repairs and changes had been made but Read had not been notified before she repudiated the contract, title would still not have passed to her, and the seller might have a claim for additional damages equal to its expenses. That would depend on whether the required changes had enhanced the value of the instrument: Crescendo should be able to recover the cost of affixing the gold monogram, but not that of repairing the bellows.

Action for the Price

When title has passed to the buyer, a seller is entitled to the full price regardless of whether the buyer has taken delivery. If the buyer rejects goods after title has passed, she is rejecting what she already owns.

ILLUSTRATION 16.10

Anderson bought a stereo on display at Burton's Appliance Store. The stereo was tagged "sold" with Anderson's name on it, and Anderson signed a form identifying the purchase and stating its price. On her way home, Anderson saw another model in the window of Modern Electronics Ltd., and decided that she would prefer it. She refused to take delivery of the stereo from Burton, and Burton sued her for the full price of the machine.

The action would succeed. At the time Anderson attempted to repudiate the contract of sale, title had already passed to her. If Burton sues for the price, however, he must be willing and able to deliver the stereo.

The conclusion in Illustration 16.10 is based on the Sale of Goods Act. It has been criticized because a seller's right to sue for the full price may be difficult to justify when the seller still has the goods. If the buyer is a consumer, the seller, as a dealer in the rejected goods, is normally in a better position to resell them. Accordingly, when a seller does not succeed in delivering the goods, it is arguable that its remedy should be limited to an action for damages even though title may have passed to the buyer. In jurisdictions in the United States that have adopted the Uniform Commercial Code, a seller may sue for the price only when the buyer has accepted the goods or when the seller is unable after a reasonable effort to resell the goods at a reasonable price. In virtually all other circumstances, a seller may sue only for damages for non-acceptance, regardless of whether title has passed.

Many retail businesses make it a practice, for reasons of good customer relations, to waive contracts of sale upon the customer's request and, even when the goods have already been delivered, to take them back. The waiver of the original contract transfers title back to the seller, who may then transfer the title to another buyer.

When a seller does sue, he usually sues for the price or, in the alternative, for damages for non-acceptance. This strategy is appropriate when the seller prefers a simple action for the price (as it normally would), but when it is not clear whether title has passed to the buyer at the time of repudiation. If the court decides that title has passed, the seller will recover the price. If the court decides that title has not passed, the seller will still recover damages for non-acceptance.

Retention of Deposit

In a contract of sale, as in any contract, the parties may provide that, in the event of breach, the party in default shall pay the other a specified sum of money by way of liquidated damages. As we have seen in Chapter 15, the court will enforce such a term if the amount specified is a genuine estimate by the parties of the probable loss. Depending upon the circumstances, an amount paid by a buyer as a deposit may be treated as liquidated damages in the event of her default. In many contracts of sale, the reason why the seller demands a deposit is to protect himself at least to that extent in the event of the buyer's non-acceptance. The intention is clear that the deposit will be forfeited upon breach by the buyer.[40]

However, we must distinguish between a **deposit**, which is intended primarily to provide a sanction to induce performance of the contract by the buyer, and a **down payment**, which constitutes a part payment of the purchase price and is unrelated to the seller's probable loss in the event of breach by the buyer. If the title to the goods has already passed to the buyer at the time the buyer repudiates, the seller is entitled not only to retain the down payment, but also to sue for the balance of the price. If title has not yet passed, the seller is entitled to retain out of the down payment any damages for non-acceptance that he can prove and is accountable to the buyer for any remaining surplus.[41] If the seller can prove damages that exceed the down payment, he may retain that sum and sue for additional damage.

deposit
a sum of money paid by the buyer to the seller, to be forfeited if the buyer does not perform its part of the contract

down payment
a sum of money paid by the buyer as an initial part of the purchase price

THE SELLER'S LIABILITY

Misrepresentation

We have considered the remedies for misrepresentation in Chapter 9; a review of that chapter is worthwhile at this point. We noted there that when a misrepresentation is innocent, the only remedy, rescission, is often impossible or at least impractical. To have the more extensive remedies available for misrepresentation, the buyer must establish either fraud or negligence. The type of statement that comes within the definition of misrepresentation has two important characteristics for our present

40. See *Stockloser* v. *Johnson*, [1954] 1 Q.B. 476. If the contract provides for a non-refundable deposit but the deposit has not been paid, for example, when the purchaser has stopped payment on the cheque, the vendor is entitled to recover the agreed sum: *Vanvic Enterprises Ltd.* v. *Mark*, [1985] 3 W.W.R. 644.
41. *Stevenson* v. *Colonial Homes Ltd.* (1961), 27 D.L.R. (2d) 698.

purposes. First, the statement must be part of the preliminary bargaining and must not be incorporated as a term in the contract of sale—if it were embodied in the contract, the buyer's recourse would be for breach of contract. Second, the statement made by the seller must be made as a statement of fact—the law provides no remedy for a buyer induced to enter into a contract by a mere expression of opinion or commendation of the goods.

Apart from liability at common law, a variety of federal and provincial statutes regulate misrepresentations, especially in misleading advertisements, and impose penalties on those making them. This aspect of a seller's liability is dealt with under the heading "Consumer Protection" in Chapter 32.

Breach of a Term

Generally, a breach of a condition entitles the injured party to discharge the contract as well as to sue for damages for any loss suffered. The Sale of Goods Act, however, sets down circumstances where a buyer will *not* be entitled to terminate the contract and return the goods even though the seller has been guilty of a breach of condition. The Act reads as follows:

> Where a contract of sale is not severable and the buyer has accepted the goods or part thereof, or where the contract is for specific goods the property in which has passed to the buyer, the breach of any condition to be fulfilled by the seller can only be treated as a breach of warranty and not as a ground for rejecting the goods and treating the contract as repudiated, unless there is a term of the contract, express or implied, to that effect.[42]

This section means, first, that the buyer must keep the goods and be content with damages when the broken contract of sale does not contemplate delivery by instalments (is not severable) and the buyer has indicated an intention to keep the goods or treated them in a way inconsistent with the seller's ownership of them.

The section seems to contemplate a second situation where the right to repudiate would be lost when the contract is for specific goods, the property in which has passed to the buyer even though the goods are still in the seller's possession. However, when the seller has committed a breach of condition by allocating unsatisfactory goods to fill the contract, such a result would seem surprising. It is difficult to see how title would pass to the buyer in that situation, short of the buyer's acceptance of the goods. Courts avoid applying this part of the section and sometimes even seem to ignore it as inappropriate to modern selling practices.

ILLUSTRATION 16.11

A sales agent for Agrarian Implements Ltd. showed to Macdonald, a farmer, a catalogue containing pictures of agricultural equipment that his firm had for sale. The agent told Macdonald that they had just taken into stock "one brand new" combine of a type pictured in the catalogue. Macdonald agreed to buy it and signed the necessary papers.

When the combine was delivered, a neighbour of Macdonald recognized it as the one with which the same sales agent had earlier given him an extensive demonstration, and which the sales agent had referred to as "a demonstrator model that we could let you have at a bargain." Macdonald at once shipped the combine back to Agrarian Implements and the firm then sued him for the price.

The combine was a specific article at the time Macdonald agreed to buy it. Nevertheless, he would be entitled to treat the contract as discharged and to refuse to accept the combine. Agrarian Implements was guilty of breach of the condition as to description (that the combine was new), and title did not pass to Macdonald.[43] If, however, Macdonald took delivery of the combine and used it for farm work, he could not subsequently, upon learning that it was not new when he bought it, insist he had a right to return it. He must be content with damages.

---

42. Ont., s. 12(3): see also Alta., s. 13(4); B.C., s. 15(4); Nfld., s. 13(4).
43. See *Varley* v. *Whipp*, [1900] 1 Q.B. 513.

In Case 16.9, we can see the consequences for the buyer when the seller is guilty of a breach of condition but the buyer has accepted the goods.

CASE 16.9

Leaf purchased a painting of Salisbury Cathedral that the seller, International Galleries, represented to him as the work of the famous artist Constable. When Leaf attempted to resell the picture five years later, it was discovered that it had not been painted by Constable but by a much less-famous artist. Its value was consequently only a small fraction of what both the seller and buyer had thought.

Leaf tried to return the picture to International Galleries and recover the purchase price. The court held that the Sale of Goods Act applied, so that Leaf did not have the right to treat the contract as being at an end. Since he did not sue for damages, as he might have done, his action failed.[44]

It is interesting that the court regarded the representation as having been incorporated into the contract of sale as a term. Its decision does not answer the question whether, had the case been treated as one of either innocent misrepresentation or mistake, the equitable remedy of rescission might still have been available at that late date.

Wrongful Withholding or Disposition by the Seller

When the title to goods has already passed to the buyer, a seller who refuses to deliver them according to the terms of the contract is guilty of a tort: the buyer may sue the seller for damages for **wrongful detention**. Moreover, the buyer may occasionally obtain a court order for the delivery of the goods. If, in addition to a failure to deliver, the seller transfers the goods to a third party, he will have disposed of goods that do not belong to him; the buyer may sue for damages for the tort of conversion—that is, for converting the buyer's goods to his own use or purposes.

wrongful detention
the refusal by the seller to deliver goods whose title has passed to the buyer

REMEDIES OF THE BUYER

A buyer has a range of possible remedies, in contract, in tort, and under consumer protection legislation. Remedies in tort, such as for conversion or for deceit, were discussed in Chapter 3. Consumer protection is dealt with in Chapter 32.

In contract, a buyer's usual remedy will be to claim damages. In Chapter 15, under the heading "Expectation Damages," we discussed the measure of damages available to a buyer when the seller fails to deliver. If delivery is merely delayed and the buyer still accepts the goods, the measure of damages is the value the goods would have had for the buyer if they had been delivered on time less their actual value when delivered.

A seller may be guilty of breach for reasons other than non-delivery: for example, breach of any of the implied terms as to title, description, suitability, and merchantability, or compliance with sample; or breach of an express term as to the quality or capability of the goods. Damages sustained by a buyer from the seller's breach of a term may sometimes be greater than the price of the goods. To recover the loss, the buyer must take the initiative and claim it from the seller. When the damages amount to less than the contract price, the buyer may tender to the seller the price less the amount of the damages. If the seller refuses the tender and sues for the full price, the buyer may defend by claiming to set off her damages against the price.[45]

---

44. *Leaf* v. *International Galleries*, [1950] 2 K.B. 86.43.

45. To reduce the risk of having to pay court costs, the buyer should pay into court the amount tendered to the seller.

As an alternative to damages, a buyer may be able to claim the equitable remedy of specific performance or of rescission; both of these remedies were discussed in Chapter 15. The Sale of Goods Act gives the court discretion to order specific performance of a contract for the sale of goods—that is, to order the seller to deliver the goods to the buyer. Generally, the court does not grant this remedy when a seller refuses to deliver, because money damages are nearly always an adequate remedy. Where the goods have a unique value for the buyer, however, the court may exercise its discretion in her favour and order specific performance. As we have seen, in the preceding section under "Breach of a Term," the Sale of Goods Act restricts the right to rescind. Nevertheless, rescission remains a possible remedy for the buyer when the seller fails to deliver goods that have been prepaid in whole or in part.

INTERNATIONAL ISSUE

International Sale of Goods

In 1980, the United Nations Commission on International Trade Law (UNCITRAL) developed a set of uniform rules for international sale of goods. The Convention on Contracts for the International Sale of Goods (CISG) establishes substantive rules relating to the formation of a contract, buyers' and sellers' obligations, and remedies. Its goals are to overcome the problems associated with conflicting principles of law between buyer and seller jurisdictions and provide certainty and consistency in the resolution of international trade disputes. It applies to sales of commercial goods between businesses in different countries (providing the countries subscribe to the convention). It does not apply to sales for personal or household use (consumer transactions).

In 1992, the convention became law in Canada, and federal and provincial legislation has been adopted to implement its terms.[46] This means that when a dispute arises in a contract covered by the convention, a Canadian court should apply the rules of the convention rather than the domestic laws relating to sale of goods. Parties may specifically opt out of the application of CISG by inserting a term in their contract (article 6). The United States has implemented the convention but the United Kingdom has not.

QUESTIONS TO CONSIDER

1. If the goal of the convention is to create uniformity and certainty, why is "opting out" allowed?

2. What would be a business's rationale for contractually opting out of CISG?

Sources: *CSIG Canada*, www.osgoode.yorku.ca/cisg/; "International Sale of Goods (CISG) and Related Transactions," *UNCITRAL*, www.uncitral.org/uncitral/en/uncitral_texts/sale_goods.html; R. Sharma, "The United Nations Convention on Contracts for the International Sale of Goods: The Canadian Experience" (2005), 36 *Victoria University of Wellington Law Review* 847–858, available online at www.yorku.ca/osgoode/cisg/writings/documents/CISGandCanadabyR.Sharma.pdf.

46. International Sale of Goods Contracts Convention Act, S.C. 1991, c. 13; International Conventions Implementation Act, S.A. 1990, c. I-6.8; International Sale of Goods Act, R.S.B.C. 1996, c. 236; International Sale of Goods Act, R.S.N. 1990, c. I-16; International Sale of Goods Act, R.S.O. 1990, c. I.10.

QUESTIONS FOR REVIEW

1. What was the principal purpose of the original Sale of Goods Act?

2. Distinguish between ownership and possession.

3. How are "goods" defined in the Sale of Goods Act? What types of personal property are not within the definition?

4. Is a contract for the installation of a central heating system a contract for the sale of goods?

5. What is the distinction between a sale and an agreement to sell?

6. What is meant by a "consignment"?

7. When does the *caveat emptor* principle apply to the sale of goods?

8. What is meant by "quiet possession"?

9. Distinguish between the implied term as to fitness and the implied term of merchantable quality.

10. What is the significance of an article being sold under its trade name?

11. What terms are implied in the case of a sale by sample?

12. What does it mean to say that the courts interpret the time set for payment as a warranty unless the parties have expressed otherwise?

13. If the seller delivers a greater quantity of goods than the buyer ordered, what choices does the buyer have?

14. What determines who bears the risk of loss when goods that are the subject matter of a contract of sale are destroyed?

15. When does title pass in the case of specific goods that are in a deliverable state?

16. In what circumstances can a person who is not the owner of goods pass a good title to them?

17. What is the distinction between unascertained goods and future goods?

18. What is a "bill of lading"?

19. When does an unpaid seller have a lien on the goods sold? When is there a right of repossession?

20. What is the appropriate measure of damages when the buyer refuses to accept the goods?

21. *A* offered to sell his goat to *B* for $10, and *B* accepted. *B* put a $10 bill on the table and suggested they have a beer to celebrate the deal. While they were drinking the beer, the goat ate the $10 bill. (News item, May 13, 1961.) Who owns the goat?

CASES AND PROBLEMS

1. On a Friday afternoon Harris went into a store owned by Kabul Karpets Inc. and saw a large Uzbek carpet which she immediately decided would be perfect on the wall of her sitting room. She promptly bought the carpet for $2000, paying by credit card.

   Because of the large size of the carpet—and the smallness of her car—she asked the store to deliver it and was told that they would do so on the following Monday. The sales assistant attached a "sold" notice to the carpet, with a small piece of adhesive tape, leaving the carpet prominently displayed on the wall of the store.

   The following Monday morning, Lewis saw the carpet through the store window and at once realized it was just what he was looking for to hang on his study wall. He entered the store, paid $2000 by credit card, and had the carpet loaded into his large van. The shop assistant who served Lewis was not the same one who had been on duty on the Friday, and the "sold" notice had somehow become detached from the carpet and presumably had been swept up by the cleaners. On the Tuesday, Harris phoned the store to inquire why her carpet had not been delivered.

Who owns the carpet?

2. Thrasher was an experienced farmer who, over more than 10 years, had successfully grown several crops including wheat, canola, and barley. Three years ago he purchased a quantity of "QR5" granular herbicide from the manufacturer, Treflan Ltd. QR5 is a well-known product, widely used as an agent to control weed infestations, particularly those found in fields sowed to canola. The herbicide was labelled with the following warning: "To cover the possibility of injury to rotational crops, seed the crops shallow into a warm, moist seedbed."

In the fall of that year, Thrasher applied the QR5 by aerial spraying to 300 acres of his land, and sowed it to canola in the following spring. After the seed germinated, Thrasher noticed large areas of weed choking out his crop. The canola crop produced at harvest only half as much as had been expected. Thrasher consulted Treflan, who advised him to sow the land the following year with wheat, as a rotational crop. He did so, but the crop was so poor that it had to be ploughed in.

Thrasher contended that the herbicide had been properly applied but failed to kill the weeds in the canola crop as it should have, and that it left a high residue that ruined the following year's wheat crop. Treflan's position was that Thrasher was at fault for the damage to the canola crop because he did not follow the application instructions properly, the herbicide was not applied uniformly, and the next year's wheat seed had been planted too deep, contrary to the instructions and warnings that came with the herbicide.

Based on the evidence presented to it, the Court found that Thrasher had applied the herbicide correctly—it had failed to kill the weeds as it should have done and had contaminated the soil. However, Thrasher had ignored the manufacturer's warning and planted the wheat seed too deep.

Should Treflan be held liable for the loss of (a) the canola crop and (b) the wheat crop?

3. Horvat agreed to purchase a 1970 Cessna 180 aircraft from Balinder. Balinder explained that he no longer owned the Cessna, having just traded it to Hidden Valley Aviation Ltd. for a newer model, but that he had agreed to find a buyer for the plane. In answer to questions from Horvat, Balinder assured her that the plane was a "little beauty" that had never given a minute of trouble, and that it had been regularly serviced. He invited Horvat to check the plane out thoroughly, but she replied that she was not a qualified mechanic and contented herself with a cursory inspection and a trial flight accompanied by Balinder.

A price was agreed on and Horvat handed over a certified cheque, made payable to Hidden Valley. The sales invoice showed Hidden Valley as the seller.

Horvat soon discovered that the Cessna's engine required major repairs to make it safe and airworthy. She brought an action against both Balinder and Hidden Valley, claiming damages for the cost of repairs.

Is Horvat entitled to recover?

4. Gabrieli bought a truck from a dealer, Transit Inc. Gabrieli signed a "purchase order" on May 12, at which time Transit ordered the truck from the manufacturer. It was agreed that the sale was subject to Gabrieli being able to arrange suitable financing.

Three weeks later, Gabrieli informed Transit that she had been able to obtain a loan from her bank and was in a position to let them have a bank draft for the full price. Transit confirmed that the arrangement was satisfactory. On August 2 the truck was delivered to Transit from the manufacturer. Transit called Gabrieli, telling her "your truck is here and ready for you to collect." Gabrieli went straight to the Transit premises, handed over the bank draft, and received the keys, papers, and the truck. At that time, Transit's sales manager also handed her a number of other documents, including one that the manager described as "your warranty," which he asked Gabrieli to sign. Gabrieli did so. The document gave a limited one-year warranty for defects but excluded implied warranties and excluded liability for consequential damages.

The truck proved to be defective and soon developed a number of faults. Gabrieli took the truck back to Transit on numerous occasions for various repairs, but these were mostly unsuccessful. Finally, after more than two years of unsatisfactory operation, Gabrieli returned the truck to Transit and demanded her money back.

Transit denied liability, pointing to the one-year warranty that excluded the statutory implied warranties. Is Gabrieli entitled to any remedy?

5. Benner's Sawmill Inc. entered into a contract with Chen to purchase a quantity of timber growing on land leased by Chen. A price of $150 per cubic metre was agreed, and the quantity set at approximately 600 cubic metres. Chen was to cut and trim the timber ready for collection by Benner's, who paid an initial deposit of $15 000. Benner's asked its insurance company about insuring the timber and was told that the timber could not be insured until it had been felled, trimmed, and "timbermarked" (that is, marked with a provincially registered mark applied by swinging a timber hammer and striking the wood surface at both ends).

Some weeks later, Chen phoned Benner's and informed them that the timber had been cut, trimmed, and stacked. The total price was $94 000 (the quantity being a little more than 600 cubic metres). When asked if the timber had been timbermarked, Chen replied that it had not. He was going away on a short vacation but would see to it as soon as he returned. In accordance with the contract, Benner's sent Chen a cheque for the full price, less the deposit already paid.

Before Chen returned from vacation, his sheds were destroyed by fire. When Benner's demanded the timber or their money back, Chen replied: "Sorry, but it was your timber that burnt."

Advise Benner's.

6. The Granite County School Board placed an order with Borough Furniture Ltd, a furniture manufacturer, for 2500 folding chairs. Before placing the order, an officer of the Board had examined a number of chairs produced by Borough (as well as chairs of other manufacturers). Eventually, they settled upon one particular model, but required a number of modifications to be made. Borough produced a prototype of the chair, which was examined by the officer, who expressed satisfaction.

Borough delivered a first batch of 500 chairs and continued with the manufacture of the remaining 2000. A few days after the first delivery, it was found that the chairs tipped rather easily and were unsuitable for use in classrooms. The Board refused to take delivery of any more chairs and demanded that Borough take back the 500 that they had delivered. Borough claimed that they had made the chairs according to the Board's specifications and demanded payment for the full 2500.

Which party has the better claim?

7. In December, Winnipeg Seafoods Ltd. orally agreed to purchase from Lakehead Fish Wholesale Co. 1000 five-kilogram boxes of frozen Lake Superior herring at $1.40 per kilogram. The fish were being stored in the cold storage warehouse of a third party, the Bailey Co. of Thunder Bay. The Bailey Co. operated as a storage company that processed and stored fresh fish. At the time it held some 1500 boxes of this type of fish in storage.

Because Winnipeg Seafoods was short of storage space, it did not want the fish shipped to it but preferred to have it remain in the warehouse at Thunder Bay. Lakehead Fish then arranged with Bailey to transfer the storage account to the name of Winnipeg Seafoods in respect of the 1000 boxes, and Lakehead Fish sent an invoice for $7000 to Winnipeg Seafoods. The invoice indicated that the merchandise was in storage at Bailey's in Thunder Bay. Immediately afterwards, Bailey sent its invoice to Winnipeg Seafoods for one month's storage charges, payable in advance. Winnipeg Seafoods did not pay either of these accounts. The price of frozen herring started to fall in the middle of January. The fish were held in storage until the end of January and then processed to prevent spoilage. On February 2, Winnipeg Seafoods returned the invoice of Lakehead Fish with an accompanying letter to the effect that it had decided to "cancel the order." Lakehead Fish then sued Winnipeg Seafoods Ltd. for the price of the fish, $7000, or in the alternative for damages for non-acceptance.

Should it succeed?

ADDITIONAL RESOURCES FOR CHAPTER 16 ON THE COMPANION WEBSITE *(www.pearsoned.ca/smyth)*

In addition to self-test multiple-choice, true–false, and short essay questions (all with immediate feedback), application exercises, and links to useful web destinations, the Companion Website provides the following resources for Chapter 16:

- **British Columbia:** Consumer Protection Legislation; Lien; Passing of Property; Sale of Goods Act; Stoppage in Transit; Tender of Payment; Tender of Performance; Terms Implied by Statute
- **Alberta:** Sale of Goods
- **Manitoba/Saskatchewan:** Sale of Goods Act
- **Ontario:** Consumer Protection Act 2002; Sale of Goods Act

Leasing and Bailment

In discussing contracts of sale in Chapter 16, we saw that ownership and possession of goods do not always go together. In this chapter, we examine two common types of contract in which ownership and possession are separated: leasing and bailment. Leasing of personal property is a form of bailment, although from a business point of view, leasing has a very different function from other forms of bailment. A lease of personal property—a chattel lease—is frequently regarded as a form of financing or an alternative to sale. By contrast, most types of bailment involve parting with possession of an item for a relatively short time—for storage, repair, or transportation. Legally, however, they share the same essential features.

In this chapter we examine such questions as:

- What are the principal types of chattel lease?

- Why are leasing contracts used, and why have they become so important?

- What are the terms that are commonly found in leasing contracts?

- What are the respective rights of the lessor and the lessee?

- What is the legal nature of bailment?

- What are the principal types of bailment contract?

- What are the rights and duties of the parties to a contract of bailment?

LEASING

Leasing is a major growth industry and has become a multi-billion-dollar business in both Canada and the United States. At the consumer level, automobile leasing has become a common alternative to purchasing on credit. In business, it is common to lease capital equipment, such as heavy machinery and aircraft.

The widespread use of leasing in business is a relatively recent development, although the concept of a **lease** is a very ancient one. The essence of a lease is that the owner of an item of property, referred to as the **lessor**, rents the property to the **lessee**—that is, allows the lessee to have possession and use of the property for a stipulated period, in return for the payment of rent. Leasing traditionally has been associated with real estate—leasing, or renting, a house, an apartment, or office space for a business has always been an alternative to purchase. We consider leases of land in Chapter 24, "Landlord and Tenant."

Although the possibility of renting personal property, or chattels, has long existed and been recognized by the law, such contracts were comparatively rare until recently. A major reason was the risk that an owner ran when he parted with possession of personal property. A person who obtains a lease of land cannot remove it, and if she fails to pay the rent, the owner can repossess it. But chattels are transportable, and there was, until modern systems of registration of property rights were developed, an obvious danger that a lessee might simply disappear with the leased property and stop paying rent for it.

The other factor that led to the great increase in the leasing of personal property was the realization that a lease could be used as a security device. This was first recognized in England more than 100 years ago, in the leading House of Lords decision of *Helby* v. *Matthews*,[1] which recognized a hiring agreement with an option to purchase at the end of the hiring term as an effective method of selling goods on credit. It opened the way for the popular type of transaction known in Britain as **hire-purchase**. In a typical hire-purchase agreement, the lessee/purchaser agrees to lease an item of property—for a specified number of years, paying a monthly rental—with an option to purchase it at the end of the term, provided the rent has been paid in full, for a nominal amount, such as $1.

This type of transaction is well known in Canada, principally as a means of marketing automobiles. In reality, it is a method of purchasing on credit, and, as such, is an alternative to the conditional sale and to the *chattel mortgage*.[2] However, not all chattel leases are intended as security devices.

> **lease**
> an arrangement where the owner of property allows another person to have possession and use of the property for a stipulated period in return for the payment of rent

> **lessor**
> the owner of the leased property

> **lessee**
> the person who takes possession of the leased property

> **hire-purchase**
> an agreement to lease an item of property with an option for the lessee to purchase it at the end of the stipulated term

TYPES OF CHATTEL LEASE

Two main types of chattel lease exist: *operating leases*, or "true" leases, where the intention is that possession will revert to the owner at the end of the term; and purchase leases, where it is anticipated that the lessee will eventually become the owner. Purchase leases can be further subdivided into *security leases*, where the credit is provided by the lessor/vendor, and *finance leases*, where a third party finances the transaction on credit.

Operating Leases

> **operating lease**
> a lease under which there is no intention to transfer ownership

In an **operating lease**, since there is no intention to transfer ownership, the term tends to be relatively short—substantially less than the expected working life of the property leased. Examples include a car rental for a weekend or a month and the renting of specialized machinery for the duration of a construction contract or of farm machinery for the harvest season.

---

1.   [1895] A.C. 471.

2.   Those transactions are discussed in Chapter 30. The 2008 economic crisis has made leasing less popular with the automobile industry.

Purchase Leases

In *Helby* v. *Matthews*,[3] the House of Lords distinguished between a "true" lease and a hire-purchase agreement according to whether the lessee/purchaser was obliged to pay the full price for the chattel and whether she became the owner on completing the payments. That test now appears to be too simplistic. A more modern approach was adopted in Ontario by Henry, J., who considered that in order to determine the true nature of a lease, it is necessary to have regard to the position of the parties, their intention, and the true effect of the transaction.[4] In practice, however, this test has been difficult to apply and has led to contradictory results. The accounting profession has developed a more objective approach to determine whether to classify a lease as an operating lease or a purchase lease. A lease is treated as a **purchase lease**, or "capital lease,"[5] if one of three conditions exists:

purchase lease
a lease whereby ownership is intended to change hands at the end of the lease term

- Title passes automatically to the lessee at the end of the lease *or* on the exercise of a "bargain purchase option."
- There is a non-cancellable term for at least 75 percent of the economic life of the asset.
- The present value of the minimum lease payments exceeds 90 percent of the market value of the asset at the time the lease commences.[6]

The distinction between an operating lease and a purchase lease is important for accounting purposes. If it is a purchase, or "capital," lease, the asset and the accompanying liability must be recorded in the balance sheet of the lessee/purchaser. From a taxation perspective, the distinction determines whether the lease payments are rental payments—and thus deductible by the lessee in determining the profits of the business—or are instalments of the purchase price and not deductible (apart from any interest element). It also determines which party is regarded as the true owner and entitled to claim capital cost allowances in respect of depreciation of the asset. From a legal perspective, all lessor's interest should be registered under Personal Property Security legislation.[7]

Security and Finance Leases

In the typical purchase lease arrangement, it is the lessor who effectively provides the credit. The lessee pays what is, in reality, the purchase price by instalments—in the form of "rent." Until the price is paid in full, the lessor has a security interest by virtue of his continued ownership of the leased property—hence the expression **security lease**.

security lease
a purchase lease in which the lessor provides the credit

An alternative that is becoming increasingly common is for a third person, such as a financial institution, to provide the credit financing. In this type of transaction, commonly known as a **finance lease**, the supplier of the goods sells them to the financer, who in turn leases them to the lessee. The financer is technically the owner of the goods, even though it probably has never had possession of them and will ultimately pass title to the lessee.

finance lease
an arrangement where a third person provides credit financing, becomes the owner of the property, and leases it to the lessee

The major auto manufacturing companies commonly establish their own leasing companies to provide consumer financing in this manner.

---

3. *Supra*, n. 1.
4. *Re Speedrack Ltd.* (1980), 1 P.P.S.A.C. 109. In *Adelaide Capital Corp.* v. *Integrated Transportation Finance Inc.* (1994), 111 D.L.R. (4th) 493 (Ont. Gen. Div.), the court attached particular importance to the fact that the lessor was in the business of providing credit financing.
5. That is, a lease that acquires a capital asset. Another term commonly used to describe the transaction is "lease-to-own."
6. *CICA Handbook*, section 3065. Somewhat different guidelines have been published by the Canada Revenue Agency in Interpretation Bulletin IT-233R.
7. *Mitsui & Co. (Canada) Ltd.* v. *Royal Bank of Canada* (1995), 123 D.L.R. (4th) 449; *Adelaide Capital Corp.* v. *Integrated Transportation Finance Inc., supra*, n. 4. See the discussion of this issue in Chapter 30.

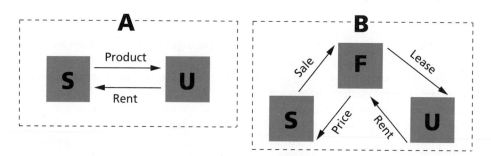

FIGURE 17.1

FIGURE 17.1

Comparing Purchase
Lease and Finance
Lease

In (A), a conventional purchase lease, the supplier, S, leases the property to the user, U, who pays rent in return. In (B), a finance lease, the supplier, S, sells the property to the financer, F, who in turn leases it to the user, U. U pays rent to F.

Sale-and-Leaseback

sale-and-leaseback
a transaction in which the owner of property sells it and immediately leases it back from the new owner

A business with cash-flow problems may enter into a **sale-and-leaseback** transaction to raise working capital. The business sells assets for cash, and leases them back in return for future rental payments. The leaseback may take the form of an operating lease or of a purchase lease. In the latter case, the effect is similar to raising cash by mortgaging the asset.

REASONS FOR CHATTEL LEASING

The reasons for operating leases are obvious. A person is likely to be reluctant to go to the expense of purchasing an item that may be used only for a limited period, even though it may be possible to resell that item when it is no longer needed. Leasing will normally be a more convenient, and frequently less expensive, alternative to outright purchase.

The advantages of purchase leases and finance leases are less obvious. The lessor's perception may be that continued ownership of the asset, until payment has been made in full, provides more security in the case of default or insolvency of the lessee than would a conditional sale or chattel mortgage, though that view is questionable under modern Personal Property Security legislation.[8] The lessee may sometimes find it preferable to lease assets, as a form of *off-balance-sheet* financing; that is, since the asset is not owned by the business, it does not appear on the balance sheet, but neither does the future rental obligation appear as a liability. The net result is to record a lower debt-to-assets ratio than would be the case if the asset had been purchased with borrowed funds. Whether that is, in fact, the case depends upon the proper classification of the lease for accounting purposes.

Initially, the main reason for preferring leasing lies in the way the transaction was treated for tax purposes. Some of these tax advantages have been countered by legislation, but it is nevertheless true that the rapid growth of leasing, and especially of international leasing, owes much to ingenious tax planning.

COMMON TERMS IN CHATTEL LEASES

What follows are the more important of the terms that are commonly found in chattel leases.

---

8.   See *Re Giffen*, [1998] 1 S.C.R. 91. This issue is considered further in Chapter 30.

Duration

The lease normally sets out the time period during which it is intended to continue in force. In purchase lease arrangements, this is usually a fixed number of years. Operating leases may not contain a fixed term, but rather provide for termination by one or other party on giving notice. If the term of the lease is shorter than the period for which the lessee is likely to want to use the asset, it is common to include an option for renewal.

Rent

Most leases provide for equal monthly or quarterly payments of rent, usually payable in advance. In a lease-to-own contract, the rent is calculated with reference to the normal selling price of the asset, with an additional "interest" element to take account of the period over which it is payable. Operating lease rentals take more account of the probable depreciation of the asset over the period of the lease and of the cost to the lessor of the asset, with an appropriate profit margin.

Insurance and Other Costs Payable by the Lessee

In short-term operating leases, the lessor normally insures the leased asset and bears the costs of maintenance and repairs. In longer leases, and especially in purchase leases, the lessee is usually required to covenant to keep the asset insured, to maintain it properly, and to pay the costs of maintenance and repairs. Sometimes the lessee is required to provide a "residual guarantee"—that is, a guarantee that the lessor will receive a minimum resale value at the end of the lease or if not, the lessee will be responsible for the difference.

Purchase Option

A purchase lease inevitably contains an option for the lessee to purchase the asset at the end of the term, usually for a relatively nominal amount. In practice, a distinction is often made between fair-market-value (FMV) leases and lease-to-buy (LTB) leases. In FMV leases, the purchase option corresponds to an estimate of the value of the asset at the end of the lease term; in LTB leases, the price is nominal (for example, $1). This difference is reflected in the rental payments—an FMV lease will have lower monthly payments than an LTB lease. Operating leases sometimes also include a purchase option, at a price to be agreed, with the price reducing over the lease term to offset depreciation.

Early Termination—Minimum Payment

Where the leased asset is new, or relatively new, the decrease in its value due to depreciation will often be greater than the amount of rent payable in the early part of the lease term. Consequently, it is usual for the lessor to insist on a minimum rental payment, to act as a deterrent against default or early termination. In England, hire-purchase agreements at one time contained harsh minimum payment clauses, requiring payment of two-thirds of the full price, or even the entire balance, if the lessee defaulted on even one monthly payment, with no reduction for the value of the asset that reverted to the lessor. Sometimes, such clauses were struck down as disguised penalties, but more effective protection to consumers was later provided by statute. In Canada, by contrast, relatively little statutory protection is provided, and in a number of provinces consumer protection legislation does not apply to leasing transactions.[9]

---

9. For example, the cost of credit disclosure provisions apply only in Alberta, British Columbia, Manitoba, and Ontario.

> ## CHECKLIST   Terms in a Lease Contract
>
> A lease contract will normally state
>
> - the duration of the lease
> - the rent payable
> - the party responsible for maintenance and insurance
> - whether there is an option to renew
> - whether there is an option for purchase and, if so, the terms of the option
> - what is to happen if the lease is terminated before the end of its prescribed term

Implied Terms

It is remarkable that there is very little law in Canada relating expressly to chattel leasing. Whereas England has its hire-purchase legislation going back to the 1930s and several U.S. states have legislation adopting article 2A of the Uniform Commercial Code, which applies to leases, there is no Canadian legislation specifically dealing with chattel leases. Nor, rather surprisingly, is there much case law. Perhaps this is because the contracts expressly cover most eventualities, there is little room for additional implied terms.

quiet possession
a warranty that there will be no interference with the lessee's possession or use of the asset

Nevertheless, it seems clear that the courts will, by analogy with the law on leases of real property, imply on the part of the lessor a warranty of **quiet possession**—that is, there will be no interference with the lessee's possession or use of the asset so long as the rent is paid and other terms are complied with. It is also likely that implied warranties, such as the warranty of fitness, are equally applicable to purchase lease contracts as they are to sales.[10] It has been held that the lessor impliedly warrants that leased equipment is reasonably fit for the purpose for which it was hired.[11] Some doubt exists as to whether this warranty is limited to defects of which the lessor ought to have been aware. If an analogy is drawn with the corresponding implied term in a contract of sale, a lessor, like a seller, should be liable even if the offending defect in the chattel is something it could not have detected. A number of provinces have resolved these doubts by extending to consumer leases the implied warranties that apply in the case of sale of goods. For example, in British Columbia the warranties implied under the Sale of Goods Act apply equally to retail leases,[12] and in Manitoba and Saskatchewan the implied warranties under the Consumer Protection Act are expressly made applicable to consumer leases.[13]

The standard of care required of a lessee who hires equipment is to take such care as a prudent person would exercise in the use of her own property.

> ## CASE 17.1
>
> Roxburgh rented a portable steam engine from Reynolds to power a wood-cutting saw. The engine exploded immediately after it was put into use, killing one worker and injuring another. Reynolds sued Roxburgh for the value of the destroyed engine and boiler. He alleged that Roxburgh had not tested the steam gauge and safety valve before running the machine. The court applied the rule that "the hirer of a chattel is required to use . . . the degree of diligence which prudent men use . . . in keeping their own goods of the same kind." However, the court held that this standard of care did not require the lessee to test the safety gauge and valve. Accordingly, the defendant was not in breach of his duty as a lessee and was not liable to pay for the destroyed steam engine.[14]
>
> The question of who was liable for the injuries to the workers—the lessor or the lessee—was not raised in the case.

---

10. This has been the case in England; see *Astley Industrial Trust Ltd.* v. *Grimley*, [1963] 1 W.L.R. 584.
11. *Griffith S.S. Co.* v. *Western Plywood Co.*, [1953] 3 D.L.R. 29.
12. R.S.B.C. 1996, c. 410, s. 20. These implied terms cannot be excluded: see Chapter 16.
13. R.S.M. 1987, c. 200, s. 58; S.S. 1996, c. 30.1., s. 48.
14. *Reynolds* v. *Roxburgh* (1886), 10 O.R. 649, per Armour, J., at 655.

RIGHTS OF THE PARTIES

The Lessor

The rights of the parties under a lease contract are, of course, governed by the terms, express and implied, of the contract. The principal remedies available to the lessor are the right to sue for rent that is due and unpaid and the right to retake possession of the leased property at the end of the lease or in the event of earlier default by the lessee. When a lessee contracts to hire a chattel for a given period, she remains liable for the whole rental even if she finds that she has overestimated the time needed to use the equipment. (In the same way, a tenant of a building is liable for rent for the full period of the lease whether she occupies or uses the premises or not.) A lessor may agree to take equipment back ahead of time and to reduce the rental charges; when he does so, he is consenting to a discharge of the original lease contract and to replacing it with a substituted agreement. But it seems that the lessor is entitled *both* to retake possession of the chattel *and* to sue for damages for loss of bargain in respect of the rent that would have been payable if there had been no default, or for any minimum rent stipulated in the contract.[15] Additionally, if the lessee is in breach of her duty to take proper care of the leased property, the lessor will have an action for damages for the loss. Damages should be calculated in accordance with the general principles of contract law.

The Lessee

As noted above, the lessor impliedly warrants that the lessee shall have quiet possession and, probably, that the goods are fit for the purpose for which they are hired. Consequently, the lessee is entitled to sue for damages if she is wrongfully dispossessed during the term of the lease, or if she suffers loss because of some defect in the goods.

The law is less clear in the case of finance leases where the supplier sells an article to the financer, who in turn leases it to the actual user, the lessee. The lessee's contract is with the financer, although most of her dealings will have been with the supplier, with whom she has no contract. Where the supplier has made express representations to the lessee to induce her to enter into the contract, a collateral contract may be implied between supplier and lessee—that is, in return for the supplier's warranty that the goods conform to a particular quality or have a particular characteristic, the lessee agrees to enter into the contract with the financer—a contract which is of benefit to the supplier.[16]

The lessee would have the usual contractual remedies against the financer, although in practice finance leases routinely exclude all implied warranties on the part of the lessor.

ETHICAL ISSUE

Consumer Leases

A common complaint about leasing contracts is that the consumer lessee rarely understands the terms of the contract—how much is she really paying, and what happens if she wishes to terminate the lease? According to one recent report,

> People sometimes confuse leasing with renting—when they don't want the car anymore, they think they can just walk away from their monthly payments. . . . In fact, they cannot, without incurring adjustment costs.[17]

continued

---

15. *Keneric Tractor Sales Ltd.* v. *Langille* (1987), 43 D.L.R. (4th) 171 (S.C.C.).

16. See *Hallmark Pool Corp.* v. *Storey* (1983), 144 D.L.R. (3d) 56. This is consistent with the principle established in *Shanklin Pier Ltd.* v. *Detel Products Ltd.*, discussed in Chapter 12, "Exceptions to the Privity of Contract Rule."

17. Ken Shaw, "Lease penalties offset costs," *Toronto Star*, July 24, 2004, p. G10.

During the term of the lease, circumstances may change. The lessee may lose her job and be unable to keep up the payments, or may move and find that the leased article is no longer suited to her needs. It is then that she discovers that she cannot just stop payments and return the article. In the majority of cases the lease terms are quite fair—it is simply that the terms were never properly explained to the lessee. But in some cases, the terms that apply on early termination can be quite harsh.

Some provincial consumer protection legislation (including that of Ontario, British Columbia, Alberta, and Manitoba) specifically addresses the harshness of consumer leasing contracts through the following requirements and limitations:

- a written disclosure statement showing the itemized costs of the lease, including the financed amount, interest rates and calculations, and implicit financing charges

- caps on termination penalties equal to three months of average payments (British Columbia and Alberta cap this amount if the goods have been returned)

- disclosure and restrictions on form and content of advertising (not in the B.C. statute)

QUESTIONS TO CONSIDER

1. Does a disclosure requirement provide sufficient protection? Should there be a set of statutory implied terms to protect consumers, as in some provincial Sale of Goods Acts?

2. Does capping the termination penalties unfairly penalize lessors?

3. Why is leasing less popular with the auto industry since the 2008 economic crisis?

BAILMENT

Definition

bailment
a transfer of possession of personal property without a transfer of ownership

bailor
owner or transferor of the goods

bailee
party accepting possession of goods from a bailor

A **bailment** is a transfer of possession of personal property without a transfer of ownership, usually on the understanding that the party receiving the property will return it at a later time or dispose of it as directed. The transferor of the property, usually its owner, is called the **bailor** and the party that receives the custody of it, the **bailee**.

Nature of Bailment

The nature of bailment can be illustrated by comparing it to other common transactions or relationships to which it bears some similarities, in particular sale, trust, debt, and licence:

- **sale** A sale transfers ownership, although (as Chapter 16 has shown) it need not involve a change in possession. By contrast, a bailment does not alter ownership but does require a change in possession.
- **trust** A transfer of property to a trustee for the benefit of one or more persons does not create a bailment. The creation of a trust gives legal ownership to the trustee, and the beneficiary acquires an equitable interest in the subject of the trust.
- **debt** A deposit of money in a bank or trust company creates a creditor–debtor rather than a bailor–bailee relationship. By contrast, a deposit of specific items of personal property for safekeeping with a bank or trust company does create a bailment.[18]

---

18. *Royal Bank of Canada* v. *Reynolds* (1976), 66 D.L.R. (3d) 88; *Cuvelier* v. *Bank of Montreal* (2002), 212 N.S.R. (2d) 17.

■ **licence** A bailment requires a transfer of possession and a voluntary acceptance of the common law duty of safekeeping. A licence amounts to no more than a grant of permission to make use of the licensor's land on the understanding that possession of any chattel is not transferred and responsibility for guarding the chattel is not accepted.[19] For example, the owner of a parking lot normally does not accept responsibility for storage of the vehicle and grants only a licence to use the lot.[20] By contrast, where a vehicle is left at a garage for servicing, the garage owner does assume responsibility for its safekeeping.[21]

Most bailments are contractual, but a bailment can also occur without there being any contract between a bailor and bailee. The essential elements of bailment are delivery of possession without the intention to transfer title and with the intention that the property shall be returned to the bailor. These elements may exist without a contract, as when the owner of a car lends it gratuitously to a friend or neighbour. A bailment may also be *involuntary*; if a customer leaves a coat behind in a restaurant, the restaurateur becomes a bailee of the coat and cannot refuse to return it at the customer's request.

Bailments may be for the benefit of the bailor or the bailee, or for the benefit of both parties. By their nature, contractual bailments are intended to be of benefit to both parties: one party obtains the service desired and the other receives payment. Non-contractual, or **gratuitous bailments**, may be for the benefit of either party. In the examples given above, the bailment of the coat benefits the bailor, whereas the loan of a car benefits the bailee.

gratuitous bailment
a bailment where one party provides no consideration, or where there is no intention to create a contractual relationship

Sub-bailment

As we have noted, a relationship of bailment may exist without any contract between bailor and bailee. The relationship may also exist between a bailor and a **sub-bailee**, even when there has been no contract or communication between them.

sub-bailee
a person who receives a bailment of property from a bailee

CASE 17.2

Punch took her diamond ring, worth $11 000, to Savoy Jewellers in Sault Ste. Marie for repair. Savoy was unable to make the repair, so they sent it to Walker Jewellers in Toronto. Savoy sent the ring by registered mail and stated the value for insurance purposes as $100. Apparently, this was normal trade practice.

When Walker had repaired the ring, it decided to return the ring to Savoy using a delivery service operated by Canadian National (CN). Again, the value was declared as $100. The contract between Walker and CN limited CN's liability for loss or damage to the declared value of $100. The ring was never delivered to Savoy.

Punch sued Savoy, Walker, and CN. The court found that Savoy was a bailee, and both Walker and CN were sub-bailees. All three owed a duty of care to Punch, and the burden on each of them was to show it was not responsible for the loss or for inadequately insuring the ring.[22]

In *Punch* v. *Savoy Jewellers* (Case 17.2) the court held that the clause in the contract between CN and Walker, which limited CN's liability, could not be relied on by CN against either Savoy or Punch, since they were not parties to the contract. All three parties were found liable. The question of whether a sub-bailee may rely on a term of its contract with the (head) bailee against the original

---

19. A licence has been described as the grant of authority to enter upon land for an agreed purpose where such entry would otherwise be a trespass: *Heffron* v. *Imperial Parking Co. et al.* (1974), 3 O.R. (2d) 722 at 727.

20. *Bata* v. *City Parking Canada Ltd.* (1973), 2 O.R. (2d) 446. The situation is probably different where the parking lot operator parks the car and retains the keys: *Heffron* v. *Imperial Parking Co. et al., supra,* n. 19.

21. *Hertz Canada Ltd.* v. *Suburban Motors Ltd.* [2000] B.C.J. No. 830.

22. *Punch* v. *Savoy Jewellers Ltd.* (1986), 26 D.L.R. (4th) 546.

bailor, who was not a party to that contract, is not a straightforward one.[23] Suppose, for example, that Punch had agreed that Savoy's liability should be limited to $100 when it sent the ring by registered mail; why should CN and Walker not be entitled to rely on a similar limitation in their contracts? The Privy Council considered that question in *The Pioneer Container* (Case 17.3).

CASE 17.3

The plaintiffs contracted with a shipping firm, Hanjin Container Lines, to have goods shipped from the United States to Hong Kong. The contract with Hanjin contained a term that "the carrier shall be entitled to sub-contract *on any terms* the whole or any part of the handling of the goods" (italics added). Hanjin contracted with the defendants, the owners of *The Pioneer Container*, to ship the goods on the last leg of their journey, from Taiwan to Hong Kong. The goods were lost in a collision off the coast of Taiwan. The bill of lading contract between Hanjin and the defendants contained a term that the contract should be governed by Chinese law and any dispute should be determined in Taiwan.

The plaintiffs sued the defendants in Hong Kong. The defendants objected that, under the terms of the bill of lading, they could be sued only in Taiwan. The court ruled that, although there was no contract between the plaintiffs and the defendants, the plaintiffs had authorized the sub-bailment and they had effectively consented to the terms of the sub-bailment.[24]

RIGHTS AND DUTIES OF A BAILEE

Liability Under Contract and Tort

Sometimes bailed goods are lost, damaged, or destroyed while in the possession of a bailee. The question then arises whether the bailee is liable for the loss suffered. When the bailment is the result of a contract, its terms, either express or implied by trade custom, set out the duties and liabilities of the bailee for the goods in its possession. All bailees are, however, under a duty to take care of property bailed to them. The duty of care required by the law of torts applies in circumstances not covered expressly or impliedly by the bailment contract, and applies also to gratuitous bailments involving no contract at all. The required standard of care does vary, as we shall see, according to the type of bailment.

Sometimes, a contract of bailment includes a term that the bailee shall not be liable for damage to the goods while in her custody, even when the damage is caused by negligence in the course of performing the contract. The courts construe this type of exemption clause very strictly against the bailee, just as we have seen them do against the seller in a contract of sale. If the goods are damaged for any reason not related to the actual performance contemplated by the contract, the bailee is not protected by the exemption clause.[25]

CASE 17.4

An army officer took his uniform to a firm of dry cleaners to be cleaned. The cleaners gave him a receipt in which they disclaimed all liability for damage arising in the course of "necessary handling." The uniform was never returned, and when the officer sued for its value, the cleaners pleaded the exemption clause. It was established that the loss arose when the cleaning firm had sent the uniform to someone else for cleaning. The court found that the wording of the contract required personal performance by the bailee. Thus, the damage had not taken place during "necessary handling." The exemption clause did not apply, and the cleaners were held liable for the loss.[26]

23. *Contrast London Drugs Ltd.* v. *Kuehne and Nagel International Ltd.* (1992), 97 D.L.R. (4th) 261, in which the Supreme Court of Canada held that employees of a warehouse firm, sued personally for negligently damaging goods stored in the warehouse, were entitled to the protection of a clause in the storage contract limiting liability to a stated amount. See the discussion in Chapter 12 under the heading "Vicarious Performance."
24. *The Pioneer Container*, [1994] 2 A.C. 324 (P.C.).
25. *Solway* v. *Davis Moving & Storage Inc.* (2002), 62 O.R. (3d) 522.
26. *Davies* v. *Collins*, [1945] 1 All E.R. 247.

Although the law of bailment has elements of both tort and contract law, bailment is a distinct relationship governed by its own rules. For example, when goods are damaged or lost while in the possession of a bailee, it is often difficult for the bailor to ascertain exactly how the harm occurred. Since a bailee is better able to establish the facts, the law of bailment places on the bailee the burden of showing that she was not negligent. She must offer some reasonable alternative explanation for the loss. Consequently, it may be easier for a bailor to sue under the rules of bailment than under the ordinary rules of tort.

The Standard of Care

As noted above, the required standard of care varies according to the type of bailment. The standard is least exacting upon a bailee when the bailment is both gratuitous and for the benefit of the bailor, as when *A* permits *B* to leave her car in *A*'s garage. After all, the bailee is doing the bailor a favour; but even a gratuitous bailee is liable for gross negligence.

The standard of care is highest on a bailee when the bailment is gratuitous and for the benefit of the bailee, as when one borrows a friend's car for personal use. The bailor receives no valuable consideration, so it is fair that, in such circumstances, the bailee should compensate the bailor when damage to the goods results from even slight carelessness on the bailee's part. In **bailments for value**, the standard of care falls between that of gratuitous bailments for the benefit of the bailee and of those for the benefit of the bailor. (Thus, a bailee who allows a friend to leave her car in the bailee's garage is not under as high a duty of care as would a warehousing firm being paid to store the car.) Generally, a bailee for value is expected to take the same care of goods as a prudent and diligent person should take of goods belonging to those with whom she transacts business—a standard of care that is at least as high and probably higher than she might choose to apply to her own goods.

bailments for value
contractual bailment

CASE 17.5 A car rental firm left one of its cars at a garage for routine servicing. The car was locked and left overnight in an unsecured parking lot adjacent to the garage. During the night, a thief broke into the locked office where the car keys were kept (with tags on them in order to identify the car), stole the key to the rental car, and drove it away.

The rental firm claimed damages for the loss of the car. The court held that there had been no breach on the part of the garage of its duty of care. It had taken reasonable precautions to prevent loss. The loss was a result of the efforts of a "truly determined thief."[27]

CASE 17.6 Duckworth owned a classic sports car that was damaged in an accident. He took the car to Superior Autobody to have repairs done, and left a deposit of $500. The shop did not have an alarm system and did not have padlocks on the latches of the overhead doors. The

shop's practice was also to leave the keys in cars to allow easy removal. Thieves broke in and stole the car, which was never recovered. The court held that the repairers were bailees for reward and were liable for the loss since they had failed to take appropriate care of the car while it was in their charge.[28]

The standard also varies according to the type of goods bailed and the extent of the promise to look after the goods. In interpreting both express and implied promises of the bailee, the courts consider all the circumstances. If the property is very valuable and easily damaged, the standard of

27. *Hertz Canada Ltd.* v. *Suburban Motors Ltd., supra,* n. 21.
28. *Duckworth* v. *Armstrong* (1996), 29 C.C.L.T. (2d) 239.

care required will be higher: one must take greater care with expensive jewellery than with a bicycle stored in one's shed. In the words of one judge, "The substantial question must always be, whether that care has been exhibited which the special circumstances reasonably demand."[29]

Two special classes of bailee are subject to higher standards of care because they deal with the public generally. These are common carriers and hoteliers or innkeepers, whom we shall discuss later in this chapter.

Rights and Remedies

Damages and *Quantum Meruit*

In a contractual bailment, the bailee has the usual contractual remedies for breach by the bailor. Because of the character of bailment, the main concern of a bailee is to receive compensation for services rendered.

When a bailee has completely performed her part of a contract, as when a warehouse returns goods that have been stored with it, the usual remedy is an action for the contract price. Occasionally a bailee may not be able to complete performance, as when a carrier has contracted to transport goods in several instalments but the bailor delivers only part of the goods for shipment. The carrier may then sue **quantum meruit** for the value of the services it has performed and for damages compensating it for its loss of profits.

> **quantum meruit**
> an amount a supplier deserves to be paid for goods or services provided to the person requesting them (also described as the fair market value of the benefit conferred)

Lien

An important additional remedy available to a bailee is a *lien* on the bailed goods in its possession. This gives the bailee a right to retain possession of the goods until the bailor pays what is due for the services. The bailor cannot repossess the goods until he has paid the sum due. Generally, a right of lien arises only when the services have been performed and payment is already due.

ILLUSTRATION 17.1

Pliable Plastics Ltd. has very little storage space for its manufactured products. It enters into an arrangement with Stately Storage Limited whereby Pliable Plastics delivers its products for storage on a daily charge basis, and when they are sold, picks them up again for delivery to the buyer. Storage charges are billed and become payable every three months.

Stately Storage has no lien upon the goods stored with it until the end of the three-month period and until it has billed Pliable Plastics. If, after two-and-one-half months have passed, Pliable Plastics sells a portion of the stored goods, Stately Storage must surrender the goods on demand to Pliable Plastics or to a buyer who presents proper documents. When three months have expired and Stately Storage bills Pliable Plastics, Stately Storage has a lien for all the accrued storage charges upon the goods remaining in the warehouse at that time.

In our discussion of the rights of an unpaid seller in Chapter 16, we saw that a lien is a possessory remedy: an unpaid bailee loses her lien on the bailed goods as soon as the bailor obtains possession of them without deceit or fraud.

A right of lien under common law rules is available to bailees who perform services such as repairs or improvements to goods bailed with them, to innkeepers, to common carriers, who are

---

29. *Fitzgerald* v. *Grand Trunk Railway* (1880), 4 O.A.R. 601, per Moss, C.J.A., at 624. For a recent example, see *Solway* v. *Davis Moving & Storage Inc., supra* n. 25.

under a duty to accept goods from anyone so long as they have space for them, and also to professional people like lawyers and bankers, who have a common law right of lien over documents in their possession when they have performed services related to the documents. Various statutes have created liens in other types of bailment and, even though they may have a common law or statutory right of lien, many businesses acting as bailees expressly provide for the right as a term in their contracts with customers.

The Right of Sale

The right of lien is valuable to a bailee because the bailor usually needs to recover his goods, and to do so he must first pay off overdue charges. If, however, the bailor is unable to pay off the charges, as when he becomes insolvent, the bailee is left with goods she cannot use because she has no title to them, and yet she has the burden of storing them. The bailment contract may contain a right of sale, and various statutes give bailees who have a lien upon goods stored with them an additional right to sell the goods.

The provisions of the statutes vary in detail, but generally they require (1) that a certain time elapse after payment falls due; (2) that advance notice be given to the bailor of the bailee's intention to sell; (3) that the sale be advertised; and (4) that it be held by public auction. Until the time of sale, the owner of the goods (or other person entitled to possession) is usually entitled to recover them on payment in full of the bailee's charges.[30] The proceeds of the sale are used, first, to reimburse the bailee for her costs of holding the sale and, second, to pay the overdue charges for her services. Any surplus belongs to the bailor.

TYPES OF BAILMENT

As we have noted, there are various types of bailment, and both the common law and the statutory rules vary to some extent according to the type of bailment.

Storage and Safekeeping

A warehousing firm that accepts goods for storage and a bank that rents a safety deposit box are bailees for storage or safekeeping and are under a duty to take care of the goods stored with them.

The terms of a contract may reduce liability; for example, if the bailor specifically directs where the goods are to be placed, the liability of the warehouse keeper will be restricted to complying with those instructions.

A warehouse firm is not customarily obliged to insure goods stored with it against loss by fire unless it has expressly contracted to do so.[31] Ordinarily, a bailee must return to the bailor the exact goods stored. When, however, the goods stored are **fungible** (that is, replaceable with identical goods also in storage), the bailee's liability is discharged when she returns to the bailor goods of the exact description in the warehouse receipt. For example, when a quantity of grain of a specific grade is stored in a grain elevator in bins containing other grain of the same grade, the elevator company is bound to deliver not the exact grain that was bailed with it, but an equivalent quantity of the same grade.

fungible goods
goods that may be replaced with different but identical goods

---

30. For example, Warehouse Lien Act, R.S.B.C. 1996, c. 480, s. 7; Repair and Storage Liens Act, R.S.O. 1990, c. R-25, s. 22.

31. See *Neff* v. *St. Catharines Marina Ltd.* (1998), 155 D.L.R. (4th) 647. But the warehouse firm's failure to install alarm and sprinkler systems may amount to failure to exercise due care of the goods: *Hogarth* v. *Archibald Moving & Storage Ltd.* (1991), 57 B.C.L.R. (2d) 319.

At common law, a warehousing firm did not obtain a right of lien on goods stored with it unless it had specifically bargained for the lien. In Canada, however, we have legislation passed by all the common law provinces giving a warehouse a right of lien on goods stored with it for the amount of its charges.

The statutes contain words such as "every warehouser has a lien on goods deposited with the warehouser for storage whether deposited by the owner of the goods, or by the owner's authority or by any person entrusted with the possession of the goods by the owner or by the owner's authority."[32] The statutes further provide that "a warehouser may sell by public auction, in the manner provided in this section, any goods on which the warehouser has a lien for charges which have become due."[33] The statutes set out the details of the notice that must be given and the way in which the sale is to be advertised and held. The aim is to give adequate protection to the bailor or owner while giving the bailee a reasonably prompt method of obtaining payment.

Repairs and Work on a Chattel

Bailment is often a normal consequence of contracts made for the maintenance of, or repairs to, various articles, as when a truck is delivered to a garage for repair, or when an electronics firm receives business machines for servicing. A repairer who works on these articles on its own premises is a bailee for value. In accepting the work, the repairer undertakes to do it in a competent manner employing the skill it professes to have and to have it done by the time it promises. The bailee is also under a duty to take care of the article while it is in her possession, in the same way as is a warehousing company.[34] Failure to do these things is a breach of contract on its part, and, depending on the circumstances, a breach may entitle the bailor to not pay for work already done or to sue for damages. The bailor is also entitled to the return of the chattel.

As noted earlier, the common law gives a repairer a lien for the value of the work done upon goods left with him. The common law right does not extend to the right to sell the goods, but some of the provinces give an additional statutory right to the repairer to sell the goods when the repair charges are three months overdue.[35]

Transportation

The law identifies three types of carriers. A *gratuitous* carrier is anyone who agrees to move goods from one place to another without reward. A *private* carrier is a business that undertakes on occasion to carry goods for reward, but reserves the right to select its customers and restrict the type of goods it is willing to carry. A **common carrier** is a business that holds itself out to the public as a transporter of goods (or passengers) for reward. The public nature of a common carrier is that it does not discriminate among those who request its services, nor does it reserve the right to refuse an offer of goods for shipment when it has the means of shipping them. However, it may be a common carrier on the terms that its services are restricted to a certain area and to those kinds of goods that are suitable for carriage by its equipment. Most railway and steamship companies are common carriers, as are some trucking companies and even gas and oil pipeline companies. Airlines may repudiate the status of a common carrier by reserving the right to refuse goods. A proprietor of an amusement ride is not a common carrier because the ride's purpose is not to *transport* but rather to

common carrier
a business that holds itself out to the public as a transporter of goods for reward

---

32. Warehouse Lien Act, R.S.B.C. 1996, c. 480, s. 2; Warehousemen's Lien Act, R.S.N.S. 1989, c. 499, s. 3. In Ontario, the former Warehousemen's Lien Act has been repealed and replaced by the Repair and Storage Liens Act, R.S.O. 1990, c. R-25. Section 4(1) gives a similar lien to a "storer" of goods.

33. R.S.B.C. 1996, c. 480, s. 4; R.S.N.S. 1989, c. 499, s. 5. In Ontario, a storer has a similar right: Repair and Storage Liens Act, R.S.O. 1990, c. R-25, s. 4(7).

34. *Letourneau* v. *Otto Mobiles Edmonton* (1984) Ltd., [2002] A.J. No. 825.

35. See, for example: Repairers' Lien Act, R.S.B.C. 1996, c. 404, s. 2; Repair and Storage Liens Act, R.S.O. 1990, c. R-25, s. 3(3) (60 days overdue).

thrill.[36] Alternatively, the operator of an escalator may be a common carrier when it moves passengers between destinations.[37]

A carrier's liability for damage to goods in the course of transit depends upon the type of carrier it is. All carriers are bailees and always have *some* responsibility for the goods under their control. Even a gratuitous bailee must exercise at least the diligence and care to be expected of a reasonable person in handling his or her own property. The duty of care required of a private carrier is greater. It owes a degree of care commensurate with the skill reasonably expected of a competent firm in its line of business. The liability of a common carrier is still greater, although it may take advantage of certain recognized defences.

A common carrier undertakes to indemnify the shipper (the bailor) against loss whether the loss occurs through the carrier's fault or not. The carrier is, therefore, an insurer as well as a bailee. The historical reason for this special liability was to prevent the practice, once frequent in England, of collusion between carriers and highwaymen: the highwayman would "rob" the carrier of the shipper's goods, and the carrier would plead that it was not its fault that the goods were taken. Although this reason seems amusing when applied to the modern railroad, steamship, and trucking companies, there is good sense in the rule itself: its practical effect is to relieve the shipper of the burden of producing evidence that it was the common carrier's lack of care that caused the loss or damage. In most circumstances, it would be impossible for the carrier to gather this evidence. The shipper need only prove (1) that the carrier received the goods in good condition and (2) that the carrier delivered them in bad condition or failed to deliver them at all. The burden is then on the carrier to establish that the cause of the loss was within one of the recognized defences available to common carriers. These defences are

- an act of God;
- inherent vice in the goods; and
- default by the shipper.

It is not enough for a common carrier to show that it was not negligent—it has only those three defences. An "act of God," as we saw in Chapter 13, refers to a natural catastrophe; fire is not an act of God unless caused by lightning. Even when the cause of the loss is a natural catastrophe, the carrier may still be liable if it has negligently contributed to the loss, for example, by putting to sea during a severe storm. A common carrier may also avoid liability if it can show that the goods had an **inherent vice** at the time of shipment; for example, the goods may have been in a combustible condition or may have had latent defects that made them more susceptible to breakage than is typical of goods of their category.

inherent vice
a latent defect or dangerous condition of goods

A common carrier can offer a third defence: that the shipper has been guilty of a breach of duty or is in some way at fault. A contract for the transportation of goods includes an implied promise on the part of the shipper that the goods are safe to carry. The shipper's breach of this duty releases the carrier from its part of the bargain and, if the goods cause damage to the carrier's equipment, for instance by exploding, the carrier may successfully sue for damages.

Unless otherwise agreed, a common carrier is liable for the full value of goods lost or destroyed. However, the carrier may, and frequently does, limit the amount of its liability when the shipper does not declare the value of the goods. Where the shipper declares less than the full value of the goods to the carrier, in order to pay a lower freight charge than it would have paid had it declared their true value, the carrier is not released from its duty, but its liability is limited to the declared value.

Contractual terms limiting the liability of carriers who operate interprovincial or international routes are enforceable only if approved by the Canadian Transport Commissioners. As a result there is some public control over the extent to which common carriers may contract themselves out of their special liability.

---

36. *Mallais* v. *D.A. Campbell Amusements Ltd.* (2007), 84 O.R. (3d) 687 (C.A.).

37. *Kauffman* v. *Toronto Transit Commission*, [1960] S.C.R. 251.

INTERNATIONAL ISSUE

International Transport of Goods

The global marketplace has created an explosion in international transportation of goods. Often multiple carriers move the goods across borders and over roads, rail, and water. Sometimes a "multimodal transport operator" coordinates the movement of the goods from one carrier to the next. Goods may be in sealed containers, unavailable for inspection by any of the carriers.

If the goods arrive damaged, it is very difficult to determine when (or in which carrier's possession) the damage occurred and what jurisdiction's rules or laws should be applied in the circumstances.

The global community has been trying to unify the liability rules for international carriage but with little success. The 1980 United Nations Convention on International Multimodal Transport of Goods failed to attract support and never came into force. The United Nations Conference on Trade and Development (UNCTAD) produced rules in 1992 but their effectiveness depends on the private sector incorporating the terms into their agreements. In 2002, the United Nations again embarked on a new effort which may or may not succeed.

QUESTION TO CONSIDER

1. How should liability be assigned when the point of damage cannot be established and multiple carriers are involved?

Sources: United Nations Commission on International Trade Law (UNCITRAL) website, www.uncitral.org; UNCTAD website, www.unctad.org; M. Faghfouri, "The International Regulation of Liability for Multimodal Transport – In Search of Uniformity" (2006), 5(1) *WMU Journal of Maritime Affairs* 95–114.

Innkeepers

innkeeper
a person or firm that maintains an establishment offering lodging to any member of the public

At common law, the word "**innkeeper**" refers to a person or firm that maintains an establishment offering lodging to any member of the public. An inn, or hotel, differs from a boarding-house, whose owner may pick and choose whom he or she is willing to accommodate, and also from a restaurant, which does not offer lodging to guests. Some provincial statutes, however, have broadened the definition considerably.

All businesses offering accommodation to the public are under a duty to take reasonable care of the belongings of their guests and patrons. Like warehousing firms, they are liable for damage or loss caused by their negligence or the negligence of their employees. Under the common law, however, innkeepers are also liable for the *loss or theft* of their guests' goods. The historical reason is similar to that for the liability of a common carrier—to prevent collusion between the innkeeper and thieves. There is, however, an important difference between goods bailed to a common carrier and goods left in the room of a hotel guest: the bailor of goods to a common carrier gives them over completely to the care of the carrier, whereas the hotel guest shares the responsibility with the hotel, since he or she has control over the goods when occupying the room. Accordingly, a hotel may avoid liability if it can show that the disappearance was due to the carelessness of the guest. And a hotel is liable for damage to the goods of its guests—as distinct from its liability for their disappearance through loss or theft—only if the damage was caused by the negligence of the hotel's employees.

The strict liability of an innkeeper at common law has been modified by legislation in most provinces. Usually, the innkeeper is liable only where the goods have been stolen, lost, or injured through the wilful act, default, or neglect of the innkeeper or an employee, or where the goods have been deposited expressly for safe custody with the innkeeper.[38] The Innkeepers Acts of the various provinces usually also give the right to sell the goods of guests by public auction if their bills remain unpaid for a specified period.[39]

Pledge or Pawn

While these two terms have the same legal significance, a pawn refers only to transactions with a pawnbroker. A **pledge** or **pawn** is a bailment of personal property as security for repayment of a loan. The borrower is the *pledgor* and the creditor the *pledgee*. The subject matter of a pledge may be goods left with a **pawnbroker**, for example, or share certificates left with a bank.

A pledgee is a bailee for value and must exercise such care as is reasonable in the ordinary and proper course of its business. A pledgee obtains a lien on the personal property pledged with it, and the pledgor cannot recover possession of the goods until it repays the debt for which they are security. In addition, by pledging the goods, the pledgor gives authority to the pledgee to sell the pledged goods upon default and to reimburse itself out of the proceeds of the sale for any costs incurred as a result of the default and for the amount of the unpaid loan. The surplus, if any, belongs to the borrower.[40]

pledge or pawn
a bailment of personal property as security for repayment of a loan where possession passes to the bailee

pawnbroker
a business that loans money on the security of pawned goods

CHECKLIST   Types of Bailment

The most common types of bailment are

■ storage and safekeeping

■ repairing

■ transportation

■ innkeeping

■ pledge or pawn

QUESTIONS FOR REVIEW

1. What is the principal difference between an operating lease and a purchase lease?

2. Distinguish between a security lease and a finance lease.

3. What warranties will normally be implied in a chattel lease?

4. What are the main perceived advantages of leasing capital assets as opposed to borrowing in order to purchase them?

5. Why would a business enter into a sale-and-leaseback transaction?

6. If a lessee defaults in paying the rent, is the lessor entitled to retake possession of the leased property as well as to sue for the rent owing?

---

38. See, for example: Hotel Keepers Act, R.S.B.C. 1996, c. 206, s. 3; Tourist Accommodation Act, S.N.S. 1994–95, c. 9, s. 11; Tourism Industry Act, R.S.P.E.I. 1988, c. T-3.3, s. 9. In some provinces, strict liability is retained but only up to a fixed amount: Innkeepers Act, R.S.N. 1990, c. I-7, s. 3 ($200); Innkeepers Act, R.S.O. 1990, c. I-7, s. 4 ($40).

39. R.S.B.C. 1996, c. 206, s. 2; R.S.O. 1990, c. I-7, s. 2; S.N.S. 1994–5, c. 9, s. 10; R.S.P.E.I. 1988, c. T-3.3, s. 8.

40. Some provincial statutes provide that ownership passes to a pawnbroker after a specified period; see, for example, Pawnbrokers Act, R.S.O. 1990, c. P. 6, ss. 20–2.

7. Give an example of (a) a non-contractual bailment and (b) an involuntary bailment.

8. Distinguish between a bailment and a licence. In what circumstances is the distinction especially important?

9. What factors determine the standard of care to be expected of a bailee?

10. What is a "sub-bailment"?

11. In what circumstances may a bailee claim a lien on bailed goods?

12. What does it mean that goods are "fungible"? How does that affect a bailee's liability?

13. Who normally bears the loss if goods left in a warehouse are stolen or destroyed?

14. Distinguish between a common carrier and a private carrier.

15. What does it mean to say that a common carrier "is an insurer as well as a bailee"?

16. What are the principal defences available to a common carrier when goods in its possession are damaged or lost?

17. Is a hotelkeeper liable if a guest has property stolen from his or her room?

18. What is meant by a "pledge"?

CASES AND PROBLEMS

1. Intrepid Exploration Inc. is a comparatively small corporation engaged in exploring and drilling for oil in shallow coastal waters, usually as a subcontractor for major companies. Intrepid's owners recently entered into a contract with Globres Inc., one of the major companies, to provide specialized drilling services in a project off the New Brunswick coast. They anticipated making a substantial profit on the contract.

Intrepid found that, to perform the contract, it would need a high-pressure drilling unit of a particular type that it did not own. Normally such units are custom-made, cost about $500 000, and take about six months to construct. Fortunately, Intrepid was able to locate such a unit, which was owned by Banditoil, a rather larger corporation in the same line of business as Intrepid. The unit was not in use at the time and was unlikely to be needed by Banditoil for at least 18 months.

Intrepid negotiated a contract with Banditoil, under which it would lease the drilling unit for 12 months, with an option to extend the lease for a further 6 months, at a monthly rental of $15 000. Shortly thereafter, and before Intrepid took delivery of the drilling unit, Globres informed Intrepid that it was unwilling to have Intrepid do the work contracted for, and was awarding the contract to another corporation, Cutprice Inc. Globres claimed to be entitled to do so under a clause in the contract, a claim that Intrepid contested. Intrepid immediately informed Banditoil that it no longer needed the drilling unit. Banditoil acknowledged receiving the information and replied that it was considering what action, if any, to take.

Intrepid has now received a demand from Banditoil for payment in full of the sum of $180 000 under the lease contract. Intrepid has also learned that Cutprice has agreed to rent the same drilling unit.

What is the extent of Intrepid's liability towards Banditoil?

2. Thames Pharmacies Ltd. entered into a contract with Koenig & Nebel Inc. (K&N) to have a large three-tonne transformer stored in the K&N warehouse for a few weeks, until the transformer could be installed in Thames's own new premises, which were still under construction. A written contract was drawn up, which contained the following provision:

The warehouse's liability on any one package is limited to $40 unless the holder has declared in writing a valuation in excess of $40 and paid the additional charge specified to cover warehouse liability.

Thames chose not to declare a higher value and pay the extra charge, relying instead on its own insurance.

When the time came to deliver the transformer to Thames's new premises, two employees of K&N, Kupfer and Vanwijk, were instructed to load the transformer on to a truck. They attempted to do so using two forklift trucks, when safe practice would have required the transformer to be lifted in chains from above and lowered on to the truck. The transformer toppled over, causing extensive damage.

Thames then discovered that its own insurance did not cover the damage and brought an action against K&N, and against Kupfer and Vanwijk personally, alleging breach of their duty of care and claiming damages of $34 000.

Is Thames entitled to succeed?

3. Firth contracted with Dave the Mover Inc. to have her furniture and household effects moved from her house, stored for a week (until she moved into her new home), and then delivered to the new home. Firth told Dave's manager that she was particularly concerned about security, since the effects included some rare and valuable antiques and artifacts. She was told there was nothing to worry about. The articles would remain in the trailer until delivery at her new home, and the trailer would be locked at all times and parked in their yard, which was securely fenced, locked at night, and kept under regular supervision.

The trailer was kept in the yard as promised for several days, but one night, after a heavy snowfall, it was moved and parked, unattended, on a public street while the yard was being snowplowed. While it was parked on the street it was stolen.

Firth claimed damages for the full value of the goods lost. Dave's admitted liability, but pointed out that the bill of lading limited damages to $0.60 per pound weight of the goods, which came to just over $7000, a small fraction of their true value.

Firth admitted she was aware of the limitation when she entered into the contract, but claimed she only agreed to it because of the assurance that the trailer would be properly supervised at all times.

Should Dave's be allowed to rely on the limitation clause?

4. Nerdley is a skilled interior designer who decided to go freelance after years of being employed by a large construction company. Although accustomed to using a computer in her work, she understands very little about their characteristics and specifications, having always relied in the past on other specialist employees of the company for advice and assistance.

Nerdley realized that she would need to acquire her own computer equipment. She was told by a friend that Millennium Electronics had "the best prices in town" and a competent sales staff. She visited their local store, briefly explained what she perceived to be her needs to Boffin, a salesperson, and eventually decided to acquire two computers, a printer, and various other items of equipment. Boffin assured her that they were "state of the art" and should be able to do everything she needed them to do.

The total price came to around $11 000. Nerdley then asked about credit and was told that Millennium recommended a leasing agreement with a finance company that it normally used in such cases. Under the agreement, Millennium sold the equipment to the finance company for $10 500, and Nerdley entered into a lease agreement with the finance company under which she agreed to make 36 monthly payments of $400, with an option at the end of the three-year period to buy the equipment for a further $400. The lease was on a standard printed form, and included the following clause:

> The lessee acknowledges that the equipment hereby leased was personally selected by the lessee for business purposes and purchased by the lessor at the lessee's request from a supplier designated by the lessee. The lessee takes full responsibility for such selection and waives all defences predicated on the failure of the said equipment to perform the function for which it was designed or selected and further acknowledges that such failure shall not be deemed to be in breach of this lease.

Nerdley very soon discovered that the computer did not have sufficient memory to operate some of the sophisticated design programs that she used, and that the printer did not have sufficiently high definition to reproduce her designs adequately.

When she attempted to take the equipment back to Millennium she was told that it was nothing to do with them and she should take it up with the finance company. Advise her.

5. 4D Enterprises Ltd. hired Jung to design and develop a website for its business. According to the agreement, Jung was to install the servers and all necessary software and to test the system fully. To enable him to do so, 4D delivered to him the two computers that would be used.

During the following three weeks, 4D phoned Jung several times to ask how the work was going. Each time, Jung assured them that it was "coming along fine" and would be ready soon. 4D started to become anxious, as they had expected the work to be done within two or three days. They made some enquiries and heard a few rather negative reports about Jung's work. As a result, they decided to find someone else to do the work and asked Jung to return their computers. Jung refused, claiming that he had done a substantial amount of work on the project, and demanded payment in full of the agreed amount.

Is Jung entitled to keep the computers until he has been paid?

ADDITIONAL RESOURCES FOR CHAPTER 17 ON THE COMPANION WEBSITE *(www.pearsoned.ca/smyth)*

In addition to self-test multiple-choice, true–false, and short essay questions (all with immediate feedback), application exercises, and links to useful web destinations, the Companion Website provides the following resources for Chapter 17:

- **British Columbia:** Hotel Keepers; Lien; Repairers' Lien; Warehouse Lien
- **Alberta:** Common Carriers; Innkeepers' Liability; Mechanics' Liens; Possessory Liens; Warehouse Liens
- **Manitoba/Saskatchewan:** Common Carriers; Innkeepers; Warehouse Storage
- **Ontario:** Common Carriers; Consumer Protection Act 2002; Innkeepers' Liability; Pawnbrokers; Repair and Storage Liens; Warehousing

Insurance and Guarantee

This chapter deals with two types of contract whose aim is to distribute risk. Insurance enables a business to shift the risk of loss—from damage to its property or from being held liable for damage to someone else's person or property—to an insurance company. In return the business pays for that protection. A contract of guarantee allows a lender or creditor to reduce the risk of non-payment by obtaining a promise from a third person to pay the debt if the debtor defaults.

In this chapter we examine such questions as:

■ What is the nature of the contract of insurance?

■ What role does insurance play in risk management?

■ What types of insurance protect against liability or loss in the operation of a business?

■ What are the special characteristics of insurance contracts?

■ What is the legal nature of a guarantee?

■ How may a guarantee be discharged?

■ What are the rights and liabilities of a guarantor?

INSURANCE AND THE MANAGEMENT OF LEGAL RISK

Insurance is a method of purchasing protection against a possible loss. The insured agrees with an insurance company that, in return for the payment of a premium or regular premiums, the company will compensate the insured if a specified loss occurs. The insurance company calculates the amount of payment required based on experience with the type of risk in question. In Chapter 3, we saw that a business faces two main types of "legal" risk:

- the risk that its property or assets may be destroyed or damaged as a result of an accident or due to the fault of some other person, and
- the risk that it may be held liable for some loss or injury caused to another person.

In the first type of risk there may be no one to hold responsible, as in the case of storm damage, for example. Or, where the loss was caused by another person, it may be impossible to trace that person, or he may have insufficient funds to pay compensation. Even when it is possible to recover, legal proceedings are likely to be time-consuming and expensive. With this type of risk, it is possible to estimate the extent of the possible loss—one cannot lose more than the total value of all one's assets.

The second type of risk is more open-ended. A very large business may be able to make an estimate of its potential liability: if one sells 100 000 cars of a particular model, it may be possible to calculate, based on experience, that a given number of defects will pass the inspection system and, of those, a certain percentage will cause serious injury. For a small business, however, such a calculation will be impossible—a shopper may trip on an uneven floor tile and suffer a crippling injury, resulting in a damage award of hundreds of thousands of dollars. (By contrast, an insurance company can make the calculation, based on the experience of thousands of similar businesses.)

What steps can a business take to guard against these risks, apart from the obvious one of taking all possible care to minimize the chances of their occurring? One possibility is to set aside a reserve or contingency fund to meet future expenses—in effect, to act as one's own insurer. That course, however, is not feasible for most businesses. The unfortunate event may occur before it has been possible to build up a sufficient reserve, and in any case, the business cannot afford to tie up so much capital to cover a risk that may never materialize. The more realistic alternative is to take out insurance coverage.

INSURANCE TERMINOLOGY

insurance policy
the written evidence of the terms of a contract of insurance

premium
the price paid by the insured to purchase insurance coverage

An **insurance policy** is a document that provides written evidence of the terms of an insurance contract. The insurance company providing the protection is called the *insurer*; the party contracting for the insurance protection is the *insured*.[1] The **premium** is the price paid by the insured for the insurance coverage specified in the policy. The premium may be paid in a single sum, but more often it is paid yearly or at some other shorter interval throughout the term of the insurance.

The four basic aspects of an insurance contract are:

- the nature of the risk covered
- the amount for which it is insured
- the duration of the protection
- the amount of the premium

1. In life insurance we must distinguish between the insured and the life insured when the subject of the insurance is the life of someone other than the party contracting for insurance.

The terms of a policy may require the insurer to pay the insurance money, in the event of a claim, either to the insured, to the insured's estate, or to some other person designated as **beneficiary**. When an insured requires supplementary coverage, that is, wider protection than is available under the insurer's standard form policy, additional clauses are incorporated in the contract by attaching them to the policy in a **rider**. When the parties agree to a change in the terms of an existing insurance contract, they may do so without rewriting the entire policy by attaching a separate **endorsement** to the policy.

An **insurance agent** is an employee or agent of the insurance company whose function is to arrange contracts with persons seeking insurance protection for themselves. By contrast, an **insurance broker** conducts an independent business and generally acts for the insured rather than for the insurer.[2] A broker is a specialist in insurance problems who advises on the coverage required and arranges insurance with the companies best suited to provide it. However, the distinction between an agent and a broker is not always a clear one. In practice, an insurance agent often gives advice to the insured about the appropriate coverage, and it is possible in some cases for an agent, or a broker, to be considered to be acting as agent for both the insurer and the insured and to owe a duty to both.[3]

beneficiary
the person entitled to receive insurance monies

rider
additional provisions attached to a standard policy of insurance

endorsement
written evidence of a change in the terms of a policy

insurance agent
an agent or employee of an insurance company

insurance broker
an independent business that arranges insurance coverage for its clients

---

CASE 18.1

Miller was injured in a motor vehicle accident caused by the negligence of a person who was underinsured. Miller had purchased an insurance policy from an agent of the Guardian company. He had requested full coverage, but the agent did not suggest that the policy should contain an "underinsured motorist endorsement," which was available at a modest premium. As a result, Miller was not fully covered for the accident that occurred.

The court held that the agent had a duty to advise the insured on suitable coverage, and since the agent was acting as the agent of the insurance company, the company was also liable.[4]

An **insurance adjuster** is an expert in the appraisal of property losses and provides these services to insurance companies for a fee. When a claim has been made, the adjuster gives an opinion to the insurer about whether the loss is covered by the insurance contract and, if so, what the amount of the loss is.

Insurance falls into two main classes: **personal insurance** and **property insurance**. Personal insurance, as the name implies, covers risk to life and health, and includes life insurance, medical insurance, accident and disability insurance, and workers' compensation. All other types of insurance are property insurance. Life insurance is unique in that the risk insured against is certain to materialize eventually, though in the case of **term insurance**, it may not occur during the period covered by the policy.

insurance adjuster
a person who appraises property losses

personal insurance
insurance against death, injury, or ill health of an individual

property insurance
insurance against damage to property

term insurance
personal insurance that provides coverage for a limited period only

REGULATION OF INSURANCE BUSINESS

Each province has one or more statutes regulating the practice of insurance business within its borders. The main purpose of these statutes is to protect the public by requiring responsible operation on the part of insurance companies and others in the business. Among other matters, the statutes authorize the appointment of a superintendent of insurance to oversee the operations and financial responsibility of licensed insurers within the province, describe the terms that must be included in insurance policies,

---

2. See *Adams Eden Furniture Ltd.* v. *Kansa General Insurance Co.* (1996), 141 D.L.R. (4th) 288.

3. See the discussion of an agent's duty in Chapter 19.

4. *Miller* v. *Guardian Insurance Co. of Canada* (1997), 149 D.L.R. (4th) 375. Contrast *Planidin* v. *Insurance Corporation of British Columbia* (2004), 245 D.L.R. (4th) 511, where it was held that the insurer owes no duty to provide advice on the extent of the coverage of a policy.

and define the extent to which an insurer may limit its liability. In addition to these provincial statutes, the federal Insurance Companies Act[5] provides for compulsory registration of federal and foreign insurance companies wishing to carry on insurance business in Canada and for voluntary registration of provincial insurance companies. Its aim is to ensure financial stability in the insurance industry by providing a system of inspection and by requiring statements and returns from these companies.

TYPES OF INSURANCE

Insurance Against Loss or Damage

Just as risk can be divided into two categories, so can business insurance: one can insure against loss or damage to one's own property or assets, and one can insure against liability to others. Until quite recently, it was usual to insure against different risks in separate insurance policies: some types of insurance—for example, fire insurance and marine insurance—go back several centuries. Typically, a business will insure against:

- damage to buildings and contents (inventory, fixtures, and equipment) due to fire or storm
- loss due to theft
- loss of, or damage to, vehicles used in the business

In addition, it may take out insurance against:

- loss of profit due to interruption of business activities
- bad debt losses (credit insurance)
- losses caused by theft or fraud of employees (fidelity insurance)
- loss due to injury to, or death of, important personnel (key-person insurance)

The precise extent of the coverage will vary from policy to policy, and from one insurance company to another. Consequently, it is of crucial importance to determine precisely what types of losses are covered and in what circumstances. One should always read the "small print." For example, does fire insurance also cover relocation expenses or loss of profit while the business is unable to operate? Does it include damage to a client's property that happens to be on the premises at the time of the fire? Does insurance against storm damage include damage by flooding? In one recent case it was held that insurance against accidental damage to the insured's photocopying machines did not cover damage due to faulty manufacture.[6]

In most instances, the insurer is liable either for the cost of repairing damaged property or for the value of the destroyed property. Value takes into account the condition of the property immediately before destruction. One may purchase insurance for full replacement value, but this higher protection is more expensive. In any event, it is sensible to review the replacement value from time to time in order to make sure that protection is adequate.

deductible clause
a clause requiring the insured to bear the loss up to a stated amount

An insurance contract frequently contains a **deductible clause**, under which the insured is required to pay the first $500 (or some higher amount) in respect of each claim. A deductible feature gives the insured a greater incentive to take care of the insured property and, by eliminating small claims, makes the insurance cheaper.

Insurance Against Liability

As we saw in Chapters 3 and 4, businesses may be held liable in various ways. These include liability for their own acts, or the acts of their employees, that cause damage to their customers, distributors, suppliers, and the general public. This type of insurance (often referred to as public liability insurance)

5. S.C. 1991, c. 47.
6. *Celestica Inc. v. ACE INA Insurance* (2003), 229 D.L.R. (4th) 392.

obligates the insurer to defend the insured against lawsuits and pay the amount of any judgment, up to the policy limit.

Consequently, businesses will normally insure against

- liability for negligent acts and omissions
- liability for defective products
- liability for the dangerous state of their premises
- liability for breach of their professional duty of care[7]

Additionally, provincial legislation makes it compulsory for operators of motor vehicles to be insured against third-party liability, and liability to employees is covered under statutory workers' compensation schemes (see Chapter 20).

Comprehensive Insurance

Rather than issue a variety of policies, each providing protection against specific risks, the modern tendency has increasingly been to issue *comprehensive* general insurance, covering most types of damage to the insured's property as well as liability to others. Because of its broader scope, such insurance tends to be expensive, though it may well turn out to be cheaper than purchasing a series of separate policies insuring against specific risks. The great advantage to the insured lies in the comprehensiveness of the coverage—unexpected risks are insured against rather than falling between the cracks of two or more separate policies.

CASE 18.2

Goderich had insured grain stored in their elevator under an "all risks" insurance policy, which covered "all risk of direct physical loss or damage . . . except as excluded." The policy excluded "loss or damage caused directly or indirectly by . . . dryness of atmosphere, changes of temperature, heating, shrinkage, evaporation. . . . " Some batches of grain were found to contain an excessive quantity of damaged grain, known as "heated grain," which was of less value. The cause of the heated grain could not be established, but there was no evidence of external causes. Goderich's claim under the insurance policy was contested by the insurance company. The court held that the loss was covered by an "all risk" policy, and the insurance company had not shown that the cause was specifically within the exclusion.[8]

INTERNATIONAL ISSUE

Medical Malpractice Insurance

Many professions require their members to insure against liability for malpractice, or breach of their duty of care. Those professionals who are not so required usually find it advisable to do so. Unfortunately, the cost of malpractice insurance, or professional indemnity insurance, has been escalating rapidly—and that cost must be passed on to the client.

In the United States, some doctors now pay $100 000 a year or more in premiums. Premiums are assessed based on the physician's specialty and location. In Florida, rates increased by 60 percent between 2000 and 2004, and an obstetrician's premium in Dade County (Florida) was $201 376 in

continued

---

7. Liability insurance is compulsory for most professions.
8. *Goderich Elevators Ltd.* v. *Royal Insurance Co.* (1999), 169 D.L.R. (4th) 763. The court applied one of the "general principles of interpretation of insurance policies" set out by McLachlin, J. in *Reid Crowther & Partners Ltd.* v. *Simcoe & Erie General Insurance Co.* (1993), 99 D.L.R. (4th) 741 (S.C.C.), namely, that "coverage provisions should be construed broadly and exclusion provisions narrowly."

2003.[9] By contrast, an obstetrician's premium in Minnesota was only $17 431. There is concern that this difference in rates will have an impact on the availability of care and specialist expertise in certain areas. Some states have introduced tort reform including damage award caps and limits on plaintiffs' lawyer fees.

Things are not quite so bad in Canada—an Ontario obstetrician's premium was $78 120 in 2005.[10] In 2004, the Canadian Health Research Foundation reported that the number of medical malpractice lawsuits was steadily declining: such lawsuits peaked in 1996 but had declined by 23 percent by 2004. As in the United States, however, the size of the average settlement is increasing.[11] Other professions face similar problems: accountants, in particular, have been hit with astronomical damages awards that increase their insurance costs.

QUESTIONS TO CONSIDER

1. Which of the following do you consider to be most responsible for the differences between the Canadian and American malpractice insurance situations? Explain your choice.
   (a) high legal fees
   (b) excessive damages awards
   (c) lack of competition in the insurance industry

2. Can you suggest other ways of tackling the problem of skyrocketing malpractice insurance premiums?

SPECIAL ASPECTS OF THE CONTRACT OF INSURANCE

Legality of Object—Wrongful Act of the Insured

It is a general principle of insurance law that the courts will not enforce a contract of insurance when the claim arises out of a criminal or *deliberate* wrongful act of the insured.[12] Two reasons are commonly given for this rule: it would be contrary to public policy to allow the insured to profit from his own crime, and it would be contrary to the purpose of insurance to allow the insured to recover compensation for a loss that he had deliberately caused himself. Thus, a beneficiary under a life insurance policy who murders the person whose life is insured is not entitled to claim,[13] and an arsonist is not entitled to recover under a policy of fire insurance.[14] However, the courts have been careful to restrict the scope of the public policy exception, and the fact that the loss occurred as a consequence of the insured's deliberate wrongful act will not prevent recovery if that consequence was not intended.[15]

---

9. U.S. General Accounting Office, "Medical Malpractice, Excerpts from Medical Malpractice and Access to Health Care (GAO-03-836)," *Almanac of Policy Issues*, August 2003, www.policyalmanac.org.
10. Canadian Medical Protection Association, *2005 Fee Schedule*, www.cmpa-acpm.ca.
11. "Myth: Medical Malpractice Lawsuits Plague Canada," MythBusters, *Canadian Health Service Research Foundation*, March 2006, www.chsrf.ca.
12. *Beresford* v. *Royal Insurance Co.*, [1938] A.C. 586.
13. *Demeter* v. *Dominion Life Assurance Co.* (1982), 132 D.L.R. (3d) 248, where the husband who was convicted of the murder of his wife was the owner and beneficiary under personal policies issued on the life of his wife. See also *Brisette Estate* v. *Westbury Life Insurance Co.*, [1992] 3 S.C.R. 87; *Lachman Estate* v. *Norwich Union Life Insurance Co.* (1998), 40 O.R. (3d) 393.
14. See *Scott* v. *Wawanesa Mutual Insurance Co.* (1989), 59 D.L.R. (4th) 660.
15. *Oldfield* v. *Transamerica Life Insurance Co. of Canada* (1998), 43 O.R. (3d) 114 Aff'd. (2002), 210 D.L.R. (4th) 1.

CASE 18.3

A dentist died as a result of a form of substance abuse, the dangers of which were obvious and were presumably known by him. The insurance company refused to pay under a policy of insurance which he had taken out on his life, claiming that his death resulted from his own intentional act. The court held that, although the act of administering the substance was deliberate, the deceased had no intention of committing suicide. His estate was consequently entitled to claim under the policy.[16]

Insurance companies tend not to rely upon the common law principle and frequently insert an express provision that coverage does not extend to damage or injury resulting from an intentional or criminal act of the insured.[17]

Insurable Interest

In Chapter 7 we distinguished an insurance contract from a wager by the fact that the insured has an insurable interest, so that the contract shifts a genuine risk of loss from the insured to the insurer. An **insurable interest** is the measure of loss that may be suffered by the insured from damage to or destruction of the thing insured, or from the death of, or injury to, the person insured. This is not always easy to determine. In one British case, the House of Lords held that a shareholder who owned most of the shares in a company had no insurable interest in its principal asset, a quantity of timber destroyed in a fire, because he was not the owner. The loss was solely that of the company itself.[18] However, in Canada, a person who owns all the shares in a corporation does have an insurable interest in its property; the Supreme Court of Canada held that an insurable interest exists where an insured can demonstrate a relation to or concern in the insured property so that damage to it will cause a loss to the insured.[19] Obviously, damage to the property of the corporation would necessarily reduce the value of his shares. Similarly, a tenant may have an insurable interest in leased premises that he uses for his business, since he may suffer financial and other loss if the premises are destroyed or damaged.[20] Although the insured need not be the owner of the insured property, he must have some form of interest in that property.[21]

When must the insurable interest exist? The answer depends upon whether the insurance is on property or on a life. When the contract is for life insurance, the person buying the insurance must either obtain the written consent of the person whose life is to be insured or have an insurable interest at the time the contract is formed, though not necessarily at the time of death of the person whose life is insured. When the contract is for property insurance, the insured must have an insurable interest at the time the contract was formed; otherwise the contract is void. And, since the purpose of insurance is to indemnify for loss suffered, the insured must still have an interest at the time the claim arises; otherwise there will be no loss to be recovered by the insured.

insurable interest
genuine risk of loss that may be suffered from damage to the thing insured

16. *Bertalan Estate* v. *American Home Assurance Co.* (2001) 196 D.L.R. (4th) 445. The Supreme Court of Canada reached a similar conclusion, on similar facts, in *American International Assurance Life Company Ltd.* v. *Martin* (2003), 223 D.L.R. (4th) 1.

17. For recent examples, see *British Columbia Insurance Corp.* v. *Kraiger* (2002), 219 D.L.R. (4th) 49 (arson); *Hodgkinson* v. *Economic Mutual Insurance Co.* (2003), 235 D.L.R. (4th) 1 (defamation).

18. *Macaura* v. *Northern Assurance Co.*, [1925] A.C. 619.

19. *Kosmopoulos* v. *Constitution Insurance Co.* (1987), 34 D.L.R. (4th) 208. The Court's reasoning suggests that any person holding a substantial proportion of a corporation's shares would have an insurable interest in its property; it is unclear whether a holder of only a small proportion would be found to have an interest.

20. *Evergreen Manufacturing Corp.* v. *Dominion of Canada General Insurance Co.* (1999), 170 D.L.R. (4th) 240.

21. See *Assaad* v. *Economic Mutual Insurance Group* (2002), 214 D.L.R. (4th) 655.

The owner of mortgaged premises insured them against damage by fire. Subsequently, the owner failed to keep up the mortgage payments and the mortgagee foreclosed. While the mortgagor was still in possession, the premises were destroyed by fire. On a claim by the mortgagor under the insurance policy, the Court held that the foreclosure had extinguished all rights and interest of the mortgagor in the property and had vested the title in the mortgagee. Therefore, the mortgagor no longer had an insurable interest in the premises.[22]

Formation of the Contract

A proposal drafted by an insurance agent is usually a mere invitation to treat, not an offer. The offer to purchase insurance coverage is made by the party seeking the insurance protection—the prospective insured—by signing an application form. What constitutes acceptance by the insurer? We need to know so that we can tell when the insurance is in force. These questions are usually answered by provincial legislation or the offer itself.

With life insurance, the applicant's offer is not accepted until the insurance company delivers the policy. It is a condition precedent to delivery of the policy that the first premium shall be paid by the insured.[23]

Making contracts for property insurance is typically less formal than for life insurance. An agent dealing in property insurance may have agency contracts with a number of insurance companies. Each contract gives the agent authority to sign and deliver policies and renewal certificates and generally to bind the company concerned; thus, a business seeking property insurance can obtain the desired protection immediately, before paying the premium or receiving a policy. The agent need only prepare a memorandum or *binder* for the agency's records as evidence of the time and nature of the request for insurance. When immediate protection is required, an insured should be satisfied that the agent has an agency contract with the proposed insurer.

Renewal

Property insurance is written for a limited period (usually for one year). Frequently, the intention is that the insurance should be renewed at the end of the period, and it is not uncommon for the insured to fail to renew it in time. What is the situation in the meantime? A common practice is for an insurance company, or its agent, to prepare a renewal policy or memorandum and send it to the insured shortly before the current policy expires. This acts as a reminder that the insurance protection is about to cease if not renewed. But unless there is evidence of an agreement between the company and the insured that they intend the delivery of a renewal policy or memorandum to create a new contract of insurance, or such an agreement can be inferred from their past dealings with one another, the act of delivering the renewal policy amounts to no more than making an offer to the insured. No contract is formed until the insured communicates acceptance, and because the offer is open at most for a reasonable time, the insured cannot wait indefinitely.

---

22. *Walton* v. *General Accident Assurance Co. of Canada* (2000), 194 D.L.R. (4th) 315.

23. See, for example: Insurance Act, R.S.B.C. 1996, c. 226, s. 38; R.S.O. 1990, c. I-8, s. 180; R.S.N.S. 1989, c. 231, s. 182. Depending upon the wording of the application form, there may be some form of temporary coverage pending issue of the policy.

CASE 18.5

The insured's auto insurance policy expired on February 5, 1989. About a month before, the insurance company sent him an offer to renew if the premium was paid before February 5, and a "pink slip" certifying that the insurance was in effect until August 5, 1989. The insured did not pay the renewal premium and was injured in an accident on February 20.

The Supreme Court of Canada held that the pink slip did not amount to a renewal of the contract. It was sent to the insured for convenience only and did not bind the company.[24]

CASE 18.6

Under a life insurance policy, a premium payment became due on July 26, 1984. The grace period expired and the company sent a "late payment offer," offering to receive late payment under certain conditions. Four months later, the company sent a letter to the insured, saying that the policy was "technically out of force" and that immediate payment of the premium was required. In February 1985 the company sent a further letter, stating that the insurance had lapsed. The letters did not come to the insured's attention until April 1985, and in July, he sent a cheque. By then, his life had become uninsurable and he died a month later.

The Supreme Court of Canada held that the July payment was too late. The company had offered to renew the policy, but that offer was open only for a reasonable time.[25]

Terms of the Contract

Chapter 5 referred to an insurance policy as an example of a standard form contract since it is prepared unilaterally in advance by one of the contracting parties (the insurer). To offset this advantage for insurers, the courts subject such contracts to a strict interpretation: they construe words most strongly against the party using them, as we noted in Chapter 11. They take the view, for example, that clauses exempting an insurer from liability in specific circumstances must be stated in clear and unambiguous terms if they are to be binding.[26]

CASE 18.7

A group of tenants brought a class action against the owner of an apartment complex, claiming that they had become ill through breathing carbon monoxide leaking from the apartment furnace. The apartment owner had a commercial liability insurance policy, but the policy contained an exclusion clause for "pollution liability." The insurance company claimed that the clause exempted them from liability.

The court held that, although carbon monoxide could be considered a pollutant, the clause was intended to exclude coverage for damages from environmental pollution. The clause should be strictly and narrowly interpreted against the insurer: it was not intended to apply to circumstances such as a leak from a faulty furnace.[27]

Disclosure

In our discussion of misrepresentation in Chapter 9, we noted that an insurer may avoid liability if it can show that the insured did not exercise the *utmost good faith* in the application for insurance. In particular, full disclosure must be made of all material facts and circumstances that are known, or should have been known, to the insured.

24. *Patterson* v. *Gallant* (1994), 120 D.L.R. (4th) 1.
25. *Saskatchewan River Bungalows Ltd.* v. *Maritime Life Assurance Co.* (1994), 115 D.L.R. (4th) 478.
26. See, for example: *British Columbia Ferry Corp.* v. *Commonwealth Insurance Co.* (1985), 40 D.L.R. (4th) 766.
27. *Zurich Insurance Co.* v. *686234 Ontario Ltd.* (2002), 222 D.L.R. (4th) 655.

A corporation took out a fidelity insurance policy to protect it against losses caused by dishonest employees. The corporation's accountant stole over $20 million over a 10-year period. The fraud should have been easily detected from the corporation's financial statements. The Court held that the insured corporation had constructive knowledge of the fraud and had a duty to disclose it. Therefore, it was not entitled to recover under the policy.[28]

The disclosure requirement has traditionally been applied strictly. For example, it has been held that an insured may be unable to collect for a claim even when the loss arose from causes unrelated to the facts that the insured should have disclosed.[29] However, some Canadian decisions have adopted a more flexible approach. For example, a statement by the insured that a night watchman would be present on the premises every night was held not to be material when the actual loss occurred in the afternoon.[30] And the insured need not disclose information of a general nature that should be well known to the insurer: an asbestos manufacturer was not required to inform its insurer that there were health risks related to working with asbestos, so long as the likelihood of exposure to asbestos was disclosed.[31]

In *Coronation Insurance Company* v. *Taku Air Transport Ltd.*,[32] the Supreme Court of Canada went even further, holding that the utmost good faith principle should not apply at all in the highly regulated field of aviation insurance. The requirement that air carriers have insurance for their passengers was primarily intended for the benefit of the public, whose protection should not depend entirely on the good faith of the carrier. Consequently, the failure of a carrier to fully disclose its past safety record did not invalidate the policy. The insurance company had a duty at least to check its own files and the public records.[33]

An insurer may insert terms in an insurance contract to extend the obligation of the insured even beyond that imposed by the requirement of utmost good faith. The application form signed by the party seeking insurance may contain a provision that the applicant warrants the accuracy—not merely the *truthfulness*—of any declarations made. If in these circumstances an applicant for life insurance replies in the negative to the question "Have you any disease?" and proves later to have had a disease of which he or she was unaware, the insurer may avoid its liability. The courts dislike this type of provision and insist on strict proof by the insurer that the question was answered inaccurately.

Insurance contracts other than for life insurance contain a statutory term that the insured shall notify the insurer promptly of any change that is material to the risk and within the control or knowledge of the insured. Such a term then gives the insurer some options. It may either cancel the insurance and return the unexpired portion of the premium, or inform the insured that the insurance will continue only on payment of an increased premium. Prompt notice by the insured in these circumstances is a condition precedent. An insurer is absolved from liability under the policy if it does not receive such notice. Insurance contracts normally also contain a term requiring the insured to notify the insurer promptly of any loss that occurs. Failure to give notice promptly may free the insurer from liability to pay the claim.

28. *jjBarnicke Ltd.* v. *Commercial Union Assurance Co. of Canada* (2000), 5 B.L.R. (3d) 199.
29. See *Lachman Estate* v. *Norwich Union Life Insurance Co.* (1998), 40 O.R. (3d) 393.
30. *Case Existological Laboratories Ltd.* v. *Century Insurance Co.* (1982), 133 D.L.R. (3d) 727.
31. *Canadian Indemnity Co.* v. *Canadian Johns Mansville Co.*, [1990] 2 S.C.R. 549.
32. [1991] 3 S.C.R. 622.
33. Unfortunately, the crash victims still did not recover compensation. The aircraft was carrying more passengers than provided for in the policy, and the policy was consequently void.

ETHICAL ISSUE

Bad Faith

Frequently an insurance company disagrees with the insured over the entitlement to compensation or the amount of compensation. The manner in which an insurance company proceeds in cases of disagreement was dramatically changed in 2002. In that year, the Supreme Court of Canada released its decision in *Whiten* v. *Pilot Insurance*.[34] It held that Pilot acted in bad faith during the management of the claim and this entitled the insured to $1 000 000 in punitive damages. Pilot alleged arson with little or no evidence to support such an allegation. Pilot rejected independent advice that the claim should be paid and even influenced an independent investigator to change his opinion. In the circumstances, the Court held that Pilot breached its duty of good faith. This duty requires promptness and fairness to the insured.

In 2006, the Supreme Court set aside punitive damages awarded against an insurer for unreasonable denial of disability benefits but allowed mental anguish damages that stemmed from the long delay in receiving benefits.[35] Since *Whiten*, insurers are required to balance their entitlement to investigate with the responsibility to not unduly delay the processing of claims, to not pursue unfounded defences, and to treat the insured fairly.

QUESTIONS TO CONSIDER

1. What strategies should an insurance company employ to avoid allegations of bad faith?

Subrogation

If a storeowner has obtained fire insurance for her premises and suffers a loss because of a fire negligently caused by her neighbour, she can recover from her own insurance company without having to sue the neighbour. On the other hand, she cannot recover twice. If she were subsequently to sue the neighbour and recover damages that, when added to her insurance compensation, would give her a sum in excess of her loss, she would hold that excess in trust for her insurer. As a result, as long as she is fully insured, she will have no incentive to sue her neighbour. If that ended the matter, many tortfeasors would escape liability for their careless acts. However, under general principles of insurance law, when an insurer has paid a claim it is entitled to "step into the shoes of the insured" and sue the person liable for the loss. But the right of subrogation cannot place the insurer in a better position than the insured.

CASE 18.9

A fire broke out in leased premises, apparently due to the negligence of the tenant. The landlord was fully indemnified by its insurer who brought an action for damages against the tenant by way of subrogation. In the lease, the landlord had covenanted to insure against damage by fire, and the tenant had agreed to pay a proportionate share of the landlord's cost of insuring. The tenant covenanted to repair the premises, except for insured fire damage.

The court held that the terms of the lease indicated that the tenant had bargained for the right to be free of liability for fire arising from its negligence. Regardless of the terms of the policy between the insurer and the landlord, the insurer could have no better claim against the tenant than the lease gave to the landlord.[36]

---

34. [2002] 1 S.C.R. 595.

35. *Fidler* v. *Sun Life Assurance Co.* [2006] 2 S.C.R. 3.

36. *Amexon Realty Inc.* v. *Comcheq Services Ltd.* (1998), 155 D.L.R. (4th) 661. But an agreement between the insured plaintiff and the defendant (for example, not to sue for more than the amount of the defendant's own insurance cover) does not bind the plaintiff's insurer and cannot restrict its right of subrogation: *Somersall* v. *Friedman* (2002), 215 D.L.R. (4th) 577 (S.C.C.).

Recovery

In many types of insurance, property is insured for a stipulated amount (usually the estimated value of the property), and the insurer's liability is limited to that amount. However, it is a basic principle of insurance law that the insured may not recover more than the amount of the actual loss. For example, if a business insures its warehouse against damage by fire for $300 000, but the warehouse is actually worth only $275 000, that lower amount is the maximum that may be recovered. A person or business might think of saving premium costs by insuring property for less than its total value, since fires and accidents rarely result in total loss. Insurance companies often insert a clause in the contract stating that an insured that does not purchase coverage of at least a stated percentage of the value of the property (usually 80 percent) will become a "co-insurer" proportional to the lower coverage, along with the insurance company, for any loss that results. The insured would not then recover the total loss, even though the loss itself was less than the face value of fire insurance policy.

It sometimes happens that the same loss is covered by two or more separate insurance policies (especially where different risks are insured separately rather than under a single comprehensive policy): that does not permit the insured to recover twice for the same loss, and where the policies are issued by different insurance companies, they will have to determine which one must bear the loss or how it must be shared.[37]

Assignment

A life insurance policy of the type that accumulates a cash surrender value is an item of property—a chose in action—which the insured may assign for value, for example, by giving a conditional assignment of the policy to a bank as security for a loan. If the insured defaults on the loan, the bank is entitled to the cash surrender value up to the amount due on the loan. The insurer's consent to an assignment of life insurance is not necessary, although the insurer is entitled to notice. The risk of the insurer is not affected by an assignment of the benefits of a life insurance contract.

In contrast, property insurance is not assignable without the consent of the insurer. The reason for this rule is that an assignment substitutes a new person as the insured, and the personal qualities of the insured may be relevant to the risk assumed by the insurer. When a person sells a house or an automobile, there is usually unexpired insurance on the property; the purchaser must therefore renegotiate the insurance with the insurer, possibly at different premium rates. On the other hand, *after* a risk materializes and an insurance claim is established, an insured may assign the claim (say, to creditors) without the consent of the insurer.

GUARANTEE

The Nature of a Guarantee

guarantee
a promise to perform the obligation of another person if that person defaults

A **guarantee** usually arises in one of three common business situations:

- A prospective creditor may refuse to advance money, goods, or services solely on the prospective debtor's promise to pay for them.
- A creditor may state that it intends to start an action against its debtor for an overdue debt unless the debtor can offer additional security to support a further delay in repayment.
- A prospective assignee of rights under a contract may be unwilling to do so if it has nothing more to rely on than the undertaking of the promisor in the original contract.

---

37. Their respective liability will depend upon the precise terms of the policies: see *Family Insurance Corp.* v. *Lombard Canada Ltd.* (2002), 212 D.L.R. (4th) 193; *Unger* v. *Unger* (2003), 234 D.L.R. (4th) 119.

In each of these circumstances, the creditor or assignee may be satisfied by a third party promising to perform the obligation of the debtor if the debtor defaults. The debtor is then called the *principal debtor*, and his obligation is known as the *principal* or *primary debt*. The person who promises to answer for the default of the principal debtor is called the *guarantor* or *surety*, and her promise is a *guarantee* or *contract of suretyship*.

ILLUSTRATION 18.1

(a) Crown Autos Ltd. agrees to sell a sports car to Tomins provided that her uncle, Gilmour, guarantees payment of the instalments. Gilmour agrees to assist his niece, and both join in signing an instalment purchase agreement whereby Tomins promises (as principal debtor) to make all payments promptly, and Gilmour promises (as guarantor) to pay off the debt if Tomins defaults payment.

(b) Arthurs purchases a delivery truck from Bigtown Trucks Ltd. under an instalment agreement. After Arthurs has made more than half his payments, he defaults because of business difficulties. Bigtown threatens to retake possession of the truck. Arthurs asks Bigtown to give him an extra six months to pay if he can obtain a satisfactory guarantor. Bigtown agrees, and Arthurs' friend Campbell signs a contract of guarantee, promising to pay the balance in six months if Arthurs fails to do so.

(c) Perez buys a freezer from Quincy and gives a promissory note payable in 60 days for the full purchase price. Quincy is in need of cash and takes the note to her banker who agrees to give her cash for it, less a 5 percent charge. Quincy endorses the note in favour of the bank—that is, she signs it when assigning it to the bank, and thereby guarantees payment if Perez defaults.

There are three important characteristics of a guarantee. First, a guarantor makes a promise to the *creditor*, not to the principal debtor. A promise made to a debtor to assist in the event of default is not a guarantee, and since the promise is not made to the creditor, the creditor cannot recover on it. Second, a guarantee is a secondary obligation arising only on default of the primary debt. For this reason it is a *contingent* liability in contrast to the absolute liability of the principal debtor. A creditor has no rights against the guarantor until default by the principal debtor.[38] Third, a guarantor's duty to pay arises immediately on default by the principal debtor. The creditor need not first sue the debtor. Strictly speaking, the creditor need not even notify the guarantor of the default before starting an action to enforce the guarantee. As a practical matter, however, the creditor always makes a demand on the guarantor before suing. Of course, when giving a guarantee, a guarantor may stipulate that the creditor must first have sued the debtor. It is more common that the guarantee specifically releases the creditor from any obligation to proceed against the debtor first. Figure 18.1 illustrates the relationships involved in a guarantee.

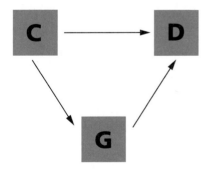

The creditor, *C*, may sue either the principal debtor, *D*, or the guarantor, *G*, once *D* has defaulted. Normally, *G* will be entitled to sue *D* to recover what she has paid on *D*'s account.

FIGURE 18.1
Liability on a Guarantee

---

38. See Chapter 11 for the distinction between a guarantee and an indemnity; an indemnifier promises absolutely to pay the debt of another person.

ILLUSTRATION 18.2

Williams tries to rent a launch from Boat Rentals Ltd. but is refused because of her youth. Williams' father, a reputable businessman, informs the manager of Boat Rentals that if the company rents the launch to his daughter, he will be responsible for any damage caused by her negligent acts if his daughter does not reimburse the company for any such damage. Boat Rentals accepts his offer.

indeminity
primary obligation to pay

In Illustration 18.2, the guarantee is rather like a contract of insurance in which the father is the counterpart of an insurer, and the boat rental firm is the counterpart of the insured. If Williams' father had undertaken absolutely (without reference to a failure by his daughter to make good the loss herself) to assume any costs of his daughter's possible negligence, his promise would have been an **indemnity** and even more like a contract of insurance.

The distinction between guarantee and indemnity is important in that the liability of a guarantor depends on the continuing existence of the liability of the principal debtor, whereas the liability under a promise of indemnity stands alone.[39] If a person guarantees the debt of a consumer debtor and the obligation is not binding under consumer legislation (for example, for failure to deliver a written statement of the terms of credit), the guarantor is not bound to pay either. On the other hand, a promise of indemnity is independent of any obligation of the person who benefits from that promise.

Continuing Guarantee

A continuing guarantee covers a series of transactions between a creditor and its principal debtor. A guarantor may, for example, agree to guarantee X Co.'s account with supplier Y up to an amount of $5000. In a series of purchases by X Co. and payments by it, X Co.'s indebtedness to Y will fluctuate considerably. At any given date during the currency of the guarantee, the guarantor is contingently liable for the debt, to a maximum of $5000. A continuing guarantee is often given for a specific length of time, and debts contracted afterwards are not the liability of the guarantor. In any event, the death of a guarantor ends liability with respect to further transactions, although the guarantor's estate remains contingently liable for the debt existing at death.

A guarantor may limit liability under a continuing guarantee until a specified date: if the principal debtor has not defaulted or been sued by that date, then the guarantor's liability terminates. The variety of terms of a guarantee is virtually limitless, and they depend only upon the ability of the parties to reach agreement.

Consideration

We have said that a guarantee is a promise, and we know that a promise is not enforceable unless it is given either under seal or for a consideration. Occasionally a guarantor does make the promise under seal but generally does not. What then constitutes the consideration for a guarantee?

The consideration is clearest when the guarantor receives an economic benefit—when she obtains a higher price as an assignor of an account receivable because she is willing to guarantee payment by the debtor. More frequently the guarantor does not receive any economic benefit for her promise; but as we have already noted (Chapter 6), consideration need not confer an economic benefit on the *promisor*. The essential element of consideration is simply that the promisee pays a price for the promise of the other party. The creditor gives sufficient consideration for the promise of the guarantor by performing some act or forbearing to do some act at the request of the guarantor. The guarantor's request need not even be express; it may be implied from the circumstances.

---

39. It may also be relevant with respect to the requirement of writing; see Chapter 10.

ILLUSTRATION 19.3

A, without authority from P, purports to accept T's offer to sell a large quantity of canned goods to P. Before the delivery date, T learns that A had no authority. Because the market is uncertain, T is unwilling to wait for P's ratification and makes a contract to sell the same goods to X. Ratification by P will now be ineffective because X has acquired rights to the goods.

Again, a principal cannot ratify when the rights of an outsider are affected.

Illustration 19.3 raises a further problem. Suppose the market value of the goods is rising rapidly when *T* learns that *A* had no authority to buy them. Can *T* revoke its offer and sell the goods to someone else at a higher price? The answer turns on the legal effect of *A*'s acceptance. If *A*'s acceptance is ineffective until ratification by *P*, then *T* can revoke its offer before that time and sell the goods to *X*. If *A*'s acceptance creates a binding contract, then *T* is bound while *P* has a choice to bind himself (by ratifying) or not. This situation arose in a 19th-century English case, *Bolton Partners* v. *Lambert*,[23] where the court held that *T*'s revocation was ineffective and he was bound by *P*'s subsequent ratification.

It is questionable whether the Bolton case applies in Canada.[24] Even if it does apply, it is subject to the important qualifications that ratification must not prejudice the rights of an outsider and that the principal must ratify within a reasonable time.

Finally, a principal cannot ratify if, at the time the agent made the contract, she failed to name the intended principal or at least mention the existence of a principal whose identity could then be ascertained. An *undisclosed principal* cannot afterwards ratify a contract made without his authority.

When an agent purports to accept an offer "subject to the ratification of my principal," the later ratification will not be retroactive. This apparent exception is simply an application of the rules of offer and acceptance: a conditional acceptance by an agent is not acceptance at all. The offeror may revoke the offer at any time before acceptance. In these circumstances the eventual "ratification" of the principal is really only an acceptance of the original offer.

CHECKLIST   Ratification

An agent's contract with a third party may be ratified:

- expressly or impliedly,
- within a reasonable time,
- by a named principal,
- if the rights of an outsider are not affected, and
- if at the time of creation and ratification, the principal was capable of making the contract.

---

23. (1889), 41 Ch. D. 295.

24. *Bolton* has been followed in other English cases although it has been criticized. The point has not often come before the Canadian courts, but in one case the court impliedly disapproved of the decision in the *Bolton* case: *Goodison Thresher Co.* v. *Doyle* (1925), 57 O.L.R. 300.

RIGHTS AND LIABILITY OF PRINCIPAL AND AGENT

When an agent makes a contract on behalf of her principal with a third party, the question arises as to who is liable on the contract—the agent or the principal? The answer depends upon a number of factors: Was the agent acting within the scope of her authority in making the contract? Was the identity or existence of the principal disclosed to the other party? There are three possible solutions:

- The principal alone is liable on the contract.
- The agent alone is liable.
- Either the principal or the agent may be held liable.

The Principal Alone Is Liable on the Contract

An agent is not liable on contracts made for her principal when the agency relationship is functioning as intended. After creating the contract, the agent steps out of the picture: the principal is liable for performance and is the one able to enforce it against the third party. Further, an agent has no liability to the third party even when she acts outside her real authority so long as she acts within her apparent authority. She may be liable to the principal for breach of the agency agreement.

To ensure that she has no liability in contracts made for her principal, an agent should indicate that she acts as agent and should identify the principal. The following are examples of signatures that accomplish this purpose:

"The Smith Corporation Limited, per W.A. Jones"

"W.A. Jones, for The Smith Corporation Limited"

Sometimes, an agent may persuade a third party to enter into a contract with her principal, without disclosing the identity of the principal.[25] She may describe herself as agent for a party that does not want for the time being to reveal his name. For example, an agent may negotiate in this way in order to obtain options for the purchase of individual pieces of land intended for assembly into a large block. The reasoning is that if the prospective purchaser is a large developer, the disclosure of his identity and purpose might induce some owners to hold out for much higher prices. In this situation, although the principal was not named in the contract, it was nevertheless made on his behalf and with his authority, and he alone is liable on, and entitled to enforce, the contract. The third party has no rights against the agent.[26]

THE AGENT ALONE IS LIABLE ON THE CONTRACT

When an agent contracts on terms that she is the real contracting party, though she is in reality acting or intending to act for an undisclosed principal, the agent alone has rights and liabilities relative to the third party. The principal can neither sue nor be sued on the contract. As we shall see in the next section, the situation is different where the existence of a principal is not mentioned, even if the third party believed it was contracting with the agent personally.[27]

---

25. This situation differs from that where the existence of a principal is not disclosed. Here, the third party knows that there is a principal but does not know who he is. The problem of the undisclosed principal is discussed later.
26. See *QNS Paper Co.* v. *Chartwell Shipping Ltd.* (1989), 62 D.L.R. (4th) 36; *Lang Transport Ltd.* v. *Plus Factor International Trucking Ltd.* (1997), 143 D.L.R. (4th) 672.
27. *Jade West Holdings Ltd.* v. *Canada Zau Fu Trade Ltd.*, [2002], B.C.S.C. 420.

Either the Principal or the Agent May Be Held Liable on the Contract

Sometimes a person who is an agent does not mention her status, and deals with a third party without it being apparent that she is acting as an agent. In that case, the third party is entitled to sue the agent on the contract. That is fair, since the third party may have been influenced by the personal credit and character of the agent. What are the third party's rights if and when it discovers the existence and identity of the principal? If the contract was one that the agent had authority to make, the third party has the option of holding either principal or agent liable for performance of the contract, but not both. If the third party sues and obtains judgment against the agent before it learns of the real principal, it has no rights against the principal.[28] If, however, the fact of agency emerges during litigation, the action may be discontinued and fresh proceedings taken against the principal. In that case, the principal may treat the contract as being made with him and has all of the defences, as well as the liabilities, of a contracting party.

Rights of the Undisclosed Principal

Can an undisclosed principal enforce a contract made on his behalf and with his authority? Generally, the answer is "yes"; he may normally intervene and enforce the contract against the other party.[29]

To succeed, an undisclosed principal must show that the contract was made with his authority. If the agent had no real authority, the undisclosed principal cannot ratify the contract and enforce it. If he were allowed to do so, he would be in a position to choose whether to be bound by the contract. Nor can the third party hold the principal liable in such a case. See Figure 19.1 for an illustration of liability in various agency situations.

CASE 19.3

A Co. was a management company controlled by the owner of a shopping mall. It had entered into a contract to rent an electronic sign from T for use in the shopping mall. In 1983, P Co. acquired ownership of the mall; A Co. continued to manage the mall as its agent. T was unaware of the change of ownership. In 1985, T entered into a new contract with A Co. to renew the rental of the sign. At the time, no mention was made of P Co.'s ownership. The contract was one that A Co. had no authority to make. P Co. refused to honour the contract and was sued by T.

The British Columbia Court of Appeal held that P Co., the undisclosed principal, was not liable on the contract. The agent had no authority, and the plaintiff had no knowledge of the principal's existence. The plaintiff's right of recovery was limited to A Co.[30]

Liability for Torts

When an agent is guilty of fraudulent misrepresentation in making a contract, even though the principal did not authorize the misrepresentation or had forbidden it, the third party may rescind the contract, just as if the principal had made the misrepresentation himself. If the agent was acting within her apparent authority, the third party may sue the principal as well as the agent for the tort of deceit.[31] An agent may also be liable to a third party for negligent misrepresentation. For

28. *Kendall* v. *Hamilton* (1879), 4 App. Cas. 504.

29. A major exception to this rule are contracts that are essentially personal in nature: *Collins* v. *Associated Greyhound Racecourses*, [1930] 1 Ch. 1.

30. *Sign-O-Lite Plastics Ltd.* v. *Metropolitan Life Insurance Co.* (1990), 49 B.C.L.R. (2d) 183.

31. *Lloyd* v. *Grace, Smith & Co. Ltd.*, [1912] A.C. 716. If the principal was innocent of the fraud, he may in turn sue the agent for damages to compensate for the loss.

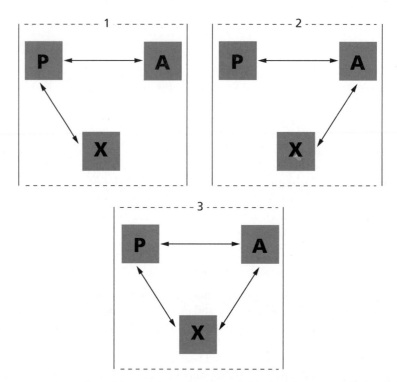

FIGURE 19.1

Liability on Agency Contract

In the most common type of case (1), an agency contract exists between the principal (*P*) and the agent (*A*). *A*, acting within her authority, actual or apparent, negotiates a contract with a third person (*X*). But that contract is one between *P* and *X*. In case (2), *A* describes herself as principal and does not disclose the existence of *P*. The result is that the contract is between *A* and *X*. In case (3), *A* says nothing about her status as agent. *X* is entitled to assume that *A* was acting on her own account and can sue *A*. But if *A* was in fact acting on behalf of *P*, *X* can choose to sue *P* instead.

example, Canadian courts have held that a real estate agent, though engaged and paid by the vendor, also owes a duty of care in the statements she makes to the purchaser.[32]

More generally, a principal is vicariously liable for torts committed by his agent while acting within the scope of her actual or apparent authority. This is so, whether the agent is an employee or an independent contractor.[33] As we have seen in Chapter 3, the actual tortfeasor (in this case the agent) remains liable for her torts, even though the principal is liable as well.

CASE 19.4

D was an agent for an insurance company, contracted to sell annuities. He persuaded *W* to buy an annuity, and *W* paid the purchase money by cheque, made out to *D*. *D* failed to purchase the annuity and made off with the money. *W* sued the insurance company for a return of the money he had paid.

The court held that the insurance company was liable, on the grounds that (1) *D* had received the money as their agent,

acting within the scope of his authority to sell annuities; (2) *D* had committed the tort of deceit, and although he was a self-employed contractor, the company was vicariously liable since *D* was acting within the scope of his contract; (3) the company was directly liable for its own negligence in hiring *D* and putting him in a position of trust, since it was known that he had a history of improper dealings.[34]

32. See *Avery v. Salie* (1972), 25 D.L.R. (3d) 495.

33. *Thiessen v. Mutual Life Assurance Co. of Canada* (2002), 219 D.L.R. (4th) 98.

34. *Wilson v. Clarica Life Insurance Co.* [2002] B.C.J. No. 292.

Breach of Warranty of Authority

There is no contract when a person holds herself out to be an agent but has no authority, actual or apparent, and the named principal does not ratify. The situation may arise because the alleged agent has acted fraudulently; for example, she may give the name of a reputable party as principal in order to obtain goods on credit. The seller will have an action in tort for deceit against the fraudulent agent, though the action may not be worth pursuing. An action in tort will also lie where an agent makes a *negligent* misrepresentation that she has an authority that she does not possess.[35]

An agent may innocently act without authority when she mistakenly believes she has the necessary authority, or, unknown to her, her principal has become bankrupt or insane or has died. No contract between a third party and the principal can be formed after the principal has lost contractual capacity or has ceased to exist. And no contract is formed between the agent and the third party either, because there was no intention that the agent should be a party to the contract. In such a case, however, the third party may bring an action against the agent for breach of **warranty of authority**.

warranty of authority
a person who purports to act as agent represents that she has authority to contract on behalf of the principal

We have seen that an agent may be liable if she acts in anticipation of a ratification that she never receives or if she contracts on behalf of a non-existent principal. These are examples of breach of warranty of authority. The measure of damages will be that which is necessary to put the other party in the position in which he would have been had the representation been true.[36]

CASE 19.5

The plaintiff owned shares in a corporation of which he was the treasurer. He was dismissed from that position and, in the course of negotiations, the defendant, a solicitor, purportedly acting on behalf of the majority shareholders, made an offer to buy out the plaintiff's shares. The solicitor did not have authority to make the offer, and the majority shareholders refused to go through with the purchase. In the meantime, the shares were de-listed and became worthless.

The solicitor was held to be in breach of warranty of authority, and the plaintiff was entitled to damages representing his loss of bargain—namely, the difference between the price offered and their new value, which was zero.[37]

TERMINATING AN AGENCY RELATIONSHIP

An agent's authority may be terminated on any of the following occasions:

- at the end of a time specified in the agency agreement
- at the completion of the particular project for which the agency was formed
- on notice by either the principal or the agent that he or she wishes to end the agency
- on the death or insanity of either the principal or the agent
- on the bankruptcy of the principal
- on an event that makes performance of the agency agreement impossible

Where no specific time is fixed for an agency relationship, it is implied that either party may end the relationship by giving reasonable notice to the other. If, however, the agreement is for a

---

35. *Alvin's Auto Service Ltd.* v. *Clew Holdings Ltd.*, [1997] S.J. No. 387.

36. *Delta Construction Co. Ltd.* v. *Lidstone* (1979), 96 D.L.R. (3d) 457. It is not entirely clear whether breach of warranty of authority is a tort or a breach of an *implied* contract between the agent and the third party in which, in return for the third party agreeing to contract with the principal, the agent impliedly promises that she has authority to act.

37. *Salter* v. *Cormie* (1993), 108 D.L.R. (4th) 372 (Alta. C.A.).

specified time, premature withdrawal by either principal or agent without the consent of the other constitutes a breach of contract.

When an agency arrangement ends for any reason other than the bankruptcy, death, or insanity of the principal, the principal may be bound by the former agent continuing to act within her apparent authority. In his own interest, a principal ought to bring the termination to the attention of all third parties likely to be affected. This precaution is especially important when a partnership is dissolved and will be discussed in Chapter 26.

FRANCHISING

At first glance, agency and franchising appear to have much in common. Both are methods that permit a business to expand rapidly. In both, the proprietor of the original business—the principal or the franchisor—employs the assistance of other persons or business entities in order to reach out to a wider public. Independent agents are engaged to market the principal's products, just as franchisees are used to market the franchisor's products. In law, however, there are significant differences between the two relationships.

The Nature of Franchising

Franchising has become a major business form in Canada. Franchises now account for close to 50 percent of all retail sales in Canada, through over 100 000 franchise operators, and the numbers are growing rapidly. When people are asked about franchising, most think of fast food, yet franchising has become common in many sectors—from hotels and restaurants to office supplies, real estate agencies, and video stores.

Despite its economic importance, there is remarkably little "law" on the subject in Canada. In many provinces, the law applicable to franchising must be found in the general principles of contract and tort law and more specific areas of law, such as consumer protection and intellectual property law.[38]

The essential characteristic of the franchising relationship is that one party, the *franchisor*, grants a *licence* to the other party, the *franchisee*, to market its product and use its name and trademark in return for payment of a *franchise fee*. However, a franchise normally amounts to considerably more than the mere granting of a licence: it involves a substantial degree of control by the franchisor over the franchisee's business. The franchisee nevertheless operates as an independent business and is not simply an employee or agent of the franchisor. As described by one judge:

> . . . franchising promises to provide the independent merchant with the means to become an efficient and effective competitor of large integrated firms. Through various forms of franchising, the manufacturer is assured qualified and effective outlets for his products, and the franchisee enjoys backing in the form of know-how and financial assistance.[39]

When it operates well, franchising provides benefits to both the franchisor and the franchisee. However, to quote from a 2001 judgment:

> ". . . To say that franchising is a risky business is, if anything, an understatement. . . ."[40]

---

38. Legislation governing franchising has been adopted in Alberta, Ontario, Prince Edward Island, and New Brunswick and is discussed in the last part of this chapter.

39. Stewart, J. of the U.S. Supreme Court, in *United States* v. *Arnold, Schwinn & Co.*, 388 U.S. 365, at 386 (1967), quoted by Stark, J. in *Jirna Ltd.* v. *Mister Donut of Canada Ltd.* (1970), 13 D.L.R. (3d) 645, at 646 (Ont. H.C.).

40. *Country Style Food Services Inc.* v. *Hotoyan* [2001] O.J. No. 2889, per Dilks J.

In theory, franchises offer the investor an opportunity to reduce the risk of business failure by providing a proven business concept, and it is true that franchises tend to fail less frequently than independent businesses that are started from scratch. But franchising is not a guarantee of success, and potential investors need to do their homework carefully. Far too many investors have embarked on a franchising venture with unreasonably optimistic expectations and have lost their life savings.

Contents of a Franchising Agreement

A franchise is created when the franchisor and franchisee enter into a contract, referred to as the **franchise agreement**. Since the franchisor normally makes a substantial number of such agreements—Subway has more than 20 000 franchises worldwide, including more than 2000 in Canada alone—whereas the franchisee normally enters into only one such agreement, the agreement is usually the franchisor's standard form contract, often accompanied by an operating manual for the franchisee. Typically, the agreement will deal with the following subjects.

franchise agreement
an agreement under which a franchisor grants to the franchisee a right to market the franchisor's products

Consideration Provided by the Franchisor

The essential feature of the agreement is the grant to the franchisee of a right, or licence, to market goods or services supplied by, or made to specifications provided by, the franchisor. The agreement further allows the franchisee to use trademarks, trade names, logos, secret processes, and so on that belong to the franchisor.

While the above features are also found in simple licensing agreements, a franchise agreement goes further. It normally provides for training the franchisee in the operation of the business, and for ongoing supervision, assistance, and management services. The franchisor frequently assists in the design of the business premises—usually to a standard design—and in establishing accounting, inventory control, and purchasing systems. It is also common for the franchisor to provide financial assistance to the franchisor, through loans or guarantees.

One of the main purposes of franchising is to enable a comparatively large number of small, independent entrepreneurs to take advantage of well-known and widely recognized trade names and reputations. Thus, the franchisor usually undertakes to provide advertising and promotion on a national or regional scale.

Consideration Provided by the Franchisee

For its part, the franchisee is required to provide an initial contribution of capital to what is, after all, the franchisee's own business. The size of the contribution varies widely, according to whether premises and equipment are purchased (and perhaps custom built) or leased from the franchisor or from some other person. Additionally, the franchisee agrees to pay for the services and assistance provided by the franchisor. Normally, there is a basic franchise fee and there are ongoing payments, which may take the form of a percentage of the revenues of the franchise, rentals for premises or equipment, payments for management services, or contributions to the cost of advertising campaigns.

A further source of profit to the franchisor is often derived from exclusive supply arrangements. In some types of franchise, the franchisee essentially acts as a retailer for products manufactured or supplied by the franchisor; the franchisee normally undertakes to sell only the franchisor's products. In other types of franchise, the franchisor is primarily selling an idea or a process; the actual goods sold to the public may be manufactured locally according to a set formula, and usually the franchisee may purchase the components only from suppliers approved by the franchisor.

Conduct of the Business

As noted above, a franchise agreement commonly provides for a substantial degree of supervision by the franchisor. The franchisee must consequently agree to give the franchisor right of access to carry out inspections and to provide proper accounts and regular information. Usually, the franchisee is required to covenant that the business will be carried on only in accordance with the franchisor's regular operating instructions and that no other competing business will be carried on by the franchisee. Since it is the franchisor's reputation that is the basis of the entire arrangement, the franchisee further covenants to protect the goodwill, trademarks, and trade secrets of the franchisor.

CASE 19.6

Robin's Foods was a franchisor of donut stores. One of its franchises was held by a numbered Ontario corporation. The numbered corporation, in addition to operating the franchise, supplied wholesale donuts to other shops for resale. The packaging did not identify the donuts as Robin's donuts, and the donut mix used was not the same mix required by Robin's. The sale of the wholesale donuts was done secretly on a cash basis and not recorded in the accounts provided to Robin's.

The court ruled that the secret activity constituted a breach of the franchising agreement, entitling Robin's to treat the agreement as terminated.[41]

Termination of the Franchise

As Case 19.6 illustrates, it is common to provide that serious breaches of the franchising agreement constitute a repudiation of the agreement, allowing the other party to treat it as terminated. Additionally, the agreement normally contains detailed provisions regarding the duration and termination of the relationship. Franchising usually involves a substantial investment by both parties and an expectation that the relationship will continue for a number of years. Consequently, one would expect the agreement to provide for a substantial fixed duration, normally with an option to renew, and to require a substantial period of notice to terminate, with penalties for premature termination.

It is an unfortunate fact that not all franchises are successful and that not all franchisees are capable of running successfully what should be a viable business. As a result, some franchises change hands quite regularly. To protect the franchisor against assignment of the franchise to an unsuitable operator, it is normal for the franchise agreement to stipulate that any assignment of the franchisee's interest may only be made with the consent of the franchisor.[42]

Restrictive Covenants

Franchises are usually territorial in nature: a franchisee is assigned a particular area—a county, city, or part of a city—in which to operate, and the franchisor often undertakes not to grant any other franchise within the same territory. In return, the franchisee agrees not to carry on business outside that territory.

An obvious risk taken by franchisors is that their franchisees, having operated a franchise successfully, will have acquired valuable experience and information, and have established relationships with customers and suppliers that they could put to their own use in an independent business. To guard against this danger, the franchisee is normally required to covenant that it will not, for a given number of years after termination of the agreement, carry on a similar or competing business within a stipulated radius from the franchise location. As we have noted in Chapter 7, such covenants may be unenforceable if they constitute an unreasonable restraint on trade.

---

41. *1017933 Ontario Ltd.* v. *Robin's Foods Inc.*, [1998] O.J. No. 1110.

42. For an interesting example, see *Kentucky Fried Chicken Canada* v. *Scott's Food Services Inc.* (1998), 41 B.L.R. (2d) 42.

CASE 19.7   Hohnjec had been the holder of a franchise granted by Yesac Foods to operate a restaurant in Barrie, Ontario. Subsequently, after termination of the franchise, Hohnjec opened a restaurant in Toronto. The new restaurant was not similar in concept to the Yesac franchise.

Yesac sought to enforce a provision in the franchise agreement, which purported to prevent the franchisee from engaging "in any other business . . . related to the food, beverage or restaurant business." The court held that the clause, which had no time or geographical limitations, was invalid and unenforceable.[43]

Dispute Resolution

Franchising agreements are intended to run for a number of years and contain a substantial number of provisions, each of which could become the subject of dispute. To avoid the expense and the possible ill will involved in litigation, it is not uncommon for franchise agreements to contain a provision establishing a procedure for resolving disputes that may arise during the operation of the franchise. Such a provision may, for example, oblige the parties to submit to mediation before the contract may be terminated for alleged breach by one of the parties.[44]

CHECKLIST Contents of a Typical Franchise Agreement

Franchise agreements usually cover the following:

- nature and location of franchise
- services to be provided by franchisor (training, management services, advertising, etc.)
- licensing of trademarks, know-how, etc.
- provision of financial assistance
- capital to be provided by franchisee
- franchise fee
- ongoing payments by franchisee (percentage of receipts, payments for services, etc.)
- arrangements for supply of materials and inventory
- provisions governing conduct of business (supervision, accounting, etc.)
- duration of relationship
- termination of relationship (notice, restrictions on assignment, penalties, etc.)
- restrictive covenants
- procedures for resolving disputes

43. *Yesac Creative Foods Inc.* v. *Hohnjec* (1985), 6 C.P.R. (3d) 398. See also *Kardish Food Franchising Corp.* v. *874073 Ontario Inc.*, [1995] O.J. No. 2849; *Cash Converters Pty. Ltd.* v. *Armstrong*, [1997] O.J. No. 2659; *Nutrilawn International Inc.* v. *Stewart*, [1999] O.J. No. 643.
44. See, for example, *Toronto Truck Centre Ltd.* v. *Volvo Trucks Canada Inc.* (1998), 163 D.L.R. (4th) 740; *Ellis* v. *Subway Franchise Systems of Canada Ltd.* [2000] O.J. No. 3849 (where the contract provided for arbitration in the state of Connecticut).

Legal Relationships Created by Franchising

The relationship between franchisor and franchisee is a contractual one between independent entrepreneurs. The Supreme Court of Canada has held that the relationship between the parties is not a fiduciary relationship.[45] Nevertheless, the ongoing nature of the relationship imposes upon them a duty of the utmost good faith.[46] As explained in a recent case:

> Franchisors are not required to act selflessly in placing the interests of the franchisee ahead of their own. However, it appears clear from the case law that a franchisor is subject to the duty to act in the utmost good faith towards a franchisee.

In particular:

> Part of the obligations in this special relationship with the franchisee includes a positive obligation to disclose accurate financial information to a prospective franchisee at the time of entering into a franchise agreement. Misrepresentations may result from silence or omissions.[47]

CASE 19.8

Neish entered into a franchise agreement with Melenchuk. He was provided with financial statements that purported to be historical records for the franchise. In fact, the records did not relate to the particular outlet but rather consisted of reconstructed records of other outlets. The records significantly misrepresented the profit and loss situation of the outlet. Neish's bank provided financing based upon the financial records provided.

Subsequently, Neish found that he had to borrow more money to keep the business alive. When he could not borrow any further he simply walked away from the business. He brought an action seeking compensation for his losses.

The court found that there was no evidence that Melenchuk knew that the records put together were actually misleading so as to constitute fraud. However, he had been negligent in putting the records together and was liable for negligent misrepresentation and breach of contract. Neish was entitled to damages for his lost investment.[48]

With respect to customers, it is important to remember that franchising is entirely different from agency. The franchisee contracts with members of the public on its own behalf, not as agent for the franchisor. There is thus no contract between the customer and the franchisor, though the franchisor might be considered, in some cases, as having held the franchisee out as having authority to act on its behalf and consequently be estopped from denying an agency relationship. When defective goods have been manufactured or supplied by the franchisor, it may, of course, be liable in tort.

Franchise Legislation

To date, four provinces, Alberta, Ontario, Prince Edward Island, and New Brunswick have enacted legislation expressly regulating franchising.[49] The most important features of these laws, which are broadly similar in effect, are as follows.

Disclosure

Franchisors are required to give every prospective franchisee a copy of the franchisor's *disclosure document* at least 14 days before the signing of any agreement or the payment of any consideration. The

---

45. *Jirna Ltd.* v. *Mister Donut of Canada Ltd.* (1973), 40 D.L.R. (3d) 303.

46. A recent decision of the Ontario Court of Appeal held that the franchisor owes a duty of good faith in the sense of an obligation to have regard to the franchisee's legitimate interests and to deal promptly, honestly, fairly, and reasonably with the franchisee: *Shelanu Inc.* v. *Print Three Franchising Corp.* (2003), 226 D.L.R. (4th) 577.

47. *Machias* v. *Mr. Submarine Ltd.* [2002] O.J. No. 1261. The Alberta and Ontario legislation require the parties to a franchise agreement to deal fairly with each other; see "Fair Dealing" in the next section.

48. *Neish* v. *Melenchuk* (1993), 120 N.S.R. (2d) 239. See also *Nutrilawn International Inc.* v. *Stewart, supra,* n. 43.

49. Franchises Act, R.S.A. 2000, c. F-23; Arthur Wishart Act (Franchise Disclosure), S.O. 2000, c. 3; Franchises Act, S.P.E.I. 2005, c. 36; Franchises Act, S.N.B. 2007, c. F-23.5. Quebec has some provisions in its Civil Code.

disclosure document must comply with the requirements of regulations and contain detailed information about the business and the franchise system, including financial statements and reports (s. 4 (Alta.); s. 5 (Ont., P.E.I., N.B.)).[50] Failure to provide a disclosure document as required gives the franchisee the right to rescind the agreement within two years, and misrepresentation in the document entitles the franchisee to compensation. The disclosure requirements generally do not apply in the case of a sale of a franchise by a franchisee.

Fair Dealing

Both acts provide that every franchise agreement imposes on each party a duty of fair dealing in its performance and enforcement (s. 7 (Alta.); s. 3 (Ont., P.E.I., N.B.)). This probably does no more than codify the position at common law.[51]

Right to Associate

In the past, some franchisors have tried by various means to prevent their franchisees from getting together to "compare notes" and, perhaps, to take concerted action against what are perceived to be unfair practices. The Alberta and Ontario Acts (s. 8 (Alta.); s. 4 (Ont., P.E.I., N.B.)) expressly recognize a "right of association" among franchisees; a franchisor may not prohibit or restrict its franchisees from forming an organization and may not penalize them in any way for doing so.

INTERNATIONAL ISSUE

Resolving Franchise Disputes

Despite the fact that most franchising agreements are carefully drafted, franchising seems to give rise to an excessive number of disputes. The termination of a franchise, in particular, is often a very contentious matter. Frequently it is not until a franchise is terminated that the franchisee really understands the nature of the agreement that he has signed. There is an obvious inequality in bargaining power between the franchisor, often a very large international corporation, and the franchisee, usually a small local business.

This inequality sometimes results in the insertion of unfair terms in the franchising contract.[52] It is common for franchise agreements to contain a choice of law clause designating the foreign franchisor's jurisdiction as the choice of law. As well, a dispute resolution clause may require mandatory arbitration with a foreign arbitrator. It also means that, when there is a dispute, the franchisor is far more able to finance the costs than is the franchisee.

The American congress is currently considering legislation that would prevent a franchisor from forcing a franchisee into arbitration. If passed, the Arbitration Fairness Act 2007 would render pre-dispute arbitration clauses in franchise agreements void and unenforceable.[53]

QUESTIONS TO CONSIDER

1. Should franchise agreements be required to contain certain standard terms that protect franchisees against unfair termination and other harsh conditions?
2. Should a mandatory requirement to submit all franchising disputes to arbitration be enforceable?

---

50. It is not possible to contract out of the disclosure requirement; *MAA Diners Inc.* v. *3 for 1 Pizza & Wings (Canada) Inc.* [2003] O.J. No. 430.
51. See *Machias* v. *Mr. Submarine Ltd.*, supra, n. 47.
52. See, for example, *B.B.J. Enterprises Ltd.* v. *Wendy's Restaurants of Canada Inc.* [2004] N.S.J. No. 81.
53. A bill to amend chapter 1 of title 9 of United States Code with respect to arbitration, S. 1782, 110th Congress, 1st Session.

QUESTIONS FOR REVIEW

1. Distinguish between dependent agents and independent agents.

2. Is a "real estate agent" a true agent?

3. What is a power of attorney?

4. What is the effect when a principal ratifies a contract made on its behalf by an agent who lacked the authority to enter into the contract?

5. What are the limits of ratification by a principal?

6. How does an agent acquire actual authority?

7. How does an agent acquire apparent authority?

8. What is meant by "holding out"?

9. Is an agent entitled to delegate his or her duties to some other person?

10. Why should an agent not act for both parties to a transaction? What are the probable legal consequences of doing so?

11. In what circumstances may an agent be held liable on a contract that he or she has negotiated?

12. Can an undisclosed principal enforce a contract made on his or her behalf?

13. What is meant by "breach of warranty of authority"?

14. Distinguish between a franchise and a licence.

15. What restrictions are usually placed on a franchisee carrying on other business activities?

16. What is the relationship between a franchisor and the eventual customer of the franchisee?

17. Is the relationship between franchisor and franchisee a fiduciary relationship?

18. What are the principal additional protections given to franchisees by the Alberta, Ontario, P.E.I., and New Brunswick legislation?

CASES AND PROBLEMS

1. Halloran entered into a contract with Scallop Petroleum Ltd. to manage one of Scallop's gas stations. The contract set out detailed arrangements for the operation of the station. It provided that all inventory should be the property of Scallop until sold, and that all proceeds of sale belonged to Scallop, out of which Halloran was to receive a fixed percentage as commission. Halloran was required to maintain two bank accounts, to pay all sales receipts into one of those accounts, and to provide Scallop with regular records of all transactions.

   At first, the relationship seemed to be working well. Then Halloran became less diligent in furnishing accounts, and Scallop began to notice various other irregularities. Halloran's records were inadequate, and an investigation revealed a shortfall in the sales account of about $80 000, which appeared to have accrued over more than a year. Scallop suspected Halloran of theft and the police were called in. Their investigation was inconclusive; it seemed probable that the money had been stolen by a former employee of Halloran, who could not be traced.

   Halloran was cleared of all involvement in the theft. However, it became clear that he had not been operating the station in accordance with the instructions set out in the contract. For example, he had been keeping cash and credit card receipts in a freezer and in a locked tin box, instead of paying them into the bank as required.

Scallop gave Halloran notice that it was terminating their relationship; it refused to pay Halloran commission on the previous month's sales, and brought an action against him for the balance of the $80 000.

Is Scallop entitled to succeed?

2. Da Silva entered into a franchising agreement with Snacks Unlimited, Ltd. to operate a fast-food outlet in Regina. Under the contract, the store was to make and sell hot dogs and hamburgers, the ingredients were to be of a specified quality, and the products were to be made to uniform standards. The premises were to be equipped and maintained according to a prescribed format and would have the decor and distinctive sign of "Snacks." Large sales were anticipated since Snacks was already a well-known operation and had carried on extensive advertising.

The franchising agreement signed by Da Silva required him to do five things:

- pay a franchise fee of $40 000
- pay a royalty of 2 percent on gross sales
- pay an annual fee of $10 000 for advertising services provided by Snacks
- buy his store equipment from Snacks
- buy his ingredients from sources indicated by Snacks

The agreement set out detailed provisions as to how the business was to be conducted and concluded with the words, "The relationship between the parties is only that of independent contractors. No partnership, joint venture, or relationship of principal and agent is intended."

Da Silva operated the business successfully for two years and showed a reasonable profit. Last year, he discovered that the firms from whom he was required to purchase his supplies were paying substantial rebates to Snacks. On the question of whether he had paid prices higher than the prevailing market prices for comparable supplies, it was difficult to generalize. For some materials, this was true; for others, he paid much the same price and in some instances even a somewhat lower price. In any event, Snacks had instructed all the suppliers to have no dealings or negotiations with its franchisees that might indicate the true nature of the arrangements made with them for rebates.

Da Silva sued Snacks for an accounting of these undisclosed profits and rebates and an order requiring them to be paid over to him.

Discuss the merits of his case, and indicate with reasons whether his action should succeed.

3. On July 2, Curran, a sales representative for the Bright Lighting Company, obtained a written order from Watts for a generator suitable for his farmhouse. A few hours later Watts phoned Curran and told him that he had changed his mind and wanted to cancel the order.

Curran told Watts that it was too late, since the order had already been mailed to the offices of the Bright Lighting Company. Watts replied that as far as he was concerned, "the deal is off."

On July 10 Bright Lighting Company wrote to Watts acknowledging receipt of his order. The equipment was shipped to Watts on July 30, but Watts refused to accept delivery. Bright Lighting Company then sued Watts on the contract it claimed to have with him.

Discuss the main arguments that could be made by each side and the probable result.

4. Keycorp was an insolvent corporation that had defaulted in payment of its mortgage to its banker, the Lusitania Bank. Keycorp instructed the bank to try to find a buyer for its commercial premises. A real estate agent engaged by the bank approached Carl's Cars Ltd. as a potential purchaser of the building. Carl's Cars submitted an offer to purchase, and a counter-offer was returned to them; in each case Lusitania Bank was described as the vendor (although the property still belonged to Keycorp). Over the next two weeks, there were further negotiations, and a price was finally agreed.

The bank was about to approach the chief executive officer of Keycorp to obtain her approval of the deal when it received a substantially higher offer from another corporation, Lockley Ltd. The bank put both offers to Keycorp, which accepted the Lockley offer and sold the property to it.

Carl's Cars eventually found another building, but its planned business relocation was delayed for several months, resulting in lost profits.

Does Carl's Cars have any cause of action against (a) Keycorp or (b) Lusitania Bank?

5. On a number of occasions over the past two years, Longhaul Transport Ltd. had carried goods belonging to Factorplus Products Inc. The shipments were arranged by a broker, Transshipments Inc. Longhaul invoiced Transshipments, which in turn invoiced Factorplus. The normal procedure was for Transshipments to pay Longhaul out of funds received by it from Factorplus. Longhaul was aware that the goods belonged to Factorplus and was under the mistaken impression that Transshipments was simply a division or subsidiary of Factorplus, rather than an independent broker.

Following one major shipment, Longhaul invoiced Transshipments but was not paid; Transshipments had received no payment from Factorplus in respect of the shipment and refused to pay the shipping charges.

Advise Longhaul whether it should sue (a) Transshipments, (b) Factorplus, or (c) both.

6. Strauss, an experienced business administrator, became unemployed six years ago when his firm "downsized." He was unable to find suitable similar employment and decided to set up his own business. He was especially attracted to the lawn care business, which he considered to have excellent growth potential. He also thought that a franchised operation provided the best chance of establishing a successful business quickly.

After examining a number of lawn care franchises, Strauss concluded that a firm called Sodmaster Inc. was the franchisor best suited to his requirements. Strauss contacted Sodmaster and had several discussions with their area manager for Eastern Ontario. Strauss was provided with a vast amount of information about Sodmaster's operations, including various projections of costs and profits based on the operation of other Sodmaster franchises. Strauss also visited other franchisees and talked with them about their experiences.

According to the financial projections in the booklet given to him by Sodmaster, a franchise with a gross annual revenue of $200 000 would normally make a small loss (after allowing for a modest management fee); one with revenue of $400 000 would show a reasonable profit, and one with revenue of $800 000 or more would show an excellent profit. Potential franchisees were warned that it was unusual to break even in the first year of operation. The projections were essentially accurate, based on the actual experience of Sodmaster franchises, though the booklet omitted to point out that only one of the franchises actually grossed more than $800 000 per year.

Strauss also made his own projections of his probable revenues and decided to go ahead and purchase a franchise for Frontenac County, Ontario. He agreed to pay a franchise fee of $40 000 ($25 000 payable immediately and the balance after two years) and to pay royalties of 6 percent on gross revenues. He also entered into the usual restrictive covenants not to carry on a competing business within 30 km of the franchise area for a period of five years after termination of the franchise. In order to get started, Strauss borrowed money on the security of his home and, in all, invested about $100 000 of his own money.

The business did not work out nearly as well as Strauss had expected. In his first year he had sales of only $60 000 (when he had anticipated twice that figure) and he made a loss of $75 000. The second year's sales reached $100 000 (with a loss of $12 000); by the third year, sales had risen to $180 000, still with a small loss; in the fourth and fifth years, Strauss' sales levelled out at a little more than $200 000, and he was still making a loss.

Because of his financial problems, Strauss never paid the remaining $15 000 owing on the franchise fee, and he also fell behind early on in the payment of the royalties. Relations between Strauss and Sodmaster became strained, and eventually Sodmaster informed Strauss that they would not be prepared to renew the franchise at the end of its five-year term. Strauss then abandoned the franchise and set up his own lawn care business in the same area.

Sodmaster brought an action against Strauss, claiming payment of the balance of the franchise fee, the unpaid royalties, and an injunction to restrain the breach of the restrictive covenant. Strauss counterclaimed for damages, alleging that he had been misled into entering into the franchise agreement in the first place.

Who should succeed?

ADDITIONAL RESOURCES FOR CHAPTER 19 ON THE COMPANION WEBSITE *(www.pearsoned.ca/smyth)*

In addition to self-test multiple-choice, true–false, and short essay questions (all with immediate feedback), application exercises, and links to useful web destinations, the Companion Website provides the following resources for Chapter 19:

- **British Columbia:** Real Estate Agents
- **Alberta:** Agency by Necessity; Enduring Power of Attorney; Franchises; Liability for Agent's Tortuous Conduct; Personal Directives; Real Estate Agents
- **Manitoba/Saskatchewan:** Real Estate Agent Legislation
- **Ontario:** Agency by Necessity; Fiduciary Duty; Franchising Legislation; Parental Liability; Power of Attorney; Real Estate Agents

CHAPTER

20

The Contract of Employment

We review the extensive area of employment law both for individual employees and for those who are members of trade unions that bargain terms of employment on their behalf. We begin by distinguishing employment from other arrangements, such as agency, and describing the nature of the employment relationship at common law. We next examine legislation that protects workers. Finally, we discuss trade unions, the collective bargaining process, and the system of regulation in place to facilitate resolving disputes. In this chapter we examine such questions as:

- What is the difference between an employer's liability in contract and in tort?

- What are the grounds for dismissal "with cause"?

- What is "wrongful dismissal," and what are its consequences?

- What are the effects of human rights requirements, and pay and employment equity statutes?

- What are the consequences of regulation on general working conditions?

- How is mandatory retirement affected by the Canadian Charter of Rights and Freedoms?

- How are employment conditions affected by workers' compensation and occupational health regulation?

- What are the implications of a collective agreement for the individual employee?

- What is the legal status of trade unions?

DEVELOPMENT OF THE LAW GOVERNING EMPLOYMENT

The principles of modern employment law are derived from the common law rules defining the **relationship of master and servant**. This law developed in an early business environment where the employer (master) had a separate contract with each employee (servant); welfare legislation and trade unions were unknown. Today, the individual contract of employment remains the most common employment relationship, and the law of master and servant continues to be important. Nevertheless, the economic and social changes of the past century and a half have greatly affected the common law in two respects:

relationship of master and servant

the contractual relationship between an employer and an employee

- *First*, statutes have been passed to establish minimum standards of working conditions; we shall refer to this branch of the law as employee welfare legislation.
- *Second*, the organization of labour into trade unions has led to the evolution of the collective agreement—a whole separate body of law known as the law of collective bargaining—to govern the relationship between employers, trade unions, and their members.

In this chapter we discuss the individual employment relationship, employee welfare legislation, and collective bargaining.

We begin with a note of caution. We cannot cite all the relevant statutes in the space available, and in any event it might be dangerous to do so: this part of the law frequently changes, and statutes may soon become obsolete. The purpose of the chapter is simply to acquaint the reader with the general approach of the law in another main area of business administration. For further discussion of specific labour problems, the reader should consult the works that have been specially prepared in this field, cited from time to time in footnotes.[1]

RELATIONSHIP OF EMPLOYER AND EMPLOYEE

Compared with Agency

The relationship of employer and employee is established by a contract that gives one party, the employer, authority to direct and control the work of the other party, the employee. The services that are contracted for may or may not include making contracts with third parties as agent for the employer.

The distinction between agent and employee is one of function. The same person is often both an employee and an agent. Indeed, an employee's chief duty may be to make contracts with third parties on behalf of the employer: for example, a purchasing agent for a company has a duty to order goods on the company's credit and has authority to do so within the limits of her agency. She is also a company employee and subject to the direction of its senior officers. Other employees may have very limited duties as agents of their employer: The driver of a delivery truck is an employee who may act as an agent when taking the truck into a garage for servicing and binding the employer to pay the charges. In many types of employment, an employee has no reason to enter into contracts on behalf of the employer and no authority, express or implied, to do so—a lathe operator, for instance. As we noted at the beginning of Chapter 19, the functions may be completely separate, as when a business engages an agent who is not an employee at all.

In Chapter 19 we learned that when an agency agreement is of indefinite duration, an agent may have no recourse against a principal that terminates the agreement without notice. By contrast, an employee, as we shall see, often has a right of action for damages for wrongful dismissal in comparable circumstances.

1. See, especially, G.W. Adams, *Canadian Labour Law*, 2nd ed. (Toronto: Canada Law Book, 1993); J.R. Sproat, *Wrongful Dismissal Handbook*, 3rd ed. (Toronto: Thomson Canada, 2004).

Both principals and employers may be liable in tort for the acts of their agents and employees, respectively. However, for various reasons, some historical and some related to the different functions of agents and employees, the liability of an employer may be wider than that of a principal; the basis for vicarious liability is not the same for principals and employers. Accordingly, when a third party is injured, it may be important to establish whether the wrongdoer was acting as an employee or as an agent of a firm.

Compared with an Independent Contractor

An independent contractor undertakes to do a specified task such as building a house. The contract between the parties does not create an employer–employee relationship because the contractor is not subject to the supervision of the person engaging him. His job is to produce a specified result, but the means he employs are his own affair.

It is not always easy to distinguish between an independent contractor and an employee. Occasionally the two functions are combined in a single person: the owner of a building may hire a building contractor to do certain repairs for a fixed price, but the agreement may also require the repairs to be made under the supervision of the owner. It may be difficult to decide whether the person doing the work is primarily an independent contractor or an employee.

When a firm undertakes work as an independent contractor, any liabilities it incurs in carrying out its task are almost entirely its own.

ILLUSTRATION 20.1

Imperial Contractors contracted with Parkinson Corp. to erect an administration building. During the construction work, Miss Chance, walking on the sidewalk far below, is injured by a falling brick. The accident is the result of inadequate protection for pedestrians provided by Imperial Contractors. Imperial Contractors—not Parkinson Corp.—would very likely be liable for the injury so caused.

On the other hand, Parkinson does have a duty to take reasonable care to hire a competent contractor. Also, if by the nature of the work undertaken, the possibility of damage to adjoining property is apparent—for example, through blasting with dynamite[2]—or if the work is inherently dangerous to third parties, Parkinson has an obligation to see to it that the contractor takes reasonable precautions to avoid such damage.

As is described in Chapter 31, a business engaging a building contractor may have to follow certain procedures in paying the contractor in order to avoid having its land and buildings subject to liens filed by employees of the contractor or by subcontractors such as suppliers of materials. Apart from this complication, a person engaging an independent contractor is not generally responsible for the contractor's obligations.[3]

The Relationship at Common Law

In defining the relationship of employer and employee, the courts have developed rules about

- the employer's liability to third persons
- the notice required to terminate the relationship
- grounds for dismissal
- assessment of damages for wrongful dismissal

These rules are part of the common law as it continues to apply to individual employment contracts, and we shall deal with them in turn.

2. *Savage* v. *Wilby*, [1954] S.C.R. 376; *Sin* v. *Macioli* (1999), 43 O.R. (3d) 1.
3. See *Vic Priestly Landscaping Contracting Ltd.* v. *Elder* (1978), 19 O.R. (2d) 591 at 601–5.

THE EMPLOYER'S LIABILITY

Liability in Contract

As we noted in Chapter 12 under the heading "Vicarious Performance," parties to a contract often understand that they will not perform personally—corporations cannot do so—and that either employees or an independent contractor will perform. The promisor remains liable for satisfactory performance, as when a construction firm undertakes to erect a building according to specifications, although it hires a subcontractor to put up the structural steel and the subcontractor does defective work. So, too, will it be liable for breach of contract should its own employees do improper work.

Liability in Tort

In our discussion of vicarious liability in Chapter 3, we noted that a business is liable for damages to a third party for the consequences of any tort an employee may commit in the course of employment. The employer may not have authorized the wrongful act: it is liable even though it has forbidden such conduct. All the injured party need establish is that the employee caused the damage while engaged at work. If, however, the harm results while the employee is not engaged in the employer's work, as when he takes time off from his duties to attend to some personal matter, the employer is not liable: the employee alone is liable. Nor is the employer liable if the employee delegates the work to someone else without the employer's consent.

ILLUSTRATION 20.2

Adair is employed by Magnum Computers as a sales agent. While driving a company van on his rounds, he negligently collides with another vehicle. He has committed a tort in the course of his employment; the owner of the damaged car may sue both Magnum Computers and Adair.

ILLUSTRATION 20.3

Adair injures a pedestrian as a result of negligent driving while using the company van to take his family to the theatre after hours, without permission or knowledge of his employer. In the words of a Nova Scotia judgment in a similar case, Adair has "departed from the course of his employment and . . . embarked upon an independent enterprise—'a frolic of his own'—for purposes wholly unconnected with his master's business."[4] He alone is liable; Magnum Computers is not.

ILLUSTRATION 20.4

While delivering a computer, Adair becomes embroiled in an argument with a customer about the quality of the product. He pushes the customer who falls and injures himself. Is Magnum Computers vicariously liable to the customer for the assault?

4. *Hall* v. *Halifax Transfer Co. Ltd.* (1959), 18 D.L.R. (2d) 115, per MacDonald, J., at 120. See also *Longo* v. *Gordie's Auto Sales Ltd.* (1979), 28 N.B.R. (2d) 56.

Of the three examples in Illustrations 20.2, 20.3, and 20.4, the last is the most difficult to resolve. As one judge put it, "Before the employer can be held liable, the blow complained of must be closely connected with a duty being carried out in the authorized course of employment and not delivered at a time when the servant has divested himself of his character as a servant."[5] We must ask whether the unauthorized and wrongful act of the employee is "so connected with the authorized act as to be a mode of doing it" or whether it is "an independent act."[6]

If having conversations about his employer's product at the time of delivery is an authorized incident of Adair's employment so as to be a way of carrying out his duties, his employer is also liable for the assault; but if his conversation is an independent act, Adair alone is liable. The court will hear evidence of trade practice in this matter before reaching its decision.

When an employer has been held liable for the negligence of an employee, it has a right to be indemnified by the employee;[7] it may, if it thinks it worthwhile, sue the employee.

NOTICE OF TERMINATION OF INDIVIDUAL EMPLOYMENT CONTRACTS

notice
advance warning that the employment relationship will end

fixed term
a contract of employment with defined start and end dates

indefinite hiring
a contract of employment for an undetermined length of time, with no expectation of termination or described end date

reasonable notice
the acceptable length of notice of termination considering the nature of the contract, intentions of the parties, circumstance of the employment, and characteristics of the employee

Notice of termination involves telling an employee in advance that the employment relationship will end. How much advance warning, or **notice**, an employee should receive depends upon a number of factors including the type of employment contract. When an employer has hired an employee for a **fixed term** and that term has elapsed, no notice of termination is necessary on the part of either party. Neither one has a right to expect anything more from the other at the end of the specified time: each has been aware of the end date from the beginning as, for example, where a student expects summer employment to terminate on the Friday before Labour Day.[8]

Often employers and employees do not discuss when the employment relationship is to end, nor do they expressly agree on the length of notice required to terminate employment. They may intend the hiring to be by the week, the month, or some other length of time, renewable for successive periods, and possibly lasting for many years; or as more often happens, they may simply regard the employment as a general or **indefinite hiring**.

In the absence of an express term about termination in a contract of employment, the common law rule is that **reasonable notice** shall be given. Sometimes a court can determine the length of reasonable notice from evidence of an established customary practice followed by the particular employer for the type of employee in question. In other circumstances, the court will ask what type of hiring the parties intended when they made the employment contract. The usual minimum reasonable notice for a weekly hiring is one clear work week, and for a monthly hiring, one clear work month.[9] If the hiring is general or indefinite, reasonable notice depends upon all the circumstances of the employment; it usually varies between three and six months and occasionally is as long as one year or more.[10] Key considerations are the length and nature of employment, the age of the employee, and the availability of similar employment given the educational and experiential background of the

5. *Wenz* v. *Royal Trust Co.*, [1953] O.W.N. 798, per Aylen, J., at 800.

6. R.F.V. Heuston and R.A. Buckley, eds., *Salmond and Heuston on The Law of Torts*, 20th ed. (London: Sweet & Maxwell, 1992) at 457.

7. *Finnegan* v. *Riley*, [1939] 4 D.L.R. 434.

8. See, for example: Employment Standards Act, S.O. 2000, c. 41.

9. The notice required to terminate a weekly or monthly hiring is similar to the notice required to terminate a weekly or monthly tenancy. For a fuller explanation, see Chapter 24 under "Termination and Renewal of a Tenancy."

10. See *Bardal* v. *The Globe and Mail Ltd.* (1960), 24 D.L.R. (2d) 140; *Stevens* v. *Globe and Mail et al.* (1992), 86 D.L.R. (4th) 204; *Minott* v. *O'Shanter Development Company Ltd.* (1999), 42 O.R. (3d) 321.

employee.[11] Executive compensation settlements are often for as much as several years' salary.[12] In most provinces, and at the federal level as well, the minimum length of required notice is specifically set down by statute, and any attempt by an employer to impose a term shorter than the minimum is void.[13] Since the legislative provisions are minimum requirements only, reasonable notice periods and contractual notice terms are usually substantially longer.

When no other evidence about the intention of the parties is given to the court, it may infer a weekly or a monthly hiring from the mere fact that the employee receives pay by the week or the month. A court may consider other factors and rule, for example, that a hiring is indefinite even though the employee is paid by the week. As stated in *Lazarowicz* v. *Orenda Engines Ltd.*:

> Upon all the circumstances of this case I have come to the conclusion that the plaintiff, despite the fact that his wages were stated to be a weekly sum only, was employed upon a general or indefinite hiring only, and for these reasons: Firstly, the plaintiff was a graduate engineer. . . . At the time he was employed by the defendant corporation [he] had been employed . . . at a monthly salary of $450. He was secure in that position and there seems little reason to conclude that he would have left that position to accept one with the defendant company if he were to be merely a weekly servant. A more important circumstance is the actual work performed by the plaintiff. . . . The evidence . . . shows that he was in a position of some considerable importance, requiring a great deal of mechanical and technical experience.[14]

If an employer dismisses an employee without notice, it may satisfy its obligation to give reasonable notice if it tenders an additional amount of pay for a period equal to the time required for reasonable notice. This is known as **payment in lieu of notice**. Employers commonly terminate this way to avoid friction with the now-terminated employee. In the *Lazarowicz* case, the court held that reasonable notice in the circumstances was three months. Since the employee had been given only one week's salary in lieu of notice, it held that the employee was entitled to the balance of three months' salary.

An employee who decides to leave voluntarily has a contractual obligation to give the employer the same amount of notice as he himself would be entitled to receive for dismissal. If he does not do so, the employer may, if it considers it worthwhile, sue the employee for damages equal to the loss caused by this breach of contract.[15]

An employee is justified in leaving without giving the usual notice if he can show that he was obliged to work under dangerous conditions that the employer refused to correct. Here the employer has broken the contract, freeing the employee from his obligations, for it is an implied term in the contract that the employer will maintain a safe place to work. An employee also has grounds for leaving immediately if he is ordered to do an illegal act. If an employer substantially changes an employee's job, for example by a **demotion** or a geographic transfer, the employee is not obliged to accept the change. Under such circumstances, the change amounts to **constructive dismissal** and the employee is entitled to reasonable notice.[16]

payment in lieu of notice
payment of the amount of compensation the employee would have earned during the reasonable notice period

demotion
transferring an employee to a job with less responsibility and/or income potential

constructive dismissal
a substantial change to an employee's job that amounts to termination of the existing employment

---

11. These considerations are often referred to as the "Bardal factors." Although they are not to be considered an exhaustive list, they are to be given significant weight: *B.C. Hydro & Power Authority*, [1986] 4 W.W.R. 123 (S.C.). The relative importance of each factor is not uniformly accepted. See, for example, comments relating to the significance of "character of employment" in *Bramble* v. *Medis Health & Pharmaceutical Services Inc.* (1999), 175 D.L.R. (4th) 385 (N.B.C.A.) and B. Fisher, "Is Occupation Still a Relevant Factor in Determining Notice Periods in Wrongful Dismissal Cases?" (1995), 6 C.C.E.L. (2d) 29.

12. Eric Dash, "Executive Pay: Has the Exit Sign Ever Looked So Good?" *New York Times*, April 8, 2007, www.cslproductions.com/scrapbook/NYTimes-Executive-Pay-4-8-07/.

13. See, for example: Labour Standards Act, R.S.S. 1978, c. L-1, ss. 43–4; Labour Standards Code, R.S.N.S. 1989, c. 246, s. 72; Employment Standards Act, S.O. 2000, c. 41, as applied in *Machtinger* v. *HOJ Industries Ltd.* (1992), 91 D.L.R. (4th) 491 (S.C.C.) and *Rizzo & Rizzo Shoes Ltd.* (Re), [1998] 1 S.C.R. 26. For contrary finding see *A.A. Waters & Brookes* v. *Lachini*, [2001] O.L.R.B. Rep. 1119.

14. (1960), 22 D.L.R. (2d) 568, per Robertson, C.J.O., at 573; affirmed on appeal (1962), 26 D.L.R. (2d) 433.

15. *RBC Dominion Securities Inc.* v. *Merrill Lynch Canada Inc.*, 2008 SCC 54.

16. *Farber* v. *Royal Trust Co.*, [1997] 1 S.C.R. 845.

GROUNDS FOR DISMISSAL WITHOUT NOTICE

The Contractual Basis

dismissal for cause
dismissal without notice or further obligation by the employer when the employee's conduct amounts to breach of contract

An employer need not give notice when it can show that the employee was dismissed for cause. **Dismissal for cause** is an example of the general law of contract: when an employee's conduct amounts to a breach of the contract of employment, the employer may be entitled to consider itself discharged from any further obligations and to terminate the contract at once. As we know, in contract law, generally not every petty breach would have this result.[17] The common law has classified the kinds of breach that are sufficient grounds for dismissal without notice, and the collective bargaining process has developed the idea further. In some jurisdictions, employees have gained additional protection by statute.[18]

Misconduct

Misconduct may be a crime associated with employment, such as embezzlement, or it can be dismissal for cause related to conduct outside of employment.[19] An employee guilty of grossly immoral conduct that might bring the employer's business into public disrepute, disturb the morale of other employees, or cause the employer direct financial loss may be dismissed at once. Conviction for a crime is grounds for immediate dismissal, especially when it involves immoral conduct such as stealing or fraud.[20]

A firm is entitled to place confidence in its employees, and, depending on the nature of the employment, evidence of a lack of integrity is often grounds for instant dismissal. An employee's deception need cause no financial loss to his employer: it is enough that the employer can no longer trust him.[21]

Employers also set their own standards of conduct or misconduct. Codes of conduct addressing activities such as harassment, discrimination, privacy, and use of technology are used to set standards of appropriate behaviour for employees. Provided the employee is made aware of the code, he or she may be dismissed for code violations.

Disobedience

job description
a description of the responsibilities of a position including objectives, qualifications, and supervisor

Wilful disobedience of a reasonable and lawful order from an employer is grounds for immediate dismissal without notice. An accurate **job description** and identified chain of command help an employer avoid employee confusion about expected behaviour and disobedience. The concept of disobedience is broad enough to include situations where the employee does not directly disobey but acts in a manner inconsistent with the usual loyalty expected of that kind of employee. In the old case of *Ridgway* v. *Hungerford Market Co.*,[22] a clerk wrote in a company minute book a protest against a resolution of the directors calling a meeting to appoint his successor. He was dismissed at once and forfeited the right to any reasonable notice that would normally have been implied in the directors' resolution.

---

17. See Chapter 14, "The Effect of Breach."

18. See, for example: Employment Standards Act, S.O. 2000, c. 41.

19. In the times of Henry VIII and Elizabeth I, the law treated any violence by a servant against her master as a minor form of treason and subjected the employee to the grisly methods of execution reserved for that most wicked of offences. Even wishful thinking by an employee was hazardous while witchcraft remained an offence. This attitude of the law, demanding of employees complete obedience and loyalty, lingered on; until as late as the end of the 19th century a strike was regarded as a form of conspiracy. See E.M. Smith, ed., *A Treatise on the Law of Master and Servant*, 6th ed. (London: Sweet & Maxwell, 1906) at 390. We have followed the classification of grounds for dismissal outlined by Smith at pp. 102–15.

20. *Pliniussen* v. *University of Western Ontario*, (1983), 2 C.C.E.L. 1.

21. *Werle* v. *Saskenergy Inc.* (1992), 103 Sask. R. 241.

22. (1835), 111 E.R. 378. See also *Hodgkin* v. *Aylmer* (Town) (1996), 23 C.C.E.L. (2d) 297.

Incompetence

The degree of skill an employer may demand depends partly on the representations made by the employee when seeking the position and partly on the degree of skill ordinarily to be expected of an employee of that category and rate of pay. Again, accurate job descriptions and recruitment activities reduce the likeliness of hiring an incompetent applicant. If an employee accepts a position on the understanding that he is capable of doing a particular kind of work and it becomes apparent that he cannot, in fact, do this work satisfactorily, the employer may then dismiss him without notice. On the other hand, incompetence as a cause for dismissal becomes more difficult to justify the longer an employee has been employed.[23] An employer must make an effort to remedy incompetence with training and education. If these efforts fail then the employer may dismiss without notice.

Illness

Permanent disability or constantly recurring illness entitles an employer to consider the contract at an end, regardless of any terms in the contract requiring notice. An employer cannot, however, recover damages from an employee for breach of contract in these circumstances: the contract is discharged by frustration and not by breach. Human rights legislation imposes a duty on employers to accommodate an employee's disability. A disabled person's employment may only be terminated after all reasonable efforts to accommodate the disability have been exhausted.

Effect of Dismissal

Any of the four grounds for dismissal set out above permits an employer to treat the contract of employment as discharged. Misconduct, disobedience, or incompetence amounts to discharge by the employee's breach, but illness discharges the contract by frustration. Discharge for any one of these personal failures of performance by an employee relieves the employer of the duty to give notice, but it must still pay the dismissed employee any wages earned until the time of dismissal.

Sometimes an employer has such a general dissatisfaction with or mistrust of an employee that it dismisses him apparently without cause. If the employer should later discover that there was in fact cause for dismissing the employee without notice, it could use these grounds to defeat an action by the employee for wrongful dismissal.[24]

Failure to Warn

Only the most serious events entitle an employer to terminate an employee after the first incident. Most circumstances require an employer to warn the employee that the offending conduct is unacceptable and further occurrences will result in termination.[25] Even a series of events may not justify dismissal if the employer has failed to warn the employee. Ignoring the initial events may be seen as condoning or accepting the behaviour and the employer may forfeit the right to complain later.[26] Therefore, most employers take a structured approach to employee discipline, noting all infractions and warnings on an employment record. As noted above, an employer must be able to establish that training or education was attempted when relying on incompetence.

There is an increasing tendency to view an employee's interest in a job as being something more than just contractual. In particular, the growing remedy of reinstatement, discussed in the next section, suggests that the interest is almost a kind of ownership. With this view in mind, it has been

23. See *Duncan* v. *Cockshutt Farm Equipment Ltd.* (1956), 19 W.W.R. 554; *Bardal* v. *The Globe and Mail Ltd., supra*, n. 10.
24. The courts admit such evidence even if it becomes known after the action has been started. See, for example: *Lake Ontario Portland Cement* v. *Groner* (1961), 28 D.L.R. (2d) 589; *Bannister* v. *General Motors of Canada Limited* (1998), 40 O.R. (3d) 577.
25. *Rajakaruna* v. *Peel (Regional Municipality)* (1981), 10 A.C.W.S. (2d) 522 (Ont. Co. Ct.).
26. *Varsity Plymouth Chrysler (1994) Ltd.* v. *Pomerleau* (2002), 23 C.C.E.L. (3d) 148 (Alta. Q.B.).

claimed that before an employee can be dismissed—and thus deprived of an "interest" in his job—he is entitled to a fair hearing. Accordingly, before dismissing an employee, the employer should confront him with a charge of misconduct and give the employee an opportunity to clear himself or at least to explain his acts and minimize their significance.[27]

Adverse Economic Conditions

Adverse economic conditions do not excuse an employer from its implied obligation to give employees reasonable notice of termination. An employer might overcome this implied obligation by getting his employee to agree expressly that in adverse economic conditions he may be dismissed without notice. However, when a right to notice is required by statute, even an express agreement to give it up is ineffective; the statute prevails, and the employer must still give notice or wages in lieu of notice.

Some statutes now permit an employer to temporarily lay off employees without notice for periods as long as three months under certain economic conditions prescribed by regulation.[28]

WRONGFUL DISMISSAL

Damages

For an employee to succeed in an action against her employer for damages for wrongful dismissal, she must show that the employer has broken the contract, as when it fails to give the employee the notice to which she is entitled. An employer often defends its actions either by claiming that the employee was dismissed for cause or that reasonable notice was given. If the employer's defence fails, the court is left with the task of assessing damages.

The measure of damages for wrongful dismissal is a particular application of the rules for assessing damages in contracts generally. In Chapter 15, we saw that the purpose of an award of damages is to place an injured party in the position it would have been in if the contract had been completed. In an employment contract, we must ask what amount of damages will compensate the employee for failure to receive the required notice of termination.

The first task for the court is to determine what length of time would have been reasonable notice in the circumstances. Once the length of reasonable notice is determined, the court multiplies the employee's rate of pay and the value of fringe benefits by the length of reasonable notice to calculate the damages. As noted earlier, the court has considerable discretion when the contract is for a general or indefinite hiring and each case must be decided on its own facts after consideration of the following factors:

> There can be no catalogue laid down as to what is reasonable notice in particular classes of cases. The reasonableness of the notice must be decided with reference to each particular case, having regard to the character of the employment, the length of service of the servant, the age of the servant and the availability of similar employment, having regard to the experience, training and qualifications of the servant.[29]

Many wrongful dismissal cases have applied this classic quotation and have expanded its scope, especially in circumstances where the employer has acted in bad faith. Employers are under an obligation to behave fairly, honestly, candidly, and reasonably when dismissing an employee. When the bad faith of the employer has added to the harm caused—as where the employer falsely makes

---

27. See *Reilly* v. *Steelcase Canada Ltd.* (1979), 26 O.R. (2d) 725; *Pulsifer* v. *GTE Sylvania Canada Ltd.* (1983), 56 N.S.R. (2d) 424; *Pilato* v. *Hamilton Place Convention Centre* (1984), 45 O.R. (2d) 652.
28. Canada Labour Code, R.S.C. 1985, c. L-2; Canada Labour Standards Regulation, C.R.C. 1978, c. 986, s. 30; Employment Standards Act, 2000, S.O. 2000, c. 41, s. 56.
29. *Bardal* v. *The Globe and Mail Ltd.*, per McRuer, C.J.H.C., *supra*, n. 10, at 145.

it appear that the employee was dismissed for serious misconduct—additional damages may be assessed against the employer.[30] Damages for mental anguish or pain and suffering may be awarded or, in extreme circumstances, punitive damages.

Finally, the court will consider any other damage that flows naturally from the employer's breach. For example, the employee may have incurred travelling expenses in seeking other employment.

Mitigation

We must remember that a party injured by breach of contract is expected to act reasonably in order to mitigate her loss. Accordingly, the employer may be able to defeat or reduce the employee's claim for damages by proving that she has not made a serious attempt to obtain reasonably comparable work elsewhere. If the employer shows that the employee had such an opportunity to work elsewhere but declined it, the court will reduce the award of damages by the amount the employee might have earned during the required term of notice. However, a dismissed employee is not required to take any work simply to mitigate her loss; if the only work available is substantially below what she might reasonably expect based on her qualifications and experience, she may refuse it without fear that the court will reduce an award of damages. Nor need she move to a distant location, requiring her to give up her current residence and find another. If she does accept a lower-paid job, she will be entitled to the lost difference in remuneration during the term of notice.

In rare circumstances, the employee may be expected to mitigate by accepting alternate employment with the dismissing employer.[31] This is most common in constructive dismissal situations. Employees are not expected to work in hostile or humiliating environments and this precludes returning to the same workplace in most situations.

Reinstatement

The emphasis on damages for wrongful dismissal as the sole remedy of employees would seem to deny the use of other remedies such as *reinstatement*—a form of specific performance by which the court orders the employer to continue to employ the aggrieved employee. We noted in Chapter 15 the great reluctance of courts to order specific performance of contracts of service against an employee. Based on common law principles alone,[32] they are as unlikely to award reinstatement. However, the impersonal nature of most employment in large business enterprises has diminished the strength of argument against reinstatement based on the personal aspect of services. Unions have long bargained for arbitration procedures in cases of dismissal and for reinstatement in appropriate cases. Indeed, reinstatement has become the norm as the remedy for wrongful dismissal under collective agreements. Another example of the use of reinstatement occurs at universities; professors who have been wrongfully dismissed are ordinarily entitled to reinstatement.

Similar protection has become available to non-union employees in industries within the legislative jurisdiction of the federal Parliament. The Canada Labour Code provides that

245 . . . any [dismissed] person

(a) who has completed twelve consecutive months of continuous employment by an employer, and

(b) who is not a member of a group of employees subject to a collective agreement may make a complaint. . . . [33]

---

30. For a detailed discussion by the Supreme Court of Canada of additional factors affecting damage awards for wrongful dismissal, see *Wallace* v. *United Grain Growers Ltd.*, [1997] 3 S.C.R. 701. See also, *Fidler* v. *Sun Life Assurance Co. of Canada*, [2006] 2 S.C.R. 3, and *Honda Canada Inc.* v. *Keays*, 2008 SCC 39.

31. *Evans* v. *Teamsters Local Union No. 31*, 2008 SCC 20.

32. For an exception arising out of unusual circumstances, see *Hill* v. *Parsons*, [1971] 3 All E.R. 1345.

33. R.S.C. 1985, c. L-2, s. 245.

If an adjudicator decides that the person has been "unjustly dismissed," she may order the employer to reinstate the employee. The Quebec Labour Standards Act and the Nova Scotia Act create a similar right for employees, but in Quebec, only after two years of uninterrupted service with one employer, and in Nova Scotia, only after 10 years.[34]

ETHICAL ISSUE

Protection of Employee Privacy

With the advent of the electronic workplace, employees have become increasingly worried in recent years about their right to privacy. Employers provide their employees with telephone, facsimile, and e-mail facilities in order to communicate with colleagues and customers, but employers are increasingly concerned about how their employees are using this technology. To justify surveillance, employers argue that telephones and computers are company property. Therefore, the employer has the right to ensure they are only used for work rather than personal purposes, and that employees are not jeopardizing the security of confidential information. Employers also cite their duty to maintain a safe workplace—including the protection of employees against sexual harassment—as justification for monitoring employees.

Common forms of technological monitoring include:

- data shadowing,
- video surveillance, and
- GPS tracking.

One of the most controversial forms of monitoring involves biometrics. Biometrics use digital scans of personal features such as fingerprints and retinas to control access to computers, work premises, and so on.

Monitoring of employees is becoming commonplace. The American Management Association, in conjunction with The ePolicy Institute, has been surveying the use of employee monitoring for over 15 years. In 1993, only 33 percent of employers reported using some form of monitoring. However, by 2001 usage had risen to 79 percent.[35]

The federal Personal Information Protection and Electronic Documents Act (PIPEDA) provides that "organizations" must obtain consent of "individuals" to the collection, use, and disclosure of personal information, except where it would be "inappropriate" to do so. Section 4 extends the application of PIPEDA to personal information collected in some employment relationships (except an employee's name, title, business address, or telephone number). Surveillance of employees is not expressly forbidden by PIPEDA, but employers must use the least invasive form of surveillance and should give the employee advance notice.

The Office of the Privacy Commissioner of Canada has had several opportunities to consider the appropriateness of workplace surveillance under PIPEDA. In PIPEDA Case #279 (issued July 26, 2004), the Assistant Privacy Commissioner found that an Internet Service Provider's use of web cameras to monitor its employees was inappropriate. The employer's stated purposes for use of

continued

---

34. Labour Standards Act, R.S.Q. 1991, c. N-1.1, ss. 124–8; Labour Standards Code, R.S.N.S. 1989, c. 246, ss. 71(1) and 26(2)(a).

35. American Management Association, *Electronic Monitoring & Surveillance Survey*, Executive Summary 2001, 2005, 2007, http://press.amanet.org/category/press-releases/.

the cameras were: security of the workplace, especially from theft, and to monitor employee productivity. The Assistant Commissioner commented that there were less intrusive ways for the employer to have achieved these purposes. She further noted that "Continuous, indiscriminate surveillance of employees . . . was based on a lack of trust and treats all employees with suspicion when the underlying problems may rest with a few individuals or with a management plan that may not be entirely sound." In other words, the position of the Assistant Commissioner was that the "cost to human dignity," in the form of the right to privacy, must also be a factor in the assessment of the appropriateness of surveillance.

QUESTIONS TO CONSIDER

1. Should employees have the right to know they are being monitored and how? Should an employee have the right to object to surveillance?

2. Is it appropriate to "reduce privacy to a contractual right," as one commentator has put it? If a prospective employee is asked in a job application if she would consent to the electronic monitoring of her work by the employer, and she declines to give her consent, is the employer entitled to dismiss her application?

3. Is personal privacy a "fundamental human right"?

Sources: Privacy Commission of Canada, Commissioner's Findings, August 14, 2002, and Case Summary #279 (July 26, 2004) www.privcom.gc.ca; Anik Morrow, "Privacy and Data Protection," Paper for Ontario Bar Association Institute, January 24, 2002; B. McIsaac, R. Shields, and K. Klien, *Privacy Law in Canada, 2007 Student Edition,* (Toronto: Thomson Canada, 2007); *Eastmond* v. *Canadian Pacific Railway*, [2004] F.C.J. No 1043; M.A. Geist, "Computer and E-mail Workplace Surveillance in Canada: The Shift From Reasonable Expectation Of Privacy To Reasonable Surveillance" (2003), 82(2) *The Canadian Bar Review* 152–189.

CHECKLIST Employer Risk-Management Strategies

- Include precise notice requirements in employment contracts for an indefinite term.
- Create clear job descriptions and codes of conduct describing employee responsibilities.
- Follow consistent warning and discipline processes that allow employees to respond to allegations.
- Offer incompetent employees training or education.
- Document infractions and responses.
- Dismiss employees in the most sensitive, fair, and respectful manner possible.

EMPLOYEE WELFARE LEGISLATION

Background

Employee welfare legislation grew out of a desire to protect workers from unfair and harmful working conditions. The reform movement faced strong opposition from the proponents of freedom of contract. Nevertheless, the pressures of a changing society were irresistible: they resulted in a series of acts of Parliament commencing just before the mid-19th century. These statutes marked a new role for the state—active intervention on the side of the employees.

Initially, reform statutes dealt with the minimum age of workers, maximum hours of work, the presence of safety devices for machinery, the maintenance of safe premises in which to work, and the definition of the liability of employers when an employee was injured in the course of employment. These statutes were only a beginning. A review of the statute law considered in this section illustrates the degree to which our legislatures have limited the freedom of contract between individual employers and employees.

A number of statutes also provided special rules affecting women in respect to both working hours and working conditions. Some have been repealed in the name of equality between the genders, and it is yet to be seen how the remainder will be judged in relation to the guarantees of equality in section 15 of the Canadian Charter of Rights and Freedoms.

To the extent that employees are now represented by trade unions, the disparity in bargaining power between employer and employees has largely been removed. There remain, however, important categories of work in which employees typically are not unionized: they still negotiate contracts of employment on an individual basis with their employers. Accordingly, legislation enacted for the welfare and protection of employees continues to provide a minimum standard of working conditions for many people.

Legislative Jurisdiction

In Canada, the activities of a comparatively small but very important group of businesses bring them under federal jurisdiction, and for them the rights and duties of employers and employees are governed by federal labour legislation. These industries include shipping, air transport, interprovincial transportation and telephone systems, radio, banking, and the operations of federal Crown corporations.[36] The remainder of our economic activity—the bulk of what we think of as industrial and commercial enterprise—is subject to provincial rather than federal legislation.

Employee Rights

Human Rights

Enhancing the rights of employees through human rights legislation began in the 1970s, before the Canadian Charter of Rights and Freedoms was enacted in 1982. However, the process was accelerated by the words in section 15 of the Charter:

> Every individual . . . has the right to the equal protection and equal benefit of the law without discrimination and, in particular without discrimination based on race, national or ethnic origin, colour, religion, sex, age or mental or physical disability.

Section 28 emphasizes that Charter rights "are guaranteed equally to male and female persons."

As we noted in Chapter 1, the Charter does not apply to the private sector, but human rights legislation passed by every province and the federal Parliament does apply to that sector. Most complaints under the provincial legislation relate to employment. The wording varies considerably but, generally speaking, the acts make it an offence to engage in

> a discriminatory practice . . . to refuse to employ or continue to employ an individual, or . . . to differentiate adversely . . . on a prohibited ground,[37]

that is, on the basis of

> race, national or ethnic origin, colour, religion, age, sex, sexual orientation, marital status, family status, disability and conviction for which a pardon has been granted.[38]

---

36. Constitution Act, 1867, s. 91.
37. Canadian Human Rights Act, R.S.C. 1985, c. H-6, s. 7(a) and (b).
38. *Ibid.*, s. 3(1), amended to include "sexual orientation," by S.C. 1996, c. 14.

Human rights legislation has increased the awareness of both public and private sector employers. To employers who are sensitive to the issues of non-discrimination, there is little or no additional cost of doing business. Indeed, it has been argued that employers who seek the most competent people and comply with the legislation by ignoring the listed personal characteristics of prospective employees benefit in terms of increased efficiency.

Pay Equity

Pay equity legislation is directed towards eliminating gender discrimination in remuneration. There are two ways of assessing the wage gap between men and women. The more traditional is through the principle of "equal pay for equal work." The law prohibits different levels of pay for substantially the same kind of work performed in the same establishment, requiring substantially the same skill, effort, and responsibility, and performed under similar working conditions.[39]

The second approach requires a focus not on the similarity of the jobs done by women and men, but on their **comparative value** to the employer—the concept of "equal pay for work of equal value" or "comparable worth."[40] The legislation requires employers to pay employees performing jobs traditionally done by women the same as those performing jobs done by men if the jobs are of equal or comparable value. The main task is to give a meaning to the word "value." It must mean something more than current market value of work, for if women are being hired at a traditionally lower wage than men receive, then an employer can argue that the market shows it can hire women at that lower wage: according to this argument, they are already being paid what they are "worth." Instead, the effort and training of the worker must be taken into account. Accordingly, while a secretary's job may require less physical effort and she may have better working conditions than a groundskeeper, her job may require taking more responsibility, applying more mental effort, and having greater skills training. Assessing the relative value of different kinds of work can be the subject of much debate.

comparative value
"equal pay for work of equal value"

Once a job evaluation results in a finding that one group of employees is paid too little in comparison with another, almost always it is unacceptable to reduce the wages of the more highly paid group. The pressure to increase the wages of the lower-paid group may substantially raise the labour costs of an employer, making it likely that the employer will contest the job evaluation.

Under traditional legislative reform, someone must file a complaint in order to trigger enforcement of the legislation's general prohibitions. An important difficulty with implementing pay equity results from reliance on a complaints system because it assumes that violations are the exception, not the rule, and it is effective only if breaches are infrequent. However, if wage discrimination is *systemic* and pervasive throughout the economy, then a complaints system of enforcement has two flaws: either it may easily be overwhelmed with individual cases, or employees may feel intimidated and fear making a complaint. To overcome this problem, the most recent pay equity legislation is based on **systemic discrimination**. It abandons the complaint system in favour of a regulatory model that not only prohibits wage discrimination but also places positive obligations on employers to scrutinize their pay practices and ensure that these practices comply with the legislation.

systemic discrimination
discrimination that is pervasive throughout an employer's work force

At present, the latest regulatory model applies to the public sectors in Manitoba, New Brunswick, Newfoundland, Nova Scotia, and Prince Edward Island, and in Ontario to both the public sector and to private sector employers who employ 10 or more persons. Throughout the rest of Canada, the complaints system alone remains in force.

Employment Equity

The newest development in employment rights goes beyond requiring employers to treat individual applicants for jobs equally, regardless of personal characteristics. Employers may be required to

---

39. At present, the standard of "equal pay for equal work" applies federally and in all provinces.

40. This standard applies to both sectors in areas of federal jurisdiction and in Quebec. See Canadian Pay Equity Compliance Guide (North York, ON: CCH Canadian Ltd., 1990).

strive towards making their work force reflect the various underrepresented classes of disadvantaged persons in the general population.

In 1986, the federal Parliament passed the Employment Equity Act,[41] which applies to all employers with 100 or more employees, "in connection with federal work, undertaking or business as defined in section 2 of the *Canada Labour Code* . . ." Employers are required to conduct a "work-force analysis"—that is, to obtain relevant information about the personal characteristics of their current employees, in order to determine underrepresentation of designated groups—women, visible minorities, Aboriginals, and persons with disabilities—in the work force generally. In addition to information from their current employees, employers must seek the same information from job applicants before determining whether certain applicants should be given preference. Employers are required to review their formal and informal hiring policies in order to remove all systemic discrimination against the designated groups, and to set goals and timetables for achieving representation based on the working-age population within each employer's community. Finally, they must prepare a plan to carry out their goals, including monitoring systems to assess their progress.

Although there was debate about intrusiveness in obtaining information about the personal characteristics of both employees and job applicants, and also about the weight employers will be required to give to the designated characteristics in making hiring decisions, the federal legislation has remained in force. In December 1993, the Ontario legislature passed a bill similar to the federal Act,[42] which applied to all public sector employment and to private sector employers with more than 50 employees. It became a major issue in the 1995 provincial election; the Progressive Conservative Party vowed to repeal the legislation, and did so after it was elected to power.[43] No other provinces have passed similar legislation.

Regulation of Working Conditions

General Working Conditions

Each province has enacted a variety of statutes prohibiting child labour, regulating the hours of work of young persons, and providing for the health and safety of employees while at work. Provinces may appoint inspectors to see that these requirements are complied with. Other statutes specify a minimum age at which children may leave school and accept full-time employment.

All provinces and the federal government provide by statute for minimum-wage rates, and grant discretionary power to certain government agencies to fix a minimum wage that varies with the industry. The legislation sets limited working hours, with some exceptions, of eight hours a day and a maximum of 40 or 48 hours a week. These statutes also require overtime rates if the number of hours worked exceeds the specified maximum.

All provinces provide for annual vacations with pay. The most frequent requirement is for employers to grant their employees one week's paid vacation after one year of work. Some provinces also require public holidays with pay.

Mandatory Retirement and the Charter of Rights and Freedoms

For many years, Canadians accepted mandatory retirement schemes as desirable and humane social institutions: workers were expected to leave their jobs, usually at age 65, and enjoy retirement on an adequate pension. However, increasing good health and life expectancy have meant that many people approaching their 65th year, who feel vigorous and enjoy their work, wish to continue working. Moreover, rapid inflation over a 30-year period until the mid-1990s has led to an unexpected

41. S.C. 1995, c. 44.

42. Employment Equity Act, S.O. 1993, c. 35.

43. Job Quotas Repeal Act, S.O. 1995, c. 4.

diminishing in the value of pensions available to many people reaching retirement age; they feel they must continue to work to maintain a reasonable standard of living. On the other hand, employers and others—especially young people seeking work—want employees to retire at the established compulsory retirement age. Some employers have insisted that they do so.

Since section 15 of the Charter of Rights and Freedoms guarantees "equal protection and benefit of the law without discrimination . . . based on . . . age," public sector employees wishing to remain in their jobs have challenged mandatory retirement provisions. The Charter has also been used to challenge provincial human rights legislation that condones mandatory retirement. Challengers claim that mandatory retirement based solely on age, without regard to the health or competence of an employee, is arbitrary and discriminatory and therefore offends the Charter. A similar argument was made successfully under the Manitoba Human Rights Code in 1981; the court held that a mandatory retirement provision at the University of Manitoba offended the provincial Code and was void.[44] The province of Quebec abolished compulsory retirement by statute in 1982.[45] In 1985, the federal government abolished mandatory retirement in its civil service. Ontario abolished it in 2005.

Defenders of mandatory retirement schemes claim that, because the schemes are socially desirable, under section 1 of the Charter they are valid because they are a "reasonable limit prescribed by law" and "can be demonstrably justified in a free and democratic society." The British Columbia human rights statute prohibits discrimination based on age but only between the ages of 18 and 65 years, and so allow mandatory retirement at 65. The Supreme Court of Canada allowed such schemes in a group of four decisions dealing with complaints made by employees of hospitals, community colleges, and universities.[46] Mandatory retirement schemes may also be upheld when they are a genuine occupational requirement.

Employment Insurance

The Employment Insurance Act[47] manages a federal employment insurance fund to which both employers and employees must contribute through payroll deductions according to a published schedule of rates. Coverage is not extended to persons receiving retirement pensions, self-employed, employed by a spouse, and employed by provincial governments, foreign governments, and international organizations.[48] The employer must account for all employee contributions and, along with its own contributions, regularly send them to the government. Benefits are payable out of the fund to workers who have contributed in the past and are currently unemployed. These benefits are not available in some circumstances, one of which is loss of work caused by a labour dispute in which the employee is on strike. Other employees, not on strike but "locked out" because a plant or business is shut down by a strike, remain eligible for benefits.

Most important, especially if an employee is unhappy with his or her treatment at work and voluntarily leaves employment without just cause—or is justifiably dismissed for misconduct—he or she will not be eligible for benefits.

44. *McIntyre* v. *University of Manitoba* (1981), 119 D.L.R. (3d) 352, followed by *Newport* v. *Government of Manitoba* (1982), 131 D.L.R. (3d) 564. Both cases held that section 6(1) of the Human Rights Code, S.M. 1974, c. 65, made mandatory retirement provisions void.

45. Abolition of Compulsory Retirement Act, S.Q. 1982, c. 12.

46. *McKinney* v. *University of Guelph*, [1990] 3 S.C.R. 229; *Harrison* v. *University of British Columbia*, [1990] 3 S.C.R. 451; *Stoffman* v. *Vancouver General Hospital*, 3 S.C.R. 483; *Douglas/Kwantlen Faculty Association* v. *Douglas College*, 3 S.C.R. 570. Provincial human rights codes and the federal Human Rights Act apply to all employment contracts within their jurisdiction, both in the public and private sectors. In contrast, section 15 of the Charter applies to all employment contracts made in the public sector—contracts made by governments at all levels, by Crown corporations, school boards, community colleges, etc.; it does not bind the private sector, including universities (see the McKinney case), even though they may receive a high proportion of their funding from governments.

47. Employment Insurance Act, S.C. 1996, c. 23 E-5.6.

48. *Ibid.*, s. 5(2).

Workers' Compensation

Harshness of the Common Law

While the common law recognized that an employer could be liable to an employee for injury sustained in the course of employment, it was notoriously difficult for the employee to recover damages. The employer might defend the action successfully if it could show that the injury:

(a) resulted from the contributory negligence of the employee, as discussed in Chapter 3, showing that he was partly responsible for the accident, even in a small degree;

(b) was caused by the negligence of a fellow employee (or **fellow servant**), provided the employer took reasonable care to hire competent workers, the usual result being that the employer escaped liability for the negligence of one employee that caused injury to another;

(c) was an **assumed risk**, accepted by the employee as a normal incident of the type of work he had agreed to do—and broadly interpreted, it might defeat almost any action by an employee, for it could be argued that every risk is a risk an employee assumes in accepting a particular employment.

It would also be difficult for dependants of an employee who had been killed at work to obtain the necessary proof to meet the burden of proof.

fellow servant
fellow employee

assumed risk
risk assumed by an employee in accepting a particular employment

Statutory Reform

Each of the provinces has replaced the common law action with a statutory compensation scheme.[49]

The statutes create Workers' Compensation Boards to hear employees' claims and also establish funds to which employers subject to the Act must contribute regularly and which are used to pay claims. Such payment replaces any personal action against an employer. To succeed, an employee need only show that the injury was caused by an accident in the course of employment. The defences of contributory negligence, negligence of a fellow servant, and assumed risk no longer apply. An employee's claim will fail only if it is shown that the accident was caused substantially by his wilful misconduct. Even then, the employee or the dependants will recover if the accident has caused death or serious disablement. The requirement of proving negligence by the employer, so long a barrier to compensation for injury, no longer exists. There is also a major advantage in avoiding the costs and hazards of litigation. As well, since an employee claims recovery from a compensation board and not from his employer, he need *not* fear prejudicing his future with the employer.

Variations in Provincial Reforms

Coverage varies somewhat among the provinces. Generally included are workers in the following industries: construction, mining, manufacturing, lumbering, fishing, transportation, communications, and public utilities. Industries are classified according to the degree of hazard. Exemptions may include casual employees and employees of small businesses employing fewer than a stated number of workers. For employees excluded from the usual workers' compensation benefits, several provinces have added a second part to their legislation defining the employer's liability for injuries caused by defective plant or equipment, or by the negligence of other employees, and granting employees a right to damages in spite of contributory negligence on their part. In other jurisdictions, the common law rules still apply to casual employees and to those in small businesses.

49. See, for example: Workers' Compensation Act, R.S.B.C. 1996, c. 492; S.N.S. 1994–95, c. 10; Workplace Safety and Insurance Act, S.O. 1997, c. 16.

Occupational Health

An area of growing concern and controversy closely related to occupational safety is occupational health. There are several reasons for the increasing awareness of health standards in the workplace. First, the general concern over environmental hazards to health has made the public much more sensitive to the special problems of the work environment: if a chemical dispersed in the atmosphere can harm people at a great distance, how much more dangerous is it for the workers who handle it and are directly exposed? Second, improvement in the general level of public health has drawn attention to the fact that persons in particular occupations suffer from certain illnesses to a greater degree than does the general public. Third, improvement in the quality of medical records and the sophistication of medical diagnosis have made it easier to connect certain diseases with some occupations. This last aspect has received great prominence in industries where large numbers of workers have been found to have very high rates of some illnesses 20 or 30 years after starting work.

Many questions concerning occupational health in the workplace remain unanswered. Should the general system of workers' compensation be responsible for research into potential health hazards, for policing work conditions in plants, and for financial aid to affected workers? Should special legislation be enacted to make industries legally responsible for specific illnesses (keeping in mind that it may be very difficult to prove in a court that the workplace actually caused a particular illness)?

Provincial occupational health and safety legislation takes a proactive approach to prevent injury in the workplace.[50] It requires a business to establish an in-house committee to identify, investigate, and correct dangers in the workplace. Government inspections are randomly carried out and companies may be fined for failing to remedy a dangerous situation. Injuries in the workplace automatically trigger an investigation.

INTERNATIONAL ISSUE

Global Employment Standards

Wide variation in wages and employment conditions around the world have led to a number of initiatives aimed at harmonizing and improving standards in developing nations. Two of the most prominent are:

- the United Nations (UN) Global Compact, and
- the Organization for Economic Co-operation and Development (OECD) Guidelines for Multinational Enterprises.

Both initiatives take a corporate social-responsibility approach. The UN Global Compact is a set of 10 principles addressing human rights, labour, the environment, and corruption. A business voluntarily undertakes to participate in the compact and in so doing agrees to adopt policies and operations furthering the compact's objectives and to publicize the results of their progress. The four principles dealing with labour are:

- freedom of association and the right to collective bargaining,
- elimination of all forms of forced and compulsory labour,
- effective abolition of child labour,
- elimination of discrimination in respect of employment and occupation.

continued

---

50. Some provinces, such as British Columbia, cover this issue in the workers' compensation legislation while others have separate legislation: Occupational Health and Safety Act, R.S.O. 1990, c. O.1.

Many of Canada's largest companies participate in the Global Compact including Alcan Inc., Bombardier, Enbridge, Hydro Quebec, and Petro Canada.

The OECD guidelines are also voluntary standards but they are the recommendations of the participating governments to the multinationals within their respective jurisdictions. Canada is a participating country. The Guidelines include eight standards addressing employment and industrial relations that are more detailed than those in the Global Compact.

QUESTIONS TO CONSIDER

1. Do you think voluntary compliance with these international codes of conduct is more likely to be achieved through the business-network approach of the Global Compact or the government-backed approach of the OECD? Why?

2. Discuss the pros and cons of the broad general principles of the Global Compact as distinct from the more detailed set of standards of the OECD.

Sources: "The Ten Principles," *The United Nations Global Compact,* www.unglobalcompact.org/AbouttheGC/ TheTENPrinciples/index.html; Organisation for Economic Co-operation and Development, *The OECD Guidelines for Multinational Enterprises* (Paris: OECD Publications, 2000), www.oecd.org/dataoecd/56/36/ 1922428.pdf; The UN Global Compact Office and OECD Secretariat, *The UN Global Compact and the OECD Guidelines For Multinational Enterprises: Complementarities and Distinctive Contributions,* Investment Division, Organization for Economic Co-operation and Development, April 26, 2005, www.oecd.org/dataoecd/23/2/ 34873731.pdf.

collective bargaining
establishing conditions of employment by negotiation between an employer and the bargaining agent for its employees

certification
an acknowledgment by an administrative tribunal that a particular union commands sufficient membership to justify its role as exclusive bargaining agent for the employees

labour relations board
an administrative tribunal regulating labour relations

bargaining agent
a union that has the exclusive right to bargain with the employer on behalf of the bargaining unit

bargaining unit
a specified group of employees eligible to join the union

COLLECTIVE BARGAINING

The Process

The process of establishing terms of employment through negotiations between a business and the bargaining agent for its employees is known as **collective bargaining**. For those industries within federal jurisdiction, a federal statute regulates collective bargaining.[51] Statutes passed by each of the provinces regulate all other industries.[52] These acts state that all employees are free to belong to trade unions and that membership in a trade union does not provide the employer with grounds for dismissing an employee. The acts also require employers to recognize the representative union as the bargaining agent for employees for reaching an agreement on the general terms of their employment.

If an employer is unwilling to recognize a trade union voluntarily, as often happens, the union may have to apply to be certified before it can proceed to bargain for the employees. **Certification** is an acknowledgment by an administrative tribunal (called in some provinces a **labour relations board**) that a particular union has won sufficient membership to justify its role as exclusive bargaining agent for the employees. This arrangement has the practical advantage of confining the negotiations to a single representative of the employees, and it avoids the confusion of rival unions claiming the right to act as bargaining agents for a group of employees. We must distinguish between a bargaining agent and a bargaining unit: a **bargaining agent** is a union that has the exclusive right to bargain with the employer on behalf of the **bargaining unit**: the bargaining unit includes a specific group of employees eligible to join the union, whether they join or not.

---

51. Canada Labour Code, R.S.C. 1985, c. L-2.

52. See, for example: Labour Relations Code, R.S.B.C. 1996, c. 244; Labour Relations Act, S.O. 1995, c. 1; Trade Union Act, R.S.N.S. 1989, c. 475.

Content of a Collective Agreement

When an employer and union reach an agreement, they place the terms in a contract called a *collective agreement*. The terms usually include a definition of the employees covered, an acknowledgment by the employer that the contracting union is their recognized bargaining agent, an outline of the steps that both parties must take in settling grievances, seniority provisions in the promotion and laying off of employees, wage rates, hours, vacation periods and other fringe benefits, the duration of the collective agreement, and the means by which it may be amended or renewed. Often there is a clause acknowledging that maintaining discipline and efficiency of employees is the exclusive task of the management of the company, subject to the right of an employee to lodge a grievance. The agreement almost invariably forbids strikes or lockouts as long as the agreement continues to operate; indeed, most provinces require that such a term be included. The employees covered do not generally include those employed in a confidential capacity, those who have managerial responsibilities such as the authority to hire or discharge others, or those employed as guards or security police in the protection of business property. Some provinces have also excluded certain professional groups such as engineers, although the recent tendency has been to include more of the professions.

The terms of a collective agreement generally prescribe in detail the procedure for dismissing employees, replacing the common law rules for notice of dismissal and grounds for dismissal. To the extent that the collective agreement prescribes working conditions above the level required by existing legislation, it replaces employee welfare legislation in protecting the interests of workers.

First Collective Agreement

Frequently the most difficult collective agreement to reach is the first one after certification: the union is new and its local members are inexperienced (even if they have advice from other union officials); management is unaccustomed to working with a union; and often there has been some hostility and bitterness between employer and employees during the certification campaign. In response to the problem, first British Columbia in 1973, followed by the federal government, Quebec, Manitoba, and Ontario, passed legislation providing for "first contract arbitration."[53] If the parties cannot reach agreement on a contract within the time stated in the Act, then the provincial or federal labour board concerned may, after hearing the parties in an arbitration, impose a first contract on them.

LABOUR DISPUTES

Types of Disputes

There are four major types of disputes affecting trade unions: jurisdictional disputes, recognition disputes, interest disputes, and rights disputes.

(1) A **jurisdictional dispute** is a disagreement between unions competing for the right to represent a group of employees. For instance, the type of work they do may seem to bring them within the terms of reference of two different trade unions. A single operation of drilling a hole through both metal and wood might raise a question of whether the worker should belong to the metalworkers' or the woodworkers' union.

jurisdictional dispute
two or more unions compete for the right to represent a particular group of employees

(2) A **recognition dispute** arises between an employer and a union when the employer insists on negotiating employment contracts directly with its employees and resists a union demand that it be recognized as the employees' bargaining agent.

recognition dispute
an employer refuses to recognize the union as the employees' bargaining agent

---

53. R.S.B.C. 1996, c. 244, s. 55; R.S.Q. 1991, c. C-27, s. 93.1; R.S.M. 1987, c. L-10, s. 75; S.O. 1995, c. 1, Sch. A, s. 43.

interest dispute
an employer and the union disagree about the particular terms to be included in the collective agreement

rights dispute
an employer and the union differ in their interpretation of terms in an existing collective agreement

(3) An **interest dispute** arises when an employer and a union cannot reach agreement about the terms to be included in a collective agreement.

(4) A **rights dispute** is a difference of opinion between employer and union on the interpretation of terms in a collective agreement already in existence.

Legislative Regulation

As we have noted, the regulation of labour disputes is a field of study in its own right, and we cannot do more than indicate a few of the basic methods used. For an adequate treatment of the law, it is necessary to consult recognized works in the field; a few are listed in the bibliography at the end of this book.

Statutes now provide machinery that either eliminates or minimizes the need to resort to strike action in each of the four main types of dispute mentioned above. Certification procedure, briefly considered in the preceding section, has done much to resolve jurisdictional disputes and is the only legal means of settling recognition disputes.

Provincial statutes require both employer and employees to follow a series of procedures designed to aid in the settlement of interest disputes:

conciliation procedure
bargaining with the help of a conciliation officer or board

cooling-off period
a time during which the employer cannot declare a lockout nor can the union begin a strike

arbitration procedure
the procedure in a rights dispute that binds the parties to accept the interpretation of the collective agreement by an arbitrator

- *First*, they require a genuine attempt over a specified period to bargain to reach agreement.[54]

- *Second*, if the parties fail to agree, they must submit to **conciliation procedure**—that is, continue to bargain with the help of a conciliation officer or board.

- *Third*, if the parties still fail to agree, the employer cannot declare a lockout or the union begin strike action until a further specified **cooling-off period** has elapsed.

For the fourth type, a rights dispute, the law imposes **arbitration procedure**: the parties are bound by the interpretation placed on the collective agreement by an arbitrator. In conciliation procedure, the parties are not bound to accept the solution proposed by the conciliation officer, but in arbitration procedure, the decision of the arbitrator is binding.

We can see that only in interest disputes is there the possibility of lawful strike action, and then only after the prescribed conciliation procedure and cooling-off period. A strike is illegal if the preliminary grievance procedures set down by statute have not been followed or, even when they have been followed, if the strike is not conducted according to carefully defined rules. The conduct of a strike by the union must be free of compulsion, intimidation, and threat. Furthermore, a strike may become unlawful if it is undertaken with an intent to injure another party and not with the intent of improving the employment interests of the strikers.

Although strikers are entitled to picket at or near the place of the employer's business, they must do so peaceably and only for the purpose of obtaining or communicating information. Statements made on placards or in literature distributed at the scene of the picketing must be correct and factual. Mr. Chief Justice McRuer of the Ontario Supreme Court outlined the scope of these rights as follows:

> It is one thing to exercise all the lawful rights to strike and the lawful rights to picket; that is a freedom that should be preserved and its preservation has advanced the interests of the labouring man and the community as a whole to an untold degree over the last half-century. But it is another thing to recognize a conspiracy to injure so that benefits to any particular person or class may be realized. Further, if what any person or group of persons does amounts to a common law nuisance to another what is being done may be restrained by injunction.[55]

---

54. In Canada, an employer need not bargain with a union that has not been certified and with which it has not previously made a collective agreement. In the United States, an employer must bargain with a union representing the majority of its employees, whether it is certified or not.

55. *General Dry Batteries of Canada Ltd.* v. *Brigenshaw*, [1951] O.R. 522, per McRuer, C.J.H.C., at 528. See also *O.K. Economy Stores* v. *R.W.D.S.U., Local 454* (1994), 118 D.L.R. (4th) 345.

IMPLICATIONS OF THE COLLECTIVE AGREEMENT FOR THE INDIVIDUAL EMPLOYEE

The parties to a collective agreement are the employer and the representative union; generally, each party is a large organization or institution, and the individual employee does not actively participate in negotiating the terms of employment. Since nearly all the bargaining is done by the union, comparatively little ground is left for an employee to negotiate with the employer at the time of making an individual contract of employment.

Labour unions have, of course, been an important means for workers collectively to obtain a bargaining power that they do not have individually, and unions have secured many improvements in conditions of work. On the other hand, the process is one that necessarily makes individual employee preferences less important than the collective goals of an organization. An individual's terms of employment are determined by his status as a member of the bargaining unit, rather than by any personal bargaining efforts:

> . . . contract becomes largely the technique of group manipulation and use. Professional managements speak for the large corporation, and professional labor leaders speak for workers; the contract thus arrived at becomes a contribution to a code of administrative behavior by which the individual's personal right to contract is considerably diminished. As a working proposition, then, we are prepared to assert that contract is meaningful today more in terms of its use by organizations and less in terms of its use by individuals.[56]

The province of Quebec has a unique piece of legislation that takes this process a stage further: the terms of a collective agreement may apply even to workers who are not members of the bargaining unit for which the union was entitled to negotiate.[57] Under the legislation, when a union has bargained for a certain rate of pay with one or more large employers within the industry, the parties may apply to the Minister of Labour for a decree extending the provisions of the collective agreement to all other employers and employees within the industry or trade in the province or within a region of the province. To succeed, the application must show that the collective agreements already written have acquired a dominance and importance for establishing conditions of labour within the industry or region. The effect is to establish a minimum wage law within the area covered by the decree, and to extend the terms of the collective agreement to workers within the industry not represented when the contract was made.

And unions have more than the dominant role in bargaining on behalf of individual workers; often workers do not have the freedom to choose whether to belong to the union. In *Bonsor* v. *Musicians' Union*,[58] the plaintiff, who had been wrongfully expelled from the union and found it impossible to earn a livelihood as a musician without being a member, testified as follows:

> I would like to tell his lordship that if I could earn my living forthwith without being a member of this so-called Musicians' Union I would not want to join it, but I have got to join it in order to work because it is a closed shop. I will always pay my subscriptions, but I will not take any active part in union matters. I will be a member by force because I am forced to be a member.[59]

After quoting the above statement of the plaintiff, Lord Denning commented:

> When one remembers that the rules are applied to a man in that state of mind, it will be appreciated that they are not so much a contract as we used to understand a contract, but they are much more a legislative code laid down by some members of the union to be imposed on all members of the union. They are more like by-laws than a contract.[60]

---

56. R.S.F. Eells and C. Walton, *Conceptual Foundations of Business*, 2nd ed. (Homewood, IL: Richard D. Irwin, 1969) at 260–1.
57. Collective Agreement Decrees Act, R.S.Q. 1991, c. D-2.
58. [1954] Ch. 479. (The dissenting judgment of Denning, L.J., was approved on appeal to the House of Lords: [1956] A.C. 105.)
59. *Ibid.*, at 485.
60. *Ibid.*

Trade unions are, of course, only one of the modern institutions that have this effect on contract. Contracts between existing businesses that restrict competition by fixing prices or output effectively diminish the freedom of contract of the consuming public; we shall consider the law dealing with this problem in Chapter 32. In addition, as we have seen, many financial institutions (insurance companies and finance companies, for example) present those to whom they sell their services with a standard form contract. It contains the terms of the agreement set down in advance on a take-it-or-leave-it basis—diminishing or even eliminating the opportunity for the other contracting party to bargain for terms it would prefer.

THE LEGAL STATUS OF TRADE UNIONS

We touched briefly on the legal status of trade unions when discussing capacity to contract in Chapter 7. We noted that trade unions are recognized as legal entities before labour relations boards in order to bind them to the board's rulings; but this recognition is for a limited purpose, and we must not infer from the fact that unions have a separate existence before an administrative tribunal that they necessarily have comparable standing before the courts. We noted also that using a representative action provides a possible means by which unions may sue or be sued in the courts.

For various reasons, our legislatures have avoided the otherwise obvious path of requiring trade unions to come within existing legislation for corporations, and so conferring on them a corporate existence comparable with that of other business organizations. Nevertheless, the legislatures seem to be moving in that direction, and when there is no decisive statutory authority, the courts are able to cite the reasoning in the famous *Taff Vale* case, a decision handed down by the House of Lords in 1901.[61]

CASE 20.1

During a strike, two agents of a union "put themselves in charge . . . and . . . illegally watched and beset men to prevent them from working for the company, and illegally ordered men to break their contracts." The court interpreted the strike as a conspiracy in restraint of trade under the then-existing law of England. As a result, the company suffered business losses and sued the union. But even though there was an admitted wrong, could the union as such be sued for damages? The House of Lords found the trade union to be a "quasi-corporate" body that could be sued. It held the union liable in damages for the company's losses.

Although the result of the *Taff Vale* case was nullified shortly afterwards by an act of Parliament,[62] and although this act was adopted by provinces in Canada, the judicial reasoning concerning the legal personality of trade unions survived and persisted.

The Supreme Court of Canada in 1960 made extensive use of the *Taff Vale* decision in the case of *International Brotherhood of Teamsters* v. *Thérien*.[63]

---

61. *Taff Vale Railway Co.* v. *Amalgamated Society of Railway Servants*, [1901] A.C. 426.

62. See Trade Disputes Act, 1906, 6 Ed. VII, c. 47, s. 1, declaring that actions of a trade union in furtherance of its interests would not thenceforth be interpreted as a restraint of trade.

63. (1960), 22 D.L.R. (2d) 1. This decision has been followed in a Manitoba case: *Dusessoy's Supermarket St. James Ltd.* v. *Retail Clerks Union Local No. 832* (1961), 34 W.W.R. 577.

CASE 20.2

Thérien was the owner of a Vancouver trucking business and had been doing business with City Construction Company for some years when the company entered into a collective agreement with the Teamsters' Union requiring, as one of its terms, that all employees be union members (a **closed-shop agreement**). Thérien agreed then to hire only union members for the operation of his trucks. However, he declined to join the union personally because he wished to maintain his relationship as an independent contractor in dealings with City Construction. He further claimed that in the capacity of an employer in his own right, he was forbidden by the Labour Relations Code of British Columbia from participating in union activities.

The union opposed that view, and because of its threats to picket City Construction, the general manager of the company informed Thérien that the company must terminate his services. Thérien suffered a significant loss of business, and he sued the union, claiming damages for its wrongful conduct. The union defended on the grounds that it was not a legal entity and so could not be sued and, second, that in any case it had not been guilty of conduct that might constitute a tort.

On the first argument of the union, the court noted that the union had been certified as a bargaining agent under the terms of the Labour Relations Act, and stated:

> It is necessary for the exercise of the [statutory] powers given that such unions should have officers or other agents to act in their names and on their behalf. The Legislature, by giving the right to act as agent for others and to contract on their behalf, has given them two of the essential qualities of a corporation in respect of liability for tort since a corporation can only act by its agents.[64]

The court quoted with approval the remarks of Lord Halsbury in the *Taff Vale* case:

> If the Legislature has created a thing which can own property, which can employ servants, and which can inflict injury, it must be taken, I think, to have impliedly given the power to make it suable in a Court of Law for injuries purposely done by its authority and procurement.[65]

Having identified the union as a suable legal entity, the court found, first, that the union had threatened to resort to picketing instead of following the grievance procedure set out in the collective agreement, and second, that the consequence of its conduct was the injurious termination of Thérien's arrangement with City Construction Company. The court awarded damages to Thérien and ordered an injunction restraining the union from interfering with him in the operation of his business.

The *Thérien* decision is one of a succession of Canadian cases developing the common law on the subject of the legal status of trade unions.[66] It does not apply, of course, in provinces whose statutes specifically define the circumstances in which trade unions may be sued. In particular, Ontario has a statutory provision that restricts the possibility of an action against a trade union for torts.[67]

closed-shop agreement
a collective agreement requiring all employees to be union members

---

64. *International Brotherhood of Teamsters* v. *Thérien, ibid.*, per Locke, J., at 11.

65. *Taff Vale Railway Co.* v. *Amalgamated Society of Railway Servants, supra*, n. 58, per Halsbury, L.C., at 436.

66. See, for example: *U.N.A.* v. *Alberta (Attorney-General)* (1990), 89 D.L.R. (4th) 609.

67. Rights of Labour Act, R.S.O. 1990, c. R.33, s. 3. For legislation expressly making unions suable entities, see Labour Relations Code, R.S.B.C. 1996, c. 144, s. 154; Labour Relations Act, R.S.M. 1987, c. L-10, s. 127; Industrial Relations Act, R.S.N.B. 1973, c. I-4, s. 114(2); Trade Union Act, R.S.S. 1978, c. T-17, s. 29, as amended by S.S. 1983, c. 81, s. 9.

QUESTIONS FOR REVIEW

1. Briefly describe two employees, each of whom has varying degrees of responsibility as agent.

2. How does an independent contractor differ from an employee?

3. Give an example of circumstances where an employee commits a tort but his employer is not liable. What element is necessary to make the employer liable?

4. After earning his B.Comm. degree, Bruce was hired as a junior accountant by Cargo Wholesale Inc. He received favourable assessment letters and salary increases after year one and year two. At the end of his third year, he received his final paycheque with a letter stating that he was dismissed for incompetence. What points might Bruce argue to show that he was wrongfully dismissed?

5. Norman is hired as a waiter in a restaurant at a summer resort without any discussion about the length of his employment contract. He receives a weekly paycheque. He is let go without notice at the end of the summer. Explain whether he has been wrongfully dismissed.

6. On what grounds is a business justified in dismissing its employees without notice?

7. What are the main factors to be taken into account when assessing damages for wrongful dismissal?

8. When is reinstatement an unlikely remedy for wrongful dismissal?

9. Why is it not effective to define pay equity solely in terms of the market value of comparable jobs?

10. Describe briefly the benefits of and problems with compulsory retirement.

11. Why was it difficult before the passing of the Workers' Compensation Act for an employee injured at work to obtain a remedy against her employer?

12. Under workers' compensation legislation, who pays compensation to an injured employee? How are the funds raised?

13. Describe some of the main elements in a collective agreement.

14. In certain provinces and in federal jurisdiction, what happens when the parties do not succeed in making a deal for their first collective agreement?

15. What is the difference between a jurisdictional dispute and an interest dispute?

16. Collective agreements have been described by some commentators as being more like legislation for individual workers. Explain.

17. Quality Meat Packers Ltd. has major factories and warehouses from coast to coast. How does this fact complicate the company's collective bargaining with its employees?

CASES AND PROBLEMS

1. Taxi drivers owned their own taxis and worked for Welcome Taxis Ltd. The taxi company called them "independent contractors" and distinguished them from employees in that they were not covered by the Employment Insurance Act. Although the company neither owned nor leased the vehicles, the drivers were required to comply with the company's directions about the dispatch services and how the vehicles were operated. They were also obligated to use the company's bookkeeping and fuel provision services— and the company could suspend or discharge the drivers for any breach of its rules.

   The Ministry of National Revenue decided to assess Welcome and require it to pay premiums for each of its drivers as an employee. Welcome appealed to the court, and the trial judge concluded that such a degree of control was exercised by the taxi company over the drivers that all the drivers were in insurable employment, pursuant to section 6(e) of the Act. The taxi company brought an application for judicial review to the Federal Court of Appeal. The following arguments were made:

   By Welcome Taxis Ltd.—The drivers were owners or operators of their own businesses within the meaning of section 6(e) of the Regulations. The trial judge erred in considering only the factor of control to the exclusion of other relevant factors. Another consideration was who owned the tools of the trade. Not only did the drivers own the vehicles, but they were in a position to gain a profit or suffer a loss from the operation of the business. The degree of financial risk taken by the drivers was considerably more than that taken by the company. The drivers were in a position to delegate their driving duties, which indicated independent status. Given the chance of profit, the relative degree of financial risk, and the ability of the drivers to "operate their own business," they were not employees of the company.

By the Ministry of National Revenue—Under a traditional employee/independent contractor analysis, the drivers appeared to be in business for their own account, as independent contractors. However, the breadth of section 6(e) was broad enough to extend the conventional meaning of "employment." The company exercised a great deal of control over the drivers. Although it did not own or lease the vehicles, it retained the right to cancel the lease agreement or exercise its option to purchase the vehicle if the drivers should fail to observe its rules. The trial judge had not erred in applying a liberal interpretation of section 6(e) and finding that the drivers were included in insurable employment.

Which argument do you think should succeed in the Court of Appeal? Give reasons for your opinion.

2. Benson had been manager of the Kilnnok Pub for 10 years. The owner, James, learned that Benson had behaved inappropriately at work, insulting several customers after he had had too much to drink. James made it clear to Benson that if he drank alcohol again during work, it would be grounds for dismissal. Two years later, there was another incident at work when Benson was rude to customers. James had had enough: he dismissed Benson and gave him three weeks' severance pay.

Benson sued James for damages for wrongful dismissal, claiming 12 months' salary.

James did not defend by pleading that he dismissed Benson for drinking while on duty; in fact, James was not aware of such conduct. However, at the trial, evidence of other employees and patrons of the pub established that Benson had been drinking on duty on many occasions.

Should Benson's action succeed?

3. C.W. Jonas was a conductor employed by the East-West Railway Company. While the passenger train on which he was working was standing in a railway station, it was struck by another train. Because of the negligent operation of the train, Jonas was severely injured. He sued the East-West Railway Company for damages for negligence.

In defence, the railway company produced its copy of an employment contract signed by Jonas. The contract included the following clause:

> The employee, C.W. Jonas, agrees that in consideration of employment and wages by the Great East-West Railway Company, he will assume all risks of accident or casualty incident to such employment and service whether caused by the negligence of the Company or of its employees or otherwise, and will forever release, acquit, and discharge the said Company from all liability. The employee waives all rights to worker's compensation that might otherwise arise under this contract.

Without rendering a decision, discuss the public policy considerations inherent in a dispute of this kind.

4. Devellano operated a retail food supermarket that bought 60 percent of its merchandise from Prairie Wholesale Grocers Limited. Because of a wage dispute, the employees of Prairie Wholesale Grocers, who were members of the Office & Shop Clerks Union, went on strike. An official of that union then telephoned Devellano to enlist her support and apply economic pressure on Prairie Wholesale Grocers by reducing purchases from it. When Devellano refused, members of the union picketed her supermarket. They stopped cars on their way into the parking lot of the supermarket and distributed leaflets, intimating, inaccurately, that Devellano's store was controlled by Prairie Wholesale Grocers. The placards used while picketing contained the words "Devellano's Supermarket" and "Strike" in large letters, although none of Devellano's own employees were on strike. As a result, Devellano lost customers and sued the union for damages and an injunction to restrain the picketing of her premises.

Discuss the defences available to the union, and state whether they would succeed.

5. Lucy Anang was hired as a chemist by the Plastic Toy Co. Her employment contract stated that, following termination of her employment with the company, she would not work for any competitor in the province for five years or at any time in the future disclose to anyone any information about secret processes used by Plastic Toy Co. Anang had worked in the laboratory of the company for a period of about three years when she was given two months' notice of dismissal.

After her dismissal, Anang tried to earn a living as a consulting chemist. The plant supervisor at Plastic Toy then learned that she was disclosing certain information about manufacturing processes to one of the company's chief competitors. Specifically, it appeared that she had disclosed secret processes related to the production of equipment used in the colouring of toys, processes of value to the company.

Plastic Toy Co. sued Anang for damages and for an injunction restraining her from disclosing further information. One of Anang's defences was that no injunction could be granted to deprive her of the right to practise her profession as a chemist. What is the likelihood that the action will succeed?

Suppose instead that Anang had left Plastic Toy Co. because she had received an offer of a higher salary from a competitor of Plastic Toy. The management of Plastic Toy had no evidence that she disclosed any of its secret processes to her new employer, but was concerned that she might do so. Is it likely that Plastic Toy could obtain an injunction restraining Anang from working for its competitor? What conflicting policy issues must the court resolve?

6. In May 1986, the directors of Universal Printing Co., publishers of a newspaper with a large circulation, approached Bell to persuade him to become their assistant advertising manager. They suggested that if he accepted, he would probably succeed the present advertising manager upon his retirement. At the time, Bell held a responsible position with an advertising agency and was 42. During the discussions, Bell emphasized that his present position was a very satisfactory one, that it was important at his age that his employment be permanent, and that he would not consider a change that did not offer the prospect of a position lasting for the balance of his working life.

After careful consideration Bell accepted the position offered at a salary of $65 000 a year. He was promoted to advertising manager in 1994, and in the period from May 1986 to July 2002, his salary was increased regularly until it reached an annual sum of $160 000. In addition, every year he received a discretionary Christmas bonus approved by the directors and a special distribution pursuant to a profit-sharing plan confined to selected employees and made under the sole direction of the principal shareholder of Universal Printing Co. Ltd. Bell's receipts under the profit-sharing plan were $23 600 in 1999, $20 400 in 2000, and $17 000 in 2001.

In August 2002, the President of Universal Printing Co. Ltd., T.G. Dodds, called Bell into his office and, after some opening pleasantries about Bell's prowess in golf, told Bell that he thought another advertising manager he had in mind could produce better results for the company. Dodds told Bell that if he could see his way clear to resigning forthwith, he might have three months' salary in lieu of notice. Bell replied that he could not afford at this stage in his career to admit to the incompetence implied in a resignation and refused. Later in the afternoon, his secretary brought him the following letter:

August 8, 2002

Dear Mr. Bell:

This is to confirm the notice given to you today of the termination of your employment with Universal Printing Co. Ltd. as of this date. Enclosed is a cheque for your salary to date. Your pension plan has been commuted to a paid-up basis that will pay you $3500 a month commencing at age 65.

T.G. Dodds.

Bell at once made efforts to secure other employment, and by December 8, 2002, found a position with an advertising agency at a salary of $42 000 a year. If he had remained a further year with Universal Printing Co. Ltd., the paid-up value of his pension would have increased to $6500 per month.

Bell brought an action against Universal Printing Co. Ltd. for damages for wrongful dismissal. What amount of damages, if any, should he recover? Are there any additional facts you would like to know?

7. In September, Knowles, the owner of a professional hockey club, began negotiations with Meyer, a professional hockey player, for Meyer's services for the following two years. The two agreed orally to a salary of $3000 a week for Meyer during the training and playing seasons. At the time, Meyer asked whether players would be covered by workers' compensation insurance if injured. Knowles replied that the club's lawyer had advised that players were not covered, but that in any event he was having written contracts drawn up by the lawyer in which a clause would provide that every player would be insured against injury and that if a player were disabled he would be looked after.

Written contracts were then prepared and presented to all the players (including Meyer) for signing. The contracts in their written form stated the agreed salary for each individual player, and outlined the usual conditions regarding the player's obligations to the club, but there was no reference to insurance protection against injury or to the employer's obligation in the event of a player being disabled.

Meyer played for the team for six weeks and then received a serious injury to his eye during a hockey game. He was immediately taken to the hospital. At the end of the game, Knowles announced to Meyer's teammates in the dressing room that he would pay Meyer's salary to the end of the season.

Knowles paid Meyer's salary to the date of his injury and refused to pay any additional sum. Meyer brought an action for damages claiming $45 000 representing his salary for the remaining 15 weeks of the playing season; $500 for the cost of an artificial eye; and $100 000 general damages as compensation for the loss of his eye.

Discuss the issues raised by these facts, and explain whether Meyer's action is likely to succeed.

ADDITIONAL RESOURCES FOR CHAPTER 20 ON THE COMPANION WEBSITE *(www.pearsoned.ca/smyth)*

In addition to self-test multiple-choice, true–false, and short essay questions (all with immediate feedback), application exercises, and links to useful web destinations, the Companion Website provides the following resources for Chapter 20:

- **British Columbia:** Child Employment; Collective Bargaining; Discrimination in the Workplace; Employment Standards Act; Essential Services; Leave of Absence; Mediation and Arbitration; Minimum Wage; Occupational Health and Safety; Privacy Rights; Strikes, Lockouts, and Picketing; Temp Agencies; Termination and Layoff of Full-time and Part-time Employees; Termination of Probationary Employees; Unfair Labour Practices; Union Certification and Decertification; Worker Pay; Workers' Compensation

- **Alberta:** Conditions of Employment; Constructive Dismissal; Cooling-Off Period for Employees; Duty to Accommodate; Employment Standards; Labour Relations; Labour Relations Act; Summary Dismissal; Termination and Layoffs; Workers' Compensation; Wrongful Dismissal

- **Manitoba/Saskatchewan:** Employment Standards—Minimum Standards in Legislation; Human Rights; Labour Relations Boards; Reasonable Notice—Statutory Minimums; Vicarious Liability and Motor Vehicles; Vicarious Liability of Employers; Workers' Compensation

- **Ontario:** Bad Faith; Discrimination; Duty to Accommodate; Employment Equity; Employment Standards; Human Rights; Labour Relations; Mandatory Retirement; Occupational Health; Pay Equity; Public Sector and Essential Services; Workers' Compensation

21

Negotiable Instruments

For centuries negotiable instruments have been the main method of paying debts and financing transactions in both domestic and international business. We shall discuss the nature and uses of these devices under the Bills of Exchange Act. In this chapter we examine such questions as:

- What types of negotiable instrument are governed by the Act, and how are they utilized?

- What is meant by negotiability?

- What are the methods, purposes, and consequences of endorsement?

- What is the liability of various parties to a negotiable instrument?

- What is a "holder in due course"?

- What are the three defences available to the parties?

- How do these defences differ?

- How are consumer bills and notes treated differently?

HISTORY

In the last section of Chapter 12, we outlined the special nature of negotiable instruments. That section should be reread before proceeding with the present chapter.

Negotiable instruments began as a form of **bill of exchange**, a document made by a merchant or banker in one city instructing a colleague elsewhere to make a payment to a certain person or to the bearer of the document. They were probably used by the merchants of ancient Greece and Rome, and the practice was passed on to the medieval Islamic world. Later they came into wide use to meet the needs of merchants in the great age of discovery and trade.

bill of exchange
a written order by one party to another party to pay a specified sum of money to a named party or to the bearer of the document

By means of a bill of exchange a merchant in London, for instance, who had bought goods from a merchant coming from Hamburg, could arrange for the goods to be paid for by a banker in Hamburg, making it unnecessary for the Hamburg merchant to risk carrying coins or bullion back with him. The London merchant would pay a sum to a London firm dealing in bills of exchange, and the firm would draw a bill on its agent in Hamburg instructing him to pay the Hamburg merchant in local currency on a certain date. The Hamburg merchant would accept the bill in exchange for his goods.

With trade taking place in both directions, the credits collecting in Hamburg would be set off by similar credits in London through goods sold by English merchants to others in Hamburg. In place of purely bilateral settlements, money-changing firms and merchants later learned to set off credits on a multilateral basis among several of the great trading cities. At regular intervals, usually at annual fairs held in the trading cities, they would get together and tally the paper they had honoured and pay each other any difference owing. The money changers were able to charge fees because of the savings to merchants who would not have to transport gold back and forth. Today, this form of setting off credits still exists in a much more sophisticated form through "clearing house" arrangements.

The rules governing negotiable instruments developed as part of the Law Merchant,[1] and as economic activity increased, the ordinary courts also adopted the rules. Eventually, a very large and complex body of case law developed around the subject. The British Parliament codified the rules in the Bills of Exchange Act (1882). In Canada, the subject of negotiable instruments is within federal jurisdiction. Our Bills of Exchange Act[2] follows the English act closely.

MODERN DEVELOPMENTS

Change is an ongoing process. As noted above, negotiable instruments became an important substitute for transporting coins and other valuables. Next, transmitting funds by telegraph, cable, and later by telex grew to take over a significant portion of transfers in business-to-business transactions. Beginning in the 1950s and 1960s, largely in consumer transactions, credit cards began to replace both cash and cheques—particularly for paying bills while travelling. As online systems developed, merchants preferred credit cards because they could be more easily assured that funds were available than if they accepted payment by cheque. In the past decade, direct debit cards have displaced credit cards in an increasing proportion of transactions; more and more consumers prefer to use these cards rather than to carry cash with them.

According to a report of the Canadian Bankers Association (October 2008), the percentage of Canadians who bank primarily through the Internet has skyrocketed, increasing from 8 percent (in 2000) to 35 percent (in 2008). In 2007, Canadians were among the world's top users of debit cards, completing 393.9 million Internet banking transactions. Only 7 percent of Canadians use cheques as their primary bill payment method.[3]

---

1. *Supra*, Chapter 2, under the heading "The Sources of Law."
2. The Bills of Exchange Act, R.S.C. 1985, c. B-4. When a footnote mentions a section only, the reference will be to this Act.
3. Statistics obtained from the Canadian Bankers Association website, www.cba.ca/en/ section.asp?fl=3&sl=251&tl=252&docid= (accessed October 18, 2008).

Does this mean that electronic transfers of funds will soon replace the traditional paper methods and make bills of exchange and cheques obsolete? Answering this question involves both international and ethical considerations.

INTERNATIONAL ISSUE

Electronic Transfers of Funds: Are Negotiable Instruments Becoming Obsolete?

A 2002 report of the Organization for Economic Co-operation and Development entitled *The Future of Money* concluded that the disappearance of physical money is inevitable; it is just a question of time. It suggested that a quicker transition to digital payments would be good for the world economy for a number of reasons, including:

- the elimination of the high costs associated with the transfer and protection of physical forms of money including cash, cheques, bills of exchange, etc.,

- the decrease in underground, illegal, and even terrorist activities as a result of the ability to track the movement of money.

If countries proceed at their own pace without a co-ordinated timetable or approach, international transactions will be cumbersome and less secure. A uniform international approach and commitment to digitization could make the inevitable transition much easier.

QUESTIONS TO CONSIDER

1. How will a move to digital transactions affect developing or emerging economies?

2. Do you think digital transactions increase the likeliness of fraud?

Source: Organization for Economic Co-operation and Development, *The Future of Money* (Paris: OECD Publications Service, 2002), www.oecd.org/dataoecd/40/31/35391062.pdf.

ETHICAL ISSUE

Should All Transfer of Funds be Digital?

If all transactions were digital, there would be a comprehensive record of all the financial activities of each of us. It would track where we went, what we earned, and how we spent it. It would reveal personal information about our preferences, religious and charitable affiliations, and medical conditions. As will be discussed in greater detail in Chapters 34 and 35, the potential for abuse and misuse of this record has privacy advocates and ethicists very concerned. Should the government be allowed to use this record to assess income tax? Should the police be allowed to view this record to investigate suspected criminal activity? Should a business be able to use this record in order to target a market? What security measures would be necessary to protect the record from abuse?

QUESTIONS TO CONSIDER

1. Contrast the advantages and disadvantages of electronic money transfers as compared with traditional methods.

2. Should individuals have a right to keep their financial activities private?

Despite the speed and efficiency of electronic payment methods, Canadian banks still maintain physical branches, which are used by 82 percent of Canadians. Banks also continue to process about 1.5 billion cheques each year.[4] The greater certainty in using negotiable instruments continues to make them attractive in particular transactions. In addition, as we shall see in this chapter, negotiable instruments play an important role in many credit arrangements through the use of drafts, promissory notes, and post-dated cheques. While the law governing negotiable instruments is rather technical, it functions efficiently and causes few problems. We limit our discussion to a broad outline of what the law aims to do and how it accomplishes its purpose.

NATURE AND USES OF NEGOTIABLE INSTRUMENTS

As Personal Property

In Chapter 12 we discussed the rights to intangible property—*choses in action*—and noted that negotiable instruments are a special kind of chose in action. In this chapter we consider the distinctive characteristics of negotiable instruments that have made them a significant and useful business tool.

Every negotiable instrument contains an express or implied promise made by one or more parties to pay the amount stated in the instrument. In the absence of evidence to the contrary, the promisee is presumed to have given good consideration for it. A negotiable instrument is normally a self-contained contract with all the necessary written evidence of its terms stated on its face. In practice, a negotiable instrument is usually a part of a contract in which one side satisfies its promise to pay for goods or services by giving the other side the instrument. Delivery of the instrument is only a **conditional discharge** because if the debtor dishonours it, the promisee's rights remain under the original contract. Promisees generally choose to sue on the negotiable instrument rather than on the original contract because it is simpler to do so.

conditional discharge
the debtor is discharged under the original contract only if the negotiable instrument given in payment is honoured

Types of Instruments

The Bills of Exchange Act governs three common types of negotiable instrument—bills of exchange (or drafts), promissory notes, and cheques. There are other kinds of instruments with the special quality of negotiability, but disputes concerning them are resolved by common law and not by the Bills of Exchange Act. For instance, bearer bonds have also been held to be negotiable instruments.

Following U.S. practice, there is a growing tendency to treat share certificates as negotiable instruments. Jurisdictions using the certificate of incorporation system, explained in Chapter 27, state expressly that a share certificate whose transfer is not restricted by words printed on its face is a negotiable instrument.[5]

We confine our discussion to the three common forms of negotiable instruments governed by the Bills of Exchange Act.

Bill of Exchange (Drafts)

A *bill of exchange* (see Figure 21.1) is a written order by one party, the **drawer**, addressed to another party, the **drawee**, to pay a specified sum of money to a named party, the **payee**, or to the bearer, at a fixed or determinable future time or on demand. A bill of exchange originates with a creditor (drawer) that requests its debtor to acknowledge indebtedness and to agree to pay according to the terms stated

drawer
the party who draws up the bill of exchange

drawee
the party who is required to make payment on the bill of exchange

payee
the party named to receive payment on the bill of exchange

---

4. *Supra*, n. 3.
5. Canada Business Corporations Act, R.S.C. 1985, c. C-44, s. 48(3).

ACCEPTED
OCT. 4, 2004
Payable at
The Regal Bank
Tower Branch,
London
G. Fawkes
for G. Fawkes & Co.

DUE Nov. 5, 2004 NO. 531

The Sterling Bank
Norwich Branch
Norwich, Ontario Oct. 3, 2004

Thirty days after date pay to the order of
the undersigned drawer $150.00
One hundred and fifty xx/100

value received and charged to the account of

TO G. Fawkes & Co. THE CROWN CO. LTD.
Parliament Street Per
Edward Cole

FIGURE 21.1
A Bill of Exchange (Accepted Time Draft)

in the instrument. A drawer sometimes designates itself as a payee. At other times it may direct that some other person or business to whom it owes money shall be the payee instead. The drawer expects the debtor (drawee) to consent by signing the instrument together with the word "accepted" and the date; the drawee then becomes an **acceptor**. A bill of exchange may circulate among a number of holders as an item of valuable personal property even *before* it has been accepted. It has value for a holder because the drawer, by drawing and delivering it, has made an implied promise guaranteeing its payment.[6] Its subsequent acceptance adds the express promise of the acceptor.

acceptor
the drawee who consents to the bill of exchange by signing it together with the word "accepted" and the date

An acceptor may indicate that the bill is to be paid out of its bank account. The drawer (or a subsequent holder) may then leave the instrument with its own bank for collection and have it deposited in its account. That bank will present the bill to the acceptor's bank for payment out of the acceptor's account. After the amount is deducted from the acceptor's account, the cancelled bill of exchange is returned to the acceptor as evidence of payment just as cancelled cheques are returned.

There are three types of bill of exchange, depending upon the time at which they are to be paid:

(a) **Demand drafts**, payable immediately upon presentation without any days of grace before payment. The cheque is the leading example of a demand draft and we treat it separately below.
(b) **Sight drafts**, which the drawee is ordered to pay "at sight." In Canada, three days of grace for making payment are allowed after presentation for acceptance.
(c) **Time drafts**, payable a stipulated number of days, months, or other period "after date" (after the date stated on the instrument) or "after sight" (after presentation for acceptance). Three days of grace should be added in fixing the maturity of a time draft. A bill payable at a given time after sight is a time draft, not a sight draft.

demand draft
a bill of exchange payable immediately upon presentation without any days of grace

sight draft
a bill of exchange payable "at sight"—three days of grace are allowed after presentation

time draft
a bill of exchange payable within a stipulated period after the date stated on the instrument or after presentation

Presentation for acceptance is necessary whenever a bill is payable at sight or after sight, so that the time at which payment is due may be determined.[7]

Sight drafts can be used as a collection device. Instead of employing a collection agency to recover its slow accounts, a business may draw sight drafts on difficult customers and have the drafts presented for acceptance and payment through the bank. The drawees will have a new incentive to accept and pay, not wanting to become known to the bank as poor credit risks.

6. S. 129.
7. S. 74.

Time drafts can be used as a means of finance for the business drawing them. By discounting them at a bank or by pledging them as security for a bank loan, the drawer can obtain cash in advance of the time when payment is due from the customer. Instead of waiting to be paid until the credit term granted to a customer expires, a business may draw a time draft on the customer immediately following the sale and discount or pledge the draft. As we see in Chapter 30, however, there are other means of achieving this result. For example, a business may borrow from a bank by conditionally assigning its accounts receivable, it may sell its accounts to a factor, or it may assign them to a finance company.

Drafts and bills of lading often complement one another when goods sold on credit are shipped to the buyer by common carrier. Their joint use permits the seller to withhold possession of the goods from the purchaser when they reach their destination until the purchaser accepts a draft drawn on it for the price. The purchaser can examine the goods but cannot obtain possession from the carrier until the seller or its agent transfers the bill of lading to the purchaser.

Promissory Note

A **promissory note** (see Figure 21.2) is a written promise by one party, the **maker**, to pay a specified sum of money to another party, the payee, at a fixed or determinable future time or on demand. The maker is usually a debtor of the payee, and it prepares the instrument itself, though it may do so at the request of the payee.

Unlike a bill of exchange, a promissory note is not presented for acceptance. It contains an express promise to pay. To a subsequent holder, a promissory note that has been endorsed by the payee has the same effect as an accepted bill of exchange. The Bills of Exchange Act applies both to accepted bills and to notes, but the provisions relating to the acceptance of bills of exchange do not apply to promissory notes.

A maker of a note may word it so that it will be payable out of the maker's bank account at maturity; it is then paid through its bank and returned cancelled to the maker.

promissory note
a written promise to pay a specified sum of money to another party at a fixed or determinable future time or on demand

maker
the party who signs and delivers a promissory note

FIGURE 21.2
A Promissory Note

Cheque

A **cheque** (see Figure 21.3) is a bill of exchange drawn against a bank and payable on demand. From the point of view of the holder, a cheque contains the implied promise of its drawer that the drawer has funds on deposit at the bank sufficient to meet its amount, or that the amount is within the terms of a line of credit granted by the bank. For this reason it is sometimes convenient to think of the drawer of a cheque as a "promisor." The bank on which the cheque is drawn is called the drawee bank.

cheque
a bill of exchange drawn against a bank and payable on demand

SUPERIOR PRODUCTS LIMITED   **No. 80013**

Calgary, Alberta   April 26, 2004

To
THE STERLING BANK
Lethbridge, Alberta

Pay to the
order of _____ C.B. BOWEN & CO. LTD. _____ $ 400.00

FOUR HUNDRED _____ **DOLLARS**

· ·XX/100

SUPERIOR PRODUCTS LIMITED
Per: *J. B. Riches*
Per: *J.B. Walker*

Branch 0752
Account 987654

FIGURE 21.3
A Cheque

Certification

certification
an undertaking by the bank to pay the amount of the cheque to its holder when later presented for payment

Since a cheque is payable on demand, the payee does not ordinarily present it to a bank for acceptance, but cashes it or deposits it to the credit of its own account. The Bills of Exchange Act does not expressly authorize the acceptance of cheques by the bank, nor does it refer specifically to the current banking practice of *certifying* cheques.[8] **Certification** amounts to an undertaking by the bank to pay the amount of the cheque to its holder when later presented for payment and, to ensure this result, the bank immediately deducts the amount of the cheque from the drawer's account. Certification takes the form of the bank's stamped acknowledgment, with date, on the face of the cheque.

Occasionally a supplier will refuse to release goods until paid by certified cheque. The buyer prepares a cheque payable to the supplier, has the drawee bank certify it, and then delivers it to the supplier. Or a payee may receive the cheque uncertified and, before releasing the goods, will have the bank certify it. Such a cheque is safer to hold than cash—a thief would have to forge an endorsement before being able to cash it. In addition, certification *at the request of the holder* also prevents any attempt by the drawer to stop payment on the cheque: since the payee could have cashed it instead of having it certified, the act of certifying makes the drawee bank liable directly to the payee.[9]

Certification of a cheque is comparable to the acceptance of other types of bills of exchange.[10] The bank concerned is the drawee to whom the instrument is addressed. Once having undertaken certification, it assumes a liability to the holder for the amount of the cheque.

Postdated Cheques

postdate
give a cheque a date later than the time when it is delivered to the payee

The drawer may **postdate** a cheque by giving it a date later than the time when it is delivered to the payee. A cheque is an order addressed to a bank, and the bank must follow the instructions given to it on the face of the cheque—the bank is not entitled to pay the instrument before its date. While a cheque is by definition payable "on demand," a holder's right to demand payment is not effective until the date on the cheque. In the meantime, the instrument operates like a time draft, though without the benefit for the drawer of three days of grace. Postdating is convenient for a drawer who

8. See J.D. Falconbridge, *The Law of Negotiable Instruments in Canada* (Toronto: The Ryerson Press, 1955) at 43.

9. When a cheque is certified at the request of the holder, the drawer is entirely discharged by its implied promise that the bank will honour the cheque. See B. Crawford and J.D. Falconbridge, *Banking and Bills of Exchange*, 8th ed. (Toronto: Canada Law Book, 1986) at 1791.

10. The difference between certification and acceptance is confined to the circumstance where the drawee bank fails, and even then relates only to certification at the request of the holder (rather than of the drawer).

expects to be unavailable at the time a debt is due and who does not wish to pay in advance. It is common for a drawer to give a series of postdated cheques to meet instalment payments.

"Stop Payment"

After delivering a cheque, the drawer may learn that the payee is in serious breach of the contract between them. Before the cheque has been charged against its account, the drawer may counter-mand or "**stop payment**" by instructing its bank not to pay the cheque. The bank may require the drawer to agree that it will not be held responsible if, through its inadvertence, the cheque is paid out of the drawer's account in spite of the countermand.

stop payment
an instruction from the drawer of a cheque to the bank not to pay the cheque

Even a cheque certified at the request of its drawer and not yet delivered to the payee may be countermanded and the amount returned to the drawer's account at the bank. Since the bank has a liability on the certified cheque, it will reject the countermand unless the cheque is surrendered by the drawer for cancellation or the drawer agrees to indemnify the bank should the bank be sued for refusing to honour the cheque.

The Use of Cheques

Although payments can be made from current bank accounts by means of sight drafts, time drafts, and promissory notes, cheques have largely superseded them. This development is due to the prac-tice of paying accounts once each month. Suppliers that once relied heavily upon the acceptance of drafts as immediate acknowledgments of indebtedness now depend upon the creditworthiness of their buyers. In any event, they can easily monitor the reliability of their buyers on a monthly basis. A good credit reputation is a prized business resource, and its reputation is quickly lost when a busi-ness issues cheques that prove to be "n.s.f." (not sufficient funds). The greater simplicity of payment by cheque has proved to be justified in all but a few instances. There are still a few trades in which the routine use of sight and time drafts persists by tradition, and in the field of international trade, where the parties are often unknown to one another and have to deal at great distance, drafts retain some advantage. The promissory note, particularly the demand note, survives as the common method by which a borrower provides evidence of its indebtedness for a bank loan.

Most people have become accustomed to expect payment by cheque. The risks inherent in handling large amounts of cash are eliminated; cheques also afford an easy and relatively safe method of making payments by mail.

A cheque, even one certified by a bank, is not legal tender. Strictly speaking, a creditor is enti-tled to payment in Bank of Canada notes and in coins up to the designated amounts for each denomination. However, to insist upon payment in cash would be inconvenient to both parties, and if a creditor refused a reasonable tender of payment by cheque and sued for payment in cash, court costs would likely be awarded against it.

CHECKLIST Classes of Negotiable Instruments

There are two classes of negotiable instruments:

(1) Those governed by the federal Bills of Exchange Act:
   - bills of exchange (or drafts)
   - promissory notes
   - cheques

(2) Those governed by other statutes and common law rules in some jurisdictions:
   - bearer bonds
   - share certificates

PREREQUISITES FOR LIABILITY

Until an instrument is delivered, a drawer, acceptor, or maker has no liability, and even after signing it may reconsider and tear it up before delivering it. A drawee has no liability in respect of a bill of exchange before accepting and delivering it.

Delivery may be "actual"—the instrument being issued directly by the promisor to the payee; or it may be "constructive"—simply by notice to the payee that the instrument is complete and ready for delivery.[11] Once an instrument has been delivered, the term "negotiation" is used to describe any subsequent transfer of it by the payee to a new holder as well as any later transfers to other holders.

NEGOTIABILITY

Meaning of Negotiability

negotiability
the special quality possessed by negotiable instruments as a distinct class of assignable contract

Negotiability is the special quality possessed by negotiable instruments as a distinct class of assignable contracts. As noted in Chapter 12, their transfer is distinguished from ordinary assignments of contracts by three features:

(a) A negotiable instrument may be transferred (or assigned) from one holder to another without the promisor being advised about each new holder; the promisor becomes liable to each successive holder in turn.

(b) An assignee may sometimes acquire a better right to sue on the instrument than its predecessor (assignor) had.

(c) A holder may sue in its own name any other party liable on the instrument without joining any of the remaining parties.

The above legal qualities give a high degree of transferability to negotiable instruments that regular assignments lack. As a practical matter, ease of transfer enables negotiable instruments to meet business needs, because on their face they are sufficiently reliable for transferees to accept them without hesitation.

For negotiable instruments to acquire these desirable qualities, they must meet the following criteria:

(a) The promise or order must be set out in writing—otherwise the transferee would hold no evidence of the promise.

(b) The obligation must be for a money payment only, requiring no further inquiry into its value. Other types of obligation—to perform services or transfer ownership of a chattel—would require a prospective assignee to investigate the value of what is being promised.

(c) The money promised must be a "sum certain." It may be repayable in instalments or with interest and still be a "sum certain."[12] But a promise to pay "the balance owing to you for services rendered" is not a sum certain because it is not possible from the face of the instrument to quantify the value of the promise.

---

11. S. 38.

12. Ss. 27 and 186. Problems arise where the instrument provides for payment of a fixed sum plus a variable or "floating" rate of interest, for example, "prime rate plus 2 percent." The Supreme Court of Canada has held that the sum must be capable of being ascertained by numerical calculation from the information contained in the instrument itself: *MacLeod Savings & Credit Union Ltd.* v. *Perrett*, [1981] 1 S.C.R. 78. The courts have had difficulty in applying this test with consistency. See also *Canadian Imperial Bank of Commerce (CIBC)* v. *Morgan* (1993), A.R. 36.

(d) The promise or order must be unconditional so that the holder need not look outside the instrument to learn the implications of some qualifying phrase such as, "if the goods are delivered in good condition" or "subject to an allowance for poor material." A contract subject to a condition, though it may be valid between the immediate parties, lacks the certainty needed for a negotiable instrument: any attempt to transfer rights under it would be a mere assignment.

(e) The negotiable instrument must be payable at a fixed or determinable future time or on demand.[13] The value of a contractual right can be appraised only when it indicates the time at which it is to be performed.

(f) Negotiation must be of the whole instrument, not for part of the amount.

(g) The negotiable instrument must be signed by the drawer (or authorized signing officers of a drawer business)[14] if it is a draft or cheque, or by the maker if a promissory note.

Consequences When a Document Is Not Negotiable

Suppose *A* Co. draws a bill on *B* Ltd. payable to *C* Inc. and *B* Ltd. refuses to accept. Does drawing the bill nevertheless serve as notice to *B* Ltd. that it must now pay *C* Inc. instead of *A* Co.? The Bills of Exchange Act states that the act of presenting an instrument for acceptance does not of itself amount to notice of an assignment of the stated sum.[15] Accordingly, if *B* Ltd. refuses to accept, it owes nothing to *C* Inc.

Although a document may not amount to a negotiable instrument (where, for example, the order or promise is conditional), it may still be enforceable between the original parties and be capable of assignment as an ordinary contractual right. In these circumstances, the **Bills of Exchange Act** does not apply, and the parties' rights are subject to the general rules governing contractual assignments as discussed in Chapter 12. Accordingly, a holder of the instrument cannot enforce the promise until the condition is met.

METHODS OF NEGOTIATION

By Endorsement and Delivery

An order instrument is one expressed to be payable "to *A*," "to *A* or order," or "to the order of *A*." To negotiate it, *A* must endorse as well as deliver it to a new holder. Endorsement may take a number of forms, which we shall examine below, but essentially it is the signature (traditionally on the reverse side of the instrument) of the payee.

A party that purchases an order instrument without the proper endorsement on it acquires a very limited legal right, probably confined to recourse against the transferor, and has no rights against any prior parties.[16] In any event, a new holder cannot acquire a better legal right than the transferor had until it has obtained the transferor's endorsement on the instrument. A new holder has a right to require the transferor to make the needed endorsement.[17]

---

13. It is difficult to justify the uncertainty introduced by the definition of "determinable future time" in section 23(b), viz., "on or at a fixed period after the occurrence of a specified event which is certain to happen though the time of happening is uncertain." It seems that a promissory note payable "at my death" would be a valid negotiable instrument. The provision is of little practical importance in business.

14. The signer is personally liable unless he states that he signs in a representative capacity: section 51. The usual practice for a corporation is for its name to be printed on the instrument and for the officer to sign "per *X*" or "*X*, director." For an interesting case, see *Allprint Co. Ltd.* v. *Erwin* (1982), 136 D.L.R. (3d) 587.

15. S. 126.

16. See Crawford and Falconbridge, *supra*, n. 9, p. 1503.

17. S. 60.

By Delivery Only

Endorsement is not necessary for an instrument in "bearer" form. It is in bearer form when initially it is made payable "to bearer," or "to *A* Co. or bearer," or when no payee has been named and a space is left blank for the insertion of a name. It is also in bearer form when it is payable to an abstraction (for example, "Pay to Petty Cash") or to a fictitious or non-existent person.[18] In addition, an order instrument becomes a bearer instrument when the named payee endorses it without any qualifying words. Unless and until a subsequent payee endorses it payable to order, it may be negotiated by delivery alone.

An order instrument is safer because any attempt to negotiate it dishonestly amounts to the criminal offence of forgery.[19] The Bills of Exchange Act makes forgery one of the exceptions to the rule that a holder may acquire a better right than the transferor had. Forgery is a defence to the parties liable on an order instrument. By contrast, because a bearer instrument may be negotiated by delivery only, a thief may successfully negotiate it without resorting to forgery. As a result, even if a bearer instrument was lost or stolen at some previous time, its holder can require the party liable to pay—but only if he can show that he acquired the instrument without knowledge of the loss or theft.[20]

Businesses rarely prepare negotiable instruments in bearer form, although, as we have noted, order instruments may be converted into bearer form by their holders. An employee, for example, may endorse her paycheque before taking it to the bank. If her endorsement is simply her signature, she has converted the cheque into a bearer instrument and it becomes subject to the risks discussed above.

At one time bank notes were promissory notes in bearer form, but now they simply state that they are legal tender and are freely negotiable by virtue of the Bank of Canada Act.[21]

ENDORSEMENT

Types of Endorsement

Endorsement in Blank

The payee on an order instrument signs his name—and nothing else—by way of endorsement, thus making it payable to bearer.

Special Endorsement

The payee specifies the next person to whom payment is to be made. For example:

Pay to Prometheus

(signed) *M. Zeus*

Restrictive Endorsement

By endorsing an instrument "for deposit only," the payee makes it non-negotiable. There is a risk that, if an instrument is stolen from a payee, the thief may forge the payee's endorsement and sell the instrument to a new holder—for example, by cashing it at a bank. When endorsed "for deposit only," an instrument can then only be deposited to the credit of the payee's account at the bank. It is no longer possible for a thief to cash the stolen instrument.

---

18. S. 20(5). See *Westboro Flooring & Decor Inc.* v. *Bank of Nova Scotia* (2004), 241 D.L.R. (4th) 257.

19. The Criminal Code, R.S.C. 1985, c. C-46, s. 374.

20. N. Elliott, J. Odgers, and J.M. Phillips, eds., *Byles on Bills of Exchange*, 27th ed. (London: Sweet & Maxwell, 2001) at 231 and 445.

21. Bank of Canada Act, R.S.C. 1985, c. B-2, s. 25.

Conditional Endorsement

The payee specifies a party to whom payment is next to be made, provided he has lived up to the terms of a contract between them as, for example, "pay to the order of Bacchus if sober." Such a condition differs from a condition written into the instrument by a drawer, an acceptor, or a maker because it does not make the original promise in the instrument conditional. The party primarily liable may disregard a conditional endorsement in making payment, but the endorser may recover from the endorsee (Bacchus) if the condition was not satisfied.

Qualified Endorsement

The payee transfers rights in a way that denies liability as an endorser—for example, "Jane Bond, without recourse." Anyone giving value for the instrument is on notice that no remedy is available against Ms. Bond should the party primarily liable default. (As we shall see, in the absence of a qualified endorsement, an endorser normally is liable to subsequent endorsees.) Manufacturers or wholesalers that "factor" their accounts receivable sometimes use a qualified endorsement. A **factor** may be willing to purchase drafts drawn on customers and endorsed over to it "**without recourse**"; the factor bears the risk of collection, without recourse to its client (the manufacturer or wholesaler).

factor
a party who purchases drafts drawn on customers at a discount and then collects directly from the customer

without recourse
no ability to claim against the endorser

Anomalous Endorsement

Suppose a party to a negotiable instrument is not sufficiently creditworthy to persuade a prospective holder to buy it. For instance, a purchaser starting up a new business wishes to pay for goods by draft but the seller is unwilling to accept the purchaser's signature alone. The purchaser then obtains the signature of his sister. As a person with a recognized credit standing, she signs the instrument solely to add her liability, as endorser (guarantor), to that of her brother who is primarily liable. The endorsement is "**anomalous**" or exceptional because it is not added for the purpose of negotiating the instrument; the endorser was not a holder in her own right.

Bills endorsed in this manner are called "**accommodation bills**." The acceptor or endorser usually signs to accommodate the drawer—that is, to make it easier for the drawer to obtain credit on the bill. An anomalous endorser contributes to negotiability because of her good credit standing.

anomalous endorsement
an endorsement that is not added for the purpose of negotiating the instrument but as a guarantee to make it easier for the drawer to obtain credit on the bill

accommodation bill
bill of exchange that contains an anomalous endorsement

Purposes of Endorsement

An endorsement may be the means of carrying out one of the following purposes:

(a)   transferring title to an instrument payable to order

We examined the first of these purposes above when we looked at the methods of negotiation and the types of endorsement. Most endorsements serve simply as the method of transferring ownership in the instrument.

(b)   giving increased security to the payee (or subsequent holder)

We have also seen that an anomalous endorsement can make a negotiable instrument more marketable because the endorsement makes the endorser liable if the party with primary liability defaults. This is so, even though the endorser has never owned the instrument and has not negotiated it to someone else.[22] An anomalous endorsement is a means of guaranteeing a debt, with the endorser in the role of guarantor.[23]

---

22. S. 130. The endorser is liable to the payee even though the payee has not himself endorsed. *Robinson* v. *Mann* (1901), 331 S.C.R. 484. Also, *Byles on Bills of Exchange, supra*, n. 20, p. 203.

23. The same effect may be had without endorsement if both the guarantor and debtor sign in the first instance as joint makers of a promissory note.

(c)   identifying the party entitled to payment

A holder of a negotiable instrument has no claim against the drawer if an intermediate holder has forged a signature. When a bank has cashed a cheque containing an endorsement forged by the person cashing it, the bank becomes a holder with no right to claim the amount from the drawee customer's account. To protect itself, a bank may (rarely) require an endorsement from someone known to it for the purpose of identifying the person seeking to cash a cheque. For instance, it may require an endorsement in the following form:

T. Smith is hereby identified

(signed) *R. Jones*

As endorser, Jones is not liable for payment as are other endorsers should the party primarily liable default. Her liability is limited to the loss that would follow from having identified someone as T. Smith who later proved not to be that person.

(d)   acknowledging a partial payment

If the maker of a note is to pay her debt by instalments, it is up to her to see that every time she makes a partial payment she obtains an endorsement on the instrument by its holder for the amount paid. Otherwise she remains liable for the full, face amount of the instrument if it is subsequently negotiated to a holder who is unaware of the partial payments. An example of this type of endorsement is the following:

May 12, 2005

Received in part payment, $175.00

(signed) *B. Brown*

As an alternative arrangement, the debtor may make a series of separate notes bearing the dates of the various instalments and require the surrender of the related note each time she pays an instalment.

LIABILITY OF PARTIES

An Endorser

dishonour
the failure by the party primarily liable to pay the instrument according to its terms

"**Dishonour**" is the failure by the party primarily liable to pay the instrument according to its terms. If the instrument is a draft, dishonour may take the form of either the drawee's refusal to accept or, if he accepts, of his later refusal to pay.[24] We have noted that an endorser is liable to any holder for the amount of the instrument should the party primarily liable dishonour it, but this statement needs to be qualified. If an endorser does not receive prompt notice of the dishonour from the holder, the endorser will be freed from liability.

In the rare event that an order instrument is negotiated several times, a particular endorser's liability extends to any subsequent endorser as well as the current holder. He has no liability to prior endorsers—indeed, they are liable to him. The holder has a choice of endorsers to require payment from when the instrument is dishonoured, provided each of them has received the necessary notice of dishonour.[25] In turn, an endorser who is held liable has recourse against any prior endorser but not against any subsequent one.[26] Assuming he cannot recover from the party primarily liable, the ultimate loser will be the first endorser (or the drawer if the instrument is a draft).

---

24. S. 132(a).

25. Alternatively, the holder may sue all the endorsers as co-defendants in a single action and leave them to work out their individual liability among themselves.

26. S. 100. Each endorser has, after receiving notice of dishonour, the same period for giving notice to earlier endorsers that the holder had after dishonour.

When an instrument contains a forged endorsement, the drawer and any endorser prior to the forgery are freed of liability. The only holder who can recover from an endorser in these circumstances is one who has satisfied the conditions for qualifying as a "holder in due course," as explained later. When such a holder suffers a loss arising from a forged endorsement or the forged signature of the drawer, unless the forger can be caught and made to pay, the loss will ultimately be borne by the person who acquires the instrument immediately following the forgery.[27]

ILLUSTRATION 21.1

A knew that C maintained an account at the B Bank. She drew a cheque on the B Bank payable to herself, forging C's signature as drawer. She then endorsed the cheque with her own signature and cashed it at a hotel operated by D. D endorsed the cheque and deposited it in the hotel account at the X Bank. The X Bank presented the cheque for payment to the B Bank through the bank clearing system. The B Bank recognized the forgery and refused to pay the cheque out of C's account. The cheque was then returned to the X Bank.

The X Bank is entitled to recover the amount that it had previously credited to D's account in respect of the cheque. The X Bank is the holder (in fact, a holder in due course), and D, as the endorser immediately after the forgery, is liable.[28] In this illustration there is no other endorser between D and A, the perpetrator of the fraud. The loss must fall upon D unless A can be apprehended and the funds recovered from her.

An endorser also warrants to any later party that she had a good title to the instrument.[29]

Finally, unless a holder "duly presents" the instrument for payment, endorsers will not have any liability to him. Accordingly, an instrument payable on demand must be presented for payment within a reasonable time after its endorsement, and an instrument that is not payable on demand must be presented on the day it falls due.[30]

A Drawer

The drawer of a draft undertakes that on duly presenting the draft it will be accepted and paid according to its terms, and that if it is dishonoured the drawer will compensate the holder or any endorser who is compelled to pay it.[31] The drawer of a cheque undertakes that the cheque will be paid from his account on demand. If there are insufficient funds in his account, he is liable to the holder or to any endorser from whom the holder may recover. Because the parties to a cheque do not ordinarily expect a formal acceptance of it by the drawee bank, the drawer of the cheque becomes for practical purposes "the party primarily liable" comparable to the acceptor of a draft or the maker of a note.

A bank follows instructions from its customer in disposing of the funds on deposit with it. Its authority to pay a cheque ends when its customer stops payment or when it receives notice of the customer's death.[32] While a holder cannot then hold the bank liable, his rights against the drawer remain unaffected by the countermand. By stopping payment a drawer dishonours the instrument and may be sued by the holder. The death of the drawer makes the amount of the cheque a charge against the drawer's estate, and it becomes one of the debts the personal representative (executor or administrator) must settle.

27. S. 132(b).
28. S. 49(1) and (2).
29. S. 132(c).
30. S. 85.
31. S. 129.
32. S. 167.

Notice of Dishonour

We have noted that neither an endorser nor a drawer will be liable in the absence of prompt, express notice of dishonour from the holder—it is not enough for the holder to show that the endorser or drawer heard about the dishonour from some other source.[33] Notice must be given not later than the business day next following the dishonour.[34] If notice is mailed, the time limit applies to the time of depositing it in the post office and not to the time it is received.[35]

No special form of notice is required as long as it conveys the essential message. In two instances, however, a special form of notice of dishonour known as *protest* is required. Protest is required if the instrument is drawn, payable, or accepted outside Canada.[36] The services of a notary public—or justice of the peace where no notary public is available—are required to confirm the dishonour, prepare a notice of the protest in prescribed form,[37] and deliver it to the endorsers and drawer within the same time as for a notice of dishonour generally.[38] The holder is responsible for contacting a notary public and is entitled to be reimbursed for the notary's fee by the endorser or drawer to whom the notice of protest is delivered.[39] An endorser may waive the right to any notice of dishonour, and avoid the expense of the fee, by including the words "No Protest" in his endorsement.[40]

A Transferor by Delivery

The term "transferor by delivery" describes anyone who negotiates an instrument in bearer form. Since no endorsement is required, a transferor by delivery is not liable on the instrument *as an endorser* if the party primarily liable simply proves financially incapable of paying it.[41] However, he may be liable to the one person to whom he has negotiated the instrument, his *immediate transferee*, but only for such loss as that transferee would sustain if the instrument were not genuine—that is, if the instrument is not what the transferor represented it to be, or he was aware that it was valueless, or if he had no right to transfer it.[42]

An Acceptor or Maker

By accepting a bill, a drawee undertakes to pay it according to the terms of his acceptance.[43] Similarly, the maker of a promissory note undertakes to pay it according to its terms.[44] On the death of either the maker or acceptor, his liability passes to his personal representative.

Limitation Periods

We have seen that the holder of a negotiable instrument must duly present the instrument for payment and, when necessary, give the required notice of dishonour in order to establish his legal rights against all prior parties to the instrument. He must then also prosecute his legal rights, by court

---

33. S. 98. See also Crawford and Falconbridge, *supra*, n. 9, p. 1576.
34. S. 96. Under some circumstances, a delay in giving notice may be excused (s. 104).
35. S. 102(2).
36. S. 111.
37. The prescribed forms are set out at the end of the Act.
38. S. 125.
39. S. 123.
40. S. 105(1)(b).
41. S. 136(2).
42. S. 137.
43. S. 127.
44. S. 185. If the party seeking payment is a "holder in due course" as defined below, the maker of a note cannot refuse to pay on the grounds that the payee who he has named in his note either does not exist or lacks capacity to endorse.

action if necessary, within the time prescribed by the relevant provincial legislation.[45] The limitation period begins to run from whichever is the latest date—the maturity of the instrument; the time of the most recent payment made in respect of it; or any written acknowledgment from which a promise to pay may be implied.

HOLDER IN DUE COURSE

Negotiation Compared with Assignment of a Chose in Action

In Chapter 8 we learned that an innocent purchaser of goods can often retain them even when the transferor, who had obtained them fraudulently, would have had to surrender them to the original vendor. We have also noted that an innocent transferee of a negotiable instrument may be able to enforce payment when the transferor himself could not do so. In this sense, a transfer of a negotiable instrument more closely resembles a transfer of title to goods than an assignment of a chose in action—negotiation is an exception to the general principle that an assignee of a chose in action takes no greater rights than the assignor had. Accordingly, a negotiable instrument may become more valuable when it is transferred. The greater rights available to innocent third-party holders of negotiable instruments make them useful tools of commerce.

Requirements to Become a Holder in Due Course

For the holder of a negotiable instrument to acquire something more than the transferor himself had, the holder must satisfy four conditions:[46]

(a) The holder must have taken the instrument complete and regular on its face.
(b) She must have acquired it before it was overdue and without notice of any prior dishonour.
(c) She, or someone through whom she claims, must have given consideration ("value") for the instrument.[47]
(d) She must have taken the instrument in good faith and without notice of any defect in the title of the person who negotiated it.

A holder who satisfies these conditions becomes a *holder in due course*.[48] Business experience has shown that the concept of negotiability has a convenience far outweighing the cost of its occasional abuse. In any event, the possibility of abuse is greatly reduced by confining the legal advantage to a holder in due course.

Purpose of the Requirements

Notice

The rule that a person cannot be a holder in due course if she has taken the instrument with knowledge of its previous dishonour, or in bad faith, or with notice of a defect of title, has one purpose—to deprive a holder of any advantage in conspiring with a transferee to take the instrument from him with a view to evading the defences of the party liable. Such a transferee does not qualify as a

---

45. In most provinces the relevant period is six years, but in some it has been reduced to two years; see the discussion of limitation periods in Chapter 31.

46. S. 55.

47. S. 55 requires that she shall have taken the instrument "for value," but section 53 states that where value has been given at any time for a bill, the holder is deemed to be a holder for value.

48. A subsequent holder will succeed to the rights of a holder in due course whether or not he himself satisfies all the essential conditions, unless he was a party to fraud or illegality affecting the instrument: section 56.

holder in due course and can be defeated by any of the defences that the party liable might have used against the transferor. The transferee gains nothing by the maneuver.

When the instrument is a time draft or note, a prospective holder of it can tell at a glance whether it is overdue or not. If it is already due, an obvious question to ask is why the present holder is trying to negotiate it instead of presenting it for payment. A prospective holder will have more difficulty deciding whether a demand draft is overdue. If it has been outstanding for an "unreasonable" length of time (which varies with the circumstances), it is deemed to be overdue,[49] and a new holder does not then become a holder in due course.

An outstanding demand note may have a different significance from a demand draft. A demand note is sometimes given as evidence of long-term indebtedness and may remain outstanding a long time without necessarily raising doubts about its collectability. Consequently, the criterion of an unreasonable length of time used in other areas of the law may be unsuitable in determining whether a demand note is overdue.[50]

Advantages

An important benefit of the concept of a holder in due course is that banks are willing to discount drafts and cash cheques drawn on other banks with relatively little delay and at much reduced risk to themselves, since they acquire the instruments in the capacity of a holder in due course. If the law did not recognize the concept, banks would be reluctant to purchase negotiable instruments and hold them as assets. They would first have to make exhaustive inquiries to be sure that valuable consideration was given for an instrument and that it was free of fraud, illegality, duress, or undue influence. Banks would not risk acquiring instruments that might be subject to such defences when the time came to collect from the party primarily liable.[51]

DEFENCES

Meaning of Defence

The term "defences" is a legal description for the various arguments that a party liable on an instrument may put up against a holder who demands payment. In determining whether a defence will succeed, there are two aspects to consider: (a) the status of the holder relative to the party liable and (b) the type of defence of the party liable. The following is an overview of legal actions in which the plaintiff is the holder of the instrument and the defendant an acceptor, maker, drawer, or endorser.

Types of Holders

immediate parties
the holder of an instrument and the party alleged to be liable on it who have had direct dealings with each other

remote parties
parties to an instrument who have not had direct dealings with one another

First, it is important to examine the relationship between the holder and the party alleged to be liable on the instrument. When a holder has had direct dealings with that party, the two of them are **immediate parties**. If they have not had direct dealings with one another and yet are parties to the same instrument, they are **remote parties**. Since a holder in due course is, by definition, a party who acquires the instrument by negotiation from the payee or from a subsequent endorser, he is always a party remote from the acceptor of a draft, maker of a note, or drawer of a cheque.

---

49. S. 69(2).

50. S. 182. See also Crawford and Falconbridge, *supra*, n. 9, pp. 1510–11.

51. As an additional protection, a bank will require the endorsement of the person from whom it acquires the instrument; but recourse against endorsers is at best a second resort, which banks naturally wish to avoid.

ILLUSTRATION 21.2

A draws a cheque in favour of B. B endorses it to the order of C. C endorses it to the order of D. D is the present holder of the cheque.

A (Drawer) ⟶ B (Payee)   C (Endorsee)   D (Endorsee)

(Endorser)   (Endorser)   (Holder)

A and B, B and C, and C and D are immediate parties of each other. The remote party relationships are A and C, A and D, and B and D. Whether the present holder, D, is a holder in due course will depend upon whether he satisfies the four essential conditions.

Types of Defences

A holder's chance of success in collecting from an immediate party is no better than his contractual rights under the agreement between them. The negotiable instrument does not increase the holder's rights. Against an immediate party, the party liable can use a line of *mere personal defences*, usually not available against remote parties.

By contrast, a remote party who is a holder in due course has the best chance of success in collecting payment. The party liable has a greatly reduced list of possible defences, termed *real defences*, with which to resist the demands of a holder in due course.

If a remote party fails to meet the standards of a holder in due course, his position lies between an immediate party and a holder in due course. He is subject not only to real defences but also to *defect of title* defences. He is not, however, subject to mere personal defences. Since this area is quite detailed and technical, we shall simply list the defences.[52]

Mere Personal Defences

All the defences—real, defect of title, and mere personal—are available to the defendant when the contestants are immediate parties, but the mere personal defences are available *only* when they are immediate parties. Defences that are good only against an immediate party are (a) lack of consideration and (b) the right of set-off, as discussed in Chapter 12.

Defect of Title Defences

We have seen that a holder in due course must have taken the instrument without knowledge of any defect in title and, when he has done so, defences based on such defects will fail. Generally speaking, when an instrument is **regular on its face**, there is no defence against a holder in due course. But if a holder takes the instrument *with* knowledge of one or more defects, or when there is an irregularity on the face of the instrument, he is *not* a holder in due course, and a defence based on a defect will be successful.[53] Such defects are:

regular on its face
nothing appears out of order on the document itself

(a) incapacity to contract as a result of drunkenness or insanity[54]
(b) discharge of the instrument by payment, or renunciation of a holder's rights in it
(c) absence of delivery when the instrument was complete at the time
(d) fraud, duress, undue influence, illegality
(e) want of authority in an agent to complete the instrument on behalf of the party primarily liable

52. For a full discussion see Crawford and Falconbridge, *supra*, n. 9.

53. Ss. 55 and 57(2).

54. Depending upon the circumstances, insanity might instead be interpreted as a real defence. See Crawford and Falconbridge, *supra*, n. 9, pp. 1348–51.

Real Defences

The following defences are good against any holder, even a holder in due course:

(a) incapacity to contract because of infancy
(b) cancellation of the instrument
(c) absence of delivery where the instrument is incomplete when taken
(d) fraud as to the nature of the instrument when the promisor is blind or illiterate
(e) a forged signature on the instrument
(f) want of authority, in someone who has represented himself as an agent, to sign on behalf of the party liable
(g) alteration of the instrument

CONSUMER BILLS AND NOTES

The modern concept of negotiability is a highly refined one, developed over the centuries and adapted to the convenience of business. Its advantages have had to be restricted, however, because of certain abuses. One abuse, in particular, related to consumer sales where the price was to be paid by instalments. The seller might assign the contract to a finance company and receive immediate payment: the buyer would receive notice of assignment and make the instalment payments to the finance company. The general rule about assignment of contractual rights, as we have seen in Chapter 12, is that an assignee acquires no better claim than the assignor had. Therefore, if the buyer had some claim against the seller, for breach of warranty or because the contract was induced by some misrepresentation, that claim can normally be asserted against the assignee. However, merchants and finance companies found a way around the general rule about assignments by using a negotiable instrument. The buyer was required to sign a promissory note for the balance of the purchase price plus finance charges, and this note, along with the conditional sale contract, was endorsed by the merchant to the finance company. The finance company became *a holder in due course* of the note, immune to any personal defences the buyer might have against the merchant.

This abuse was remedied by an amendment to the Bills of Exchange Act,[55] removing the protection otherwise accorded to a holder in due course in consumer credit arrangements where a finance company acts in concert with a seller of goods on the instalment plan. The Act requires that every consumer bill or consumer note be prominently and legibly marked on its face with the words "consumer purchase" before or at the time the instrument is signed by the purchaser or by anyone signing to accommodate the purchaser (that is, a guarantor).[56] It is further provided that the right of the holder of a consumer bill or consumer note to have the whole or any part thereof paid by the purchaser or a guarantor is subject to any defence or right of set-off, other than counterclaim, that the purchaser would have had in an action by the seller on the bill or note.[57]

Therefore, a buyer on consumer credit can now use against a finance company that sues him as holder of his promissory note all the personal defences formerly available only against the seller.

---

55. See also the discussion of this issue in Chapter 32, under the heading "Consumer Protection."
56. S. 190(1). If not so marked, the instrument is void in the hands of either the seller or the finance company (s. 190(2)).
57. S. 191.

QUESTIONS FOR REVIEW

1. Describe the nature of "clearing house" arrangements.

2. In addition to bills of exchange, promissory notes, and cheques, describe two other types of negotiable instruments.

3. Describe briefly the respective uses of demand drafts, sight drafts, and time drafts in commercial practice.

4. What is the difference in legal effect between a drawer having her cheque certified and a payee later having the cheque certified?

5. Describe the three qualities of negotiable instruments that distinguish them from ordinary assignments and how these qualities make them commercially useful.

6. Donna draws a cheque payable to Edgar for "a maximum of $1000 for carpentry work." Edgar completes the work while Donna is out of town and takes the cheque to his bank to cash it. The bank refuses on the ground that it is not a valid cheque. Is the bank correct? Explain.

7. Describe the difference between a "bearer" instrument and an "order" instrument.

8. Explain the significance of a party transferring a negotiable instrument endorsed "without recourse." When is this type of endorsement used?

9. *J* delivers a cheque for $500 in payment for a second-hand computer purchased from *K. K* inadvertently leaves the cheque on a restaurant table. *Q* picks it up from the table, forges *K*'s name, and cashes the cheque at the *L* Bank. *K* reports the loss of the cheque to *J*, who immediately informs her bank to stop payment. What rights does the *L* Bank have?

10. *W* delivers a cheque for $1000 in payment of a debt owed to *X. X* endorses the cheque to *Y*'s Second Hand Shop to purchase a television set. *Y* endorses the cheque to her landlord, *Z*, in part payment of her monthly rent. When *Z* takes the cheque to his bank, the teller recognizes *W*'s signature and has heard that he is in financial difficulty. She contacts *W*'s bank and learns that there are not sufficient funds in *W*'s account. What should *Z* do to protect his claim?

11. Describe the requirements for a party to be considered a holder in due course.

12. You are the maker of a note in which you undertake to pay $500 to a moneylender on demand. Subsequently you pay an instalment of $200 to the moneylender on this liability. What steps should you take to ensure that you will not have to pay a further $500 at some later time?

13. Gower has drawn a time draft on Cohen payable three months after sight to Jenkins. The draft is complete and regular with the possible exception of a clause that Cohen, the drawee, is "to pay the amount of this draft out of money due me on December 31 for professional services rendered." If Cohen refuses to accept the draft, does he owe its amount in future to Gower or to Jenkins?

14. The endorsements appearing on the back of each of three negotiable instruments are reproduced below. An asterisk following a name indicates an actual signature. Identify each of the endorsements by type, and explain its effect for the parties concerned:

    (a) Pay to John Factor, Without Recourse
        The Synthetic Textile Co. Ltd.
        per *Terry Lean*,*/Manager.
        *John Factor**

    (b) Pay to James Hawkins,
        *S. Trelawney**
        For deposit only,
        *James Hawkins**

(c) Pay to Archibald Grosvenor only
No Protest *Reginald Bunthorne**
*Archibald Grosvenor**
Archibald Grosvenor is hereby identified,
*Ralph Rackstraw**

15. Wilma purchased a used minivan, including a three-month warranty on parts and labour, from Xenon Used Cars Inc. for $10 000. She paid $1500 down and signed a promissory note for $8500, payable in monthly instalments of $285 for three years. If any payment is missed by Wilma, the entire sum will fall due at once because of her default. Xenon immediately transferred the note to Yarrow Finance Corp. and received payment of $7750. Wilma received notice of the transfer with a request to make her monthly payments directly to Yarrow Finance. The van broke down repeatedly within the first month, and Wilma was unable to obtain proper repairs from Xenon. She refused to make the payments to Yarrow Finance, and it sued her for the full sum due. Describe the nature of Wilma's defence against Yarrow Finance and whether she will succeed.

CASES AND PROBLEMS

1. On April 28, the University of Penticton made a note payable to the Baroque Construction Co. Ltd., three months after date. The amount of the note was expressed simply as "the balance due to you for construction of our Arts Building." On May 2 following, the Baroque Construction Co. Ltd. sold the note to a private financier, R. Jay, for $47 500, having shown him accounts and vouchers indicating a balance of $50 000 due from the university. On July 31, R. Jay presented the note to the treasurer of the university for payment and was advised by him that the construction contract with the Baroque Construction Co. Ltd. contained a guarantee clause and that serious defects had developed in the foundation of the Arts Building. The treasurer stated that the university was not prepared to pay the note for this reason. R. Jay countered with the argument that the defective work was not the slightest concern of his, and that the proper officer of the university had signed the note. He then sued the University of Penticton on its note. Should he succeed? Give reasons.

2. On the afternoon of October 27, Connor supplied office furniture valued at $48 000 to Osmond. When the furniture was delivered, Connor received a certified cheque for $48 000 from Osmond. The cheque, drawn on Osmond's account at the Kelsey Bank, had been certified earlier that afternoon by the bank at Osmond's request. That morning Osmond had deposited a cheque from a customer for $76 000; the cheque had not yet been cleared, but the bank took the risk that it would be honoured by the Portage Bank, where Osmond's customer had his account.

   On October 28, after having been informed by Portage that it would not honour the $76 000 cheque, the Kelsey Bank called Connor to say that certification had been revoked and that she should not attempt to negotiate the cheque. The next day, Connor presented the certified cheque for payment. The Kelsey Bank refused payment, and Connor sued the bank.

   Is the Kelsey Bank legally bound to honour the cheque? Explain.

3. Elston owned all the issued common shares of Ham Ltd. He lent Ham Ltd. $160 000 of his personal funds and obtained in return a promissory note from the company payable to his order.

   For personal reasons Elston subsequently had to borrow money on his own account from the Atlas Bank. To secure this loan he delivered the Ham Ltd. promissory note to the bank, but without endorsing it. The bank gave no notice to Ham Ltd. that it was the transferee.

THE NATURE OF INTELLECTUAL PROPERTY

Forms of Intellectual Property

Intellectual property is intangible property that is the product of mental activity. The four most recognized forms of intellectual property are trademarks, copyright, patents, and industrial designs. Each type of intellectual property deals with ideas or inventions of which individuality or originality is an essential feature. Each category comprises a particular type of property that is protected according to its own rules.

As a result, intellectual property law is a very complicated subject. Some property rights are protected solely by statute, while others are also protected by common law rules. For some interests, registration is essential, while other rights arise upon creation. Some types of intellectual property may fall within two different categories, while others may fall into gaps between the categories so that no protection is provided at all. In addition, since intellectual property is essentially concerned with knowledge, information, and above all, innovation, it is linked to technological progress. New methods of storing, presenting, and transmitting information and ideas are constantly being devised, and some of these techniques do not fit neatly into the traditional categories of intellectual property that were established 100 or more years ago. Currently, the rules are evolving to address the new challenges. It is important to note that of all the different areas of law, intellectual property law is one of the most complex and technical, and perhaps the most specialized. The registration of trademarks and patents, for example, is normally dealt with by a small and select body of experts. This chapter is designed to present a general overview of intellectual property rights and protections and some guidance on how to avoid infringing the rights of others.

Not all ideas, information, or knowledge qualify as intellectual property: confidential information, trade secrets, and what is commonly referred to as "know-how," though they may be protected by law, are not regarded as forms of property. Some recently introduced statutory rights provide protection for new concepts without fitting them into any of the established categories.

CHECKLIST Forms of Intellectual Property

Canadian law recognizes the following basic forms of intellectual property:

- trademarks
- copyright
- patents
- industrial designs

Should Intellectual Property Be Protected?

The proposition that ideas should receive legal protection as a form of property has not always been universally accepted. As discussed in Chapter 3, the common law protected ideas with torts such as passing off and product defamation. The increasing value of intellectual property motivated legislative protection.

Advocates of protection claim that creators, such as writers, inventors, and designers, have a right to the rewards arising from their efforts and that without protection, creativity is discouraged. By contrast, opponents of protection claim that ideas and inventions, or at least some ideas and inventions—especially those concerning matters such as health, medicine, food production, and education—properly belong to the whole world. They point to the heavy social costs of protection— higher prices due to the payment of royalties and licence fees, and inefficient use of resources resulting from restrictions on the use of new techniques and from the exercise of monopoly power. Excessive protection, as much as lack of protection, may hinder economic and social progress.

The problem, especially for a country such as Canada, which is both an exporter and importer of cultural and technological innovation, is to find the right balance. While the United States seems to be moving towards greater protection of "ownership rights," for example, by lengthening the period of copyright protection and criminalizing infringement (mostly for the benefit of large corporations),[1] Canadian courts have recently shown more concern for what may be termed "user rights."[2]

TRADEMARKS

Nature of Trademarks

trademark
an identifiable feature that is used by a person for the purpose of distinguishing their goods or services from those of others

Section 2 of the Trade-marks Act[3] defines a **trademark** as

(a) a mark that is used by a person for the purpose of distinguishing or so as to distinguish wares or services manufactured, sold, leased, hired, or performed by him from those manufactured, sold, leased, hired, or performed by others
(b) a certification mark
(c) a distinguishing guise

Although the Act does not define the word "mark," it is generally accepted that virtually any visual characteristic of goods or their presentation that serves to distinguish them from goods that do not have the same trade connection can be considered a "mark."

certification mark
a special type of trademark used to identify goods or services that conform to a particular standard

distinguishing guise
the shaping of goods or their containers, or a distinctive mode of wrapping or packaging

A **certification mark** is a special type of trademark used to identify goods or services that conform to a particular standard, a typical example being the "TRUSTe" mark for internet security. The owner of the certification mark may register it and license its use to other persons whose goods or services meet the defined standards. A **distinguishing guise** usually refers to the shaping of goods or their containers, or to a mode of wrapping or packaging that is distinctive—a Coca-Cola bottle, for example.[4]

Business Names

Today, businesses operate using a variety of business names, domain names, and trade names. Each of these names involves trademark issues. The name of an established business is a valuable asset that forms part of the goodwill of the business. A trademark may be and frequently is part of a business name, but the entire name is not itself a trademark. For example, the word "Ford" is a trademark of the Ford Motor Company, but the full name is not a trademark. Common words such as "company" or "limited" are not trademarkable. Similarly, only portions of a domain name are eligible for trademark protection. Although a domain name is technically only an address, that portion of the name that is uniquely linked to goods or services may be registered as a trademark.[5] Businesses often register separate trade names to market different product lines or represent different divisions of a business (sometimes referred to as brands). For example, Cara Operations Limited owns the trademark

1. The Sonny Bono Copyright Extension Act of 1998, which extends U.S. copyright protection by 20 years, to 70 years after the creator's death, is commonly known as the "Mickey Mouse Act," because of the benefit it conferred on the Walt Disney Company.

2. See the Supreme Court of Canada decisions in *Theberge* v. *Galerie d'Art du Petit Champlain*, [2002] 2 S.C.R. 336, *Canadian Association of Internet Providers* v. *SOCAN* (2004), 240 D.L.R. (4th) 193.

3. Trade-marks Act, R.S.C. 1985, c. T-13. (Unless otherwise stated, statutory references in this part of the chapter are to this Act.)

4. In order to qualify as a trademark, a distinguishing guise must be more than purely functional: see *Kirkbi AG* v. *Ritvik Holdings Inc.* (2003), 228 D.L.R. (4th) 297 affd. [2005] 3 S.C.R. 302 (Lego Block case).

5. For an interesting examination of this topic, see L.K. Jones, "Trademark.com: Trademark Law in Cyberspace" (1999), 37 *Alta. L. Rev.* 991. This problem is discussed further in Chapter 34.

"Harvey's" for its fast-food restaurant brand.[6] A business should investigate trademark protection and availability for its name, domain name, and any trade names before investing heavily in them.

As we shall see in Part 6, the names of all corporations, and those of some unincorporated businesses, must be registered. However, separate registers are maintained for corporations and for unincorporated businesses, and each province keeps its own registers. Unfortunately, that means that a search of the relevant provincial registry may not reveal other users in other provinces. In addition, registration of a business name does not give a business the right to carry on business under that name if to do so would infringe the trademark of some other business. The government specifically excludes any suggestion that granting incorporation under a particular name guarantees the use of that name and specifically warns applicants of this limitation.[7] Therefore, a separate trademark search and registration should be completed. Since section 40(2) of the Trade-marks Act allows a proposed trademark to be registered, a business can gain trademark protection before it invests too heavily in its names.

Protection of Trademarks

Common Law: The Tort of Passing-off

The common law protects a trademark owner through the tort of passing-off. A person commits the tort of **passing-off** when he misrepresents goods, services, or a business in such a way as to deceive the public into believing that they are the goods, services, or business of some other person, and thereby causing damage to that person. The main purpose of a passing-off action is to protect the trademark owner from what is, in effect, a theft of goodwill.

The legal definition of **goodwill** is "the benefit and advantage of the good name, reputation, and connection of a business."[8] Consider goodwill as the difference between the market value of a business as a going concern and its break-up value—that is, the sum that could be obtained by selling off all of its fixed assets and inventory piece by piece. The name of the business and any mark clearly associated with it forms part of a business's reputation and goodwill.

passing-off
misrepresenting goods, services, or a business in such a way as to deceive the public into believing that they are the goods, services, or business of some other person

goodwill
the benefit and advantage of the good name, reputation, and connections of a business

CASE 22.1

Ray Plastics Ltd. manufactured a successful tool—a combined snow brush, ice scraper, and squeegee—called "Snow Trooper." It supplied the tool to a number of large retailers, including Canadian Tire. Canadian Tire suggested to another of its suppliers, Dustbane Products Ltd., that it consider producing a similar type of tool. Dustbane did so, producing a tool that was virtually identical and at a lower price; it thereby obtained all of Canadian Tire's snow-brush business.

The court found that the design of the "Snow Trooper" was very distinctive, that it had been intentionally copied, and that this constituted the tort of "passing-off." It awarded an injunction and damages to Ray Plastics.[9]

The elements of the tort of passing-off are:

- The plaintiff's goods, services, or business must enjoy a reputation that is of some value worth protecting.

6. Canadian Trademark Registration Number TMA147423.

7. When applying for federal incorporation with a specific name, the federal government requires a NUANS (Newly Upgraded Automated Name Search) search. Names likely to cause confusion are rejected. The federal government limits its investigation to the contents of this search and applicants are warned to complete a trademark registration and monitor ongoing applications. See the Industry Canada website: www.ic.gc.ca/epic/site/cd-dgc.nsf/en/cs02060e.html.

8. *Inland Revenue Commissioners* v. *Muller* [1901] A.C. 217 at 223.

9. *Ray Plastics Ltd.* v. *Dustbane Products Ltd.* (1994), 57 C.P.R. (3d) 474. See also *Eli Lilly and Co.* v. *Novopharm Ltd.* (2000), 195 D.L.R. (4th) 547, in which the shape and colouring of a drug capsule were held to be a distinctive get-up. However, the combination of shape and colour must be unique or sufficiently unusual to clearly distinguish the product from other products: *Novopharm Ltd.* v. *AstraZeneca AB* (2003), 233 D.L.R. (4th) 150.

- The defendant must have misrepresented its goods, service, or business as those of the plaintiff.
- There must either be actual confusion or a likelihood of confusion in the public's mind between the goods, services, or business of the plaintiff and those of the defendant.
- The plaintiff must suffer or be likely to suffer damage in consequence of the passing-off.[10]

CASE 22.2

The plaintiff, Greystone Capital Management, was a firm of real estate and investment managers conducting business in British Columbia. The firm was well regarded and enjoyed an excellent reputation in the real estate industry in the province. The defendant company also operated as property developers and managers in British Columbia. It changed its name to Greystone Real Estate Corporation, even though they were aware of the plaintiff's existence.

The court ordered the defendant to change its name and to refrain from using the word "Greystone" in any future name. It also awarded damages to the plaintiff. The plaintiff established the existence of goodwill associated with its name. The defendant's use of the name "Greystone" was likely to mislead the public and to cause injury to the plaintiff.[11]

In some recent cases, plaintiffs have argued that the definition of passing-off should be expanded to include situations where one person makes use of a well-known trade name or mark in order to obtain a benefit, even though the owner cannot show any damage and there is no likelihood of confusion in the minds of the public.[12] To date, this view has had only limited success in the courts and the argument is more effective under the statutory causes of action.

CASE 22.3

The defendant named its new hotel in Edmonton the "Fantasyland Hotel." An injunction was sought by Walt Disney Productions, which had for some years used the name "Fantasyland" in connection with its amusement parks. The Alberta Court of Appeal confirmed the trial judgment, dismissing the action. According to the court:

Passing-off cases fall into two broad categories. In the first are those where competitors are engaged in a common field of activity and the plaintiff has alleged that the defendant has named, packaged or described its product or business in a manner likely to lead the public to believe the defendant's product or business is that of the plaintiff. The second, and nowadays perhaps more common type of passing-off, is where it is alleged that a defendant has promoted his product or business in such a way as to create the false impression that his product or business is in

some way approved, authorized or endorsed by the plaintiff or that there is some business connection between the defendant and the plaintiff. By these means a defendant may hope to cash in on the goodwill of the plaintiff. The appellant says this case is of the second type because the respondent, in using the name "Fantasyland" for its hotel, is creating the false impression that it is authorized or connected with the appellant—in other words, the respondent is "cashing in" on the appellant's goodwill. The appellant's theory of the law of passing-off contains a fatal weakness. Even the "more common type of passing-off" referred to requires proof of the essentials of goodwill: misrepresentation or confusion, which the trial judge found, as a fact, did not exist in this case. In other words, the allegation or even the belief that the respondent is benefiting from the use of the name "Fantasyland" is not enough to found the tort of passing-off.[13]

10. See *Ciba-Geigy Canada Ltd.* v. *Apotex Inc.* (1992), 44 C.P.R. (3d) 289 (S.C.C.), per Gonthier, J. See also *Kirkbi, supra* n. 4.

11. *Greystone Capital Management Inc.* v. *Greystone Properties Ltd.* [1999] B.C.J. No. 514.

12. In rare circumstances when the passing-off deliberately suggests an association with another's product, it may not be necessary to show damage. For example, an advertising campaign that incorrectly associates a product with another's product may actually benefit that other product, but might still amount to passing-off: see *National Hockey League* v. *Pepsi-Cola Canada Ltd.* (1995), 122 D.L.R. (4th) 412.

13. *Walt Disney Productions* v. *Fantasyland Hotel Inc.* (1998), 85 C.P.R. (3d) 36, affd. (2000), 4 C.P.R. (4th) 370. Similarly, the use of the trademark "Playboy," in connection with magazine and hotels, was held not to be confusing with the same name for hair stylists: *Playboy Enterprises Inc.* v. *Germain* (1978), 39 C.P.R. (2d) 32 affd. (1979), 43 C.P.R. (2d) 271 (Fed. C.A.). See also *Toyota Jidosha Kabushiki Kaisha* v. *Lexus Foods Inc.* (2000), 194 D.L.R. (4th) 491.

Section 7 of the Trade-marks Act

The Trade-marks Act provides additional statutory causes of action that are closely related to the common law action of passing-off. Section 7 prohibits

- making a false or misleading statement tending to discredit the business, wares, or services of a competitor
- directing public attention to one's wares, services, or business in such a way as to cause or be likely to cause confusion in Canada between those wares, services, or business and the wares, services, or business of another
- passing-off other wares or services as and for those ordered or requested
- making, in association with wares or services, any description that is false in a material respect and likely to mislead the public as to their character, quality, origin, or mode of production
- doing any other act or adopting any other business practice contrary to honest industrial or commercial usage in Canada

Although section 7 appears to restate the common law, it gives wider protection in some cases, since it applies to the whole of Canada and appears to be broader in scope than the common law action.

Registered Trademarks

Unregistered trademarks are protected by the passing-off tort and under section 7 of the Trade-marks Act. However, additional advantages are available if a business registers its trademarks under the Trade-marks Act.

When a registered mark is used, there is no need to indicate that it is registered in order to obtain the benefits of registration, but it has become common practice, on labels and in advertisements, to use the symbol ® or ™, frequently accompanied by words such as ". . . is the registered trademark of XYZ Inc."

Rights Obtained by Registration

Section 19 of the Act gives the owner of a valid registered trademark the exclusive right to its use throughout Canada in respect of the goods and services for which it was registered. No unauthorized person may then sell, distribute, or advertise any goods or services in association with a confusing trademark or trade name (section 20), or otherwise use the mark in a manner that is likely to have the effect of depreciating the value of the goodwill attached to it (section 22). Registration provides a complete defence to a passing-off action. If another person claims that he had already been using the mark, or a deceptively similar mark, before the registration, his only recourse is to attack the validity of the registration.[14] If, after a trademark has been registered, it is discovered that some other person had been using a similar trademark before the registered owner first used it, the first user may bring proceedings to have the registration "expunged," that is, removed (section 17).

Registration gives the owner other advantages; normally it applies to the whole of Canada so that the right of exclusive use is not restricted to the area in which the owner actually does business and has established a reputation. A trademark that has been registered in Canada may also be registered in other countries that adhere to the International Convention for the Protection of Industrial Property. Although a separate foreign application must be filed, the Canadian registration creates a presumption in favour of validity, distinctiveness, and ownership.

14. *Molson Canada* v. *Oland Brewery Ltd.* (2002), 214 D.L.R. (4th) 473.

Duration

A trademark registration is valid for a period of 15 years and may be renewed indefinitely. The Registrar may from time to time request evidence that the trademark is still being used, and if it has been abandoned or is not renewed at the end of the 15-year period, it may be expunged from the register (sections 44, 45).

Requirements for Registration

The Mark

In order for a trademark to be registered, it must satisfy a number of conditions (section 12). In particular, the mark must *not* be

(a) a word that is primarily merely the name or surname of an individual who is living or died within the preceding 30 years
(b) clearly descriptive or deceptively misdescriptive of the character or quality of the wares or services, or of their place of origin
(c) the name of any of the wares or services in connection with which it is used
(d) likely to be confused with another registered trademark
(e) a mark that is prohibited by sections 9 or 10 of the Trade-marks Act

Prohibitions (a), (b), and (c) ensure that the names of people and places and descriptive words that are in common usage are not taken out of circulation through registration by giving a monopoly to the registered owner. The intention of prohibition (d) is to carry out the main purpose of the Act: trademarks are designed to be distinctive, and such distinctiveness would be lost if two or more persons were allowed to register confusingly similar marks. Although each case must be determined on its own facts with regard to all the surrounding circumstances, section 6 provides a list of relevant considerations including the nature of the wares, the degree of resemblance, and the nature of the trade. Finally, sections 9 and 10 prohibit registration of marks that suggest an association with royalty, the government, or certain international organizations or professional groups or that are scandalous or obscene.

Selecting and designing a suitable trademark is difficult. Ideally, the mark should be distinctive and eye-catching and should quickly become associated in the public mind with the goods or services of its owner. It must be original so that it does not offend against condition (d) by being confusingly similar to some other registered mark, but should not be one that is likely to be rejected under one of conditions (a), (b), or (e). The normal practice is to make a search of the Trade-marks Branch of the Canadian Intellectual Property Office for other marks that are visually or phonetically similar to the mark being proposed for registration;[15] in some cases it may also be advisable to make searches in the United States. In practice, the application to register is normally prepared and filed by a specialist trademark agent, who will give advice on the likelihood of an application being accepted; such advice is important, since the case law on this subject is extremely complicated.

---

15. This may now be done by means of a NUANS search, a system operated by Industry Canada that provides a computerized search for all federally (and some provincially) registered companies and trademarks. *The Canadian Intellectual Property Office CanadianTrade-marks Database* website also has database search capabilities: http://strategis.ic.gc.ca/app/cipo/trademarks/search/tmSearch.do?language=eng.

ILLUSTRATION 22.1

(a) A mark consisting of the name of a historical figure, such as "William Shakespeare" or "John A. Macdonald," would probably be acceptable, even though it is very likely that there are living persons with those names. Similarly, fictitious names, such as "Captain Kirk" or "Darth Vader," are registrable because the public would not identify the names with living individuals. In one instance, an invented name, "Marco Pecci," was held to be registrable in the absence of evidence that such an individual actually existed, despite the possibility that there might somewhere be a person of that name.[16]

(b) Words, especially adjectives, that are merely descriptive (or misdescriptive) of the quality of the goods are not acceptable. "Instant" or "Super" would be rejected, though "Kold One" has been accepted when applied to beer.[17] The word "Golden" was held to be descriptive of a beer and therefore not registrable.[18]

(c) The use of a place name as descriptive of the quality or origin of goods is normally not permitted. The mark "Toscano," applied to wine, was disallowed since that is the Italian name for wine from a famous region.[19] In another case, however, a producer was permitted to register the mark "Oberhaus" in relation to wine, despite the fact that there is in Germany a small village called Oberhausen where wine is produced. It was considered unlikely that the Canadian wine-buying public would know of the place.[20]

(d) A proposed trademark will be confusing if a casual consumer somewhat in a hurry is likely to draw a mistaken inference. An applicant was allowed to register the trademark "Barbie's" for restaurant, take-out, catering, and banquet services despite the objections of Mattel Inc., owners of the famous "BARBIE" mark in association with dolls and doll accessories. The Supreme Court of Canada held that the doll and restaurant businesses appeal to different consumers and confusion was unlikely.[21]

Ownership and Use

Registration creates a presumption of ownership. It does not make a person the owner of a trademark; that person must already be the owner at the time of registration. Even in the case of an approved application based upon proposed use, the mark will be registered only after the applicant has filed a declaration that it has started to use the mark in Canada.

The application to register may be based upon any one of the following grounds (section 16):

- the mark has been previously used or made known in Canada
- the mark has been registered and used abroad, in a country that is a party to the international convention
- it is proposed to use the mark in Canada

Generally, the advertising of a trademark is not sufficient to constitute "use"; the goods to which the mark relates must have been sold or the services performed. However, advertising alone may be sufficient to amount to "making known" the mark in Canada.

16. *Gerhard Horn Investments Ltd.* v. *Registrar of Trade Marks*, [1983] 2 F.C. 878.
17. *Registrar of Trade Marks* v. *Provenzano* (1978), 40 C.P.R. (2d) 288.
18. *John Labatt Ltd.* v. *Molson Cos.* (1987), 19 C.P.R. (3d) 88 (Fed. C.A.).
19. *Jordan & Ste Michelle Cellars Ltd.* v. *Gillespies & Co.* (1985), 6 C.P.R. (3d) 377. In that case, the words were also deceptively misdescriptive, since the wine was Canadian.
20. *Stabilisierungsfonds fur Wein* v. *T.G. Bright & Co. Ltd.* (1985), 4 C.P.R. (3d) 526. Sections 11.11 to 11.19 of the Act now contain detailed provisions regarding the names and geographical descriptions that may be used in connection with wines and spirits. Those provisions are intended to comply with Canada's obligations under the World Trade Organization rules.
21. *Mattel, Inc.* v. *3894207 Canada Inc.*, [2006] 1 S.C.R. 772. For an expanded discussion about the determination of confusion see *Veuve Clicquot Ponsardin* v. *Boutiques Cliquot Ltee*, [2006] 1 S.C.R. 824.

Opposition Proceedings

The initial obstacle in registering a trademark is to satisfy the Registrar that the chosen mark is eligible for registration. If the Registrar refuses registration, the owner may appeal that decision to the courts. If there is no objection by the Registrar, or an objection has been overcome, the Trade-Marks Office issues a notice that the application has been approved for advertisement in the *Trade-Marks Journal*, and, subsequently, the application must be advertised. Any person may file a notice of opposition within two months of the advertisement. Registration may be opposed on any of the following grounds:

- the application did not comply with the various formal requirements for filing
- the mark is not registrable
- the applicant is not the person entitled to registration
- the mark is not "distinctive" (sections 37, 38)

The opponent must describe the reason for the opposition in sufficient detail to allow the applicant to reply to the objection. However, the onus of satisfying the Registrar that the trademark should be registered still rests on the applicant. This is so, even though the Registrar has in effect already reached a preliminary decision in favour of the application by permitting it to be advertised. Opposition proceedings are determined in the first place by hearing officers, with appeal to the Trial Division of the Federal Court.

An objection that the mark is not registrable may be based on any of the elements set out in section 12 of the Act. The motivation behind a challenge is usually to prevent a business competitor from gaining an advantage by being granted the exclusive right to use the mark. The other common reason is that the objector claims pre-existing rights to an identical or confusingly similar mark, whether or not it is registered. Determining what is "confusing" depends on all the surrounding circumstances including the nature of the business concerned and the goods or services supplied.[22]

CASE 22.4

A small Ontario corporation, Pink Panther Beauty Corp., applied to register the name "Pink Panther" as a trademark for hair-care and beauty supplies that it proposed to market. The application was opposed by United Artists, the well-known movie studio that owns the Pink Panther movies, the Pink Panther cartoon character, and the accompanying music. United Artists has its own "Pink Panther" registrations for movie-related services. It argued that the application by the Ontario corporation should not be granted because of the risk of confusion with its existing marks. Further, it claimed that the applicants were simply trying to cash in on their famous name.

The court allowed the application by the Ontario corporation to register the mark. There was no likelihood of confusion, since the applicant sold beauty products, not movies.[23]

Actions for Infringement

Unauthorized Use

One major advantage of registration is that unlike passing off, a registered trademark may be infringed by *any* unauthorized use of that mark or a confusingly similar mark by some other person.

22. Section 6(5) contains a non-exhaustive list; whether confusion is likely is determined on a balance of probabilities: *Dion Neckwear Ltd.* v. *Christian Dior S.A.* (2002), 216 D.L.R. (4th) 451.

23. *Pink Panther Beauty Corp.* v. *United Artists Corp.* (1998), 80 C.P.R. (3d) 247. (The dissenting judge would have disallowed the application: the applicant was simply attempting to cash in on the goodwill associated with the name.) The Supreme Court of Canada has held that this case should not be followed to the extent that it may suggest that some resemblance of linkage to the wares in question is necessary for confusion to exist; the wares or services in question do not have to be of the same general class: *Mattel, supra* n. 21.

What constitutes "use" is sometimes difficult to determine. Sections 2 and 4 of the Act indicate that a trademark is "used" when it distinguishes someone's wares or services from those originating from someone else. To appropriate another's name or mark, even without any intent to deceive, is to "use" another's mark.[24] It is not necessary for the defendant to have attempted to pass off its products as those of the owner of the mark. Comparative advertising, where one firm attempts to demonstrate that its product is superior to a rival's, may constitute a "use" of the rival's mark if the advertisement refers to the name or mark of the rival product.[25] An infringement may be accidental or deliberate; it is not necessary to show an intention to damage the goodwill of the owner of the mark,[26] though such an intention may persuade a court to award punitive damages.

In *Coca-Cola Ltd.* v. *Pardhan*[27] the well-known soft-drink company brought an action alleging infringement of its trademark on the ground that the defendant bought quantities of the beverage in Canada and then exported it for resale without the consent of the manufacturer. Coca-Cola argued that the defendant's export amounted to infringement because exporting is deemed to be use under the Act.[28] The Federal Court of Appeal rejected the argument, and found that improperly distributing authentic goods did not amount to infringement.[29] The court held that "goods which originate in the stream of commerce with the owner of a trademark are not counterfeit."[30]

Jurisdiction and Remedies

Both the civil provincial courts and the Federal Court of Canada have jurisdiction to hear an action for infringement. The appropriate provincial court may deal with both passing-off and Trade-marks Act claims but the resulting judgment will be enforceable in the specific province only. On the other hand, if an action is brought in the Federal Court, the judgment is enforceable anywhere in Canada. However, the Federal Court only has jurisdiction to deal with statutory actions brought under the Trade-marks Act. Normally, that should not cause any difficulty since, as we have seen, section 7 of the Act seems to provide greater protection to even unregistered trademark owners than does the common law tort of passing off.

The remedies that either court may grant are essentially the same. If there is injury to the goodwill of the owner, then damages may be awarded; if the defendant has profited from the infringement, an account of profits may be ordered. The defendant may be restrained from further infringement by an injunction and may be required to deliver up or dispose of infringing materials. The court may also order the defendant to allow the plaintiff to search for and seize offending wares and relevant books and records,[31] and in a statutory action, may impose a ban upon further imports of offending products.[32]

24. *Walt Disney Productions* v. *Triple Five Corp.* (1993), 113 D.L.R. (4th) 229. In *Pro-C Ltd.* v. *Computer City Inc.* (2001), 205 D.L.R. (4th) 568, the Ontario Court of Appeal held that a trademark was not "used" simply because it appeared on a passive website. This case is considered further in Chapter 34.

25. *Eye Masters Ltd.* v. *Ross King Holdings Ltd.* (1992), 44 C.P.R. (3d) 459. Contrast *Future Shop Ltd.* v. *A & B Sound Ltd.* (1994), 55 C.P.R. (3d) 182.

26. Even a "spoof" upon a trademark may be actionable: see *Source Perrier S.A.* v. *Fira-Less Marketing Co. Ltd.* (1983), 70 C.P.R. (2d) 61.

27. (1999), 85 C.P.R. (3d) 489.

28. Section 4(3).

29. The purpose of section 4(3) is not to equate exporting with "use," but rather to enable Canadian producers who do not make local sales but simply ship their goods abroad to establish "use" in Canada for the purposes of obtaining Canadian trademark registration. See also *Molson Cos.* v. *Moosehead Breweries Ltd. et al.* (1990), 32 C.P.R. (3d) 363.

30. Stayer J. relied on the Federal Court of Appeal decision in *Smith & Nephew Inc.* v. *Glen Oak Inc. et al.,* (1996), 68 C.P.R. (3d) 153.

31. This is the so-called "Anton Piller" relief: see *Anton Piller KG.* v. *Manufacturing Processing Ltd.*, [1976] Ch. 55.

32. The power to ban imports has been restricted by the North American Free Trade Agreement Implementation Act, S.C. 1993, c. 44, s. 234.

Assignment, Licensing, and Franchising

Historically, common law rules only allowed an owner to transfer a trademark if the transferee was taking over the whole business. Section 48 of the Trade-marks Act substantially modifies the common law so that an owner may now transfer a trademark (a) whether or not it is registered, (b) either as part of or separately from the goodwill of the business, and (c) in respect of either all or some of the goods and services with which it is associated. An owner may also license the use of a registered trademark under specific conditions set out in the licence (section 50).

Special care must be taken when assigning or licensing a trademark to ensure that the rights of either or both parties are not lost. Generally, when a business is sold, the rights in a trademark with which it is associated pass to the purchaser—a transfer of the business operates to assign the trademark. If the mark is registered, the fact of the assignment may be entered on the register, but an assignment may be valid even if unregistered. If a mark is unregistered, the new owner may seek to register it after having commenced to use it. A more difficult situation occurs when an owner keeps the business but assigns the trademark, perhaps because the business is to discontinue production of the particular line of goods with which the mark is associated. An example occurs when a foreign company that has previously marketed its goods in Canada and has established rights to a trademark here forms a subsidiary company in Canada to take over the manufacture or distribution of its goods. The difficulty arises because, in the eyes of the public, the trademark may remain distinctive of the goods of the previous owner rather than those of the new owner, who consequently will not immediately have an established right to it.[33]

When licensing a trademark, the owner often wants to continue to use the mark and also to allow use by one or more other businesses, usually in return for payment of a fee or royalty. This may be done by giving notice to the public that the use is under licence. In that case use by the licensee is deemed to be use by the registered owner itself so as to preserve the distinctiveness of the mark (section 50). A licensed user cannot transfer the right to use a mark, and a breach of any of the terms of the licence will normally constitute an infringement of the trademark.

Although a *franchise agreement*, as discussed in Chapter 19, usually involves much more than the licensing of a trademark, the franchiser will in most cases require that the franchisee market goods or services under the franchiser's trademark. Franchisers normally insist on strict conditions in the franchise agreement, relating to such matters as quality control, purchasing of supplies and equipment, advertising, and the use of trademarks, trade names, designs, and the like. Breach of the agreement by a franchisee normally terminates its right to use the trademark, so that continued use would amount to infringement.

COPYRIGHT

Statutory Origin

Unlike the law of trademarks, copyright is entirely the creation of statute. There is no common law action for infringement of copyright. Interest in copyright developed after the invention of the printing press, and the first known copyright law was the Statute of Queen Anne, adopted in England in 1709. For many years copyright was associated almost exclusively with the written word, though its scope grew to cover drawings, paintings, and musical scores. In modern times, with the advent of motion pictures, sound recording, radio and television broadcasting, computer software, and the Internet, it has become a central feature of several major industries.

In Canada, the law of copyright is governed by the Copyright Act,[34] originally adopted in 1924 and substantially amended in 1988, 1993, and 1997.

---

33. See *Wilkinson Sword (Canada) Ltd.* v. *Juda*, [1968] 2 Ex. C.R. 137.
34. R.S.C. 1985, c. C-42. Unless otherwise stated, references in this part of the chapter are to this Act, as amended.

International Treaties

Canada is a signatory to the Berne Convention, an agreement to which more than 150 countries adhere. An author who is a citizen of a Convention country has copyright protection in Canada, and Canadian authors enjoy protection in other Convention countries. Canada also adheres to the Universal Copyright Convention. The Universal Copyright Convention enables a citizen of a contracting state to enjoy the same copyright protection in another contracting state as does a national of that state. Therefore, a Canadian national can obtain protection in the United States simply by following the American practice of marking the work with the symbol © or the word "copyright," followed by the name of the copyright owner and the year of first publication. Similar benefits are also provided by a number of reciprocal agreements that Canada has entered into with other countries. In 1997, Canada also became a signatory of two treaties developed by the **World Intellectual Property Organization** that are especially concerned with the impact of new technologies and the Internet on creator's rights: the WIPO Copyright Treaty (1996) and the WIPO Performances and Phonograms Treaty (1996). These treaties came into force on May 20, 2002 and require participating countries to adopt domestic legislation creating copyright enforcement remedies with significant infringement deterrence effect. As of 2008, Canada has not adopted legislation to implement the 1996 WPIO treaties.[35]

World Intellectual Property Organization
a specialized agency of the United Nations dedicated to harmonizing intellectual property laws and regimes worldwide

Reform

As will be discussed in Chapter 34, computer technology and the Internet have created unparalleled access to copyrighted material. They have also created the ability to instantaneously copy, distribute, and alter that material, and this has led to tension between owners and users. All parties support the movement for copyright reform but they disagree on how the reforms should balance owners' and users' rights.

Since the signing of the 1996 WIPO treaties, the Canadian government has talked of copyright reform to address such activities as downloading, uploading, burning, copying, and storing electronic material. The 1996 WIPO treaties prioritize owners' rights by calling for criminalization of these activities, strong enforcement procedures and remedies, and support for **Digital Rights Management Technology** (DRMT) and Technological Protection Measures (TPM). Users argue that these activities have become commonplace and DRMTs violate privacy rights and do not distinguish between acceptable and unacceptable copying.

Digital Rights Management Technology
a system collecting data about the licensing, payment, use, and authenticity of a work

In June 2005, Canada's Liberal government introduced Bill 60, largely in conformity with the WIPO treaty obligations, but the bill died on the table when the Liberals fell to the Conservative Party in the 2006 federal election. The new minority Conservative government proposed copyright reform in the throne speech and introduced a bill (Bill C-61, an Act to amend the Copyright Act) on June 12, 2008, but the parliament was dissolved for an October 2008 election. It remains to be seen whether the new minority Conservative government will resurrect Bill C-61. The ongoing reform debate focuses on three key areas: downloading, fair dealing, and the role of DRMTs.[36]

35. Canada is not the only signatory country that has failed to implement the corresponding domestic legislation. France, Germany, the European Community, and the United Kingdom have also failed to implement the treaty provisions. The United States has adopted the 1996 treaty provisions in the Digital Millennium Copyright Act (DMCA).

36. For a thorough review of Canadian copyright reform issues see Michael Geist (ed.), *In the Public Interest: The Future of Canadian Copyright Law* (Toronto: Irwin Law Inc., 2005).

INTERNATIONAL ISSUE

Canada–U.S. Tension

Arguably, the Canada–United States border is the easiest border to cross in the world and in the Internet age, information flows invisibly across the boundary. This is cause for concern for copyright owners and users as each country has a very different set of rules governing the protection and use of copyrighted material. The United States copyright regime is dominated by the Digital Millennium Copyright Act, which puts the rights of creators first. Unauthorized downloading of copyrighted material is illegal, including peer-to-peer software and music transfers. The use of DRMTs is supported and ISPs are required to turn over the names of their subscribers that download and share material illegally. In addition, the Sony Bono Copyright Extension Act provides copyright owners with 70 years of posthumous protection compared to Canada's 50 years.

Canada, on the other hand, has not enacted domestic legislation in line with the WIPO treaties. As will be discussed later in this section, the current Canadian copyright regime supports user rights, in contrast to the U.S. approach. Some private-use downloading is legal in Canada.[37] In an apparent acceptance of the fact that blank CDs may be legally used to duplicate copyrighted material, the government collects a levy on each blank CD and this money is distributed to copyright owners.[38] The Canadian Privacy Commissioner opposes the use of DRMTs to monitor private usage.[39] Canadian privacy laws forbid the arbitrary release of subscribers' names by ISPs, which has protected Canadians from the type of infringement lawsuits music producers have launched in the United States.

These conflicting regimes have led some American critics to call Canada a haven for online piracy. The Office of the United States Trade Representative has placed Canada on its Watch List of countries it feels could improve their copyright enforcement policies.[40]

QUESTIONS TO CONSIDER

1. Should Canada attempt to co-ordinate its copyright regime with the United States in order to reduce tension between the countries?

2. Did Canada lose the ability to independently determine its own copyright direction when it signed the 1996 WIPO treaties?

Nature of Copyright

Rights of Owner

What is commonly referred to as "copyright" is really a collection of distinct rights conferred by statute. The basic rights of the owner of copyright are:

- the right to produce or reproduce the work in question, or any substantial part of it, in any material form
- the right to perform or deliver the work in public
- the right to publish an unpublished work

---

37. Section 80 specifically exempts private-use copying of music from infringement provisions and the Federal Court suggested that peer-to-peer private-use downloading did not infringe copyright. *BMG* v. *John Doe* (2004), 239 D.L.R. (4th) 726, partially affirmed (2005), 252 D.L.R. (4th) 332 (F.C.A.).

38. Section 82.

39. Letter from Jennifer Stoddart, Privacy Commissioner of Canada, to the Industry Minister, dated January 18, 2008.

40. Office of the United States Trade Representative, *2007 Special 301 Report*, www.ustr.gov/Document_Library/ Reports_Publications/2007/2007_Special_301_Review/Section_Index.html.

There are also a number of more specific rights:

- the right to translate the work
- the right to convert the work from one form into another (for example, to convert a novel into a play, or vice versa)
- the right to make a recording or film of the work
- the right to communicate the work by telecommunication
- the right to exhibit the work in public
- the right to authorize any of the above (section 3)

The nature of copyright is best understood as the power of the owner of the copyright to restrain others from doing any of those things that only the owner has the right to do.

In all works in which copyright exists, it arises *automatically*, without any registration or publication. The private act of creating a work gives rise to copyright protection without the need to publish the work to a wider audience. The author or creator of the work is the original owner and may assign the copyright. Copyright may be owned by the author of a book or by the firm that publishes it, by the composer of a piece of music or by the recording company, or it may be owned by some person not connected in any way with the creation or production process, such as an heir or creditor of the author. However, there are other rights, generally referred to as **moral rights**, that are personal to the author or creator and cannot be assigned to others.

moral rights
the permanent rights of an author or creator to prevent a work from being distorted or misused

Moral Rights

These include

- the right to integrity of the work
- the right to prevent distortion or mutilation of the work
- the right to prevent it from being used in association with some product, service, cause, or institution
- where the work is copied, published, or performed, the right to be associated with the work as author or to remain anonymous

The author of a play is entitled to have the authorship properly attributed to her when it is performed or, if she wishes to remain anonymous or use an alias, the right not to have her true identity revealed. An artist who paints a picture is entitled not to have it defaced.

CASE 22.5

A sculptor who created a flock of flying geese, to be displayed in a shopping centre, is entitled not to have them decorated with red ribbons at Christmas time.[41] This is the case whether or not he still owns the copyright.

Limits to Copyright

There is no copyright in any work unless and until it is created. There is no copyright in a mere idea or thought. Copyright attaches to the expression of an idea in a material form. As was stated in one leading case:

> It is . . . an elementary principle of copyright law that an author has no copyright in ideas but only in his expression of them. The law of copyright does not give him any monopoly in the use of the ideas with which he deals or any property in them, even if they are original. His copyright is confined to the literary work in which he has expressed them.[42]

---

41. *Snow* v. *Eaton Centre Ltd.* (1982), 70 C.P.R. (2d) 105. In *Theberge* v. *Galerie d'Art du Petit Champlain Inc.* (2002), 210 D.L.R. (4th) 385, the Supreme Court of Canada ruled that moral rights are infringed only if the work is modified in a manner that is prejudicial to the honour or integrity of its creator.

42. *Moreau* v. *St. Vincent*, [1950] Ex. C.R. 198, per Thorson, P., at 202.

A playwright could "borrow" the plot from another person's novel, provided the play is expressed entirely in her own words. Such conduct might be considered to be unprofessional and to amount to plagiarism, but it would not by itself constitute an infringement of copyright.

Works in Which Copyright Exists

Copyright exists in every original literary, dramatic, musical, and artistic work (section 5). It must be emphasized that the requirement of *originality* applies to each of these four categories. "Originality" means that the work must have originated from its creator; there is no requirement that it must be particularly imaginative, novel, or skillful. Nevertheless, for a work to be "original," it must be work independently created by its author and must display at least a minimal degree of skill and judgment. The fact that it may have involved substantial effort does not by itself mean the work has originality.

CASE 22.6

Tele-Direct Publications Inc., an affiliate of Bell Canada, brought an action against American Business Information Inc., claiming copyright on its "Yellow Pages" directories because of the extra work it did to arrange phone number information from Bell Canada and add other data, such as fax numbers. The Federal Court of Appeal ruled that compilations of this nature, which simply rearrange existing data, do not make it subject to copyright.

According to the court, the Yellow Pages, taken as a whole and given the visual aspects of the pages and manner of their arrangement, are protected by copyright. The information that they contain is not. The court concluded that Tele-Direct had exercised only a minimal degree of skill, judgment, or labour in its overall arrangement, which was insufficient to support a claim of originality so as to be entitled to copyright protection.[43] This logic is similar to that of the 1996 WIPO Copyright Treaty which include databases if the data selection or arrangement amounts to an "intellectual creation."

Literary Works

The Copyright Act gives a very broad meaning to "literary work." The expression includes any work that is reduced to writing or printing, and "includes tables, computer programs and compilations of literary works" (section 2). There must, however, be some reduction into a tangible form, such as writing, film, or sound recording. There is no copyright in spoken words as such.

CASE 22.7

A book was published about the late classical pianist Glenn Gould. The book was largely based on private interviews between Gould and the author, Jock Carroll. Gould's estate sued claiming, among other things, that copyright in the interviews belonged to Gould. The court held that Carroll was the sole author and owner of the copyright in the notes and recordings of his interviews of Gould, and that Gould (and his estate) had no copyright in the spoken words.[44]

As well as the obvious items such as books and magazine and newspaper articles, the term "literary works" has been held to include income tax tables, street directories, examination papers, insurance forms, parts catalogues, and the like. From this list it is apparent that literary merit is not

---

43. *Tele-Direct (Publications) Inc.* v. *American Business Information, Inc.*, [1998] 2 F.C. 22. See also *Edutile Inc.* v. *Automobile Protection Association* (2000), 188 D.L.R. (4th) 132. Prior to the 1993 amendments to the Copyright Act (introduced to implement NAFTA, Art. 1705), compilations were protected only insofar as they could be characterized as literary works. Compilations may now also be related to artistic, dramatic, and musical works. In the Tele-Direct case, the court warned that earlier cases regarding compilations should be applied with caution.

44. *Gould Estate* v. *Stoddart Publishing* (1998), 161 D.L.R. (4th) 321. Contrast *Hager* v. *ECW Press Ltd.*, [1999] 2 F.C. 287.

an essential element of a "literary work." Machine drawings and sketches have sometimes been treated as literary works, though it is more common for them to be classified as artistic works; the actual classification is usually unimportant.

Computer Software

Amendments to the Act made in 1988 added computer programs to the list of protected literary works. Prior to that year, the situation in Canada regarding computer programs had been uncertain. A program is usually first written in a computer "language." This "source code" is humanly readable. It is then translated into "object code," consisting of a series of 0s and 1s, readable by the computer. The object code may in turn be embodied in a computer chip. It is reasonably clear that the humanly readable source code qualifies as a literary work. However, in *Apple Computer Inc.* v. *Mackintosh Computers Ltd.*[45] the defendants were accused of copying the plaintiff's chips and, in doing so, substantially reproducing the programs embodied in the chips. The defendants argued that the program is merely a "specification" and that by copying the chip the defendants were simply carrying out the specification, just as is done when one makes a pie from a recipe. The plaintiffs responded that the defendants' conduct was more like copying the recipe itself. The Supreme Court of Canada agreed and held that copyright exists in computer programs embodied in a chip, or in other machine-readable forms, and that the copying of a chip constitutes an infringement of the copyright in the program itself. The 1988 amendment reinforces this position, defining "computer program" to mean instruction or statements expressed, fixed, embodied, or stored in any manner, for use directly or indirectly in a computer in order to bring about a specific result. However, not every part of a software program is necessarily protected by copyright; some parts of the program may be purely functional, and to copy those parts would not constitute an infringement.[46] The statutory provisions also contain certain exemptions, permitting the making of single copies for a specific purpose, such as making a back-up copy or reproducing the program in another form in order to render it compatible with a particular computer.

Dramatic Works

A "dramatic work" is defined to include "any piece for recitation, choreographic work, or mime, the scenic arrangement or acting form of which is fixed in writing or otherwise," "any cinematographic work, and any compilation of dramatic works" (section 2). The category is sufficiently wide to include not only the older forms of drama, such as plays, operas, and ballets, but also most new forms of entertainment. The key words in the definition are "fixed in writing or otherwise." The text of a play and score of a musical comedy are protected since they are fixed in written form. But so are films, video recordings of dramatic works, and sound recordings of an interview or of a poetry reading.

Although an event such as a street riot or a plane crash, or perhaps even a football game, occurs independently of a person making a record of it, and is not itself a "dramatic work," recording such an event, for example, on film, can constitute the dramatic work of the photographers and film editors. Copyright can subsist in such a film, and to copy the film would constitute an infringement of copyright. Before 1988, a "live" broadcast of such an event was considered not to be protected by copyright because it was not "fixed."[47] This rule has been amended, in part to comply with Canada's obligations under the Canada–U.S. Free Trade Agreement and NAFTA, and mainly to

---

45. (1990), 71 D.L.R. (4th) 95. The litigation in the United States between these two corporations reputedly cost $30 million in legal expenses!

46. *Delrina Corp.* v. *Triolet Systems Inc.* [2002] O.J. No. 3729.

47. *Canadian Admiral Corp.* v. *Rediffusion Inc.*, [1954] Ex. C.R. 382. In *Robertson* v. *Thompson Corp.* (2006), 274 D.L.R. (4th) 138 the Supreme Court of Canada held that CD-ROMs were faithful to the collective works of newspapers but the articles were so removed from their original placement and context in the body of the newspapers that they were rendered individual works. In the leading Australian case of *Victoria Park Racing and Recreation Grounds Co. Ltd.* v. *Taylor* (1937), 58 C.L.R. 479, it was held that no copyright was infringed when the defendants broadcast a radio commentary on horse races organized by the plaintiffs from a platform erected on land adjoining the racetrack.

deal with a number of problems relating to cable retransmissions of television signals. The amendment makes it an infringement of copyright to communicate a work to the public by any form of telecommunication unless the retransmission complies with the Broadcasting Act. The rule deals with the problem of "live" broadcasts by providing that a work is considered to be "fixed" even if it becomes fixed simultaneously with its transmission.

Musical Works

A "musical work" refers to a musical composition that is printed or otherwise graphically produced or reproduced. A performance of a musical work is not within the definition. However, separate protection is given to sound recordings. The recording is itself regarded as a work in which copyright subsists, whether or not the work being performed also has its own copyright (section 18). A recording of a live performance by a jazz musician, in which a new work is improvised, is protected by copyright even though the music itself was never written down. A recording of a performance of a symphony by Beethoven is similarly protected, even though any copyright in the symphony itself would long ago have expired.

Artistic Works

An "artistic work" is defined by section 2 to include "paintings, drawings, maps, charts, plans, photographs, engravings, sculptures, works of artistic craftsmanship, architectural works, and compilations of artistic works." Architectural work means "any building or structure, or model of a building or structure." For architectural works, copyright is restricted to the artistic character and design and does not extend to the processes or methods of construction. A trademark of distinctive design may also qualify as an artistic work and may be protected by copyright. In addition, plans and drawings of machinery or other devices may be protected by copyright as artistic works, and at the same time may depict or describe an invention that is protected by *patent*. It is also frequently difficult to determine whether a particular piece of work is an artistic work, protected by copyright, or an *industrial design*, which may receive a different form of protection.

The Protection of Copyright

Registration

Copyright comes into existence automatically on the creation of a work. Registration of copyright is not necessary, but the Act provides for registration (section 54), and it does confer certain advantages on the registered owner. In particular, the certificate of registration creates a presumption that copyright subsists in the work and that the person registered is the owner of the copyright. Still, the advantages to be gained from registration are relatively small, and the practice is not widely used except by performing rights societies.

Duration of Copyright

In Canada, a work is usually protected by copyright during the life of its author and for a further period of 50 years after the author's death (section 6). The deceased author's estate or an assignee of the copyright, for example, a publisher, may use the protection. The Act prescribes different terms for the following:

- photographs are protected for 50 years from the making of the original negative or plate
- posthumous works—works not published before the death of the author—are protected for 50 years from the date of first publication
- jointly authored works are protected for 50 years after the death of the last surviving author
- Crown copyright persists for 50 years from the date of first publication

Ownership of Copyright

Normally, copyright belongs initially to the author or creator of a work. Copyright in a work may be jointly owned by two or more authors, such as the joint authors of a book. However, it is also possible for separate copyrights to exist in different parts of the same complete work; for example, the writer of the lyrics of a song may hold copyright in the words (as a literary work), and the composer may hold copyright in the music.

There are a number of exceptions to the general rule. When photographs have been commissioned, copyright belongs to the person who ordered the photograph to be taken rather than to the photographer, unless otherwise agreed.[48] Works that have been prepared or published by or under the direction of the government belong to the Crown, subject to contrary agreement. Most important is the rule that where the author of a work was employed by some other person and the work was made *in the course of employment*, copyright belongs to the employer—again, unless otherwise agreed.[49]

As discussed in the next section, copyright may be assigned by the original owner to some other person. Section 14 provides that, when an author has assigned a work, copyright in it reverts automatically to the author's estate 25 years after the death of the author. This rule cannot be varied by agreement. However, the rule applies only in cases of sole authorship where the original copyright belonged to the author.

Assignment and Licensing

An owner of copyright may assign it, for value or by way of gift, or it may pass to heirs upon the death of the owner. The so-called moral rights of an author, as already noted, are not capable of being assigned. An owner may also assign only part of a copyright in a work or divide it territorially. For example, one person might own the copyright of a book in Canada and another in the United States. Copyright could even be divided between Western and Eastern Canada. Authors often assign the copyright in a book to their publishing company in return for the payment of a royalty—for example, 10 percent of total sales revenue. The parties may attach a variety of conditions to an assignment, dealing with such matters as publication in other countries, translations, and reproduction in other forms.

Alternatively, an author may retain the copyright in a work but give the publisher a licence to print or reproduce and sell it, again normally in return for a royalty. Licences may also be much more restricted. An author may grant a licence for the single performance of a play or musical work, on a specified date at a particular theatre, or for the reproduction of an extract from a work in some other work—for example, in an anthology of poetry, a collection of essays, or a set of teaching materials.

In some circumstances, a person wishing to perform or reproduce a copyrighted work may do so without obtaining the consent of the owner by paying a prescribed royalty. This may be done, for example, when the author has been dead for 25 years and copyright has reverted to the author's estate, or when the author cannot be traced.

A special arrangement is available for musical and dramatic works. An author may assign the performing rights of the work to a **performing rights society**. In turn, the society grants licences for performance for a fee, pays part of the fee to the author, and retains the remainder to cover the society's costs. A Copyright Board has authority to approve and to regulate the rates set by their collectives. A performing rights society can, of course, only impose a fee for what would otherwise amount to an infringement of copyright.

performing rights society
a society to which authors of musical and dramatic works assign performing rights and which grants licences for performances

---

48. Senate Bill S-9, introduced in October 2004, proposed a change to the ownership of photographs but it was never adopted.

49. In *Hanis* v. *Teevan* (1998), 162 D.L.R. (4th) 414, copyright in computer software developed by an employee was held to belong to the employer university. A special rule (art. 13) applies to employees of newspapers: see *Robertson* v. *Thomson Corp.* (2004), 243 D.L.R. (4th) 257.

CASE 22.8

In 1995, the Society of Composers, Authors and Music Publishers of Canada (SOCAN) applied to the Copyright Board for approval of a special tariff applicable to Internet transmissions of copyrighted music (the so-called Tariff 22). The tariff was to be imposed on Internet Service Providers (ISPs) located in Canada. SOCAN's application was opposed by the Canadian Association of Internet Providers, which argued that ISPs did not commit any breach of copyright by transmitting or caching copyrighted music.

The dispute eventually reached the Supreme Court of Canada, which ruled that the ISPs committed no breach of copyright and could not be required to pay the tariff.[50]

Infringement of Copyright

What Constitutes Infringement?

Copyright consists of a number of exclusive rights vested in the owner. An infringement occurs when another person, without the consent of the owner, does an act that only the owner has the right to do. An unauthorized public performance, publication, or reproduction of a copyrighted work constitutes an infringement, as does the translation of a work or its conversion into some other form, or recording, broadcasting, or exhibiting it in public. A person who purports to authorize some other person to do any of those acts, without the owner's consent, is also guilty of infringing copyright.

CASE 22.9

SOCAN alleged that offering musical ringtones to wireless telephone customers was "communicating a musical work to the public by telecommunication" and amounted to copyright infringement. It requested a tariff from the wireless telephone carriers. The wireless providers argued that each transmission of a ringtone is a private communication and therefore cannot be considered communication to the public. The Federal Court of Appeal disagreed, holding that the all the customers had access to all the ringtones offered by the wireless carrier, and this qualified as offering to the public.[51]

It is not necessary for the entire work to be copied to constitute an infringement of copyright; the unauthorized copying of a substantial part is sufficient. What amounts to a "substantial" part is a question of fact and degree. A quotation of a few lines from a written work, especially if attributed to its author, does not constitute an infringement, but the quotation of several pages might. The offending copy need not be identical to the original work, and one cannot avoid liability simply by arranging the copied work in a different format or by making minor changes.

CASE 22.10

Hager was the author of a book about famous Canadians of Aboriginal heritage, which included a nine-page chapter about country music star Shania Twain. The chapter was based on Hager's interviews of Twain and included many quotations from those interviews. Subsequently, Holmes was commissioned by ECW Press to write a book about Twain. The ECW book was found to contain substantial portions of Hager's work, including most of the direct quotations from the interviews with Twain. Hager sued ECW for breach of copyright.

continued

---

50. *Canadian Association of Internet Providers* v. *SOCAN, supra*, n. 2. Bill C-60 would have, in part, reversed that decision.

51. *Canadian Wireless Telecommunications Association, Bell Mobility Inc. and Telus Communications Company* v. *SOCAN*, [2008] FCA 6.

ECW argued that the quoted words of Twain were not protected by copyright because they were not the original work of Hager. They also claimed that the copying was not substantial (it amounted to about one-third of the Hager chapter) and that it constituted fair dealing for research purposes.

These defences were rejected, and Hager was awarded damages, plus an accounting equal to 10 percent of ECW's profits from the sale of their book. The court held that Hager's work was protected by copyright because it was a product of her skill, judgment, and labour. Twain's quoted words were in response to Hager's questions, and had been selected by Hager for inclusion in her book. The copying was substantial and could not be said to have been done for research purposes.[52]

A person may also infringe copyright by reproducing a work in an altogether different form. For example, making a three-dimensional object from a designer's drawings may infringe the copyright in those drawings.[53]

CASE 22.11 The plaintiffs, a film production company, produced a popular TV series based on a fictional suburban Quebec couple. The defendants made a pornographic film in which the TV characters were readily identifiable by their costumes and mannerisms. None of the dialogue was taken from the plaintiffs' productions. The court held that this constituted a breach of the plaintiffs' copyright.[54]

The person who actually makes the copy is not the only one who may be liable for infringement of copyright. A theatre owner who permits the theatre to be used by a group of actors or musicians for a performance that infringes the author's copyright is as guilty of infringement as are the performers. Also, a bookseller who imports and sells a "pirated" edition of a copyrighted book is as guilty as the illegal publisher. It is an infringement of copyright to authorize a person to do something that the owner of the copyright has the sole right to do. A person who buys a book and lends it to a friend for the purpose of photocopying it infringes the copyright in the book as much as does the friend. However, the manufacturing and selling of tape recorders, which can be used for "dubbing" prerecorded tapes onto blank tapes, has been held not to constitute authorizing an infringement.[55]

"Fair Dealing" and Other Permitted Uses

Certain acts that would otherwise amount to infringements of copyright are expressly permitted by the Copyright Act, and the exemptions have been expanded by the 1997 amendments to the Act. The most important exemption allows the fair use of copyright works for the purpose of research or private study (section 29), for criticism and review (section 29.1), or for news reporting (section 29.2). Subject to a number of conditions, educational institutions are permitted to copy and reproduce works for purposes of instruction (section 29.4).[56]

---

52. *Hager* v. *ECW Press Ltd.*, *supra*, n. 44.

53. *Hanfstaengl* v. *H.R. Baines & Co.*, [1895] A.C. 20; *Theberge* v. *Galerie d'Art du Petit Champlain Inc.* (*supra*, n. 41). A majority of the Supreme Court of Canada held that there was no infringement when a painting, a reproduction of which had been licensed for posters, was printed on a different material (canvas). Also see *Robertson* v. *Thomson Corp.*, [2006] 2 S.C.R. 363.

54. *Productions Avanti Cine-Video Inc.* v. *Favreau* (1999), 177 D.L.R. (4th) 568. The court also held that the film could not be described as a "parody" and come within the "fair dealing" exception.

55. *CBS Songs Ltd.* v. *Amstrad Consumer Electronics*, [1988] 2 All E.R. 484. The Act now imposes a levy on the sale of blank cassette tapes and compact discs (sections 82, 83).

56. It does not permit the reproduction of an entire work or a substantial portion thereof: see *Boudreau* v. *Lin* (1997), 150 D.L.R. (4th) 324.

CASE 22.12

A provincial law society provided various services to its members. These included providing photocopying machines in the library so that members could make copies of law reports and other documents and, for an additional fee, have library staff make copies of documents on request and fax or courier them to members. A publisher of law reports claimed that these practices constituted infringements of its copyright in the reports.

The Supreme Court of Canada agreed that the publishers owned the copyright in the reports. Although the actual judgments of the courts are in the public domain, the reports contained headnotes and annotations that met the requirement of originality.

However, the Court held that there was no infringement of that copyright by the law society. In particular, (1) the mere provision of photocopiers, which might be used to infringe copyright, did not constitute authorization to infringe; (2) the fax transmission of a single copy of a work to a single individual does not constitute "communication to the public" under the Act; and (3) under the fair dealing provisions of the Act, a person is permitted to use and copy copyrighted works for purposes of research. Research is not limited to non-commercial use, and lawyers carrying on their profession conduct research within the meaning of the Act.[57]

Copying of a musical work or performance of a musical work for the private use of the copier is also not infringement (section 80). Instead, a levy is imposed on blank CDs and the money collected is distributed to musical work copyright owners. (section 82)

CASE 22.13

In 2003, the Copyright Board approved a tariff on MP3 storage devices proposed by the Canadian Private Copying Collective as an extension of the CD levy. The Federal Court of Appeal disallowed the tariff. In 2007, the Canadian Copying Collective brought a similar iPod levy forward, and again the Copyright Board approved the levy on the basis that without it, common "**format shifting**" falls outside the private copying exception.

The Federal Court of Appeal overturned the decision, confirming that imposing such a levy falls outside the Copyright Board's current legislative authority. Although consumers may be excited about the cost savings, the logical interpretation of the judgment is that common consumer practices may constitute infringement.[58]

format shifting
transferring purchased material, such as music, from one of the owner's devices to another

Remedies for Infringement

The usual civil remedies are available in cases of infringement of copyright:

- *damages* for profit or income lost by the owner, or for conversion of the owner's property[59]
- *account* for profits made by the defendant as a result of the infringement (normally an alternative to damages)
- *injunction*, to restrain the defendant from further infringement and to require the delivering up of any offending copies

---

57. *Law Society of Upper Canada* v. *CCH Canadian Ltd.* (2004), 236 D.L.R. (4th) 395. Section 30.2(1) of the Act provides that a library or person acting under its authority does not infringe copyright to do anything on behalf of a patron that the patron could personally have done under the fair dealing exception. The library must not be established or operated for profit.

58. *Canadian Private Copying Collective* v. *Canadian Storage Media Alliance* (C.A.) [2005] 2 F.C.R. 654; *Apple Canada Inc. et. al.* v. *Canadian Private Copying Collective* [2008] FCA 9. Intellectual property rights in relation to the Internet are also discussed in Chapter 34.

59. Improper copies are deemed to be the property of the copyright owner. However, they are essentially worthless, so that where an offending publisher destroyed improper copies it was not liable for additional damages in conversion: *Editions JCL Inc.* v. *91439 Canada Ltée* (1994), 120 D.L.R. (4th) 225.

The 1997 amendments to the Act also introduced fines up to $20 000 to deter bootlegging and pirating of copyrighted materials.

Of course, many infringements of copyright go unpunished. While it may be a breach of copyright to photocopy a book or article other than for purposes of study or research, or to videotape a television broadcast of a copyrighted work for later viewing,[60] it is most unlikely that the offences will be discovered or, if they are, that it will be worthwhile for the owner to sue the offender.[61]

ETHICAL ISSUE

Music Downloading

As this section identifies, it is difficult for the law to control music downloading. Technology has made this practice so easy, quick, and untraceable that alternative measures such as levies are being adopted to compensate the copyright owners. Opponents complain of a significant loss to the music and entertainment industries. Still, does anyone argue that photocopying in libraries should be illegal?

QUESTIONS TO CONSIDER

1. Where is the ethical line in music sharing?

2. Is there an ethical difference between downloading, uploading, burning a CD, or lending a CD?

PATENTS

At common law, an inventor had no inherent right to the fruits of his or her creation, and no law was broken by merely making use of another's invention. Like copyright but unlike trademarks, the law of patents is entirely based upon statute. However, a patent differs fundamentally from copyright: while copyright comes into existence *automatically* upon creation of the work, a patent exists only after a grant from the appropriate government body.

Patent legislation was introduced as early as 1824 and 1826, in Lower and Upper Canada, respectively. The first federal Patent Act was adopted in 1869, largely based upon the existing American legislation. This American influence prevailed until just a few years ago. The current Patent Act,[62] originally enacted in 1935, was substantially amended in 1987, in part to bring Canada's law into conformity with international practice under the Patent Cooperation Treaty. The 1987 amendments changed a number of the specifically American features of our law. These amendments came into effect on October 1, 1989; patents granted or applied for prior to that date remain subject to the earlier law. Further substantial amendments, notably in respect of pharmaceutical products, were introduced in 1992 and 1993.

---

60. *Tom Hopkins Int'l. Inc.* v. *Wall & Redekop Realty Ltd.* (1984), 1 C.P.R. (3d) 348. Time shifting on cable television is also an issue for copyright reform.

61. In *BMG Canada Inc.* v. *John Doe* (2004), 32 C.P.R. (4th) 64, the Federal Court rejected a request from a music producer that five major ISPs disclose the identity of customers who traded music downloaded from the Internet. In May 2005, the Federal Court of Appeal dismissed an appeal from that decision, but without prejudice to the plaintiffs' right to commence a further action for disclosure based on clearer evidence (*supra* n. 37).

62. R.S.C. 1985, c. P-4. (Unless otherwise stated, references in this part are to that Act, as amended.)

International Treaties

The concept of a patent is now almost universally recognized. Over 120 countries now adhere to the Patent Cooperation Treaty adopted by the World Intellectual Property Organization. It provides for the filing of a single international patent application, which then gives patent protection in all the signatory countries.[63] More than 160 countries belong to the Paris Union and adhere to the International Convention for the Protection of Industrial Property, which gives an applicant one year from the date of filing in Canada to file in a member country. Canada belongs to both treaties.

The Nature of Patents

An inventor or the legal representative of an inventor may obtain a patent that gives the applicant exclusive property in the invention for a period of 20 years (section 44).[64] This property comprises the "exclusive right, privilege and liberty of making, constructing and using the invention and selling it to others to be used" (section 42).

In return for this right, the inventor must make the invention public, by filing an adequate description of the invention, so that others will be able to duplicate the invention freely when the statutory period of monopoly has expired.[65] Therefore, an inventor has a choice. He or she can keep the invention entirely secret and continue to exploit it indefinitely but run the risk that some other person will sooner or later stumble upon the same invention or unravel the secret; or the inventor can reveal it and enjoy exclusive rights for a limited period only. Given the speed at which technological advances are now being made, and the perhaps over-generous period of protection, applying for a patent would seem advisable for inventions that are likely to prove lucrative. However, obtaining a patent is a complex and fairly expensive business, and if an invention is likely to have only a short productive life, secrecy may be the better option. The alternatives of registering the invention as an industrial design or relying upon copyright protection of the plans or specifications should also be considered. But it must be remembered that while copyright provides protection for a much longer period, that protection is more limited, since it extends only to the method of expression and not to the idea itself.

Patentable Inventions

Only "inventions" qualify for patent protection. The Patent Act defines an invention as "any new and useful art, process, machine, manufacture or composition of matter, or any new and useful improvement in any art, process, machine, manufacture or composition of matter" (section 2). Three elements in the definition must be present for an invention to be patentable. It must be:

- an art, process, machine, manufacture, or composition of matter or an improvement to such
- new
- useful

As well, inherent in the notion of an invention is the requirement that it is something that possesses the quality of ingenuity and is not simply an obvious step that any person with ordinary skill in the field might have taken.

---

63. In 2008, Canada and the United States started the Patent Prosecution Highway Pilot Program designed to accelerate patent application processing in one country if the application had already been favourably examined in the other country.

64. For patents issuing from applications filed before October 1989, the period is 17 years. The new 20-year period runs from the date of the patent application; the previous period ran from the date of the grant.

65. Some aspects of the patented invention may continue to be protected after the expiry of the patent, for example, under trademark law. Thus, others may be free to use the invention, but not to copy a distinctive shape or format. See *Eli Lilley and Co.* v. *Novopharm Ltd.* (*supra*, n. 9); *Thomas & Betts Ltd.* v. *Panduit Corp.* (2000), 185 D.L.R. (4th) 150. Contrast *Kirkbi AG* v. *Ritvik Holdings Inc.*, *supra* n. 4.

Art, Process, Machine, Manufacture, or Composition of Matter

For an invention to be patentable, it must fall within one of these categories. The word "art" refers to the manual or productive arts, as distinct from the fine arts. A "process" means a method of manufacture or operation designed to produce a particular result—for example, a new process for the chemical cleaning of fabrics. "Machine" and "manufacture" are given their usual meanings, and a "composition of matter" refers to such things as chemical formulae that produce new compounds and substances.

A patent will not be issued solely for a scientific principle or abstract theorem, such as a mathematical formula (section 27(8)). For these purposes, a computer program is equated to an abstract theorem and is *not* by itself patentable,[66] though a patent may be granted for an invention that involves the use of a computer program as an essential part to achieve a particular result.

CASE 22.14

Researchers at Harvard College developed a method of genetically altering mice to make them more likely to develop cancer following exposure to chemicals. This made the mice valuable for experimentation purposes. The invention was registered as a patent in the United States (and in a number of European countries) by the college. The college applied to register a patent for the "Harvard mouse" (or "oncomouse," to give it its technical name) in Canada.

Registration was refused by the Patent Appeal Board, and the refusal was upheld by the Federal Court. The court considered that the insertion of the foreign gene into the genetic fabric of the mouse was largely uncontrollable and unpredictable. The process lacked the element of reproducibility required of a patent.

The Federal Court of Appeal, however, allowed the application. It held that the oncomouse could be considered a "composition of matter" within the meaning of section 2 of the Act. The offspring of the original mouse would still bear that particular genetic trait, which does not occur in nature, even though there might be no control over other traits that might occur naturally.

The decision of the Federal Court of Appeal was appealed to the Supreme Court of Canada, which (by a 5–4 majority) allowed the appeal and held that the oncomouse could not be patented.[67] Although some "lower" forms of life have been held to be patentable,[68] the majority considered that patenting higher life forms would involve a radical departure from the traditional patent regime and was a highly contentious matter that raised a number of extremely complex issues. If higher life forms were to be patentable, it must be under the clear and unequivocal direction of Parliament. The fact that the Patent Act was ill-equipped to deal with the patentability of higher life forms was an indication that Parliament never intended the definition of "invention" to extend to this type of subject matter.

Novelty

An essential element of an invention is that it be "new." A patent will not be granted for a machine or process that is already known or in use, even if it has not been patented by some other person.[69]

Until 1989, Canada had a "first-to-invent" system; that is, if two or more persons applied for a patent for the same invention, only the first inventor was considered the true inventor and entitled to the patent. The present law adopts the more common "first-to-file" system; in cases of conflicting applications, the application with the earlier filing date prevails.

---

66. *Schlumberger Canada Ltd.* v. *Commissioner of Patents*, [1982] 1 F.C. 845.

67. *Harvard College* v. *Canada (Commissioner of Patents)* (2002), 219 D.L.R. (4th) 577.

68. Genetically modified yeast has been patented; see *Re Application of Abitibi Co.* (1982), 62 C.P.R. (2d) 81. However, in *Pioneer Hi-Bred Ltd.* v. *Canada (Commissioner of Patents)* (1987), 14 C.P.R. (3d) 491 (F.C.A.); affd (1989), 25 C.P.R. (3d) 257 (S.C.C.), it was held that a soybean variety developed by traditional plant cross-breeding was not patentable subject matter. The rights of plant breeders may now be protected under the Plant Breeders' Rights Act; see below, under the heading "Technological Change and Intellectual Property Law."

69. The discovery of a new use for a known compound is patentable: see *Apotex Inc.* v. *Wellcome Foundation Ltd.* (2002), 219 D.L.R. (4th) 660.

An invention for which a patent is claimed must be one that has not been disclosed to the public anywhere in the world before the filing date. There is an exception to this rule when the inventor himself makes the disclosure, but even then he must file the application within one year of making the disclosure.

Utility

For an invention to qualify as "useful" it must possess industrial value—for example, by making a process easier, cheaper, or faster. Also implied is that it be usable; that is, it should be reproducible and operable, so that a skilled worker, by following the specifications published in the patent, should be able to reproduce the invention and obtain the desired result.

Ingenuity

An invention requires an element of ingenuity. As we have noted, it must be more than an obvious step. As has been said:

> The question to be answered is whether at the date of invention . . . an unimaginative skilled technician, in light of his general knowledge and the literature and information on the subject available to him on that date, would have been led directly and without difficulty to [the] invention.[70]

In reaching such a conclusion, the patent office or court must be careful not to be influenced by hindsight. Great inventions often seem deceptively simple and obvious in retrospect.

Obtaining a Patent

Only the inventor or the legal representatives of the inventor may apply for the grant of a patent. "Legal representatives" include not only heirs and executors, but also persons claiming through the inventor. If an inventor has assigned the rights to an invention to another person or to a corporation, the assignee may apply. An employer usually owns inventions made by its employees, and thus is entitled to apply for a patent.[71]

Applications for patents are made to the Commissioner of Patents and are processed by the Patent Office, a branch of the Canadian Intellectual Property Office. Individual inventors may pursue their own applications, but any other applicants must use the services of a registered **patent agent**. In practice, making an application is a highly complex and specialized matter and is almost invariably handled by a patent agent.

The agent first makes a search of the register of patents, and frequently also a search at the U.S. Patent Office, to ensure that no patent has already been granted in respect of the invention. The next major task is to draft the application, in a form prescribed by the Patent Rules. The most important part of the application has two elements: (a) the **specification**, providing a full description of the invention, its use, operation, or manufacture, and (b) the **claim**, setting out the features claimed to be new and in respect of which the applicant claims an exclusive right. Particular care must be taken to ensure that the claim is sufficiently broad to obtain the maximum benefit from the invention. At the same time, it must not be excessively wide so as to include matters that are obvious or already known, and thus render the claim invalid.

When an application has been filed, a further application must be made for the claim to be examined. The Patent Office then appoints an Examiner to consider the application. The Examiner makes searches of patents, and frequently of technical publications, to ensure that the claimed invention is indeed novel and otherwise complies with the requirements of the Patent Act. The Examiner scrutinizes the specification and claim to ensure that complete disclosure has been

patent agent
a registered agent who pursues applications for patents on behalf of individual inventors

specification
the description of the invention, its use, operation, or manufacture

claim
a statement of the features claimed to be new and in respect of which the applicant claims an exclusive right

---

70. *Beecham Canada Ltd.* v. *Proctor & Gamble Co.* (1982), 61 C.P.R. (2d) 1 at 27, per Urie, J.A.
71. *Techform* v. *Wolda* (2001), 206 D.L.R. (4th) 171.

made and that the invention is described in a way that would enable other persons to utilize it once the period of protection has elapsed. During this stage, the applicant may make amendments to the application in order to satisfy objections raised by the Examiner. When the process is complete, the Examiner determines whether or not a patent shall be granted. An appeal from a rejection of the application may be made to the Patent Appeal Board and then to the courts.

When the application is successful, the Patent Office issues a "Notice of Allowance," and on payment of a fee (which is additional to the application fee), it issues the patent. Since 1989, the Act has required that a further yearly fee be paid in order to maintain the patent. The fees, however, are relatively modest and vary according to the nature of the applicant entity: for an applicant that qualifies as a "small entity,"[72] the government fees to obtain a patent and to maintain it for the full 20-year period could be less than $2500. The cost of protection for a five-year period could be as little as $500. However, the services of a skilled patent agent will cost considerably more than the fees paid to the Patent Office.

Protection of Patent Rights

As we have seen, patent rights may now be preserved for a period of 20 years, so long as the yearly maintenance fee is paid. A patent confers on its owner the exclusive right of constructing and using the invention and selling it to others to be used. An owner may assign patent rights to others or grant a licence for their limited or exclusive use. An assignment must be in writing and registered with the Patent Office, as must a grant of an exclusive licence.

Any unauthorized act that interferes with the full enjoyment of the exclusive rights conferred by the patent is an infringement. The usual remedies of damages, injunction, and accounting for profit are available to the patentee and to anyone (for example, an assignee or licensee) claiming under him. An action to protect or enforce a patent right may be brought in the Federal Court or in the appropriate provincial court.

Patents and the Public Interest

The granting of a patent is a serious matter, since giving an exclusive right to use and exploit an invention, for a period of up to 20 years, in effect creates a *monopoly*. The result is to confer a considerable advantage over business competitors and sometimes, if the patentee chooses not to exploit the invention, to deprive the public of the use of the invention. There are many stories—most of them probably fabrications—of large corporations buying up inventions (such as everlasting light bulbs) that threaten their business in order to suppress the invention.

Patent legislation attempts to protect the public in a number of ways, which are discussed below.

Scope of the Claim

The law seeks to ensure that only genuine inventions qualify for the grant of a patent, and disallows claims that are too broad in scope. One of the most important functions of the patent examiner is to enforce these policies. In addition, third parties, such as business competitors or rival researchers, may challenge the validity of a patent by bringing an **action for impeachment** in the Federal Court. The Attorney General of Canada may also bring such an action.

action for impeachment
an action challenging the validity of a patent

For patent applications filed after October 1, 1989, an alternative form of challenge is available. Any person may apply to the Commissioner of Patents for re-examination of any claim of a patent. Upon receiving such a request, the Commissioner establishes a Re-examination Board to examine the request.

---

72. A "small entity" means an individual inventor or a business concern that employs 50 or fewer persons, or is a university, and that meets a number of other conditions. The fees payable by other applicants are twice as high.

CASE 22.15 Research in Motion (RIM) found itself embroiled in a patent dispute in the United States that highlights the complications associated with multiple dispute resolution venues. NTP Inc. claimed that RIM's BlackBerry infringed NTP's patent rights and started an infringement action in the U.S. federal court in Virginia. In addition to defending the court action, RIM challenged the validity of the NTP patents through the patent reexamination process of the U.S. Patent and Trademark Office. RIM found itself in the confusing position of losing the court action[73] while achieving preliminary success in the patent challenges. RIM eventually settled both actions with a payment of over US$600 million for a licence of the NTP patents.

Abuse of Patent Rights

Another form of protection allows the Attorney General or any interested person to apply to the Commissioner of Patents when it is alleged that patent rights are being abused. An abuse occurs, for example,

- if demand for the patented article in Canada is not being met to a reasonable extent and on reasonable terms
- if the patentee is hindering the creation of new industries or damaging the public interest by refusing to grant licences
- if any trade, industry, or person engaged therein is unfairly prejudiced by the conditions attached to a patent
- if the existence of a patent has been used so as to unfairly prejudice in Canada the manufacture, use, or sale of any materials

Compulsory Licensing

The aim of patent law is not only to encourage new inventions by protecting them, but also to encourage the working of those inventions in Canada without undue delay. Thus, a patentee cannot simply hold a patent for the purpose of blocking trade. If it does not exploit the invention itself in a reasonable manner, it must sell it or grant a licence on reasonable terms. Where there is abuse, some other person who wishes to make use of the invention may apply for the grant of a **compulsory licence**, which may be ordered on terms that allow the applicant to work the patent while giving the patentee a fair return. Normally this arrangement involves the payment of a stipulated rate of royalty on products manufactured under the licence.

compulsory licence
a licence granted to a person to work a patent without the consent of the owner of the patent

For pharmaceutical products protected by patent in other countries, a system of compulsory licensing existed, prior to 1987, that allowed Canadian firms to manufacture or import drugs upon payment of a low royalty to the patentee. This system led to the development of a thriving generic drug industry in Canada, to the economic benefit of the Canadian consumer but to the detriment of foreign pharmaceutical companies. It also arguably acted as a deterrent to research and development of pharmaceutical products within Canada. It became a controversial issue that featured prominently in the debates on the Free Trade Agreement between Canada and the United States and in the subsequent NAFTA negotiations; American pressure has in part been responsible for the changes that have been made in the law.

The 1987 and 1993 amendments to the Act replaced the compulsory licensing scheme for patented medicines with special regulations that established a framework for allowing generic drug companies to obtain the right to produce patented drugs on payment of a royalty to the patent

---

73. *NTP, Inc.* v. *Research in Motion Ltd.*, (2005) 418 F. 3d. 1282 (U.S. App.); (2006) 546 U.S. 1157.

owner. The regulations are extremely complex and have produced one of the most hotly contested areas of litigation.[74] In part due to the problems highlighted by this litigation, the regulations were amended in 1999.

Competition Law

The Competition Act[75] provides a further form of protection of the public interest. It prohibits the exploitation of a patent in such a way as to unduly restrain trade or prevent or lessen competition, and authorizes the Federal Court to grant appropriate relief.

ETHICAL ISSUE

Drugs for AIDS

Almost 5 million people are infected with AIDS in Africa; fewer than 100 000 are receiving treatment. The key reason is cost: the patented drugs necessary to treat AIDS cost between $8000 and $15 000 per person, per year. Generic drugs could reduce that cost to a few hundred dollars.

The World Health Organization has urged that countries be allowed to produce generic drugs to counter the AIDS epidemic, and the World Trade Organization has now agreed to allow its members to do so in times of health crises.

Canada's Access to Medicines Regime (CAMR) was enacted in May 2004. It amends the Patent Act (and the Food and Drugs Act) to approve the production of generic drugs in Canada, for export to countries that could not otherwise afford drugs to fight AIDS, malaria, tuberculosis, and other diseases. In September 2007 the first authorization was granted to a generic drug company to produce a patented HIV/AIDS drug for export to Rwanda.

QUESTIONS TO CONSIDER

1. Why should Canadians not also be entitled to benefit from cheaper drugs?

2. Should there be any restrictions on the production of generic drugs for fighting potentially fatal illnesses and diseases?

INDUSTRIAL DESIGNS

Industrial designs comprise the fourth type of intellectual property, registrable under the Industrial Design Act.[76] Originally enacted in 1868, the Act has been amended on a number of occasions. Despite the amendments, the Act remains a somewhat archaic and rather unsatisfactory piece of legislation.

---

74. See the decisions of the Supreme Court of Canada in *Eli Lilly and Co.* v. *Novopharm Ltd.* (1998), 161 D.L.R. (4th) 1; *Merck Frosst Canada Inc.* v. *Canada* (1998), 161 D.L.R. (4th) 47.

75. R.S.C. 1985, c. C-34. See further Chapter 32. The assignment of a patent may lead to an undue lessening of competition: see *Apotex Inc.* v. *Eli Lilly and Co.* (2004), 240 D.L.R. (4th) 679.

76. R.S.C. 1985, c. I-9. (Unless otherwise stated, references in this part are to this Act, as amended.)

Meaning of "Industrial Design"

The Act (section 2) defines "industrial design" as:

> features of shape, configuration, pattern or ornament and any combination of those features that, in a finished article, appeal to and are judged solely by the eye.

Features that are solely utilitarian or functional are not protected, nor is any method or principle of manufacture or construction. For many years it was thought that the Act referred only to designs placed on an article, such as a decorative design on a dinner service, a crest or emblem on a sports shirt, or a design on a roll of wallpaper. More recently, however, it has been held to also apply to the design of the shape of the article itself, insofar as the design is ornamental and not dictated by the function of the article. The shape of a stacking chair or a knife handle may be registered. In order to secure registration some degree of originality is required.

Protection by Registration

The Act permits the proprietor of an industrial design to register it and obtain exclusive rights to its use in Canada for a term of five years, with the possibility of renewing the registration for one further term of five years. At common law there is no property in an industrial design, except insofar as it may qualify for protection as a trademark. Protection is consequently dependent upon registration. A proprietor may apply to register a design with the Commissioner of Patents. Application must be made within one year of the first publication of the design. "Publication" in this sense means making the design available to the public—for example, by selling an article to which the design has been applied.

The only person entitled to apply for registration is the "proprietor," who is usually the designer, but if a client or customer commissioned and paid for the design, that person is considered to be the proprietor. If the design was produced by an employee in the normal course of employment, the employer will normally be the proprietor.

Registration gives the proprietor the exclusive right to apply the design to any article for the purpose of sale. However, in order to protect the design, each article to which the design is applied must be marked with the name of the proprietor, the word "Registered" or its abbreviation, "Rd," and the year of registration. A proprietor may assign or grant a licence for the use of a registered design, but the assignment or licence must be recorded on the register in order to preserve the exclusive right.

During the existence of the exclusive right, no other person may apply the design, or any imitation of it, to any article for the purpose of sale without the written consent of the proprietor. The usual remedies of damages, injunction, and account for profits are available to the proprietor; in addition, the Act prescribes a number of summary offences, punishable by fine, for infringement of industrial design rights.

As we have seen, both industrial designs and patents may be protected only by prompt registration. Normally, it will not be difficult to decide whether a design qualifies for patent protection or should be registered as an industrial design. Industrial designs are essentially ornamental, whereas a patentable invention must be useful. In cases of doubt, the advice of a qualified patent agent should be sought.

Industrial Designs, Trademarks, and Copyright

The same design or logo that may be applied to an article as an industrial design may also be considered a trademark. Similarly, the ornamental shape of a container or wrapper may be registered as an industrial design as well as protected under trademark law as a "distinguishing guise." Protection as a trademark is clearly superior, since property rights in a trademark are not dependent upon registration and are not limited to a maximum period of 10 years. However, the two forms of protection do not conflict: a proprietor may register an industrial design and still claim protection for the design as a trademark.

The situation with respect to copyright is more complex. The Copyright Act originally refused copyright protection for designs capable of being registered under the Industrial Design Act. An exception was made for designs that were not used or intended to be used as models or patterns to be multiplied by any industrial process. This provision was revised in 1988, though the intention of the new provision remains essentially similar. Now, if the design is applied to a useful article and the article is reproduced in a quantity of more than 50, some other person does not infringe copyright in the design simply by reproducing the article. Thus, protection for the design can only be secured by registering it under the Industrial Design Act.[77]

CONFIDENTIAL INFORMATION, TRADE SECRETS, AND KNOW-HOW

The description "intellectual property" should properly be restricted to the four forms—trademarks, copyright, patents, and industrial designs—that we have discussed in this chapter. Mere ideas or knowledge, however valuable, are not regarded as "property" in the strict sense of the word. The Supreme Court of Canada has ruled that confidential information is not property that can be the subject of theft under the Criminal Code.[78]

Confidential information may nevertheless have commercial value. A secret manufacturing process—if it can be kept secret—may be more valuable not patented than patented. And a uniquely efficient way of operating a business, though not capable of being patented at all, may be worth millions in extra profits to its owner. Similarly, a list of customers or clients may constitute an important part of the goodwill of a business. Information can also be valuable to people other than its owner. Although not property in the strict sense, information can still be sold to others as, for example, where data is made available to subscribers to a computerized data retrieval service.

The possessor of confidential information, trade secrets, or know-how is not entirely without legal protection, though such protection normally arises out of a contractual or fiduciary relationship rather than from any proprietary interest. A seller may supply machinery or equipment to a buyer and at the same time license the buyer to use the seller's know-how or some secret process. In such a case it is usual to stipulate in the contract that the buyer will not divulge the secret to anyone else.[79] Similarly, as discussed in Chapter 20, some contracts of employment include a restrictive covenant restraining the employee, if she leaves the employment, from making use of the employer's confidential information or divulging it to someone else. The employer may claim breach of contract and seek an injunction to prevent the employee from joining a competitor. As well, the employer may sue the competitor for the tort of inducing breach of contract as discussed in Chapter 3.

As will be discussed in Chapter 28, officers, company directors, and partners stand in a *fiduciary relationship* to their employers, corporations, or co-partners. To misuse or divulge confidential information acquired in the course of such a relationship may constitute a breach of trust, which can be restrained by injunction or punished by an award of damages or an accounting for profits made as a result of the breach.[80]

---

77. Copyright Act, s. 64. See *Bayliner Marine Corp.* v. *Doral Boats Ltd.* (1986), 10 C.P.R. (3d) 289.

78. *R.* v. *Stewart*, [1988] 1 S.C.R. 963.

79. In *Cadbury Schweppes Inc.* v. *FBI Foods Ltd.* (1999), 167 D.L.R. (4th) 577, the Supreme Court of Canada held that a manufacturer under licence who produced a competing product after the termination of the licence, using confidential information, was liable in damages for the loss suffered by the licensor.

80. See *LAC Minerals Ltd.* v. *International Corona Resources Ltd.* (1989), 61 D.L.R. (4th) 14. Misuse of confidential information by corporate directors or officers is discussed further in Chapter 28.

CASE 22.16 A former employee of Apotex took up a new position with a competing firm, Novopharm. He brought with him confidential information about a process for making the drug Lovastatin. Apotex brought an action for an injunction restraining Novopharm from carrying out further research on the drug and for damages against the employee and against Novopharm.

The court held both the employee and the new employer liable. Novopharm knew, or ought to have known, that the information was confidential and had been obtained from Apotex. They were consequently liable for the breach of trust of their new employee.[81]

TECHNOLOGICAL CHANGE AND INTELLECTUAL PROPERTY LAW

Intellectual property protection has become increasingly important to business in the technological age. Firms and nations now spend vast amounts on research and development, aware that inventiveness is the key to competitiveness in the international economy. Entertainment, for which copyright is the raw material, is a multibillion-dollar industry. In corporate mergers and takeovers, trademarks and brand names are frequently valued in millions, or even billions, of dollars. Information, it seems, knows no frontiers. Of the total number of patents now registered each year in the United States, approximately one-half are registered by foreign inventors. Intellectual property has become internationalized.

New technologies have created new problems, not all of which are easily solved by analogy to old situations. The "Harvard Mouse" case, discussed earlier in this chapter, illustrates this point. The case highlights the ongoing debate about the legitimacy of, and possible limitations that should be imposed upon, genetic engineering, especially of human life forms. Another related issue concerns the genetic modification of foods: are genetically modified foods a great benefit to humankind that should be protected by patent law, or are they a potential cause of uncontrollable catastrophe? This debate was given a new focus in the recent case of the Saskatchewan farmer accused of infringing a patent for genetically modified canola.[82]

Technological change has also led to two relatively recent statutes, enacted to protect the rights of plant breeders and the designers of integrated circuits. The Plant Breeders' Rights Act[83] provides exclusive rights, similar to patent rights in respect of new varieties of plants, including genetically modified plants. To qualify, a plant variety must be clearly distinguishable from all other commonly known varieties of the species, be both stable and homogeneous, and be of a variety not yet sold in Canada. Application is made to a Commissioner of Plant Breeders' Rights, who may require or conduct such tests as are necessary to establish the novelty of the variety. A grant is for a term of 18 years, subject to payment of an annual fee, and confers the exclusive right to sell, produce, and use the variety.

The Integrated Circuit Topography Act[84] also provides exclusive rights similar to patent rights in the "topography" or design of integrated circuits (semiconductor chips) and in the circuits that incorporate such designs themselves. Registration is required, and protection is for a period of 10 years.

New technologies have not only given rise to the creation of new types of intellectual property and new rights; the ways in which existing rights may be exercised and infringed is also changing.

---

81. *Apotex Fermentation Inc.* v. *Novopharm Ltd.* (1998), 162 D.L.R. (4th) 111.
82. *Schmeiser* v. *Monsanto Canada Inc.* (2004), 239 D.L.R. (4th) 271. The farmer had claimed that the genetically modified seed had blown onto his land. The Supreme Court of Canada upheld the grant of a patent for the seed, but held that the farmer had obtained no benefit from its use and was not liable to compensate the patent owner.
83. S.C. 1990, c. 20.
84. S.C. 1990, c. 37.

New questions are constantly being raised, to which simple answers cannot be given. As noted, trademark and copyright laws have been challenged by the development of e-mail and the Internet. (This issue is discussed further in Chapter 34.) To quote the Economic Council of Canada:

> . . . new technology and the movement towards an increasingly knowledge-based economy and society are throwing up issues of such scale and significance that no part of the existing policy structure can remain unaffected.[85]

QUESTIONS FOR REVIEW

1. What types of intellectual property are protected by law?
2. What are the principal costs and benefits of protecting intellectual property?
3. What is a "trademark"?
4. What are the essential elements of the tort of passing-off?
5. Are there any advantages to be gained in registering a trademark?
6. What is a "certification mark"?
7. On what grounds may the registration of a trademark be opposed?
8. What are the principal rights possessed by an owner of copyright?
9. In relation to copyright, what are "moral rights"?
10. Does copyright exist in computer software?
11. For how long does copyright usually last?
12. In what ways may a person become an owner of copyright?
13. What constitutes "fair dealing" in relation to copyright?
14. What qualities must an invention have in order to be patented?
15. Why might an inventor choose not to register a patent?
16. What is meant by an "industrial design"?
17. How may "know-how" be protected?

CASES AND PROBLEMS

1. In 1955, a successful novel entitled *Lolita*, authored by Vladimir Nabokov, was published. The novel recounts the story of how a middle-aged man, Humbert Humbert, becomes infatuated with his 12-year-old stepdaughter, Lolita, eventually descending to rape, murder, and madness. The story is narrated by Humbert himself.

   In 1995, the Italian author Pia Pera wrote a book entitled *Lo's Diary*, which was subsequently translated into English. The book purports to tell the story of the affair as experienced by Lolita herself. The principal events of the earlier parts of the story are the same as described in the Nabokov book, though described from the very different perspective of the young girl. (Ms. Pera's book goes on to describe events that occurred after the parting of the two protagonists.)

85. *Report on Intellectual and Industrial Property*. Ottawa: Economic Council of Canada, 1971, pp. 5–6.

The late Mr. Nabokov's son and executor threatened action for infringement of copyright. Should the action succeed?

2. A small Canadian corporation, Lexus Foods Inc., applied to register the name Lexus as a trademark for its range of canned fruit products.

The application was opposed by the Japanese manufacturer of the well-known Lexus model of automobiles. It argued that the application by the Canadian corporation should not be granted because of the risk of confusion with its existing marks. Further, it claimed that the applicants were simply trying to cash in on their famous name.

Is the objection a valid one?

3. Shamrock Homes Inc. is a major construction company that specializes in the construction of large residential developments. Brendan, their chief engineer, has worked out an entirely new method of planning a development, requiring the construction of a factory in which prefabricated components for houses are manufactured and assembled to speed up the construction of houses. The factory is specially designed to be converted into a shopping mall when all the houses are completed. Shamrock estimates that the new method reduces construction costs by as much as 15 percent.

Shamrock wishes to patent this new method, fearing that competitors will easily be able to copy it otherwise. Give your opinion as to whether the method is patentable.

4. Bouchard was a part-time university student in an MBA program. As part of his work for one course, he wrote a term paper based on his experience of dealing with a particular problem in the course of his full-time employment, and using data that he had collected there. His employer consented to his use of that material.

Without Bouchard's knowledge, Lam, the professor who had supervised the paper, had it published (with some revisions) in a casebook sold by the university to MBA students. In the casebook, Lam was named as the author, and no mention was made of Bouchard.

When Bouchard saw his paper in the casebook, he brought an action for infringement of copyright. Should his action succeed? What defences might be raised by Lam?

5. McCoy's Restaurants Ltd. is a large firm incorporated under the Canada Business Corporations Act. It operates a chain of 60 restaurants across Canada under the name of "McCoy's," and is well known nationally due to its extensive advertising campaigns.

Angus McCoy recently bought a restaurant, previously known as "Sam's Diner," situated at a busy truck stop near Brandon, Manitoba. He formed a company under the name of Angus McCoy (Brandon) Ltd., incorporated under the Manitoba Business Corporations Act, and renamed the restaurant "The Real McCOY's." The decor and furnishings of Angus's restaurant are not at all like those of the McCoy chain, but the external appearance bears some similarity.

The president of McCoy's Restaurants Ltd. is angry because she has been planning to open a branch in Brandon. She alleges that Angus is attempting to deceive the public, is trading on her company's reputation, and is benefiting from its advertising. She has written to Angus, insisting that he change the name of his company and his restaurant; otherwise McCoy's Restaurants will commence legal proceedings.

Angus maintains that no one is confused, that he chose the name "The Real McCOY's" deliberately to distinguish his restaurant from those of the chain, and that, since the principal owners of McCoy's Restaurants Ltd. are called Angelotti and Zbigniewsky, they are the ones who are trading under false colours.

Advise Angus what legal actions might be taken against him and whether or not they might succeed.

6. Dolphin Marine Ltd. is a well-established firm with an excellent reputation for building racing boats. It has recently produced a new 12-metre model, the DM35X, with a fibreglass hull of novel design, which has been highly successful in a number of important races.

Kopikat Inc. is a small firm that has been building catamarans for a number of years with little success, either sporting or financial. Kenny, the controlling shareholder and president of Kopikat, buys one of the new Dolphin models, constructs a mould of the hull, and commences to produce a racer with a hull identical to the DM35X and with other features that are very similar. Kopikat is planning to market it at a price $8000 lower than the DM35X.

Has Kopikat infringed any right of Dolphin?

7. Richards, a freelance writer, wrote a long article on the devastating effects of the tsunami in Asia, and submitted it to the *Global Post*, a leading newspaper that had published other articles by her. The newspaper agreed to publish her article in their edition of December 29, 2004.

Some weeks later, the *Global Post* published on their website a number of extracts from what they described as "the best GP articles of 2004." Included was Richards' tsunami article. Richards complains that (1) she had never agreed to the publication on the Internet, and (2) in editing the article, the newspaper had omitted important details so that the edited version did not properly represent the original work.

Does Richards have an action against the newspaper?

ADDITIONAL RESOURCES FOR CHAPTER 22 ON THE COMPANION WEBSITE *(www.pearsoned.ca/smyth)*

In addition to self-test multiple-choice, true–false, and short essay questions (all with immediate feedback), application exercises, and links to useful web destinations, the Companion Website provides the following resources for Chapter 22:

- **British Columbia:** Business Names
- **Alberta:** Copyright Act; Trade name/Trademark
- **Manitoba/Saskatchewan:** Business Names
- **Ontario:** Business Names

23

Interests in Land and Their Transfer

Since land remains the most long-lasting business asset and the "ultimate platform of human activity," the ownership of land is a primary concern both in private life and in carrying on business. It is, therefore, important to understand land ownership. In this chapter we examine such questions as:

- What is land or real property?
- How is land owned?
- What are the various levels of ownership in land?
- How is ownership shared?
- What are the legal characteristics of "estates" and "interests less than estates"?
- How is condominium ownership structured?
- How are interests in land transferred and protected?

THE NATURE OF INTERESTS IN LAND

The Definition of Land

Ordinarily, when we think of land, we think of the surface and its contours. This is adequate for everyday conversation, but a purchaser who buys land must know more about what the term includes. In law, **land** includes not only the surface but all that is under the surface, including the natural resources such as minerals or oil, and everything above the surface, including the buildings on the land—and the air above it. Today, a landowner's entitlement to the air above the surface has been severely restricted. Various statutes, international treaties concerning air travel, and municipal by-laws limiting the use of land have reduced ownership of the air.[1] Aircraft may pass freely over the land at a safe altitude, and buildings must not exceed a certain height.

Perhaps most important to remember is that land includes all things permanently attached to it—trees, buildings, fences—known as **fixtures**. When *A* transfers her house and lot to *B*, the document describes the land only, according to its location and dimensions, but it is also presumed that everything affixed to the land goes with it. Lawyers do not draw a distinction between land and buildings as do businesses and accountants. Although for business purposes we report the depreciation of buildings but not of land, the two are lumped together in law when determining or transferring ownership.

land
comprises the surface, all that is under the surface, including the minerals and oil, and everything above the surface, including buildings

fixtures
all things permanently attached to land are deemed part of the land

Real Property

The Meaning of "Property"

Land is usually referred to as *real property* or *real estate*, two important terms that need some explanation. We are familiar with the term "**property**" from our earlier discussions of personal property, intangible property, and intellectual property. Its common definition is "everything which is the subject of ownership . . . everything that has exchangeable value or which goes to make up wealth. . . ."[2] By this definition, property means the thing itself, whether it be a piece of land or a piece of cheese, or a bill of lading or a share certificate, or the tangible things these documents represent.[3] The person or entity that holds the ownership to the property is said to have **title** to the property: "ownership *of* a thing," or "title *to* a thing."

property
(1) everything that is the subject of ownership or (2) the legal interest in a thing

title
holding ownership of a thing

The Meaning of "Real"

The word "real" refers to an ancient remedy; certain interests in land gave the owner a remedy by way of **real action**—an action to repossess the interest interfered with—rather than a remedy by way of *personal action*, an action for money damages without a right to recover the interest. Eventually the term "real" property came to refer to interests in land generally.

real action
an action to repossess an interest in land that had been interfered with

The Meaning of "Estate"

Land is permanent, except on the rare occasions when a piece of it slides into the sea. Its value may drop but it exists perpetually. We must consider each owner of land as a temporary owner because

---

1. In *Didow* v. *Alberta Power Ltd.* [1988] A.J. No. 620, the Alberta Court of Appeal held that power lines, about 50 feet above the ground, which crossed a corner of the plaintiff's field, constituted a trespass into his airspace. A subsequent amendment to the Hydro and Electric Energy Act, R.S.A. 2000, c. H-16, permitted this type of intrusion without compensation.

2. *Black's Law Dictionary*, 6th ed. (St. Paul: West Publishing, 1990) at 1216.

3. The lesser-known meaning of property is not the thing itself but the legal interest in the thing—the right or rights that the law will recognize and protect. Property in this sense has been called "ownership, the unrestricted and exclusive right to a thing; the right to dispose of a thing in every legal way, to possess it, to use it, and to exclude everyone else from interfering with it." *Ibid.*

eventually the land will pass to another owner. As a result, the law defines ownership of land based on the length of time that the owner is entitled to exclusive possession of the land and calls such ownership arrangements **estates in time**. Any interest in land that gives someone exclusive possession for some period of time is known as an estate.

During an owner's exclusive possession of the land, he or she may change the nature or use of the land for those that come after them. For instance, if the owner of land grants to a city the right to lay watermains across the land and to maintain and repair them, that right could affect a subsequent owner who would like to tear up the pipes and erect a building. If, over many years, successive owners of the land were to grant away more of their rights, eventually there would be a complex bundle of rights held by various persons. Each subsequent holder of an estate in time would own the land minus the rights granted away. Rights dealing with the use of the land and not exclusive possession to it are referred to as **interests less than estates**. Land use is also controlled by all three levels of government, as we shall discuss later in this chapter.

estates in time
the right to exclusive possession of the land for a period of time

interests less than estates
interests in land that do not give the right to exclusive possession

ESTATES IN TIME

Freehold Estates

The first category of estates is freehold estates. A **freehold estate** is indeterminate in time; it cannot be predicted how long the interest of the owner will last.

freehold estate
an interest in land that is indeterminate in time

Fee Simple Estate

This estate, usually referred to as the **fee simple**, is the longest interest a person can own in land and is as close to complete ownership as the law comes. When we speak of land ownership, we mean fee simple. The holder of the fee simple holds it for all time present and future. The holder of the fee simple may designate the next owner by selling it, transferring it, or leaving the property to someone in a will. Even if there is not a will, the relatives of a deceased owner are entitled to inherit it. If the owner dies without relatives or a will, then it is transferred to the government. He may grant the whole of the fee simple away; he may grant away a lesser interest keeping the rest for himself; or he may grant the whole of it in various portions to different persons.

fee simple
the interest in land closest to complete ownership

ILLUSTRATION 23.1

(a) *A*, the holder of the fee simple in Blackacre, may grant it to an older brother *B* for the rest of *B*'s life. At *B*'s death it returns to *A* or to *A*'s heirs if *A* dies before *B*. *A* retains the fee simple subject to a life estate to *B*.

(b) *A* may grant Blackacre to a brother for life with the rest of the fee simple going to a niece, *C*, at the brother's death.

The holder of a fee simple may carve up the estate in other ways and grant them to other persons; the situations in Illustration 23.1 serve merely as examples.

Life Estate

A **life estate** is an estate in land for the life of one person—usually for the life of the person who holds the estate, but not necessarily: a person may hold an estate, measured by the life of another person. *A* may grant Blackacre to *B* for the rest of *A*'s own life—if *A* dies within a few months, the life estate ends. *B* retains no interest in Blackacre. This type of life estate, however, is quite rare. The more usual life estate is for the life of the person to whom the interest is given and often arises under the terms of a will. For example, the owner of a fee simple may, by the terms of her will, give a life estate in the family home to her brother, who becomes the **life tenant**; or a widow may give a life estate to her eldest child. In either of these situations she may also direct that the rest of the fee simple pass to the grandchildren.

life tenant
a holder of a life estate

The balance of the fee simple, after a life estate has been carved out, is called either a reversion or a *remainder*. It is called a **reversion** when the grantor of the life estate reserves the balance of the fee simple for herself and her heirs (that is, it *reverts* back to the grantor or her heirs after the life estate ends). It is called a **remainder** when it goes to some third person. The balance of the estate in example (a) in Illustration 23.1 above is a reversion and in example (b) a remainder.

reversion
the balance of a fee simple reserved to the grantor and her heirs at the end of a life estate

- *First*, it is difficult to sell land subject to a life estate. Very few people will buy only the remaining years of a life tenant's interest, an uncertain period of time. Similarly, they will rarely buy a reversion or remainder because it is impossible to tell how long the life tenant will live. Only if both the life tenant and the **remainderman** join in the sale and together grant the whole of the fee simple will it be relatively easy to sell the land.

remainder
the balance of a fee simple that goes to a third person at the end of a life estate Unfortunately, life estates create many problems.

- *Second*, a life tenant is limited in the changes she can make on the land without the consent of the remainderman. She cannot tear down buildings or cut down trees without the permission of the remainderman even if she wishes to replace them with something more valuable; she must leave the land to the remainderman substantially as she received it. On the other hand, she is under no duty to make repairs and may let buildings decay.

remainderman
a person who holds the reversion or remainder in a fee simple

- *Third*, she cannot compel the remainderman to contribute anything to the cost of substantial repairs and maintenance needed on the land though they will ultimately be of benefit to the remainderman in preserving its value.

Life estates are not commonly used in business. However, they are often used for tax planning purposes and family situations. For example, parents may wish to transfer the fee simple in the family cottage to the children but retain a life estate to enjoy until their deaths. A spouse may wish to create a life estate in the family cottage for her second spouse and leave the fee simple to the children of her first marriage. This will allow the current spouse to enjoy the cottage for life without disinheriting the children of the first marriage.

Leasehold Estates

The other major category of estates is leasehold estates. A **leasehold** estate is an interest in land for a definite period of time—a week, a month, a year, a hundred years, or any other specific period. Here we find the great distinction between a freehold and a leasehold estate: a freehold estate is either for an *infinite* time (the fee simple) or an *indefinite* time (the life estate), but the leasehold is for a definite time. In a leasehold estate, the person to whom the interest is granted is called the **lessee** or **tenant**, and the grantor of the interest is called the **lessor** or **landlord**.

leasehold
an interest in land for a definite period of time

lessee or tenant
a person to whom an interest in a leasehold estate is granted

Historically, leaseholds have always been considered lesser estates than freeholds. This was so even though it was obvious that leases for 100 years would almost invariably last longer than a life tenancy, a freehold estate. However, a leasehold interest must be derived from a freehold interest and cannot last longer than the freehold from which it is derived.

lessor or landlord
a grantor of an interest in a leasehold estate

ILLUSTRATION 23.2

In her will *T* gives *A* a life estate in Blackacre with the remainder after *A*'s death to *X* in fee simple. *A* leases Blackacre to *B* Inc. for 100 years. Several months later *A* dies. *X*, the remainderman, can take possession of Blackacre and evict *B* Inc. *X* is not bound by the lease because *A* could not create a leasehold interest in Blackacre to last longer than his own life estate.

The above result is an application of the rule that a person cannot grant to another a greater interest than he himself holds.[4]

Leasehold interests share an important characteristic with freehold interests—a lease gives a lessee the right to exclusive possession of the land described in the lease. A lessee has the right to keep all persons off the leased land *including* the lessor himself, unless the lessor has reserved the right to enter the property for inspection and repairs. The law concerning leasehold interests is the meeting-place of the strict concepts of real property, the flexible concepts of contract, and the changing policies of government regulation. Leases play an important role in commerce and industry, and in finance as an alternative to the traditional method of borrowing money on the security of mortgages. The provincial regulations dealing with leasehold interests are discussed in more detail in Chapter 24, "Landlord and Tenant."[5]

Sharing Title: "Co-Ownership"

Tenancy in Common

tenants in common
concurrent holders of equal undivided shares in an estate

Two or more persons may become co-owners of the same estate in land at the same time. They are concurrent holders of the estate whether it is a fee simple, a life estate, or a leasehold estate. In the absence of any special agreement between them or of special terms set out in the initial grant, co-owners are deemed to be tenants in common. **Tenants in common** hold equal shares in the estate; that is, each is entitled to the same rights over the property and an equal share of the income. Each interest is an *undivided* interest. One tenant cannot fence off a portion of the property for her exclusive use—each is entitled to the use of the whole property. However, tenants in common may agree expressly to hold unequal shares, transfer the share of one to another, or divide and fence the property into exclusive lots. In addition, a tenant in common may transfer her interest to any third party without the consent of the others: the transferee becomes a tenant in common with them. When a tenant in common dies, her interest goes to her heirs, who continue to hold the interest with the other tenants in common. Business partners usually hold title to real property as tenants in common.

Joint Tenancy

joint tenants
concurrent holders each of whom has a right of survivorship

right of survivorship
the right of a surviving tenant to the interest of a deceased joint tenant

probate
the process of administering and settling the estate of a deceased person

Another form of co-ownership is joint tenancy. Two or more persons become **joint tenants** only when expressly created at the time the estate is granted to them or afterwards by an express agreement among them. The feature that distinguishes a joint tenancy from a tenancy in common is the **right of survivorship**. Under the right of survivorship, the interest of a deceased joint tenant passes on his death to the surviving tenant instead of to the heirs of the deceased. If *A*, *B*, and *C* own Blackacre in joint tenancy, upon *C*'s death his interest will pass to *A* and *B*, who will continue to own Blackacre in joint tenancy between them. *C*'s interest does not go to his heirs.

Husband and wife often take title to their family home in joint tenancy. On the death of either spouse, the survivor automatically receives full title to the property. Joint tenancy is an advantage to the survivor because the house does not form part of the deceased partner's estate and become entangled in problems of **probate** (administration and settling of the deceased person's estate). Legal fees and probate costs are significantly reduced.

---

4. In 1877, England passed the Settled Estates Act creating an important exception to the rule. The statute was later enacted only in British Columbia and Ontario. Under the statute a life tenant may lease his estate for a term not exceeding 21 years, and the lease will be valid against the remainderman. If the life tenant dies, the lessee pays the rent to the remainderman for the balance of the lease and may stay in possession. The statute also provides that the rent bargained for by the life tenant must be the best reasonably obtainable.

5. Leases of personal property are discussed in Chapter 17 and Chapter 30.

Severance

A joint tenant may end the right of survivorship at any time before his death without the consent of the other joint tenants. By a procedure called **severance**, he may turn his joint tenancy into a tenancy in common. If there are two or more other tenants remaining, they continue as joint tenants with each other, but are tenants in common with the one who has severed his joint tenancy. The most common method of severance is by a joint tenant granting his interest to a third party. The grant automatically turns the interest transferred into a tenancy in common with the remaining interests. A joint tenancy is also severed by giving a mortgage on one's share. However, a joint tenant *cannot* sever his share by disposing of it in his will: the courts have held that a will speaks only at the moment a testator has died, and at that moment his share has already passed to the surviving joint tenant or tenants.

severance
a procedure that turns a joint tenancy into a tenancy in common

INTERESTS LESS THAN ESTATES

Easements

At Common Law

In addition to estates in land that are divided according to time, there are other interests distinguished by the use or benefit they confer upon the holder. None of these interests gives the right to exclusive possession.

An **easement** is a right enjoyed by one landowner over the land of another, for a special purpose rather than for the general use and occupation of land. The most common type of easement is a **right-of-way**: the holder of a right-of-way may pass back and forth over the land of another in order to get to and from her own land. She does not have the right to remain on the other's land or bring things on the land and leave them there or to obstruct others from using the land, but she can maintain an action against anyone who interferes with her right to pass. Other examples of easements are the right to hang eaves of a building over another's land and to drain water or waste materials from one piece of land over a watercourse on another's land. Adjoining landowners frequently have mutual easements over each other's land, such as a shared driveway or a narrow strip between houses to provide access for maintenance and repairs.[6] Once granted, an easement attaches to the land and binds subsequent owners—they cannot interfere with the exercise of the easement. Similarly, purchasers of the land benefiting from the easement acquire the former owner's easement rights.

An essential requirement of an easement, at common law, is that there must be a **dominant tenement** (a piece of land that benefits from the easement) and a **servient tenement** (the land subject to the easement) owned by a different person. The dominant tenement must be *close* to the servient tenement; how close is a subjective determination based on the facts of each situation.

easement
a right enjoyed by one landowner over the land of another for a special purpose but not for occupation of the land

right-of-way
an easement that gives the holder a right to pass back and forth over the land of another in order to get to and from her own land

dominant tenement
the piece of land that benefits from an easement

servient tenement
the land subject to the easement

"Statutory Easements"

The term "easement" is sometimes used to describe certain statutory rights, such as the right granted a telephone company to run wires and cables either underground or overhead on poles. The telephone company has the right to leave wires where they have been installed and to inspect and repair them when necessary—rights very similar to easements. But often the telephone company owns no land in the area. The nearest land that could be considered a dominant tenement may be many kilometres away. Therefore, strictly speaking, the right is not an easement—it is a right created by statute.[7]

---

6. For recent examples see *Rose* v. *Krieser* (2002), 212 D.L.R. (4th) 123; *Fallowfield* v. *Bourgault* (2003), 235 D.L.R. (4th) 263.

7. The example given at the beginning of this chapter of a municipality being given a right to lay watermains over a landowner's property might be an easement proper or merely a statutory right, depending upon whether the municipality owned land nearby.

Easements by Prescription

prescription
the creation of an easement over adjoining land through exercising a right continuously and openly

Simply using another person's land may give an adjoining landowner an easement over his neighbour's land without a written grant. The method is called **prescription**, and an easement is created if a person:

- continuously exercises a right for a period of at least 20 years,
- openly,
- without fraud, deceit, force, or threats against the owner of the land, and
- without consent or permission of the owner or payment to the owner.

An easement by prescription is as valid as an easement by grant and is recognized in some parts of Atlantic Canada and in parts of Manitoba and Ontario where land ownership is recorded in a registry system. Easements by prescription are not recognized in the three western-most provinces or in those parts of Manitoba and Ontario covered by *land titles* registration. Both of these systems of recording interests in land will be discussed in the last section of this chapter. In areas where easements by prescription may arise, a landowner must guard against them.[8]

CONTEMPORARY ISSUE

Conservation Easements

Past decades have seen the creation of legislation in several Canadian provinces concerning conservation easements. These statutes reflect a compromise between the legal rights of land owners (protected under statute and at common law) and the concerns of those who would like to protect environmentally sensitive land.

The easements created by this legislation, such as the Environmental Protection and Enhancement Act in Alberta (R.S.A. 2000, c. E-12), the Conservation Land Act in Ontario (R.S.O. 1990, c. C.28), and the Conservation Easements Act in Saskatchewan (S.S. 1996, c. C-27.01), more closely resemble restrictive covenants than easements in their traditional sense—although the Ontario legislation makes it very clear that such an easement shall not be deemed a restrictive covenant. Pursuant to these statutes, landowners may enter agreements with conservation organizations or bodies whereby the landowner retains ownership to the land, but the conservation body gains the right to access the land for purposes of "conservation, maintenance, restoration or enhancement" of the land. The easements can also include positive or negative covenants that bind the landowner in his use of the land—presumably to safeguard environmental sensitivities inherent in the land. The easement is to be registered against the property and once registered, shall run with the land.

The Alberta Government, in its January 3, 2005, issue of "Agri-News," heralded the use of conservation easements. It quoted Andy Murphy, of the Alberta Conservation Association: "Conservation easements are a great concept that farmers and ranchers would likely be interested

continued

---

8. One danger is that a former owner of the land may have permitted the exercise of a right for many years. The prescription period continues to run from the moment that the right was exercised, regardless of a transfer of ownership of the land. Thus, there may be only a small part of the 20 years to go, or the full 20-year period may already have elapsed when the current owner obtains title. While a prospective easement may seem inoffensive to the current owner, there is a risk that the easement may later reduce the market value of the land. See, for example, *Depew* v. *Wilkes* (2002), 216 D.L.R. (4th) 487. In some provinces the courts have power to cancel an easement if it is obsolete because of changes in the character of the land: see, for example, Property Law Act, R.S.B.C. 1996, c. 377, s. 35; *TDL Group Ltd.* v. *Harvey* (2002), 212 D.L.R. (4th) 278.

in as an easy way they can preserve precious tracts of land they have for future generations."
At the beginning of 2003, over 35 000 acres in Alberta had been brought under the protection of 52 different conservation easements. Of these easements, 15 had been "purchased" while the land under the remaining 37 had been "donated."

QUESTIONS TO CONSIDER

1. Do you think conservation easements are an effective method of protecting environmentally sensitive land?

2. Are conservation easements more effective than restrictive covenants? Why or why not?

3. Do you foresee any legal difficulties with conservation easements—for instance, will they be popular with mortgagees?

Covenants

An owner of land may wish to sell part of it yet continue to control or restrict the use of the part she proposes to sell. We can understand her motives—she may wish to see the property kept in good repair so that the area does not deteriorate, to prevent the carrying on of a noisy business that would interfere with her privacy, or to have the purchaser improve the land by planting trees and shrubs to enhance the beauty of the area. She may, of course, require the purchaser to do any or all of these things as part of the consideration for the contract of sale of the land. However, this would not bind any subsequent buyer. The solution is to create an interest in land that the law recognizes as binding upon all subsequent owners.

ILLUSTRATION 23.3

V, owner of Blackacre and Whiteacre, sells Whiteacre to *P*. As part of the consideration, he obtains a promise that *P* and all subsequent owners of Whiteacre will keep in repair all buildings on both Whiteacre and Blackacre. So long as *P* owns Whiteacre, he is bound by his promise. *P* then sells Whiteacre to *A*, who is aware of that promise. *A* refuses to carry it out, and *V* sues *A* for breach. The court would have no difficulty dismissing the promise to repair buildings on Blackacre as not binding *A*. *A* has no connection with *P*'s promise insofar as it affects Blackacre—he has no interest in that land nor was he a party to the contract between *V* and *P*. Accordingly, *A* is not bound to repair the buildings on Blackacre.

The promise concerning Whiteacre is more troublesome. It may seem reasonable for *V*, who still owns adjoining lands, to require Whiteacre to be kept in good repair so that the area will remain at high market value.

The courts have held that it is too onerous to bind subsequent owners to positive duties, and that as a matter of public policy it would be dangerous to permit the creation of interests in land requiring all subsequent owners to personally perform promises in perpetuity. Lands might eventually be tied up by multiple promises or covenants for the benefit of surrounding lands.[9]

---

9. In the middle of the 19th century, one of these covenants was questioned in the English Court of Chancery. The court decided that it was too onerous to require a subsequent holder to act positively in order to carry out covenants, but if the covenant were purely *negative*—that is, if the holder were required to refrain from certain conduct or certain use of the land—then the court would hold the covenant valid and enforceable. *Tulk* v. *Moxhay* (1848), 41 E.R. 1143. In a recent decision a majority of the Ontario Court of Appeal ruled that, although the refusal to enforce positive covenants may occasionally cause inconvenience and unfairness, the rule is well established and ought not to be changed: *Amberwood Investments Ltd.* v. *Durham Condominium Corp. No.123* (2002), 211 D.L.R. (4th) 1.

Restrictive Covenants

Courts have taken a more favourable view of covenants that require the owner to refrain from doing something. These negative covenants are known as "covenants running with the land," or **restrictive covenants**. Restrictive covenants are subject to a rule similar to that concerning easements—there must be a piece of land subject to the covenant and another piece that receives the benefit of the covenant. A covenant recognized by the courts as running with the land is enforceable *by* any subsequent holder of the land benefiting from it *against* any subsequent holder of the land subject to it.

There are a number of rules governing the types of conduct that may be regulated by restrictive covenants, how the benefits of the covenants may be transferred, and how they may be enforced.[10] Covenants found to be highly unreasonable or against public policy will not be enforced by the courts against subsequent owners.

Remedies for Breach of a Covenant

Suppose an owner of land subject to a restrictive covenant acts quickly in defiance of it—for example, by erecting a high wall or cutting a doorway through an existing wall—before an aggrieved adjacent owner manages to obtain an injunction. Is the adjacent owner without remedy? The court may exercise its discretion, especially when a deliberately provocative breach of covenant has occurred, to grant a *mandatory injunction* requiring the wrongdoer to tear down the prohibited wall, or block the doorway and restore the wall. If it is too late to restore the damage, as when the wrongdoer has cut down a row of 100-year-old oak trees, the court may award damages in lieu of an injunction.

Building-scheme Covenants

Restrictive covenants are widely used by residential housing developers to regulate the uses and look of the subdivision. Covenants are included in the deed to each builder or homeowner. Typical restrictive covenants prohibit the use of land for other than residential purposes, limit building on the land to one-family dwellings, require minimum frontage or square footage per house, specify maximum fence heights, and ban outdoor clotheslines.

If over the years the character of an area has changed and a once-reasonable covenant has become unduly restrictive, an affected landowner may apply to the court to have the covenant terminated. The court will require that the owner of the land for whose benefit the covenant was made be served with notice and given an opportunity to defend the covenant.

Restrictive covenants that regulate land use over an entire neighbourhood or a shopping centre are referred to as **building-scheme covenants**. In a building scheme, each owner mutually agrees with all other owners to be bound by the covenant in return for the promise of all neighbouring owners to be similarly bound. In order to have the court remove the covenant for the benefit of one owner, all adjoining owners must be served with notice and given a chance to state their opinions. As a result, it may be very difficult to have a restrictive covenant under a building scheme terminated.

Covenants are gradually being replaced by municipal regulations in the form of zoning and building by-laws, especially in newly developed areas. Nevertheless, covenants still play an important role in older settled parts of our cities and towns; sometimes they unduly restrict the development of an area.

---

10. Canadian courts have held that for a restrictive covenant to be enforceable, not only must the party seeking to enforce it (the covenantee) own land to be benefited by the covenant, but the land must also be identified in the instrument creating the covenant. *Re Sekretov and City of Toronto* (1973), 33 D.L.R. (3d) 257; *Canada Safeway* v. *Thompson (City)*, [1997] 7 W.W.R. 565. For statutory authority to modify or discharge a restrictive covenant see, for example: Conveyancing and Law of Property Act, R.S.O. 1990, c. C.34, s. 61(1).

Other Interests

Oil, Gas, and Mineral Leases

It is beyond the scope of this chapter to review the many other interests less than estates.[11] One interest deserves special mention—the right to take minerals, oil, and gas from under the surface of land occupied by others. The right to remove materials is usually found in an agreement commonly called a *lease*. An oil, gas, or mineral lease bears little similarity to a true leasehold interest. Rather, it combines several contractual rights and interests in land into one agreement.

- First, to the extent that the agreement permits the lessee to occupy a portion of the surface area of the land (often only a very small proportion of the area from which the oil, gas, or mineral is taken), it has elements of a true lease.
- Second, to the extent that it grants the lessee the right to travel back and forth over the owner's land, lay pipes and move equipment, it is similar to an easement.
- Third, to the extent that it permits the lessee to permanently remove materials extracted from the ground (previously the real property of the owner and now the personal property of the lessee), it is similar to a contract or sale.[12]

Obviously gas, oil, gold, or other minerals significantly increase the value of land and owners tend to keep these rights for themselves when they sell the rest of the land. As a result it is very common for these rights to be held by a former owner or even the government. Extraction may still require the grant of a right of way or easement from the current land owner. The law concerning mineral, oil, and gas leases has become highly specialized in recent years and heavily regulated by government. We simply note that such agreements are more than mere leases and that they form a highly developed field of study of their own.

---

11. See, for example, A.H. Oosterhoff and W.B. Rayner, *Anger & Honsberger's Law of Real Property* (Aurora, Ont. 1985: Canada Law Book Co.); B. Ziff, *Principles of Property Law*, 3rd ed. (Toronto, 2000: Carswell).

12. An ancient interest in land known as a *profit à prendre* that permitted the lessee to remove material extracted from the ground.

Licences

A "licence" given to another person by an owner to use his land is not, strictly speaking, an interest in land at all. If *B* gives his friend, *A*, permission to hold a garage sale on his front lawn, *A* becomes a "licensee" on *B*'s land during the garage sale; she is not a trespasser. However, she has no "right" to remain on *B*'s land, and if he should revoke permission, something he may do at any time, *A* would have only a reasonable minimum time to remove her goods and herself from *B*'s lawn. Suppose, however, that parties enter into a contractual licence.

ILLUSTRATION 23.4

The city of Brockville charges the Jazz Theatre Company a fee to use its municipal auditorium and grants it a licence to perform a play for one week. The city also provides box-office facilities and janitorial services. Revocation of permission to use the auditorium for that week would be a breach of contract. If the breach were sufficiently serious, Jazz Theatre might well obtain an injunction preventing the city from removing its stage settings and players until the end of the week. An injunction—or any other remedy—would be a contractual right enforceable only against the city. If the city sold the auditorium before the week scheduled for the performances, Jazz Theatre would have no rights against the purchaser. Its only remedy would be for damages against the city.

Contractual licences between enterprises that have entered into long-term and stable relations can have substantial business value, and they do create rights binding between the original parties. Their relative simplicity when contrasted with the formalities of creating an interest in land has made licences a useful business tool.

In summary, Figure 23.1 illustrates the various types of interests in real property that we have just discussed.

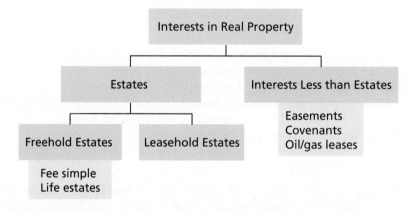

FIGURE 23.1
Interests in Real
Property

GOVERNMENT REGULATION OF LAND

Use and Development

The owner of a chattel may do as she pleases with it—she may even destroy it, and no one has the legal right to interfere. Land is not regarded in this way, especially when it is situated in a community where people live quite close to one another. From very early times, governments have assumed the power to regulate, control, and monitor landowners' activities.

Community regulation has grown rapidly in the last half-century and all three levels of government regulate land use or development. Early regulations covered only such nuisances as fire and health hazards, but the increased density and size of urban centres and the growing complexities of city life have forced municipal governments into large-scale regulation of land use. Zoning by-laws prescribe the use and type of buildings that may be erected in various districts of a municipality. Building regulations prescribe minimum standards of quality for materials and the size of all parts of structures erected within an area. Planning by-laws set out requirements for roadways and for water and sewage services, and often prescribe the amounts of land a land developer must give to the municipality for use as school and park areas.

Provincial legislation regulates land development. Land development usually involves reconfiguring large blocks of under-used land into new "more productive" parcels. The most common example is farm property that is converted into a residential subdivision. Two key components are involved: changing the allowed use, for example, agricultural to residential; and changing the size of the parcel, for example, subdividing a farm it into city-sized lots. Provincial planning legislation limits the right of an owner to subdivide his property without prior permission of the municipality. This allows a municipality to control the density of an urban centre.

Another area of concern for redevelopment projects has been the protection of historical, architectural, and archeological buildings and sites, a concern reflected in provincial "heritage" statutes. This provincial legislation allows municipalities to designate sites for preservation and monitor any proposed changes to them.

Growing public awareness and concern about long-term environmental hazards have led to provincial and federal environmental assessment and protection legislation, discussed in Chapter 32. A proposed development often requires an environmental impact assessment before development can proceed.

Federal legislation regulates land use in areas of federal jurisdiction such as airports, national parks, natural resources, military sites, and Indian lands. These matters often have interprovincial or international dimensions and involve considerations beyond those of the local community. Some land development projects involve all three levels of government, as the following recent conflict over an Indian land claim illustrates.

ILLUSTRATION 23.5

The municipal government for Haldimand County gave all necessary approvals for a residential subdivision, known as Douglas Creek Estates, in Caledonia, Ontario. In July 1995, the developer registered a plan of subdivision and began selling lots. Also in 1995, Six Nations (an organization of 13 Indian Bands) sued the federal and provincial governments claiming entitlement to Douglas Creek Estates (among other things) and warned the developer of the "dangers" associated with development. In February of 2006, Six Nations protesters took possession of the site. Occupation, protests, road blockages, and sometimes violent disruptions occurred. In March 2006, the protesters ignored a court-ordered injunction to leave the site. Negotiations between Six Nations, the Ontario government, and the federal government proceeded on an irregular basis. In June 2006, the Ontario government agreed to pay $12.3 million to purchase the land from the developer plus additional compensation for lost profit. As the new title holder of the land, the Ontario government withdrew objections to the Six Nations occupation despite the disapproval of surrounding neighbours. To date, the dispute remains unresolved.[13]

Rights in the Matrimonial Home

For many centuries a widow's principal security on the death of her husband was a right to **dower**—that is, a right to a life interest in one-third of the real property held by her husband in fee simple during their married life.

dower
a widow's right to a life interest in one-third of the real property held by her husband in fee simple before his death

13. CBC News In Depth, "Caledonia Land Claim," *CBC News*, November 1, 2006, www.cbc.ca/news/background/caledonia-landclaim/.

Common-law dower has been abolished in all provinces.[14] It is replaced by family law legislation which still recognizes the special interest that a spouse has in the family home. The legislation varies greatly from province to province and has been changing so frequently in recent years that it would not be useful to attempt a summary.[15] In particular, statutory rights go much farther than the ancient right to dower and—most importantly—include the right to refuse consent to any change in the title to the family home or to its sale (a sale without consent is void).[16]

Consequently, no transaction involving residential property should be entered into without taking into account the relevant matrimonial property legislation. This legislation complicates the use of the matrimonial home as collateral security for business loans or lines of credit.

Leasehold Estates

Provincial legislation exists in all provinces regulating the rules for landlords and tenants. Tenancies are regulated based on the nature of the use of the property: commercial or residential. Residential tenancy statutes often take the form of consumer protection legislation where rent increases are regulated, landlord remedies curtailed, and writing requirements softened. Commercial tenancy legislation is less protective and preserves many of the common law remedies available to landlords. This topic will be discussed in more detail in Chapter 24.

Condominiums

Condominiums are a provincial legislative solution to a shortage of housing and recreational areas in large urban centres. The provinces have enacted legislation recognizing a fee simple in individual **condominium units** of multiple-unit developments, such as high-rise apartments or row housing, without an interest in the surface land or ground.[17] The legislation is not restricted to residential housing and applies equally to the development of commercial and industrial buildings.

condominium unit
a unit in a multiple-unit development that may be owned in fee simple

The Nature of Ownership in a Condominium

An owner of a unit is entitled to a fee simple estate in that unit and also obtains an undivided part ownership, in common with other unit owners, of the shared areas of the development known as **common elements**. These include structures and areas external to the unit such as entrances, hallways, stairs, and elevators, and communal facilities such as laundries, recreation rooms, garages, swimming pools, tennis courts, and so forth. Each unit can be bought and sold, mortgaged, and passed to successors on death. It is separately assessed and taxed. Transfers do not affect the ownership of other units. A purchaser acquires a unit subject to several important conditions. In a multiple-unit building he must, like a tenant, allow entry to make necessary repairs to services; contribute to the cost of operation, upkeep, and in some degree to the restoration of the common property; and insure his own unit. In addition, he becomes a member of the **condominium corporation** charged with responsibility for management of the property as a whole, and he is subject to the rules and regulations governing the development. Although the corporation is not the owner of the common elements, it may own one or more units and so share in that ownership. For example, it may own units rented for janitorial and supervisory staff as well as for its own offices.

common elements
structures and areas external to a condominium unit, including communal facilities

condominium corporation
a corporation—whose members are the condominium owners—that is responsible for managing the property as a whole

---

14. It was replaced by "homesteads" legislation, giving a surviving spouse a life interest in the entire family home. Manitoba and Saskatchewan retain Homesteads Acts: C.C.S.M., c. H80; S.S. 1989, c. H-5.1. Alberta retains a Dower Act (R.S.A. 2000, c. D-15), which grants a life interest in the matrimonial home to a surviving spouse, but the common law right to one-third of the deceased husband's property is abolished: Law of Property Act, R.S.A. 2000, c. L-7, s. 3.

15. For example, the definition of "spouse" is restricted to married couples in most provinces, but extends to co-habiting partners in British Columbia, Manitoba, and Saskatchewan. The Supreme Court of Canada held that a restriction to married couples does not offend against the Charter: *Walsh* v. *Bona* (2002), 221 D.L.R. (4th) 1.

16. For example, Homesteads Act, C.C.S.M. s. H80, s. 4; Matrimonial Property Act, R.S.N.S. 1989, c. 275, s. 8; Family Law Act, R.S.O. 1990, c. F.4, s. 21.

17. See, for example: Strata Property Act, S.B.C. 1998, c. 43; Condominium Act, S.O. 1998, c. 19; R.S.N.S. 1989, c. 85.

Responsibility for Maintaining Units

The unit owner is responsible for maintaining the unit. For this reason, the definition of the boundaries of a unit is a matter of critical importance: does a unit-owner's property extend beyond the surface of the walls of the rooms? If a piece of plaster is knocked out of the wall, is the damage to the property in the unit or in the common elements? If the description of a unit included ownership of, say, the space eight centimetres beyond the surface of the wall, and plumbing in that space immediately behind the plaster failed, would the unit-owner be responsible for repairs even if the plumbing served an adjoining unit and not his own? We can see that it may be a serious disadvantage to own much of the area beyond the surface of the inner walls. The definition of the unit is established by the developer during the initial stages of condominium development.

Maintenance and Management of a Condominium

In a good-quality rental apartment building, a competent landlord is interested in maintaining this asset in good condition and will have the necessary management and technical expertise to do so. In a condominium, when the last unit has been sold the purchasers of condominium units become the owners of the complex. If the entrepreneur who built the condominium retains no further interest, the tasks of maintaining the condominium in a good state of repair, paying its bills, and having generally efficient management become the collective responsibility of unit-owners through the condominium corporation. Ordinarily, it would not be possible for individual owners to run a large development, and they would authorize the corporation to hire an expert to oversee the operation. Frequently the entrepreneur, while still controlling the condominium corporation as the owner of the unsold units, will arrange a management contract for, say, five years. Even after selling off the last unit, the entrepreneur may stay on as manager at a substantial fee. Accordingly, it is important for a prospective buyer of a unit to assess the quality of the building, the reputation of the entrepreneur, and the quality of management of the condominium development. Even when management is in competent hands, a unit-owner cannot sit back as a house-owner ordinarily can and attend only to her own property. She must remain concerned about the sound management of the condominium corporation on a continuing long-term basis. Most legislative schemes require a condominium to undertake periodic property reviews, schedule routine maintenance, and maintain a reserve fund to cover the cost of major projects and emergencies. Prospective buyers should consider the contents of the latest property review and the adequacy of the reserve fund.

Financing and Insurance

A buyer must maintain fire and liability insurance on their unit in order to comply with their mortgage requirements and the condominium rules. If something happens to the unit and/or the complex, the mortgage holders and insurers must consider the interests of the development as a whole, not just the specific unit owner. The most common method of dealing with the problem is through an "insurance trust." A trustee insures the entire building for the benefit of both the condominium corporation and every individual unit-owner; each pays part of the premium proportionate to its interest.

We can see that while there are many attractive features in the development of condominiums, there are also new problems confronting prospective purchasers that must be weighed against the advantages.

Cooperative Housing

An alternative to condominiums is cooperative housing. In a cooperative housing development a member merely buys a share in the cooperative organization which entitles the shareholder to occupy one of the units in the development. A risk of this type of home ownership is that the whole cooperative venture may flounder because of bad management and insolvency. All members are affected equally by the failure and may lose their equity investment, even though they may personally have been honouring their obligations and paying the required contributions for taxes and upkeep. Financing a share in cooperative housing presents difficulties of its own. A member buys an equity share and has rights, similar to a leasehold interest, to occupy a unit. The method of borrowing money on the value of a share in a cooperative, combined with the right to occupy a unit, is more complicated than a straight loan by way of mortgage on a private residence.

A cooperative venture usually requires a high degree of commitment to a community project and more direct involvement in management than is typical of condominium ownership. A high level of involvement in the management of the cooperative is probably the best assurance of sound management and survival.

CHECKLIST Government Regulation of Land

Municipal	Provincial	Federal
■ Zoning by-laws	■ Planning legislation	■ Environmental protection and assessment legislation
■ Property standards by-laws	■ Environmental protection and assessment legislation	■ Land regulation as part of specific areas of federal jurisdiction such as:
■ Building permit regulations	■ Heritage statutes	• National parks
	■ Family law statutes	• Natural resources
	■ Residential tenancies legislation	• Indian affairs
	■ Commercial tenancies legislation	• Airports
	■ Condominium legislation	• Military

THE TRANSFER OF INTERESTS IN LAND

By a Sale or Gift

An interest in land may be transferred in any one of several ways. The most common way of disposing of an interest in land is by a voluntary transfer between living persons, in performance of a contract for the sale of land or, less commonly, as a gift. The methods used to transfer land developed over hundreds of years into a comparatively uniform form of *grant*. It contains a description of the grantor, the grantee, and the interest being transferred and was originally signed and sealed by the grantor before a witness. Since the document was under seal, it is often called a **deed of conveyance**—frequently shortened to **deed**. The equivalent of a grant under the land titles system, used in an ever expanding number of jurisdictions as described in the next section, is called a **transfer** and is effective without being made under seal. As we shall discuss later in this chapter, modern title conveyancing is handled electronically without seals or even signatures.

deed of conveyance or deed
a document under seal that transfers an interest in land from the owner to another party

transfer
under the land titles system the equivalent of a grant; not required to be made under seal

A holder of an interest may grant the whole of it or only part, reserving the rest of it to himself. When he grants only part of it, the balance remains his. For example, when a landlord grants a lease for five years he retains the *reversion*. Possession returns to him at the end of the lease—just as we have already seen, when the holder of a fee simple grants a life estate, the reversion stays with him and his heirs. When a person grants an easement over his land, he retains the remaining interest in the land (the servient tenement).

The transferor of an interest may wish to transfer almost all his interest, retaining only a small part for himself. In these circumstances, the *form* of the grant changes. He conveys away his whole interest except that he expressly reserves the part he wishes to keep. So, if *A* owns both Blackacre and Whiteacre and wishes to sell Whiteacre to *B* but retain an easement over it in order to get to and from Blackacre, *A* will grant Whiteacre to *B*, at the same time *reserving* a right-of-way over it. Such **reservations** are quite common in grants of land. As noted earlier in this chapter under Government Regulation of Land, some grants of only part of the land require prior approval of the municipality under planning control legislation.

> **reservation**
> that part of an interest in land expressly retained by the transferor

In summary, a transfer of an interest in land can have two results. First, if it is a transfer of the *whole interest*, then the interest remains unaltered but is in the hands of another person. Second, if it is a transfer of only *part of an interest*, the interest is divided into two parts and there are two holders—the grantee with the interest he has obtained under the grant and the grantor with the interest he has retained because he did not transfer it by the grant.

On Death of the Owner

Interests in land are also transferred on the death of the owner, either by will or according to the rules of intestate succession. The owner may dispose of her property by will according to her wishes and the claims she feels she should satisfy.[18] If she dies *intestate* (without leaving a will), the interest passes according to statutory rules of inheritance to the holder's heir or heirs; that is, the interest passes automatically to the closest relatives. If, for example, a widow holds a fee simple in Blackacre and at her death she is survived by two daughters, they will become the owners of the fee simple. As noted earlier, if the title is held in joint tenancy, the land will pass automatically to the surviving joint tenant.

By Compulsory Sale

The holder of an interest in land may be compelled to transfer it against her will. A creditor may hold a mortgage or obtain judgment against her in court and eventually have the land sold in order to satisfy the debt. More will be said about mortgage remedies in Chapter 25. A second type of compulsory transfer of land is **expropriation**. When a public body such as the federal government or a local school board requires land for its activities, it may proceed under statute to force the transfer of land to itself. It must, of course, pay compensation for taking the land, and if the parties cannot agree upon a price, the statute provides for arbitration or judicial proceedings to determine the price to be paid.

> **expropriation**
> a compulsory sale and transfer of land to a public body

> **extinguish the title**
> end the title of the owner and the owner's right to regain possession

Adverse Possession

Just as we saw with easements of prescription, at common law the continuous exclusive use of land may create an interest in it. An unauthorized occupant of land can **extinguish the title** of an owner and gain the title for himself. This is known as **adverse possession** and it requires the following conditions:

> **adverse possession**
> the exclusive possession of land by someone who openly uses it like an owner and ignores the claims of other persons including the owner

> **limitation period**
> the time period within which a right of action must be pursued or it is lost forever

- open, notorious, exclusive possession of the land[19]
- without the permission or consent of the owner
- for the legislated **limitation period** for real property claims (for example, 10 years, longer against the Crown)[20]

---

18. Subject to any rights that a surviving spouse may have under matrimonial home legislation, discussed above.

19. See for example: *Wallis's Ltd.* v. *Shell-Mex and BP*, [1974] All E.R. 575; *Teis* v. *Ancaster (Town)* (1997), 35 O.R. (3d) 216; *Leichner* v. *Canada Attorney General* (1996), 31 O.R. (3d) 700.

20. See, for example: Real Property Limitations Act, R.S.O. 1990, c. L.15, s. 4 (10 years); Limitations of Actions Act, R.S.N.S. 1989, c. 258, s. 10 (20 years).

Most jurisdictions using the land titles system of registration have eliminated the extinguishment of title by adverse possession.[21]

REGISTRATION OF INTERESTS IN LAND

First in Time

We have seen that interests in land are varied and complex and they may be transferred in a variety of ways. Determining who owns the property and what other claims or interests non-owners may have is of key importance when valuing, purchasing, developing, or mortgaging land. In Canada, title to real property is established through provincially regulated public registration systems that record all interests in land.[22] The validity of each interest is determined based on the order of registration, with earlier registrations having priority over subsequent registrations. Therefore, a purchaser should not rely on a properly executed grant of title unless it is registered in the public system. The date the grant was given does not establish ownership; the date *and time* of registration does. The public registration record for each parcel of land is available for review by anyone, but most often real estate lawyers and **title searchers** analyze the record to determine the state of the title to a particular parcel of land.

As has already been noted throughout this chapter, two different types of registration systems are employed throughout Canada—the registry system and the land titles system. Both systems subscribe to the "first in time" concept, also known as the **priority of registration** rule.[23] The impact of this rule encourages a purchaser to register her grant immediately on receiving it.

Registry System

The registry system is the older of the two systems and is gradually being phased out in favour of the land titles system. This is because it is a labour-intensive system that places the responsibility for establishing good title to real property on the users of the system or their real estate lawyers. Each transaction involving land requires an examination of the registered interests in order to establish the proper chain of ownership, identify any defects or other interests, and take corrective action. Each document must be examined to confirm that it meets the requirements to effectively deal with the interest. In the registry system one cannot simply rely on the record or the fact of registration to confirm title; an evaluation of all documents registered in the title search period must be undertaken. Ownership may only be relied upon if a **chain of title** can be established throughout the search period. The specific length of the search period is usually set out in the legislation. Some registry systems limit the required search period to the proceeding 40 years, which can mean hundreds of registrations.[24]

title searchers
paralegals trained in land law who study the public registration systems and produce summaries of the registered interests affecting the title to specific real property

priority of registration
priority of interests in real property are determined based on the order of registration in the public system; earlier registrations have priority over subsequent registrations

chain of title
the series of grants over the title search period that can be traced to the current owner (vendor)

---

21. See, for example: Limitation Act, R.S.B.C. c. 266, s. 12; Real Property Act, R.S.M. 1988, c. R-30, s. 61(2); Land Titles Act, R.S.O. 1990, c. L-5, s. 51. In Alberta, a claim based on adverse possession may be registered; Land Titles Act, R.S.A. 2000, c.L. 4, s. 39. Unless it is registered, it is not binding upon a transferee of the land. In Nova Scotia, adverse possession claims are allowed provided they do not affect more than 20 percent of the area of the parcel: Land Registration Act, S.N.S. 2001, c. 6, s. 75.
22. Subject to very few exceptions that will be noted later, such as adverse possession.
23. There are other variations between the systems that are discussed below.
24. Registry Act, R.S.O. 1990, c. R.20, s. 112(1); Limitations of Actions Act, R.S.N.S. 1989, c. 258, s. 20.

ILLUSTRATION 23.6

In 2008, *X* is considering the purchase of Red Oaks from *Y*. The registry system registration record for Red Oaks shows:

Registration Number	Date of Registration	Type of Document	Amount	Parties (from)	Parties (to)
112345	Jan. 1, 1945	Grant/Transfer	$100.00	A	B
276654	Feb. 2, 1960	Grant/Transfer	$9 000.00	M	N
325671	May 1, 1982	Grant/Transfer	$50 000.00	N	P
399871	May 1, 1992	Easement (South 2 metres)	$1.00	P	Hydro Commission
423567	June 1, 1999	Grant/Transfer	$150 000.00	P	Y

(a) There is a continuous chain of title to the present holder, *Y*. *X* need not worry about the transfer from *A* to *B* or any subsequent transfer by *B*. The fact that *M* conveyed the land to *N* more than 40 years ago and there was no subsequent difficulty with the title establishes a chain of title upon which *X* can rely.

(b) *X* should be concerned about the easement granted in 1992. It is inside the 40-year search period, and, therefore, the subsequent grant to *Y* is subject to this easement. *X* should examine the document to determine how it affects Red Oaks. Given that the grantee is a utility company, the easement is likely for the supply of electrical power. *X* must decide if he is willing to accept the title subject to the Hydro Commission's easement.

Searching the title to a real property under the registry system can be a laborious and sometimes hazardous task. An error in one of the documents that has gone undetected may later be discovered and disclose an outstanding interest, creating serious consequences for the current owner. If harm results through the negligence of a lawyer, he or she must compensate the client. Lawyers carry liability insurance to compensate clients in case such an error occurs. The registry system is still in use in some parts of the Atlantic provinces, Manitoba, and Ontario.

searching a title
to examine the title to a piece of land

Land Titles System

The risks inherent in the registry system have triggered the movement to the newer **land titles system**.[25] It was adopted in western provinces long ago, and it is now moving across the rest of Canada.[26] The distinctive feature of the system is that as each new transaction concerning a piece of land is submitted for registration, the land titles office carefully examines and approves the document before recording it. Lawyers need not review individual documents to detect errors; the record of registration acts as a **certificate of title**. Section 23(2) of the British Columbia Land Titles Act specifically states that the certificate of title is conclusive evidence in any court that the person named in the certificate is the holder in fee simple of the property.[27] In effect, the government guarantees the accuracy of the title as shown on the record. There are variations from jurisdiction to jurisdiction in the methods of recording and in the type of guarantee given by the government. The great advantage of the system is that a purchaser need not search through 40 or more years of records to discover the state of the title. The land titles office produces a complete statement, valid

land titles system
a system of land registration where the land titles office brings all outstanding interests in the land up-to-date and certifies them as being correct

certificate of title
summary of registered interests in a property, showing the owner and any mortgages, easements, or other interests held by others, which may be relied upon by the public

---

25. The system was also adopted in some states of the United States and is now in use in most of England. It is now in use in most of Ontario, New Brunswick, and parts of Nova Scotia.
26. In Ontario, the old paper system is rapidly being converted to an electronic title registry.
27. In British Columbia, the Land Titles Act, R.S.B.C. (1996) c. 406, s. 23(2).

to the moment the statement is issued. If errors occur, land titles systems have "assurance" funds available to compensate injured parities. A land titles system does not completely eliminate the need to search title; there are exceptions to the certificate that must be separately searched, but it drastically reduces the work involved.

As we have seen, the land titles system attempts to do away with the risks of adverse possession and to give absolute and concise information on the state of the title.[28] The older registry system makes no attempt to do this: its purpose is simply to provide an inventory of all title documents and let the searcher assess their validity.

Electronic Registration

The shift from registry to land titles systems has been expedited by the automation of land registration. Historically, paper documents were created in duplicate and one original copy was maintained in the system. In the registry system (unlike the land titles system) access to original documents is essential since users must assess the validity of the documents themselves. Storage issues led to standardization of forms for both registry and land titles, microfilming of documents, and less use of formalities such as seals and witnesses.[29] Now, all provinces are moving to electronic systems with three key components:

- electronic record keeping—a computerized data bank of registered interests in land
- electronic search capabilities—the ability to electronically search existing registrations using assigned "property identifier numbers" (called PINs or PIDs)
- electronic registration of documents—paperless registration of interests completed online[30]

As part of the automation process, most registry lands are being converted to the land titles system. During this transitional time, properties are mapped and issued an identification number. In New Brunswick any sale or new mortgaging of a property requires it first be converted into the land titles system. Subdivision of lots triggers immediate conversion in Nova Scotia.

There are advantages and disadvantages to electronic registration systems. The electronic system is far more accessible. Searches may be completed online and there is no longer a need to physically travel to the local registry or land titles office in order to complete a title search. Similarly, electronic systems can handle a much higher volume of searches and registrations with virtually no physical storage requirements. However, the electronic system faces new problems such as capacity, viruses, and crashes. One of the most serious threats is fraud. The elimination of signatures, witnesses, and paper, together with the wide access to the electronic system has led to **title fraud**—the fraudulent transfer or mortgaging of land by a non-owner. This has led some provinces to restrict access to electronic registration.

title fraud
fraudulent transfer or mortgaging of land by a non-owner

---

28. See for example the British Columbia Land Titles Act, *ibid.*, s. 24 or the Ontario Land Titles Act, R.S.O. 1990, c. L.5, s. 51.

29. The Ontario Land Registration Reform Act abolished the need for seals or witnesses in the registry system so that the same form of transfer could be used in both registry and land titles and to make documents shorter to microfilm. The POLARIS forms implied standardized covenants into the document so they need not be printed in each form.

30. See British Columbia Land Titles Act, *supra* n. 27; Ontario Land Registration Reform Act, R.S.O. 1990, c. L.4 (applies to both registry and land titles systems); Land Registration Act, S.N.S. 2001, c. 6.

ETHICAL ISSUE

Real Estate Fraud Prevention

Part of the Ontario Real Estate Fraud Prevention Plan involves restricting access to electronic registration. In order to register any document, one must be an account holder. Account applications are screened on the following criteria:

- identity of applicant—is the applicant entitled to access?
- financial resources—does the applicant have resources to compensate victims of fraud?
- good character/accountability—does the applicant have integrity?

Registrations for the transfer (grant) of title are further restricted to lawyers only and each lawyer (one acting for the vendor and one for the purchaser) must confirm completeness of the transfer registration. The rationale for these restrictions is that lawyers are governed by a self-regulating profession with discipline and investigatory powers. Requiring the consent of two lawyers on opposing sides of the transaction will further reduce the likelihood that fraud will go undetected. Search-only accounts will remain widely available.

QUESTIONS TO CONSIDER

1. Consider the role of self-regulating law societies in inspiring integrity in the legal profession.

2. Does restricting access to electronic registration undermine the goals of the automated system generally?

Source: Ontario Ministry of Government and Consumer Services, "New Access Requirements for ELRS; Registration Requirements for Transfers and Powers of Attorney," Bulletin No. 2008-02, *ServiceOntario*, March 7, 2008, www.gov.on.ca/ont/portal/!ut/p/.cmd/cs/.ce/7_0_A/.s/7_0_GTS/_s.7_0_A/7_0_GTS/_l/en?docid=200385.

Claims That Are not Registered on Title

It is possible for some unregistered claims or interests to affect a landowner's title in both the registry and land titles systems. Therefore, in addition to a title search, potential purchasers often undertake "off title" searches or investigations.

Adverse Possession

We have already noted that in jurisdictions where the registry system is still in use, a purchaser cannot rely solely on the records because the vendor's title may have been extinguished by adverse possession. Adverse possession is also still possible in some land titles systems: for example, adverse possession claims of less than 20 percent of the parcel of land are allowed in the Nova Scotia land titles system.[31]

---

31. Land Registration Act, S.N.S. 2001, c. 6, s. 75.

Small encroachments may not be detectable by a purchaser. A **survey** of the real property is one way to uncover problems. It is a detailed drawing or map of the real property showing all the boundaries of the land and the location of all fixtures, encroachments, or overhangs. A survey can be used to:

- confirm that the buildings are actually on the land being purchased (something the registration system does not confirm),
- confirm that the location of all buildings comply with the municipal zoning by-laws
- identify any possible claims for adverse possession
- locate fences, driveways, etc. in relation to the boundaries of the property

Arrears of Taxes

Two other claims against lands not ordinarily registered under either the registry or the land titles system are arrears of municipal tax on the land and, in some provinces, arrears of tax against corporations accruing while they hold the land. Tax arrears attach to the real property as if they had been registered. If any of these claims appears after a purchaser has paid the vendor, the purchaser must pay them in order to protect her interest in the land. A prospective purchaser should request a tax certificate from the municipality showing any taxes outstanding and evidence from the provincial government of any arrears of corporation taxes. This information cannot be obtained from the registry or land titles office but only from the government concerned.

Creditor's Claims

A claim against land may arise when the vendor is a judgment debtor at the time of the sale—that is, he has been sued successfully by a creditor who has filed its judgment with the sheriff for the county or district. If a claim of this kind is outstanding (unpaid) at the time the land is sold, the judgment creditor may still require the sheriff to **levy execution** against the land—that is, seize and hold a sale of the land in order to recover the amount due under the judgment. The purchaser will then have to pay the debt to save the land. Accordingly, a purchaser should also make a search for executions in the sheriff's office to ensure that there are none before completing the sale. Various other claims against a vendor, such as debts owed to public bodies for fines or taxes, may be registered with the sheriff's office, according to each province's own rules. In order to facilitate a search for these claims, the sheriff's office and the land registry office are often in the same building, or special facilities are provided in the registry office to search the execution records. These records may also be searched electronically.

Tenant in Possession

Another hazard to a purchaser may be created by a tenant in possession of the land. In most jurisdictions, short-term leases—usually for three years or less—need not be registered or even be in writing and are valid against purchasers that buy the interest of the landlord. A purchaser must inspect the property to see whether there are any tenants, and if there are, she should obtain an acknowledgment from them of the type of tenancy they claim to hold.

Title Insurance

We can see that the transfer of an interest in land is a complex transaction requiring careful examination of the registry or land titles records, the municipal and provincial by-laws and regulations, the local sheriff's office records, and an inspection of the land itself. These complicated search requirements, as well as the risk of title fraud in electronic registration, have increased the popularity of **title insurance**. Title insurance allows a potential purchaser or lender to buy insurance covering defects in the title to the real property. Though many variations exist, basic title insurance usually covers:

- title (fee simple estate) in the subject land
- a defect, charge, lien, or other interest (discoverable in the public record)
- lack of access to the property
- costs of defending the title to the property

Additional coverage is available for such things as off-title risks, known defects in title, and survey-related issues. Title insurance takes away the need to prove negligence against a real estate lawyer for a subsequently discovered defect in title. However, it does not eliminate the need for a lawyer during a real estate deal; lawyers play a pivotal role in negotiating coverage, exclusions, and premiums associated with title insurance. In some provinces, lawyers are specifically required to explain and offer title insurance to prospective purchasers.[32]

INTERNATIONAL ISSUE

Title Insurance

Although it is a relatively recent phenomenon in Canada, title insurance has been considered almost essential in the United States for decades. One reason for this is the fact that U.S. lawyers are not required to carry mandatory public liability insurance. Therefore, even proven claims of negligence may go unsatisfied. In addition, state-run land registration systems vary widely across the United States. Most are registry-style systems lacking any certification of title from the government, and some even record interests by name of grantor and grantee rather than property description. Recording by name rather than property description makes it difficult to detect a fraudulent conveyance. The very active U.S. secondary mortgage market has also contributed to the popularity of title insurance. A lender's title insurance policy makes the mortgage more saleable, and, in fact, many lenders make title insurance a condition of granting the mortgage.

Recent criticism of the American $15 billion secondary mortgage industry focuses on the high profit margin and questionable sales tactics of the title insurance industry. In 2003, only 4 percent of the total premiums collected were paid out as compensation.[33] Usually, real estate agents or mortgage brokers select the title insurance company rather than the purchaser and the industry markets to these groups using incentives such as free vacations.[34] Iowa prohibits private-sector title insurance and offers a cheaper state-run program.

QUESTION TO CONSIDER

1. What lessons should Canada learn from the American experience?

Sources: Joyce Dickey Palomar, "Title Insurance Companies' Liability for Failure to Search Title and Disclose Record Title" (1987), 20 *Creighton L. Re.* 455; Deborah J. Cook, "Iowa's Prohibition of Title Insurance—Leadership or Folly" (1983–84), 33 *Drake L. Rev.* 883.

---

32. Law Society of Upper Canada, *Rules of Professional Conduct*, Rule 5.01.

33. Les Christie, "Title Insurance: Getting Ripped Off?" *CNNMoney.com*, January 11, 2006, http://money.cnn.com/2006/01/11/real_estate/title_insurance_exposed/index.htm.

34. *Ibid.*

QUESTIONS FOR REVIEW

1. Define the terms title, real, land, property, and estate.

2. What factors have encouraged the growth of public regulation of land use?

3. Describe the two main classifications of interests in land. Distinguish between freehold and leasehold estates.

4. How does the existence of a life estate make it difficult to sell land?

5. Describe the nature of the interest that a spouse has in the family home. How did this interest evolve?

6. In what ways may title to land be acquired?

7. What are the principal differences between joint tenancy and tenancy in common?

8. Describe the two elements of ownership in a condominium and how they affect responsibility for maintenance.

9. What is the special nature of insurance for a high-rise condominium building?

10. In cooperative housing, who owns the property?

11. What are the reasons for limitation periods generally? How do they apply to land?

12. Distinguish between the circumstances under which an easement may be obtained by prescription and a title may be extinguished by adverse possession.

13. Describe the three typical characteristics of oil, gas, and mineral leases.

14. Distinguish between a restrictive covenant in a grant, a building-scheme covenant, and a zoning by-law.

15. For decades, each winter Timson has openly entered the fields of an uninhabited farm adjoining his home and cross-country skied several times a week. He knows the Abel family that used to farm there, but they have moved to a town 25 kilometres away. The Abels have just sold the farm to Belsen, and he has erected a sign at the gate, "No Trespassing." Does Timson have a right to continue his cross-country skiing?

16. What is expropriation and how does it take place?

17. What is the main difference between the registry system of registration and the land titles system?

18. How is electronic registration connected to the expansion of the land titles system?

19. What must a prospective purchaser of land do to ensure that the vendor has the right to transfer the property clear of any claims? Does the purchase of title insurance change this answer?

20. What is the purpose of a survey?

CASES AND PROBLEMS

1. Rumford College was established in the centre of the city in the late 19th century when the city was still small. It was granted 20 acres at the time—about nine hectares—and occupied two hectares with its buildings and lawns, expanding to about four hectares over the years. By the 1960s, as the city grew, the remaining five hectares became extremely valuable, and Rumford ultimately agreed to sell certain portions for commercial development. It sold one hectare to each of three developers, including a restrictive covenant with each grant limiting the height of any buildings to 20 metres so as to protect the view of Rumford's college towers. Two of the three developers erected buildings complying with the restriction. The third, Townhouse Inc., kept the land vacant.

   Savvy Developers Inc. wished to erect a 25-storey luxury apartment building in the area to a height about five times more than the 20-metre limit. In addition to paying market value to Rumford for one-half hectare of land, it offered to donate $500 000 to the college's endowment fund if it would forgo the restrictive covenant to allow the construction of the apartment building. Rumford agreed and sold the land. When

Townhouse learned about the deal with Savvy, it resold its hectare to Upper Developments Ltd., deliberately omitting the restrictive covenant from the grant.

Upper Developments then sought a declaration from the court that the restrictive covenant no longer applied because of the concession made to Savvy. How do you think this dispute should be resolved by the court?

2. Peter Green owned and operated Green's General Hardware as well as the lands and buildings where he carried on business. His younger brother John worked for him as manager, as did his daughter, Susan. Peter died leaving a will in which he gave the business and real property to John for life, with the remainder to Susan at John's death. John and Susan could not agree on how to run the business. John wanted to push sales and expansion as quickly as possible; Susan feared that such action would make the business unstable—she preferred to build more slowly, consolidating the gains of the business. The dispute became heated, and John fired Susan. Within a few years the business was in serious financial difficulty. John had allowed several buildings, including a warehouse, to fall into disrepair. Susan sought by court action to force John to keep the buildings in good repair. Should she succeed? Why?

John died and left a will giving his whole estate including the business and buildings to his wife. Who is entitled to the business and why?

3. Ferrand owned a summer cottage near Fredericton, New Brunswick. He sold it and delivered a grant to Simpson in exchange for $35 000 cash on June 10. On June 11, Simpson received a telephone call to return home to Newfoundland where her mother was seriously ill. She left without registering her grant to the cottage. When Ferrand learned that Simpson had left the area, he called an acquaintance, Entwistle, and asked him whether he was interested in buying the cottage at a bargain price of $26 000. Entwistle had offered Ferrand that amount several months before and Ferrand had refused. Entwistle eagerly accepted the offer on June 20 and paid Ferrand. On the same day, Entwistle received a grant to the cottage and registered it without knowledge of its prior sale to Simpson. Ferrand then absconded with the money from both sales.

Several weeks later, Simpson returned to find Entwistle occupying the cottage. When Entwistle refused to move, Simpson brought an action to have Entwistle put out and herself declared the owner.

The Registry Act, R.S.N.B. 1973, c. R-6, contains the following provision:

19. All instruments may be registered in the registry office for the county where the lands lie, and if not so registered, shall . . . be deemed fraudulent and void against subsequent purchasers for valuable consideration whose conveyances are previously registered.

Will Simpson succeed in her action? Would the result be different if Entwistle had heard that Simpson had purchased the cottage before he paid Ferrand the $26 000? Give reasons.

4. Don Wellman owned his own home, subject to a mortgage, when he married Victoria Selva. The two lived in the house for 20 years. Since Victoria earned a higher salary than Don, she made most of the payments on the house mortgage and also financed various improvements as well as an addition to the house. They had two children. Don suffered from severe depression, and as he aged he became violent during arguments with Victoria. One day, during a fit of rage, he killed her and was convicted of manslaughter and sentenced to prison.

Her estate sued Don, claiming a transfer of one-half the value of the house for the benefit of her heirs, including the two children. Give your opinion of the arguments that might be made for both sides and whether the action would succeed.

5. For over 30 years Montgomery owned two farms—Green Gables, on which he lived, and Wildwood. The two were separated by a farm owned by Cavendish. Montgomery continually used a road across the Cavendish farm to go to and from Green Gables and Wildwood. The access to the road was through a gate on the boundary of the Cavendish property. During most of these years Montgomery gave Cavendish a

large turkey for New Year's, presumably as a gesture of goodwill and appreciation for the use of the road.

Three years ago Montgomery sold Wildwood to Radoja. Radoja made relatively little use of the road over the Cavendish property (going across twice yearly to visit Montgomery with mortgage payments) until last year, when she also bought Green Gables. The old road then became valuable to Radoja as the most convenient access between her two properties. In the meantime, however, the Cavendish family had extended their lawn across the roadway and Radoja's suddenly increased use of the road led to a dispute about her rights.

Cavendish sought a court injunction to restrain Radoja's use of the alleged right-of-way. Indicate, with reasons, whether the court will grant the injunction.

6. Running southerly from Halifax along the Atlantic is a provincial highway approximately 300 metres from the shoreline, where Essex Oil Ltd. has owned a service station on the east side of the road since 1953. The Essex Oil property extends about 300 metres along the east side of the highway and 100 metres east to a right-of-way owned by the province for a proposed scenic highway that would run closer to the seacoast parallel to the existing highway. The oil company's land was unfenced except along the existing highway, beside the station. On the other side of the provincial right-of-way and running down to the Atlantic shore is the Webster Trailer Court and Campsite, a business that was operating there for some years before Essex Oil opened its station.

The province continually deferred construction of the new road, and the right-of-way, a strip about 50 metres wide, lay vacant. The trailer court obtained a licence from the province to use the right-of-way but made no request of Essex Oil Ltd. to use that portion of its land not occupied for the business of the service station. Beginning in 1954, without any communication with Essex Oil, Webster's employees cut the grass on both the provincial right-of-way and the oil company's land, cleared litter, planted flowers, and painted the fence on the far side of the oil company's land, adjacent to the existing road. The employees converted the whole of this land into a playground for guests, putting up tennis courts and a baseball diamond, and during the winter flooding part of the land for a skating rink.

Finally, in 1973, some 19 years after the trailer court had begun to make use of this land, the province announced that it had abandoned all plans to build a road on the proposed site. Essex Oil Ltd. then decided to dispose of its unused land and wrote to Webster Trailer Court and Campsite, offering to sell the land for $25 000.

Mr. Webster, owner of the trailer court, consulted his solicitor, who checked the title deed and confirmed that the disputed land belonged to Essex Oil Ltd. The solicitor also advised him, however, that if the trailer court were to remain in possession for another two months, it would have been using the land for 20 years and would then, under Nova Scotia law, have obtained title by adverse possession and without any payment to Essex Oil Ltd.

The Webster Trailer Court and Campsite did not reply to Essex Oil's offer and continued to make use of the land for the enjoyment of its guests. Essex Oil Ltd. wrote again in three weeks and received no reply. A week later, the local manager of Essex Oil Ltd. attempted to reach Mr. Webster by telephone. His secretary said he was out of town for another four weeks, but had left word that on his return he would be glad to discuss the offer in the oil company's first letter.

The full 20-year period had elapsed by only two or three days when the management of Essex Oil Ltd. became suspicious of what was going on and immediately had a fence constructed around the unfenced sides of its strip of land, right across a number of tennis courts and through the baseball diamond. It had no sooner done so than it received a letter from the Webster Trailer Court and Campsite solicitor stating that his client had a "possessory title" to the disputed land. Webster Trailer Court and Campsite then brought an action against Essex Oil Ltd. for a court order to the effect that it had acquired title to the land.

Discuss the validity of the plaintiff's case and the nature of the argument, if any, that might be offered by the defendant.

ADDITIONAL RESOURCES FOR CHAPTER 23
ON THE COMPANION WEBSITE *(www.pearsoned.ca/smyth)*

In addition to self-test multiple-choice, true–false, and short essay questions (all with immediate feedback), application exercises, and links to useful web destinations, the Companion Website provides the following resources for Chapter 23:

- **British Columbia:** Adverse Possession and Prescription; Builders' Liens; Condominiums; Conveyance of Land; Expropriation; Fixtures; Fraudulent Transfer of Property; Land Title and Survey Authority; Partition of Property; Power of Attorney; Property Taxes; Riparian Rights; Strata Title; Trespass to Land

- **Alberta:** Builders' Liens; Land Titles System; Spousal Interests in Land (Dower Rights); Title Insurance

- **Manitoba/Saskatchewan:** Condominiums; Land Titles System; Registry System (Manitoba)

- **Ontario:** Adverse Possession; Condominiums; Dower—Family Law Legislation; Electronic Registration; Land Registration Reform; Land Titles; Matrimonial Homes; Registry Systems; Reserve Funds; Restrictive Covenants; Title Insurance

24

Landlord and Tenant

There are many reasons why someone leases real property, whether in the form of vacant land, buildings and surrounding land, or just space within a building. The premises may be used for residential, recreational, and social or business purposes. In this chapter we examine such questions as:

■ What is the nature of the landlord-and-tenant relationship?

■ What classes of tenancies may be created?

■ What are the typical covenants put into leases, and what is their effect?

■ How are tenancies terminated and renewed?

■ What are "fixtures," and why are they important?

■ What are the consequences of a landlord transferring his or her interest?

■ What are "leasebacks," and how are they used?

■ Why are residential tenancies treated in a special way?

THE NATURE OF THE RELATIONSHIP

Definition of a Tenancy

A leasehold interest is created when a landlord (lessor) grants, and a tenant (lessee) accepts, a "term." A **term** is an interest in land for a definite period. The landlord divides the interest in the land between herself and the tenant by giving an interest to the tenant for a limited time and retaining the reversion. At the end of the term, the tenant must give up the land: the right to possession reverts to the landlord. The noun **lease** is used both as a short form for leasehold interest and to refer to the agreement or contract between landlord and tenant creating the leasehold.

As we have seen in the preceding chapter, a leasehold interest is an estate in land.[1] When parties create a leasehold, certain rights and duties automatically accrue to both the landlord and the tenant. But the requirements of land law for creating an estate are strict and do not take into account the intentions of the parties. Even though the parties clearly intend to create a leasehold interest, if they fail to fulfill these requirements, no estate in the land comes into existence, and the usual rights and duties between landlord and tenant do not arise. The consequences may be serious for either party but especially for a would-be tenant:

- he may be evicted by the owner at once
- he has no right himself to evict strangers
- he cannot acquire further interests in land such as easements

For these reasons we emphasize the essentials for the creation of a leasehold. They are, first, that the tenant must obtain the right to exclusive possession, and second, that the tenancy must be for a definite or ascertainable period of time.

It also is important to note that all provinces designate **residential tenancies** as a special class of tenancy in their landlord and tenant legislation. They do so in order to recognize the special importance of basic shelter for individuals who lease apartments and houses as their residence. The major part of the chapter applies to **commercial tenancies**, and its application to residential tenancies will be qualified by reference to the specific statutory provisions that we discuss in the final section of this chapter.

Exclusive Possession

Exclusive possession characterizes the difference between estates in land and lesser interests in land. It distinguishes control over the land from a right merely to use the land in common with others. A person who has a right to use land in common with others may have an easement, as discussed in the preceding chapter, or may be merely a *licensee*. A licensee enters upon land with the consent of the owner, as, for example, when he is allowed to go fishing in a farmer's stream. He is on the land lawfully, not as a trespasser, but he has no interest in the land. He does not have the right to exclude others from the land or to object to the activities of others.

A tenant's right to exclusive possession gives him far greater power than he would have as a contractual licensee. He may keep anyone off the land, and his landlord has no right to evict him from the land until the term ends. A tenant may prevent even the landlord from entering the land unless the lease gives the landlord a right to enter for a specific purpose, such as to view the state of repair of the property and to make repairs. The right to exclusive possession of land gives a tenant the ability to acquire other lesser rights—a tenant may acquire an easement over adjoining land for the duration of his tenancy in the same manner as the holder of a fee simple.

---

1. Estates in time were considered in Chapter 23. Leases of personal property were considered in Chapter 17.

term
an interest in land for a definite period of time

lease
(1) a leasehold interest and (2) the agreement between landlord and tenant creating the leasehold interest

residential tenancies
a lease of premises used as living accommodation

commercial tenancies
a lease of premises used for a business or non-residential purpose

There have been numerous cases about what constitutes exclusive possession. The main problem is whether a person is considered to have exclusive possession if under the terms of the lease others are given limited rights to use or have access over the land. Generally, it is not wise for a business to enter into a lease that grants a right of use to a third person or to the landlord, except (as already noted) for the limited purpose of inspecting the premises and making repairs.

Definite or Ascertainable Period

A lease must begin on a fixed date, and it must end on a fixed or ascertainable date. The final date need not be stated if the period itself is definite: a lease that begins on March 1 of a certain year to run for a week, a month, a year, five years, or 500 years is a valid leasehold interest because the date of expiry can always be worked out accurately. Long leases—for 99 years, or even for 999 years—were fairly common in England[2] but are rarely found in Canada, although terms of 25 to 50 years are not uncommon in the case of large commercial developments (see the discussion of "Leasebacks" later in this chapter).

If the parties attempt to create a term for an uncertain period, the term is void and no leasehold interest comes into existence. A lease "for the duration of the war" or "until the tenant becomes insolvent" is void. However, parties who wish to have such a lease can accomplish their purpose by a comparatively simple change in the wording. The requirement of certainty is satisfied if a lease must end *at the latest* upon a certain date, but may be brought to an end *at an earlier date* upon the happening of a particular event. A lease of Blackacre from *A* to *B* for 10 years that is to be terminated earlier "should *B* become insolvent" is a valid lease.[3]

CLASSES OF TENANCIES

Term Certain

term certain
a tenancy that expires on a specific day

overholding tenant
a tenant who remains on the premises without a new agreement with the landlord after the term of the lease expires

A **term certain** is a tenancy that expires on a specific day, the term ending without any further act by either the landlord or the tenant. A lease of a restaurant at a summer resort "from May 24 to September 15" of a particular year and a long-term lease of a cold-storage plant "from March 1, 1985, to February 28, 2005" are examples of typical commercial leases for a term certain. The tenant is expected to vacate before the end of the last day of the tenancy unless he has made new arrangements with the landlord. If he stays on without making any arrangements, he becomes an **overholding tenant** and may be evicted by the landlord. If, however, the landlord accepts further rent without protesting, a new tenancy may be created, as explained below.

Periodic Tenancy

periodic tenancy
a leasehold interest that renews itself automatically on the last day of the term for a further term of the same duration

A **periodic tenancy** is a leasehold interest that renews itself automatically on the last day of the term for a further term of the same duration, unless either the landlord or the tenant serves notice to bring the tenancy to an end. A periodic tenancy may be created by a formal agreement, but in Canada it arises more often in an informal way when a tenant moves into possession and pays an agreed rent to the landlord at regular intervals as agreed between them, either in writing or orally. If, for example, a business pays rent on the first day of each month, the tenancy renews itself for another month without further agreement between the parties. A periodic tenancy also comes into existence when a tenant remains in possession after the tenancy for a term certain has expired, and

---

2. For historical reasons. Such a lease is virtually equivalent to a fee simple.

3. Proposed amendments to bankruptcy law would void a termination clause triggered by insolvency, see the discussion in Chapter 31.

pays further rent to the landlord. The most common type of periodic tenancies are weekly, monthly, and yearly. The yearly tenancy is often called a **tenancy from year to year**.

We note here the contrast between a term certain and a periodic tenancy: a term certain ends automatically unless the parties make an arrangement to continue it; a periodic tenancy renews automatically unless either of the parties serves notice to end it. We shall discuss the requirements of notice later in this chapter, under "Termination and Renewal of a Tenancy."

tenancy from year to year
a periodic tenancy that renews itself yearly

Tenancy at Will

A tenancy at will is not a true leasehold interest because it does not last for a definite period, nor does the tenant have any right to exclude the landlord and remain on the premises. The tenant is there merely at the landlord's will, and the landlord may demand possession at any time without notice. The tenant does, however, have a reasonable time to gather up possessions and leave.

On the other hand, a tenant at will is under no obligation to remain in possession and pay rent—he may vacate possession at any time without notice. Such a tenancy may exist when the owner of real property allows a prospective purchaser to occupy the premises pending the conveyance of the title to the purchaser, or when a landlord permits a tenant to remain on a day-to-day basis pending the wrecking of the building to make way for new construction. A tenancy at will may be gratuitous, or the landlord may exact a payment without turning the arrangement into a leasehold.

Tenancy at Sufferance

A tenancy at sufferance is not a true tenancy either. The typical example is that of an overholding tenant who entered into possession rightfully under a lease but now stays in possession wrongfully after the term has expired. Since he came into possession lawfully, he is not treated as a *trespasser* unless the landlord orders him to leave and he refuses. (Ordinarily, a **trespasser** is one who enters without consent or lawful right on the lands of another or who, having entered lawfully, refuses to leave when ordered to do so by the owner.) We should contrast the position of a tenant at sufferance with that of a tenant at will. Although a tenant at will has no estate in the land and can be put out by the landlord, he is nonetheless there lawfully, by agreement. A tenant at sufferance has no agreement with the landlord: his occupation of the land is merely tolerated by the landlord until the landlord acts to put the occupier out.

trespasser
one who enters without consent or lawful right on the lands of another or who, having entered lawfully, refuses to leave when ordered to do so by the owner

COVENANTS

To Pay Rent

The **covenant** to pay rent is easily understood when we recall the nature of a leasehold interest. A leasehold is a specific period "carved out" of the fee simple and is usually sold for an agreed sum. Often leases recognize this fact by stating the total rent to be paid during the whole of the lease, and then describing how this sum is to be paid. For example, the tenant may promise to pay the sum of $120 000 to lease a suite of offices for five years in 60 monthly instalments of $2000 per month.

The promise to pay rent is unconditional and must be performed despite misconduct by the landlord. Only an act of the landlord that amounts to an eviction of the tenant discharges the obligation of the tenant to pay rent.[4] If the leased premises are destroyed, in the absence of a specific term in the lease dealing with the problem, the tenant is still liable for the rent. He has purchased a leasehold interest consisting of a certain geographically defined area, and must pay for it whether or not the building and amenities continue to exist for the full term. In certain circumstances the

covenant
a term or promise contained in a lease

---

4. *Cross* v. *Piggott* [1922] 2 W.W.R. 662.

doctrine of frustration applies to commercial leaseholds.[5] One example involves leasehold interests above the ground floor in a multi-storey building. If a 10-storey building burns down, it seems that the landlord cannot insist that a firm on the ninth floor continue to be liable for rent.[6]

When a tenant leases only a portion of the landlord's building, the landlord usually retains control over heating, repairs, and maintenance. In these circumstances it is common to state in the lease that liability to pay rent shall be suspended if the leased premises are substantially destroyed by fire or other cause, and not by the tenant's own negligence. But such a provision is not automatically implied, and unless it is expressly stated in the lease, the tenant remains liable for the rent—subject to our discussion above concerning leases of premises above the ground floor.

A tenant's covenant to pay rent is independent of any express promise by the landlord to make repairs to the property, and the tenant is not excused from paying rent on the grounds that the landlord has not performed her part of the bargain. A tenant is not, however, liable for further rent when the acts of the landlord amount to an eviction, as we shall see when we consider the covenants of "repairs" and "quiet enjoyment" below.

The terms of the covenant to pay rent are binding on both parties. During the term, the landlord cannot increase the rent unless express provision has been made, as in the case where the parties agree that the landlord may increase the rent by an amount equal to any increase in property taxes. If the landlord wishes to increase the rent, she cannot do so until the term expires. She may, of course, bargain for an increase in any subsequent lease.

Assignment and Subletting

Freedom to Assign

A tenant may wish to assign the balance of the term of a tenancy before it expires. For example, the tenant's business may have become so successful that he requires larger premises, or he may have received an offer to sell the business as a going concern provided he assigns the balance of the lease to the purchaser so that the business may continue at the same location. A tenant, as owner of a leasehold interest, has (subject to the terms of the lease) the right to assign it. A tenant does not, however, terminate his contractual obligations to the landlord by assigning: the landlord may still hold him accountable for performance of those obligations if, after the assignment, the assignee does not perform them. For this reason a tenant should make it a term of the assignment of the tenancy that the assignee shall carry out all the tenant's covenants in the lease and indemnify him against any loss caused by the assignee's default.

The Landlord's Consent to Assignment

When leasing premises, a landlord is often concerned with the reputation of the tenant as well as with his ability to pay the rent. It may be a matter of prestige, for instance, to have the head office of a large corporation as a tenant in a new building in order to encourage other prospective tenants of good quality. A landlord may also be concerned about the type of business to be carried on for any of several reasons. Here are a few examples:

- the prestige or reputation of the building
- the risk of unprofitable competition with the business of other tenants or with that of the landlord herself—a problem often arising in large business blocks and shopping centres
- noise, fumes, or traffic interfering with other tenants
- the wear and tear that certain businesses may inflict upon the premises

5. In England, the House of Lords has held that the doctrine of frustration may, in some circumstances, apply to commercial tenancies: *National Carriers* v. *Panalpina (Northern) Ltd.* [1981] A.C. 675.
6. C. Bentley, J. McNair, and M. Butkus, eds., *Williams and Rhodes: Canadian Law of Landlord and Tenant*, 6th ed. (Toronto: Carswell, 1988), at p. 6–41.

For these reasons, a landlord almost invariably requires a tenant to agree that he will not assign the lease without first obtaining consent (permission) from the landlord.

On the other hand, if a landlord were free to withhold consent for any reason, the tenant might be placed in a difficult position. A landlord could arbitrarily refuse to give consent to an assignment that would in no way be harmful to her. Accordingly, tenants often require that the words "but such consent shall not be unreasonably withheld" be added to the covenant. In the provinces of Manitoba, New Brunswick, Prince Edward Island, and Saskatchewan, these words are implied by statute as part of the covenant unless they are expressly excluded.[7] It is unusual for them to be expressly excluded, and a tenant should be cautious about entering into a lease in the provinces mentioned above when the landlord excludes the implied words—or in the other provinces when the landlord refuses to permit the addition of those words to the covenant requiring her consent to an assignment.

Subletting

A sublease differs from an assignment. An assignment is a transfer of the *whole* of the remainder of the tenant's term to the assignee; so long as the assignee performs all its covenants, the tenant has no further right or interest in the lease. A sublease is a transfer of *part only* of the tenant's term to the subtenant. If the term given to the subtenant expires just one day before the expiration of the main lease (leaving the tenant with a reversion of one day), the tenancy of the subtenant is created not by an assignment but by a sublease. The tenant becomes the landlord of the subtenant. The sublease may differ materially from the main lease in the rent payable, in any of the covenants given by either party, and in the extent of the premises sublet (the subtenant may hold only a portion of the premises leased to the tenant). In a sublease, just as in an assignment, the tenant remains liable to the landlord to perform all the covenants under the main lease. The discussion concerning the requirement of consent of the landlord for assignment applies equally to subleases—the covenant usually refers to subletting as well as to assignment.[8]

Restriction on Use of Premises

We have noted that a landlord is usually concerned with both the reputation of a tenant and the proposed use of the premises. Once a landlord has accepted a tenant, she can do little to control how the tenant carries on its business. However, by initially requiring a covenant in the lease that restricts the use of the premises to particular activities, the landlord acquires important control. Such covenants are also enforceable against the tenant's assignees and subtenants.

A tenant may, in turn, insist that the landlord give a covenant not to rent adjoining premises to a competing business, known as an **exclusive use clause**. If, however, the landlord should commit a breach by renting adjoining premises to an innocent third party unaware of the covenant, the tenant would have no rights against the other tenant. His remedy would be limited to an action for damages against the landlord.

exclusive use clause
a landlord's promise not to rent adjoining premises to any other entity in the same or competing business as the tenant

Even in the absence of an express covenant, there is an implied covenant by the tenant to treat the premises in a "tenant-like manner"—that is, use them only for those purposes for which they are reasonably intended. A tenant could not turn a cold-storage plant into a glue factory, or a restaurant into a hotel. In other words, a tenant may be prevented from carrying on activities for which the premises were not intended and that would cause excessive wear and tear.

---

7. The right to assign a leasehold interest, when it is subject to consent that may not be unreasonably withheld, is now considered to be a major term of the lease. If a landlord unreasonably withholds consent, her doing so will be a major breach and the tenant may end the relationship by cancelling the lease without further liability: *Lehndorff Canadian Pension Properties Ltd.* v. *Davis Management Ltd.* (1989), 59 D.L.R. (4th) 1 (B.C.C.A.). However, justifiable reasons for withholding consent may include economic ones, such as a prospective assignee (or a subtenant) competing with the landlord's interests. See *Windsor Apothecary Ltd.* v. *Wolfe Group Holdings Ltd.* (1996), 148 Sask. R. 234.

8. For an example of unreasonably refusing consent, see *Zurich Canadian Holdings* v. *Questar Exploration Inc.* (1999), 171 D.L.R. (4th) 457 (Alta. C.A.).

Fitness for Occupancy

At common law, there is generally no covenant of fitness implied by a lessor in granting a lease. The lessee takes the premises as he finds them and at his own risk. Unless a tenant obtained an express covenant in the lease concerning the fitness of the premises for a particular use, or unless the landlord made a misrepresentation, the tenant is responsible for his own investigation of the premises.[9] However, courts have suggested that the course of dealing between the parties may create an implied covenant that the premises will be fit for the lessee's purposes if disclosed to the lessor, much as the implied condition of fitness arises in a sale of goods.[10]

A landlord is not liable to a tenant or the tenant's customers, family, or guests for injuries caused by the unsafe condition of the premises, unless the landlord actually created the danger. However, where the landlord covenants to maintain and repair the premises, and fails to carry out that responsibility, occupiers' liability legislation generally equates her duty to visitors to that of an occupier.[11] In all other circumstances the tenant, as the party in exclusive possession of the property, bears any responsibility that arises from injuries caused to persons on the property.

Repairs

The General Rule

As a general rule, a landlord is not liable to make repairs to the property unless she expressly covenants to do so. Quite apart from law, of course, a landlord has an economic incentive to maintain her property in good condition.

A landlord may, however, be liable to repair structural defects that develop, particularly if failure to repair would amount to an indirect eviction of the tenant and consequently a breach of the covenant for quiet enjoyment, as we shall see in the next subsection. For example, if a landlord fails to repair a leak in the roof of an office building and it results in the soaking and eventual crumbling of the ceiling and walls in an office suite, the tenant has an action against the landlord even where no covenant to repair has been given. In addition, when rented premises are in a large building, the landlord is responsible to the tenants for the maintenance of corridors, stairways, and elevators.

waste
damage to the premises that reduces its value

The general rule is that a tenant is not liable to make repairs to the premises unless he has expressly covenanted to do so. The rule is subject to two exceptions. First, as we have already noted, the tenant must not make such use of the premises as will cause excessive wear. Second, he is liable for committing **waste**. Waste may be either *voluntary*—as when a tenant pulls down part of a building or otherwise damages it, or makes alterations that reduce its value. Alternatively it may be *permissive*, that is negligent, as when a tenant fails to repair a leak in the roof even though he is aware that more serious harm will result if he does not correct the problem. The law of waste is of little importance today, since parties to a lease generally make an express agreement about which of them shall keep the leased premises in good repair.

Usual Covenants in the Lease of a Building

When a tenant leases an entire building or property, the landlord frequently obtains a covenant from him to keep the property in good repair, reasonable wear and tear excepted. Accordingly,

---

9. Historically, residential tenancies came with an implied covenant relating to fitness for habitation. This has been incorporated into residential tenancy legislation.

10. *Telex (A/Asia) Proprietary Ltd.* v. *Thomas Cook & Sons (A/Asia) Proprietary Ltd.*, [1970] 2 N.S.W.R. 257 (C.A.).

11. Occupiers' Liability Act, R.S.B.C. 1996, c. 337, s. 6; C.C.S.M., c. O8, s. 6; S.N.S. 1996, c. 27, s. 9; R.S.O. 1990, c. O.2, s. 8. See the discussion of occupiers' liability in Chapter 3.

the tenant agrees to make such repairs as are necessary to keep the property in the same condition as when the lease began, except for normal depreciation. The tenant is not liable for damage caused by faulty construction or for deterioration in the property due to the normal forces of nature. Unless the lease exempts the tenant, however, the tenant's covenant to repair includes liability to make good any loss by fire or storm. Often a tenant exempts himself from liability in this respect by qualifying the covenant to repair with the words "loss by fire, lightning, and tempest excepted."

When a tenant leases only part of a building, the landlord usually undertakes to provide various services such as heat, water, and elevator service, and also to keep the premises in good repair. We should note that there is an important difference between a covenant to repair given by the tenant and one given by the landlord. A tenant is in possession of his premises and should be aware of their falling into disrepair—he is in breach of the covenant the moment he permits the premises to fall into disrepair, and it is not up to the landlord to remind the tenant.

In contrast, the landlord, not being in possession of the tenant's premises, is not presumed to be aware of any state of disrepair in them, and her duty to repair does not arise until the tenant gives her notice. A landlord who undertakes to repair the premises often reserves the right to go on the premises at reasonable hours and inspect and view the state of repair. Reserving this right, however, does not place any duty upon her to make inspections or to repair until she has received notice from the tenant.

Quiet Enjoyment

The whole purpose of a lease is to give the tenant possession and the right to "enjoy" the premises during the term of the lease. Accordingly, the landlord covenants to give **quiet enjoyment** either impliedly, simply by granting the lease, or expressly, in a specific covenant for that purpose. The covenant has two aspects. First, it is an assurance that the landlord has good title to the property at the time she gives the lease; second, it is a covenant that subsequent to the making of the lease, the landlord will not herself interfere, or permit anyone obtaining an interest in land from her to interfere with the tenant's enjoyment of the premises.

covenant of quiet enjoyment
a landlord's promise to do nothing to interfere with the tenant's possession and use of the premises

---

ILLUSTRATION 24.1

(a) Greer owns a large tract of land including some warehouses. A mining company survey shows valuable ore deposits. She grants the company a long-term mining lease, and the company begins extensive mining excavations. Subsequently, she leases the warehouses to Atkins Inc., which intends to use them to store heavy machinery. Atkins discovers that the mining operations have undermined the foundations of the warehouses, making them unsafe for use. Since the mining company is conducting its activities properly, and Greer cannot prevent its operations because she had validly granted it a mining lease before granting Atkins Inc. its lease, Greer's title was defective. Therefore, she committed a breach of her covenant to Atkins Inc. for quiet enjoyment.

(b) Mendoza leases a suite of offices to McAdam and McCollum, a firm of practising accountants. Subsequently, he leases the area on the floor directly above to a machine shop. The machine-shop operations create noise and heavy vibrations, making it impossible for the accountants to carry on their practice. Mendoza is in breach of his covenant.

Breach of the covenant of quiet enjoyment no longer requires physical interference with the enjoyment of the premises. Substantial noise or vibration that interferes with the comfort or convenience of a lessee will be recognized as a breach of the covenant of quiet enjoyment. Accordingly, a court may reduce the rent of the tenant during the period of interference.[12]

Insurance

In the absence of an express provision, neither landlord nor tenant is under a duty to insure the premises for the benefit of the other. In most cases, of course, the landlord insures the premises to protect her own investment. If the leased property consists of an entire building or a group of buildings under the complete control of one tenant, especially if the lease is for a long term, the rent may impose full responsibility for the premises including obtaining insurance on the tenant.

The complexity of liability and insurance problems increases when there is a large number of business tenants, each with its own employees, as in a large office building or a shopping mall. Who is liable for the loss if an employee should negligently cause a fire that substantially destroys a mall? Providing insurance protection and allocating risk through the use of exemption clauses requires great expertise.[13]

The question of insurance is closely tied to the problem of what should happen to the tenancy in case of severe damage to the premises by fire, flood, or storm. Failure to make proper provision can lead to great hardship, particularly for the tenant. A lease stating that if the premises are substantially destroyed, the liability to pay rent is suspended until the building is repaired may not be of much benefit to the tenant; such a clause may place the tenant at the mercy of the landlord. While the landlord decides what to do, the tenant, although not paying rent, is temporarily out of business. If he leases premises elsewhere, he may find that when the building is repaired he is liable to pay rent for both locations. A lease should state that the repairs must be made within a certain time and that if they are not made within that time, the tenant then has the option of terminating the lease rather than waiting until the premises are restored. Another possibility is to give the tenant the right to make the repairs himself and to deduct the costs from future rent.

Provision of Services and Payment of Taxes

Once more, a distinction must be made between tenancies for a whole building and those for a portion of a building. When a tenancy is for a portion of a building only and the landlord retains control over the building as a whole, it is usual for the landlord to covenant to provide heat, water, electricity, and occasionally even telephone service. When the tenancy is for the whole of the building, it is usual for the tenant to provide all these things himself.

Generally, property taxes are paid by the landlord when the tenant leases only a portion of the building. If the lease is of the whole of the building, the taxes may be paid by either party. As long as the agreement is clear, it is not important who pays. If it is the landlord, the rent will be that much higher; if the tenant, then it is that much lower. In the absence of an agreement on the matter, it is the landlord's duty to pay the taxes. Sometimes the cost of these items is passed on to the tenant in the form of **additional rent**. Some leases include a term that each tenant must pay their proportionate share of maintenance expenses, utilities, and taxes.

additional rent
a tenant's proportionate share of maintenance costs, utilities, and taxes

12. For a full review of the law in this area, see *Caldwell* v. *Valiant Property Management* (1997), 145 D.L.R. (4th) 559. A tenant's right to quiet enjoyment extends to non-interference with the guests whom she might invite to visit her: *Cunningham* v. *Whitby Christian Non-Profit Housing Corp.* (1997), 33 O.R. (3d) 171.

13. See *Greenwood Shopping Plaza Ltd.* v. *Beattie*, [1980] 2 S.C.R. 228, where employees were held personally liable and could not take advantage of an exemption clause as third parties. The subsequent Supreme Court decision in *London Drugs* v. *Kuehne & Nagel International Ltd.* (1992), 97 D.L.R. (4th) 261, appears to overturn, or at least limit, the restrictive view taken in the Greenwood case. See also *Laing Property Corp.* v. *All Seasons Display Inc.* (1998), 53 B.C.L.R. (3d) 142, affirmed by the B.C. Court of Appeal, (2000) 6 B.L.R. (3d) 206.

> **CHECKLIST** | Covenants in a Lease

This is *not* a complete list of covenants; there may be other important ones depending upon the circumstances of the lease. In every lease, however, covenants that should be checked carefully by both parties are those concerning

- payment of rent
- restrictions on assigning or subletting the premises
- restrictions on the use of the premises
- fitness for occupancy
- responsibility for repairs
- quiet enjoyment of the premises
- responsibility for insurance
- responsibility for provision of services such as access (for example, elevators), heating, electricity, etc.
- responsibility for payment of property taxes

REMEDIES OF THE LANDLORD

Damages and Recovery of Rent

A landlord may sue for damages caused by a tenant's breach of any covenant other than the covenant to pay rent. The right to recover rent requires further discussion. Suppose without excuse a tenant abandons the premises and pays no further rent. According to long-established rules concerning interests in land, the landlord is then in a predicament. On the one hand, by leaving the premises vacant and insisting on her rights under the lease, she can claim the entire rent due under it. But the tenant may be unable to pay the full amount due. (In land law, apart from any statutory provisions to the contrary, there is no duty to mitigate damages as there is in contract law.) On the other hand, the landlord may occupy the premises or lease them to another tenant at a lower rent in order to reduce her loss, but she will then be presumed to have accepted the **surrender** by the tenant, freeing the tenant from further obligations to pay rent. Only existing arrears will be recoverable.

surrender
abandonment of the premises by the tenant during the term of the lease

As already noted, a lease creates an interest in land *and* a contract between the parties. So the courts looked to the principles of contract law for a solution to the landlord's dilemma. If a landlord wishes both to resume possession and to continue to hold the tenant liable for rent, she must inform the tenant that she regards him to be in breach and that she will hold him responsible for any loss during the remainder of the tenancy even if she finds a new tenant at a lower rent. A landlord may now mitigate her losses without losing her rights against the defaulting tenant. But if the landlord chooses not to mitigate by renting the premises, it is unclear whether the tenant still remains liable for the full rent.

With respect only to *residential* tenancies, the duty to mitigate is clearer. Several provinces have amended their landlord and tenant laws as follows:

> A landlord or tenant who claims compensation for damage or loss that results from the other's non-compliance with this Act, the regulations or their tenancy agreement must do whatever is reasonable to minimize the damage or loss.[14]

14. Residential Tenancy Act, S.B.C. 2002, c. 78, s. 7(1). The wording is different in other acts but the effect is similar; see Residential Tenancies Act, C.C.S.M. c.L. 70, s. 55(2); Residential Tenancies Act 2006, S.O. 2006, c. 17, s. 16.

Does this provision lead to the implication that no similar rule exists for commercial tenancies? In 1971, the Supreme Court of Canada affirmed the rule that a landlord has no duty to mitigate if she chooses not to do so.[15] However, if the landlord does terminate the lease and seeks damages, she must mitigate her damage.[16] The law is complicated in this area and a landlord should obtain a legal opinion before acting to terminate the tenancy.[17]

Under the Bankruptcy and Insolvency Act, a landlord has priority over other creditors in the event of the tenant's bankruptcy to the amount of three months' rent in arrears.[18] For rents due in excess of this sum, she ranks only as a general creditor. The purpose of the three months' preference is to encourage landlords to be a little more patient with a defaulting commercial tenant. Inability to pay rent may be only temporary, but eviction will close the business down, probably causing greater hardship to both the tenant and other creditors of the tenant. Provincial landlord and tenant acts recognize the right of a trustee in bankruptcy to repudiate an outstanding lease without further liability[19] or, with proper notice, to continue to use the premises for so long as may serve the purpose of liquidating the tenant's assets and to pay rent at the rate specified in the lease.[20]

Eviction

right of re-entry
a landlord's remedy of evicting the tenant for failure to pay rent or breach of another major covenant

This remedy is sometimes called the landlord's **right of re-entry**. The right of re-entry for failure to pay rent is a term implied by statute if not expressly included in the lease. The period for which rent must be in arrears before a landlord is entitled to re-enter and evict the tenant varies considerably from province to province and is longer in the case of residential tenancies. Before evicting a tenant in default, the landlord must follow the procedure laid down in the legislation of the province.

Leases often provide that the landlord may re-enter and evict the tenant for breach of any of the other covenants in the lease. Since eviction amounts to a *forfeiture*—that is, to the penalty of forfeiting the remainder of term to the landlord, the court is very reluctant to permit eviction for breach of any covenant other than one relating to payment of rent, use of the property, or assignment of the lease. The court grants a tenant relief against forfeitures either under the general principles of equity or under various statutory reliefs found in provincial legislation.[21] Generally speaking, so long as the tenant subsequently makes good the breach, the court will restrain the landlord from evicting him and will declare the lease to be valid under its original terms.

Distress

distress
the right of the landlord to seize assets of the tenant found on the premises and sell them to realize arrears of rent

The landlord has a power of **distress**, or the right to *distrain* for rent—that is, she may seize assets of the tenant found on the premises and sell them to recover arrears of rent. Usually, the landlord authorizes a bailiff to distrain on the property of the tenant. The right to distrain does not arise until

---

15. *Highway Properties Ltd.* v. *Kelly, Douglas & Co. Ltd.* (1971), 17 D.L.R. (3d) 710; *607190 Ontario Inc.* v. *First Consolidated Holdings Corp.* (1992), 26 R.P.R. 298 (Ont. Div. Ct.). See also Jeffrey W. Lem, "The Landlord's Duty to Mitigate upon a Tenant's Repudiation of a Commercial Lease: A Commentary on *607190 Ontario Limited* v. *First Consolidated Holdings Corp.*," 30 R.P.R. (2d) 33 (1993).

16. B.G. Preeco 3 Ltd. v. Universal Exploration, [1987] 6 W.W.R. 127.

17. See, for example, *Smith* v. *Busler*, [1988] B.C.J. No. 2739 (S.C.); *Globe Convestra Ltd.* v. *Vucetic* (1990), 15 R.P.R. (2d) 220 (Ont. Gen. Div.). See also *Transco Mills Ltd.* v. *Percan Enterprises Ltd.* (1993), 83 B.C.L.R. (2d) 254 (C.A.); *Jade Agencies Ltd.* v. *Meadow's Management Ltd.*, [1999] B.C.J. No. 214.

18. R.S.C. 1985, c. B-3, s. 136(1)(f), as amended by S.C. 1992, c. 27. In the absence of bankruptcy proceedings, a landlord's priority under provincial legislation is usually greater than three months.

19. Repudiation does not terminate the lease. It terminates the liability of the lessee, but not of any guarantor: *KKBL No.297 Ventures Ltd.* v. *IKON Office Solutions Inc.* (2004), 243 D.L.R. (4th) 602. Where a lease has been assigned, repudiation by the assignee's trustee does not terminate the liability of the original lessee: *Crystalline Investments Ltd.* v. *Domgroup Ltd.* (2004), 234 D.L.R. (4th) 513.

20. See, for example: Commercial Tenancy Act, R.S.B.C. 1996, c. 57, s. 29; Commercial Tenancies Act, R.S.O. 1990, c. L.7, ss. 38(2) and 39(1); Landlord and Tenant Act, R.S.M. 1987, c. L-70, ss. 46(2) and 47(1).

21. Courts of Justice Act, R.S.O. 1990, c. C.43, s. 98; Law and Equity Act, R.S.B.C. 1996, c. 224, s. 24.

the day after the rent is due and a demand for payment has been made. A landlord cannot prevent the tenant from removing goods from the premises even as late as the day the rent is due. She may, however, object if the tenant is clearly removing the goods in order to avoid the landlord's power of distress. If the tenant removes the goods in spite of the landlord's objection or later removes them fraudulently to prevent the landlord from asserting her rights after the right has arisen, the landlord may follow the goods and have them seized in another location, provided they have not been sold in the meantime to an innocent purchaser.[22] The time limit within which a landlord may seize goods in this fashion varies from province to province.

A landlord is not permitted to exercise the right of eviction and simultaneously or subsequently exercise a right of distress. The right to distrain is limited to situations where the relationship of landlord and tenant still exists.[23]

Certain personal property is exempt from seizure—necessary household furniture, a limited supply of food and fuel, and mechanic's tools. If the landlord by mistake seizes the goods of third parties such as customers or consignors, they must be released on proof of ownership. The landlord may also seize equipment or appliances purchased on the instalment plan and not fully paid for, but before selling them she must first pay the balance owing to the seller.[24] A commercial lease may contain a term by which the tenant "contracts out" of its right to exemptions should the landlord distrain for rent.[25]

Injunction

If a tenant proposes or has begun to use the premises in a manner that would be in breach of a covenant restricting use, the landlord may obtain an injunction ordering the tenant to cease the prohibited use. An injunction may be obtained against certain types of use even when they are not expressly prohibited under the terms of the lease if they are inconsistent with the general design and ordinary use to which the property would be put. For example, a landlord could obtain an injunction to prevent a house ordinarily used as residential property from being turned into a medical clinic.[26]

Generally speaking, whenever a landlord is entitled to obtain an injunction, she also has the right to re-enter the property and evict the tenant. She will make her choice based on the circumstances, and in particular, on whether the lease is an otherwise desirable one from her point of view.

REMEDIES OF THE TENANT

Damages

A tenant may recover damages from the landlord arising from breach by the landlord of any of her covenants. For instance, a landlord, believing the tenant has committed a breach, may wrongfully infringe the tenant's rights; she may evict the tenant mistakenly believing that the tenant was in arrears of rent and had been served with notice. The wrongful eviction by the landlord is a breach of the covenant for quiet enjoyment. Similarly, if a landlord distrains upon more goods than were reasonably necessary to satisfy a claim for arrears of rent, the tenant may recover damages. If the

22. See *Albo* v. *Concorde Group Corp.* (2004), 235 D.L.R. (4th) 465, where the purchaser was a party to the fraud.

23. *Mundell* v. *796586 Ontario Ltd.* (1996), 3 R.P.R. (3d) 277.

24. The priority of a landlord may be superior to that of a chattel mortgagee—that is, of a different type of secured creditor. Chattel mortgages are discussed in Chapter 30, under the heading "Methods of Securing Credit."

25. We shall see in our discussion below that many of the provinces have now abolished the remedy of distress for residential (though not for commercial) tenancies.

26. *McCuaig* v. *Lalonde* (1911), 23 O.L.R. 312.

landlord or her bailiff, in attempting to distrain upon the goods of the tenant, enters the premises illegally, that is, by use of force, she will be liable for damages for trespass. A tenant is entitled to prevent an exercise of the power of distress by keeping the premises continually locked, but in these circumstances the threat of distress can be an ongoing harassment to the tenant.

If a landlord has expressly covenanted to keep the premises in good repair or to rebuild them if they are destroyed, her failure to do so will be a breach not only of the covenant to repair but also of the covenant for quiet enjoyment.

Injunction

A tenant may also obtain an injunction to restrain a landlord from a continuing breach of the covenant of quiet enjoyment. A court will grant an injunction against a landlord for interfering with quiet enjoyment caused by a continuing nuisance, such as vibrations, noise, or fumes escaping from the landlord's premises. The court will not grant an injunction, however, where it would be futile to do so—for example, where vibration caused by the landlord has so damaged the structure that it has been condemned as unsafe for occupation, destroying its usefulness to the tenant. The tenant's remedy is to vacate the premises and seek damages.

We have already noted that an important covenant often given by a landlord to a retail tenant is a promise not to lease premises in the same building or shopping centre to a competing business. When a breach occurs, an injunction restraining the second tenant from carrying on the competing business will be granted only if the second tenant was aware of the covenant.

Termination of the Lease

When a landlord's breach of the covenant of quiet enjoyment has made the premises unfit for the tenant's normal use and occupation, the tenant, in addition to any other remedy, may terminate the lease and vacate the premises. Upon vacating, the tenant ends any further liability to the landlord. The landlord's breach must make the entire premises unfit for the tenant's use—amounting to a total eviction—before the tenant has this option.

If the landlord's interference is only with part of the premises, or is only a nuisance or inconvenience rather than amounting to a total eviction, the tenant remains bound to pay the rent and cannot terminate the lease. His remedies are then an action for damages for the injury suffered and an injunction to restrain further breach.

TERMINATION AND RENEWAL OF A TENANCY

Surrender

As we noted under "Classes of Tenancies" earlier, a commercial tenancy for a term certain expires automatically without notice. Although not required by law, a landlord often delivers a reminder to the tenant that the lease is about to expire and that he must vacate on the date of expiry. Upon vacating the premises, the tenant surrenders them to the landlord.

A surrender may also take place during the term of a tenancy by express agreement between landlord and tenant, as when a tenant no longer desires to keep the premises and pays the landlord a sum of money to release him from obligations for the balance of the term. A landlord may also bargain for the tenant's surrender of the remainder of the term when she needs vacant possession in order to sell the property or wishes to make substantial alterations or to demolish the building.

Suppose a tenant abandons the premises without making an agreement to surrender to the landlord. As we have seen, a landlord may be presumed to have treated an abandonment as a surrender of the premises when she re-lets to another tenant or takes possession of the premises herself to make use of them for her own purposes. Often it may be difficult to decide from the circumstances whether the landlord has accepted an abandonment and so released the tenant from further obligation to pay rent. Since abandonment is usually committed by an insolvent tenant, the landlord's rights against the tenant may have little practical value.

Forfeiture

In our discussion of a landlord's remedies, we noted that breach of certain covenants by a tenant (such as failure to pay rent) entitles the landlord to evict the tenant and impose a forfeiture of the lease. Once the forfeiture takes place, the relationship of landlord and tenant is terminated. The tenant has no further obligations under the lease, although he may be liable because of his breach before forfeiture for damages suffered by the landlord. Similarly, if a landlord has attempted to impose forfeiture by improperly evicting her tenant—entitling the tenant to consider his obligations under the lease at an end—the relationship of landlord and tenant is terminated, but the tenant may still recover damages for the landlord's breach of covenants.

Termination by Notice to Quit

Periodic Tenancies

A periodic tenancy renews itself automatically unless either the landlord or the tenant serves **notice to quit** on the other party—that is, serves notice of an intention to bring the tenancy to an end. Notice to quit served by a tenant is sometimes called notice of intention to vacate. In weekly, monthly, or quarterly tenancies, the length of notice required to bring the tenancy to an end is *one clear period of tenancy*. In other words, one party must give the other notice *on or before the last day of one tenancy period* for the tenancy to come to an end *on the last day of the next period*.

notice to quit
notice of an intention to bring the tenancy to an end

ILLUSTRATION 24.2

West Side Corp. rents a small warehouse from Bernstein on a monthly basis, commencing March 1, at a rent of $1250 per month. The following September, West Side buys a warehouse building with possession available on November 1. West Side must serve Bernstein with notice to quit on or before September 30 if it wishes to terminate the tenancy on October 31. October is then a clear month. If, however, it does not serve notice until after September 30—say, on October 3—October is no longer a clear month, and West Side Corp. is not able to terminate the tenancy until November 30. In these circumstances, November will be the clear month.

The common law rule that six clear months' notice is necessary to terminate a yearly tenancy at the end of the first year or any succeeding year of the tenancy applies to commercial leases in all provinces except New Brunswick, Nova Scotia, Quebec, and Prince Edward Island. In these provinces only three clear months' notice is required.

ILLUSTRATION 24.3

Bok leases the Greenbrier summer hotel in Alberta from O'Brien at a yearly rental of $30 000, commencing April 1, 1997. The yearly tenancy will renew itself automatically each April 1 unless either party gives six clear months' notice before April 1—that is, on or before September 30 of the preceding year. If Bok wishes to vacate the property by March 31, 2004, he must serve notice on or before September 30, 2003. If he serves notice on October 1, 2003, it is too late; the tenancy will automatically renew itself on April 1, 2004, and continue to March 31, 2005. Thus, the maximum time that may elapse between giving notice and terminating the tenancy may be 18 months less a day, that is, from October 1, 2003, to March 31, 2005.

Tenant Remaining in Possession After the Expiration of a Term Certain

We have already noted that if a tenant remains in possession after the expiration of a term certain, he becomes a tenant at sufferance and may be evicted by the landlord at any time on demand. What happens, however, if the landlord accepts further rent from the tenant? A periodic tenancy then arises on all the terms of the original lease except those that are inconsistent with a periodic tenancy. An example of an inconsistent term would be a covenant by the landlord to redecorate the premises every three years during a term certain of 12 years. This covenant would not become part of a subsequent periodic tenancy.

Generally speaking, if a periodic tenancy arises after the expiry of a *term certain expressed in years* (for example, a lease for five years at an annual rental of $8400 payable in instalments of $700 per month), then the periodic tenancy created will be a *yearly tenancy*. If instead the term certain is stated as a *term of months* (say, a lease for eight months at a monthly rent of $700), then the periodic tenancy created will be a *monthly* one; similarly, if the term certain is expressed in terms of weeks or quarter-years, a succeeding periodic tenancy will be weekly or quarterly, respectively.

The wording used to describe the term in the original lease may be ambiguous and can result in a difficult question of interpretation about what type of succeeding periodic tenancy is created when the landlord accepts further payment of rent. Suppose, for example, in the original lease a *term certain is granted for one and a half years at a monthly rent of $700*, and the tenant remains in possession and continues to pay rent after the expiry of the original term. Is the term so created expressed in years or months? There has been conflict in the Canadian cases.[27] If such a problem should arise, it is best to seek legal advice. If the periodic tenancy following the original lease is held to be yearly, it may be impossible for either party unilaterally to bring the tenancy to an end for a period of almost 18 months; whereas if the periodic tenancy is monthly, the maximum period of notice would be just under two months.

Parties May Set Their Own Terms for Notice

The requirements for a valid notice to quit discussed above are those that apply in the absence of express agreement; the parties to a lease usually agree to vary them to suit their own needs. Landlord and tenant may agree that some period less than six months is sufficient notice for either party to terminate a yearly tenancy. Similar variations may be agreed upon for any length of tenancy.

Renewal

A lease for a term certain, particularly a lease of premises for a retail store, often provides for a renewal at the option of the tenant. Asking for such an option makes good business sense: in taking the risk of operating a retail outlet in a particular area, the tenant may not want the added burden of a long-term lease for fear that the venture may prove unprofitable. On the other hand, if the tenant takes only a short-term lease and the venture proves to be a success, he cannot count on successfully negotiating for a new lease at the expiry of the original lease. An option permits him to terminate the tenancy at the end of the original lease if he does not wish to continue, yet he has the security of exercising the option if the business proves successful. A typical option arrangement would be an initial lease for, say, three years, with an option for a further five or 10 years. Landlords are usually quite willing to grant options provided they receive some protection against inflation and sufficient notice to obtain a new tenant if the option is not exercised.

The various forms of protection a landlord may seek are numerous. In general, a landlord will require that the rent in any renewal be increased by the amount of any increase in taxes that occurs during the original lease, and sometimes will also require either a fixed increase in rent or a series of percentage increases at various intervals during the term of the renewal, often tied to the consumer

27. See Williams and Rhodes, *The Canadian Law of Landlord and Tenant*, supra, n. 6, at 4:11–3.

price index or some other measure of the rate of inflation. A landlord will usually require notice of at least three months from the tenant that he intends to exercise the option, and probably six months if the renewal is for a long period, such as 10 years.

FIXTURES

As we noted in Chapter 23, in our introduction to real property, land includes everything fixed to it. Trees, fences, and buildings form part of the land, but they are distinguished from the land itself in that they are called **fixtures**. Technically, then, an oil derrick, a grain elevator, a stand of timber, and a large office building are all fixtures, although in the everyday language of business they are not usually called fixtures. An object that is affixed to a fixture (such as a furnace installed in a building) is itself a fixture. It is in this more restricted sense that the word is often used.

fixtures
objects that are attached to the land or to a building or other fixture on the land

General Rules for Ownership of Fixtures

Whether an object is held to be a fixture may determine its owner. Generally, an object permanently affixed to a building becomes a part of the building and of the real property itself. In a sale of land the vendor cannot remove fixtures that were attached at the time of the contract of sale; they belong to the purchaser. Similarly, since fixtures belong to the landlord, a tenant cannot remove them.

The question of what is or is not a fixture does not often arise in a sale of land because the purchaser and vendor usually agree between them what fixtures remain with the land. If the vendor wishes to take certain fixtures away, he expressly reserves that right in the agreement of sale, and the sale price may be adjusted accordingly. In tenancy, however, a problem may arise *after* the lease begins. The tenant may attach objects to the premises for his own benefit without any agreement with the landlord. The question then arises whether he may take them away when he vacates the premises.

The result would be very harsh if a tenant temporarily attached valuable objects to the building, unaware of the consequences of so doing, and later discovered he could not remove them under any circumstances. In such a case the landlord would reap an unjust benefit. Understandably, the law has developed more flexible rules in these circumstances than in a sale of land. To apply the rules we must decide, first, whether the object has become a fixture and, second, if it has, whether it belongs to those classes of fixtures that may be removed by a tenant.

Determining Whether an Object Is a Fixture

To determine whether an object has become a fixture, we may ask a number of questions:

- Has the object been fastened to the building with the intention that it become a fixture?
- What use is to be made of it?
- How securely and permanently is it attached?
- How much damage, if any, will be caused to the building by its removal?

A picture hanging on a hook in the wall is quite obviously not a fixture. A partition nailed and bolted to the walls of the building is quite clearly a fixture. But what would we conclude about the following—a table that has been bolted to the floor to prevent delicate machinery on it from being jarred; machinery bolted to the floor to prevent vibration; a display stand tacked to a wall so that it will not topple over; a neon sign held in place by guy wires bolted to the roof of the building?

Ordinarily, objects not bolted or anchored in any way but merely resting on their own weight are presumed not to be fixtures. Objects affixed in any way create a presumption that they are fixtures, although this presumption may be rebutted by asking what a reasonable person would intend when attaching the object, for instance, the display stand mentioned above. When objects are held not to be fixtures, they may be removed by the tenant at any time. If the tenant should inadvertently forget to remove them from the premises when the lease expires, they still remain the property of the tenant and may be claimed afterwards.

Tenant's Fixtures

Even when it is decided that an object was affixed in such a manner that it has become a fixture, the tenant may still have the right to remove it if he can show that either (a) it was attached for the convenience of the tenant or for the better enjoyment of the object, as when it is purely ornamental, or (b) it was a **trade fixture**—that is, an article brought onto the premises for the purpose of carrying on some trade or business, including manufacturing. Both these classes of fixtures are commonly called **tenant's fixtures**. A tenant may remove them before the end of his tenancy, provided that in doing so he does not cause permanent damage to the structure of the building and he repairs what damage is done. If, however, a tenant leaves without removing his fixtures and the term expires, they are presumed to become part of the premises and the property of the landlord. We might add that a tenant's fixtures include *only* those fixtures brought onto the premises by the tenant himself. Fixtures installed by the landlord or left by preceding tenants are the landlord's property from the time of installation or from the beginning of the tenancy and may not be removed.

Advantages of an Express Agreement About Fixtures

From the above discussion, we can see that there is not a precise test to determine whether an object attached to the premises by a tenant remains his property or becomes a part of the building. The problem can often be avoided in advance by making an agreement concerning specific fixtures. If the parties expressly agree that a particular object—one that would otherwise undoubtedly be a fixture—is to remain the property of the tenant, the agreement is conclusive.

ORAL LEASES

In most jurisdictions, when a tenant is in possession under a short-term lease of three years or less, the lease need not be in writing in order to satisfy the Statute of Frauds, although, of course, a written lease is advisable in any event.[28] Leases of longer than three years are usually unenforceable if they are not in writing. If, for example, a tenant enters into an oral lease for five years and the landlord later changes her mind and refuses to let the tenant into possession, the tenant is without remedy. If, however, the tenant is already in possession and has paid rent, the doctrine of part performance, as discussed in Chapter 10 under the Statute of Frauds, will apply. Under the rules of equity, the court will order the landlord to give the tenant his lease in the terms originally agreed between them. A landlord too may obtain specific performance and hold the tenant bound to a long-term lease if, after taking possession, the tenant wishes to avoid the lease and vacate the premises.

SALE OF THE LANDLORD'S INTEREST

Relationship Between a Tenant and a Purchaser of the Landlord's Interest

As we noted at the beginning of this chapter, a landlord grants away a right to possession of her land for a term and reserves to herself the right to possession at the end of the term—that is, the reversion. She also receives the benefit of the tenant's covenants, including the promise to pay rent. When a landlord sells land subject to a lease, she parts with both the reversion and the benefits of

---

28. The enforceability of oral short-term leases may depend upon the amount of rent to be paid. See, for example: Statute of Frauds, R.S.O. 1990, c. S. 19, s. 3, and R.S.N.S. 1989, c. 442, s. 3; *Carter* v. *Irving Oil Co.*, [1952] 4 D.L.R. 128, per MacDonald, J., at 131; Williams and Rhodes, *The Canadian Law of Landlord and Tenant, supra*, n. 6, pp. 2:1–2.

the covenants given by the tenant. A purchaser acquires the whole interest in the land subject to the outstanding lease, and is bound to both the rights and duties of the former landlord. We may ask, "How can a purchaser receive both the rights and duties of the landlord when the tenant was not a party to the sale and there is no privity of contract between purchaser and tenant?" The answer is that between the tenant and the new landlord who has purchased the reversion there is **privity of estate**. The doctrine of privity of estate is much older than the doctrine of privity of contract. Although the ancient aspects of this doctrine have been abolished, privity of estate between a new landlord and the tenant has been retained and is eminently sensible. Neither landlord nor tenant can destroy the stability of the relationship by claiming that the original contract of lease does not bind them. Their respective interests in the land create the relationship between them.

privity of estate
the relationship between tenant and landlord created by their respective interests in the land that passes to a transferee of the interest

Privity of Contract with the Former Landlord

The creation of *privity of estate* with a new landlord does not bring to an end *privity of contract* with the former landlord. Although a landlord may sell her reversion, she still remains personally liable on her covenants to her tenant, in particular, the covenant for quiet enjoyment. If the new landlord should interfere with the covenant for quiet enjoyment in an irreparable manner, the tenant, if he chooses, may sue the original landlord in contract. He might well have to do so if the new landlord has subsequently become insolvent or has little in the way of assets. The doctrine of privity of estate is a concept of real property and does not apply to personal property, with the possible exception of ships.[29]

Relationship Between a Tenant and the Landlord's Mortgagee

The leasehold estate acquired by a tenant, like other interests in real property, is valid against parties that subsequently acquire an interest in the land. If *after* leasing her land the landlord borrows against it under a mortgage, the mortgagee's (that is, the lender's) interest will be subject to the rights of the tenant. If the mortgagor (the landlord–borrower) defaults, the mortgagee may claim the reversion but is not entitled to evict the tenant. So long as the tenant observes the terms of the lease, the mortgagee is bound by it and cannot obtain possession except as provided under the lease.

On the other hand, when the landlord mortgages her land *before* leasing it, the tenant is, in theory at least, at the mercy of the mortgagee if the landlord defaults, unless the mortgagee concurred in the lease at the time it was given. However, it is almost always in the best interest of the mortgagee to collect the rent rather than put the tenant out and try to obtain a new tenant. The risk to a tenant is greater if the lease is a long-term one, and at the time of default the value of the premises for leasing purposes has increased substantially beyond the current rent. For this reason, it is wise for a tenant to obtain the agreement of the mortgagee before entering into a long-term lease.

The Need to Register a Long-term Lease

To protect his interest, a tenant should register notice of a long-term lease in the land registry office. Otherwise, the interest may be destroyed if the landlord fraudulently sells to a bona fide purchaser who has no notice of the tenancy. The need for registration varies from province to province. In some provinces, leases as short as three years must be registered, while in others, only leases over seven years need be. Leases under three years need not be registered in any province.

---

29. See *Lord Strathcona Steamship Co.* v. *Dominion Coal Co.*, [1926] A.C. 108; *Port Line Ltd.* v. *Ben Line Steamers Ltd.*, [1958] 2 Q.B. 146. See also "Contracts Concerning Land" in Chapter 12 under "Exceptions to the Privity of Contract Rule."

CONTEMPORARY ISSUE

Commercial Condominium Ownership: An Alternative to Leasing?

Leasing premises is not the only option when a business does not wish to purchase or construct an entire building. Non-residential condominiums are increasingly being used for professional, office, retail, commercial, and even industrial purposes. Mixed-use condominiums might have retail stores and services at ground level, perhaps offices above them, and residential units on the higher levels.

There are several advantages to buying a commercial condominium unit rather than leasing. Among them are stability and security of tenure (no need to worry about large increases in rent or being refused renewal when the lease expires), the opportunity to own a specific location, the benefits of a sound capital investment, tax advantages of ownership, the opportunity to have a say in the operation of the building without being solely responsible for its management, and ownership of improvements. In a mixed-use condominium, the residents on the upper floors are a potential "captive audience" for the businesses below.

Nevertheless, the disadvantages of owning a non-residential condominium should also be considered. The initial capital investment and the carrying costs may be unaffordable. If the business grows and requires more space, adjacent units may not be available. Resale potential may not be good. A wise choice of location is very important; selling in a poor real estate market could be disastrous. In a mixed-use development, the developer may not have structured voting rights and cost allocations equitably. Conflict and bad feeling between residential and non-residential owners and poor management of the development might result.

QUESTIONS TO CONSIDER

1. What kinds of business would benefit most from locating in a commercial condominium? What kinds would be better off leasing space? Give your reasons.

2. What sorts of business might be best suited to a mixed-use condominium development?

3. From an urban planning point of view, what are the benefits of mixed-use developments? the drawbacks?

Source: See Margaret Fairweather and Lynn Ramsay, Q.C., *Condominium Law & Practice in British Columbia* (looseleaf), Continuing Legal Education Society of British Columbia, paragraphs 1.8–1.9.

LEASEBACKS

leaseback
a financial arrangement enabling a business to buy a building and sell it to a financial institution that, in turn, gives a long-term lease of the property back to the business

An established company with a good record of earnings is often able to arrange with a financial institution, usually an insurance company, to finance its acquisition of a new building by a long-term leasing device known as a **leaseback**, which forms part of a larger transaction. The business and the insurance company arrange the entire transaction in advance. First, the business obtains a short-term loan, usually from a bank, to finance construction of the building. As soon as the building is completed, the business sells it to the insurance company and pays off its bank loan. The insurance company then leases the building back to the business. The lease is usually for a period of 20 or 25 years, with the lessee business receiving an option to renew for additional five-year periods. The lessee business acts very much as the owner of the property rather than as a tenant, paying for all repairs, maintenance, insurance, and property taxes during the currency of the lease.

The leaseback device has several advantages for the lessee business. First, the business need not go through the relatively more expensive and elaborate procedure of issuing securities in the capital market as a means of financing its expansion. The arrangements for a leaseback are relatively simple, once a willing financial institution is found to undertake the project. Second, in terms of financing, a leaseback may be more advantageous than buying the property and mortgaging it because a mortgagee will not generally provide the full value of the project, leaving the company to raise the balance, whereas under a leaseback a financial institution provides the whole amount required. Third, there may be tax advantages for the lessee business.

From the point of view of a lessor financial institution, rented property represents an investment of funds that not only provides regular rental revenue that includes the amortization of the cost of the property, but also gives the lessor the reversionary interest and possession of the entire property at the expiration of the lease. Any improvements in the building added by the tenant and any inflation in land values accrue to the benefit of the landlord. In addition, if the lessee business gets into financial difficulty, the legal formalities in evicting it are simpler and quicker than those required for a mortgagee to foreclose on a mortgage. This advantage is seldom a major concern, however, since the leasebacks are confined in practice to large businesses with good earning records.

The leaseback, as compared with other leases, is a relatively long, detailed, and complex document, often carefully setting out the rights a tenant has in making alterations and adding fixtures to the building, as well as in the types of trade it may carry on. Sometimes the lessor may impose restrictions on the future borrowing of the lessee business, as a means of ensuring that it will not enter into obligations so great as to impair its ability to pay the rent.

Sometimes a leaseback includes an option for the lessee business to purchase the premises at the end of the term or the last renewal of the term. The price at which the option may be exercised by the lessee may be determined in a variety of ways. It may be simply a specified sum of money, or it may be calculated by a formula taking into account, for example, whether the option is exercised at the end of the original term or the end of a renewal.

RESIDENTIAL TENANCIES

The Changing Needs of Residential Tenants

Rapid urbanization after the Second World War caused Canadian cities to grow quickly and dramatically raised the cost of buying housing. Cities also attracted the vast majority of immigrants as well as Canadians from declining rural areas. The demand for housing was met by rental accommodation, especially in high-rise apartment buildings. The typical city tenant now lives in a large apartment complex and may not have even met his landlord. He has come to regard himself as a consumer of housing and to think of his relation with his landlord as based on a contract for services rather than an acquisition of an estate in land. Provincial legislation specifically addresses the needs of the residential tenant. The legislation repealed a number of the rules of landlord and tenant law that differ from the rules of contract law—but it did so only for residential tenancies; it does not affect the leasing of premises for business purposes.

ETHICAL ISSUE

Discrimination

Provincial human rights legislation protects tenants and prospective tenants against discrimination based on such things as race, colour, gender, ancestry, sexual orientation, lawful source of income, and age. However, exceptions exist; for example, British Columbia allows senior's buildings, reserved for persons over 55. Ontario allows same-gender buildings, occupied by either all men or all women. Landlords are also allowed to select tenants based on income information and credit checks.

QUESTIONS TO CONSIDER

1. Do you think these protections and exceptions are enough to prevent discrimination against students?

2. Are the poor protected? Consider the role of publicly subsidized housing.

Source: Human Rights Code, R.S.B.C. 1996, c. 210, s. 10; R.S.O. 1990, c. H-19, ss. 4, 21.

Legislated Protection for Tenants

Residential tenancy legislation varies considerably from province to province, but there are certain basic features that are commonly found in most of the laws:

- restrictions are imposed on the landlord's right to demand security deposits
- landlords are required to maintain the premises in a reasonable state of repair
- tenants are relieved from paying rent in the event of certain breaches of covenant by the landlord or if the lease contract is frustrated
- the landlord's remedy of distress is abolished
- the landlord has a duty to mitigate any loss caused by the tenant's breach
- the landlord may not arbitrarily or unreasonably withhold consent to an assignment or subletting
- it is made more difficult to evict a tenant, even for non-payment of rent
- restrictions are imposed on rents and rent increases
- special tribunals and procedures have been established to deal with disputes

As a general rule, the landlord in a residential tenancy is prohibited from requiring any security deposit in excess of one month's rent, and even that sum may only be applied to the payment of rent for the last rent period under the tenancy agreement. The landlord must also pay interest on the amount of the deposit at a specified rate.[30]

Under common law, a residential tenant was deemed to have accepted the property in its state at the time of entering into the lease. The landlord had no liability for repairs or injury caused even by hidden dangers about which the tenant could not reasonably have known. (A landlord was liable

---

30. Residential Tenancies Act, 2006, S.O. 2006, c. 17, ss. 105, 106. The protection afforded tenants with respect to security deposits varies considerably from province to province. See, for example: Residential Tenancy Act, S.B.C. 2002, c. 78, ss. 17–22; Residential Tenancies Act, C.C.S.M. c.R. 119, ss. 29–36.1.

for repairs only when renting furnished premises.) The legislation makes the landlord liable for maintaining residential premises in a good state of repair fit for habitation and further states that the tenant's knowledge of the lack of repair before the lease is irrelevant.[31]

Formerly, the failure of a landlord to perform her own covenants, even if they were major terms, did not release the tenant from the obligation to pay rent unless the landlord's breach amounted to an eviction of the tenant. The legislation makes some promises or covenants in a residential lease interdependent, so that breach by one party of a condition frees the other from his or her own obligations.[32]

The doctrine of frustration is expressly declared to apply to residential tenancies,[33] so that a tenant is no longer liable to pay rent for the balance of the term when the premises became uninhabitable through no fault of his own, or to restore the property if it was destroyed during the tenancy.

The landlord's remedy of distress has also been abolished.[34] It eases the requirements when a tenant wishes to move from the premises—a landlord may not arbitrarily or unreasonably withhold consent to an assignment or subletting.[35]

Nor can a tenant be evicted as easily. Termination by notice to quit has been changed to require notice even for a term certain tenancy that would otherwise end without any act by either landlord or tenant.[36] In the absence of notice to quit, a tenancy is deemed to continue as a periodic tenancy. In addition, the notice period has been lengthened in some provinces. In Ontario, for example, all tenancies other than weekly tenancies require at least 60 clear days' notice prior to the termination date and weekly (or daily) tenancies require 28 days, on the part of both landlord and tenant.[37] Landlords are precluded from terminating tenancies and evicting tenants except for a serious breach of the lease by a tenant; or because at the end of the current lease the landlord wishes to repossess the premises for occupation by herself or her immediate family; or because the premises are going to be torn down or substantially altered in order to be used for different purposes such as conversion to commercial premises.[38]

Finally, the legislation imposes restrictions in many cases on the amount of rent that may be charged and on increasing existing rents.[39]

INTERNATIONAL ISSUE

Rent Control

Availability of affordable housing is a necessity in a healthy community. Ensuring its supply involves balancing the interests of tenants and landlords. When housing prices or unemployment rates rise, the demand for rental units increases. In a purely supply-and-demand scenario, low vacancy rates would lead to escalating rents. Tenants could be required to move out at the end of their term

continued

31. S.B.C. 2002, c. 78, s. 32; C.S.S.M. c.R. 119, s. 59; S.O. 2006, c. 17, s. 20.
32. S.B.C. 2002, c. 78, ss. 45, 47; S.O. 2006, c. 24, ss. 12(4). Before withholding rent a tenant should review the rules; some provinces require the rent to be deposited with the tribunal pending resolution of a dispute.
33. S.B.C. 2002, c. 78, s. 92; C.S.S.M., c. R. 119, s. 105; S.O. 2006, c. 17, s. 19.
34. S.B.C. 2002, c. 78, s. 26; C.S.S.M. c.R. 119, s. 192; S.O. 2006, c. 17, s. 40.
35. S.B.C. 2002, c. 78, s. 34; C.S.S.M. c.R. 119, s. 43; S.O. 2006, c. 17, s. 95.
36. For example: S.B.C. 2002, c. 78, s. 57; S.O. 2006, c. 17, s. 47.
37. S.O. 2006, c. 17, s. 44(1), (2), and (3).
38. S.O. 2006, c. 17, ss. 48, 49, 50.
39. S.B.C. 2002, c. 78, s. 41; C.S.S.M. c.R. 119, ss. 117, 118; S.O. 2006, c. 17, ss. 110-136.

unless they are willing to pay large (unaffordable) rent increases. As a result, it is common for provinces to fix the amount of rent that can be charged or limit the amount of any rent increase. The distinction between these two controls is made clear by reviewing the recent history of rent controls in Ontario. Prior to 1998, the Ontario rent control system established a baseline legal rent for each existing or new rental unit.[40] Thereafter, only annual rent increases were allowed at the prescribed percentage (tied to the consumer price index). This cap on rent increases applied regardless of any change in tenant. Since 1998, the system provides protection from unreasonable rent increases only to existing or continuing tenants (subject to some exceptions). When a new tenant rents the unit, the landlord may set a new rent without regard to past rental rates or increases.[41]

In the United States, rent control is implemented at the municipal level in accordance with governing state legislation. As of 2003, only 125 cities had some form of rent control including New York, San Francisco, Washington D.C., and Los Angeles. Several states have banned rent control entirely, including Florida and Illinois. In 1995, California restricted rent control protection to existing and continuing tenants. In 2008, California voters defeated a proposition that would have abolished rent control entirely.

The worldwide trend is mixed: both China and Japan have eliminated rent control while countries in the Middle East seem to be embracing them. Dubai and Qatar implemented new rent control programs in 2005 and 2007, respectively.

QUESTIONS TO CONSIDER

1. What are the arguments for and against rent control?

2. Why is Ontario's current stabilization system hailed by some as a fair compromise?

Sources: Prince Christian Cruz, "The Pros and Cons of Rent Control," *Global Property Guide*, April 10, 2008, www.globalpropertyguide.com/investment-analysis/The-pros-and-cons-of-rent-control (accessed October 22, 2008); Peter Dreier, "Californians Defend Rent Control," *Rooflines*, June 5, 2008 www.rooflines.org/941/californians_defend_rent_control/ (accessed October 22, 2008).

QUESTIONS FOR REVIEW

1. Define tenancy at will, term certain, overholding tenant, subletting, eviction, forfeiture, surrender, and quiet enjoyment.

2. What are the risks for a tenant if he limits his right to exclusive possession of the premises? Explain.

3. Should a leasehold interest be shown as an asset (with an equal and offsetting liability) on the balance sheet of a business? If so, at what amount?

4. Describe the difficulty caused by the strict covenant to pay rent as it relates to frustration in contract law.

5. What are the concerns of a landlord with respect to a tenant's right to assign the remainder of a leasehold interest?

6. Lewis owns a five-bedroom house next to his own home in Niagara-on-the-Lake, and rents it to Tessa for three years. Tessa then applies for a licence to operate a bed and breakfast on the premises. Lewis objects to such use of the house. Would he have any legal recourse against Tessa?

---

40. Rent Controls Act 1992, S.O. c. 11, replaced by the Tenant Protection Act, S.O. 1997, c. 24. Landlords could apply for permission to increase rents above guidelines in prescribed circumstances.
41. Residential Tenancies Act 2006, S.O. 2006, c. 17, ss. 110-136.

7. Describe the usual responsibilities of a landlord for repairs when a tenant leases only part of a building. How does this situation differ from a lease of an entire building?

8. Turner rented a store from Lauren on the ground floor of a multi-storey building as an art gallery to sell paintings and small statues. Turner's hours of business were normal retail business hours. A few months later, Lauren leased the adjoining store to Rockbar Inc. It played very loud music from noon until Turner's closing time. The music, especially the thumping sounds, could be heard clearly in Turner's store and interfered with normal conversation. Does Turner have any remedies?

9. How would you suggest that responsibility for insuring the premises be allocated in a large shopping mall? Describe the most difficult aspects of the problem.

10. What is the dilemma for the landlord when a tenant abandons the premises during the term of the lease?

11. Describe the landlord's duty to mitigate after a tenant abandons the premises.

12. In what way may a tenant be in a difficult position when the premises burn down, even if the lease states that the rent is suspended until the premises are rebuilt?

13. What property is exempt from a landlord's right to distrain?

14. Under the common law, how long a period of notice must be given to terminate a yearly tenancy? What is the meaning of "clear" as it relates to notice?

15. Oscar leased Blackacre from Brenda for five years at a monthly rent of $1200. Neither of them seemed to notice when the lease had expired. For several months, Oscar continued to pay his rent on the first day of each month. Brenda now needs to take possession of Blackacre for a large construction project. How much notice must she give to Oscar?

16. Explain the importance of renewal clauses in business leases.

17. Thomson has rented a restaurant. He bolts a large shelf to the wall and places a television screen on the shelf. In the kitchen he bolts a small partition to the floor to separate his stoves from the refrigerator and freezer area. Define which of these objects are fixtures and the types of fixture they are.

18. How is the relationship of a tenant affected by his landlord's sale of her interest to a purchaser? What is the nature of the new relationship?

19. Stroll leases a warehouse for a term certain of five years. During the second year of the lease, the landlord, Vernon, mortgages the land. At the end of the fifth year of the lease, Stroll and Vernon enter into another lease for a further five years. Explain the difference, if any, in Stroll's position in the first term and in the second term insofar as the mortgage is concerned.

20. (a)   What are three reasons that make leaseback arrangements attractive to lessee businesses?

    (b)   What are the reasons that make them attractive to lessor financial institutions?

21. Describe briefly the reasons for treating residential tenancies differently from commercial tenancies.

CASES AND PROBLEMS

1. Ms. Bone, the owner of a downtown block of stores, rented one of them to Mr. Bull, who opened a retail china shop on the premises. Bull's tenancy was from year to year. He had a number of display cases built with glass doors to keep their fragile contents out of the reach of curious customers. The cases were secured to the wall by one-inch nails. Bull also purchased and installed heavy-duty air-conditioning equipment, which was connected to the water supply and anchored to the floor.

Several years later, Bull was adjudged bankrupt on a petition of his creditors. At the time he owed Bone $3600 for three months' rent. The trustee in bankruptcy remained in possession of the store pending liquidation of the business assets. The trustee claimed the display cases and air-conditioner for the benefit of Bull's general creditors, but Bone claimed them as lessor of the store.

Discuss the respective rights of Bone and of the trustee in bankruptcy.

2. Kruger leased a warehouse to Pool Corp. for a term certain of eight months at a rent of $3000 per month, commencing January 1 and expiring August 31. Pool did not move out on August 31 and tendered its cheque for $3000 to pay the rent for September. It was accepted by Kruger. On October 1, Pool's manager appeared at Kruger's office with another cheque for $3000. Kruger said he had inspected the warehouse and was disappointed by the rough treatment the building was receiving from Pool's employees. When the manager replied that he could hardly expect otherwise in a busy operation, Kruger stated it was not worth his while to rent it under those conditions unless he received at least $4000 per month. The manager refused to pay that much and tendered the company's cheque for $3000. Kruger refused the cheque and ordered Pool to "clear out of the warehouse at once." The manager left and mailed the cheque to Kruger, who simply held it and did not cash it.

On November 1, Kruger called Pool by telephone and asked if the company would pay $4000. The manager replied, "No." Kruger said that he was at the end of his patience and had given Pool a full month to change its mind. He sent a bailiff to evict Pool that very day, cashed its cheque for the previous month, and sent it a demand for "the $1000 still owing."

Pool was forced to move its stock to a more expensive warehouse at once and suffered some damage to its goods when they were moved into the street by the bailiff. It sued Kruger for losses of $8000 caused by the eviction. Should it succeed? Give reasons for your opinion.

3. Rogers, a dance teacher, was looking for space to operate a dance studio. She visited premises on the second floor of Hart's building four times with other people who concluded that the premises were suitable for the purposes intended. Rogers signed a lease and, with Hart's approval, she had installed a special dance floor, cabinets, dance bars, and mirrors and did painting and electrical work, including installation of light fixtures. She then began her classes.

Hart immediately noticed that the building began to vibrate. Within 24 hours, he had a special beam installed but the vibrating continued. Hart hired a structural engineer at once to examine the building. The engineer concluded that the vibration was caused by harmonic pressure created by the coordinated movement of the dancers. He stated that the vibration could not be avoided by structural changes and it could ultimately cause the building or parts of it to collapse. Hart worried about the safety of the patrons of the restaurant situated under the dance studio, as well as of Rogers herself and her students. Three days after classes had begun, he told Rogers that the classes had to stop.

Rogers immediately began to look for new premises and took the position that by preventing her from continuing dance classes, Hart terminated the lease without notice. She sued Hart for damages for the cost of all the improvements she had made, the cost of moving, and general damages for loss of business. She argued that because the defect in the premises was latent and did not become apparent until after she had begun the dance lessons, it was unreasonable to ask her to ensure the soundness and safety of the premises. It was Hart's problem as landlord to deal with.

Give your opinion of Rogers' claims and whether they should succeed.

4. Allgate Realties Ltd. constructed a new building suitable for a restaurant in a suburb of Calgary. Streeter, the manager, invited Kratinsky to examine it. Kratinsky already owned and operated a restaurant in the city and was hesitant. Streeter assured him that the suburb was growing rapidly with new businesses about to open, as well as new housing developments. He offered Kratinsky a five-year lease including a sale to him of the building at the end of the lease. Kratinsky finally accepted; he opened the restaurant three months later.

Almost no new construction took place in the area; the restaurant was isolated and business was very poor. Within six months Kratinsky closed the restaurant and refused to pay further rent, claiming that

Allgate had made serious misrepresentations and was in breach of the contract. Allgate responded that there were no covenants in the lease referring to future development in the area and that Kratinsky remained bound by the lease and sale of the property.

Whose argument do you think will prevail?

5. Ivan Drugs Inc., a drugstore chain, leased premises from Hay Investments Ltd. in its shopping mall. The lease was for 10 years, at a "base" rent of $46 200 per year in monthly instalments of $3850, plus Ivan's share of the taxes, insurance, and common expenses of the mall. Ivan also agreed to pay an additional 6 percent of gross annual sales as rent, to the extent that its gross sales exceeded $770 000 for the year ($46 200 represents 6 percent of $770 000). The lease also contained a usual covenant allowing Ivan to assign the lease with consent of Hay.

In the first three years, Ivan's sales exceeded $1 500 000, and it duly paid the additional sums to Hay. However, during the third year a much larger shopping mall was opened across the street from Hay's mall. Ivan, fearing its sales at the current location would suffer, leased larger premises at the new mall and moved from its old premises, leaving them vacant. Ivan continued to pay the "base" rent and its share of the taxes, insurance, and common expenses, but paid no additional rent based on its sales in the new mall.

Partly as a result of receiving diminished rent, Hay was unable to obtain extensions of its mortgages or new financing for the mall and was in financial difficulty. Hay served notice on Ivan to enforce the original agreement according to its terms and to pay rent based on sales that could be attributed to Ivan's business if it had remained in Hay's mall. Hay Investments Ltd. asserted that Ivan Drugs Inc. had impliedly promised to carry on business for the full term of the lease.

Give your opinion of the validity of Hay's claim and what you think the result should be.

6. John Perini purchased a house and then called on his widowed daughter-in-law, whom he admired, and said, "Mary, I want you to look at the house I have bought for you. You won't have to worry about rent any more." Mary was very pleased, and moved into the house with her children within a few days. During the first three years after he purchased the house, Perini frequently visited his daughter-in-law and grandchildren in the house, but then moved into a senior citizens' home where, except for a few special family occasions at the house, they came to visit him.

Perini died 14 years after he had purchased the house. Mary had always paid the municipal taxes and looked after the house but paid no rent to her father-in-law. Perini regularly paid the fire insurance premiums himself under a policy that specified that any claims would be paid to him as the insured. He never conveyed the title to Mary, apparently because he had once bought a house for another member of his family who had soon after sold it, wasted the proceeds, and returned to him destitute, asking for money.

An officer of the trust company that was executor for Perini's estate found the duplicate copy of the deed in Perini's name, among his papers. The executor then claimed the house from Mary as part of the Perini estate to be given to other beneficiaries under the will. Mary did not understand the legal arrangements; she could only state that she believed the house had been bought in her name and that she had lived in it continuously from the time of its purchase. She needed the house for her family and resisted the executor's demand. The trust company, as executor for the estate, sued her for possession of the property.

During the trial the court was referred to the Limitations Act of the province. The sections referred to read in part as follows:

4. No person shall make entry . . . or bring an action to recover any land or rent, but within ten years next after the time at which the right to make such entry . . . or to bring such action . . . first accrued to the person making or bringing it.

5. Where a person is in possession . . . as tenant at will, the right of the person entitled subject thereto . . . to make an entry . . . or to bring an action to recover the land or rent shall be deemed to have first accrued either at the determination of the tenancy, or at the expiration of one year after the commencement of the tenancy, at which time the tenancy shall be deemed to have determined.

8. No person shall be deemed to have been in possession of any land within the meaning of this Act merely by reason of having made an entry thereon.

Express an opinion, with reasons, about the probable outcome of this action.

7. Frost Investments Limited owned three adjoining buildings downtown that it rented to various tenants as office space. All three buildings were heated centrally from a single heating plant in Building No. 1. The Generous Loan Company occupied offices in Building No. 3 under a lease in which the lessor, Frost, covenanted to maintain the heat continuously above 60 degrees from October 1 to May 24, except for weekends. In January a serious fire occurred in Building No. 2, breaking the heating connections between Buildings No. 1 and No. 3. The damage was so serious that Frost decided to demolish Building No. 2 and rebuild.

In the meantime, Generous Loan Company suffered a significant drop in business because of very low temperatures in its offices. It eventually vacated the premises and leased other quarters at a higher rent. It then sued Frost, claiming damages of $1750 for the additional amount of rent it had to pay the new landlord for what otherwise would have been the balance of the term of its lease with Frost, and $6000 for its estimated loss of profits. Frost counterclaimed for rent for the balance of the term of the lease, seven months at $2150 per month. What do you think the decision should be?

8. Tagom rented a service station from Oil Can Limited for a term of 12 months commencing July 1, at a rent of $975 per month payable on the first day of each month. The lease contained the following clause:

If the lessee shall hold over after the term . . . the resulting tenancy shall be a tenancy from month to month and not a tenancy from year to year, subject to all the terms, conditions and agreements herein contained insofar as same may be applicable to a tenancy from month to month.

On May 28 of the following year, Oil Can sent Tagom a notice stating that he must give vacant possession on the expiry of the lease. On June 30, Oil Can representatives visited Tagom and asked him what he intended to do. He replied that he would not leave the premises "peacefully." Tagom remained in possession on July 1, and sent a cheque by registered mail to Oil Can as rent for that month. Although the area superintendent had given instructions to the accounting department not to accept any rent from Tagom, a junior clerk deposited it in the company bank account. Soon afterwards, a senior officer discovered the error, informed Tagom that the act of the clerk in accepting the cheque had been inadvertent and against instructions, and delivered a refund cheque from the company to Tagom for $975. Tagom returned the cheque.

Was a new tenancy created, or could Oil Can obtain a court order for immediate possession?

ADDITIONAL RESOURCES FOR CHAPTER 24 ON THE COMPANION WEBSITE *(www.pearsoned.ca/smyth)*

In addition to self-test multiple-choice, true–false, and short essay questions (all with immediate feedback), application exercises, and links to useful web destinations, the Companion Website provides the following resources for Chapter 24:

- **British Columbia:** Commercial Leases; Distress of Rent; Fixtures; Residential Leases
- **Alberta:** Commercial Leases; Condominiums; Distress; Fixtures; Residential Tenancies
- **Manitoba/Saskatchewan:** Residential Tenancies
- **Ontario:** Assignment of Rents; Assignments of Tenancy; Distress; Fixtures; Landlord and Tenant Legislation; Leasehold Improvements; Ontario Rental Housing Tribunal; Overholding; Tenant Protection Act

Mortgages of Land and Real Estate Transactions

A purchaser of land rarely has the resources to pay the full price at the time of completing the purchase. A mortgage plays a central role in financing the transaction. In this chapter we discuss the nature of mortgages, the rights and obligations of both lenders and borrowers, and the various stages of a typical real estate transaction. We examine such questions as:

- What is the concept of a mortgage, and what are the important mortgage terms?

- What are the rights of the mortgagor and mortgagee?

- What remedies are available to the mortgagee?

- What is a "second mortgage," and how is it used?

- In what ways are a mortgagee's rights different from those of other creditors?

- What is an "offer to purchase"?

- What are the necessary steps in proceeding with a real estate transaction?

- What is the process of "closing" the transaction?

THE ESSENCE OF MORTGAGE LAW

The Mortgage as a Contract

mortgage
a loan contract that gives the lender an interest in the borrower's land as security for a debt

mortgagor
a borrower who gives his lender an interest in his land as security for repayment of a debt

mortgagee
a lender who accepts an interest in land as security for a loan

maturity date
end of the term when debt must be repaid

calculation period
stages at which accrued interest is added to principal

amortization period
length of time it should take to repay an entire debt

term
time period during which an interest rate is fixed and principal lent

mortgage commitment
document in which parties to a mortgage initially agree to borrow and lend

acceleration clause
a clause stating that upon default of any instalment, the whole of the principal sum of the mortgage and accrued interest immediately falls due

A **mortgage** document—as well as representing an interest in land—is a loan contract containing a number of important terms. The most important term is the personal promise of the **mortgagor** (borrower) to pay off the debt and of the **mortgagee** (lender) to discharge its interest in the land upon repayment. It is useful to set out the most important covenants of each party. The mortgagor covenants:

(a) to pay the principal debt and accrued interest, either at the **maturity date** or in instalments as agreed by the parties,[1]

(b) to keep the property adequately insured in the name of the mortgagee,

(c) to pay taxes on the land and buildings, and

(d) to keep the premises in a reasonable state of repair.

The total debt that must be repaid includes the principal sum borrowed plus the interest charged by the mortgagee. Interest is expressed as an annual percentage rate and the mortgage specifies the **calculation period**—stages when interest is added to the principal. Periodic payments are usually required and they are commonly a blend of interest and principal. The amount of each payment is determined by the **amortization period**—the length of time it should take to repay the entire debt. Spreading the debt over a longer amortization period reduces the amount of the periodic payments. The interest provisions are fixed for a specific time period, known as the **term** of the mortgage. At the expiration of the term, the mortgage must be paid off, renewed at an agreed-upon interest rate, or re-financed with a new mortgagee. Together, these terms establish the financial arrangement for the mortgage loan. They are usually first described in the **mortgage commitment** letter, in which the parties initially agree to borrow and lend.

Mortgages almost always contain an **acceleration clause**, which states that upon default of any instalment, the whole of the principal sum of the mortgage and accrued interest immediately falls due. Default accelerates the maturity date, and the mortgagee may pursue all its remedies.

The mortgagee covenants:

(a) to execute the necessary discharge of the mortgage upon repayment in full, and

(b) to leave the mortgagor in possession and not interfere with his use and enjoyment of the mortgaged premises so long as the mortgagor observes all his covenants.

The mortgagor signs the mortgage and the mortgagee merely accepts the document without signing it. Since the mortgagee's promises are set out as provisos or standard charge terms—some are simply implied by the common law and statutory principles of mortgage law—its acceptance of the document binds it to the mortgage terms.

As in earlier times, real estate mortgages still frequently arise out of private transactions between two individuals. However, a very large proportion of mortgage lending to individual borrowers is now done by financial institutions—insurance companies, trust companies, and banks, for example—that have assumed the role of corporate mortgagees.[2]

---

1. Except in Alberta and Saskatchewan, where a mortgagor cannot be sued personally for the mortgage debt. See the section dealing with provincial variations, below.

2. The reverse situation, where the mortgage borrower is a corporation and the lenders individuals (bondholders), is also common, as we shall see in our discussion of the nature of corporate securities in Chapter 27 and of floating charges as security devices in Chapter 30.

Mortgage as an Interest in Land

The concept of the mortgage as an interest in land developed through the common law and is now codified in provincial legislation. Under the common law and early registry systems, a mortgage was an actual conveyance of the **legal title** to a fee simple interest in land by the mortgagor to the mortgagee as security for a debt. The transfer of title had two conditions: first, that the mortgagor could remain in possession of land as long as payments were up to date, and second, that the mortgagor was entitled to have the legal title returned to him upon full payment of the debt. However, if the appointed day passed without the debt being repaid, the conditions then expired, and the mortgagee owned the interest absolutely. The common law courts construed the condition strictly. If a mortgagor was delayed by a storm or illness and arrived with the money the day after the final day for payment, it was too late—the mortgagee could take possession of the land and keep it. The mortgagee could choose to keep the land and not sue for the outstanding debt, or to sue for the debt on condition that he would reconvey the land.

legal title
an interest in land recognized by the common law

The Mortgagor's Right to Redeem

It seemed unfair to allow a mortgagee to keep title to land in situations where only a small amount of the debt remained unpaid. The courts of equity created a remedy for these cases of hardship. If the mortgagor petitioned the court and pleaded hardship and also tendered payment of the debt in full, the court would acknowledge his interest in the land and permit him to **redeem** it. It would order the mortgagee to reconvey the land to him. This right of redemption obtained by the mortgagor from a court of equity is known as the **equity of redemption**, and it is often called simply the **equity**. This is the source of the modern business term "equity," meaning the interest of the proprietors of a business in its total assets after allowing for creditors' claims.

redeem
have the land reconveyed to the mortgagor

equity of redemption or **equity**
the right of the mortgagor to redeem mortgaged land on payment of the debt in full

The Mortgagee's Right to Foreclose

The courts of equity also recognized that limits needed to be placed on a mortgagor's equity of redemption. A mortgagor should not be entitled to redeem his property years later after the mortgagee had significantly improved the land. The courts agreed that after a *reasonable* period of time had passed, the right to redeem the property should *expire* and the mortgagee could then safely treat the land as his own. By the 19th century, the **foreclosure** period became generally accepted as six months from the date of the hearing in the case. Provincial mortgage legislation now establishes minimum time periods within which a defaulting mortgagor may redeem, after which his interest is foreclosed.

foreclosure
an order by a court ending the mortgagor's right to redeem within a fixed time

Why Mortgagees Rarely Take Possession

Although a mortgagee is entitled to take possession upon default of the mortgagor, in practice, a mortgagee rarely takes possession until after it has obtained foreclosure. There are exceptions, such as when it believes that the mortgagor has no intention of trying to redeem, the property is vacant, or the premises may become dilapidated. There are three main reasons for not going into possession:

- *First*, a mortgagee generally wants its money rather than the mortgagor's property, and it would prefer to encourage the mortgagor to pay off the debt.
- *Second*, its possession would be uncertain, since the mortgagor might at any moment tender payment, redeem his interest, and demand possession.
- *Third*, it must account for any benefits it receives from occupation of the land and deduct it from the amount owing if the mortgagor tenders payment, thus losing any material advantage gained from taking possession.

Land Titles System

The land titles system, through its governing legislation, has changed the nature of a mortgagee's interest in land. Under the land titles system (which is being used in more and more areas across Canada, as discussed in Chapter 23) mortgages are often called **charges**, mortgagors are **chargors** and mortgagees are **chargees**.[3] Charges are no longer, strictly speaking, conveyances of the legal title. Rather, they are liens or encumbrances recorded on the title to the land, for which the ordinary remedy is to force a sale of the land and then apply the proceeds towards repayment of the debt.[4] Despite this significant distinction, basic mortgage procedure remains mostly unchanged. Chargors execute a charge document containing the terms of the loan and a personal promise to pay, remain in possession of the land, and, upon payment in full, are entitled to a discharge of the charge. If there is default, the chargee may dispossess the charger, foreclose his interest, and sell the property. The chargor still has a "redemption period" during which he may tender full payment of the debt and stop the foreclosure or sale of the property.[5] We discuss the mortgagee's remedies more fully below.

Registration

Like all other interests in land, a mortgage or charge must be registered in the appropriate registry or land titles system as discussed in Chapter 23. It must be in the proper form and identify the parties and the land involved. The priority of the interest is determined by the order of registration. Consequently, if a mortgagee fails to register its mortgage, a subsequent purchaser will be unaware of the mortgage and will acquire title free from it. Similarly, a subsequent mortgagee would establish priority over the earlier mortgage if it registered first. We can see then that failure to register may result in the complete loss of the land as security, although the mortgagor's personal covenant to pay would still survive. Registration of the mortgage is public notice of its existence.

RIGHTS OF THE MORTGAGEE AND MORTGAGOR

The Mortgagee

Although the courts of common law and equity are merged and most registry systems are being converted to land titles, the interests of the mortgagee and mortgagor are still interpreted according to the remedies and principles developed before the merger.[6] If the mortgagor defaults on any of the terms of the mortgage, the mortgagee has the following remedies:

(a) It may sue the mortgagor on his personal covenant to repay, just as a creditor may sue any debtor who is in default, and obtain a personal judgment against him.
(b) It may dispossess the mortgagor and occupy the land itself (or put in a tenant). As noted above, this is not an attractive remedy until after foreclosure.
(c) It may sell the land under its contractual or statutory power of sale, as explained below.

charge
a lien or encumbrance on land

chargor
mortgagor

chargee
mortgagee

3.   Since 1984, mortgages throughout Ontario, including those regions under the registry system, have been converted to charges and no longer represent legal title to the land: Land Registration Reform Act, R.S.O. 1990, c. L.4, s. 1, 6.
4.   Land Titles Act, R.S.A. 2000, c. L-4, s. 103.
5.   *Supra* n. 3, s. 6(3);
6.   Despite these reforms and the fact that the mortgagor who gives a charge on his land retains legal title, the old terminology concerning legal and equitable title, rights, and remedies remains in common use.

(d) It may proceed with a court action for foreclosure and eventually destroy the mortgagor's right to redeem.

(e) Subsequent to foreclosure, it may again sue on the covenant to pay the debt, provided it is willing and able to reconvey the land.[7]

A mortgagee frequently chooses a combination of these remedies.

The Mortgagor

The rights of a mortgagor after default are as follows:

(a) He may repay the mortgage loan together with interest and all expenses incurred by the mortgagee up to and including the date of the order of foreclosure and obtain a release of his land.

(b) He may obtain an accounting for any benefits obtained from the land by the mortgagee and deduct them from the amount owing on redemption.

(c) If sued on his covenant to repay after foreclosure, he may require the mortgagee to prove that it is ready and able to reconvey the land upon repayment.

(d) If sued on his covenant to repay after sale of the property under power of sale, he may attack the sale price or sale expenses as unreasonable and have the amount outstanding reduced.

(e) He may also obtain relief against the consequences of an acceleration clause. If he pays all prior accrued payments, performs all other terms of which he may have been in default, and pays all costs incurred by the mortgagee, a court will permit him to continue to make regular payments under the original terms of the mortgage.[8]

(f) He may ask a court to stop the foreclosure proceedings and hold a sale (as discussed below).

THE MORTGAGEE'S REMEDIES UPON DEFAULT

As we have seen, there are advantages and disadvantages to each of the various remedies. In this section we will examine the basic procedures, benefits, and drawbacks of the primary remedies.

Foreclosure

The process of obtaining foreclosure consists of three stages:

- Upon default, the mortgagee goes to court and asks for an order establishing a time limit within which the mortgagor can redeem.
- Once the redemption period has expired, the court issues a final order of foreclosure that ends any further claim of the mortgagor and the claims of subsequent registered interests.
- Upon registration of the final order of foreclosure, the mortgagee is recognized as the owner of the property.

As the owner of the property, the mortgagee is deemed to accept the land in full satisfaction of the debt; it no longer has any right to demand payment. As noted above, most mortgagees do not want to be landowners. Therefore, foreclosure is an attractive remedy only when the value of the property is high and the amount of the debt is low. However, in these circumstances, the mortgagor is likely to redeem.

---

7. Except in Manitoba and Saskatchewan, where a final order of foreclosure extinguishes the right to sue on the personal covenant of the mortgagor: Mortgage Act, C.C..S.M. 2000, c. M200, s. 16; Limitation of Civil Rights Act, R.S.S. 1978, c. L-16, s. 6.

8. Mortgages Act, R.S.O. 1990, c. M.40, ss. 22(1) and 23(1).

In some jurisdictions, when a mortgagee starts a foreclosure action and the mortgagor believes that the land is worth more than his mortgage debt, the mortgagor or a subsequent secured creditor may request the court to hold a sale. We shall return to this topic when we discuss provincial variations later in this chapter.

Sale by the Court

A mortgagee may request that the land be sold under the supervision of the court (or in some of the western provinces, under the supervision of the registrar of titles), the sale to be either by tender or by auction. Some jurisdictions permit the mortgagee or its agent to bid; others prohibit such bidding. The sale must be advertised for a specified period and carried out according to provincial statutes and regulations. In some jurisdictions the court or registrar sets a reserve price below which no tenders will be accepted. The reserve price is not disclosed. When the tenders are opened, the highest one is accepted if it is over the reserve price. If no bid is above the reserve price, then the land remains unsold and the mortgagee may resort to its other remedies.

When a sale produces a successful bid, the mortgagee is entitled to recover the principal sum owing, accrued interest, and expenses of the court action and the sale. If the sale produces a smaller sum, the mortgagee may obtain judgment against the mortgagor for the deficiency. If the sale is for a larger sum, the surplus is returned to the mortgagor or his other secured creditors of the land.

Sale by the Mortgagee

power of sale
a right upon default to sell mortgaged land

Most mortgages, and in some jurisdictions the statutes governing mortgages, give the mortgagee a contractual and statutory **power of sale** that may be exercised privately without court action or supervision, although advance notice to the mortgagor is generally required. A mortgagee may exercise its power of sale at any time after default, subject to any statutory period of grace. By executing a proper conveyance and declaring that it is made in pursuance of a power of sale, the mortgagee may validly transfer the title to the land to any third party. The sale must, however, be a genuine sale and not amount to a fraud upon the mortgagor. A mortgagee may not sell to itself either directly or through an agent. If the mortgagee is a private lender, she may sell the land to a company of which she is a shareholder or officer, but such sales will be carefully examined by the court and may be easily cancelled if there is any evidence of taking unfair advantage by selling at an unreasonably low price. Whenever a mortgagee exercises a power of sale, it is under a duty to take reasonable steps to obtain a fair price for the land. If the mortgagor can show that the mortgagee sold for an unreasonably low price, the court will reduce the deficiency accordingly or give the mortgagor judgment for any surplus he should have received.

The same rules concerning the proceeds of a sale apply here as in a sale by the court. If there is a deficiency, the mortgagee may still sue the mortgagor for the sum; if there is a surplus, it must be returned to the mortgagor or to the remaining secured creditors.

INTERNATIONAL ISSUE

Mortgage Crisis

Recently, the United States experienced a major disruption in its mortgage industry. Homeowners defaulted on residential mortgages in record numbers and the resulting explosion in power-of-sale and foreclosure proceedings created a glut in the market and a decline in housing prices.

continued

The National Consumer Law Center reports that between 1980 and 2005, American foreclosures increased almost 300 percent, while home ownership increased by only 5 percent. The *Los Angeles Times* reported a record 47 171 foreclosures in California during the first quarter of 2008, more than four times as many as in the first quarter of 2007.

Some factors contributing to the high number of defaults were

- loans given to borrowers with poor credit,
- predatory initial lending terms that included low interest-only mortgages (teaser rates) with large balloon payments of principal required at the end of the term, and
- mortgages with no down payments, or fully financed housing purchases.

As a result, homeowners found themselves with mortgages they could not afford to maintain after the initial low-interest term. They could not refinance due to falling real estate values and they could not sell because too many other homes were already for sale at low prices.

A number of legislative initiatives are being considered to ease the crisis and to prevent future instability in the mortgage market. They include:

- regulating lending criteria,
- restricting predatory lending practices,
- extending low "teaser" rates, and
- altering foreclosure and power-of-sale procedures to provide greater protection for mortgagors.

Possible changes to foreclosure and power-of-sale procedures include longer redemption periods, restrictions on possession rights, and expanded defences available to mortgagors.

QUESTIONS TO CONSIDER

1. What measures do you think best protect both mortgagors and mortgagees?

2. In this market, which remedy best protects a mortgagee?

Sources: Peter Y. Hong, "California Home Entering Foreclosure Hit Record," *Los Angeles Times*, April 23, 2008, http://articles.latimes.com/2008/apr/23/business/fi-foreclose23; the National Consumer Law Center and the National Association of Consumer Advocates, "Comments to the Board of Governors to the Federal Reserve System Regarding the Board's Authority under HOEPA to Prohibit Unfair Acts or Practices in Connection with Mortgage Lending," Docket No. OP-1288, August 15, 2007, www.consumerlaw.org/issues/predatory_mortgage/content/HOEPA_CommentsAug07.pdf.

SALE BY A MORTGAGOR OF HIS INTEREST

Financial Arrangements

A mortgagor struggling to keep up with mortgage payments may need to sell his property before the maturity date. Alternatively, a mortgagor may want to move to a larger location during the term of the mortgage. A mortgagor may transfer the property to a new purchaser but the existing mortgage must be dealt with as part of the financial arrangements between the two.

ILLUSTRATION 25.1

Adam, the owner of Blackacre, mortgages it to BCD Trust Co. for $100 000. Subsequently, he sells Blackacre to Rona for $160 000. How is the price to be paid by Rona?

There are three possibilities:

- First, Rona may pay Adam the full $160 000 and obtain an undertaking from Adam that he will pay off the mortgage to BCD Trust Co.

- Second, Rona may pay $60 000 to Adam for Adam's equity of redemption and a further $100 000 to BCD Trust Co. in full payment of the mortgage.

- Third, Rona may pay Adam $60 000, as above, and accept Blackacre subject to the mortgage; that is, Rona will herself assume responsibility for paying off the mortgage. We can see that the third possibility is really a variation of the second: instead of paying the mortgage off at once, Rona simply pays it off as it falls due. This is known as an **assumption** of the mortgage.

assumption
a subsequent purchaser takes over the responsibility of paying off the mortgage

closed mortgage
a mortgage that does not permit early repayment of the debt without a substantial penalty

In circumstances like those in Illustration 25.1, the first possibility rarely occurs because Rona takes the risk that Adam's other creditors might obtain the purchase money through court action, or Adam might abscond so that the funds never reach BCD Trust Co., leaving Rona to pay BCD in order to redeem the mortgage. She might end up paying $260 000 for Blackacre instead of $160 000. The second option can be very expensive for two reasons. First, by the terms of the mortgage, the mortgagor may not have the right to pay off the mortgage before the due date without a substantial penalty; this is a **closed mortgage**. Also, purchasers rarely pay the full purchase price up front for land. Land transactions are almost invariably financed by a credit arrangement, usually in the form of a mortgage. If interest rates have risen, the purchaser will wind up replacing a low interest mortgage with a new higher interest mortgage. Therefore, it would likely be most convenient for Rona simply to pay $60 000 to obtain Blackacre and to *assume* the mortgage liability for making payments.

Sometimes, especially where the mortgagor (vendor) has significantly reduced the first mortgage by instalment payments—or the value of the property has risen substantially—the purchaser may not have the resources to pay fully for the vendor's equity. Accordingly, she will arrange through a financial institution for a new mortgage for a larger sum of money. She will then use the proceeds of the new mortgage to pay off the existing mortgage, with the balance going towards the cash portion of the purchase price.

Effect of Default by the Purchaser

What happens if the purchaser, Rona, defaults on payment of the original mortgage?

- The fact that Adam has sold his land to Rona does not affect BCD's rights as mortgagee of Blackacre; BCD retains all its rights against the land. It may obtain possession and sell the land. It may also recover from Adam, the original mortgagor, on his covenant—his contractual obligation—to repay the debt.

If BCD sues Adam, what rights does Adam have upon paying off the mortgage?

- Adam may successfully sue Rona for the full sum of money he was required to pay to BCD. One reason for this result is that as part of her purchase price for Blackacre, Rona assumed the mortgage and agreed to pay it off. The law implies that the promise to pay off the mortgage includes a promise to indemnify Adam—that is, to protect Adam from any liability under it. A second reason is that by paying off the mortgage Adam has, in effect, purchased the mortgagee's rights. He becomes subrogated to the mortgagee's rights and is, in effect, the mortgagee to whom Rona is now a mortgagor. At this point, Adam may use all the remedies against Rona that BCD Trust Co. might itself have utilized against the land and the mortgagor.

Instead of suing Adam, may the mortgagee BCD sue the purchaser Rona directly?

■ There is no contract between BCD and Rona that gives BCD this right. Nor do the courts recognize any privity of estate between a mortgagee and the purchaser of the land as they do in the case of landlord and tenant. Under common law rules, BCD may successfully sue Rona only if it can obtain an assignment of Adam's right to indemnity discussed in the preceding paragraph. As a practical matter, Adam will often agree to assign his right in order to avoid having the mortgagee sue him on his covenant in the mortgage. In Ontario, the Mortgages Act gives the mortgagee a statutory right to sue the purchaser, Rona, directly, without obtaining an assignment from Adam, the mortgagor, but only while Rona holds the land.[9] If she sells it to yet another purchaser, Bill, then Bill becomes liable to pay the mortgage, and Rona is released from her statutory obligation to the mortgagee.

SECOND MORTGAGES

Uses of a Second Mortgage

A prospective purchaser often finds she does not have sufficient money to buy land that is already subject to a mortgage, or sometimes the owner of land already subject to a mortgage may wish to raise an additional sum by using his equity as security. Second mortgages (that is, mortgages registered after one prior mortgage) are quite common. Less common are third and fourth mortgages. The subsequent mortgages rank behind prior mortgages and their interests may be wiped out by the remedies of the first mortgagee.

ILLUSTRATION 25.2

V offers Hillcroft for sale for $230 000 subject to a mortgage for $150 000 to *M* Co. Ltd. *P* would like to buy Hillcroft, but she has only $55 000 in cash, and she needs $80 000. She arranges to borrow $25 000 from her business associate *M2* and to give *M2* a second mortgage on Hillcroft. Having made these arrangements, *P* accepts *V*'s offer to sell, and they arrange a **closing date** (a date for completing the transaction).

On the closing day the following transactions take place:

(a) *V* delivers a transfer of Hillcroft to *P*;

(b) *P* delivers a mortgage of Hillcroft to *M2*;

(c) *M2* gives *P* $25 000;

(d) *P* gives *V* the total sum of $80 000 and also assumes the existing first mortgage given by *V* to *M* Co. Ltd.

These transactions usually take place simultaneously in the office of one lawyer or in the registry office. The parties trade the necessary documents and sums of money, and *P* and *M2* immediately register the transfer and mortgage. The net result of the transaction is as follows: *P* holds the title in Hillcroft subject to the first mortgage to *M* Co. Ltd. for $150 000 and the second mortgage to *M2* for $25 000. She is indebted in the sum of $175 000.

Rights of a Second Mortgagee

A second mortgagee has rights similar to those of a first mortgagee except that

(a) he ranks behind the first mortgagee in priority of payment, and

(b) he has the personal covenant of *P* and no personal covenant of *V*.

In Illustration 25.2, if *P* defaults payment on both mortgages, the first mortgagee may start an action for foreclosure. The second mortgagee may decide to stand by and do nothing. If the first mortgagee completes the foreclosure, the interest of both *P* and the second mortgagee is destroyed. The second mortgagee loses his security in Hillcroft and is left with only a right of action for debt against *P*,

closing date
the date for completing a sale of property

---

9. Mortgages Act, *ibid.*, s. 20(2), (3).

who may be insolvent. If the first mortgagee proceeds with a sale under power of sale or sale by the court, the proceeds will be paid, first, to satisfy the first mortgage debt and expenses of the sale, and second, to satisfy the second mortgage debt. The second mortgagee will be paid only to the extent that there is any surplus after paying off the first mortgagee. Of course, the sale may bring in more money than the total amount owed on both mortgages, and in that case the excess will go to *P*.

When the first mortgagee begins a foreclosure action, the second mortgagee may choose to redeem—that is, to pay off the first mortgage himself and receive an assignment of it. But then he will have invested an additional sum in the land. In Illustration 25.2 above, *M2* would have to pay about $150 000. With *P* insolvent, *M2* would have little hope of collecting by suing for the debt. He may, in turn, commence a foreclosure action, and, in effect, buy Hillcroft for about $175 000 (which may or may not be a good buy depending upon the current real estate market); or he may proceed with either of the two remedies of sale, taking the risk that a sale may not bring in enough to pay off the sums he has invested.

Risks for a Second Mortgagee When the Mortgagor Defaults

A second mortgage invariably provides that default on the first mortgage is also immediate default on the second mortgage—that is, a breach of the mortgagor's obligation to protect the second mortgagee's interest in the land, and the second mortgagee may immediately act upon the usual remedies. In the absence of such protection, a second mortgagee might find himself in the following position:

(a) Payment of the second mortgage is not yet due, so there is no default on it.
(b) The first mortgage, having an earlier due date, is in default and the first mortgagee promptly pursues one of its remedies against the land—foreclosure, sale by court, or exercise of the power of sale.
(c) The result of either of these remedies would be to destroy the second mortgagee's interest in the land.

In a sale either by the court or by the first mortgagee, to the extent that the sale brought in more than the debt due on the first mortgage, the second mortgagee would receive compensation, but he might well recover only a part of the debt. To avoid these risks a second mortgagee may himself act promptly to pursue his remedies.

Sometimes a mortgagor defaults on only the second mortgage, or, if he has defaulted on the first as well, the first mortgagee may be quite satisfied with the adequacy of its security and is willing to "sit tight" and see what the subsequent mortgagees and creditors intend to do. The first mortgagee need not worry since it has the prime interest in the land and no one can affect its position. If the second mortgagee forecloses, he becomes the owner of the property, subject to the prior interest of the first mortgagee. He must now make the payments and assume the responsibilities of the original mortgagor. A second mortgagee rarely proceeds by sale, but in such circumstances, the purchaser would obtain title clear of the mortgagor's interest and the second mortgage, but, of course, still subject to the first mortgage. In either case the new owner must make satisfactory arrangements with the first mortgagee.

Subsequent Mortgages After a Second Mortgage

Each successive mortgage ranks in priority according to its registration. Each subsequent mortgage gives all the usual remedies to the mortgagee, subject to the prior rights of any earlier mortgagee. Each subsequent mortgagee takes a greater risk as creditor for several reasons:

■ *First*, the land is subject to a larger financial debt, and any drop in price will injure the security of the latest mortgagee first.
■ *Second*, a succession of mortgages on one piece of land usually indicates financial instability and poor management on the part of the borrower.
■ *Third*, failure by a subsequent mortgagee to act reasonably promptly in case of default may result in the destruction of its secured interest in the land, if a prior mortgagee exercises its power of sale.

■ *Fourth*, the cost of redeeming prior mortgages may be too high—in order to prevent foreclosure of its interest, a subsequent mortgagee may have to lay out more money than it can afford.

This is why interest rates are higher on subsequent mortgages and lenders frequently demand additional security, such as mortgages on other lands or personal property, before advancing a mortgage loan.

MORTGAGEE'S RIGHTS COMPARED WITH RIGHTS OF OTHER CREDITORS

A creditor that has no security other than its debtor's promise is a **general creditor**, and its claim ranks as a general claim. A creditor that has collateral security—that is, a prior claim against one or more specified assets of the debtor, is a **secured creditor**. If the debtor becomes insolvent, the general creditors must wait until the claims of the secured creditors have been satisfied out of the assets against which they have their claims. When the sale of an asset brings in more than the amount owing to the secured creditor, the excess becomes available for the settlement of general claims. Here we may see the relation of the mortgagee's remedy of sale to other creditors' claims. A mortgagee is a secured creditor in the land. As we noted earlier in this chapter, after a sale of the mortgaged land by the mortgagee, the sale proceeds first go to satisfy the mortgage debt and sale expenses. Any surplus is returned to the mortgagor; if the mortgagor is insolvent, the surplus goes to his creditors. However, if there is a deficiency—that is, the particular security realizes less than the amount of the secured creditor's claim—to the extent of that deficiency, the secured creditor then ranks as a general creditor along with all the general creditors.

general creditor
a creditor that has no security other than the debtor's promise to pay

secured creditor
a creditor that has collateral security in the form of a prior claim against specified assets of the debtor

---

ILLUSTRATION 25.3

(a) Harper is the proprietor of a successful, small retail business with a building worth about $320 000. He has mortgaged the building for $250 000 to Commerce Trust Co. Unfortunately, his area suffers a serious recession when a large local industry closes; he has little working capital and cannot weather the indefinite loss in sales. He becomes insolvent and is declared bankrupt. A trustee is appointed, and, in due course, the building is sold. The remainder of Harper's assets are also sold. The following is a statement of Harper's financial position after all the assets are liquidated:

Assets		Liabilities	
Bank balance from:		Commerce	
sale of building	$270 000	Trust Co.	$247 000
sale of other		General	
assets	38 000	Creditors	85 000
TOTAL	$308 000	TOTAL	$332 000

The assets would distributed as follows:

Commerce Trust Co.	$247 000
General Creditors	61 000
	$308 000

We see that the mortgagee receives 100 cents on the dollar of debt owed to it from the sale of the building. In addition, the sale produces a surplus of $23 000. This sum

is added to the $38 000 realized from all other assets, and is paid out rateably to the general creditors. Here, they receive 61 000 ÷ 85 000 of each dollar of indebtedness—about 72 cents on each dollar.

(b) Suppose, however, that the sale of the building brings a much smaller sum because of the depressed market—say, $200 000. The assets and liabilities are now as follows:

Assets		Liabilities	
Bank balance from:		Commerce	
sale of building	$200 000	Trust Co.	$247 000
sale of other		General	
assets	38 000	Creditors	85 000
TOTAL	$238 000	TOTAL	$332 000

The assets would now be distributed as follows:

Creditors

	Secured	General	Total
Commerce Trust Co.	$200 000		
plus $\frac{47\,000}{132\,000}$ × 38 000		$13 530	$213 530
General Creditors			
$\frac{85\,000}{132\,000}$ × 38 000		24 470	24 470
	$200 000	$38 000	$238 000

Note: We obtain the figure of $132 000 by adding the deficiency of $47 000 on the mortgage debt to the total unse-

continued

cured debt of $85 000. In these circumstances the mortgagee receives a total of over $213 000 from a debt of $247 000—about 86 cents on each dollar of debt. On the other hand, the general creditors suffer much more severely: they receive about 24 500 ÷ 85 000 of each dollar of indebtedness—about 29 cents on each dollar. We may note that their position is worsened by the fact that the mortgagee joined them to rank as a general creditor for that portion of the debt unsatisfied by the sale of the building, thus dividing the assets among a larger group of claims.

TRANSFERRING A MORTGAGEE'S INTEREST IN LAND

Assignment

A mortgagee may wish to obtain cash by selling the mortgage rather than waiting for the mortgage debt to fall due in order to collect. The mortgage may be a sound investment, having good security and a reliable debtor, or it may be a risky investment. In either case, the mortgagee may sell its mortgage at the best price it can get. The sale of a mortgage is a transaction involving both contractual and real property aspects. The mortgagee *assigns* its rights to the covenants made by the mortgagor, and *grants* or transfers its interest in the land to the purchaser (assignee) of the mortgage. Sometimes, in order to obtain a higher price, an assignor-mortgagee guarantees payment—that is, if the mortgagor defaults in payment, the assignor, on the assignee's demand, will pay off the mortgage and take back an assignment of it. In most sales, however, a mortgagee sells the mortgage outright, and the purchaser takes the risk of default together with all the usual remedies of a mortgagee.

A purchaser of a mortgage, as an assignee of contractual rights, is bound by the usual rules of assignment in contract. As we have seen in Chapter 12, the debtor, in this case the mortgagor, is not bound by the assignment until receiving notice of it, and the assignee takes the mortgage subject to the equities and the state of the mortgage account between mortgagor and mortgagee.

Discharge of Mortgages

Effects of a Discharge

When a mortgagor or a subsequent purchaser pays off the whole of the mortgage debt at maturity of the loan, he is entitled to a discharge from the mortgagee. A discharge operates both as an acknowledgment that the debt has been paid in full and as a cancellation of the lien or encumbrance on the land. To clear his title to the property, the mortgagor promptly registers the discharge in the land titles office. A fraudulent mortgagee cannot then successfully exercise a power of sale and grant the legal title to an innocent purchaser on the pretence that the mortgage is unpaid and in arrears. A fraudulent mortgagee has been known to do just that and to deprive a mortgagor of the land when the mortgagor has neglected to obtain a discharge and register it.[10] In areas where the registry system still exists, a discharge from the mortgagee operates to reconvey the legal title of the land to the mortgagor.

Arrangements for Prepayment of Mortgage Debt

A mortgage sometimes contains a contractual term permitting the mortgagor to repay the mortgage and to obtain a discharge even before the debt matures. The term permitting such repayment may have various conditions attached to it. Often a mortgagee requires a period of notice, usually three

---

10. *Dicker* v. *Angerstein* (1876), 3 Ch. D. 395.

months, before it need accept the money. Such a requirement gives it time to find a new borrower so that the money received does not lie idle until it finds a new investment. A mortgagee usually requires payment of a bonus, for example, three months' interest in lieu of notice, or it may require both notice and a bonus. Flexible mortgage-prepayment clauses often contain various other prepayment possibilities. A mortgagor may be permitted to prepay part of the debt rather than all of it, in order to make good use of extra earnings and to reduce the interest payable on the mortgage loan. Certain types of mortgages, particularly second mortgages and short-term mortgages, permit repayment "at any time without notice or bonus." Mortgages containing such a term are usually called **open mortgages**.

Partial Discharges

A mortgage may also permit the mortgagor to prepay a specified portion of the mortgage debt and to obtain a **partial discharge**—that is, a discharge of a definite portion of the mortgaged lands. Partial discharges are common when the mortgagor is a land developer. The developer may own a large piece of undeveloped land and wish to sell off a part free from any encumbrance; or he may wish to erect a large building on a particular part of the land and require financing in the form of a large, new mortgage—which he cannot obtain except as a first mortgage. These various methods of prepaying part or all of a mortgage debt play an important role in the credit financing of land development.

open mortgage
a mortgage permitting repayment of the debt at any time without notice or bonus

partial discharge
a discharge of a definite portion of the mortgaged lands

PROVINCIAL VARIATIONS

The remedies available to mortgagees and mortgagors developed, as we have seen, over a long period. The various provinces of Canada adopted existing English law at the date each province obtained its first legislative body; the dates range from 1758 in Nova Scotia to 1870 in Alberta, Manitoba, and Saskatchewan. Accordingly, the variations in the mortgage law received by each province are considerable. After its adoption of the English law, each province developed its own procedures and made statutory amendments to meet its own needs. Although the basic provisions are similar, the specifics differ widely according to the economy of the province and the character of business within it. We present here a brief summary of the main variations in remedies.

The Mortgagee's Rights

In Alberta, British Columbia, and Saskatchewan, a mortgagee's right to sue on the covenant to repay has been restricted by statute.[11]

In British Columbia, in that portion of Manitoba under the registry system, and in Ontario, New Brunswick, Prince Edward Island, and Newfoundland, a mortgagee may foreclose the equity of redemption in the manner we have already discussed. In Alberta, Saskatchewan, and that portion of Manitoba under the land titles system, the usual remedy is sale by the court. If the sale does not produce any satisfactory bids, then the mortgagee may proceed to foreclose, but foreclosure appears to be a rare remedy in practice. In all provinces, a mortgagee may request the court or registrar to hold a sale of mortgaged land, and, except in Nova Scotia, may sell under a power of sale if it is provided for either by statute or under the terms of the mortgage. In Nova Scotia, although the court issues an order of "foreclosure and sale," foreclosure is not really permitted: the court must hold a sale.

---

11. Law of Property Act, R.S.A. 2000, c. L-7, s. 40; Property Law Act, R.S.B.C. 1996, c. 377, s. 32; Limitation of Certain Civil Rights Act, R.S.S. 1978, c. L-16, s. 2(1) and (2). See *National Trust Co.* v. *Mead*, [1990] 2 S.C.R. 410.

The Mortgagor's Rights

With the exception of New Brunswick, those provinces permitting a mortgagee to start an action for foreclosure also allow the mortgagor to request the court to hold a sale, provided he deposits a sum of money as security for the costs of the sale if it produces no acceptable bids. Accordingly, a mortgagor may prevent the mortgagee from acquiring the mortgagor's interest in the land. This right of the mortgagor can be an important protection when the land is worth substantially more than the mortgage debt. We should remember, however, that if the market value of the land does exceed the mortgage debt by a significant amount, the mortgagor, unless he is considered a bad personal credit risk, should be able to refinance the land by obtaining an extension of his mortgage or arranging for a new mortgage and paying off his old mortgage. In any event, he should be able to sell the equity of redemption at its market value. In all jurisdictions a mortgagor has the right to redeem the land by paying off the entire debt before foreclosure or sale.

REVERSE MORTGAGES

reverse mortgage
a form of mortgage under which no repayment is due until the mortgagor sells or dies

A recent development in Canadian law has been the adoption from Europe of the concept of the **reverse mortgage**. It can be a benefit, mainly to senior citizens who are retired and are "house rich and cash poor." Typically, a homeowner purchased a house many years earlier and has paid off the mortgage debt on the property; she owns it without debt. Suppose that her employment did not make provision for a generous retirement pension and she now has a meagre income. Meanwhile her house has increased substantially in market value.

Using the reverse mortgage concept, she may give a mortgage on her house and receive a lump sum or a periodic payment based on the market value of the property, prevailing interest rates, and actuarial calculations of her life expectancy. She remains in possession of the house while the principal and interest on the reverse mortgage accrue; no repayment is due until she sells the house or dies. When one of these two events occur, and if the market value of the house is greater than the accrued debt, the lender pays the excess to the owner or her estate. If the value of the house is less than the accrued debt, then the lender absorbs the deficiency.

As a result of our aging population and the increasing number of persons in the financial position we have just described, the reverse mortgage is becoming more common.[12] Some financial institutions have begun to promote this new area. There are wide variations in the design of reverse mortgages and at present little, if any, regulation.[13]

Concern has been expressed that seniors should seek advice before undertaking a reverse mortgage and consider alternatives such as selling the house and buying or renting smaller accommodation.

MORTGAGE FRAUD

In the summer of 2004, it was reported that Canada was experiencing a rise in "mortgage fraud."[14] This increased incidence of fraud was said to be linked to the "hot" real estate market in many Canadian cities, automation of the land registration systems, and the rise of the phenomenon of identity theft.

---

12. For a useful discussion of the reverse mortgage, see the Canadian Centre for Elder Law Studies, *Consultation Paper on Reverse Mortgages* (B.C. Law Institute, February 2005).

13. It seems doubtful whether either the federal Interest Act, R.S.C.1985, c. I-15 or the various provincial consumer protection laws (discussed in Chapter 32) provide a satisfactory basis for regulation. Manitoba was the first to adopt legislation directed specifically at reverse mortgages. See Part III of the Mortgages Act, C.C.S.M., c. M200.

14. In a *Toronto Sun* business column, it was reported that real estate fraud cost an estimated $300 million in Canada in the year 2001 alone: Linda Leatherdale, "Homes Fall Prey to Identity Thieves," *Toronto Sun*, August 15, 2004, http://money.canoe.ca/Columnists/Leatherdale/2004/08/15/pf-584340.html.

This mortgage fraud—which takes as its primary victim mortgage lenders but also creates costs for homeowners and society generally—can take two forms.

The first is essentially a form of identity theft, whereby one fraudster assumes the identity of a registered land title holder, while a second "conspirator" assumes the identity of a purchaser. An agreement of purchase and sale is drawn up and used to obtain mortgage financing, which is never repaid. When the mortgage goes into default, the true owner of the property is surprised to learn of power of sale proceeding by an unknown lender.

The second form of mortgage fraud involves the artificial inflation of the value of a property, through "flips" of properties (a property is purchased and then immediately resold at an inflated price, so as to increase the purported value of the property, and increase the amount of mortgage financing) or through misrepresentations of the purchase price using falsified purchase agreements or phony appraisers.

While the mortgagees are defrauded of the mortgage amount, homeowners are also affected. In the case of identity fraud, not only will the real homeowner have to convince the mortgagee that he is not the debtor, but he will likely have to spend additional money on land registry and legal fees to restore his title on the register. Additionally, the costs of mortgage fraud borne by the mortgage lenders will inevitably be passed on to mortgagors in the form of higher lending costs. The initial response by the courts was not favourable to the homeowner. In *Household Realty Corp.* v. *Liu*,[15] the Ontario Court of Appeal upheld a fraudulent mortgage against an innocent homeowner. The lender was entitled to enforce its remedies. In 2007, the court took the rare step of overruling itself. In *Lawrence* v. *Wright*, it held that only a true owner could give a valid charge so this mortgage was held invalid and the innocent homeowner's title was cleared.[16] The Ontario land titles legislation has since been amended to invalidate fraudulent documents.[17] The losing party, either the duped lender or the innocent homeowner, is entitled to make a claim against the Land Titles Assurance Fund. Alberta legislation strengthens the proof of identity requirements for the registrar of land titles and imposes a duty on the real estate industry to protect against mortgage fraud.[18]

Fraudulent registration of any document in a real property transaction is a criminal offence with a maximum penalty of 5 years in prison.

ETHICAL ISSUE

Money Laundering and Solicitor–Client Privilege

As part of a federal anti-terrorism initiative, the federal government enacted the Proceeds of Crime (Money Laundering) and Terrorist Financing Act. Under the federal legislation, professionals and financial institutions are required to report suspicious transactions or large cash payments of $10 000 or more. An independent government agency, (FINTRAC), investigates and analyzes reports and tracks cross-border movements of currency.

Lawyers were among the professionals covered by the Act and real estate lawyers were particularly affected since their work involves receiving large sums of money from their clients. The

continued

---

15. (2005), 261 D.L.R. (4th) 679 (On. C.A.)

16. [2007] 84 O.R. (3d) 94 (on. C.A.);

17. The Ontario Land Titles Act, s. 78(4.1) invalidates fraudulent documents registered after October 19, 2006. However, the amendment does not invalidate the chain of documents stemming from the document, only the initial fraud.

18. Land Titles Amendment Act, 2006, S.A. 2006, c. 21 s. 13; The Real Estate Amendment Act, 2006, S.A. 2006, c. 29, s. 2.

Federation of Law Societies of Canada launched a successful court challenge of the law. It argued that requiring lawyers to report on their clients was a violation of solicitor–client privilege and a breach of the constitutional right to independent counsel. The courts agreed with the Federation's position and restricted the application of the new law. As a result, the Minister of Finance introduced amendments to the Act exempting lawyers from its reporting requirements.

In recognition of the fact that preventing money laundering is a worthy goal, the Federation developed model rules for lawyers' codes of professional conduct. The model "know your client" rule requires lawyers to confirm their clients' identities with independent documents and collect information such as addresses and occupations. The model "no cash" rule prohibits lawyers from accepting cash payments of $7500 or more.

QUESTIONS TO CONSIDER

1. Do you think law societies are in a better position to deal with money laundering than FINTRAC?

2. This is another example of a conflict between two worthy goals. What are the arguments that justify the priority of solicitor–client privilege?

Sources: Proceeds of Crime (Money Laundering) and Terrorist Financing Act, S.C. 2000, c. 17; Committee on Anti-Money Laundering, Federation of Law Societies of Canada, "The Federation of Law Societies of Canada Submission in Response to Finance Canada's Enhancing Canada's Anti-Money Laundering and Anti-Terrorist Financing Regime Consultation," *Department of Finance Canada*, September 30, 2005, www.fin.gc.ca/consultresp/regime_14e.html; *Law Society of British Columbia* v. *Attorney General of Canada* (2002), 207 D.L.R. (4th) 736 (B.C.C.A.); Federation of Law Societies of Canada, "Model Rule on Client Identification and Verification Requirements," March 20, 2008, www.flsc.ca/en/pdf/Federation_Model_Rule_080327.pdf.

A TYPICAL REAL ESTATE TRANSACTION

The Circumstances

A real estate transaction can best be understood by following a typical sale from start to finish. We shall use for an example a fictional piece of land in Oshawa, Ontario, governed by the registry system. John Vincent owns the land and building on Main Street described in his grant as Lot 27, Plan 7654, in the City of Oshawa. The building fronting on Main Street consists of a large store at ground level and three suites of offices on the second floor. Vincent occupies the store himself and runs a men's wear shop. The offices are rented to three tenants, one to Dr. A. McAvity, dentist, the second to Happy Auto Insurance Company, and the third to C. McCollum, chartered accountant. Business has been poor; Vincent is 70 years old and wishes to retire. He has advertised without success to find a buyer of his business. Although he has received many inquiries about purchasing the building, a prime location, no one is interested in buying his rather old-fashioned stock and fixtures. He has finally decided to run a closing-down sale and then sell the building.

Listing the Property for Sale

listing agreement
contract between the vendor and his real estate agent creating the obligation to pay commission

John Vincent has decided to hire a real estate agent to help him find a buyer for the property. Vincent signs a **listing agreement** that appoints the agent and:

■ designates a list price (selling price) and term (length of the engagement);
■ gives the agent the exclusive right to advertise the property on MLS (Multiple Listing Service), and via the Internet and television during the term of the listing;

- allows the agent to show the property to prospective buyers, either individually or collectively at "open houses";
- requires Vincent to pay the agent a commission (usually a percentage of the sale price) if the agent "procures an offer" at the list price or Vincent accepts an offer at any price;[19] and
- directs Vincent's lawyer to pay the commission directly to the agent out of the sale proceeds.

The duties and responsibilities of Vincent's agent are discussed in Chapter 19.

The Offer to Purchase

Hi-Style Centres Ltd., a firm selling women's wear, operates a chain of stores and is anxious to have an outlet in Oshawa. The owners approach Vincent's agent with the proposal that he rent the store to them. However, Vincent has decided to leave Oshawa and retire to Victoria, British Columbia. He wishes to break all business connections in the East. He says he would consider an offer to purchase but not to rent. Hi-Style makes two offers to purchase, both rejected by Vincent as too low. It now makes a third offer that Vincent is considering seriously. The essential terms are:[20]

(a) Hi-Style offers to buy the premises for $645 000, payable as follows: tender $25 000 as a deposit by certified cheque attached to the offer; assume the first mortgage of about $375 000 held by the Grimm Mortgage Company; give back to Vincent a second mortgage of $125 000 (interest and other terms set out in detail); pay the balance on closing date (completion date).

(b) The sale is to be closed 90 days after the date of the offer.

(c) Hi-Style may search the title and submit **requisitions** (questions concerning claims against Vincent's title) within 60 days of acceptance of the offer. Vincent promises to deliver a copy of the survey of the lot, which he has in his possession, for examination by Hi-Style. If serious claims against Vincent's title are raised and Vincent cannot answer them satisfactorily, the contract will be terminated and the deposit returned to Hi-Style. If requisitions are answered satisfactorily or no requisitions are submitted within 60 days, it is presumed that Hi-Style accepts Vincent's title as satisfactory.

requisitions
questions concerning claims against a seller's title to property

(d) Vincent is to remain in possession and the building is to remain at his risk until closing. He promises to keep the building insured to its full insurable value. He also undertakes to give possession of the building in substantially the same condition as it was at the time of making the contract. If the building is destroyed or seriously damaged, Hi-Style may elect to take over the premises and to receive the proceeds of all insurance, or it may elect to terminate the contract, with Vincent to suffer the loss, if any.

(e) Vincent is to pay all taxes and insurance until closing and deduct from the amount due at closing all outstanding current expenses, such as accrued water and electric bills, unpaid taxes, and insurance. He will transfer all insurance policies to Hi-Style, provided the insurance companies are willing to accept Hi-Style as a satisfactory risk, and Hi-Style will pay for the prepaid unexpired portion of such policies. Alternatively, Hi-Style may arrange its own insurance to commence on the day of closing.

---

19. The standard real estate association listing agreement also contains extended commission obligations if the vendor accepts an offer after the expiration of the term of the listing from a purchaser introduced to the property by the agent.

20. An offer to purchase may also include other terms, the importance of which varies according to the circumstances, in particular, the nature of the property. For example, the vendor might be required to give a warranty that the heating plant conforms to regulations; to produce a certificate of inspection of boiler or gas installations; to warrant that the premises do not violate existing zoning by-laws; to identify all encroachments or easements in respect of which the property is either a servient or a dominant tenement; and to allow the prospective purchaser access to the premises for the purpose of checking the land survey.

(f) Vincent warrants that his three suites of offices are leased to tenants as stated at rents of $1250 monthly per suite under leases expiring two years after date of closing for Suite No. 1, two years four months after closing for Suite No. 2, and Suite 3 as a monthly tenancy only. He will deliver the original of the two leases and assignments of the leases on closing, an acknowledgment from the third tenant that she is only a monthly tenant, and signed notices to the tenants that Hi-Style is the new landlord to whom they are to pay their rent.

(g) The offer is open for two days, and acceptance must be communicated to the office of the lawyer for Hi-Style in Oshawa before 5 p.m. on the second day.

Preparations for Completing the Transaction

Accepting the Offer

The agent shows Vincent four copies of the offer. Vincent decides to accept it and signs all four copies. The agent sends two signed copies back to Hi-Style (one for Hi-Style's lawyer, Harmon), retaining the other copies for Vincent and his lawyer, Vale. The agent also sends a copy of the survey of Vincent's lot to Harmon. The manager of Hi-Style has taken the careful step of having Harmon draw up the offer in the first place. So Harmon is familiar with its terms; in particular, she has made a special note in her file of the last day to submit requisitions concerning title to the land, as well as the date of closing the transaction.

Verifying Title and Possession

As the purchaser's lawyer, Harmon takes the following steps:

(1) She discusses the purpose and availability of title insurance with the purchaser, but Hi-Style decides against title insurance.

(2) She orders an electronic search of the title to the lot and also compares the survey received from Vincent with the plan of the whole area as filed in the registry office, to make sure there are no discrepancies in the boundaries of the lot and to learn whether there are any outstanding claims registered.

(3) She conducts "off title searches" by sending letters to various agencies. For example, she writes to the city tax department asking for a certificate showing the state of real property taxes, both arrears and current, and encloses the small fee usually required for the certificate.

(4) She writes to the Grimm Mortgage Company advising them of the assumption and asking them to prepare and forward a mortgage statement showing what the exact amount outstanding on the mortgage, including accrued interest, will be on the date of closing.

(5) She examines the zoning by-law and checks with the office of the building inspector for any outstanding work orders and deficiency notices under municipal by-laws. Many jurisdictions will provide a zoning compliance letter if the survey is submitted to them with a small fee.

(6) She asks her client to examine the premises carefully to confirm that the building is occupied by the tenants and by Vincent as stated in the contract and that there are no other persons who appear to be exercising an adverse claim over any part of the premises. In the case of valuable commercial property on main streets, the boundaries are very important, especially if demolition and reconstruction are even remotely contemplated. Harmon advises Hi-Style to hire a surveyor to make a new survey and compare it with the old, thus checking whether adjacent owners are in possession of any part of the lot and have perhaps extinguished Vincent's title to portions they have occupied.

(7) She checks with the sheriff's office for any claims that may be filed there against the vendor.

(8) After collecting all the aforesaid information, Harmon writes a requisition letter to Vale identifying all discrepancies she has found in the title and off title searches and requesting

that Vale correct any problems. Harmon must make sure that Vale receives this letter by the requisition date. In the letter she asks for copies of all leases. She asks Vale to obtain tenant acknowledgements—standard form questionnaires describing the terms of the tenancy, the state of premises, and the status of rent. She also confirms who will be preparing the electronic documents.

Preparing the Documents for Closing

Within a few days Vincent's lawyer, Vale, electronically prepares a **transfer** and second mortgage, the documents both lawyers will authorize for electronic registration. Harmon examines them and approves their contents. To avoid any confusion about names or initials and the description of the land to be conveyed, both lawyers check very closely to see that all details are accurate. A few days before closing, each lawyer meets with their respective client and reviews the draft documents and statement of adjustments (discussed below). The electronic registration system no longer requires the vendor to sign the transfer. However, both vendor and purchaser are asked to sign an authorization and direction allowing their lawyers to electronically register the documents in the form presented.

There are tangible documents that are signed and delivered on closing. Vale has prepared a charge document for the second mortgage and Hi-Style will sign this. Both clients sign undertakings to re-adjust the accounts after closing if there is a mistake on the statement of adjustments (as discussed below).

transfer
an electronic grant that both lawyers will authorize for registration

Preparing the Accounts for Closing

Harmon finds that Vincent's title to the land is in good order and she is satisfied with Vale's response to her requisition letter. She receives a mortgage statement from Grimm Mortgage Company, and it agrees with the statement made by Vincent concerning the amount outstanding. A few weeks before the date of closing, Vale prepares a document called a **statement of adjustments** (see below) setting out all the items, both credits and debits, that must be adjusted between the parties to arrive at the correct amount to be paid by Hi-Style to Vincent on the date of closing. The closing date is to be April 15.

statement of adjustments
a document setting out all the items—both credits and debits—that must be adjusted between the parties to arrive at the correct amount to be paid on closing

Re: Lot 27, Plan 7654, in the City of Oshawa
Hi-Style Centres Ltd. purchase from Vincent

STATEMENT OF ADJUSTMENTS

1. SALE PRICE		$645 000.00
2. Deposit paid by purchaser	$ 25 000.00	
3. First mortgage to Grimm Mortgage Company to be assumed by purchaser	$373 580.60	
Plus interest, April 1 to 15 at 10.5%	$ 1 612.03	
	$375 192.63	
4. Second mortgage back to vendor	$125 000.00	
5. Unpaid taxes for current year, $5695.00, charged to vendor to April 15— 3½ months	$ 1 661.04	
6. Rent received in advance: Suite #1: 1½ months	$ 1 875.00	
Suite #2: 1½ months	$ 1 875.00	

continued

```
        Suite #3:
            ½ month                          $   450.00
                                                              $ 4 200.00

    7. Union Hartford Fire Insurance
          Policy no. 8953744, three years,
          expires Nov. 1, current year.
       Amount: $450 000
       Premium: $1 870
       Unexpired portion:                                     $    1 012.92

    8. Full tank of furnace oil –
          2000 litres @ 43.4¢                                 $      868.00

    9. BALANCE DUE ON CLOSING               $115 827.25
                                            $646 880.92       $646 880.92
```

The Closing

Trading Documents

Since all registrations can be completed online, the lawyers agree to close the deal without a face-to-face meeting. Each lawyer couriers a package of documents to the other's office to be held in escrow (an agreement that the documents will not be released, used, or registered without the prior authorization of the other). Vale's package includes:

(a) the undertaking to re-adjust

(b) the original copies of the leases to Suites No. 1 and No. 2

(c) the properly executed assignments of each lease

(d) the acknowledgment of the tenant in Suite No. 3 that she is a monthly tenant at a rent of $900 payable in advance

(e) the notice signed by Vincent to each tenant of Suites No. 1, No. 2, and No. 3 informing them of the change of ownership and requesting them to pay all future rent to Hi-Style

(f) the current tax bill

(g) a certified copy of the insurance policy showing the transfer to Hi-Style as purchaser and Vincent as second mortgagee

(h) keys to the building

On the morning of April 15, Harmon updates all her searches and electronically transfers $115 827.25 to Vale's trust account. Both lawyers access the electronic registration system and authorize the registration of the transfer and the charge (second mortgage).

Delivering Possession

Vale agrees not to release the funds he has received until registration is complete. On rare occasions, the vendor's lawyer may agree not to release the funds until the purchaser confirms possession. The mechanics of delivering possession to a purchaser sometimes cause great friction and even court action. To avoid such friction the vendor should arrange to be completely out of the premises by the time the deal is closed and deliver the keys to the purchaser. If this is not done, the purchaser may understandably be very upset and demand that the money not be released. Once anger replaces common sense, both vendor and purchaser may become obstinate, and the vendor's lawyer holding the funds is caught between them. In the present case, however, all goes smoothly: Vincent has vacated the premises the day before and the keys are delivered on closing. Harmon calls the manager of Hi-Style to tell her that the keys are available. The manager picks up the keys, goes to the building, and finds the store vacant. The transaction is complete.

After the Closing

Each lawyer still has several things to do besides submitting a bill. Vale will write to Grimm Mortgage Company to inform it of the sale and name the purchaser. He will also write to the city tax office to inform them of the change of ownership. He will write to the insurance company enclosing the copy of the policy and the transfer, and request the return of the policy with an endorsement noting the change of ownership and the interest of the second mortgagee in the property. He will also request that a copy of the policy be sent to the purchaser. Vale will pay the commission owed to the real estate agent from the proceeds of sale in accordance with the direction in the listing agreement.

Harmon will communicate with Vale to see that all these things have been completed. She will also write to Grimm Mortgage Company and to the city tax office asking each of them to send all further notices to the head office of Hi-Style. She will write to each of the tenants to inform them of the change of ownership, enclosing Vincent's notice and giving them the address at which Hi-Style would like the rent to be paid.

Only after all these things have been done, when the lawyers are able to return all the documents to their respective clients and to make a full written report of all details, will the transaction be complete.

The Distinctiveness of Each Transaction

It is important to stress that each sale of land is a separate and distinctive transaction: the terms should be tailored to meet the specific requirements of the parties in the circumstances. Perhaps we see the greatest degree of standardization in contracts for the sale of similar houses in a subdivision. Even there, however, significant variations in such standard contracts occur because of special credit arrangements, extra features installed by the builder, or arrangements for completion of the house after possession. In the sale of commercial property, the variations are far greater: often, possession does not pass to the purchaser on closing, as where the whole premises are already rented to tenants and are purchased for their investment value, or where the vendor stays on as a tenant. Sometimes when the sale of a business is involved, the purchaser covenants to buy goods from the vendor, or the vendor covenants to refrain from opening a competing business in the same neighborhood. Our fictional illustration set out above is not a model for other transactions, nor does it deal with every detail that might arise in the circumstances. Rather it is intended to give a picture and an understanding of a typical real estate transaction.

QUESTIONS FOR REVIEW

1. Describe the contractual aspects of a mortgage.
2. How does a mortgagee's interest in land under the land titles system differ from the type of interest a mortgagee receives under a registry system?
3. Describe the two harshest of the common law rules for mortgagors. How did equity remedy this?
4. Why does a mortgagee rarely take possession immediately on default by the mortgagor?
5. Define foreclosure; acceleration clause; legal title; charge; power of sale.
6. In a sale of mortgaged land by the court, what are the consequences for the mortgagor if there is a deficiency? If there is a surplus?
7. When a purchaser acquires land from the mortgagor and defaults, whom may the mortgagee sue? Why? Are there any exceptions to this rule?

8. What are the main options open to a second mortgagee when the mortgagor defaults?

9. In addition to timely repayment of the loan, what other duties does a mortgagor assume?

10. *M*, a mortgagee, wishes to sell you a $20 000 mortgage on Blackacre. *M* states that *Q*, the mortgagor, is already in default, but *M* needs money quickly to proceed with another transaction. *M* offers to assign the mortgage to you for $16 000. Name the two most important things you would need to verify before accepting the offer.

11. Distinguish between a general creditor and a secured creditor.

12. Greenacre, a five-hectare field in a new subdivision, is available for sale. You would like to divide it into 20 lots, develop 8 of them yourself, and eventually sell off the remaining 12 lots. Describe an important term you would want in the mortgage you need to finance the purchase.

13. Why would a mortgagor who has defaulted request the court to hold a sale of his property rather than allow the mortgagee to foreclose?

14. What is the appeal of a reverse mortgage on their home to a retired elderly couple?

15. In our "Typical Real Estate Transaction," explain why Vincent would agree to take back a second mortgage.

16. Before closing the real estate transaction, there are a number of tasks that the purchaser's lawyer must complete. Discuss three of the responsibilities.

CASES AND PROBLEMS

1. Four years ago Azoic Wholesalers Ltd. purchased a warehouse building for $550 000. To finance the purchase, the company paid $75 000 in cash, gave a 7.5 percent first mortgage to the Reliable Insurance Company for $315 000, and an 11 percent second mortgage of $160 000 to the vendor. The vendor subsequently sold the second mortgage to Sharpe Realties Ltd. for $145 000. All documents were duly registered. For the next few years Azoic Wholesalers Ltd. managed to pay interest on both mortgages and somewhat reduce the principal.

   Azoic Wholesalers Ltd. subsequently became insolvent and was declared bankrupt. A trustee in bankruptcy was appointed, and all the assets of the company sold. The statement below shows its financial condition after all assets were liquidated.

   Calculate how the available cash will be distributed to the various creditors.

Azoic Wholesalers Ltd.

STATEMENT OF CONDITION AT DATE OF DISTRIBUTION

Assets		Liabilities	
Bank balance from:		Reliable Insurance Co.	
sale of building	$425 000	(first mortgage)	$296 000
sale of all other assets	78 000	Sharpe Realties Ltd.	
		(second mortgage)	151 000
Total available cash	503 000		
Deficiency of assets	83 000	General creditors	139 000
	$586 000		$586 000

2. Fedorkow purchased a 100-hectare farm on the St. John River in New Brunswick for $90 000. He paid $12 000 cash and gave back a mortgage of $78 000 to the vendor, Bowes. The mortgage was payable over a 15-year period with interest at 8.5 percent in instalments of about $630 per month. Within a year, Bowes fell ill and decided to retire to a warm climate. She sold the mortgage to Manor Mortgage Co. with only a slight discount on the amount then outstanding because she personally guaranteed payment by Fedorkow.

A year later Fedorkow received an offer to purchase his frontage on the St. John River, an area of about 5 hectares, for $32 000. He visited the offices of Manor Mortgage Co. and asked if they would be interested in giving a discharge of the mortgage over the 5 hectares. Manor Mortgage Co. agreed to do so provided Fedorkow gave a $1000 bonus and a further $12 000 in reduction of the mortgage debt. The parties carried out the arrangement, and the 5 hectares were discharged from the mortgage, leaving the mortgage on the remainder of the farm. Subsequently, Fedorkow defaulted on the mortgage, having also let the farm fall into disrepair. Manor Mortgage Co. sued Bowes as guarantor of the mortgage debt for the balance of $31 560 then outstanding.

Should Manor Mortgage Co. succeed? Explain.

3. Expecting to make a quick profit, Pender purchased two hectares of land in a suburban community outside Fredericton for $85 000. He paid $20 000 in cash and obtained a loan for $65 000 by mortgaging the property to Quincy for two years with interest at 11 percent. Under the terms of the mortgage, Pender was to make quarterly payments of $5000 plus interest, with the balance of the principal sum and interest due at the end of two years. Pender's attempts to sell the land failed because the suburb did not develop as he had hoped. He paid the first quarterly instalment but missed the second.

Quincy took possession shortly after the default in payment and applied for foreclosure. The market for land in the area continued to weaken, and shortly after he obtained a final order of foreclosure, Quincy advertised the property for sale "under the mortgagee's power of sale." He accepted the highest offer of $50 000 and sued Pender for the deficiency of $10 000 plus accrued interest and the costs of obtaining foreclosure and conducting the sale, for a total of $15 600.

Pender defended by claiming that Quincy had given up all rights against him when he foreclosed Pender's equity of redemption, unless he could return the land. Quincy argued that he retained the choice to exercise his power of sale with a claim for any deficiency.

Which argument do you believe is more sound? Explain.

4. Keller owned and operated the Serene Bed & Breakfast near Sarnia for many years. It was a small business, and her health was not good. She decided to sell but found the market very limited. Jepson agreed to purchase Serene Bed & Breakfast from her for $195 000 if she agreed to take back a second mortgage. On March 31, Jepson paid Keller $30 000 on closing, assumed the first mortgage of $150 000 held by Huron Co-op Inc., and gave Keller a second mortgage for the balance of $15 000.

The spring and summer tourist seasons were very poor, and Jepson lost money during the first six months. He defaulted on payments to both mortgagees and informed them that he could not carry on. Huron replied that it intended to commence foreclosure proceedings immediately. Both Jepson and Keller then met several times with the manager of Huron at his office, to try to work out the most convenient arrangement and keep expenses to a minimum, avoiding court costs. They agreed to avoid court proceedings by Jepson conveying the property to Huron—and Keller would also transfer her interest as second mortgagee to Huron in return for the nominal sum of $100.

Several months later Keller learned that Jepson owned a substantial interest in a large retail hardware store; he earned a good salary there as manager. She requested that he pay the unpaid debt on the second mortgage, but he refused on the basis that Keller could no longer reconvey the interest she held, having already transferred it to Huron. Keller believed that she was entitled to repayment and sued Jepson.

Give your opinion of the defence raised by Jepson and whether Keller should succeed.

5. Lawlor purchased a small house from Cloutier at a price of $80 000. She paid $15 000 in cash and gave Cloutier a first mortgage for the balance. A year later, when Lawlor had reduced the principal amount of the mortgage to $52 000, she suffered financial reverses that made it impossible for her to continue to repay mortgage principal as required. Cloutier brought an action against Lawlor and on May 15 obtained an order for foreclosure with the deadline for payment by Lawlor specified as November 15.

On July 10, the insurance of $50 000 on the house expired and Lawlor renewed it while she was seeking to refinance with a new mortgagee. A few weeks later the house was seriously damaged by fire; the insurance adjuster appraised the loss at $35 000.

Both Cloutier and Lawlor immediately claimed the insurance money. The insurance company refused to pay Cloutier on the grounds that the insurance policy contained no mortgage clause that would have assigned to him rights in any claim "in so far as his interest may appear." The insurance company also refused to pay any part of the loss to Lawlor on the grounds that she had no insurable interest in the property.

Discuss the validity of the claims of Cloutier and Lawlor. Assume that there is no evidence to show that the fire was other than accidental in its origin.

6. Three years ago, the Lister Co. Ltd. borrowed $200 000 from the Hi-Rise Bank. Lister Co. was in the textile business and gave a real estate mortgage on one of its buildings as collateral security for the bank loan: the mortgage provided security in the land, building, and fixtures in the building.

The company was later adjudged bankrupt on a petition of its creditors. A question arose about whether a certain piece of expensive machinery in the mortgaged building was in fact a fixture against which the bank would retain priority in liquidation. The trustee in bankruptcy, representing the general creditors, claimed it was not a fixture, so that the proceeds from its sale would be applied to all creditors' claims and not solely to that of the bank as mortgagee.

An officer of the bank and the trustee in bankruptcy went personally to inspect the machine, but were unable to agree whether it could be described as being "permanently" affixed. The bank then started legal action to have its claim as mortgagee of the machine confirmed. At this point, the trustee offered as a compromise to recognize the bank's priority to the extent of $20 000, a sum much less than the probable resale value of the machine. The bank accepted the offer and withdrew its action.

A few days later the bank learned that at the time it took the mortgage on the building, the machine in question had been affixed to a cement floor in the plant in a permanent way, but that the building had since been renovated and the machine was reattached much less securely to the new floor. Neither the bank nor the trustee had this information when they contracted to substitute $20 000 in cash for the mortgage claim. The trustee refused to waive the agreement, however, and the Hi-Rise Bank brought an action asking the court for rescission of that contract and an order acknowledging its claim as a secured creditor with respect to the machine.

Discuss the nature of the argument on which the bank would base its claim and indicate whether its action should succeed.

Give an opinion on the probable outcome of this litigation with reasons.

7. Joseph Bator and Cecilia Potter met in 1990 and went out together for the next seven years. From time to time they discussed marrying but always delayed. In 1994 Joseph bought a large old residence that he converted into a rooming house.

While on a trip in the summer of 1997, Joseph met another woman and they made plans to marry. When Joseph broke this news to Cecilia, it proved to be a traumatic occasion for both of them. To soothe his conscience, Joseph promised Cecilia he would give her the rooming house. He consulted his lawyer, who reminded him that capital gains tax would become payable because of the proposed gift, but that his tax liability might possibly be deferred if Joseph were to convey the house to Cecilia and take a mortgage back for its total value of $100 000. His lawyer drafted a mortgage for $100 000 stating that the principal sum of $100 000 would be repayable without interest in instalments of $4000 per annum. Both Joseph and Cecilia understood that, as mortgagee, Joseph would not enforce payment of the annual $4000 instalments due under the mortgage; they were to be his gift to Cecilia. Cecilia gave up her apartment and moved into the rooming house and proceeded to manage it.

Joseph was married in late 1997, and a year later Cecilia also married someone else. In the late 1990s, Joseph's fortunes declined significantly; Cecilia and her husband prospered. By November 2002, Joseph was pleading with Cecilia that she begin paying him the annual instalments on the mortgage. Cecilia was sympathetic but her husband insisted that she not do so. Joseph then sued Cecilia for the full unpaid principal sum of $100 000, which, by a standard acceleration clause in the mortgage, became due upon default.

Give an opinion on the probable outcome of this litigation with reasons.

8. Victor Contractors Ltd. financed the construction of a high-rise apartment tower in Hamilton by receiving "draws" on first mortgage financing as work progressed. Rail Canada Pension Fund held the first mortgage for $10 700 000. The mortgage contained the following clause:

> The Mortgagor [Victor Contractors Ltd.] covenants and agrees with the Mortgagee [Rail Canada Pension Fund] that, except with the prior consent of the Mortgagee (which consent shall not be unreasonably withheld), it will not enter into any agreement for the sale, transfer or other disposition of the mortgaged premises.

On May 31, Victor Contractors agreed to sell the apartment building to Steel City Developers Corp. for $16 000 000. Steel City Developers paid a deposit of $75 000 and agreed to assume the existing first mortgage. The closing date was December 1, with the balance due on closing. The contract included the following clause:

> This Agreement is conditional upon the Vendor [Victor Contractors Ltd.] being able to obtain within thirty days following this date the consent of the first mortgagee [Rail Canada Pension Fund] to this sale and to the assumption of the first mortgage obligations by the Purchaser [Steel City Developers Corp.].

When Victor Contractors requested consent from Rail Canada Pension Fund, its manager stated that he would have to be satisfied with the financial capability of Steel City Developers and wished to see its audited financial statements. The secretary-treasurer of Steel City Developers refused to produce the statements on the grounds that her company had a firm policy of never disclosing its financial affairs to anyone except its bank because this policy gave it an advantage over its competitors.

With matters at an impasse, the solicitors for Steel City Developers finally wrote on June 28, informing Victor Contractors that since, as vendor, it had been unable to obtain the consent of the first mortgagee as required, "This Agreement is now null and void." In reply, Victor Contractors wrote, "It is clear that your letter of June 28 written on behalf of your client constituted a wrongful renunciation of the contract of sale and purchase."

Victor Contractors then sued Steel City Developers for specific performance or, alternatively, for damages for breach of contract. Steel City Developers counterclaimed for the return of the deposit of $75 000.

Outline what you consider to be the main issue that the court will have to resolve in this case, and offer with reasons an opinion about the probable outcome. Why would Rail Canada Pension Fund have insisted upon a right to satisfy itself of the financial capability of any purchaser of the apartment building?

ADDITIONAL RESOURCES FOR CHAPTER 25 ON THE COMPANION WEBSITE *(www.pearsoned.ca/smyth)*

In addition to self-test multiple-choice, true–false, and short essay questions (all with immediate feedback), application exercises, and links to useful web destinations, the Companion Website provides the following resources for Chapter 25:

- **British Columbia:** Conveyance of Land; Cost of Borrowing; Credit; Real Estate Agents; Reporting
- **Alberta:** Foreclosures; Personal Covenants; Real Estate Agents; Restrictive Covenants
- **Manitoba/Saskatchewan:** Mortgage Legislation
- **Ontario:** Charge; Discharge; Electronic Registration; Foreclosure; Judicial Sale; Land Registration Reform Act; Mortgages Act; Personal Covenant; Power of Sale

Business Organizations: Their Forms, Operation, and Management

Business may be carried on in one of three principal forms—sole proprietorship, partnership, or corporation. By definition, only an individual can carry on business as a sole proprietor, while it requires two or more persons to form a partnership. The corporation is the most flexible business form. An individual may incorporate a business and be the sole owner (shareholder); a small group of persons may establish a corporation to carry on their business; a large enterprise with thousands of shareholders could not carry on business except by means of a corporation.

Chapter 26 is devoted mainly to the law of partnership, but we also discuss sole proprietorships briefly. While there is no separate body of law regulating sole proprietorships and no special formalities are required to begin operations, they remain subject to many regulations that are of general application to business. For example, the owner may be required to obtain a licence in order to carry on a particular type of business. In most provinces, if business is carried on under any name other than the actual name of the proprietor, that name must be registered.

Each province regulates partnerships under its Partnership Act. These acts govern not only the relationship among partners but also their relations with the rest of the community.

The more complex law of corporations is the subject of Chapters 27, 28, and 29. In Chapter 27, we examine the nature and significance of corporations and their formation and composition. In Chapter 28, we concern ourselves with the relations between directors and shareholders, and the management of a corporation's internal affairs. Chapter 29 deals with the external business relations of a corporation—with its customers, its creditors, its potential investors, and with the general public.

26

Sole Proprietorships and Partnerships

This chapter examines unincorporated business entities—sole proprietorships and partnerships, with the main emphasis on partnerships. In this chapter we examine such questions as:

- Why are partnerships formed?
- What is the legal nature of a partnership?
- Why is it important to establish whether a partnership exists between persons carrying on a business?
- How are partnerships created?
- What are the usual contents of a partnership agreement?
- To what extent are partners liable for the acts of their co-partners and for the debts of the firm?
- What are the duties owed by partners to one another?
- How are partnerships terminated, and what happens when they are?
- What are limited partnerships?
- What are limited liability partnerships?
- What are "joint ventures"?
- What are "income trusts"?

CHOOSING THE APPROPRIATE FORM OF BUSINESS ORGANIZATION

Almost all businesses in Canada are carried on in one of the following forms:[1]

- sole proprietorship
- partnership
- corporation

A sole proprietorship or a partnership may come into existence without formality—that is, simply by the actions of the individual or group setting up a business. However, a corporation may only be formed under a statute in a prescribed manner and registered with the designated government department. Although for many years the procedure for incorporation was relatively expensive and cumbersome, a corporation can now be formed quickly and for a few hundred dollars. In addition, almost all provinces currently permit a corporation to be created with a single shareholder, so that corporations are a viable alternative not only to partnerships but also to sole proprietorships. Accordingly, when an individual or a group of persons contemplate establishing a business, an initial decision must be made whether or not to incorporate. At this point professional legal, accounting, and management advice should be sought. Many small businesses decide to incorporate at the outset, while others make the decision to do so later, or they remain unincorporated. There are now more than one million corporations registered in Canada, representing close to one-third of all businesses, most of them small and medium-sized enterprises. One factor that must be considered is that a number of professions do not permit their members to carry on their practice in the form of a corporation: in those cases, sole practice or partnership is the only option. However, as we shall see in Chapter 27, that situation is changing.

In the next chapter we shall consider the reasons why a person or group of persons might decide to incorporate their business. The subject of this chapter is those businesses that operate without incorporating.

SOLE PROPRIETORSHIPS

An individual who sets up a business has, simply by doing so, created a **sole proprietorship**. No formalities are necessary. While there is no distinct body of law regulating sole proprietorships, they are subject to many regulations that apply to all forms of business. Laws regarding public health, zoning, and, of course, taxation apply to all businesses, whether sole proprietorships, partnerships, or corporations. A sole proprietor may have to obtain a licence to carry on a particular type of business. For example, a municipal licence is normally required before one may start business as an electrician, plumber, restaurateur, or taxi driver. Provincial licensing and registration may be required for a car dealer, insurance broker, or employment agency. The proprietor must keep proper accounts for income tax purposes. She must make payroll deductions for employee income tax, employment insurance, and Canada Pension Plan. In hiring staff, she must observe human rights legislation and must comply with health and safety regulations.

In most provinces, statutes require that if business is carried on under a name other than the actual name of the owner, the name must be registered.[2]

sole proprietorship
an unincorporated business owned by a single individual

---

1. A few businesses are carried on by cooperatives, trusts, and other types of unincorporated association, but because of their limited importance we shall not consider them.

2. See, for example: Business Names Act, R.S.O. 1990, c. B.17, s. 2(2), and the discussion in Chapter 22. Saskatchewan even requires registration when an owner uses her own name as the business name: The Business Names Registration Act, R.S.S. 1978, B-11, s. 2(c).

PARTNERSHIPS

Advantages and Disadvantages

partnership
the relationship between two or more persons carrying on a business with a view to profit

A **partnership** may be formed by two or more persons, who may be natural persons (individuals) or legal persons (corporations). There are obvious advantages in carrying on a business venture as a joint undertaking. Working together, members of a group can pool their knowledge and skills, and their physical and financial resources. There are also obvious disadvantages. Disagreements may lead to stalemate; dishonesty or incompetence of one member may lead to losses suffered by other members; when a group wishes to make important decisions, it may lose valuable time in reaching agreement. None of these problems exists when a person acts solely on his or her own behalf.

The Partnership Act

Although partnerships may be established without formality, their affairs are governed by a well-developed body of laws. This is because, until the 20th century, partnership was the accepted way for two or more persons to carry on an enterprise. Problems concerning almost every aspect of partnership had become the subject of legal decisions, starting about the middle of the 18th century. By the 1880s, there was a virtually complete body of rules that were well settled, but the mass of decisions on detailed points made it difficult to discover the broader principles. To remedy this situation, the British Parliament in 1890 passed the Partnership Act,[3] which brought together the numerous cases under more general principles and codified the law. The English Act has been adopted in substantially the same form by all the common law provinces.[4] With one important exception,[5] the Act has remained virtually unchanged from its original form, and there have been comparatively few cases on its interpretation, so that it can be taken as an accurate representation of the state of partnership law today.

THE NATURE OF PARTNERSHIP

The Definition of Partnership

"Partnership is the relation which subsists between persons carrying on a business in common with a view of profit."[6]

---

3. 1890, 53 and 54 Vict., c. 39 (U.K.).

4. In Ontario, it is referred to as the "Partnerships Act" (in the plural): R.S.O. 1990, c. P.5. All the other provinces use the singular "Partnership Act" form. There are substantial differences among the provinces in the treatment of limited partnerships and the registration of business names. Alberta and British Columbia include both subjects in the Partnership Act. Manitoba and Saskatchewan include limited partnerships in the Partnership Act, but have a separate Business Names Registration Act. Prince Edward Island has a separate Limited Partnerships Act, but includes registration in the Partnership Act. New Brunswick, Nova Scotia, and Ontario each have three separate statutes, while Newfoundland and Labrador has a Limited Partnership Act and a Partnership Act but no provisions on registration.

5. The introduction of the limited liability partnership, considered later in this chapter.

6. Partnership Act, 1890, s. 1(1). The same wording is used in Canadian versions of the statute. See, for example: Partnership Act, R.S.B.C. 1996, c. 348, s. 2; R.S.N.S. 1989, c. 334, s. 4: Partnerships Act, R.S.O. 1990, c. P.5, s. 2. Subsequent references in this chapter to British Columbia, Ontario, and Nova Scotia are to these statutes.

CHECKLIST Elements of a Partnership

There are four basic elements in the definition of "partnership"; a partnership is

- a relationship
- between persons
- carrying on business in common
- with a view to profit

This definition of partnership is extremely important because of the consequences that may follow from a finding that a person is a partner. Whether two or more persons are partners depends upon all the circumstances of a case.

The Partnership Relationship

Partnership is a consensual and contractual relationship. Normally, a formal written partnership agreement is drawn up and is signed by all the partners. However, persons may be found to be partners although no written or even oral agreement exists.[7] In the absence of an express agreement, they may still be held to be partners if they have acted as such.[8] The courts look at the substance of the relationship and are not necessarily guided by what the parties may themselves choose to call it.[9]

The Business Nature of Partnership

The Partnership Act defines partnership as a relation between persons carrying on a business for profit. It does not apply to other associations, such as charitable enterprises, joint trustees of an estate, or public boards.

The term "business" is an imprecise one. It includes "every trade, occupation, or profession," but it does not include every activity carried on for a profit. For instance, owning property and collecting rent from tenants does not necessarily amount to carrying on a business. The joint ownership of property does not of itself make the owners partners. Similarly, if a group of investors forms a syndicate to hold a portfolio of securities, that arrangement does not amount to carrying on a business unless the investors engage in the trade of dealing in shares, rather than merely retaining them for investment income.

CASE 26.1

A group of persons, including a corporation (Kamex), joined together to purchase a piece of development property with a view to reselling it at a profit. One of the co-owners, March, entered into an exclusive listing agreement with a real estate agent (Le Page); in doing so, he was acting without the agreement of his co-owners.

The group sold the property, and Le Page sued the members of the group for its commission. It claimed that they had formed a partnership and that they were consequently jointly liable on the contract made by March.

The court held that there was no partnership. The members of the group were not carrying on a business, but were merely co-owners of the property. Consequently, March alone was liable for the commission.[10]

7. Conversely, the existence of a written "partnership agreement" will not create a partnership if it is found that no such intention existed: *M. Tucci Construction Ltd.* v. *Lockwood* [2000] O.J. No. 3192.

8. For example, in *Pinteric* v. *People's Bar and Eatery Ltd.* [2001] O.J. No. 499, where the plaintiff alleged the existence of an oral partnership agreement, the Ontario Court of Appeal held that the fact that he had received "advances" rather than a salary pointed to a partnership relationship.

9. In *Lansing Building Supply (Ontario) Ltd.* v. *Ierullo* (1990), 71 O.R. (2d) 173, co-developers of land entered into a "joint venture" agreement that specifically provided that they were not to be considered partners. Nevertheless, the court held that the true nature of their relationship was one of partnership.

10. *A.E. Le Page Ltd.* v. *Kamex Developments Ltd.* (1977), 78 D.L.R. (3d) 223, Aff'd.[1979] 2 S.C.R. 155.

Although a partnership must be a business relationship, not every business relationship makes the parties to the relationship partners with each other. The Act speaks of "carrying on" a business. Isolated transactions undertaken jointly do not by themselves make the parties partners. For example, if two merchants in the Atlantic provinces pool an order of goods purchased in Montreal so that they can fill one freight car and obtain a lower freight rate, that arrangement does not by itself make them partners. However, a partnership may exist for even a single venture, depending upon the circumstances.

CASE 26.2

A group of Canadian investors purchased the interests of the members of a Texas partnership that owned a large apartment building. The value of the building had declined drastically, and the whole purpose of the transaction was to realize the loss, which the Canadian investors hoped to set against their income tax liability. After the transfer of the partnership interests, the building was immediately sold.

The Supreme Court of Canada held that a tax motivation and a short duration do not by themselves negate the existence of a partnership. However, in this case there was never any intention to carry on a "business," and therefore the relationship was not one of partnership.[11]

The Profit Motive

The definition requires that the business be carried on with a view to profit. Those words might seem redundant, since profit—or the hope of it—is what business is all about. But the words have generally been taken to mean that a sharing of profits is an essential element of partnership.

Generally, the sharing of gross receipts does not create a partnership. For example, if an owner of a theatre were to rent it to a drama group and one of the terms of the contract was that she would receive 10 percent of the gross receipts, such an arrangement would not make the owner a partner of the group. Similarly, in our example of the two merchants pooling an order to reduce shipping charges, there is a sharing of costs, but not of profits.

The receipt of a share of the profits of the business is strong evidence tending to establish a partnership, though it is not by itself conclusive. In particular, it does not *by itself* amount to a partnership if the sharing of profits is part of an arrangement to

- repay a debt owed
- pay an employee or agent of the business as part of his remuneration
- pay an annuity to a widow, widower, or child of a deceased partner
- repay a loan under which the lender is to receive a rate of interest varying with the profits
- pay the seller of a business an amount for good will that varies according to the profits (B.C., s. 4; Ont. s. 3.; N.S., s. 5)

Apart from the above situations, it is difficult to imagine circumstances in which the only evidence of a partnership would be the fact that a person is sharing in the profits of a business. A person receiving a share of profits has usually contributed property or money to the business. Even though partners often share profits according to a ratio that is not based solely on capital contribution, the courts consider profit sharing that coincides with the ratio of capital contribution to be strong evidence of partnership.

---

11. *Backman* v. *Canada* (2001), 196 D.L.R. (4th) 193. Since there was no business, there was no business loss for which tax relief could be claimed. Contrast this decision with that in *Spire Freezers Ltd.* v. *Canada* (2001), 196 D.L.R. (4th) 211 (S.C.C.) (a case with a similar tax motive, decided at the same time as the Backman case), where the Canadian investors retained some of the assets of a California partnership and were held to be carrying on a business.

Another important factor is whether the person receiving the profits has taken part in the management of the business. Evidence showing that she has taken some active role in the business, particularly in making decisions on important matters, when added to the fact that she has shared in the profits, will usually suffice to establish her as a partner.

The Legal Nature of Partnership

Legal Personality

In the next chapter, on corporation law, we discuss in considerably more detail the significance of legal personality. As a matter of law a corporation has a separate personality of its own. In the law of partnership the position is less clear. The Act defines a partnership as a "relation" between persons. Strictly, a partnership has no independent existence and merely represents the collective rights and duties of all the partners. Logically, this means that whenever a partner dies or retires or a new partner is admitted, the partnership comes to an end and is replaced by a new relationship. In actual practice, however, and in some of its legal implications, a partnership does have a semi-separate existence of its own. Certainly, as an accounting matter, a partnership is treated as a separate entity with its own assets, liabilities, and financial statements.

The Continuing Relationship Between Partners

The Partnership Act itself recognizes, in a number of places, the concept of a "**firm**,"[12] which members join or leave. It speaks of a person being admitted as a partner into an existing firm, or retiring from a firm, or being expelled from a firm, and of the composition of a firm being changed. And while it provides that the death (or insolvency) of a partner dissolves the partnership, the Act accepts that the partners may agree that the partnership should continue between the survivors (B.C., s. 36(1); Ont., s. 33(1); N.S., s. 36(1)). It is consequently possible, and normally advisable, for partners to agree expressly that on the death, bankruptcy, or retirement of one of them, the partnership relation among the others will continue.

firm
collective reference to the partners in a partnership

Partnership Property

Again, it is clear from the Act that a partnership may have property that is distinct from the property of the individual partners. In particular, real property held by a partnership is treated according to the usual rules governing real property as far as the partnership is concerned, but insofar as the individual partners are concerned, their interest in the real property is considered personal property; that is, they do not own the property itself, but rather an interest in that property.

Creditors of the Firm

Partnership creditors have first call against partnership assets before the personal creditors of an individual partner. This is so because until the creditors of the partnership have been paid, it is impossible to identify and distribute the share of an individual partner. If, after these creditors are paid, no assets remain, then the partner has no share for personal creditors to seize.

Another instance of the separate existence of the firm occurs in the rule that a deceased partner's personal creditors have first call against the personal assets of her estate (B.C., s. 11; Ont., s. 10; N.S., s. 11). If the partnership assets are insufficient to pay off the partnership creditors, they must wait for the personal creditors to be paid out of the personal estate of the deceased partner before they can take what is left in order to satisfy their debt. Under the Bankruptcy and Insolvency Act, this rule also applies to the estate of a living partner who becomes bankrupt.[13]

---

12. See, for example, B.C. s. 1; Ont., s. 5; N.S., s. 7.

13. R.S.C. 1985, c. B-3, s. 142. As discussed in Chapter 31, the Bankruptcy and Insolvency Act is in the process of being revised.

Legal Proceedings

For the purposes of processing a court action, a partnership may be treated as if it were a separate entity. The partnership may bring an action in the name of the firm without naming all the partners as plaintiffs, and an outside party may sue a partnership in its firm name without naming all the partners as defendants. It is, in fact, wise to sue a partnership in the firm name rather than in the names of the individual partners, as we shall see when we consider the question of the liability of partners.

THE CREATION OF A PARTNERSHIP

The Partnership Agreement

A partnership comes into existence by the agreement, express or implied, of the partners. Generally speaking, partners may agree to whatever terms they wish, provided the terms are not illegal and do not offend public policy. A **partnership agreement** may be wholly oral and yet be valid and enforceable.[14] As we know, of course, an oral agreement is subject to the lapses of memory of the parties to the agreement, and, if only for certainty, it is important to have a written record of it.

partnership agreement
an agreement between persons to create a partnership and (usually), setting out the terms of the relationship

Business partnerships can be perilous ventures, and, probably because dissolution of a partnership is relatively easy, a high proportion of them break up after a short time. The reasons for dissolution are varied. Many are dissolved because the business venture has proved unprofitable, others because the venture has proved very profitable and the partners have gone on to form a corporation. Still others dissolve because of a conflict of personalities that the parties cannot resolve. A substantial number of profitable partnerships are destroyed by misunderstanding or mistrust. The failure to decide important issues in advance often leads to the kind of misunderstanding and mistrust that, in turn, creates an irreparable breach between the parties.

The main purpose of a partnership agreement is to set out, as carefully and as clearly as possible, the entire terms of the relationship.

CHECKLIST Contents of a Partnership Agreement

Normally, a partnership agreement will deal with the following matters. Depending upon the individual circumstances, there are likely to be other matters that should be covered as well:

- identity of the partners
- name of the firm
- nature of the business to be carried on
- duration of the relationship
- method of terminating the partnership
- rules for introducing new partners
- what is to happen on the retirement or death of an existing partner
- participation in management and in making major decisions
- contribution of each partner in terms of work and responsibilities
- capital contribution of each partner
- ownership of property used in the business
- sharing of profits and losses
- procedure for resolving disputes

14. An agreement to create a partnership may fall within the Statute of Frauds (in those provinces where that statute applies; see Chapter 10). However, once the partnership has come into existence, the statute no longer applies.

As we shall see later in this chapter, the Partnership Act sets out a number of implied terms that apply in the absence of any provision in the agreement to the contrary. It is normally advisable, however, for the parties to make express provision in respect of the matters covered by the Act.

In order to draft an effective partnership agreement, the parties must consider the most likely events that might lead to disagreement and upset the partnership or change its course of action. A well-drafted, carefully thought-out partnership agreement is of itself no guarantee of a successful partnership. The other elements—a sound business idea, reasonably good luck, mutual trust and good faith, and diligent application—must be present for a partnership to succeed, but a well-drawn agreement minimizes one major hazard.

It is usually inadvisable for partners to draft their own agreement. The usual problems of ambiguous words can create the same misunderstandings that arise in the law of contracts. In addition, individual partners may be unaware of many of the pitfalls that accumulated experience in business and learning in partnership law may avoid. For these reasons a partnership agreement is, perhaps more than any other type of agreement, one that should be drafted with expert advice and assistance. If the parties to the agreement are investing large sums in the venture, then each should have his or her own legal counsel to help protect that investment.

Registration

No particular formalities are required in order to form a partnership; by contrast, as we shall see in the last part of this chapter, a limited partnership is formed by registration. However, almost all provinces do require the filing, in a local registry office, of a declaration giving such essential information as the names and addresses of each partner and the name under which they intend to carry on business. Declarations must also be filed when there is any change in membership or when a firm is dissolved. The registration requirements do not necessarily apply to all partnerships. For example, in British Columbia only partnerships engaged in trading, manufacturing, or mining are required to register, and in Ontario a partnership is not required to register if it carries on business under a name that is composed solely of the names of all of the partners.[15]

There are penalties for failure to carry out the requirements of the statute, which vary from province to province, but non-registration in no way affects the existence of the partnership as such. The purposes of this registration system are quite clear. The register is open to the public and provides the minimum of essential information about a partnership and particularly about the partners in the firm, thus enabling a plaintiff to serve each partner with notice of an action if she wishes to do so. It is also helpful to prospective creditors or other suppliers in checking the accuracy of information given by a member of the partnership concerning the membership of the firm.

THE LIABILITY OF A PARTNER

What is the significance of deciding that a particular venture is a partnership and of identifying a person as a partner in the venture? The significance lies primarily in the partner's personal liability to outsiders who have dealt with the partnership. As a general rule, a person who is held to be a partner becomes personally responsible for the debts and liabilities of the partnership.[16]

Contractual Liability

Agency Principles

Probably the greatest risk of liability to which a partner subjects himself results from the contractual obligations of the partnership. "Every partner is an agent of the firm and his other partners for the

---

15. Partnership Act, R.S.B.C., 1996, c. 342, s. 81; Business Names Act, R.S.O. 1990, c. B.17, s. 2(4).

16. The exceptions are the limited liability partnership and the limited partnership, both considered later in this chapter.

purpose of the business of the partnership, and the acts of every partner who does any act for carrying on in the usual way business of the kind carried on by the firm of which he is a member, bind the firm and its partners" (B.C., s. 7; Ont., s. 6; N.S., s. 8). That is so unless the authority of the partner has been restricted by an agreement with the other partners *and* the third party knows of this restriction. Any acts done by a partner within the scope of his apparent authority and relied upon by an outsider bind the firm and all the partners. Thus, a restriction placed upon the authority of a partner has the same effect as a restriction placed upon the authority of an agent by his principal: it affects only those outsiders who have knowledge of the restriction (B.C., s. 10; Ont., s. 9; N.S., s. 11).

The notion of apparent authority was discussed in Chapter 19, in the context of the law of agency, and need not be repeated here.[17]

Joint Liability

"Every partner in a firm is liable jointly with the other partners for all debts and obligations of the firm incurred while he is a partner. . . . " (B.C., s. 11; Ont., s. 10; N.S., s. 12). The chief effect of this rule of **joint liability** is that each partner is personally liable for the full amount of the firm's debts. When the liabilities of a partnership exceed its assets, a creditor or injured party, having obtained judgment against the partnership and exhausted its assets in trying to satisfy judgment, may look to the personal assets of any partner or partners until the judgment has been satisfied. Accordingly, it is important for a person advancing credit to a firm to determine whether it is a partnership and, if so, who are the partners.

Another consequence of this rule is that only one cause of action arises from the obligation. If, by carelessness or ignorance of the facts, a plaintiff brings action against some of the partners and obtains judgment against them, her rights will be exhausted. If their assets are insufficient to satisfy the judgment and she later discovers that there are other partners, she will not be able to sue those others for the deficiency. This risk is eliminated if she sues the defendants in the firm name since that has the effect of suing all the persons who were partners at the relevant time.

If a partner pays the firm's debts in full, he is entitled to be reimbursed by his co-partners for their shares of the debt (B.C., s. 27(b); Ont., s. 24(2); N.S., s. 27(b)). See Figure 26.1 for an illustration. But if the other partners are insolvent, one partner may be left with payment of the full debt. It is consequently most important to choose one's partners carefully.

Apparent Partners

In principle, a person is liable only for the obligations of a partnership incurred while he is a member of the firm. Hence, "a person who is admitted as a partner into an existing firm does not thereby

joint liability
the situation where each of a number of persons is personally liable for the full amount of a debt

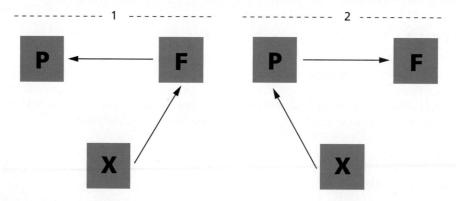

FIGURE 26.1
Joint Liability

(1) If the outsider (*X*) sues the firm (*F*), then any partner (*P*) is liable to contribute his share to the firm and may be sued by the firm for that share.

(2) If *X* instead sues *P*, *P* is fully liable but is entitled to be indemnified by the firm; that is, *P* can sue *F* or his co-partners personally.

17. See, in particular, the case of *Mercantile Credit Co. Ltd.* v. *Garrod*, [1962] 3 All E.R. 1103, discussed in Chapter 19.

become liable to the creditors of the firm for anything done before he became a partner," and "a partner who retires from a firm does not thereby cease to be liable for partnership debts or obligations incurred before his retirement" (B.C., s. 19; Ont., s. 18; N.S., s. 20). The only way he may free himself from his obligations is by novation—that is, by agreement with the partners remaining in the firm *and* with the firm's creditors.[18]

A person who, not being a partner, represents himself to be, or allows himself to be represented as a partner in a firm, is liable to any person who has given credit to the firm on the faith of that representation (B.C., s. 16; Ont., s. 15; N.S., s. 17).

CASE 26.3

A was a salaried lawyer, employed by another lawyer, *S. A* was not in partnership with *S*, and did not share in the profits of the practice. However, *A*'s name was on the "firm's" letterhead, and there was a bank account in the firm's name.

The plaintiff engaged *S* to lend some of its funds in a mortgage transaction. *S* did not register the mortgage and misappropriated the money. He was subsequently disbarred and sent to prison.

A did not perform any work for the plaintiff, but had been introduced to its senior officers, apparently as a partner of *S*.

The court held that *A* had allowed himself to be represented as a partner, and consequently was *prima facie* liable. However, the plaintiff had enjoyed a long personal relationship with *S*, and had not been induced to deal with the "firm" by *A*'s holding out. *A* was therefore not liable.[19]

Although a partner who retires is generally not liable for debts of the firm contracted after he ceased to be a partner, he may be liable by estoppel to third parties who reasonably believe he is still a member of the firm and advance credit to the firm in reliance on his membership. A retiring partner may free himself from this liability by carrying out the requirements of the Partnership Act (B.C., s. 39; Ont., s. 36; N.S., s. 39). An advertisement in the official gazette of the province is adequate notice to persons generally who had not dealt with the firm before the retiring partner left the firm, but all persons who have dealt with the firm before the partner's retirement should receive actual notice of the retirement if the retiring partner is to be fully protected. It is customary, therefore, to send notices to all those persons who have dealt with the firm more or less recently, depending upon the nature of the business. A further important precaution is to ensure that, where particulars of the partnership have been registered, the retiring partner's name is removed from the list of partners.[20]

CHECKLIST Steps to Be Taken on Retirement from a Partnership

To protect himself against possible liability for future acts of his partners, a retiring partner should

■ ensure that all existing clients of the firm are notified

■ place a notice in the official gazette of the province (and perhaps also in the local newspaper)

■ ensure that his name is removed from the register

■ ensure to the best of his ability that any letterheads are destroyed or altered to remove his name

---

18. See Chapter 13 under "Discharge by Agreement" (Substituted Agreement).

19. *Bet-Mur Investments Ltd.* v. *Spring* (1994), 17 B.L.R. (2d) 55. See also *Brown Economic Assessments Inc.* v. *Stevenson* [2003] S.J. No. 295.

20. The precise legal effects of registration are somewhat uncertain. The Nova Scotia statute provides that a statement in the register that a person is a partner is "incontrovertible"; Partnerships and Business Names Registration Act, R.S.N.S. 1989, c. 335, s. 11. The Ontario statute formerly contained the same rule, but no such provision appears in the current statute.

Tort and Breach of Trust

The liability of a firm and of its partners is not restricted to contracts. The Act makes the firm liable for "any wrongful act or omission of any partner acting in the ordinary course of the business of the firm" (B.C., s. 12; Ont., s. 11; N.S., s. 13). Therefore the firm, including all the other partners, would be liable for injuries or damage caused by a partner when driving on the firm's business, for a defamatory statement made by him in business correspondence, or for negligence in dealing with a client's affairs.[21] The principle is similar to that of vicarious liability, discussed in Chapter 3. The firm is also liable for breaches of fiduciary duty and breaches of trust committed by a partner; for example, for any misapplication by a partner of funds that have been placed in the care of the partner while acting within the scope of his apparent authority, or that have been entrusted to the firm.[22] The Act (B.C., s. 13; Ont., s. 12; N.S., s. 14) envisages two situations: see Figure 26.2.

CASE 26.4

A partner in a law firm undertook (privately) the administration of his aunt's estate. The firm's letterhead was used, and funds belonging to the estate passed through the firm's bank accounts.

The partner defrauded the estate and transferred funds to his own account.

In an action against the firm, it was held that the firm was liable, even though the other partners were not aware of the activities in relation to the estate. The partner had been acting within the scope of his apparent authority, since the administration of estates is a matter normally undertaken by lawyers.[23]

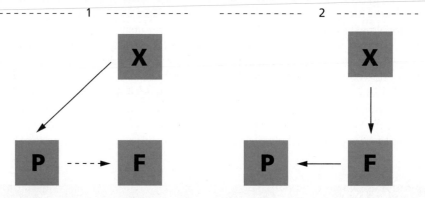

FIGURE 26.2

Misapplication of Funds

In situation 1, *X* entrusts *P* with money or property to be handed over to the firm (*F*); instead, *P* keeps the money or property for himself. In situation 2, *X* entrusts money or property to the firm, and it is subsequently misappropriated by *P*.

THE RELATION OF PARTNERS TO ONE ANOTHER

Partnership is a contractual relationship, and the relations of partners to one another is essentially governed by the terms of their contract. These terms may be found in the partnership agreement, they may be inferred from the conduct of the parties, or they may be implied from the Partnership Act.

---

21. *McDonic* v. *Hetherington* (1997), 142 D.L.R. (4th) 648.
22. See *Ernst & Young* v. *Falconi* (1994), 17 O.R. (3d) 512; see also *Strother* v. *3464920 Canada Inc.*, [2007] 2 S.C.R. 177.
23. *Public Trustee* v. *Mortimer* (1985), 16 D.L.R. (4th) 404; see also *Korz* v. *St. Pierre* (1988), 43 D.L.R. (4th) 528.

A partner who acts in a manner that is contrary to the partnership agreement commits a breach of contract and may be liable to compensate the other partners for any damage resulting from the breach.[24]

Implied Terms

The Act sets out a number of terms that will be implied if those matters are not expressly covered in a partnership agreement. The main terms that are implied are summarized below, with explanatory comment where necessary.[25] It is important to remember that the parties to a partnership agreement may, and frequently do, vary these terms either at the time of the original agreement or later by unanimous consent.[26]

Partnership Property

"All property and rights and interests in property originally brought into the partnership stock or acquired, whether by purchase or otherwise, on account of the firm or for the purposes and in the course of the partnership's business are called . . . 'partnership property' and must be held and applied by the partners exclusively for the purposes of the partnership and in accordance with the partnership agreement" (B.C., s. 23(1); Ont., s. 21(1); N.S., s. 23(1)). Additionally, the Act provides that, unless the contrary intention appears, all property bought with money belonging to the firm is deemed to have been bought on account of the firm and is available only for the use of the firm (B.C., s. 24; Ont., s. 22; N.S., s. 24).

It is not always clear whether a particular item of property is "brought into the partnership stock." Property that is used in the business is not necessarily partnership property, but may remain the property of the individual partners. Consequently, the partnership agreement should make clear precisely what property is to be considered to have been contributed as "capital."

ILLUSTRATION 26.1

A and *B* decide to go into partnership in a local delivery business. *A* owns a warehouse, valued at $50 000. *B* owns two vans, also valued at $50 000. Two years later the partnership is dissolved. The warehouse is now worth $70 000, and the vans are worth $20 000. How much is each entitled to?

(a) If the warehouse and vans were brought in as partnership property, then the total value of the assets—$90 000—would be divided equally between them and each would receive $45 000.

(b) If the assets brought into the business remained the individual property of *A* and *B*, then *A* would recover the warehouse ($70 000) and *B* only the depreciated vans ($20 000).

Either result might be fair, depending upon the original intentions of the parties, but in the absence of a clear agreement, one party might receive a windfall of $25 000 at the expense of the other.

Financial Arrangements

The Act sets out a number of basic presumptions with respect to capital and profits, which apply "subject to any agreement express or implied between the partners." It should be emphasized that these rules are more often than not varied by agreement.

(1) "All the partners are entitled to share equally in the capital and profits of the business and must contribute equally towards the losses, whether of capital or otherwise, sustained by

---

24. See, for example, *Ernst & Young* v. *Stuart* (1997), 144 D.L.R. (4th) 328 (partner leaving firm without giving proper notice and joining competitor).

25. The passages quoted are from the Ontario statute; the British Columbia and Nova Scotia versions differ slightly in a few cases.

26. See B.C., s. 21; Ont., s. 20; N.S., s. 22.

the firm" (B.C., s. 27(a); Ont., s. 24(1); N.S., s. 27(a)). Partners commonly vary this term: they contribute different proportions of capital and share profits based on other criteria such as time spent on partnership business.

(2) If a partner incurs expenses or personal liabilities "in the ordinary and proper conduct of the business of the firm," or in doing anything to preserve the business or property of the firm, the firm must indemnify him for these expenses or liabilities (B.C., s. 27(b); Ont., s. 24(2); N.S., s. 27(b)). Thus, as we have seen, if one partner is sued for the firm's debts, he is entitled to a contribution from his fellow partners.[27]

(3) A partner is not entitled, before the ascertainment of profits, to interest on the capital subscribed by him (B.C., s. 27(d); Ont., s. 24(4); N.S., s. 27(d)). In other words, if the agreement provides for the payment of "interest" on a partner's capital, the payment is not regarded as an expense of the firm, but rather as an appropriation of profits. But if a partner makes a loan to the firm in addition to what he has agreed to subscribe as capital under the partnership agreement, he is entitled to interest at the rate of 5 percent on the value of the excess contribution while it remains with the firm. The rate of interest may be varied by agreement.

(4) "No partner is entitled to remuneration for acting in the partnership business" (B.C., s. 27(f); Ont., s. 24(6); N.S., s. 27(f)). Partnership agreements frequently do provide for the payment of a "salary" to one or more partners. Sometimes, one partner is the managing partner who devotes most of his time to the partnership business, whereas the other partner or partners are merely investing partners. Their partnership agreement will likely state that the managing partner is to be paid a salary. This "salary" is normally considered as a first call on the partnership profits before any further division of profits among all the partners. A partner, however, is not an employee, and his salary is not an expense of the firm. Like interest on capital, it is considered to be a distribution of profits.

CASE 26.5

M was described as a "salaried partner" in a law firm. He was to be paid a fixed salary of £1200 per year out of profits, plus one-third of the profits of the branch office that he ran.

The firm suffered a substantial loss, due to defalcations by the senior partner. M claimed he was still entitled to his salary of £1200, which should be paid by the other partners.

It was held that M was entitled to nothing. He was a partner, not an employee. His "salary" was a first charge on the profits of the firm. Since there were no profits, his share was nothing.[28]

Normally, partners are not willing and able to wait until some time after the end of the firm's accounting year, when the year's profits have been ascertained, before enjoying any of the fruits of their labour. It is common, therefore, to provide that a partner may "draw" up to a specified amount each month out of his prospective share of profits. Such an amount will be considered merely an advance on his share of the projected profits, repayable to the firm to the extent that it exceeds his share of the actual profits when they are determined.

Conduct of the Business

The Act provides that, unless there is agreement to the contrary:

(1) "Every partner may take part in the management of the partnership business" (B.C., s. 27(e); Ont., s. 24(5); N.S., s. 27(e)). This implied term is occasionally varied. For example,

27. There is an exception in the case of a limited liability partnership, discussed at the end of this chapter.
28. *Marsh* v. *Stacey* (1963), 103 Sol. J. 512 (U.K.).

a parent who takes a child into partnership may wish to reserve the management of the firm to himself. Very large partnerships, such as large law firms, often have two or more classes of partners, and it may be that only the senior partners take part in the management of the firm.

(2) "Any difference arising as to ordinary matters connected with the partnership business may be decided by a majority of the partners, but no change may be made in the nature of the partnership business without the consent of all existing partners" (B.C., s. 27(h); Ont., s. 24(8); N.S., s. 27(h)). In cases of a serious disagreement, this provision can be troublesome. The minority may insist that the particular decision did not concern an ordinary matter but affected the nature of the partnership business. It may be advisable, therefore, to spell out clearly which matters may only be decided unanimously.

(3) "The partnership books are to be kept at the place of business of the partnership or the principal place if there is more than one and every partner may, when he thinks fit, have access to and inspect and copy any of them" (B.C., s. 27(i); Ont., s. 24(9); N.S., s. 27(i)).

Membership

Partnership is a personal relationship, a fact that is underlined by two further provisions of the Act:

(1) "No person may be introduced as a partner without the consent of all existing partners" (B.C., s. 27(g); Ont., s. 24(7); N.S., s. 27(g)). Two common variations occur—where there are senior and junior partners and the consent of only the senior partners is required, and where a partner has reserved the right to have a son or daughter join the firm at a later date.

(2) No partner may assign his share in the partnership, either absolutely or by way of mortgage, so as to permit the assignees to take over his duties or "to interfere in the management or administration of the partnership business or affairs, or to require any accounts of the partnership transactions, or to inspect the partnership books." An assignee may, however, "receive the share of profits to which the assigning partner would otherwise be entitled and the assignee must accept the account of profits agreed to by the partners" (B.C., s. 34; Ont., s. 31; N.S., s. 34).

One should note that the Act does not prohibit the assignment of a partnership interest (though the partnership agreement may do so expressly). An assignee becomes entitled to receive a share of the profits, but does not become a partner.[29]

Fiduciary Duties

The Act contains three provisions that, together, set out the fiduciary duties of partners to one another.[30] It is probably erroneous to describe these as "implied terms," since the rules are not stated to be subject to contrary agreement, and, indeed, it is doubtful to what extent partners may contract out of these duties.

Information

"Partners are bound to render true accounts and full information of all things affecting the partnership to any partner or his legal representatives" (B.C., s. 31; Ont., s. 28; N.S., s. 31).

---

29. Consequently, the assignee owes no fiduciary duty to the partnership: *Zawadzki* v. *Matthews Group Ltd.* (2001), 152 O.A.C. 3.

30. The B.C. Act (s. 22(1)) also contains a general rule that "a partner shall act with the utmost fairness and good faith towards the other members of the firm in the business of the firm."

Thus, information regarding the firm's business that is provided to any of the partners must be made available to all of them.[31] The only circumstances under which this term might be varied would be in a partnership having several classes of partners. It is possible that, by express agreement, the most junior group of partners might not have access to all the books and records of the partnership. Even such a reservation, however, would be restricted to a narrow class of information.

Secret Benefits

"Every partner must account to the firm for any benefit derived by him without the consent of the other partners from any transaction concerning the partnership or from any use by him of the partnership property, name or business connection" (B.C., s. 32; Ont., s. 29; N.S., s. 32). A partner may be given permission by his co-partners to use partnership property for his own purposes, or to take advantage of an opportunity offered to the firm. But without full disclosure and authorization, any benefit belongs to the firm.

CASE 26.6

A partner in a firm of chartered accountants had responsibility for a major corporate client. After some time, he was offered a directorship in the corporation. He disclosed this to the firm and paid his director's fees to the firm. However, he failed to disclose that he was also entitled to shares and stock options. When this was discovered, on the dissolution of the partnership, he was held liable to account to the firm for the value of the shares and options.[32]

Duty Not to Compete

"Where a partner without the consent of the other partners carries on any business of the same nature as and competing with that of the firm, he must account for and pay over to the firm all profits made by him in that business" (B.C., s. 33; Ont., s. 30; N.S., s. 33). These terms are varied occasionally according to the circumstances of the partnership. For example, an individual might be carrying on a retail business in the downtown area and subsequently enter into a partnership to carry on a similar business in a suburban shopping centre. Since the two businesses might well be considered "of the same nature and competing with" each other, the partner owning the downtown business would require, as a term of the partnership agreement, that the partners in the suburban business consent to his continuing the downtown business.

The duty to account for secret profits and the duty not to compete sometimes overlap.

CASE 26.7

Davis and Ouellette formed a partnership to secure certain mining claims. The scheme fell through, but the partnership was never formally dissolved. Ouellette subsequently acquired the opportunity to buy the shares of a corporation that owned some of the claims. He notified Davis that he was terminating the partnership and then purchased the shares on his own behalf.

It was held that when Ouellette acquired the opportunity to buy the shares, he was still a partner. The opportunity belonged to the firm, and he had derived a benefit without the consent of his partner. He was liable to account for the profit that he made.[33]

---

31. See *Dockrill* v. *Coopers & Lybrand* (1994), 111 D.L.R. (4th) 62. Legal advice on how to "downsize" the firm must be made available to the partner being "downsized."

32. *Rochwerg* v. *Truster* (2002), 212 D.L.R. (4th) 498. See also *McKnight* v. *Hutchison* (2002), 28 B.L.R. (3d) 269.

33. *Davis* v. *Ouellette* (1981), 27 B.C.L.R. 162.

CASE 26.8

Olson and Gullo were partners involved in property development and speculation. Gullo acted fraudulently. He bought a piece of land and resold it at a profit of $2.5 million. (Apparently, he also attempted to have Olson killed—which was presumably a breach of his fiduciary duty!) The trial judge awarded the whole profit to Olson. On appeal

by Gullo's estate, it was held that he was accountable for only half of the profit. It was incorrect to say that this would allow him to profit from his own wrong. As a partner, half of the profit should have belonged to him anyway. It was the other half that should go to the plaintiff.[34]

TERMINATION OF PARTNERSHIP

Express Provision

It is advisable for the partnership agreement to make express provision for what is to happen on termination—in particular, on the retirement or death of a partner. What events justify termination? How much notice must a partner give to terminate the arrangement? Will the partnership among the remaining members continue? How is the retiring partner's share to be valued? What are the arrangements for the continuing partners to buy out the share of a deceased or retired partner? These are among the most important matters that should be settled in advance.

Implied Statutory Rules

In the absence of express agreement, the Partnership Act sets out a number of rules to govern termination.

Termination by Notice or Expiry

"Where no fixed term is agreed upon for the duration of the partnership, any partner may determine the partnership at any time on giving notice of his intention so to do to all other partners" (B.C., s. 29; Ont., s. 26; N.S., s. 29). The notice so given may be oral or in writing, unless the partnership was originally formed by deed, in which case notice in writing is necessary.

A partnership may be entered into for a fixed term, or may simply be a partnership at will—that is, so long as the partners wish to continue. Where a partnership was entered into for a fixed term, but is continued after the term has expired and without any express new agreement, the rights and duties of the partners remain the same as they were at the expiration of the term (B.C., s. 30; Ont., s. 27; N.S., s. 30). Without continuing conduct, however, the partnership is dissolved by the expiration of the fixed term. Similarly, if it was entered into for a single venture or undertaking, it expires with the termination of that venture or undertaking.

Termination on Death or Insolvency

Since partnership is a personal relationship, it automatically terminates on the death of a partner, at least so far as the relationship between the deceased and the other partners is concerned. The Act, however, goes further and provides that, subject to any contrary agreement, "every partnership is dissolved as regards all the partners by the death or bankruptcy or insolvency of any partner" (B.C., s. 36(1); Ont., s. 33(1); N.S., s. 36(1)).

This term, perhaps more than any other, is varied by the partnership agreement. In a partnership having substantial assets and many members, the operation of this implied term dissolving the

---

34. *Olson* v. *Gullo* (1994), 113 D.L.R. (4th) 42, leave to appeal refused (1994), 20 B.L.R. (2d) 47 (S.C.C.).

partnership could be disastrous. Accordingly, the partnership agreement usually provides that the partnership will continue in existence upon the death or insolvency of any partner. The partnership agreement usually provides that the surviving partners will buy out the share of a deceased partner, often using life insurance purchased on the life of each partner for that purpose.

Even in a simple partnership between two persons, their agreement should provide for some means of ascertaining the value of the partnership on the death of either of them. Although the partnership will be terminated, the survivor may wish to continue the business as a sole proprietor—or find a new partner—and to buy out the share of the deceased partner.

The problem is primarily financial rather than legal. The arrangements must take into account the ability of the remaining partners to pay for the share of the deceased or insolvent partner, methods for ascertaining the value of that share, and the tax consequences of a particular method.

The Act further provides that, if a partner causes his share of the partnership property to be charged as security for his personal debts, the other partners are entitled to terminate the relationship (B.C., s. 36(2); Ont., s. 33(2); N.S., s. 36(2)).[35]

Dissolution by Law

A partnership is dissolved by any event that makes it unlawful for the business of the firm to be carried on or for members of the firm to carry it on in partnership (B.C., s. 37; Ont., s. 34; N.S., s. 37). The results here are in keeping with the general law of contract concerning illegality.

Even when there is disagreement among the partners concerning dissolution, or where dissolution at a specific time would be contrary to the terms of the partnership agreement, the court may (on an application by one or more partners) order the partnership dissolved under the following circumstances:

- where a partner is found to be mentally incompetent
- where a partner becomes permanently incapable of performing his part of the agreement
- where a partner has been guilty of conduct likely to prejudicially affect the business
- where a partner commits a breach of the agreement or otherwise conducts himself in such a manner that it is not reasonably practicable for the other partners to carry on the business in partnership with him
- where it is just and equitable that the partnership be dissolved (B.C., s. 38; Ont., s. 35; N.S., s. 38)

Effects of Dissolution

On the dissolution of a partnership, the property of the partnership is applied in payment of the debts and liabilities of the firm, and the surplus assets are applied in payment of what is due to the partners respectively (B.C., s. 42; Ont., s. 39; N.S., s. 42). The Act further provides that, subject to any contrary agreement, in settling accounts between the partners after a dissolution of the partnership, losses (including losses and deficiencies of capital) are to be paid first out of profits, next out of capital, and last, if necessary, by the partners individually in the proportion in which they were entitled to share in the profits. The Act (B.C., s. 47; Ont., s. 44; N.S., s. 47) also prescribes the sequence in which the liabilities of the firm must be met.

---

35. Under the B.C. Act, where there are three or more partners, this terminates the relationship only as between the partner whose share is charged and the other partners. The relationship between the other partners remains intact (s. 36(2)).

CHECKLIST Sequence of Payments on Dissolution

The assets of the firm must be applied in the following sequence:

(1) payment of the debts of the firm owed to non-partners

(2) repayment of loans made to the firm by partners

(3) repayment of the capital contributed by partners

(4) sharing any surplus among the partners according to their entitlement to share in profits

The above provisions may be varied, though not so as to affect the rights of non-partners. It could, for example, be agreed that any loss be borne by the wealthier partner, even though he was not entitled to all the profits. What is important to note is that deficiencies of capital are treated as a loss of the firm; this is in contrast to the situation of shareholders in a corporation, as we shall see in the next chapter.[36]

LIMITED PARTNERSHIPS

All provinces have either a Limited Partnership Act or a set of provisions in their Partnership Act permitting the carrying on of business, under certain very restricted conditions, with limited liability.[37] These Acts came into force at about the same time that the private limited company (discussed in the next chapter) also became available for general use. Since for most business ventures incorporating a company is a more effective way to obtain limited liability, very little use has been made of limited partnerships.[38]

The major requirement for the formation of a **limited partnership** is that there must be one or more general partners. A **general partner** has unlimited liability, while a **limited partner** has a liability limited to the amount paid by her to the limited partnership as capital. That is, she stands to lose what she has invested in the business but is not liable to contribute further.

All the Acts prohibit a limited partner from taking an active part in the management of the partnership. If she does so, she becomes liable as a general partner. The words of prohibition vary considerably in each of the statutes.[39] A limited partner would be "taking an active part" if she were personally to transact any business for the firm or be employed for that purpose as an agent or as a lawyer. She can examine the records of the firm, inquire into its progress, and advise on its management without incurring the liability of a general partner. The result is that a limited partner who attempts to take part in the management of the firm does so at a considerable personal risk. She may find herself in the dilemma that if she does not interfere, the business may fail completely; yet if she chooses to exercise some control in order to save the business, she will incur unlimited liability. For this reason more than any other, limited partnerships have been rarely used, except for tax-planning purposes.

limited partnership
a partnership in which some of the partners limit their liability to the amount of their capital contributions

general partner
a partner in a limited partnership whose liability is not limited

limited partner
a partner in a limited partnership whose liability is limited to the amount of his or her capital contribution

---

36. See *Garner* v. *Murray*, [1904] 1 Ch. 57, for an interpretation of this section when partners make unequal capital contributions or share losses unequally. The rule is also modified in the case of a limited liability partnership.

37. Alberta, British Columbia, Manitoba, and Saskatchewan include the limited partnership provisions in the Partnership Act; the other provinces have separate Limited Partnership(s) Acts.

38. Limited partnerships do have tax advantages in some circumstances.

39. See, for example: Partnership Act, R.S.B.C. 1996, c. 348, s. 64; Limited Partnerships Act, R.S.O. 1990, c. L.16, s. 13; R.S.N.S. 1989, c. 259, s. 17.

The limited partnership provisions set out more stringent regulations for registration than are demanded of ordinary partnerships. Failure to comply with requirements of detailed essential information also results in the loss of limited liability.

A limited partnership is not to be confused with a limited liability partnership, discussed below. A limited liability partnership makes no distinction between general and limited partners, and does not restrict contractual liability.

INTERNATIONAL ISSUE

Enron and Limited Partnerships

One of the most high-profile financial scandals in recent U.S. history involved the use of limited partnerships. As with Canadian limited partnerships, the United States requires that at least one general partner be liable for all the debts and liabilities of the operations, and no more than 35 limited partners can belong to the firm.

Enron Corp. set up many limited partnerships, parking debt in each one. Lenders became limited partners instead of creditors. Andrew Fastow, Enron's CFO and architect of the limited partnership strategy, moved the company away from the use of corporate subsidiaries. In an interview with CFO Magazine in 1999, Fastow described the benefits of the limited partnership: "You can get together with one or two investors and craft a particular structure to meet your and their objectives, which is very difficult if you have a public entity [where] you might have to go with shareholder votes and amendments of charters and the like."[40]

Amid much scandal, Enron filed for bankruptcy in late 2001. Of course, the ultimate downfall of Enron did not lie in the use of limited partnerships, but in the way those relationships were accounted for and disclosed to the public. Mr. Fastow pleaded guilty to several counts of fraud and was sent to jail. As will be discussed in the next two chapters, accounting and corporate governance rules have changed as a result of the Enron fiasco.

One interesting American variety of limited partnership is the Public Limited Partnership. An unlimited number of public investors may become limited partners if the partnership is registered with the Securities and Exchange Committee. Shares in these partnerships are sold through brokerage houses rather than on the exchange.

QUESTIONS TO CONSIDER

1. How did the layering of limited partnerships on top of a corporation nullify the effect of the general partner's liability?

2. What are the pros and cons of Public Limited Partnerships?

Sources: Ronald Fink, "Beyond Enron," *CFO Magazine*, February 1, 2002, www.cfo.com/article.cfm/3003186/ c_3036065; Richard DeGeorge, *Corporate Governance, Accounting Disclosure and Insider Trading*, Chapter 9, Business Ethics, (Upper Saddle River, NJ: Prentice Hall, 2004); "10 Enron Players: Where they Landed after the Fall," *New York Times*, January 29, 2006, www.nytimes.com/2006/01/29/business/businessspecial3/29profiles. html?_r=1&pagewanted=print&oref=slogin.

---

40. Ronald Fink, "Beyond Enron," *CFO Magazine*, February 1, 2002, www.cfo.com/article.cfm/3003186/c_3036065.

LIMITED LIABILITY PARTNERSHIPS

After remaining virtually unchanged for more than 100 years, Canadian partnership law saw a radical change in 1998 with the introduction, in Ontario, of the **limited liability partnership**(LLP).[41] Alberta followed in 1999, and Saskatchewan in 2001.[42] Since then, the LLP has also been introduced in Manitoba, New Brunswick, and Nova Scotia.[43] In those last three provinces, however, the legislation only came into effect in 2004, and at present, it is only in Ontario and Alberta that much use has been made of LLP status, principally by large accounting and law firms. Although the LLP has only a limited application for the present, the implications of the change are substantial.

As we have noted above, the Ontario Partnerships Act, like those of the other common law provinces, makes a partnership liable for torts committed by a partner in the ordinary course of the business (section 11), and makes each partner jointly liable for the debts and obligations of the firm (section 10). The 1998 amendments qualify section 10, providing:

> . . . a partner in a limited liability partnership is not liable . . . for debts, liabilities or obligations of the partnership or any partner arising from the negligent acts or omissions that another partner or an employee, agent or representative of the partnership commits in the course of the partnership business while the partnership is a limited liability partnership.[44]

A partner remains liable for his own negligent acts or omissions, and for those of a person who is under the partner's direct supervision or control.[45] It also appears that the firm itself remains liable, so that a non-negligent partner still stands to lose the entire value of his partnership share. However, an injured party may not look beyond the assets of the firm to the assets of the individual non-negligent partners.[46]

Under the Ontario law, the protection of non-negligent partners appears to extend only to the negligent acts or omissions of a partner—it does not apply to other torts or to breaches of trust, nor does it affect the contractual liability of partners. The Alberta legislation provides rather broader protection. A member of a LLP is not liable for the "negligence, wrongful acts or omissions, malpractice or misconduct" of a partner, or of an employee or agent of the firm, unless he knew of the act in question and failed to take reasonable steps to prevent its commission, or the act was committed by someone for whom he was directly responsible and he had failed to provide adequate supervision.[47]

The Saskatchewan legislation adopts an entirely different approach: partners in a LLP are personally liable for any partnership obligation for which they would be liable if the partnership were a corporation of which they were directors.[48] The Manitoba provisions on liability (s. 75) follow those of Alberta quite closely, while New Brunswick (ss. 48, 49) and Nova Scotia adopt both approaches (ss. 57, 58).

Although there are substantial differences in detail, all the provinces require a written agreement that designates the partnership as a LLP. An existing partnership may convert itself into a LLP if all the partners agree. An LLP must register its firm name, and the name must contain the words "limited liability partnership" or the abbreviation LLP or L.L.P. Those provinces that have adopted the LLP form all permit LLPs from other jurisdictions to register as extra-provincial LLPs.

limited liability partnership
a partnership in which non-negligent partners are not personally liable for losses caused by the negligence of a partner

---

41. Partnerships Statute Law Amendment Act, 1998, S.O. 1998, c. 2.

42. Partnership Act, R.S.A. 2000, c. P-3, ss. 81–104: R.S.S. 1978, c. P-3 (as amended), ss. 78–110.

43. Partnership Act, R.S.M. 1987, c. P30, ss. 51–88; R.S.N.B.1973, c. P-4, ss. 46–54; R.S.N.S. c. 334, ss. 48–71. The Ontario legislation is far less comprehensive than that of the other provinces.

44. R.S.O. 1990, c. P.5 (as amended), s. 10(2).

45. *Ibid.*, s. 10(3).

46. *Ibid.*, s. 10(4).

47. R.S.A. 2000, c. P-3, s. 12.

48. R.S.S. 1978, c. P-3 (as amended), ss. 80, 81. The liability of directors of a corporation is discussed in Chapter 29.

The most important restriction is that a LLP may carry on business only for the purpose of practising an "eligible profession."[49] In addition, that statute must expressly permit a LLP to practise the profession, and the governing body of the profession must require the partnership to maintain a minimum amount of liability insurance.

The LLP should not be confused with the limited partnership, discussed in the preceding section. In particular,

- in a limited partnership there must be at least one general partner who has unlimited liability
- limited partners, unlike partners in a LLP, lose their limited liability if they participate in management
- limited partnerships are not restricted to the professions

ETHICAL ISSUE

To Limit or Not to Limit?

Limited liability partnerships have been allowed in Canada since 1998, though they have been permitted in many states of the United States for even longer. Their use has spread to a number of other countries, especially since the Enron case. Nevertheless, there is still disagreement as to whether becoming "limited," where it is permitted, is necessarily a good move. It involves questions of trust and privacy.

In favour of LLPs, it is argued that

- it obviously makes sense to limit one's personal liability when claims in the millions of dollars are being made against accounting and law firms
- without LLP status it may be difficult to attract new partners
- all the big firms are going limited, so LLP status is a mark of success

Arguments against LLP status are

- it is a signal to clients that even the partners do not trust each other
- the conversion from unlimited to limited status poses some difficult problems and requires unanimity among existing partners
- disclosure requirements result in a loss of privacy and, perhaps, confidentiality
- it is not yet clear just how much legal protection the LLP status provides

QUESTIONS TO CONSIDER

1. Which of the above arguments do you find convincing?

2. In what circumstances, if any, would you recommend an existing partnership to "go limited"?

JOINT VENTURES

joint venture
a business venture
undertaken jointly by two or
more parties

A **joint venture** is an agreement that two or more parties (often corporations) make to contribute a part of their respective resources (particular assets and expertise) to a specific project. Sometimes a project requires a greater capital outlay than any one corporation may be prepared

---

49. In most provinces that is defined as a profession governed by statute. Alberta permits the use of LLPs by any profession that allows the formation of professional corporations; these are considered in Chapter 27.

to put at risk. A joint venture spreads the risk among the participants. In the oil and gas industry, for example, corporations have found it practical to undertake exploration expenditures jointly to discover and develop oil and gas reserves, as in the Arctic and Atlantic continental shelf explorations.

Legally, a joint venture may take a variety of forms. Its simplest form is just a contractual relationship among the participants for a specific undertaking, and is sometimes referred to as a **contractual joint venture**. An alternative method is for the parties to incorporate a separate corporation (a joint subsidiary) for the venture with each participant holding shares in it. This type of arrangement is known as an **equity joint venture** and is subject to the general rules of corporation law.

Participants typically regard a contractual joint venture as an extension of their own operations and a collaboration with other parties, rather than as a separate business. The venture is for a specific project or series of explorations, and of limited duration. Normally, profits are not retained jointly for investment in other projects, but are distributed to each of the participants in proportions set down in the joint venture agreement. The parties may also try to limit their liability by providing that their only contribution will be those things specifically set out in the agreement, that the agreement shall not be construed as a partnership, and that their liability will not be joint and several. They may also try to limit the authority of members to act as agents for one another in the operation of a joint venture and may identify one of themselves (or an independent party) as the "operator" of the joint venture. Whether such an arrangement will be effective to limit the agency of each participating member remains a question of fact to be determined by the court if a dispute arises with an outside third party. Such restrictions may not be effective if it is determined that the venture was, as a matter of fact, a partnership.[50]

contractual joint venture
a joint venture effected by agreement without the creation of any separate legal entity

equity joint venture
a corporation formed, and jointly owned, by the parties to a joint venture for the purpose of carrying on the venture

INCOME TRUSTS

Trusts are a complicated area of the law, as noted in Chapter 12, and this section will attempt only a basic explanation of their latest business application. Over the past decade, income trusts emerged as a popular Canadian business entity. This was largely due to favourable tax treatment and their unique liability structure.

The income trust structure involves the transfer of income-producing assets from the operating company to a trust. The trust is created by an agreement known as a **declaration of trust** and this document (in conjunction with trust law) governs the trust. The operating company continues to manage the assets under the supervision of the trustees, but all income (less expenses) is the property of the trust. It is then distributed by the trust to **unitholders** (rather than shareholders) and taxed only once in the hands of the unitholders. When units are offered to the public, the trust is also governed by securities legislation. New tax rules to be phased in by 2011 impose a second layer of taxation and thereby eliminate a trust's major tax advantage over corporations.

The Uniform Law Commission of Canada is currently developing a model law addressing the governance issues associated with income trusts.[51]

declaration of trust
an agreement that establishes a trust and designates the trustees

unitholders
beneficiaries of an income trust

50. *Central Mortgage and Housing Corp.* v. *Graham* (1973), 43 D.L.R. (3d) 686; *Lansing Building Supply (Ontario) Ltd.* v. *Ierullo, supra,* n. 9. A majority of the Supreme Court of Canada held, in *LAC Minerals Ltd.* v. *International Corona Resources Ltd.*(1989), 61 D.L.R. (4th) 14, that there was no fiduciary duty between parties to a joint venture (though there was a duty not to misuse confidential information). See also *Chitel* v. *Bank of Montreal* [2002] O.J. No. 2170.

51. Uniform Law Commission of Canada, *The* Uniform Income Trusts Act: *Closing the Gap between Traditional Trust Law and Current Governance Expectations,* August 2006, www.ulcc.ca/en/poam2/Uniform_Income_Trusts_Act_Report_En.pdf.

QUESTIONS FOR REVIEW

1. To what laws are sole proprietorships subject?

2. Is it necessary to have a written agreement in order to create a partnership?

3. What are the advantages and disadvantages of partnerships as opposed to sole proprietorships?

4. What are the basic elements of the partnership relationship?

5. What is the difference between sharing profits and sharing gross receipts?

6. In what circumstances may a person receive a share of the profits of a partnership business without herself being a partner?

7. Why is it important to distinguish between partnership property and the personal property of the individual partners?

8. When is it necessary for a partnership to be registered?

9. What does it mean to say "every partner is an agent of the firm"?

10. What is meant by "apparent authority"?

11. What is "joint liability"?

12. What steps should a partner take to protect herself against ongoing liability when she retires?

13. Can a partner receive a "salary" from the firm? What is the real nature of a partner's salary?

14. What are the three principal fiduciary duties imposed on partners?

15. How is partnership property distributed on the dissolution of a partnership?

16. Is there any difference between a partnership and a "joint venture"?

17. What are the principal forms that a joint venture may take?

18. What are the principal advantages and disadvantages of being a limited partner?

19. What is a "limited liability partnership"? How does it differ from a "limited partnership"?

20. In what ways is the liability of a partner in a LLP limited?

21. What was the motivation for the creation of income trusts?

CASES AND PROBLEMS

1. Angus had been a partner for some years in the accounting firm of Harty & Old, and was the head of their Vancouver insolvency department. According to the terms of the partnership agreement, each partner was required to give 12 months' notice in writing to terminate the relationship. The partnership agreement also contained a provision whereby each partner undertook not to enter into any business that was in direct competition with Harty & Old for a period of five years after leaving the firm.

   Unknown to his fellow partners at Harty & Old, Angus entered into negotiations with Sandersons, a rival accounting firm. He negotiated an agreement with them to join their insolvency department and then informed Harty & Old that he was leaving them immediately.

   Harty & Old commenced an action against Angus for breach of the partnership agreement, and also sued Sandersons for inducing the breach.

   Ought they to succeed (a) against Angus and (b) against Sandersons? What would be the most appropriate remedy?

2. Giovanni and Leporello were in partnership together under the registered name "Adventures Unlimited." The partnership was formed for the purpose of providing guided adventure vacations for rich clients. Under a clause in the partnership agreement, it was provided that neither partner incur expenditures on behalf of the firm in excess of $500 without the approval of the other partner.

Giovanni purported to enter into a contract—in the name of "Adventures Unlimited"—with Elvira Sails Ltd. (a corporation engaged in selling and leasing boats), to rent a large cabin cruiser for a period of three months, at a rent of $10 000 per month. He signed the rental agreement in his own name, paid a deposit for $1000 by a cheque drawn on the partnership's bank account, took delivery of the cruiser, and has not been seen since. The cruiser was reportedly last seen in the Virgin Islands.

What rights (if any) does Elvira Sails have against Leporello?

3. Crawford and McDougall were sisters of relatively advanced years. For some years they had entrusted their financial affairs to Watson, a lawyer, who was a partner in the firm of Heather & Co. Due to some disastrous investments that they made on Watson's advice, they lost almost $250 000.

The loss was discovered when they learned that Watson had been disbarred for misconduct. It was evident that their loss had been caused either by fraud or by negligence on the part of Watson, though it was less clear which.

The sisters brought an action against Heather & Co, claiming damages for their loss.

Should they succeed? What particular circumstances might be relevant?

4. Adders LLP is a limited liability partnership, registered in Ontario, practising as chartered accountants. It has 15 partners and over 200 employees. One of its major clients, Norne Inc., is a small but dynamic resource company, incorporated in Ontario.

Until about two years ago the Norne account was supervised by Counter, a senior partner. More recently, the corporation's account has been handled by Turner, a young accountant who is considered to be in line for a partnership. Counter still exercised "nominal" supervision, discussing the account with Turner from time to time, but increasingly Turner was left to work by herself.

Shortly after taking over the account, Turner was approached by Plotter, Norne's chief financial officer, who outlined to her a scheme to extract large sums of money from Norne through unauthorized borrowings. Turner would be able to use her position to falsify the accounts and to conceal the transactions. Turner agreed, and over the next 18 months they were able to divert over $5 million from Norne before their scheme was discovered. Turner, Plotter, and the money have all disappeared.

Adders LLP is now being sued by Norne Inc. and also by Driller, an investor resident in British Columbia, who recently purchased a 20 percent share in Norne after examining the accounts prepared by Adders.

Consider the liability of (a) Adders LLP, (b) Counter, and (c) the other partners in the firm.

5. Albinoni, Bonporti, and Corelli were partners. According to the partnership agreement, the following provisions applied:

(a) **Capital**
Albinoni and Bonporti each contributed $20 000; Corelli contributed no capital.

(b) **Advances**
Albinoni advanced $10 000 to the firm by way of loan, repayable on six months' notice or on dissolution.

(c) **Profits**
Profits were to be shared in the following proportions:
Albinoni, 40 percent
Bonporti, 40 percent
Corelli, 20 percent
They were to contribute in the same proportions (40/40/20) to make up any loss or deficiency.

(d) **Drawings**
The partners were entitled to draw, by way of an advance on their prospective shares of profits, up to $60 000 in any year.

Since the end of the last accounting period, the following drawings were made:
Albinoni, $ 8000
Bonporti, $ 7000
Corelli, $15 000

The partnership has now been dissolved. At the time of dissolution, the total value of the firm's assets, including undrawn profits, was $100 000. (This does not include the $30 000 already drawn by the partners.)

Calculate how the surplus, or deficiency, should be shared, if the total liabilities to the firm's external creditors (that is, not including debts owed to partners) are

(1) $ 10 000
(2) $ 90 000
(3) $150 000

ADDITIONAL RESOURCES FOR CHAPTER 26 ON THE COMPANION WEBSITE *(www.pearsoned.ca/smyth)*

In addition to self-test multiple-choice, true–false, and short essay questions (all with immediate feedback), application exercises, and links to useful web destinations, the Companion Website provides the following resources for Chapter 26:

- **British Columbia:** Business Names; Limited Liability Partnerships; Limited Partnerships; Partnerships; Sole Proprietorships

- **Alberta:** International Partnerships; Limited Liability Partnerships; Limited Partnerships; Partnership in Alberta

- **Manitoba/Saskatchewan:** Partnerships

- **Ontario:** Business Names; Fiduciary Duty; Limited Liability Partnerships; Limited Partnerships; Multi-Disciplinary Partnerships; Partnership Agreements; Registration of Partnerships

The Nature of a Corporation and Its Formation

This is the first of three chapters concerned with corporations. In it we discuss some of the most fundamental issues concerning the nature of the corporation and examine such questions as:

- What is a corporation?

- What are the consequences that flow from incorporation?

- What is meant by "limited liability"?

- How is a corporation formed?

- What are the usual provisions of the "corporate charter"?

- What is corporate "capital"?

- What are "shares"?

- What are the main distinctions between shares and bonds?

THE NATURE OF A CORPORATION

The corporation, or limited company, has become the dominant feature of the modern business world. Not only is it the main instrument of big business, it also rivals sole proprietorship and partnership as a means of carrying on smaller enterprises.

The Corporation as a Legal Person

legal person
an entity recognized at law as having its own legal rights, duties and responsibilities

A corporation is a person in the eyes of the law; that is, it is a **legal person**. A legal person is an entity recognized by law as having rights and duties of its own. A distinction is commonly drawn between legal persons and natural persons. Natural persons—that is, human beings—automatically have rights and obligations. Their rights and obligations may vary according to age, mental capacity, and other factors,[1] but they are all "persons." By contrast, a legal person is entirely a creation of the state. A legal person has rights and duties under the law, but it cannot insist on those rights or carry out its duties except through human agents.

corporation
a legal person formed by incorporation according to a prescribed legal procedure

Although legal systems create other legal entities, for our purposes the most important one is the **corporation**. The corporation evolved from the need to look after the common interests of a group of natural persons. It is a well-established legal principle, in both common law and civil law countries, that a corporation may be created as a separate and distinct legal person apart from its members.[2]

There are numerous types of corporations: publicly owned corporations created by governments to carry on special activities (for example, the Bank of Canada, the Canadian Broadcasting Corporation, Central Mortgage and Housing Corporation, and Canadian National Railway); municipal corporations to run local government; charitable corporations (for example, the Red Cross, the Heart and Stroke Foundation, the Ford Foundation); educational institutions; and business corporations—the most numerous type of all. For the purposes of this book, we are concerned only with business corporations.[3]

Characteristics of Corporations and Partnerships

The significance of the separate legal personality of a business corporation can be appreciated when compared with partnership.

Liability

As we saw in Chapter 26, in a partnership each partner is normally liable for the debts of the firm to the limit of his or her personal assets.[4] A corporation is liable for its own debts. If, as is usually the case, a shareholder has paid the full price for his shares, he can lose no more in the event that creditors seize the corporation's assets. It is for this reason—the limited liability of their *shareholders*—that business corporations are referred to as limited companies, although this is really something of a misnomer since the corporation itself is liable to the full extent of its assets.[5]

limited liability
the liability of shareholders is limited to the amount of their capital contributions

Limited liability is widely regarded as one of the main advantages of incorporation. However, the benefits of limited liability are sometimes over-estimated since, for a small corporation to obtain credit, its directors or shareholders are often required to give personal guarantees or mortgage their own

---

1. The contractual capacity of minors and persons of unsound mind was considered in Chapter 7.
2. See Bonham and Soberman, "The Nature of Corporate Personality," in *Studies in Canadian Company Law*, Ziegel, ed., Vol. 1, Ch. 1 (Toronto: Butterworths, 1967).
3. As we shall see later in this chapter, business corporations can be divided into a number of categories.
4. Exceptions are the limited liability partnership and limited partnership.
5. In British Columbia, Alberta, and Nova Scotia it is possible to form an unlimited company, in which the shareholders are liable for the company's debts. The main attraction of this form has been to create tax planning opportunities for U.S. businesses.

property as collateral security. In addition, as we shall see in the next two chapters, when shareholders become directors—as they often do in smaller enterprises—they are subject to a wide and increasing range of personal liability to other shareholders, to those doing business with the corporation, and to society as a whole, from which their limited liability as shareholders does not protect them.

Transfer of Ownership

A partner cannot release herself unilaterally from her liabilities—to her partners, to the firm, and to its clients—simply by retiring. She must bargain for her release with both her partners and her creditors. She may even be liable for debts contracted after her retirement, unless she has given notice to persons who regularly deal with the firm and has fulfilled the other requirements of the Partnership Act. Since a shareholder has no liability for corporate debts even while he retains his shares, creditors of the corporation have no interest and no say in what he does with his shares. The shareholder may sever all connections with the corporation simply by transferring his shares to another person. However, as we shall see later in this chapter, it is usual in closely held corporations to impose special restrictions on the transfer of shares.

Management

A partnership is unsuitable for a venture involving a large number of investors. Each partner, as an agent of the firm, may enter into contracts on behalf of the firm. By contrast, shareholders have no authority to bind their corporation to contractual obligations—only officers of the corporation may do so.

A partnership usually requires unanimity on major business decisions, a requirement that could stalemate a firm with a large number of partners. In a corporation, management is delegated to an elected board of directors that normally reaches decisions by simple majority votes. Major decisions that are referred back to the shareholders do not require unanimity, but at most a two-thirds or three-quarters majority, depending upon the issue and the requirements of the corporation law statutes in the jurisdiction.

This separation of ownership and management ranks with limited liability as a primary feature of the business corporation. These two features enable an investor to invest a specific sum of money and receive a return on it, without either taking any additional risk beyond the sum invested or having to take an active part in the management of business affairs.

Although at one time the major shareholders in a corporation were usually its managers as well, there has been an increasing separation between those who invest and those who manage.[6] The separation is, however, less pronounced in Canada than in the United States because many large Canadian corporations are still controlled by a single individual or by members of a family, or are wholly owned subsidiaries of foreign parent corporations.[7]

Duty of Good Faith

As we saw in Chapter 26, partners owe each other a duty of good faith or fiduciary duty. It would normally be a breach of duty for a partner to carry on another business independently without the consent of her other partners (especially if it were a competing business), or to enter into contracts with the firm on her own behalf. A shareholder owes no such duty to the corporation:[8] he may carry on any independent business himself and may deal freely with the corporation as if he were a stranger.

---

6. The classic study of this subject is that by Berle and Means, *The Modern Corporation and Private Property* (New York: Macmillan, 1932). It is still well worth reading.

7. Randall K. Morck, David A. Stangeland, and Bernard Yeung, "Inherited Wealth, Corporate Control, and Economic Growth:The Canadian Disease?" in *Concentrated Corporate Ownership*, Randall K. Morck, ed. (Chicago: National Bureau of Economic Research and University of Chicago Press, 2000).

8. See *Blacklaws* v. *470433 Alberta Ltd.* (2000), 187 D.L.R. (4th) 614. As we shall see in Chapter 28, directors owe a duty of good faith to their corporation.

Continuity

We have seen that in the absence of special provisions in the partnership agreement, the death or bankruptcy of a partner dissolves a partnership. Even when provisions are made in advance to continue the partnership and to buy out the share of the deceased or bankrupt partner, the procedure is often cumbersome and expensive. A corporation, by contrast, exists independently of any of its shareholders.[9] A person's shares may be transferred by gift or by sale, by will or by statute transmitting them to the personal representative on death, or by creditors seizing them, yet none of these events affects the existence of the corporation. A corporation continues in existence perpetually unless it is dissolved by order of a court or by a voluntary resolution of its shareholders, or it is struck off the register for failure to comply with statutory regulations.

Taxation

Unlike a partnership, a corporation is a taxable entity. Income of a corporation is taxed first in the corporation and again in the hands of a shareholder when a dividend is declared. To offset this double taxation, small corporations are taxed at an especially low rate and dividends receive preferential tax treatment.[10]

CHECKLIST Partnerships and Corporate Ownership Contrasted

	partnership	corporation
separate legal entity	no	yes
personal liability of owners	yes*	no
duty of good faith	yes	no
agency	yes	no
transferability of ownership	no	yes
participation of owners in management	yes	no
continuity	no	yes
taxable entity	no	yes

*There are exceptions; see Chapter 26.

Consequences of Separate Corporate Personality

Capacity

ultra vires
beyond the powers

A corporation is created by law and has the characteristics that the legislators give it. Originally, corporations were formed for specific purposes and could act only for those purposes expressly stated in their constitution. Any act outside the scope of those objects was ***ultra vires***—beyond the powers—of the corporation. Contracts made for an unauthorized purpose were invalid.

The *ultra vires* doctrine, as it applied to corporations, has now been abolished throughout Canada. Under the federal Canada Business Corporations Act,[11] and most of the provincial statutes

---

9. It survives even the death of all its shareholders: *Re Noel Tedman Holdings Pty. Ltd.*, [1967] Qd. R. 561 (Queensland S. C.).
10. The small business tax rate in Ontario was 16.5% in 2008.
11. R.S.C. 1985, c. C-44, referred to hereafter as the CBCA.

under which business corporations are formed, a corporation has the capacity and all the rights, powers, and privileges of a natural person (section 15).

As an artificial person, a corporation can, of course, act only through its human agents—its directors and officers. When a corporation purports to make a contract, it is necessary to determine whether its agent had authority. The law of agency has been considered in Chapter 19, and we shall return to it in Chapter 29, when we examine the question of the liability of corporations.

Separate Existence: Salomon's Case

As we noted in the previous section, a corporation is a legal entity distinct from its shareholders. The classic case on the existence of the corporation as a separate entity came before the House of Lords in 1897 in *Salomon* v. *Salomon & Co. Ltd.*[12] It is probably the most widely quoted decision in the whole of corporate law.

CASE 27.1

Salomon had carried on a successful business as a shoe manufacturer for many years. In 1892, he formed a corporation in which he held almost all the shares (20 001 out of 20 007, the remaining six shares being held by members of his family, in order to meet what was then the statutory requirement of seven shareholders). He then sold his business to the corporation. Soon afterwards, a downturn in the shoe industry, caused by loss of government contracts and a series of strikes, drove the corporation into insolvency, and a trustee was appointed to wind it up. The trustee claimed that the corporation was merely a sham, that Salomon was the true owner of the business and the real debtor—and, as such, he should pay off all debts owed by the corporation. The lower courts supported the trustee's position, but the House of Lords decided in favour of Salomon. The Lords said that either the corporation was a true legal entity or it was not. Since there was no fraud or any intention to deceive, all transactions having been fully disclosed to the parties and the statutory regulations complied with, the corporation was properly created and was solely responsible for its own debts.

The decision in the *Salomon* case was important because it recognized the separate legal personality of the so-called one-man company at the time when it was becoming a common form of doing business.[13] As a leading writer on the subject has said, "Since the *Salomon* case, the complete separation of the company and its members has never been doubted."[14]

For the most part, the principle of separate legal personality has worked well in the commercial world, but there are some circumstances where the shareholders' interests may be recognized. In the 1987 *Kosmopoulos* case, the Supreme Court of Canada held that a shareholder, even one who owns all the shares of a corporation, does not own its assets, but still has an insurable interest in those assets. If they are destroyed, his shares will lose value, and, consequently, he should be entitled to insure against their destruction.[15]

It remains unclear how far the principle in the *Kosmopoulos* case can be taken and whether it is restricted to insurance claims. Certainly, it does not seem to follow that, where an injury is done to a corporation, a shareholder will always have a claim for the consequent reduction in the value of his or her shares. As the Ontario Court of Appeal has since ruled, the fact that the plaintiff was the principal shareholder and directing mind of corporations that were defrauded did not entitle him to personal compensation for the losses suffered by the corporations. To hold otherwise would

12. [1897] A.C. 22.
13. The CBCA, s. 5, now allows a corporation to be formed with only one shareholder, as do the laws of almost all provinces.
14. *Gower's Principles of Modern Company Law* (6th ed.), pp. 79–80. London: Sweet & Maxwell, 1997.
15. *Kosmopoulos* v. *Constitution Insurance Co. of Canada* (1987), 34 D.L.R. (4th) 208. The concept of insurable interest is discussed in Chapter 18.

610PART 6Business Organizations: Their Forms, Operation, and Management

enable him to jump in front of the queue to the prejudice of other corporate creditors. Where a wrong is done to a corporation, a shareholder has no claim for damages in respect of that wrong.[16]

CASE 27.2

An oil exploration company had formed two subsidiaries, apparently to take advantage of government financing. One subsidiary owned a drilling rig; the other contracted to provide drilling services. The rig was damaged due to the alleged negligence of the defendant. The defendant was *prima facie* liable to the corporation that owned the rig, but not for the economic loss sustained by the service corporation. The two corporations were separate entities, and the loss to the service corporation was too remote.[17]

In other cases, the hardship is suffered not by the owners of the corporation but by the persons who deal with it.

CASE 27.3

K, a Toronto lawyer, had incorporated a real estate company, Rockwell, of which he effectively owned almost all the shares. Rockwell became involved in a contractual dispute with another corporation, Newtonbrook, and eventually brought an action against Newtonbrook for specific performance of the contract. Rockwell lost the action, and Newtonbrook was awarded costs of $4800. When Newtonbrook sought to recover the costs, it found that Rockwell's entire assets consisted of $31.85 in its bank account. Newtonbrook's attempt to recover from *K* personally failed.[18]

Limitations on the Principle of Separate Corporate Existence

When application of the *Salomon* decision leads to unfair results, should the courts refuse to follow it? Should legislation disregard the principle of separate legal identity?

Exceptions to Limited Liability

The limited liability of shareholders is not absolute. We have already noted that, in practice, shareholders of small private companies are often required to provide security or personal guarantees for loans made to their corporations. The Canada Business Corporations Act (CBCA) provides a further exception to the principle: where shareholders have received an improper distribution of corporate assets, for example, where a dividend has been paid although the corporation had made no profits, they are liable for the corporation's debts to that extent (section 45).[19] Other statutes, such as the federal Bankruptcy and Insolvency Act,[20] require shareholders who have received property from a corporation before it became insolvent to repay the amounts received in certain circumstances.

16. *Martin* v. *Goldfarb* (1998), 163 D.L.R. (4th) 639; *Meditrust Healthcare Inc.* v. *Shoppers Drug Mart* (2002), 220 D.L.R. (4th) 611.

17. *Bow Valley Husky (Bermuda) Ltd.* v. *Saint John Shipbuilding Ltd.* (1997), 153 D.L.R. (4th) 385. The question of recovery for economic loss was considered in Chapter 3.

18. *Rockwell Developments Ltd.* v. *Newtonbrook Plaza Ltd.* (1972), 27 D.I.R. (3d) 651.

19. There are also several provisions that make directors liable for the debts of their corporation; these are considered in Chapter 29.

20. R.S.C. 1985, c. B-3. See Chapter 31.

It is also important to note that the principle of limited liability does not protect persons who happen to be shareholders of corporations from *personal* liability. For example, a director who drives dangerously and causes an accident while on company business is not absolved from liability in tort, even though the corporation may also be vicariously liable.[21] And directors who make negligent misrepresentations regarding the affairs of their corporation may be personally liable for any resulting loss.[22] In Chapter 28 we will discuss the other circumstances in which officers and directors are exposed to personal liability.

Other Statutory Provisions

There are numerous examples, especially in taxation and labour law, where statutes require the separate personality of corporations to be disregarded. For example, Canadian-controlled private corporations are taxed at a lower rate on the first $400 000 of their annual income; but it is not possible to multiply this concession by forming several distinct corporations, because **associated corporations** are only entitled to a single concession between them.[23] Again, employers are not allowed to avoid statutory employment standards by transferring their assets to an associated corporation, thereby leaving the employer unable to meet employee claims for unpaid wages, vacation pay, and other benefits.[24] Nevertheless, the courts and legislature have stopped short of imposing any form of group liability. Thus, it is only in exceptional circumstances that a parent company will be held liable for the debts of its subsidiary or vice versa.

associated corporations corporations that are related either (a) vertically, as where one corporation controls the other (parent–subsidiary), or (b) horizontally, as where both corporations are controlled by the same person (affiliates)

ILLUSTRATION 27.1

Holdco is the parent company of a major marketing group. It has a number of divisions, each operated by a wholly owned subsidiary corporation. Retailco, its retailing subsidiary, recently became bankrupt, owing $100 million. At the same time, Creditco, the corporation that operates its credit financing division, has profits of $20 million. The assets of Creditco are not available to pay the creditors of Retailco.

Lifting the Corporate Veil

There have also been cases—although in Canada they have been quite rare—where the courts have been prepared to disregard the separate existence of corporations and "lift the veil" of incorporation to impose liability on those that control it. It seems that, in order to identify an individual within a corporation, three conditions must be met:

- The individual must control the corporation.
- That control must have been exercised to commit a fraud, a wrong, or a breach of duty.
- The misconduct must be the cause of the plaintiff's injury.[25]

Rather than equate a controlling shareholder with the corporation that he controls, Canadian courts have generally preferred to seek other routes to secure a just result. As we saw in the *Kosmopoulos*

---

21. See *Berger* v. *Willowdale* (1983), 41 O.R. (2d) 89.

22. *NBD Bank of Canada* v. *Dofasco Inc.* (1999) 181 D.L.R. (4th) 37; contrast *Montreal Trust Company of Canada* v. *Scotia McLeod Inc.*, (1995), 26 O.R. (3d) 481.

23. Income Tax Act, R.S.C. 1985, c. 1 (5th Supp.), s. 125. Corporations are associated where one corporation controls the other (parent–subsidiary relationship), or where both corporations are controlled by the same person or group of persons (affiliates).

24. See, for example, Employment Standards Act, R.S.O. 1990, c. E.14, which defines "employer" to include any associated corporation.

25. *W.D. Latimer Co. Ltd.* v. *Dijon Investments Ltd.* (1992), 12 O.R. (3d) 415. Courts are more likely to pierce the corporate veil when a shareholder engages in conduct amounting to fraud. See *Gilford Motor Company* v. *Horne*, [1933] Ch. 935 (C.A.).

case,[26] the Supreme Court of Canada refused to lift the veil and to hold that the corporation and the individual who owned all of its shares were one and the same person, but reached the same result by finding that he had an insurable interest in the corporation's property.

INTERNATIONAL ISSUE

Foreign Investment in Canadian Corporations

As will be discussed in Chapters 32 and 33, foreign investment in Canadian corporations is monitored and controlled by Industry Canada pursuant to the Investment Canada Act.[27] In addition, the Canada Business Corporations Act requires that 25 percent of a Canadian corporation's directors be resident Canadians (as does the Ontario, Alberta, Saskatchewan, and Manitoba legislation). However, there are variations among the provinces in the related legislation. To encourage foreign investment, British Columbia and Nova Scotia have dropped directors' residency requirements.

Another recent strategy to increase foreign investment (particularly by Americans) is the introduction of a new type of corporation: the unlimited liability corporation (ULC). As the name suggests, these corporations do not benefit from the protection of limited liability. On wind-up or dissolution, shareholders in a ULC are personally liable to the ULC's creditors for any unsatisfied debts.[28] So far, Nova Scotia, Alberta, and British Columbia have introduced ULCs in their provincial incorporation legislation. Ontario did not authorize ULCs when it amended its incorporation legislation in 2007. The attraction of ULCs for investors lies in the different tax treatment they receive in the United States. Although ULCs are taxed like any other corporation in Canada, in the United States they are viewed as "flow through" vehicles and no federal income tax is collected from them. When considering investing in this type of corporation, potential shareholders must weigh the tax benefits against the potential liability involved.

QUESTION TO CONSIDER

1. What impact will provincial variation in the availability of ULCs have on foreign investment decisions?

Sources: Geoff Kirbyson, "Alberta's Unlimited Liability Corporations Will Draw Them In," 27(41) *The Lawyers Weekly*, April 7, 2006, available online at www.lawyersweekly.ca/index.php?section=article&articleid=260; Business Corporations Act, S.B.C. c. 57 s. 51.3; Cassels Brock Lawyers, *Business Law Group e-COMMUNIQUÉ*, Vol. 7 No. 2, June 2007, corporate newsletter,,www.casselsbrock.com/publicationdetail.asp?aid=1349.

METHODS OF INCORPORATION

Early Methods of Incorporation

The oldest method of incorporation in the common law system—dating back to the 16th century—is by **royal charter** granted by the sovereign. Until the 19th century, all corporations were created by charter. Some of these are still in existence—the best known to Canadians being the Hudson's Bay Company, founded in 1670. A few royal charters are still issued today to universities, learned societies, and charitable institutions, but none to business corporations.

royal charter
a special licence given by the Crown to form a corporation for the purpose of carrying on a particular activity

---

26. *Supra*, n. 15.
27. R.S.C. 1985, c. I-21.8.
28. There is some provincial variation in the extent of shareholder liability. Alberta extends shareholder liability beyond liquidation and windup situations. Liability also applies to former shareholders.

From the end of the 18th century, corporations began to be created by **special Acts of Parliament**, especially for large projects of public interest—railroads, canals, waterworks, and other public utilities. Today, special acts are still used to create such corporations as Bell Canada and Canadian Pacific, and also to create special government corporations such as the Central Mortgage and Housing Corporation, the Canadian Broadcasting Corporation, and Air Canada. Parliament and the provincial legislatures have also passed statutes setting out procedures for the incorporation of particular types of businesses, such as banks and trust and loan companies. Such businesses may be incorporated only under those acts.

special Acts of Parliament
legislative acts creating a specific corporation

Incorporation Statutes

Today, however, almost all business (for profit) corporations are incorporated under general incorporation statutes. Under a statute of this type, any group of persons that complies with its requirements may form a corporation. In Canada, there is both federal and provincial incorporation legislation. The systems in use vary from one province to another.

Incorporation Roots: The Memorandum and Letters Patent Systems

In 1862, a system was introduced in England that depended upon Parliament rather than the royal prerogative, and that system was adopted by five provinces. It now remains in force in only one— Nova Scotia. The system requires applicants to register a document that sets out the fundamental terms of their agreement, called a **memorandum of association**. If the memorandum and certain other prescribed documents comply with the statute and the registration fee is paid, the authorized government office issues a **certificate of incorporation** and the corporation comes into existence. We shall call corporations incorporated in this manner "memorandum corporations."

memorandum of association
a document setting out the essential terms of an agreement to form a corporation

The other five provinces and the federal government employed a different system that survives today only in Quebec and Prince Edward Island. There, the incorporating document is called the **letters patent**, an offspring of the royal charter, but issued under the authority of the Crown's representative in each jurisdiction. Under the letters patent system, a general statute regulates the conditions under which the letters patent may be issued. Although in theory the granting of letters patent is discretionary, in practice, the steps taken by applicants do not differ greatly from those for registering a memorandum under the English system.

certificate of incorporation
a certificate that a corporation has come into existence

letters patent
a document incorporating a corporation, issued by the appropriate authority, and constituting the "charter" of the corporation

The Articles of Incorporation System

In 1970, Ontario passed a substantially different Business Corporations Act, creating a new method of incorporation adapted from a system in use in the United States. In 1975, the federal Parliament adopted the same system in its new statute, although many of the provisions of the federal act were quite different from those of the Ontario version. The CBCA has become the model for the new system: Alberta, Manitoba, New Brunswick, Newfoundland, Ontario, Saskatchewan, and, most recently, British Columbia[29] have followed with acts based on the federal scheme, although with local variations. Under the articles of incorporation system, persons who wish to form a corporation sign and deliver articles of incorporation to a government office and, in turn, are issued with a certificate of incorporation.

As the articles of incorporation system is now the most widely used one in Canada, our discussion will focus on it.

---

29. The memorandum system was in force in British Columbia until 2004, when the new Business Corporations Act, SBC 2002, c. 57, came into effect. The system combines features of both the memorandum and letters patent systems. Unfortunately, the terminology chosen is unnecessarily confusing in the Canadian business and legal context; the new statutes have adopted terms used in various parts of the United States, in particular, the word "articles," which has a different meaning in the memorandum system used in Nova Scotia, as well as in Britain and most Commonwealth countries. Canada Business Corporations Act, R.S.C. 1985, c. C-44; Ontario Business Corporations Act, R.S.O. 1990, c. B-16; Alberta Business Corporations Act, R.S.A. 2000, c. B-9; New Brunswick Corporations Act, S.N.B. 1981, c. B-9.1; Saskatchewan Corporations Act, R.S.S. 1977, c. B-10 and Newfoundland Corporations Act, R.S.N.L. 1990, c. C-36.

The Choice of Jurisdiction

The first decision to be made in forming a corporation is whether to incorporate federally or provincially. The CBCA is especially suitable for large businesses that carry on their activities nationwide; but even a small, local, one-person business may incorporate under it.[30]

The activities of a business incorporated under provincial jurisdiction are not restricted to that province. It may carry on business anywhere inside or outside Canada. However, corporations not incorporated within a province—and this includes federally incorporated corporations as well as those incorporated in other provinces—must comply with certain registration requirements in order to carry on business there.[31] Nevertheless, the act under which it was incorporated governs its *internal* operating rules for holding shareholder meetings, electing directors, declaring dividends, and other matters that are examined in Chapter 28. The checklist below outlines some of the considerations involved in choosing whether to incorporate under federal or provincial jurisdiction.

CHECKLIST Federal or Provincial Incorporation?

Considerations	Federal	Provincial
Type of business activity	Mandatory for federally regulated activities (s. 91) such as banking	
Location of business activity	All across the country	One province
Registered office	In Canada	In the province
Name selections	Pre-screened	Variation (many leave burden on business)
Name use	Throughout Canada	Within province
Prestige value	Increased prestige	
Initial fees	Approx. $200	Approx. $300
Directors' Canadian residency	25%	0%–25%*
Annual filings	Multiple separate	Combined

*Saskatchewan, Ontario, Alberta, Manitoba, and Newfoundland require 25 percent and British Columbia, Nova Scotia, P.E.I., New Brunswick, and Quebec have eliminated the residency requirement.

THE CONSTITUTION OF A CORPORATION

articles of incorporation

founding corporate document, often referred to as the charter or constitution of the corporation

Articles of Incorporation

Under the articles of incorporation system, a corporation is formed by filing **articles of incorporation** in the prescribed form and paying the required registration fee.[32] The articles of incorporation are often referred to as the "charter" or "constitution" of the corporation and set out essential information

---

30. Federally incorporated corporations (that is, under the CBCA) make up about one-half of the largest corporations in Canada but less than 10 percent of small corporations.

31. See, for example, the Ontario Extra-Provincial Corporations Act, R.S.O. 1990, c. E. 27. The formalities that must be complied with vary to some extent according to whether the corporation is incorporated federally, elsewhere in Canada, or abroad; for example, only non-Canadian corporations require a licence to do business in Ontario. The Corporations Information Act, R.S.O. 1990, c. C.39, requires registration of certain information—for example, place of registered office, names of directors, and place within the province where notice may be served.

32. The incorporation fee under the CBCA is $250 (reduced to $200 for electronic filing). The corresponding Ontario fee is $360 ($300 for electronic filing).

about the corporation. In those provinces that have not adopted the articles of incorporation system, the corresponding "charter" document is the letters patent or the memorandum of association.

CHECKLIST   Content of the Articles of Incorporation

- name of the corporation
- place where the registered office is situated
- classes and any maximum number of shares that the corporation is authorized to issue
- if there are two or more classes of shares, the rights and restrictions attached to each class
- any restriction on the transfer of shares
- number of directors
- any restrictions on the business that may be carried on
- other provisions that the incorporators choose to include

Occasionally, matters not usually found in a charter will also be included. This may be done in order to give certain "entrenched" rights to minority shareholders. Normally, the charter can only be altered by a special resolution, requiring the approval of a two-thirds majority of the shareholders,[33] and the filing of the amended charter. In most circumstances, however, the charter is an unsuitable instrument for reflecting special arrangements among the shareholders. Instead, shareholders enter into a separate shareholders' agreement outside the corporate constitution, setting out how they will exercise their powers. This topic will be discussed further in the next chapter.

The Corporate Name

As noted above, the articles must include the name of the proposed corporation. The registration of corporate names is closely regulated. The appropriate government office must approve the name and will refuse to register the corporation if it falls within certain prohibited categories (in particular, those that falsely suggest an association with the government or with certain professional bodies, or that are scandalous or obscene), or if it is likely to be confused with the name of some other existing corporation. In order to avoid the inconvenience and delay caused by the rejection of a chosen name, intending incorporators normally first make a "name search" to check that no existing corporation is registered with a similar name and undertake trademark searches. Records of corporations are now computerized,[34] which greatly facilitates such checks. If the name is not important to the incorporators, the problem can be avoided by using a "number name," where the registry simply assigns a number to the new corporation.[35]

By-laws

Nature of By-laws

Incorporators generally keep the incorporating documents as short as possible to gain flexibility in the operation of the corporation, but detailed operating rules are needed for its day-to-day affairs. Under both the articles of incorporation and letters patent systems, these operating rules are called

---

33. The procedures for altering letters patent or a memorandum tend to be more cumbersome than those under the newer articles of incorporation system.

34. The NUANS (newly upgraded automated name search) system, operated by Industry Canada, provides a computerized search system for all federally (and some provincially) registered companies and trademarks. See the discussion under "Trademarks" in Chapter 22.

35. CBCA, s. 11(2). A number name may be subsequently changed to a "normal" name without the usual formality that is required to amend the articles: CBCA, s. 173(3).

by-laws
the internal working rules of
a corporation

by-laws.[36] By-laws are flexible, requiring confirmation by only a simple majority of shareholders, although corporation acts do specify some matters that must be dealt with by special resolution requiring a two-thirds majority.

It is not strictly necessary to have by-laws at all. However, it is normal and convenient to have them, and they may be amended or new by-laws may be adopted, as and when required, with a minimum of formality. Usually, the directors amend by-laws or adopt new ones, but the new or amended by-laws need confirmation at the next general meeting of shareholders in order to remain valid. By-laws fall into two main categories: general operating rules and specific director authorizations.

General Operating Rules

The first category provides general operating rules for the business of the corporation that are usually passed at the first meeting of the shareholders. The first by-laws are often quite long and elaborate, dealing with such matters as the election of directors, their term of office, the place and required notice for meetings of directors, the quorum necessary (that is, the minimum number who must be present) before a meeting of directors can act on behalf of the corporation, the categories of executive officers, provisions for the allotment of shares and for the declaration of dividends, and procedures for holding the annual general meeting and other meetings of shareholders.

CHECKLIST   Provisions Included in Typical By-laws

- The qualification of a director shall be the holding of at least one share in the capital stock of the corporation.
- A director shall hold office until the third annual general meeting following his appointment.
- Notice of a meeting of directors shall be given in writing to each director not less than seven days before the meeting.
- Three directors shall constitute a quorum for the transaction of any business, except as otherwise provided in these by-laws.
- Questions arising at any meeting of directors shall, except as herein provided, be decided by a majority of votes: in the event of an equality of votes, the Chair of the meeting shall have a second or casting vote.
- Any contract entered into by the corporation that involves the expenditure or the incurring of a liability in excess of $10 000 must be approved by a majority of all the directors.
- Written notice of not less than 28 days, in the case of an annual general meeting, and 21 days, in the case of other shareholder meetings, shall be given to all shareholders entitled to vote at the meeting.
- A quorum is present at a general meeting of shareholders if not less than 10 shareholders, together holding a majority of the shares entitled to vote at the meeting, are present in person or by proxy.
- Shares in the corporation shall be allotted by resolution of the board of directors, approved by not less than two-thirds of all directors, on such terms, for such consideration, and to such persons as the directors determine.
- The directors may at any time by resolution, approved by not less than two-thirds of all directors, declare a dividend or an interim dividend, and pay the same out of the funds of the corporation available for that purpose.

---

36. For a memorandum corporation they are called articles of association, which causes confusion. The one really important difference is that, in the memorandum system, articles of association can only be altered by a special resolution of the shareholders, requiring a three-quarters majority.

Authorization to Directors

Most statutes no longer require a by-law to be passed in order to confer any particular power on the directors (unless the corporation's own constitution does).[37] Certain matters, such as the sale of substantially all of a corporation's property or the amalgamation with another corporation, are required to be approved by special resolution of the shareholders, and although directors now normally have the power to borrow money on the security of the corporation's assets without special authorization, it is common for them to ask the shareholders to confirm a major loan transaction, because creditors may insist upon such confirmation. Shareholder resolutions of this type are still often referred to as "by-laws."

TYPES OF BUSINESS CORPORATIONS

Public and Private Corporations

Initially, legislators believed that limited companies would be used primarily for large undertakings having many shareholders (i.e., be public corporations). Consequently, the regulations focused on protection of the general public through disclosure and publication obligations. By the end of the 19th century, it became evident that incorporation was also a useful and fully effective tool for family businesses. Since these small corporations did not seek investment from the general public, the disclosure and publication requirements were unnecessary.

In 1908, the British Parliament enacted provisions to permit the formation of **private companies**, which were not permitted to offer shares to the public and in which the right to transfer shares had to be restricted in some manner. Those provisions found their way into Canadian incorporation statutes, but now exist only in Prince Edward Island and Nova Scotia. The CBCA and most other provincial statutes now permit even a single shareholder to form a corporation, and do not maintain a formal distinction between public and private corporations. Instead, a more realistic distinction is made between those corporations that issue their shares to the general public[38] and those that do not. The two types of corporation are commonly referred to, respectively, as "widely held" and "closely held."

private company
a corporation with a restricted number of shareholders prohibited from issuing its shares to the general public

Widely Held Corporations

Incorporation statutes, such as the CBCA, apply to both widely and closely held corporations but draw a number of distinctions between them. The CBCA, for example, imposes various obligations upon what it terms a "**distributing corporation**" with respect to such matters as proxy solicitation, the number of directors, and the need for an audit committee. These requirements are considered further in Chapter 28. But the most important difference is that distributing corporations are also subject to regulation under the relevant provincial securities acts in those provinces in which their securities are issued or traded. Increasingly, and especially since the Enron affair, securities legislation and the policies of securities regulators and of stock exchanges have come to play an important role in the way in which Canada's larger corporations are structured and conduct their business and affairs. Those topics are considered in Chapters 28 and 29.

distributing corporation
a corporation that issues its securities to the public; also referred to as issuing corporations, reporting issuers, and publicly traded corporations

Closely Held Corporations

The main use of the closely held corporation is to incorporate small- and medium-sized business enterprises where the number of participants is small. A closely held corporation is a true limited company with the same legal significance and corporate independence as the widely held corporation. In fact, when a large corporation creates a subsidiary, it usually does so by incorporating a closely held corporation. Many large U.S. and other foreign corporations operate wholly owned subsidiaries in Canada

---

37. See CBCA, s. 16(1).

38. The CBCA describes these as "distributing" corporations. Securities legislation refers to these as issuing corporations or reporting issuers.

that are closely held. All the shares are held by the parent corporation, except for a few that may be held here by corporate officers. A number of these subsidiaries rival our own large public corporations in size.

The vast majority of corporations are closely held—over 90 percent in Canada. It is therefore rather surprising that they are largely neglected as a subject of study in business administration. The literature of economics, finance, accounting, and management directs its attention to widely held corporations. Closely held corporations have been permitted the luxury of operating in an atmosphere of relative privacy. In a closely held corporation, the owners are usually the managers as well, thus focusing questions of management and ultimate decision making within a small group. We shall examine the legal implications of this characteristic of closely held corporations in the next chapter.

Corporate Groups

The largest businesses, in Canada and internationally, frequently comprise a group of corporations, one or more of which is widely held, with shares held by the public and listed on one or more stock exchanges, together with a number of subsidiaries that are closely held, in the sense that they are often wholly owned by their parent company. For example, the corporate structure of the Hollinger companies and related entities (formerly controlled by Lord Black) involved over 60 companies—some public, some private—and were subject to a number of different jurisdictions.[39] Groups of this nature can give rise to extremely complex relationships and to possible conflicts, as we shall see in Chapter 28.

Professional Corporations

As we saw in the previous chapter, members of many of the leading professions have been prohibited from incorporating their practices, either by the rules of the professional body to which they belong or under the statute governing the profession. They have consequently been restricted to practising as sole proprietors or in partnership with the disadvantage, in the latter case, of being liable for obligations incurred by their co-partners. One response to that problem, which we have already discussed, has been the adoption of legislation permitting the establishment of limited liability partnerships (LLPs).

professional corporation (PC)
a special type of business corporation that may be formed by members of a profession

Most provinces now allow for the incorporation of the **professional corporation (PC)**.[40] Under the legislation, members of listed professions may form a PC, provided it is permitted by the rules of the profession itself and the professional controls the voting shares.[41] The Saskatchewan act provides:

> One or more members of an association may incorporate a corporation pursuant to the Business Corporations Act for the purpose of carrying on, in the name of the corporation, the business of providing professional services that may lawfully be performed by members of the association.[42]

The words "Professional Corporation" or the abbreviation "PC" must appear in the name of the corporation,[43] and all members of the corporation must be members of the profession.[44] Regarding liability, the act provides:

> The liability of a member of an association to a person who receives services from the member is not affected by the fact that the services were provided by the member as an employee of, or on behalf of, a professional corporation.[45]

---

39. See *Catalyst Fund General Partner I Inc.* v. *Hollinger Inc.* [2004] O.J. No. 4722.

40. Alberta has allowed the creation of PCs for more than 20 years. The Ontario and Saskatchewan legislation only came into effect in 2001. Manitoba adopted a rather different approach, by amending the relevant statutes governing those professional bodies that are now allowed to incorporate: Professional Corporations (Various Acts Amendment) Act, S.M. 1999, c. 41. Quebec still does not allow professional corporations for dentists, doctors, or engineers.

41. In Ontario, for example, the Chartered Accountants Act, the Public Accountants Act, and the Law Society Act have been amended to permit the formation of PCs. The legislation is contained in the oddly named Balanced Budgets for Brighter Futures Act, S.O. 2000, c. 42.

42. Professional Corporations Act, S.S. 2001, c. P-27.1, s. 4(1).

43. *Ibid.*, s. 4(2).

44. *Ibid.*, ss. 5(2), 6(1). Thus, multi-disciplinary PCs are not (yet) permitted.

45. *Ibid.*, s. 15.

In effect, a member of a profession who incorporates (either alone or together with other members) remains responsible for her own negligence or misconduct towards clients, although the principle of limited liability does seem to provide protection against the claims of other creditors—for example, lessors of premises or suppliers of equipment. The principal advantage of professional incorporation is not to obtain a degree of limited liability, but rather to enjoy a number of tax advantages that are not available to sole proprietorships and partnerships.[46]

Only members of listed professions may form a PC, but one should remember that not all professions are prohibited from incorporating. For example, engineers and geophysicists are not "listed" and consequently cannot form a PC; however, that is no disadvantage since they are able to establish a "normal" corporation.

ETHICAL ISSUE

Undermining Professional Standards?

Recent legislative changes have introduced the LLP and the professional corporation as alternative vehicles for conducting professional activities, and the concept of multi-disciplinary partnerships is also gaining ground. This has led to fears, in some quarters, that professional standards are being undermined. In particular, it is argued that such developments may lead to the destruction of the professional–client relationship. Would you really want to have your teeth pulled by a corporation?

Others would argue that there are adequate safeguards to ensure that professional standards are maintained, and that there is no valid reason for denying to professionals the benefits of incorporation that are enjoyed by other businesspersons (and by some professions).

QUESTIONS TO CONSIDER

1. Are the recent changes discarding the traditions of a century, or are they simply keeping up with the times?

2. Is there any reason why professionals, such as accountants, doctors, and lawyers, should not be allowed to incorporate in the "normal" way?

CORPORATE CAPITAL

Equity and Debt

There are two principal ways in which a corporation can raise funds: by issuing shares (equity) and by borrowing (debt). A third method—financing the corporation's activities out of retained profits—is really akin to the first, since the shareholders are effectively reinvesting part of their profit. Although borrowing increases the funds that are at the disposal of the corporation's management, it is really misleading to speak of "debt capital," since borrowing increases both assets and liabilities. A corporation's true capital is its "equity capital" or "share capital."

---

46. In particular, the lower rate of income tax on small corporations and greater flexibility in providing for retirement pensions. However, there may also be tax disadvantages, so the decision to form a PC must be considered very carefully.

Share Capital

Every business corporation must have a share capital.[47] The word "capital" has different meanings in different contexts. In letters patent and memorandum jurisdictions, when a corporation is incorporated, its charter places an upper limit on the number or money value of shares it may issue. This limit is called the **authorized capital**. A corporation need not issue all its authorized share capital. The **issued capital** and **paid-up capital** of a corporation are, as their names indicate, the parts of the authorized capital that have been issued and paid for.

In articles of incorporation jurisdictions, by contrast, a corporation may state the maximum number of shares that can be issued if it so wishes, but does not have to do so. A corporation must, however, still keep a **stated capital account** disclosing the consideration received for each **share** issued. Shares must be fully paid for at the time of issue.[48] Consequently, there is no difference between issued capital and paid-up capital.

There are several ways of becoming a shareholder:

- by being one of the original applicants for incorporation
- by buying shares issued by a corporation subsequent to its incorporation, or
- by acquiring (by purchase or gift) previously issued shares from another shareholder

The first two ways result from contracts between the shareholder and the corporation, and the transactions increase the issued capital as shown in the accounts of the corporation. The third way is the result of a transfer to which the corporation is not a party at all, and does not affect its accounts.

Par Values

Until the early part of the 20th century, all shares had a nominal or **par value**—a fixed value established in the charter like a bank note or a bond. Shares were issued by the corporation at their par value. However, par value provided little indication of a share's real value; once issued a share rarely had a market price identical with its par value.

A corporation was prohibited from issuing its shares for less than their par value (that is, at a "discount"). If a corporation's shares were selling on the market below their par value and the corporation required additional capital, investors would not purchase a new issue at par. In order to make an issue, the corporation would be compelled to reduce the par value of the shares to a more realistic figure and to reduce its capital accordingly by obtaining an amendment to its charter, causing delay and expense.

The United States introduced **no par value shares**—that is, shares that represent a specific proportion of the issued capital of the corporation, rather than a fixed sum of money. The advantages of no par value shares, in particular, the fact that they may be issued from time to time at prices that correspond to their current market value, resulted in their adoption by all the jurisdictions in the United States; soon afterwards they were permitted in Canada. The articles of incorporation system has now abolished par value shares entirely.

---

authorized capital
the maximum number (or value) of shares that a corporation is permitted by its charter to issue

issued capital
the shares that have been issued by a corporation

paid-up capital
the shares that have been issued and fully paid for

stated capital account
the amount received by a corporation for the issue of its shares

share
a member's proportionate interest in the capital of a corporation

par value
a nominal value attached to a share at the time of issue

no par value share
a share that has no nominal value attached to it

ILLUSTRATION 27.2

Pliable Plastics Inc. is incorporated under the articles of incorporation system. Its articles contain no restriction on the total number of shares that may be issued, and its shares have no par value. Initially, it issued 50 000 shares at $100 each, giving it a stated capital of $5 000 000. The directors wish to raise a further $3 000 000.

If the current market price of the shares has fallen to $60, they can raise $3 000 000 by issuing 50 000 new shares at that price. On the other hand, if the market price has risen to $120, they will need to issue only 25 000.

---

47. Charitable and non-profit corporations need not have a share capital.

48. CBCA, s. 25(3). Previously, shares could be issued "partly paid," with the corporation being able to make a subsequent "call" for the remainder of the price.

Until the introduction of the articles of incorporation system, **preferred shares** were almost always issued with a par value. They paid a preferred dividend expressed as a percentage of the par value and the corporation could redeem them at par value. For example, a share might have a par value of $100 (and be redeemable at that price) and pay a dividend of 8 percent (that is, $8 per share). With the abolition of par values, preferred shares are now stated to have a redemption price ($100), with a preferred dividend expressed simply as a sum of money ($8).

preferred share
a share carrying preferential rights to receive a dividend and/or to be redeemed on the dissolution of the corporation

CORPORATE SECURITIES

The Distinction Between Shares and Bonds

A corporation may borrow money in a number of ways, but when it borrows substantial sums on a long-term basis it normally does so by issuing **bonds**. The classic distinction between shares and bonds (or "debentures," as they are sometimes called) is that the holder of a share is a member of, and owner of an interest in, the corporation. The holder of a bond is a creditor. In the business world, there is no such clear-cut distinction. In the language of modern business, the true *equity* owner of a corporation, and the person who takes the greatest risk, is the holder of **common shares**. From this end of the scale, we proceed by degrees to the person who is a mortgagee or bondholder, where the holder takes the least risk. In between we may have the holders of preferred shares. Today, most larger corporations have, in addition to an issue of common shares, one or more classes of bonds or debentures and probably also a class of preferred shares.

bond
a document evidencing a debt owed by a corporation

common share
a share carrying no preferential right

When deciding whether to invest in the shares or the bonds of a corporation, an individual usually does not make a conscious choice between becoming a member (that is, an equity owner) and becoming a creditor. She regards herself in both instances as an investor. Her investment decisions are determined primarily by economic considerations. Bonds provide a fixed and guaranteed return (provided the corporation remains solvent), in the form of regular interest payments and the right to be redeemed in full at their maturity date. Common shares carry no guarantee that their holders will receive anything, either in the form of dividends or on dissolution, but their holders participate in any "growth" of the corporation. Preferred shareholders come somewhere in between. They are entitled to receive dividends and to have their shares redeemed on the dissolution of the corporation, before payments are made to the holders of the common shares, but those rights are often restricted to a fixed dividend and a fixed amount payable on redemption.

The line between shareholder and bondholder is nonetheless a distinct and important one in its legal consequences for a corporation. First of all, since bondholders are creditors, interest paid to them is a debt of the corporation. It must be paid whether or not the corporation has earned profits for the year. Shareholders are not creditors and receive dividends only when the directors declare them. One consequence, especially important for taxation, is that interest payments are normally an expense of doing business and are deducted before taxable income is calculated; dividends, on the other hand, are payable out of after-tax profits. Second, bonds are usually secured by a mortgage or charge on the property of the corporation (see the discussion in Chapter 30 under "Floating Charges"). If a corporation becomes insolvent, its secured bondholders are entitled to be repaid not only before the shareholders but also before the general creditors. They are secured creditors, and the trustee acting for them can sell the corporation's assets to satisfy the debt owed to them.

Rights of Security Holders

Bondholders

Bondholders do not normally have a direct voice in the management of the corporation unless it is in breach of the terms of the trust deed or indenture under which the securities were created. Only when a corporation gets into financial difficulty or is in breach of the trust deed may the trustee step in and take part in management on behalf of the bondholders. It is true, however, that bondholders do exert an indirect form of control over management in the restrictive clauses commonly written into bond indentures, which may place a ceiling on the further long-term borrowing of the corporation, on the amount of dividends it may pay, and even, in smaller corporations, on the salaries it pays to its officers.

Common Shareholders

By contrast, common shareholders have, in theory at least, a strong voice in the management of the corporation. As we shall see in the next chapter, it is they who elect the board of directors and who must approve major changes in the corporation's activities. Otherwise, however, their rights are limited. They have no entitlement to a dividend and can receive one only after bondholders and preferred shareholders have been paid. And, on the liquidation of the corporation, their entitlement is to share what is left after the claims of creditors and preferred shareholders have been satisfied.

Preferred Shareholders

Preferred shareholders are in an intermediate category. Usually, they are entitled to be paid a fixed dividend before any dividend is paid to the common shareholders, and they are entitled to be paid the fixed redemption price of their shares on liquidation of the corporation before any surplus is distributed to the common shareholders. Frequently, they have no right to vote unless the payment of dividends to them is in arrears. In this respect they are more like creditors than investors. However, payment of preferred dividends is not a contractual commitment of a corporation as is bond interest; a preferred shareholder must enforce her rights as an individual and is not dependent upon a trustee taking action, as a bondholder normally is.

Class Rights

cumulative right
the right of the holder of a preferred share to be paid arrears from previous years before any dividend is paid on the common shares

participating right
the right of a holder of a preferred share to participate in surplus profits or assets of the corporation in addition to the amount of the preferred dividend or redemption price

Where a corporation issues more than one class of shares—for example, common shares and preferred shares—the precise rights of each class must be set out in its constitution.[49] The various combinations of rights and privileges that may attach to a class of shares are extensive and may relate not only to dividend rights and rights of redemption, but also to voting rights, rights to appoint directors, and sometimes to the right to convert a security of one class into a security of another class.

Problems of interpretation arise in the drafting of rights for various classes of shareholders. Two questions with respect to preferred shareholders' rights to dividends are particularly important. The first is whether the rights are **cumulative**: if the full preferred dividend is not paid in one year, do the arrears accumulate so that they must be paid in a subsequent year or on winding up the corporation, before the common shareholders are entitled to anything? The second is whether on winding up, their rights are **participating**: if after the preferred shareholders have been fully paid, do they still participate in any remaining surplus along with the common shareholders? This uncertainty makes it all the more important to draft class rights with the greatest care.

CHECKLIST   Priority of Payment on Liquidation of a Corporation

On liquidation of a corporation its assets must be distributed in the following sequence. (Note that bondholders are creditors—and usually they are secured creditors.)
(1) secured creditors
(2) unsecured creditors
(3) preferred shareholders
(4) common shareholders

49. See CBCA, s. 6(1)(c).

The Transfer of Corporate Securities

Negotiability

We have seen in Chapter 12 that share and bond certificates are a type of personal property subject to different rules of transfer and ownership from those that apply to sales of goods. We noted further in Chapter 21 that these choses in action may in some circumstances be treated as negotiable instruments. Thus, bond certificates in bearer form may be considered as a type of negotiable instrument at common law. Articles of incorporation statutes expressly treat share certificates as a type of negotiable instrument.[50]

In theory, if bonds and shares are to serve the purposes of a capital market, they should be readily transferable (that is, "liquid"). When bonds and shares are treated as negotiable instruments, an innocent holder for value may often acquire a better title than his predecessor had, as, for example, when he purchases bonds or share certificates that have been stolen. However, two unfortunate results have also flowed from this development: first, there has been an increased temptation to indulge in theft as it is easy to sell stolen certificates; second, it has become easier to pass off forged (and therefore worthless) certificates on purchasers. The innocent holder of a forged negotiable instrument, as we have seen, obtains no title.

Restrictions on Share Transfer

In a widely held corporation, shares are almost always freely transferable; if they are not, the shares will not be accepted for listing on a stock exchange. In contrast, closely held corporations almost invariably restrict the transfer of shares; otherwise, it would be difficult for them to remain closely held.

Restrictions on share transfer are required to be set out in the corporation's constitution,[51] and can take almost any form. Such restrictions must also be noted on the share certificate; otherwise, they are not binding on a purchaser who has no notice of the restriction.[52] In practice, the most common restriction is to require the consent of the board of directors to any transfer, but there are other varieties, such as giving the right of first refusal to existing shareholders or directors before a shareholder can sell to an outsider, or giving a major shareholder the right of veto. Requiring the consent of directors gives them the discretion to approve or reject a proposed member of the corporation, much as partners determine whether they will admit a new partner.

QUESTIONS FOR REVIEW

1. What is meant by a "legal person"?
2. What is meant by "limited liability"? Whose liability is limited?
3. What are the main differences between partnerships and corporations?
4. What were the principal arguments made by the creditors in the Salomon case in attempting to make Salomon personally liable?
5. In what ways may two or more corporations be said to be "associated"?
6. What is meant by "lifting the corporate veil"?

---

50. Unless there are restrictions on transfer noted on the certificate: CBCA, s. 48(3).
51. See, for example, CBCA, s. 6(1)(d).
52. CBCA, s. 49(8). See *Bank Leu AG* v. *Gaming Lottery Corp.* (2003), 231 D.L.R. (4th) 251.

7. How does the articles of incorporation system of forming a corporation differ from (a) the letters patent system and (b) the memorandum and articles system?

8. What information must be set out in articles of incorporation?

9. Why must care be taken in selecting a corporate name? What is a "number name"?

10. What is the main function of a corporation's by-laws?

11. What are the principal characteristics of closely held corporations?

12. What are the main advantages of forming a professional corporation?

13. What is the function of a corporation's stated capital account?

14. In what way are par values for shares likely to be misleading?

15. What special rights are normally carried by preferred shares?

16. What are the usual rights of bondholders?

17. What factors influence an investor's choice between shares and bonds?

18. In what sequence should a corporation's assets be distributed on liquidation of the corporation?

19. In what circumstances are restrictions on the transfer of shares binding on purchasers of the shares?

CASES AND PROBLEMS

1. Oakdale Motors Inc. is a corporation, incorporated under the Canada Business Corporations Act, engaged in the selling, repairing, and servicing of automobiles. All of its shares are owned by Faulkner, who is also the sole director. Faulkner acts as the general manager of the corporation and supervises its day-to-day operations.

   One day last winter, Hill visited the premises of Oakdale Motors to look at a used car that she had seen advertised and that she was interested in purchasing. The area outside the sales office was extremely slippery, being covered by ice that was, in turn, covered by a thin layer of snow that had fallen overnight. Faulkner was working at the Oakdale premises that day and knew of the dangerous state of the premises, but had made no effort to have the danger removed.

   Hill slipped on the ice, fell, and broke her leg. The injury was a serious one and has left her with a permanent disability.

   She has learned that Oakdale Motors Inc. is in severe financial difficulties and is likely to be made bankrupt. However, Faulkner appears to be quite wealthy.

   Would Hill have any claim against Faulkner?

2. Macbeth, the owner of 20 hectares located on the outskirts of Niagara Falls, decided to sell, and on January 2 signed an exclusive listing agreement with Ross, a real estate broker. Macbeth agreed to pay Ross a commission of 5 percent on the sale of the property, which he listed at $350 000.

   On January 19, Ross filed articles of incorporation for a new corporation, Burnam Woods Properties Ltd., of which he was the sole shareholder. He appointed his friend Lennox as general manager.

   Several weeks later, Ross introduced Macbeth to Lennox as general manager of Burnam Woods but said nothing to suggest that he, Ross, had any interest in the corporation. Within a few days Lennox submitted an offer on behalf of the corporation to purchase Macbeth's property for $240 000. Macbeth rejected the offer but made a counter-offer to sell at $290 000. Burnam Woods accepted the counter-offer, and the deal was closed on March 15, when Macbeth paid Ross his commission of $14 500.

   Shortly afterwards, Burnam Woods entered into negotiations with another corporation, Castle Hall Developments Ltd., and sold the 20 hectares to it for $450 000, realizing a quick profit of $160 000.

On April 24 following, Macbeth learned of the resale by Burnam Woods and also learned about Ross's share ownership in the Burnam Woods company. Macbeth immediately sued Ross and Burnam Woods jointly for recovery of the real estate commission of $14 500 and for the $160 000 profit realized on the second sale by Burnam Woods Properties Ltd. to Castle Hall Developments Ltd.

Examine the validity of Macbeth's claim, and offer an opinion about its chances for success.

3. Rosina has recently developed a highly original computer program that, she claims, will revolutionize the practice of landscape architecture. She has been advised by a consultant that marketing the software is likely to be a highly profitable venture. However, to develop and market the project will require working capital, which Rosina does not have. Fortunately her uncle, Bartolo, has agreed to put $100 000 of his savings into the project.

With the help of a lawyer friend (who has advised them that they should each obtain independent legal advice), they have worked out a rough structure for their project, as follows:

(a) They will form a corporation, of which they will be the sole shareholders.
(b) Rosina will assign her copyright in the program to the corporation and will work full-time in developing and marketing it.
(c) Bartolo will contribute $100 000 in cash as working capital and will participate in major management decisions but will not be responsible for the day-to-day running of the business.

Since Rosina will be giving up a fairly well-paid job in order to develop the new business, she is concerned that she should not be left entirely without income during the initial period (when there would be no sales revenue). In turn, Bartolo would like there to be some sort of guarantee of a reasonable return of income on his investment.

What form of capital structure for the corporation, and what other possible arrangements, would you consider to be appropriate?

4. Stick and Twist are lawyers who have practised in partnership for a number of years. With the introduction of legislation permitting the formation of professional corporations in their province, they decided to convert their partnership into a PC.

The new corporation, "Stick and Twist Lawyers PC," was formed with a share capital of $1000, Stick and Twist each holding one share. They are the sole directors. The corporation has very few tangible assets, since its office is rented, as is much of its office equipment.

Twist "disappeared" a few months ago, and Stick has discovered that

(a) a client is claiming $200 000 from the corporation in respect of money which she had entrusted to Twist for the purchase of a condominium; and
(b) the landlord is claiming $12 000 in respect of rent owing on the premises. Twist had assured Stick that the rent had been paid.
To what extent are (1) the corporation and (2) Stick liable?

5. Pliable Plastics Inc. issued 50 000 common shares at $100 each. Some years later, in order to raise additional finance, it issued 20 000 Class "A" preferred shares, also at $100 each. The preferred shares were stated to have a redemption price of $100, and were entitled to receive a first dividend of $8 per share. The following year, to raise further funds, the corporation made an issue of bonds, in the sum of $2 000 000, secured by a floating charge on all of its assets.

Soon afterwards, Pliable Plastics found itself in serious financial difficulties. Although it had substantial assets, these were not readily realizable, and it was unable to pay its debts as they fell due. It appeared that the situation could only get worse. The directors resolved to sell off the corporation's assets and to wind up the corporation.

The sale of the assets realized $7 000 000, and after paying off its creditors (other than the bondholders) the corporation was left with $5 500 000. How much will each common share receive?

ADDITIONAL RESOURCES FOR CHAPTER 27 ON THE COMPANION WEBSITE *(www.pearsoned.ca/smyth)*

In addition to self-test multiple-choice, true–false, and short essay questions (all with immediate feedback), application exercises, and links to useful web destinations, the Companion Website provides the following resources for Chapter 27:

■ **British Columbia:** Business Corporations; Corporate Name Registration; Incorporation

■ **Alberta:** Business Corporations Act; Income Trusts; Incorporation; NUANS Reports; Other Incorporated Bodies; Pre-incorporation Contracts; Professional Corporations; Taxation of Corporations; Unlimited Liability Corporations

■ **Manitoba/Saskatchewan:** Non-Share Capital Corporations; Officers; Process of Incorporation; Separate Legal Entity; Shareholders

■ **Ontario:** Articles of Incorporation; Not-for-Profit Corporations; Ontario Corporations; Professional Corporations; Promoters; Reporting Issues; Securities Legislation

Corporate Governance:

THE INTERNAL AFFAIRS OF CORPORATIONS

This chapter and the next address corporate governance. They discuss the internal and external affairs and the business of a corporation. In this chapter we examine such questions as:

■ How is a corporation organized and managed?

■ What is the function of the board of directors?

■ How are the directors appointed and removed?

■ Who is an officer?

■ What are the duties of directors and officers?

■ What are the consequences of a breach of duty by a director or an officer?

■ What defences are available to directors and officers?

■ What are the rights and duties of shareholders?

■ How are the rights of minority shareholders protected?

WHAT IS CORPORATE GOVERNANCE?

Corporate governance
the rules governing the organization and management of the business and affairs of a corporation in order to meet its internal objectives and external responsibilities

Corporate governance refers to the organization and management of the business and affairs of a corporation in order to meet its internal objectives and external responsibilities. Where do we find the rules of corporate governance? As discussed in Chapter 27, the incorporating documents—the articles of incorporation and the by-laws—create the management structure within the corporation and this is one set of corporate governance standards. Also, as noted earlier, each incorporating jurisdiction—Canada and each province—has corporation legislation that must be followed. It is in this legislation that we find the legal rules of corporate governance.

The Canada Business Corporations Act (CBCA)[1] and the corresponding provincial statutes draw a broad distinction between two aspects of a corporation's activities. Section 102 states that "the directors shall manage, or supervise the management of, the *business* and *affairs* of a corporation" (italics added). The difference between these two terms is explained in section 2(1), where "affairs" are defined as "the relationships among a corporation . . . and the shareholders, directors and officers . . . but *does not include the business carried on* [by the corporation] . . ." (italics added). The distinction, which is helpful in understanding the complex activities of corporations, is between

(a) the *affairs*: the internal arrangements among those responsible for running a corporation—the directors and officers—and its main beneficiaries—the shareholders—which we discuss in this chapter; and

(b) the *business*: the external relations between a corporation and those who deal with it as a business enterprise—its customers, suppliers, and employees—as well as relations with government regulators and society as a whole; discussed in Chapter 29.

There is at least one group for which the distinction is blurred: the shareholders in a publicly traded corporation. An invitation to the public to invest in a corporation is directed towards those who may not yet be part of its internal relations, but if the members of the public accept an offer to buy shares, they will subsequently become involved in its "affairs." These potential public shareholders are protected through special provincial securities regulations imposed on only those companies issuing shares to the public and so we discuss securities regulation in both Chapters 28 and 29. In this chapter we will review the basic legal rules of corporate governance and the liability arising from their breach. The rules discussed in this chapter apply to both *privately* and *publicly held* corporations and are codified in federal and provincial legislation. Breach of the rules may give rise to civil, regulatory, or even criminal liability or a combination of all three.

CORPORATE GOVERNANCE OF PUBLICLY TRADED CORPORATIONS

publicly traded corporations
corporations that issue shares to the public, also known as public corporations, widely held corporations, reporting issuers, and issuing corporations

Recent public corporate scandals such as those involving Enron and WorldCom led securities regulators to tighten the rules of corporate governance for **publicly traded corporations** (this chapter will also use the CBCA term, *distributing corporation*). First, the United States passed the Sarbanes-Oxley Act of 2002 (SOX), and next, the Securities and Exchange Commission introduced new rules, policies, and recommendations for the internal operations of public companies.[2] Canadian

---

1. R.S.C. 1985, c. C 44. The Act was substantially amended by Bill S-11, S.C. 2001, c. 14. Unless otherwise stated, statutory references in this chapter are to that Act, as amended. Corresponding provincial legislation: Business Corporations Act, S.B.C. 2002, c. 57; Business Corporations Act, R.S.A. 2000, c. B-9; Business Corporations Act, R.S.S. 1978, c. B-10; Corporations Act, C.C.S.M. c. C225; Business Corporations Act (OBCA) R.S.O. 1990, c. B-16; Companies Act, R.S.N.S. 1989, c. 81; Companies Act, R.S.N.B. 1973, c. C-13; Companies Act, R.S.P.E.I. 1988, c. C-14; Corporations Act, R.S.N.L. 1990, c. C-36. Most provincial legislation is similar to the federal legislation. Relevant major departures will be noted.

2. 15 U.S.C. s. 7201 et. seq.

securities regulators adopted some of the SOX standards.[3] This means publicly traded companies are required to meet the standards in both the CBCA (or the relevant provincial incorporating legislation) *and* the provincial securities legislation. These rules increase the protection available to the public stakeholders—public shareholders, creditors, employees, and lenders. The general themes of the legislation are independence of decision makers, transparency, disclosure, accountability, and organizational checks and balances.[4] Some of the recommendations include:

- A majority of directors should be independent.
- The CEO should not also hold the position of chair of the board.
- The corporation should establish separate, independent committees of the board to regulate executive compensation and nomination of board members.
- The corporation should adopt and publish a "code of ethics."
- The board should perform regular self-assessments.

Many privately held corporations choose to comply with the higher standard of corporate governance in order to meet their ethical responsibilities and in preparation for a **public offering** in the future. Where relevant, this chapter will identify the heightened requirements for public companies.

public offering
selling shares to the public, which must be done in compliance with provincial securities regulations

THE STRUCTURE OF THE MODERN BUSINESS CORPORATION

Business corporations differ greatly from one another in their size and composition. Modern legislation tries to take these differences into account. However, there are certain elements that are essential to all corporations.

The three basic groups common to all corporations are the shareholders, the **board of directors**, (generally referred to as "the board") and the **officers**. In small private corporations, such as family companies, it often happens that most or even all of the shareholders are also directors and officers. Even if the distinction between shareholders and directors may sometimes become blurred in practice—for example, when they get together to discuss business, they may not specify whether the meeting constitutes a directors' meeting or a shareholders' meeting—the distinction remains important legally.

In a large corporation, by contrast, the board of directors may have as many as 15 or 20 members who are elected by shareholders. Generally, in such cases the board will appoint or hire a *chief executive officer* (CEO, also often called the president or managing director) or a smaller committee of directors (the *management committee* or *executive committee*) to direct the affairs and business of the corporation and to supervise its other officers and employees. CEO's are most often full-time employees of the company who, together with other officers, manage the corporation. It is this team, not the board, that are known collectively as "the management." The management refers only the important policy matters to the full board of directors. In turn, the board of directors usually calls no more than the required annual meeting of shareholders, at which it reports to them on the state of the corporation's affairs and holds elections to determine the board of directors for the coming year.

Public or distributing corporations are required to have an **audit committee**, whose members include at least three directors. Originally, the audit committee's task was only to review the financial statements of the corporation before they were submitted to the full board for approval.[5] Recent provincial securities regulations expand the responsibilities of the committee and require *all* audit

board of directors
the governing body of a corporation, responsible for the management of its business and affairs

officers
high-ranking members of a corporation's management team as defined in the by-laws or appointed by the directors, such as the president, vice-president, controller, chief executive officer, chief financial officer, general counsel, and general manager

audit committee
a group of directors responsible for overseeing the corporate audit and the preparation of financial statements. The committee has wider responsibilities in a distributing corporation.

---

3. National Policy Instrument 58-201. Although securities regulation is a matter of provincial jurisdiction and each province has its own legislation and Securities Commission, the 13 provincial and territorial regulators cooperate on most regulation through the Canadian Securities Administrators (CSA). The result is nationally consistent instruments, guidelines, and policies that are adopted under the same numbering system.

4. Richard DeGeorge, Chapter 9, "Corporate Governance, Accounting Disclosure and Insider Trading," in *Business Ethics*, 6th ed. (Upper Saddle River, NJ: Prentice Hall, 2006).

5. CBCA, s. 171. Any other corporation (that is not public or distributing) may have an audit committee.

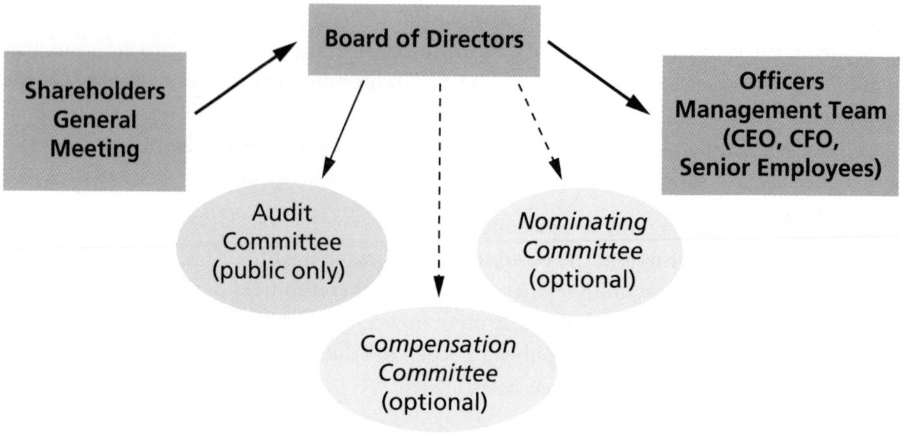

FIGURE 28.1
Corporate Structure

Power originates with the general meeting of shareholders. The shareholders elect a board of directors to manage the corporation. The directors, in turn, appoint or hire a chief executive officer, who is the highest-ranking employee in charge of the day-to-day running of the corporation.

compensation committee
committee responsible for setting director and officer pay

nominating committee
committee responsible for proposing and recruiting new directors

committee members to be independent directors; the auditor must be retained by and report to the audit committee rather than the board or corporate management.[6] A **compensation committee**, responsible for setting director and officer compensation, and a **nominating committee**, responsible for finding new directors, are also recommended but not mandatory.[7] Figure 28.1 illustrates the general structure of a corporation.

INTERNATIONAL ISSUE

Sarbanes-Oxley Act of 2002

The U.S. Sarbanes-Oxley Act of 2002 (SOX) set new standards for the internal organization of publicly traded companies. These standards go beyond the Canadian regulations and include mandatory codes of ethics and compensation committees, expanded disclosure requirements, and CEO and CFO compensation clawbacks. Compliance does not come cheaply: American businesses are complaining about the high cost of implementing SOX standards.

SOX has also had a large influence on the corporate governance of Canadian businesses. Its reach extends beyond American geographic borders and applies to many Canadian corporations. Canadian corporations trading on an American stock exchange must comply with SOX, as must Canadian subsidiaries of U.S. parent corporations. If Canadian corporations want to find investors internationally, they must be aware of the corporate governance rules in foreign jurisdictions.

QUESTION TO CONSIDER

1. Should public corporate governance rules be those of the incorporating jurisdiction or those of the jurisdiction where the shares are sold? Or both?

Sources: L. McCallum and P. Puri, *Canadian Companies' Guide to the Sarbanes Oxley Act* (Toronto: Butterworths, 2004); Kevin Drawback, "Reform Backlash Gathers Momentum: Restriction on Class-action Suits Part of a Trend," *National Post*, February 21, 2005.

---

6. National Instrument No. 52-110, s. 2.3, 3.1. This instrument also creates an expanded definition of "independent" that means free of "any direct or indirect material relationship." Previously, only the majority of the directors on this committee had to be independent.

7. National Policy No. 58-201; Multilateral Instrument 58-101.

DIRECTORS

The Role of the Directors

Section 102 of the CBCA provides that the directors shall manage, or *supervise* the management of, the business and affairs of the corporation. In addition to the general power of management, the Act confers a number of specific powers on the directors. The most important of these are:

(a) to issue shares—subject to the corporation's constitution, the directors may issue shares at such times, to such persons, and for such consideration as they may determine (section 25).

(b) to declare dividends—the directors determine whether, or to what extent, profits should be distributed to the shareholders or retained in the corporation.

(c) to adopt by-laws governing the day-to-day affairs of the corporation—the directors may adopt new by-laws or amend existing ones. Although they must be submitted for approval at the next meeting of shareholders, the by-laws remain effective until then (section 103).

(d) to call meetings of shareholders (section 133). The directors must call an annual general meeting each year, but they may call additional meetings whenever they wish.

(e) to delegate responsibilities (except those outlined in (a) to (d)) and appoint officers (sections 115 and 121). Officers do not have to be directors.

CHECKLIST Powers of Directors

In relation to the internal affairs of the corporation, the most important powers given to the directors are:

■ to issue shares

■ to declare dividends

■ to adopt by-laws

■ to call meetings of shareholders

■ to delegate responsibilities and appoint officers

A corporation is required to have one or more directors.[8] A distributing corporation must have a minimum of three directors, at least two of whom must be *independent*; that is, they must not be officers or employees of the corporation (section 102(2)). Provincial securities regulations define "independent" more broadly as "no direct or indirect material relationship with the corporation."

Where a corporation has more than one director, decisions of the board of directors are normally taken by majority vote, unless the corporate constitution requires a higher special majority or unanimity. Usually, the by-laws make provision for the holding of meetings of the board, the election of a chairperson, rules on voting, quorums, and like matters.

Shareholders play little or no part in management. They have certain rights, the most important being to vote at meetings, but generally, once the shareholders have elected a board of directors, they have no further power to participate in management. If they do not like the way the directors are running the corporation's business and affairs, they cannot interfere. Legally, their

8. Even a corporation with only a single shareholder must have one or more directors, though there is no reason why the shareholder should not also be the sole director. The articles of incorporation are required to state the number (or the minimum and maximum number) of directors that the corporation is to have (section 6(1)(e)).

main course of action is to dismiss the directors and elect new ones in their place.[9] It is consequently of vital importance that the shareholders select competent and trustworthy individuals as their directors.

CASE 28.1

The majority shareholder of a corporation wanted the corporation to sell its main asset. At his request the directors called a general meeting of shareholders, which passed a resolution (over the opposition of some of the minority shareholders) instructing the board of directors to go ahead with the sale.

The board refused to do so, believing that the sale was not in the best interests of the corporation. The majority shareholder sought a declaration that the board was bound to carry out the instructions of the general meeting of shareholders.

The court refused to grant the declaration, ruling that it is the directors who manage the business of a corporation and, until such time as they are replaced, they must act as they think best for the corporation and are not bound to follow instructions from the shareholders.[10]

One very important effect of this rule is that the shareholders cannot compel the directors to declare a dividend, unless there is an express requirement in the corporation's constitution that a dividend be paid in particular circumstances.

Appointment and Removal of Directors

A director of a corporation must be a minimum of 18 years of age, be of sound mind, and not have declared bankruptcy (section 105). In addition, at least 25 percent of the directors of a corporation must be resident Canadians.[11] Unless required by the articles of incorporation, a director need not hold shares in the corporation.

A corporation's first directors are appointed at the time of incorporation and hold office until the first meeting of shareholders, which must be held not less than 18 months after the corporation comes into existence (section 133). Subsequently, directors are elected, re-elected, or replaced on a regular basis. Normally this occurs at the annual general meeting of the corporation, but elections may be held at any time at a special meeting called for that purpose. Casual vacancies on the board—for example, where a director dies or becomes seriously ill—may normally be filled by the remaining directors.

Directors are elected by ordinary resolution of the shareholders (section 106(3)); that is, a simple majority vote is sufficient.[12] The effect of this rule is that a single shareholder or a group of shareholders, holding anything more than 50 percent of the total votes, is able to elect the entire board of directors. (Conversely, complete equality between two competing groups can lead to deadlock—as sometimes happens when two equal partners incorporate their business.) An exception to the general rule may be made by providing, in the articles of incorporation, that directors be elected by a system of **cumulative voting**—a form of proportional representation designed to ensure that any substantial minority of shareholders will be represented on the board. Such systems, however, are quite rare in Canadian corporations.[13]

cumulative voting
a method of electing directors by a form of proportional representation

9. If dissatisfied shareholders hold a sufficient proportion of the shares, they need not wait until the next meeting called by the directors; they may requisition a meeting (s. 143) to elect a new board. As will be discussed under the section called Protections of Minority Shareholders, in some situations there may be court remedies available.

10. *Automatic Self-Cleansing Filter Syndicate Co. Ltd.* v. *Cuninghame*, [1906] 2 Ch. 34 (U.K.C.A.).

11. S. 105(3), as amended. Prior to November 2001, the CBCA required a majority of directors to be resident Canadians. Some provinces still require a majority of directors to be resident Canadians, while others have no residence or citizenship requirement. If there are fewer than four directors, at least one director must be a resident.

12. The Alberta and Saskatchewan statutes allow for directors to be appointed by a class of shareholders, or by creditors or employees, if the articles so provide: Business Corporations Act, R.S.A. c. B-9, s. 106(9); R.S.S. c. B-10, s. 101(8).

13. Except in New Brunswick, where cumulative voting is mandatory: Business Corporations Act, R.S.N.B. c. 9.1, s. 65.

A director's term of office may not exceed three years, and even during that term a special meeting may be called to vote on the removal of a director (section 109). Except where cumulative voting is provided for, an ordinary resolution (simple majority) is sufficient for the removal of any director, and the articles may not prescribe a greater majority (section 6(4)).

OFFICERS

As noted, officers are responsible for the day-to-day "hands on" management of the corporation. Officers derive their power from the directors. The CBCA defines an officer as "someone appointed by the directors" with functions similar to "a president, vice-president, secretary, treasurer etc . . ." (section 2(1)). It is for the directors to define and designate responsibilities of each officer (section 121) and this is usually done in the by-laws. The only statutory requirement is that the officer be of "full capacity." Officers may be removed by the directors. In most corporations, officers exercise tremendous power and, as will be discussed in the next section, they are subject to the same duties as directors. The responsibilities of officers of distributing corporations are attracting more attention from provincial regulators, which now require CEO's and CFO's to certify contents of a corporation's audited financial statements.

CHECKLIST Corporate Governance Legislative Overview

	Private Corporations	Public Corporations	
	CBCA	CBCA	Securities Regulation
Minimum directors	1 s. 102(2)	3 s. 102(2)	3
Independent directors	Not required	2	Majority Recommended NP 58-201 s. 3.1
Financial statements	Unaudited s. 163(1)	Audited s. 161	Audited by Public Accountant and certified by CEO/CFO
Annual general meeting of shareholders	Required	Required	Required
Audit committee	Optional	Required s. 171	Required All members must be financially literate, independent directors NI 52-110 s. 3.1
Compensation committee	Not required	Not required	Optional Disclose alternate method if used NP 58-201 s. 3.15
Nominating committee	Not required	Not required	Optional NP 58-201 s. 3.10
Disclosure of corporate governance practices	Not required	Not required	Required NI 58-101 F1
Code of ethics	Not required	Not required	Recommended NP 58-201 s. 3.8

ETHICAL ISSUE

Who Is "Independent"?

When Bill Gates was appointed to Berkshire Hathaway Inc.'s Board of Directors in 2004, he was designated by the board as an independent director. His only pre-existing relationship with the corporation was as a shareholder. Still, critics complained about the designation, citing his long friendship with chairman Warren Buffet.[14]

What does independent mean? The commonly understood meaning of the word is that an independent party is free of any conflicting interests or ties. The CBCA definition designates only employees and officers of the corporation as being non-independent. The provincial securities regulation definition excludes anyone with a "direct or indirect material relationship with the corporation" and it leaves the determination of what a "material relationship" is up to the directors themselves to decide with some minor direction.

The regulation suggests that a material relationship is one that could "reasonably interfere with the exercise of independent judgment." It goes on to suggest that examples include employees, officers, and their immediate family members. But what about friends, distant relatives, or competitors?

QUESTIONS TO CONSIDER

1. Should a director be free of any potential conflict of interest to be considered independent?

2. Is it appropriate to let the board of directors determine its own members' independence?

3. How can a nominating committee or a code of ethics help with this issue?

Sources: National Instrument 52-110 s. 1.4; Belle Kaura, "The Corporate Governance Conundrum: Re-inventing the Board of Directors and Board Committees," in P. Puri and J. Larson (Eds.), *Corporate Governance and Securities Regulation in the 21st Century* (Toronto: Butterworths, 2004).

DUTIES OF DIRECTORS AND OFFICERS

Section 122 of the CBCA describes the statutory duties of directors and officers:

(1) Every director and officer of a corporation in exercising their powers and discharging their duties shall
  (a) act honestly and in good faith with a view to the best interests of the corporation; and
  (b) exercise the care, diligence and skill that a reasonably prudent person would exercise in comparable circumstances.
(2) Every director and officer of a corporation shall comply with this Act, the regulations, articles, by-laws and any unanimous shareholder agreement.

To fully understand these responsibilities we must consider *what* duties are owed and also *to whom* the duties are owed.

What Duties Are Owed?

Section 122(1)(a): Fiduciary Duties

The CBCA requires that directors and officers "act *honestly* and in *good faith* with a view to the *best interests* of the corporation" (section 122(1)) (italics added). This is the language associated with

---

14. David Pauly, "Just How "Independent" Is Berkshire's Board?" *National Post*, January 26, 2005.

fiduciary duty, a duty with which we are already familiar. It imposes a high standard of conduct on directors and officers involving loyalty, integrity, and trust.[15] This duty addresses the motives, considerations, and factors that influence decision-making separately from the decisions themselves. We will discuss particular examples of common conflicts of interest in the section called Specific Conduct. All of the examples involve, in one way or another, situations where there is a conflict, at least potentially, between a director's personal interest and that of the corporation. However, it is important to understand that Section 122 (1) (a) imposes a general duty on directors and officers to avoid any *conflict of interest* with their corporation.

Section 122 (1) (b): Duty of Care, Diligence and Skill

Section 122 (1) (b) of the CBCA requires directors and officers to exercise the care, diligence, and skill that a *reasonably prudent person* would exercise in *comparable circumstances*. A director or officer owes a duty not to be negligent in carrying out his or her duties. This is an objective standard; no greater diligence is required of a director than is required of the average person. We have not yet developed standards for a professional class of directors.[16] By contrast, a director who is also *employed* by a corporation, for example, as its chief executive officer, its treasurer, or its chief engineer, will normally owe a professional duty of care, but that duty is owed in respect of the employment, not as a director.

Directors are not expected to give continuous attention to the affairs of the corporation and, unless there are suspicious circumstances, they are entitled to rely on information received from the officers of the corporation.[17] However, they may not willfully close their eyes to mistakes and misconduct. If they acquiesce in such matters, they may be liable in damages to the corporation for any losses that result.

To Whom Are Directors' and Officers' Duties Owed?

To the Corporation

Although the Act does not expressly say so, it is implicit, especially in the words "with a view to the best interests of the corporation," that the duties of directors and officers are owed, at least primarily, to the corporation. The interests of "the corporation" are normally taken to mean the interests of the corporate legal entity, *present and future*. Directors and officers may—and should—consider the long-term interests of the corporation and not merely the present interests or wishes of the shareholders. But do directors and officers owe duties to anyone other than the corporation? How should they balance competing interests?

To the Shareholders and Other Stakeholders

Although directors are elected and can be removed by a majority of the shareholders, it would be wrong to conclude that their first duty is to those shareholders who have elected them—as was demonstrated in Case 28.1. The duty of a director is owed to the corporation *as a whole*.

However, this does not answer the question whether, in addition to the duties owed to the corporation as a whole, any duty is owed to *individual* shareholders or other stakeholders. Modern corporate governance theory recognizes that the conduct of a corporation's business affects not only shareholders but many other sectors of the public as well. If a large corporation is badly managed,

---

15. It may also extend to senior employees. See *MacMillan-Bloedel Ltd.* v. *Binstead* (1983), 22 B.L.R. 255.

16. The members of the audit committee of a distributing corporation are required to be "financially literate." That is not a statutory requirement but a rule adopted by Canadian securities regulatory authorities under Multilateral Instrument 52-110. Financial literacy means that the individual "has the ability to read and understand a set of financial statements."

17. *Dovey* v. *Corey*, [1901] A.C. 477.

the well-being of many people and even the national interest may be seriously affected. Creditors of a bankrupt corporation go unpaid. Employees may lose their jobs, as may other members of the community where the corporation carries on business. A corporation that produces defective products may injure consumers, and one that does not take effective measures to prevent pollution may cause severe damage to the environment. Consequently, the public in general has a "stake" in good corporate management.

The traditional English and Canadian answer to the question is *no:* directors' and officers' duties are owed to the corporation only, and it is the corporation that may seek a remedy if the duties are breached.[18]

The *Peoples* v. *Wise* Distinction

Recently, the Supreme Court of Canada considered the duties in section 122 and drew a clear distinction between the fiduciary duty and the duty of skill and care.[19]

CASE 28.2

Wise Stores Inc. (Wise) bought Peoples Department Stores Inc. (Peoples). The three sons of the Wise founder (Wise brothers) were the majority shareholders, officers, and directors of Wise. After the purchase they also became the sole directors of Peoples. The integration of the two operations did not go smoothly, especially in the area of inventory control and bookkeeping. The Wise brothers reviewed the inventory problems and accepted the recommendation of the Vice-President of Administration and Finance. They implemented a joint inventory procurement policy which divided purchasing responsibilities between the two operations. Peoples would make purchases from North America and Wise would make all other international purchases. Within a year of implementation the inventory system was in total chaos; suppliers went unpaid. Eventually both Wise and Peoples declared bankruptcy and Peoples' bankruptcy trustee

sued the Wise brothers personally, claiming they breached the duties owed to Peoples' creditors.

The Supreme Court of Canada held that there was no fiduciary duty owing to the creditors or other stakeholders, stating "At all times directors and officers owe their fiduciary obligation to the corporation. The interests of the corporation are not to be confused with the interests of the creditors or those of any other stakeholders."[20] However, the Court held that the duty of skill and care was not limited to the corporation: "the identity of the beneficiary of the duty of care is much more open-ended, and it appears obvious that it must include creditors."[21]

On the facts, the Court held that the Wise brothers met the required objective standard of skill and care by acting prudently and on a reasonably informed basis. The creditors were denied a remedy.

To the Public

In *Peoples* v. *Wise*, the Supreme Court extended the duty of skill and care to other stakeholders including shareholders, creditors, and employees. In refusing to extend the fiduciary duty the same way, the Court noted the broad protection afforded to these groups under other statutory provisions. Some of that legislation will be discussed later in this chapter, in Chapter 29, and in Chapter 32

---

18. *Percival* v. *Wright*, [1902] 2 Ch. 421. The conduct described in this case is now forbidden by statute but the general principle remains. Only if the directors offer to act on behalf of other shareholders, thereby creating an agency relationship, or if they stand in some other fiduciary relationship, will they be under a duty to them: *Allen* v. *Hyatt* (1914), 17 D.L.R. 7; *Malcolm* v. *Transtec Holdings Ltd.* [2001] B.C.J. No. 413. Under securities legislation, directors are required to disclose to the shareholders information relating to takeover offers; see the discussion in Chapter 29.

19. *Peoples Department Stores Inc.* v. *Wise* (2004), 244 D.L.R. (4th) 564, at p. 582. In Alberta, a director who is appointed by a particular class of shareholders (or by creditors of employees) may give special (but not exclusive) consideration to the interests of that class: R.S.A. c. B-9, s. 122(4). There may be special circumstances in which directors owe a fiduciary duty to others—for example, to clients of the firm; see *Air Canada* v. *M & L Travel Ltd.* (1993), 108 D.L.R. (4th) 592.

20. *Ibid.,* at para. 43–44.

21. *Ibid.,* at para. 57.

where we examine other aspects of the external relations of corporations. As we shall see, corporate directors must manage their corporations in conformity with the law, and they may incur personal liability if they fail to do so.

In *Peoples*, the Court also noted that it may be in the best interests of the corporation to consider the interests of others.[22] A corporation that promotes good labour relations by considering the welfare of its employees, enjoys good customer and community relations, and is perceived as socially responsible and responsive to environmental concerns is likely to prosper better in the longer term than one that does not. A corporation's management rightly devotes considerable attention to its public image and relations. It may even be argued that directors owe a duty to the corporation to do so.[23]

The situation is different in Ontario. In August 2007, possibly in response to the *Peoples* decision, the Ontario Business Corporations Act was amended to make it clear that both the fiduciary duty and the duty of skill and care are owed *only* to the corporation.[24]

Defences to Breach of Duty

Directors and officers are personally liable for a breach of duty. If the corporation goes bankrupt, disgruntled shareholders, employees, and creditors often accuse officers and directors of breach of duty or "mismanagement." How can directors and officers protect themselves? What defences are available? What risk-management strategies should be in place? Both legislation and the common law provide some guidance.

The CBCA includes the following defences and risk-management strategies:[25]

(a) Reasonable diligence, also known as the **due diligence defence**: By establishing that the required degree of care was taken, directors and officers can defend themselves against claims of breach of the articles, by-laws, and the act (section 123(4)).

due diligence defence
establishing that an acceptable standard of care and skill was exercised by a director or officer

(b) Good faith reliance: Good faith reliance on audited financial statements or expert reports is a defence to breach of fiduciary duty or duty of skill and care (section 123 (5)). Therefore, obtaining expert reports prior to key decisions is a good risk-management strategy.

(c) Corporate indemnity: An agreement with the corporation to reimburse a director or officer for any costs associated with liability for breach of duty is enforceable provided that the director acted honestly, reasonably, and in good faith (section 124). Naturally, the effectiveness of this risk-management strategy depends on the financial health of the corporation.

(d) Directors' and officers' liability insurance: A corporation may purchase directors' liability insurance on behalf of its board (section 124(6)). These policies have many exclusions, including bad faith and fraud, and are very expensive.

The key common law defence available to directors and officers is known as the **business judgment rule**. Under this rule, courts will grant business experts the benefit of the doubt and not easily criticize a business decision. Judges recognize that they are not business experts and even sound decisions may ultimately be unsuccessful. Therefore, courts focus on the process used to arrive at the decision; as long as directors and officers exercise an appropriate degree of prudence and diligence while making the decision, the court will hold that the duty of skill and care is met. As was noted in

business judgment rule
courts will defer to the business decisions of directors and officers provided they are arrived at using an appropriate degree of prudence and diligence

22 *Ibid.*, at para. 42.

23. *Re Olympia & York Enterprises Ltd.* and *Hiram Walker Resources Ltd.* (1986), 59 O.R. (2d) 254 at 271 (On. Div. Ct.).

24. Section 134 (1).

25. There is some provincial variation: Ontario's reasonable diligence and good faith defence extends to interim financial reports and reports or advice of an officer or employee (section 135(4)).

Peoples, establishing and *following* good corporate governance rules can protect directors and officers from allegations that they have breached their duty of care.[26]

The business judgment rule has its limits. It will not protect a director from liability for a failure to comply with specific legal obligations such as mandatory disclosure under securities legislation.[27]

Strict Liability

Directors may also be subject to strict liability, where no breach of duty need be established. The CBCA and corresponding provincial statutes make directors liable to their corporation when they vote at meetings of the board on specified matters that cause financial losses to the corporation, such as the improper redemption of shares or the payment of a dividend in circumstances that leave the corporation unable to meet its liabilities (section 118(2)). In addition, if the corporation becomes insolvent, the directors are personally liable to all employees of the corporation for unpaid debts for services performed while they were directors, up to the amount of six months' wages (section 119).[28] Directors may also become liable for failure to comply with other statutes. For example, if the corporation is insolvent, the federal government may collect from the directors the income tax that the corporation was required to withhold from the wages and salaries of employees.[29] Even the volunteer directors of a non-profit corporation have been held liable under this provision.[30]

Specific Conduct Involving Conflicts of Interest

Contracts with the Corporation

Perhaps the most important fiduciary obligation is the duty to disclose any interest that the director may have in contracts made with the corporation. This duty arises where a director negotiates the sale of her own property to the corporation, or the purchase of property from the corporation. It may arise indirectly, for example, a director may be a shareholder in another corporation that is selling to or buying from her corporation. The problem occurs frequently among related corporations, where a director of one corporation is a shareholder and perhaps a director of a second corporation.

ILLUSTRATION 28.1

Brown holds a large number of shares in each of World Electric and Universal Shipbuilding, and is a director of each of these corporations. Universal Shipbuilding requires expensive turbo-generator sets for two large ships under construction. World Electric is one of several manufacturers of turbo-generators.

Brown is faced with an obvious conflict of interest: can she encourage or even support a contract between the two corporations? On one side, it is in Brown's interest to see Universal Shipbuilding obtain the equipment at the lowest possible price. On the other side, it is in her interest to see World Electric get the contract and obtain the highest possible price.

Under section 120 of the CBCA, a director who has an interest in a contract must disclose this fact at a meeting of the board of directors that considers the contract and must not vote on the matter. If, after learning of the interest, the remaining independent members of the board still wish to

---

26. *Peoples, supra* note 19, at para 64.

27. *Kerr* v. *Danier Leather Inc.*, 2007 SCC 44 at para 55.

28. Section 119 uses the word "debts," though it limits the amount to 6 months' wages. It is, however, not necessary to establish that the debt claimed is for "wages," provided it was incurred for services performed. The section 123(4) defence of reasonable diligence applies to both section 118 and section 119. In *Proulx* v. *Sahelian Goldfields Inc.* (2001), 204 D.L.R. (4th) 670, the Ontario Court of Appeal (considering s. 131 of the Ontario act) held that vacation pay owing constituted a debt, whether or not it should be regarded as "wages," and was within the section.

29. Income Tax Act, R.S.C. 1985, c. 1 (5th Supp.), s. 227.1.

30. *MNR.* v. *Corsano* (1999), 172 D.L.R. (4th) 708.

go through with the contract, they may enter into a binding contract. If the remaining independent directors are not enough to form a quorum, the contract should be ratified at a general meeting of the shareholders. Failure by a director to disclose an interest gives that director's corporation the right to rescind the contract upon learning of the interest.

One type of contract in which a director clearly has a personal interest is the contract providing for their own remuneration, so it is perhaps surprising that the CBCA simply provides that the directors may fix the remuneration of the directors, officers, and employees of the corporation (section 125). There is an obvious risk that the directors will be excessively generous to each other or to their CEO.[31] Securities regulations require distributing corporations to disclose executive compensation and to develop independent methods of establishing executive compensation, and the creation of compensation committees is recommended.

Interception of Corporate Opportunity

A different situation arises when it is a director's duty to acquire a particular item of property for the corporation or to give the corporation the chance of first refusal, and instead she acquires the property for herself. In that case, she has *intercepted* an opportunity belonging to the corporation and has committed a breach of duty. If a director has received a mandate to act as agent for the corporation to purchase a specific piece of property or a particular type of property, she is under the same duty as that placed upon any agent to acquire property for her principal. If she buys the property for herself, she has breached her duty. The property is deemed to be held in trust for the corporation, as is any profit made.

Corporate Information

A rather different situation arises when a director receives information about a profitable venture or an opportunity to buy property at an advantageous price. She may be under no duty to acquire the property for the corporation, but if the information is received in her capacity as a director of the corporation, then it is her duty to give the corporation first chance of acquiring an interest in the venture or property. If the corporation decides not to acquire the property, the director is probably free to do so. But she makes a dangerous decision if she assumes that the corporation would not want the property anyway, and then acquires it in her own name without consulting the corporation. In practice, it is sometimes difficult for a court to decide whether in the circumstances the information came to the director personally or in her role as a director of the corporation. But once the court decides that the opportunity belonged to the corporation, the result is quite clear: purchasing on her own behalf is a breach of duty.

CASE 28.3   *R* was a director of a large corporation that was in the process of expanding its chain of retail grocery stores. A major part of his duties was to travel around the country looking for suitable independent stores for the corporation to purchase. *R* entered into an arrangement with a friend to buy those stores that seemed especially good bargains and to resell them to the corporation, concealing the fact of his ownership. When this was later discovered, the corporation brought proceedings against him.

The court held that *R* was under a duty to acquire the stores for the corporation, and therefore was held to have done so as its agent.[32]

---

31. See *UPM-Kymmene Corp.* v. *UPM-Kymmene Miramichi Inc.* (2002), 214 D.L.R. (4th) 496, where the board approved a "compensation agreement" for the chairman that included a "signing bonus" of 25 million shares. The court held that there had been inadequate disclosure and set aside the agreement.

32. *Canada Safeway Ltd.* v. *Thompson*, [1951] 3 D.L.R. 295. Note that in reselling the stores to the corporation, the director was also in breach of his duty to disclose his interest. The corporation could have chosen instead to rescind the contracts. See also *Slate Ventures Inc.* v. *Hurley* (1998), 37 B.L.R. (2d) 138.

CASE 28.4

C was a director of a corporation involved in exploration and natural resource development. C was approached by a prospector, who asked if the corporation would be interested in acquiring certain claims. He reported this at a meeting of the board of directors. A majority of the board considered that the corporation was already over-committed financially and decided against taking up the offer.

When the prospector approached C again, C decided to take up the claims for himself. He later left the corporation, after a disagreement. The corporation learned of his acquisition of the claims and brought proceedings against him.

The court held that, once the corporation had rejected the opportunity, it no longer belonged to the corporation and C was free to take advantage of it.[33]

Competing with the Corporation

Another aspect of the conflict of interest principle is the rule that a director may not carry on a business competing with that of her corporation, except with the permission of the corporation.

The corporation is entitled to claim all the profit made by the director and to obtain an injunction prohibiting the director from any future competition.

CASE 28.5

O'Malley was a director of Canaero, a corporation specializing in aerial surveying. He had been engaged on a project for the corporation in Guyana, during which he learned a lot about the terrain and made some useful contacts. He subsequently resigned from Canaero,

formed his own corporation, and successfully tendered for a surveying contract with the government of Guyana.

O'Malley was held to be in breach of his duty to Canaero and accountable to them for his profit on the contract.[34]

Related Party Transactions

As noted in the previous chapter, large businesses often operate through a group of related corporations. Those corporations deal with each other on a regular basis. Frequently, they share some of the same directors. The potential for conflicts of interest is obvious. Almost inevitably, some inter-group contracts or arrangements will be more beneficial to one party than to the other. The situation becomes especially perilous where the two or more corporations concerned do not have the same shareholders or creditors.

The likelihood of impropriety (or at least of perceptions of impropriety) is further increased where the corporate group is effectively controlled by a single individual or family—a situation that is quite common in Canada.

CASE 28.6

Hollinger Inc., a corporation in which 12 percent of its voting shares were held by the public and the remainder were owned by Lord Black and his associates, made a loan of $1.1 million to Ravelston Corp., all of whose shares were owned or controlled by Lord Black. Minority

shareholders in Hollinger alleged that the loan had not been properly approved.[35] In related proceedings it was alleged that improper payments totalling $32 million were made from one Hollinger corporation to another corporation and its directors. The court appointed an inspector to investigate.[36]

33. *Peso Silver Mines Ltd.* v. *Cropper* (1966), 56 D.L.R. (2d) 117 (S.C.C.). In contrast, where a majority of the directors (and shareholders) of a corporation purported to pass a resolution rejecting a contractual opportunity offered to the corporation and then took it for themselves, that was held to be a breach of their duties. The resolution was not adopted in good faith: *Cook* v. *Deeks*, [1916] A.C. 554.

34. *Canadian Aero Service Ltd.* v. *O'Malley* (1973), 40 D.L.R. (3d) 371 (S.C.C.).

35. *Catalyst Fund General Partner I Inc.* v. *Hollinger Inc.* [2004] O.J. No. 4722 aff'd. [2006] O.J. No. 944 (On. C.A.).

36. *Ibid.*, O.J. No. 3886. In criminal proceedings initiated by the American Securities and Exchange Commission, Lord Black was convicted of fraud and obstruction of justice arising from redirection of sale proceeds from Hollinger corporations to directors through artificial non-competition agreements.

Insider Trading

Insider trading is one type of conduct for which English and Canadian courts were reluctant to impose liability, so the legislatures intervened to create a duty. Insider trading attracts all three types of liability: civil liability, regulatory liability, and criminal liability.

Insider trading occurs when a director or officer of a corporation, or some other person (for example, a shareholder or employee of the corporation), buys or sells the corporation's shares or other securities, making use of confidential inside information in order to make a profit or avoid a loss.

insider trading
the use of confidential information relating to a corporation in dealing in its securities

---

ILLUSTRATION 28.2

(a) The directors of a small family company are approached by a large public corporation that offers to buy all the shares of the family company at a price considerably above that at which the shares had previously been valued. The next day, one of the directors is approached by her uncle, who is a shareholder and who offers to sell some of his shares to her. Without disclosing the proposed takeover, she buys the shares at a price well below that of the offer.

(b) The directors of a mining corporation receive a confidential report from their surveyor that very valuable mineral deposits have just been discovered. One of the directors immediately instructs her broker to buy as many of the corporation's shares as possible on the stock exchange, before the good news is released and forces up the price.

(c) The directors of a corporation learn that their major customer has just declared bankruptcy, owing the corporation a large sum of money. Default on the account by their customer is likely to result in the corporation showing a substantial loss in the forthcoming half-yearly accounts. One of the directors promptly sells her shares just before the news becomes public and the shares drop in value.

In each of the hypothetical cases in Illustration 28.2, a director has made use of information that came to her in her capacity as a director for her own benefit.

Originally, at common law, courts did not see this conduct as harmful to the corporation and so it did not consider it a breach of the fiduciary duty owed to the corporation. The legislatures stepped in to fill the void. Securities legislation imposes strict disclosure requirements whenever a director or other insider trades in the securities of her own corporation, and has made insider trading a criminal offence, punishable by fines or imprisonment or both. Under the Ontario Securities Act, for example, fines of up to $5 million and prison terms of up to 5 years may be imposed.[37] A recent amendment to the Criminal Code has increased the potential penalty to 10 years' imprisonment.[38] Despite the heavy penalties, however, the number of prosecutions for insider trading seems to be increasing, both in Canada and in the United States.

The above provisions apply principally to corporations whose securities are publicly traded as a way of promoting public confidence in the markets. However, section 131 of the CBCA provides that, even in the case of a private corporation, an insider who purchases or sells a security of the corporation with knowledge of specific, confidential, price-sensitive information is liable

(a) to compensate the seller or purchaser (as the case may be) for any loss suffered as a result of the transaction, and

(b) to account to the corporation for any benefit or advantage obtained.

For the purposes of the legislation, "insider" includes a director or officer, an employee, any shareholder who holds more than a prescribed percentage of the corporation's securities, and a "tippee"—that is, a person who knowingly receives confidential information from an insider.

---

37. Securities Act, R.S.O. 1990, c. S. 5, s. 122. An offender may also be required to pay back three times the amount of any profit made. In *R. v. Harper* (2003), 232 D.L.R. (4th) 738, a fine of almost $4 million was imposed, though it was reduced to $2 million on appeal.

38. Criminal Code, R.S.C. 1985, c. C-46, s. 382.1, as amended by S.C. 2004, c. 3. In Canada, few inside traders are given jail time. Most receive fines and are banned from the securities industry and public boards.

CHECKLIST Directors' Liability

A director faces the following types of personal liability for breach of her duties:

Type of Personal Liability	Available Remedy
(a) Civil liability	
(i) to the corporation	
• breach of fiduciary duty, s. 122(1)(a)	• damages for losses arising from breach
• specific conduct involving conflicts of interest, s. 120	• accounting of amounts paid for improper dividends or share redemption
• breach of duty of skill, diligence, and care, s. 122(1)(b)	• rescission of contract involving conflict of interest
	• constructive trust of property
	• accounting of profits
	• injunction to restrain breach of duty
(ii) to others	
• breach of duty of skill, diligence, and care, s. 122(1)(b)	• damages for losses arising from the liability
• liability for unpaid wages	
• liability for unpaid taxes	
• liability for insider trading	
(b) Regulatory and criminal liability	
• insider trading	• fines and imprisonment (Criminal Code)
• other statutory offences discussed in Chapter 29	• fines and imprisonment (Securities Act)

SHAREHOLDERS

The Role of Shareholders

Publicly Traded Corporations

In large, publicly traded corporations, shareholdings may be widely distributed with no single shareholder or group holding more than 5 percent of the voting stock. Less frequently, one entity may control a majority of shares. Both situations make changing management difficult. Management may respond to calls for change with a piece of practical advice to investors: "If you don't like the management, sell!" In other words, "Do not get into costly corporate struggles. Cut your losses by getting out and reinvesting in a corporation more to your liking." All that may be changing with the recent attempts to strengthen corporate governance and the role of independent directors. However, the new rules do not directly expand the shareholders' power or influence over the affairs of the corporation.

Private Corporations

In private corporations, shareholders' problems are radically different. The usual problem is a serious disagreement among the principal shareholders, who are frequently also directors and senior employees of the corporation. In the absence of careful contractual arrangements providing safeguards, a minority shareholder may find himself "locked in" and "frozen out" at the same time.

The minority shareholder is "locked in" in the sense that he probably cannot sell his shares except at a fraction of what he believes they should be worth. There are two reasons for this. First, in most private corporations the transfer of shares is restricted, usually requiring the consent of the board of directors. They may be unwilling to agree to the transfer of his shares except to someone of their own choosing. Second, even if the minority shareholder is free to sell the shares, he will have great difficulty in finding a buyer who would consider acquiring a minority position in a private corporation.

The minority shareholder may be "frozen out" in the following manner. First, the majority directors may fire him from his job with the corporation, or, at the very least, refuse to renew his employment contract when it expires. Second, they may remove him from the board of directors or elect someone else in his place at the next election. Third, they may increase salaries to themselves, so that the corporation itself earns no apparent profit. Even if a profit is shown, it may be retained by the corporation, since dividends are payable only at the discretion of the board of directors. Therefore, a minority shareholder may find himself deprived of his salary-earning position, his directorship, and his prospect of any dividends on his investment. Worse, he is often left without a marketable security.

In these circumstances the majority shareholders may not have broken any law, and no remedy existed at common law. However, a number of statutory provisions empower the courts to give relief to minority shareholders. We will discuss these, as well as strategies to avoid the problem, under "The Protection of Minority Shareholders" later in this chapter.

Rights Attached to Shares

Shareholder rights come from two principal sources—the rights attached to their shares by the articles of the corporation and the rights conferred on them by the relevant corporate legislation.

As we saw in Chapter 27, the corporate constitution sets out the rights attached to each class of shares. For example, the CBCA requires that the articles state the classes of shares that may be issued and, if there are to be two or more classes of shares, the rights, privileges, restrictions, and conditions attaching to each class (section 6(1)(c) and section 24(4)). If there is only one class of shares, the rights of the shareholders include the rights

- to vote at any meeting of shareholders
- to receive any dividend that is declared
- to receive the remaining property of the corporation (after payment of its debts) on dissolution (section 24(3))

Additional rights may be attached to shares, and, if there are different classes of shares, rights may be granted to some shares and not others; but the three basic rights must exist and be exercisable by one or other class of shares.

Meetings and Voting

Notice and Attendance at Meetings

If shareholders wish to voice their objections about the management, they need a forum to do so. The forum provided under all statutes is the **general meeting of shareholders**. The corporation may hold other meetings of shareholders in the course of the year, but it is required by statute to hold at least one **annual general meeting**.[39] Shareholders are entitled to advance notice of all general meetings and are entitled to receive copies of the financial statements before the annual general meeting. They may attend the meetings, question the directors, and make criticisms of the management of the corporation.[40]

general meeting of shareholders
a formal meeting of shareholders at which they are able to vote on matters concerning the corporation

annual general meeting
the general meeting of shareholders that is required by law to be held each year to transact certain specified business

---

39. CBCA, s. 133. The Act requires that an annual meeting be held not more than 15 months after the previous annual meeting and no more than 6 months after the end of the corporation's financial year; thus it is possible for a calendar year to pass without a meeting.

40. The CBCA (ss. 132(4),(5)) now makes provision for shareholder meetings to be held by electronic means. A corporation's by-laws may provide for voting by means of telephonic or electronic communications facilities.

The Right to Requisition Meetings

What if shareholders want to call a meeting and the board of directors refuses to do so? All the provinces provide in their statutes that the shareholders themselves may call a meeting. However, these provisions require a relatively large proportion of the shareholders to petition for the meeting, a requirement that is virtually impossible to meet in large corporations where even a large number of shareholders may hold only a small percentage of the total shares.[41] The right to requisition a **special meeting** is therefore of limited use in large corporations, but is especially valuable in the smaller, private companies.

special meeting
any general meeting of shareholders other than the annual general meeting

The Right to Vote

The right to attend meetings and to criticize must ultimately be backed by some form of power in the hands of the shareholders. This power is found in the right to vote. The collective power of the shareholders is exercised through the passing (or defeating) of resolutions—an **ordinary resolution**, which is adopted by a simple majority of votes cast, and a **special resolution**, which requires a two-thirds majority.[42] The CBCA sets out a number of matters that must be approved by either an ordinary or a special resolution, the most important being

ordinary resolution
a resolution adopted by the general meeting and passed by a simple majority

special resolution
a resolution of the general meeting required to be passed by a special (usually two-thirds) majority

(a) the approval of alterations to the articles of incorporation—special resolution (section 173)
(b) the approval of certain other fundamental changes, such as amalgamation with another corporation (section 183) or the sale of all, or substantially all, of the corporation's property—special resolution (section 189)
(c) the approval of any amendments made by the directors to the by-laws—ordinary resolution (section 103)
(d) the election of the auditor—ordinary resolution (section 162)
(e) the election or removal of directors—ordinary resolution (sections 106, 109)

Excepting the items described in (a) and (b), the most important matter voted upon by the shareholders is the election of directors, since, as we have seen, it is the directors who control the management of the corporation's affairs.

Class Voting Rights

Not all shareholders necessarily have the right to vote. A corporation's shares may be divided into different classes, with different voting rights. Common shares almost invariably carry the right to vote; preferred shares often carry a right to vote only in specified circumstances, such as when preferred dividends are in arrears. The founders of a corporation may create several classes of shares and weigh the voting heavily in favour of a small group of shares held by themselves. For example, they could give Class "A" shares 100 votes per share and Class "B," issued to a broader group of shareholders, only one vote per share. It would be virtually impossible for a publicly traded corporation to have such a share structure today. Securities commissions, stock exchanges, and underwriters would probably refuse such an issue, and without their concurrence a public offering is impossible. Virtually all common stock offered on the public market today carries one vote per share. By contrast, in private corporations there is no restriction upon the different rights that may be attached to various classes of shares, provided at least one class has voting rights. Within a particular class, however, all shares must enjoy the same rights (section 24).

---

41. CBCA, s. 143, requires a requisition to be made by 5 percent of shareholders, and this is the requirement in most provinces. Prince Edward Island specifies the impossibly high figure of 25 percent.
42. S. 2. In Nova Scotia, a special resolution requires a three-quarters majority.

Class rights, which may relate not only to voting but also to other matters such as rights to priority in payment of dividends or to receive the surplus on liquidation of the corporation, must be set out in the articles of incorporation. Consequently, they may only be varied by special resolution of the shareholders. In addition, to alter the rights of a particular class requires approval by the votes of two-thirds of that class and of any other class that may be adversely affected (section 176).

class rights
special rights attached to a particular class of shares

Proxies

In most publicly traded corporations, only a small proportion of shareholders actually attend general meetings. All corporation statutes permit a shareholder to nominate a **proxy** to attend a general meeting and to cast that shareholder's votes at the meeting as instructed. This is done by signing a form, naming the proxy, and sending it to the corporation before the meeting. Most jurisdictions now go further and require all corporations, except the smallest private ones, to send a **proxy form**, the contents of which are prescribed in detail, to all shareholders at the same time as notice of a meeting is given.

proxy
a person appointed to attend a general meeting of shareholders and to cast the votes of the shareholder appointing him or her

proxy form
a form required to be circulated to shareholders before a general meeting, inviting them to appoint a proxy if they so wish

In the event of a proxy fight between two groups of shareholders—usually the board of directors and a dissenting group—each group solicits all the shareholders by mail in order to persuade them to give their proxy forms to the group making the solicitation. The dissenting group may go to the corporation's head office to obtain lists of all the shareholders from the share register in order to make their solicitations. Here the board of directors has a great advantage. As a matter of practice, they include proxy forms, offering one of themselves as the proposed proxy, with the mailed notice of the annual general meeting.[43]

Financial Rights

Shareholders expect to receive a return on their investment in one or both of two forms—earnings distributed regularly in the form of dividends and growth that can be realized by selling the shares or on dissolution of the corporation. Holders of common shares may be satisfied with smaller dividends if there is capital appreciation in the corporation's assets or if a significant part of the profits is retained within the business and has the effect of increasing the value of the shares. Preferred shares, as we saw in Chapter 27, often do not participate in growth, and their holders are primarily concerned with receiving dividends.

Dividends

A fundamental right attached to shares is the right to receive any **dividend** that is declared by the corporation. The declaration of dividends is entirely within the discretion of the board of directors. Shareholders normally have no right to be paid a dividend, even when the corporation makes large profits.

dividend
a distribution to shareholders of a share of the profits of the corporation

There can be no discrimination, however, in the payment of dividends among shareholders of the same class. Each shareholder is entitled to such dividends as are declared in proportion to the number of shares of that class held. In addition, directors are bound to pay dividends in the order of preference assigned to the classes of shareholders. They may not pay the common shareholders a dividend without first paying the whole of any preferred dividends owing to preference shareholders.

Distribution of Surplus

On the dissolution of a corporation, provided it has assets remaining after paying off all its creditors, shareholders are entitled to a proportionate share of the remaining net assets. The distribution of these net assets among the various classes of shareholders must also be made in accordance with the respective priorities of each class.

---

43. This advantage is only partly offset by disclosure requirements and by compelling management to provide shareholders with a means to nominate a different proxy.

Pre-emptive Rights

One of the more important powers given to the board of directors is the power to issue shares. The issue of new shares involves two possible risks for existing shareholders. First, the issue of shares to some other person will necessarily reduce the proportion of the total number of shares that a shareholder holds. Second, there is the risk of "stock watering"; if new shares are issued for a price that is less than the value of the existing shares, the value of the existing shares will be diluted.

ILLUSTRATION 28.3

A owns 34 of the total of 100 shares issued by *XYZ* Inc. The assets of *XYZ* Inc. are worth approximately $1 million. The directors wish to raise additional capital and resolve to issue 20 new shares to *T*, at a price of $5000 per share. As a result, *A* will now own only 28.3 percent of the total shares and can no longer block the adoption of a special resolution. A's shares, previously worth $10 000 each, will be worth only $9167.

---

pre-emptive right
a right to have the first opportunity to purchase a proportionate part of any new shares to be issued

American courts have held that a shareholder has a **pre-emptive right** to retain his proportionate holdings in a corporation, but this right is subject to various qualifications. When a corporation proposes to issue more shares, it must normally offer each shareholder a proportion of the new issue equal to the proportion he holds of the existing shares. A shareholder who has 3 percent of the issued shares of a corporation is entitled to purchase 3 percent of any further issue. A right of pre-emption preserves the balance of power in the corporation. It also ensures that, if the new shares are issued at a price that is less than the value of the existing shares, the existing shareholders are not prejudiced, at any rate, if they exercise their right of pre-emption. Any reduction in the value of their existing shares will be exactly balanced by the gain they receive in buying the new shares at an undervalue.

Canadian courts have never recognized a general principle of pre-emption. In limited circumstances, however, they have recognized rights somewhat similar to pre-emptive rights. Directors have the right to issue authorized share capital of the corporation at their discretion, but they must issue shares only for the purpose of raising capital or for purposes that are in the best interest of the corporation. If they have a bona fide intention of raising capital, they may distribute the shares to whomever they wish upon payment of a fair price. But if directors issue shares not for the benefit of the corporation but to affect voting control, the issue may be declared void. For example, if directors were to issue shares to themselves for the purpose of out-voting shareholders who, up to that point, had a majority of the issued shares, the extra share issue could be set aside by the court.

CASE 28.7

Bonisteel was a director of Collis Leather Co. and the owner of 458 of a total of 1208 issued shares. He entered into an agreement with another shareholder to buy that shareholder's 150 shares. The purchase would have given him control of the corporation. Collis, the general manager and the person most responsible for the corporation's success, threatened to leave if Bonisteel took control. In order to forestall Bonisteel, the directors resolved to issue 292 new shares, and each director was asked how many shares he wished to subscribe for. Most of the new shares were taken up by directors other than Bonisteel, with the result that he would be left with less than 50 percent of the total shares. Bonisteel brought an action to restrain the directors from making the allotment.

The court held that such an allotment would be invalid. The corporation was not in need of additional funds, and it was improper to issue new shares for the purpose of altering the balance of control.[44]

---

44. *Bonisteel v. Collis Leather Co. Ltd.* (1919), 45 O.R. 195.

CASE 28.8

Afton was a "junior" mining company, incorporated in British Columbia. As was common in the industry, it was looking for a "major" company to help finance a large drilling program. Teck, a large resource corporation, became interested in Afton and made an offer to buy a controlling block of its shares. The directors of Afton, led by its chief engineer, Millar, rejected the offer and preferred to enter into an arrangement with Canex, the subsidiary of another Canadian corporation, even though Canex was not prepared to match the Teck offer. Following the rejection, Teck started buying Afton shares on the stock exchange, and soon announced that it had acquired more than 50 percent of the issued shares. The Afton directors then entered into a long-term contract with Canex, which involved issuing a large block of new shares to Canex. This arrangement reduced the Teck holding to less than 50 percent.

The share issue was challenged by Teck but upheld by the court. The Afton directors had entered into the arrangement with Canex and had issued the new shares, because they genuinely believed that the interests of Afton would be better served as a "partner" of Canex than as a subsidiary of Teck.[45]

While not required to do so, most corporations give shareholders a pre-emptive right. When it proposes to issue further shares, it may first issue subscription rights or share rights to all existing shareholders, giving each shareholder one right for each share held. The shareholder then has an option to purchase a new share at a specified price for a specified number of subscription rights. For example, a shareholder owning 50 shares may receive 50 rights entitling him to buy 10 shares (one share for every five rights) at a specified price per share. Subscription rights are normally made transferable, and if the market value of the existing shares significantly exceeds the specified price for the new shares, the rights themselves will have a market value; they may be sold to anyone who wishes to purchase them and exercise the option.

The Right to Information

Disclosure is one of the fundamental principles of modern corporate governance. Disclosure of relevant information enables investors to evaluate the effectiveness of management, and publicity may be an effective deterrent to high-handed behaviour or misconduct in management.

The Financial Statements

Annual **financial statements** must be presented to the shareholders prior to the annual general meeting. All corporation acts require that basic information be part of the financial statements, though the detailed requirements vary. Generally, the basic items required are:

financial statements
annual accounts that are required to be presented to the shareholders at the annual general meeting

- the income statement, showing the results of operations for the financial year
- the balance sheet, showing the corporation's assets as of the financial year-end (including details of changes in share capital during the year)
- a statement of changes in financial position, analyzing changes in working capital
- a statement of retained earnings showing changes during the year, including the declaration of dividends
- a statement of contributed surplus

The annual financial statements should be in comparative form, showing corresponding data for the preceding financial year. In addition, some statutes require that shareholders be sent comparative interim quarterly financial statements. New securities regulations require CEOs and CFOs of distributing companies to certify that the statements fairly reflect the financial condition of the corporation.[46]

---

45. *Teck Corp.* v. *Millar* (1973), 33 D.L.R. (3d) 288.

46. Multilateral Instrument 52-109; full compliance for year ending December 31, 2005.

Documents of Record

documents of record
documents that a corporation is required to keep and make available to shareholders

A corporation must maintain certain documents of record at its head office, which may be inspected by any shareholder during usual business hours. These **documents of record** include:

- minutes of shareholders' meetings
- a register of all transfers of shares, including the date and other particulars of each transfer
- a copy of the corporation's charter, a copy of all by-laws (or articles) and special resolutions, and a register of shareholders
- a register of the directors

These documents may often be useful to a minority group of shareholders attempting to collect evidence to support a claim of misconduct or ineffectiveness on the part of the directors. Access to the share register permits a dissentient group to obtain the names and addresses of all other shareholders so that they may communicate with them, explain their complaints, and attempt to enlist their support.

Another document of record is the collection of minutes from directors' meetings. Unlike the other documents of record, however, directors alone, not the shareholders, have a right of access to it.[47]

The Auditor

To assist in the analysis and evaluation of the financial statements, and to ensure their accuracy so far as possible, the acts provide for the appointment of an independent auditor by the shareholders. Private companies may dispense with this requirement, but only if the shareholders unanimously agree to do so. The auditor must be an independent person who is not employed by the corporation.[48] In order to confirm the accuracy of the financial statements, the auditor examines all the records and books of accounts of the corporation. The auditor provides an opinion on whether the statements fairly present the financial position of the corporation in accordance with generally accepted accounting principles.[49] Both the auditor's report and the financial statements must be sent to all shareholders before the corporation's annual general meeting; the period usually specified is at least 21 days before the meeting. These items are included in the corporation's **annual report** to shareholders.

annual report
the report on the business and affairs of the corporation, which the directors are required to present at the annual general meeting

Only the auditor and the directors have the right to examine the books of account; shareholders as such do not have access to them. If a shareholder suspects that something is wrong, he may communicate his information to the auditor, but the auditor has no duty to undertake a special examination at the request of a shareholder; the auditor's duty is owed to the corporation itself rather than the shareholders.[50] As a last resort, a shareholder may apply to a court for the appointment of an inspector.

In a distributing corporation, the audit must be completed by an auditor registered with the Canadian Public Accountability Board. The audit committee, made up of independent directors, supervises the auditor and must create a process to receive anonymous complaints and reports of irregularities in the financial affairs of the corporation, often referred to as whistleblower protection.[51]

---

47. Ss. 20, 21. An exception is made in the case of minutes that record the disclosure of a director's interest in a contract with the corporation: s. 120 (6.1), introduced in 2001.

48. Although the shareholders appoint the auditor, they do so as an organ of the corporation (the general meeting), and the auditor's contract is with the corporation, not with the shareholders: see *Roman Corp.* v. *Peat Marwick Thorne* (1992), 8 B.L.R. (2d) 43. The auditor's duty is owed to the corporation, not to the shareholders who appointed her: see *Hercules Managements Ltd.* v. *Ernst & Young* (1997), 146 D.L.R. (4th) 577 (S.C.C.).

49. See section 5400, *CICA Handbook* (Canadian Institute of Chartered Accountants), for a complete statement of the form and content of the auditor's report.

50. *Hercules, supra*, n. 48.

51. National Instruments 52-108 and 52-110.

Appointment of Inspector

Case 28.6 provides an example of the typical situation where an inspector is appointed. All the jurisdictions, with the exception of Prince Edward Island, have statutory provisions enabling shareholders to apply to the courts to appoint an **inspector** to investigate the affairs of the corporation and to audit its books. The statutes give inspectors sweeping powers of inquiry, and the remedy can be a very effective one. In some jurisdictions there are a number of obstacles that undermine this effectiveness; in particular, a substantial proportion of shareholders may be required to join in the application, and the applicant may be required to give security to cover the costs of an investigation, which may be very high. However, the CBCA and most of the provincial acts based on it now permit a single shareholder to apply, and they expressly state that the applicant is not required to give security for costs (section 229). A concerned shareholder may choose either of two options: he may request the Director—a government official appointed to supervise the affairs of corporations—to apply to the court to order an investigation, or he may apply directly to the court himself. In either event, it is necessary to make out a *prima facie* case—that is, produce sufficient evidence of the probability of serious mismanagement to warrant further investigation.

inspector
a person appointed by the court to investigate the affairs of a corporation

Duties of Shareholders

We have seen that directors of corporations are under strict duties of good faith. They must use their own best judgment as to what is in the best interests of the corporation and are not bound to follow the instructions of the shareholders. However, when there is a controlling shareholder (or group of shareholders)—with the power to call a general meeting, dismiss directors, and appoint new ones in their place—it is usually the controlling shareholder who determines corporate policy, and the directors often merely act as a "rubber stamp." That being the case, one must ask whether shareholders—and especially controlling shareholders—owe any duty to their corporation.

Unlike some U.S. courts, Canadian courts have consistently held that a majority shareholder owes no positive duty to act for either the welfare of the corporation itself or the welfare of his fellow shareholders.[52] His obligation ends when he has paid the full purchase price for his shares. He has no obligation to attend meetings or to return proxy forms, and he is free to exercise his vote in whatever way he pleases and for whatever purposes he desires. His share is an item of property that he is free to use as he pleases, even if that is against the interests of the corporation or of his fellow shareholders. This freedom may be complicated if the shareholder is himself a director of the corporation. A director owes a duty to act honestly and in good faith with a view to the best interests of the corporation (section 122), but when he votes as a shareholder he is entitled to consider his own personal interests.[53]

THE PROTECTION OF MINORITY SHAREHOLDERS

Majority Rule

At the very least, a shareholder's freedom to use his vote as he chooses means that the courts will not substitute their judgment for his when his actions are based upon business considerations. As a consequence, a controlling group of shareholders, through its ability to determine the composition of the board of directors, to approve their actions or decline to do anything about their misdeeds, and even (if they have a two-thirds majority) to amend the corporation's constitution, could ensure that

---

52. See *Brant Investments Ltd.* v. *Keeprite Inc.* (1991), 3 O.R. (3d) 289.
53. *North-West Transportation* v. *Beatty* (1887), 12 App. Cas. 589.

the affairs of the corporation were managed entirely for their own benefit and to the detriment of the minority. As we saw when we considered the dilemma of the "frozen-out" shareholder, these things can happen without any law being broken.

ILLUSTRATION 28.4

A, B, C, and D are the equal shareholders and directors of a corporation, Traviata Trattoria Ltd. The articles of incorporation restrict the business of the corporation to the operation of one or more restaurants. Contrary to D's wishes, A, B, and C decide to sell the restaurant to a property developer and to invest the proceeds in a casino business. They use their votes to pass two special resolutions: (1) approving the sale of the restaurant (substantially the only asset of the corporation) and (2) amending the articles to remove the restriction on the business that may be carried on by the corporation.

In this example, no wrong has been done to the corporation, and the majority has acted within its rights. Nevertheless, D may justifiably feel aggrieved since the whole basis upon which he became a shareholder in the corporation has been changed.

ILLUSTRATION 28.5

Sixty percent of the shares of Figaro Ltd. are held by Almaviva Inc., a large public corporation, and 40 percent by its original founder, Susanna. Following a disagreement over company policy, Almaviva used its majority voting power to appoint three of its own directors to be directors of Figaro. The new directors subsequently sell an important piece of Figaro's property to Bartolo Ltd., a corporation wholly owned by Almaviva. The sale is at a gross undervalue.

Here, the directors of Figaro have probably been in breach either of their duty of care and skill or their duty to act in good faith and in the interests of their corporation. The corporation, Figaro, has been injured, since the value of its assets has been reduced, but the loss falls entirely on its minority shareholder, Susanna, since the majority shareholder, Almaviva, gains more as shareholder of the purchaser, Bartolo (100 percent of the undervalue), than it loses as shareholder of the vendor, Figaro (60 percent of the undervalue). Consequently, Almaviva, as controlling shareholder of Figaro, will not complain about any breach of duty by its directors.

ILLUSTRATION 28.6

The shares in Jenufa Ltd. are held in equal proportions by A, her husband B, and his two sons by a previous marriage, C and D, all of whom had until recently been directors. After an acrimonious divorce, B, C, and D use their majority voting power to remove A from the board. Subsequently, instead of distributing the profits as dividends, they decide to reinvest them in a fund to provide for the long-term capital needs of the corporation. They also refuse to consent to A transferring her shares to any third party.

In this example, A is locked in and frozen out. But the corporation has not been injured, and, unless it can be shown that B, C, and D acted in bad faith, there may have been nothing improper in their actions.

Under traditional principles of corporation law, the aggrieved minority shareholders in the above illustrations received little or no help from the courts. However, special statutory remedies have greatly improved the situation of the minority. In examining the more important of these, we shall concentrate upon the remedies provided in the CBCA, bearing in mind that almost all the provinces have adopted essentially similar rules.

The Appraisal Remedy

In some situations, where the majority shareholders make fundamental changes to the corporation, section 190 offers a procedure whereby a dissenting shareholder need not go along with the change. He may elect instead to have his shares bought out by the corporation. If a price cannot be agreed, the court will fix a fair price. However, this **appraisal remedy** is limited to specific actions by the majority, the most important of which are:

appraisal remedy
the right to have one's shares bought by the corporation at a fair price

- changing any restriction on the issue, transfer, or ownership of shares
- changing any restriction on the business that the corporation may carry on
- amalgamating or merging with another corporation
- selling, leasing, or exchanging substantially all the assets of the corporation
- "going private" or "squeezing out" transactions

The remedy is of most use in private corporations, where no ready public market exists for minority shareholdings, since a dissenter in a public corporation would normally just sell his shares on the stock exchange. However, the procedure is a complicated one, and the dissenter must comply with every step prescribed by the Act in order to take advantage of it. If, instead, the shareholder can show that his interests have been "unfairly disregarded," he is more likely to resort to the "oppression remedy" discussed below.

The Derivative Action

When a corporation has suffered an injury, as in Illustration 28.5 or, for example, where directors have made a secret profit for themselves by exploiting a "corporate opportunity," the corporation may sue the wrongdoer to recover its losses.

Ordinarily, an action on behalf of the corporation must be started by its directors—it is part of the management function. However, if the directors are the wrongdoers, they are hardly likely to commence an action against themselves. The common law recognized the right of a minority shareholder to start an action on behalf of the corporation, frequently called a **derivative action**— but it was procedurally difficult.

derivative action
proceedings brought by one or more shareholders in the name of the corporation in respect of a wrong done to the corporation

The modern statutory derivative action (section 239) overcomes most of the procedural barriers. It permits a shareholder to obtain leave from the court to bring an action in the name and on behalf of the corporation. To do so he need only establish that the directors refuse to bring the action themselves, that he is acting in good faith, and that it appears to be in the interests of the corporation or its shareholders that the action be commenced. If he establishes these things, then the court may make an order to commence the action. The acts prohibit the court from requiring the shareholder to give security for costs. At any time, a court may order the corporation to pay to the complainant costs, including legal fees and disbursements (sections 242(4) and 240(d)). The court may also direct "that any amount adjudged payable by a defendant in the action shall be paid, in whole or in part, directly to former and present shareholders of the corporation . . . instead of to the corporation . . ." (section 240(c)). In Illustration 28.5 above, Susanna could receive direct compensation for her loss, rather than being compensated only indirectly through an increase in the assets of the corporation.

Although the statutory derivative action has substantially improved the position of minority shareholders, the remedy has been somewhat overshadowed by the oppression remedy, discussed below.

Winding Up

Minority partners have better protection than most minority shareholders. They are entitled to an accounting of profits and to receive their share of them regularly. In the event of a total breakdown in relations, they can normally insist on a dissolution and sale of the assets and receipt of a proportionate part of the proceeds. Since the other partners cannot continue to use the partnership assets for their sole benefit, they must either face dissolution or come to a reasonable settlement. Not so in a private corporation. In the absence of a separate agreement among the shareholders, a minority shareholder has none of the rights of a partner.

winding up
the dissolution (or liquidation) of a corporation

Corporation statutes have, however, followed partnership law in one important respect. They give the courts discretion to make an order **winding up** a corporation where it is "just and equitable" to do so.[54] But because of the drastic nature of the remedy, the courts have been reluctant to use it if the corporation is flourishing or is fairly large. Typically, the remedy is available where the corporation is a small family business or an "incorporated partnership," where there is deadlock, where relations between the participants have broken down, or where a "partner" has been frozen out. In these cases, the remedy has proven quite effective, since the mere threat of its use has often been sufficient to persuade the majority to reach a compromise.

CASE 28.9

G Corp. was a joint venture corporation with two shareholders—*J*, who owned 52 percent of the shares, and *P*, who owned the remaining 48 percent. The relationship between *J* and *P* broke down, largely as a result of different expectations that they had with respect to the objectives and operation of the venture. *P* applied for an order directing the winding-up of the corporation and its sale as a going concern. *J* responded by offering to purchase *P*'s shares, but *P* rejected the offer, and instead made a counter-offer. No agreement was reached.

The court found that the circumstances justified winding up the corporation, since the parties had lost confidence in each other, but since each party would prefer to continue the business alone, it ordered a "buy/sell shotgun" solution.[55]

Oppression Remedy

oppression remedy
a statutory procedure allowing individual shareholders to seek a personal remedy if they have been unfairly treated

Beginning in the 1970s, an alternative remedy—usually called the **oppression remedy**—was introduced and widely adopted in Canada. It is by far the broadest and most flexible remedy available to shareholders. In fact, it is available to more than just shareholders; section 238 of the CBCA describes a "complainant" as any person the court approves. Courts will approve persons with a legitimate interest. It is not necessary to establish wrongdoing; complainants need only show that they been treated *unfairly or oppressively*. Courts are empowered to make *any* order they consider just and appropriate to remedy the situation.

The oppression remedy is typically sought where a minority shareholder is frozen out, as in Illustration 28.6,[56] but it has also been applied in cases of deadlock or breakdown in the relations between shareholders or directors;[57] in a few cases, the oppression remedy has been used where a wrong has been done to the corporation and a minority shareholder has suffered in consequence, even though a derivative action would seem to be more appropriate in such circumstances. It is possible that Susanna, in Illustration 28.5, might seek an oppression remedy rather than bring a derivative action.[58]

To justify the making of an order under section 241, a complainant[59] must show that the action complained of has been "oppressive or unfairly prejudicial or . . . unfairly disregards the

54. CBCA, s. 214(1)(b)(ii). The "just and equitable winding up" rule has been a feature of English and Canadian company law statutes since around the end of the 19th century.

55. *Patheon Inc.* v. *Global Pharm Inc.* [2000] O.J. No. 2532.

56. *Re Ferguson and Imax Systems Corp.* (1983), 150 D.L.R. (3d) 718; *Daniels* v. *Fielder* (1989), 52 D.L.R. (4th) 424.

57. *Eiserman* v. *Ara Farms* (1989), 52 D.L.R. (4th) 498; *Tilley* v. *Hailes* (1992), 7 O.R. (3d) 257.

58. See, for example: *Journet* v. *Superchef Food Industries Ltd.* (1984), 29 B.L.R. 206. However, it seems that the plaintiff must still show that he has been affected in a way different from that of other shareholders: *NPV Management Ltd.* v. *Anthony* (2003), 231 D.L.R. (4th) 681; *Pasnak* v. *Chura* [2004] B.C.J. No. 790. For discussion of this issue, see MacIntosh, "The Oppression Remedy: Personal or Derivative?" (1991), 70 Can. Bar Rev. 29.

59. In some circumstances a creditor has been held to be a proper "complainant" for the purposes of the section: *Piller Sausages & Delicatessen Ltd.* v. *Cobb International Corp.* [2003] O.J. No. 2647; *Dylex Ltd.* v. *Anderson* (2003), 63 O.R. (3d) 659.

interests" of the complainant. However, the courts have emphasized that the conduct need not be wrongful or in bad faith, though this will be a factor to take into account.[60] It is particularly well suited to deal with the breakdown of family companies, where both or all sides allege wrongdoing by the others.

CASE 28.10

Elaine brought an application against her brother, Abraham, and nephew, Matthew, each of whom owned or controlled one-third of the shares of the furniture company built up by their deceased parents (or grandparents). It was the ninth piece of litigation involving those parties commenced during a period of two years. The judgment delivered by Herold J. of the Ontario Superior Court of Justice paints a graphic picture of the dispute:

> Each time one reads a judgment involving an oppression remedy claim or hears a case with respect to the same, one wonders if one hasn't considered the worst possible corporate scenario—this case is no different. There is a great deal of animosity amongst the various protagonists and there is a great deal of disagreement with respect to both the facts and the inferences and legal conclusions to be drawn therefrom. . . . A portion of the complaint by Elaine . . . involves the lack of what were referred to as the "corporate niceties", such mundane things as annual meetings of shareholders and directors, minutes of same, formal resolutions and the like. The reality is that there were no such corporate niceties. . . .

Among Elaine's allegations of oppressive conduct were the following:

- She never received any dividends (in fact, no dividends were ever paid to anyone).

- Abraham took $210 000 from the corporation without authority. (Abraham responded that maybe he did but Elaine took money too.)

- Abraham and Matthew increased six-fold the rent paid by the corporation to another corporation owned by themselves.

- There were numerous instances of improper loans and payments for personal expenses (by all three parties).

- Abraham and Matthew were financing the litigation, to the tune of $65 000, out of corporate funds—in effect using Elaine's money to sue herself.

The judge found that there had been an irreconcilable breakdown in relations. The parties had not spoken to each other for two years. Not only could the parties not agree on the time of day, "I don't believe they could even agree on what day it was." In the event, it was unnecessary to decide who had been oppressed and how. It was sufficient that there had been a breakdown, which triggered the statute. The only real question was, "What are the appropriate terms of disentanglement?" Since Abraham's whole life was wrapped up in the business, and it was Matthew's main livelihood, whereas Elaine had nothing to do with its operation, the respondents were ordered to buy out Elaine's shares at a fair value to be determined by an independent auditor.[61]

Section 241(3) allows the court to make any order it thinks fit. By far the most common remedy granted has been to require the majority to buy out the minority interest at a fair price, but a wide range of other orders may be made.[62] Judges may customize a solution that suits the particular needs of the corporation. Because of its great flexibility and the absence of technical obstacles, the oppression remedy is quickly becoming the most widely used shareholder remedy in Canada.

---

60. *Brant Investments Ltd.* v. *Keeprite Inc., supra,* n. 41; *Westfair Food Ltd.* v. *Watt* (1991), 79 D.L.R. (4th) 48 (leave to appeal refused).

61. *Viner* v. *Poplaw* (2003), 38 B.L.R. (3d) 134. For another example of a protracted family dispute under the oppression procedure, see *Waxman* v. *Waxman* [2004] O.J. No. 1765 (leave to appeal refused).

62. In some cases the court has allowed the minority petitioner to buy out the majority oppressor: see *Tilley* v. *Hailes, supra,* n. 57.

CASE 28.11

In proceedings related to the improper loan described in Case 28.6, Catalyst, a Hollinger non-voting minority shareholder, sought an oppression remedy removing 8 of the 10 Hollinger directors. Lord Conrad Black resigned prior to the hearing. The trial judge ordered the removal of every Hollinger director who was also associated with Ravelston except Peter White. Although Mr. White's conduct was found to be oppressive, he was allowed to remain on the board "at the pleasure" of the remaining independent Hollinger directors. The trial judge felt that Mr. White's continued service as an officer and director of Hollinger was in the best interests of the corporation "at least on a transitional basis." Approximately six months later, at the request of the independent Hollinger directors, the judge ordered Mr. White's permanent removal. Mr. White appealed both orders, arguing that the trial judge had stripped the shareholders of their right to select directors and changed the nature of his director's duties when the independent directors were given the power to remove him.

The Ontario Court of Appeal upheld both of the orders declaring that section 241 gives the court the power to "directly interfere with the corporate governance of a corporation and the rights and obligations of directors, officers and shareholders."[63]

SHAREHOLDER AGREEMENTS

Advantages

Although the oppression remedy has greatly increased the protection given to the minority shareholder, it still depends on the court exercising its discretion in their favour. A shareholder is still in a less secure position than is a partner.

This uncertainty is a factor to be considered if a small group of equal partners propose to transform their business into a corporation. It may make good business sense to incorporate because of the nature of the business, its growth, and its tax position. Yet each of the partners, if aware of the dangers of being a minority shareholder at odds with the others, might well hesitate to give up the protection of partnership law.

Fortunately, it is possible to approximate the protection available to partners with two agreements. One agreement is a long-term employment agreement between the corporation and the shareholder. The second is an agreement among the shareholders that is outside the constitution of the corporation. This process is not simple because, as we have seen, directors owe their primary duty to the corporation. They must not compromise their duty to act in the best interests of the corporation. Subject to an important exception to be discussed below, any agreement among shareholders must be restricted to their role as shareholders and must not infringe on their role as directors.[64] This danger can be avoided in a well-drafted **shareholder agreement**. Each agreement must be tailored to the needs of the individual business, but it may be useful to examine briefly the chief elements normally included in a shareholder agreement.

shareholder agreement
an agreement between two or more shareholders that is distinct from the corporation's charter and by-laws

Right to Participate in Management

The shareholders promise to elect each other to the board of directors at each annual meeting and not to nominate or vote for any other person. They may also promise not to vote for any major change in the corporation's capital structure or in the nature of its business except by unanimous agreement.

---

63. *Catalyst Fund General Partner 1 Inc.* v. *Hollinger Inc.* (2006), 79 O.R. (3d) 288 (On. C.A.) at para. 50. In *BCE Inc.* v. *1976 Debenture Holders,* 2008 SCC 69, the Supreme Court denied an oppression remedy to debenture holders objecting to the leveraged buyout of BCE, saying no single set of stakeholders' interests has priority over others.

64. *Motherwell* v. *Schoof,* [1949] 4 D.L.R. 812.

Right to a Fair Price for a Share Interest

The shareholders may agree to a regular method of valuation of their shares. They may agree not to sell their shares to an outsider without giving the right of first refusal proportionately to the remaining shareholders. If one of them commits a major breach of the shareholder agreement and remains unwilling to remedy it, he can be required to sell his interest to the others at the appraised value. In addition, if any shareholder is wrongfully expelled or dismissed by the others, he may require them to buy out his interest at the appraised value. This provision may also state that in the event of a dispute about appraisal, a named person, usually the auditor, will arbitrate and assess the value of the interest.

Unanimous Shareholder Agreements

The CBCA and most provincial statutes formally recognize **unanimous shareholder agreements** and permit them to govern relationships among shareholders in a private corporation in much the same manner as in a partnership. The CBCA states that "an agreement among all the shareholders . . . that restricts in whole or in part the powers of the directors to manage the business and affairs of the corporation is valid" (section 146(2)), and that the shareholders who are given the power to manage "have all the rights, powers, duties and liabilities of a director . . . and the directors are thereby relieved of their rights, powers, duties and liabilities to the same extent" (section 146(5)).

unanimous shareholder agreement
a shareholder agreement to which all shareholders are parties

The Act also states that "a purchaser or transferee of shares subject to an unanimous shareholder agreement is deemed to be a party to the agreement" (section 146(3)). Thus, on the sale of a share interest in a private corporation that is subject to such an agreement, the transferee not only receives an assignment of rights as a shareholder, but is also bound to carry out the duties of the transferor. A unanimous shareholder agreement must be "noted conspicuously" on the face of a share certificate in order to bind subsequent transferees (section 49(8)).

These provisions modify the common law rule that no agreement may fetter the discretion of directors. However, only *unanimous* agreements have special status under the acts. The CBCA makes frequent reference to unanimous shareholder agreements and treats them almost as if they were part of the corporate constitution, rather like by-laws. In doing so, it has provided the opportunity to develop a new, flexible device for business planning in private corporations.

QUESTIONS FOR REVIEW

1. What is the distinction between the "business" and the "affairs" of a corporation?

2. Where are the rules of corporate governance found?

3. What are the principal powers given to the board of directors of a corporation incorporated under the CBCA?

4. How are directors appointed? How may they be removed?

5. To whom are directors' and officers' duties owed?

6. What defences are available to a director accused of breach of duty?

7. When a director enters into a contract with his or her own corporation, what precautions should be taken to ensure the validity of the contract?

8. What is meant by "intercepting a corporate opportunity"?

9. In what circumstances might a director have a conflict of interest?

10. What is "insider trading"?

11. Who is an "insider"?

12. What is meant when one says that a minority shareholder is (a) "locked in" and (b) "frozen out"?

13. What are the principal rights attached to shares in a corporation?

14. What is the difference between an ordinary resolution and a special resolution?

15. What are "class rights"?

16. What is a "proxy"? How are proxies appointed?

17. Do shareholders have any right to receive a dividend if the corporation is profitable?

18. What are "pre-emptive rights" in relation to a corporation's shares?

19. Are there any restrictions on the directors' powers to issue new shares?

20. What information must be provided in a corporation's annual financial statement?

21. What is the role of a corporation's auditor? To whom is the auditor's duty owed?

22. What are a corporation's "documents of record"?

23. Do shareholders owe any duty to their corporation?

24. What is the "appraisal remedy"?

25. What is meant by a "derivative action"?

26. What are the principal differences between the "just and equitable" winding-up procedure and the oppression remedy?

27. What matters are commonly dealt with in shareholder agreements?

28. What are the main effects of a unanimous shareholder agreement?

CASES AND PROBLEMS

1. Ten years ago, Davidson and Farmer formed a corporation to develop a fishing lodge that they had bought (in the name of the corporation). They each owned 50 shares in the corporation. There were no other shareholders, and Davidson and Farmer were the only directors.

   They worked hard to develop the business, which became quite successful. No dividends were ever paid by the corporation, but Davidson and Farmer had paid themselves generous salaries for their work as directors.

   Last year Davidson died. In his will he left his entire estate to his sister, Eriksen. Before her marriage Eriksen had occasionally worked at the lodge (for a salary), but recently had not been involved in the business.

   Shortly after Davidson's death, Farmer (as the sole surviving director) purported to appoint his niece, Greenberg, as a director to fill the vacancy on the board. Next, Farmer and Greenberg passed a resolution issuing one share in the corporation to Greenberg for a consideration of $10 000 (which was estimated to be approximately 1 percent of the value of the business).

   In response to requests from Eriksen, Farmer has agreed to register the transfer of Davidson's shares to her, but has made it clear that he will not agree to her becoming a director and that he intends to continue running the business together with Greenberg.

   Does Eriksen have any remedy?

2. Petrescu is a director of Dracula Fashions Ltd., a small but successful corporation operating a boutique in Calgary. She also owns 25 percent of the corporation's shares.

Petrescu recently inherited some property from her aunt, including a bookstore in downtown Calgary. The bookstore was not very successful, but Petrescu realized that the store premises would be ideal for Dracula, which was seeking to expand.

At the next board meeting she informed her fellow Dracula directors that she had heard of a suitable property that had just come on the market. The chief executive officer, Vlad, agreed to inspect the property, and when he reported back that the property seemed very suitable and was reasonably priced, the board unanimously approved the purchase of the property from the estate of Petrescu's aunt.

Petrescu at no time disclosed the fact that the estate was that of her aunt or that she was the main beneficiary under the aunt's will. However, Vlad has since discovered that fact.

Was Petrescu in breach of her duty to the corporation? Does the corporation have any remedy?

3. Until three years ago, Slater was the sole shareholder and director of Lockley Quarries Ltd., a small corporation that owned a quarry and produced trimmed limestone blocks. Then an opportunity arose to purchase a second quarry at a very good price. Slater did not have sufficient funds and persuaded Mason to come into business with him and to help finance the purchase of the new quarry. As a result, Mason became a 40 percent shareholder and a director of Lockley Quarries. Slater and Mason got on well together and the business prospered.

A few months ago, Slater was approached by an old friend, Chalker, who proposed that they—Chalker and Slater—purchase and operate a gravel pit that had come on the market. Slater agreed and a new corporation was formed to acquire the gravel pit, with Chalker and Slater as equal shareholders and directors.

Mason has learned of the dealings between Slater and Chalker. He considers that he should have been given the opportunity to participate in the new gravel pit venture. Do you agree? Does Mason have any remedy against Slater?

4. Normin Inc. is a large mining corporation, incorporated under the CBCA, the shares of which are publicly traded and are listed on the Toronto Stock Exchange. It has recently been conducting extensive exploration on land acquired in the Canadian Arctic.

Late in the afternoon of March 31, Normin's chief executive officer, Baffin, received a fax from the mineralogist in charge of the explorations. The fax, headed "Highly Confidential," informed Baffin that a giant deposit of tin had been discovered. It appeared that it would be fairly easy to extract and would be extremely profitable.

Baffin at once informed as many of the directors and senior officers as he could contact. After some discussion they agreed to prepare a press release the next morning. However, on the evening of March 31:

(a) One of the directors, Banks, telephoned his broker, Charles, and, without giving any reason, instructed Charles to buy as many Normin shares on his account as he could, provided the price did not exceed $30 per share. The following morning, Normin shares opened on the exchange at $28.75. Charles bought 10 000 shares for Banks, at prices between $28.75 and $29.50.

(b) Another director, Melville, contacted her brother, Parry, and offered to buy his shares in Normin. Parry had acquired the shares some years before, but had since lost interest in the investment and had several times asked Melville if she would like to buy them. Melville offered to pay $29 per share, and Parry accepted and transferred his 15 000 shares to his sister.

(c) Hudson, a senior executive of Normin, told his bridge partner, Frobisher, that she should tell no one and buy Normin shares as soon as possible. Frobisher bought 2000 shares on the exchange the following morning, at $29.25 per share.

At midday on April 1, the press release was published, giving details of the find. Trading on the exchange became brisk, and by the end of the day the price of Normin shares had reached $47.50.

Discuss the possible liability of any of the individuals mentioned, and the remedies, if any, that Parry and other shareholders who sold their shares before midday on April 1 might have.

5. For many years Sergei (a widower) owned and ran a large farm, initially by himself and later with the help of his four children. Eight years ago, on the advice of his accountant and his lawyer, he decided to transfer the farm to a corporation and, with a view to keeping the farm in the family (and to saving taxes), to make his children shareholders in the corporation.

   A corporation, Eisenstein Farms Inc., was formed with two classes of shares. As consideration for the transfer of the farm to the corporation, Sergei received 1000 Class "A" preferred shares, each share carrying one vote. The four children, Galina, Ivan, Oleg, and Tanya, each received 100 Class "B" common shares, also carrying one vote per share, for which they paid $10 per share. Two of the children—Galina and Ivan—had left home and no longer took an active part in running the farm. The other two—Oleg and Tanya—continued to live with their father and work on the farm, and were made directors and employees of the corporation along with Sergei. No dividends were paid by the corporation in respect of the common shares (Sergei received dividends on his preferred shares), but Sergei, Oleg, and Tanya all received salaries.

   A year ago things started to turn sour. Oleg married, and neither Sergei nor Tanya got on with his wife. They complained that he was neglecting the farm and spending most of his time helping his wife with her business. (Oleg denied this.) After a series of heated arguments, Oleg threatened to resign from the board of directors and to quit his employment with the corporation. Sergei and Tanya immediately accepted his "resignation." Since then, relations between them have deteriorated further. Oleg is no longer receiving any remuneration from the corporation, either as a director or employee, has been excluded from directors' meetings, and has been given no information about the corporation's business or affairs.

   Oleg considers that he has been treated unfairly. Does he have any remedy?

6. Aldeburgh Inc. is a corporation incorporated under the CBCA. It has never issued shares to the public. It owns a large piece of land and a number of vacation cottages fronting on a lake some distance north of Queensville, Ontario. The property has produced relatively little income in the past.

   Until recently, Aldeburgh had four shareholders—Balstrode, Crabbe, Orford, and Swallow—who each owned 25 percent of the issued shares. Balstrode, Crabbe, and Orford are the directors of the corporation. Swallow is retired and has taken little interest in the business.

   A few months ago, the three directors received a tip from Grimes (a friend of theirs and a prominent local politician) that a large corporation, Maltings Developments Inc., was proposing to establish a major recreational complex along the lake and was almost certain to get permission for the development. When the news became public, he suggested, the price of land in the area would soar.

   Balstrode, Crabbe, and Orford held a directors' meeting and resolved that Aldeburgh should try to buy up as much property in the area as possible. They did not tell Swallow the good news. Aldeburgh borrowed as much money as it was able to and bought a number of lots.

   During the same period, the following events occurred:

   (a) Balstrode approached Swallow and persuaded Swallow to sell her his shares. She said nothing about the proposed development.
   (b) Crabbe personally bought one lot for herself (without disclosing the fact to anyone), which she was later able to resell to Maltings at a large profit.
   (c) Orford bought one lot (in the name of a numbered company) that she resold to Aldeburgh at a quick profit, without disclosing that she was the beneficial owner.
   (d) Grimes bought several lots himself, which he later sold to Maltings at a large profit.

   Soon afterwards, Maltings offered to buy all the land owned by Aldeburgh or, alternatively, to buy all its shares. An agreement was reached to sell the shares, with the result that all the Aldeburgh shares are now owned by Maltings, and the shareholders of Aldeburgh all made large profits on the sale of their shares.

   Maltings has now discovered the secret activities of Balstrode, Crabbe, Orford, and Grimes. Swallow has learned about the profit that Balstrode made on the resale of his shares.

   Who is liable for what? to whom? on what grounds? How can liability be enforced?

ADDITIONAL RESOURCES FOR CHAPTER 28 ON THE COMPANION WEBSITE *(www.pearsoned.ca/smyth)*

In addition to self-test multiple-choice, true–false, and short essay questions (all with immediate feedback), application exercises, and links to useful web destinations, the Companion Website provides the following resources for Chapter 28:

- **British Columbia:** Corporate Dissolution; Derivative Action; Due Diligence Defence and Limited Liability; Liability of Management; Oppression Remedy; Shareholder Remedies
- **Alberta:** Corporate Management; Directors' Liability; Oppression Remedy; Shareholders Remedies
- **Manitoba/Saskatchewan:** Corporate Internal Liability
- **Ontario:** Business Judgment Rule; Code of Conduct; Conflict of Interest; Corporate Governance; Directors' and Officers' Duties; Directors' and Officers' Liability; Disclosure; Fiduciary Duty; Insider Trading; Oppression Remedy; Sarbanes Oxley

CHAPTER

29

Corporate Governance:
EXTERNAL RESPONSIBILITIES

This chapter examines the relationship between the corporation and the outside world—its customers, creditors, employees, competitors, potential investors, and the general public. We must remember that a corporation is an artificial person that is responsible for its own actions. Still, it can act only through its directors, officers, and agents, and so requires multiple layers of accountability. In this chapter we examine such questions as:

- In what ways does legislation protect creditors, investors, and other persons who deal with, or are affected by, corporations?

- To what extent is a corporation liable for the acts of its directors, officers, and agents?

- How do corporations enter into contracts?

- Can a corporation be negligent?

- Can a corporation commit a crime?

- To what extent may directors, officers, or agents be held personally liable for acts done, or not done, in the name of a corporation?

- What liability is imposed on corporate officers under environmental legislation?

LIABILITY ARISING FROM BUSINESS RESPONSIBILITIES

The business activities of a corporation affect many external groups or **stakeholders**. The most commonly identified stakeholders include the corporation's creditors, employees, consumers, competitors, potential public investors, and the public at large. In this chapter we discuss the principal legislative measures that have been enacted for the protection of these stakeholders, and the potential liability arising at common law and under various regulatory schemes.

> **stakeholders**
> groups affected by the business activities of a corporation

The common law and legislative measures often impose liability on the corporate entity itself, as well as its directors and senior officers. Recent measures have expanded the circle of liability to include outside experts working on behalf of the corporation such as accountants, underwriters, and lawyers.

Types of Liability

Stakeholders are protected by a variety of measures. Proactive measures establish preemptive requirements such as disclosure of information or licensing of professionals, and stakeholders are empowered to enforce these standards through civil causes of action. Chapter 28 focused primarily on proactive standards of internal corporate governance enforced through civil causes of action. This chapter expands on the civil causes of action available to stakeholder groups and considers the criminal and regulatory offences created to punish corporations, directors and officers, and others when wrongdoing occurs.

Criminal liability arises from an offence contained in statute, most often (but not always) the Criminal Code.[1] Criminal offences address the most serious types of misconduct and result in the most serious form of punishment: imprisonment.

As discussed first in Chapter 1, regulatory liability stems from subordinate legislation where specialized government agencies and tribunals are assigned the task of implementing programs, monitoring conduct, or investigating misconduct. The fulfillment of this responsibility requires establishing rules that set the standard of acceptable conduct. These rules often assign a penalty for failure to comply. The rules and penalties are known as **regulatory offences**.

> **regulatory offences**
> less-serious offences created by government regulation through specialized legislation, agencies, and tribunals

Regulatory offences resemble traditional criminal law because, in order to protect the public interest, they punish those who ignore the rules. Therefore, regulatory offences derive their standards from criminal law.[2]

The Requirement of *Mens Rea*

For most offences, the prosecution must prove *beyond a reasonable doubt* that not only did the accused actually commit the act described in the offence, but also that he had the "intent." It must establish that the accused had *mens rea* (a guilty mind)—that is, a guilty intention or guilty knowledge. For example, a person who is found to be in possession of stolen goods has not committed an offence if he did not know that they were stolen.

---

1. The federal government is given legislative jurisdiction over criminal law, and the Criminal Code R.S.C. 1985 c. C-46 is the comprehensive legislation containing most criminal offences. Other statutes may contain offences dealing with the subject matter of the legislation.

2. Some statutory regulations also create civil liability, so that a wrongdoer may have to compensate a party harmed by its breach. See, for example, liability for insider trading, discussed in Chapter 28. Section 131 of the CBCA makes "insiders" (usually directors or employees of a corporation) who use confidential information to profit from a transaction in the corporation's securities (a) liable to compensate any person who suffered loss and (b) accountable to the corporation for the profits. In addition, such regulations almost invariably authorize the appropriate government agency to prosecute and to exact punishment. Section 251 of the CBCA makes a person who contravenes section 131 "guilty of an offence punishable on summary conviction."

The Presumption of Intent

For regulatory offences, we find that the courts and statutes tend to broaden the concept of *mens rea*. It may be enough to show that if any ordinary person would or *should* have realized that his conduct was an offence, the wrongdoer will be convicted. For instance, if a person drove his car at 100 km/h through a crowded shopping area, he would very likely be convicted of careless or dangerous driving even if he did not believe that he was endangering anyone.

For these strict liability offences, the courts hold that there is a presumption that the accused, in committing the wrongful act, had the requisite *mens rea*. However, the accused can overcome the presumption by persuading the court that he acted with reasonable care in the circumstances.

Absolute Liability

No *mens rea* at all is required for a conviction of an absolute liability offence. It is enough for the prosecution simply to prove that the accused committed the wrongful act—for example, a driver in a vehicle with a faulty speedometer who is unaware that he is exceeding the speed limit. Usually, absolute liability is confined to statutes dealing with public health and safety.

CHECKLIST Classification of Offences

The Supreme Court of Canada has divided offences into three classes depending upon the language of the statute. They may be summarized as follows:[3]

- **■** *Mens rea* **offences**, where the prosecution must demonstrate the existence of some positive state of mind such as intent, knowledge, or recklessness.
- **■** **Offences of strict liability**, where the commission of the prohibited act raises a presumption that an offence has been committed, leaving it open to the accused to avoid liability by proving that he took all reasonable care (due diligence).
- **■** **Offences of absolute liability**, where it is not open to the accused to excuse himself by showing that he was free of fault. Simply doing the act makes one guilty of the offence.

---

mens rea offence
an offence where the prosecution must establish a "guilty mind" on the part of the defendant

strict liability offence
an offence where there is a presumption of guilt unless the defendant can show that he or she took reasonable care

absolute liability offence
an offence where the absence of fault is no defence

This third class remains a very limited one. The Supreme Court of Canada has held that an absolute liability offence is unconstitutional when conviction may lead to an accused being imprisoned.[4]

This chapter will examine situations where various types of liability (civil, regulatory, and criminal) and various types of offences (*mens rea*, strict liability, and absolute liability) are used to protect stakeholders.

PROTECTION OF CREDITORS

Implications of Limited Liability

When an unincorporated business becomes insolvent, the creditors are entitled to whatever assets are available. If a deficiency remains, they may look to the personal assets of the sole proprietor or

---

3. See *R. v. City of Sault Ste. Marie* (1978), 85 D.L.R. (3d) 161 (S.C.C.).
4. *Reference re s. 94(2) of the B.C. Motor Vehicle Act*, [1985] 2 S.C.R. 486; *R. v. Transport Robert (1973) Ltee* (2003), 234 D.L.R. (4th) 546.

partners. In those forms of business organization, a debtor's liability is not limited to her business assets—her personal assets may be seized as well. In a corporation, however, a creditor's rights are limited to the assets held by the corporation. If those assets are inadequate, the creditor normally has no further remedy against the shareholders.[5] Assuming no wrongdoing, a creditor's only protection is the fund of assets owned by the corporation itself. For this reason, legislatures and courts have tried to establish rules to assure creditors that those assets will not be wasted. As noted in Chapter 28, if the assets are wasted, a creditor may have a claim against the directors and officers personally for breach of their duty of skill and care but not for breach of fiduciary duty.

Preservation of Capital

Except for financial institutions such as banks and insurance companies, the law requires no minimum issued capital for corporations.[6] Legally, a corporation may carry on business with a share capital of $1. Of course, it would be difficult to obtain credit with only a nominal equity investment, but even so, such a corporation could become liable to pay a large sum of money as a result of, say, the negligent conduct of one of its employees.

It is difficult to devise legal rules that will protect creditors from the risk of extending credit to a corporation that becomes unable to pay. The primary concern of the law has therefore been to ensure that a corporation's stated capital is not improperly reduced by preferring the rights of shareholders over those of creditors.

On the winding-up of a corporation, its creditors are entitled to have the assets applied in satisfaction of their claims before any surplus is returned to the shareholders. Historically, a corporation's capital could not be returned to its shareholders except on a winding-up, and only after all creditors had been paid in full. That principle resulted in the following rules:

- Dividends could be paid only out of profits.
- A corporation was not allowed to buy back its own shares.
- A corporation was not allowed to lend money to assist a purchaser to acquire its shares.
- A corporation could not normally lend money to its shareholders.
- A **reduction of capital** required approval of the courts.

reduction of capital
writing down (reducing) the stated amount of a corporation's capital

Over time, these rules became confusing and inflexible so the legislature intervened to eliminate the difficulties.

The CBCA (and those provincial statutes modelled on it) set out rules that are relatively simple to understand and to apply. The rules are divided into two types—rules that prohibit any payment by the corporation to its shareholders that renders the corporation's liquid assets insufficient to pay the existing claims of creditors, and rules that restrict the return of capital to shareholders even when the corporation might still be left with sufficient liquid assets to pay its creditors. Any improper payment of dividends or return of capital will trigger personal liability of the directors.

The Solvency Test

Shareholders usually receive money from the corporation by way of dividends, or, in certain circumstances, through redemption or repurchase by the corporation of its own shares. If payments by the corporation in either of these instances are made when the corporation is insolvent, or would have the effect of making the corporation insolvent, the directors may be held personally liable to the corporation for the deficiency.[7]

---

5. There are a few limited exceptions to this principle: see the discussion under "Exceptions to Limited Liability" in Chapter 27. As discussed in Chapter 28, creditors may claim against directors and officers personally if the insolvency arises from breach of their duty of skill (except in Ontario): See *Peoples* v. *Wise,* [2004] 3 S.C.R. 461; Ontario Business Corporations Act, R.S.O. 1990, c. B.16, s. 134.

6. In most countries outside North America, corporations must have a minimum capital prescribed by law.

7. See, for example: CBCA, ss. 42 and 118(2)(c).

insolvency
having liabilities in excess of the realizable value of one's assets or being unable to pay one's debts as they fall due

The effectiveness of this rule depends upon the definition of **insolvency** that is used. Two factors must be considered: a corporation is deemed insolvent if the realizable value of its assets has become less than its total liabilities, or if it is unable to pay its debts as they become due.[8]

The Maintenance of Capital Test

In theory, the money paid into the corporation by shareholders should be preserved as far as possible within the corporation as a capital fund, available for absorbing business losses so that creditors (and in some cases, preferred shareholders) may be paid in full. The maintenance of capital test therefore goes beyond the solvency test. It applies in the following cases.

(i) Dividends

The CBCA, section 42, provides that a corporation may not pay a dividend if there are reasonable grounds for believing that (a) the corporation is, or would be after the payment, unable to pay its liabilities as they become due (the solvency test), *and* (b) if the realizable value of the corporation's assets would thereby be less than the aggregate of its liabilities *and* its stated capital of all classes (maintenance of capital test). In other words, after the dividend has been paid, the corporation's net assets must not be less than the amount of its stated capital. This rule effectively restates (in a less ambiguous manner) the old rule that dividends may only be paid out of profits. A corporation's net assets will only exceed its stated capital if either it has undistributed profits or its assets have increased in value.

ILLUSTRATION 29.1

A corporation originally issued shares for a total of $5 million. For several years it has traded at a profit, in the sense that its revenues exceeded its expenditures. However, its capital assets have depreciated in value. It now has net assets of exactly $5 million. Despite having a trading profit, it cannot pay a dividend. Payment of a dividend in these circumstances will expose the directors to personal civil liability.

(ii) Return of Capital

A corporation may return a part of its capital to its shareholders either by making a *pro rata* payment to each shareholder—in which case the effect is essentially the same as the payment of a dividend—or by buying back the shares of some of its shareholders. A return of capital, like the payment of a dividend when there are no profits or capital gain out of which to pay it, reduces the funds available to meet the claims of creditors and, if the corporation should subsequently become insolvent, would give a preferred repayment to shareholders before the creditors' claims are met.

The CBCA provides that a corporation may repay capital to its shareholders provided that it will be able to satisfy the solvency and maintenance of capital tests.[9] This rule is reasonable, since shareholders may have contributed substantially more capital than the corporation really needs. So long as creditors are protected, there is no reason to insist that excess capital remain in the corporation.

---

8. The federal Bankruptcy and Insolvency Act provides, additionally, an "after the fact" test that permits a trustee in bankruptcy to apply for a court inquiry in respect of dividends paid within 12 months preceding bankruptcy to determine whether the dividend rendered the corporation insolvent, and that authorizes the court to give judgment to the trustee against the directors, jointly and severally, in the amount of such dividend: Bankruptcy and Insolvency Act, R.S.C. 1985, c. B-3, s. 101.

9. CBCA, s. 38. To do so requires a special resolution.

Corporations may also redeem or purchase their own shares for a number of specified reasons, subject to solvency requirements to protect creditors.[10]

Loans to Shareholders, Directors, and Employees

The old rules against return of capital were reinforced by a prohibition against a corporation making loans of any kind to its shareholders, directors, or employees. The idea behind the prohibition was that such loans might amount to an indirect return of capital and might deprive the corporation of liquidity. The CBCA has eliminated those rules.[11] Recent focus on ethics in corporate governance has revived this concern.

PROTECTION OF EMPLOYEES

Chapter 20 dealt with employee/employer relationships in detail and so we will only make brief mention of some employee protections here. In Chapter 28, we discussed the personal liability of directors for up to six months' wages of employees. Employee safety is protected through Occupation Health and Safety legislation, which requires ongoing monitoring and creates regulatory offences for unsafe workplaces. Injured employees are covered by no-fault insurance through Workplace Safety legislation. Human Rights legislation and tribunals create civil liability and regulatory offences to promote non-discriminatory work environments.

PROTECTION OF CONSUMERS AND COMPETITORS

Businesses compete with each other for customers so the protection of these two stakeholder groups naturally fits together. Their protection involves multiple provincial and federal statutes. Consumer protection is a matter of provincial jurisdiction, and all provinces have legislation limiting unfair business practices and creating regulatory offences and civil causes of action. The federal Competition Act addresses unfair conduct among competitors and improper marketing and advertising strategies. The Competition Act creates both regulatory and criminal offences. Chapter 32, Regulation of Business, deals with the competitive business environment in detail.

PROTECTION OF INVESTORS

Securities Legislation

In contrast to the United States, Canadian securities regulation is a matter within provincial jurisdiction. Each Canadian province has a Securities Act, under which a government board is created, known in most of the provinces as the **securities commission**. The securities commission operates as the enforcing agency charged with ensuring that the requirements of the Act are complied with.[12] All thirteen provincial and territorial securities commissions now cooperate on regulation, policy, and administration through a single organization known as the Canadian Securities Administrators.

securities commission
the statutory authority appointed to supervise the issue of securities to the general public, the operation of the securities industry, and the stock exchange

---

10. Ss. 30 to 37. Since the prohibition against a corporation holding its own previously issued shares has been relaxed, the rule against giving financial help to any person to buy shares has also become unnecessary. An actual return of capital to its shareholders must be distinguished from a reduction in the amount of a corporation's stated capital. A reduction generally does no more than recognize a state of affairs that has occurred: the corporation's net assets have decreased in value. As such, it is not objectionable (s. (s38(1)(c) and (3)).

11. Prohibitions or restrictions still exist in some provincial statutes.

12. Through the Canadian Securities Administrators the provincial securities commissions have adopted a number of National Rules and Policies that have a common number identification system.

CONTEMPORARY ISSUE

One Federal Securities Regulator

Over the past decade there has been a push to change Canadian securities regulation. Proposed reforms would see the 13 provincial securities commissions replaced by a single federal regulator. Advantages include consistency, efficiency, lack of duplication, and cost effectiveness.

The recent chaos in world financial markets has given new life to this proposal. On October 29, 2008, federal Finance Minister Jim Flaherty announced that "it was time to move toward a single securities regulator . . . [that] reflects regional interests, yet can quickly respond with a single voice to market developments."[13]

QUESTIONS TO CONSIDER

1. Under what constitutional power could the Federal Government implement this reform?

2. How could this reform improve Canada's position when dealing with international financial issues?

Sources: Eion Callan and Barabara Schecer, "Crisis Used to Push for Single Regulator," *National Post*, October 30, 2009, p. 1, reporting speech by Jim Flaherty on October 29, 2008; Wise Persons' Committee (Committee to Review the Structure of Securities Regulation in Canada), *It's Time—WPC Final Report*, December 17, 2003, available online at www.wise-averties.ca/main_en.html.

Objectives of Securities Legislation

The securities legislation asserts governmental control over the public offering of shares. The goals of the legislation are to ensure the integrity, fairness, and efficiency of the market and promote investor confidence in it.[14] To accomplish these goals, securities commissions have three key areas of responsibilities:

- the securities industry,
- the corporations offering their shares to the public, and
- the stock exchanges within the provinces (for example, the Toronto Stock Exchange in Ontario).[15]

Canadian securities legislation employs several devices to achieve the objectives described above. We will examine the following devices:

(1) registering or licensing those engaged in various aspects of the securities business,

(2) requiring the issuer of securities to the public to file a prospectus with the securities commission,

(3) regulating continuous disclosure by public corporations, and

(4) as discussed in Chapter 28, setting standards of corporate governance for public corporations.

---

13. Eion Callan and Barabara Schecer, "Crisis Used to Push for Single Regulator," *National Post*, October 30, 2009, p. 1, reporting speech by Jim Flaherty on October 29, 2008.

14. Securities Act, R.S.O. 1990, c. S-5, s. 1.1.

15. *Ibid.*, ss. 21 to 21.11. It is beyond the scope of this chapter to review the detailed regulations governing stock exchanges.

The Securities Industry: Licensing

The registering of persons engaged in the securities industry is an important device for ensuring ethical conduct. Licensing is on an annual basis, and each securities commission has authority under its provincial statute to revoke, suspend, or refuse to renew the licence of anyone when, in its opinion, such action is in the public interest. Operating without a licence is a criminal offence. Depending upon the jurisdiction, a licence may be required of persons engaged in a wide variety of activities. Those affected include brokers (who buy and sell securities as agents), investment dealers (who buy and sell securities as principals), broker dealers (who may act as either principal or agent in the promotion of companies), securities issuers (companies issuing their securities directly to the public without the intermediate services of investment dealers), salespeople employed by any of these businesses, and investment counsel and securities advisers. Self-regulating organizations such as the Investment Dealers Association of Canada (IDA) and the Mutual Fund Dealers Association of Canada (MFDA) work with their members to meet requirements of the securities commission.

The Public Corporation: Public Offering

Corporate Governance

Before any company may make a public offering, the internal structure of the company must meet the high standards of corporate governance required by the securities regulations. As discussed in detail in Chapter 28, the internal structure requirements include a larger board of directors, mandatory independent compensation-setting, and audited financial statements, among other things. The specific requirements are based on the following fundamental principles:

- *Independence:* Decision makers should be free of conflicts.
- *Transparency:* Decisions should be made through an open process.
- *Disclosure:* Information should be available to the public.
- *Accountability:* Decision makers should be responsible for their conduct.
- *Checks and Balances:* Internal structures should bring irregularities to light.

Prospectuses

No corporation, partnership, or other form of business organization may issue securities to the public unless a **prospectus** has been filed with and approved by the securities commission of the province or territory in which the securities are to be sold. Prospectus requirements are an attempt to ensure that prospective investors have access to the relevant facts about a corporation before deciding to invest in it. In most instances, an investor is entitled to a copy of the prospectus before buying securities and may rescind the contract of subscription if he or she does not receive the prospectus.

> **prospectus**
> the document that a corporation is required to publish when inviting the public to subscribe for its securities

The contents of a prospectus are prescribed by statute or in regulations and are too detailed to describe here. It is sufficient to note that the prospectus must include, among other things:

- a full description of the securities to be offered (either shares or bonds) with a statement of their voting rights, preference, conversion privileges, and rights on liquidation;
- the nature of the business carried on;
- the names, addresses, and occupations of the directors;
- the proposed use of the proceeds from the issue of securities;
- details of any share options to be given by the corporation;[16]

---

16. A share (or stock) option is a right to subscribe for shares in the corporation at a fixed price within a specified time, given by a corporation as consideration for the payment of money, the rendering of services (often the services of directors), or any other valuable consideration. The option becomes valuable at any time before expiry that the market price exceeds the option price.

- the remuneration of the underwriter;
- the dividend record of the corporation;
- the particulars of property and services to be paid for out of the proceeds of the issue;
- recent audited financial statements; and
- a certificate of accuracy signed by the CEO, CFO, the promoter, and two directors.

The prospectus must contain full, true, and plain disclosure of all material facts. Failure in this regard is a strict-liability regulatory offence, punishable by a fine of up to $5 million dollars and/or 5 years in prison; knowingly falsifying a prospectus is a criminal offence.[17] It also triggers civil liability on behalf of the corporation and personal liability for the directors, officers, underwriters, and any person that signed the prospectus.[18] There are some exceptions to the requirement of a prospectus for sales to **non-public purchasers**.

non-public purchasers
purchasers that are not members of the general public such as banks, insurance companies, and municipal corporations

Continuing Disclosure

Control by the securities commission extends not only to issues of new securities but also to trading in already outstanding securities. Public corporations must make annual and quarterly filings[19] with the securities commissions disclosing financial and other material information, including:

- audited financial information with management's discussion and analysis;[20]
- notice of any change in auditor;
- notice of any change in corporate structure and inter-corporate relationships;
- descriptions of internal corporate governance practices including details of directors' identities and independence, compensation-setting and nomination processes, existence of a code of ethics, and ongoing assessment of governance effectiveness;[21]
- notice of material changes relating to the business, operations, or capital of an issuer that would reasonably be expected to effect the share price;[22] and
- acquisitions of other businesses.

CEOs and CFOs must certify the accuracy of all information contained in the annual filing. The Canadian Securities Administrators operate the System of Electronic Disclosure for Analysis and Retrieval (SEDAR) that gives the public electronic access to the filings of public companies. Other provisions contained in the legislation

- make the proxy a more effective means of registering shareholders' opinions,[23]
- require publication of insiders' transactions involving their corporation's shares[24] (as noted in Chapter 28),
- authorize civil actions against insiders, and
- make insider trading a regulatory and criminal offence.[25]

The Canadian Securities Administrators operate the SEDI, the System of Electronic Disclosure by Insiders, where insiders may submit their reports online and the public may view the reports.

---

17. Securities Act, R.S.O. 1990, c. S-5, s. 122; Criminal Code, R.S.C. 1985, c. C-46, s. 400.

18. *Ibid.*, s. 130. The Supreme Court of Canada recently declined to impose civil liability under the Ontario Securities Act with respect to a forecast contained in a prospectus: *Kerr* v. *Danier Leather Inc.* 2007 SCC 44.

19. This filing is called the Annual Information Filing (AIF) and its contents are prescribed by National Instrument 51-102.

20. Securities Act, R.S.O. 1990, c. S-5, ss. 75 to 83.1.

21. National Instrument 58-101, Disclosure of Corporate Governance Practices.

22. The Supreme Court of Canada considered the distinction between material change and material fact in a 2007 decision: *Kerr, supra,* n. 17.

23. Securities Act, R.S.O. 1990, c. S-5, ss. 84 to 88.

24. *Ibid.*, ss. 106 to 111.

25. *Ibid.*, ss. 76, 122(1)(c), and 134.

The Public Accounting Industry

Reliable financial information is at the heart of investor protection. In 2004, the Canadian Securities Administrators introduced new requirements for accountants engaged in public accounting or auditing. National Instrument 52-108 created the Canadian Public Accountability Board (CPAB), responsible for setting new standards for public accountants and overseeing their work. The CPAB carries out regular inspections of audit firms as a means of quality control and has disciplinary power. Only those public accountants recognized by and in good standing with the CPAB may provide an auditor's report for the purposes of the securities commission.

Secondary Market Liability

Civil liability for inaccurate information extends beyond the initial public offering to secondary trades in securities. The word secondary refers to the "re-sale" of shares between investors as distinct from initial purchases from the corporation. Securities legislation[26] creates a civil cause of action for any person who trades in a corporation's shares while inaccurate public information remains uncorrected. The corporation, its directors, officers, and influential insiders may all be held liable for damages suffered by a shareholder or former shareholder. Independent experts such as lawyers, accountants, or financial analysts may also be liable if their reports contain misrepresentations. The plaintiff need not prove that he or she relied on the misrepresentation, just that it existed at the time of the transaction. A due diligence defence is available and damage awards are capped.

Takeovers and Reorganizations

Another important objective of securities legislation is to give shareholders who have received a **takeover bid** for their shares sufficient information and time to assess the merits of the bid.[27] Takeover provisions include a requirement for disclosure of the number of shares in the offeree corporation held by the offeror corporation and its officers, and details of recent trading in those shares. In addition, the directors of an offeree corporation are required to issue a **directors' circular** to the shareholders setting out, among other things, their own intentions with respect to the takeover offer, and details of any arrangements made with the offeror corporation concerning their continuance in office or compensation for loss of office. However, this legislation does not apply to all corporations; in particular, takeovers of small private corporations are not regulated.

Both corporate and securities legislation contain detailed and complex rules dealing with mergers, with various types of corporate reorganization, and with winding-up. Needless to say, no one should make a decision in one of the above areas without expert assistance. The problems involved usually concern creditors' rights, the effects of taxation, the relevance of competition legislation, and the rights of various classes of shareholders, in addition to the general economic consequences for the corporations involved.

takeover bid
an offer by one corporation to acquire all or a substantial part of the shares of another corporation

directors' circular
a document required to be issued to the shareholders by the board of directors when a takeover of a widely held corporation is proposed

PROTECTION OF THE PUBLIC INTEREST

Protecting the public interest is a difficult challenge that involves balancing the interests of multiple stakeholders. Usually government is responsible for protecting the public, and the interests of the public are diverse. For example, it is in the public interest that people are employed, that employees earn a competitive wage, that business has access to foreign markets, that domestic products are competitive

---

26. Securities Act, R.S.O. 1990, c. S-5, s. 138.1; Ontario was the first province to create secondary market liability. Others have followed: B.C. (s. 140.1) Nov. 22/07; Alta.(s. 211.03) Dec. 31/06; Sask. (s. 147) Feb. 15/08; Man. (s. 174) Nov. 11/06; Que. (s.225.3) Nov. 9/07; N.S. (s. 146) Nov. 15/07; N.B. (s. 161.1) May 30/07; Nfld. (s. 138.1) Jun. 1/07; P.E.I Nov. 2/07.

27. *Ibid.*, ss. 89 to 105.

with imports, and that the environment is preserved. It is impossible to establish standards that protect all of the interests of the public and difficult choices must be made. Government uses regulation to balance the interests of business, stakeholders, and the public at large. The remaining part of this chapter will examine civil, regulatory, and criminal liability in place to protect the public interest without designating a particular stakeholder. By way of example, this chapter will look at the environmental regulatory scheme. The legal requirements should be viewed as a minimum standard of behaviour that management is encouraged to exceed.

ETHICAL ISSUE

Corporate Social Responsibility and Executive Compensation

As discussed in Chapter 1, corporate social responsibility is a management theory that suggests that corporate management should consider not only what is profitable and legal but also what is ethical. Corporations should consider the interests of the communities in which they operate and the public as a whole. Over time, these ideas appear to be gaining support within the business community. According to one commentator, "hard-edged capitalism is falling out of favour in the nation's executive suites."[28]

One explanation for this change, again, is the Enron debacle, which demonstrated the dangers of corporate greed. Another lies in the collapse of the market in hi-tech stocks, which suggests that the "bottom line" is not necessarily an accurate measure of corporate success and viability. Hopefully, the lesson will finally be learned from the worldwide collapse of the credit- and asset-backed paper markets in the fall of 2008.

The Canadian Democracy and Corporate Accountability Commission's 2002 report made a series of recommendations, including the following:

- The law should make it clear that social responsibility considerations may be taken into account by corporate management.

- The structure of corporate governance should be modified to include a corporate social responsibility committee of the board of directors.

- Large corporations should be required to publish a "social audit."

- The law should provide protection to employees against adverse action taken against them for "whistle-blowing."

- Canadian corporations should be required to adhere to a core set of human rights standards in their operations overseas.

- Business schools should develop mandatory courses focusing on corporate social responsibility.

Unfortunately, few of the above described recommendations were implemented. Many blame the continued primacy of the profit motive on the structure of executive compensation. Traditionally, executive compensation schemes link performance bonuses to the profitability of the company rather than long-term stability or corporate social responsibility. Bonuses are often in the form of stock options, whose value rise with the price of corporate shares. This structure reinforces "bottom-line" decision making with a view to short-term profit and may even encourage inflated financial reporting.

continued

28. *Toronto Star*, May 18, 2002, p. H6.

The US$700 billion Wall Street bailout, approved by Congress in October 2008, may forever change executive compensation. Some of the conditions attached to the bailout are limits on executive severance packages and clawbacks of bonuses. Yet, some critics argue that no bailout at all would be the best way to teach a lesson about greed.

QUESTIONS TO CONSIDER

1. Are these recommendations realistic? Can ethics be legislated?

2. Is there really a conflict between the long-term interests of a corporation and a requirement of social responsibility?

3. How should executive compensation be restructured to encourage socially responsible behaviour?

Sources: Canadian Democracy and Corporate Accountability Report, *The New Balance Sheet: Corporate Profits and Responsibility in the 21st Century,* January 2002; Brenda Bouw, "Preventing 'Bad Social Behavior': Curbing Wall Street CEO Pay Could Improve Canadian System, Rights Group Says," *The Chronicle Herald.ca,* September 27, 2008, http://thechronicleherald.ca/Bisomess/1081398.html; Stephen Gandel, "How Washington's Bailout Will Boost Wall Street Bonuses," *Time Magazine,* October 27, 2008, www.time.com/time/business/article/0,8599,1853846,00.html?imw=Y.

CIVIL LIABILITY OF CORPORATIONS

As already noted, corporations are exposed to *civil liability*—liability towards a plaintiff, typically to pay damages for harm done through committing a tort, breaking a contract, or breaching a statutory duty. In the early parts of this chapter and in Chapter 28, we focused on civil liability triggered by statute. Now we will complete this discussion by commenting on key issues in tort and contract.

Liability in Tort

A corporation acts through its human agents. Where a corporation is held liable in tort, it is almost invariably on account of a negligent or wrongful act committed by an employee, agent, or officer, and its liability is *vicarious.*[29] As with any defendant, liability depends on the plaintiff proving each element of the tort. It is possible that the corporation will be the only defendant liable if the elements of the tort are committed by separate employees. As noted in Chapter 2, class actions have levelled the playing field between business and the small stakeholder. Business can no longer ignore minor consequences of its actions.

Contractual Liability

Generally speaking, a corporation is liable for the contracts made by its agents in the ordinary course of business under the rules of agency (discussed in Chapter 19). Agents of a corporation acting within their actual or apparent authority[30] bind the corporation to contracts made with third parties.

---

29. Vicarious liability is discussed in Chapter 3. As noted there, it is possible for a corporate employer to have primary liability in tort, without the employee being personally liable: see *Edgeworth Construction Ltd.* v. *N.D. Lee & Associates* (1993), 107 D.L.R. (4th) 169.

30. Where a director or officer acts within the scope of her usual, or apparent, authority, even though she has no actual authority to do so, the corporation will be bound unless the third party knew (or ought to have known) of the lack of authority.

indoor management rule

the principle that a person dealing with a corporation is entitled to assume that its internal procedural rules have been complied with unless it is apparent that such is not the case

The by-laws and other internal corporate documents will describe agency powers and the proper process for contract ratification. Still, the courts have held contracts to be enforceable even when the proper rules were not followed. In the absence of notice of an irregularity or of suspicious circumstances, everything that appears normal may be relied upon by an outsider and the contract will bind the corporation.[31] This principle is known as the **indoor management rule**,[32] and is really just an application of the apparent authority principle in agency law. An innocent third party may rely upon the regularity of a corporate act, just as he may rely upon the apparent authority of an agent, if it is reasonable for him to do so in the circumstances.

ILLUSTRATION 29.2

W, the chief executive officer of *A* Ltd., negotiates a contract to buy equipment from *B* Inc. for $1 million. The by-laws of *A* Ltd. provide that any contract involving expenditure of more than $50 000 must be approved by the board of its Japanese parent company. That approval had not been obtained. Consequently, *W* was acting outside the scope of her actual authority. Can *B* Inc. enforce the contract?

The answer is "yes" unless *B* Inc. knew of the restriction in the by-laws and that the approval of the parent board had not been obtained.

As we saw in the preceding chapter, certain corporate documents must be filed in a government office and are available to the public for examination. At one time, the public was deemed to have notice of the contents of those documents whether they had read them or not. If the documents prohibited either the corporation or one of its officers from carrying out certain acts, a third party could not rely upon what otherwise might be the officer's apparent authority to perform those acts. That rule often led to substantial injustice and has now been abolished by statute. For example, section 17 of the Canada Business Corporations Act (CBCA) provides:

> No person is affected by or is deemed to have notice or knowledge of the content of a document concerning a corporation by reason only that the document has been filed by the Director or is available for inspection at an office of the corporation.

A contracting third party who actually has read or knows the contents of a restriction will be bound by it, but in saying this we are merely restating the common law rule of agency—a third party who knows of an express restriction between the principal and agent cannot claim to rely upon an apparent authority that ignores the restriction. For large or important contracts, one should not take the indoor management rule for granted. Third parties usually hire corporate lawyers to review the corporation's documents of record and ensure that all necessary authorizations have been obtained.

Pre-Incorporation Contracts

pre-incorporation contract

a purported contract made in the name of a corporation before it comes into existence

We noted in Chapter 19 that, at common law, a corporation could not ratify a **pre-incorporation contract**—that is, a contract made on its behalf before it came into existence. If a "contract" was made in the name of a corporation even one day before it came into existence, the purported contract is of no effect and a new contract would have to be negotiated once the corporation was formed. Further, the individual who purported to contract on behalf of the corporation normally could not be held to the contract either, since the intention was to contract with the corporation.[33]

The CBCA and the provincial statutes based on it have changed this, by providing that a person who enters into, or purports to enter into, a written contract in the name of or on behalf of a

---

31. *Royal British Bank* v. *Turquand* (1856), 119 E.R. 886.

32. This rule receives statutory recognition in the Canada Business Corporations Act (CBCA), R.S.C. 1985, c. C-44, s. 18. Subsequent references in this chapter are to the CBCA unless otherwise stated.

33. See *Delta Construction Co. Ltd.* v. *Lidstone.* (1979), 96 D.L.R. (3d) 457. The individual may be liable for breach of warranty of authority: this is discussed in Chapter 19. Contrast *Kelner* v. *Baxter* (1866), L.R.2 C.P. 174, where the court found that there was an intention that the individual contractor be bound.

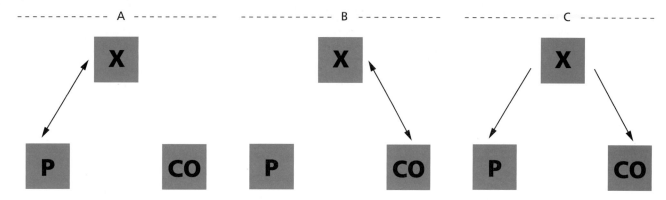

In situation **A**, the promoter, *P*, has entered into a contract with a third party, *X*, in the name of corporation *CO*, before it has come into existence. The effect is to create a contract between *P* and *X*. In situation **B**, the corporation has since been formed and has adopted the contract. There is now a contract between *CO* and *X*, and *P* is no longer a party to it. In situation **C**, the court has, on an application by *X*, apportioned liability, and both *P* and *CO* are liable.

FIGURE 29.1

Pre-Incorporation Contracts

corporation before it comes into existence is personally bound by the contract and is entitled to its benefits.[34] In addition, a corporation may, within a reasonable time after it comes into existence, adopt a written pre-incorporation contract. In that event, the corporation is bound by the contract and is entitled to its benefits, and the person who purported to act in the name of the corporation ceases to be liable.[35]

The clear intention is that, whether or not the contract is adopted, it will be enforceable by the other party. To prevent unfair manipulation by a corporation and a contractor, the Act (section 14(3)) gives the court power to apportion liability between the corporation and the contractor in any manner it thinks fit.

A promoter acting on behalf of a corporation before it comes into existence may avoid personal liability and waive any benefits under the contract when the contract includes an express term that the promoter will not be bound by the agreement.[36] Figure 29.1 illustrates some of the possible relationships involved in pre-incorporation contracts.

CRIMINAL LIABILITY OF CORPORATIONS

A corporation can be charged with, and convicted of, an offence under the Criminal Code in the same way as a natural person.[37] For example, in one of the leading Canadian cases on corporate criminal liability, a number of corporations were convicted of conspiracy in rigging bids for a construction contract.[38]

---

34. S. 14(1).

35. S. 14(2). There are some variations from province to province. For example, Ontario does not restrict the rule to written contracts. In the case of a corporation incorporated under the CBCA, it would seem that the effect of an oral pre-incorporation contract would be decided under the common law rules: see *Kettle* v. *Borris* (2000), 10 B.L.R. (3d) 122.

36. S. 14(4). To be effective, there must be an express exclusion of liability: see *Szecket* v. *Huang* (1999), 168 D.L.R. (4th) 402; *1394918 Ontario Ltd.* v. *1310210 Ontario Inc.* (2002), 57 O.R. (3d) 607.

37. There are some crimes that it would seem to be impossible for a corporation to commit, for example, bigamy. Corporations have been convicted of manslaughter in some common law jurisdictions.

38. *Canadian Dredge & Dock Co. Ltd.* v. *R.* (1985), 19 D.L.R. (4th) 314 (S.C.C.). The judgment of Estey, J. provides an excellent overview of the issue of corporate criminal liability.

The Nature of Corporate Criminal Liability

How Can Corporations Commit Crimes?

The characteristics of corporations present special problems for criminal liability:

(a) As we have seen, most criminal offences require the prosecution to prove both that the accused actually committed the act and that there was some level of intent—but a corporation has neither a physical body with which to carry out the offence nor a "mind" of its own capable of forming an intent.

(b) If convicted, a guilty person's punishment is often imprisonment—but a corporation cannot be imprisoned.

The consequences of (b) merely limit sanctions against a corporation to fining it or ordering it to refrain from certain conduct, or, in some cases, to dissolving the corporation—a relatively painless form of punishment. The prosecution may also lay charges personally against directors and senior officers of a corporation, a topic considered later.

With regard to (a), the courts did not find it easy to apply the principles of criminal law to corporations. Regulatory offences, which are most often strict or absolute liability, are much more popular vehicles to address corporate conduct. However, the public interest demands that serious corporate misconduct attract criminal consequences, and so the courts and legislature (through the Criminal Code) have created rules that attribute individual acts and intent to the corporation.

The "Directing Mind" Principle

The earliest test used to establish corporate criminal liability was the "directing mind" principle. It held that corporate *mens rea* existed if a guilty mind could be found in an "active director" or the "directing mind or will" at the "the centre of the personality of the corporation."[39] This meant a person with policy-making authority rather than just supervisory or implementation responsibilities.

What if the wrongful act is committed not by a senior officer or director, but by a person lower down in the hierarchy? Canadian courts have generally tended to find an act committed by an employee who has significant responsibilities, such as the head of an important department or a branch, to be an act of the corporation itself. But the courts would not hold the act of a low-level employee, for example, a clerk who cheated a customer, to be the act of the corporation. However, drawing the line between those employees and officers whose acts will be identified as acts of the corporate employer and those whose acts will not be so identified is not an easy task.

CASE 29.1

A corporation was charged with fraud, contrary to section 338 of the Criminal Code, as a result of the activities of the manager of its used-car sales division in turning back odometers. Although the corporation had issued written instructions that such practices should not occur, the corporation was convicted. The manager had sole responsibility for managing the division and, in that respect, was "the directing will" of the corporation: his acts were those of the corporation.[40]

---

39. *Lennard's Carrying Co. Ltd.* v. *Asiatic Petroleum Co. Ltd.*, [1915] A.C. 705: a ship owner was sued for damages under a statute that stated an owner would not be liable for harm caused by his vessel "without his actual fault." Speaking for the House of Lords, Viscount Haldane found that Mr. Lennard was "the active director" of the corporation, and that it was "impossible . . . to contend . . . that he did not know or can excuse himself for not having known" that the ship was unseaworthy. He went on to call the director "the active spirit," the "directing mind and will," and "the centre of the personality of the corporation." While this was a civil case and not a criminal prosecution, it was seen as opening the door for courts to find the actions of senior officers and directors of corporations to be those of the corporation itself both with regard to the actual committing of the acts and the required guilty or negligent mind.

40. *R.* v. *Waterloo Mercury Sales Ltd.* (1974), 49 D.L.R. (3d) 131.

By contrast, it has been held that a truck driver employee of a waste disposal corporation was not a "directing mind" of the corporation, and his conduct did not make the corporation liable for an offence that required *mens rea.*[41]

The Criminal Code: The New Test

Recent amendments to the Criminal Code have clarified the situation and increased corporate exposure to criminal liability.[42] The important changes are:

- First, the physical act and mental intent of any offence are no longer required to be found in the same person. Now, corporate criminal liability can be established in multiple employees with different responsibilities.
- Second, the physical act may be committed by virtually any employee or contractor or an aggregate of them.
- Third, corporate *mens rea* may be found not only in those with policy-making authority but also in those **senior officers** with operational responsibilities.[43]

The type of intent required by the offence will determine the rule:

(1) In the case of an offence that requires the prosecution to prove negligence (e.g., criminal negligence causing death), an organization is a party to the offence if (a) one of its representatives, acting within the scope of his authority, is a party to the offence, and (b) the senior officer responsible for that aspect of the organization's activities departs markedly from the standard of care that could reasonably be expected to prevent the representative from being a party to the offence;

(2) In the case of an offence that requires the prosecution to prove intent (other than negligence), an organization is a party to the offence if one of its senior officers (a) acting within the scope of her authority, and with the intent, at least in part, to benefit the organization, is a party to the offence, or (b) with the required intent directs the work of other representatives of the organization so that they commit the specified act or omission, or (c), knowing that a representative of the organization is about to be a party to the offence, does not take all reasonable measures to stop them.

senior officer
a representative who plays an important role in establishing an organization's policies or is responsible for managing an important aspect of its activities, including the directors, the CEO, and the CFO of a corporation

Criminal Code Offences

As already noted, an organization may be charged with any offence, but the Criminal Code contains some offences that are particularly applicable to corporate conduct:

- fraud (section 380) and fraud affecting the public markets (section 380(2))
- market manipulation—false market activity or manipulating share prices (section 382)
- distributing false prospectuses, statements, or accounts (section 400)
- criminal negligence causing bodily harm—any duty imposed by common law or statute may form the basis of this offence (section 219). Section 217.1 specifically imposes a duty on those who direct (or supervise) work to protect workers and the public
- whistle-blower retaliation—includes threatening, disciplining, demoting, or firing a whistle-blower or potential whistle-blower (section 425.1)

---

41. *R. v. Safety-Kleen Canada Inc.* (1997), 145 D.L.R. (4th) 276. The corporation was found guilty of another strict liability, regulatory offence.
42. Criminal Code, R.S.C.1985, c. C-46, ss. 22.1, 22.2. A broader range of organizations are now exposed to criminal liability including partnerships, trade unions. and municipalities (s. 2).
43. *Ibid.*, s. 2 (as amended).

Sentencing

Criminal sentences should denounce the conduct, protect the public, deter the offender and others, repair the harm done, rehabilitate the offender, encourage assumption of responsibility by the offender, and promote public confidence (section 718). Sentencing a corporation is a challenge: it cannot be imprisoned, and a fine is a punishment ultimately borne by the shareholders. The Criminal Code addresses corporate penalties in the following ways:

- criminal fines cannot be deducted as a cost of doing business
- specific aggravating and mitigating factors for organizations include degree of planning, public costs, depletion of corporate assets, other regulatory offences, and convictions of corporate representatives (section 718.21)
- probation for corporations may involve the development of policies and procedures and supervision of management by a court-appointed compliance officer (section 732.1)

CRIMINAL LIABILITY OF DIRECTORS AND OFFICERS

As we noted in Chapter 27, the principle of limited liability does not protect directors from liability for torts or breaches of fiduciary duty that they personally commit. In principle, directors, like employees, are liable for their own torts that are committed in the course of performing their duties, even though the corporation may also be vicariously liable.[44]

The question we address here is whether directors (and officers) should be held criminally liable for offences committed by their corporation while under their supervision.

One view is that simply holding corporations liable is not in itself a strong enough deterrent to ensure effective enforcement of regulatory schemes. A large corporation with sufficient assets might consider the penalty merely a "licence"; it pays the fine and carries on with its activities. The corporation's manager may pass the costs on to the consumer through higher prices or to the corporation's shareholders through lower dividends. At the other extreme, a corporation may be merely a "shell" with virtually no assets to pay its fine; those who control the enterprise walk away from it and start up a similar activity using a new corporation.

A strong argument can be made that effective deterrence requires that, as well as the corporation, the individuals responsible for the offence be punished directly. Directors and senior officers should be personally liable for offences committed by their corporation. As has been said, ". . . the threat of jail sends a clear message to corporate executives that they are not immune to criminal sanctions. . . . Incarceration is one cost of business that you can't pass to the consumer."[45]

However, there are problems in attempting to prosecute individuals. In complex organizations, where responsibility is shared among a number of persons, it is often difficult to identify with any certainty who is responsible and who can—and should—be convicted of committing an offence. These two factors—a belief that directors and officers and not just corporations should be made liable and that it may be difficult to obtain convictions—have led legislatures

- to enact express provisions making senior officers and directors liable,
- to require CEO's and CFO's to certify annual filings, and
- to make the grounds for individual liability much broader.

---

44. The fact that they are acting in the corporation's interest does not by itself protect them from personal liability; see *ADGA Systems International Ltd.* v. *Valcom Ltd.* (1999), 43 O.R. (3d) 101; *Lana International Ltd.* v. *Menasco Aerospace Ltd.* (2000), 190 D.L.R. (4th) 534. For a comprehensive analysis, see Flannigan, "The Personal Tort Liability of Directors" (2002), 81 Can. Bar Rev. 247.

45. See Nelson Smith, "No Longer Just a Cost of Doing Business . . ." (1992), 53 *La. L. Rev.* 119 at 126.

LIABILITY FOR ENVIRONMENTAL OFFENCES

Liability for environmental offences provides a good illustration of the wider general issue of corporate and director liability, as well as being a question of major practical concern to corporations and their officers. Environmental protection involves air, water, and land pollution; preservation of natural resources; acceptable use, transportation and disposal of waste, toxins and dangerous goods; and assessment of the environmental impact of any activity. These topics are regulated by municipal, provincial, and federal governments. The Canadian Environmental Protection Act, 1999, as well as most of the corresponding provincial statutes, create strict liability offences for corporations and their directors and officers when the Act or its regulations are breached. For these offences, establishing due diligence is the only defence.[46] It is beyond the scope of this chapter to review the voluminous federal and provincial legislation[47] on this topic; instead, we will discuss basic principles common to many environmental offences.

What Standard of Skill and Care Must Be Met?

The challenge for the accused is to meet what is generally acknowledged to be a steadily rising standard of care. The enterprise must demonstrate that it has an effective system to prevent offences, must monitor the results of the system, and must improve the system if problems occur. A corporation cannot escape liability simply by delegating responsibility to an employee. Any employee's actions may be treated as those of the corporation itself. If not, the corporation will have failed to put in place an effective system of control.

Each enterprise whose activities may pose a risk must show that it reviews its current monitoring system frequently and makes reasonable efforts to keep up-to-date on technological change in the field.

The Expertise Required of Directors and Senior Officers

Another aspect of the problem relates to the expertise of directors and senior officers. Are they held to higher standards of care and skill if they have expertise in the area where a hazardous activity is carried on? Suppose a senior officer is an engineer with long experience in the field. Would she be expected to take precautions against a risk that an accountant would unlikely be aware of? A common-sense view would say "yes," and there is some support for it in a 1983 case, *R. v. Placer Developments Ltd.*,[48] where the accused corporation allowed diesel fuel to escape into fishing waters. The court seemed to expect greater diligence from the corporation's experienced senior officers:

> The accused was required to possess, and did possess sufficient expertise to be aware of the potential risk to the environment posed by a fuel system in northern mining camps. . . . [T]he accused had the opportunity and knowledge in the field, through their employees Mr. Morganti with thirty two months' field experience and Mr. Goddard with twenty five years' experience, to influence the offending conduct on the site.[49]

---

46. See, for example: *R. v. MacMillan Bloedel Ltd.* (2002), 220 D.L.R. (4th) 173.

47. Examples: Federal Legislation: Canadian Environmental Protection Act, 1999 (CEPA 1999) and the Canadian Environmental Assessment Act (CEAA); British Columbia: Environmental Management Act, 2003, Environmental Assessment Act, 2002, Waste Management Act, 1996, Water Act, 1996; Alberta: Environmental Protection and Enhancement Act, 2000, Natural Resources Conservation Board Act, 2000, Climate Change and Emissions Management Act, 2003, Water Act, 2000; Ontario: The Environmental Protection Act, 1990, The Environmental Bill of Rights, 1993, The Environmental Assessment Act, 1990, The Waste Diversion Act, 2002, The Ontario Water Resources Act, 1990.

48. (1983), 13 C.E.L.R. 42 (Y.T. Terr. Ct.).

49. *Ibid.*, at 49.

On the other hand, the court suggested that even if the accused firm did not possess that expertise, it would still be liable for the offence:

> The greater the likelihood of harm, the higher the duty of care. . . . Anyone choosing to become involved in activities posing danger to the public or to the environment assumes an obligation to take whatever measures may be necessary to prevent harm. . . . Unless equipped with appropriate professional skills, no one ought to undertake any activity involving a danger to the public. . . . Mining in the north requires not only an expert knowledge of mining, but equally important, an expert appreciation of the special problems caused by remote operations in northern environments.[50]

These observations suggest that the accused corporation was caught in one of two ways. Either it failed to employ the expertise it ought to have known that it needed in order to manage the hazardous activity, or if it did employ the necessary expertise, then the person with that expertise failed to use the professional care and skill attributed to him. Perhaps an unskilled employee who had been sent to the site would not be found personally liable because he could not have been expected to anticipate the risk, but the employer enterprise would then be caught by its failure to send an employee with the necessary skills to carry out the task.

Who Should Be Found Liable?

Those in Charge of an Activity

We have already noted that, apart from the liability of an enterprise itself, any person who actually commits an offence is personally liable, even when he was acting within the scope of his authorized activities. The issues become more difficult when legislatures enact regulations to make senior officers and directors liable because they are considered to be in charge of an activity, even though they have not participated directly in the offence. The task is to find appropriate language, sufficient to capture those who should bear the blame and yet absolve those who were innocent. With this purpose in mind, our legislatures have tended to use two phrases: the first makes liable those who "cause or permit" a hazardous substance to be discharged;[51] the second makes liable "any officer, director or agent . . . who directed, authorized, assented to, acquiesced in, or participated in the commission of an offence."[52]

So, who are these persons? In order to "permit" or "acquiesce in" an activity such as disposing of hazardous materials, one must have a significant role in controlling those who actually carry it out. Permitting or acquiescing has no meaning if the person charged is merely one who learned about the activity but could do nothing to affect it. Accordingly, the prosecution must first persuade a court that a person charged had effective powers and responsibility. A senior officer and director who is personally in charge of a hazardous procedure (that is, she is the person to whom those performing the activity report on a regular basis) presents a clear case of effective control and responsibility for the activity.

The Difficulty of Determining Responsibility

What about an independent or "outside" director—a person who was elected to the board because of his experience in financial services and who faithfully attends board meetings twice a year? He reads all the material sent to him and asks probing and useful questions at meetings. However, when it comes to environmental concerns, he relies on the reports and assurances given by the senior officer, the "inside" director, who is in charge. Should the independent director also be considered to share in control? Did he "permit" or "acquiesce in" an offence that occurred under the supervision of the inside director?

Since the law is not intended to punish innocent and reasonably diligent people, it would seem that ordinarily an independent director in those circumstances ought not to be held personally

---

50. (1983), 13 C.E.L.R. 42 (Y.T. Terr. Ct.), at 52.

51. See, for example: Fisheries Act, R.S.C. 1985, c. F-14, s. 36(3).

52. Canadian Environmental Protection Act, S.C. 1999, c. 33, s. 280.

liable for the offence. This view seems to be confirmed by the current case law: virtually all the charges brought under Canadian legislation have been against inside directors. However, in many situations there is not a clear-cut division between insider and outsider: for instance, did the outsider receive any reports that disclosed questionable practices to a reasonable person in his position? Were answers to his questions evasive? What should an outsider do when he feels uneasy with the information provided?

We should also note that not all insiders are in control of an operation, or directly involved in it, simply because they are directors and senior officers within the enterprise. Should an inside director who learns secondhand about a potential problem in another branch of the enterprise be expected to undertake a personal investigation, outside her normal responsibilities? These questions remain very difficult and depend upon the degree of involvement of the specific director in the particular circumstances of each case.

CASE 29.2

A corporation's premises contained a large, toxic, chemical waste storage site with many decaying, rusting, and uncovered containers; soil samples revealed concentrations of various dangerous chemicals. The prosecution charged the corporation with permitting the discharge of liquid industrial waste that could impair the quality of the groundwater and contaminate the environment. Charges were also laid against three directors.

All the defendants argued that they had shown due diligence in carrying out their duties. Ormston, J. found that the corporation—Bata Industries—did not establish a proper system to prevent the escape of toxic substances and did not take reasonable steps to ensure the effective operation of even their faulty system. The corporation was found guilty.[53]

With respect to the directors, the court provided a useful summary of the questions that should be asked in assessing a director's defence of having shown "due diligence" in his particular circumstances:

(a) Did the board of directors establish a pollution-prevention "system"—that is, was there supervision or inspection?
(b) Did each director ensure that the corporate officers had been instructed to set up a system sufficient within the terms and practices of the industry of ensuring compliance with environmental laws, to ensure that the officers report back periodically to the board?
(c) The directors are responsible for reviewing the environmental compliance reports provided by the officers, but are justified in placing reasonable reliance on reports.
(d) The directors should substantiate that the officers are promptly addressing environmental concerns brought to their attention by government agencies or other concerned parties including shareholders.

(e) The directors should be aware of the standards of their industry and other industries that deal with similar environmental pollutants or risks.
(f) The directors should immediately and personally react when they have notice that the system has failed.

Of the directors, Mr. Bata was found to be "the director with the least personal contact with the plant" where the offence occurred. His responsibilities were at other plants and "he attended on-site . . . once or twice a year to review the operation and performance goals. . . . " Although Mr. Bata did not personally review the operation when he was on site,

> He responded to the matters brought to his attention promptly and appropriately. He had placed an experienced director on site and was entitled in the circumstances to assume that . . . [the on-site director] was addressing the environmental concerns. . . . He was entitled to rely upon his system . . . unless he became aware the system was defective.[54]

Accordingly, Mr. Bata was acquitted.

In contrast, another director, Mr. Marchant, was found to have more responsibility than Mr. Bata but less than a third director who was held to be "on site." Mr. Marchant came to the facility once a month and toured the plant. The court found that the problem was brought to his "personal attention" and that

> . . . he had personal knowledge. There is no evidence that he took any steps after having knowledge to view the site and assess the problem. . . . [D]ue diligence requires him to exercise a degree of supervision and control that demonstrate that he was exhorting those whom he may be normally expected to influence or control to an accepted standard of behaviour.

Mr. Marchant was found guilty.

---

53. *R. v. Bata Industries Ltd.* (1992), 9 O.R. (3d) 329 at 362.
54. *Ibid.*, at 364.

What Should the Punishment Be?

A further question is: what punishment should a court impose? Generally, corporations are fined according to the seriousness of the breach and the harm caused. Directors and officers receive somewhat smaller fines, but in extreme cases, they may be sentenced to prison terms.[55]

CASE 29.3

A corporation, Varnicolor Chemical Ltd., reprocessed and disposed of industrial wastes. Waste materials escaped from its toxic disposal site into the groundwater, and moved towards a river that was used as a source of drinking water for downriver communities. The corporation took no action to clean up the spill; rather, it was the Ministry of the Environment that did so at an estimated cost of $2.5 million. Both the corporation and one of its directors, Mr. Argenton, were charged with offences.[56]

Mr. Argenton was "the only officer and director to take an active part in the operations and actual management of . . . [Varnicolor]. He was clearly, at all relevant times, the sole directing mind of the company. . . ." Accordingly, his actions were the actions of the corporation. Mr. Argenton pleaded guilty. Charges against the corporation were stayed. The court discussed in detail the criteria for sentencing Mr. Argenton. It described the purposes of sentencing as protecting the public, deterring and rehabilitating offenders, promoting compliance with the law, and expressing public disapproval.

It summarized the factors that should affect the severity of a sentence as follows:

- *The nature of the environment affected:* The concern is both with the sensitivity of the environment affected and the gravity of the risk. In this case, the drinking water of residents in the area would be contaminated.

- *The extent of the damage actually inflicted:* Here, there was a high cost of cleanup.

- *The deliberateness of the offence:* In considering this factor, the court stated:

Not only was Mr. Argenton involved on site in the operations of the company, but he was as well involved in the negotiations which preceded the issuance of the certificate of approval by the Ministry . . . for the Varnicolor site. . . . Therefore, as a result of this active involvement and in depth knowledge of the business operations, it is clear that Mr. Argenton was uniquely in a position to be aware . . . of . . . the requirements of the Ministry. Mr. Argenton has indicated that he found these requirements to be unclear and ambiguous; however, it was at all times open to . . . [him] to seek clarification. . . . There is no indication . . . that he made any attempts to do so. In a number of respects, Mr. Argenton acted in defiance of the requirements. . . . Such violations are in effect a breach of trust on the part of the person to whom such a certificate has been granted and, as such, jail terms are an appropriate penalty to ensure compliance with the law by both the person being sentenced and society in general.

- *The attitude of the defendant:* In this case, Mr. Argenton did not voluntarily report the escape of toxic waste, nor did he show a co-operative attitude.

- *Attempts to comply with the regulations:* There was no evidence of a cleanup at the site by Varnicolor or by Mr. Argenton, and indeed, the corporation had become inactive.

The maximum sentence under the Environmental Protection Act was 12 months. The court found that the conduct of the defendant amounted to a serious breach of the Act and sentenced him to 8 months in jail.

The Business Consequences

What conclusions can we draw from these developments, and how will they affect the conduct of business? Clearly, there is a public consensus that protecting the environment is a high priority, in response to which legislatures have created extensive regulatory schemes. Meeting the standards under these schemes imposes substantial costs on many businesses, especially on resource industries

---

55. For a case in which both a fine ($76 000) and a jail sentence (30 days) were imposed, see *R. v. Romaniuk* (1993), 112 Sask. R. 129 (Q.B.).

56. *R. v. Varnicolor Chemical Ltd.* [1992] O.J. No. 1978.

and manufacturing and transportation enterprises. The most important challenge is to meet the requirements effectively and efficiently.

How may this be done? First, businesses need to review their practices to learn whether any of their activities create a concern about health, safety, or the breach of regulations. They must seek the best advice available and keep up-to-date with current technology. They are expected to take every reasonable precaution to meet the latest standards.

Second, once they are informed about the risks, they should review their insurance coverage with a view to obtaining the maximum risk protection that is available and affordable. The cost of insurance coverage leads to the third stage. If after obtaining the best advice for implementing safety systems and obtaining insurance a particular business activity ceases to be competitive, then it becomes necessary to decide whether to continue that branch of operations.

INTERNATIONAL ISSUE

International Environmental Regulation

Environmental protection is a global problem because we share the environment with the rest of the world and pollutants move invisibly across national boundaries. Unfortunately, standards vary by jurisdiction, but there are a number of strategies being employed to establish universal standards of environmental protection. The Canadian Environmental Protection Act, 1999, attempts to extend its reach beyond Canadian borders by addressing international air and water pollution (Part 7 Division 6). The Minister is empowered to regulate polluters and collect clean-up costs. Section 166(4) recognizes the jurisdictional limits of this power:

> If the air pollution referred to in paragraph (1)(a) is in a country where Canada does not have substantially the same rights with respect to the prevention, control or correction of air pollution as that country has under this Division, the Minister shall decide whether to act under subsections (2) and (3) or to take no action at all.

Governments try to create uniform standards around the world by entering into conventions and treaties, such as the Kyoto Protocol. The Kyoto Protocol (an amendment to the United Nations Framework Convention on Climate Change, ratified by Canada in 2002) requires greenhouse gas emissions to by reduced by 6 by (from 1990 levels) by 2012. In May 2006, the Environment Minister announced that Canada would not meet the Kyoto target. The United States is a signatory of Kyoto but never ratified it.

The International Organization for Standardization, a non-governmental organization, has also created an environmental standards program. It established a voluntary certification standard for environmental management systems (ISO 1400). Participating organizations complete environmental audits of their business processes and design customized systems for effective environmental management.

The United Nations Global Compact designates 10 guiding principles of corporate social responsibility, 3 of which relate to environmental issues:

- to encourage the development of environmentally friendly technologies
- to support the precautionary principle (prove activity does no harm)
- to promote greater environmental responsibility

Organizations voluntarily agree to comply with the principles and publicly report their progress. Canadian participants in the Global Compact include Bell Canada Enterprises, Enbridge, Hydro Quebec, Talisman Energy Inc., and Petro Canada.

continued

QUESTIONS FOR REVIEW

1. What is meant by the "indoor management rule"?

2. Is a person dealing with a corporation expected to know the contents of the corporation's articles of incorporation? Or its by-laws?

3. Can a corporation adopt a pre-incorporation contract? What is the effect of its purporting to do so?

4. Is a corporation required to have any minimum amount of capital?

5. Are there any restrictions on a corporation paying dividends to its shareholders?

6. Why are there restrictions against a corporation returning capital to its shareholders?

7. What are the principal objectives of securities legislation?

8. What is a prospectus?

9. What liability is triggered by a false or misleading prospectus?

10. What is the difference between strict liability and absolute liability?

11. Can a corporation be convicted of a criminal offence? How?

12. Does the principle of limited liability protect a director from criminal liability in the course of performing her duties?

13. Should directors be held personally liable for environmental offences committed by their corporation?

14. What standard of care and skill is expected of corporate directors in relation to environmental offences?

15. Who may perform an audit for a public corporation?

CASES AND PROBLEMS

1. About a year ago, MacIntosh, a qualified accountant with substantial business experience, met Kellerman, the owner of a number of business ventures. Kellerman persuaded MacIntosh that her experience would be valuable to him in his own business activities, which he was seeking to expand. He persuaded MacIntosh to invest a substantial proportion of her savings in his ventures, in return for which it was agreed that she would become a shareholder and director of Kellerman's corporation, "AJP Enterprises Inc." In the course of their discussions, MacIntosh was shown books of account and other records that appeared to relate to AJP Enterprises.

   MacIntosh transferred $50 000 into a bank account in the name of AJP Enterprises Inc. In return, Kellerman gave her a document assigning to her one-half of his shares in that corporation.

Soon afterwards, MacIntosh negotiated an arrangement with an advertising agency, Occidental Broadcasts Ltd., to provide radio and television advertising for the AJP business in return for monthly payments of $2000. Occidental was paid (out of the AJP Enterprises bank account) for the first three months, but has not been paid since then, although the company continued to provide advertising services for a further five months.

When Occidental eventually demanded payment of a further $10 000, MacIntosh discovered that

(a) the AJP Enterprises bank account contained only $1.73

(b) Kellerman had disappeared

(c) there was no record of any corporation by the name of "AJP Enterprises Inc.," or any similar name, having been incorporated in any jurisdiction in Canada

Can MacIntosh be held personally liable for the $10 000 claimed by Occidental?

2. Rainbow Sails Ltd. is a corporation incorporated under the CBCA. It has three shareholders, Brown, Green, and White, who are also the directors of the corporation. White acts as CEO, though he has never been formally appointed to that position.

The articles of the corporation contain (*inter alia*) the following provisions:

■ The business of the corporation is restricted to the manufacture, buying, and selling of sailboats, and under no circumstances is the corporation to engage in the manufacture, buying, or selling of mechanically powered boats or other craft.

■ Any contract or proposed contract involving an expenditure in excess of $5000 must be approved unanimously by the Board of Directors.

Some months ago, White sold on behalf of Rainbow a new sailboat that they had manufactured to a customer, Mermaid Marinas Inc. White agreed to accept from Mermaid a small motor boat in part exchange. Although White had no difficulty reselling the motor boat, Brown and Green were angry when they learned of the transaction since they both had an aversion to power boats. They warned White not to enter into any other similar transactions; otherwise, they would deprive him of his powers as CEO.

Some weeks later, Mermaid's sales manager asked White if Rainbow would be interested in buying a floatplane that Mermaid no longer had much use for. White thought the plane was an excellent bargain and agreed to pay $15 000 for it. White took delivery of the plane, and the next day he crashed it.

Brown and Green refuse to countersign any cheque to Mermaid, and Mermaid is now threatening to sue for the price of the plane.

Is Rainbow liable to pay for the plane? If so, does Rainbow have any right of action against White personally?

3. Queensville Quality Cars Ltd. is a large automobile dealership specializing in the sale of both new and used cars and light trucks. Until recently its used-car division was managed by Murphy, who was in charge of a dozen salespersons and mechanics. Murphy was not a director of the corporation.

Following several complaints from customers, alleging, among other things, that the odometers on used cars appeared to have been altered, the managing director of the corporation, Patel, sent written instructions to all division heads (including Murphy) warning them that tampering with odometers is a serious offence and that any officer or employee of the corporation found doing so would face instant dismissal.

Notwithstanding the warning, Murphy instructed one of his mechanics, Ferreira, to change the odometer on a car that the corporation had recently obtained as a trade-in. Ferreira did so, the car was resold, and the purchaser subsequently complained about the condition of the car.

When questioned, Ferreira admitted to having changed the odometer and was dismissed. At about the same time, Murphy disappeared, taking with him a substantial amount of cash belonging to the corporation. Patel reported both the theft and the tampering with odometers to the police.

Queensville Quality Cars Ltd. has now been charged with an offence under the Criminal Code in respect of altering an odometer. Should the company be convicted?

4. Gigantic Forestry Inc., one of Canada's largest pulp and paper enterprises with 12 mills in various locations across the country, operates a pulp mill on the Grizzly River in British Columbia. It has a government permit to discharge up to 18 200 kg of suspended solids per day into the river. The main suspended solids consist of a lime mud, ash, wood bark, clay, sand, and pulp fibre. Gigantic was charged with exceeding the permitted levels of discharge and pleaded guilty. There had been a previous conviction 18 months earlier, with a fine of $50 000 against the corporation. Two directors, described below, were also charged.

On February 27, Gigantic discharged suspended solids at a level significantly in excess of its permit. The spill resulted from a mechanical failure causing an overflow of lime mud from the storage tank into an emergency spill pond. The pond, being near to capacity when the emergency occurred, overflowed to the river. The suspended solid emission was 35 483 kg per day, almost double the permitted level.

Aggravating factors are as follows: (1) Prior to the spill, Gigantic had prepared a "response manual" to deal with spills but with no specific guidelines in place to deal with this type of event. Since then, guidelines have been created, including reduction of production in relevant areas and, if machinery cannot be repaired, shutting down production completely. (2) The emergency spill pond had not been cleaned for five or six days. (3) The high-level alarm in the storage tank was not working that evening.

On the day of the spill, during the day shift, it was noted that the mud filter drive tripped out three times. The night shift supervisor checked the filter at approximately 19:45 hours that day, just after the start of his shift. The filter drive was not working. Millwrights were called, and they set to work to repair the mud filter drive at 20:30 hours, and by 04:25 hours the next day, February 28, mud was again being pumped from the storage tank to the mud filter.

Initially during the shutdown of the mud system, mud continued to flow from the mud washer to the storage tank. The shift supervisor instituted procedures to minimize the flow of mud from the mud washer to the storage tank. He had noted a large amount of clear liquid in the pond when he came on shift.

The shift supervisor then made certain that everything was done to minimize the overflow of the storage tank to the pond. The shift supervisor's judgment that mud was not escaping from the pond to the sewer was unfortunately incorrect. To the recollection of the plant people interviewed following this incident, this was the first time the pond had overflowed to the sewer.

Blinkov is a director and president of Gigantic. He resides in Vancouver where the corporation has its head office and visits the Grizzly River site several times a year, but spends most of his workdays in Vancouver or visiting the other 11 mills. His assistant, Crowe, is in charge of environment control systems at all 12 mills and regularly prepares detailed reports on each plant for Blinkov to review. Charbonneau is a director and manager of the Grizzly River mill. She lives in a nearby town and spends most of each day at the mill. The supervisors report to her at least once each month and are instructed to report any problems immediately. She had not personally examined the storage tank or emergency spill pond for several months before the spill. At 22:00 hours the day of the spill, the night shift supervisor telephoned Charbonneau and told her of the problem. She said she would examine the situation the following morning.

The court fined Gigantic $200 000. Should either or both directors, Blinkov and Charbonneau, be found guilty? If so, suggest a penalty.

ADDITIONAL RESOURCES FOR CHAPTER 29 ON THE COMPANION WEBSITE *(www.pearsoned.ca/smyth)*

In addition to self-test multiple-choice, true–false, and short essay questions (all with immediate feedback), application exercises, and links to useful web destinations, the Companion Website provides the following resources for Chapter 28:

- **British Columbia:** British Columbia Environmental Legislation; Liability of Management
- **Alberta:** Environmental Legislation; Securities Commission
- **Manitoba/Saskatchewan:** Business Practices Act; Environmental Liability; Personal Liabilities of Directors and Officers; Securities Commission
- **Ontario:** Directors' Liability, Environmental Protection; Legislation Imposing Directors' Liability; Prospectus; Secondary Market Liability

Creditors and Debtors

Modern businesses rarely operate without "credit." Credit may be long-term, as when a corporation raises part of its capital by issuing bonds or debentures, or it may be short-term, as when a business purchases supplies to be paid for within 30 days.

A reputable business generally has little difficulty obtaining credit to manage its normal day-to-day needs. For purchases of more substantial items, a lender may require "security" in addition to the borrower's contractual promise to pay. The creditor may require collateral security in the form of a mortgage of the borrower's land, as discussed in Chapter 25. More often, a buyer will give collateral in the form of a security interest in other types of property—the items purchased from the creditor, other chattels, or stocks and bonds.

In Chapter 30 we discuss the different methods of securing credit. Most provinces have comprehensive legislation called Personal Property Security Acts, regulating various kinds of credit arrangements. In addition, special rules apply to certain types of bank loans under the federal Bank Act. The relationships and conflicts that may arise among these different types of security form one of the issues we consider in that chapter.

Some businesses inevitably fail, become insolvent, and are unable to meet the claims of all their creditors. In Chapter 31 we consider the rights of creditors when a business becomes bankrupt—an area under federal legislation—and we also examine the protection given to creditors by provincial legislation, in particular, by statutes dealing with builders' liens.

30

Secured Transactions

Almost all businesses operate on credit to some extent. Most businesses have debts, and most have accounts receivable. As we shall see in this chapter, an important distinction is drawn—in law and in business practice—between secured and unsecured credit. In this chapter we describe the various legal devices for securing credit and examine such questions as:

- What is meant by "security"?

- What is the nature of a conditional sale?

- What is a chattel mortgage, and how does it differ from a conditional sale?

- How are consignments and leases used as security devices?

- What is a floating charge?

- How do the Personal Property Security Acts operate to protect secured creditors?

- How are secured creditors' rights enforced?

- How do secured interests affect the rights of third parties?

- What additional protection is given to banks as secured creditors?

THE MEANING OF "SECURITY"

Types of Security Interest

The best security for a debt is the good credit rating and strong earning power of the debtor. But over and above a debtor's willingness and ability to pay back the debt, various legal devices give a creditor additional assurance that debts owing will be repaid. Most of these devices are agreed to in advance as terms in the contract by which they are created. They are often called *consensual security interests* and typically give a creditor **collateral security**—that is, a right to take possession of and to sell specified assets of the debtor in satisfaction of the debt. Security agreements can be very broad, and modern legislation makes it theoretically possible to cover virtually all existing and future property owned by a debtor.

There are also security interests that arise as a normal consequence of a transaction, not because the parties to a credit transaction have bargained for them, but because of rules of the common law or express statutory provisions. They may be described as *non-consensual security interests*. We have examined examples of such interests as rights of lien and resale available to unpaid sellers of goods and repair services in earlier chapters[1] and will examine other interests in the next chapter. In this chapter our main concern is with consensual security interests.

Security Practices

Suppliers generally do not require collateral security when extending credit to trade customers. Unsecured transactions are simpler and cheaper to record, their risk is relatively small because trade credit is usually short-term, and competition may make it unwise for a supplier to offend customers by demanding security. If a supplier loses only a small proportion of its sales revenue by defaults in payment, it may well be better off accepting the loss than incurring added administrative costs and perhaps losing sales by requiring security for each sale and then having to take possession of and sell the secured assets if default occurs.

Collateral security is not a good substitute for a sound debtor. However, security reduces risk and is often required in large transactions and in consumer sales. In particular, it establishes a creditor's *priority* relative to other creditors in the event of a debtor's bankruptcy.

In consumer transactions, security devices operate primarily as a form of incentive to pay the money owing and avoid repossession of the article purchased. The right of repossession is most likely to be used for expensive durable goods. Even then, the resale value will often be less than the amount owing. It is common for goods in the hands of a defaulting debtor to deteriorate considerably before repossession.

Rights of a Secured Creditor

An **unsecured creditor**—that is, a general creditor with no security interest in any of the debtor's assets—may ultimately acquire an interest like a security interest through a court action to collect an overdue debt. When a creditor obtains judgment for the amount of the debt and the debtor fails to pay, the creditor can then obtain an execution order authorizing the seizure and sale of certain of the debtor's assets.[2] By contrast, a **secured creditor** does not need a judgment or an execution order, but can proceed on its own to enforce its rights over the security. In this sense, a security interest provides a creditor with a self-help remedy. More important, as we shall see, an unsecured judgment creditor generally has no right to seize any assets already subject to a security interest of another creditor. The secured creditor has **priority**.

collateral security
an interest in property of a debtor that gives a creditor the right to seize and sell it in the event of non-payment of the debt

unsecured creditor
a creditor who has no security interest in any of the debtor's property

secured creditor
a creditor who has a security interest in the property of the debtor

priority
a first, or prior, right to be repaid out of the debtor's asset

---

1. See Chapter 16 for an explanation of an unpaid seller's rights of lien and resale and Chapter 17 for similar rights available to warehousing and repair service businesses and common carriers.
2. See the discussion of "Methods of Enforcing Judgment" in Chapter 15.

However, even when a debt is stated to be payable "on demand," the debtor must normally be given time to raise the funds to repay the debt. If the creditor seizes property without giving reasonable notice, it may be liable in damages.[3]

CASE 30.1

Murano operated a video store financed in part by a loan from the Bank of Montreal. The bank became concerned about the financial affairs of the store and wrote to Murano, indicating their intention to liquidate if adequate arrangements were not made within the next six weeks. In fact, the bank took no further steps for three months, when the parties met to discuss a request by Murano for a new financing arrangement. The bank agreed to consider the request, but one week later, without giving notice, it appointed a receiver and took possession of the store. It also informed other creditors of Murano of its actions.

Murano lost his entire business, including another store that was not included in the bank's financing arrangement. The court held that the bank had failed to give reasonable notice, that it was in breach of duty to its client in disclosing information to other creditors, and that it was liable in damages to Murano.[4]

Unfortunately for the creditor, when a debtor's financial position has deteriorated to the point that the creditor decides it must act, the secured assets in the possession of the debtor may already be in a deteriorating condition or may even have disappeared, and other creditors may also have designs on them. Consequently, security agreements frequently require a debtor to waive any right to notice. After a creditor takes possession, however, statutes generally require the creditor to give notice to the debtor of the time and place at which the goods are to be sold in order to satisfy the debt.[5]

METHODS OF SECURING CREDIT

Credit Devices Previously Considered

Historically, the law affecting credit devices has been drawn from a combination of real estate mortgage law and the law of the sale of goods. Several of these credit devices have already been considered in previous chapters. In particular:

Mortgages Although this chapter deals with collateral security in the form of *personal* property rather than real property, the concept of priority in relation to land mortgages and to other creditors' claims explained in Chapter 25 remains relevant.

Leases Leases of equipment were examined as an example of bailment in Chapter 17, and leases of land as an interest in real property in Chapter 24. As we saw in Chapter 17, leases may also serve as a type of security device, where items of personal property are acquired on credit.

---

3.   *Ronald Elwyn Lister Ltd.* v. *Dunlop Canada Ltd.* (1982), 135 D.L.R. (3d) 1. At least 10 days' notice must be given before enforcing security in the property of an insolvent debtor; see Chapter 31.

4.   *Murano* v. *Bank of Montreal* (1998), 163 D.L.R. (4th) 21. In *Royal Bank of Canada* v. *W. Got & Associates Electric Ltd.* (1999), 178 D.L.R. (4th) 385, where the bank failed to give notice before foreclosing on a loan, the bank was held to be in breach of contract and to have committed the tort of conversion. The Supreme Court of Canada upheld an award of punitive damages.

5.   See, for example: Personal Property Security Act (hereafter PPSA), R.S.O. 1990, c. P.10, s. 63(4); S.M. 1993, c. 14, s. 59(6); S.S. 1993, c. P-6.2, s. 59(6).

Consignments The distinction between a consignment of goods and a sale of goods was discussed in Chapter 16. A consignment may also amount to an indirect type of secured credit. As we have seen, retailers may not have sufficient capital to carry all the inventory they need and may bring in a stock of goods shipped on consignment by a manufacturer or wholesaler. The merchandise remains the property of the manufacturer or wholesaler, who effectively provides financing in the form of goods rather than money.

Other Credit Devices Earlier chapters also dealt with assignments of book debts (Chapter 12) and with pledges (Chapter 17), both of which can be considered methods of securing credit. A third-party guarantee (considered in Chapter 18) is slightly different because the "security" consists of a promise by a person, rather than a legal interest in an item of property.

Among the more important forms of security we have yet to consider are those created by conditional sale contracts, chattel mortgages, and floating charges.

Conditional Sales

A close parallel exists between a lease and a conditional sale. In a lease, the hirer (lessee) undertakes to pay rent for a specified period and at the end of that period can elect to buy the item, applying rent already paid towards the purchase price. In a conditional sale, the transfer of title to the buyer is usually conditional upon the buyer's completion of a series of scheduled instalment payments. In the meantime, the buyer has possession of the goods, and the seller retains the title to them as security for the full payment of the purchase price. Both a lessee and a conditional buyer are *bailees* of the goods.[6]

A conditional sale contract serves two main functions as a security device: it gives the secured party a right to look to the goods in satisfaction of the debtor's obligation, and it gives the secured party priority in the goods over the interests of third parties, especially other creditors.

As a creditor, the conditional seller has the ordinary contractual remedy of suing the debtor for the unpaid balance of the debt. In addition, a conditional seller invariably makes it a term of the agreement that he may retake possession of the goods on default by the buyer. **Repossession** does not affect the ownership of the goods since the seller has retained title from the outset.

repossession
the act of taking back possession of property that is in the possession of a defaulting debtor

A conditional seller is not entitled to use force in recovering the goods. The proper course of action is to obtain a court order authorizing the necessary steps to regain possession. In some provinces a seller is not entitled to repossess goods except by court process.

A majority of the provinces permit a conditional seller not only to repossess the goods upon default but also to sue the buyer for any deficiency arising because the amount still owed by the buyer exceeds the amount realized on resale of the goods.[7] In other provinces a conditional seller has to make a choice—either to sue the conditional buyer for the amount owing or to repossess the goods, but not both.[8] Consumer protection legislation in some provinces provides that a term in the conditional sale contract allowing the conditional seller to repossess and resell the goods on default is unenforceable once the conditional buyer has paid a certain proportion (for example, two-thirds) of the purchase price.[9]

redeem
reclaim the goods and continue with the conditional sale

The rights of a conditional buyer also vary considerably from one province to another. Some provinces permit a conditional buyer to **redeem** within specified periods upon payment of the

---

6. A conditional sale contract often places the conditional buyer under a higher duty by making her responsible for damage to the article whether caused by her or not.

7. For example: PPSA, S.N.S. 1995–96, c. 13, s. 61(6); s. 63(5)(f) (Ont.).

8. For example: PPSA, R.S.B.C. 1996, c. 359, s. 58.

9. For example: Consumer Protection Act 2002, S.O. 2002, c. 30, Sch. A, s. 25; PPSA, s. 58(3) (B.C.). However, a court may still grant the right to repossess and resell on special application by the conditional seller.

instalments in arrears plus interest and any costs incurred by the seller in repossessing.[10] Other provinces require a conditional buyer who has defaulted to pay the whole unpaid balance of the price—not merely the amounts in arrears—when an **acceleration clause** is included in the conditional sale contract.[11] In most jurisdictions a conditional buyer has a statutory right to receive any surplus realized by a conditional seller that repossesses and resells the goods for more than the amount owed by the buyer plus costs of reselling.[12]

acceleration clause
a provision whereby the full outstanding amount of a debt becomes immediately payable if the debtor defaults in making any instalment payment

Many merchants who sell goods on the instalment plan do not finance the credit transactions themselves. Instead, they sell or assign their conditional sale agreements to finance companies that collect the instalments and administer the contracts. Conditional sale contracts also play an important role in financing wholesale purchasers. A retailer or dealer may finance its purchases of stock-in-trade from a manufacturer by buying them from the manufacturer under a conditional sale contract. As a conditional seller, the manufacturer acquires an asset in the form of an account receivable, which it almost invariably assigns to a finance company. As an assignee, the finance company stands in the position of the manufacturing company, with title in the goods withheld from the dealer or merchant (the conditional buyer) until the account is paid in full.

Chattel Mortgages

As we saw in Chapter 25, when discussing mortgages of land, a mortgage is a transfer of an interest in property by the mortgagor (borrower) to the mortgagee (lender) as security for a debt, with a condition that if the debt is repaid by a specified date, the interest in the property reverts to the mortgagor. However, it is not only interests in land that may be the subject of a mortgage. An interest in personal property may be similarly charged, by what is commonly referred to as a **chattel mortgage**.

chattel mortgage
a mortgage of personal property

As with mortgages of land, there are two basic uses of chattel mortgages. In the first type of case, the vendor of an article of property "takes back" a mortgage on the property sold. The effect is essentially similar to a conditional sale, except that in a conditional sale the article remains the property of the vendor until the debt is paid, whereas in a chattel mortgage it is transferred to the buyer and immediately re-transferred to the vendor. In the second case, the owner of an article mortgages it to the lender—usually a bank or financial institution—as security for a loan. That loan may be used either to pay for the article that is being mortgaged or to purchase an entirely different article.

A chattel mortgage may be contrasted with a pledge. In a chattel mortgage, the borrower retains possession of the property, and the lender's security interest is in the title to specific goods or in after-acquired property. By contrast, a pledge is a form of bailment. The lender takes possession of the assets or documents evidencing the borrower's ownership, while the title remains with the borrower.

A chattel mortgage is often used in the sale of a business as a going concern where office equipment, machinery, or vehicles are included in the sale transaction.

Another common use of the chattel mortgage occurs in the sale of a building with equipment, such as a furnished office building or apartment building. Frequently the price includes both real property and equipment in the building. Not only may the vendor take back a real estate mortgage for the unpaid balance of the purchase price, but he may also take back a concurrent chattel mortgage on all moveable equipment. The chattel mortgage (so long as it is duly registered) avoids any question about whether certain equipment is a fixture; a real estate mortgage would cover only fixtures, but with a concurrent chattel mortgage covering furniture and equipment, the question becomes irrelevant.

More commonly, chattel mortgages are used as security for loans made by financial institutions. In particular, banks use chattel mortgages as a device for securing credit in the field of consumer financing.

---

10. For example: PPSA, s. 62(1) (Man. and Sask.).

11. For example: PPSA, s. 66(2)(a) (Ont.).

12. For example: PPSA, s. 64 (Ont.).

When a person borrows to finance a purchase of goods and gives a chattel mortgage, the effect may not seem much different from buying the goods under a conditional sale contract. However, in a conditional sale, it is the actual goods purchased that comprise the collateral. In a chattel mortgage, the debtor may give security in the form of other personal property and even in property acquired after the chattel mortgage has been executed.

A chattel mortgage that includes **after-acquired property** is a very flexible device. It may cover inventories that fluctuate during its term, as some goods are bought and added to inventory while others are sold and subtracted from inventory. The mortgage does not transfer title to specific goods to the creditor, and buyers acquire good title to goods sold by the debtor in the ordinary course of business. The creditor's security interest remains as a suspended priority against general creditors. If the debtor defaults, the secured creditor may then seize whatever property is covered by the chattel mortgage and sell it to satisfy the debt. A chattel mortgage may also cover goods not yet in a deliverable state, such as goods in production and growing crops.

after-acquired property
property acquired by the debtor after the debt has been incurred

A chattel mortgagee has remedies similar to those of a conditional seller. As a creditor, he may sue on the mortgagor's covenant to pay the debt, and he may take possession of the mortgaged goods upon default by the mortgagor. A chattel mortgagee invariably reserves the right upon default to resell the goods to a third party. In exercising this right of sale, he must act reasonably and fairly to obtain a good price for them. If he fails to do so, he may be accountable to the mortgagor for the difference between the price obtained and what would have been a fair price for the goods. If on selling at a fair price the mortgagee obtains less than the debt outstanding, he may obtain judgment against the mortgagor for the deficiency, but if there is any surplus he must return that surplus to the mortgagor.

Floating Charges

As we saw in Chapter 27, it is common for a corporation to borrow money by issuing bonds to the public, using its assets as security. Each certificate issued to a bondholder is evidence of an interest in a **trust deed**—an elaborate form of mortgage on the lands and buildings of the company. The parties to a trust deed are the borrowing corporation (as mortgagor) and a trustee for the bondholders (as mortgagee). Generally, a trust company acts as trustee for the bondholders.

trust deed
a document evidencing a mortgage on the property of a corporation

Bonds issued by Canadian corporations frequently provide additional security over and above the mortgage of real property through the creation of a **floating charge**. A floating charge adds those remaining corporate assets not already mortgaged or pledged to the security. When a trust deed includes a provision for a floating charge, the trustee also has access to business assets, including chattels and choses in action, ahead of the unsecured creditors of the corporation.

floating charge
a form of mortgage on all the assets of a corporation other than those already specifically charged

A floating charge nicely complements a mortgage of real property because it provides security over the whole of the assets as a working unit. If the corporation defaults in the payment of its bond obligations, the trustee may then more easily place the corporation in the hands of a receiver and manager who can operate it in the interest of the bondholders.

Corporations sometimes issue bonds secured by a floating charge alone and without a mortgage of specific assets. Such bonds are commonly called **debentures**.

debenture
an alternative term to describe a corporate bond

All provinces require mortgages and floating charges to be registered. As with conditional sales and chattel mortgages, failure to register makes the trust deed void against creditors and subsequent purchasers or mortgagees. The statutory registration requirements vary from province to province. Some are found in corporations acts, while others are in separate acts. In addition, the interests that are secured by floating charges fall within the general scope of personal property security legislation and are protected by registration in the normal way (see below).[13]

---

13. In Ontario, it was for some time unclear whether a floating charge on a corporation's assets needed to be registered under the Corporate Securities Registration Act (CSRA), the PPSA, or both. Since 1989, registration under the PPSA alone is required and the CSRA was repealed. However, charges registered under the CSRA prior to October 10, 1989, remain protected: S.O. 1989, c. 16, s. 84; PPSA, s. 78.

> ### CHECKLIST Types of Personal Property Security Interests
>
> Personal property security interests may take any of the following forms:
>
> - conditional sales
> - chattel mortgages
> - floating charges
> - chattel leases
> - consignments
> - pledges
> - assignments of accounts receivable[14]

PERSONAL PROPERTY SECURITY LEGISLATION

Jurisdiction and Application

Section 92 of the Constitution Act, 1867 assigns "Property and Civil Rights in the Province" to provincial jurisdiction. Each of the provinces and territories has a Personal Property Security Act (PPSA) in substantially the same form.[15] This single act applies "to every transaction . . . that in substance creates a **security interest**";[16] it governs not only conditional sale contracts, chattel mortgages, and assignments of book debts, but also floating charges, pledges, leases and consignments intended as security, and other less common forms. These forms of security are now collectively referred to as **security agreements**.

We should note that the legislative schemes are not completely harmonious. Although the provinces are working to reduce the minor variations among the Acts, some inconsistencies still exist.[17] Additionally, as we shall see, conflicts may arise between the relevant provincial legislation and federal laws, such as the Bank Act. Finally, the Act does not apply to non-consensual security interests; nor does it apply to interests in real property.

The very nature of personal property means that it is moveable and may cross jurisdictional boundaries. Each Act contains conflict-of-law provisions that determine which province's law applies in various circumstances.

security interest
an interest in goods, intangible property, or personal property that secures payment of a debt or performance of an obligation

security agreement
an agreement that creates a security interest, including chattel mortgages, conditional sales contracts, etc.

CASE 30.2

Xtra, a corporation with its head office in Ontario, leased 75 truck trailers to TCT, a corporation located in Alberta. The truck trailers were used throughout the country. TCT became bankrupt. Xtra claimed its truck trailers back. The claim was opposed by GMAC, which had a security interest over all the assets of TCT. The security interest was registered in Alberta. Xtra's lease was not registered.

At the time, Ontario law did not require the registration of a "true lease," whereas the Alberta PPSA did. However, the Ontario PPSA (section 7(1)) provides that "the validity, perfection

continued

---

14. These are considered later in this chapter.

15. In 1976, Ontario introduced a Personal Property Security Act (PPSA), modelled rather loosely on the provisions of the U.S. Uniform Commercial Code, and since then all the common-law jurisdictions have followed suit. The Civil Code of Quebec contains broadly similar provisions to the PPSAs.

16. Security interest is a defined term under each of the Acts: PPSA, s. 2 (Ont.), s. 1 (Alta., Man.).

17. For example, Ontario recently eliminated the distinction between true leases and financing leases made only in the Ontario Act.

and effect of perfection . . . of a security interest in an intangible, or goods that are normally used in more than one jurisdiction . . . shall be governed by the law of the jurisdiction where the debtor is located at the time the security interest attaches." As the debtor's main place of business was in Alberta, the law of that province applied, and GMAC's claim prevailed.[18]

Purpose of PPSA Legislation

When parties create a security interest, they create a relationship that may take priority over the interests of others. The PPSA legislation works to instill confidence in lenders, borrowers, buyers, and owners by establishing a uniform public system that deals with all types of security interests and priority questions. The Acts themselves are complex and technical. Here, we will provide only a general description of how the legislation works.

The Acts recognize that all security devices have the same purpose—to secure repayment by the debtor. They set out to establish a single unified system with common rules for the following purposes:

- to define a secured party's remedies against a defaulting debtor
- to create one system of registration to record all secured interests
- to define priorities between a secured party on the one hand, and third party purchasers, subsequent secured parties, and general creditors on the other

The legislation does not prohibit businesses from using their old contract forms to create security interests or from continuing to refer to them by such traditional labels as "conditional sale contracts" or "chattel mortgages." The legislation does not distinguish between the particular forms of security interest—all are considered security agreements. The public is given notice of the interest through the registration of a common form of **financing statement**.

The Acts recognize that both leases and consignments of goods can be used as forms of security. However, as we saw in Chapters 16 and 17, these arrangements are frequently used quite apart from any intention to create a security interest. Most provinces have adopted an approach that effectively avoids the difficulty of distinguishing between the two purposes. A consignment or a lease that secures payment or performance of an obligation is within the scope of the Act.[19] Additionally, the Act applies to commercial consignments and to leases for a term in excess of one year, whether or not they are intended to create a security interest.[20]

financing statement
the document summarizing the details of a security interest that is filed in order to protect that interest

---

CASE 30.3

Telecom Leasing leased a car to the B.C. Telephone Company, which in turn leased the car to one of its employees, Giffen, who subsequently became bankrupt. The lease was for a term of more than one year and gave the lessee the option of purchasing the vehicle. Telecom failed to register a financing statement under the (B.C.) PPSA.

It was accepted that the lease was a genuine lease, rather than a security arrangement. Nevertheless, the lessor's interest was required to be perfected under the PPSA, and since it had not been, Telecom had no right to retake possession of the vehicle.[21]

---

18. *GMAC Commercial Credit Corp.* v. *TCT Logistics Inc.* (2004), 238 D.L.R.(4th) 487. See also *Gimli Auto Ltd.* v. *BDO Dunwoody Ltd.* (1998), 160 D.L.R. (4th) 373.

19. For example, s. 1(1) (B.C.); s. 4(1)(b) (N.S.); S.N.B. 1993, c. P-7.1, s. 3(1)(b). Ontario had a particularly troubling distinction between financing leases (subject to the PPSA) and "true" leases (not subject to PPSA), R.S.O. 1990, c. P.10, s. 2(a)(ii). Manitoba had adopted a similar approach, but this was changed in 1993. Several cases illustrate the complication associated with this distinction: *Re Stephanian's Persian Carpets Ltd.* (1980), 1 P.P.S.A.C. 119; *Standard Finance Corp.* v. *Coopers & Lybrand Ltd.*, [1984] 4 W.W.R. 543; *Adelaide Capital Corp.* v. *Integrated Transportation Finance Inc.* (1994), 111 D.L.R. (4th) 493. Ontario removed this distinction on August 1, 2007 (S.O. 2006 c. 34).

20. *Ibid.*, s. 3(c) (B.C.); s. 3(2) (N.B.); s. 4(2) (N.S.).

21. *Re Giffen*, [1998] 1 S.C.R. 91.

PPSA legislation also recognizes that assets subsequently acquired by a debtor can be added to a security interest already in existence and permits the use of chattel mortgages to cover after-acquired property such as inventories. This is practical in the business setting because goods in inventory are always changing. However, in consumer transactions the security interest of sellers or creditors is confined to the exact goods financed and does not extend to any other after-acquired assets of the consumer.

Where the property charged as collateral is disposed of by the debtor, the Acts provide that the security interest attaches to the proceeds.[22]

CASE 30.4

Cardinali bought a boat from a marina under a conditional sale agreement. The marina assigned the contract to a financing company. The boat was defective, and the marina gave Cardinali a new boat in its place. When Cardinali subsequently defaulted in his payments, the finance company repossessed the boat, sold it, and sued Cardinali for the deficiency.

The trial judge found that the new boat represented proceeds of the disposal of the first boat and that the finance company had a security interest in it. On appeal, the Ontario Court of Appeal held that the new boat had not been exchanged for the first boat and consequently did not represent proceeds of disposal.[23]

Key Components of the Personal Property Security Act

The Act is organized around three key components:

- creation of a security interest,
- attachment of the security interest, and
- perfection of the security interest.

As we have already noted, a security interest is created when the creditor and debtor enter into some form of security agreement that gives the creditor an interest in the debtor's personal property to secure repayment of a debt or satisfaction of an obligation.

attachment
the moment in time when a debtor's property becomes subject to a security interest

Attachment occurs only upon *performance* of the security agreement by both debtor and creditor. A security interest cannot attach to an asset until the debtor has acquired an ownership interest in it. Nor does a security interest attach until the creditor has performed his part of the bargain by giving the value promised to the debtor.

perfection
the moment in time when a creditor's security interest becomes protected

Perfection protects and establishes priority of the security interest and it may occur one of two ways:

- when the secured party takes *possession* of the asset(s)—as in a pledge—ending any false impression of ownership given by the debtor's possession, or
- most often, when a secured party *registers a financing statement* in the PPSA system. The financing statement gives details of the security interest and provides public notice of the creditor's interest.[24]

A perfected security interest is one that has all three components: creation, attachment, and perfection, as illustrated in Figure 30.1.

---

22. For example, R.S.A. 2000, c. P-7, s. 28(1); s. 28(1) (N.B.); s. 25(1)(b) (Ont.). Consequently, a secured creditor will be able to trace the proceeds into the debtor's bank account: *Massey-Ferguson Industries Ltd.* v. *Bank of Montreal* (1983), 4 D.L.R. (4th) 96, varied (1985) 21 D.L.R. (4th) 640 (Ont. C.A.).

23. *General Motors Acceptance Corp. of Canada* v. *Cardinali* (2000), 185 D.L.R. (4th) 141. However, the court found in favour of the finance company on the ground that the purchaser had agreed to an alteration of the original contract.

24. The two alternatives are not available for every form of security interest. A security interest in negotiable instruments is perfected only by possession (holding) of the instruments, and a security interest in book debts is perfected only by registration.

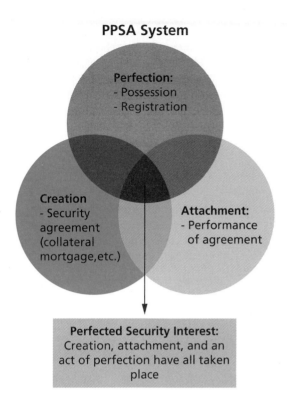

PPSA System

Perfection:
- Possession
- Registration

Creation
- Security agreement (collateral mortgage,etc.)

Attachment:
- Performance of agreement

Perfected Security Interest:
Creation, attachment, and an act of perfection have all taken place

FIGURE 30.1
The PPSA System

Registration

If security interests are to be protected by the law, then an effective system of alerting third parties to those interests, whatever their form, needs to be in place. As described above, the Acts establish a centralized registration system within each province for recording security interests. By using computer facilities to record and revise security information and by enlarging the geographic area over which a search can be made, a large database is established and maintained. However, there is at present no comprehensive nation-wide system of registration comparable to the NUANS system of corporate registration, and searches are completed on a province-by-province basis.[25]

The registration system operates rather like the land titles system except that the search is usually made against the name of a particular debtor, whereas under the land titles system it is made against a described parcel of land.[26] The provincial government maintains a compensation fund to reimburse losses caused by incorrectly processed information, and the system provides a guaranteed certificate of search.

Priority and Competing Interests

The three stages of creation, attachment, and perfection are necessary to protect the security against competing **unperfected security interests** of others.

unperfected security interest
a security interest that is not attached or perfected

---

25. See Chapter 26.

26. A search may also be made against the property charged. In particular, it is advisable to search against the V.I.N. of any vehicle that may be subject to a security interest; see *Re Lambert* (1994), 119 D.L.R. (4th) 93. This provides additional protection in cases where the debtor's name is incorrectly spelled.

ILLUSTRATION 30.1

X Co. borrows money from *Y* Bank in order to buy a truck. *X* Co. gives *Y* Bank a chattel mortgage on the truck and takes delivery of it. The security interest is *created* by the loan contract and chattel mortgage. The interest *attaches* when *Y* Bank hands over the money to *X* Co. and *X* Co. uses it to obtain delivery of the truck from the dealer. After handing over the money, the bank *registers* a financing statement. The interest is *perfected* when *Y* Bank registers a financing statement.

It is important to pinpoint the exact moment of perfection in order to determine priority between two perfected security interests in the same asset. Generally, the legislation assigns priority to the creditor that first perfects his interest. In practice, this generally means that priority goes to the first to register. A creditor who first creates and attaches his interest may nevertheless lose his priority if he delays perfecting that interest and a subsequent creditor perfects first. The subsequent creditor might be aware of the unperfected security interest of the first creditor; even so, by registering first, that interest is perfected and obtains priority.

CASE 30.5

BMP Corp. sold the assets of its donut business to a numbered corporation and took back a chattel mortgage. The mortgage was guaranteed by a Mr. Trafford, whose wife was the sole shareholder of the numbered corporation. Due to an oversight, the financing statement was not registered. Subsequently, Mrs. Trafford registered a financing statement regarding shareholder advances to protect herself against any unsecured creditors of the purchaser. She had actual notice of the guarantee given by her husband and of BMP's security interest. When BMP discovered the oversight, it registered its financing statement and brought an application for an order setting aside Mrs. Trafford's financing statement or postponing her interest.

The court held that, notwithstanding her knowledge of the chattel mortgage, Mrs. Trafford's interest had priority.[27]

Perfection or attachment need not occur in any particular order. For example, some lenders register the financing statement (the act of perfection) before the loan money is advanced to the debtor (the act of attachment). Once the loan attaches, perfection dates back to the time of registration.

There are some exceptions to the general priority rule. Consider a situation where one creditor takes security in after-acquired property and a subsequent creditor supplies new assets to the same debtor, taking back a security interest in them. Although the new assets become after-acquired property of the debtor, a good case can be made for giving the one who supplies later credit a priority over the existing perfected security interests. Otherwise, a business in financial straits will find it difficult to obtain additional credit needed to rehabilitate itself and survive. The debtor's assets have been increased by the value of the new assets financed by credit, so that the first creditor has not had the value of his security diminished.

purchase-money security interest (PMSI)
the interest that arises when goods purchased by a debtor are charged as security for a loan made to enable those actual goods being acquired

In recognition of this problem, the Acts give special priority to a **purchase-money security interest (PMSI)**. This interest arises when a seller (for example, a conditional seller) reserves a security interest in the actual goods sold to the debtor, or when a lender (for example, a chattel mortgagee) finances a debtor's acquisition of the same assets that are used as collateral. The rule is a necessary qualification to a system that makes it easy to include after-acquired assets and their proceeds in a security interest.

---

27. *BMP & Daughters Investment Corp.* v. *941242 Ontario Ltd.* (1993), 7 B.L.R. (2d) 270.

Rules for determining priorities among competing perfected security interests are potentially very complex, especially for the financing of business inventories. Fortunately, in practice, a business often has only a single source of financing for its inventories, in which case the need to establish priorities does not arise. In financing other business assets, however, competition is more likely between one secured creditor claiming a charge on after-acquired assets and another claiming a purchase-money security interest, as when a company gives a floating charge over all its assets and then acquires new equipment under a conditional sale contract. In these circumstances, the legislation gives priority to the PMSI of the conditional seller.[28]

EFFECT OF SECURITY INTERESTS ON PURCHASERS

Separation of Possession and Ownership

The existence of security arrangements typically separates possession of property from formal legal ownership of it. For example, a consignor ships goods to a consignee while retaining title under a consignment contract; a conditional seller gives possession of goods to a conditional buyer while retaining title under a conditional sale contract; a mortgagee acquires title but leaves possession of the goods with a mortgagor under a chattel mortgage. Since possession of goods usually creates an appearance of ownership to a third party, the effect of a credit device may be to mislead an innocent third person. A debtor left in possession of goods may appear to own assets that she, in fact, does not own.

Under the common law, a seller cannot transfer title to goods that she does not own. A creditor whose existence is not known to the buyer may have legal title to the goods and subsequently assert his right to repossess them from the buyer. The buyer is unaware of the risk of not acquiring title and of losing the goods.

Legislatures have generally been more sympathetic to the interests of innocent purchasers than have the courts of common law. As we saw in Chapter 16, a measure of protection is provided under the Factors Act and the Sale of Goods Act. However, the principal safeguard for purchasers now lies in the PPSA requirement that a security interest in goods left in the possession of a debtor must be perfected by registration.

Effect of Registration

A properly registered security interest is generally effective against third parties, except for specified classes of good-faith transferees.[29]

ILLUSTRATION 30.2

Peng purchases a computer from Federchuk's Ltd. under a conditional sale agreement. He makes a down payment and agrees to pay the balance plus finance charges in 18 equal monthly instalments. Two months later Peng sells the computer to Tse without disclosing the existence of the conditional sale contract. Can Federchuk's gain possession of the computer from Tse despite the fact that she is an innocent purchaser?

---

28. Provided, of course, that that interest has been perfected; see *Canadian Imperial Bank of Commerce* v. *Otto Timm Enterprises Ltd.* (1995), 130 D.L.R. (4th) 91.

29. See, for example, s. 9(1) (Ont.).

According to the Personal Property Security Acts, in Illustration 30.2 Federchuk's would be able to recover the computer from Tse if it had properly registered its security interest before Peng resold the machine to Tse, since she would have had the opportunity to find out about the security interest before making the purchase by making the appropriate search. She is not in a stronger position because of her ignorance. Federchuk's claim takes priority because it was perfected before the purported sale to Tse. The same effect would be achieved if, instead of buying on credit by means of a conditional sale, Peng had borrowed the money from a bank, given a chattel mortgage as security, and used the proceeds of the loan to buy the computer. The bank would then have been in a position analogous to Federchuk's for the purposes of registration and of maintaining its rights of repossession against third parties.

The Mercantile Agency Rule

There is one common type of business transaction in particular in which a conditional seller clothes a conditional buyer with an appearance of ownership. Manufacturers often sell their goods to dealers or merchants under wholesale conditional sale contracts. If a retail business finances its inventories under a wholesale conditional sale contract registered by the manufacturer, is the retailer able to give a good title to its customers when it does not itself have title? A negative answer would fly in the face of consumer expectations. This type of financing arrangement invites consumers to rely on a merchant's apparent ownership of its inventories. The PPSA provides that when a conditional seller delivers goods to a conditional buyer, who resells them *in the ordinary course of business*, a retail buyer acquires a good title to the goods.[30] If the dealer fails to meet its obligations, the manufacturer or a finance company holding a registered wholesale instalment account receivable cannot seize the goods from the retail buyer.

The above rule does *not* protect buyers of goods from someone who is not a regular seller of those goods. An unfortunate buyer may find that the conditional seller or his assignee can lawfully seize the goods purchased. The buyer's only remedy is to sue the seller for breach of an implied promise to convey good title. Unfortunately, a seller's warranty in a private sale is likely to be of little value. It can be argued that an innocent purchaser in a private sale needs more protection than she would have in a sale by a regular dealer. Yet she has less protection. Therefore, purchasers should undertake a PPSA search before completing a private sale.

Registration Practice

PPSA legislation does not *require* registration in the sense that failure to register is an offence; nor does it invalidate the creditor's interest. If a secured creditor (or his assignee) chooses not to register, his interest continues as an unperfected security interest and he simply takes a risk that third parties may acquire interests that prevail over his own. Why might a creditor choose not to register? The answer turns on the nature of the creditor's business. Suppose that a creditor's business is primarily one of selling relatively low-value goods to many different customers. He may not find it worthwhile to trace goods wrongfully disposed of by a debtor and then to sue in order to recover them from an innocent purchaser. Instead, he may decide to save the trouble and expense of registering the security interest in the first place. In practice, disputes do not often arise between a secured creditor and a subsequent transferee of goods, and, except for more expensive durable goods, retail conditional sellers (or finance companies as their assignees) may decide not to register conditional sale contracts.

30. For example, s. 28(1) (Ont.).

On the other hand, sales by a manufacturer or wholesaler often involve taking a security interest in assets of a business that has other creditors as well. For instance, a truck manufacturer may sell a fleet of vehicles under a conditional sale agreement to a large retail business. The retail business purchases stock-in-trade from suppliers who also provide credit. If the business becomes insolvent, a dispute may arise over the truck manufacturer's claim to repossess the vehicles and thus to deprive the other creditors of an important asset from which to realize their own claims. Risk of this kind of dispute provides the main incentive for registration, since registration of a security interest is essential for a creditor to maintain priority against other creditors.[31]

EFFECT OF SECURITY INTERESTS ON OTHER CREDITORS

Assignment of Book Debts

In this chapter we have examined two of the principal ways in which a security interest may arise— as a result of a sale of goods on credit and as a result of a loan to purchase goods. In these circumstances a debtor's increased liabilities are offset by the newly acquired assets. A third use of security devices arises when an existing creditor requires additional collateral as a condition for leaving a loan outstanding. For this purpose, businesses often provide a conditional **assignment of book debts** to a bank or other creditor. As we saw in Chapter 12, an assignment of this kind is conditional in two respects. First, the amount of the accounts receivable used as security fluctuates with the state of accounts between the borrowing business (assignor) and its customers. Second, the assignment is only a potential one as long as the borrowing business keeps its loan in good standing: the security arrangement does not materialize in an actual assignment, with notice to the borrowing business' customers, unless the borrowing business defaults on its loan.

> **assignment of book debts**
> security interest in the debtor's accounts receivables

If default occurs, however, the lender, as assignee, may collect directly on the book debts owed to the assignor in priority to the assignor's general creditors. An assignment of book debts may seriously prejudice the position of the general creditors, and prospective general creditors need a means of ascertaining whether an assignment has been made. Again, registration of a creditor's security interest provides the necessary information.

Under the PPSA, an assignment is ineffective against creditors of an assignor and against subsequent assignees of the book debts unless it is properly registered.[32] The object is to assure prospective creditors of a business that, unless there is registered public notice to the contrary, the assets of the business in the form of accounts receivable will be available to meet their claims. Registration provides public notice that those accounts are not available to satisfy debts.

While registration of an assignment may provide information to assist the decisions of a prospective creditor, it does nothing for existing *unsecured* creditors whose decisions to give the debtor credit have already been made. The effect of an assignment is to deprive them of a part of the assets to which they might otherwise have been able to look for payment of their claims. Knowledge of the assignment does not help them. When a major creditor such as a bank insists on obtaining and registering an assignment of book debts, unless the assignment provides a significant benefit to the debtor in exchange, the assignee obtains its new priority at the expense of the general creditors, for whom no relief is available.[33]

---

31. For example, s. 20 (Alta., B.C., Ont. and Sask.).

32. An assignment of book debts is also void as against a trustee in bankruptcy unless it has been properly registered: Bankruptcy and Insolvency Act, R.S.C. 1985, c. B-3, s. 94. The reform of the bankruptcy legislation will remove this section because it is the provincial PPSA scheme.

33. See, for example: *Bank of Nova Scotia* v. *Keough* (2000), 188 D.L.R. (4th) 494.

Conflicting Priorities

We have seen that other creditors of a debtor may be affected by a security interest claimed by a particular creditor. Priorities among creditors become of crucial importance when the proceeds from a liquidation of all the assets of a debtor are insufficient to pay in full the claims of all creditors, as we have seen in our discussion of land mortgages. Information about the existence of security interests is therefore essential in making decisions about granting credit: a prospective creditor needs to know the extent to which an applicant has already given collateral security to other creditors before deciding whether to grant further credit of his own.

The PPSAs, by extending to a wide variety of methods of securing credit and by adopting a simple "first to register" system, have done much to make the necessary information available, though, as we have seen, there may still be problems in interprovincial situations. Unfortunately, the Acts do not cover the entire field of personal property security, and conflicting claims between different types of creditors remain all too common and are often difficult to resolve.[34] Conflicts may arise, for example, where a landlord of premises distrains for arrears of rent and claims fixtures that are subject to a security interest that has been registered under the PPSA.[35] Or the conditional seller of a vehicle may have an interest, protected by the PPSA, that conflicts with the lien of a repairer.[36] As we shall see in the next chapter, conflicting claims to priority frequently arise in bankruptcy proceedings,[37] and, as we shall see in the final part of this chapter, conflicts exist between provincial PPSA laws and the federal Bank Act.

CHECKLIST   Priority Rules of the PPSA

(a) First to *perfect* has priority

(b) When all competing interests have been perfected by registration: first to *register* has priority

(c) The first security interest perfected by registration may still lose priority to:

    (i) a security interest perfected by possession,

    (ii) a purchase-money security interest,

    (iii) a statutory lien (landlord/tenant; repairer's lien, bankruptcy),

    (iv) a consumer purchasing goods in the *ordinary course of business*, or

    (v) a subsequent registered interest if the first registration expires (each registration lasts for a fixed time period and must be renewed to maintain priority)

---

34. See, for example: *GMS Securities & Appraisals Ltd.* v. *Rich-Wood Kitchens Ltd.* (1995), 121 D.L.R. (4th) 278, in which a conflict existed between the (Ontario) Mortgages Act, the Registry Act, and the Personal Property Security Act.

35. *859587 Ontario Ltd.* v. *Starmark Property Management Ltd.* (1999), 42 B.L.R. (2d) 16.

36. See *Canadian Imperial Bank of Commerce* v. *Kawartha Feed Mills Inc.* (1998), 41 O.R. (3d) 124; *General Electric Capital Canada Inc.* v. *Interlink Freight Systems Inc.* (1998), 42 O.R. (3d) 348 (not followed in *Riordan Leasing Inc.* v. *Veer Transportation Services Inc.* (2002), 61 O.R. (3d) 536).

37. See, for example: *Royal Bank of Canada* v. *Sparrow Electric Corp.* (1997), 143 D.L.R. (4th) 385, in which the trustee in bankruptcy was faced with claims under the Alberta PPSA, the federal Bank Act, and the Income Tax Act.

INTERNATIONAL ISSUE

Mobile Equipment

Large mobile equipment presents a financing challenge. Lenders involved in financing the purchase of things like aircraft equipment often take an interest in the equipment as security for the loan, knowing that the equipment will often be in foreign jurisdictions. Creditors need reassurance that their security will be protected and have priority over other interests even when the equipment is far from home.

In 2001, 53 member states of the United Nations International Institute for the Unification of Private Law (UNIDROIT) adopted the Convention on International Interests in Mobile Equipment (the Cape Town Convention), which addressed the creation, perfection, and priority of security in large mobile equipment.[38] The convention proposes a system similar to the domestic PPSA system with the creation of an "international interest" and a searchable electronic registration system. Priority is determined on a "first in time" registration basis. Creditors with priority in the international system are entitled to repossess the secured equipment even when it is in a foreign (member) jurisdiction. The convention came into force on March 1, 2006 after ratification by eight countries. Canada, the United States, the United Kingdom, France, and Germany have ratified the convention and are introducing domestic legislation to implement its terms with respect to aircraft equipment.[39] The international priority regime would override PPSA rules, so provinces across Canada are also in the process of adopting corresponding legislation. The international registry is supervised by the International Civil Aviation Organization.

QUESTIONS TO CONSIDER

1. An international interest would override the domestic rules of priority for PPSA and Bankruptcy. What is the rationale for this position?

2. How do you think this convention will affect lending decisions and terms?

3. What is the incentive for a developing nation to adopt the convention?

Sources: Sean D. Murphy, *United States Practice in International Law*, Vol. 2, (Cambridge: Cambridge University Press, 2005) at 383–390; "Cape Town Convention on Financing of High-Value, Mobile Equipment" (2004), 94(4) *American Journal of International Law* 852–854. www.unidroit.org/english/conventions/mobile-equipment/mobile-equipment.pdf.

SECURITY FOR BANK LOANS

Loans Under the Bank Act

The right to lend to primary producers against the security of their products has long been a distinctive feature of Canadian banking practice. The production of raw materials dominated the early Canadian economy. Typically the producers—usually small-scale farmers—have always required short-term financial assistance to help defray costs through the growing season. Farmers must wait

---

38. UNIDROIT, Convention on International Interests in Mobile Equipment, November 16, 2001, available online at www.unidroit.org/english/conventions/mobile-equipment/main.htm

39. International Interests in Mobile Equipment (Aircraft Equipment) Act, S.C. 2005, c. 3. The Convention was extended beyond aircraft equipment to include railway and space assets.

several months to recoup costs through sales of their produce, and generally they lack sufficient capital to finance themselves in the meantime. Appropriate financing is a short-term *self-liquidating loan*—that is, a loan that must be repaid from the proceeds from sale of the goods whose production the loan is financing. Over the years, successive revisions of the Bank Act have expanded the types of assets that may serve as security and the types of borrowers who may qualify for this type of bank loan, but their underlying self-liquidating character has remained substantially the same.

Section 427 of the current federal Bank Act,[40] empowers Canadian chartered banks to lend to the following types of borrower:

- wholesale or retail purchasers or shippers of, or dealers in (i) products of agriculture, the forest, the quarry and mine, the sea, lakes, and rivers; and (ii) wares and merchandise whether manufactured or not
- manufacturers
- aquaculturalists
- farmers
- fishermen

The types of security that banks are authorized to take vary with the type of borrower and have become quite diverse. At the retail and wholesale level, a bank may take primary produce or manufactured items of inventory held in stock pending resale. For example, a grain-elevator company may borrow under section 427 to permit it to pay farmers on receipt of their grain for storage. Manufacturers may borrow under the section on the security of inventories of raw materials, work-in-process, and finished goods. When lending to farmers, a bank may accept as security crops growing or produced on the farm, livestock, or agricultural equipment. The section permits advances to a farmer for the purchase of seed, fertilizer, or pesticides with future crops serving as security for the loan; the purchase of feed with the livestock as security; the purchase of agricultural equipment with the equipment itself as security; and repairs, improvements, and additions to farm buildings on the security of agricultural equipment. Fishermen may obtain loans on the security of fishing vessels, equipment, supplies, or products of the sea. Similarly, forestry producers can borrow on the security of fertilizer, pesticide, forestry equipment, or forest products.

Rights of a Lending Bank

The security taken by a bank is neither a pledge nor a chattel mortgage. The borrower does not physically transfer the assets to the bank as security, and the bank does not acquire title to the property as security.

A borrower under section 427 signs an agreement containing the following promises:

- to keep the property insured and free from claims
- to account to the bank for the proceeds of sales
- to give the bank a right to take possession in the event of default or neglect
- to grant a power of attorney to the bank
- to consent to the sale of the security without notice or advertisement if the borrower defaults

While the loan is in good standing, the borrower must apply the money realized from the sale of the goods towards a reduction of the loan. As a further assurance that the proceeds from sales are applied against the loan, a bank frequently takes a conditional assignment of the borrower's accounts receivable. If the borrower defaults and the bank takes possession of the goods in the

---

40. Bank Act, S.C. 1991, c. 46. Section 427 came into effect in 1992, and is the successor to section 178 of the previous Bank Act, which in turn replaced section 88 of an earlier act in 1980. It is common to encounter in the literature on this subject the expression "section 178 loan," or even "section 88 loan."

borrower's hands and sells them, the bank is entitled to retain out of the proceeds whatever amount will repay the balance owing on the loan plus costs.[41] Any surplus belongs to the borrower, and any deficiency represents a debt still due.

To protect its security against a borrower's unsecured creditors and subsequent purchasers or mortgagees in good faith, a bank must insist that the borrower file a standard form of notice expressing an intention to give this type of security. Filing of a notice of intention constitutes constructive notice of the bank's interest to other persons dealing with the borrower and preserves the bank's authority.[42] The place for filing is the local or nearest office of the Bank of Canada.[43] In order to protect the value of the security itself, a bank may also require borrowers other than farmers or fishermen to submit at frequent intervals a statement showing the current value and location of the goods comprising the security.

Other Forms of Collateral Security for Bank Loans

The Bank Act also authorizes chartered banks to employ many of the devices for securing credit that we have considered earlier in this chapter. In addition to, or instead of, security under section 427, a bank may require any of the following types of security as a condition for granting credit:

- an assignment of a warehouse receipt, representing title to goods while held in storage, or of an order bill of lading representing title to goods while in the course of transit
- a pledge of shares or bonds, accompanied by a power of attorney signed by the borrower authorizing the bank to sell them as the borrower's agent if need be
- a pledge of drafts drawn by the borrower against his customers
- an assignment of book debts
- an assignment of the cash surrender value of a life insurance policy
- a chattel mortgage
- a real estate mortgage[44]
- a guarantee by a third party

While not expressly authorized by the Bank Act, judicial decisions permit a bank, in addition to holding collateral security provided by the borrower, to exercise a right of lien on other personal property belonging to the borrower in the bank's possession.[45] A bank may apply against a loan any draft that the borrowing business has left with it for collection.[46] It may apply in settlement of the loan any deposit balances kept with it by the borrowing business if it has not previously earmarked these balances for some particular purpose.[47] A bank lien does not extend to property left with the bank for safekeeping.[48]

Conflicts Between the Bank Act and Personal Property Security Acts

As the preceding sections have shown, banks may utilize a wide range of security devices. They can take advantage of the provisions of section 427 of the Bank Act, or they can use the more common forms of security such as chattel mortgages and floating charges. The range of options available,

---

41. Employees of the borrower take priority over the bank to the extent of three months' arrears of wages. Bank Act, S.C. 1991, c. 46, s. 427(7).

42. See *Royal Bank of Canada* v. *Lions Gate Fisheries Ltd.* (1991), 76 D.L.R. (4th) 289.

43. Bank Act, s. 427(4), (5).

44. Normally, a mortgage loan is limited to 80 percent of the value of the property; further restrictions apply to loans made on the security of residential (as opposed to commercial) property: Bank Act, s. 418(1).

45. *Re Williams* (1903), 7 O.L.R. 156.

46. *Merchants Bank* v. *Thompson* (1912), 26 O.L.R. 183.

47. *Riddell* v. *Bank of Upper Canada* (1859), 18 U.C.Q.B. 139.

48. *Leese* v. *Martin* (1873), L.R. 17 Eq. 224.

however, can pose a dilemma for banks and can lead to conflicting claims between them and other creditors.

One problem is that a degree of overlap exists between section 427 of the Bank Act and the credit devices more generally available. For example, while section 427 does not extend to all forms of property that can be the subject of a security interest under personal property security acts, it is unclear to what extent security interests under section 427 fall within the scope of the provincial acts and are protected by registering under those acts.[49]

Second, the Bank Act and the provincial acts each have their own system of registration, which can result in conflict between creditors, each claiming priority under a different scheme.[50]

Third, since the Bank Act is federal legislation but other personal property security legislation is within provincial jurisdiction, neither level of government can resolve the problems alone. Although the operation of section 427 cannot be made subject to provincial legislation,[51] the respective spheres of operation of the different laws remain unclear.

ETHICAL ISSUE

Is the Law Too Favourable Towards Secured Creditors?

What about the interests of other stakeholders? According to one commentator, "Nowhere in the world is there a system for the regulation of secured financing that is more accommodating to secured creditors than the Canadian PPSAs."[52] It has been estimated that in most insolvencies at least 90 percent of the debtor's assets go to satisfy the claims of secured creditors—mainly the banks—leaving little or nothing for unsecured creditors, such as suppliers, contractors, and employees.

The problem has been highlighted by a number of recent high-profile bankruptcies. Often, employees have been left with unpaid wages and have lost their accrued pension benefits while the banks walk away with all the assets. What is perhaps even worse are those cases where the secured creditors are the owners of the business themselves. In 2004, a pulp plant closed down in a small New Brunswick mill town. About 400 people lost their jobs when the owners of the pulp mill decided to close the plant and declare bankruptcy. Most employees also lost their pensions. Many of them had worked at the plant for over 20 years. The primary secured creditor, with claims exceeding $34 million, was the New York corporation that owned all the company's shares.

QUESTIONS TO CONSIDER

1. Are secured creditors given too much protection?

2. Should the owners of a business be allowed to be its secured creditors?

49. See *Rogerson Lumber Co. Ltd.* v. *Four Seasons Chalet Ltd. and Bank of Montreal* (1980), 113 D.L.R. (3d) 671; *Re Bank of Nova Scotia and International Harvester Credit Corp. of Canada Ltd.* (1990), 73 D.L.R. (4th) 385. For a full discussion of this issue, see Cuming (1992), 20 C.B.L.J. 336.

50. For example: *Bank of Montreal* v. *Pulsar Ventures Inc. and City of Moose Jaw*, [1988] 1 W.W.R. 250; *Royal Bank of Canada* v. *Sparrow Electric Corp.* (1997), 143 D.L.R. (4th) 385.

51. *Bank of Montreal* v. *Hall*, [1990] 1 S.C.R. 121.

52. R.C.C. Cuming, "Canadian Bankruptcy Law: A Secured Creditor's Heaven" (1994–5), 24 C.B.L.J. 17 at 21.

QUESTIONS FOR REVIEW

1. What is meant by "collateral security"?

2. Why might a creditor choose not to take security for a debt?

3. In what way do security devices act as an incentive to repay one's debts?

4. What are the principal types of security interest?

5. Why is a lease of personal property commonly treated as a security interest?

6. What is an "acceleration clause"?

7. Distinguish between a chattel mortgage and a pledge.

8. What is the principal difference, in practice, between a conditional sale agreement and a chattel mortgage?

9. How can a creditor obtain a security interest in property that the debtor does not yet possess?

10. What is a "floating charge"?

11. How is priority determined in the PPSA system?

12. What is the function of a "financing statement"?

13. What does it mean that a security interest must be "perfected"?

14. What is a "purchase-money security interest," and why is it given special priority?

15. What allowance is made for a consumer buying goods from a seller in the business of selling those goods?

16. What types of loan receive special protection under the Bank Act?

17. How is a security interest protected under the Bank Act?

CASES AND PROBLEMS

1. In May 1994, SIS Ltd. leased two large, portable, tent-like structures to Cansaw Services Inc. for a term of 24 months, at a monthly rental of $11 000. In December of the same year, Cansaw negotiated a loan from the Regal Bank and executed a general security agreement, which gave the Bank a security interest in:

> . . . the undertaking of Cansaw and all of Cansaw's present and after-acquired personal property including, without limitation, in all goods, intangibles, money, and securities now owned or here- after owned or acquired by or on behalf of Cansaw . . . and in all proceeds and renewals thereof, accretions thereto and substitutions therefore . . . , and including, without limitation, all of the fol- lowing now owned or hereafter owned or acquired by or on behalf of Cansaw: all equipment (other than inventory) of whatever kind and wherever situate, including, without limitation, all machinery, tools, apparatus, plant, furniture, fixtures, and vehicles of whatsoever nature or kind . . .

The Bank registered its security interest under the (Alberta) Personal Property Security Act on the same day.

By May 1996, Cansaw's business was in severe financial difficulties. It had not paid rent to SIS for almost six months and owed them $65 000 in arrears. Its debts to the Bank now totalled almost $1 million.

On May 3, 1996, the Bank delivered a written notice to Cansaw that it was in breach of the financ- ing agreement and gave it one week to remedy its breach. On May 16, 1996, the Bank demanded payment of the outstanding debt and delivered a notice of intention to enforce its security (under section 244 of the Bankruptcy and Insolvency Act). A few days later, the directors of SIS learned of Cansaw's problems with the Bank and gave instructions to a civil enforcement company to enter Cansaw's premises and to disman- tle and repossess the structures. At the same time, acting on the advice of their lawyer, SIS registered a security interest in the structures.

The Bank demanded that SIS return the structures, claiming that their general security agreement covered the structures and had priority over the claim of SIS. SIS replied that they were the owners of the structures and were entitled to repossess them since Cansaw had defaulted on payment of the rent. Who has the better claim?

2. Clarkson purchased an automobile from Easyprice Autos for $17 000, under a conditional sale agreement. Easyprice assigned the conditional sale contract to CVF Inc., which advanced Clarkson the bulk of the purchase price. CVF immediately registered its security interest under the (Ontario) Personal Property Security Act.

   Six months later, Clarkson entered into a second conditional sales contract with Sonmax Corp. for the purchase and installation of stereo equipment in the vehicle at a cost of $3500, including financing charges. CVF was not informed of this second contract. Sonmax promptly registered a lien against the vehicle under the Repairs and Storage Liens Act.

   A few months later, when Clarkson fell into arrears with his repayments, Sonmax repossessed the vehicle, and gave Clarkson notice of its intention to sell the vehicle to secure repayment of what was owed them. At that point, CVF learned of the action by Sonmax and also claimed the vehicle.

   Which firm has the prior claim?

3. Silver was the proprietor of the "Sick Parrot," an exotic but eventually unsuccessful restaurant. The premises were originally leased from Desai, who sold the property to Ramesh in 1996.

   In order to finance the purchase of new furniture and fittings, Silver had borrowed $20 000 from McTavish in 1995; in doing so he had entered into a general security agreement, giving McTavish a security interest in ". . . all inventory, furnishings, and fitments . . ." of the business. McTavish did not register her interest at the time, and Ramesh was unaware of the interest when he purchased the property.

   Around the end of 1997, it became clear to Silver that the restaurant business had failed. He was six months in arrears with his rent and still owed McTavish $15 000. He decided simply to abandon the business and has disappeared. When Ramesh learned that the restaurant had gone out of business, he re-entered the premises and took possession of all the inventory, furniture, and so forth. A few days later, McTavish also learned of Silver's departure. She immediately registered her security interest and demanded that Ramesh return all the items he had seized.

   Ramesh agreed to return the inventory and furniture, which were worth very little, but claimed that, as the landlord, he was entitled to keep the bar, shelving, refrigerators, light fitments, and other "fixtures." Is Ramesh correct?

4. Avila purchased a second-hand Cadillac from Better Buy Motors Ltd. under a conditional sale agreement. She used the car for several months in her work as a sales representative and paid her instalments regularly. When she had only two instalments left to pay, the car was towed out of her driveway and delivered to Fancy Finance Corp., on instructions of that company. Avila had never heard of Fancy Finance before. It informed her that it had "repossessed" the car under a prior, properly registered chattel mortgage that it held, and that the chattel mortgagor had fraudulently sold the car to Better Buy Motors.

   Examine the nature of Avila's rights and indicate against whom they are available. What factors should be taken into account in assessing her loss?

5. Holmes purchased a refrigerator and stove from Watts Electric Ltd. under a conditional sale agreement. Watts Electric Ltd. discounted the contract with Domestic Finance Co. Neither Watts Electric nor Domestic Finance registered the agreement.

   Several months later Holmes sold the appliances to Fischer for cash without disclosing that there was still an unpaid balance owing to Domestic Finance, and left the province. After Holmes defaulted payment, Domestic Finance discovered that Fischer had possession of the appliances and repossessed them. Fischer then sued Domestic Finance for wrongful seizure of the appliances.

   State the arguments for the plaintiff and the defendant. What should the decision be?

6. Oliver purchased a used car from Hardy Motors Ltd. for $5500 and paid $3800 in cash as a down payment on the understanding that he would have 30 days to pay the balance. The manager of Hardy Motors Ltd. stated that 30-day credit was unusual for this type of purchase and that he would still have to get Oliver's signature on a conditional sale agreement "as a matter of form." Oliver signed the agreement, which included a term that Oliver would pay the balance of the purchase price over 24 months in monthly instalments of $89.50 each. The manager told Oliver that he would hold the conditional sale agreement for 30 days so that Oliver would have that time to raise the balance of the purchase price.

Hardy Motors Ltd. was in financial trouble. In breach of its understanding with Oliver, the company at once discounted (assigned) the conditional sale contract with Vanguard Finance Co. The finance company informed Oliver of the assignment and requested payment to it of the monthly instalments specified in the conditional sale agreement. Oliver ignored the notice, and before the expiration of the 30 days, paid the balance of $1700 directly to Hardy Motors Ltd. Soon after Hardy Motors Ltd. was adjudged bankrupt, and the manager absconded with the cash assets of the business. Vanguard Finance seized the car from Oliver, who then sued the finance company for wrongful seizure, asking for a court order for return of the car to him.

Should Oliver's action succeed?

ADDITIONAL RESOURCES FOR CHAPTER 30 ON THE COMPANION WEBSITE *(www.pearsoned.ca/smyth)*

In addition to self-test multiple-choice, true–false, and short essay questions (all with immediate feedback), application exercises, and links to useful web destinations, the Companion Website provides the following resources for Chapter 30:

- **British Columbia:** Enforcement of Security Interests; Perfection and Priority of Security Interests; Personal Property Registry; Personal Property Security Act
- **Alberta:** Builders' Lien Act; Debt Collections; Garnishment; Liens; Loan Transactions; Personal Money Security Interest; Personal Property Registry; Personal Property Security Act; Seizure
- **Manitoba/Saskatchewan:** Personal Property Security Acts; Seizing Goods
- **Ontario:** Assignment of Rents; Attachment; Bulk Sales; Financing Statement; Personal Property; Personal Property Security Act; Purchase Money Security Interest; Registration; Sale of Collateral; Security Interest

31

Creditors' Rights

In this chapter we examine the various ways in which the rights of creditors are protected and enforced. The main focus is on the Bankruptcy and Insolvency Act, but consideration is also given to other statutes, in particular, the various provincial laws regarding builders' liens, also known as mechanics' liens or construction liens in some provinces. We consider such questions as:

- What are the principal objectives of bankruptcy law?

- How does bankruptcy law distinguish between different types of debtors—and why?

- What constitutes an "act of bankruptcy"?

- What principles govern the administration of a bankrupt's assets?

- What is a builders' lien?

- How are the interests of contractors and subcontractors protected?

- What is the effect of limitation periods on creditors' rights?

STATUTORY ARRANGEMENTS FOR THE PROTECTION OF CREDITORS

In Chapter 15 we examined two of the most important methods by which a creditor's rights may be enforced—levying execution against the goods of the debtor and garnishing his wages. These methods work more or less satisfactorily where the debtor has sufficient assets or income to satisfy the debt and where there is only one creditor. We considered, in Chapter 30, the rights of a secured creditor to recover what is owing by taking possession of the debtor's property, which constitutes the security for the debt, and selling it. We also saw that where there are a number of creditors with conflicting claims, problems of priorities arise.

The great majority of business persons are honest and pay their debts reasonably promptly if they are able to do so. Consequently, resorting to legal procedures to collect money owed by solvent debtors is comparatively unusual. But in some cases a debtor's financial position may become so hopeless that it is unwise or impossible for him to continue to carry on business. A person becomes insolvent when he is unable to pay his debts as they fall due or when his liabilities exceed his realizable assets. When a debtor finds himself in that condition, at least some of his creditors will go unpaid.

A businesses is usually both a creditor and a debtor. It uses credit to grow the business and extends credit to customers in the ordinary course of doing business. Therefore, it is important to understand the rules of debt collection. A number of statutes have as their main purpose the protection of creditors' claims. These acts set out the rights of creditors both against their debtors and against each other. In this chapter, we will review the ways in which the Bankruptcy and Insolvency Act (BIA), the Companies' Creditors Arrangement Act, and the Builders' Lien Acts assist in this purpose.

THE BANKRUPTCY AND INSOLVENCY ACT

Background

Jurisdiction over bankruptcy is assigned to the federal Parliament under the Constitution Act, 1867. The first federal Bankruptcy Act was adopted in 1919 and remained in force until replaced by the Bankruptcy Act of 1949. That Act remains the basis of our current bankruptcy law, though it has been substantially amended on a number of occasions, most notably in 1992, when it was renamed the Bankruptcy and Insolvency Act.[1] Further major reforms were undertaken in 2005 and 2007. It is expected that the latest revisions will be proclaimed in force in the near future.

In the period prior to 1919, some provinces passed legislation governing procedures for "assignments" and prohibiting certain types of fraudulent conduct by debtors,[2] but no legal machinery existed for the compulsory division of an insolvent debtor's property among his creditors. There was no formal way of giving an honest debtor a formal discharge from his obligations once all his assets had been distributed to his creditors; they could continue to pursue him for payment, subject only to limitations statutes.

The Bankruptcy and Insolvency Act performs a number of functions:

■ It establishes a uniform practice in bankruptcy proceedings throughout the country and attempts to do so as inexpensively as possible.

1. Bankruptcy and Insolvency Act, R.S.C. 1985, c. B-3, as amended by S.C. 1992, c. 27, S.C. 2005, c. 47 (Bill C-55) and S.C. 2007, c. 36 (Bill C-12). The 2005 and 2007 reforms received royal assent on December 14, 2007 but only some of the reforms have been proclaimed in force; the remaining proclamations are expected in 2009. Unless otherwise stated, statutory references in this part of the chapter are to this Act.

2. Some provincial legislation remains in effect; see, for example: the Assignments and Preferences Act, R.S.O. 1990, c. A.33. In case of a conflict between provincial and federal legislation dealing with insolvency, the latter prevails: *British Columbia* v. *Henfrey Samson Belair Ltd.* (1989), 59 D.L.R. (4th) 726.

■ It attempts to provide for an equitable distribution of the debtor's assets among his various creditors.

■ It provides a framework for preserving and reorganizing the debtor's business or affairs by working out an arrangement with the agreement of his creditors in order to avoid a total liquidation of a debtor's estate, if possible.

■ It provides for the release of an honest but unfortunate debtor from his obligations and so permits him to make a fresh start free of debts.

INTERNATIONAL ISSUE

Cross-border Insolvency

In 1997, the United Nations Commission on International Trade Law adopted a Model Law on Cross-border Insolvency.[3] It addresses the jurisdictional issues associated with multinational corporations and foreign bankruptcy proceedings. The model law proposes that international co-operation in trans-border insolvency be achieved using three strategies:

■ authorizing courts to coordinate and cooperate with each other;

■ restricting the scope of local (domestic) bankruptcy proceedings; and

■ granting local relief to representatives of foreign proceedings.[4]

Canada's 2007 reform of insolvency law incorporates the general concepts advanced by the model law with some modification in form. One interesting variation is the inclusion of a provision that allows a court to refuse to make an order that is not in compliance with Canadian law or if doing so would be contrary to public policy. Also, Canadian courts are not obligated to enforce an order made by a foreign court.[5]

QUESTIONS TO CONSIDER

1. Why is international co-operation important?

2. What circumstances might be considered contrary to public policy?

3. How do these limitations respect domestic sovereignty?

Competing Policy Issues

There are many stakeholder interests to consider: creditors, debtors, consumers, business, government, and the public as a whole. It is helpful in bankruptcy law to distinguish the public interest from that of the parties to a bankruptcy proceeding, even though their interests often coincide. Business confidence and respect for the law are reinforced if creditors are able to recover what is lawfully owing to them. But their interests may diverge from that of society generally in a number of ways. The chief concern of most creditors is to quickly collect as much as possible of what is owed to them. They will normally have little interest in whether a debtor's business can be saved and

---

3. Available online at www.uncitral.org/uncitral/en/uncitral_texts/insolvency/1997Model.html.

4. Industry Canada, "Backgrounder: Government Announces Reform of the Bankruptcy and Insolvency Act and the Companies' Creditors Arrangement Act," June 3, 2005, www.ic.gc.ca/epic/site/ic1.nsf/en/02282e.html.

5. Bill C-12: An Act to amend the Bankruptcy and Insolvency Act, the Companies' Creditors Arrangement Act, the Wage Earner Protection Program Act and chapter 47 of the Statutes of Canada 2005, LS-584E, Legislative Summaries, Library of Parliament, December 14, 2007, (clauses 60 and 81), available online at www.parl.gc.ca/common/bills_ls.asp?lang=E&ls=c12&source=library_prb&Parl=39&Ses=2.

turned around. Bankruptcy law, however, contains provisions whereby creditors may be encouraged, and sometimes compelled, to accept an arrangement designed to save a business and therefore the jobs it provides. Again, a creditor normally wishes to preserve the possibility of recovering in full what she is owed, even if this is not possible in the debtor's present financial circumstances. However, it is in the public interest to allow an honest but unfortunate debtor to be discharged from his debts once he has paid as much as possible and to give him a fresh start.

Where a debtor has virtually no assets available to meet his debts, the natural instinct of his creditors may be simply to cut their losses and not waste time and money in a fruitless attempt to recover something. One of the aims of bankruptcy legislation, however, is to promote an atmosphere of confidence in business relations, and confidence would be undermined if bankruptcy fraud went unpunished. Therefore, the Act contains provisions to punish dishonest debtors and to prevent them from re-engaging in business activities.

There are, of course, limits to what even well-drafted legislation can achieve. In many situations, the damage done to creditors' claims by the time bankruptcy occurs is largely irreparable. The best protection for creditors is to be careful in granting credit. To assist prospective creditors by making more information available to them, the Act requires certain information to be filed concerning bankrupt debtors and the directors and officers of bankrupt corporations.

Government Supervision

The Act (section 5) creates the position of Superintendent of Bankruptcy, who keeps a record of all bankruptcy proceedings in Canada and has a general supervisory function over all bankrupt estates. The Superintendent is responsible for investigating the character and qualifications of persons applying for licences to act as trustees and has the power to suspend or cancel a trustee's licence. He or she may issue directives to trustees or receivers regarding the administration of a bankrupt estate, intervene in any court proceeding, and investigate situations where a bankruptcy offence may have been committed (section 10(1)). Over the last 15 years the powers of the Office of the Superintendent have gradually expanded.

For the purposes of administration, the Act makes each province and territory a bankruptcy district. Each district may be divided into two or more divisions, according to the size of the province or territory. For each division, one or more **official receivers** are appointed. Official receivers are officers of the court and are required to report to the Superintendent all bankruptcies originating in their divisions (section 12).

official receiver
a public official responsible for the supervision of bankruptcy proceedings

The Act designates the highest trial court in each province or territory as the court for hearing bankruptcy proceedings (section 183). Usually a particular judge or judges of the provincial court are designated to deal with bankruptcy matters, and their courts are commonly referred to as the Bankruptcy Court, though strictly speaking no separate bankruptcy tribunal exists. The courts hear creditors' **petitions** for the bankruptcy of their debtors and determine whether or on what terms certain debtors should be discharged after their affairs have been wound up.

petition
a request to commence bankruptcy proceedings against a defaulting debtor

The actual administration of a debtor's estate is placed in the hands of a licensed **trustee in bankruptcy**, who is normally an accountant and is appointed by the court or, in the case of a voluntary assignment in bankruptcy, by the official receiver. In either case, in appointing the trustee regard must be paid to the wishes of the creditors, who retain the power to appoint a substitute trustee (section 14). The creditors also appoint one or more (but not exceeding five) inspectors to instruct and supervise the trustee (section 116).

trustee in bankruptcy
the person appointed to administer the property of a bankrupt

Persons to Whom the Act Applies

Bankrupts and Insolvent Persons

The Act applies, in general, to debtors who are individuals, partnerships, and corporations—apart from banks, insurance companies, and trust, loan, and railway companies. A "**bankrupt**" is defined as a person who has made an assignment or against whom a receiving order has been made; that is,

bankrupt
a person who has made a voluntary assignment in bankruptcy or against whom a receiving order has been made

a formal legal step must be taken in order to declare a person bankrupt. A distinction is made between debtors who voluntarily declare bankruptcy and those who are petitioned into bankruptcy by their creditors.

insolvent person
a person who is unable to meet (or has ceased to pay) his or her debts as they become due, or whose debts exceed the value of his or her realizable assets

The Act, as its title indicates, applies to insolvent persons as well as to bankrupts. An **insolvent person** is defined, for the purposes of the Act, as a person who is not bankrupt, whose liabilities to creditors amount to at least $1000, and who either

- is unable to meet his obligations as they generally become due,
- has ceased paying his current obligations in the ordinary course of business as they generally become due, or
- has debts due and accruing due, the aggregate of which exceeds the realizable value of his assets (section 2).

The Act distinguishes between two basic types of person—those who are potential candidates for bankruptcy (insolvents) and those who have been declared bankrupt (bankrupts). A person may be insolvent without having been declared bankrupt, and a bankrupt may turn out not to be insolvent.

Consumer Debtors

consumer debtor
an individual who is insolvent but whose aggregate debts do not exceed $75 000 (soon to be changed to $250 000)

An important distinction is drawn in the Act between "consumer debtors" and other debtors. It defines a **consumer debtor** as an insolvent natural person (that is, an individual) whose aggregate debts, excluding any debt secured by the person's principal residence, do not exceed $75 000 (section 66.11). The 2007 reforms will change the maximum amount to $250 000. Consumer bankruptcies already represent the vast majority of all bankruptcies (79 796 in 2007), while business bankruptcies have fallen by 46 percent over the last 15 years (6307 in 2007).[6]

The relevance of the distinctions—between insolvent persons and bankrupts, and between commercial and consumer debtors—will be considered when we discuss the various procedures provided for under the Act.

Corporations

income trust
a trust with assets in Canada and whose units are traded on a prescribed stock exchange

As we saw in Chapter 27, the principle of limited liability means that the shareholders of a corporation are not liable for its debts. The corporation is liable for its own debts to the full extent of its assets, but these may be very few. Notions of punishment and rehabilitation have little meaning for a bankrupt corporation. A group of individuals may form a corporation with a very small capital sum and, if the corporation becomes bankrupt, they lose very little (unless they have personally guaranteed its debts). To make a fresh start in business, they may simply form a new corporation. However, the worst abuses—for example, where the assets of a corporation are drained by the payment of excessive dividends or by redeeming shares—are governed by provisions that allow such transactions to be reviewed and set aside. Further, where a corporation commits a bankruptcy offence, any director or officer who authorized, participated in, or acquiesced in the offence is liable to punishment for the offence (section 204).[7] The 2007 amendments make bankruptcy and insolvency protection available to **income trusts**, and trustees have similar liability to a director.

---

6. "Canadian Bankruptcy Statistics (1980–2008)," *BankruptcyCanada.com*, www.bankruptcycanada.com/bankstats1.htm (sourced from Industry Canada).

7. An individual who is a bankrupt is not permitted to be a director of a corporation; see, for example: Canada Business Corporations Act, R.S.C. 1985, c. C-44, s. 105(1)(d).

Procedures Under the Act

The Act makes provision for three distinct types of procedure, applicable in different circumstances and each with its own special consequences:

(1) a **proposal**—a procedure to avoid formal liquidation of the debtor's estate, at least temporarily, by allowing the debtor time to attempt to reorganize and save a viable business or, in the case of a consumer debtor, to reorganize his affairs;

(2) an **assignment**—a voluntary application by a debtor to institute bankruptcy proceedings;

(3) a **receiving order**—initiated by creditors' petition to have their debtor declared bankrupt by the court.

Proposals

The Act makes provision for two types of proposal—commonly referred to as *commercial proposals* (Division I) and *consumer proposals* (Division II)—the latter being a simplified procedure available to individual consumer debtors. For corporations, an alternative method of avoiding liquidation is provided under the Companies' Creditors Arrangement Act. That Act is considered later in this chapter, under the heading "Other Methods of Liquidation and Reorganization."

Commercial Proposals   A Division I proposal may be made by an insolvent person, a liquidator of an insolvent person's property, or by a receiver in relation to an insolvent person. A proposal may also be made by a bankrupt or by the trustee of a bankrupt's estate, provided the estate has not yet been wound up (section 50(1)).

A proposal constitutes an offer made by the debtor to his creditors, providing for the orderly repayment of his debts or of some part of his debts,[8] over a period of time. If the proposal is accepted by a sufficient proportion of the creditors, application may be made to the court to have it declared binding upon all the creditors.

Where a proposal is made before bankruptcy, the debtor files a copy of the proposal with the official receiver in the debtor's district. The proposal must be accompanied by a statement showing the debtor's financial position, verified by affidavit of a licensed trustee. An insolvent person can gain additional time by filing a notice of intention with the official receiver, stating his intention to make a proposal (section 50.4). If the debtor has already been made bankrupt, the proposal and statement of financial position are delivered to the existing trustee. The proposal must be approved by the inspectors (appointed by the creditors to supervise the trustee) before any further action is taken.

The next stage is to obtain approval for the proposal at a meeting of the creditors. One of the most important changes introduced in the 1992 amendments was to bring secured creditors within the scope of the Act. Now, a proposal may be made to secured creditors or to one or more classes of secured creditors, as well as to unsecured creditors. Acceptance of a proposal requires the approval of a majority in number, and two-thirds in value, of the unsecured creditors, and a similar proportion of each class of secured creditors. Secured creditors not included in the proposal, or whose class has rejected the proposal, continue to enjoy the protection provided by their security.

If the proposal is accepted by a sufficient proportion of creditors, the next step is for the trustee to apply to the court for approval. Although the court will be reluctant to refuse approval to a proposal that is acceptable to the majority of creditors, it must be satisfied that the terms of the proposal are reasonable and for the benefit of the general body of creditors (section 59(2)). In particular, it may withhold approval if the proposal fails to provide reasonable security for repayment of at least 50 cents on the dollar to unsecured creditors, or if the debtor has been guilty of a bankruptcy offence.

proposal
a procedure whereby a debtor, by agreement with the creditors, reorganizes his or her affairs without being made bankrupt

assignment
a voluntary declaration of bankruptcy

receiving order
a court order made in proceedings instituted by creditors, whereby a debtor is declared bankrupt

---

8. Certain debts, notably those to the Crown and to employees, must be paid in full; section 60(1.1), (1.3).

Once approved by the court, the proposal is binding on all unsecured creditors and on all secured creditors of a class that has given its approval. Unless the proposal provides to the contrary, the debtor retains control of his property. However, monies payable under the proposal must be paid to the trustee for distribution to the creditors. Where the debtor defaults in the performance of any provision of the proposal, the trustee is required to notify all creditors and the official receiver. Application may then be made, by any creditor or by the trustee, to have the proposal annulled (section 63(3)). The effect of annulment is that the debtor is deemed to have made an assignment (see below).

Consumer Proposals An insolvent individual who owes no more than $75 000 (soon to be $250 000), not counting any debt secured by mortgage on a principal residence, may make a proposal to his creditors for the reduction of, or extension of time for the payment of, his debts (section 66.12). It should be noted that the provisions do not apply to individuals who have already been declared bankrupt. Bankrupt consumers are subject to the general provisions of the Act, though they presumably may make a proposal under Division I.

A Division II proposal must be prepared with the assistance of an "administrator," a licensed trustee or other person appointed by the Superintendent to administer consumer proposals. The administrator is responsible for investigating the debtor's financial affairs and for providing counselling. Procedures are simplified, and a formal meeting of creditors is not required unless requested by creditors representing 25 percent in value of the proven debts. Where no meeting is requested, the proposal is deemed to be accepted by the creditors. A proposal that has been accepted or is deemed to be accepted does not require approval of the court.

An important consequence of filing a consumer proposal is that the debtor also obtains protection against lease terminations, acceleration of instalment payments, or having utilities shut off (section 66.34).

Assignments

By making an assignment an insolvent person may voluntarily declare himself bankrupt. A debtor who is no longer able to meet his debts as they fall due may prefer to initiate bankruptcy proceedings himself, rather than wait for his creditors to do so. By making an assignment he puts an end to an unsatisfactory situation and makes an earlier rehabilitation possible. Also, to continue to carry on a business once he knows he is insolvent might well involve him in the commission of a bankruptcy offence and jeopardize his eventual discharge (section 173(1)(c)).

A debtor makes an assignment by filing a petition with the official receiver, accompanied by a sworn statement listing his property and his debts and creditors (section 49).[9] When the official receiver files the petition, she appoints a trustee, who becomes responsible for the administration of the debtor's estate and to whom the debtor's property is assigned. From that point on, the debtor ceases to have any right to dispose of or deal with his property.

The estate of a bankrupt who has made an assignment is administered in the same manner as one administered under a receiving order (the procedure will be dealt with in the next section). However, a special simplified form of administration is provided in the case of an individual bankrupt who has made an assignment and whose realizable assets, after deducting the claims of secured creditors, do not exceed $5000 in value (section 49(6)).

Receiving Orders

act of bankruptcy
a prescribed act of a debtor that must be proved before the debtor may be declared bankrupt

A creditor or group of creditors may file a petition with the court in the judicial district where the debtor is located in order to have the debtor declared bankrupt, provided the creditor (or group) is owed not less than $1000, and the debtor has committed an **act of bankruptcy** within the previous six months (section 43). A secured creditor may initiate a petition, but to the extent that she makes a claim in bankruptcy, she is considered to have abandoned her security.

9. As already noted, a person who defaults on a proposal may also be deemed to have made an assignment.

It should be noted that, unlike the rules for making proposals and assignments, there is no requirement that the debtor be insolvent; it is sufficient that he has committed an act of bankruptcy. An act of bankruptcy, as we shall see in the next section, may be committed by a person who is not insolvent. However, in the great majority of cases where a receiving order is made, the debtor is likely to be insolvent.

Subject to a few exceptions, a petition may be filed in respect of any debtor, whether an individual, partnership, or corporation. No petition may be made against an *individual* who is engaged solely in fishing or farming, or against a wage earner who does not earn more than $2500 a year and does not carry on any business on his own account (section 48).[10]

Bankruptcy proceedings are considered penal in nature, and the burden of proving the facts alleged is on the petitioning creditors, who must comply with all the formalities required by the Act. The petition may be opposed by the debtor, who may dispute the existence of the debt or of an alleged act of bankruptcy. Even where the petitioning creditors succeed in establishing facts that would justify the making of a receiving order, the court has a general discretion to refuse to make the order or to grant a stay of proceedings. For example, it may decline to make an order if it considers that, given a fair chance, the debtor will be able to meet his obligations within a reasonable period. It may also decline to make an order where the debtor has no assets to divide among the creditors and there is no likelihood that he will have assets in the future.

Where a receiving order is made, its effect is to vest the bankrupt's property in the trustee appointed by the court to administer the estate.

Acts of Bankruptcy

We have noted that before creditors can succeed in having their debtor declared bankrupt and a receiving order issued, they must prove that he has committed an act of bankruptcy. The Bankruptcy and Insolvency Act sets out in detail the various types of conduct that constitute an act of bankruptcy by a debtor (section 42). In summary they are as follows:

- An assignment of assets to a trustee. If a debtor makes an assignment of his property to a trustee for the benefit of his creditors, whether it is an authorized assignment or not, and the arrangement is not satisfactory to the creditors, they may cite the assignment as an act of bankruptcy and petition to have a receiving order issued. They might choose to do so, for example, when the debtor has transferred his assets to a trustee who is not acceptable to them.
- A fraudulent transfer of assets to a third party other than a trustee. A transfer of property by a debtor in anticipation of bankruptcy in order to withhold assets from distribution to creditors is a fraudulent transfer. As we shall see when discussing "Powers and Duties of the Trustee" below, any attempt to deprive creditors of access to assets by transferring them to a third person (including the debtor's spouse or child) is void if the transfer takes place within a specified period prior to bankruptcy.
- A fraudulent preference. Any payment by a debtor that has the effect of settling the claim of one creditor in preference to the outstanding claims of other creditors is a fraudulent preference.
- An attempt by the debtor to abscond, with intent to defraud creditors.
- A failure to redeem goods seized under an execution issued against the debtor.[11] As we have seen in Chapter 15, a creditor may sue a debtor, obtain judgment, and seek to satisfy the judgment by having the debtor's assets seized. When a debtor's assets are few, a seizure may well benefit the judgment creditor to the disadvantage of other creditors. Accordingly, if a

---

10. Such an individual may, however, make a voluntary assignment. A corporation engaged in farming or fishing may be petitioned.

11. More specifically, a debtor commits an act of bankruptcy if he permits an execution to remain unsatisfied for fifteen days after seizure by the sheriff, until within five days of the time fixed for sale by the sheriff, or in a variety of other circumstances set out in section 42(1)(e).

debtor fails to take steps to prevent the sale of his property under an execution order, he commits an act that entitles his creditors to apply to the court for his bankruptcy. If they do so, all the debtor's property, including the property subject to the execution order, is put in the hands of a licensed trustee for distribution to all the creditors.[12]

- The presentation at a meeting of creditors of (a) a statement of assets and liabilities disclosing the debtor's insolvency, or (b) a written admission by the debtor that he is unable to pay his debts.
- An attempt to remove or hide any of his property, with intent to defraud creditors.
- Notice to any of the creditors that the debtor is suspending payment of his debts.
- A default in any proposal that the debtor has previously persuaded the creditors to accept as a means of forestalling bankruptcy proceedings.
- A failure to meet liabilities generally as they become due.

The most common of these acts of bankruptcy are failing to pay debts as they become due and failing to redeem goods seized under an execution.

ADMINISTRATION OF A BANKRUPT'S AFFAIRS

Powers and Duties of the Trustee

The appointment of a trustee is the first step in establishing creditor control. The trustee takes possession of the assets of the bankrupt debtor and all books and documents relating to his affairs. She becomes in effect a temporary manager of the business, subject to the supervision of inspectors appointed by the creditors. She may carry on the business or, alternatively, sell the assets. She can do such things as employ a lawyer, borrow further money for the business by pledging or mortgaging its remaining free (unsecured) assets, and negotiate with creditors for the acceptance by them of specific assets in lieu of money settlement of their claims. She may even engage the bankrupt debtor himself to assist in the administration of the bankrupt estate. To do these things she must have specific authority from the inspectors (section 30). The principal duties of a trustee, however, are to recover all property that under bankruptcy law should form part of the debtor's estate, and to apply that property in satisfaction of the claims of creditors (sections 16(3), 25).

Recovery of Property

The trustee takes possession of those assets of the debtor that are in the debtor's possession and also seeks to recover any other assets, for example, by collecting debts owed to the debtor. As a general rule, the trustee cannot obtain a better title to property than the debtor himself possessed in that property. Consequently, the trustee's interest is subject to the claims of persons who own property that is in the possession of the debtor or of secured creditors who have interests in that property. However, the Personal Property Security Acts (PPSAs) have introduced an exception to the general principle. If someone has leased personal property to the debtor and has failed to register that interest, the security interest may be ineffective and subordinate to the claim of the trustee.[13] As will be discussed further in later sections, some property (such as household goods) is exempt from seizure by the trustee.

In addition, there may be property that the debtor has disposed of and that by law should form part of his bankrupt estate and be available to satisfy the claims of creditors. Thirteen sections of the Act under the heading "Settlements and Preferences" are needed to set out the complex rules for the recovery of property (sections 91–101.2).

---

12. It is possible that, instead of petitioning for a receiving order, all the debtor's major creditors may choose to obtain individual judgments and execution orders. In Ontario, the Creditors Relief Act, R.S.O. 1990, c. C.45, provides for a scheme of rateable distribution of the proceeds of sale among execution creditors.

13. *Re Giffen*, [1998] 1 S.C.R. 91; not followed in *Re Ouellet*, [2004] 3 S.C.R. 348.

Settlements

The term "**settlement**" refers to gifts of property made by the debtor before becoming bankrupt. The intention of the rules is to prevent a person who is insolvent or on the verge of insolvency from prejudicing the claims of his creditors by giving his property away—usually to members of his family or to friends.

> **settlement**
> a gift of property made by a debtor before becoming bankrupt

In general, any gratuitous transfer of property[14] by a debtor that occurred within a year before his bankruptcy becomes void and recoverable by the trustee. In addition, the trustee may impeach a transfer of property made as long as five years before the bankruptcy, but the burden is then on the trustee to show that at the date of the transfer the debtor was unable to pay his debts in full without the aid of such property (section 91).[15]

A settlement may be attacked not only under the provisions of the Bankruptcy and Insolvency Act but also under provincial laws dealing with **fraudulent transfers**;[16] it is not unusual for a trustee in bankruptcy to pursue both kinds of remedies.

> **fraudulent transfer**
> a transfer of property by a debtor with the intention of putting that property out of the reach of creditors

CASE 31.1

A husband and wife had jointly owned their home since 1974. In 1978, the husband gave a personal guarantee to a bank in respect of a debt owed by the corporation of which he and his wife were the sole shareholders. In 1990, the husband transferred his half-interest in the home to his wife for $1. Shortly thereafter the bank demanded repayment of the debt and, when the husband was unable to meet the guarantee, it appointed a receiver. The husband died insolvent in 1991.

The bank successfully claimed that the transfer of the interest in the home was a fraudulent conveyance and was consequently void under the (Ontario) Fraudulent Conveyances Act. The bank was entitled to a 50 percent interest in the property.[17]

CASE 31.2

The Chans obtained a judgment against the Stanwoods for an amount exceeding $250 000 and were pressing for immediate payment. In an attempt to avoid the seizure of their family home and other assets, the Stanwoods consulted a lawyer, Davis, who recommended a complex scheme that involved the creation of a corporation with an elaborate share structure and voting rights. The home and assets were transferred to the corporation, but the Stanwoods remained in effective control of the corporation through their power to appoint "friendly" directors.

The Chans commenced proceedings under the (B.C.) Fraudulent Conveyances Act and were successful in having the transfer to the corporation set aside. Their claim for damages against the lawyer who devised the scheme failed. The court held that to advise someone to commit a breach of the Act is not a civil wrong.[18]

The provisions of the provincial legislation differ from those of the Bankruptcy and Insolvency Act in a number of respects, and the trustee may rely on the provincial act to supplement the normal bankruptcy remedies.[19] In particular, it is not necessary to be an established creditor in order to bring proceedings under the Fraudulent Conveyances Acts to have a transaction set aside. Decisions have held that a claimant in a tort action (who had not yet obtained a judgment) could

---

14. The rule does not apply to property transferred in a genuine business transaction; *Re Dowswell* (1999), 178 D.L.R. (4th) 193. Nor does it apply to transfers of property that would otherwise be exempt from execution, such as a RRIF; see, for example: *Royal Bank of Canada* v. *North American Life Assurance Co.* (1996), 132 D.L.R. (4th) 193 (S.C.C.).

15. In practice, it is almost impossible for a trustee to establish the exact financial status of a bankrupt debtor at a time as long as a year or more before the bankruptcy.

16. See, for example: Fraudulent Conveyances Act, R.S.B.C. 1996, c. 163; R.S.N.L. 1990, c. F-24; R.S.O. 1990, c. F.29.

17. *Bank of Montreal* v. *Bray* (1997), 36 O.R. (3d) 99; not followed in *Stone* v. *Stone*, [2002] W.D.F.L. 615, (Ont. SCJ). See also *Mutual Trust Co.* v. *Stornelli* (1999), 170 D.L.R. (4th) 381.

18. *Chan* v. *Stanwood* (2002), 216 D.L.R. (4th) 625.

19. *Flightcraft Inc.* v. *Parsons* (1999), 175 D.L.R. (4th) 642.

challenge a transfer of property to relatives, designed to defeat the claim,[20] and that a wife could challenge a secret transfer of property by her husband to his children that would have the effect of depriving her of her rights under the Family Law Act.[21]

Preferences

A solvent debtor is entitled to pay his creditors in any order he pleases. He may choose to pay one creditor before he pays another—that is, to give preference to the claim of the first creditor over the second—perhaps because he depends upon the prompt services or delivery of goods from the first creditor. (Another reason is this: if the debtor is a corporation, the directors may have given personal guarantees of one or more of the debts.) By contrast, in bankruptcy the guiding principle is that creditors of the same class should be treated equally.

A debtor facing imminent bankruptcy should consequently not be permitted to unfairly favour certain creditors over others. The Act deals with this situation by providing that (a) a payment of money or a transfer of property to a creditor, (b) by an insolvent debtor, (c) within three months preceding bankruptcy, and (d) with a view to giving that creditor preference over other creditors amounts to a **fraudulent preference** and is recoverable (section 95). The time limit extends to 12 months where the creditor who received the preference is a related person (section 96). The provisions are intended to nullify transactions that would otherwise defeat the legitimate claims of creditors. They do not invalidate payments made in good faith to creditors who were unaware of the impending bankruptcy, or other transfers of property such as the sale of inventory or other business assets in the normal course of business (section 97).[22]

fraudulent preference
the payment of money or transfer of property to a creditor with a view to giving that creditor preference over other creditors

CASE 31.3

Green Gables Manor Inc., a corporation operating a nursing home, made payments of $13 000 to each of its two controlling shareholders and directors. The payments were stated to be in respect of management fees owed to them. It also executed a general security agreement in their favour in respect of outstanding claims. The following day, a receiving order was granted, and Green Gables was declared bankrupt.

The trustee claimed repayment of the sums and a declaration that the security agreement was void. The court found that the two directors were "related" to the corporation for the purposes of the Bankruptcy and Insolvency Act, that the transactions represented a "preference," and that they should accordingly be set aside.[23]

Reviewable Transactions

A third source of potential abuse is that category of transactions where a debtor has entered into a contract with a relative or a corporation in which he has a major interest. Since he was not dealing at **arm's length** with that other party, there is a risk that the interests of his creditors may have been harmed. The debtor may have sold property at an undervalue or bought at an excessive price. The effect is as if he had made a gift of the difference between the sum actually received or paid and the fair market value of the property. Persons related to each other are deemed not to deal at arm's length. The Act defines "related" broadly so that it includes not only personal relationships through blood, marriage, or adoption, but also the relationship between a corporation and its controlling shareholders or between two or more corporations with a common controlling person or group (section 4).

Under the Act, transactions that were not at arm's length are reviewable. If entered into by the debtor within 12 months preceding bankruptcy, the trustee may apply to the court for an inquiry

arm's length
a transaction between persons who are not related or associated in any way

20. *Hamm* v. *Metz* (2002), 209 D.L.R. (4th) 385.

21. *Stone* v. *Stone* (2001), 203 D.L.R. (4th) 257.

22. Several provinces also have a Fraudulent Preferences Act; for example: R.S.A. 2000, c. F-24; R.S.B.C. 1996, c. 164; R.S.S. 1978, c. F-21.

23. *Re Green Gables Manor Inc.* (1998), 41 B.L.R. (2d) 299. Contrast *Sheraton Desert Inn Corp.* v. *Yeung* (1998), 168 D.L.R. (4th) 126.

into whether or not the debtor gave or received, as the case may be, fair market value for the property or services that were the subject of the transaction (sections 3, 100).[24] If the price paid in the transaction was substantially greater or less than fair market value, the court may award the difference gained by the other party to the trustee in bankruptcy.

Payment of Claims

Having taken possession of a bankrupt's property, the trustee's duty is to apply the property in payment of the lawful claims against the bankrupt estate. However, not all the bankrupt's property is subject to seizure. The 2007 reforms **exempt** RRSPs from bankruptcy seizure save and except the previous year's contribution. Section 67 provides that "the property of a bankrupt divisible among his creditors shall not comprise . . . any property that . . . is exempt from execution or seizure under the laws of the province within which the property is situated and within which the bankrupt resides." Provincial laws provide exemption from seizure for such items as household furnishings and appliances, tools of the bankrupt's trade, some farm property, and insurance policies and RRSPs, though these exemptions vary considerably from one province to another.

> **exempt**
> property that is not subject to seizure by the trustee as a result of an exception in a federal or provincial statute

Having taken possession of the bankrupt's property, the trustee's duty is to apply that property in satisfaction of the claims of creditors. That normally involves selling the property and distributing the cash proceeds among the creditors. In appropriate cases the trustee may distribute **liquidating dividends** (payments on account) to the creditors from time to time as required by the inspectors and as realization of the debtor's assets permits. In doing so she must, of course, be careful to take account of the claims of the secured and preferred creditors.

> **liquidating dividends**
> payments made from time to time by a trustee in bankruptcy to creditors on account of the full amount due to them

Because the assets are almost certainly insufficient to satisfy all the claims in full, the priority of claims is important. A trustee must act with great care in the administration and liquidation of the debtor's affairs. She may be personally liable to creditors for losses caused them by her failure to pay the claims in the proper order of priority. As we saw in Chapter 30, the determination of priorities can be an extremely difficult matter, especially where the claims of secured creditors are involved. The trustee must determine whether a claim to a secured interest is effectively protected (for example, by registration under the PPSA).[25] Where there are two or more such claims, the trustee must determine their respective priority. That may prove especially difficult where the claims are made under different statutes, such as a provincial PPSA and the federal Bank Act.[26]

In such cases, it is normally advisable for the trustee to seek a ruling from the court.

Super Priority

Super priority entitles a creditor to have their claim satisfied before the claims of any secured creditor. The Bankruptcy and Insolvency Act (and proposed amendments) designates specific creditors with this status.

> **super priority**
> entitlement to be paid before secured creditors

i) Unpaid Sellers   An unpaid seller has a right to repossess goods sold and delivered to a bankrupt in relation to the bankrupt's business (section 81.1). The supplier must make a demand within 30 days of the delivery of the goods, and the goods must still be in the possession of the purchaser, be identifiable, and be in the same condition as when sold. The claim ranks above any other claim to the goods, except that of a bona fide purchaser of the goods for value without notice of the supplier's right. A supplier who repossesses goods cannot subsequently claim against the bankrupt for any deficiency in respect of those goods.

---

24. A similar inquiry can be made where a bankrupt corporation has paid dividends to its shareholders or has redeemed shares; section 101.

25. See *Re Giffen, supra,* n. 13.

26. See, for example: *Royal Bank of Canada* v. *Sparrow Electric Corp.,* [1997] 1 S.C.R. 411; *Abraham* v. *Canadian Admiral Corp.* (1998), 39 O.R. (3d) 176.

CASE 31.4 Thomson Electronics had supplied goods to Consumers Distributing, for which it had not been paid. Consumers Distributing was declared bankrupt, and Thomson claimed recovery of the goods that it had supplied in the preceding month. The goods were not in the possession of Consumers Distributing but were being stored in a warehouse belonging to Tibbett and Britten Inc., which was also a creditor of Consumers Distributing.

The court held that for section 81.1 to apply, the goods had to be in the actual physical possession of the bankrupt. Thomson's claim to recover the goods failed.[27]

An additional priority is created for farmers, fishermen, and aquaculturalists who have supplied their products to a bankrupt and have not been paid. The claims of such suppliers extend not only to the goods supplied but are also secured by a charge on the entire inventory of the purchaser. This charge ranks above any other claim against that inventory, except that of an unpaid seller of specific goods (section 81.2).

ii) Wage Earners   The 2007 amendments to the BIA give wage earners super priority for up to 6 months unpaid wages (to a maximum of $2000) out of the **current assets** (liquid) of the debtor. The priority extends to wages, commissions, salary, and compensation for services rendered. This claim ranks behind the unpaid seller but ahead of secured creditors. The amendments also create a government-backed compensation scheme known as the Wage Earner Protection Program. Employees are entitled to claim from the fund up to $3000 (or 4 weeks) of arrears of wages.

current assets
cash or cash equivalent assets such as negotiable instruments, demand deposits, and accounts receivables

iii) Interim Financing   Sometimes it is necessary for an insolvent business to obtain credit while it tries to reorganize and survive as a going concern. Naturally, it is difficult to convince a lender to extend credit in such circumstances. The 2007 amendments allow a court to prioritize interim financing given during reorganization above any existing secured interest in an asset. The debtor and creditor must obtain permission of the court prior to making the loan. This type of financing is also known as **debtor-on-possession financing**.

debtor-on-possession financing
court-sanctioned secured loans advanced during reorganization and given priority over pre-existing secured creditors

Secured Creditors

Secured creditors, as we have seen, may be included in a proposal made by an insolvent person and may also be affected by the rights of unpaid sellers, agricultural suppliers, wage earners, and interim financing creditors. The Act requires a secured creditor to give at least 10 days' notice to an insolvent person before enforcing her security (section 244) and contains provisions governing the conduct of a receiver, appointed by a secured creditor, insofar as that conduct relates to the administration of a bankrupt estate (sections 245–7).

Subject to these provisions, however, a secured creditor is entitled to enforce her security to obtain payment of what is owing. A secured creditor must pay to the trustee any surplus if the security she holds is worth more than the debt owing to her. When the trustee and secured creditor cannot agree on the value of the security, it may be necessary to sell it and pay the secured claim out of the proceeds (sections 127–34). The bankrupt estate is entitled to any surplus for the benefit of other creditors. When the value of the security is less than the secured debt, the creditor receives the full value of the security and, in addition, ranks as a general claim along with other unsecured creditors for the deficiency. When the trustee and secured creditor agree on the value of the secured assets without having to sell them, the creditor may accept the security in settlement of her account, either by paying any excess value to the trustee or by making a claim against the trustee as a general creditor for the deficiency.

27. *Thomson Consumer Electronics Canada, Inc.* v. *Consumers Distributing Inc.* (1999), 170 D.L.R. (4th) 115.

Preferred Creditors

Out of the free assets remaining after payment or settlement of priority and secured claims, the trustee must next pay the **preferred creditors**. Preferred creditors are listed in section 136 of the Act. The following is a summary of preferred claims, in the order of their priority;

preferred creditors
unsecured creditors whose claims are given preference over those of other unsecured creditors

(1) When the bankrupt debtor is deceased, his reasonable funeral expenses and legal expenses related to his death.

(2) Expenses and fees of the licensed trustee in bankruptcy and her legal costs.

(3) A levy for the purpose of defraying the expense of the supervision of the Superintendent in Bankruptcy.

(4) Up to six months' arrears of wages of employees of the bankrupt debtor to the extent of $2000 for each employee. This preference is available to satisfy remaining wages owed that were not paid under the super-priority over current assets. (The Act postpones all claims for wages by spouses, former spouses, parents, children, brothers, sisters, uncles, and aunts of the debtor until all other claims have been satisfied.)

(5) Spousal or child support arrears (s. 136 (d.1)); the 2007 amendments exempt any tax refund owing to the debtor from seizure by the trustee if it is subject to a claims for arrears of spousal or child support.

(6) Municipal taxes levied within the two years preceding bankruptcy.

(7) Arrears of rent due to the landlord for a period of three months preceding bankruptcy.

(8) The costs of the first execution or attachment creditor. (A creditor obtains an execution order against tangibles, such as land or goods, and an attachment against choses in action, such as accounts receivable or bank deposits.)

(9) Indebtedness of the bankrupt under the Canada Pension Plan, the Employment Insurance Act, and the Income Tax Act for amounts required to be deducted from employees' salaries.

(10) Claims for certain injuries sustained by employees.

General Creditors

After settling the priority, secured and preferred claims, the trustee pays the **general creditors** rateably to the extent of the funds remaining.

general creditors
creditors whose claims are not secured or preferred

Deferred Creditors

The BIA takes the claims of some creditors out of their presumptive class and delays payment of their claims until after all other creditors. As noted above, wages claims of spouses are deferred until after all other claims are paid (s. 137(2)). Similarly, silent partner loans (s. 139) are deferred until after all other creditors are paid.

CHECKLIST Priority of Payment of Claims

Claims against the property of a bankrupt debtor are paid in the following sequence:

(1) super-priority claims

(2) secured creditors

(3) preferred creditors

(4) general creditors

(5) deferred creditors

Proving Debts

To rank as a claim against the bankrupt estate, all creditors must "prove" their debts. They do so by submitting declarations to the trustee outlining the details of their accounts and specifying the vouchers or other evidence by which they can substantiate these claims. The declaration states whether or not the claim is a secured or preferred claim.

Duties of the Bankrupt Debtor

Following a receiving order or authorized assignment, the debtor must submit himself for examination by the official receiver to explain his conduct, the causes of his bankruptcy, and the disposition of his property. He must submit a sworn statement of his affairs to the trustee, together with a list of the names and addresses of his creditors and the security held by them, attend the first meeting of creditors, and supply the information they require. He must also hand over possession of his property to the trustee, co-operate with the trustee, and "aid to the utmost of his power in the realization of his property and the distribution of the proceeds among his creditors" (section 158(k)).

Bankruptcy Offences

A bankrupt debtor and any other person who commits an offence listed in the Act is liable to imprisonment or a substantial fine. These offences include failing to perform any of the duties considered above, making a fraudulent disposition of his property before or after bankruptcy, giving untruthful answers to questions put to him at an examination, concealing, destroying, or falsifying books or documents, and obtaining any credit or property by false representations before or after bankruptcy (section 198).

Discharge of the Bankrupt Debtor

discharge
a court order whereby a person who has been declared bankrupt ceases to have the status of a bankrupt person

As we have noted, an important object of our bankruptcy legislation is to clear an honest but unfortunate debtor of outstanding debts and to leave him free to resume business life. The **discharge** of a bankrupt debtor usually cancels the unpaid portion of his debts remaining after they have been reduced by payment of liquidating dividends, and gives the debtor a clean slate with which to start business again.

ETHICAL ISSUE

Discrimination Against Students

When a bankrupt person is discharged, the effect is normally to cancel or immediately discharge all his or her outstanding debts and to give him or her a fresh start. There are, however, some debts that are not cancelled (section 178). These include fines, penalties, damages for sexual assault, alimony, and student loans. The Canadian Federation of Students launched an unsuccessful challenge to this rule under the Charter.[28]

The 2007 amendments to the Bankruptcy and Insolvency Act modify but do not eliminate the harsh treatment of student loans. The new rule delays discharge of a student loan until 7 years after completion of school (formerly 10 years) and students could apply to further reduce it to 5 years after completion of their studies for hardship reasons.

continued

---

28. *Chenier v. Canada (Attorney General)* 2005 CanLII 23125 (Ont. Sup. Ct.).

> ### QUESTIONS TO CONSIDER
>
> 1. Do students deserve to be lumped together with criminals and deadbeat parents, as the *Toronto Star* put it (April 3, 2004, p.C2)?
>
> 2. Are students (or ex-students) as a class entitled to the protection of the Charter?
>
> 3. What policy rationale justifies the different treatment of student loans?

Historically, the discharge of a debtor has been an official act of the court. In deciding whether to grant or refuse a debtor's application for discharge, the court consults the report of the trustee (sections 170–2). One of the more important reasons why a court may refuse or suspend the debtor's discharge is that his assets have proved to be insufficient to pay the unsecured creditors at least 50 cents on the dollar. He may still obtain a discharge, however, if he can show that he cannot reasonably be held responsible for this circumstance. Other reasons for refusing to give a discharge are the following:

- the bankrupt debtor neglected to keep proper books
- he continued to trade after he knew he was insolvent
- he failed to account satisfactorily for any loss or deficiency of assets
- he caused the bankruptcy by rash speculation or extravagant living
- within three months preceding bankruptcy he gave an undue preference to a creditor
- he was bankrupt or made a proposal to his creditors on a previous occasion
- he is guilty of any bankruptcy offence or has failed to perform his duties

Other related reasons are set out in the Act (section 173).[29]

The 2007 amendments to the BIA propose drastic change to the discharge process with the introduction of automatic discharges. Most debtors (who have completed mandatory counselling) would be eligible for automatic discharge unless an objection is filed or if tax arrears make up more than 75 percent of the debtor's unsecured debts. The chart below illustrates when automatic discharge may be obtained under the amended BIA:

	No Surplus	Surplus	75% of Unsecured Debts are Tax Arrears
First Bankruptcy	discharge after 9 months	discharge after 21 months	hearing required
Second Bankruptcy	discharge after 24 months	discharge after 36 months	hearing required

Until obtaining his discharge, a bankrupt debtor is subject to a fine or imprisonment if, without disclosing his status, he obtains credit of $500 or more for a purpose other than the supply of necessaries for himself and his family, or if he recommences business and fails to disclose to those with whom he deals that he is an undischarged bankrupt (section 199).

OTHER METHODS OF LIQUIDATION AND REORGANIZATION

Corporate Winding-Up

We have seen that the Bankruptcy and Insolvency Act provides a means for liquidating insolvent corporations, partnerships, and sole proprietorships. There are, in addition, a variety of ways in which the affairs of a solvent corporation may be wound up, but it is shareholders rather than the corporation or creditors who initiate the proceedings.

---

29. In *Bank of Montreal* v. *Giannotti* (2000), 197 D.L.R. (4th) 266, the Ontario Court of Appeal refused a discharge to a bankrupt who had been "uncooperative, evasive and untruthful" about his financial affairs.

Each of the provinces has a separate statute or a part in its corporations act to provide a means of winding up solvent corporations.[30] The legislation may authorize the shareholders to appoint a liquidator (who may be a director, officer, or employee of the corporation) to wind up the affairs of the corporation without recourse to the court; alternatively, it may authorize them to apply to the court for a winding-up order and the appointment of a liquidator.

In addition, the federal Winding-Up and Restructuring Act[31] outlines a procedure by which the shareholders of a solvent, federally incorporated corporation may petition the court to issue a winding-up order. The court may issue a winding-up order if the capital of the corporation has been impaired to the extent of 25 percent, or if a substantial proportion of the shareholders petition for winding-up because of a lack of integrity or responsibility on the part of the corporation's management.

A corporation may also surrender its charter, apart from proceedings under either the Bankruptcy Act or a Winding-Up Act. For example, the Canada Business Corporations Act permits dissolution, if a corporation has no property and no liabilities, by special resolution of the shareholders. "Articles of dissolution" are then sent to the director of the office that regulates federally incorporated corporations, and she issues a certificate of dissolution.[32] A corporation may wish to dissolve in this way when it has sold all its assets to another corporation and has distributed the proceeds to its shareholders, and when the purchasing corporation has assumed all its liabilities, with the consent of its creditors.

The Companies' Creditors Arrangement Act

compromise and arrangement

an agreement made by a debtor corporation with its creditors whereby arrangements are made for repayment of debts without liquidating the corporation

As we have already noted, the Bankruptcy and Insolvency Act provides an alternative to the formal liquidation of a debtor's estate by means of a "proposal." For corporations, another method of avoiding liquidation is by means of a **compromise and arrangement** with the creditors, approved by the court, under the Companies' Creditors Arrangement Act (CCAA).[33] That act and the Bankruptcy and Insolvency Act are distinct statutes and provide alternative procedures, though many of their provisions are broadly similar.[34]

The CCAA allows a corporation in financial distress to seek court protection in order to reorganize its affairs and to avoid what might be an unnecessary and undesirable bankruptcy. If value of a corporation as a going concern exceeds its break-up value, a reorganization of its debts is usually preferable to the corporation itself, its creditors, and its employees. The Act was used infrequently until the mid-1980s, when the benefits of reorganizations and workouts become more widely appreciated. The mechanism is somewhat similar to that found in Chapter 11 of the U.S. Bankruptcy Code.

The purpose of the CCAA is to permit a corporation to restructure its affairs so that it can eliminate some of its debt and resume business in a leaner, more efficient form that will have a greater chance of returning to profitability. During the reorganization, the corporation's creditors are restrained from taking action except through the reorganization process.

vulture funds

large investors who purchase the debt or shares of a corporation in the course of its reorganization

A relatively recent development has been the emergence of "**vulture funds**"—large investors who are prepared to purchase substantial portions of the debtor corporation's debts or its shares at

30. See, for example: Company Act, R.S.B.C. 1996, c. 62, ss. 267–96 (it still has limited application although repealed by the Business Corporations Act, S.B.C. 2002, c. 57); Corporations Act, R.S.M. 1987, c. C225, Part XVII; Business Corporations Act, R.S.O. 1990, c. B.16, Part XVI; Companies Winding-Up Act, R.S.N.S. 1989, c. 82.

31. R.S.C. 1985, c. W-11.

32. R.S.C. 1985, c. C-44, s. 210. Some provincial statutes also provide for dissolution of companies formed under their acts. See, for example: Corporations Act, R.S.M. 1987, c. C225, Part XVII; Business Corporations Act, R.S.O. 1990, c. B.16, s. 239.

33. R.S.C. 1985, c. C-36. Although a federal statute, this act applies to both federally and provincially incorporated corporations.

34. The previously discussed 1997, 2005, and 2007 amendments to both the Bankruptcy and Insolvency Act and to the Companies' Creditors Arrangement Act are bringing the provisions of the two acts much closer to each other.

a heavily discounted price, hoping that the reorganization will be successful. This development seems in some ways to be contrary to the true intention of the Act, since these investors are clearly far more concerned with realizing a quick profit on their investment than in securing the rehabilitation of the debtor. However, one advantage is that the process provides a market in which smaller creditors may sell their claims without having to wait for the reorganization to be completed.

The differences between the CCAA and the proposal procedures under the Bankruptcy and Insolvency Act have been substantially lessened, though some significant differences remain. In particular, the CCAA applies only if the total of creditor claims exceeds $5 million. When a court grants a stay of proceedings under the CCAA, it appoints a **monitor** to supervise the business and financial affairs of the debtor corporation. The position of the monitor is essentially similar to that of a trustee in bankruptcy. The final arrangement must be approved by a two-thirds majority of the creditors.[35]

monitor
a person appointed to supervise the reorganization of a debtor corporation under the Companies' Creditors Arrangement Act

BUILDERS' LIENS

Nature of Builders' Liens

We noted in Chapter 17 that a bailee who makes repairs or improvements on goods obtains a possessory lien on the goods for the value of her services. By contrast, when a person extends credit by performing work or supplying materials in the construction of a building or other structure affixed to land, it is physically impossible for him to exercise a possessory lien. In any event, under the law of real property, when goods are affixed permanently to land they become fixtures: the supplier of the goods is not permitted to sever them from the property. In these circumstances, a creditor had no recourse at common law except to sue for the debt owing and obtain judgment and an order for execution against the land. However, a substantial degree of protection is provided by statute.

Contractors and Subcontractors

In all provinces of Canada, persons who have extended credit in the form of goods and services to improve land now have a statutory remedy under **builders' lien** legislation. Although the title and wording of the acts vary from province to province,[36] each act provides substantially the same protection for creditors. Its basic purposes are to give creditors who have provided work and material for the improvement of land an interest in the land as security for payment and "to prevent multiplicity of actions for small claims, in which the cost would be enormously out of proportion to and in excess of the sums claimed. . . ."[37]

The provisions of builders' lien acts operate in two rather different ways, which can best be understood by an example.

builders' lien
an interest that builders and others involved in construction work may have in a building as security for money owed to them for work done (also known as a **mechanics' lien** or a **construction lien**)

ILLUSTRATION 31.1

O Co. owns a piece of land on which it plans to have an apartment building constructed. *O* Co. hires *C* Co. to erect the building for an agreed price. *C* Co., in turn, subcontracts the specialized tasks of supplying and erecting the structural steel, installing the plumbing and heating systems and electrical wiring, and supplying and installing elevators to various firms specializing in these trades.

---

35. CCAA, s. 6, as amended by S.C. 1997, c. 12.

36. In Alberta, British Columbia, Manitoba, Nova Scotia, and Saskatchewan the statute is now called the Builders' Lien Act, and in Ontario, the Construction Lien Act. Newfoundland, New Brunswick, and Prince Edward Island retain the original name, Mechanics' Lien Act.

37. *McPherson* v. *Gedge* (1883-4), 4 O.R. 246, per Wilson, C.J., at 257.

In Illustration 31.1 we have two types of contracts, a master contract between *O* Co., the owner of the property, and the main contractor, *C* Co., and a series of subcontracts between the main contractor, *C* Co., and the various specialized firms. In respect to the master contract, *O* Co. is liable for the whole amount of the contract price as a contractual debt. *C* Co. has a builders' lien—that is, an interest in *O* Co.'s land and building as it is erected—for the total value of work and materials (to the maximum of the contract price) provided by *C* Co. and its subcontractors. In turn, the subcontractors and suppliers have a right of action against *C* Co. for the value of the work and materials supplied for the project under the terms of the subcontracts. There is, however, no privity of contract between the subcontractors and suppliers and *O* Co. Nevertheless, the legislation also gives liens against the land to the subcontractors and suppliers.

Holdback

holdback

an amount that the owner who contracts for construction work may withhold from payments made to the principal contractor to protect against claims from subcontractors and suppliers

The value of these liens is limited to a specified proportion of the price due from the owner, *O* Co., to the main contractor, *C* Co., under the master contract. This proportion, called a **holdback**, varies somewhat from province to province but is generally from 10 to 20 percent.[38] Where the value of the work and materials exceeds the holdback, the subcontractors and suppliers have no security in the land for the excess sum.

O Co. fully protects itself against liens of the subcontractors and suppliers by retaining the holdback during construction and for a specified period afterwards. If *C* Co. should become insolvent during this period, *O* Co. would pay the holdback into court for the benefit of the lienholders. The court would then supervise the payment of this money among the lienholders, and neither *O* Co. nor its land would be subject to their claims.

Who Is Protected?

A builders' lien is available only to creditors who participate directly as workers or supply material for use directly in the construction work. In *Brooks Sanford Co.* v. *Theodore Tieler Construction Co.*, the court said:

> While the objects and policy [of the Act are] . . . to prevent an owner from obtaining the benefits of the labour and capital of others without compensation, it is not the intention to compel him to pay his contractor's indebtedness for that which does not go into or benefit his property.[39]

The courts have held that an architect who prepares the plans for a building comes within this definition and is entitled to a lien.[40] Some provincial statutes give a lien to a lessor who rents equipment for use on the contract site for the price of the rental of the equipment.[41] On the other hand, a party that sells tools or machinery to a contractor is not entitled to a lien against a building constructed with the use of the tools or machinery it has supplied; the tools and machinery remain the property of the contractor and can be used in other projects as well.[42] Nor can suppliers obtain a lien against property where the contractor has ordered materials for the building and has had them delivered to its own

---

38. See, for example: Builders' Lien Act, S.B.C. 1997, c. 45, s. 4(1); Construction Lien Act, R.S.O. 1990, c. C.30, s. 1(1). (Subsequent references to these particular acts in footnotes will be simply to B.C. and Ont., followed by section number.)

39. (1910), 22 O.L.R. 176, per Moss, C.J.O., at 180.

40. The right to a lien does not arise until construction actually begins: *Chaston Construction Corp.* v. *Henderson Land Holdings* (Canada) Ltd. (2002) 214 D.L.R. (4th) 405. By contrast, a land-use consultant, engaged by a developer to advise on zoning issues, was not entitled to a lien. His work contributed to the project as a whole, but did not constitute "work on" any particular improvement: *Kreuchen* v. *Park Savannah Development Ltd.* (1999), 171 D.L.R. (4th) 377.

41. This type of lien is available in Ontario, Alberta, Newfoundland, and Saskatchewan: see, for example, Ont., ss. 1(1) and 14(1).

42. *Crowell Bros.* v. *Maritime Minerals Ltd.*, [1940] 2 D.L.R. 472.

premises, unless the supplier can prove that the supplies were later used in the construction of the building. Where, however, a supplier delivers the goods directly to the building site, it obtains a lien immediately, whether the materials are eventually used in the structure or not.[43] The reason for this provision is that a supplier who delivers materials to the building site reasonably assumes that they will be used there and relies upon the property as security for his claim.

Suppliers of materials may, if they choose, waive their right of lien by contract. They may find an advantage in doing so when the effect is to persuade a mortgagee to lend additional funds for the completion of a project. The suppliers may then realize their claims out of the proceeds of a sale of the completed building.

Employees' Rights

Provincial legislatures have acknowledged that the bargaining power of wage earners may be unequal to that of the builders and contractors who employ them, and that these wage earners may not fully understand the nature of their rights. As a result, the various Acts contain a provision that a term in a contract of employment waiving the employee's right of lien is void. However, in some provinces this provision does not apply to employees whose wages exceed a specified amount per day.

The Acts give wage earners a priority for approximately one month's arrears of wages over all other liens derived through the same contractor or subcontractor.[44] This priority recognizes the fact that wages often provide the sole means of subsistence of wage earners, while suppliers of materials and lessors of equipment probably carry on business with several construction projects at once, and usually have larger capital funds to depend on if a single contractor or owner defaults in payment.

Procedures Under Builders' Lien Legislation

Registration

A builders' lien arises immediately upon work being done or materials being used in the improvement of property or (in some provinces) upon the supply of rented equipment for use on a contract site. To make a lien legally actionable, the lienholder must register it. It may be registered during the performance of the work or services or supply of material or within a specified period of time (usually 45 days) after completion or abandonment of performance. If a lien is not registered within the time specified, it ceases to exist. Registration gives a lienholder a period within which it must commence a legal action—usually 90 days after the work has been completed or the materials have been placed or furnished, or after the expiry of the period of credit.[45] For this purpose provinces have interpreted "completion of the contract" to mean "substantial performance of the contract."[46] Registration also gives a contractor or subcontractor a lien against the property itself.

In most of the provinces, an action brought by one lien claimant is deemed to be brought on behalf of all other lien claimants, and it is unnecessary even to name other lien claimants as participants since they must be served with notice of the trial.[47]

A lien may be registered against land in the same way and same place as are other interests in land. Registration provides public notice of a lienholder's claim and establishes the lienholder's priority over unsecured creditors of the owner of the property and over subsequent mortgagees and purchasers of an interest in the property. After registration, a lien expires unless the lienholder brings an action to enforce the claim within the prescribed time and registers a certificate stating that the action has been started, or unless another lienholder starts an action within this period.

43. Ont., s. 15.
44. B.C., s. 37; Ont., s. 81.
45. B.C., s. 14 (one year); Ont., s. 36.
46. B.C., s. 1; Ont., s. 2.
47. Ont., ss. 50(3) and 59.

Lienholders' Rights

A builders' lien does not give a lienholder the right to personally take possession of or to sell land and buildings to realize a claim. In fact, if the lienholder is a subcontractor and if the owner pays the statutory holdback into court, the lienholder's rights are limited to its share in this fund: it has no rights against the land and buildings of the owner. Even if an owner fails to pay the statutory holdback into court, the lienholder's claim against the land is limited to the amount the owner should have paid into court. To realize its claim against the land, a lienholder, whether a main contractor or a subcontractor, must first bring an action and obtain a court order appointing a trustee. The trustee then has the power to manage the property and to sell it for the benefit of the lienholder and other creditors.

If eventually the trustee does sell the property, she must pay the proceeds to satisfy, first, the claims for municipal taxes; second, those of mortgagees who have prior registered mortgages; third, lienholders' claims for wages regardless of the order in which they filed their liens; fourth, all other lienholders' claims regardless of the order in which they filed their liens; fifth, subsequent mortgagees or other persons who have a secured interest in the land; and, finally, if there are any proceeds left, claims of the general creditors of the owner. After all creditors are paid, any balance remaining belongs to the owner.

Progress Payments

During the construction of a building and for the specified statutory period afterwards, the owner may safely make progress payments to the contractor for all amounts except the statutory holdback.[48] However, if the owner receives notice from subcontractors or suppliers that liens are outstanding and unlikely to be paid by the contractor, she should cease payments to the contractor at once and ascertain the extent of the liens. If there is some doubt whether the holdback is sufficient to satisfy the claims for liens, she should seek legal advice immediately; as soon as she has knowledge of these claims, she loses the protection of the Act to the extent that she continues to make payments to the contractor. On the other hand, she must not make the error of wrongfully withholding payment due to a solvent contractor because of an unfounded claim for a lien.

In some jurisdictions, all money received by contractors and subcontractors on account of the contract price are deemed to be trust funds held for the benefit of those who have performed work or services or furnished materials. The contractor or subcontractor, accordingly, cannot divert those funds to its own use until all the claims against it are satisfied.[49]

Once the statutory period has elapsed and no claims have been registered, the owner may pay the amount withheld to the contractor and so complete her obligations under the contract.

Practical Application of Builders' Liens

Mortgage Lenders

An owner of land usually finances a construction project by mortgaging the land to a mortgagee who advances the mortgage money as work progresses on the building. Some builders' lien laws require a mortgagee to withhold from the mortgage advances an amount equal to the sum that the owner should withhold from the contractor. Even if the Act does not have such requirements, it is sensible for a mortgagee to do so to protect the mortgagor (owner), who is liable to subcontractors and suppliers for the amount of the holdback if the contracting firm does not pay its accounts.

---

48. B.C., s. 6(3); Ont., s. 22(1).
49. Ont., s. 8(1). See *Rudco Insulation Ltd. v. Toronto Sanitary Inc.* (1998), 42 O.R. (3d) 292.

Tenants

When a tenant contracts to have a building erected on his landlord's property or, perhaps more commonly, to have improvements made to existing buildings, a builders' lien is not enforceable against the landlord's interest in the property unless the lienholder can establish that the work was undertaken either expressly or impliedly at the request of the landlord.

General Contractors

The party that takes the greatest risk in the construction industry is normally the general contractor. Most large contracts are awarded by tender to the lowest bidder with a sound reputation. In this highly competitive business, contractors often cut their margin both for errors and profit to a very small sum in order to win a contract. Bad luck in the form of unexpectedly difficult foundation work, bad weather delaying the project, a breakdown of essential equipment, an accident seriously injuring key personnel, or a labour dispute may leave a contractor in a deficit position.

Subcontractors

Even when her contractor is in financial difficulty, an owner incurs no liability herself if she follows the procedures of the Builders' Lien Act. The subcontractors, on the other hand, take the risk that the holdback will not be sufficient to pay their claims. Where the subcontract is for a large sum of money, they generally protect themselves by receiving progress payments from the contractor: they do not let themselves get too far ahead in the work without being paid a proportion of the price.

Contractors Who Own the Land

Contractors often undertake to construct buildings on land owned by themselves, especially residential buildings. Usually a builder erects such a building with a view to selling it soon after its completion. If bad luck or mismanagement cause his insolvency, his "subcontracts" with specialized trades are really main contracts with himself as owner. Accordingly, the land is subject to liability for the total value of the liens, and the holdback provisions do not apply. Often a builder will have obtained mortgage money on the land; the mortgagee will have priority over the lienholders for only the money already advanced to the builder before the liens arose.

OTHER STATUTORY PROTECTION OF CREDITORS

Provisions protecting the rights of creditors, or of particular types of creditors, are found in many statutes, in most of which creditor protection is merely incidental to the main aim of the statute. In addition to the measures discussed above, two other statutes merit a brief mention.

Bulk Sales Acts

All the common law provinces initially had a statute called the Bulk Sales Act, modelled on legislation commonly adopted in the United States. The purpose of the statute was to protect the creditors of a person making a "**bulk sale**"—that is, a sale of all, or substantially all, the inventory of a business or the fixtures and goods with which the business was carried on. The statute called for notice to and consent by a creditor before a bulk sale would be effective. Most provinces have repealed their Bulk Sales Acts, apparently taking the view that with the adoption of comprehensive Personal Property Security Acts, the Bulk Sales Acts no longer served any useful purpose.

bulk sale
a sale of all or substantially all the assets of a business

The main exception to this trend has been Ontario, which still retains its Bulk Sales Act,[50] though even there the Act is rarely used.

Business Corporations Acts

A fairly recent development has been the use by a corporation's creditors of the "oppression remedy," provided in the Canada Business Corporations Act (CBCA) and the various provincial acts. The oppression remedy was discussed in Chapter 28, under the heading "The Protection of Minority Shareholders," and it is clear that the primary intention behind the remedy was to protect shareholder rights. However, the CBCA[51] includes, in the definition of a "complainant" who may seek a remedy for oppression, the holder of a "security" of the corporation (which includes a debt obligation) and "any other person who, in the discretion of the court, is a proper person to make an application" under that part of the Act.

The remedy may be granted where the court is satisfied that the actions of a corporation have been oppressive or unfairly prejudicial to the interests of "any security holder, creditor, director, or officer" of the corporation. The various provincial statutes contain essentially similar provisions.

In a number of cases, most notably in the Ontario courts, it has been held that creditors, both secured and unsecured, have standing to complain of oppression by the managers of their debtor corporation, and are entitled to seek any of the wide range of remedies that the court has discretion to order.[52]

CASE 31.5

SCI Systems had advanced money to GTL Co. in return for a promissory note for $800 000. GTL defaulted when the note became due, and SCI obtained a default judgment against GTL. GTL still failed to pay, claiming that it was unable to do so. SCI discovered that, shortly before the note became due, GTL had paid dividends amounting to $850 000 to its three directors, who were also its sole shareholders, and had also transferred to them further assets worth $250 000.

In an action under section 248 of the (Ontario) Business Corporations Act, the court held that the conduct of the directors had resulted in protecting the company from its payment obligation to SCI Systems. The acts of GTL Co.'s directors were oppressive to SCI, and the directors were personally liable for the full amount of the judgment.[53]

Although the courts have occasionally warned that debt actions should not be routinely turned into oppression actions,[54] the practice of using the oppression remedy as a means of enforcing creditors' rights is growing rapidly. This trend is perhaps unfortunate, since it seems that the oppression remedy can be used to allow one creditor to gain an advantage over other creditors with competing claims, creditors who are not parties to the action and whose interests are not required to be considered by the court. It also adds yet another form of action to the already bewildering confusion of potentially conflicting creditors' remedies.

50. R.S.O. 1990, c. B.14. Newfoundland and Labrador also has a Bulk Sales Act.

51. R.S.C. 1985, c. C-44, ss. 238 and 241.

52. See, for example: *Sidaplex-Plastic Suppliers Inc.* v. *Elta Group Inc.* (1995), 131 D.L.R. (4th) 399; *Levy-Russell Ltd.* v. *Shieldings Inc.*, [1998] O.J. No. 3932. See also the learned judgment of Macdonald, J. in *First Edmonton Place Ltd.* v. *315888 Alberta Ltd.*, [1988] A.J. No. 511 (Alta. Q.B.). Section 248(3) of the Canadian Business Corporations Act empowers a court to make an order as it thinks fit upon a finding of oppression.

53. *SCI Systems, Inc.* v. *Gornitzki Thompson & Little Co.* (1997), 147 D.L.R. (4th) 300. The applicant also relied on the provisions of the Fraudulent Conveyances Act, R.S.O. 1990, c. F.29, and the Assignments and Preferences Act, R.S.O. 1990, c. A.33, but having found oppression, the court considered it unnecessary to deal with that issue.

54. See *Royal Trust Corp. of Canada* v. *Hordo* (1993), 10 B.L.R. (2d) 86. A creditor does not have an automatic right to bring an action for an oppression remedy. The remedy is discretionary and should probably not be granted where ordinary bankruptcy proceedings provide a satisfactory resolution: see *C.C. Petroleum Ltd.* v. *Allen* (2003), 36 B.L.R. (3d) 244.

LIMITATIONS STATUTES

We noted in Chapter 13 that when a person has a right of action against someone who defaults payment on a debt or who is in breach of contract, she must begin an action within a prescribed period or lose the right to sue. In most provinces the normal limitation period is now two years.[55] A plaintiff must start court proceedings within the two-year period or lose the right to resort to the courts. Such limitations on actions are justified on the grounds that a person who fails to pursue a claim leaves the other party in a state of uncertainty that ought not to continue permanently, and because, as the years pass, it becomes more difficult to produce the evidence concerning the facts of the case.

The limitation period runs from the time that the claim is "discovered." A right of action does not arise until there has been a breach or default. Thus, in a contract for the sale of goods on credit, the seller's right of action does not arise until the price becomes due and the buyer fails to pay. A trade account receivable often comprises a number of charges for goods or services invoiced at different times in the past and since paid in part. A customer (debtor) is entitled to specify the particular purchases against which a payment on account is to be applied, but in the absence of such instructions the supplier (creditor) is entitled to treat each payment as discharging the oldest outstanding purchases and so keep the debt current.

The limitation period for an action for breach of contract starts over again if the debtor makes a part payment or delivers a written promise to pay. However, if the debtor makes a new promise to pay the debt, he is bound by that promise and may be sued upon it.

A debtor need not make an express promise to pay; his promise to pay may be implied from the circumstances of the part payment. Normally, a presumption of a new promise to pay arises from the mere fact of making a part payment or from a written acknowledgment of the debt, without other evidence to contradict the presumption.

Each province has a general limitations statute governing limitation periods for a number of different classes of actions, and limitation periods are often also prescribed in other statutes. The limitation periods vary considerably. For this reason, when considering starting an action or defending one under the provisions of a statute, a lawyer first checks to see if a limitation period may affect the rights of the parties.

QUESTIONS FOR REVIEW

1. What objectives does the Bankruptcy and Insolvency Act seek to achieve?

2. What are the functions of the Superintendent of Bankruptcy, the Official Receiver, and the Trustee in Bankruptcy?

3. Distinguish between a bankrupt and an insolvent person.

4. How is a "consumer debtor" defined?

5. What is the difference between an assignment and a receiving order?

6. What is the effect, in bankruptcy law, of a proposal?

7. Distinguish between an act of bankruptcy and a bankruptcy offence.

8. Distinguish between a fraudulent transfer and a fraudulent preference.

9. What is a "reviewable transaction"?

10. What special right does an unpaid seller of goods have when the buyer is bankrupt?

---

55. See, for example: Limitations Act, R.S.A. 2000, c. L-12, s. 3; Limitation Act, R.S.B.C. 1996, c. 266, s. 3; Limitations Act, S.O. 2002 c. 24, s. 4. In some provinces, the period for actions in contract is still six years; for example, Limitation of Actions Act, R.S.N.S. 1989, c. 258, s. 2(1)(e).

11. What is a "preferred creditor"? What are the principal categories of preferred claims?

12. How does a bankrupt become "discharged"?

13. What is the aim of the Companies' Creditors Arrangement Act?

14. What is the purpose of a "holdback" under builders' lien legislation?

15. Whose interests are protected by a builders' lien?

16. How do the Business Corporations Acts protect creditors of corporations?

CASES AND PROBLEMS

1. Griffiths entered into a contract with Vic's Karsales Ltd. under which it was agreed that she would lease a new Moskvitch car for a period of three years, at a monthly rent of $350. The contract contained an option for Griffiths to extend the term of the lease or to purchase the car at the end of the term for $5000. Both parties were under the impression that Griffiths intended to keep the car for no more than three years and to lease another new car at the end of the lease period.

   One year later, Griffiths became bankrupt. By that time, she had missed three monthly payments on the lease. Vic's Karsales demanded the return of their car. The trustee in bankruptcy refused, on the ground that Vic's had not registered a security interest.

   Who is entitled to the car?

2. Leung was in serious financial difficulties. She owed $150 000 to Desert Rose Inc., in respect of a business venture. She also owed $100 000 to Kwan. She entered into an agreement with Kwan whereby she sold her house to Kwan for $500 000, which was approximately its fair market value. The debt of $100 000 was set off against the purchase price, and it was further agreed that Kwan would lease the house back to Leung for a period of two years at a rent of $30 000 a year. That sum of $60 000 was also set against the purchase price. The balance of $340 000 was paid on completion of the transfer and was mostly used by Leung to pay off debts to her other creditors.

   When Desert Rose sought to collect the debt owed to it, Leung was unable to pay. Does Desert Rose have grounds for impugning the transaction between Leung and Kwan?

3. On April 1, Greenfingers Garden Centre Ltd. was declared bankrupt as a result of a petition entered by the Agricultural Bank Ltd. The Bank was owed $250 000 by Greenfingers and had registered a security interest pursuant to a general security agreement that covered all of Greenfingers' inventory and other business assets.

   On the preceding March 1, Snow White Ornaments Inc. had supplied Greenfingers with 120 garden gnomes, to the value of $2500. On March 12, Bauer, a farmer, supplied a number of fruit trees to Greenfingers for $1000. And on March 15, Spreaders Inc. supplied Greenfingers with a quantity of bags of fertilizer for $800. None of them has been paid. Some of the trees and fertilizer, and almost all the gnomes, remain unsold.

   What claims do the respective creditors have?

4. Buckhouse Inc. is the owner of a large office building in the downtown area of a major Canadian city. It entered into a 10-year lease, at a monthly rental of $8000, with Justitia Ltd. As an inducement to enter into the lease, Buckhouse granted Justitia an 18-month rent-free period, a leasehold improvement allowance of $100 000, and a cash payment of $150 000.

   Justitia Ltd. is a corporation formed by two lawyers, Straight and Narrow, as a management company for their law practice. Straight and Narrow are the sole shareholders and directors of Justitia.

   The law practice occupied the premises for a period of 21 months, though Straight and Narrow never entered into a written lease with Justitia Ltd. At the end of that period, rent having been paid for only three months, they moved out of the building and found other premises.

Justitia has ceased to pay rent to Buckhouse and, apart from the lease, has no assets. The inducement payment of $150 000 was paid out as a dividend to Straight and Narrow.

Does Buckhouse have any claim against Straight and Narrow?

5. The N.S.F. Manufacturing Co. Ltd. was adjudged bankrupt on a petition of its creditors, and the trustee in bankruptcy realized the following amounts from the sale of its business assets:

Cash in bank	$ 1 000
Accounts receivable	52 000
Inventories	25 000
Land and buildings	74 000
	$ 152 000

The liabilities of the business were as follows at the time of the receiving order:

Bank loan secured under section 427 of the Bank Act	$ 40 000
Trade accounts payable	65 000
Municipal taxes payable	5 000
Wages payable (five months at $3000 per month for one employee)	15 000
First mortgage on land and buildings	50 000
Second mortgage on land and buildings	25 000
	$ 200 000

The expenses of liquidation were $5000. The trustee's fee was $3000.

How many cents on the dollar should the general creditors receive? Show the order in which the trustee in bankruptcy made payments to the various types of creditors. Assume that all secured creditors had taken the necessary steps to protect their security.

6. Yorkville Construction Inc. was the main contractor on a large construction project on land owned by Mayfair Properties Ltd. Yorkville engaged Rodwell Ltd. to provide piping insulation services for the project. Yorkville received a series of payments from Mayfair under the contract, and used all the monies to pay its general overhead expenses, including advertising and promotion expenses, bank charges, insurance, lease payments on its vehicles, office rent, and utilities. It did not pay Rodwell for its work.

Yorkville became insolvent.

Does Rodwell have any claim against (a) Mayfair or (b) the directors of Yorkville?

ADDITIONAL RESOURCES FOR CHAPTER 31 ON THE COMPANION WEBSITE *(www.pearsoned.ca/smyth)*

In addition to self-test multiple-choice, true–false, and short essay questions (all with immediate feedback), application exercises, and links to useful web destinations, the Companion Website provides the following resources for Chapter 31:

- **British Columbia:** Bankruptcy and Insolvency; Fraudulent Conveyances; Fraudulent Preferences
- **Alberta:** Builders' Liens; Collection Agents; Creditor Assistance Act; Debt Collection
- **Manitoba/Saskatchewan:** Builders' Liens; Exempt Property in Bankruptcy; Fraudulent Transfers and Conveyances
- **Ontario:** Assignment and Preferences; Bulk Sales; Construction Liens; Debt Collection Process; Fraudulent Conveyances; Limitation Periods

The Modern Legal Environment for Business

T he preceding parts of this book have been concerned primarily with private law—in particular, with the laws of torts, contracts, and property and with the forms of business organization. But business is increasingly becoming affected by public law and by international law. In the following chapters we look at two of the most important influences on modern business activity—the ever-increasing scope of government regulation and the impact of globalization. We conclude our study with an examination of the legal aspects of electronic commerce and privacy.

The most onerous task for modern business managers is complying with the never-ending flow of new government regulations. Chapter 32 examines the process of regulation and looks at some of the more important specific aspects of regulation—consumer protection, competition, and environmental law.

Chapter 33 is concerned with international business transactions by way of foreign trade and foreign investment. When a business operates internationally, it must be concerned with far more than just the contractual relationships with its customers and suppliers. International business is extensively regulated by governments, so the legal relationship between an importer or exporter and the governments of the affected countries is of key importance. Therefore, international business involves both private law and a public law through the examination of the private relationships between parties to contracts, and the public relationships between those parties and the governments. There is also a third dimension to consider—the international relationships among governments or public international law—and so we examine the major treaties and agreements ratified by the Canadian Government.

Finally, we address the legal implications of electronic commerce (e-commerce). E-commerce is a relatively new development, and it is still not always clear how existing legal principles will adapt to the complex challenges that it poses. In Chapter 34, we examine its impact on traditional areas of the law such as contract, tort, and intellectual property. In Chapter 35 we consider how government regulation addresses the privacy concerns highlighted by electronic commerce.

32

Government Regulation of Business

Government regulation affects many aspects of business activity and governs business's relationships with key stakeholders, such as customers, competitors, and the public. In this chapter we examine the regulatory framework within which Canadian business must operate, concentrating on three of the most important areas of regulation from the point of view of business: consumer protection, competition, and the environment. We examine such questions as:

- Who has the power to regulate?

- How are specific business sectors regulated?

- How can business use the courts to eliminate oppressive regulation?

- What are the consequences of consumer protection law for the consumer and for business?

- How does competition law affect business arrangements?

- What are the main elements of environmental protection law?

THE LEGAL FRAMEWORK FOR DOING BUSINESS IN CANADA

As we noted in Chapter 1, for business to operate fairly and efficiently, it is necessary to have an adequate legal and regulatory framework in place. However, excessive regulation can impose heavy and unnecessary costs and inhibit business activity. The challenge is to strike an appropriate balance.

During the 1980s and early 1990s, "deregulation" was a popular notion—business should be freed from excessive government control. In many instances direct government interference was merely replaced by a different sort of regulation, social regulation. *Direct regulation* occurs when the government controls such matters as prices, rates of return, and production levels. *Social regulation*, on the other hand, lays down standards that business must observe, in such areas as health, safety, and the environment.

Previous chapters already examined regulations protecting some key stakeholders. Chapter 20 described the extensive regulation dealing with employees, including social regulation such as employment standards legislation and direct regulation such as workers' compensation regimes. Chapters 28 and 29 reviewed securities and corporate governance regulation in place to protect public investors and the public at large. In this chapter we examine some of the more important aspects of direct and social regulation protecting three key stakeholders: consumers, competitors, and the public.

THE POWER TO REGULATE BUSINESS

Division of Powers Under the Constitution

In Canada, all three levels of government—federal, provincial, and municipal—regulate business activities according to the powers allocated to them by the Constitution Act, 1867 (as shown in the Checklist, below). Court interpretation of the powers has often left all levels of government dissatisfied. However, agreeing on constitutional changes has proven elusive and perhaps impossible. The complexity and rapid change of the business environment make it unrealistic to expect that a magic formula to allocate powers between the different levels of governments can be found.

CHECKLIST The Constitution Act, 1867: Constitutional Power to Regulate Business Activities

Federal Powers, Section 91
- Regulation of trade and commerce
- Specific industries such as banking, shipping and navigation, air transportation, and radio and television
- Taxation
- Intellectual property
- Interest, currency, and promissory notes

Provincial Powers, Section 92
- Property and civil rights
- Municipalities (this section allows a province to delegate the power to regulate to a municipality)
- Direct taxation within the province
- All matters of a private nature within the province
- Specific industries such as road transportation, including trucking; and stock exchanges and securities trading

Inevitably there is overlap between the categories, and sometimes there are even conflicting rules, making it difficult for businesses and their lawyers to determine which regulations apply in a particular situation, especially when business is carried on in more than one province.[1]

Both the federal and provincial legislatures have created regulatory schemes in many areas. When a business wishes to challenge the validity of a particular scheme, it begins by asking whether the legislature that passed the law had jurisdiction. This is not always an easy question for courts to answer, since some of the powers in section 91 overlap those listed in section 92. The courts have interpreted the provincial power over "property and civil rights" to mean virtually the whole body of private law, including contracts and most business transactions—matters that we might well think are included in federal jurisdiction over "trade and commerce." Conversely, the federal power has been interpreted quite narrowly to mean trade and commerce *among several states*.[2] Therefore, it applies to matters of interprovincial and international commerce and not to matters conducted wholly within a single province.[3] For example, section 91 has been interpreted to give the federal government exclusive jurisdiction over banks and banking; deep sea, coastal, and Great Lakes shipping and navigation; air transportation; radio and television broadcasting; and atomic energy. The production, storage, sale, and delivery of oats, barley, and wheat is in federal hands through the monopoly given to the Canadian Wheat Board by Parliament on the basis that its major activity is international.

On the other hand, two sectors with a large interprovincial element remain almost exclusively within regulatory schemes of the provinces—road transportation, including trucking, and stock exchanges and securities transactions in general. The federal government has stayed out of these areas and left them to the provinces. Despite the above described conceptual distinction, business activities in many sectors fall within both federal and provincial jurisdiction. Questions of interpretation are not always easily resolved.

When interpreting the Constitution, courts adopt a two-stage approach to the task. First, they identify the true subject-matter—the "pith and substance"—of the law in question, and second, they assign it to the appropriate area or "head" of legislative power. If a court decides that the subject-matter of a law more properly belongs under a head of jurisdiction of the other legislature, then it will declare the law invalid.

concurrent powers
matters in which both the federal and provincial governments have power to legislate

In some instances, the Constitution expressly confers **concurrent powers** on both levels of government, as in section 95, which grants shared jurisdiction over agriculture and immigration. More often, both levels of government will have passed laws in the same area, relying on their respective powers in section 91 and section 92. The court may find that the subject-matter has a "double aspect"—that is, it clearly falls within both a federal and a provincial head of power. If there is no conflict between the federal and provincial laws, then both are valid.[4]

1. For example, section 95 provides that both the federal and provincial governments have concurrent jurisdiction over agriculture and immigration, and section 92A gives the provinces concurrent powers to make laws regulating the export of natural resources.
2. *Citizen's Insurance Co.* v. *Parsons* (1881), 7 App. Cas. 96: the Privy Council ruled that a provincial statute regulating fire insurance was within the provincial power; it did not affect the federal trade and commerce power because the federal power did not extend to matters wholly within the boundaries of a single province. The Supreme Court of Canada has continued to question the federal power to legislate in general commercial matters where the application of a law falls within the boundaries of a province. See, for example: *MacDonald* v. *Vapour Canada*, [1977] 2 S.C.R. 134, and *Labatt Breweries* v. *Attorney-General of Canada*, [1980] 1 S.C.R. 914.
3. It is interesting to note that U.S. Constitution's equivalent to our trade and commerce provision is "commerce among the several states." The U.S. Supreme Court has given these words a much wider interpretation and has expanded the powers of Congress, despite the interstate requirement of the words themselves.
4. See, for example: *Multiple Access* v. *McCutcheon*, [1982] 2 S.C.R. 161. The court found no conflict between federal and provincial laws concerning insider dealing in corporate securities.

But what if there is a conflict? In that event, the principle of **federal paramountcy** applies. In order to preserve the same law across the country in an area of federal jurisdiction, the federal law prevails over a contrary provincial law.[5]

federal paramountcy
the principle that a federal law prevails over a conflicting provincial law

Restrictions on Government Powers: The Charter

Even if a law is declared valid on a jurisdictional basis, it may still be challenged. As we noted in Chapter 1, the rights entrenched in the Canadian Charter of Rights and Freedoms cannot be infringed by legislation, federal or provincial, unless it is justifiable in a free and democratic society. To the extent a law offends a right in the Charter, it will be declared invalid.

CASE 32.1

A firm was prosecuted for opening its store on a Sunday, contrary to the federal Lord's Day Act. In its defence it claimed that the law was unconstitutional. The Supreme Court of Canada first considered whether the law should be characterized as criminal law (and therefore within federal powers), enacted for a religious purpose (preserving "the sanctity of the Christian Sabbath"), or as a law regulating business (and accordingly within provincial powers over property and civil rights in the province) to ensure that workers enjoyed "a uniform day of rest."

The Court concluded that the purpose was religious and that the law was properly within federal power to enact criminal law. However, it struck the law down as being contrary to the Charter, which prohibits discrimination on the basis of religion.[6]

As a general rule, the Charter is intended to protect the rights and freedoms of individuals, not corporations. However, as Case 32.1 illustrates, there are occasions when corporations may invoke its protection. In particular, a corporation should be allowed to rely on the Charter where it is charged with an offence or is the defendant in civil proceedings instigated by the government. Just as no one should be convicted of an offence under an unconstitutional law, no one should be subject to any proceedings or sanction authorized by an unconstitutional law.[7]

Although Charter rights are essentially personal in nature, they nevertheless do have an important application to some business situations. In particular, the fundamental freedoms of expression and association may be invoked to protect business activities.[8] The Supreme Court of Canada has ruled, on a number of occasions, that "commercial speech" is protected under section 2(b).[9]

Restrictions on advertising, of products or of professional services, are *prima facie* contrary to the Charter, though such restrictions may be justified under section 1 provided they are reasonable

5. See, for example: *Bank of Montreal* v. *Hall*, [1990] 1 S.C.R. 121, which was considered in Chapter 30. In one case it was held that, since the federal government has exclusive jurisdiction over aeronautics, provincial building code legislation and municipal zoning by-laws were not applicable to the construction of airport buildings: *Greater Toronto Airports Authority* v. *City of Mississauga* (2000), 192 D.L.R. (4th) 443.

6. *R.* v. *Big M Drug Mart*, [1985] 1 S.C.R. 295. Subsequently, in *R.* v. *Edwards Books and Art*, [1986] 2 S.C.R. 713, the court held that an Ontario law prohibiting stores from opening on Sundays was a valid exercise of the province's power over property and civil rights, since the purpose of the law was to ensure that workers had a uniform day off each week. Sunday opening has since been legalized in Ontario.

7. *Canadian Egg Marketing Agency* v. *Richardson*, [1998] 3 S.C.R. 157. In that case, a national egg marketing scheme was held (by the Supreme Court of Canada) not to be contrary to the Charter.

8. Charter of Rights and Freedoms, section 2(b) and (d). By contrast, in *Canadian Egg Marketing Agency* v. *Richardson*, *supra*, n. 7, the mobility rights (under section 6) were held to be essentially private in nature; they do not extend to the right to conduct one's business anywhere in Canada without restriction. See also *Archibald* v. *Canada* (2000), 188 D.L.R. (4th) 538, concerning the legality of restrictions on grain farmers under the Canadian Wheat Board Act, R.S.C. 1985, c. C-24.

9. *Irwin Toy Ltd.* v. *Quebec* (1989), 58 D.L.R. (4th) 577; *Rocket* v. *Royal College of Dental Surgeons of Ontario* (1990), 71 D.L.R. (4th) 68. In *UL Canada Inc.* v. *Attorney General of Quebec* (2003), 234 D.L.R. (4th) 398, the Quebec Court of Appeal held that a ban on the sale of yellow-coloured margarine did not violate the Charter freedom of expression.

and do not go beyond what is necessary to promote a legitimate objective.[10] However, arbitrary or unreasonable restrictions will be struck down.[11]

CASE 32.2

In 1988, the federal government introduced legislation prohibiting all advertising and promotion of tobacco products. The prohibition was challenged by one of the leading cigarette manufacturers.

The Supreme Court of Canada held that the legislation violated section 2(b) of the Charter and was not justifiable under section 1. The objective of the legislation—to discourage the use of tobacco—was legitimate, but there was no direct scientific evidence showing a causal link between advertising bans and decreased tobacco consumption. The government had failed to show that a partial advertising ban would be less effective than a total ban. The impairment of the complainant's rights was more than minimal, and the offending provisions of the legislation were declared to be of no force and effect.[12]

As a result of the court's ruling, the federal government adopted new legislation[13] restricting tobacco advertising, but in a way that is intended to be consistent with the ruling. The new law has, in turn, been challenged by the manufacturers, but has so far been found not to infringe the Charter.[14]

The freedom of association, protected by section 2(d) of the Charter, may also have some applications to business situations.

CASE 32.3

Pursuant to the Optometrists Act, R.S.B.C. 1996, c. 342, the Board of Examiners in Optometry adopted rules prohibiting business associations between optometrists and non-optometrists. Two optometrists, who had been cited by the board for violating the prohibition, petitioned for judicial review of the validity of the board's rules. They argued that the rules violated their freedom of association guaranteed by section 2(d) of the Charter.

The court held that the rules were of a public nature. Section 2(d) applies to a wide range of associations, including those of an economic nature, and a business relationship is an association protected under the section. The prohibition could not be justified under section 1 of the Charter. The board had failed to establish that the rules were proportional to the objective of maintaining high standards of professional conduct and independence free of any real or apparent conflicts of interest that would undermine the public's confidence in the profession. The absolute prohibition against any business relationship between optometrists and non-optometrists was excessively broad.[15]

Although the Charter is applicable to business situations, the tendency of the courts is to deny its application to claims that are based solely on economic grounds. As was said in one case:

> . . . because there is an economic aspect to a Charter claim does not, for that reason alone, disqualify it . . . there have been numerous Charter cases in which there was an economic component or implication to a claim. On the other hand, where a claim is based solely on economic grounds, I think it unlikely that a Charter claim could succeed.[16]

10. See *Griffin* v. *College of Dental Surgeons of British Columbia* (1989), 64 D.L.R. (4th) 652; *Urban Outdoor Trans Ad* v. *City of Scarborough* (2001), 196 D.L.R. (4th) 304; *Vann Niagara Ltd.* v. *Town of Oakville* (2002) 214 D.L.R. (4th) 307; (2004) 234 D.L.R. (4th) 118 (S.C.C.).

11. See the recent decision of the Supreme Court of Canada in *R.* v. *Guignard* (2002), 209 D.L.R. (4th) 549. See also *Carmichael* v. *Provincial Dental Board of Nova Scotia* (1998), 169 N.S.R. (2d) 294.

12. *RJR-MacDonald Inc.* v. *Canada* (1995), 127 D.L.R. (4th) 1.

13. Tobacco Act, S.C. 1997, c. 13.

14. *J.Y.I. MacDonald Corp.* v. *Canada* (2002), 102 C.R.R. (2d) 189. See also *Rothmans, Benson & Hedges Inc.* v. *Saskatchewan* (2003), 232 D.L.R. (4th) 495.

15. *Costco Wholesale Canada Ltd.* v. *British Columbia* (1998), 157 D.L.R. (4th) 725.

16. *Archibald* v. *Canada, supra,* n. 8, at 545–46, per Rothstein, J.A. See also *Longley* v. *Canada* (2000), 184 D.L.R. (4th) 590.

JUDICIAL REVIEW OF GOVERNMENT REGULATION

Legislation that confers regulatory powers on government ministers or agencies frequently also expressly provides for review of, and appeals against, executive decisions and actions. In many cases, the legislation establishes special boards or tribunals for that purpose, and may also make provision for appeals to the courts from decisions of the board or tribunal. As well, federal and provincial legislation commonly gives the courts a power of review. The Federal Court has a general jurisdiction to review the exercise of powers by federal boards and commissions,[17] and several of the provinces have enacted similar provisions with respect to provincial boards.[18] Even without such legislation, the courts traditionally assert a general right to review the legality of administrative acts and decisions.

In addition to the validity challenges already mentioned, an administrative act or decision may be challenged on a number of grounds:

■ *Lack of authority*—Although the relevant legislation itself may be valid, the official or agency acted outside the scope of the authority conferred by the statute.

■ *Procedural irregularity*—The official or agency proceeded in a manner inconsistent with the requirements of the statute; for example, public meetings required by the legislation were not held, or the prescribed notice was not given.

■ *Procedural unfairness*—Even when the legislation does not prescribe appropriate procedures, an official or agency is not entitled to act in a purely arbitrary manner. As Professor Mullan states:

> In general, whenever a person's 'rights, privileges or interests' are at stake, there is a duty to act in a procedurally fair manner.[19]

This means that persons likely to be affected have a right to be heard and to have access to relevant documents, that adequate notice must be given of any public hearings, and that the decision-maker must act impartially and not have a personal interest in the subject-matter.

CHECKLIST Strategies to Prevent or Limit the Application of Government Regulation

(1) Challenge the validity of the legislation on the basis of constitutional jurisdiction.

(2) Challenge the validity of the legislation because it violates the Charter of Rights and Freedoms.

(3) Appeal the decision of the administrative decision-maker on one of the grounds set out in the legislation.

(4) Seek judicial review of the administrative decision because it was outside the scope of the legislation or the process was flawed.

---

17. Federal Court Act, R.S.C. 1985, c. F-7, s. 18.

18. For example: Judicial Review Procedure Act, R.S.B.C. 1996, c. 241; R.S.O. 1990, c. J.1.

19. D.J. Mullan, *Administrative Law*, 3rd ed. (Toronto: Carswell, 1996) at 200.

CONSUMER PROTECTION

Background

consumers
individuals who purchase goods and services from a business for their personal use and enjoyment

Consumers are broadly defined as individuals who purchase goods and services from a business for their personal use and enjoyment. The definition does not include businesses or individuals using goods or services for a business activity or resale. The idea that consumers need to be protected by the courts and legislatures is relatively new. A few specific laws to remedy abuses by merchants and moneylenders sufficed until the late 19th century. Retail trade was carried on by relatively small local merchants who dealt directly with customers in an ongoing relationship. If sellers did not treat their customers fairly, customers would go elsewhere. Goods were simpler and most buyers could check the quality of what they bought. In this simpler trading environment, the available remedies in tort and contract law, considered in Chapters 3 and 16, were generally adequate.[20]

Why is Consumer Protection Legislation Necessary?

Legislation is needed now because business has changed. Figure 32.1 shows some of the ways modern developments have affected consumers.

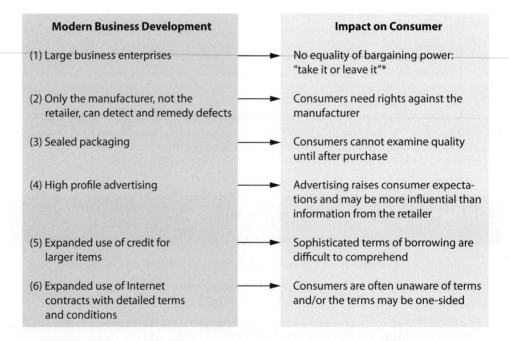

Modern Business Development	Impact on Consumer
(1) Large business enterprises	No equality of bargaining power: "take it or leave it"*
(2) Only the manufacturer, not the retailer, can detect and remedy defects	Consumers need rights against the manufacturer
(3) Sealed packaging	Consumers cannot examine quality until after purchase
(4) High profile advertising	Advertising raises consumer expectations and may be more influential than information from the retailer
(5) Expanded use of credit for larger items	Sophisticated terms of borrowing are difficult to comprehend
(6) Expanded use of Internet contracts with detailed terms and conditions	Consumers are often unaware of terms and/or the terms may be one-sided

FIGURE 32.1
The Modern Business Environment

George Mitchell (Chesterhall) Ltd. v. *Finney Lock Seeds Ltd.*, [1983] 1 All E.R. 108 at 113; In the words of Lord Denning: ". . . the freedom was all on the side of the big concern. . . . The big concern said 'Take it or leave it.' The little man had no option but to take it."

---

20. There are isolated earlier examples of consumer protection legislation; for example, provisions against false and misleading advertising were introduced in the Criminal Code as early as 1914.

In response to specific problems, each Canadian province, as well as the federal government, passed legislation. There was little, if any, consultation, and no overriding theory or policy about consumer protection was initially developed. The result is a collection of individual statutes that often overlap. In 2008, the federal government announced plans to organize its legislation under a comprehensive Consumer Protection Action Plan.[21]

Legislative intervention to protect consumers against exploitative contractual arrangements has proven to be a controversial topic. It may be justified by demands for a more equitable economic system—consumers are perceived as typically having less bargaining power than the businesses with which they deal. But consumer protection regulation is criticized as ineffective—consumers are rarely aware of their rights, and government agencies make little effort to enforce the law. Consumer protection is also seen by some as paternalistic—overruling private contracts, substituting the government's view of what is in the consumer's best interest, and adding to the cost of doing business. This cost may be absorbed by sellers and creditors, in reduced profits, or is more likely passed on to consumers themselves in the form of higher prices.

Principal Types of Consumer Legislation

Some consumer protection legislation can best be understood in the context of discussions of other topics. We have dealt in Chapter 9 with the prohibition on charging excessive rates of interest; with the requirement of written evidence of the terms of consumer sales contracts in Chapter 10; and with the prohibition of exempting clauses in consumer sales contracts in Chapter 15. In Chapter 16 we noted that some provinces have made the implied terms in the Sale of Goods Act mandatory in the case of consumer sales.[22] Changes in the law affecting residential tenancies were dealt with in Chapter 24 and restrictions on the repossession of goods purchased under instalment contracts in Chapter 30.

The purpose of the present section is to provide an overview of the five main categories of consumer protection. They are:

- regulation of misleading advertising
- regulation of quality standards affecting labelling, safety, performance, and availability of servicing and repairs
- regulation of business conduct towards consumers
- disclosure of the effective cost of credit
- supervision of specific businesses that deal with the public through licensing, bonding, and inspection

Virtually all consumer protection statutes apply to both the sale of goods to consumers and the sale of services such as home repairs, carpet cleaning, and the preparation of income tax returns.

Misleading Advertising and Other Representations of Sellers

More and more legislation addresses misleading representations by sellers of goods and services—a trend that probably reflects reservations about the ability of the courts to adapt and apply the common law to new selling practices. Statutes not only govern the representations that can be made about particular products, but also regulate the quality of goods, allow for inspection of the industry,

21. CBC News, "Ottawa Strengthens Outdated Product Safety Legislation," *CBCnews.ca*, April 8, 2008, www.cbc.ca/canada/story/2008/04/08/safety-bill.html. This plan includes toughening the Food and Drugs Act and introducing new recall and reporting obligations in the Canada Consumer Product Safety Act. *Infra* n. 37. The Bill (C-52) died on the table when Parliament was dissolved for the October 2008 election.

22. In this context, "consumer" means a person who bought a consumer product from a retail seller, but does not include a person who intended to use the product primarily for business purposes: *Colhoun* v. *Ford Motor Co. of Canada* [2004] S.J. No. 543.

regulatory offences
less serious offences that do not require *mens rea* (mental intent) and usually allow due diligence as a defence

criminal offences
most serious offences that require proof of mental intent (*mens rea*)

and create **regulatory** and **criminal offences** for non-compliance. The best known of these statutes is the Food and Drugs Act, which prescribes penalties for the sale of any article of food or any drug that is adulterated or that is manufactured, packaged, or stored under unsanitary conditions. The Act also provides in part:

> No person shall label, package, treat, process, sell or advertise any food in a manner that is false, misleading or deceptive or is likely to create an erroneous impression regarding its character, value, quantity, composition, merit or safety.[23]

The federal Competition Act is the most comprehensive legislation regulating business conduct and it includes advertising. It contains a section[24] that begins with a general prohibition of misleading representations made for the purpose of promoting the supply or use of a product or of any business interest. More specifically, the section makes it an offence to make false or misleading representations about the qualities of a product or the "regular" price at which it is sold. When reading the section we should also bear in mind that the Act defines the word "product" as referring equally to goods and services. The section, as amended in 1999, reads as follows:

> (1) No person shall, for the purpose of promoting, directly or indirectly, the supply or use of a product or for the purpose of promoting, directly or indirectly, any business interest, by any means whatever, knowingly or recklessly make a representation to the public that is false or misleading in a material respect. . . .
>
> (2) For the purposes of this section, a representation that is
>
> (a) expressed on an article offered or displayed for sale or its wrapper or container,
>
> (b) expressed on anything attached to, inserted in or accompanying an article offered or displayed for sale, its wrapper or container, or anything on which the article is mounted for display or sale,
>
> (c) expressed on an in-store or other point-of-purchase display,
>
> (d) made in the course of in-store, door-to-door or telephone selling to a person as ultimate user, or
>
> (e) contained in or on anything that is sold, sent, delivered, transmitted or made available in any other manner to a member of the public,
>
> is deemed to be made to the public by and only by the person who causes the representation to be so expressed, made or contained. . . .

Subsection (2.1) extends the prohibition to persons outside Canada who market their products in Canada and is clearly aimed at American telemarketers who target Canadian consumers.

dual offence
an offence of the Competition Act that may be either a criminal or regulatory offence, depending upon the seriousness of the conduct

bait-and-switch advertising
advertising a product at a bargain price but not supplying it in reasonable quantities

Misleading advertising is a **dual offence**. Depending upon the seriousness of the non-compliance, it may constitute either a criminal or regulatory offence. The criminal offence carries a maximum penalty of five years' imprisonment, a substantial fine, or both. It is likely to be reserved for serious misconduct or for repeat offenders. By contrast, several other advertising-related offences under the Act were decriminalized by the 1999 amendments and are now exclusively regulatory offences included in a category of reviewable "deceptive market practices."[25] These include **bait-and-switch advertising**, making performance claims that lack proper substantiation, and making misleading savings claims. Such practices are subject to review by the Competition Tribunal, which may order the offender to refrain from such conduct for up to 10 years and may impose fines of up to $100 000.

---

23. R.S.C. 1985, c. F-27, s. 5(1). Other provisions regulating labels and advertising are found in the Weights and Measures Act, R.S.C. 1985, c. W-6. An identical provision applies to deception in the sale of drugs. There are separate federal statutes regulating the sale of meat, livestock, fruit, vegetables, and honey.

24. Competition Act, R.S.C. 1985, c. C-34, s. 52.

25. *Ibid.*, ss. 74.01 to 74.07.

CASE 32.4

In 2000, Alan Benlolo and his brothers Elliot and Simon were the principals in two Internet directory scams known as yellowbusinesspages.com and yellowbusinessdirectory.com. Between May and August they sent out four different bulk "advertising" mailings to over 600 000 prospects. The mailings looked remarkably like a Bell Canada invoice and some contained a version of the Yellow Pages "walking fingers" logo. Each "invoice" requested payment of $25.52 by a specific date. After several warnings from the Competition Bureau, the brothers were convicted of the criminal offence of making false and misleading representations contrary to s. 52(1) of the Competition Act. Alan and Elliot were sentenced to three years in federal jail and fined $400 000.

The brothers appealed the sentences claiming that the conduct should have been characterized as a deceptive market practice and dealt with as regulatory offence, thereby eliminating any possible federal jail time. In 2006, the Court of Appeal upheld the sentences saying that criminal charges and significant jail time were appropriate because these individuals opened bank accounts for their "business," incorporated the operating corporations, designed the mailings, and arranged for their distribution. They were intentional architects of a fraud, not legitimate business people who stepped over a line.[26]

The provinces have also passed various forms of legislation dealing with misleading advertising. In addition to prohibiting such advertising and imposing fines against sellers, consumers affected by misleading statements have civil remedies. For instance, Ontario's Consumer Protection Act declares it to be an "unfair practice" to make "a false, misleading or deceptive consumer representation" which may include a wide variety of representations about the "sponsorship, approval, performance characteristics, accessories, uses, ingredients, benefits or quantities" that the goods or services do not have.[27] There is a long list of examples of deceptive representations. The Act also creates "an unconscionable consumer representation" as a type of unfair practice that includes such conduct as simply asking a price that "grossly exceeds the price at which similar goods or services are readily available to like consumers."[28] A consumer subjected to an unfair practice may terminate the contract and "where rescission is not possible . . . the consumer is entitled to recover any payment exceeding the fair value of the goods or services received under the agreement or damages, or both" (section 18(2)). In addition, the court may award exemplary or punitive damages against the business. Similar protection exists in other provinces.[29]

The above provisions demonstrate the overlap of federal and provincial jurisdictions in the Constitution; both levels of government seem to have concurrent powers to regulate these types of selling practices, and this has led to some confusion.

ETHICAL ISSUE

Corporate Social Responsibility and Self-Regulation

It can be difficult to determine when an ad is misleading and therefore only the most obvious abuses are acted upon by the government. In an effort to raise the level of professionalism in advertising and foster public confidence, Advertising Standards Canada (ASC), an industry body formed in the 1960s, developed the Canadian Code of Advertising Standards. The code goes far

continued

26. *R. Benlolo*, (2006), 81 O.R. (3d) 440 (On. C.A.).

27. Consumer Protection Act, 2002, S.O. 2002 c. C.30, s.14.

28. *Ibid.*, s. 15 (2)(b).

29. For example: Trade Practice Act, R.S.B.C. 1996, c. 457; Fair Trading Act, R.S.A. 2000. c. F-2.

beyond inaccurate or misleading ads and addresses advertisements targeting children, containing violence, playing on fears, or offending public decency. This voluntary code of conduct is widely adopted by advertisers, advertising agencies, and the media. A dispute resolution process is also available to resolve consumer and competitor complaints.

QUESTIONS TO CONSIDER

1. How is compliance with the Canadian Code of Advertising Standards a demonstration of Corporate Social Responsibility?

2. What are the arguments in favour of and against endorsing the ASC code?

3. How should the ASC determine when an ad is too violent or offends public decency?

Regulation of Labelling, Product Safety, and Performance Standards

There is a lot of federal legislation establishing public health and safety standards for consumer products. Some standards focus on the quality of the product itself while other standards ensure the consumer is informed about the product. For example, the Consumer Packaging and Labelling Act[30] sets out comprehensive rules for packaging and labelling consumer products, including requirements for identifying products by their generic names and stating the quantity of the contents. The Act also provides for standardized package sizes to avoid confusion.

The Textile Labelling Act[31] requires labels bearing the generic name of the fabric to be attached to all items of clothing. The federal care-labelling program encourages manufacturers to include recommended procedures for cleaning and preserving the fabric. In view of the pervasive use of synthetic fibres, these labels give us important information.

The Hazardous Products Act[32] divides products into two classes. Part I lists products considered so dangerous that their manufacture is banned in Canada. The list includes such items as children's articles containing lead. Part II lists products that must be manufactured and handled in conformity with regulations under the Act and includes such items as bleaches, hydrochloric acid, and various glues containing potent solvents. The Minister of Industry[33] has broad discretion in banning products deemed to be a threat to public health or safety.

The Food and Drugs Act[34] is a comprehensive statute regulating many aspects of foods and medical and cosmetic products, since virtually all of them, if improperly processed, manufactured, stored, or labelled, may adversely affect consumers' health or safety. Provisions deal with such matters as sanitary production, contamination prevention, the listing of ingredients contained in products, and the dating of products having a shelf life of less than 90 days. The Act is administered jointly by Canadian Food Inspection Agency and Health Canada. They have the power to search, seize, examine, and recall products including imports.

---

30. R.S.C. 1985, c. C-38.

31. R.S.C. 1985, c. T-10.

32. R.S.C. 1985, c. H-3.

33. The former Department of Consumer and Corporate Affairs was merged with the Department of Trade, Industry and Technology in 1993 and now functions as Industry Canada.

34. R.S.C. 1985, c. F-27.

ILLUSTRATION 32.1

The 2008 tainted meat outbreak involving Maple Leaf Foods illustrates the importance of effective inspection and recall procedures. Over 30 people died from eating various products containing tainted meat and a $100 million class action lawsuit was commenced.

Previously, the Canadian Food Inspection Agency came under heavy criticism when the contents of a 2005 report were made public. The report identified problems in the system including irregular inspections, delays in warning the public, unclear recall protocols, and limited resources.[35]

The Motor Vehicle Safety Act[36] provides for the adoption of regulations setting national safety standards for motor vehicles whether manufactured in Canada or imported. It also requires manufacturers to give notice of defects in vehicles to the Department of Transport and to all purchasers of the defective vehicles. All of the above described federal statutes create regulatory and/or criminal offences for non-compliance.

In April 2008, the federal government introduced the Canada Consumer Product Safety Act[37] which, if passed, will expand mandatory recall power beyond food products:

> 32. (1) If an inspector believes on reasonable grounds that a consumer product is a danger to human health or safety, they may order a person who manufactures, imports or sells the product for commercial purposes to recall it.

It also requires mandatory disclosure of defects, increases penalties for non-compliance, and expands liability to corporate officers.

Provincial statutes provide further protection for consumers. As we have noted in Chapter 16, implied terms under the Sale of Goods Act with respect to merchantability and fitness are made binding on sellers in contracts with consumers; sellers cannot escape liability by requiring buyers to sign exemption clauses.[38]

This approach, of imposing contractual liability on sellers by inserting compulsory terms in consumer contracts, has been taken further in the Saskatchewan and New Brunswick statutes, which imply additional warranties and extend protection to third persons who were not parties to the contract, such as members of the buyer's family.[39]

Regulation of Business Conduct Towards Consumers

Regulations dealing with business conduct are found in many different statutes that take a variety of approaches. In this section we will look at problematic business conduct and the strategies used by regulators to combat it.

Pressure Selling   As a response to high-pressure door-to-door selling methods, most provinces enacted legislation making certain types of contracts non-binding on consumers.[40] Consumers are

---

35. Robert Cribb, "Food Alarms Rang in '05," *TheStar.com*, September 24, 2008, www.thestar.com/News/Canada/article/504671; Joanna Smith, "Two More Firms Jointly Launch Class Action Against Maple Leaf," *TheSpec.com*, August 27, 2008, www.thespec.com/News/BreakingNews/article/425810.

36. S.C. 1993, c. 16.

37. Canada Consumer Product Safety Act, 2nd Session, 39th Parliament 2007/2008, Bill C-52, first reading April 8, 2008. The Bill died on the table when the 2008 election was called, but since the Conservative government was re-elected, the Bill may be reintroduced.

38. For example: Consumer Protection Act, R.S.N.S. 1989, c. 92, s. 26(3); S.O. 2002, c. C.30, s. 9(3).

39. Consumer Protection Act, S.S. 1996, c. C-30.1; Consumer Product Warranty and Liability Act, S.N.B. 1978, c. C-18.1.

40. For example: Business Practices and Consumer Protection Act, S.B.C. 2004, c.2, s. 10.

cooling-off period
a specified period following a contract of sale during which a buyer may terminate the contract by giving written notice to the seller

given a **cooling-off period** after contracting. During this period they may terminate the contract by giving written notice to the seller. Upon doing so, he or she has no further obligation under the contract and may recover any money already paid. This marks an important departure from the common law rule that the rights and liabilities of the parties are established at the time the contract is formed.

In these statutes the cooling-off period varies from two to ten days. In some provinces it is based on the time when the contract is entered into; in others, from the date on which a written memorandum of the contract is received by the buyer. The legislation applies to both goods and services, but in some provinces it does not apply to sales under $50. Cooling-off periods are also being used to address the inequities of Internet and distance contracting.

Unsolicited Goods   Pressure selling can take the form of sending goods not ordered by the consumer, hoping to induce the recipient to pay for them. Consumer protection statutes expressly state that use of the goods by the recipient does not amount to an acceptance of the seller's offer. Accordingly, a recipient of unsolicited goods may use them without becoming liable for their price. The purpose of the provision is to discourage sellers from sending unsolicited goods to consumers, and it seems to have been quite effective. Some provinces have taken a similar approach to unsolicited credit cards.[41]

telemarketing
the use of telephone communications for promoting the supply of a product or for promoting a business interest

Telemarketing   Concerns about fraudulent **telemarketing** led to major amendments in the federal Competition Act, which took effect in March 1999.[42] "Telemarketing" is defined as "the practice of using interactive telephone communications for the purpose of promoting, directly or indirectly, the supply or use of a product or for the purpose of promoting, directly or indirectly, any business interest."[43] Deceptive telemarketing is made a criminal offence, punishable by a maximum of five years in prison and a fine within the discretion of the court; a fine of up to $200 000 may be imposed on summary conviction. The provisions also extend criminal responsibility to directors and officers of a corporation when its employees are found guilty of deceptive telemarketing. In 1999, a Quebec court imposed a record $1 million fine for deceptive telemarketing and imposed the first-ever jail sentences. The firm's president and several of the firm's sales agents were sentenced to six months in jail.[44]

The rules require agents to disclose the name of the company they represent, the purpose of the call, the kind and value of the product or service being promoted, the terms or restrictions relating to delivery of the product to customers, and other specified information. Additionally, the provisions prohibit telemarketers from conducting contests where the participant can receive prizes only after they make some kind of prior payment, or from offering gifts or prizes for buying a product unless the value of the gift is disclosed. It is also illegal for telemarketers to offer a product for sale at a price grossly in excess of its fair market value, where delivery of the product is conditional on prior payment by the customer.

In 2008, a National Do Not Call List was established by the Canadian Radio-television and Telecommunications Commission.[45] Once a consumer registers his or her number, telemarketers must not call them to solicit unless the telemarketer is a registered charity, a political party, or has an existing business relationship with the consumer. Registration is effective for a period of 3 years. Corporations face a possible $15 000 fine for each violation.

---

41. See Consumer Protection Act, R.S.B.C. 1996, c. 69, s. 47; R.S.N.S. 1989, c. 92, s. 23; S.O. 2002, c. C.30, s. 13 (although use of the card triggers an agreement s. 68).

42. Competition Act, R.S.C. 1985, c. C-34, s. 52.1.

43. Internet communications, automated pre-recorded messages, and consumer-instigated calls to a customer relations line are not covered.

44. American Family Publishers et. al., *Competition Bureau Annual Report 98/99.*

45. An Act to Amend the Telecommunications Act, S.C. 2005, c. 50; Telecom Decision CRTC 2008-6.

Repossession A standard form consumer contract may contain a term asserting that the lender or seller has some form of self-help remedy should the consumer default. For example, the contract may authorize the seller to repossess the goods from the consumer if instalment payments are not kept up, or to sue for the entire balance due under the contract if the consumer defaults in a single instalment payment. Consumer protection statutes in some provinces state that the seller's remedy of repossession is lost once the buyer has paid a specified proportion (for example, two-thirds) of the purchase price, and other statutes limit the circumstances in which a seller or creditor can enforce an **acceleration clause**, which is a provision in the contract that stipulates that the unpaid balance of the price is immediately payable should the buyer default. A further example occurs in the law of landlord and tenant, where some provinces have abolished a landlord's self-help remedy of seizing a residential tenant's goods for arrears of rent.[46]

acceleration clause
a contractual provision whereby the unpaid balance of the price becomes payable immediately in the event of default by the buyer

Financing Arrangements Many vendors who sell durable goods to consumers on the instalment plan "discount" their consumer credit contracts to finance companies. Typically, a vendor assigns the contract to a finance company and receives immediate payment of a sum that is less than the full amount to be paid by the buyer. The buyer then receives notice of assignment and makes the instalment payments to the finance company. The general rule about assignment of contractual rights, as we have seen in Chapter 12, is that an assignee "takes subject to the equities" and acquires no more enforceable claim than the assignor had. There is little doubt that a vendor can more readily find an assignee to buy its instalment receivables if the assignee acquires rights against the buyer that are *not* subject to any complaints the buyer (consumer) may have about the goods.

Vendors and finance companies found a way around the general rule about assignments by using a negotiable instrument: a buyer was required to sign a promissory note for the balance of the purchase price plus finance charges, and this note, along with the conditional sale contract, was endorsed by the vendor to the finance company. As a result, the finance company became a *holder in due course* of the note, immune to any "personal defences" the buyer might have against the vendor. Until the matter was corrected by legislation, a consumer might be liable to a finance company with no opportunity to refuse to pay for the goods if they proved defective or if the dealer refused to perform its warranties. An amendment to the Bills of Exchange Act made finance companies subject to consumers' defences against sellers.[47]

Another way around the rule was to use the contract of sale itself to waive the consumer's rights by a rather special kind of exempting clause: the consumer was asked to sign a standard form contract of sale containing a clause (sometimes referred to as a "cut-out clause") agreeing that any assignee of the contract (for example, a finance company), when seeking to enforce the debt, would not be subject to the defences that the debtor (consumer) might have against the assignor (dealer). As noted in Chapter 30, most consumer protection acts now state that an assignee of a consumer credit contract shall have no greater rights than the assignor and is subject to the same obligations.[48]

Disclosure of the True Cost of Credit

The federal Interest Act requires that interest rates in written contracts be expressed in annual percentages.[49] Consumer protection statutes also contain disclosure requirements for all contracts where a buyer of goods or services or a borrower of money repays the debt by instalments. They require sellers and lenders to give their customers a detailed statement of the terms of credit in dollars

46. See, for example: Residential Tenancy Act, S.B.C. 2000, c. 78, s. 26(3)(a).
47. R.S.C. 1985, c. B-4, s. 191.
48. For example: Consumer Protection Act, R.S.B.C. 1996, c. 69, s. 3(1); R.S.N.S. 1989, c. 92, s. 25; S.O. 2002, c. C.30, s. 83.
49. R.S.C. 1985, c. I-18, s. 4.

and cents and in percentage terms as an effective annual rate of interest, as well as any charges for insurance and registration fees. A customer is not bound by the contract if the seller fails to comply with the requirements.[50]

The purpose of this legislation is to make the costs of obtaining credit clearer to the prospective debtor, who is then able to compare offers of credit and to shop around for the lowest effective rate of interest.

Some provincial consumer legislation imposes higher standards of financial disclosure on particular industries. Under the Ontario Consumer Protection Act, time share, personal development, leasing, and motor vehicle repair contracts are required to contain special terms including detailed financial disclosure and cost-of-borrowing calculations.

Regulation of Specific Businesses by Licensing, Bonding, Inspection, or Other Regulation

Licensing of businesses is another common method of protecting consumers. We have discussed the licensing of many professions in Chapter 4. Licensing is also used to regulate the providers of a variety of goods and services. A familiar example is the inspection and licensing of restaurants by municipal authorities to ensure sanitary conditions in the preparation of food.

Consumer protection acts may enable regulatory boards to suspend or revoke registration and to hear complaints. All provinces prohibit door-to-door traders from continuing to sell unless they are registered so that sanctions, if actively pursued, can be effective. Collection agencies—often accused of using high-pressure tactics and harassment to collect outstanding debts—are also subject to similar registration requirements.

After some highly publicized failures of travel agencies in the 1970s in which consumers who had paid for holiday packages lost their money, some provinces passed legislation to license travel firms in much the same way as door-to-door sellers and collection agencies. In addition, they required travel agents to be bonded in order to guarantee consumers against loss of prepaid travel and accommodation, or established Travel Assurance Funds to accomplish the same purpose.

ILLUSTRATION 32.2

The payday loan industry provides an interesting illustration of provincial and federal co-operation in consumer protection regulation. In 2004, the questionable lending practices of the payday loan industry caught the attention of the press. The *Toronto Star* reported that the combination of administrative charges, interest, and insurance fees typically collected on a two-week payday loan amounted to the equivalent of an annualized interest rate of between 390 to 891 percent, even though it is a criminal offence to charge more than 60 percent per annum.

Since banking and interest are matters of federal jurisdiction, the federal government acted first by amending the Criminal Code to allow provinces to regulate this lending industry and set their own interest rate caps. Since then British Columbia, Manitoba, Nova Scotia, and Saskatchewan have passed legislation regulating the industry. New Brunswick and Ontario are in the process of adopting legislation. Licensing, bonding, reporting, and disclosure requirements are common to most of the provincial schemes, but not all have capped the interest rates. Manitoba set a cap of 17 percent. Ontario's bill does not call for a cap. Quebec bans payday loan outlets completely.[51]

50. For example: Consumer Protection Act, R.S.B.C. 1996, c. 69, s. 41; S.O. 2002, c. C.30, Part VII.

51. Legislative Summary of Bill C-26, September 2007, available online at www.parl.gc.ca/common/bills_ls. asp?lang=E&ls=c26&source=library_prb&Parl=39&Ses=1; Service Alberta, *Alberta Payday Loan Business Regulation Proposal*, accessed at www.servicealberta.ca/payday.cfm (link no longer active); Joanna Smith and Robert Benzie, "Payday Loan Crackdown," *TheStar.com*, April 1, 2008, www.thestar.com/News/Ontario/article/407813.

CHECKLIST Summary of Relevant Consumer Protection Legislation				
Misleading Advertising	**Labelling, Product Safety, and Performance**	**Business Conduct Towards Consumers**	**Disclosure of Cost of Credit**	**Specific Industry Regulation (Licensing, etc.)**
■ Food and Drugs Act ■ Competition Act ■ Provincial consumer protection statutes	■ Food and Drugs Act ■ Consumer Packaging and Labelling Act ■ Textile Labelling Act • Hazardous Products Act ■ Motor Vehicle Safety Act ■ Proposed Canada Consumer Product Safety Act ■ Provincial Sale of Goods Acts	■ Provincial consumer protection statutes ■ Competition Act	■ Interest Act ■ Bills of Exchange Act ■ Provincial consumer protection Statutes	■ Provincial consumer protection statues Specific Industries: ■ Provincial payday loan legislation ■ Provincial travel industry legislation

COMPETITION

Background

The essential characteristic of an efficient market economy is competition. If consumers and customers have a choice between the goods or services of competing firms, prices will be lower or quality better, or both. But an entirely unregulated market has within it the seeds of its own destruction. The most efficient firms will ultimately drive the less efficient out of business—at least in certain sectors of the market. They will then enjoy a monopoly, there will be no competition, and the benefits of a free market will be lost. The same may occur where two or more firms coordinate their actions and strategies in such a way as to divide up the market rather than competing for it. Where such market imperfections exist or are likely to occur, governments must intervene in order to preserve competition.

The Common Law

As we saw in Chapter 8, the common law has long recognized the desirability of promoting free and fair competition, in particular, by refusing to enforce contracts that unreasonably restrain trade. The courts have struck down provisions in contracts where one party agrees not to compete with the other and where the scope of that restriction is unreasonably wide. Typical provisions restrict a former employee from establishing his own business or working for a competitor firm for a certain period after termination of the employment. Similar restrictions on franchisees, partners, shareholders in small corporations, or vendors of businesses prevent them from competing with their former associates. Such provisions are not always invalid, but the courts will not enforce them if they unreasonably restrict competition. However, the common law principle operates only to prevent a party from enforcing a contract that is in restraint of trade. It has no application to situations where the parties voluntarily enter into and abide by contracts that restrict competition.

The torts of conspiracy and of unlawful interference with trade may also provide a remedy for a business injured by unfair competition, as noted in Chapter 3. The actions are very limited in scope, applying only where two or more parties deliberately conspire to cause injury to another's business, or where one person uses unlawful means to induce another to breach a contract with a third person. Such actions are very rare in Canada.[52]

The Competition Act

The Competition Act was enacted to supplement the common law.[53] As noted earlier in this chapter, the Competition Act also contains various provisions relating to matters such as misleading advertising, deceptive marketing practices, and to consumer protection generally. As for anti-competitive practices, the provisions of the Act can be grouped under three main headings, dealing with

- conspiracies
- monopolizing
- mergers

Before examining these provisions, two other aspects of the Act should be considered briefly: exemptions and enforcement.

Exemptions

The Act does not apply to certain classes of persons or to certain types of restrictive practice. In particular, the basic prohibition against conspiracies generally does not apply to the professions. Governing bodies of professions such as law, medicine, and public accountancy may establish agreements among their members dealing with such matters as qualifications, provided they are reasonably necessary for the protection of the public. Also exempt are agreements or arrangements among underwriters and others involved in the distribution of securities, and among members of a shipping conference.

Enforcement

The entire administration of the Act is the responsibility of the Commissioner of Competition, as head of the Competition Bureau. Less serious regulatory offences known as civil matters or reviewable matters are managed by the Deputy Commissioner, Civil Matters and are ultimately referred to the Competition Tribunal (see Figure 32.2). This specialized tribunal has the power to order a variety of civil remedies. More serious cases involving criminal offences are investigated by the Deputy Commissioner, Criminal Matters and prosecuted through the courts by the Attorney General. The Act creates a number of criminal offences, punishable by heavy fines and by imprisonment for up to five years. In 1999, fines totalling almost $90 million were imposed on a number of producers of vitamins participating in an international price-fixing cartel (see definition of cartel below); a Swiss businessman was personally fined $250 000, and in another case, a Canadian businessman was jailed for nine months.

Normally, a person who is adversely affected by conduct that is prohibited by the Act lodges a complaint, leaving it with the Commissioner to investigate and take the appropriate procedure. However, section 36 also provides that an individual may bring an action for damages resulting from prohibited conduct or from contravention of an order of the Tribunal.[54] This is rarely done because it is difficult and expensive to prove damage or even that an offence has been committed.

---

52. For an interesting (but unsuccessful) action, see *Ed Miller Sales & Rentals Ltd.* v. *Caterpillar Tractor Co.* (1996), 30 C.C.L.T. (2d) 1 (Alta. C.A.). See also *Manos Foods International Inc.* v. *Coca-Cola Ltd.* (1999), 180 D.L.R. (4th) 309.

53. R.S.C. 1985, c. C-34. References to section numbers in this part of the chapter are to this Act, as amended. The Competition Act replaced the Combines Investigation Act, which was the first legislative attempt to protect competition.

54. The constitutionality of this provision was upheld by the Supreme Court of Canada in *City National Leasing Ltd.* v. *General Motors of Canada*, [1989] 1 S.C.R. 641. For a recent example of such an action, see *Culhane* v. *ATP Aero Training Products Inc.* (2004), 238 D.L.R. (4th) 112, in which the plaintiff failed to substantiate a claim of predatory pricing.

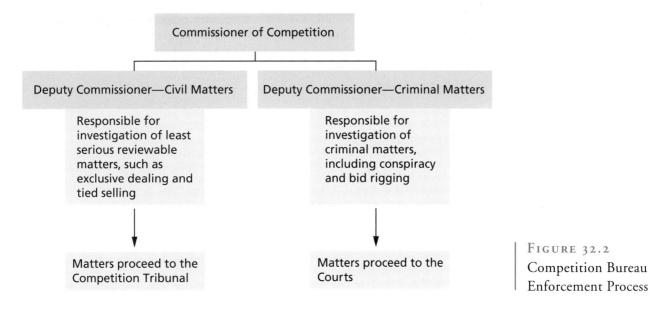

FIGURE 32.2
Competition Bureau
Enforcement Process

Conspiracies

Section 45 of the Competition Act

Section 45 of the Act sets out the basic prohibition against **cartels**, which are arrangements between enterprises designed to lessen competition. Cartels are known as "trusts" in the United States—hence the expression *anti-trust* law. (The word "trust," when used in this sense, is not to be confused with the equitable concept of the trust, described in Chapter 12.)

cartel
an agreement or arrangement between enterprises to lessen competition

Section 45 provides:

(1) Every one who conspires, combines, agrees or arranges with another person

    (a) to limit unduly the facilities for transporting, producing, manufacturing, supplying, storing or dealing in any product,

    (b) to prevent, limit or lessen, unduly, the manufacture or production of a product, or to enhance unreasonably the price thereof,

    (c) to prevent or lessen, unduly, competition in the production, manufacture, purchase, barter, sale, storage, rental, transportation or supply of a product, or in the price of insurance upon persons or property, or

    (d) to otherwise restrain or injure competition unduly,

is guilty of an indictable offence and is liable to imprisonment for a term not exceeding five years or to a fine not exceeding ten million dollars or to both.

The section creates a criminal offence so the matter proceeds to court rather than the tribunal. In order to secure a conviction, it is necessary for the Crown to prove that the conduct of the accused was intentional, that is, there was *mens rea*.[55]

"Conspires, Combines, Agrees or Arranges . . ."

The essential requirement of section 45 is that two or more persons conspire together; that is, they enter into some sort of agreement. The great difficulty lies in proving it. Restrictive agreements are rarely in writing. There would be little point in drawing up a formal written agreement since it would not be enforceable and would constitute damning evidence of a criminal conspiracy. In

---

55. For a fuller discussion of *mens rea*, see Chapter 29.

investigating suspected offences under the Competition Act, the Competition Bureau has wide powers to search premises and computer records, and to seize documents (sections 15 and 16). Consequently, the existence of an agreement must usually be inferred from the actual behaviour of the parties and surrounding circumstances, unless one of the conspirators can be induced to testify.

CASE 32.5

Members of the Canadian Steel Pipe Institute were concerned about the lack of price stability in their market, following a period during which there had been wide fluctuations and various attempts by some firms to undercut their competitors and fellow members. Public meetings were held and industry reports circulated, urging members to adopt an open pricing policy. The policy involved publication of price lists and notification of price changes.

The Institute emphasized that the policy was a voluntary one, and each member was free to adopt its own pricing policy. Nevertheless, the evidence was that after the open price policy was instituted, bids submitted by members of the institute were frequently identical.

The evidence to support the existence of an actual agreement comprised the following:

(1) the various public statements that had been made

(2) the publication of price lists

(3) the fact of identical pricing

(4) a communication from one firm to another to the effect that a third firm, which had been awarded a contract at a substantially lower price, was "not playing ball"

On that evidence the court inferred that a tacit agreement had, in fact, existed among the members of the Institute.[56]

A distinction must be drawn between a tacit agreement and conduct that is sometimes described as "conscious parallelism." The fact that prices among competitors in a particular industry tend to go up or down at the same time, and by approximately the same amount, does not necessarily mean that there is a conspiracy or agreement. Within the industry, prices of competitors will tend to be similar for similar products, a practice called **parallel pricing**; otherwise, those with higher prices would lose sales. One firm may tend to be the "price leader," so that if it raised or reduced its prices, the others would quickly follow suit even though they had made no commitment to do so. Thus parallel pricing by itself is not evidence of conspiracy.

parallel pricing
the practice, among competing firms, of adopting similar pricing strategies

Undue Lessening of Competition

One method of reducing or eliminating competition, as Case 32.5 demonstrates, is parallel pricing. Other common examples of anti-competitive practices are:

- imposing limits on production (that is, setting quotas)
- market-sharing, where firms agree to divide up the market on a territorial basis
- product specialization, where firms agree that each will manufacture or sell a different type of product

The Competition Act does not prohibit all lessening of competition; it only addresses conduct that "unduly" lessens it. This rather vague distinction suggests that some lessening of competition is acceptable. But how much? The courts have interpreted it to mean that there must be a serious or significant reduction in competition.[57] In order to determine the seriousness of the effect, the relevant market must first be defined, with regard both to the product and to its geographical scope. Then the court must determine whether the accused parties possessed a sufficiently large share of that market ("market power") to injure competition. For example, a number of small firms could legitimately combine together to protect their share of the market from one or more larger competitors without unduly limiting competition.

56. *R. v. Armco Canada Ltd.* (1976), 70 D.L.R. (3d) 287.

57. *R. v. Nova Scotia Pharmaceutical Society*, [1992] 2 S.C.R. 606.

CASE 32.6

A number of pool car operators entered into an agreement whereby each agreed not to undercut prices charged by other members of the cartel to existing customers on shipments from Toronto to the West. The question was whether their agreement was likely to reduce competition unduly.

The court accepted that there was a significant reduction of competition among pool car operators. However, that was only one method of shipping goods. There were other methods, such as trucking and intermodal freight forwarding, to which potential customers could easily switch. Consequently, competition was not significantly affected.[58]

Other Specific Offences

Apart from the general conspiracy offence, under section 45 the Act expressly specifies a number of types of anti-competitive behaviour that constitute separate offences. In particular, it is an offence

- to agree not to submit a bid or to agree in advance what bids will be submitted in response to a call for bids or tenders (**bid-rigging**) (section 47)
- to limit unreasonably the opportunities for any person to participate in professional sport or to play for the team of her or his choice in a professional league (section 48)
- to implement in Canada a directive or instruction from a person outside Canada, giving effect to a conspiracy that, if it had been entered into in Canada, would constitute an offence under the Act (section 46)

bid-rigging
agreeing not to submit a bid or agreeing in advance what bids will be submitted in response to a call for bids or tenders

This last provision is aimed at multi-national corporations carrying on business in Canada, where the Canadian subsidiary carries out improper instructions from a foreign parent.

Monopolizing

The offence of conspiracy requires that two or more persons agree to restrict competition. However, a single person or firm that enjoys a monopoly, or even a very powerful position, in a particular sector of the market may also abuse its power in a manner that is contrary to the public interest. The Act deals with such conduct in a variety of ways. Certain types of conduct, especially in relation to pricing and distribution, are made illegal. More generally, the Act identifies some anti-competitive behaviour as an **abuse of dominant position**, which, though not a criminal offence, may be prohibited by order of the Tribunal.

abuse of dominant position
taking an unfair advantage of possessing a monopoly or dominant position in the marketplace

ILLUSTRATION 32.3

One of the most famous illustrations of tied selling and abuse market dominance is Microsoft's bundling of its Windows operating software with its Internet browser and media player. Bundling new software products with its operating software meant Windows consumers could not get one product without the other. This had a devastating effect on other software suppliers. Microsoft's practice has been challenged not only in the United States, but all around the world. In the European Union, Microsoft was ordered to separate the products, offer unbundled software, and share codes that would allow compatibility with other products. It was also fined $690 million plus costs. In February 2008 Microsoft was fined an additional $1.325 billion for failure to comply with the earlier rulings.[59]

58. *R. v. Clarke Transport Canada Inc.* (1995), 130 D.L.R. (4th) 500.

59. *United States* v. *Microsoft*, 87 F. Supp. 2d 30 (D.D.C. 2000); Kevin O'Brien, "Microsoft Rejected in Antitrust Appeal," *International Herald Tribune*, September 17, 2007, www.iht.com/articles/2007/09/17/business/msft.php?page=2; Bo-Mi Lim, "Microsoft Loses Antitrust Case Before S. Korean Regulator," *Washinton Post*, December 7, 2005, www.washingtonpost.com/wp-dyn/content/article/2005/12/07/AR2005120700137.html.

Pricing Practices

discriminatory pricing
where a seller makes a practice of discriminating between purchasers with respect to the price charged for goods or services

Section 50 prohibits three types of pricing practices: discriminatory pricing, regional price discrimination, and predatory pricing. **Discriminatory pricing** occurs where a seller knowingly makes a practice of discriminating between purchasers who are in competition with each other, with respect to the price charged for goods of like quality and quantity. To constitute an offence, there must be a systematic pattern of behaviour. Practices such as granting volume discounts and loyalty bonuses or rebates are allowed, so long as they are made available to all competing customers on the same terms. Vendors are, of course, permitted to change their prices from time to time.

regional price discrimination
where a seller charges lower prices in one region than it charges elsewhere, with the aim of eliminating competition

Regional price discrimination occurs where a vendor of products charges lower prices in one part of Canada than elsewhere in the country, resulting in lessened competition or elimination of a competitor. **Predatory pricing** involves selling products at unreasonably low prices, again with the effect of significantly lessening competition or eliminating a competitor. Although the statute does not expressly say so, an essential element of both offences is that the vendor must possess substantial market power. In order to be able to reduce competition or to drive out a competitor by artificially lowering the price of one's product, a firm needs to have both a large share of the market and deep pockets. This was certainly so in the *Hoffmann-LaRoche* case,[60] in which the manufacturer of Valium distributed the drug to Canadian hospitals free of charge for a period of a year. The court held that this constituted an attempt to prevent other manufacturers of tranquillizers from entering the market.

predatory pricing
where a seller temporarily reduces prices to an unreasonably low level with the aim of driving competitors out of business

resale price maintenance
where a supplier of goods attempts to control their resale price

Section 61 applies to the practice of **resale price maintenance**. It is an offence for the supplier of a product, "by agreement, threat, promise or any like means," to attempt to influence upwards, or to discourage the reduction of, the resale price of the product. Usually the offence takes the form of a refusal to supply, or some other form of sanction against, cut-price and "discount" retailers. Manufacturers and wholesalers are entitled to suggest or recommend to their customers a particular resale price, but if they do, they should make it clear that the customer is under no obligation to follow that suggestion and will not be prejudiced by a failure to do so. A supplier may raise a number of defences specifically recognized by section 61; in particular, that the customer has used the products as "loss leaders," has engaged in "bait-and-switch selling," has been guilty of misleading advertising, or has provided poor service to its own customers.

CASE 32.7

In 2004, John Deere Ltd. was investigated for price maintenance concerns arising from its refusal to allow its dealers to sell the Series 100 lawn tractor below a certain price. John Deere settled the matter by consenting to a prohibition order that required John Deere to make a 5 percent rebate payment to each customer who purchased a Series 100 lawn tractor between January 1, 2003 and August 31, 2003.[61]

Distribution Practices

The Act deals less strictly with other types of distribution practices. Generally, a supplier is entitled to choose its customers and is free to decide whether to supply a particular person or not, except where that refusal is part of a conspiracy or is related to a pricing offence. However, in circumstances where a product is not in short supply, and a potential customer is willing to meet the usual trade terms and cannot otherwise obtain adequate supplies of the product because of a lack of competition among suppliers, the Tribunal may order a supplier to supply that customer (section 75).

---

60. *R.* v. *Hoffmann-LaRoche Ltd.* (1980), 28 O.R. (2d) 164. As that case illustrates, "pricing" may be predatory where no price is charged at all: see also *Culhane* v. *ATP Aero Training Products Inc., supra* n. 52.

61. *Competition Bureau.*v. *JohnDeere*, October 19, 2004. Summary available on the Competition Bureau website at www.competitionbureau.gc.ca/epic/site/cb-bc.nsf/en/01863e.html.

Other distribution practices, such as exclusive dealing, tied selling, and market restriction, are also reviewable. A supplier may make it a condition that the buyer deals only or primarily in the supplier's products (**exclusive dealing**); it may be a condition for the supply of one type of product that the buyer also deals in other products of the supplier (**tied selling**); or it may be a condition of supplying a customer that the customer markets the product only within a prescribed area (**market restriction**). Such practices are not forbidden, but section 77 provides that the Tribunal may, on application by the Commissioner, make an order prohibiting the practice or requiring it to be modified.

Abuse of Dominant Position

Under the former Combines Investigation Act, monopolizing was a criminal offence; however, the statute was worded and interpreted in such a way that it was all but impossible to secure a conviction. The Competition Act decriminalized monopolizing (apart from certain specific offences considered above) and introduced the concept of reviewable conduct amounting to an abuse of a dominant position. To obtain an order remedying an abuse of dominant position, the Commissioner must show that the firm against which the order is sought is in substantial control of a particular business sector and has engaged in an anti-competitive practice that has prevented, or is likely to prevent or substantially lessen, competition (section 79). Section 78 sets out a non-exhaustive list of practices that are regarded as anti-competitive, such as the buying up of products to prevent the erosion of existing price levels, the pre-emption of scarce facilities or resources, and the requirement that a supplier refrain from selling to a competitor or sell only to certain customers.

The applicability of section 79 depends largely upon the identification of the relevant product and market. The firm usually argues for a broad definition, while the Commissioner proposes a narrower definition so that fewer products or a smaller geographic area will be taken into account.[62]

exclusive dealing
where a supplier of goods makes it a condition that the buyer should deal only or primarily in the supplier's products

tied selling
where a supplier makes it a condition that, to obtain one type of product, the buyer must also deal in other products of the supplier

market restriction
where a supplier makes it a condition that the buyer markets the product only within a prescribed area

---

CASE 32.8

NutraSweet accounted for more than 95 percent of all sales in Canada of the sweetener aspartame—a product used mainly in the soft-drink industry. One other firm, Tosoh, accounted for the rest of the market.

Tosoh complained to the Competition Bureau that NutraSweet had entered into exclusive purchasing contracts with its customers: if they wished to buy aspartame from NutraSweet, they had to agree to buy *only* from NutraSweet.

This raised the question of defining the relevant market: was it the market for aspartame or for sweeteners generally, and was the market Canada or the world?

The Tribunal considered the evidence of cross-elasticity of demand between the various types of sweeteners and concluded that there was, at most, only weak evidence of competition between aspartame and other sweeteners. Customers were unlikely to switch to other sweeteners on account of the conditions imposed by NutraSweet. Similarly, although aspartame was available in other countries, transportation costs were low, and there were no tariff barriers, the Tribunal concluded that the relevant market was Canada. Prices in Canada differed significantly from prices in other countries, suggesting that Canada was a distinct geographic market and that customers were unlikely to switch to imported aspartame.

Having defined the market, the Tribunal found that NutraSweet had used its market power to keep other suppliers out of Canada, with the effect of lessening competition significantly.[63]

---

62. See *Canada (Director of Investigation and Research, Competition Act)* v. *Southam Inc.*, [1997] 1 S.C.R. 748.

63. *Director of Investigation and Research* v. *NutraSweet Co.* (1990), 32 C.P.R. (3d) 1.

> **CHECKLIST**   Restricting Competition
>
> Competition may be restricted by conspiracies between a number of producers, or by monopolizing on the part of a single producer (abuse of dominant position).
>
> Common examples of conspiracies are
>
> - price fixing
> - parallel pricing
> - bid-rigging
>
> Common examples of monopolizing are
>
> - discriminatory pricing
> - predatory pricing
> - regional price discrimination
> - resale price maintenance
> - exclusive dealerships
> - tied selling arrangements
> - marketing restrictions

Mergers

One way to combat monopolizing is to try to prevent monopolies from coming into existence in the first place. To this end, section 92 of the Competition Act gives the Tribunal power to prevent a merger from proceeding, in whole or in part, and to make various other orders, where it concludes that the merger is likely to prevent or significantly lessen competition in Canada. The Tribunal may act only on a reference from the Commissioner, after the Commissioner has carried out a full investigation of a proposed merger or of one that has taken place.

merger
the amalgamation of two or more businesses into a single business entity

"**Merger**" is broadly defined (by section 91) to include the acquisition, by the purchase of shares or assets, or by amalgamation, combination, or other means, of control over, or of a significant interest in, the business of a competitor *(horizontal merger)*, supplier, customer *(vertical merger)*, or other person *(conglomerate or diversification merger)*. "Control" apparently means legal control—that is, ownership of more than 50 percent of the shares or voting rights of another corporation, but a "significant interest" may be something less than legal control.[64] Most likely to lessen competition are horizontal mergers between competing firms, since the number of competitors is effectively reduced when one such firm obtains control over another. But vertical mergers, where a firm takes control of its suppliers or its distributors, may also reduce competition by increasing the market control of large firms. Diversification will only rarely have an anti-competitive effect.

In determining whether a merger is likely to have a significant effect on competition, the Tribunal is required (by section 93) to have regard to a variety of factors: in particular, it should consider whether

- the existence of foreign competition is likely to ensure that a reduction of competition within Canada will not have adverse consequences
- the "target" firm is in poor economic health and would likely not have continued in business
- acceptable substitutes exist for the products affected
- there are barriers that might prevent new competitors from entering the market

---

64. Normally, an interest of 10 percent or less will not be considered significant.

■ effective competition will still exist after the merger

■ the merger will eliminate a vigorous, effective, and innovative competitor

Even where it is determined that a proposed merger will substantially and detrimentally lessen competition, it may still be justified on grounds of economic efficiency (section 96). The creation of a larger firm, pooling the assets and skills of the parties, may produce gains—such as improved products, increased exports, or reduced reliance on imports—that offset any detrimental effects resulting from a reduction in competition.[65]

Although the Tribunal has the power to "unscramble" a completed merger, such an event is unlikely for two reasons. First, there are pre-notification requirements for large mergers, involving firms whose combined revenues exceed $400 million per year, or whose assets exceed $35 million. A party proposing a large acquisition must inform the Bureau before proceeding with the transaction.[66] Consequently, the mergers most likely to affect competition are reviewed before they take place. Second, where it is reasonably clear that a merger will not have anti-competitive consequences, the review process can be avoided by obtaining an advance ruling from the Commissioner.

ENVIRONMENTAL PROTECTION

Environmental law is one of the fastest-growing areas of law and regulation in Canada. In a five-year period to mid-2002, there were over 20 000 government environmental inspections, and around 600 prosecutions for offences against federal environmental laws. Despite this, many consider that the Canadian environment is not adequately protected. According to the organization Friends of the Earth, most environmental crimes go undetected and unpunished. At current rates, biotech companies are inspected only twice a century, and PCB storage sites every 20 years.

Both federal and provincial governments regulate the environment. Municipalities also pass by-laws to provide local environmental protection and to restrict activities deemed to be harmful. As a result, a large proportion of enterprises must now seek professional advice about which regulatory schemes may apply to their industry.

Growing Concern for the Environment

The common law, in particular the tort of nuisance, has a very limited application to pollution problems, as we saw in Chapter 3. Generally, an owner was entitled to do as he chose on his land. However, an owner is liable for damage arising from the escape of any harmful substance stored on his land. But, except in the most direct of injuries, the proof of damage is difficult.

A few regulatory schemes were introduced many years ago in order to prevent the most obviously harmful disregard of the environment. As far back as the 19th century, there were laws prohibiting the dumping of dangerous substances into rivers, lakes, and harbours. However, at that time, and indeed until quite recently, there was limited appreciation of the cumulative effects of pollution; governments made very little effort to enforce the early schemes, and offending industries often ignored them entirely.

Increased awareness made enforcement a major public issue, and the need for legislation and regulation to remedy the deficiencies of the existing statutory and common law became very apparent. Major environmental disasters, such as the running aground of the Exxon Valdez off the coast of Alaska and the Bhopal chemical spill in India, and the worldwide concern about climate change and depletion of the earth's ozone layer, have made the public much more aware of the dangers associated with many activities in industry, transportation, and natural resource exploitation.

---

65. This involves a balancing of positive and negative effects: see *Commissioner of Competition* v. *Superior Propane Inc.* (2001), 199 D.L.R. (4th) 130.

66. As noted in the next chapter, additional requirements, under the Investment Canada Act, apply in the case of acquisition of a Canadian firm by a foreign firm.

The Modern Legislative Framework

Environmental law is another of the areas in which the federal Parliament and provincial legislatures have concurrent jurisdiction. The protection of the environment is clearly within the competence of the provinces, but matters such as air and water pollution are national problems and require national solutions.

CASE 32.9

The Manitoba government established a scheme to compensate fishermen for loss suffered as a result of mercury contamination. In addition to Manitoba firms, corporations operating in Ontario and in Saskatchewan were found to have discharged mercury into rivers that drained into Manitoba. The Supreme Court of Canada held that Manitoba did not have power to impose liability in respect of acts done outside the province.[67]

Federal Legislation

The most important federal legislation is contained in the Canadian Environmental Protection Act (CEPA);[68] it is augmented by a number of separate statutes relating to particular types of pollution or dangers to the environment.[69]

The CEPA applies to all elements of the environment—air, land, and water, all layers of the atmosphere, all organic and inorganic matter and living organisms, and any interacting natural systems that include components of the foregoing. The Act requires the Minister of the Environment to formulate environmental quality objectives, guidelines, and codes of practice relating to the environment in general and to such specific matters as recycling, storing, and disposing of substances, and activities for the conservation of natural resources and promotion of sustainable development (section 8). Separate parts of the CEPA deal with subjects such as toxic substances, hazardous wastes, nutrients, international air pollution, and ocean dumping. Amendments made in 1999 introduced stricter controls over the use of toxic substances, gave significant new powers to enforcement officers to deal with polluters, and increased the maximum fines and sentences for offenders.

Provincial Legislation

All the provinces have a "general" environment protection law,[70] supplemented by various statutes referring to specific types of environmental protection. Examples are statutes relating to air pollution,[71] water conservation and pollution,[72] transportation of dangerous goods,[73] and waste management.[74]

---

67. *Interprovincial Corp. Ltd.* v. *R.*, [1976] S.C.R. 477.

68. S.C. 1999, c. 33. The Act consolidated a number of earlier statutes, among them the Clean Air Act, the Environmental Contaminants Act, the Ocean Dumping Control Act, and parts of the Canada Water Act.

69. Most notably in the Nuclear Energy Act, R.S.C. 1985, c. A-16; the Fisheries Act, R.S.C. 1985, c. F-14; the Pest Control Products Act, R.S.C. 1985, c. P-9; and the Transportation of Dangerous Goods Act, S.C. 1992, c. 34.

70. For example: Environment Management Act, R.S.B.C. 1996, c. 118; Environment Act, S.N.S. 1994–95, c. 1; Environment Protection Act, R.S.O. 1990, c. E-19.

71. For example: Clean Air Act, S.S. 1986–87–88, c. 12.1; Environmental Protection and Enhancement Act, R.S.A. 2000, c. E-12.

72. For example: Environmental Protection and Enhancement Act, R.S.A. 2000, c. E-12; Environment Act, S.N.S. 1994–5, c. 1.

73. For example: Dangerous Goods Handling and Transportation Act, R.S.M. 1987, c. D-12; Dangerous Goods Transportation Act, R.S.O. 1990, c. D.1.

74. For example: Waste Management Act, R.S.B.C. 1996, c. 482.

Environmental Impact Assessment Review

It is much better to prevent injury to the environment than to try to remedy it after it has occurred. Environmental impact assessment review processes have been introduced at the federal level by the Canadian Environmental Assessment Act,[75] and in all provinces. Usually, the initiator of a development project is required to undertake an environmental assessment of the proposed project and submit it to the appropriate government agency. Major projects are subject to public review by an independent review board, and public hearings are held in the communities likely to be affected. The review board submits its findings to the minister responsible or to the whole Cabinet, which makes the final decision.

The scope and the procedures of the review process vary from one jurisdiction to another. In some, the process applies to both the private and the public sectors. In others, only public authorities are required to comply with the process. However, that is not as important an omission as it might seem, since few, if any, major private development projects can occur without the involvement of one or more government agencies. For example, the federal environment assessment and review process applies only to "federal projects," but federal projects include not only those initiated by federal departments and agencies, but also those for which federal funds are solicited and those involving federal property.

Enforcement and Liability

Although private enforcement of environmental standards is possible using the common law tort of nuisance or negligence, the enforcement of environmental laws is primarily a public matter. Legislation provides public authorities with a wide variety of enforcement tools. Polluters may be ordered to refrain from harmful activities, to remedy existing situations, and to pay for the costs of cleanup. Owners of contaminated property may be forbidden from dealing with that property, even where they were not responsible for causing the contamination. Most important, environmental legislation normally creates a number of offences, punishable by fines and, in serious cases, by imprisonment. And, as we saw in Chapter 29, since most major polluters are corporations, which cannot be sent to prison, the statutes frequently provide for the punishment of corporate directors and officers who are personally responsible for pollution offences.

INTERNATIONAL ISSUE

Foreign Bribery

This chapter has dealt with a number of regulations that require businesses to seek government approval. Would a Canadian business ever consider bribing the Commissioner of Competition to obtain approval for a merger? Of course not; in Canada, bribery of Canadian public officials is unacceptable and government corruption is prohibited through a number of Criminal Code offences including bribery, fraud, influence peddling, and money laundering.

Internationally, attitudes concerning the bribery of government officials vary widely. In some cultures, it is considered normal, if not acceptable, to bribe an official to get a favourable or at least more rapid response.

continued

---

75. S.C. 1992, c. 37.

In 1997, the Organization for Economic Cooperation and Development (OECD) adopted the Convention on Combating Bribery of Foreign Public Officials in International Business Transactions. This treaty called for member nations to adopt domestic legislation that criminalized bribery of foreign officials. Canada ratified the treaty and passed the Corruption of Foreign Public Officials Act (CFPOA) in 1999. This Act criminalizes any benefit conveyed directly or indirectly to a public official "in order to obtain or retain an advantage in the course of business." It covers any bribery where there is a real and substantial link between the offence and Canada. The maximum penalty under the Act is five years in prison. Progress on the fight against corruption must be reported to Parliament on an annual basis.

In recognition of the cultural variation in bribery standards, "facilitation payments" made to expedite or secure the performance of a "routine" act by a public official are exempt for the CFPOA.

In 2002, Hector Remeriez Garcia, a U.S Immigration Officer working at the Calgary airport, was sentenced to six months in jail and deported to the United States after accepting bribes from an Alberta Company, Hydro Clean Group Inc, in violation of the CFPOA. The company was also convicted and received a $25 000 fine.

The United States has similar legislation known as the Foreign Corrupt Practices Act. The OECD visits participating countries to evaluate anti-corruption progress and makes recommendations about further measures. Other Canadian steps taken to reduce bribery include inserting anti–money-laundering provisions in the Income Tax Act and amending the Criminal Code to expand its applications to organizations.

QUESTIONS TO CONSIDER

1. Should Canada attempt to regulate international business conduct by extending the reach of its criminal law beyond its borders?

2. Facilitation payments are not acceptable in Canada so why should they be exempt from the Corruption of Foreign Public Officials Act?

Sources: Department of Justice Canada, "The Corruption of Foreign Public Officials Act A Guide," May 1999, www.justice.gc.ca/eng/dept-min/pub/cfpoa-lcape/index.html; Foreign Affairs and International Trade Canada, *Corporate Responsibility Report – Bribery and Corruption: Sixth Report to Parliament*, October 21, 2005, www.international.gc.ca/foreign_policy/internationalcrime-old/6-report_parliament-en.asp.

QUESTIONS FOR REVIEW

1. What strategies are available to business to avoid the application of government regulation?

2. How does the Constitution divide the power to regulate business among the various levels of government in Canada?

3. What is meant by "concurrency" and by "paramountcy"?

4. Which provisions of the Charter have particular application to business activity?

5. What changes to the business environment strengthened the need for consumer protection legislation?

6. How are consumer protection standards enforced?

7. What are the principal forms of misleading advertising that are prohibited by the Competition Act and what are the consequences?

8. What is the purpose of a "cooling-off period"?

9. How does the Competition Act attempt to prevent fraudulent telemarketing?

10. What is a cartel? How do cartels operate against the public interest?

11. How does a court determine if competition has been "unduly" lessened?

12. Give examples of the principal types of abuse of dominant position.

13. Why is it thought necessary for governments to control mergers?

14. Why are "horizontal" mergers more likely to affect competition than other types of merger?

15. Why is the determination of the relevant "market" essential to the application of competition law?

16. What is the purpose of environmental impact assessment review?

CASES AND PROBLEMS

1. Dr. Carpenter relocated her dental practice to premises in a new shopping mall and placed an advertisement to that effect in the local newspapers. The notice conformed with the advertising standards of the dental profession in the province, but one of the newspapers decided to print a "human interest" story and did an interview with Dr. Carpenter. The story was printed without first having been shown to Dr. Carpenter, and a number of advertisements for dental supplies appeared on the same page. At the same time, Dr. Carpenter ordered a sign announcing the change of premises, which she intended to be displayed in the window of her old premises. Instead, by mistake, the sign was displayed in a public area of the shopping mall.

   The professional association considered that the sign and the advertisements that accompanied the newspaper article constituted breaches of the professional advertising code, and gave notice to Dr. Carpenter of a disciplinary hearing, which could result in the cancellation or suspension of her licence to practise.

   On what grounds, if any, can the validity of the disciplinary hearing and the professional regulations be challenged?

2. Ebrahim bought a used car from Cival Autos Inc. for $8000. The car was described by Cival as follows: "one careful owner only, low mileage, excellent condition." In fact, Cival's manager was aware that the car had had three previous owners, the most recent of whom had been convicted of dangerous driving following a collision in which the car had sustained serious damage. He also knew that the odometer had been altered and that the car was generally in very poor condition.

   Very soon after Ebrahim took delivery, the car started to develop problems. At first he took the car back to Cival, where he was told that the problems were minor and that they had "fixed" them. After three such visits to Cival, Ebrahim took the car to an independent garage, and the true facts about the car became known.

   Apart from the normal remedies in contract and tort, is there any other legal action that Ebrahim can take against Cival?

3. Red Square Records Inc. is a Canadian corporation holding the sole rights to import and distribute in Canada discs and tapes produced by a Russian company, Krasnayadisk. For some years Red Square has been importing two labels that have proved very popular, partly because of their low price. It has been selling the discs to dealers at $4.99 each, and they are retailed at prices ranging from $6.99 to $8.99.

   Recently, Krasnayadisk introduced a new label, on which it is releasing previously unavailable archive recordings that are of great interest to collectors. Red Square has started to import the discs and makes them available to retailers at $18.99 each.

Steve's Records Inc., a Canadian firm that owns a large chain of record stores across Ontario, had been selling large quantities of the cheaper Krasnayadisk recordings, and its customers had shown a lot of interest in the new label. However, many were deterred by the high price. Steve's found another source for the new label—a dealer in the United States, who was prepared to supply Steve's at a price of $11.99 per disc. This enabled Steve's to sell the new label at a much lower price than any of its competitors.

Some months ago, Steve's received a letter from Red Square informing it that, if Steve's did not stop purchasing the new label from the United States, Red Square would no longer be willing to supply it with the two cheaper labels. Steve's ignored the warning and continued to import the new label.

A few weeks ago, Steve's ordered some discs from Red Square and was informed that Red Square would no longer supply Steve's. The cheaper labels are also available in the United States, but at the same price of $4.99, and with higher shipping costs.

Is there any action that Steve's can take against Red Square's refusal to supply it?

4. Truenorth Press Inc. owned both of the daily newspapers in Bayville. The papers were relatively unsuccessful compared to Truenorth's other dailies throughout Canada and faced stiff competition for advertising revenue from a large number of small community newspapers that circulated in the same distribution area. Those community newspapers contained local news stories, advertisements from mainly local firms, appeared once or twice a week, and were distributed free of charge.

Truenorth embarked on a campaign to acquire the community papers and, within one year, obtained control of 20 publications, including the two papers with the largest circulation.

A group of citizens—readers, who feared that there would be fewer "local" stories, and small firms, who feared that their advertising rates would be increased once Truenorth gained control of the remaining papers—held a number of public meetings to express their concern.

Is there any legal action that they could take?

ADDITIONAL RESOURCES FOR CHAPTER 32 ON THE COMPANION WEBSITE *(www.pearsoned.ca/smyth)*

In addition to self-test multiple-choice, true–false, and short essay questions (all with immediate feedback), application exercises, and links to useful web destinations, the Companion Website provides the following resources for Chapter 32:

- **British Columbia**: Business Practices and Consumer Protection Act; Collection Agents; Consumer Protection Legislation; Consumer Taxes; Cooling-off Period; Credit Cards; Credit Reporting; Direct Sales Contracts; Dishonest Trade Practices; Distance Sales Contracts; British Columbia Environments Legislation; Sale of Goods Act

- **Alberta**: Dishonest Trade Practices; Fair Trading Act; Occupational Health and Safety

- **Manitoba/Saskatchewan:** Consumer Protection Legislation; False or Exaggerated Claims

- **Ontario:** Agreements to Share Power; Consumer Protection Act 2002; Environmental Protection Regulation; Unfair Business Practices

International Business Transactions

As previous chapters have identified, both law and business administration in Canada often involve international issues. Increasingly, the world is becoming a single giant marketplace in which businesses from different countries compete against and sometimes co-operate with each other. This chapter provides an overview of the legal framework within which international business is conducted, discussing various aspects of foreign trade, foreign investment, and the resolution of international business disputes. We examine such questions as:

- What are the common features of export contracts?

- How are such contracts interpreted and enforced?

- How do governments regulate international trade?

- How is international trade affected and promoted by international bodies such as the World Trade Organization (WTO) and the North American Free Trade Association (NAFTA)?

- What are the legal forms available to foreign investors?

- How do governments regulate foreign investment?

- In what ways does international law apply to investment?

- How are international business obligations enforced by the courts?

- What is the role of international commercial arbitration?

- How are trade disputes resolved within NAFTA and the WTO?

Canadian Business in a Global Economy

Law and International Business

Foreign Trade

Foreign Investment

The Resolution of International Business Disputes

CANADIAN BUSINESS IN A GLOBAL ECONOMY

For Canada, the international dimension of business is especially important. Canada's exports of goods amount to over one-third of the nation's gross domestic product.[1] Canada ranks among the top ten of the world's trading nations and is a major exporter of goods and services. In 2007, its total exports amounted to $532 billion, and imports to $502 billion. To put these figures in perspective, one of the world's largest exporters, the United States, exports only approximately three times as much as Canada, and Japan not even double.

Canada's largest trading partner is the United States, which takes over three quarters of our exports and provides over half of our imports. In turn, Canada is one of the largest trading partners of the United States. The United States exports more to Canada than to any other trading partner and imports more from Canada than from anywhere else except the European Union and China.[2] Canada also has substantial trading relations with countries as diverse as Japan, the United Kingdom, Germany, Korea, China, the Netherlands, France, and Russia.

Traditionally, Canada's strength is as an exporter of raw materials, minerals (and indeed remains the world's second-largest exporter in those categories), and resource-based products, but in more recent years we have also become an important exporter of manufactured goods, chemicals, and transport and telecommunications equipment.

Perhaps of equal importance is the fact that, of the world's major industrialized economies, Canada ranks among the world's top ten countries as both an exporter and importer of investment capital. By the end of 2007, total foreign direct investment (FDI) in Canada amounted to $500 billion, and Canadian FDI abroad to $514 billion.

LAW AND INTERNATIONAL BUSINESS

Conducting an international business involves a wide variety of legal issues. To understand them, it is useful to consider how firms become international or multinational. Traditionally, establishment of international business operations was viewed as a progression. First, a business established a single location and marketed its products to the surrounding community. Eventually, it expanded, creating substantial regional or national presence. At some stage, it found its first customer in another country and its operations became international. This is the **foreign trade** stage. The e-commerce revolution has allowed many modern businesses to skip the natural progression. Launching a business online may mean that the very first customers of a new business could be international, accelerating the new business to the foreign trade stage.

foreign trade
the buying and selling of goods and services between parties from different countries

foreign presence
placing representatives of a business in foreign markets

As the business' foreign markets grow, it may find it worthwhile to have a **foreign presence** by appointing an *agent* in the other country or establishing a *representative office* there. Gradually, its activities may expand from simply seeking customers and providing information to supplying spare parts, repairs, and maintenance services.

The final stage occurs when the firm commences other activities abroad, such as processing its products. Initially those activities may be modest ones, such as labelling, packaging, or assembling components. Eventually, however, the operations may develop into full-scale manufacturing, and a

---

1. Office of the Chief Economist of Foreign Affairs and International Trade Canada, Table 4-2, *Canada's State of Trade and Investment Update 2008*, Catalogue no. FR2-8/2008, available online at www.international.gc.ca/economist-economiste/performance/state-point/2008.aspx?lang=eng. The statistics in this section are taken from the aforesaid report and the World Trade Organization's Canadian trade profile, available online at http://stat.wto.org/CountryProfile/WSDBCountryPFView.aspx?Language=E&Country=CA.

2. According to the WTO, the European Union supplied 18 percent of the total imports to the United States in 2007, China supplied 16.9 percent of total U.S. imports, and Canada was a close third at 15.7 percent. The United States sent 21.4 percent of its exports to Canada, while the European Union received 21.3 percent.

branch or *subsidiary* may be established. The business has graduated from foreign trade to **foreign investment** and has become, by definition, a multinational enterprise.

Foreign trade and foreign investment result in a wide variety of legal relationships. There are contractual relationships of many different types—sale of goods and services, carriage of goods, bailment, insurance, agency, and employment. Questions arise regarding the law of negotiable instruments, intellectual property, partnerships and corporations, secured transactions, and creditors' remedies. There is an additional complication—international business transactions, by definition, involve parties in two or more different countries: Which country's law will apply to a transaction? This is a question of **private law**—the law that governs transactions between private parties, such as a seller and buyer of goods.

Virtually every government regulates foreign trade and investment to some extent. Therefore, international business involves legal relationships between private persons or entities and governments. This raises questions of **public law**. Finally, in an effort to open international markets for their businesses and secure domestic markets, governments often make bilateral agreements (such as double taxation treaties, investment protection treaties, or free trade agreements) or multilateral agreements (such as the General Agreement on Tariffs and Trade [GATT], the North American Free Trade Agreement [NAFTA], and the International Convention for the Protection of Industrial Property). As a result, issues of **public international law**, involving relations between states, also arise. On January 25, 2008, the Canadian government announced a new policy of introducing all proposed international treaties in the House of Commons to allow for debate before Canada formally ratifies a treaty.[3]

Throughout this chapter we will make reference to various **non-governmental organizations** and **super-governmental organizations** that work to establish common standards and laws around the world. Member countries of super-governmental organizations send government representatives to voice their positions and negotiate on their country's behalf. Examples include the World Trade Organization, the United Nations Commission on International Trade Law, and the Organization for Economic Cooperation and Development. Some standards are introduced as codes of conduct, guiding principles, and suggested contractual language with the hope that private business will voluntarily adopt them. Other times, suggested legislative models are produced to influence governments as they implement domestic legislation. These organizations play a major role in the development of international business law.

foreign investment
conducting operations in a foreign market

private law
the law that governs transactions between private parties, such as a seller and buyer of goods

public law
law governing the relationship between private individuals and the state

public international law
law involving relations between states

non-governmental organizations
voluntary, non-profit associations of private entities working to influence policy, raise awareness, and affect change, such as the International Chamber of Commerce

super-governmental organizations
non-profit associations of governments from around the world working to find common solutions to international issues

FOREIGN TRADE

Export/Import Contracts

Export/import contracts generally fall into one of two categories: contracts for the international sale of goods and contracts for the supply of services abroad. Goods or services may be supplied in one of three main ways:

- The supplier may deliver directly to the customer in the other country.
- Delivery may be made through the supplier's own marketing organization established in the other country.
- The customer may accept delivery in the supplier's home country and himself arrange to ship the goods home.

---

3. Foreign Affairs and International Trade Canada Press Release, "Canada Announces Policy to Table International Treaties in House of Commons," January 25, 2008, No. 20, www.news.gc.ca/web/view/en/index.jsp?articleid=374729.

Whichever method is adopted, the contract between supplier and customer constitutes the essence of the transaction. The following discussion concentrates upon the most common type of export transaction—contracts for the international sale of goods.

The Contract of Sale

Much of what has been written in earlier chapters of this book with respect to the law of contracts and, in particular, to contracts for the sale of goods, applies equally to export contracts as it does to contracts with a purely domestic scope. However, contracts with an international element present special problems due to the simple fact that the goods are to be delivered to, or services supplied to, a customer in another country.

Usually, the international sale of goods involves a number of parties and consists of several distinct though related contracts. In addition to the basic agreement for the sale of the goods, the parties normally arrange for the transportation of the goods, for their insurance during shipment, and, frequently, for the financing of the transaction. Carriers, insurers, banks, or finance houses may be involved as well as the buyer and seller. Since export transactions require special expertise, the parties commonly employ the services of specialist **export houses** or **freight forwarders**, who make the arrangements for shipment, insurance, and financing.

export houses or **freight forwarders**
specialist firms that make the arrangements for shipment, insurance, and financing in export sales

The Proper Law of the Contract

As we have noted, an export contract by definition involves two or more countries. A question that frequently arises is, "Whose law governs the contract or its various component parts?"

ILLUSTRATION 33.1

A Canadian manufacturer sells goods to a Hungarian customer. The goods are to be shipped by a German airline, insured by a British insurance company, and financed by a Swiss merchant bank.

Several contracts make up the entire transaction in Illustration 33.1, and each one might be governed by a different law. The laws of the different countries may vary considerably with respect to such matters as the rights of unpaid vendors or carriers, the terms to be implied as to quality or fitness of the goods, and the circumstances in which a contract will be frustrated.

proper law of the contract
the law of the country or jurisdiction by which the provisions of a contract are to be interpreted and its effect determined

To determine which law applies—that is, the **proper law of the contract**—it is necessary to refer to a body of principles known as the **conflict of laws**, or **private international law**. Canadian courts, and the courts of most other countries, hold that the proper law of the contract is the law that the parties intended to govern. The clearest method of establishing the proper law is for the parties themselves to make express provision.[4] A contract might state that it is subject to the law of Ontario, England, or Switzerland. The choice of law need not be that of the location of one of the parties or be related to the place where the contract is to be performed—sometimes the parties choose a "neutral" law.

conflict of laws or **private international law**
the principles of law that apply to resolve questions concerned with private relationships that are affected by the laws of two or more countries

Where the parties do not expressly state the proper law, the court will attempt to determine the intention of the parties from the surrounding circumstances. For example, if the contract states that any dispute is to be submitted to arbitration in a particular country, or that the courts of a particular country shall have jurisdiction, then it is probable that they also intended the law of that country to govern the contract.[5] An intention may also be inferred from the use of particular legal

4. *Vita Food Products Inc.* v. *Unus Shipping Co. Ltd.*, [1939] A.C. 277.
5. *Hamlyn & Co.* v. *Talisker Distillery*, [1894] A.C. 202.

terminology or the form of the document. Where the court cannot draw such an inference, it will apply the system of law that it considers to be most closely connected with the contract. In making this determination, it will have regard to all the circumstances and pay special attention to such factors as the place where the contract was made, the place where it is to be performed, the subject-matter of the contract, the place of business of the parties, and the place of acceptance of the risk.[6] And since the contract may comprise a number of distinct elements, it is possible that different laws may apply to different parts.[7]

Contractual Terms

Another difficulty is that terms or expressions may have different meanings in different legal systems, or to parties from different countries. In practice, the problem is not so severe as it might seem. Over the centuries a widely accepted standard terminology has evolved. Initially, the meaning of terms such as "FOB" and "CIF," which we encountered in Chapter 16, became largely standardized through mercantile custom. More recently, a set of standard terms (known as **Incoterms**) adopted by the International Chamber of Commerce, have come to be widely used. The original Incoterms were first published in 1936, and the current version dates from 2000.

Another important development has been the publication and widespread adoption of standard form contracts, published by various trade associations and by international bodies such as the United Nations Economic Commission for Europe. Super-governmental organizations, such as the International Institute for the Unification of Private Law (**UNIDROIT**), the United Nations Commission on International Trade Law (**UNCITRAL**), and the Organization for Economic Cooperation and Development (**OECD**) have encouraged the harmonization of national commercial laws or the adoption of uniform laws. For example, the 1980 Vienna Convention on Contracts for the International Sale of Goods, implemented in Canada in 1991,[8] standardized sale-of-goods terms and practices resulting in an international standard of interpretation. Canadian e-commerce legislation, discussed in Chapter 34, follows the template of the UNCITRAL model law. The process of harmonization is an ongoing one, continually evolving in order to keep up with new developments.

The Documentation

An export sale normally requires at least four documents:

- the contract of sale
- the bill of lading
- the insurance policy or certificate
- the invoice

We have already discussed the contract of sale and bills of lading in Chapter 16, and insurance in Chapter 18. A bill of lading, as we have seen, is an acknowledgment by the carrier that the goods have been delivered for shipment. It operates as a document of title to the goods, facilitating the financing of the transaction. The insurance policy, similarly, is evidence that the goods are insured against loss or damage during transit and is usually necessary in order to obtain financing.

The invoice is of special importance in international sales of goods and must be correct in every respect, since it provides information not only for the parties to the transaction but also for the customs authorities of the country of importation. The invoice states the names and addresses of the

Incoterms
a set of standard contractual terms adopted by the International Chamber of Commerce

UNIDROIT
the International Institute for the Unification of Private Law, founded by the League of Nations in 1926 to harmonize laws, currently has 61 member states including Canada

UNCITRAL
United Nations Commission on International Trade Law established by the United Nations General Assembly in 1966 to further harmonization and unification in international trade through conventions, model laws, and guidelines

OECD
the Organization for Economic Cooperation and Development, established in 1961, has 30 member countries including Canada and promotes world trade and sustainable economic growth by setting standards for best practice

---

6. *Imperial Life Assurance Co. of Canada* v. *Colmenares*, [1967] S.C.R. 443.

7. *M.W. Hardy Inc.* v. *A.V. Pound & Co. Ltd.*, [1956] A.C. 588.

8. International Sale of Goods Contracts Convention Act, S.C. 1991, c. 13. It has also been adopted by several of the provinces; see, for example: International Sale of Goods Act: S.N.S. 1988, c. 13; R.S.O. 1990, c. I.10.

buyer and seller, the date of the order, a full description of the goods sold, details of packaging, and the price (on the basis of which customs duty is normally calculated). It must conform to the requirements of the importing country, which may insist upon the production of additional documents, such as certificates of value, origin, quality, or inspection.

In recent years these tangible forms of documentation have begun to be replaced by computerized communications. Bodies such as the Comité Maritime International have devised uniform sets of rules dealing with electronic data exchange in international business transactions.

Shipment and Insurance

Since it is the shipment of goods to another country that distinguishes the international sale of goods from purely domestic transactions, transportation arrangements are an essential element of an export sale. The parties may agree that the buyer will collect the goods from the seller's factory and make its own arrangements for transportation, or that the seller will deliver the goods to the buyer's premises in the other country, or that each will be responsible for some stage of the transportation. Usually, too, the goods will be insured against loss or damage during transit, and either the buyer or the seller may assume responsibility for arranging insurance. The contract price reflects whether it is the seller or the buyer who arranges and pays for shipment and insurance, and up to which stage of the journey.

A seller may quote a price *ex works* (that is, at the factory gate); if it is agreed to deliver the goods to the buyer's own premises, the total price will be correspondingly higher. As we saw in Chapter 16, the precise arrangements for shipment may determine the point at which title to the goods, or the risk of loss, passes from the seller to the buyer.

Over the centuries a number of standard terms have evolved to describe the more common types of arrangements for shipment. Examples of these terms (with the corresponding Incoterm abbreviations) are:

- EXW (*ex works*);
- FOB (free on board);
- CIF (cost, insurance, and freight)
- DDP (delivery duty paid)

These terms broadly correspond to the various stages of shipment and the extent of the obligations undertaken by the seller. Figure 33.1 illustrates the four contract types listed above. In EXW contracts, the seller's responsibility is only to make the goods available to the buyer at the seller's own works or warehouse. The buyer bears the cost and the risk of transportation, though the seller is still obliged to furnish the necessary invoice and to provide all reasonable assistance to obtain any export licence or other authorization necessary for exporting the goods.

Under an FOB contract, the buyer arranges shipment, and the seller's obligation is to deliver the goods to the carrier named by the buyer. The seller's responsibility ends when the goods are safely on board the ship or aircraft. Other variants are the FCA (free to carrier) and FAS (free alongside ship) contracts, where the seller's duty is, respectively, to deliver to the first carrier (for example, where the goods are collected by the carrier and loaded into a container for shipment to a cargo terminal) and to deliver to a specified pier or warehouse at the port of shipment.

A CIF contract represents a major extension of the seller's obligations. Here, the seller assumes responsibility for shipping the goods to the country of destination. The seller is responsible not only for shipment to the port of destination but also for insuring the goods.[9]

A final category of contracts extends the obligations of the seller still further, with the seller bearing the risks and costs of transporting the goods to an agreed destination and sometimes (as in a DDP contract) even paying the import duties.

---

9.   Under a CFR (cost and freight) contract, the seller pays carriage, but the buyer arranges its own insurance.

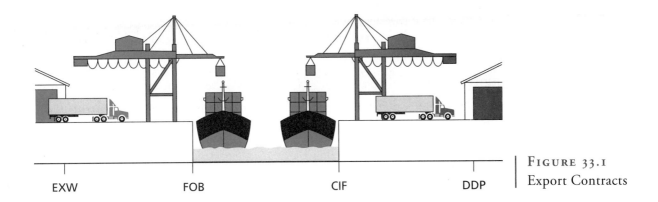

FIGURE 33.1
Export Contracts

As new methods of goods transportation are developed, so also are new types of contractual terms. The use of pallets, roll-on/roll-off ferries and, especially, containers has revolutionized the carriage of goods and, in turn, has led to the development of new legal terms, such as full container load (FCL) and less than a full container load (LCL). Where the consignment comprises a full container load, shipment may be made door to door in a sealed container. If there is less than a full container load, the goods are consolidated with the goods of other exporters in a "groupage container" and are loaded and separated at a container freight station.

Payment

A basic element in any contract of sale is the payment of the price. In an international contract the currency used to denominate the price and to make payment is important. The price may be denominated in one currency but paid in some other currency. Generally, a seller does not mind in which currency the price is paid, so long as that currency is freely convertible. However, it will state the price in a stable currency, especially if there is to be a substantial time lag between contract and payment; if the buyer's country imposes **exchange controls** or does not permit its currency to be freely converted—as is often the case in developing countries—the seller will also require actual payment to be made in a "hard" currency. An exporter or importer may also "hedge" against the risk of currency fluctuations by using a method of **foreign exchange risk management**, such as borrowing in foreign currency or taking an option to buy or sell foreign currency.

exchange controls
restrictions on the conversion or export of currency

foreign exchange risk management
methods of reducing the risk involved in currency fluctuations

Financing

Financing is especially important in international sales, partly because the time between the goods leaving the seller and reaching the buyer tends to be longer than in domestic sales, and partly because the amounts involved in international sales tend to be larger. A seller would like to receive payment as soon as its goods leave the factory or warehouse, whereas the buyer would prefer to postpone payment until the goods have been safely delivered. To accommodate both preferences normally requires the services of a banker.

For a long time the bill of exchange (see Chapter 21) was the most important method of payment in export sales. In recent years, other methods of financing have been devised, the most important of which are the **collection arrangement** and the **letter of credit**. Under a collection arrangement the seller employs the services of its bank to collect payment by depositing the documents with the bank and receiving credit for the price (less the bank's charges). By contrast, a buyer obtains a letter of credit from its bank and uses it to pay the seller.[10] More recently, banks and

collection arrangement
an arrangement whereby the seller employs the services of its bank to collect payment by depositing the documents with the bank and receiving credit for the price

letter of credit
a document that the buyer of goods obtains from the bank and uses to pay the seller

---

10. An alternative method is for the buyer to obtain a banker's guarantee.

finance houses have developed other highly flexible methods of financing, such as non-recourse finance, factoring, and financial leasing, methods that require more detailed explanation and are beyond the scope of this book.

Countertrade

countertrade
a form of barter, under which a seller agrees to accept payment in goods produced or procured by the buyer

In its simplest form, **countertrade** is a form of barter. A seller agrees to accept, instead of money, payment in goods produced or procured by the buyer. Another increasingly common arrangement is for a corporation that sells machinery to a firm in a developing country to agree to accept part of that firm's production as the price; thus it might sell modern cutting and sewing equipment and receive finished clothing in return. The forms of countertrade are virtually unlimited, but countertrade involves greater risks than do simple sales, since the "seller" will have to find a way of disposing of the goods acquired in exchange.

Export of Services

The "export" of services can take a number of forms. A buyer may come to a seller, as where a foreign tourist stays in a hotel or attends a concert in Canada. Transactions of this nature generally do not involve any element of foreign law. Or a seller might go to a buyer, as where a Canadian bank or insurance company opens a branch in another country to serve customers there. It is also possible for services to be "transmitted" to customers in other countries. Data, legal or financial advice, or technological expertise may be supplied to customers in other countries. Property in one country may be insured by an insurance company in another country. Banks may lend money to foreign clients. In 2007, world service exports grew faster (17.8%) than merchandise exports (14.8%).

Much of what has been said in relation to the international sale of goods applies equally to the provision of services—for example, the importance of determining the proper law of the contract and the problems of payment. Of particular importance in contracts involving the transfer of technology are the local rules governing the protection of intellectual property. A Canadian corporation that licenses a patent or a trademark or supplies "know-how" to an enterprise in another country will want to ensure that its rights are protected by the laws of that country and that its trade secrets do not become public knowledge.

Government Regulation of International Trade

Ever since foreign trade first evolved, governments have sought to regulate it by controlling exports and imports and by imposing customs duties. Countries consider trade relations a matter of national importance, and although many countries, such as Canada and most of its major trading partners, are broadly committed to the principle of free trade, they still maintain barriers that a would-be exporter must overcome. A particular concern of governments is the preservation of a reasonable balance of trade with other countries. Consequently, the tendency is to encourage exports and discourage imports.

Export Promotion

Governments provide a variety of services to their own producers in order to assist them to compete in the global market. An important function of Canadian embassy staff abroad is to collect commercial information and disseminate it to Canadian business. More tangible support, mostly in the form of insurance, guarantees, and financial services, is provided by the Export Development Corporation, a Crown corporation whose purpose is to facilitate and develop Canada's export trade, and by other specialist bodies such as the Canadian Wheat Board. Government support is especially important with respect to exports to less-developed countries, by providing loan guarantees and long-term credit. International aid programs may also provide indirect assistance to exporters. For example, programs funded by the Canadian International Development Agency frequently require a substantial Canadian content.

Export Controls

Although the general policy of most countries is to encourage exports, restrictions upon exports remain common. Export controls in Canada date back to the Export Act of 1897,[11] which regulated the export of a number of commodities, notably lumber. The federal government introduced further controls for reasons of national security during the First World War, and created a more comprehensive system following the Second World War and the commencement of the Cold War in 1947 by the Export and Import Permits Act.[12] The Act introduced a system of licensing for exports of certain listed products and for most exports to listed countries. Among the listed products are armaments, munitions, and other strategic materials. Listed countries were mostly confined to members of the then Communist bloc. Further regulations and other statutes have added to the lists both of products and of countries. Restrictions have been imposed on the export of certain types of cultural property and of some energy and agricultural products, and from time to time countries such as South Africa, Iran, Libya, Iraq, and Yugoslavia have joined the list of proscribed countries. Canadian membership in NATO (North Atlantic Treaty Organization) has also led to restrictions on exports of high-tech products to Communist and some other countries on the "COCOM list" (Coordinating Committee for Multilateral Export Controls). More recently, the Special Economic Measures Act[13] contains a general power to make orders and regulations restricting or prohibiting the exportation by Canadians of goods, whether from Canada or anywhere else in the world, to designated foreign states or to persons in such states.

An added problem, which has probably affected Canada more than any other country, has been the extra-territorial application of U.S. legislation. That legislation is intended to prevent the re-export (from Canada and other countries) of products originating in the United States to countries such as Cuba, and also prohibits dealings with those countries by foreign subsidiaries of U.S. corporations. The so-called Helms-Burton law[14] carries the process still further, potentially rendering Canadian (and other) firms with investments in Cuba liable to penalties in U.S. courts.

Import Duties

Customs duties on imports have been in existence almost as long as international trade itself. Originally these duties provided an important source of revenue for many countries—in 1867 customs duties constituted the major part of federal revenue in Canada. The growth of other sources of government revenue, especially income tax, and the worldwide movement to tariff reduction, have steadily reduced the fiscal importance of import duties. Their most important function nowadays is to protect domestic products against competition from cheaper imports.

Two statutes contain most of Canada's import duty legislation—the Customs Act[15] and the Customs Tariff.[16] The first deals with the administration of the system by the Canada Customs and Revenue Agency, and provides the basis for regulations that classify products and determine their dutiable value and country of origin. The Customs Tariff sets out the rates of duty (tariff) imposed on each category of products.

The setting of tariffs is no longer determined unilaterally by governments, but is largely regulated by international agreements, such as the GATT and the NAFTA. For goods imported into Canada, various preferences are granted, notably for products coming from Commonwealth, Caribbean, and less-developed countries and from our NAFTA partners, Mexico and the United

11. S.C. 1897, c. 17: see now R.S.C. 1985, c. E-18.
12. S.C. 1947, c. 17; now R.S.C. 1985, c. E-19.
13. S.C. 1992, c. 17. (See especially section 4.)
14. The Cuban Liberty and Democratic Solidarity Act of 1996, 22 U.S.C. s. 6021–6091.
15. R.S.C. 1985, c. 1 (2nd Supp.).
16. S.C. 1997, c. 36.

States. Determining the origin of goods consequently becomes very important, since goods may be manufactured in one country from raw material or components originating in another country, and may be routed via a third country.[17]

Import Restrictions

non-tariff barriers
national rules, other than import duties, that restrict or prevent the importation of goods

With the decline in the importance of import duties over the years, the existence of **non-tariff barriers** has become more significant as an obstacle to international trade. Countries often impose restrictions on imports. Sometimes they are overt; in other instances they are less visible. By Canadian law, some goods (for example, narcotics) may not be imported at all; others may be imported only under licence and subject to particular conditions.

quotas
restrictions on the quantities of goods that may be imported

Generally, Canada adopts a relatively liberal policy towards imports from other countries and adheres to the principles established by the GATT. Nevertheless, Canada does impose import **quotas**, or quantity restrictions, on certain products,[18] particularly textiles and agricultural products. A wide variety of other statutes impose restrictions on imports in order to protect public health, public safety, and the environment and for other reasons of public policy. Other countries impose their own restrictions, and a Canadian manufacturer wishing to export its products must always check to ensure that the products will be allowed to enter the other country.

Frequently, national rules on the marketing of products are just as important as restrictions on importation. There is little point exporting products to a country if they cannot legally be resold there. National health and safety standards and labelling requirements must be complied with, and they are sometimes formulated in such a way that, although ostensibly applicable to domestic and imported products alike, in practice they discriminate against imports.[19]

Dumping and Subsidies

The desire to promote exports, by producers themselves and by their governments, sometimes leads to two types of practice that are generally regarded as unfair—dumping and export subsidies. **Dumping** occurs where a firm sells goods abroad at prices lower than those at which similar goods sell in the domestic market. In effect, the firm uses the profits on its domestic sales to subsidize its exports and undercut its competitors. **Export subsidies** occur where the government of a country provides special benefits, financial or otherwise, to its producers in order to assist them to export. Benefits may take a wide variety of forms, such as reduced freight charges, income tax rebates, or unusually favourable credit terms or guarantees.

dumping
selling products abroad at prices below those charged on domestic sales

export subsidy
the granting by governments of financial assistance to promote exports

anti-dumping duties and **countervailing duties**
special duties imposed on imported products to counter the advantage obtained from dumping or export subsidies

Dumping and export subsidies, by reducing the price of imported goods, confer a benefit on the consumers of the importing country. Not surprisingly, however, such practices are resented by domestic manufacturers of competing products. Where domestic competition exists, and it appears that material injury has been or is likely to be caused to domestic producers of similar goods, importing countries often impose counter-measures to nullify the benefits of foreign subsidies. Counter-measures take the form of **anti-dumping duties** and **countervailing duties**, designed to increase the cost of imports by the amount of the margin of dumping or of the export subsidy. In Canada, such duties are imposed under the Special Import Measures Act (which was substantially amended in 1999). Many Canadian exporters have encountered difficulties with the corresponding measures

---

17. The dispute between Canada and the United States regarding the origin of Honda cars manufactured in Canada, using components made in Japan and sold in the United States, is a good example. See Frederic P. Cantin and Andreas F. Lowenfeld, "Rules of Origin, The Canada–U.S. FTA, and the Honda Case" (Jul. 1993), 87(3) *The American Journal of International Law* 375–390.

18. See Export and Import Permits Act, R.S.C. 1985, c. E-19. Other restrictions are contained in the Customs Act and the Special Import Measures Act, R.S.C. 1985, c. S-15.

19. A recent example is the ban imposed in some European countries on the sale of genetically modified agricultural products.

imposed by the United States.[20] We shall return to this issue later, when considering the impact of the WTO, NAFTA, and the softwood lumber trade dispute.

The International Law of Trade

In theory, national governments are free to adopt whatever measures they choose to regulate imports into, and exports from, their own territories. Of course, in doing so they are aware that other countries may retaliate. If Country *A* imposes restrictions on imports from Country *B*, it can hardly expect Country *B* to accept Country *A's* exports freely. The international law of trade is based to a large extent upon the principle of reciprocity, an approach generally followed in negotiating agreements between states, sometimes bilaterally and sometimes on a multilateral basis. Canada is a party to many such agreements, two of which—the General Agreement on Tariffs and Trade (GATT) and the North American Free Trade Agreement (NAFTA)—are of particular importance.

The GATT and the World Trade Organization (WTO)

The GATT is the principal instrument that lays down agreed rules for international trade. It came into force on January 1, 1948, with nine original members, one of which was Canada. The number of members has since risen to 151 (as of July 2007); others, including most notably Russia, have applied for membership.

The original intention, immediately after the Second World War, was to establish an International Trade Organization (ITO), as a part of the United Nations. This object was only partly achieved, since the ITO as such did not come into existence. Instead, a multilateral agreement was negotiated—the GATT. Despite its title, the GATT was far more than just an "agreement." It had its own Secretariat (in Geneva), a Council of Members, and the capacity to establish Tribunals (or "Panels") to adjudicate disputes between member countries. Over the years its scope was extended and its rules augmented by agreements reached in a series of "rounds." The "Uruguay Round" commenced in 1986 and finally concluded in December 1993. A new "Millennium Round" was scheduled to begin in Seattle in December 1999. The Seattle meeting, which was disrupted by wide-scale protests, failed to reach any agreement even as to the agenda for further talks. However, new talks started in 2000, and a broader agenda was agreed at the ministerial conferences held in Doha, Qatar, in 2001 and in Cancun, Mexico, in 2003.[21]

The Uruguay Round proposed the creation of a new organization, the WTO, which came into existence on January 1, 1995, and supersedes the GATT as an organization. The actual GATT agreement, however, remains in effect, together with the various "side agreements."

Probably the most serious shortcoming of the GATT was that it applied only to the international trade in goods, and even then did not apply to most agricultural products or to textiles. The Uruguay Round extended GATT arrangements to include trade in some farm products, textiles, some services, and to the protection of intellectual property rights. It also extended its application to include **trade-related investment measures** (TRIMs), and considerably strengthened the mechanisms available for the settlement of disputes. Subsequently, in 1997, further agreements were negotiated in relation to financial services, information technology, and telecommunications services. However, disagreements among WTO members still remain with respect to a number of sectors, in particular, agricultural products, "cultural" products, transportation services, electronic commerce, and environmental and labour standards.

trade-related investment measures
national measures regulating investment that have an impact upon international trade

---

20. For an interesting example, see *IPSCO Inc. & IPSCO Steel Inc.* v. *United States & Lone Star Steel Co.* (1990) 899 F.2d 1192 (U.S. Court of Appeals), and the commentary by McConnell (1991), 70 Can. Bar Rev. 180.

21. Ministerial conferences are held every two years. Following the Cancun meeting, a decision was adopted by the General Council on August 1, 2004, setting out a framework for resolving outstanding issues. Negotiations continued at ministerial meetings in Geneva in 2004 and Hong Kong in 2005.

In addition to providing a forum for negotiations and for the resolution of trade disputes, the most important functions of the GATT and WTO have been the harmonization of customs rules and the progressive reduction of customs duties. In addition, the GATT sets out a code of rules governing international trade and such matters as the transportation of goods, customs procedures, and valuation.

The fundamental principle that underlies the WTO is that of non-discrimination. That principle, in turn, has two elements: first, goods originating from one contracting state should not be treated more or less favourably than goods from another state—that is, all should receive **most-favoured-nation (MFN) treatment**;[22] second, goods from other member states should, once the appropriate tariff has been paid, be treated no less favourably than corresponding domestic goods— that is, they should receive **national treatment**. In accordance with these basic principles, the WTO generally prohibits quotas and other forms of non-tariff barriers, export subsidies, and, except under strict conditions, the imposition of anti-dumping duties and countervailing duties.

The GATT and WTO have had a two-way impact upon Canadian law and the laws of the other contracting states. First, membership imposes a positive duty to enact laws to implement the obligations agreed to within the framework of the organization. Therefore, Canada has implemented the GATT tariff schedule through the Customs Tariff. Second, there is a negative duty not to apply laws that are contrary to the obligations undertaken as a member. Consequently, insofar as Canada imposes anti-dumping and countervailing duties, it may do so only within the limits prescribed by the GATT. If Canada is found to be in breach of its WTO obligations, it is required to take the necessary steps to amend its legislation in order to comply.

most-favoured-nation (MFN) treatment
the principle that goods imported from one country should not be treated less favourably than those imported from any other country

national treatment
the principle that goods from another country should not be treated less favourably than domestic goods

CASE 33.1

The United States complained that Canada was in violation of the GATT by prohibiting or restricting the importation into Canada of certain American periodicals and magazines through discriminatory tax treatment of so-called split-run periodicals, and by applying favourable postage rates to certain Canadian periodicals. A WTO Panel found that the Canadian measures were incompatible with the GATT. As a result, Canada was required to change its legislation.[23]

CASE 33.2

In 2002, the United States and New Zealand complained to the WTO that Canada was illegally subsidizing its dairy industry by allowing Canadian processors to buy lower-priced milk to manufacture cheese and other products for export under a scheme known as the Commercial Export Milk program. A WTO Panel concluded that the scheme amounted to an illegal subsidy; as a result, Canada agreed to discontinue the scheme.[24]

North American Free Trade

free trade area
group of countries within which customs duties are eliminated

An exception to the MFN principle, accepted under WTO rules, permits the creation of regional **free trade areas**, within which customs duties may be eliminated entirely. The most important and best known of such areas is the European Union (EU), a customs and economic union of 27 European states (as of 2008). In 1988, another free trade area was created, with the signing of the Canada–United States Free Trade Agreement. This agreement, which came into force at the beginning of 1989,[25] provided for the phasing out of tariffs in trade between the two nations over a period of ten years. Four years later, on December 17, 1992, the leaders of Canada, Mexico, and

---

22. By way of exception, reduced rates of duty are applied to many goods coming from less-developed countries.

23. See *United States v. Canada: Certain Measures Concerning Periodicals*, WTO panel report WT/DS31/R, March 14, 1997.

24. WTO panel report WT/DS103/33, May 15, 2003.

25. It takes effect in Canada by virtue of the Canada–United States Free Trade Agreement Implementation Act, S.C. 1988, c. 65.

the United States signed the North American Free Trade Agreement (NAFTA), bringing into existence the world's largest free trade area, with more than 360 million consumers.[26] The NAFTA also contains a clause permitting other countries on the American continent to join, and a Free Trade Area of the Americas (FTAA) has been proposed.[27]

Although the NAFTA is based upon essentially the same principles as the WTO, in many respects it goes considerably further in liberalizing trade and investment. All tariffs on goods between the three countries were eliminated in three stages. The final stage was implemented on January 1, 2008 and removed the last remaining trade restrictions on certain agricultural commodities. The NAFTA streamlines customs procedures and eliminates user fees. Agricultural products are within the scope of the NAFTA, which provided for the elimination of import barriers, export subsidies, and domestic support. Special rules apply to energy and natural resources, and export restrictions will generally not be permitted. Services, including financial services, are dealt with in the agreement, with providers of services entitled to receive national treatment (or MFN treatment, if that is better) in the other member countries. Government procurement—the purchase of goods and services by governments—is partly opened to competition. Of major significance are the rules on intellectual property. All principal intellectual property rights—copyright, patents, and trademarks—are recognized and protected, and laws are to be harmonized to secure broadly equivalent protection in each country.[28] Finally, the NAFTA is not restricted to trade in goods and services; it also contains provisions relating to investment (discussed later in this chapter).

Recently, many countries have been negotiating new free trade agreements (FTAs). In December 2008, Central America, Chile, Mercosur and Israel signed an FTA. Chile and China entered into an FTA on February 5, 2008, and Canada and member states of the European Free Trade Association signed an FTA on January 26, 2008.[29]

FOREIGN INVESTMENT

Forms of Foreign Investment

A distinction is commonly drawn between *portfolio investment* and *direct investment*. Portfolio investment is essentially "passive" investment, normally in government or corporate bonds or listed securities. Foreign direct investment (FDI), by contrast, occurs as part of active business operations. It can be defined as

> . . . investment made to acquire a lasting interest in an enterprise operating in an economic environment other than that of the investor, the investor's purpose being to have an effective voice in the management of the enterprise.[30]

It may involve the acquisition of property, such as a factory or hotel, or of all or a substantial part of the shares[31] in an existing corporation in the "host" country. FDI may also involve the establishment of an entirely new business ("greenfield" investment), and also includes the reinvestment of earnings in the host country.

---

26. The NAFTA is implemented in Canada by the North American Free Trade Agreement Implementation Act, S.C. 1993, c. 44, and came into effect on January 1, 1994. The Canada–United States agreement is effectively superseded, being suspended during the operation of the NAFTA.

27. Canada has also entered into bilateral free trade agreements with Chile, Costa Rica, and Israel, and an agreement with Singapore is under negotiation.

28. This has required changes to be made in Canadian laws, such as those governing the compulsory licensing of pharmaceutical patents; see Chapter 22. As of 2008, Canadian intellectual property law is not yet harmonized with the United States.

29. Member states of the EFTA are Iceland, Liechtenstein, Norway, and Switzerland.

30. United Nations, World Investment Directory 1992. New York: UNCTC, 1992.

31. To be classified as direct rather than portfolio investment, the acquisition must normally be of at least 10 percent of the shares of the host country corporation.

Normally, FDI is conducted through the establishment of

- a branch
- a subsidiary
- a joint venture

branch
a business carried on by the owner in its own name at a location distinct from its head office

subsidiary
a separate corporation owned or controlled by its "parent" corporation

joint venture
a form of partnership between two or more independent enterprises, or a corporation jointly owned by them

Where it establishes a **branch**, the investor carries on business in the host country in its own name, the foreign branch being an integral part of its global business, with the assets of the branch owned directly by the foreign investor. By contrast, a **subsidiary** is a separate corporation, incorporated in the host country and owning assets there. The parent investor owns the shares in the subsidiary (or a majority of them), but not the assets. The distinction can sometimes be very important. For example, some countries do not allow foreign ownership of land, but permit a local corporation to do so, even if a majority of its shares are held by foreigners.

A **joint venture** is formed by two or more parties, at least one of which is normally from the host country. It can take the form either of a type of partnership (contractual joint venture) or of a jointly owned subsidiary corporation (equity joint venture). Canadian investors overseas generally prefer the subsidiary or equity joint venture forms, principally for tax reasons, and some host countries permit foreign investment only in those forms.

Government Regulation of Foreign Investment

A firm wishing to invest and carry on business in another country must, of course, comply with the laws of that country. For example, a foreign corporation that carries on business in Canada through a branch may be required by the laws of the province where the branch is located to obtain a licence and to register certain information.[32] If it wishes to incorporate a subsidiary in Canada, it may be required to have a certain number of directors who are resident Canadians.[33] In the same way, a Canadian firm seeking to establish a branch or subsidiary abroad will have to comply with the local laws. Some countries do not permit foreign corporations to conduct business through a branch. Others do not allow foreigners to own a majority of the shares in a domestic corporation, at least in some economic sectors, making a joint venture (with a local partner) the only feasible method of carrying on business.

Many countries have a somewhat contradictory attitude towards foreign investment. On the one hand, they see foreign investment as desirable because it brings much-needed capital into the economy, creates employment, opens up export markets, and introduces modern technology and management skills. On the other hand, they regard it with suspicion as a form of economic imperialism, likely to cause social and environmental damage, to stifle the development of local business, and to exert undue political influence. Consequently, they seek both to attract foreign investment and to control it, by a mixture of incentives and restrictions. They offer inducements such as tax holidays, but at the same time exclude foreign investors from participating in certain activities (such as finance, communications, and transportation), forbid them to own real estate, or require them to meet specific conditions with regard to matters such as creating jobs or utilizing domestic raw materials.

Like many other countries, Canada subjects certain types of inward direct investment to review and to prior general authorization. Until 1985, Canada took a rather restrictive attitude to foreign investment, reflecting concern over the high level of foreign ownership of Canadian industry and resources. The Foreign Investment Review Agency (FIRA) could refuse to authorize investment it considered not to be in the national interest, or it could attach conditions to an investment. In 1985, FIRA was replaced by a new agency, Investment Canada, which is now the Investment Review Division of Industry Canada.[34] Although it retains most of the powers of FIRA, it has adopted a more positive approach to

---

32. See, in Ontario, Corporations Information Act, R.S.O. 1990, c. C-39 and Extra-Provincial Corporations Act, R.S.O. 1990, c. E.27.

33. See, for example: Canada Business Corporations Act, R.S.C. 1985, c. C-44, s. 105(3).

34. Investment Canada Act, S.C. 1985, c. 28 (1st Supp.). Investment Canada was dissolved in 1995 and its responsibilities assumed by Industry Canada under the direction of the Director of Investments, 1995 S.C., c. 1, s. 45.

the promotion of foreign investment. The establishment of a new business is generally not reviewed; it requires only that Industry Canada be notified. The acquisition of larger, existing Canadian businesses requires authorization[35] and must be "of significant benefit to Canada"; in practice, authorization is almost always granted. In certain cases, the approval of provincial governments and of other bodies may also be required. For example, the 1999 takeover of MacMillan-Bloedel by the U.S. company Weyerhaeuser required the approval of the British Columbia and Ontario governments, the Canadian Competition Bureau, the Canadian Ministry for International Trade, and Investment Canada, in addition to court approval and the support of two-thirds of the MacMillan-Bloedel shareholders.

A more restrictive approach to foreign investment is taken in some sectors. All acquisitions or investments to establish a new business in cultural sectors such as book publishing and film making are subject to review, regardless of the amount involved. A variety of federal, and in some cases

CONTEMPORARY ISSUE

BCE and the Ontario Teachers' Pension Fund

The Ontario Teachers' Pension Fund (OTPF) sought approval for a $51.7 billion purchase and privatization of BCE Inc., the country's largest telecommunications company and Bell Canada's parent. The proposal involved significant foreign investment through three private American equity partners, and therefore required the approval of many different agencies including the Canadian Radio-television and Telecommunication Commission, the Competition Bureau, and Industry Canada.

Legislation requires that foreign control of telecom companies must not exceed 46.9 percent. The CRTC voiced a concern that future Canadian control of BCE should be protected. On March 27, 2008, the CRTC approved the deal on conditions including the following corporate governance provisions:

1. The number of directors be fixed at 13.

2. Six Canadian directors must be nominated by Canadian investors, while non-Canadian investors may nominate only 5.

3. The Chairman and CEO must be Canadian and cannot be the same person.

4. A second OTPF delegate must sit on the Executive Committee.

5. Independent Programming Committee members must be Canadians not affiliated with the non-Canadian investors.

The deal collapsed in December 2008 when BCE could not obtain an acceptable financial opinion.

QUESTIONS TO CONSIDER

1. Why do you think the telecom industry is required to be under Canadian control?

2. Do you think the conditions are enough to ensure the company remains under Canadian control? Consider the concept of control separate from ownership.

Source: Broadcasting Decision 2008-69 [CRTC Application 2007 1117-8, decision released March 27, 2008], available online at www.crtc.gc.ca/archive/ENG/Decisions/2008/db2008-69.htm; Teresa Tedesco, "BCE Takeover Deal Falls Through," *Financial Post*, December 10, 2008, available online at www.financialpost.com/most_popular/story.html?id=1059612.

---

35. Originally, the acquisition of businesses with assets of more than $5 million was subject to review. For NAFTA members this was raised to $150 million, and this was extended to WTO members in 1995. The review threshold is now determined by a formula.

provincial, statutes restrict foreign ownership of banking, financial, and telecom services, and business involved in insurance, transport undertakings, fishing and fish processing, oil, gas, and uranium. The existence of public monopolies, such as the post office, electricity, and liquor sales, further restricts the potential for foreign investment.

Foreign Investment and International Law

As we noted in our discussion of foreign trade, prior to the conclusion of the Uruguay Round the GATT applied only to the international trade in goods and consequently had no general application to foreign investment. However, certain types of investment rules can clearly have an impact upon trade. If, in granting approval to a foreign investment, a host country attaches conditions (usually called **performance requirements**)—for example, that the investor must use local raw materials or components, or that it must export a stipulated percentage of its total production— those conditions will interfere with the investor's freedom to trade. The legality of such TRIMs was considered by a Panel of the GATT, in a complaint referred to it in 1982.[36] The United States, at the request of a number of American corporations that had invested in Canada, complained that conditions imposed by FIRA, requiring the investors to buy components and materials from local Canadian sources, was in effect imposing restrictions on the importation of similar goods. The Panel upheld the complaint, ruling against Canada.

Probably the greatest fear of a potential foreign investor is that its assets might be expropriated by the host country government or nationalized without adequate compensation. **Expropriation** has been one of the more controversial issues in international law. Some industrialized countries would like to see expropriation entirely prohibited, whereas many developing countries consider the power to nationalize to be essential to their economic development. The United Nations supports a state's right to nationalize, expropriate, or transfer ownership of foreign-owned property, but declares that appropriate compensation must be paid.[37]

The 1985 Convention establishing the Multilateral Investment Guarantee Agency, under the auspices of the World Bank, provides some protection against the consequences of expropriation, but probably of greater importance are the numerous **bilateral investment protection treaties** entered into between capital-importing and capital-exporting countries. These treaties usually provide that foreign investment receive national treatment—that is, it should be treated no less favourably than a comparable domestic enterprise. It is usual to provide that a host country may not expropriate or nationalize the property of an investor from the other country "except for a public purpose, under due process of law, in a non-discriminatory manner," and that any such expropriation "must be accompanied by prompt, adequate, and effective compensation."[38]

The NAFTA significantly relaxes the general rules of the Investment Canada Act as they apply to Mexican and U.S. investment in Canada. Performance requirements regarding such matters as exporting or local sourcing of goods or services are not permitted, and, as a general principle, investors are entitled to national treatment or to MFN treatment, if that is better.[39] Canadian investment in Mexico and the United States enjoys similar privileges and protection.

performance requirements
conditions attached by the host country in granting approval to a foreign investment

expropriation
a state's right to assume ownership of private property within its geographic borders

bilateral investment protection treaty
a treaty entered into between two countries, whereby each country undertakes to protect investors from the other country and to give them certain rights

---

36. *United States v. Canada: Administration of the Foreign Investment Review Act*, report of February 7, 1984 (Case No. 108, GATT Doc. L/5308).

37. United Nations Charter of Economic Rights and Duties of States, adopted December 12, 1974, GA Res. 3281 (xxix), UN GAOR, 29th Sess. Sup. No. 31 (1974) 50. Canada abstained from voting on this proposition.

38. See, for example, Art. VI of the "Agreement between the Government of Canada and the Government of the Republic of Poland for the Promotion and Reciprocal Protection of Investments," signed in Warsaw on April 6, 1990 (Canada Treaty Series 1990, No. 43).

39. Sometimes a country imposes restrictions upon its own investors that do not apply to foreign investors. In such a case, MFN treatment may be more favourable than national treatment.

In January 2008 MacDonald Dettwiler and Associates Ltd., a British Columbia company involved in satellite technology, announced it would sell its space and satellite division to an American company, Alliance Techsystems, for $1.325 billion. The proposed sale drew immediate reaction because this division includes the "Canadarm" used on the space shuttle. Many Canadians consider the Canadarm a source of national pride. The Canadarm technology was developed by McDonald Dettwiler with the help of grant money from the Canadian government.

To add to the controversy, Alliance Techsystems supplies arms such as land mines and cluster bombs to the U.S. Military. Concern is being expressed that the Canadarm, taxpayer-funded technology, may now be used to weaponize space and contravene Canada's position on the Mine Ban Treaty. Pursuant to the Investment Canada Act, the proposed sale requires Industry Canada approval. On March 14, 2008, the Industry Minister stated that the sale would only be approved if there was a net benefit for Canada. In April 2008, the Minister blocked the sale.

QUESTIONS TO CONSIDER

1. Could it be argued that there was a "net benefit" to Canada and should the possible use of the technology to weaponize space have been a factor in Industry Canada's decision?

2. Should government grants of money include conditions about future use or sale of the developments made using grant money?

Sources: Petti Fong, "Canadarm Sale Sparks Revolt," *TheStar.com*, January 18, 2008, www.thestar.com/News/Canada/article/295280; The Canadian Press, "Proposed Canadarm Sale Must Yield Net Benefit to Canada: Prentice," March 13, 2008, available online at http://cnews.canoe.ca/CNEWS/Canada/2008/03/13/pf-4994361.html.

THE RESOLUTION OF INTERNATIONAL BUSINESS DISPUTES

Like all other business activities, foreign trade and foreign investment can give rise to disputes. These may be based in private law, as, for example, between parties to an international contract for the sale of goods. Or disputes may be primarily about public or administrative law, between governments on the one hand and importers or investors on the other. In addition, questions of public international law may arise where it is alleged that one state is in breach of its treaty obligations to another. Disputes may be resolved before a national court, an arbitrator, or some form of international tribunal.

Courts

In principle, Canadian courts, and those of most other countries, are open to the world, in the sense that one need not be a Canadian citizen or resident in order to be able to sue or be sued in them. Nevertheless, a number of problems may arise in disputes with an international element.

ILLUSTRATION 33.2

A Canadian manufacturer contracts to sell electrical equipment to a Korean construction company, with delivery to be made at a construction site in Saudi Arabia. The price is stated to be payable in Swiss francs. The manufacturer ships the equipment to Saudi Arabia, but the Korean company refuses to take delivery, claiming that the equipment does not meet the contract specifications.

The Canadian firm wishes to sue for the price; perhaps the Korean party will claim damages. But in which country should the action be brought? In Canada, Korea, Saudi Arabia, Switzerland, or perhaps somewhere entirely different? What if the contract had stipulated that it is governed by the laws of New York State?

In determining the questions in Illustration 33.2, a number of issues must be considered.

Jurisdiction

The question of whether or not a court will hear an action is essentially one for the court itself to decide. Courts do not encourage "forum shopping"—that is, allowing a plaintiff to seek out a jurisdiction most likely to view its claim favourably. Courts insist that the issue have some "connecting factor" with the country in which a party seeks to bring the action. The grounds upon which the courts exercise jurisdiction vary from country to country, and are not even identical in each province within Canada. As a general rule, courts of a country or province will normally assert jurisdiction over foreign defendants if

- a tort was committed there
- a contract was to be performed there
- damage from a tort or breach of contract was sustained there
- the dispute concerned property or goods situated there
- the activities complained of were conducted there
- the contract stipulated that it should be governed by the laws of the country or province
- the parties to a contract specified that those courts should have jurisdiction in the event of a dispute

There is a general discretion to exercise jurisdiction where there is some other "real and substantial connection" with the country or province. However, this broad jurisdiction is limited in two ways. The court may decline jurisdiction, even though it might exercise it on one of the above grounds, if it considers that there is some other forum that is more appropriate or is more closely connected to the matter in dispute—the *forum non conveniens* principle.[40] Or the court may decline jurisdiction if it considers that the courts of other provinces or states concerned might refuse to enforce its judgment. British Columbia, Nova Scotia, and Saskatchewan have passed legislation consolidating the rules.[41]

---

40. There are two distinct issues: does the court have jurisdiction (a real and substantial connection to the case), and, if so, is there some other more suitable jurisdiction? See *Lemmex* v. *Bernard* (2002), 213 D.L.R. (4th) 627. See also, *Unifund Assurance Co.* v. *Insurance Corp. of British Columbia*, [2003] 2 S.C.R. 63.

41. Court Jurisdiction and Proceedings Transfer Act, S.B.C. 2003, c.28 (in force May 4, 2006); S.N.S. 2003, c.2 (in force June 1, 2008); S.S. 1997, c. C-41.1 (in force March 1, 2004); these acts are based on the model law produced by the Uniform Law Conference of Canada.

CASE 33.3

A Barbados corporation owned an Internet domain name of which an Ontario corporation was the registrar. A Delaware corporation with the same trademark tried to acquire the domain name but the Barbados corporation demanded huge compensation.

The Delaware corporation obtained an order from the Pennsylvania courts (where it had its principal place of business) that the Barbados corporation transfer the domain name to it. The Ontario registrar honoured the order and transferred the name to the Delaware corporation. The Barbados corporation responded by bringing an action in Ontario for damages from the Delaware company and an order that the Ontario registrar transfer the domain name back to it.

The Ontario court declined jurisdiction because it was not the appropriate forum to hear the dispute; the Delaware corporation had not done any act or completed any transaction in Ontario. In addition, it would be unreasonable for an Ontario court to exercise jurisdiction over a Delaware corporation at the request of a Barbados corporation. Even if Ontario could exercise jurisdiction, it should not do so, since none of the factors to be considered in determining the issue of *forum non conveniens* established Ontario as the convenient forum.[42]

Standing

Although parties need not be residents or citizens of a country in order to have access to its courts, some restrictions may apply. A foreign corporation that has not been licensed or registered in Canada cannot be a plaintiff in Canadian courts. Foreign plaintiffs without assets within the jurisdiction may be required to post **security for costs**. A further problem arises where the defendant is not present or does not have an establishment within the jurisdiction and cannot be served with the writ or originating process. Although courts may give leave to serve the defendant outside the jurisdiction, they are generally reluctant to grant judgments against absent defendants unless there is a very strong connection between the cause of action and the country concerned.

security for costs
money deposited into the court in case an unsuccessful foreign plaintiff is ordered to pay the legal costs of the successful defendant

Choice of Law

We have already discussed the question of the proper law of the contract. It is important to recall that it is not unusual, in international trade disputes, for the courts of one country to apply the law of another. Thus, in Illustration 33.2, if the contract had stipulated that the law of New York was to apply, that clause might in itself be adequate reason for a Canadian court to decline jurisdiction to a Canadian plaintiff.[43] Even so it might be possible for the Korean party to sue a Canadian defendant in a Canadian court for damages for non-performance, in which case the court would determine the rights of the parties according to New York law.

Enforcement of Foreign Judgments

Even if a plaintiff persuades a court to accept jurisdiction in a dispute of an international nature and succeeds in obtaining a judgment against the defendant, the matter does not necessarily end there. If the defendant has assets within the jurisdiction, judgment may be levied against those assets by court order. But, to return to our example in Illustration 33.2, a Canadian judgment against the Korean contractor, or a Korean judgment against the Canadian manufacturer, might be of little value if the losing party has no assets in the country where judgment is granted.

---

42. *Easthaven Ltd.* v. *Nutrisystem.com Inc.* (2001), 202 D.L.R. (4th) 560. For discussion of the *forum non conveniens* principle, see *Eastern Power Ltd.* v. *Azienda Comunale Energia & Ambiente* (1999), 178 D.L.R. (4th) 409; *Western Union Insurance Co.* v. *Re-Con Buildings Products Inc.* (2001), 205 D.L.R. (4th) 184.

43. The Supreme Court of Canada has ruled that, where the parties themselves have provided that disputes be referred to a particular forum, effect should normally be given to that agreement: *Z.I. Pompey Industrie* v. *Ecu-Line N.V.* (2003), 224 D.L.R. (4th) 577.

The question then arises of whether a Korean judgment may be enforced in Canada, and vice versa. Unfortunately, this is a complex legal issue, often without a clear answer. At common law a local judgment, provided it is for a sum of money, is considered to be a debt, and a creditor can ask a Canadian court to enforce payment.[44] But a foreign judgment debt will normally only be recognized so long as the foreign court was exercising proper jurisdiction according to the standards of the local courts (the "forum"). Ordinarily, the standards require that there was a "real and substantial connection" between the substance of the action and the country in which judgment was granted; the judgment was not obtained by fraud; and it does not offend against natural justice or public policy.[45]

CASE 33.4

Shore Boat Builders Ltd., a corporation incorporated in British Columbia, built a boat for Moses, a fisherman residing in Alaska. Moses later brought an action in an Alaska court, alleging that the boat was defective in a number of respects and claiming damages for breach of warranty. Shore considered that they had a good defence to the action, since Moses had himself carried out certain modifications to the boat. However, on the advice of their lawyer, Shore did not enter an appearance in the Alaska proceedings. In default, judgment was given against Shore for damages of $58 000.

Moses then brought an action in British Columbia, claiming enforcement of the Alaska judgment. The British Columbia Court of Appeal held that the Alaska default judgment was enforceable.

Shore had sold their product directly to an Alaska client; they therefore assumed the burden of defending their product in Alaska and could reasonably assume that they might be sued in Alaska in respect of that product. Alaska was the place where the loss was suffered and that was entitled to exercise jurisdiction.[46]

CASE 33.5

In 1981, the Beals bought a building lot in Florida for US $8000 from the Saldanhas, who were residents of Ontario. By mistake, the wrong lot was sold, and the Beals built a home on a lot they did not own. The Beals brought an action for damages, for breach of contract, in a Florida court.

The Saldanhas did not defend the action, apparently because they feared that the costs of defending the action, even if they won, would greatly exceed any award against them (which they did not expect would be much more than the $8000 paid for the land). In 1991, a Florida jury awarded triple compensatory damages of $210 000 and additional punitive damages of $50 000. The Beals sought to enforce the judgment in Ontario, by which time, with judgment interest at 12 percent and the fall in the value of the Canadian dollar, the claim had risen to CDN $800 000.

The Ontario trial judge refused to enforce the judgment, holding that the Florida judgment had been obtained by fraud and that it would be contrary to public policy to enforce it in Ontario. That judgment was reversed by the Ontario Court of Appeal. On a further appeal, the Supreme Court of Canada ruled that the Florida judgment should be enforced. Since the land was situated in Florida, the courts of that state were a proper forum. Although there were some procedural features that would not have been allowed in Ontario (for example, the defendants were not notified of the actual amount claimed by the plaintiffs, merely that it exceeded $5000), there was no evidence of fraud or a denial of natural justice. International comity required that the Florida judgment be respected.[47]

44. Most Canadian provinces have adopted legislation providing for the enforcement of foreign judgments on a reciprocal basis. However, only a few reciprocal agreements with other countries have been entered into, the ones with the United Kingdom being the most important; see, for example: Reciprocal Enforcement of Judgments (U.K.) Act, R.S.O. 1990, c. R.6.

45. *Morguard Investments Ltd.* v. *de Savoye* (1990), 76 D.L.R. (4th) 256. That case concerned the recognition by a British Columbia court of an Alberta judgment. However, the principles enunciated by the Supreme Court of Canada have subsequently been applied to judgments by foreign courts.

46. *Moses* v. *Shore Boat Builders Ltd.* (1993), 106 D.L.R. (4th) 654. Contrast *Brower* v. *Sunview Solariums Ltd.* (1998), 161 D.L.R. (4th) 575.

47. *Beals* v. *Saldanha* (2003), 234 D.L.R. (4th) 1.

Commercial Arbitration

Arbitration, sometimes referred to as private justice, is an alternative dispute resolution process in which disputing parties select an independent neutral adjudicator to privately decide their dispute. The parties agree in advance to be bound by the decision of the arbitrator with very limited rights to appeal. Parties design their own process through the selection of the arbitrator, the procedural rules, and the choice of law to be applied in determining the outcome. This control over the process, or **party autonomy** as it is often described, is considered a major benefit of arbitration.

party autonomy
the parties' freedom to determine how their dispute will be resolved

The delays, costs, publicity, and uncertainties surrounding international litigation have increasingly led parties in international commercial contracts to select binding arbitration for resolution of any disputes arising from their relationship. Rather than risk a dispute being heard before the "home" court of one party, parties usually insert an **arbitration clause** into the contract at the time of agreement. The arbitration clause designates the arbitrator, the location or forum, the choice of law to be applied, and the procedural rules to be followed. Sometimes it specifically names an arbitrator, but more commonly it nominates an organization that provides arbitration services such as the International Chamber of Commerce. There are now many private providers of international arbitration services located in all major commercial centres around the world. Countries such as Sweden and Switzerland are popular arbitration venues because of their long-standing traditions of neutrality. As part of an international trend, Canadian legislation and courts support a policy in favour of arbitration and generally refuse to accept jurisdiction over commercial disputes covered by a valid arbitration clause.[48]

arbitration clause
a term in a commercial contract designating arbitration as the process for resolution of any disputes arising between the parties

One major advantage of arbitration, as opposed to litigation, is the ability to select an arbitrator with great experience in the specific area of the dispute, a right not available in the public courts. Other advantages are the non-public nature and confidentiality of the proceedings, especially important where the dispute concerns trade secrets, and usually costs are lower and decisions are speedier. Most modern commercial arbitration employs standard procedures, such as those adopted in the United Nations Commission on International Trade Law (UNCITRAL) model, which are generally better adapted to international disputes than regular court procedures.

Perhaps the greatest advantage of commercial arbitration, as opposed to litigation, lies in the relative ease with which awards may be enforced. Unlike litigation, arbitration is consensual: the parties to the original contract have agreed to submit any dispute to arbitration and to abide by the award. As a result, there is no valid reason for a court to refuse to enforce an arbitration award should one of the parties fail to comply with it. Canada has legislation, at both the federal and provincial levels, which implements the 1958 United Nations Convention on the Recognition and Enforcement of Foreign Arbitral Awards and adopts the 1985 UNCITRAL Model Law on International Commercial Arbitration.[49]

Disputes Involving Governments

Generally, governments cannot be compelled to appear as defendants before the courts of another country or to submit to arbitration. An individual or corporation that wishes to challenge the actions or decisions of a government—for example, the refusal of an import licence or the expropriation of an investment—may normally do so only in the courts of that country.

---

48. *Ontario Hydro* v. *Denison Mines Ltd.*, [1992] O.J. No. 2948; *Deluce Holdings Inc.* v. *Air Canada*, [1992] O.J. No. 2382; *Buck Bros. Ltd.* v. *Frontenac Builders*, [1994] O.J. No. 37; *Onex Corp.* v. *Ball Corp.*, [1994] 12 B.L.R. (2nd) 151; *Canadian National Railway Co.* v. *Lovat Tunnel Equipment Inc.* (1999), 174 D.L.R. (4th) 385 (Ont C.A.); *Diamond & Diamond* v. *Srebrolow*, [2003] O.J. No. 4004. As noted in Chapter 2, courts and legislators are retreating from the policy in favor of arbitration in the area of consumer disputes.

49. Commercial Arbitration Act, R.S.C. 1985, c. 17 (2nd Supp.); United Nations Foreign Arbitral Awards Convention Act, R.S.C. 1985, c. 16 (2nd Supp.); International Commercial Arbitration Act: R.S.B.C. 1996, c. 233; R.S.O. 1990, c. I.9.

However, where a complainant alleges that a state is in breach of a treaty obligation owed to one or more other states, a number of procedures exist for the resolution of the dispute. Most often the treaty or convention designates a process to be followed for dispute resolution. For example, bilateral investment protection treaties usually provide that the parties agree to submit to binding arbitration any dispute concerning the expropriation of assets or payment of proper compensation, such arbitration to be conducted by the International Centre for the Settlement of Investment Disputes, or according to the UNCITRAL rules.[50] Most important from a Canadian perspective are the procedures provided for in the WTO and the NAFTA.

The GATT and WTO

From its inception in 1948, the GATT contained a mechanism for the resolution of disputes between states that are parties to the agreement. The mechanism was revised and strengthened when the WTO was created in 1995.

We should note that only states that are contracting parties may raise a complaint against another contracting party. Private persons have no standing as such, though an individual or firm that considers it has been injured by an action of a foreign government in violation of the GATT may request its own government to bring proceedings.

The WTO contains two types of proceedings for the settlement of disputes. There is provision for consultation between the parties and, if necessary, a conciliation procedure—essentially a diplomatic solution. Alternatively, a contracting state that considers that the proper operation of the rules is being "nullified or impaired" by the actions of another contracting state may request the WTO Council to appoint a panel to adjudicate the dispute. After hearing the submissions of the parties, the panel makes recommendations, which may require an offending state to remove a provision of law or an administrative practice found to be contrary to the rules or, in certain cases, to compensate an injured party. Under the new WTO procedures, a panel decision may be appealed to a special appellate panel.

Since 1948, over 300 cases have been submitted to GATT or WTO panels, more than 90 percent of those involving four parties—Canada, the European Union, Japan, and the United States. Not surprisingly, considering the volume of trade between the two countries, disputes between Canada and the United States have been common. Among the more notable are those by the United States in respect of Canadian countervailing duties on grain corn and in respect of provincial rules on the marketing of alcoholic beverages, and by Canada against the United States in respect of countervailing duties on Canadian pork and on softwood lumber. The Canada–United States disputes concerning the Canadian treatment of "split-run" American magazines and the subsidies given to the Canadian dairy industry have already been mentioned (Cases 33.1 and 33.2), and, as we saw, the adverse findings of the panel have led to changes in the Canadian legislation. In other recent high-profile proceedings:

- 1999—The WTO ruled against Canada's "autopact" agreement, in proceedings brought by the European Union and Japan, because the rules gave preferential treatment to automobiles imported from the United States.
- 2000—A WTO ruling compelled Canada to change its rules on drug patents, increasing protection from 17 to 20 years.
- 2001—In a dispute brought by Brazil, a WTO panel found that Canada had provided export subsidies to aircraft manufactured by the Bombardier firm. (It also found Brazil guilty of subsidizing their manufacturer, Embraer.)

50. See, for example, the Canada–Poland Treaty, *supra*, n. 37, Art. IX. Federal Bill C-9, An Act to Implement the Convention on the Settlement of Investment Disputes between States and Nationals of Other States (ICSID Convention) received royal assent on March 14, 2008. British Columbia, Newfoundland and Labrador, Ontario, and Saskatchewan have already passed similar legislation.

- 2002—In a dispute brought by the United States, some practices of the Canadian Wheat Board were held to constitute an export subsidy, though other features of the Canadian system, of which the United States complained, were ruled legitimate.
- 2004—Canadian import duties on hormone-treated beef from the European Union (EU) were held to be no longer legitimate, after the EU had changed its rules following an earlier adverse panel ruling, in which Canada had been a complainant.

Canada has also been a successful complainant in a number of WTO dispute proceedings.

- 2005—The WTO Appellate Panel ruled in Canada's favour in the infamous softwood lumber dispute against the United States. This dispute proceeded under both the WTO and NAFTA dispute resolution processes and is considered in the next section.[51]
- 2008—a continuation of the hormone-treated beef dispute resulted in a ruling upholding the Canadian and America retaliatory sanctions imposed against EU products as a result of the EU's continued improper restrictions on Canadian and American beef.
- 2008—a WTO panel held that Chinese import duties on Canadian, EU, and American automotive parts were illegal.

NAFTA Chapters 19 and 20

The NAFTA contains dispute resolution provisions that are rather similar to those of the WTO, though the NAFTA may have more effective implementation. When a dispute arises under both the NAFTA and the WTO, the complainant may choose under which set of procedures it should be settled.[52]

In the event of a dispute, Chapter 20 of the NAFTA[53] provides for the holding of consultations at the request of either party. Should no mutually satisfactory agreement be reached, the dispute is then referred to a Free Trade Commission. If, in turn, the Commission fails to find an acceptable solution, either party may request the Commission to appoint an Arbitral Panel. A panel is composed of five members, two of whom are appointed by each of the parties from lists of experts in trade law or practice, with a chairperson selected by agreement or by lot. The panel hears the submissions of the parties and produces a report, published by the Commission. The parties must implement the report within 30 days; if a party fails to do so, an aggrieved party may withdraw benefits in retaliation. A party may appeal a panel decision to an Extraordinary Challenge Committee.

Chapter 19 of the NAFTA, which is based upon the chapter of the same number in the Canada–United States Agreement, contains separate provisions for the resolution of disputes concerning the imposition of anti-dumping and countervailing duties. Such disputes occur frequently and are often more important, at least in financial terms, than the general disputes that are dealt with under Chapter 20. In particular, U.S. countervailing duties are widely perceived as constituting the most serious threat to Canadian exports.

Currently, each country applies its own anti-dumping and countervail laws, though in the longer term the parties are required to establish common rules on subsidies and on anti-competitive practices such as dumping. Under the NAFTA, the parties are entitled to ensure that the national laws are correctly applied. The nature of a complaint, consequently, is that the country imposing the anti-dumping or countervailing duty has incorrectly or improperly applied its own law. The complaint procedure has already been used on a number of occasions, most controversially in the softwood lumber case.

---

51. Both sides had previously claimed victory in that dispute. In 2004 a WTO Panel ruled that the Canadian system of charging "stumpage fees" did constitute a subsidy, but that the U.S. method of calculating countervailing duties was improper.

52. There are a few exceptions, where the NAFTA procedures must be used.

53. Chapter 20 is the successor of Chapter 18 of the Canada–United States Free Trade Agreement. Among disputes resolved under that chapter are those against Canada, in respect of rules requiring the landing in Canada of West Coast salmon caught by U.S. fishing boats, and against the United States concerning the minimum size requirements for importation of lobsters.

CASE 33.6

The softwood lumber dispute between Canada and the United States has been dragging on for almost twenty years. In the United States, most forestry land is privately owned, whereas in Canada it is largely owned by the provinces, which grant long-term licences to lumber firms in return for the payment of "stumpage" rates. The United States claims that the Canadian system operates as a subsidy to Canadian lumber producers, who are thus able to undercut their American competitors. At the request of the American lumber industry, the United States had imposed countervailing duties on Canadian lumber. A Canadian complaint against those duties was upheld by a NAFTA panel in 1992, and confirmed on appeal two years later. Following fresh complaints from U.S. producers, new countervailing duties were imposed in 2002, leading to a fresh round of complaint procedures, both in the WTO and in NAFTA (under both Chapters 19 and 20).

Through decisions in September 2004 and March 2006, NAFTA tribunals again ruled that the countervailing duties were improper and should be refunded. In December 2005, the WTO Appellate division also held that the U.S. countervailing duties were improperly collected and Canada was entitled to take retaliatory measures. A separate arbitration was scheduled to determine the amount of retaliation. Canadian softwood lumber companies have paid approximately $3.7 billion dollars in countervailing duties. Despite the many adverse trade rulings, the United States government did not revoke the duties.

Finally, in April 2006, the United States and the newly elected Canadian government arrived at a negotiated settlement. The agreement revoked the duties, provided for the return of at least 80 percent of the deposits collected since 2002, and ensured seven years of stability in the industry. The agreement was implemented in October 2006 and Export Development Canada began processing refunds. The Softwood Lumber Products Export Charge Act, 2006 received royal assent on December 14, 2006, by which time 98.9 percent of refunds had been paid to Canadian softwood lumber companies.[54]

NAFTA Chapter 11

Chapter 11, which deals with foreign investment, is unique and innovative. It provides a means whereby Canadian, Mexican, and U.S. businesses that invest in another NAFTA country may sue the host government directly for infringement of the rights guaranteed by the Agreement. The investor rights were included in the NAFTA primarily to protect firms from illegal expropriation by a government. However, several firms have used, or threatened to use, Chapter 11 to sue governments when their foreign operations have been affected by government measures that are "tantamount to expropriation" decisions, since those measures make it effectively impossible for the firm to carry on its normal operations.[55] Several of the more controversial NAFTA tribunal rulings, or threatened actions, have involved challenges to environmental or health legislation.[56] For example:

- 1998—Canada withdrew its ban on the gasoline additive MMT and paid $13 million in damages to the U.S.-based Ethyl Corporation, which had brought a NAFTA challenge against the prohibition, claiming compensation of $250 million.
- 2000—A NAFTA tribunal ruled that Mexico had violated the agreement and ordered its government to pay $16.7 million to the U.S.-based Metalclad corporation. The company had wanted to open a hazardous waste treatment and disposal site in central Mexico, but local government said the project violated environmental protection laws.

---

54. The agreement will refund more than $5 billion to Canadian companies. For a review of the history of the dispute, see the press releases issued by the Minister of International Trade on December 5, 2005; March 17, 2006; April 27, 2006; October 6, 2006; October 30, 2006; and December 14, 2006, available on the Foreign Affairs and International Trade Canada website (www.international.gc.ca).

55. Two of the most recent actions have been by Canadian softwood lumber manufacturers claiming damages as a consequence of the illegal U.S. countervailing duties.

56. For an excellent review, see Soloway (2000) 33 C.B.L.J. 92.

- 2000—S. D. Myers, a U.S. corporation, sued the Canadian government for $75 million because Canada banned the export of PCBs to the United States. The ban was subsequently lifted. The tribunal found in favour of the company on two counts of the complaint and awarded damages of $6 million.
- 2001—A U.S. corporation, Crompton (now known as Chemtura Corporation), filed a suit, claiming compensation of $100 million against the Canadian government in respect of a ban on the use of the pesticide lindane for use on crops of canola (although lindane is not permitted in the United States or in Europe). The case is still pending.
- 2005—the Canadian-based company Methanex failed in its claim against the United States, which alleged that the state of California's decision to phase out the use of its gasoline additive, MTBE, cost the company $970 million. Methanex was ordered to pay the United States costs, valued at approximately $4 million.[57]
- 2007—Canada successfully defended a $160 million claim brought by UPS which alleged that Canada Post received preferential treatment due to its government ownership, especially from Canadian Border Services.[58]

The tribunal proceedings have been strongly criticized by Public Citizen, a consumer watchdog group in Washington, on the ground that they are mostly conducted in secret. In Canada, the Canadian Union of Postal Workers and the Council of Canadians launched an unsuccessful legal challenge against the Chapter 11 tribunal process, claiming that the secrecy of the proceedings violates the Canadian Charter of Rights and Freedoms.[59]

QUESTIONS FOR REVIEW

1. Distinguish between foreign trade and foreign investment.
2. Distinguish between public international law and private international law.
3. What is meant by the "proper law of the contract"?
4. What are "Incoterms"? Give examples.
5. What documentation is usually involved in an international sale of goods?
6. What is the purpose of foreign exchange risk management?
7. How can services be "exported"?
8. In what ways do governments attempt to promote exports? Are export subsidies permissible?
9. What is meant by "non-tariff barriers"? Give examples.
10. What is "dumping"?
11. What are countervailing duties?
12. What is the relationship between the GATT and the WTO?
13. What are "TRIMs"?
14. Distinguish between most-favoured-nation treatment and national treatment.

---

57. *Methanex Corporation* v. *United States of America,* available online at: www.state.gov/documents/organization/51052.pdf.
58. *United Parcel Service of America, Inc. ("UPS")* v. *Government of Canada,* available online at www.international.gc.ca/assets/trade-agreements-accords-commerciaux/pdfs/MeritsAward24May2007.pdf.
59. *Council of Canadians* v. *Canada (Attorney General),* [2006] 277 D.L.R. (4th) 527. The Ontario Court of Appeal dismissed the appeal, holding that NAFTA had received parliamentary approval as an international treaty, but this did not incorporate it into domestic law.

15. Distinguish between portfolio investment and direct investment.
16. Distinguish between (a) a branch, (b) a subsidiary, and (c) a joint venture.
17. What are "performance requirements"?
18. What purposes are normally served by bilateral investment protection treaties?
19. What is "forum shopping"? Why is it considered objectionable?
20. What is meant by "*forum non conveniens*"?
21. What are the principal advantages of commercial arbitration as opposed to litigation?
22. How are disputes resolved within the WTO? within the NAFTA?
23. Explain how the softwood lumber dispute demonstrates both the strengths and the weaknesses in the WTO and NAFTA dispute resolution processes.
24. In what way is Chapter 11 of the NAFTA novel?

CASES AND PROBLEMS

1. ABC Inc., a manufacturing company located in Hamilton, Ontario, agrees to sell machine tools to a customer in Belgium. The contract price is stated to be "$50 000, FOB the S.S. Lusitania in Halifax, Nova Scotia." ABC Inc. arranges for the goods to be shipped from its factory and loaded on the Lusitania by Titanic Transporters Ltd., an Ontario shipper. ABC Inc. does not insure the goods, believing that Titanic's insurance provides adequate coverage.

   (a) What, if any, will be the liability of ABC Inc. if the goods are

      (1) damaged in a road accident, caused by the negligence of Titanic's driver, en route to Halifax?
      (2) damaged due to the negligence of a crane operator while being loaded onto the Lusitania?
      (3) lost at sea in mid-Atlantic?

   (b) What difference would it make if the price had been stated "CIF Antwerp"?

2. XYZ Ltd., a large Canadian mining corporation, entered into an agreement three years ago with the government of the Republic of Utopia to develop the mining and processing of the rich zinc deposits in that country. A joint-venture corporation, Cantopia Ltd., was established (under the law of Utopia), in which XYZ held 49 percent of the shares and the government of Utopia held the remainder. XYZ invested $25 million in the project, in the form of machinery, technology, and capital to finance the operation of mines and smelters; the Utopian government's contribution to the project took the form of a lease, at nominal rent, of a large tract of land where valuable deposits had been discovered. It was agreed that Cantopia would mine the zinc, process it, and export it through XYZ's worldwide marketing organization. Profits would be shared in the ratio 49/51 percent.

   Recently, following a military coup, the new government of Utopia enacted a law requiring all mining enterprises to sell their total output to the newly established National Resources Corporation, wholly owned by the Utopian government, at prices to be established by a government agency. Under the prices established for zinc, it has become impossible for Cantopia to operate at a profit.

   Are there any steps that XYZ can take to protect its investment?

3. Canadian production of widgets is almost entirely in the hands of three corporations—Altawidge Ltd., Ontwidge Ltd., and Scotiawidge Ltd. All three corporations export a substantial volume of their products to the United States.

Two years ago, as a result of increased competition from Malaysian widget producers, two of the Canadian corporations—Ontwidge and Scotiawidge—experienced financial difficulties. As a result, the governments of Ontario and Nova Scotia stepped in to help save the widget industry. They provided long-term, low-interest loans to the corporations and granted other benefits, such as research grants and exemption from property taxes. By contrast, Altawidge has received no government support, but has been able to compete with its rivals because its operations are more advanced technologically.

Recently, there have been complaints from widget producers in the United States that they have lost a substantial share of the American market to imports from Canada and Malaysia. They allege that widget production in both countries is heavily subsidized. As a result of these complaints, the U.S. Department of Commerce has introduced a countervailing duty of 17 cents for each widget imported from Canada. The effect of the duty is to make Canadian widgets more expensive in the United States than domestically produced widgets.

Altawidge has in turn complained that, whether or not the Nova Scotia and Ontario producers receive an improper subsidy, their own products enjoy no such benefit and should not be subjected to the duty.

Discuss the issues raised, and suggest what steps might be taken to resolve the dispute.

4. Maxrevs Ltd. is a corporation incorporated in Manitoba, which manufactures small gasoline-powered motors for use in a variety of power tools. It sells its motors directly to tool manufacturers throughout North America, and also sells in substantial quantities to wholesale dealers in motor parts and components. One of those dealers supplied a number of Maxrevs motors to "weedeater" manufacturer Snapper Inc., a corporation incorporated in Michigan.

Gonzalez, a resident of Texas, purchased a Snapper weedeater and subsequently sustained a severe injury to his leg and hand when the tool malfunctioned. He brought an action in a Texas court against both Snapper and Maxrevs. Although Maxrevs was served with notice of the proceedings, it did not enter an appearance and did not defend the action.

The Texas court found that the connection between the motor and the revolving blade was defective, and held Snapper liable. It also found that Maxrevs had been negligent in failing to provide adequate instructions for installation of their motors in tools of that kind and awarded damages against Maxrevs amounting to US $5 million.

Gonzalez has now filed a claim in the Manitoba court to enforce his judgment against Maxrevs. Is it likely that the Manitoba court will enforce the judgment?

ADDITIONAL RESOURCES FOR CHAPTER 33 ON THE COMPANION WEBSITE *(www.pearsoned.ca/smyth)*

In addition to self-test multiple-choice, true–false, and short essay questions (all with immediate feedback), application exercises, and links to useful web destinations, the Companion Website provides the following resources for Chapter 33:

- **British Columbia**: Comity in the Enforcement of Foreign Judgments; International Arbitration; Reciprocal Enforcement

- **Alberta**: International Arbitration; Reciprocal Enforcement

- **Ontario**: Commercial Arbitration; Enforcement of Foreign Judgments; Interprovincial Enforcement; Jurisdiction; Security for Costs

34

Electronic Commerce

Electronic commerce (e-commerce) is the most rapidly growing sector of the economy, along with information technology. Increasingly, business is being conducted through the Internet and through other electronic means. This creates problems of applying existing legal rules and principles to new situations and raises some entirely new legal issues. In this chapter we examine such questions as:

- What is e-commerce?

- How is the law changing to accommodate the challenges of e-commerce?

- How are contracts made on the Internet?

- What law governs those contracts?

- How are consumers protected in e-commerce transactions?

- How has the Internet affected the law of defamation?

- How do trademark and copyright laws apply to the Internet?

- How can, or should, e-commerce be regulated by government?

- Which courts have jurisdiction over Internet disputes?

- To what extent is international co-operation necessary in order to devise an effective legal framework for e-commerce?

E-COMMERCE

What is E-commerce?

Electronic commerce, often referred to as **e-commerce**, is most broadly defined as "the delivery of information, products, services, or payments by telephone, computer, or other automated media."[1] More commonly, e-commerce is understood to refer to commercial activity that makes use of computer networks, including the **Internet** or **intranet** systems.[2]

According to one report, "the Internet has done for electronic commerce what Henry Ford did for the automobile—converted a luxury for the few into a relatively simple and inexpensive device for the many."[3]

The Impact of E-commerce on Business

Prior to 1995, e-commerce was almost non-existent. It was in that year that firms such as Amazon.com, Cisco, and Dell first began to use the Internet extensively for commercial transactions. The worldwide volume of e-commerce grew from $28 billion in 1998 to more than $1 trillion by 2003. In Canada, the value of sales made via the Internet exceeded $62 billion in 2007, with private-sector business-to-business (B2B) transactions accounting for $36 billion and business-to-consumer (B2C) sales for more than $22.1 billion. More than 87 percent of Canadian businesses have Internet access.[4] B2B transactions account for about two-thirds of all e-commerce. They include intranet activities—between branches of the same company or between related companies in a multinational group—and arm's-length transactions with other businesses involving Internet supply of services or products, technical support, invoicing, or payment. B2C transactions most often involve electronic retailing where a consumer accesses a business website to purchase or license tangible or electronic goods or services.

E-commerce has brought fundamental change to the business world in three key areas:

- existing business practices,
- new industries, and
- the business environment.

Existing Business Practices

Traditional businesses are adapting all facets of their operations to the online model. The hard copy, tangible processes of the past are rapidly being replaced by the instantaneous movement of intangible bits of electronic data. The use of Internet and intranet systems is transforming B2B and B2C relationships, as well as relationships with employees, government, and the public. As a result, businesses are supplying their products to customers through **electronic retailing (e-retailing)**, electronically monitoring their supply-chain management and record-keeping processes, and using **electronic transfer of funds** to bank, make payments, and collect account receivables online.

electronic commerce or **e-commerce**
the use of computer networks to facilitate commercial activities including the production, distribution, sale, and delivery of goods and services

Internet
the interconnected logical networks that link computers worldwide

intranet
closed systems linking specific users internal to a company or group; commonly used for data exchange

electronic retailing (e-retailing)
the supply of tangible or electronic goods or services over the Internet. Supply of tangible goods involves a conventional mode of delivery; electronic goods are downloaded directly to the customer's computer.

electronic transfer of funds
payment made through electronic (intangible) media such as telephone or Internet rather than by cash or cheque. Payment may take the form of credit card charges, debit of bank accounts, or even e-cash. Often, customers can access these forms of payment on the business's website.

---

1. "Electronic Commerce and Canada's Tax Administration: A Report to the Minister of National Revenue from the Minister's Advisory Committee on Electronic Commerce," Ottawa, April 1998.

2. M. Frecenko and A. Huntley, *Ecommerce Corporate–Commercial Aspects*, (Markham, ON: Lexis Nexis, 2003) at 3. The use of the Internet raises other legal issues that are not related to e-commerce, as defined here. These are not considered in this chapter. For a comprehensive survey, see M. Geist, *Internet Law in Canada*, 3rd ed. (North York, ON: Captus Press, 2002).

3. "The Economic and Social Impacts of Electronic Commerce: Preliminary Findings and Research Agenda" (Paris: OECD, 1998), at 10, available online at www.opec.org.

4. Data from "Electronic Commerce in Canada," available from the Industry Canada website, http://e-com.ic.gc.ca.

Another obvious business use of the Internet is as an advertising medium. One reason why so much free information is available online is that websites and search engines also frequently carry advertising. Even those businesses not involved in e-retailing maintain websites as a form of advertising. Misleading online advertising may trigger criminal and/or civil liability under the Competition Act.[5]

Establishing a Website for Online Business

When a business decides to go online, especially when it seeks to advertise and market its products or services, a number of steps must be taken. Each step usually involves the negotiation of an agreement. Generally, the business will have to

- negotiate a website development agreement—creating a website involves obtaining various development services (content, graphics, software, etc.), raises intellectual property issues, and usually requires professional assistance.
- negotiate a website-hosting agreement—once developed, the site must be installed and operated on a web server, usually operated by an Internet service provider.
- negotiate an Internet access agreement with the Internet service provider.
- register a domain name[6] and protect the intellectual property associated with the website.

Additionally, if the site is to be used for more than just advertising, it must be secure, and encryption services will be required.

New Industries

In addition to transforming the way traditional business operates, e-commerce has created entirely new industries. Obvious examples of new industries include Internet service providers (ISPs); network infrastructure support and outsourcing, including data management and security; and countless new online products and services.

e-cash
an online payment system that enables the anonymous transfer of money over the Internet

One innovation is **e-cash** (or cybermoney)—an online payment system that enables the secure and anonymous transfer of money over the Internet or other networks. E-cash has an advantage in that it may be used in small-value transactions that are not cost-effective when conventional credit cards are used. It also has a disadvantage from the point of view of the government, as it is difficult to monitor and may facilitate criminal activity. Another recent development, smart cards, are set to replace today's plastic credit and debit cards. Smart cards use an embedded integrated circuit chip in place of the conventional magnetic strips, and consumers can use them to make secure purchases over the Internet.

Other common business uses of the Internet are for investment broking, share trading, gambling, and disseminating pornography—all of which can be considered forms of e-commerce.

Business Environment

The business environment has been positively and negatively influenced by e-commerce. The global nature of the Internet offers businesses access to customers and suppliers from around the world. E-commerce is one of the major reasons why business has "gone global." Even small, local businesses are able to do business internationally via e-commerce, and the marketplace has expanded exponentially. Unfortunately, the explosion in e-commerce has also attracted abuse. E-commerce faces concerns about public safety, fraud, invasion of privacy, identity theft, money laundering, and tax evasion. Governments

---

5. Competition Act, R.S.C. 2985 c. 34 is discussed in Chapter 32. The Competition Bureau has issued an Information Bulletin discussing the application of the Competition Act to representations made on the Internet, available online at www.competitionbureau.gc.ca.

6. It may be necessary to register multiple domain names. See domain names under the heading "Intellectual Property."

have responded with increased regulation of the business environment and businesses must protect themselves and their stakeholders with increased awareness, security, and proactive measures.

The Impact of E-commerce on the Law

Electronic commerce is such a recent phenomenon that its legal implications are still unfolding. It presents new challenges and issues requiring the re-examination and adaptation of a broad range of traditional legal principles involving contract, tort, intellectual property, and international law. In addition, e-commerce is responsible for the development of new legal principles in areas such as privacy and consumer protection. Courts, legislatures, and the international community have responded to the e-commerce challenge and a new body of law is emerging based on case decisions, new legislation, and international treaties.

Regarding e-commerce law, the first question we must ask is: To what extent can existing legal rules and principles be applied to situations that arise in e-commerce? Cases involving e-commerce issues are coming before the courts and judges are adapting long-held principles to the new environment. This body of case law is slowly developing but pressing issues require the immediate response of government. The second question is: Should there be government regulation of e-commerce? The federal government has the power to regulate e-commerce, and indeed all uses of the Internet within Canada, under its general power to regulate intra-provincial communication.[7] In addition, provincial governments have power to regulate e-commerce under various constitutional categories including property and civil rights.[8] Initially there was broad consensus, in Canada and internationally, that the Internet (as it relates to e-commerce)[9] was functioning fairly well for the most part, that a system of self-regulation appeared to exist, and that excessive government regulation would impede the development of international e-commerce. In 1999, the chairperson of the Canadian Radio-television and Telecommunications Commission (CRTC) announced that there was no intention on the part of the CRTC to exercise general supervision of the Internet in Canada. There was fear that, given the transnational nature of cyberspace, any attempt by one country to regulate e-commerce might simply result in business migrating to less-restrictive regimes.[10]

However, since this initial position was expressed, several concerns have emerged. First, as has been noted, the development of case law was slow and gaps and inconsistency in existing legal principles appeared. This left business and consumers functioning in an uncertain legal environment. Second, international B2B and B2C transactions triggered the application of more than one country's laws and regulations. Harmonization was required. Finally, illegal e-commerce activity caught the attention of government. As a result, both federal and provincial governments have responded with legislation governing e-commerce.

The final question is: How can law address the transnational nature of e-commerce? A consistent global approach to e-commerce law is considered the best way to facilitate its smooth development, but both courts and legislatures face jurisdictional boundaries. Non-governmental organizations such as the Organization for Economic Co-operation and Development (OECD), the World Trade Organization (WTO), the United Nations Commission on International Trade Law (UNCITRAL), and the World Intellectual Property Organization (WIPO) are working towards standardization through international guidelines, treaties, conventions, and model laws. Member nations are encouraged to adopt domestic legislation consistent with international guidelines. Unfortunately, not all countries follow the international standards and businesses face jurisdictional variation in e-commerce law.

---

7. Constitution Act, 1867, s. 92(10)(a). It is somewhat less clear to what extent Internet usage constitutes "broadcasting" under the Broadcasting Act, S.C. 1991, c. 11.

8. *Ibid*, (Constitution) s. 92 (13)(14).

9. There are other aspects of the Internet that cause greater concern and are leading to calls for greater government regulation. See the section headed "Illegal Activities."

10. For an interesting review of the major issues regarding Internet regulation, see Geist, "The Reality of Bytes: Regulating Economic Activity in the Age of the Internet" (1998), 73 *Wash. L. Rev.* 521.

E-COMMERCE AND THE LAW

Contract Law

Electronic commerce, like any other form of commerce, is principally about making contracts. To what extent can traditional contract law be applied to e-commerce? Both the courts and the legislatures have addressed contract law issues.

Formation of Contracts

As we saw in Chapter 5, the key elements in the formation of a contract are offer and acceptance. When does a contract come into existence in a typical e-commerce transaction?

ILLUSTRATION 34.1

Elektra visits her favourite online CD store, clicks on "browse," and chooses the classical music category.

Following the website's instructions, she selects five CDs, each time clicking on "add this to my shopping basket." She then clicks on "Order," types in her credit card number, her name, and postal address, and finally clicks on "Confirm."

Has any contract been made and, if so, when? Does the store's website constitute an offer to sell the listed CDs, or is it simply an advertisement or an invitation to treat?[11] Is the offer made when Elektra clicks on "Order" or on "Confirm"? At what point is her order accepted by the store? Does that acceptance have to be communicated to Elektra before a contract comes into existence?[12] Would it make any difference if Elektra had ordered the CDs to be paid for COD, rather than on her credit card? Could she change her mind and refuse to take delivery?

These are some of the questions that arise in even the very simplest type of e-commerce transaction. To answer these questions, courts refer to similar cases where communication has been by mail, phone, or fax. Any firm planning to engage in e-commerce should design its website to spell out very clearly the legal consequences of clicking on each icon. It has become common practice to use "**web-wrap agreements**," or "click-wrap agreements," which require the consumer to click on the appropriate box to indicate agreement with the terms of sale.[13]

web-wrap agreement
a website document setting out contractual terms, the acceptance of which is indicated by clicking on the appropriate icon (also called a click-wrap agreement)

CASE 34.1

A group of law students in Ontario entered into an agreement through the Internet to subscribe to the Microsoft Network. In doing so, they were directed to the "membership rules," and before concluding the agreement they were required to click on a box indicating that they had read and accepted those membership rules. They subsequently brought an action in Ontario against Microsoft, alleging that Microsoft had taken payments from their credit cards in breach of contract and had failed to provide reasonable and accurate information concerning their accounts.

One of the conditions set out in the membership rules was that all disputes should be decided under the law of, and by the courts of, the State of Washington. The Ontario court held that the membership rules had been agreed to and formed part of the contracts. Consequently, the Ontario courts had no jurisdiction.[14]

---

11. See Chapter 5, under "The Nature of an Offer."

12. See Chapter 5, under "Transactions Between Parties at a Distance from Each Other."

13. The use and validity of web-wrap agreements is discussed by Sigel, Ling, and Izenberg in a paper prepared for the Uniform Law Conference of Canada, accessible at www.ulcc.ca/en/cls.

14. *Rudder* v. *Microsoft Corp.* [1999] O.J. No. 3778. See also *Kanitz* v. *Rogers Cable Inc.* (2002), 58 O.R. (3d) 299.

Web-wrap agreements need to be designed to ensure that all intended terms and conditions are brought to the attention of potential customers. In 2007, the Supreme Court of Canada stated that hyperlinks to "terms and conditions" must be visible, functional, and accessible.[15]

The Law Governing the Contract

Determining if and when a contract is made is of primary importance. But the moment when the contract is made may also determine where it is made, which in turn may determine the law that governs the transaction.[16]

ILLUSTRATION 34.2

Assume the same facts as in Illustration 34.1.

Elektra is resident of British Columbia. The CD firm is incorporated in Delaware. The website is operated through a server located in the Cayman Islands. On receiving Elektra's order, the server automatically notifies a warehouse in Alberta that the firm uses to dispatch goods ordered by Canadian customers.

Where was the contract made? Is it governed by the laws of British Columbia, Delaware, the Cayman Islands, or Alberta? Why might this be important? The law of the contract may determine such matters as:

- the capacity of the parties to contract
- the legality of the contract
- the formal requirements governing the contract
- any terms that are to be implied
- the effects of, and remedies for, breach of contract
- the applicability of consumer protection legislation

For example, the customer may be considered a minor in one jurisdiction but not in another, or a minor may have a restricted capacity to contract in one jurisdiction but not in another. Certain types of contract—for example, off-course betting on horse races—may be lawful in one jurisdiction but not in another. Particular types of contract may be required to be in writing or to be notarized. One jurisdiction may imply a warranty of fitness; another may not. A contract may be terminated by frustration in one jurisdiction but not in another.

Again, many of these and similar problems can be avoided by a clear statement of the law that is intended to govern, though that will not always protect the merchant. For example, consumer protection legislation in the customer's country may still apply, regardless of such a statement.

Formal Requirements

As just noted, the law that governs a contract may impose certain formal requirements—in particular (as noted in Chapter 10), that certain types of contract must be in writing. This raises the question of whether electronic contracts can be said to be in writing, and whether an electronic signature constitutes a true signature. The federal government resolved these problems for individual-to-government contracts in the Personal Information Protection and Electronic Documents Act (PIPEDA), enacted in 2000.[17]

---

15. *Dell Computer Corp.* v. *Union des consommateurs* [2007] S.C.J. No. 43 (Q.L.), 2007 SCC 34; In *Rogers Wireless Inc.* v. *Muroff,* 2007 SCC 35, para 15 (citing *Dell* at para 229) the Supreme Court accepted that Internet consumers must have a certain level of computer competence.

16. See Chapter 5, under "Determining the Jurisdiction Where a Contract Is Made." The place where a contract is made is one of a number of factors that may determine the law governing the contract: see Chapter 33, under "The Proper Law of the Contract."

17. S.C. 2000, c. 5.

This law adapts existing federal statutes and regulations to the electronic environment, allowing the use of electronic alternatives where the legislation contemplates the use of paper to record or communicate information or transactions (section 32), and recognizing electronic documents and signatures.[18]

In Canada, the law of contract falls almost exclusively within provincial jurisdiction, so the provinces have enacted their own legislation governing B2B and B2C electronic contracts.[19] The provincial legislation adapts contract law to the Internet environment by addressing topics such as acceptance by clicking an icon, communication of acceptance, electronic signatures, and writing.

The provincial legislation is based upon the Uniform Electronic Commerce Act, a model statute prepared by the Uniform Law Conference of Canada in accordance with the principles of the UNCITRAL model law.[20]

The Uniform Electronic Commerce Act provides:

s. 5. Information shall not be denied legal effect or enforceability solely by reason that it is in electronic form.[21]

s. 7. A requirement under law that information be in writing is satisfied by information in electronic form if the information is accessible so as to be usable for future reference.[22]

s. 8. A requirement under law for the signature of a person is satisfied by an electronic signature.[23]

s. 20(1). Unless the parties agree otherwise, an offer or the acceptance of an offer, or any other matter that is material to the formation or operation of a contract, may be expressed

(a) by means of an electronic document; or

(b) by an action in electronic form, including touching or clicking on an appropriately designated icon or place on a computer screen or otherwise communicating electronically in a manner that is intended to express the offer, acceptance or other matter.[24]

Consumer Protection Legislation

Consumer protection is primarily an area of provincial jurisdiction, although particular industries may also fall under federal protection, such as banking. In an attempt to offer Canadian consumers uniform online protection and provide international consistency, Industry Canada, together with the governments of Ontario, Alberta, and Quebec, and representatives of business, developed eight principles entitled *The Canadian Code of Practice for Consumer Protection in Electronic Commerce.*[25] The principles incorporate the OECD *Guidelines for Consumer Protection in the Content of Electronic Contracts.*[26] The Industry Canada code of practice and the OECD guidelines reflect the developing international standards of consumer protection in online contracting.

---

18. See, especially, sections 41, 43, and 46.

19. The relevant acts are the Electronic Commerce Act, S.N.L. 2001, c. E-5.2; S.N.S. 2000, c. 26; S.O. 2000, c. 17; S.P.E.I. 2001, c. 31; Electronic Commerce and Information Act, S.M. 2000, c. E-55; Electronic Information and Documents Act, S.S. 2000, c. E-7.22; and Electronic Transactions Act, S.A. 2001, c. E-5.5; S.B.C. 2001, c. 10; S.N.B. 2001, c. E-5.5.

20. The text of the Uniform Electronic Commerce Act is available from the Uniform Law Conference of Canada website: www.ulcc.ca.

21. For corresponding provisions in the provincial legislation, see, for example, s. 3 (B.C.); s. 6 (N.S.); s. 4 (Ont.).

22. See s. 5 (B.C.); s. 8 (N.S.); s. 5 (Ont.).

23. See s. 11 (B.C.); s. 11 (N.S.); s. 11 (Ont.).

24. See s. 15 (B.C.); s. 21 (N.S.); s. 19 (Ont.).

25. The Canadian Framework for Consumer Protection in Online Commerce has three goals: equivalent protection, harmonization, and international consistency. The eight principles will be subject to periodic review and are available at http://cmcweb.ca/epic/site/cmc-cmc.nsf/en/fe00064e.html.

26. The OECD *Consumer Guidelines* cover fair business practices, advertising, and marketing and are available online at www.oecd.org/document/51/0,3343,en_2649_34267_1824435_1_1_1_1,00.html.

In 2001, federal, provincial, and territorial consumer affairs representatives endorsed a model for B2C Internet consumer protection legislation.[27] Some provinces have adopted consumer protection legislation based on the model law.[28] Protective measures include mandatory disclosure of terms, cancellation rights or cooling-off periods, and printable consumer copies.[29] Consumer protection laws may apply to transactions completed outside their specific jurisdiction. The Ontario legislation applies to all consumers located in Ontario, no matter where the vendor or the goods are based. Alberta's protections apply when either the consumer or vendor is a resident of Alberta, or the offer or acceptance is made in Alberta.[30] Quebec consumers are protected from waivers of Quebec authority.[31] An online vendor needs to be familiar with the specifics of the consumer protection laws in relevant jurisdictions.

CHECKLIST Precautions to be Taken by Vendors When Contracting Online

Where a website is to be used to sell goods and services, the trader should take the following precautions:

- Become familiar with the e-commerce and consumer protection laws of provinces, countries, or jurisdictions in which it intends to do business.
- Where necessary, customize contract terms for the specific jurisdiction.
- Design the website so that the terms of the contract are brought to the attention of customers before any contract is concluded. Ensure any hyperlinks are visible, easily accessible, and functional.
- State clearly which law and jurisdiction apply to any contracts formed.
- Avoid giving customers too much freedom to amend terms—use yes/no or accept/decline options wherever possible.
- Maintain full back-ups of all contracts made via webpages.
- Generate and forward a printable customer copy of the contract at the time of purchase.

Torts

The tort most closely associated with the Internet is that of defamation, which is usually personal, rather than commercial, in nature. The courts have held that posting defamatory material on a website is publication for the purposes of the law of libel and may constitute "broadcasting" for purposes

27. Canada's Office of Consumer Affairs, Internet Sales Contract Harmonization Template, available online at http://strategis.ic.gc.ca/epic/site/oca-bc.nsf/en/ca01642e.html.
28. Consumer Protection Act, S.N.L. c.92, ss. 21V–21AF; Consumer Protection Act, 2002, S.O. 2002, c.30, ss. 37–40; Consumer Protection Act, C.C.S.M. c. C200, ss. 127–135; Consumer Protection Act, S.S. 1996, c. C-30.1, ss. 75.5–75.91; Fair Trading Act, R.S.A. 2000, c. F-2, s. 42.
29. See "Consumer Protection Rights in Canada in the Context of Electronic Commerce," Office of Consumer Affairs, August 31, 1998; Deturbide, M., *Consumer Protection Online*, (Markham: Lexis Nexis Canada, 2006). The details of disclosure, notice, and cancellation protections are usually set out in the regulations rather than the legislation: Alberta Regulation 81/2001 (Internet Sales Regulation) passed pursuant to the Fair Trading Act, *ibid.* Particular industries may be subject to additional regulation: Alberta Regulation 246/2005 (Energy Marketing Regulation), Part 3: Internet Marketing Contracts.
30. S. 2, Ontario Consumer Protection Act, 2002, *supra* n. 28; Alberta Regulation 81/2001, s. 2.
31. Article 3149 CCQ; (58.) Quebec law requires websites of firms whose place of business is in the province to be in the French language.

of libel and slander legislation.[32] Some courts have taken an especially serious view of defamation on the Internet and have increased damage assessments due to its potential to reach a very large audience.[33] An important issue in several defamation suits has been that of jurisdiction, a topic that will be considered later in this chapter. Another important issue relates to limitation periods; the British Columbia Court of Appeal held that each Internet publication extends the limitation period.[34]

An important question that has been raised, notably in a number of U.S. cases, is whether Internet service providers (ISPs) can be held responsible for material placed on the Internet through their servers. Can they be considered to have "published" a libel, to have made a misrepresentation, to be guilty of false advertising or of breach of copyright, or to have committed crimes such as the dissemination of child pornography or hate literature?

ISPs are an integral part of the e-commerce system. They have been described as the "gatekeepers" to the Internet. It is through an ISP that a person may place information on the Internet or access information placed there by some other person.

The ISPs generally take the view that they should be likened to a postal service or phone company and should not be responsible for any material transmitted by them. But others argue that their role is not always so passive and that they do, in practice, exercise a degree of control over their clients. In the *SOCAN* case described in Chapter 22,[35] the Supreme Court of Canada essentially agreed with the position taken by the ISPs. That case was concerned with copyright law, and turned, in part, on the interpretation of the Copyright Act, but it would seem to indicate that ISPs are not considered parties to a tort so long as their activities are restricted to the transmission of information.[36]

E-commerce can give rise to claims in tort in other ways. For example, many e-commerce services depend upon the use of sophisticated computer programs, which can go wrong—sometimes very wrong. In one recent case an investor was awarded damages against a discount electronic trading broker when faults in the broker's data entry system caused the posting of multiple transaction records in the plaintiff's account, and resulted in the plaintiff selling securities he did not own.[37] In another tort example, a student successfully sued Laurentian University for misrepresentations made on the university website.[38]

Intellectual Property

As one might expect, e-commerce and the use of the Internet give rise to many difficult questions concerning intellectual property rights and their possible infringement. For example, although the components of a website may be quite standard or ordinary, the specific organization, presentation, and content of a website are often unique and attract both copyright and trademark protection. In this section, we review the main issues that have emerged to date. However, ever-changing technology means that new issues are continuously emerging.

32. *Janssen-Ortho Inc.* v. *Amgen Canada Inc.*, [2005] O.J. No. 2265 (dealing with an Internet radio broadcast); *Bahlieda* v. *Santa* (2003), 233 D.L.R. (4th) 382 (ON. C.A.). In the context of the Ontario Libel and Slander Act, the finding of "broadcasting" was a triable issue and the act requires written notice of intended legal action; see Chapter 3.

33. See, for example: *Barrick Gold Corporation* v. *Lopehandia* (2004), 71 O.R. (3d) 416 ON. C.A.: damages were increased from $15 000 to $75 000 based on the "Internet factor." Publishing a libel in a limited number of personal e-mails is likely to be less harmful than posting it on a website: *Ross* v. *Holley*, [2004] O.J. No. 4643; *Newman* v. *Halstead*, 2006 A.C.W.S.J. LEXIS 651, 2006 A.C.W.S.J. 14. The recent popularity of blogs and social networks such as Facebook increase the likelihood of large defamation awards: *Newman* v. *Halstead*, 2006 BCSC 65.

34. *Carter* v. B.C. *Federation of Foster Parents Association*, 2005 B.C.C.A. 398.

35. *Canadian Association of Internet Providers* v. *SOCAN* (2004), 240 D.L.R. (4th) 193 (S.C.C.).

36. The Supreme Court of Canada also ruled that the practice of "caching" information is "content neutral" and is simply a consequence of the improvement of Internet technology and did not give rise to liability.

37. *Robet* v. *Versus Brokerage Services Inc.* (2001), 104 A.C.W.S. (3d) 988.

38. *Olar* v. *Laurentian University* (2007), Carswell Ont 3595. The same representation was also contained in the hard copy of the university calendar.

Trademarks

As we saw in Chapter 22, a **trademark** may be infringed by **passing-off**, or by any unauthorized use of the mark or of a confusingly similar mark, whether or not the infringement is intentional. Trademark infringement may occur in e-commerce in the same way as in ordinary commerce. However, the nature of the Internet greatly increases the probability of infringements, their potential seriousness, and the likelihood of their detection. It is quite possible for two businesses in different countries, or in different jurisdictions within the same country, to have the same name or to have confusingly similar names. Where neither of them is making a deliberate attempt to "steal" the business of the other, the possible trademark infringement is unlikely to give rise to problems and, in "normal" business, may well go undetected. But that may not be so where the infringement occurs on the Internet.

trademark
an identifiable feature that is used by a person for the purpose of distinguishing their goods or services from those of others

passing-off
misrepresenting goods, services, or a business in such a way as to deceive the public into believing that they are the goods, services, or business of some other person

---

ILLUSTRATION 34.3

Caitlin, the owner of the "Enchanted Florist" flower shop in Toronto, decides to create and maintain a website on the Internet to enable her customers to order flowers for delivery in Toronto and the surrounding area. On this website, she posts photographs of her more popular flower arrangements and takes orders over the phone from regular customers with account numbers. A month later, Caitlin receives notice that Halifax and Victoria flower shop owners—of shops named the "Enchanted Florist"—are claiming that she is infringing their trademarks.[39]

Without the Internet, the potential conflict would probably never have come to light. Each shop would have advertised in local newspapers and in the local "Yellow Pages" and would have been oblivious to the existence of the others. If the three parties are sensible, it is probable that the situation will be settled amicably; it is most unlikely that any of them would be able to show damage resulting from the infringement by the others if, indeed, there is any infringement. But, in the United States, there have been instances of parties being involved in expensive litigation in similar situations.[40] In such a case, the court would have to decide which of the parties was in fact entitled to use the "Enchanted Florist" trademark, and whether it was entitled to sole use. As we shall see later, the question also arises as to which court should hear the dispute.

Of course, trademark infringement on the Internet is not always accidental. Two Canadian cases have concerned the alleged infringement of the "Yellow Pages" and "Pages Jaunes" trademarks.

CASE 34.2

Bell Actimedia Inc. produces and distributes trade and telephone directories in Canada, and provides business listings on the Internet. It also owns the Canadian rights to the trademarks "Yellow Pages" and "Pages Jaunes." It learned that Globe Communications, a partnership registered in Quebec, had established a website with the address www.lespagesjaunes.com and was advertising itself as the "business directory of the French-speaking world."

Bell, which itself had registered several Internet sites, including www.yellowpages.ca, www.canadayellowpages.com, www.pagesjaunes.ca, and www.pagesjaunescanada.com, sought an injunction to restrain Globe from using its "Pages Jaunes" trademark, alleging passing-off and unfair competition.

The Court held that Bell was entitled to the injunction sought; a *prima facie* case of infringement had been made out, and Bell had established that it would suffer irreparable harm if an interlocutory injunction was not granted.[41]

---

39. The example, with changes to the locations, is taken from Kalow, "From the Internet to Court: Exercising Jurisdiction over World Wide Web Communications" (1997), 65 Fordham L. Rev. 2241.

40. See, for example: *Bensusan Restaurant Corp.* v. *King* (1996), 937 F. Supp. 295; *Cybersell Inc. (Arizona)* v. *Cybersell Inc. (Florida)* (1997), US App. LEXIS 33871.

41. *Bell Actimedia Inc.* v. *Puzo* (1999), 166 F.T.R. 202.

In the other case, owners of the "Yellow Pages" trademark obtained an award of damages against two corporations, one incorporated in Canada and the other a Nevada corporation, for infringement of its mark (as well as of the "walking fingers" logo), by advertising their business directory service as "Canadian Yellow Pages on the Internet" on their website, www.cdnyellowpages.com.[42]

CASE 34.3

"The Software Guy" was established in 2002 as an online retailer of business application software. In 2003 another firm, "The Software King," started up a similar business, with a remarkably similar webpage. The two domain names were also very similar: www.thesoftwareguy.com and www.thesoftwareking.com. The proprietors of the two businesses had had previous contacts and had even discussed setting up business together.

Software Guy sought an injunction to restrain Software King from using that name and from using text from its website.

The court dismissed the application. To the extent that the names were confusingly similar, the confusion arose from the word "software," which is a generic term to which the applicant had no claim. As to the website, it seemed to have obviously been "pirated," even reproducing an obvious grammatical error. However, there was a strong suggestion that the applicant had itself pirated the design from elsewhere. It was not the creator and had no copyright in the design.[43]

Unauthorized **linking** of websites may be trademark infringement if it suggests affiliation, endorsement, or sponsorship. Infringement is most likely when the link is opened in its own frame within a single browser window so that both websites are visible at the same time.

CASE 34.4

Showmax Inc. intended to open a big-screen movie theatre. Its website contained an unauthorized link to a picture of an IMAX theatre from the IMAX website. The

Federal Court found that the linkage incorrectly conveyed the impression that the two businesses were associated.[44]

---

linking
(or hyperlinking) an electronic connection of one website to another website. Links may be automatic or activated by the user. The new website may replace the original website or open in its own frame or browser window.

domain name
the registered Internet address of a website

Domain Names

As the above cases demonstrate, trademark infringement often results, intentionally or not, because of the close similarity of Internet addresses, or **domain names**.

In order to understand the legal implications of domain names, a basic understanding of the current system is necessary.[45] Theoretically, each website on the Internet is unique; no two domain names are exactly the same.

Domain names always have two or more parts, separated by dots. The part on the left is the most specific. The part on the right is the most general and is referred to as the "top-level domain." Top-level domains are either "generic," such as commercial (.com), educational (.edu), or organizational (.org), or they are "national," such as Canada (.ca). Generic names are assigned by authorized

---

42. *Tele-Direct (Publications) Inc.* v. *Canadian Business Online Inc.* (1998), 85 C.P.R. (3d) 332.

43. *Software Guy Brokers Ltd.* v. *Hardy*, [2004] B.C.J. No. 95.

44. *IMAX Corp.* v. *Showmax Inc.* (2000), 5 C.P.R. (4th) 81 (F.C.T.D.). It was also argued that linking infringed copyright. See also Fecenko, *supra*, n. 2, at 177.

45. The present domain name system has evolved over the past twenty years or so. For a full description of the system and its legal implications, see Gole, "Playing the Name Game: A Glimpse at the Future of the Internet Domain Name System" (1999), 51 *Fed. Com. L. J.*403. A useful description is given in "Developments—The Law of Cyberspace" (1999), 112 *Harv. L. Rev.* 1575.

registrars, whose activities are supervised by the Internet Corporation for Assigned Names and Numbers (ICANN), a non-profit body established in 2000; national names are assigned by national authorities. In Canada, the ".ca" domain has been controlled by the Canadian Internet Registration Authority (CIRA) since 1999.

Although no two domain names are identical, domain names can still be confusingly similar. For example, many Canadian business corporations are registered in the ".com" top-level domain, but there is nothing to prevent some other person registering the same name in the ".ca" domain— or in the domain of some other country. Registering a domain name costs very little, so there is a strong likelihood that there will be many instances of confusingly similar names. Traffic to a site may determine its advertising value, and this may motivate registrants to choose domain names very similar to existing high traffic sites in hopes of diverting web traffic.[46] To avoid this problem, many businesses register their name with as many generic and national top-level domains as possible.

Although domain names originated simply as addresses, it is now common for a domain name to include an existing trademark or trade name. Consequently, the use of an exclusive domain name may amount to the infringement of another's trademark. Many businesses register their domain names as trademarks and the Canadian Intellectual Property Office is accepting the registrations, provided the generic or national portion (.com, .ca, etc.) is disclaimed. Examples of trademarked domain names are ctvnews.com and tsn.ca.[47]

CASE 34.5

ITV Technologies Inc., a corporation incorporated in British Columbia, was a web services provider and in 1995 had registered the domain name www.itv.net. WIC Television Ltd., an Edmonton-based corporation, had been in the business of television broadcasting since 1974 and owned a number of stations throughout Canada. WIC owned several registered trademarks using the letters "ITV" and had registered a website with the domain name itv.ca. In 1996, WIC contacted ITV and asked it to stop using the ITV domain name.

Instead of waiting for WIC to sue for trademark infringement, ITV launched a pre-emptive strike and brought an action for an order expunging WIC's "ITV" trademarks, on the ground that they were not registrable. WIC counterclaimed, alleging infringement of its trademarks and seeking an injunction.

After a nine-year court battle, both sides eventually lost.[48] There was nothing unlawful about WIC's marks, which were well-known and distinctive in Alberta, and there was no reason for them to be expunged. On the other hand, there was no evidence, or likelihood, of confusion between the products of the two companies so the mark was not infringed.

In Case 34.5, the infringement of the trademark seems to have been innocent, at least initially, with no intention to "steal" business from its owner. In other instances, such as that in Case 34.2, there seems to have been a clear intention to derive a benefit from the use of a well-known trademark and to divert business away from the owner of the mark.[49] This type of passing-off is facilitated by the fact that Internet users, when trying to locate the website of a well-known firm, will often "intuit" the address by trying the trade name plus ".com," or will type in an incorrect address using the wrong top-level domain.

46. In one trademark validity case, the court considered evidence of the number of website hits and advertising expenses: *Candrug Health Solutions Inc.* v. *Thorkelson* (2007), FC 411. Another way to divert traffic and infringe trademark is to place a trademark in a "meta tag" used by search engines to compile search results. See Fecenko, *supra*, n. 2 at 175.

47. Registered Canadian Trade Mark TMA594391 by CTV Inc; TSN.ca was registered by The Sports Network Inc. (TMA551540). The generic portions were disclaimed because they lack distinctiveness.

48. *ITV Technologies, Inc.* v. *WIC Television Ltd.* (2003), 239 F.T.R. 203, affirmed by the Federal Court of Appeal, [2005] F.C.J. No. 438.

49. See also *Peinet Inc.* v. *O'Brien* (1995), 61 C.P.R. (3d) 334; *Molson Breweries* v. *Kuettner* (1999), 94 A.C.W.S. (3d) 550.

CASE 34.6

The plaintiffs were the publishers of one of the oldest and most widely read newspapers in Saskatchewan. They also maintained a website, www.thestarphoenix.com, that reproduced the front page of their newspaper with the current day's lead stories, and contained advertising paid for by their customers. The defendant created a website, www.saskatoonstarphoenix.com, that looked very much like that of the plaintiffs, but substituted his own advertising.

The court awarded damages to the plaintiffs. The defendant's actions amounted to passing-off. There was a misappropriation of the plaintiff's goodwill, an intention to mislead the public, and actual or potential damage to the plaintiffs.[50]

Some strange uses, or abuses, of the domain name system have evolved. A U.S. court granted an injunction for trademark infringement in a case where an anti-abortion activist registered the domain name www.plannedparenthood.com in order to promote his views.[51] More recently, the British Columbia Supreme Court granted an injunction and awarded damages against an individual using the domain name lawsocietyofbc.ca to direct people to a website containing "adult content."[52]

cybersquatting
the registration of a domain name containing the trademark of another person, with the intention of selling the domain name to the owner of the mark

One of the more notorious practices is that of **cybersquatting**, where a person registers a domain name that includes a well-known trademark or brand name, and then offers to sell the domain name to the owner of the mark or brand. Such action almost certainly constitutes a trademark infringement and may have serious consequences for the infringer, who may be ordered to relinquish the domain name and to pay court costs.[53] However, cybersquatters normally rely on the fact that the trademark owner may find it less expensive and more convenient simply to buy the domain name from the registrant.

CASE 34.7

A travel retailer had a website, located at www.itravel2000.com, and had registered the name "itravel" under the Ontario Business Names Act. It applied to the CIRA to register the domain name itravel.ca, but was informed that the name had already been registered. The registrant was an individual who had no connection with the travel business, and had acquired the name with the sole purpose of selling it to the highest bidder.

On application by the travel retailer, the court granted an injunction, preventing the defendant from using or selling the name.[54]

alternative dispute-resolution
the use of private procedures such as arbitration and mediation to resolve disputes

Domain name disputes may be resolved in the courts—for example, by actions for trademark infringement. Alternatively, in the case of generic names, ICANN has established an **alternative dispute-resolution** policy, with a list of approved dispute-resolution service providers, and CIRA has a similar policy for names within the ".ca" domain.[55] The World Intellectual Property Office operates an arbitration and mediation centre.

50. *Saskatchewan Star Phoenix Group Inc.* v. *Noton* [2001] S.J. No. 275.

51. *Planned Parenthood* v. *Bucci* (1997), US Dist. LEXIS 3338. Other examples are discussed in the article by Gole, *supra*, n. 45.

52. *Law Society of British Columbia* v. *Canada Domain Name Exchange Corp.* (2004), 243 D.L.R. (4th) 746, affirmed by the British Columbia Court of Appeal (2006), 259 D.L.R. (4th) 171.

53. See, for example: *Panavision International Inc.* v. *Toeppen* (1996), US Dist. LEXIS 19698. Mr. Toeppen reportedly registered some 240 names and then attempted to sell them for exorbitant fees.

54. *itravel2000.com Inc.* v. *Fagan* (2001), 197 D.L.R. (4th) 760.

55. Details of the ICANN uniform domain-name dispute-resolution policy can be obtained from the ICANN website at www.icann.org/udrp/udrp.htm. For the CIRA dispute-resolution policy, see www.cira.ca/en/cat_Dpr.html.

CASE 34.8

Bill Cosby owns all the trademarks associated with the television show *Fat Albert and the Cosby Kids*, which was the basis for the December 2004 feature film entitled *Fat Albert*. Six months prior to the movie's release, Sterling Davenport registered the domain name fatalbert.org. After release of the movie, Davenport linked the domain name to a website selling sexually explicit products. Davenport had registered over 500 other domain names, often using celebrity names.

In July 2005, Bill Cosby filed an e-mail complaint with the World Intellectual Property Office Arbitration and Mediation Center. Davenport never responded to the complaint and the arbitrator found that the domain name was confusingly similar to the Cosby trademark, that Davenport registered the domain name in order to trade on Cosby's fame, and that both Davenport's registration and use of the domain name were done in bad faith. The arbitrator ordered that the domain name be transferred to Bill Cosby.[56]

Copyright

It is generally accepted that copyright laws apply to the publication and reproduction of materials on the Internet or in e-mail communications. A website is recognized as an artistic work and linking websites may associate the work with someone other than the creator. The Internet makes infringement of copyright, whether deliberate or unintentional, a very easy matter.[57] Anything that can be copyrighted can be converted into digital form and sent across the Internet, permitting a perfect copy to be downloaded onto another computer or storage device.

Internet users have traditionally embraced the view that "information wants to be free," and copyright is routinely infringed as material posted on the Internet is copied and forwarded to other users without the knowledge or consent of the copyright owner. Indeed, it is widely—though incorrectly—believed that by posting material on a website, the author or owner impliedly consents to its being copied and reproduced. In some instances, that may be true and, even where it is not, copyright owners rarely take action against infringements that are non-commercial in nature. For example, a student finding an interesting piece of information on the Internet downloads it and forwards it to a friend, or a teacher edits materials from the Internet and incorporates them into teaching materials. Such actions may or may not constitute "fair dealing,"[58] or may impliedly be consented to by the copyright owner; but even if they are not, the owner is unlikely to sue. By contrast, if material posted on the Internet is used for a commercial purpose, or in a manner that is offensive to the copyright owner, legal proceedings are far more likely. Businesses should clearly state the acceptable terms of use of material placed on their websites.

CASE 34.9

Sotramex, a firm specializing in cleaning up mining and forestry sites, prepared a technical description (written by one of its employees) to appear on the website of the International Centre for the Advancement of Environmental Technologies. A year or so later, Sorenviq, another firm engaged in reforestation, posted a virtually identical item on

its own website without acknowledging the true authorship. The two firms were competitors.

The court found that the author's copyright had been infringed and ordered Sorenviq to remove the text from its website and to pay $10 000 damages plus $5000 exemplary damages.[59]

---

56. *William H. Cosby, Jr.* v. *Sterling Davenport*, WIPO Arbitration and Mediation Center Case No. D2005-076, available online at www.wipo.int/amc/en/domains/decisions/html/2005/d2005-0756.html.

57. For a basic review of the challenges that the Internet has caused with respect to copyright, see: Charlotte Waelde and Hector MacQueen, "Entertainment to Education: The Scope of Copyright" (2004), 3 I.P.Q. 259–283. The Supreme Court of Canada ruled, in the *SOCAN* case, *supra*, n. 35, that the practice of "caching" (that is, making temporary copies of webpages to speed up delivery) does not of itself constitute an infringement of copyright. Other practices, such as "linking," also raise copyright problems: it may infringe an author's moral right to association. Infringement may depend on whether the link is user activated, automatic, or "deep." For further discussion, see Geist (*supra*, n. 2), Ch. 16 and *IMAX*, *supra*, n. 44.

58. The concept of "fair dealing" is discussed in Chapter 22 and includes research, private study, and news reporting: Copyright Act R.S.C. 1985, c. C-42, ss. 28–29 as amended.

59. *Sotramex Inc.* v. *Sorenviq Inc.,* [1998] A.Q. No. 2241 (Quebec Superior Court—Civil Division).

Although "private" infringements of copyright are usually ignored, if they occur on a large scale they can be costly to copyright owners.

CASE 34.10

Canada's largest recording company, BMG, brought an action for copyright infringement against persons unknown. It claimed that the defendants traded music downloaded from the Internet by sharing directories on their computers using peer-to-peer (P2P) file-sharing programs. BMG's evidence was that 29 users had each downloaded over 1000 songs over which it held copyright. As a result of sharing, music revenues in Canada had fallen by over 40 percent in the past five years.

BMG could not identify the defendants and therefore asked the court to order five major ISPs to disclose the identity of those of their customers who traded downloaded music. The Federal Court denied BMG's motion on privacy grounds and stated that there was no evidence of copyright infringement. Downloading a piece of music for personal use was not a breach of copyright, nor did placing a copy on a shared directory amount to authorizing infringement. Although the judgment was upheld on appeal, the statements relating to downloading for personal use were criticized as premature by the Court of Appeal, which noted that the *private use exception*[60] is not always available.[61]

technical protection measures (TPMs)
access locks or use locks for electronic material: An access lock requires a password to access the work; a use lock blocks particular uses of the work such as copying

digital rights management system (DRMS)
a system collecting data about the licensing, payment for, and authenticity of a work.

The *BMG* and *SOCAN* decisions have been hailed as major victories for Internet users. The music industry is urging legislative intervention while resorting to **technical protection measures** (TPMs) and **digital rights management systems** (DRMS) to protect their works.[62] The industry's favoured solution would be to impose a duty on ISPs to withdraw their services from subscribers if they are notified that a subscriber is infringing copyright.[63]

The World Intellectual Property Organization has responded to Internet copyright infringement with several treaties: WIPO Internet Treaties, The WIPO Copyright Treaty (WCT), and WIPO Performances and Phonograms Treaty (WPPT). These treaties call for domestic legislation that will create legal remedies for circumvention of TPMs or DRMS, impose obligations on ISPs, and entrench a copyright holder's exclusive right to make a work available over the Internet. Under these provisions, unauthorized temporary or permanent storage and unauthorized access to a shared drive on a personal computer would all constitute infringement.[64] Although reform of Canadian copyright law has been proposed, to date, Canada has not amended its Copyright Act to incorporate the WIPO treaties' provisions.[65]

---

60. The private use exception: Section 80 of the Copyright Act allows private copying of sound recordings of musical works onto audio recoding media for the private use of the person making the copy. When this exception was created, a levy was imposed on the sale of blank audio recording media. The Canadian Private Copying Collective was established to collect and distribute the levy to artists, songwriters and copyright holders.

61. *BMG Canada Inc.* v. *John Doe* (2004), 239 D.L.R. (4th) 726 affirmed by the Federal Court of Appeal (2005), 252 D.L.R. (4th) 342. The issue was whether P2P sharing was personal use. Initially, the personal copying levy focused on blank CDs. In 2004, the Federal Court of Appeal ruled that MP3s and iPods were not subject to the levy: *Canadian Private Copying Collective* v. *Canadian Storage Media Alliance*, 2004 FCA 424 (leave to appeal to the Supreme Court was refused). Recently, the Copyright Board approved a levy on iPods for 2008–2009 and even suggested cell phones and personal computers could be next. See Copyright Board of Canada, "Copying for Private Use, Copyright Act, Subsection 83(8): File: Private Copying 2008–2009," available online at www.cb-cda.gc.ca/decisions/c19072007-b.pdf. See also, Michael Geist, "iPod Levy May Yet Face the Music," *Toronto Star*, August 6, 2007.

62. These measures are not without their critics. Access-to-information concerns have been raised because these systems do not distinguish between legal uses and infringing "conduct." See C.M. Correa, "Fair Use in the Digital Era," *UNESCO INFOethics 2000*, http://webworld.unesco.org/infoethics2000/papers.html#correa.

63. Somewhat similar legislation has been enacted in the United States legislation to deal specifically with the liability of Internet intermediaries for breach of copyright: Digital Millennium Copyright Act, 1998.

64. The United States implemented the WIPO treaty provisions in 1998, *ibid.*, and the European Union Copyright Directive, passed May 22, 2001, adopts WIPO treaty provisions.

65. Canada agreed to implement the WIPO treaties. Bill C-60 proposed the required changes, but it died on the order table on November 29, 2005 when the 2006 election was called. Bill C-61, introduced in June 2008, died on the table when the 2008 election was called. For a discussion of copyright reform, see Sara Bannerman, "Canadian Copyright Reform: Consulting With the Copyright's Changing Public" (2006), 19 *I.P.J.* 271. According to government press releases, copyright reform remains a priority of the government: www.tbs-sct.gc.ca/rpp/0708/pch/pch02_e.asp#name2.

Privacy

There is growing concern over the fact that organizations—government and business—have accumulated vast amounts of electronic information about private individuals, which may be used for purposes not contemplated by the individual who originally supplied it. Electronic commerce greatly increases the amount of information that is made available, and, being in computerized form, that information is easily edited and transmitted. It can also be sold to marketers and others. Failure to properly safeguard private information may expose a business to tort liability.

The Personal Information Protection and Electronic Documents Act (PIPEDA), which has already been referred to in the context of contract law and will be discussed in greater detail in Chapter 35, imposes restrictions on the use, and misuse, of personal information. The Act applies to every organization that collects, uses, or discloses personal information in the course of commercial activity. Organizations are required to develop and publish privacy policies. Probably its most important feature is the requirement to obtain an individual's consent to use or disclose information collected. In addition, individuals will have the right to inspect their personal information held by a company and to have it corrected. According to some critics, the Act does not go nearly far enough; individuals will usually be unaware that information about them is being used improperly. Proposed amendments to PIPEDA include the obligation to disclose any breach of privacy.[66] Some provinces have adopted their own privacy legislation, in which cases affected organizations may be exempt from the federal legislation.[67]

ETHICAL ISSUE

Employee Technology Use

The Internet is part of everyday business activity, and the majority of employees have access to the Internet at work. In their personal lives, employees use the Internet as a form of social networking and expression. Social networking sites allow members to chat, post biographical information, pictures, and personal opinions, and share all of this information with fellow members. Business is struggling with the level of acceptable personal Internet use in the workplace. Employers are concerned about issues such as wasted time, viruses, security, confidentiality, harassment, and illegal activity including gambling and accessing pornography.

A 2007 survey of employers conducted on behalf of the American Management Association reported that 66 percent of employers monitor employee Internet activities, 43 percent retain and review employee e-mail, and 30 percent of employers have fired an employee for misuse of the Internet.

Many employers have developed codes of conduct for technology use, but there is no uniform position on the use of social networking sites. Some employers have banned their use entirely, while others allow unlimited access.

continued

---

66. Section 29 required a review of PIPEDA five years after enactment. The findings of the review were reported to Parliament on May 2, 2007 and can be found at www.e-com.ic.gc.ca/epic/site/ecic-ceac.nsf/en/gv00401e.html. On August 1, 2007, the Privacy Commissioner issued guidelines for businesses to follow when a privacy breach occurs, available online at www.privcom.gc.ca/media/nr-c/2007/nr-c_070801_e.asp.

67. Personal Information Protection Act, S.A. 2003, c. P-6.5; Personal Information Protection Act, S.B.C. 2003, c. 63; *An Act Respecting the Protection of Personal Information in the Private Sector*, R.S.Q., c. P-39.1.

QUESTIONS TO CONSIDER

1. Should employees access social networking sites while at work?

2. Should employers be entitled to monitor employee Internet use?

3. When making employment decisions, should employers (or potential employers) make use of information available on potential employees' personal or social networking sites?

Sources: American Management Association and The ePolicy Institute, *2007 Electronic Monitoring & Surveillance Survey*, http://press.amanet.org/press-releases/177/2007-electronic-monitoring-surveillance-survey; Virginia Galt, "Firms Develop Codes of Conduct to Curb Porn Surfing on Internet," *Globe and Mail*, July 19, 2004, p. B4; Virgina Galt, "Keyword for Workplace Messaging? Caution," *Globe and Mail*, October 7, 2006, p. B14; Dianne Stafford, "Employers Limiting Use of Internet By Staff," *National Post*, February 28, 2007 p. WK 7.

Another privacy-related issue is whether persons are, or should be, protected from electronic junk mail, or "spam," as it is commonly known. Arguably, spam constitutes an invasion of privacy and might be actionable under the common law of trespass. However, it would normally not be worth suing, even if the action were likely to succeed. In one Ontario case, a firm brought an action against its ISP, seeking an injunction to have its service restored. The ISP had discontinued the service following complaints that the plaintiff firm had been sending out up to 200 000 unsolicited messages each day to promote the sale of its furniture. The court ruled that spam is a breach of "netiquette"—the Internet's unwritten rules of conduct—and refused the injunction.[68]

INTERNATIONAL ISSUE

What to Do About Spam?

Spam, at one time considered to be a minor irritant, has become a major worldwide concern. Canada has been named the sixth-largest source of spam in the world and more than 86 percent of the e-mails sent globally are junk mail.[69] Time is wasted, hard-drive space used up, computers can be paralyzed, and money is spent on special programs designed to block spam. And that is just the nuisance spam.

A substantial proportion of spam is intended to defraud. There can be few Internet users who have not received a "Nigeria letter," offering millions of dollars in return for the temporary use of their bank accounts. Spam is also used to sell suspect pharmaceuticals and other bogus products.

A number of countries have adopted specific legislation to combat spam. Norway adopted legislation in 2001. United Kingdom's legislation, in place since 2003, has been criticized for exempting work addresses. Similarly, the United States' CAN-SPAM Act has been denounced for being too soft on spammers. Industry Canada set up a task force on spam that recommended legislation in 2005, but as of 2008, no new spam legislation has been enacted. Instead, existing legislation is being used to tackle the problem. Privacy legislation applies to spam because e-mail addresses are considered personal information and therefore use without consent is a privacy violation. The

continued

---

68. *1267623 Ontario Inc.* v. *Nexx Online Inc.* (1999), 45 O.R. (3d) 40. It is normal for ISP contracts to include a "netiquette clause," so that the dissemination of spam would constitute a breach of the contract with the ISP.

69. Brock Smith and Shauna Towriss, "Tougher Legislation Needed to Fight Spam," *The Lawyers Weekly*, Vol. 28, No. 25, April 13, 2007. The top five countries are the United States, China, Russia, the United Kingdom, and Japan.

Criminal Code addresses unauthorized use of computers and fraudulent activities. Deceptive or misleading e-mails may be violations of the Competition Act. Still, Canada remains the only G-8 nation without specific anti-spam legislation.

In a widely reported case in April 2005, an American spammer, Jeremy Jaynes, became the first spammer to be convicted of violating anti-spam law and was sentenced to nine years in prison. Jaynes was alleged to have sent as many as 10 million e-mails per day, using addresses stolen from AOL, and to have made $24 million out of his fraudulent schemes. However, in September 2008, after multiple appeals, the Virginia Supreme Court overturned the conviction and declared Virginia's anti-spam law unconstitutional as an overly broad infringement on free speech.[70]

QUESTIONS TO CONSIDER

1. If anti-spam legislation is adopted in Canada, should it include criminal or regulatory offences?

2. Should ISPs have a duty to prevent their customers from sending spam?

3. Should the right to free speech protect spam?

Sources: Industry Canada, *The Digital Economy. An Anti-Spam Action Plan for Canada*, May 2004; Industry Canada, *The Digital Economy. International Spam Measures Compared*, May 2004, both available at www.ic.gc.ca; Canadian Internet Policy and Public Interest Clinic, *Spam*, June 2, 2007, http://cippic.ca/spam/.

Illegal Activities

Spam is just one of the potentially illegal activities undertaken on the Internet. The Internet facilitates "identity theft" and "phishing," the practice of using fraudulent e-mails and fake websites to induce recipients into disclosing personal financial data. Virus attacks can disable computers, destroy files, and cause millions of dollars of damage. Many countries are concerned about the use of the Internet to facilitate other activities, such as the dissemination of hate literature and child pornography. Pornography, in fact, is one of the most important sectors of e-commerce in financial terms. The Internet provides an easy method of distribution and one that makes detection and prosecution extremely difficult.

Another activity, which, if not illegal, is often strictly regulated by governments, is gambling. Again, the Internet provides a means of circumventing local laws by establishing offshore "virtual casinos" and betting offices. In 1998, a British company established what was claimed to be the first worldwide online betting service at www.sportingbet.com, based in the tax-haven island of Alderney. The principal attraction of offshore, online gambling—to both bookmakers and punters—is that it enables the taxes that governments often impose on gambling to be avoided, increasing profits and pay-outs. The objection—from the point of view of the rest of the population—is that it undermines what is often an important source of government revenue.

This brings us to what is perhaps the greatest concern that governments have with respect to e-commerce—tax evasion. One of the most important and comprehensive studies made of e-commerce in Canada is that prepared for Revenue Canada (now the Canada Customs and Revenue Agency) in 1998.[71] Tax administrators have a number of concerns:

■ Sales taxes and customs duties are easy to evade in e-commerce transactions, especially where goods or services are delivered electronically.[72]

---

70. *Jaynes* v. *Commonwealth of Virginia*, Supreme Court of Virginia No. 062388, September 12, 2008.

71. "Electronic Commerce and Canada's Tax Administration."

72. Canada Customs and Revenue Agency GST/HST Technical Information Bulletin B-090 explains the Agency's position on GST and electronic commerce, available online at www.cra-arc.gc.ca/E/pub/gm/b-090/b-090-e.pdf.

- Income tax (especially corporate income tax) may be avoided by moving operations offshore.
- Electronic commerce commonly reduces the number of persons involved in a transaction, cutting out the intermediary, which in turn eliminates the usual "audit trail" and makes tax evasion more difficult to detect.
- The use of e-cash also facilitates fraud and evasion.

INTERNATIONAL ASPECTS OF E-COMMERCE

As we have noted throughout this chapter, the international nature of the Internet is one of the great potential advantages of e-commerce, and it is also the cause of many headaches for government officials, business persons, and their lawyers. Businesses are uncertain about which laws apply to their contracts and other activities, which courts have jurisdiction to resolve their disputes, and what liabilities they may be subject to. Governments are unsure to what extent they should attempt to regulate e-commerce, and even less sure whether such attempts would be effective. For example, if Canadian businesses are subjected to stricter privacy regulation than their American competitors, they may lose out in the race to develop e-commerce. However, the European Union's privacy legislation bans foreign firms from conducting e-business in most of Europe unless they are subject to equally strict privacy rules at home. Therefore, Canada must draft legislation that is sufficiently strict to satisfy the Europeans, without losing out in the American market.

Jurisdiction

jurisdiction
the right of a court to hear and resolve a dispute

Chapter 33 briefly discussed the principles applied by courts to determine whether they have **jurisdiction** to hear a dispute with international aspects. These principles are complex, even when applied to conventional business transactions that cross provincial, state, or national borders. Jurisdictional issues in the context of online transactions present an even greater challenge.[73] To quote from one study:

> Traditional rules relating to jurisdiction and competence incorporate a notion of territoriality. But Internet communications are not geographically dependent. The very origin of an e-mail message may be unknown. Web site information cannot be confined to a target audience, but is disseminated simultaneously to a global market. It may affect individuals in a myriad of jurisdictions, all of which have their own particular laws.[74]

As a general rule, the courts of most countries accept jurisdiction if the defendant is resident or domiciled there. In the case of an extra-territorial defendant, jurisdiction is accepted only where there is a real and substantial connection with the country (or province or state).

The general rule is often unsatisfactory in e-commerce situations, especially those involving consumer transactions. The vendor may be resident in another country or province, and it may be quite impractical to expect the consumer to commence legal proceedings in a distant jurisdiction with, perhaps, a very different legal system. Sometimes it may not even be possible to determine where the defendant is resident, since its web address does not necessarily indicate its physical location. This difficulty has led some provinces to assert jurisdiction over all residents' consumer disputes.[75] But that solution is not without problems. An electronic retailer could find itself liable to

---

73. According to Professor Geist, "Lurking in the background of virtually every Internet law issue is the question of jurisdiction" (*supra*, n. 2, at 43).

74. Ogilvy Renault, "Jurisdiction and the Internet: Are Traditional Rules Enough?" The study is reproduced on the website of the Uniform Law Conference of Canada at www.ulcc.ca/en/cls.

75. See the report "Consumer Protection Rights in Canada in the Context of Electronic Commerce," *supra*, n. 29. Also see the section on Consumer Protection, *supra*, notes 30 and 31.

be sued anywhere in the world, unless it states clearly that its offer to sell is restricted to certain countries only. To do business internationally, the retailer would have to comply with the consumer laws of many different jurisdictions, some of which might regard a simple disclaimer of liability as ineffective. Also, from the point of view of the consumer, a judgment against a foreign supplier might be useless if the supplier has no assets in the customer's country, and the courts of the supplier's country might not be willing to enforce a judgment obtained by the customer in his or her own country.

Similar problems exist in the case of trademark and copyright violation. The question of jurisdiction in such cases has been considered by American courts on a number of occasions, and what has been called a **level-of-interactivity test** (also called an active-versus-passive test) has evolved. In *Zippo Manufacturing Co.* v. *Zippo Dot Com, Inc.*,[76] the plaintiff Pennsylvania corporation, manufacturer of the well-known brand of cigarette lighters, brought an action against a California corporation, which provided an Internet news service, for infringement of its "Zippo" trademark. Reviewing the jurisdictional principles, the court ruled that three types of situation exist:

(1) where the out-of-state defendant is carrying on substantial business within the jurisdiction

(2) where the defendant maintains an interactive site

(3) where the defendant's site provides purely passive advertising site

In case (1), there is jurisdiction where the business is being carried on; in case (3) there is no jurisdiction; case (2) remains an uncertain "grey area." In the particular case, the court found that the California corporation was doing substantial business in Pennsylvania, and that the Pennsylvania courts were entitled to exercise jurisdiction.[77]

Some Canadian courts have adopted the level-of-interactivity test, and the *Zippo* case was referred to with approval in a case before the British Columbia Court of Appeal.[78]

Jurisdiction issues also arise in tort actions, such as defamation. Traditionally, Canadian courts have taken the view that jurisdiction may be exercised in the state or province where the tort is committed. Defamation is committed where the defamatory statement is "published"—that is, where it is made available to be seen, heard, downloaded, or read. But a defamatory statement posted on the Internet could be said to have been published everywhere.[79] That would seem to suggest that a plaintiff alleging libel might sue anywhere in the world, choosing a jurisdiction where the law of defamation is most favourable and where damages are likely to be highest.

level-of-interactivity test
a review of the features of a website to determine if it is active or passive; only active sites will be considered connected to the jurisdiction (also called the active-versus-passive test)

CASE 34.11

Braintech Inc., a corporation that designs and develops advanced pattern-recognition technologies for use in industrial robot applications, was incorporated in Nevada in 1987 (under a different name). It had moved its head office to Arizona, to Texas, and then, in 1996, to Vancouver, though apparently it still maintained a research and development facility in Texas.

continued

76. (1997), 952 F. Supp. 1119 (W.D. Pa.).

77. Contrast *Cybersell Inc. (Arizona)* v. *Cybersell Inc.* (Florida) (1997), US App. LEXIS 33871, where the Florida-incorporated defendant was found to be engaging solely in "passive" advertising, and the Arizona court declined jurisdiction.

78. *Braintech, Inc.* v. *Kostiuk* (1999), 171 D.L.R. (4th) 46. See also *Pro-C Ltd.* v. *Computer City Inc.* (2000), 7 C.P.R. (4th) 193; *Wiebe* v. *Bouchard*, [2005] B.C.J. No. 73; *Desjean* v. *Intermix Media, Inc.* (2006), 57 C.P.R. (4th) 314. In *Easthaven Ltd.* v. *Nutrisystem.com Inc.* (2001), 202 D.L.R. (4th) 560, the Ontario Superior Court declined to accept jurisdiction in a dispute between a Barbados corporation and a Delaware corporation, where the only connection with Ontario was the fact that the domain name in question had been registered through an Ontario corporation. See Case 33.3, in Chapter 33. According to Professor Geist, "the Canadian courts' approach to internet jurisdiction has remained somewhat of a mystery," *Toronto Star*, February 16, 2004, and *Toronto Star*, September 26, 2005.

79. For an analysis of this problem, see Gosnell, "Jurisdiction on the Net: Defining Place in Cyberspace" (1998), 29 *C.B.L.J.* 345. Without evidence that someone in the jurisdiction downloaded or read the statement, the tort was not committed in the jurisdiction: *Crookes* v. *Yahoo* (2007) BCSC 1325.

Braintech alleged that it had been libelled by Kostiuk, a resident of British Columbia, in material that he had posted on an Internet chat forum about potential investments in hi-tech firms. Braintech brought an action against Kostiuk in Texas. Kostiuk did not defend the suit, believing that the Texas court had no jurisdiction. The Texas court found in favour of Braintech and awarded damages of US$409 680. Braintech then sought to have the Texas judgment enforced in British Columbia. At the trial level, Braintech succeeded, the court holding that it was bound to enforce the Texas judgment.[80] That judgment was overturned by the British Columbia Court of Appeal, which held that the Texas court had no jurisdiction to hear the original case and that its judgment should therefore not be enforced.[81]

An alternative approach is to take the view that defamation is committed where the injury is suffered. Normally, that will be where the plaintiff lives, for that is where her reputation is harmed. Some level of foreseeability must be applied to this test, otherwise a defendant could be sued anywhere.

CASE 34.12

Bangoura had been employed by the United Nations and had worked in a number of African countries. After he retired, he settled in Ontario and became a Canadian citizen. The *Washington Post* published a story on its website alleging that Bangoura had been removed from his position with the U.N. Drug Control Programme because of a scandal that had occurred in Kenya.

Bangoura commenced a libel action against the *Post* in the Ontario Superior Court. The *Post* brought a motion to have the claim set aside on the ground that the Ontario court did not have jurisdiction. Initially, the court ruled that even though the libel was published in Washington, D.C., injury was suffered by the plaintiff in Ontario, and the Ontario court could assume jurisdiction.[82] Reversing the trial court, the Court of Appeal held that the Washington court had jurisdiction; it was unreasonable to expect the newspaper to foresee that Bangoura would be a resident of Ontario three years later.[83]

Non-governmental Organizations

At present, different countries or groups of countries are each going their own way, and some countries are making a point of not regulating—and not taxing—e-commerce, with the aim of attracting business. The result is a mass of conflicting rules that impede the development of e-commerce by responsible enterprises and encourage the growth of more dubious activities. It is becoming increasingly obvious that concerted action is necessary at the international level, but just as obviously, different countries have different concerns and interests, making an international consensus difficult to achieve. The contribution of **non-governmental organizations** is vital to building international harmony.

The OECD has developed guidelines for domestic legislation in the areas of consumer protection, multinational corporate governance, bribery, and taxation.[84] The UNCITRAL model laws on international commercial arbitration and enforcement of foreign arbitral awards aim to standardize commercial dispute resolution around the world.[85] The 2005 United Nations Convention on the

non-governmental organization
private groups or associations that are not part of a state, nation, or political structure—they are usually not-for-profit and focus on societal issues

---

80. Applying the principle enunciated in *Morguard Investments Ltd. v. de Savoye* (1990), 76 D.L.R. (4th) 256; see "Enforcement of Foreign Judgments" in Chapter 33.

81. *Braintech Inc.* v. *Kostiuk, supra,* n. 76. The Supreme Court of Canada refused leave to appeal: [2000] 1 S.C.R. 7.

82. *Bangoura* v. *Washington Post* (2004), 235 D.L.R. (4th) 564. Although enforcement of an Ontario judgment might be a problem, Pitt J. pointed out that a defamation action is often more about character vindication than about money. See also *Burke* v. *NYP Holdings Inc.* (2005), 48 B.C.L.R. (4th) 363 (BC S.C.).

83. *Bangoura* v. *Washington Post* (2005), 258 D.L.R. (4th) 341; the Supreme Court of Canada refused leave to appeal.

84. OECD guidelines for regulation of multinational corporations are available online at www.oecd.org/department/ 0,3355,en_2649_34889_1_1_1_1_1,00.html.

85. See Chapter 33; the United Nations created UNCITRAL to harmonize international trade law around the world.

Use of Electronic Communication in International Contracts addresses contract formation and jurisdiction issues, and as has been noted, WIPO has multiple treaties addressing intellectual property. Governments may choose to adopt these international standards completely, partially, or not at all. Therefore, we are still a long way from international harmony in the regulation of e-commerce.

QUESTIONS FOR REVIEW

1. What contracts are normally involved in establishing a business website?

2. What is a web-wrap agreement?

3. How has legislation addressed the formation of contracts made over the Internet?

4. Why is it important to ascertain which legal system governs a contract?

5. How are consumers protected in online transactions?

6. What is e-cash?

7. How is it possible for a domain name to infringe some other person's trademark?

8. What is cybersquatting?

9. What is the level-of-interactivity test?

10. What factors influence jurisdiction over an Internet libel case?

11. How does Canada protect an individual's privacy in e-commerce transactions?

12. Why are non-governmental organizations important to e-commerce?

13. In what ways does the Internet facilitate illegal activities?

14. What proposals are being made to reform the Copyright Act?

CASES AND PROBLEMS

1. On Saturday at 10:00 p.m., Jane (a resident of Manitoba) ordered a computer online from SMART Computers for $49 plus tax and delivery charges. Jane entered her credit card information and her e-mail address, and clicked "BUY NOW." At 10:04 p.m. she received an e-mail confirmation of her purchase showing a credit card charge of $75. Jane placed the order after she was told by a friend that the SMART website mistakenly priced the computer at $49 instead of $449. Although SMART blocked the order page when it discovered the error on Friday, Jane successfully bypassed the block and also the webpages disclosing the terms and conditions of the sale. The order page indicated that the purchase was subject to terms and conditions but there was no hyperlink to the terms. SMART refused to supply the computer, indicating that the computer was not available for $49. Jane started a breach of contract action in Manitoba. The terms and conditions stated that supply of the computer was subject to availability and that all disputes must be settled in the courts of Michigan in the United States.

    Consider the principles of offer, acceptance, consideration, and intention, and determine if there is a valid contract. If so, do the terms and conditions form part of the sale contract? What information will be important in order to determine the status of the contract and the terms and conditions?

2. Altanet Inc. is incorporated in Alberta, and carries on the business of providing Internet access and related services to its clients. In March 2007, it registered the domain name altanet.ca. One of its employees, O'Connor, had developed a new technique for designing webpages for clients. He tried to persuade Altanet's management to adopt the technique, and, when they decided not to, he resigned from the corporation and decided to go into business on his own. In May 2007, he established a corporation, Rocky Netservices Inc., and registered the domain name alta.net.

When Altanet's managers discovered the existence of the Rocky website, they wrote to O'Connor, alleging that he was attempting to pass his business off as that of Altanet in order to lure its clients away, and they demanded that he cease to use the alta.net domain name. O'Connor replied that the two domain names were different and equally legitimate, that no similarity existed between the names of the two corporations, and that Altanet had no cause to complain about his using the new webpage technique since it had declined to adopt it when given the opportunity.

How should the issue be resolved?

3. Dan's Discs Inc., a corporation incorporated in Ontario, operates a number of retail record stores in Ontario, as well as a Canada-wide CD mail-order business. It has registered, in Canada, the trademark "Dan's Discs." In October 2008, it established an Internet site, dansdiscs.com, and since then has been soliciting and accepting orders for CDs through its Internet site.

It recently discovered the existence of another website, dansCDs.com, established by a corporation also called "Dan's Discs Inc.," which was incorporated in December 2008 under the laws of the state of Delaware, but which operates out of an office in Buffalo, N.Y. That website advertises:

Canadian clients—we guarantee to ship you your favorite disks at prices lower than any Canadian supplier.

The Canadian "Dan's Discs" considers that the actions of the Delaware firm constitute a blatant and deliberate attempt to steal its customers and, further, that the Canadian company has the sole right to the trademark "Dan's Discs." It has obtained evidence that the Delaware firm has already shipped more than 20 000 CDs to addresses in Canada. Its investigations have also revealed that another corporation, also called Dan's Discs Inc., was incorporated twenty years ago in New Mexico, and operates a small retail store there. It has no website and has never done business in Canada. Nevertheless, the Canadian firm fears that the New Mexico corporation could be taken over by some unscrupulous person who might then use it to compete against them.

Does the Canadian firm have any legal remedy against either of the U.S. corporations? In which jurisdiction should it attempt to seek a remedy?

4. Green is a biologist and an environmental activist. He has recently become extremely concerned about the use of a poultry-feed additive, which he describes as "recycled chicken poop," being marketed by a multinational corporation, Hollyhill Inc. He claims that it causes genetic defects in poultry and may cause cancer in humans. When he went public with his claims, Hollyhill categorically denied them and posted on its Internet site a lengthy report commissioned from an independent scientific foundation, purporting to find that the product was entirely safe.

In turn, Green reproduced the complete report on his own website, but this time interspersed with his own comments and those of several like-minded colleagues. The comments point out alleged weaknesses in the report and, in some places, pour scorn on the authors of the report.

Hollyhill have now written to Green, demanding that he remove the report and comments from his website, claiming that his actions amount to an infringement of their copyright.

Advise Green.

5. Midas Prospecting Inc. is a corporation incorporated in British Columbia that is engaged in mineral exploration. Goldfinger, its CEO, lives in Vancouver.

From time to time Goldfinger likes to search the Internet for references to his company. One day, using his favourite search engine, "Gargle," he discovers a story written by Sleaze, a university professor from New Zealand, and published on the website of a little-known Australian journal that deals with environmental issues. The story, entitled "The Poisoners of Paraguay," alleged that Midas had discharged tons of cyanide into a river in Paraguay and that Goldfinger had managed to suppress the news by bribing that country's Minister of the Environment. Although there is evidence that some such event may have taken place, the story was clearly incorrect since neither Midas nor any other corporation with which it is associated has ever carried on operations in Paraguay.

The journal offered to publish a full retraction, and the offer was accepted by Goldfinger. Sleaze, however, insists that his story is substantially true and refuses to apologize.

Midas and Goldfinger have commenced an action for defamation in British Columbia against Sleaze, and against Gargle (which is based in California), which they claim has published the libel by providing the link to the story.

Consider (a) whether the B.C. court has jurisdiction to try the action and (b) whether the claim against Gargle has any validity.

ADDITIONAL RESOURCES FOR CHAPTER 34 ON THE COMPANION WEBSITE *(www.pearsoned.ca/smyth)*

In addition to self-test multiple-choice, true–false, and short essay questions (all with immediate feedback), application exercises, and links to useful web destinations, the Companion Website provides the following resources for Chapter 34:

- **British Columbia**: Electronic Transactions
- **Alberta**: Electronic Transactions
- **Manitoba/Saskatchewan:** Consumer Protection Act; Electronic Transactions; Internet Agreement Legislation
- **Ontario:** Amending Electronic Contracts; Consumer Protection Legislation; E-Commerce Legislation; Privacy Legislation

35

Privacy

In this age of technological advancement, individual privacy is more and more difficult to protect. Privacy law is evolving to meet the new challenges and now regulates everyday business activities. A maze of overlapping federal and provincial privacy legislation imposes civil, regulatory, and even criminal liability to protect the privacy of individuals. In this chapter we examine such questions as:

- What aspects of a person's life are considered private?

- Is privacy a human right?

- What level of privacy should individuals expect?

- What provincial and federal regulatory regimes exist to supervise public-sector activities?

- What legislation governs private-sector personal information management?

- What laws govern privacy in the workplace?

- What concerns exist for personal information that is transferred to another country?

- How has tort law responded to invasion of privacy?

- How does criminal law address privacy issues?

- What risk-management strategies should a business employ?

PRIVACY

What Is Privacy?

Early legal scholars described privacy as "the right to be left alone" and considered it essential to a person's "autonomy, liberty, and integrity."[1] Modern **privacy** has three key dimensions: personal privacy, territorial or spatial privacy, and privacy of personal information.[2] **Personal privacy** involves issues of bodily integrity such as surveillance, search, and seizure. **Territorial privacy** covers the protection of one's home, business, and other personal spaces. **Privacy of personal information** involves protection of the trail of information left behind as we go about our daily lives. Protection of personal information is necessary because it can be used to identify us or reveal our personal habits, opinions, behaviours, beliefs, or characteristics.

Participation in normal society means complete privacy is impossible. Privacy law and, to some extent, individuals themselves, determine how much privacy citizens will sacrifice. For example, how much private information is revealed on a personal website is entirely the individual's choice. Some people post pictures and blog about personal relationships while others would never dream of such disclosure. On the other hand, residents are required by law to file a tax return containing very personal information. The law of privacy involves balancing the needs of society with the individual's right to privacy.

Privacy as a Human Right

Government must respect people's privacy. In 1984, the Supreme Court of Canada declared that the right to privacy was a fundamental human right protected by section 8 of the Charter of Rights and Freedoms.[3] It held that the right to privacy was not absolute; individuals were only entitled to as much privacy as would be reasonable to expect in the circumstance. This standard of protection, commonly referred to as the **reasonable expectation of privacy**, requires a subjective and objective assessment of privacy expectations in each situation.

Section 7 of the Charter, dealing with life, liberty, and security of person, has also been interpreted as establishing constitutional authority for a right to privacy: "privacy is at the heart of liberty."[4] The combined effect of sections 7 and 8 is to limit the government's ability to interfere with an individual's privacy rights. Government invasion of privacy is acceptable only when no reasonable expectation of privacy exists, or despite the reasonable expectation, the invasion itself is reasonable and the principles of **natural justice** are respected. As we shall discuss later in this chapter, the federal government and most provinces have enacted privacy legislation to protect individual privacy during public-sector activities.

There is also federal and provincial human rights legislation that prohibits private sector discrimination and harassment based on race, gender, religion, age, marital status, sexual orientation, ethnic origin, and disability.[5] Although privacy issues are not specifically addressed in the human

privacy
has three key dimensions: personal privacy, territorial or spatial privacy, and privacy of personal information

personal privacy
the respect of bodily integrity free from unreasonable surveillance, search, and seizure

territorial privacy
lack of intrusion in one's home, business, and other personal spaces

privacy of personal information the protection of the trail of information left behind as we go about our daily lives

reasonable expectation of privacy
the subjective and objective assessment of reasonable privacy expectations in a given situation

natural justice
procedural fairness or due process

---

1. Alysia Davies, "Invading the Mind: The Right to Privacy and the Definition of Terrorism in Canada" (2006), 3(1) *U. Ottawa Law & Tech. J.* 249 at 261.

2. The three aspects of privacy were first discussed in *R* v. *Dyment*, [1988] 2 S.C.R. 417 and most recently in *R.* v. *Tessling*, [2004] 3 S.C.R. 432. The Federal Court of Appeal described privacy as connoting "concepts of intimacy, identity, dignity and integrity of the individual": *Canada (Information Commissioner)* v. *Canada (Transportation Accident Investigation & Safety Board)*, 2006 FCA 157 (C.A.).

3. *Hunter* v. *Southam Inc.*, [1984] 2 S.C.R. 145; section 8 of the Charter protects against unreasonable search and seizure.

4. *Supra* n. 2, *Dyment* at 427–428. See also, *R.* v. *O'Connor*, [1995] 4 S.C.R. 411 and *R.* v. *Beare*, [1988] 2 S.C.R. 387.

5. Canadian Human Rights Act, R.S. 1985, c. H-6; Alberta Human Rights, Citizenship and Multiculturalism Act, R.S.A. 1980, c. H-14; British Columbia Human Rights Code, R.S.B.C. 1996, c. 210; Manitoba Human Rights Code, C.C.S.M., c. H-175; New Brunswick Human Rights Act, R.S.N.B. 1973, c. H-11; Nova Scotia Human Rights Act, R.S.N.S. 1989, c. 214 as am.; Ontario Human Rights Code, R.S.O. 1990, c. H-19; Human Rights Act, R.S.P.E.I. 1988, c. H-12; Saskatchewan Human Rights Code, S.S. 1979, c. S-24.1 as am.; Human Rights Code, R.S.N.L. 1990, c. H-14.

rights legislation, the collection or use of personal information relating to a prohibited ground may lead to discriminatory or harassing behaviour.[6] As a result, human rights and privacy complaints often arise out of the same circumstances.

Privacy and Technology

data shadows
electronic records of the Internet activity of a user

biometrics
technological analysis of physical characteristics, such as fingerprints

Technological advancements such as computers, the Internet, **data shadows**, digital cameras, **biometrics**, and digital storage devices are the newest and greatest threats to privacy. The technological ability to collect, store, transmit, and alter personal information has transformed privacy risks. Also expanded is the ability to track movements, surveil subjects, and reveal findings to an expansive audience. Personal information may be used for obviously criminal purposes, such as identity theft, or more subtle activities, such as targeted marketing or employment decisions. As early commentary colourfully describes: "The electronic computer is to privacy what the machine gun was to the horse cavalry."[7]

In addition to making violation of privacy interests much easier, technology has made protection of privacy rights much more difficult. Data flows freely across geographic borders. The creator, host, and user of a website could all be in different jurisdictions. Canadian laws protecting electronic personal information may be impossible to enforce when the website, its server, and creator are located in another country.

CASE 35.1

Ms. Lawson discovered that her personal information was being used by Accusearch Inc., an American company in the business of selling background checks and other tracing services. This use was without her consent, and she believed it violated the federal Personal Information Protection and Electronic Documents Act (PIPEDA).[8] She filed a complaint with the Privacy Commissioner, who declined to investigate stating that she lacked jurisdiction to investigate an American company. In reviewing this decision, the Federal Court held that the Privacy Commissioner was wrong; she did have jurisdiction to investigate. The complainant was Canadian, the source of the information was Canadian, the request for the background check originated in Canada, and the website displayed a Canadian presence with a ".ca" domain name. The court acknowledged that the non-resident status of the operator of the website might frustrate the success of the investigation, but that it should not be confused with a lack of jurisdiction.[9]

Privacy and Business

Governments are not the only institutions dealing with privacy-related issues. Businesses constantly collect, use, store, and transfer personal information about their employees, customers, consumers, suppliers, and competitors. Technology has enhanced an employer's ability to monitor employee conduct and customer behaviour through video surveillance, e-mail and telephone monitoring, and key-card access systems. All of this means that privacy is also a private-sector concern. The Personal Information Protection and Electronic Documents Act (PIPEDA) is the primary piece of federal legislation regulating privacy issues in the private sector. Common law and criminal laws also expose businesses to liability for invasion of privacy.

---

6. The Canadian Human Rights Act did initially made reference to the need for privacy of personal information, but this provision was repealed in 1983.

7. Allan W. Scheflin and Edward M. Opton, Jr., *The Mind Manipulators: A Non-fiction Account* (London: Paddington Press, 1978), as reported by McIsaac, Shields, and Klein, *The Law of Privacy in Canada*, (Toronto: Thomson Carswell, 2007) at 1–4.2. See also: "RFID and Privacy: Tracking Your Patterns?" *CBC News Online*, May 31, 2006, www.cbc.ca/news/background/privacy/.

8. S.C. 2000, c. 5, as amended.

9. *Lawson* v. *Accusearch Inc.* 2007 FC 125 (F.C.); The Court agreed that PIPEDA did not have extraterritorial effect.

INTERNATIONAL ISSUE

Outsourcing and Transborder Data Flow

In the global business environment, outsourcing specialized operational tasks has become a common practice. When outsourcing involves the transfer of personal information, issues of security and privacy are raised. Customers may consent to the collection of personal data without realizing that their information could be shared with another company located halfway around the world and subject to different disclosure and protection rules. In recognition of international privacy concerns, the Organization for Economic Cooperation and Development created guidelines to enhance privacy protection during transborder data exchanges. Guideline 10 suggests that personal data should not be used or disclosed without the consent of the owner or authority of law.

Canadian outsourcing to the United States has become even more controversial since the enactment of the USA PATRIOT Act.[10] This legislation allows U.S. law-enforcement officials to obtain personal records or information from any source in the country without the data owner knowing. As a result, there have been several Canadian challenges of personal data outsourcing to the United States. In *B.C.G.E.U.* v. *British Columbia (Minister of Health)*, union members argued that the Ministry of Health was violating patients' rights to privacy under s. 7 of the Charter by outsourcing physician billing data that contained personal patient information to a private U.S. company.[11] The B.C. Supreme Court disagreed, holding that the contractual arrangement authorized under the Canada Health Act ensured that a reasonable expectation of privacy was protected. British Columbia now restricts public sector transborder outsourcing.[12]

The Privacy Commissioner rejected a similar complaint against the Canadian Imperial Bank of Commerce.[13] The bank outsourced the processing of credit card transactions to an American company. The specific confidentiality and security provisions contained in the outsourcing agreement were approved by the Office of the Superintendent of Financial Institutions and this satisfied the Commissioner. Both decisions turned on the specific terms of the outsourcing agreement and prior regulatory approval of the terms.

When considering sending sensitive information across the border and outsourcing to American firms, businesses should

- undertake a security analysis of the American company prior to contracting,
- inform the affected customer/data owner,
- include specific confidentiality, security, and reporting provisions in the outsourcing agreement,
- seek regulatory approval of the agreement, if available, and
- regularly audit the privacy practices of the outsource company.

continued

10. Uniting and Strengthening America by Providing Appropriate Tools Required to Intercept and Obstruct Terrorism (USA PATRIOT) Act of 2001.

11. *B.C.G.E.U.* v. *British Columbia (Minister of Health Services)* 2005 BCSC 466 (S.C.)

12. British Columbia Freedom of Information and Protection of Privacy Act (FOIPPA), R.S.B.C. 1996, c. 165, s. 30.1 makes it an offence to store, access, or disclose personal information outside Canada. Alberta is considering the issue: Office of the Information and Privacy Commissioner, Alberta, *Public-sector Outsourcing and Risks to Privacy* (February 2006), www.cr-international.com/2006_Canada_Alberta_Public-Sector_Outsourcing_and_Risks_to_Privacy_February.pdf.

13. Office of the Privacy Commissioner, PIPEDA Case Summary # 313, October 19, 2005, available online at www.privcom.gc.ca/cf-dc/2005/313_20051019_e.asp.

QUESTIONS TO CONSIDER

1. If Canadian data is at greater risk of disclosure when transferred to the United States, why not ban outsourcing to the United States?

2. Are there certain types of information that should remain within Canadian borders?

Sources: Donna L. Davis, "Case Comment: Tracking Cross-border Data Flows: A Comment on *Lawson* v. *Accusearch Inc.*," 6(2) *Canadian Journal of Law and Technology*; OECD Guidelines on the Protection of Privacy and Transborder Flows of Personal Data, available online at www.oecd.org/document/18/ 0,3343,fr_2649_34255_1815186_1_1_1_1,00.html; "Frequently Asked Questions: USA PATRIOT Act Comprehensive Assessment Results," *Treasury Board of Canada Secretariat*, March 28, 2006, www.tbs-sct.gc.ca/ pubs_pol/gospubs/TBM_128/usapa/faq_e.asp; "Explanatory Notes for the Privacy Protection Checklist," *Treasury Board of Canada Secretariat*, October 24, 2006, www.tbs-sct.gc.ca/pubs_pol/gospubs/TBM_128/gd-do/ notes_e.asp.

GOVERNMENT REGULATION OF PRIVACY

Privacy is the subject of a maze of regulation. There are federal and provincial statutes. There is legislation of broad application that sets general standards applicable to most public and private activities. Other legislation targets specific conduct such as telemarketing. Some statutes focus on particular industries such as health care or credit reporting. It is not the goal of this chapter to provide an exhaustive review of all privacy legislation. Instead, we focus on the statutes of general application with some examples of legislation targeting specific conduct and industries.

Regulation of Privacy in the Public Sector

In the public sector, privacy is protected by both federal and provincial legislative regimes. The federal legislation governs the conduct of the federal government, its agencies, and public institutions. Similarly, provincial legislation regulates the provincial government, agencies, and public institutions.

government institutions
government departments and agencies listed in Schedule 1 of the Privacy Act

As we have already noted, the Charter of Rights and Freedoms establishes constitutional protection of privacy and it, along with the Criminal Code, protects privacy during law-enforcement activities of government.

The collection, use, and disclosure of personal information by federal **government institutions** are regulated by the Privacy Act.[14] The definition of personal information covers recorded information about an identified individual. The Act also includes a non-exhaustive list of examples such as information about a person's educational, financial, medical, criminal, or employment history, and the personal opinions *about* the individual expressed by *another* person (s. 3).

purpose of collection
a need for collecting personal information that must be related directly to an operating program or activity of the institution

consent
approval of the person to whom the collected information relates

The **purpose of collection** must relate *directly* to an operating program or activity of the institution (s. 4), and information should be obtained directly from the individual (s. 5(1)) after disclosure of the purpose (s. 5(2)). An institution need not comply with section 5 if to do so might compromise the purpose of collection or the accuracy of the information (s. 5(3)). **Consent** of the individual is only required in order to use the information for a purpose other than the one for which it was collected (s. 7).

---

14. R.S.C. 1985, c. P-21.

The Privacy Act controls the disclosure of recorded personal information under its control (i.e., under its administrative management). Society expects government to be open and transparent, so institutions have broad power to disclose information without the consent of the individual, (s. 8) including:

- for the purpose it was collected,
- for any purpose in accordance with a statute,
- in compliance with a subpoena or court order,
- in legal proceedings involving the government,
- to a regulatory investigative body,
- for research or statistical purposes,
- when the head of the institution believes that disclosure is in the public interest and *clearly outweighs* the invasion of privacy.

In the last case above, notice of disclosure must be given to the Privacy Commissioner who may notify the individual affected (s. 8(5)).[15]

Individuals are entitled to access information about themselves in the possession of government and have inaccuracies corrected (s. 12). The institution must **retain** personal information for at least two years after its last use so that the individual has time to access it (s. 6).[16] However, the right of access is complicated in the public sector, given the overriding responsibilities associated with law enforcement, national security, and public confidence. Therefore, there are a number of exceptions to the right of access to personal information. Access may be refused if the information is:

retain (retention)
keep information available for subsequent access by the individual

- contained in designated exempt data banks (s. 18),
- obtained in confidence from another government (domestic or international) (s. 19),
- injurious to federal–provincial relations (s. 20),
- injurious to international affairs (s. 21),
- prepared for or injurious to law enforcement or policing (s. 22),
- obtained by the Privacy Commissioner (s. 22.1),
- obtained as part of the Public Servants Disclosure Protection Act (s. 22.2),
- about someone other than the individual (s. 26),
- a threat to safety (s. 25),
- subject to solicitor–client privilege, or
- medical in nature and access would not be in best interests of the individual (s. 28).

Compliance with the requirements of the Privacy Act is monitored by the Privacy Commissioner, who has the power to investigate and initiate complaints; compel written, oral, or documentary evidence; and assess whether or not the complaint is well founded. After completion of a private investigation, a report of the findings, together with any corrective recommendations, is given to the head of the government institution under review and the complainant. Reports relating to a denial of access to personal information are reviewable by the Federal Court (s. 41).

---

15. Public access to government records may be requested under the Access to Information Act, R.S. 1985, c. A-1. This statute allows the head of an institution to refuse public access to any record of personal information (s. 19). In a recent Supreme Court of Canada Case, the privacy of personal information was given priority over the right of access: *H. J. Heinz Co. of Canada Ltd.* v. *Canada (Attorney General)*, [2006] 1 S.C.R. 441.

16. Privacy Regulations, SOR/83-500, s. 4.

ETHICAL ISSUE

Government Transparency and Accountability

The Office of the Privacy Commissioner of Canada has identified a number of deficiencies in the current Privacy Act that reduce the transparency and accountability of the federal government. The following items are some of the changes that are recommended for immediate adoption:

- require an institution to meet a necessity or "needs" test before collecting personal information;
- expand the review powers of the Federal Court to include all privacy complaints, not just those involving a denial of access;
- give the Federal Court the power to award damages against offending institutions;
- allow the Privacy Commissioner to make public the reports of the privacy practices of government institutions; and
- strengthen the provisions governing the disclosure of personal information by the Canadian government to foreign states.[17]

The importance of the last recommendation is highlighted by the findings of Justice O'Connor during the Commission of Inquiry into the Actions of Canadian Officials in Relation to Maher Arar.[18] He found that it was very likely that American authorities detained and deported Mr. Arar to Syria (where he was subsequently tortured) because of inaccurate information supplied to them by the RCMP.

QUESTIONS TO CONSIDER

1. Under what circumstances should the Canadian government release personal information to a foreign government?

2. How do these recommendations enhance transparency and accountability?

3. Why are transparency and accountability important in government?

Sources: Office of the Privacy Commissioner of Canada, *Government Accountability for Personal Information: Reforming the* Privacy Act, June 5, 2006, www.privcom.gc.ca/information/pub/pa_reform_060605_e.asp; Office of the Privacy Commissioner of Canada, *Addendum to Government Accountability for Personal Information: Reforming the* Privacy Act, April 17, 2008, www.privcom.gc.ca/information/pub/pa_ref_add_080417_e.asp.

CHECKLIST   Privacy Act

Government institutions dealing with personal information should:

- only collect information that directly relates to the operation of a government program or activity,
- collect information directly from the individual,
- keep information secure and up to date,

continued

---

17. Office of the Privacy Commissioner of Canada, "*Privacy Act* Reform: 10 Quick Fixes," May 16, 2008, www.privcom.gc.ca/legislation/pa/pa_reform_e.asp.

18. Commission of Inquiry into the Actions of Canadian Officials in Relation to Maher Arar (Arar Commission): Report of Events Relating to Maher Arar, (Ottawa: Canadian Government Publishing, 2006).

- use or disclose information only for purpose it was collected (some exceptions),
- obtain consent for any other use,
- allow access to information by individual (broad exceptions), and
- respond to complaints of individuals and recommendations of Privacy Commissioner.

Provincial Variation

All of the provinces have enacted legislation that deals with public-sector handling of personal information and access to information held by provincial agencies. Most provinces combine these topics into one "Freedom of Information and Protection of Privacy" (FIPPA) statute.[19] Some provinces designate a provincial information and privacy commissioner (B.C., Alta., Ont.), while others leave supervision in the hands of the provincial ombudsman (Man., N.B.). It is beyond the scope of this chapter to review the specific variations among provinces, but some important distinctions from the federal legislation are as follows:

- British Columbia and Alberta: The Privacy Commissioner can make binding orders and comment on the privacy implications of proposed legislation.
- Ontario and Saskatchewan: Separate legislation covers municipal governments.
- Ontario: The provincial Crown can be held liable for damages arising from negligent disclosure of a record.

In addition, some provincial public sectors are regulated by specialized legislation.

Municipalities

As noted above, Saskatchewan and Ontario have enacted separate privacy legislation covering municipal governments, boards, and agencies.[20] The form and substance of the municipal statutes mirror the FIPPA protection and access standards. Supervision of compliance is also managed by the provincial privacy commissioners.

The Saskatchewan Local Authority Freedom of Information and Protection of Privacy Act applies to boards of education, universities, colleges, and hospitals. The right of access under this Act has priority over confidentiality provisions. In Ontario, universities, colleges, boards of education, and hospitals fall under the provincial, not municipal, legislation.

Health Care

Health Care is an area of provincial jurisdiction involving both public-sector and private-sector stakeholders. For example, most hospitals are government institutions (already covered by FIPPA), while pharmacies and medical labs would be considered private-sector commercial activities (subject to private-sector legislation, as will be discussed later). Some (but not all) hospice,

19. British Columbia Freedom of Information and Protection of Privacy Act, *supra* n. 12; Alberta Freedom of Information and Protection of Privacy Act, R.S.A. 2000, c. F-25; Saskatchewan Freedom of Information and Protection of Privacy Act, S.S. 1990–91, c. F-22.01; Manitoba Freedom of Information and Protection of Privacy Act, S.M. 1997, c. 50; Ontario Freedom of Information and Protection of Privacy Act, R.S.O. 1990, c. F.31; Nova Scotia Freedom of Information and Protection of Privacy Act, S.N.S. 1993, c. 5; Newfoundland Access to Information and Protection of Privacy Act, S.N.L. 2002, c. A-1.1; Prince Edward Island Freedom of Information and Protection of Privacy Act, R.S.P.E.I. 1988, c. F-15.01. One exception is New Brunswick, which has two separate statutes: Protection of Personal Information Act, S.N.B. 1998, c. P-19.1, and the Right to Information Act, S.N.B. 1978, c. R-10.3.
20. Saskatchewan Local Authority Freedom of Information and Protection of Privacy Act, S.S. 1990-91, c. L-27.1; Municipal Freedom of Information and Protection of Privacy Act, R.S.O. 1990, c. M.56.

personal health information
information relating to the physical or mental health of an identifiable individual that is used or obtained primarily for the purpose of providing health care

PHIPA
Personal Health Information Protection Act (in Alberta and Saskatchewan, simply HIPA)

counselling, and support services are private-sector, not-for-profit organizations. All have access to very sensitive **personal health information** about individuals. Therefore, specific provincial legislation focusing on health care providers and custodians of health information is evolving to address the highly sensitive nature of this information. So far, Alberta, Manitoba, Saskatchewan, and Ontario have adopted legislation specifically addressing the protection of health information across all sectors of the health care industry (**PHIPA**).[21] Non-compliance with personal health legislation can result in fines ranging from $50 000 in Manitoba to $500 000 for corporations in Saskatchewan. Organizations continue to be subject to general privacy legislation for non-health personal information such as financial or employment records. Classifying the type of information can be difficult.

CASE 35.2

An Ontario Divisional Court was asked to review the release of a nurse's occupational health records by the employer hospital. The records were released to the College of Nurses without her consent and used in an investigation of the nurse. The hospital identified the primary purpose of the record as employment. The court characterized the records as personal health information entitled to the protection of PHIPA. However, a PHIPA exception exists for release of information to a regulatory body.[22]

In addition, many of the individuals participating in the health care sector are licensed professionals bound by provincial legislation and professional codes of ethics requiring confidentiality. Doctors, nurses, and pharmacists are just a few examples. Breach of confidentiality by these professionals triggers investigation and discipline by the professional licencing body.

Naturally, both the legislation and professional standards make exceptions for non-consensual collection, use, and disclosure of personal health information when it is necessary for the effective delivery of health services or public safety. Individuals must be notified of disclosure.

Education

Education is also an area of provincial jurisdiction that involves public- and private-sector participants. Privacy issues in this sector are regulated by multiple statutes:

- Public schools (elementary and secondary), boards, universities, and colleges are covered by the provincial Freedom of Information and Protection of Privacy Act(s) (FIPPA)
- Private schools (as private-sector commercial activities) are covered by PIPEDA
- In Manitoba, school boards, universities, and colleges are subject to the Personal Health Information Act[23]
- Both public and private schools (and boards) are subject to provincial Education Act(s) that regulate the use and disclosure of pupil records[24]

---

21. Personal Health Information Act, S.M. 1997, c. 51; Health Information Act, R.S.A. 2000, c. H-5; Health Information Protection Act, S.S. 1999, c. H-0.021; Personal Health Information Protection Act, S.O. 2004, c. 3. In other provinces, the privacy of health information is addressed through the standard federal and provincial public- or private-sector privacy statutes.

22. *Hooper* v. *College of Nurses of Ontario*, 2006 CanLII 22656 (ON S.C.D.C.).

23. *Supra* n. 21, s.1.1

24. For example, s. 266 the Ontario Education Act.

ETHICAL ISSUE

Privacy versus Security: The Virginia Tech Shooting

Seung Hui Cho, a student at Virginia Polytechnic Institute (Virginia Tech), walked into the West-Amber Johnston Hall co-ed residence at 7:15 a.m. on April 16, 2007 and started shooting. Police were called to the scene and proceeded with their investigation on the assumption that it was a domestic incident. Two hours later, after returning to his apartment to re-arm, Cho entered the Norris Hall Engineering building, chained the doors shut, and continued his shooting spree. When it was all over, 33 people, including Cho, were dead and 23 others were injured.

Obviously, the primary responsibility for the shootings lies with Cho, but victims' families are questioning the conduct of the school administrators. A subsequent investigation revealed that Cho was a deeply disturbed young man who struggled with mental illness his whole life. Problems surfaced in elementary and high school; school administrators became involved and Cho received treatment that seemed to help. However, this medical history was not passed on to Virginia Tech when Cho enrolled in post-secondary education. Cho purchased his guns legally from a registered fire arms dealer who was also unaware of Cho's mental condition. At Virginia Tech, some students and faculty expressed concern about Cho's violent writings but no action was taken.

QUESTIONS TO CONSIDER

1. Who is served by keeping medical information private?

2. Does keeping medical information secret further stigmatize the illness or does it prevent discrimination?

3. When should society's needs override individual privacy rights?

Sources: Marc Fisher, "Did Privacy Laws Play a Part in the Virginia Tech Massacre?" *Kitchener Record*, September 5, 2007, available online at http://news.therecord.com/article/237586.

Regulation of Privacy in the Private Sector

Private-sector privacy is a matter of both federal and provincial legislative jurisdiction. Federal jurisdiction stems from the general power over trade and commerce and the interprovincial and international nature of data flow, as well as major privacy concerns in key federally controlled industries such as banking and telecommunications.[25] Provincial authority to regulate privacy stems from the property and civil rights power. Therefore, in addition to federal legislation, some provinces have enacted their own comprehensive private-sector privacy legislation.

PIPEDA

As noted above, the Personal Information Protection and Electronic Documents Act (PIPEDA) is the comprehensive private-sector federal legislation controlling the collection, **use**, and **disclosure** of

use
(of personal information) any access, change, or destruction of data within the organization

disclosure
(of personal information) transfer of data to third parties outside the organization

---

25. The federal power over trade and commerce was defined by five questions: *General Motors of Canada Ltd.* v. *City National Leasing* (1989), 58 D.L.R. (4th) 255 (S.C.C.). Section 7 of the Telecommunications Act empowers the CRTC to take steps to protect the privacy of persons. The Bank Act does not have special privacy provisions so banks are governed by PIPEDA.

commercial activity
any general or particular activity performed or in the objectives of an organization that has a commercial aspect

personal information during a **commercial activity** (s. 4(1)(a)).[26] It applies to all persons, corporations, individuals, organizations, associations, partnerships, and trade unions operating in Canada that are not already covered by the Privacy Act. However, if a province has adopted substantially similar legislation, businesses covered by the provincial legislation will be exempt from compliance with the federal statute. As discussed below, three provinces have taken this step.

Enforcement The federal Privacy Commissioner monitors compliance with PIPEDA. The Privacy Commission receives and investigates complaints, following which a report must be issued. The Commissioner lacks the power to make orders, but a report may be reviewed by the Federal Court and appropriate orders made. In addition, the Commissioner may undertake research, educational initiatives, and audits of an organization to determine its level of PIPEDA compliance. The Act creates offences for destruction of requested information (s. 8(8)), whistle-blower retaliation (s. 27.1), and obstruction of an investigation or audit (s. 28).

CASE 35.3

A dismissed employee requested access to her employment file and complained to the Privacy Commissioner when the employer refused to make full disclosure. The Privacy Commissioner ordered production of all documents, even those for which solicitor–client privilege was claimed; section 12 of PIPEDA gives the Commissioner power to order production in the same manner as a court. The Federal Court of Appeal overturned the production order and the Supreme Court of Canada agreed. It held that solicitor–client privilege was a fundamental part of the Canadian justice system, and section 12 does not confer a right of access to solicitor–client documents.[27]

personal information
recorded and unrecorded information about an identifiable individual, including that supplied by the individual and created by the organization

individual
natural person, not a corporation

Requirements PIPEDA covers **personal information** about an identifiable **individual** *whether recorded or not*, excluding the name, title, business address, or telephone number of an employee. Personal information includes information supplied to the organization, such as birth dates and marital status, and information created by the organization, such as employee identification numbers and performance evaluations. The legislation regulates the reasonable handling of personal information according to the following 10 guiding principles of the Canadian Standards Association Model Code:[28]

Principle 1: Accountability (Clause 4.1)

- *Policies & Procedures*—organizations shall create, implement and publicize internal policies and procedures that will assist it in complying with PIPEDA.
- *Complaints Process*—the policies must include a simple and accessible process for responding to and investigating complaints.
- *Compliance Monitor*—every organization shall identify a person to be responsible for compliance with the Act.
- *Data Transfers*—the organization is responsible for data transferred to third parties and must ensure its protection using contractual or other methods.

26. The legislation was initiated to satisfy data protection requirements of European Union (EU Data Protection Directive). The 1996 Model Code for the Protection of Personal Information developed by the Standards Council of Canada served as the model for PIPEDA.
27. *Canada (Privacy Commissioner)* v. *Blood Tribe Department of Health*, 2008 SCC 44.
28. Model Code for the Protection of Personal Information, CAN/CSA Q830-96; It is incorporated into PIPEDA as a schedule: S.C. 2000, c. 5, Schedule 1. Sections 5 (1) and (2) require mandatory compliance with all obligations in the Schedule using the word "shall;" when the word "should" is used, the Act considers the statement a recommendation.

CASE 35.4

A bank customer complained to the Privacy Commissioner when a market research firm contacted her to participate in a survey. The surveyor revealed that her information was obtained from the bank's database. The bank hired the market research firm to survey on its behalf, and the firm subcontracted the telephone calling to a third party.

The bank had a confidentiality agreement with the market research firm, but no agreement existed with the third party. The Privacy Commissioner found that the bank's confidentiality agreement "was deficient in that it made no provision for sub-contracting." The bank was in violation of the accountability principle.[29]

Principle 2: Identifying Purpose (Clause 4.2)

■ *Collection*—an organization may only collect information that is necessary for an expressly identified purpose.
■ *Communication*—the purpose of collection should be communicated to the data owner at time of collection but must be communicated before use.
■ *Reasonableness*—the purpose must be one that a reasonable person would consider appropriate in the circumstances (s. 5(3)).

CASE 35.5

In 2001, Canadian Pacific Railway installed six video surveillance cameras in the mechanical facility of its Scarborough maintenance yard, focusing on entrances and exits. The railway posted signs warning of the security system and identifying the purpose of the cameras as protection against "theft, vandalism, unauthorized personnel, and incidents related." An employee alleged that the cameras

were being used to track punctuality of employees and were a violation of PIPEDA. The Privacy Commissioner agreed that the use of the cameras was unreasonable (in contravention of s. 5(3)). The Federal Court disagreed with the Commissioner and found the use of cameras reasonable for the identified purpose.[30]

In Case 35.5, the Court applied a four-part test to determine reasonableness:

(a) Is the measure demonstrably necessary to meet a specific need?
(b) Is it likely to be effective in meeting that need?
(c) Is the loss of privacy proportional to the benefit gained?
(d) Is there a less privacy-invasive way of achieving the same end?

Principle 3: Consent (Clause 4.3)

■ *Collection, use, and disclosure* require the knowledge and consent of the data owner.
■ *Meaningful consent* requires that the organization explain the purpose of the collection, use or disclosure in understandable language prior to obtaining consent and once given, consent may be withdrawn.
■ *Exceptions* – Section 7 describes situations when collection, use or disclosure of data without knowledge or consent is acceptable.
■ *Reasonableness* (s. 5(3)) may cure a lack of consent but consent will not cure unreasonableness.

29. Office of the Privacy Commissioner of Canada, *PIPEDA Case Summary #35*, November 6, 2003, available online at www.privcom.gc.ca/cf-dc/2002/cf-dc_020110_02_e.asp.
30. *Eastmond* v. *Canadian Pacific Railway* 2004 FC 852 at para. 127.

CASE 35.6

A credit bureau collected Social Insurance Numbers not from the data owners but from the data owners' banks. The data was to be used for identification purposes. The Privacy Commissioner held that this indirect collection was acceptable if the credit bureau received contractual confirmation from the banks that they had received all necessary consents from the data owners. Reliance upon the banks' consents was reasonable in the circumstances because a large volume of data was being processed on a daily basis.[31]

opt-out consent
data-owner consent is implied from a failure to refuse consent

Consent is a very controversial issue because it can take so many forms and the requirements vary given the circumstances and sensitivity of the information. Consent may be oral or written, express or implied. In particular, the popular practice of **opt-out consent**, considered a form of implied consent, has been the subject of much scrutiny.

CASE 35.7

Air Canada intended to share Aeroplan member data with third parties for various marketing and surveying purposes, so it sent 60 000 of its 6 000 000 members a brochure describing 5 scenarios involving data sharing. Members could check a box to "opt out" of the activity. When investigating complaints arising from this form of opt-out consent, the Privacy Commissioner found that:

- It was unreasonable to imply consent after contacting only 1 percent of the membership.
- Express (not implied opt-out) consent was necessary for targeted marketing associated with the specific member's purchasing behaviour. This personal information was too sensitive for opt-out consent.
- A lack of confidentiality agreements with the third parties violated the accountability principle.

In consultation with the Privacy Commissioner's office, Air Canada redrew its information-sharing policy, which now excludes individualized member profiles, includes confidentiality agreements, and identifies an easy process for members to block the sharing of their data.[32]

Subsequent reports of the Privacy Commissioner developed four criteria to determine if opt-out consent is acceptable in a particular circumstance:

- Personal information must be non-sensitive in nature and context;
- Information sharing must clearly define the precise limits of use or disclosure;
- The identified purpose must be clear, well defined, and brought to the attention of the data owner; and
- An easy, inexpensive, and convenient process for withdrawing consent must be available and communicated to the data owner.[33]

31. Office of the Privacy Commissioner of Canada, *PIPEDA Case Summary #194*, July 16, 2003, available online at www.privcom.gc.ca/cf-dc/2003/cf-dc_030716_e.asp.
32. Office of the Privacy Commissioner of Canada, *PIPEDA Case Summary #42*, January 1, 2005, available online at www.privcom.gc.ca/cf-dc/2002/cf-dc_020320_e.asp.
33. Office of the Privacy Commissioner of Canada, *PIPEDA Case Summary #192*, July 23, 2003, available online at www.privcom.gc.ca/cf-dc/2003/cf-dc_030723_01_e.asp.

> ## CHECKLIST Summary of Section 7 Exceptions to the Need for Consent
>
> **Section 7(1): Collection of information without consent must be:**
>
> (a) in the interests of the owner and in a circumstance when consent cannot be obtained in a timely manner,
>
> (b) for the purpose of investigating a breach of law where it is reasonable to believe consent would compromise accuracy or availability,
>
> (c) for journalistic, literary, or artistic purposes,
>
> (d) of publicly available information and specified in regulations, or
>
> (e) in compliance with a legal obligation to disclose
>
> **Section 7(2): Use of information without consent must be:**
>
> (a) for the purpose of investigating a breach of law (committed or about to be committed),
>
> (b) in an emergency that threatens the life, health, or security of an individual,
>
> (c) for statistical or scholarly research or study,
>
>   (c.1) of information publicly available and specified in regulations, or
>
> (d) of information collected under s. 7 (1)(a)(b) or (c)
>
> **Section 7(3): Disclosure without consent must be:**
>
> (a) to a lawyer for the organization,
>
> (b) for the purpose of collecting a debt owed by the individual to the organization,
>
> (c) required by a subpoena, warrant, or rules of a court,
>
> (d) made to a government agency for national security or law enforcement purposes,
>
> (e) during an emergency that threatens the life, health, or security of an individual,
>
> (f) for statistical or scholarly research or study,
>
> (g) made to a historic conservationist for the above purpose,
>
> (h) made 100 years after the record was created or 20 years after the death of the data owner,
>
>   (h.1) of information publicly available and specified in regulations,
>
>   (h.2) made by an investigative body arising from an investigation of breach of law, or
>
> (i) required by law

Principle 4:   Limiting Collection (Clause 4.4)

- *Identified purpose*—only information necessary to fulfill the purpose may be collected.
- Collection must use *fair and lawful means* without deception.

Principle 5:   Limiting Use, Disclosure and Retention (Clause 4.5)

- *Use and Disclosure*—information shall be used or disclosed only for the identified purpose and with the consent of the data owner.
- *Retention*—information may be kept for only as long as is necessary for the identified purpose.
- *Destruction*—the organization shall have policies and guidelines governing the safe and secure destruction of the information.

CASE 35.8

A movie theatre chain offered accessibility equipment to assist disabled persons when viewing movies. The names, addresses, and phone numbers of people using the equipment was recorded on a sheet of paper held at the counter and was sometimes verified against personal identification. The identified purpose of the collection was to allow for follow-up with the patron if the equipment was returned damaged or not at all. The company believed this collection discouraged vandalism, damage, and theft.

An investigation by the Privacy Commissioner found that the collection was reasonable for the identified purpose; however, practices varied among specific theatres, and there were no policies with respect to safeguarding, retaining, or destroying the information. The breach of the retention and destruction requirements was remedied by implementing a policy of releasing the original record of the information to the patron when the equipment was returned in good repair.[34]

Principle 6:   Accuracy (Clause 4.6)

■ Information must be *complete*, *accurate*, and *current*.

The challenge of this principle is that organizations are not to collect more information than required for their purpose—they cannot unnecessarily update personal information. This appears to conflict with the need for accuracy and currency. One solution is to clearly display the date up to which the information is accurate.

Principle 7:   Safeguards (Clause 4.7)

■ *Security* shall be appropriate for the type of information and shall include *physical, organizational*, and *technological* measures.
■ Measures must protect against *theft, loss, unauthorized access, copying, or alteration*.
■ *Employee confidentiality* is one necessary component.

CASE 35.9

CIBC's privacy safeguards were found to be inadequate when it was discovered that loan applications containing personal information about applicants were being mistakenly faxed to unintended recipients in the United States and Quebec. Even more troubling was the fact that the misdirected faxes continued over several years (2001–2004), even after the bank was repeatedly notified by the recipients. Eventually, one of the unintended recipients

contacted the media. The interim efforts of the bank were deemed insufficient by the Privacy Commissioner because they did not involve retrieval of the customer data, confirmation of destruction, or notification of affected customers. In the wake of negative publicity and criticism from the Privacy Commissioner, CIBC banned all branch faxing across Canada pending the implementation of a new fax policy.[35]

Case 35.8 highlights an important gap in PIPEDA; it does not require an organization to notify an affected individual when a breach of privacy or security occurs. Despite calls for amendments to include breach notification, no change has been made.[36] In the CIBC case, the Commissioner recommended implementation of an immediate notification mechanism as part of an effective safeguard policy.

---

34. Office of the Privacy Commissioner of Canada, *PIPEDA Case Summary #304*, June 20, 2005, available online at www.privcom.gc.ca/cf-dc/2005/304_20050607_e.asp.

35. Office of the Privacy Commissioner of Canada, *Incident Summary #2: CIBC's Privacy Practices Failed in Case of Misdirected Faxes*, April 18, 2005, available online at www.privcom.gc.ca/incidents/2005/050418_01_e.asp.

36. Breach notification was recommended during the five-year review of PIPEDA completed in 2007, but the recommendation has yet to be acted upon.

Principle 8: Openness (Clause 4.8)

- *Availability*—information about policies and practices shall be available to the public.
- *Disclosure*—information about who has access to personal information shall be available to the public.

This principle is limited by the safeguard principle. Obviously, organizations are not required to publicize any part of their policies and practices that would compromise the effectiveness of the security.[37]

Principle 9: Access (Clause 4.9)

- *Accuracy*—a data subject shall have access to the recorded personal information and shall be able to dispute the accuracy of the record.
- *Correction*—the data subject is entitled to have the record corrected once the inaccuracy or incompleteness is established.

Despite this principle, individuals are not entitled to access information that is subject to solicitor–client privilege, doctor–patient confidentiality, or other legal proprietary interests. The safeguard principle requires that the organization confirm that the individual requesting the information is entitled to access it. Organizations are not entitled to charge the individual for access unless prior notice is given and even then, the cost should be minimal.

Principle 10: Challenging Compliance (Clause 4.10)

- *Complaints process*—each organization must have an internal process to handle complaints.

In order to satisfy the Privacy Commissioner during any subsequent investigation or audit, a record of the internal investigation process and outcome should be maintained. Modifications made to privacy policies should be documented in order to establish responsiveness to concerns of the public.

Provincial Variation

Three provinces, British Columbia, Alberta and Quebec, have passed provincial legislation acknowledged to be "substantially similar" to the federal statute.[38] Therefore, private sector protection of personal information in these provinces is governed by the provincial statutes (not PIPEDA), with two key exceptions. First, federal agencies, works, and undertakings within the province still need to comply with PIPEDA. Second, extra-provincial transfer of the personal information continues to be governed by the federal legislation.

The provincial statutes broaden privacy protection to include not-for-profit activities and expand the authority of the provincial privacy commissioners to include order-making powers. They also extend protection to employees working in businesses within provincial constitutional jurisdiction, as discussed below.

Specific Stakeholders

Employers and Employees   Privacy in the workplace involves balancing employees' reasonable expectations of privacy with the relevant business and property interests of the employer. Legislative protection varies depending upon the nature of the employment relationship. Personal information

---

37. Office of the Privacy Commissioner of Canada, *PIPEDA Case Summary #183*, July 10, 2003, available online at www.privcom.gc.ca/cf-dc/2003/cf-dc_030710_03_e.asp.

38. Personal Information Protection Act, S.B.C. 2003, c. 63; Personal Information Protection Act, S.A. 2003, c. P-6.5; Act Respecting the Protection of Personal Information in the Private Sector, R.S.Q., c. P-39.1.

covert surveillance
the employee is unaware of surveillance and has not consented to it

disclosed surveillance
the employee is given advance notice of surveillance but does not consent to it

consensual surveillance
the employee is aware of and consents to the surveillance

of public-sector employees is protected by the Privacy Act or its provincial equivalent. Private-sector employee information is protected by PIPEDA if the employment is in a business within federal jurisdiction or crosses provincial boundaries. For employees of businesses within provincial jurisdiction, only British Columbia, Alberta, and Quebec (as described above) have legislation protecting their data. In other provinces, protection must be found in the employment contract, collective agreement, or the common law.[39]

Countless privacy issues arise in the workplace. One of the most controversial is surveillance of employees by employers. It can take many forms: electronic, video, or observational tracking, and it can be **covert**, **disclosed**, or **consensual**. As Case 35.5 demonstrates, video surveillance of employees in the workplace is an extremely privacy-invasive practice and will only be considered reasonable if it meets the four criteria described in the case. Other forms of surveillance may still be too invasive, especially when surveillance is covert.

CASE 35.10

An employee filed a complaint after being terminated for cause associated with the employee's conduct during washroom visits. The complainant alleged that monitoring his washroom visits was a breach of privacy under PIPEDA.

After receiving a Health and Safety complaint about the "messy" condition of the men's washroom, the employer began secretly monitoring washroom visits. A log was kept by branch staff recording who used the washroom, when, and the condition in which it was left. Within three days, it was determined that the washroom only needed attention after visits by the complainant and the monitoring ceased. The complainant was interviewed, issued a disciplinary letter, and warned that continued conduct would result in dismissal.

The Privacy Commissioner agreed that the covert surveillance was unreasonable in the circumstances (in violation of s. 5(3)). Washrooms are places where a high expectation of privacy exists. The employer could not rely on the section 7 exceptions to the need for consent for an unreasonable invasion. The employer did not exhaust all less-invasive measures first.[40]

Case 35.10 suggests that employer surveillance practices should reflect that:

- surveillance is a last resort,
- should be undertaken only after all other methods of collecting information have been unsuccessful, and
- should be limited to the least intrusive form possible.

Monitoring of employee e-mail involves not only privacy, but also property issues. The hardware, software, and network used in the workplace are company property, and communications using an employer's network could be considered by the recipient as communications from the employer. It is unlikely that any reasonable expectation of privacy exists when using a company asset.[41] No expectation of privacy exists if the employer gives notice of the monitoring to the employee.[42] Common forms of notice include codes of conduct, privacy policies, and collective agreements.

39. *International Association of Bridge, Structural, Ornamental and Reinforcing Iron Workers and its Local 736* v. *E.S. Fox Ltd.*, 2006 CanLII 468 (ON L.R.B.) para 14, affirmed 2006 CanLII 6007; *Re: McKesson Canada and Teamsters Chemical Energy* and *Allied Workers Union, Local 424*, 136 L.A.C. (4th) 102; *Rodgers* v. *Calvert*, (2004), 49 B.L.R. (3d) 53.

40. Office of the Privacy Commissioner of Canada, *PIPEDA Case Summary #379*, May 21, 2008, available online at www.privcom.gc.ca/cf-dc/2007/379_20070404_e.asp.

41. *Camosun College* v. *CUPE*, [1999] B.C.C.A.A.A. No. 490 (an arbitrator upheld a dismissal based on the contents of an e-mail sent using the employer's system). See also, *Johnson* v. *Bell Canada*, 2008 FC 1086, where personal e-mails about an employee saved in Bell's computer system were not subject to disclosure under PIPEDA because they were not business related.

42. *Briar et al.* v. *Treasury Board* (2003), P.S.S.R.B. 3, summary available online at http://pslrb-crtfp.gc.ca/decisions/summaries/31092_e.asp (the system gave notice of monitoring at log-in). Covert monitoring will require reasonable cause. See: Alberta Office of the Information and Privacy Commissioner, *Parkland Regional Library*, Review Number 3016, June 24, 2005, available online at www.oipc.ab.ca/ims/client/upload/F2005-003.pdf.

CASE 35.11

Imperial Oil's dismissal of an employee for personal use of company e-mail was upheld. The contents of the employee's e-mails could be considered sexist and racist, and, therefore, violated the harassment policy of the employer. The employee was aware of Imperial Oil's technology-use policy, prohibiting personal use of the company's e-mail system.[43]

Consumers   Much of the focus of the private-sector legislation is on the protection of personal information, but this is not the only area of concern for consumers and potential consumers. Telemarketing has become a major intrusion on territorial privacy. Consumers are bombarded in their homes with unwanted solicitation calls disguised as market surveys and free giveaways. As a result, the federal Telecommunications Act was amended in 2005 to empower the Canadian Radio-television and Telecommunications Commission(CRTC) to establish a National Do Not Call List (DNCL).[44] Any telemarketers contacting consumers whose names are on the DNCL may be subject to fines of up to $15 000 per offending call. It is the obligation of the telemarketer to regularly check the list. Registered charities, political parties, and businesses with a pre-existing relationship with the consumer are exempt from the DNCL rules.

Other telemarketing controls implemented under the CRTC's authority to regulate telemarketers and its general responsibility for protecting privacy require that

- calls and faxes be confined to designated time periods such as 9:00 am to 9:30 p.m. on weekdays,
- a consumer's request to not be called made during a telemarketing call must be processed without further contact, and
- upon request a telemarketer must provide a toll free number that the consumer can call to speak to an employee of the telemarketer or client.[45]

Specific Businesses   Some private-sector businesses are subject to specific privacy regulation:

- Private investigators and security guards have specific privacy and confidentiality obligations.[46]
- Credit reporting agencies' disclosure of information is controlled by provincial consumer-protection legislation.[47]
- Airline and airline reservation system operators may be ordered to share passenger information with various government agencies in the interest of national security under the provisions of the Aeronautics Act.[48]

As we can see, privacy issues are heavily regulated in both the private and public sectors. Businesses should familiarize themselves with the legislation that affects their industry before they develop a privacy policy.

---

43. Bhamre Employment Insurance Claim Appeal, (September 23, 1998) CUB42012A.

44. S.C. 1993 c. 38, s. 41.1. Some provinces also regulate the conduct of telemarketers. See, for example, British Columbia Business Practices and Consumer Protection Act, Telemarketer Regulation 290/05.

45. Canadian Radio-television and Telecommunications Commission, "Fact Sheet: New and Revised Unsolicited Telecommunications Rules," available online at www.crtc.gc.ca/eng/INFO_SHT/t1022.htm.

46. See, for example, the Ontario Private Security and Investigative Services Act, O. Reg. 363/07.

47. See, for example, the British Columbia Business Practices and Consumer Protection Act, S.B.C. 2004, c.2, Part 6.

48. R.S.C. 1985, c. A-2, s. 4.81.

CHECKLIST Summary of Key Privacy Legislation

Legislation	Public Sector	Private Sector
Federal	• Charter of Rights and Freedoms • Criminal Code • Privacy Act	• Personal Information Protection and Electronic Documents Act (PIPEDA)
Provincial	• Freedom of Information and Protection of Privacy (Acts) • Municipal Freedom of Information and Protection of Privacy (Sask., Ont.) • Health Information Protection • Education (Acts) • Health Information Protection (Alta., Man., Sask., and Ont.)	• Telecommunications Act • Personal Information Protection (Acts) (B.C., Alta., Que.) • Education (Alta., Man., Sask., and Ont.)

CIVIL LIABILITY

Failure to meet privacy obligations can give rise to civil liability in both contract and tort. As already noted, security obligations and confidentiality terms are standard in outsourcing contracts. In addition, employment contracts now commonly include confidentiality agreements. Consumer-protection laws imply privacy obligations into consumer agreements. Damages arising from any failure to comply with these terms may be recovered in a breach-of-contract action. As the following sections describe, tort liability is less clear.

Tort: Invasion of Privacy

Common Law

Historically, the right to privacy has been protected through existing property-based torts such as trespass, nuisance, and defamation. For example, the Alberta Supreme Court found that harassing collection calls so invaded the privacy of the debtor that an action in private nuisance was successful.[49] Whether the common law recognizes an independent tort of invasion of privacy, separate from any property interest, is still the subject of debate.[50] In 2005, the English Court of Appeal recognized a breach of privacy as part of the law of confidentiality.[51]

---

49. *Motherwell* v. *Motherwell* (1976), 73 D.L.R. (3d) 62 (Alta. C. A.).

50. Invasion of privacy recognized in Australia: *Grosse* v. *Purvis,* [2003] QDC 151. Invasion of privacy was rejected as a stand-alone tort in *Secretary of State for the Home Department* v. *Wainwright* (2003), 4 All E.R. 969 (H.L.). The United States has recognized a common-law right of privacy covering four specific situations: (1) intrusion upon the plaintiff's solitude; (2) public disclosure of embarrassing facts; (3) publicity placing plaintiff in an false light; and (4) appropriation of plaintiff's identity. For a comparison of international privacy law, see: A. Levin and M. J. Nicholson, "Privacy Law in the United States, the EU and Canada: The Allure of the Middle Ground" (2005), 2(2) *U. Ottawa L. Tech. J.* 357.

51. England: *Douglas* v. *Hello! Ltd.,* [2005] EWCA CIV 595 (C.A.); *OK!* magazine also sued *Hello!* for breach of confidence and unlawful interference; this matter proceeded to the House of Lords where *OK!* prevailed and received damages of over £1 000 000: [2007] UKHL 21.

CASE 35.12

The unauthorized publication of six wedding pictures in *Hello!* magazine caused Michael Douglas and Catherine Zeta Jones to sue *Hello!* for breach of privacy. Prior to the wedding, both *Hello!* and *OK!* magazines approached the couple to obtain the exclusive rights to their wedding photographs. After intense negotiations, the couple selected *OK!* magazine as the exclusive publisher in exchange for $1 000 000 and picture approval. In compliance with the agreement, the private ceremony was the subject of strict security measures, and guests were prohibited from taking photographs. Still, *Hello!* obtained and published unauthorized pictures taken by a freelance photographer posing as a wedding guest or waiter. In the following days, the *Sun* and the *Daily Mail* also published the unauthorized pictures.

The Court of Appeal held that the publication was a breach of privacy and was compensable as a breach of confidentiality. *Hello!* knew that the wedding was private and the photographs were confidential. This placed *Hello!* under an obligation to keep the photographs secret. The Court accepted that the European Convention on Human Rights placed an obligation on member countries to take positive steps to protect privacy. In the absence of legislation, the Court was required to act. It awarded damages to Douglas and Zeta Jones.[52]

Although Case 34.12 falls short of declaring an independent tort of invasion of privacy, it does recognize the right to privacy protection separate from a property right or contractual interest. The law of confidentiality was extended to protect disclosure of aspects of the defendants' private lives.[53]

To date, no Canadian court has awarded compensation based solely on a common law tort of invasion of privacy, although many courts have accepted the possibility that it might exist.[54] For example, a privacy action against an Ontario employer arising from an unauthorized credit check was allowed to proceed to trial.[55]

Statutory Cause of Action

As a result of the slow progress of the common law, several provincial governments have created civil causes of action. British Columbia, Manitoba, Saskatchewan, and Newfoundland each have statutory causes of action for **wilful invasion of privacy**.[56] The legislation includes a list of considerations to be taken into account when determining liability, including the nature of the action, the effect of the action, the relationship between the parties, the conduct of the parties, and any apology. In Manitoba, these factors are used to assess damages. Some situations are exempt from liability, including those where there is consent or the invasion is lawfully authorized or part of a lawful right of defence. Some provinces exempt news-gathering activities undertaken in the public interest.

wilful invasion of privacy
a person knew or should have known that their actions would invade the privacy of another

Tort: Negligence

Protecting personal information is part of complying with privacy legislation and this involves security measures. Inadequate security may allow internal or external unauthorized access to private

---

52. The Court relied on *Campbell* v. *MGN* [2004] UKHL 22 and *Von Hanover* v. *Germany* App. No 59320, June 24, 2004. See also Gillian Black, "Douglas v. Hello! – An OK! Result" (2007), 4(2) SCRIPT-ed 161.

53. *Supra* n. 47, para. 95, 102.

54. Many defendants have unsuccessfully sought to have lawsuits claiming invasion of privacy thrown out of court without a trial on the basis that no such cause of action exists; in denying these requests, courts across the country have suggested that such a cause of action should exist.

55. *Somwar* v. *McDonald's Restaurants of Canada Limited*, [2006] O.J. No. 64 (Ont. S.C.J.). Similarly in British Columbia, the Court of Appeal allowed a breach of common law privacy rights to proceed to trial long after the statutory claim expired: *Lord* v. *McGregor* (1999), 119 B.C.C.A. 105 (C.A.). In Newfoundland, an invasion of privacy action involving repeated calls to collect an unpaid debt failed because the circumstances of the subject case did not amount to invasion of privacy: *Dawe* v. *Nova Collection Services (NFLD) Ltd.* (1998), 160 Nfld. & PEIR 266 (Nfld. Prov. Crt.). The court seemed ready to accept that a common law tort existed.

56. Privacy Act, R.S.B.C. 1996, c. 373, s. 1; Privacy Act, R.S.M. 1987, c. P125, s. 2; Privacy Act, R.S.S. 1978, c. P-24, s. 2; Privacy Act, R.S.N. 1990, c. P-22 s. 3.

information. As discussed in Chapter 3, the tort of negligence imposes liability when a duty of care is owed, the standard of care is not met, and damage is caused as a result. PIPEDA imposes a duty on businesses to protect personal information. If security measures are inadequate when compared to the reasonable efforts undertaken by other similar businesses, then liability will follow. This tort imposes liability on the custodian of the information, even when someone else actually accesses or misuses the information. In some circumstances, even breach of fiduciary duty could impose liability for improper use or disclosure of personal information.

CASE 35.13

In late 2006, TJX, the parent company of Winners and HomeSense stores, experienced one of the largest personal information security breaches in history, affecting approximately 45 million debit and credit cards (including Canadian customers). An intruder placed unauthorized software on the TJX computer system through a wireless connection based outside two stores in Florida. Using this connection, the intruder was able to access credit card information, driver's licence data, and provincial identification numbers. Upon investigation, the Privacy Commissioner found that:

- it was not reasonable for TJX to collect driver's licence data and provincial identification numbers,

- indefinite retention of the information unreasonably increased the risks to the customer, and although TJX had physical, administrative, and technical protection measures in place (locks,

swipe cards, employee training, and codes of conduct), its technical measures were below standard because

- it relied on a "weak" (wired equivalent) encryption protocol,

- the industry standard of Wi-Fi protected access was preferred in 2003 and *required* by September 2006, and

- there was inadequate monitoring of the system.

Therefore, TJX was in breach of its obligations under PIPEDA.[57] Consumer class-action lawsuits were commenced in Canada and the United States alleging negligence associated with inadequate security. Terms of settlement of the lawsuits included providing consumers with identity theft insurance and credit report monitoring.[58] Banks also sued for costs associated with issuing new credit cards.

CRIMINAL LIABILITY

Criminal liability is a common way of dealing with privacy violations resulting in identity theft. General Criminal Code offences such as fraud (s. 383) and impersonation (s. 402) are effective measures to deal with the perpetrators of identity theft. Unauthorized intruders may be charged with unauthorized use of a computer (s. 342.1), theft of telecommunications (s. 326), or mischief in relation to data (s. 430(1.1)).

Proposed amendments to the Criminal Code[59] would impose criminal liability more broadly by focusing on the custodian of the personal information and creating offences for the transfer or sale of data capable of being used for identity theft. The offence would cover situations where the transferor knows, believes, or is reckless about whether the information can be used to commit an offence. This recklessness element could potentially expose situations of inadequate security measures to criminal liability.

57. Office of the Privacy Commissioner of Canada and Office of the Information and Privacy Commissioner of Alberta, Report of an Investigation Into the Security, Collection and Retention of Personal Information: TJX Companies Inc./Winners Merchant International L.P., September 25, 2007, available online at www.privcom.gc.ca/cf-dc/2007/tjx_rep_070925_e.asp.

58. Robert Westervelt, "TJX Should Have Had Stronger Wi-Fi Encryption, Say Canadian Officials," *SearchSecurity.com*, Sept. 25, 2007, http://searchsecurity.techtarget.com/news/article/0,289142,sid14_gci1273889,00.html.

59. Reckless Handling of Data Bill C-27, An Act to Amend the Criminal Code, 39th Parliament, 2nd Session. This Bill died on the table when the fall 2008 election was called.

Part VI of the Criminal Code deals specifically with invasion of privacy through the offence of wilful interception of private communications (s. 184). Private communications may be intercepted with the consent of *either party* involved or with court authorization. What is considered a private communication is central to the offence, and this involves the concept of reasonable expectation. Most often these provisions are used in consideration of admissibility of criminal evidence and authorization of law enforcement interception. They have not been tested in the employee e-mail context.

CODES OF CONDUCT

The principles used as the basis for the federal Privacy Act were drawn from the Organization for Economic Cooperation and Development guidelines. One of the motivations behind the development of PIPEDA was the desire to meet the standards set by the European Directive on Protection of Data. Although Canada was not legally required to comply, the desire to do business with the European Union and to be perceived as a responsible government encouraged voluntary compliance.

It is this same motivation that gives credibility to voluntary codes of conduct developed by industry associations and international organizations. In order to be respected and competitive within their industries, businesses comply with standards that may be more rigorous than those required by law. The Canadian Association of Internet Providers has a Privacy Code developed around the Canadian Standards Association's model code. The Canadian Bankers Association Privacy Code governs more than 50 domestic and foreign banks operating in Canada. The Insurance Bureau of Canada has a Model Personal Information Code available for use by is 120 member companies. The Canadian Marketing Association requires members to follow their Code of 7 Privacy Principles.[60]

As discussed earlier in the Health Care section, certain professional associations govern the privacy practices of their members through professional codes of conduct or ethics. Violations trigger investigation and possible discipline by the self-regulating body. The Health Information Privacy Code of the Canadian Medical Association covers most of the physicians in Canada.

BUSINESS RISK-MANAGEMENT STRATEGIES

As this chapter demonstrates, privacy is a complicated legal issue involving a maze of provincial and federal legislation, voluntary codes of conduct, and potential civil or criminal liability. In order to develop effective and legally compliant privacy policies, a business should:

- identify a person responsible for privacy within the organization;
- become familiar with the privacy legislation, industry standards, and codes of conduct applicable to its activities;
- complete an audit of the company's activities to determine
  - what personal information is collected, used, disclosed, and retained and for what purposes,
  - what privacy risks exist, and
  - what security measures and policies are currently in place;

- assess each type of information, practice, and risk based on
  - degree of sensitivity,
  - relevance to purpose,
  - invasiveness, and
  - seriousness of potential damage;

---

60. All of the voluntary codes of conduct referred to in this section may be accessed through the Industry Canada website (Office of Consumer Affairs) at www.ic.gc.ca/epic/site/oca-bc.nsf/en/ca01364e.html.

- develop and implement privacy polices and codes of conduct that comply with the legislation, meet or exceed industry standards, and reduce the likelihood of breach;
- develop a response protocol for privacy breaches that includes incident reporting, immediate containment of the breach, preservation of evidence, and notification of the affected individuals, police, or privacy commissioner (where relevant);
- educate and train employees;
- communicate policies to relevant stakeholders: customers, suppliers, and the public; and
- regularly review and update policies and procedures.

QUESTIONS FOR REVIEW

1. What are the three key components of modern privacy?
2. What is the constitutional authority for declaring the right to privacy a human right?
3. What is the standard of protection that the Charter gives to privacy?
4. What federal legislation protects privacy in the public sector and how is compliance monitored?
5. What federal legislation protects personal information held in the private sector and what does this statute require businesses to do?
6. What test does a court apply to determine if a privacy-invasive activity is reasonable?
7. Does a common law tort of invasion of privacy exist in Canada?
8. How does inadequate security expose business to civil and possibly criminal liability?
9. What steps should be followed by a business considering outsourcing data processing to an American company?
10. How does the requirement of "consent" for collection, use, and disclosure of personal information differ in the public and private sectors?
11. What protection is available for employee personal information?

CASES AND PROBLEMS

1. KDP Limited operates a pool-servicing business in Vancouver. In the summer, KDP has 8 service vans on the road; each van has 2 employees and 12 of the employees are students. It seems that fewer and fewer service calls are being completed each day and the manager is concerned about productivity. The employees say it is the increased traffic in the city; it just takes longer to get to and from each call. It also seems that the gas expenses are rising. The cost of gas is high and the vans are on average 8 years old, so the manager is wondering whether more fuel-efficient vehicles should be leased.

Before making such a big investment, the manager decides to collect work-productivity information. He wonders if the vans are making unauthorized stops or not taking the most efficient routes to service calls. GPS units are installed in each van to track the start and stop times, speed, locations, routes taken, and mileage. The units cannot be turned off by the driver.

After secretly tracking each van for one week, it is discovered that Jim and Jeff, summer students operating van 3, are spending each afternoon at Jim's parents' backyard pool. They are dismissed. Jeff files a complaint with the Privacy Commissioner.

What should the Privacy Commissioner consider when investigating this complaint? Would your answer be different if the business is located in Winnipeg?

2. In 2005, Primtel Ltd., a wireless telephone company, decided to publish a telephone directory including all the telephone numbers of their subscribers except those numbers that were "unlisted." The directory was available to the public on the company's website. Customers were advised of the pending directory by way of an insert in the December 2004 billing. The fine print on the back of the insert advised those customers not wishing to appear in the directory to contact the company and arrange for "unlisted" status. Primtel charged an additional $2 per month fee for unlisted service.

Mary contracted with Primtel in 2002; at the time, she declined the unlisted option because of the additional fee. This was long before there was public access to her number online. She does not notice Primtel's bill insert and, after receiving several annoying phone calls from a former boyfriend, she discovers that her phone number is now available online. She complains to the Privacy Commissioner because she believes her private information has been disclosed without her consent.

What are the relevant rules relating to consent and how should the Privacy Commissioner decide this case?

3. Ticketmarketer is a company that sells tickets online for concerts, plays, and sporting events. Payment is by credit card but purchasers are asked to provide their home address, phone number, and e-mail. The company uses this information for verification of identity when tickets are picked up at the venue.

Joan is a marketing manager at Ticketmarketer and has started tracking what type of event each customer attends. She then uses the information for promotional purposes: Once repeat customers' preferences are identified, they receive advance notification of similar events by e-mail.

Is there any privacy concern about this practice? If so, how should Joan revise the plan to become privacy compliant?

ADDITIONAL RESOURCES FOR CHAPTER 35 ON THE COMPANION WEBSITE *(www.pearsoned.ca/smyth)*

In addition to self-test multiple-choice, true–false, and short essay questions (all with immediate feedback), application exercises, and links to useful web destinations, the Companion Website provides the following resources for Chapter 35:

- **British Columbia:** Personal Information Protection Act; Privacy Rights
- **Alberta:** Personal Information and Electronic Documents Act (PIPEDA); Privacy Act; Office of the Information and Privacy Commissioner of Alberta (OPIC)
- **Manitoba/Saskatchewan:** FIPPA; Personal Health Information; Privacy Act
- **Ontario:** Freedom of Information and Privacy Legislation; Personal Health Information Protection Legislation

BIBLIOGRAPHY

General References

Black, H.C. *Black's Law Dictionary*, 8th ed. (St. Paul, MN: West Publishing Co., 2004).

Denning (Lord). *The Discipline of Law* (London: Butterworth & Co., 1979).

Driedger, E.A. *The Construction of Statutes*, 2nd ed. (Toronto: Butterworth, 1983).

Jackson, R.M. *Jackson's Machinery of Justice*, 8th ed. (Cambridge: Cambridge University Press, 1989).

Posner, R.A. *Economic Analysis of Law*, 5th ed. (Toronto: Little Brown and Company, 1998).

Waddams, S.M. *Introduction to the Study of Law*, 6th ed. (Toronto: Carswell Company, 2004).

Part 1: The Law in Its Social and Business Context

Emond, D. Paul. *Commercial Dispute Resolution: Alternatives to Litigation* (Aurora: Canada Law Book, 1989).

Friedmann, W. *Law in a Changing Society*, 2nd ed. (New York: Columbia University Press, 1972).

Hart, H.L.A. *The Concept of Law*, 2nd ed. (London: Oxford University Press, 1994).

Hogg, P.W. *Constitutional Law of Canada*, student ed. (Scarborough: Thomson Carswell, 2005).

Lederman, W.R. *Continuing Canadian Constitutional Dilemmas* (Toronto: Butterworth & Co., 1981).

Magnusson, D.N. and Soberman, D.A. *Canadian Constitutional Dilemmas Revisited* (Kingston: Institute of Intergovernmental Relations, 1997).

Pirie, A. *Alternative Dispute Resolution: Skills, Science and the Law* (Toronto: Irwin Law Inc., 2000).

Watson, G.D., et al. (eds.). *Civil Litigation Cases and Materials*, 4th ed. (Toronto: Emond Montgomery Publications Ltd., 1991).

Part 2: Torts

Fleming, J.G. *The Law of Torts*, 9th ed. (Sydney: Law Book Company, 1998).

Fridman, G.H.L. *Introduction to the Canadian Law of Torts*, 2nd ed. (Markham: LexisNexis Butterworths, 2003).

Hart, H.L.A. and Honoré, A.M. *Causation in Law*, 2nd ed. (Oxford: Oxford University Press, 1985).

Linden, A.M. *Canadian Tort Law*, 7th ed. (Toronto: Butterworth & Co., 2001).

Osborne, P.H. *The Law of Torts*, 3rd ed. (Toronto: Irwin Law Inc., 2007).

Waddams, S.M. *Products Liability*, 4th ed. (Scarborough: Carswell, 2002).

Part 3: Contracts

Beaston J., *Anson's Law of Contract*, 27th ed. (Oxford: Oxford University Press, 1998).

Corbin, A.L. *Corbin on Contracts*, rev. ed. by Perillo J.M. (St. Paul: West Publishing Co., 1993) (supplemented annually).

Cross, R. and Tapper, C. *Cross on Evidence*, 9th ed. (London: Butterworths, 1999).

Fridman, G.H.L. *The Law of Contract in Canada*, 4th ed. (Toronto: Carswell Company, 1999).

Furmston, M.P. *Cheshire, Fifoot and Furmston's Law of Contract*, 14th ed. (London: Butterworth & Co. Ltd., 2001).

Guest, A.G. and Lomnicka, E. *An Introduction to the Law of Credit and Security* (London: Sweet & Maxwell, 1978).

Hailsham, *Halsbury's Laws of England*, 4th ed. revised, Vol. 5(2) 24 (London: Butterworths, 1993).

Lewison, K. *The Interpretation of Contracts*, 3rd ed. (London: Sweet & Maxwell, 2004).

McCamus, J.C. *The Law of Contracts* (Toronto: Irwin Law Inc., 2005).

Miller, R.L., and Jentz, G.A. *Business Law Today*, Standard Edition, 7th ed. (Florence, KY: South-Western College/West, 2006).

Palmer, G.E. *Mistake and Unjust Enrichment* (Columbus: Ohio State U. Press, 1962).

Posner, R.A. *Economic Analysis of Law*, 3rd ed. (Boston: Little, Brown & Co., 1977).

Waddams, S.M. *The Law of Contracts*, 5th ed. (Aurora: Canada Law Book, 2005).

Williston, S. *A Treatise on the Law of Contracts*, 4th ed. (New York: Lawyers Cooperative Publishing, 1993).

Part 4: Special Types of Contract

Sale of Goods

Atiyah, P.S. *The Sale of Goods*, 10th ed. (Harlow: Longman, 2001).

Fridman, G.H.L. *Sale of Goods in Canada*, 4th ed. (Toronto: Carswell Company, 1995).

Guest, A.G. (ed.). *Benjamin's Sale of Goods*, 6th ed. (London: Sweet & Maxwell Ltd., 2002).

Leasing and Bailment

Selby, R.F. *Leasing in Canada: A Business Guide*, 3rd ed. (Toronto: Butterworth & Co., 1999).

Insurance and Guarantee

Crawford, B., Baer, M.G., and Rendall, J.A. (eds.). *Cases on the Canadian Law of Insurance*, 6th ed. (Toronto: Carswell Company, 2000).

McGuiness, K.P. *The Law of Guarantee*, 2nd ed. (Toronto: Carswell Company, 1996).

Agency and Franchising

Fridman, G.H.L. *The Law of Agency*, 7th ed. (London: Butterworth & Co., 1996).

Employment

Adams, G.W. *Canadian Labour Law*, 2nd ed. (Toronto: Canada Law Book Company, 1998) (updated with looseleaf supplements).

Arthurs, H.W., et al. *Labour Law and Industrial Relations in Canada*, 4th ed. (Toronto: Butterworth & Co., 1993).

Eells, R.S.F and Walton, C. *Conceptual Foundations of Business*, 2nd ed. (Homewood, IL: Richard D. Irwin, 1969).

Heuston, R.F.V. and Buckley, R.A. (eds.). *Salmond and Heuston on The Law of Torts*, 20th ed. (London: Sweet & Maxwell, 1992).

Organisation for Economic Co-operation and Development. *The OECD Guidelines for Multinational Enterprises* (Paris: OECD Publications, 2000).

Sproat, J.R. *Wrongful Dismissal Handbook,* 3rd ed. (Toronto: Thomson/Carswell, 2004).

Negotiable Instruments

Crawford, B. and Falconbridge, J.D. *Banking and Bills of Exchange*, 8th ed. (Toronto: Canada Law Book, 1986).

Elliott, N., Odgers, J., and Phillips, J.M. (eds.). *Byles on Bills of Exchange*, 27th ed. (London: Sweet & Maxwell, 2001).

Falconbridge, J.D. *The Law of Negotiable Instruments in Canada* (Toronto: The Ryerson Press, 1955).

Part 5: Property

General

Burn, E.H., (ed.). *Cheshire & Burn's Modern Law of Real Property*, 14th ed. (London: Butterworth & Co., 1988).

Oakley, A.J. *A Manual of the Law of Real Property*, 8th ed. (London: Butterworth & Co., 2002).

Oosterhoff, A.H. and Rayner, W.B. *Anger & Honsberger's Law of Real Property* (Aurora, ON: Canada Law Book Co., 1985).

Sinclair, A.M. *Introduction to Real Property Law*, 4th ed. (Toronto: Butterworth & Co., 1997).

Ziff, B. *Principles of Property Law*, 3rd ed. (Toronto: Carswell, 2000).

Intellectual Property

Cairns, D.J.A. *Remedies for Trademark Infringement* (Toronto: Carswell Company, 1988).

Geist, M. (ed.). *In the Public Interest: The Future of Canadian Copyright Law* (Toronto: Irwin Law Inc., 2005).

Hughes, R.T. *Hughes on Copyright and Industrial Design* (Toronto: Butterworth & Co., 1984) (updated with looseleaf supplements).

Hughes, R.T. and Ashton, T.P. *Hughes on Trademarks* (Toronto: LexisNexis Canada Inc., 2005).

Hughes, R.T. and Woodley, J.H. *Hughes and Woodley on Patents* (Toronto: Butterworth & Co., 1984) (updated with looseleaf supplements).

Landlord and Tenant

Bently, C., McNair, J., and Butkus, M. (eds.). *Williams and Rhodes: Canadian Law of Landlord and Tenant*, 6th ed. (Toronto: Carswell, 1988).

Fleming, J. *Ontario Landlord & Tenant Law Practice 2007* (Toronto: LexisNexis Canada Inc., 2007).

Lamont, D.H. *Residential Tenancies*, 6th ed. (Toronto: Carswell Company, 2000).

Rhodes, F.W. *Williams' The Canadian Law of Landlord and Tenant*, 6th ed. (Toronto: Carswell Company, 1988).

Mortgages

Canadian Centre for Elder Law Studies. *Consultation Paper on Reverse Mortgages* (B.C. Law Institute, February 2005).

Traub, M.W. *Falconbridge on Mortgages*, 5th ed. (Aurora: Canada Law Book, 2004).

Part 6: Business Organizations: Their Forms, Operation, and Management

Sole Proprietorships and Partnerships

DeGeorge, R. *Corporate Governance, Accounting Disclosure and Insider Trading*, (Upper Saddle River, NJ: Prentice Hall, 2004).

Corporations

Berle, A. and Means, G. *The Modern Corporation and Private Property* (New York: Macmillan, 1932).

Davies, P.L. *Gower and Davies' Principles of Modern Company Law*, 7th ed. (London: Sweet & Maxwell Ltd., 2003).

DeGeorge, R. *Business Ethics*, 6th ed. (Upper Saddle River, NJ: Prentice Hall, 2005).

DeGeorge, R. *Corporate Governance, Accounting Disclosure and Insider Trading* (Upper Saddle River, NJ: Prentice Hall, 2004).

McCallum, L. and Puri, P. *Canadian Companies' Guide to the Sarbanes Oxley Act* (Toronto: Butterworths, 2004).

Morck, R. K. (ed.). *Concentrated Corporate Ownership* (Chicago: National Bureau of Econcomic Research and University of Chicago Press, 2000).

Gower, L.C.B. *Gower's Principles of Modern Company Law*, 6th ed. (London: Sweet & Maxwell, 1997).

Pritchard, B. and Vogt, S. *Advertising and Marketing Law in Canada* (Toronto: LexisNexis Canada Inc., 2004).

Puri, P. and Larson, J. (eds.). *Corporate Governance and Securities Regulation in the 21st Century* (Toronto: Butterworths, 2004).

Underhill, A. *Underhill's Principles of the Law of Partnership*, 12th ed. by Ivamy, H. and Jones, D.R. (London: Butterworth & Co., 1986).

Van Duzer, J.A. *Law of Partnerships and Corporations* (Concord, Ont.: Irwin Law, 1997).

Welling, B. *Corporate Law in Canada*, 2nd ed. (Toronto: Butterworth & Co., 1991).

Ziegel, J.S. (ed.). *Studies in Canadian Company Law*, Vol. 1 (Toronto: Butterworth & Co., 1967) and Vol. 2 (Toronto: Butterworth & Co., 1973).

Part 7: Creditors and Debtors

General

Dunlop, C.R.B. *Creditor-Debtor Law in Canada*, 2nd ed. (Toronto: Carswell Company, 1995).

Murphy, S.D. *United States Practice in International Law*, Vol. 2 (Cambridge: Cambridge University Press, 2005).

Bankruptcy

Houlden, L.W. and Morawetz, C.H. *Bankruptcy and Insolvency Act, 1994* (Toronto: Carswell Company, 1993).

Mechanics' Liens

Macklem, D.N. and Bristow, D.I. *Construction and Mechanics' Liens in Canada*, 6th ed. (Toronto: Carswell Company, 1990).

Personal Property Security

McLaren, R.H. *Personal Property Security: An Introductory Analysis*, 5th ed. (Toronto: Carswell Company, 1992).

Part 8: The Modern Legal Environment for Business

Government Regulation of Business

Cotton, R. and Lucas, A. *Canadian Environmental Law*, 2nd ed. (Toronto: Butterworths & Co., 1992) (updated with looseleaf supplements).

Dunlop, J.B., McQueen, D., and Trebilcock, M.J. *Canadian Competition Policy: A Legal and Economic Analysis* (Toronto: Canada Law Book Company, 1987).

Flavell, C.J.M. *Canadian Competition Law: A Handbook* (Toronto: Carswell Company, 1997).

Noziak, R.S. *The 1999 Annotated Competition Act* (Toronto: Carswell Company, 1998).

Estrin, D. *Business Guide to Environmental Law* (Toronto: Carswell Company, 1993).

Mullan, D.J. *Administrative Law* (Toronto: Irwin Law, 2001).

Thompson, G., McConnell, M.L., and Huestis, L.B. *Environmental Law and Business in Canada* (Aurora, ON: Canada Law Book, 1993).

Ziegel, J.S., Geva, B., and Cuming, R.C.C. *Commercial and Consumer Transactions: Cases, Text and Materials*, 3rd ed. (Toronto: Emond Montgomery Publications, 1995).

International Business Transactions

Castel, J.-G. *Introduction to Conflict of Laws*, 4th ed. (Markham: Butterworths, 2002).

Castel, J.-G., de Mestral, A.L.C. and Graham, W.C., et al. *The Canadian Law and Practice of International Trade with Particular Emphasis on Export and Import of Goods and Services*, 2nd ed. (Toronto: Emond Montgomery, 1997).

Magnus, U. (ed.). *Global Trade Law: International Business Law of the United Nations and UNIDROIT Collection of UNCITRAL's and UNIDROIT's Conventions, Model Acts, Guides and Principles* (Munchen, Germany: Sellier European Law Publishers, 2004).

Raworth, P. *Legal Guide to International Business Transactions* (Calgary: Carswell Company, 1991).

Trebilcock, M.J. and Howse, R. *The Regulation of International Trade*, 2nd ed. (London: Rutledge, 1999).

Electronic Commerce

Campbell, D. (ed.). *Law of International On-line Business: A Global Perspective* (London: Sweet & Maxwell, 1998).

Fencenko, M.J. and Huntley, A.M. *E-commerce Corporate Commercial Aspects* (Toronto: LexisNexis Canada Inc., 2003).

Gahtan, A.M., Kratz, M., and Mann, J.F. *Electronic Commerce: A Practitioner's Guide* (Toronto: Carswell, 2003).

Geist, M.A. *Internet Law in Canada*, 3rd ed. (Concord: Captus Press, 2002).

Privacy

McIsaac, B., Shields, R., and Klein, K. *The Law of Privacy in Canada*, (Toronto: Thomson Carswell, 2007).

McNair, C.H.H and Scott, A.K. *A Guide to the Personal Information Protection and Electronic Documents Act* (Toronto: LexisNexis Canada Inc., 2005).

Office of the Privacy Commissioner of Canada. *Leading by Example: Key Developments in the First Seven Years of the Personal Information Protection and Electronic Documents Act (PIPEDA)* (Ottawa: Minister of Public Works and Government Services Canada, 2008).

Scheflin, A.W. and Opton, E.M., Jr. *The Mind Manipulators: A Non-fiction Account* (London: Paddington Press, 1978).

WEBLINKS

Part 1

www.justice.gc.ca/eng/
dept-min/pub/just/09.html
Canada's System of Justice

http://laws.justice.gc.ca/en/charter
The full text of the Canadian Charter of Rights and
Freedoms

www.efc.ca
Electronics Frontier Canada (materials on the Charter,
including recent cases)

www.ethics.ubc.ca
The W. Maurice Young Centre for Applied Ethics (at the
University of British Columbia)

www.ethicscentre.ca/EN/index.cfm
Canadian Centre for Ethics and Corporate Policy

http://dsp-psd.pwgsc.gc.ca/Reference/
queens-e.html
How a bill becomes law

www.scc-csc.gc.ca/court-cour/sys/index-eng.asp
The structure of the Canadian court system

www.lawsociety.mb.ca
The Law Society of Manitoba (each province has its own
law society with its own website)

www.flsc.ca
The Federation of Law Societies

www.legalaid.ab.ca
Alberta legal aid (several other provinces have similar
addresses, e.g., www.legalaid.mb.ca and www.legalaid.on.ca)

www.adrcanada.ca
ADR Institute of Canada

Part 2

www.law-lib.utoronto.ca/resources/topic/torts.htm
Bora Laskin Law Library links to various sites on tort law

www.fsco.gov.on.ca/english/insurance/auto/
Financial Services Commission of Ontario overview of
no-fault automobile scheme (similar sites exists in other
provinces with some form of no-fault compensation
scheme)

www.insurance-risk-mgmt.utoronto.ca
Risk management and insurance

www.worksafebc.com
Workers Compensation Program British Columbia
(similar sites exist in other provinces)

http://law.unb.ca/cpwala/toclegal.htm
University of New Brunswick's Legal Guide to The
Consumer Product Warranty and Liability Act

In the context of Chapter 4, students may wish to examine
the websites of various professional bodies—and in particular,
their codes of professional conduct. Among the more interesting sites are

www.cica.ca
The Canadian Institute of Chartered Accountants

www.cga.org
The Canadian Association of Certified General
Accountants

www.cma.ca
The Canadian Medical Association

www.pharmacists.ca
The Canadian Pharmacists Association

For other codes of professional conduct, try

www.ethicsweb.ca/resources
Applied Ethics Resources

Part 3

www.law-lib.utoronto.ca/resources/topic/cont.htm
Bora Laskin Law Library links to contract law

www.ic.gc.ca
Industry Canada website

www.bcli.org/bclrg/projects/proposals-contract-
law-reform-act
B.C. Law Institute Proposal for a Contract Law Reform Act

www.cca-acc.com/documents/ccalist_e.asp
Canadian Construction Association standard form
documents

Part 4

www.ulcc.ca/en/cls
Uniform Law Conference of Canada (commercial law
projects)

www.cfla-acfl.ca
Canadian Finance and Leasing Association

www.cfa.ca
Canadian Franchise Association

http://bsa.canadabusiness.ca
Business Start-Up Assistant (information on starting a
business, franchising, employment law, etc.)

www.ibc.ca
Insurance Bureau of Canada

www.hrsdc.gc.ca
Employment Standards Legislation in Canada

www.bank-banque-canada.ca
The Bank of Canada

Part 5

www.law-lib.utoronto.ca/resources/topic/
property.htm
Bora Laskin Law Library links to property law materials

www.cipo.ic.gc.ca
Canadian Intellectual Property Office

http://trademarkscanada.ca
Order form for NUANS business name search

www.cb-cda.gc.ca
Copyright Board of Canada

www.accesscopyright.ca
Canadian Copyright Licensing Agency

http://patents1.ic.gc.ca
Industry Canada's Canadian Patents Database

www.wipo.int
World Intellectual Property Organization

www.servicealberta.ca/LandTitles.cfm
Overview of land titles system in Alberta
(most provinces have similar sites)

www.ltb.gov.on.ca
Reference Guide to Residential Landlord and Tenant Law
in Ontario
(most provinces have similar sites)

Part 6

www.ic.gc.ca
Industry Canada's business and consumer site

http://businessgateway.ca
Canada Business (government services for business
including information on business start-ups and links to
provincial sources)

http://rc.lsuc.on.ca/jsp/membershipServices/
limitedLiabilityPartnerships.jsp
Information on limited liability partnerships from the
Law Society of Upper Canada

www.fin.gov.on.ca/english/publications/2001/
ibprof.html
Ontario Ministry of Finance Information Bulletin on
professional corporations

www.ethicscan.ca
Resource centre for consumer and corporate affairs

www.tsx.com
Toronto Stock Exchange

British Columbia, Nova Scotia, and Ontario have particularly good sites on setting up a business, at

www.bcbusinessregistry.ca
www.novascotiabusiness.com
http://incorporationontario.ca

Provincial securities commissions have useful sites, for
example

www.albertasecurities.com
www.bcsc.bc.ca
www.osc.gov.on.ca
www.csa-acvm.ca
Canadian Securities Administrators

Part 7

www.ulcc.ca/en/poam2
Uniform Law Conference of Canada (materials on
personal property security law)

www.ppsa.net
PPSA Legislation (explanation of how the system works)

http://strategis.ic.gc.ca/epic/internet/inbsf-
osb.nsf/en/home
Office of the Superintendent of Bankruptcy Canada

http://strategis.ic.gc.ca/epic/internet/inbsf-
osb.nsf/en/h_br01011e.html
Canadian bankruptcy statistics

www.law-lib.utoronto.ca/resources/topic/
bankrupt.htm
Bora Laskin Law Library links to materials on bankruptcy law

www.bankruptcycanada.com
Information on declaring bankruptcy

Part 8

For Chapter 32:

www.ic.gc.ca
Industry Canada's main site

www.competitionbureau.gc.ca
Competition Bureau of Canada

www.ec.gc.ca
Environment Canada

www.sierraclub.ca
Sierra Club of Canada Environmental News

For Chapter 33:

www.investincanada.gc.ca
Investment Canada news and information

www.dfait-maeci.gc.ca
Foreign Affairs and International Trade Canada

www.chamber.ca
The Canadian Chamber of Commerce

www.citt.gc.ca
The Canadian International Trade Tribunal

www.wto.org
The World Trade Organization

www.naftanow.org
NAFTA site operated jointly by the three NAFTA parties

www.oecd.org
The Organisation for Economic Cooperation and Development (OECD)

www.iccwbo.org
The International Chamber of Commerce

www.edc.ca
Export Development Canada

For Chapter 34:

http://e-com.ic.gc.ca
Industry Canada: Digital Economy in Canada

www.it-can.ca
Canadian IT Law Association

www.ulcc.ca/en/cls
Uniform Law Conference of Canada e-commerce project, including draft Uniform Electronic Commerce Act

www.piac.ca
The Public Interest Advocacy Centre (also addresses privacy issues)

http://europa.eu.int/information_society/topics/ebusiness/ecommerce
The European Union e-commerce site

www.econsumer.gov
International project on consumer protection in e-commerce

www.cippic.ca
Canadian Internet Policy and Public Interest Clinic (also addresses privacy issues)

For Chapter 35:

www.privcom.gc.ca
Office of the Privacy Commissioner of Canada

www.oipc.ab.ca
Office of the Information and Privacy Commissioner of Alberta

www.privacyinfo.ca
Privacy site maintained by Professor Michael Geist of the University of Ottawa Faculty of Law

www.oipcbc.org
Office of the Information and Privacy Commissioner for British Columbia

www.ipc.on.ca
Information and Privacy Commissioner for Ontario (most other provinces have a similar site)

GLOSSARY

Aboriginal peoples Indian, Inuit, and Métis peoples of Canada   147

absolute liability offence an offence where the absence of fault is no defence   662

absolute privilege complete immunity from liability for defamation   69

abuse of dominant position taking an unfair advantage of possessing a monopoly or dominant position in the marketplace   757

acceleration clause a provision whereby the full outstanding amount of a debt becomes immediately payable if the debtor defaults in making any instalment payment   554, 692, 751

acceptance any conduct by the buyer in relation to the goods that amounts to recognition of an existing contract of sale   214

acceptor the drawee who consents to the bill of exchange by signing it together with the word "accepted" and the date   446

accommodation bill bill of exchange that contains an anomalous endorsement   453

accord and satisfaction a compromise between contracting parties to substitute a new contractual obligation and release a party from the existing one   264

act of bankruptcy a prescribed act of a debtor that must be proved before the debtor may be declared bankrupt   716

act of God the raging of the natural elements   268

action for impeachment an action challenging the validity of a patent   491

actual authority the authority given expressly or impliedly to the agent by the principal   395

additional rent a tenant's proportionate share of maintenance costs, utilities, and taxes   534

adjudicate hear parties and deliver a decision with reasons   43

administrator the personal representative of a person who dies intestate   255

admissible evidence evidence that is acceptable to the court   39

ADR alternative dispute resolution—using private procedures instead of the courts to resolve disputes   43

adverse possession the exclusive possession of land by someone who openly uses it like an owner and ignores the claims of other persons including the owner   515

advocate a barrister in Quebec   46

after-acquired property property acquired by the debtor after the debt has been incurred   693

age of majority the age at which a person is recognized as an adult according to the law of his or her province   142

agency agreement the agreement between principal and agent whereby the agent undertakes to act on behalf of the principal   391

agent a person acting for another person in contractual relations with third parties   391

agreement to sell a contract of sale in which the transfer of goods is deferred to some future time   326

alien non-citizen   147

alternative dispute-resolution the use of private procedures such as arbitration and mediation to resolve disputes   806

amortization period length of time it should take to repay an entire debt   554

annual general meeting the general meeting of shareholders that is required by law to be held each year to transact certain specified business   643

annual report the report on the business and affairs of the corporation, which the directors are required to present at the annual general meeting   648

anomalous endorsement an endorsement that is not added for the purpose of negotiating the instrument but as a guarantee to make it easier for the drawer to obtain credit on the bill   453

anti-dumping duties and **countervailing duties** special duties imposed on imported products to counter the advantage obtained from dumping or export subsidies   776

anticipatory breach a breach that occurs in advance of the time agreed for performance of a contract   287

apparent authority the authority that a third party is entitled to assume that the agent possesses   396

appellant the party who petitions for an appeal   28

appraisal remedy the right to have one's shares bought by the corporation at a fair price   651

arbitration a form of ADR where a dispute is referred to an arbitrator who adjudicates the matter and the parties agree to be bound by the arbitrator's decision, although there may be a right to appeal to the courts   43

arbitration clause a term in a commercial contract designating arbitration as the process for resolution of any disputes arising between the parties   787

arbitration procedure the procedure in a rights dispute that binds the parties to accept the interpretation of the collective agreement by an arbitrator   434

arm's length a transaction between persons who are not related or associated in any way   720

articles of incorporation founding corporate document, often referred to as the charter or constitution of the corporation   614

assault the threat of violence to a person   68

assignee a third party to whom rights under a contract have been assigned   247

assignment a transfer by a party of its rights under a contract to a third party   247

assignment a voluntary declaration of bankruptcy   715

assignment of book debts security interest in the debtor's accounts receivables   701

assignor a party that assigns its rights under a contract to a third party 247

associated corporations corporations that are related either (a) vertically, as where one corporation controls the other (parent–subsidiary), or (b) horizontally, as where both corporations are controlled by the same person (affiliates) 611

assumed risk risk assumed by an employee in accepting a particular employment 430

assumption a subsequent purchaser takes over the responsibility of paying off the mortgage 560

attachment the moment in time when a debtor's property becomes subject to a security interest 696

attorney a lawyer in the United States, encompassing the roles of both barrister and solicitor 46

audit committee a group of directors responsible for overseeing the corporate audit and the preparation of financial statements. The committee has wider responsibilities in a distributing corporation. 629

authorized capital the maximum number (or value) of shares that a corporation is permitted by its charter to issue 620

bailee party accepting possession of goods from a bailor 358

bailment a transfer of possession of personal property without a transfer of ownership 358

bailments for value contractual bailment 361

bailor owner or transferor of goods 358

bait-and-switch advertising advertising a product at a bargain price but not supplying it in reasonable quantities 746

bankrupt declared insolvent by the court 255

bankrupt a person who has made a voluntary assignment in bankruptcy or against whom a receiving order has been made 713

bargain each party pays a price for the promise of the other 123

bargaining agent a union that has the exclusive right to bargain with the employer on behalf of the bargaining unit 432

bargaining unit a specified group of employees eligible to join the union 432

barrister a lawyer in England who accepts cases from solicitors and presents them in court, and also acts as consultant in complex legal issues 46

basic law a constitution that is habitually obeyed by the citizens of a country and that they regard as legitimate and binding 10

battery unlawful physical contact with a person 68

beneficial contracts of service contracts of employment or apprenticeship found to be for a minor's benefit 143

beneficial owner a person who, although not the legal owner, may compel the trustee to provide benefits to him 243

beneficiary a person who is entitled to the benefits of a trust 243

beneficiary the person entitled to receive insurance monies 373

bid-rigging agreeing not to submit a bid or agreeing in advance what bids will be submitted in response to a call for bids or tenders 757

bilateral contract a contract where offeror and offeree trade promises and both are bound to perform 114

bilateral investment protection treaty a treaty entered into between two countries, whereby each country undertakes to protect investors from the other country and to give them certain rights 782

bill of exchange a written order by one party to another party to pay a specified sum of money to a named party or to the bearer of the document 443

bill of lading a document signed by a carrier acknowledging that specified goods have been delivered to it for shipment 340

biometrics technological analysis of physical characteristics, such as fingerprints 820

board of directors the governing body of a corporation, responsible for the management of its business and affairs 629

bond a document evidencing a debt owed by a corporation 621

branch a business carried on by the owner in its own name at a location distinct from its head office 780

brief a case handed by a solicitor to a barrister 46

builders' lien an interest that builders and others involved in construction work may have in a building as security for money owed to them for work done (also known as a **mechanics' lien** or a **construction lien**) 727

building-scheme covenant a restrictive covenant that regulates land use over an entire neighbourhood or a shopping centre 508

bulk sale a sale of all or substantially all the assets of a business 731

burden the requirement that, unless a party can establish facts and law to prove its case, it will lose 13

business judgment rule courts will defer to the business decisions of directors and officers provided they are arrived at using an appropriate degree of prudence and diligence 637

by-laws the internal working rules of a corporation 616

calculation period stages at which accrued interest is added to principal 554

canon law law created by the Church, which had its own jurisdiction and courts in matters pertaining to itself, family law, and wills 26

cartel an agreement or arrangement between enterprises to lessen competition 755

case law a collection of individual cases decided by the courts that develop and shape legal principles 10

causation injury resulting from the breach of the standard of care 56

cause of action an event or set of events that gives rise to legal liability 37

caveat emptor let the buyer beware 190, 328

certificate of incorporation a certificate that a corporation has come into existence 613

certificate of title summary of registered interests in a property, showing the owner and any mortgages, easements, or other interests held by others, which may be relied upon by the public 517

certification an acknowledgment by an administrative tribunal that a particular union commands sufficient membership to justify its role as exclusive bargaining agent for the employees   432

certification an undertaking by the bank to pay the amount of a cheque to its holder when later presented for payment   448

certification mark a special type of trademark used to identify goods or services that conform to a particular standard   468

chain of title the series of grants over the title search period that can be followed up to the current owner (vendor)   516

charge a lien or encumbrance on land   556

chargee mortgagee   556

chargor mortgagor   556

chattel mortgage a mortgage of personal property   692

chattels tangible personal property   327

cheque a bill of exchange drawn against a bank and payable on demand   447

choses in action rights to intangible property such as patents, stocks, and contracts that may be enforced in the courts   247

choses in possession rights to tangible property that may be possessed physically   247

civil law the system of law involving a comprehensive legislated code, derived from Roman law that developed in continental Europe and greatly influenced by the Code Napoléon of 1804   22

civil liability responsibility arising from a breach of a private law enforced through a lawsuit initiated by the victim   5

claim a statement of the features claimed to be new and in respect of which the applicant claims an exclusive right   490

class action an action in which an individual represents a group of possible plaintiffs and the judgment decides the matter for all members of the class at once   35

class rights special rights attached to a particular class of shares   645

closed mortgage a mortgage that does not permit early repayment of the debt without a substantial penalty   560

closed-shop agreement a collective agreement requiring all employees to be union members   437

closing date the date for completing a sale of property   561

code of conduct a common standard of behaviour that may take the form of a values statement or a prescribed set of rules   8

code of conduct rules of a professional organization setting out the duties and appropriate standards of behaviour to be observed by its members   90

codify set down and summarize in a statute the existing common law rules governing a particular area of activity   24

coercion improperly forced payment under protest   195

collateral agreement a separate agreement between the parties made at the same time as, but not included in, the written document   228

collateral contract an implied contract that binds a party who made a representation or promise that induced a person to enter into a contract with another party   245

collateral security an interest in property of a debtor to which a creditor may look in the event of non-payment of the debt   689

collection arrangement an arrangement whereby the seller employs the services of its bank to collect payment by depositing the documents with the bank and receiving credit for the price   773

collective bargaining establishing conditions of employment by negotiation between an employer and the bargaining agent for its employees   432

commercial activity any general or particular activity performed or in the objectives of an organization that has a commercial aspect   828

commercial tenancies a lease of premises used for a business or non-residential purpose   527

commission agent one who sells on behalf of a principal to third parties and receives compensation through commissions   391

common carrier a business that holds itself out to the public as a transporter of goods for reward   364

common elements structures and areas external to a condominium unit, including communal facilities   512

common law the case-based system of law originating in England and covering most of the English-speaking world—based on the recorded reasons given by courts for their decisions   21

common share a share carrying no preferential right   621

community legal services or **legal clinic** a model of legal aid where legal services are delivered by community law offices with full-time staff lawyers and managed by boards elected by residents of the community   41

comparative value "equal pay for work of equal value"   427

compensation committee committee responsible for setting director and officer pay   630

compliance officers employees that monitor regulatory and legislative requirements applicable to the business and ensure that the business complies   47

compromise and arrangement an agreement made by a debtor corporation with its creditors whereby arrangements are made for repayment of debts without liquidating the corporation   726

compulsory licence a licence granted to a person to work a patent without the consent of the owner of the patent   492

conciliation procedure bargaining with the help of a conciliation officer or board   434

concurrent powers matters in which both the federal and provincial governments have power to legislate   11, 740

condition a major or essential term of the contract, the breach of which may relieve the injured party from further performance   285, 328

condition precedent any set of circumstances or events that the parties stipulate must be satisfied or must happen before their contract takes effect   229

condition subsequent an uncertain event that brings a promisor's liability to an end if it happens   267

conditional discharge the debtor is discharged under the original contract only if the negotiable instrument given in payment is honoured   445

condominium corporation a corporation—whose members are the condominium owners—that is responsible for managing the property as a whole 512

condominium unit a unit in a multiple-unit development that may be owned in fee simple 512

conflict of interest a situation where a duty is owed to a client whose interests conflict with the interests of the professional, another client, or another person to whom a duty is owed 79

conflict of laws or **private international law** the principles of law that apply to resolve questions concerned with private relationships that are affected by the laws of two or more countries 770

consensual surveillance the employee is aware of and consents to surveillance 834

consent approval of the person to whom collected information relates 822

consideration the price for which the promise of the other is bought 123

consignment the transfer of goods from one business to another for the purpose of sale 326

constructive dismissal a substantial change to an employee's job that amounts to termination of the existing employment 419

constructive fraud the unconscientious use of power by a dominant party to take advantage of the weakness of the other party 191

constructive trust a relationship that permits a third party to obtain performance of a promise included in a contract for his benefit 243

construing interpreting 221

consumer debtor an individual who is insolvent but whose aggregate debts do not exceed $75 000 (soon to be changed to $250 000) 714

consumers individuals who purchase goods and services from a business for their personal use and enjoyment 744

contempt of court a finding by a court that a party has refused to obey it and will be punished 27

contingent or **contingency fee** a fee paid for a lawyer's services only if the client is successful; there is no charge if the client is unsuccessful 42

contra proferentem a rule of contract interpretation that prefers the interpretation of a clause that is least favourable to the party that drafted the clause 224

contractual joint venture a joint venture effected by agreement without the creation of any separate legal entity 601

contributory negligence negligence of an injured party that contributes to her own loss or injury 60

conversion dealing with the goods of another in a manner that is inconsistent with the other's ownership 67

cooling-off period a time during which the employer cannot declare a lockout nor can the union begin a strike 434

cooling-off period a specified period following a contract of sale during which a buyer may terminate the contract by giving written notice to the seller 750

corporate governance the rules governing the organization and management of the business and affairs of a corporation in order to meet its internal objectives and external responsibilities 628

corporate social responsibility a concept that suggests business decision-makers consider ethical issues including the interests of customers, employees, creditors, the public, and other stakeholders in addition to legal and financial concerns 8

corporation a legal person formed by incorporation according to a prescribed legal procedure 606

costs funds paid by litigants to cover a portion of the government's expenses in maintaining the court system 39

counsel lawyer representing a plaintiff or defendant 37

counterclaim a claim by the defendant arising from the same facts as the original action by the plaintiff to be tried along with that action 38

countertrade a form of barter, under which a seller agrees to accept payment in goods produced or procured by the buyer 774

courts of chancery a system of courts under the king's chancellor and vice-chancellors developed from the hearing of petitions to the king-courts of equity 26

covenant a serious promise 134

covenant a term or promise contained in a lease 529

covenant of quiet enjoyment a landlord's promise to do nothing to interfere with the tenant's possession and use of the premises 533

covenantor one who makes a covenant 134

covert surveillance the employee is unaware of surveillance and has not consented to it 834

criminal liability responsibility arising from commission of an offence against the government or society as a whole 5

criminal offences most serious offences that require proof of mental intent (*mens rea*) 746

cumulative right the right of the holder of a preferred share to be paid arrears from previous years before any dividend is paid on the common shares 622

cumulative voting a method of electing directors by a form of proportional representation 632

current assets cash or cash equivalent assets such as negotiable instruments, demand deposits, and accounts receivables 722

cybersquatting the registration of a domain name containing the trademark of another person, with the intention of selling the domain name to the owner of the mark 806

deceit the making of a false statement with the intention of misleading another person 82

deposit a sum of money paid by the buyer to the seller, to be forfeited if the buyer does not perform its part of the contract 343

damages a money award to compensate an injured party for the loss caused by the other party's breach 58, 300

data shadows electronic records of the Internet activity of a user 820

debenture an alternative term to describe a corporate "bond" 693

debtor-on-possession financing court-sanctioned secured loans advanced during reorganization and given priority over pre-existing secured creditors 722

deceit knowingly making a false statement with a view to its being acted upon by another person   67

declaration of trust an agreement that establishes a trust and designates the trustees   601

deductible clause a clause requiring the insured to bear the loss up to a stated amount   374

deed of conveyance or **deed** a document under seal (which today is usually a small, red, gummed wafer) that transfers an interest in land from the owner to another party   134, 514

defamation making an untrue statement that causes injury to the reputation of another person   69

demand draft a bill of exchange payable immediately upon presentation without any days of grace   446

demotion transferring an employee to a job with less responsibility and/or income potential   419

dependent agent an agent who acts exclusively, or mostly, for a single principal   391

derivative action proceedings brought by one or more shareholders in the name of the corporation in respect of a wrong done to the corporation   651

digital rights management system (DRMS) a system collecting data about the licensing, payment for, and authenticity of a work   808

Digital Rights Management Technology a system collecting data about the licensing, payment, use, and authenticity of a work   477

directors' circular indoor management rule the principle that a person dealing with a corporation is entitled to assume that its internal procedural rules have been complied with unless it is apparent that such is not the case   672

disbarred expulsion from the law society and loss of the privilege of practising law   46

discharge a court order whereby a person who has been declared bankrupt ceases to have the status of a bankrupt person   724

discharge a contract cancel the obligations of a contract; make an agreement or contract null and inoperative   263

disclaimer an express statement to the effect that the person making it takes no responsibility for a particular action or statement   84

disclosed surveillance the employee is given advance notice of surveillance but does not consent to it   834

disclosure (of personal information) transfer of data to third parties outside the organization   827

discriminatory pricing where a seller makes a practice of discriminating between purchasers with respect to the price charged for goods or services   758

dishonour the failure by the party primarily liable to pay the instrument according to its terms   454

dismissal for cause dismissal without notice or further obligation by the employer when the employee's conduct amounts to breach of contract   420

distinguish identification of a factual difference that renders a prior precedent inapplicable to the case before the court   23

distinguishing guise the shaping of goods or their containers, or a distinctive mode of wrapping or packaging   468

distress the right of the landlord to seize assets of the tenant found on the premises and sell them to realize arrears of rent   536

distributing corporation a corporation that issues its securities to the public; also referred to as issuing corporations, reporting issuers, and publicly traded corporations   617

dividend a distribution to shareholders of a share of the profits of the corporation   645

doctrine of frustration the law excuses a party from performance when external causes have made performance radically different from that contemplated by the parties   270

document under seal a covenant recorded in a document containing a wax seal, showing that the covenantor adopted the document as his act and deed   134

documents of record documents that a corporation is required to keep and make available to shareholders   648

domain name the registered Internet address of a website   804

dominant tenement the piece of land that benefits from an easement   505

dower a widow's right to a life interest in one-third of the real property held by her husband in fee simple before his death   511

down payment a sum of money paid by the buyer as an initial part of the purchase price   343

drawee the party who is required to make payment on the bill of exchange   445

drawer the party who draws up the bill of exchange   445

drawing party the contracting party that prepared the agreement and/or the particular clause   293

dual offence an offence of the Competition Act that may be either a criminal or regulatory offence, depending upon the seriousness of the conduct   746

due diligence defence establishing that an acceptable standard of care and skill was exercised by a director or officer   637

dumping selling products abroad at prices below those charged on domestic sales   776

duress actual or threatened violence or imprisonment as a means of coercing a party to enter into a contract   195

duty of care a relationship so close that one must take reasonable steps to avoid causing harm to the other   54

duty to account the duty of a person who commits a breach of trust to hand over any profits derived from the breach   82

duty to warn to make users aware of the risks associated with the use of the product   64

e-cash an online payment system that enables the anonymous transfer of money over the Internet   796

earnest a token sum or article given to seal a bargain—now a rare practice   214

easement a right enjoyed by one landowner over the land of another for a special purpose but not for occupation of the land   505

electronic commerce (e-commerce) the use of computer networks to facilitate commercial activities including the production, distribution, sale, and delivery of goods and services   795

electronic retailing (e-retailing) the supply of tangible or electronic goods or services over the Internet. Supply of tangible goods involves a conventional mode of delivery; electronic goods are downloaded directly to the customer's computer.   795

electronic transfer of funds payment made through electronic (intangible) media such as telephone or Internet rather than by cash or cheque. Payment may take the form of credit card charges, debit of bank accounts, or even e-cash. Often, customers can access these forms of payment on the business's website.   795

endorse sign one's name on a negotiable instrument   256

endorsement written evidence of a change in the terms of a policy   373

entering (filing) an appearance filing notice of an intention to contest an action   37

equitable assignment an assignment other than a statutory assignment   250

equitable relief a discretionary remedy first developed by the courts of equity to undo an injustice   166

equitable remedies special non-monetary remedies given only when damages alone will not adequately compensate for a loss   27, 310

equity rules developed by the courts of equity as exceptions to existing rules of common law   27

equity joint venture a corporation formed, and jointly owned, by the parties to a joint venture for the purpose of carrying on the venture   601

equity of redemption or **equity** the right of the mortgagor to redeem mortgaged land on payment of the debt in full   555

estates in time the right to exclusive possession of the land for a period of time   502

estopped prevented   130

examination for discovery processes allowing either party to examine the other in order to narrow the issues   38

exchange controls restrictions on the conversion or export of currency   773

exclusive dealing where a supplier of goods makes it a condition that the buyer should deal only or primarily in the supplier's products   759

exclusive listing agreement an agreement by the client of a real estate agent to pay commission on any sale of a property whether it is sold by the client, the agent, or some other agent   394

exclusive use clause a landlord's promise not to rent adjoining premises to any other entity in the same or competing business as the tenant   531

execution order an order that gives the sheriff authority to levy execution   316

executor the personal representative of a deceased person named in his or her will   255

exempt property that is not subject to seizure by the trustee as a result of an exception in a federal or provincial statute   721

exemption clause a clause in a contract that exempts a party from liability   224, 242, 291

exercise an option to accept the offer contained in an option   107

expectation damages an amount awarded for breach of contract based on expected profits   302

expert opinion an opinion given by a person who purports to have specialized knowledge of a subject   188

export houses or **freight forwarders** specialist firms that make the arrangements for shipment, insurance, and financing in export sales   770

export subsidy the granting by governments of financial assistance to promote exports   776

express repudiation a declaration by one of the contracting parties to the other that it does not intend to perform as promised   286

expropriation a compulsory sale and transfer of land to a public body   515

expropriation a state's right to assume ownership of private property within its geographic borders   782

extinguish the title end the title of the owner and the owner's right to regain possession   515

factor a party who purchases drafts drawn on customers at a discount and then collects directly from the customer   453

false arrest causing a person to be arrested without reasonable cause   68

false imprisonment unlawfully restraining or confining another person   68

federal paramountcy the principle that a federal law prevails over a conflicting provincial law   741

fee simple the interest in land closest to complete ownership   502

fellow servant fellow employee   430

feudal law a system of land ownership rooted in sovereign ownership: land was handed down to lords who gave possession of parcels of land to lesser "royals" in exchange for military service and loyalty   26

fiduciary duty a duty imposed on a person who stands in a special relation of trust to another   78

finance lease an arrangement where a third person provides credit financing, becomes the owner of the property, and leases it to the lessee   353

financial statements annual accounts that are required to be presented to the shareholders at the annual general meeting   647

financing statement the document summarizing the details of a security interest that is filed in order to protect that interest   695

firm collective reference to the partners in a partnership   585

fixed term a contract of employment with defined start and end dates   418

fixtures all things permanently attached to land are deemed part of the land   501

fixtures objects that are attached to the land or to a building or other fixture on the land   541

floating charge a form of mortgage on all the assets of a corporation other than those already specifically charged   693

foreclosure an order by a court ending the mortgagor's right to redeem within a fixed time   555

foreign exchange risk management methods of reducing the risk involved in currency fluctuations   773

foreign investment conducting operations in a foreign market   769

foreign presence placing representatives of a business in foreign markets   768

foreign trade the buying and selling of goods and services between parties from different countries   768

format shifting transferring purchased material, such as music, from one of the owner's devices to another   486

franchise agreement an agreement under which a franchisor grants to the franchisee a right to market the franchisor's products   405

fraudulent misrepresentation an incorrect statement made knowingly with the intention of causing injury to another   83

fraudulent preference the payment of money or transfer of property to a creditor with a view to giving that creditor preference over other creditors   720

fraudulent transfer a transfer of property by a debtor with the intention of putting that property out of the reach of creditors   719

free trade area group of countries within which customs duties are eliminated   778

freehold estate an interest in land that is indeterminate in time   502

fundamental breach a breach that is so significant that it deprives the innocent party of most (if not all) of the benefit of the contract   294

fungible goods goods that may be replaced with different but identical goods   363

future goods goods that have not yet been produced   338

garnishee order an order requiring the debtor's employer to retain a portion of the debtor's wages each payday and surrender the sum to the creditor   316

general creditor a creditor that has no security other than the debtor's promise to pay; creditors whose claims are not secured or preferred   563, 723

general damages damages to compensate for injuries that cannot be expressed in monetary terms   71

general meeting of shareholders a formal meeting of shareholders at which they are able to vote on matters concerning the corporation   643

general partner a partner in a limited partnership whose liability is not limited   597

goods personal property, other than money and choses in action   326

goodwill the benefit and advantage of the good name, reputation, and connections of a business   469

government institutions government departments and agencies listed in Schedule 1 of the Privacy Act   822

gratuitous bailment a bailment where one party provides no consideration, or where there is no intention to create a contractual relationship   359

gratuitous promise a promise made without bargaining for or accepting anything in return   123

guarantee a promise to perform the obligation of another person if that person defaults   202, 382

guardian a person appointed to manage the affairs of a minor in the place of his or her parents   142

hearsay words attributed by a witness to a person who is not before the court   39

hire-purchase an agreement to lease an item of property with an option for the lessee to purchase it at the end of the stipulated term   352

holdback an amount that the owner who contracts for construction work may withhold from payments made to the principal contractor to protect against claims from subcontractors and suppliers   728

holder a party who acquires a negotiable instrument from the transferor   256

holding out representing by words or conduct that a person is one's agent or has a particular authority   397

human rights recognized entitlements encompassing traditional freedoms associated with civil liberty and basic human necessities   12

immediate parties the holder of an instrument and the party alleged to be liable on it who have had direct dealings with each other   458

implied term a term not expressly included by the parties in their agreement but which, as reasonable people, they would have included had they thought about it   230

implied term as to description it is implied that goods sold by description will conform to the description   329

implied term as to title it is implied that the seller has a right to sell the goods   329

implied term of fitness it is implied that the goods are of a type that is suitable for the purpose for which they are bought   330

implied term of merchantable quality it is implied that the goods are in reasonable condition and free from defects that would make them unsuitable for use   331

implied term that goods correspond with sample it is implied that, when a sample of the goods to be sold has been provided, the actual goods supplied will correspond to that sample in type and quality   332

in-house counsel a lawyer who provides legal services to a business as a full-time employee of the business   47

income trust a trust with assets in Canada and whose units are traded on a prescribed stock exchange   714

Incoterms a set of standard contractual terms adopted by the International Chamber of Commerce   771

indefinite hiring a contract of employment for an undetermined length of time, with no expectation of termination or described end date   418

indemnity a promise by a third party to be primarily liable to pay the debt   202

indeminity primary obligation to pay   384

indemnity or **compensation** a money award given as a supplement to rescission for loss sustained in performing a contract   186

independent agent an agent who carries on an independent business and acts for a number of principals   391

individual natural person, not a corporation   828

inducing breach of contract intentionally causing one person to breach his contract with another   67

inherent vice a latent defect or dangerous condition of goods   365

injunction a court order restraining a party from acting in a particular manner, such as committing a breach of contract   71, 312

injurious reliance loss or harm suffered by a promisee who, to his detriment, relied reasonably on a gratuitous promise   132

innkeeper a person or firm that maintains an establishment offering lodging to any member of the public   366

insider trading the use of confidential information relating to a corporation in dealing in its securities   641

insolvency having liabilities in excess of the realizable value of one's assets or being unable to pay one's debts as they fall due   664

insolvent person a person who is unable to meet (or has ceased to pay) his or her debts as they become due, or whose debts exceed the value of his or her realizable assets   714

inspector a person appointed by the court to investigate the affairs of a corporation   649

insurable interest an interest where a person has a financial benefit from the continued existence of the property or life insured or would suffer financial detriment from its loss or destruction   151, 377

insurance adjuster a person who appraises property losses   373

insurance agent an agent or employee of an insurance company   373

insurance broker an independent business that arranges insurance coverage for its clients   373

insurance policy the written evidence of the terms of a contract of insurance   372

intentional torts torts involving conduct that was not accidental   67

interlocutory injunction a temporary restraining order   313

interest dispute an employer and the union disagree about the particular terms to be included in the collective agreement   434

interests less than estates interests in land that do not give the right to exclusive possession   502

Internet the interconnected networks that link computers worldwide   795

intestate when a person dies without leaving a will   255

intranet closed systems linking specific users internal to a company or group; commonly used for data exchange   795

invitee a person permitted by an occupier to enter premises for business purposes   65

inviting tenders seeking offers from suppliers   110

issued capital the shares that have been issued by a corporation   620

issuing commencing the lawsuit by filing a copy of the statement of claim with the court office   37

job description a description of the responsibilities of a position including objectives, qualifications, and supervisor   420

joint liability the situation where each of a number of persons is personally liable for the full amount of a debt   588

joint tenants concurrent holders each of whom has a right of survivorship   504

joint venture a business venture undertaken jointly by two or more parties; a form of partnership between two or more independent enterprises, or a corporation jointly owned by them   600, 780

judgment creditor a party who has obtained a court judgment for a sum of money   315

judgment debtor a party who has been ordered by the court to pay a sum of money   315

judicare a model of legal aid in which lawyers agree to be paid according to government fee schedules for serving clients who qualify for legal aid   41

jurisdiction the province, state, or country whose laws apply to a particular situation   113

jurisdiction the right of a court to hear and resolve a dispute   812

jurisdictional dispute two or more unions compete for the right to represent a particular group of employees   433

labour relations board an administrative tribunal regulating labour relations   432

land comprises the surface, all that is under the surface, including the minerals and oil, and everything above the surface, including buildings   501

land titles system a system of land registration where the land titles office brings all outstanding interests in the land up-to-date and certifies them as being correct   517

lapse the termination of an offer when the offeree fails to accept it within a specified time, or if no time is specified, then within a reasonable time   105

lease an arrangement where the owner of property allows another person to have possession and use of the property for a stipulated period in return for the payment of rent   352

lease (1) a leasehold interest and (2) the agreement between landlord and tenant creating the leasehold interest   527

leaseback a financial arrangement enabling a business to buy a building and sell it to a financial institution that in turn gives a long-term lease of the property back to the business   544

leasehold an interest in land for a definite period of time   503

legal not offensive to the public good and not violating any law   148

legal aid a system where the government pays for many legal services provided to low-income litigants   39

legal audit a review of each area, action, and interaction of the business to identify potential legal liability and legal compliance risks   7

legal capacity competence to bind oneself legally   142

legal liability responsibility for the consequences of breaking the law   5

legal person an entity recognized at law as having its own legal rights, duties, and responsibilities   606

legal risk business activities, conduct, events, or scenarios that could expose a business to any type of legal liability; a business risk that may involve legal proceedings   6, 72

legal risk-management plan a plan developed by a business that identifies potential legal liability and provides preventive and remedial strategies   6

legal title an interest in land recognized by the common law   555

lessee or **tenant** the person who takes possession of the leased property; a person to whom an interest in a leasehold estate is granted   352, 503

lessor or **landlord** the owner of the leased property; a grantor of an interest in a leasehold estate   352, 503

letter of credit a document that the buyer of goods obtains from the bank and uses to pay the seller   773

letters patent a document incorporating a corporation, issued by the appropriate authority, and constituting the "charter" of the corporation   613

level-of-interactivity test a review of the features of a website to determine if it is active or passive; only active sites will be considered connected to the jurisdiction (also called the active-versus-passive test)   813

levy execution seize and sell a debtor's chattels or arrange for a sale of his lands; to seize and hold a sale of land in order to realize the amount due under a judgment registered against the owner   315, 520

libel written defamation   69

liberal approach statutory interpretation that considers the legislative intent, purpose, and history of the statute, as well as the context of the language; an approach that looks to the intent of the parties and surrounding circumstances, and tends to minimize, but does not ignore, the importance of the words actually used   25, 221

licensee a visitor (other than an invitee) who enters premises with the consent of the occupier   66

lien a right of a person in possession of property to retain that property until payment   340

life tenant a holder of a life estate   503

limitation period the time period within which a right of action must be pursued or it is lost forever   515

limited liability the liability of shareholders is limited to the amount of their capital contributions   606

limited liability partnership a partnership in which non-negligent partners are not personally liable for losses caused by the negligence of a partner   599

limited partner a partner in a limited partnership whose liability is limited to the amount of his or her capital contribution   597

limited partnership a partnership in which some of the partners limit their liability to the amount of their capital contributions   597

linking (or hyperlinking) an electronic connection of one website to another website. Links may be automatic or activated by the user. The new website may replace the original website or open in its own frame or browser window.   804

liquidated damages an amount agreed to be paid in damages by a party to a contract if it should commit a breach   305

liquidating dividends payments made from time to time by a trustee in bankruptcy to creditors on account of the full amount due to them   721

listing agreement contract between the vendor and his real estate agent creating the obligation to pay commission   568

major breach a breach of the whole contract or of an essential term so that the purpose of the contract is defeated   285

maker the party who signs and delivers a promissory note   447

malicious prosecution causing a person to be prosecuted for a crime without an honest belief that the crime was committed   68

mandatory injunction an order requiring a person to do a particular act   71

market restriction where a supplier makes it a condition that the buyer markets the product only within a prescribed area   759

material could reasonably be expected to influence the decision of a party to enter into a contract   185

maturity date end of the term when debt must be repaid   554

mediation a form of ADR where a neutral third party who is acceptable to both sides acts as a mediator, assisting the parties to reach a settlement   43

memorandum of association a document setting out the essential terms of an agreement to form a corporation   613

mens rea **offence** an offence where the prosecution must establish a "guilty mind" on the part of the defendant   662

merchant law rules and trade practices developed by merchants in medieval trade guilds and administered by their own courts   26

merger the amalgamation of two or more businesses into a single business entity   760

minor or **infant** a person who has not attained the age of majority according to the law of his or her province   142

minor breach a breach of a non-essential term of a contract or of an essential term in a minor respect   285

miscarriage an injury caused by the tort of another person   203

mitigate duty to act reasonably and quickly to minimize the extent of damage suffered   61

mitigation action by an aggrieved party to reduce the extent of loss caused by the breach of the other party   301

monitor a person appointed to supervise the reorganization of a debtor corporation under the Companies' Creditors Arrangement Act   727

moral cause moral duty of promisor to perform his promise   126

moral rights the permanent rights of an author or creator to prevent a work from being distorted or misused   479

mortgage a loan contract that gives the lender an interest in the borrower's land as security for a debt   554

mortgage commitment document in which parties to a mortgage initially agree to borrow and lend   554

mortgagee a lender who accepts an interest in land as security for a loan   554

mortgagor a borrower who gives his lender an interest in his land as security for repayment of a debt   554

most-favoured-nation (MFN) treatment the principle that goods imported from one country should not be treated less favourably than those imported from any other country   778

national treatment the principle that goods from another country should not be treated less favourably than domestic goods   778

natural justice procedural fairness or due process   819

necessaries essential goods and services   142

negative covenant a promise not to do something   312

negligence the careless causing of injury to the person or property of another   54

negligent misrepresentation an incorrect statement made without due care for its accuracy   83

negotiability the special quality possessed by negotiable instruments as a distinct class of assignable contract   450

negotiable instrument a written contract containing a promise, express or implied, to pay a specific sum of money to the order of a designated person or to "bearer"   256

negotiation the process of assigning a negotiable instrument   256

nemo dat quod non habet no one can give what he does not have   336

new trial a case sent back by the appeal court for retrial by the lower court   29

no-fault insurance a system of compulsory insurance that eliminates fault as a basis for claims   53

no par value share a share that has no nominal value attached to it   620

nominating committee committee responsible for proposing and recruiting new directors   630

non est factum "it is not my doing"   177

non-governmental organization voluntary non-profit associations of private individuals or groups working together to influence policy, raise awareness or affect change; private groups or associations that are not part of a state, nation, or political structure—they are usually not-for-profit and focus on societal issues   6, 769, 814

non-public purchasers purchasers that are not members of the general public such as banks, insurance companies, and municipal corporations   668

non-tariff barriers national rules, other than import duties, that restrict or prevent the importation of goods   776

notary a solicitor in Quebec   46

notice advance warning that the employment relationship will end   418

notice to quit notice of an intention to bring the tenancy to an end   539

novation the parties to a contract agree to terminate it and substitute a new contract   265

OECD the Organization for Economic Cooperation and Development, established in 1961, has 30 member countries including Canada and promotes world trade and sustainable economic growth by setting standards for best practice   771

offer a tentative promise made by one party, subject to a condition or containing a request to the other party   101

offeree the person to whom the offer is made   101

offeror the person making the offer   101

officers high-ranking members of a corporation's management team as defined in the by-laws or appointed by the directors, such as the president, vice-president, controller, chief executive officer, chief financial officer, general counsel, and general manager   629

official receiver a public official responsible for the supervision of bankruptcy proceedings   713

open mortgage a mortgage permitting repayment of the debt at any time without notice or bonus   565

operating lease a lease under which there is no intention to transfer ownership   352

opportunity cost the lost chance of making a similar contract with a different promisor   303

oppression remedy a statutory procedure allowing individual shareholders to seek a personal remedy if they have been unfairly treated   652

opt-out consent data-owner consent is implied from a failure to refuse consent   830

option a contract to keep an offer open for a specified time in return for a sum of money   107

ordinary resolution a resolution adopted by the general meeting and passed by a simple majority   644

outside counsel self-employed lawyers who work alone, in small partnerships, or in large national firms, and bill the business for services rendered   47

overholding tenant a tenant who remains on the premises without a new agreement with the landlord after the term of the lease expires   528

overrule to declare an existing precedent no longer binding or effective   23

paid-up capital the shares that have been issued and fully paid for   620

par value a nominal value attached to a share at the time of issue   620

paralegal a non-lawyer who provides some form of legal service to the public   47

parallel pricing the practice, among competing firms, of adopting similar pricing strategies   756

parol evidence rule a rule preventing a party to a contract from later adding a term previously agreed upon but not included in the final written contract   226

part payment something tendered by the buyer and accepted by the seller after formation of the contract, to be deducted from the price   214

part performance performance begun by a plaintiff in reliance on an oral contract relating to an interest in land, and accepted by the courts as evidence of the contract in place of a written memorandum   210

partial discharge a discharge of a definite portion of the mortgaged lands   565

participating right the right of a holder of a preferred share to participate in surplus profits or assets of the corporation in addition to the amount of the preferred dividend or redemption price   622

partnership the relationship between two or more persons carrying on a business with a view to profit   582

partnership agreement an agreement between persons to create a partnership and (usually) setting out the terms of the relationship   586

party and party costs an award that shifts some of the costs of litigation to the losing side according to a published scale of fees   40

party autonomy the parties' freedom to determine how their dispute will be resolved   787

passing-off misrepresenting goods, services, or a business in such a way as to deceive the public into believing that they are the goods, services, or business of some other person   70, 469, 803

past consideration a gratuitous benefit previously conferred upon a promisor   126

patent agent a registered agent who pursues applications for patents on behalf of individual inventors   490

pawnbroker a business that loans money on the security of pawned goods   367

payee the party named to receive payment on the bill of exchange   445

payment in lieu of notice payment of the amount of compensation the employee would have earned during the reasonable notice period   419

penalty clause a term specifying an exorbitant amount for breach of contract, intended to frighten a party into performance   305

perfection the moment in time when a creditor's security interest becomes protected   696

performance requirements conditions attached by the host country in granting approval to a foreign investment   782

performing rights society a society to which authors of musical and dramatic works assign performing rights and which grants licences for performances   483

periodic tenancy a leasehold interest that renews itself automatically on the last day of the term for a further term of the same duration   528

personal health information information relating to the physical or mental health of an identifiable individual that is used or obtained primarily for the purpose of providing health care   826

personal information recorded and unrecorded information about an identifiable individual, including that supplied by the individual and created by the organization   828

personal insurance insurance against death, injury, or ill health of an individual   373

personal privacy the respect of bodily integrity free from unreasonable surveillance, search, and seizure   819

petition a request to commence bankruptcy proceedings against a defaulting debtor   713

PHIPA Personal Health Information Protection Act (in Alberta and Saskatchewan, simply HIPA)   826

plaintiff the party that commences a private (civil) legal action against another party   35

pleadings documents filed by each party to an action providing information it intends to prove in court   38

pledge or pawn a bailment of personal property as security for repayment of a loan where possession passes to the bailee   367

postdate give a cheque a date later than the time when it is delivered to the payee   448

power of attorney a type of agency agreement authorizing the agent to sign documents on behalf of the principal   392

power of sale a right upon default to sell mortgaged land   558

pre-emptive right a right to have the first opportunity to purchase a proportionate part of any new shares to be issued   646

pre-incorporation contract a purported contract made in the name of a corporation before it comes into existence   672

predatory pricing where a seller temporarily reduces prices to an unreasonably low level with the aim of driving competitors out of business   758

preferred creditors unsecured creditors whose claims are given preference over those of other unsecured creditors   723

preferred share a share carrying preferential rights to receive a dividend and/or to be redeemed on the dissolution of the corporation   621

premium the price paid by the insured to purchase insurance coverage   372

prescription the creation of an easement over adjoining land through exercising a right continuously and openly   506

prima facie at first sight; on the face of it   192

principal the person on whose behalf the agent acts   391

priority a first, or prior, right to be repaid out of the debtor's asset   689

priority of registration priority of interests in real property are determined based on the order of registration in the public system; earlier registrations have priority over subsequent registrations   516

privacy has three key dimensions: personal privacy, territorial or spatial privacy, and privacy of personal information   819

privacy of personal information the protection of the trail of information left behind as we go about our daily lives   819

private company a corporation with a restricted number of shareholders prohibited from issuing its shares to the general public   617

private law law that regulates the relations between private persons and groups of private persons; the law that governs transactions between private parties, such as a seller and buyer of goods   3, 769

private nuisance interference with an occupier's use and enjoyment of her land   67

private rights individual rights arising from private law   12

privilege the right of a professional to refuse to divulge information obtained in confidence from a client   93

privity of contract the relationship that exists between parties to a contract   239

privity of estate the relationship between tenant and landlord created by their respective interests in the land that passes to a transferee of the interest   543

probate the process of administering and settling the estate of a deceased person   504

procedural law law that deals with the protection and enforcement of substantive rights and duties   21

product defamation making false and damaging statements about the products of another person   70

professional corporation (PC) a special type of business corporation that may be formed by members of a profession   618

promisee a party who has the right to performance according to the terms of the contract   115

promisor a party who accepts an obligation to perform according to the terms of the contract   115

promissory estoppel or **equitable estoppel** the court's exercise of its equitable jurisdiction to estop a promisor from claiming that she was not bound by her gratuitous promise where reliance on that promise caused injury to the promisee   130

promissory note a written promise to pay a specified sum of money to another party at a fixed or determinable future time or on demand   447

proper law of the contract the law of the country or jurisdiction by which the provisions of a contract are to be interpreted and its effect determined   770

property (1) everything that is the subject of ownership or (2) the legal interest in a thing   501

property insurance insurance against damage to property   373

proposal a procedure whereby a debtor, by agreement with the creditors, reorganizes his or her affairs without being made bankrupt   715

prospectus a statement issued to inform the public about a new issue of shares or bonds; the document that a corporation is required to publish when inviting the public to subscribe for its securities   190, 667

proxy a person appointed to attend a general meeting of shareholders and to cast the votes of the shareholder appointing him or her   645

proxy form a form required to be circulated to shareholders before a general meeting, inviting them to appoint a proxy if they so wish   645

public international law law involving relations between states   769

public law law that regulates the conduct of government and the relations between government and private persons   3, 769

public nuisance interference with the lawful use of public amenities   67

public offering selling shares to the public, which must be done in compliance with provincial securities regulations   629

publicly traded corporations corporations that issue shares to the public, also known as public corporations, widely held corporations, reporting issuers, and issuing corporations   628

punitive or **exemplary damages** damages awarded with the intention of punishing a wrongdoer   71

purchase lease a lease whereby ownership is intended to change hands at the end of the lease term   353

purchase-money security interest (PMSI) the interest that arises when goods purchased by a debtor are charged as security for a loan made to enable those actual goods being acquired   698

purpose of collection a need for collecting personal information that must be related directly to an operating program or activity of the institution   822

qualified privilege immunity from liability for defamation provided a statement was made in good faith   69

quantum meruit an amount a supplier deserves to be paid for goods or services provided to the person requesting them (also described as the fair market value of the benefit conferred)   134, 362

quasi-contract an obligation that may arise, not as a result of contractual relations, but because one party has received an unfair benefit at the expense of the other   178

quiet possession a warranty that there will be no interference with the lessee's possession or use of the asset   356

quotas restrictions on the quantities of goods that may be imported   776

ratification subsequent adoption by the proposed principal of a contract made by an agent acting without authority   398

ratify acknowledge and promise to perform   145

real action an action to repossess an interest in land that had been interfered with   501

reasonable expectation of privacy the subjective and objective assessment of reasonable privacy expectations in a given situation   819

reasonable notice the acceptable length of notice of termination considering the nature of the contract, intentions of the parties, circumstance of the employment, and characteristics of the employee   418

rebut overcome   157

receiving order a court order made in proceedings instituted by creditors, whereby a debtor is declared bankrupt   255, 715

recognition dispute an employer refuses to recognize the union as the employees' bargaining agent   433

rectification correction of a written document to reflect accurately the contract made by the parties   168

redeem have the land reconveyed to the mortgagor; reclaim the goods and continue with the conditional sale   555, 691

reduction of capital writing down (reducing) the stated amount of a corporation's capital   663

regional price discrimination where a seller charges lower prices in one region than it charges elsewhere, with the aim of eliminating competition   758

regular on its face nothing appears out of order on the document itself   459

regulations administrative rules implemented by government as a result of authorization given in a statute   10

regulatory or **quasi-criminal liability** responsibility arising from breaches of less serious rules of public law often enforced through specialized regulatory tribunals set up by the government for specific purposes   5

regulatory offences less-serious offences created by government regulation through specialized legislation, agencies, and tribunals; less serious offences that do not require *mens rea* (mental intent) and usually allow due diligence as a defence   661, 746

relationship of master and servant the contractual relationship between an employer and an employee   415

remainder the balance of a fee simple that goes to a third person at the end of a life estate   503

remainderman a person who holds the reversion or remainder in a fee simple   503

remote unrelated or far removed from the conduct   57

remote parties parties to an instrument who have not had direct dealings with one another   458

repossession the act of taking back possession of property that is in the possession of a defaulting debtor   691

representative action an action brought by one or more persons on behalf of a group having the same interest   147

repudiate reject or declare an intention not to be bound by   142

requisitions questions concerning claims against a seller's title to property   569

res ipsa loquitur the facts speak for themselves   60

res judicata a case that has already been decided by a court and cannot be brought before a court again   35

resale price maintenance where a supplier of goods attempts to control their resale price   758

rescind set the contract aside and put the party back in her pre-contract position   185

rescission an order by a court to rescind; setting aside or rescinding a contract in order to restore the parties as nearly as possible to their pre-contract positions   171, 186, 313

reservation that part of an interest in land expressly retained by the transferor   515

reserve judgment postpone giving a decision after the hearing ends   39

residential tenancies a lease of premises used as living accommodation   527

residual powers powers that fall within federal jurisdiction because they are not expressly allocated to the provinces by the Constitution   11

respondent the party who defends on an appeal   28

restitution an order to restore property wrongfully taken; repayment or recovery of a loss   71, 178

restrictive covenant a term in restraint of trade; a covenant requiring the holder of the land to refrain from certain conduct or certain use of the land   156, 508

retail sales sales of consumer goods by retail businesses, in the ordinary course of their business, to private individuals   328

retain or **retainer** the contract between a lawyer and client that describes the work that will be done and the fee that will be charged   47

retain (retention) keep information available for subsequent access by the individual   823

reverse mortgage a form of mortgage under which no repayment is due until the mortgagor sells or dies   566

reversion the balance of a fee simple reserved to the grantor and her heirs at the end of a life estate   503

rider additional provisions attached to a standard policy of insurance   373

right of re-entry a landlord's remedy of evicting the tenant for failure to pay rent or breach of another major covenant   536

right of survivorship the right of a surviving tenant to the interest of a deceased joint tenant   504

right-of-way an easement that gives the holder a right to pass back and forth over the land of another in order to get to and from her own land   505

rights dispute an employer and the union differ in their interpretation of terms in an existing collective agreement   434

Roman law the system of law codified by the Eastern Roman Emperor Justinian in the 6th century   22

royal charter a special licence given by the Crown to form a corporation for the purpose of carrying on a particular activity   612

rule of law established legal principles that treat all persons equally and that government itself obeys   3

rules of civil procedure the provincial regulations that set out the steps in a private lawsuit, including forms, fees, and timelines   34

sale-and-leaseback a transaction in which the owner of property sells it and immediately leases it back from the new owner   354

searching a title to examine the title to a piece of land   517

secured creditor a creditor that has collateral security in the form of a prior claim against specified assets of the debtor   563, 689

securities commission the statutory authority appointed to supervise the issue of securities to the general public, the operation of the securities industry, and the stock exchange   665

security agreement an agreement that creates a security interest, including chattel mortgages, conditional sales contracts, etc.   694

security for costs money deposited into the court in case an unsuccessful foreign plaintiff is ordered to pay the legal costs of the successful defendant   785

security interest an interest in goods, intangible property, or personal property that secures payment of a debt or performance of an obligation   694

security lease a purchase lease in which the lessor provides the credit   353

self-induced frustration a party wilfully disables itself from performing a contract in order to claim that the contract has been frustrated   272

senior officer a representative who plays an important role in establishing an organization's policies or is responsible for managing an important aspect of its activities, including the directors, the CEO, and the CFO of a corporation   675

servient tenement the land subject to the easement   505

serving providing a copy of the issued claim to each defendant   37

set aside or **rescinded** cancelled or revoked to return the parties as nearly as possible to their original positions   171

set off the right of a promisor to deduct an existing debt owed to it by the promisee   253

settlement an out-of-court procedure by which one of the parties agrees to pay a sum of money or perform an act in return for a waiver by the other party of all rights arising from the grievance   36

settlement a gift of property made by a debtor before becoming bankrupt   719

severance a procedure that turns a joint tenancy into a tenancy in common   505

severed removed from the contract   148

share a member's proportionate interest in the capital of a corporation   620

shareholder agreement an agreement between two or more shareholders that is distinct from the corporation's charter and by-laws   654

sight draft a bill of exchange payable "at sight"—three days of grace are allowed after presentation   446

slander spoken defamation   69

sole proprietorship an unincorporated business owned by a single individual   581

solicitor an "office" lawyer in England who interviews clients, carries on legal aspects of business and family affairs, and prepares cases for trial   46

solicitor–client fee payment for the time and expenses of a lawyer in preparing a case and representing the client in negotiations to settle or in court   39

solicitor–client privilege a client's right to have all communications with his or her lawyer kept confidential   46

special Acts of Parliament legislative acts creating a specific corporation   613

special damages damages to compensate for quantifiable injuries   71

special meeting any general meeting of shareholders other than the annual general meeting   644

special resolution a resolution of the general meeting required to be passed by a special (usually two-thirds) majority   644

specific goods goods in existence and agreed on as the subject-matter of the sale   337

specific performance an order by a court of equity to carry out a binding obligation; an order requiring a defendant to do a specified act, usually to complete a transaction   27, 311

specification the description of the invention, its use, operation, or manufacture   490

stakeholder a person or organization that manages a betting arrangement for a fee and redistributes winnings   150

stakeholders groups affected by the business activities of a corporation   661

standard form contract an offer presented in a printed document or notice, the terms of which cannot be changed by the offeree, but must be accepted as-is or rejected   103

standard of care the level of care that a person must take in the circumstances   55

standing offer an offer that may be accepted as needed from time to time   110

stare decisis to stand by a previous decision   23

stated capital account the amount received by a corporation for the issue of its shares   620

statement of adjustments a document setting out all the items—both credits and debits—that must be adjusted between the parties to arrive at the correct amount to be paid on closing   571

statement of defence a reply to a statement of claim, admitting facts not in dispute, denying other facts, and setting out facts in support of the defence   37

statute barred an action that may no longer be brought before a court because the party wishing to sue has delayed beyond the limitation period in the statute   278

statute a piece of legislation passed by government   10

statutory assignment an assignment that complies with statutory provisions enabling the assignee to sue the other party without joining the assignor to the action   250

stop payment an instruction from the drawer of a cheque to the bank not to pay the cheque   449

stoppage in transit the right of a seller to order a carrier not to deliver to the buyer   341

strict or **plain-meaning approach** an approach that restricts interpretation to the ordinary or dictionary meaning of a word   221

strict interpretation courts apply the provisions of a statute only where the facts of the case are covered specifically by the statute   25

strict liability liability that is imposed regardless of fault   51

strict liability offence an offence where there is a presumption of guilt unless the defendant can show that he or she took reasonable care   662

sub-bailee a person who receives a bailment of property from a bailee   359

subordinate legislation law created by administrative agencies whose authority is granted by statute in order to carry out the purposes of the legislation   24

subrogation where one person becomes entitled to the rights and claims of another   61

subsidiary promise an implied promise that the offeror will not revoke once the offeree begins performance in good faith and continues to perform   114

subsidiary a separate corporation owned or controlled by its "parent" corporation   780

substantial performance performance that does not comply in some minor way with the requirements of the contract   290

substantive law the rights and duties that each person has in society   21

super priority entitlement to be paid before secured creditors   721

super-governmental organizations non-profit associations of governments from around the world working to find common approaches to international issues, such as the World Trade Organization or United Nations   6, 769

surrender abandonment of the premises by the tenant during the term of the lease   535

survey detailed drawing or map of the real property showing all the boundaries of the land and the location of all fixtures, encroachments, or overhangs   520

system of courts the organization of courts into a hierarchy that designates the responsibilities of the court and determines the importance of the precedent; the standard system has three levels: trial, appeal, and final appeal   26

systemic discrimination discrimination that is pervasive throughout an employer's work force   427

takeover bid an offer by one corporation to acquire all or a substantial part of the shares of another corporation   669

technical protection measures (TPMs) access locks or use locks for electronic material: An access lock requires a password to access the work; a use lock blocks particular uses of the work such as copying   808

telemarketing the use of telephone communications for promoting the supply of a product or for promoting a business interest   750

tenancy from year to year a periodic tenancy that renews itself yearly   529

tenant's fixture a trade fixture or any other fixture attached for the convenience of the tenant or for the better enjoyment of the object   542

tenants in common concurrent holders of equal undivided shares in an estate   504

tender of performance an attempt by one party to perform according to the terms of the contract   263

term an interest in land for a definite period of time   527

term time period during which an interest rate is fixed and principal lent   554

term certain a tenancy that expires on a specific day   528

term insurance personal insurance that provides coverage for a limited period only   373

territorial privacy lack of intrusion in one's home, business, and other personal spaces   819

third party a person who is not one of the parties to a contract but is affected by it   239

third-party liability liability to some other person who stands outside a contractual relationship   81

tied selling where a supplier makes it a condition that, to obtain one type of product, the buyer must also deal in other products of the supplier   759

time draft a bill of exchange payable within a stipulated period after the date stated on the instrument or after presentation   446

title holding ownership of a thing   501

title fraud fraudulent transfer or mortgaging of land by a non-owner   518

title insurance a policy of insurance that compensates the policy holder for defects in a title   520

title searchers paralegals trained in land law who study the public registration systems and produce summaries of the registered interests affecting the title to specific real property   516

tort a wrongful act done to the person or property of another   51

trade fixture an object attached to the premises for the purpose of carrying on a trade or business   542

trade-related investment measures national measures regulating investment that have an impact upon international trade   777

trademark an identifiable feature that is used by a person for the purpose of distinguishing their goods or services from those of others   468, 803

transfer under the land titles system, the equivalent of a grant; not required to be made under seal   514

transfer an electronic grant that both lawyers will authorize for registration   571

trespass unlawful entering, or remaining, on the land of another   68

trespasser one who enters without consent or lawful right on the lands of another or who, having entered lawfully, refuses to leave when ordered to do so by the owner   66, 529

trust an arrangement that transfers property to a person who administers it for the benefit of another person   242

trust agreement the document that conveys property to a trustee to be used for the benefit of a third party beneficiary   243

trust deed a document evidencing a mortgage on the property of a corporation   693

trustee a person or company who administers a trust   242

trustee in bankruptcy the person appointed to administer the property of a bankrupt   713

ultra vires beyond the powers and therefore void   11, 608

unanimous shareholder agreement a shareholder agreement to which all shareholders are parties   655

unascertained goods goods that have not been set aside and agreed upon as the subject of a sale   338

UNCITRAL United Nations Commission on International Trade Law established by the United Nations General Assembly in 1966 to further harmonization and unification in international trade through conventions, model laws, and guidelines   771

unconscionable contracts contracts between parties of unequal bargaining power that result in an unfairly advantageous bargain for the powerful party   193

undisclosed principal a contracting party who, unknown to the other party, is represented by an agent   244

undue influence the domination of one party over the mind of another to such a degree as to deprive the weaker party of the will to make an independent decision   191

unenforceable contract a contract that still exists for other purposes but neither party may obtain a remedy under it through court action   207

UNIDROIT the International Institute for the Unification of Private Law, founded by the League of Nations in 1926 to harmonize laws, currently has 61 member states including Canada   771

unilateral contract a contract in which the offer is accepted by performing an act or series of acts required by the terms of the offer   114

unincorporated collectivity a group of persons that in most cases is not recognized by the courts and that may not sue or be sued   34

unitholders beneficiaries of an income trust   601

unjust enrichment an unfair benefit   178

unlawful interference with economic relations attempting by threats or other unlawful means to induce one person to discontinue business relations with another   69

unperfected security interest a security interest that is not attached or perfected 697

unsecured creditor a creditor who has no security interest in any of the debtor's property 689

use (of personal information) any access, change, or destruction of data within the organization 827

utmost good faith a duty owed when a special measure of trust is placed in one party by the other 189

vicarious liability the liability of an employer to compensate for harm caused by an employee 53

vicarious performance a third party performs on behalf of the promisor who remains responsible for proper performance 241

void never formed in law 145

voidable a contract that a court may set aside in an attempt to restore the parties to their original positions 174

voidable contract a contract that may be rendered unenforceable at the option of one of the parties 145

vulture funds large investors who purchase the debt or shares of a corporation in the course of its reorganization 726

wager an agreement between two persons in which each has some probability of winning or losing 150

waiver an agreement not to proceed with the performance of a contract already in existence 264

warranty a lesser or non-essential term that does not relieve the injured party from performance 285, 328

warranty of authority a person who purports to act as agent represents that she has authority to contract on behalf of the principal 403

waste damage to the premises that reduces its value 532

web-wrap agreement a website document setting out contractual terms, the acceptance of which is indicated by clicking on the appropriate icon (also called a click-wrap agreement) 798

wilful invasion of privacy a person knew or should have known that their actions would invade the privacy of another 837

winding up the dissolution (or liquidation) of a corporation 652

without recourse no ability to claim against the endorser 453

workers' compensation a scheme in which employers contribute to a fund used to compensate workers injured in industrial accidents regardless of how the accident was caused 53

World Intellectual Property Organization a specialized agency of the United Nations dedicated to harmonizing intellectual property laws and regimes world wide 477

writ an ancient form required in order to take a grievance to court 26

wrongful detention the refusal by the seller to deliver goods whose title has passed to the buyer 345

INDEX

EXPLANATION OF ABBREVIATIONS

Throughout the text and footnotes, references occur to reported decisions of the courts, to statutes, and to legal periodicals. Listed below are the abbreviations for frequently cited source materials.

Canada

REPORTS

A.J.	Alberta Journal
A.R.	Alberta Reports
Alta L.R.	Alberta Law Reports
B.C.J.	British Columbia Journal
B.L.R.	Business Law Reports
C.C.C.	Canadian Criminal Cases
C.C.E.L.	Canadian Cases on Employment Law
C.C.L.I.	Canadian Cases on the Law of Insurance
C.C.L.T.	Canadian Cases on the Law of Torts
C.E.L.R.	Canadian Environmental Law Reports
C.P.R.	Canadian Patent Reports
C.R.	Criminal Reports
C.S.	Cour Supérieure (Québec)
D.L.R.	Dominion Law Reports
D.T.C.	Dominion Tax Cases
Ex.C.R.	Exchequer Court Reports
F.C.	Federal Court Reports
F.T.R.	Federal Court Trial Reports
M.J.	Manitoba Journal
M.P.R.	Maritime Provinces Reports
N.B.R.	New Brunswick Reports
N.S.R.	Nova Scotia Reports
O.A.C.	Ontario Appeal Cases
O.A.R.	Ontario Appeal Reports
O.J.	Ontario Journal
O.L.R.	Ontario Law Reports
O.R.	Ontario Reports
O.W.N.	Ontario Weekly Notes
P.P.S.A C.	Personal Property Security Act Cases
S.C.R.	Supreme Court Reports
S.J.	Saskatchewan Journal
Sask.R.	Saskatchewan Reports
W.L.R.	Western Law Reports
W.W.R.	Western Weekly Reports

STATUTES

Revised Statutes of

R.S.A.	Alberta
R.S.B.C.	British Columbia
R.S.C.	Canada
R.S.M.	Manitoba
R.S.N.B.	New Brunswick
R.S.Nfld.	Newfoundland
R.S.N.S.	Nova Scotia
R.S.O.	Ontario
R.S.P.E.I.	Prince Edward Island
R.S.Q.	Quebec
R.S.S.	Saskatchewan

(Statutes for individual years are cited as S.A., S.B.C., S.C., S.M., S.N.B., S.Nfld., S.N.S., S.O., S.P.E.I., S.Q., S.S., respectively.)

S.O.R.	Statutory Orders and Regulations

PERIODICALS

C.B.L.J.	Canadian Business Law Journal
Can. Bar Rev.	Canadian Bar Review
Can. B.A.J.	Canadian Bar Association Journal
Osg.H.L.J.	Osgoode Hall Law Journal
UBC L. Rev.	University of British Columbia Law Review
U.T.L.J.	University of Toronto Law Journal

JUDGES

J.	Justice
J.A.	Justice of Appeal
JJ.	Justices
C.J.	Chief Justice
A.G.	Attorney-General

United Kingdom

REPORTS

All E.R.	All England Reports
E.R.	English Reports (Reprint)
I.R.	Irish Reports
L.J. Ex.	Law Journal Exchequer